BY SEA, BY LAND
THE
ROYAL MARINES
1919–1997

BY SEA, BY LAND

THE

ROYAL MARINES

1919–1997

JAMES D. LADD

An Authorised History

HarperCollins*Publishers*

HarperCollins*Publishers*
77–85 Fulham Palace Road
Hammersmith
London
W6 8JB

The HarperCollins website address is:
www.fireandwater.com

First published in the United Kingdom as *Royal Marines 1919–1980* by
Jane's Publishing Limited
238 City Road
London EC1V 2PU

ISBN 0–7106–0011–9

Revised and updated edition published in the United Kingdom as *By Sea, By Land* by
HarperCollins*Publishers* 1999

3 5 7 9 8 6 4 2

ISBN 0 00 472366 X

Set in Linotype PostScript Sabon and Gill Sans by
Rowland Phototypesetting Ltd, Bury St Edmunds, Suffolk

Printed and bound in Great Britain by
Clays Ltd, St Ives plc

CONTENTS

Right: The Commandant General Royal Marines, Major General R. H. G. Fulton.

BY 1943 THE FUNCTIONS OF THE
ROYAL MARINES ... WERE TO PROVIDE:

(1) detachments for service in HM Ships which, while fully capable of manning their share of the gun armament, are specially trained to undertake such landing operations as the Naval Commander-in-Chief may find it necessary to order.

(2) units to undertake, in co-operation with other services, special amphibious operations.

(3) units for the rapid establishment and temporary defence of Naval and Fleet Air Arm bases.

History of Combined Operations Organisation
Amphibious Warfare Headquarters, London 1956

By 1997 these functions had changed only in that all Royal Marines were trained as commandos, their 3 Commando Brigade RM was a part of the British Rapid Reaction Force and individual reinforced Commando units might each be deployed as an Expeditionary Force. Service in ships was considerably reduced from the levels in 1943.

FOREWORD

BUCKINGHAM PALACE.

Her Majesty's Royal Marines have served their
Sovereign and country with courage and distinction
since 1664. At fairly regular intervals during the
intervening years some willing soul has been found
to bring the record of their activities up-to-date.
The last official history brought the record up to
1919. After 60 years it was obviously time to add
another volume, and this is it.

60 years out of over 300 may not seem very much,
but in terms of action and development the period
between 1919 and 1980 will surely rank as one of the
most important the Corps is ever likely to experience.
The primary role has changed from providing detachments
to man part of the armament of the major units in fleet,
to the organisation of an amphibious and air transportable
raiding force trained to cope with warfare in all
conditions from the Arctic to the jungle and desert.
But in between came the Second World War, and once
again in Kipling's words ' "It's Tommy this, and Tommy
that" and "Chuck him out, the brute!" but it is "Saviour
of his country when the guns begin to shoot." ' And
during the years of that war, the Corps undertook a
quite remarkable variety of tasks with its traditional
measured discipline and calm confidence.

If you read this book in conjunction with its
predecessors you cannot fail to notice the continuity
of steadfast service whatever the demands, whatever the
conditions and whatever the equipment. As the story
unfolds it becomes increasingly plain that the thread which
runs through it all is the very best of the character and
quality of the British people.

1980

PREFACE
By Major General Robert Fulton,
Commandant General Royal Marines

This lastest edition of James Ladd's book brings the story of the Royal Marines up to date, not only by recording events but also by shedding new light on earlier ones. In his preface to the previous edition, Lieutenant General Sir John Richards KCB, then Commandant General, wrote:

> 'The history of the Royal Marines up to 1919 has been well documented in three volumes of *Britain's Sea Soldiers* and although several books in recent years have summarised our history up to recent times, this one by James Ladd fills a long felt need for an authoritative and detailed account of the Royal Marines over the past 60 years. It shows the changing nature of warfare between 1919 and the present day and the way in which the Corps' major involvement in sea service and naval gunnery in the 1920s and 1930s was subsequently replaced by amphibious and commando service. No comparable period in our history has seen so many changes in our roles and commitments or has better demonstrated our versatility.'

That was in 1980. Since then, the operations to recover the Falklands Islands in 1982 and to assit the Kurds in Northern Iraq in 1991 have taken place and are covered here in detail, while the Emergency in Northern Ireland is a thread running through the later years.

Throughout the period covered by this book, the Royal Marines have played a leading role in evolving the United Kingdom's ability to project power from the sea. While the role of gunnery has waned, the landing parties of the early years have developed into the Commando forces of the later ones. Now a new generation of amphibious ships is becoming the primary means not only of delivery to a theatre of opererations but also of extending the influence of the maritime force throughout that theatre. Harnessing technology remains as important as ever but this book clearly demonstrates that the key battle-winning factor has been, and remains, the quality of the individual Royal Marine.

Royal Marines have always understood the importance of sea, land and air, excelling in operations requiring the close integration of all 3 Services. Nevertheless, this is a story of a maritime Corps, steeped in the culture and traditions of the Royal Navy, yet with our own highly individual and distinctive ethos; and ethos that is firmly rooted in 335 years of history but which also pays tribute to the remarkable men who first wore the Green Beret – the wartime Commandos. It is the blend of the maritime foundation of the Royal Marines with the Commando heritage and spirit that inspires the members of the Corps today.

James Ladd, who served in the Corps during World War II, has been diligent in his research work not only in our museum archives but also through is many contacts with serving and retired members of the Corps. His book achieves a balance between the regimental aspects of the Corps and the wider background of military history. I believe that, like its predecessor, it will be welcomed by a wide range of readers.

AUTHOR'S NOTE
to *Royal Marines 1919–1980*

To Sir Robert Bruce Lockhart the Royal Marines appeared as 'a more united family than any other branch of the fighting services'.[1] For although they are not necessarily born as Marines, they seldom die outside the spirit of the Corps if they do not die in its service. This sentiment is apparent in the many hundreds of contributions from serving and ex-members of the Corps, who helped to make this book a family as well as a military history.

The Royal Marine's probably unique adaptability has taken him in the 20th century through the last great battles of capital ships, raiding ashore as a commando, and spearheading the defence of NATO's northern flank, to name but a few of the many roles he has fulfilled in the past 60 years. Roles that mirror many aspects of the development of warfare in this century, and which have involved him in so many operations that only examples can be shown in detail. An appendix of unit histories summarises these operations, however, showing that there have only been brief periods over the sixty years when elements of the Corps were not in action or deployed for it. In describing such actions words have been used in their everyday sense for the benefit of the general reader, rather than in the more specialised definitions such words may have in military reports. Equipment is also described in non-technical terms for readers who may not be familiar with the particular techniques of warfare described, and metric equivalents to knots etc are shown for those readers unfamiliar with Imperial measure. [On revision many of these 'equivalent' measurements have been eliminated, as they tended to make the reading difficult and by 1997 metric measurements are more familiar to readers than they were in 1980 – JDL 1999]

The narrative carries forward the record of the Corps' actions described in General Sir H. E. Blumberg's *Britain's Sea Soldiers*[2] covering the World War of 1914–1918. But, because of the 30-year rule which prohibits access to certain State papers relating to matters since 1949, not all the political implications of some policies can be included for no official records are available covering operations since that date, but there is reason to believe that no significant events have been omitted. The Corps can be seen to be meeting the changing nature of warfare with as versatile a force of Royal Marines in the 1980s, as faced those unexpected tasks in earlier years: by RM divers of 1940; by landing craft crews in 1944 who were fighting as infantry in 1945; or of the RM helicopter pilots of 1961.

J.D. Ladd
Royal Marines Museum
Eastney
March 1980

AUTHOR'S NOTE
to *By Sea, By Land*

Seventeen years have passed since the publication of *Royal Marines 1919–1980*, years in which the Corps has continued to meet the many varied demands on its services. It provided a major element of the forces defending NATO's northern flank. Its 3 Commando Brigade RM spearheaded the recovery of the Falkland Islands in the South Atlantic, in a war which had more similarities to those of the 19th century than of earlier in the 20th century. This is dealt with in some detail as it may well be the pattern of hostilities in the next few decades. The lessons of that Falklands War, operation 'Corporate', have been studied and applied not only in the Corps but in a wider sphere of British military and political thinking.

Titles in the last half of the 20th century showed minor but possibly confusing changes. For example: before the mid-1950s a typical Commando's title was 40 Royal Marine Commando, but thereafter in unit titles the plural Royal Marines was placed after the unit description as in 40 Commando Royal Marines.

The Corps by 1997 was as integrated with the Royal Navy as it had been in earlier centuries, and the concept of amphibious operations had assumed a greater political importance by 1997 than it ever had before in the closing decades of the 20th century. Therefore in setting out the history in chapters 11 to 13 the subjects have been dealt with by showing: the events of operation 'Corporate' in chapter 11; some aspects of training, organisation and weapons in chapter 12; and examples of deployments for operations and overseas training in chapter 13. All of which explain the Corps' continued ability to meet the changing nature of warfare and the military needs of the British people.

J. D Ladd
Topsham
June 1999

ACKNOWLEDGEMENTS
for *Royal Marines 1919–1980*

The author is most grateful to His Royal Highness Prince Philip for his foreword to this book, and for the help and encouragement of the Commandant General, Lieutenant General Sir John Richards, KCB, and his predecessor, General Sir Peter Whiteley, GCB, OBE. He would also like to thank the many hundreds of Royal Marines, their families and friends who kindly wrote or met him to provide an unequalled source of eyewitness accounts of life in the Corps, and in other ways helped him, as did Mr J. McDonald in memory of his friend, a 'Royal killed early in World War II'. My fellow members of the RM Historical Society have been unstinting in their help – the late Major General J.L. Moulton, CB, DSO, OBE, has been most generous in his help, Major Alan Marsh's detailed research into Marines of the Fleet Air Arm is the principal source for Fleet Air Arm references, Mr John Trendell's *Operation Music Maker* (privately published) a comprehensive study of the bands is the source of Appendix 5, Mr Leslie Garrett, Mr Tony Perrett and other members have also been generous in their help.

The staff of the Museum under their Director Major Tony Brown MBE in 1980, their Curator Mr Paul Fauset, the archivist Miss Bridget Spiers, and Keeper of the Photographic Library Mr Harry Playford have given unstinted help. He is particularly indebted to the Corps' Historical Records Officer, Major Alastair Donald, who has given the author so much advice from his unequalled knowledge of the Corps' history and for his work on the appendix on uniforms. He thanks Capt Derek Oakley, editor of the *Globe and Laurel*, and members of the Public Relations and News Teams including Capt Roger Spiers, C/Sgt Bob Cawley and C/Sgt Bob Brown for their help on more recent aspects of the Corps' history, and others who have helped with revision of the text including Maj A.C.J. Sharland, Maj T.K. Courtenay with the editors of the RMR history, Maj A.J. Gowan, Capt D.G. Sayers, Mr J.D. Brown (Naval Historical Branch), Sgt M.S. Alexander. The crest on the dust jacket [for the 1st edition] was drawn by Mr Paul Fauset.

The following have kindly read the text or those major parts of it on which they had special knowledge: Capt D. Oakley, Major A.J. Donald, Maj Dan Flunder (World War II), Maj John Hawley (serving), Capt Ian Leslie (serving in 1980), the late Maj Jimmy Powell (L Craft). The author hopes others who kindly read sections of the book will accept his general thanks and excuse his not naming them individually. He is grateful to them all for their suggestions and improvements but any errors are entirely his. The opinions expressed in this book (whether attributed or not) are not those of Her Majesty's Government.

He also wishes to thank Mr T. Charman, Mrs Tina Baines and Miss S.K. Connet for preparing the typescript, Mrs Rosemary Donald for her secretarial services, Mr Anthony Preston, the staffs of the Imperial War Museum, the Ministry of Defence Naval Historical Branch, the Public Record Office, Mr Michael Stevens the editor of the 1980 edition, for his encouragement and advice, and C/Sgt K. Kelly, the artist assisted by WO C.R. Ridgway.

General acknowledgement is made to the following for permission to reproduce photographs and drawings: the Royal Marines Museum archives and the Trustees of the Corps' property for all photograph items; and drawing by Lt D. Tong RM with Introduction to chapter 4.

ACKNOWLEDGEMENTS
for *By Sea, By Land*

In addition to those who contributed to the first edition (*Royal Marines 1919–1980*) the author is grateful for the contributions made by officers and men of 3 Commando Brigade RM who kindly agreed to be interviewed in 1982. He also wishes to thank those who commented on the text of chapters 11 to 13: Lt General Sir Steuart Pringle Bt, KCB; Major General Julian Thompson CB, OBE and for permission to quote from his book *No Picnic*; Major General Nick Vaux CB, DSO and for permission to quote from his book *March to the South Atlantic*; Major General Andrew Whitehead CB, DSO; Major General M. P. J Hunt OBE; Lieutenant-Colonel Ewen Southby-Tailyour OBE RM and for permission to quote from his book *Reasons in Writing*. Major Mark Bentinck RM the Corps Historical Records Officer; Captain D. Oakley MBE RM and for permission to quote from his book *A Pictorial History of the Royal Marines*, Major A.J. Donald RM for information on 1990s uniforms, for advice on general matters and corrections to the original text of *Royal Marines 1919–1980* which have been incorporated in this edition. He also wishes to thank: Major Ralph Howard-Williams RM for his considerable assistance with the 'new' text; the staff of Exeter Central Library; Mr Matthew Little and the Director of the Royal Marines Museum; Miss Angela Patric the librarian at CTCRM; and those serving officers and men who provided information which give this history its authenticity.

The opinions expressed in this book (whether attributed or not) are not those of Her Majesty's Government.

THE ROYAL MARINES
MUSEUM

The history of the Royal Marines from 1664 comes alive in this award winning Museum, with its exhibits and displays. Many of these are explained with videos and figures and others have detailed label captions.

These sea solders raised during the time of the Dutch Wars, with their tawny yellow coats and flintlock muskets began the first 90 years of what became Maritime Regiments, followed by the formation of 50 Companies of Marines. Shown in displays and pictures of these early periods are Marines in Australia, at Bunker Hill (Boston, USA) and in the Napoleonic Wars. Their dress, weapons and battles are explained in graphic detail.

The Royal Marine Artillery and the Royal Marines Light Infantry from the early 19th century until they were amalgamated in 1923, can be seen in their many battles afloat and ashore with examples of how they lived through these times. With, for example, a section of a World War I trench and the raid on Zeebrugge explained in exhibits, including a diorama.

Actions of World War II at sea and on land are displayed with Commando assaults graphically illustrated. The Korean War, the withdrawal from Empire and the Suez landings are explained. Wars of the 1980s and 1990s provide more modern exhibits as does the detail on training in the 1990s.

The exhibits are housed in what was once the officers mess at Eastney, home of the Portsmouth Grand Division and Portsmouth Marines until the late 1960s. The interiors have been restored to show what the mess was like in the early 20th century.

How to get there – by car take the A3(M) or the M27 and follow the sign posts for SOUTHSEA on the A2030. The Museum lies at the east end of the promenade.
– by rail to one of the Portsmouth stations and then by bus or taxi.
– For details of buses please telephone 01329 232208.

Opening times – 10am to 5pm Whitsun to August and 10am to 4.30pm for the rest of the year. The Museum closes for a few days each Christmas and in exceptional circumstances.

Tel: 01705 819385   Fax: 01705 838420
information compiled in September 1998

SEA SOLDIERS

An icy wind made breathing difficult and chilled the bones despite the lieutenant's Arctic clothing. As he trudged over frozen snow by the railway to Kandalaksha (Murmansk) on New Year's day 1919, North Russia was a place of many uncertainties. In the next 75 years or more Royal Marines would be protecting British lives and interests in equally difficult circumstances. Over 1,000 miles from the sea, up the river Yangtze (modern Chang Jiang) in China during the 1920's and 1930's, Royal Marines from the decks of gunboats held off pirate armies exacting unlawful tolls on British ships. In Greece and elsewhere they gave help to local communities at times of natural disasters – 'the only angels in our calamity' as the Royal Navy were once described. They saw service in major wars and many smaller ones – aboard HMS *Exeter* 'an 11-inch shell came through the port side . . . below the Marines' mess deck' at the battle of the River Plate (13 December 1940), and five months later 400 anti-aircraft gunners and searchlight crews fought as infantry in the rearguard on Crete. The following December a small raiding force of Marines landed behind the Japanese lines in Malaya to ambush enemy staff cars. In August 1942 40 RM Commando landed at Dieppe 'with a courage terrible to see', and later in that War Marine commandos were in many fierce actions from Normandy and the rivers of north-west Europe to the jungles of Burma. They landed in tanks in Normandy (6 June 1944); they provided assault craft crews and manned the guns of close-support craft coming into the beaches at Walcheren (November 1944) and elsewhere, under heavy fire from undefeated coast batteries. They patrolled the jungles of south-east Asia in the 1950s and 1960s, when they also fought in the mountain deserts of Aden, in Korea and to keep the peace in troubled lands around the world. In 1982 the 3 Commando Brigade RM spearheaded the recapture of the Falkland Islands after an Argentinean invasion. In 1991 they were deployed in northern Iraq and during the UN operations in Yugoslavia, Royal Marines served with peace keeping forces as they did elsewhere in that decade.

But in 1919 the majority of Royal Marines were serving in ships, with a strength which had been reduced from 55,603 on 15 November 1918[1] to 15,000 by the end of 1919.[2] At that time the Corps was divided into two arms: the Royal Marine Artillery (RMA), whose gunners served on all capital ships; and the Royal Marine Light Infantry (RMLI), whose privates also served as gunners in ships from their home ports. After these arms were amalgamated in 1923, the strength fell to around 10,000. The Marines' role was later defined as follows: 'In war and peace ... while fully capable of manning their share of the gun armament of ships ... [to be] especially trained to be a striking force ... for amphibious operations such as raids ... or the seizure of temporary bases'[3] for the fleet. They were, as Kipling wrote, '... a kind of giddy harumfrodite – soldier and sailor too ...'.[4]

For the detachment of HMS *Dauntless* (4,850 tons), manning two of her six 6-in guns, these duties led to a number of actions in the Baltic against Russian ships disputing the coastal waters of the emerging Latvian and Estonian states after World War I. The origins of this undeclared war are confused but the political decisions were made by the Supreme War Council of the Allies, meeting at Versailles, who in mid-February 1919 gave Britain the main responsibility for the Baltic. Aboard *Dauntless* the RM detachment, under their Senior Royal Marine Officer (SRMO), Captain C.R.W. Lamplough (later Major General, CBE, DSC),[5] provided a gun crew for one of her Mark XII 6-in guns on a PXIII* mounting. This crew worked in the open behind the gun shield, where the pitching and rolling gun platform made it difficult to keep your feet in rough weather, never mind carrying through the drill for loading and firing the gun. In this the crew would normally follow the dial pointers giving information from the director through the Transmitting Station (T/S), but if communications were cut or electric power failed the gun would be fired in 'local control' to commands from the captain of the gun or the officer commanding its turret.

Dauntless was in commission for most of the next 20 years and later saw service in World War II. During peacetime her detachment usually completed 2½-year commissions, before leave and a posting to duties ashore, possibly in Stonehouse Barracks, as she was a Plymouth ship. Each ship had a Port Division – Chatham, Portsmouth or Plymouth – from which her seamen and Marines were drawn, with Plymouth Marines, for example, only serving in Plymouth ships in normal circumstances. At sea the Marines normally manned 'X' or 'B' turret of capital ships and a portion of the secondary armament, but on the signing of the Washington Treaty in 1922 the Americans sank more British battleships 'than were ever lost in a battle at sea';[6] 20 battleships were scrapped, and four in building were cancelled. With them went some 4,500 berths for Royal Marines at sea and in training posts, although the Treaty had the unexpected effect in raising the size of cruisers to 10,000 tons[7] with 8-in guns, as such ships were capable of the long Pacific voyages made by American fleets. Few limits were placed on aircraft carriers, but as these had no heavy armament, their Marine detachments were small, and although the Washington Treaty allowed the signatories to have as many small warships as they wished, this did not affect the Corps since Marines did not serve at that time in destroyers or other small ships.

A further limitation on the size of the Corps was the Ten Year Rules maintained by successive British Governments, and which in various forms restricted all military planning by the assumption that there would be no major war within the next decade. As a result of this, the proposed Raiding Force of Marines was not created, although in the 1920s the Admiralty had wanted such a force to seize temporary bases for the fleet. In a wider context the Rule made the Admiralty's task more difficult in balancing fleet commitments between the Far East and European waters, for the Navy wanted to avoid fighting a war in Europe at the same time as it faced one in the East. But in the inevitable compromises which had to be made detachments of Marines had to be found for service afloat with few opportunities for 'square numbers' (those pleasant jobs in barracks).

During the 1920s and early 1930s the Corps' strength remained around 10,000 with the majority at sea, typically on the China station, which was a popular draft for which many volunteered to do a second commission on completing their first. But this station was not all rice wine and mahjong, as the detachment aboard the old cruiser HMS *Despatch* found after they crossed the silt-dulled waters of the Yangtze River's outflow some 150 miles out to sea from the great river's estuary. *Despatch* made the passage of 1,000 miles across the central plains of China to moor-up at Hankow (modern Hankou) in the winter of 1926.

Here the Marines were landed to patrol the warehouse area of the British concession, under rights granted to British, French and American warships under 19th-century treaties with China. These privileges angered the 20th-century Chinese and on 22 December a mob tried to break into the concession area.[8] They smelt unwashed, a stench of garlic and urine emanating from them in their excitement, for the Chinaman of those days appears to have been indifferent to hygiene. But they were repulsed by strong will rather than strong arm tactics, the Marines holding steady until the mob dispersed. After Christmas, on 2 January 1927, Chinese soldiers picked flowers in the 'no Chinese allowed' gardens of the Race Club,[9] and in more forceful efforts the mob tried to pluck Marines from their strongpoint on the Bund. This riverside wharf of the concession became the centre of Chinese resentment against foreigners, as bricks and jagged bits of gutter were hurled at the landing party of 35 Marines from *Despatch*. With fixed bayonets, they held off the mob, knowing that to open fire would precipitate a major skirmish, although three Marines were injured by flying bricks before the local police took charge of the situation. Later there were some grumblings by authorities in London, because the local consul had arranged the withdrawal of the landing party and the resulting loss of the concession, yet only some five years earlier a few rounds from the gunboat HMS *Widgeon* had recovered wool cargoes improperly confiscated from a British ship higher up the Yangtze.

The days of gunboat diplomacy were drawing to a close with the resurgence of Chinese and other nationalism. Nevertheless the practice of maintaining an old cruiser in Hankow during the 'dry' season continued until the river was closed in the Sino-Japanese war, and when the river was in flood with sufficient water to manoeuvre more modern cruisers, these went 1,200 miles or more up river from the sea. Marines were transferred from the larger ships' detachments to serve on the gunboats from time to time. Others volunteered, as did Marine Claude Flambard from HMS *Caradoc*, to sail as armed guards on a British merchantman.[10] On a previous voyage her captain had been waylaid by pirates, who, no doubt, had moved the buoys the River Inspectorate placed to mark 'crossings' where river channels swung from one bank to the other. The guards sailed to Ichang (modern Yichang) some 300 miles up river from Hankow. *Caradoc* had been in the Mediterranean fleet and her sailing to the China station – one of the Admiralty's balancing of forces – was in response to the increasing friction over local taxes.

For young Marines joining ships in China the voyage out could be full of incident. In HMS *Hawkins* after coaling-ship, a 6-hour dust-choking slog with coal bags, one young Marine was posted as keyboard sentry standing guard over the ship's keys.[11] A few days later in the Bay of Biscay, the same youngster was persuaded he should wish the Commander a Merry Christmas. He did so by chalking the greeting on the deck of the keyboard flat (ship's space), and for his cheek had to scrub this deck for two hours every night for a week. 'It's a good job I didn't hang my stocking up' sums up the philosophy with which punishments were accepted. He was to serve 2½ years aboard HMS *Hawkins* before returning home.

In the unstable political situation of a Russian inciting the Southern army (of what became Chiang Kai-shek's forces) against foreigners, the 'E' class cruiser HMS *Emerald* on 23 March 1927 put ashore 14 Marines at Nanking (modern Nanjing), 300 miles down river from Hankow.[12] They were to protect the consulate from looters of the retreating Northern army of the Chinese government, but were refused permission to enter the city gates after marching a mile from the river. In twos and threes they had to get through the gate in taxis. Next morning firing broke out in the town. At 1014 hours the Consul reported by wireless that there were looters in the building, and for the next 36 hours the consulate party was subjected to numerous searches and harassment by Southern army soldiers, as the Consul's staff wisely prohibited any defensive fire.[13] Disarmed, the Marines had to watch the building being looted and they decided to stay with the wounded Consul, although they might have escaped back to the ship. Looking for help in the surrounding streets, three Marines found a Southern army officer who ordered the looters away; a car was then found to take the Consul back to the *Emerald*, where he later died of his wounds. Meanwhile a party of Marines with a Lewis gun Section on the Bund had held off the mobs for three hours before the Marines were withdrawn.

They had to return the following day, after Chinese troops attacked American property. That afternoon two of *Emerald*'s officers brought the American consul to temporary safety, after a couple of salvos of shrapnel from the ship had dispersed soldiers attacking the American consulate. Later two platoons of seamen and Marines were landed under a covering bombardment of 76 rounds of shrapnel and high-explosive (HE) from *Emerald* and 19 from the American destroyers USS *Noa* and *William F. Preston*. The platoons rescued 48 expatriates, and looting stopped in the town.[14] Further threats of bombardment, later reported as an effective deterrent, prevented more attacks on British and American residents, 500 of whom were safely evacuated. About the same time in March (1927) the 12th RM Battalion was landed in Shanghai to reinforce such deterrents, as explained in Appendix 4.

Throughout the early 1930s Royal Marines were engaged in many minor incidents on the rivers of China, often against bandits, but after August 1937 they were bombed by Japanese planes, despite the large Union Jacks spread over the ships' awnings. In October 1937 even the railway line was bombed in an attempt to prevent a troop train – well marked with Union Jacks – evacuating British crews from ships trapped on the Yangtze. But by this date the Mediterranean deployments had been made against Italy and rearmament was under way. As the Corps was – and is – engaged in such varied and far-flung operations, the narrative of their history at times must move sharply from one scene to another and breaks in the text are intended to show where such changes are made.

The British tradition of cutting armed forces in peacetime had been sustained in the 1920s and early 1930s by a faith in the League of Nations. This, for many Marines like John Hopkins,[1] meant 10 years abroad during his first 'twelve', although he made no complaint. Few left the service in this time of economic depression, for there were bed, board and some lively times in the Corps, not only on the China station in the decades between the world wars. There was the annual Spring Cruise, when ships from the Home and Atlantic Fleets sought 'more favourable conditions for training than in the inclement weather ... in home waters',[2] and in 1921 two forces, the Red and the Blue fleets sailed for Spain. Five battleships, six light cruisers, five K-class submarines and the 3rd Destroyer Flotilla (13 V and W class) made up the Red fleet. The Blue had three battle-cruisers – HMS *Hood*, *Tiger* (built 1912) and *Repulse* – the 2nd and 4th Destroyer Flotillas 'with 24 boats', and four L-class submarines. They came down the Channel at 9 knots on 17 January,[3] seaplanes scouting with two of the light cruisers of Red fleet. Then the two fleets sought shelter as the weather deteriorated.

The first phase of this cruise was intended to test the 'comparative fighting values of the submarine and dreadnought'. But on the morning of 20 January, some 72 hours after the exercise began, K5 was lost as she dived under Blue fleet's battle-cruisers approaching her at 18 knots. All 57 of her crew were lost and she was never found despite an intensive search. The loss overshadowed the rest of the cruise, but the fleets had carried out an hour-long mock action off Cape Finnisterre before reaching north-west Spain for the Admiral's annual inspection, which that year was held in Arosa Bay. On the return passage the battleship squadrons at times moved in two divisions so that gunnery officers, rangetakers, and crews were given practice in ship-to-ship gunnery. Other exercises followed: in submarine attacks; live-firing practice, *Revenge* firing three rounds from each 15-inch gun at three-quarter charge while steaming at 21.3 knots; musketry courses; and concentrated gunfire practice with all the war drills, although live rounds were not fired.

An epidemic of influenza throughout the fleets had been nipped in the bud by the medical officers while the ships were in Spanish waters, and the regattas in 12-oared cutters and 5-oared whalers could, therefore, be held as usual. In one of these two RMLI privates pulled in a winning crew when the total stakes on the race were £324.[4] Although Marines did not carry out seamen's duties 'when picked for a racing boat's crew . . . they were not likely to be defeated', which puzzled – and continues to puzzle – seamen who thought a boatload of Jollies was 'an occasion for pointed pleasantries'.[5] By the time the fleets anchored in their UK bases, on 21 March, they had sailed 3,000 miles and paid a final tribute to the crew of K5.

Marines, frequently referred to individually aboard ship as 'Royal', were to spend more time at sea than many seamen of the 1920s and 1930s. For these Marines' detachments there were many ceremonials, from the morning parade for 'Colours', when the ensign was raised each day, for guards when local dignitaries visited ships and on the visits of Admirals for inspections or other reasons. The Marines blue uniforms and white helmets were worn for such ceremonies after 1923 (see Appendix 3), but when HMS *Renown* took the Prince of Wales (later King Edward VIII) to the Far East in 1921–2, the detachment wore pre-1914 full service dress of a blue tunic with scarlet facings for the RMA, and scarlet tunics with the royal blue facings for the RMLI.[6] Other major cruises included the voyage of the Special Service Squadron formed for a cruise around the world in 1924, with 600 Marines in the ships' detachments.[7] On such cruises the ships' officers had opportunities to become familiar with foreign waters and to bring back intelligence, as those visiting Tientsin did in 1937 when they first saw a Japanese Landing Ship which was able to launch small assault craft.[8]

Other voyages, like those on the Yangtze, included actions to protect British nationals. HMS *Colombo* stood by off Nicaragua during a revolution before sailing home through three successive hurricanes.[9] No doubt such ravages of the sea are the source in part of all seafarers' calm indifference to the brickbats of a crowd. More often, however, they were praised in the manner of the delegate's plea on behalf of the citizens of Ierossos in north-east Greece, which summed up for many 'very poor . . . who in our great distress' – after an earthquake of 1932, – '[saw] the only angel in this calamity has been the British Fleet . . . [which] is our only hope . . . while the earthquake shocks continue . . .'.[10]

Not all the wild water was found in foreign parts, however, for early in 1924 the young Lord Mountbatten was on duty in *Revenge*.[11] He was called on deck 'when a tornado of rain hit the ship as she lay anchored in Torbay'. It had been a calm night and the awnings were spread, but in the squall the seamen were nipping this way and that to up-boats, drop a second anchor and slope the awnings. But where was Royal? He was on parade, for the detachment fell-in despite the storm and gales of laughter from the seamen, the RM officer reporting his men ready for duty as required.

In the 1920s there were still many hundreds of coaling stations around the world whose stocks were reported in Admiralty orders, and 'Royal' coaled ship with the rest of the crew. He also took part in many other routines of ship life.

Marines, like seamen, lived and ate in their allotted part of the ship, which was their mess decks and known in the Marines' case as 'the barracks'; although anything less spacious than a shore establishment is hard to imagine, for the casings of ventilator shafts, ships' machinery and the low deck-head (ceiling) made the spaces cramped. In these circumstances personal cleanliness was essential, so Royal took a bath daily if there was sufficient water, after which he did his dhobi (laundry). The ship's forced-air draught blew noisily from nozzles along the ducting and sometimes there were no ports opening for fresh air. Nevertheless the mess deck was a cheerful place where Marines made their home, and when possible there were two Sections of the Marines, some fourteen to sixteen men, living as a group in their mess as part of the 'barracks'. This helped to build up the teamwork essential when the Sections landed for action.[1] Each day two Marines took their turn as cooks of the mess, responsible for keeping the mess clean and collecting meals from the galley.

Before 1921 these cooks prepared the food and the galley staff merely cooked it, but after a trial period in HMS *Hawkins*.[2] among other ships, all meals were *prepared* and cooked in the galley. This system was used for the next 40 or so years, until ships were equipped with cafeterias and men no longer ate and slept in their mess. Corporals, as mess supervisors, did not take a turn as 'cook', while sergeants lived and slung their hammocks in the 'horse box', which had a stable-like door to an area partitioned off from the mess deck. The sergeants' messman, an old Marine, kept the 'Box' clean and tidy, and boy buglers slept there to protect them from bullying or worse in a general mess. Otherwise Royal kept clear of the 'Box'.

The ships' companies were divided into Watches, so that in a two-Watch system those in the Port Watch could relieve the Starboard Watch turn and turn about every four hours at sea. Half the ship's company at other times, the Starboard Watch, say, might be sent on leave. But the system varied and in some capital ships there were three Watches – Red, White and Blue. Some men in each detachment were also designated as watch keepers, who for a three-month period would do special duties, as explained later, but in normal harbour routine Royal would have lashed up and stowed his hammock before turning-to at 0600 hours for an hour scrubbing the officers' flats – those passages and landings around the officers' cabins aft. Between 0700 and 0800 he shaved and had breakfast before falling in with the other non-watchkeepers of the detachment, when the ship's company paraded at 0800 Divisions. The men would be inspected and then fall out to go to 'Cleaning quarters'. Royal might be a gun-sweeper responsible for the general cleanliness of a gun, or a turret- or magazine-sweeper among other duties. In this way each Marine had a specific general duty if he was not a watch-keeper, and whatever his routine duties he had an action station – when a turret-sweeper might be a gun-loading number or a magazine-sweeper have his position in loading charges into the hoist.

In the daily routine, however, he was piped – a boatswain's pipe shrilled for attention before orders over the Tannoy when no bugler was aboard – at 1000 hours to 'stand easy' for ten minutes. This was the time for a smoke and to read your mail, before the pipe 'hands to quarters clean guns' that sent every man to his action station for half an hour.[3] The rest of the morning was spent at general cleaning quarters, the cooks of the mess collecting the rum ration at noon after 1100 pipe for 'up spirits' (an issue which ceased in 1970). In the 1920s and 1930s afternoons from 1400 to 1600 hours were spent in gun drill, cleaning and sport, while on Wednesdays in harbour all the ship's company had a make-and-mend when you darned your socks or took part in sports. Tea at 1630 hours was often slices of bread, jam, 'herrings-in' on Saturdays and that sugary sweet tea made from condensed milk that had its own special flavour from a china dish.

In his free time Royal might play Uckers, a form of Ludo on a board 4ft square with 'dice and other appurtenances . . . in proportion'. In one match 'after opening ceremonies, i.e. muscle exercise and war dance, we lost the toss'.[4] This Team from *Warspite* also lost the game against *Iron Duke*, attributing the defeat to 'bad visibility, probably caused by coal dust; inability of our dice to accustom itself to chunks of fuel lying about . . . and marking . . . our marker has since studied theories to try and obtain "Six" from "Five"'. The last meal of the day was supper – cold meat and salad perhaps – served at 1830.[5] At 2100 (2030 at sea) came evening rounds, when the Duty Officer in harbour or the Commander at sea went through the ship to check all was in order. On Saturday mornings the ship's captain made these rounds, with a thorough inspection of all quarters and hands in the ship. Then it was extra duties for any Royal who had left his washing to dry on a steam pipe, although this was a rare event as the OCRM's daily rounds of the 'barracks' made sure Royal knew what the ship's captain expected. Sunday was a day of rest after Divisions (the morning church parade on the upper deck). A day of rest, that is, for all but the watch keepers.

The watch keepers included keyboard sentries, guarding four keyboards in HMS *Hood*.[6] From these were issued magazine keys to named officers, but not accepted on return if the indicator light at the board was lit to show that the magazine had not been locked. There were 'X' keys for compartments normally used only in working hours and other groups of keys, all of which had to be entered in a register on any issue or return. Other watch keepers included the corporal-of-the-gangway who helped the duty Regulating Petty Officer search men coming aboard, making it harder to get a bottle into a ship than a ship into a bottle. In harbour the corporal – often a Marine given the authority of a corporal for these duties – had other administrative work to carry out, while at sea he was the captain's messenger. Watch keepers who were sentries included the jetty sentry in harbour. At sea he was a lifebuoy sentry stationed aft, where he could release one or two life buoys if he saw a man in the water, or was ordered by the officer of the watch to release the port or starboard buoy.[7] He had also to make sure at night that the stern light was burning. Other sentries were posted from time to time, as was the focsle sentry on *Sussex* with 20 rounds of .303-in during the night hours to prevent boats making fast to the mooring cable and buoy, although he was not to open fire without orders from the Officer of the Watch.[8]

The round of watches for a sentry or other watch keepers was based on periods of 4 hours 'on' and 4 hours 'off' during one period of 24 hours, followed by a day's stand-off. The third day he did four 'on' and four 'off', followed by 36 hours stand-off. There were, therefore, four Marines required for each watch keeper's duty covering every 24 hours. A man might then stand the 'forenoon' (0800 to 1200 hours), the 'dogs' (1600 to 2000) and the 'middle' (2359 to 0400) and be on stand-off until the next 'afternoon' watch (1200 to 1600), followed by duty on the 'first' (2000 to 2359) and the 'morning' (0400 to 0800), after which he could go ashore on the 0900 liberty (leave) boat if he was not required for ceremonial guards or gun drills.[9] At sea or in a two-Watch system, the 'dogs' were used to prevent a man standing the same watches every 24 hours – he stood the 1st dog (1600 to 1800) one day and the last (1800 to 2000) the next, (this last dog watch was known as the 2nd dog watch in the Merchant Navy). During the 36 hours he was not watch keeping, Royal in the Mediterranean in the 1930s did not have to be back aboard until 1100 hours the following day. He might take a 'run' ashore in his best rig with a swagger cane and belt, for civilian clothing was not worn by the lower-deck personnel when going ashore until the 1950s. 'Runs ashore', not physical marathons in the run-with-your-feet sense, although perhaps exhausting in other ways, were the Navy's term for short-leave periods. In Malta the 'run' might take Royal down Strada Stretta, the Gut in Valetta. 'Come inside, Royal' was the plea here from cheerful girls touting for bar business. 'All your crew are here', she would call, although there might only be a couple of *matelots* in the gloom of the bar behind the brightly lit café front, one of the dozens stretching either side of the street. Beer was 2d ($^2/_3$p) a pint here in 1936 and a bed cost 6d (2½p) when a Marine's pay was 3/-s (15p or 30 US cents) a day.[10] Royal, if he went inside a bar, was jostled by the girls in horseplay or more fleshly delights if he chose. Although the girls to many a young Marine appeared older than they were, this did not deter the suitors from brawls when in their cups. Riots would be too provocative a description of these fracases, but Provost Marshals like Major D.A.C. Shephard with his boxer's appearance quelled such disturbances in the 1930s without fuss, as did his Assistant Provost Captain C.S. Watson. Both were Physical Training Officers, well able to look after the most cantankerous stoker or 'stroppy' Marine.

The ship's detachment also provided Marine Officer's Attendants (MOAs) and Wardroom Attendants (WRAs), who kept their officers' cabins clean and valeted their clothes. As gunnery ratings they also took part in practically all gun drills, and when the detachment landed they might act as field orderlies to the OCRM (Officer Commanding RMs) and his lieutenants. The officer/MOA relationship was one of personal friendship, and at least one has been heard to swear at his officer's incompetence in getting a dress tunic wet – man to man in the officer's cabin. In flag ships of battle fleets the Marines also provided three Admirals' orderlies and three orderlies to fetch and carry messages for his office staff.

Officers between the Wars of 1918 and 1939 found in the Mediterranean Fleet a lingering Edwardian gaiety. There was polo in Malta – HMS *Warspite* carried some ponies[11] there in the early 1930s – and later in Alexandria there was a craze for roller-skating hockey.

The more serious purposes of the crews were tested in 'General Drills' held when all the ships of a fleet were assembled in an anchorage, on a Monday forenoon in the 1920s but on any unexpected day in later years. The Admiral would signal 'Weigh anchor by hand' or 'Prepare to take a tow' or – for Royal's special delight – 'Land a platoon of Marines in full kit at . . .'. 'Prepare for collision' brought 30 or so of *Hood*'s Marines to the rails with a many-tonned collision mat they had to manhandle into position, for this great 'rug' could cover a gash in the ship's side after a collision. These evolutions were almost a sport, although no less keenly executed even if the order was 'Two fried eggs to the flag ship'. For Joey, the RM junior officer, his service future might hang on the outcome of his detachment's efforts; and a ship's commander, as executive officer, put his future on the line in every evolution. Mention of young Joey leads to those confusions of titles by which Royal Marine officers and NCOs were frequently known: the senior marine captain was known aboard as 'Major', and the senior sergeant as 'Sergeant Major' – although seamen frequently referred to this NCO as 'Major'.

Gunnery exercises from 1919 were directed towards improving gunnery control and the concentration of fire in the target area. Live firing exercises always had – and have – their dangers, as when HMS *Devonshire* was carrying out single ship firing with her main armament on 26 July 1929, the first broadside from her twin 8-inch being fired at about 1000 hours.[12] Almost simultaneously a sheet of flame rose from 'X' turret manned by Marines, blowing the turret roof into the sea. Captain J.A. Bath, DSC, and 15 men were killed outright or died of their injuries, as did a Naval ordnance artificer, and all but one of the rest of the gun's crew were seriously injured. The uninjured survivor, Marine Albert Streams, clambered out of the smoke over the turret top after the first shock of the explosion, but he went back into the suffocating darkness of the billowing smoke and fumes. He ignored the obvious risk of further explosions from the charges in the hoist and handling room 'deliberately endangering his own life to save others',[13] a gallant act for which he was awarded the Albert Medal. He was later killed in action with 40 Commando in 1943.

The cause of the accident was probably a hang-fire – when the cordite did not explode immediately – in one gun, which the crew had not realised in their reflex actions of a well-drilled team firing every 8 or 10 seconds, although the gun had not recoiled before the breach was opened at the moment the charge exploded after a hung-fire delay. Subsequently a hang-fire latch was fitted to prevent any breech being opened accidentally in action until after the gun had recoiled. At other times Royal took some chances to be sure his turret excelled in firing practice. For instance, when the air blast mechanism clearing the fumes from a turret after a round was fired broke down in a live-round shoot by HMS *Hood*, the Marine crews, despite the fumes and smoke that choked the turret, got off three salvos to match the seamen's fire from other turrets.[14] By 1930 the Mediterranean Fleet had established an RM Strike Force of two battalions drawn from ships' detachments.[15] Each company of these battalions was provided by pairing battleships. Every year, when fleet deployments allowed, a Strike Force landing was practised, but understandably the captains of ships disliked losing the major portion of their Marine gunners for landings, a problem we shall see becoming a crucial factor in the Corps' commitments at the start of World War II.

The Marines were usually landed in oared cutters, and typically, in a night landing on 2 July 1929, they came ashore with their own Signals Section and two Naval wireless sets for contact with the fleet. They were ashore for three days, although each night they came off before sunset to avoid malaria-carrying mosquitoes. Their only transport was specially designed folding handcarts for medium machine guns, and in a similar exercise the following year the companies ran out of water by noon on the day they landed.[16] But by 1931 general training in the fleets was restricted by cuts in government expenditure which limited rounds for live firing, the fuel for sea-time, and had more serious consequences.

The Government's cuts must be understood against the background of a world-wide trade depression, which in 1926 had led to the British general strike. In this the Marines guarded sailors operating essential services, with, for example, a machine gun from *Warspite* mounted at a Glasgow dockyard gate,[1] and a hastily raised RM Battalion[2] protecting the ammunition wharf in Portsmouth. The men received supplementary allowances while standing by in such industrial emergencies.[3]

By 1931 there were 2½ million unemployed.[4]

Wage cuts proposed by the May Committee that year fell more heavily on the lower-deck seamen and Marines than on senior officers.[5] For those Marines who had joined after 1921, with 'X' numbers and known as 'Jixxers',[6] their pay at 4/6d (22½p) a day after 6 years' service[7] would be cut by 1/-s (5p), as was the pay of those on the higher pre-1921 rates. The resulting hardship to their families understandably put seamen (on similar rates) and the Marines in an ugly mood. The tune, if not the words, of 'The Red Flag' was heard by one corporal-of-the-gangway, and ashore there were meetings in the canteen at Inver-gordon (Ross and Cromarty), although these were not the organised affairs some participants later claimed.[8] On Monday night, 13 September 1931, an RN lieuten-ant with a shore patrol from HMS *Valiant* came into one of these meetings and 'a pint pot was thrown at the lieutenant by some idiot but did no damage'.[9] The men went off to their ships but next morning aboard *Valiant* no one turned-to, and the Commander told the RM Officers to leave their men on the mess deck. Some other ships also mutinied, although the Marines and seamen then went about their duties without supervision. But in the next day or so an Admiralty Fleet Order was read to the effect that '... the Admiralty is fully alive to ... [the] special hardship ... from the reduction of pay ... [and] investigations ... [will be] made ... with a view to necessary alleviation ...',[10] for these investi-gations the ships were to sail to their own ports. Whether or not the individual Marines who refused duty were set back in their careers is hard to prove, but there is no evidence of bitterness nor overreaction by officers or men at the time of the mutiny or later.

The mutiny had resulted as much from a series of inept communications as from the unfairness of the cuts. For the men had first heard about these over the BBC radio, as cuts affecting 71 per cent of the Royal Navy but far fewer other service personnel and only 20 per cent of the Civil Service.[11] The outcome was a smaller reduction for the seamen and Marines than had been proposed; subsequently any sweeping changes in conditions of service were considered with growing understanding, as when senior officers in the Corps took steps to meet the needs of Marines' home commitments in the late 1930s when there were fewer UK postings.

Whether or not the Ten Year Rule of 1919 to 1932 created a fixed state of mind in defence departments, as Lord Hankey later suggested, there is no doubt that in the inter-war years British 'planning lacked the point of reference which military action or its prospect provides'.[1] The initial rearmament was mainly directed at increasing the size of the RAF 'as other countries were increasing spending on air power'.[2] Naval plans were hedged about by various treaty negotiations – the London Conferences of 1929–30 and 1935, the Anglo-German Agreement of June 1935 – but when the prospect of war became clear, five *King George V*-class battleships were ordered. Their keels were laid in the years 1936–8 and each would require a Marine detachment of 250 or more as additional anti-aircraft defences were added.[3] Further plans for four *Lion*-class battleships to follow the KGVs were made and not abandoned until 1940. The Admiralty, therefore, expected an additional 2,500 Marines – five wartime Commandos' worth – would be required by 1940 for sea service in capital ships.[4] The cruisers added to the fleet would also require some 1,500 Marines, absorbing most if not all the increased manpower when the Corps' strength was raised in 1938.

General Sir William W. Godfrey, KCB, CMG, who was Adjutant General of the Royal Marines from 1936 until the outbreak of World War II, was only once approached by senior Naval Officers for an opinion on the employment of Royal Marines in wartime.[5] At this meeting the First Sea Lord explained that the Admiralty required a Mobile Naval Base Defence Organisation (MNBDO) and a striking force of a brigade to be ready for action in 1939, but the bulk of the Corps would be deployed at sea when the Naval staffs were 'contemplating war as an affair on the High Seas'.[6] The Adjutant General in those years was on the staff of the Second Sea Lord, whose responsibilities were mainly concerned with personnel,[7] an indication of the Admiralty's view of the Corps as a source of manpower for ships' guns, at a time when senior Naval Officers were less ready to discuss with their staffs matters of policy than they were during World War II.[8] Such attitudes in part explain why the Admiralty – responsible up to 1940 for all amphibious operations – failed to make use of Marines in this role, although General Sir William Godfrey was a firm believer in the value of raids by 'a striking force of Marines *to work with the fleet*' (his italics),[9] a role he had planned for a Marine battalion in 1916, but not carried through when they were withdrawn from the Mediterranean.[10] Typical of Adjutant Generals of those years, Sir William had been one of the three Marines to attend the *first* Naval staff course in 1912.[11] He served on the planning staff in the Dardanelles in 1915–16, and in the Admiralty Plans Division during 1924–7, and therefore like many senior Marine officers had seen service outside the Corps. He had also been a Royal Marine ADC to the King from 1934 to 1935. But no senior officer above the rank of major serving in 1939 – except Brig Tripp, as mentioned in Chapter 2 – had held operational command of more than a detachment. However, that is not to say they did not fully appreciate the rigours of war, for almost without exception they had served in World War I.

For junior officers there were the prospects of action against the Italians in the 1930s. This had helped to sharpen their detachments' training, but many had found shipboard life a little flat if enjoyable.[12] The Navy had moved the nucleus of the MNBDO units to Alexandria in 1935, when the Admiralty was contemplating the use of Port 'X', probably in the Greek Bay of Navarino, if French ports were not available and Italian air raids neutralised Malta. Before the MNBDO could be moved to Port 'X', however, the Admiralty abandoned the plan, as Italian aircraft could put any ships there at needless risk.[13] Major exercises and cruises were also cancelled, for ships were needed in strategic centres – HMS *Devonshire* had passed through the Hellespont when she was recalled 'at all speed' before she could show the flag in Black Sea ports.[14] The annual joint exercise by the Atlantic and Mediterranean Fleets was also cancelled that spring of 1936,[15] although to placate the Maltese traders a token force visited the island, deprived as it was of the usual fleet visits after a spring cruise.

The groundwork for British Naval victories of World War II had been largely prepared by this time, in particular in techniques for night actions, which the Grand Fleet had avoided in 1916–17.[16] By the 1930s the use of star shells and controlled searchlights lessened the risks of major ships' exposure to unseen MTBs or destroyers suddenly streaking through the night to launch torpedoes. Fleets also now turned into an enemy's torpedo attack to present a narrow target as quickly as possible, and the coordination of ships' activities by wireless had been revolutionised by Lord Mountbatten when he was Mediterranean Fleet Signals Officer. Marines served as signallers in the fleets, and before 1923 flag battleships had carried an RMLI signals instructor and an RMA signaller; other capital ships carried two RM signallers and all vessels 'allowed an RM Officer' carried at least one signaller 'proficient in flag signals, semaphore, buzzer [W/T], lamp and shuttered [searchlight] signalling'.[17] Marine signallers also had to be familiar with the signal procedures of the Naval Examination Service (NES), whose small craft inspected merchantmen entering harbours in time of war.

Royal saw other actions in the Mediterranean – refugees were rescued from the ravages of the Spanish Civil War; ashore there were security duties in Palestine. There was also a worldwide commitment in the protection of Empire trade routes. By 13 September 1938, for example, in addition to ships in home waters, in the Mediterranean and in China, there were one or two cruisers in San Francisco (California), in Antigua (West Indies), Colombo (Ceylon, modern Sri Lanka),

Montevideo (Uruguay) and Simonstown (South Africa).[18] In those years there were about seven weeks' food stocks in the British Isles, which were dependent on sea routes for its replenishment,[19] a fact not always appreciated by those nations and individuals questioning the size of British fleets. Only the American navy was of comparable size, and in striving in the 1920s to ensure her major warships at least equalled the number and power of those in the Royal Navy, some friction arose between the two services. One Marine remembers HMS *Renown*'s visit to the Philippines in 1922 when 'the US Navy . . . just ignored us'.[20] But these rivalries of the 1920s were largely forgotten by the time war broke out. One British Marine, serving 'as a kind of "lease lend" aboard USS *Alabama*', found the gunnery of a high standard but missed the mess routine of his own ship; for the Americans ate in two sittings in cafeteria style and 'if you hadn't finished when the whistle blew after the first sitting: bad luck'.[21]

Preparations for war, which accelerated in 1939, included the Navy's 'rapid and smooth mobilisation . . . a longstanding tradition', for which exercises had been regularly carried out at all the Grand Divisions (Chatham, Portsmouth and Plymouth) before 1939. RM Reservists and pensioners under 55 were recalled and the fleet's detachments placed on a war footing; the numbers in many detachments were as much as 25 per cent below their peacetime complement, so that the increases were larger than the planned increases, which raised peacetime complements by 30 to 50 per cent.[22] Nevertheless, among the Marines, with some 275 years of sea soldiering behind them, there was the quiet confidence of highly trained men. All those exercises and evolutions, the parade ground drills and ceremonials, had taught Royal the way to go to war. His experience ranged from life in tropical climates to that north of the Arctic Circle. He had learnt to look after himself and his messmates in the minor battles of North Russia, in skirmishes along the banks of the Yangtze, and a hundred other incidents – experiences of sea service which so ably prepared the Marine for his far wider roles in the coming war.

'From Admiralty, most immediate: Commence hostilities at once with Germany.'[1] This signal at 1248 hours on 3 September 1939 opened the Royal Navy's war at sea. Within hours the German submarine U33 sank the liner *Athenia* and 112 lives were lost.[2] There was to be nothing phoney about this war at sea, for within the month some fifty Allied and neutral merchant ships were lost and an aircraft carrier had been torpedoed.

On the day war was declared Winston Churchill returned to the Admiralty as First Lord, a post he had held 25 years previously. Venerating tradition but ridiculing convention he was a champion of the Royal Marines and once described the Corps as having a 'rough tough history'.[3] The Marines' mood was expressed in a cheer by HMS *Curlew*'s detachment at Chatham on hearing war had been declared.[4] They were soon ammunitioning this anti-aircraft cruiser and proud to be the first gun's crew to finish loading their magazine. Within hours they left Chatham to begin the long voyages protecting merchant ships which were the lot of many Naval ships throughout World War II, interspersed – as they were for *Curlew* in Norwegian waters – by hard fought actions.

Among other steps taken to counter enemy submarines – before they began to hunt in packs on 10 October – was the formation of groups to hunt down U-boats. Aircraft carriers in these groups included HMS *Ark Royal*, which on 14 September was attacked west of the Hebrides by U39, unsuccessfully – 'due to torpedo defects'.[5] Meanwhile *Ark* had flown off three Skuas in answer to the SOS of SS *Fanad Head*, and as they flew in over her position, U30 was attempting to sink the merchant ship by gunfire. The submarine crash-dived, and Lieutenant G.B.K. Griffiths, a Royal Marine pilot, and Lieutenant Thurston RN, dived to the attack.[6] As their 100lb bombs hit the water, both exploded on impact – the delay mechanisms were faulty. As the planes were not clear of these blasts, the aircrafts' tail planes were damaged. They crashed. Both pilots swam to the abandoned *Fanad Head* but the two air gunners were unable to escape from the planes before they sank. The submarine resurfaced and a boarding party looking for papers took both pilots prisoner, despite further attacks by Swordfish from *Ark Royal*. Guy Griffiths tried to get a message home to explain the faulty bomb fuse but this defect was not discovered for some months.

The answer to U-boat attacks would be well-defended convoys rather than hunting groups, but before this policy was adopted, the carrier HMS *Courageous* was operating in the Western Approaches and had flown off her planes 300 miles SW of Ireland. As she turned into wind to land them on, Marine Tom Spence was on the mess deck, a narrow passage alongside a hangar.[7] He pulled on his jersey to go on watch manning the 4.7-in HA (High Angle) gun forward high on the bow. There was a dull clang, followed almost immediately by 'all hands prepare to abandon ship'. The 18-year-old Tom Spence scrambled up the ladders to the flight deck as the ship listed to 40 degrees, dodged some rolling aircraft bombs, and went down a line on the ship's side. Other men jumped but some were killed as they hit the ship's side. 'Barnacles ripped my hands . . . but I made it to the swirling water and swam to a raft', he writes. This contraption of canvas-covered buoyancy roped to a lattice-wood floor enabled men to stand waist deep in water inside the raft. For desperate moments Tom Spence was held head down in the press of men already aboard, after they had pulled him inboard over the buoyancy containers. Then the ropes broke and he surfaced to cling on to the raft for an hour before a destroyer picked them up. A corporal had paraded his men from the detachment, these Marines leaning against the heel of the ship to keep their balance until a Naval Officer bellowed 'Royal Marines . . . Shun . . . Dis . . . Miss!' sending them over the side at the double. *Courageous*, hit by two torpedoes from U29, sank in 15 minutes with the loss of the lives of her Captain and 518 crew.[8] All carriers were then withdrawn from the U-boat search. Not until 1943 would the screening of convoys become fully effective, after the key factor was found to be the ratio of escorts to a convoy's perimeter, not to the number of ships.[9] Until then the ships often sailed in relatively small convoys.

Only the supreme courage of their merchant seamen saved the British from defeat in the first two years of total war. They had been joined in the autumn of 1939 by Royal Marine and Royal Naval pensioners who looked after the one or two guns fitted high over the stern of most cargo ships. Their department was DEMS (Defensively Equipped Merchant Ships), which initially provided a single 4.7-in or 4-in gun for most cargo ships to discourage submarines on the surface,[1] although some ships, like SS *Brookwood* (8,500 tons), carried two guns – a 4-in breech loader with a range of 13,500yds and a 12-pounder for anti-aircraft defence with a range of 6,000yds. Her gunner was Harry 'Shiner' Wright, a pensioner, recalled at 50 years of age in August 1939, after 10 years in schools' administration.[2] He saw some paradox in a 28-year-old taking his civilian job, for within 10 weeks of recall Harry Wright was 'out on the exposed gun platform – none too safe a place in a high wind', with the ship rolling at 8 knots through the Bay of Biscay. She was in a Gibraltar-bound convoy of 46 ships, and sailing to Ceuta (Spanish Morocco) with a cargo of coal. Harry Wright liked the Merchant Navy crew – 36 officers and men – 'happy . . . generous to the extreme and very kind hearted', their ages ranging from 18 to 75. John Hopkins, who at one time had served in China, was recalled and served in DEMS, where he was not as happy as in Naval ships. But he stayed a gunner for several voyages although torpedoed twice.[3]

On sailing in ballast to Halifax (Nova Scotia) *Brookwood* had her first live firing practice – a round at 2,000yds, at 6,000yds and at 12,000yds from the 4-inch gun, three rounds from the 12-pounder – all completed in seven minutes from sounding the alarm,[4] a fast time in which the seaman crew had shown an enthusiasm and efficiency that delighted their gunner. Harry Wright was the layer, the Chief Steward was trainer, and an apprentice or other crewman operated the sight-setting wheel to the gunner's command, after the gunner had spotted the fall of shot. The rest of the gun crew were seamen who passed and loaded the ammunition from boxes lashed on the gun platform. When the ship reached Nova Scotia, without any issue of winter clothing, Harry Wright was cold and his guns froze so that a bare hand touching the steelwork would be skinned. Her cargoes of wheat from Halifax, coal to Gibraltar, sugar from Trinidad (West Indies), steel from Sydney (Australia) meant many weeks at sea and some action. Coming down the Channel in mid-July 1940, *Brookwood* was attacked by bombers in one of a series of air attacks that sank 40 Allied ships that month.[5] Harry Wright found his crew 'were splendid in action especially the young apprentices' and the ship was not hit.

On the next voyage, one night at 2315 hours (23 August 1940) he was blown out of his bunk – 'the cabin sides were bulging in and the bulkhead was falling . . . [after] struggling into a few clothes and my life-jacket, I rushed on deck'.[6] The night was dark and heavy waves were washing the only undamaged lifeboat against the ship's side. But the seamen got her away with 31 men aboard the 27ft boat and five men in a jolly boat towed astern. They had 700 miles to sail to Ireland and were five days making 250 miles, each existing in agonies of thirst on two beakers of water and one and a half biscuits a day. Being off the trade routes, they did not expect anyone to see 'our signals . . . wet to the skin . . .

sometimes with the sea dashing us about, at others hardly moving in the dead calm . . . we were pretty well all in . . .'.[7] But, in the oily grey of a calm dawn, a lookout on SS *Clan MacBean* scanned his sector of the horizon, his powerful binoculars picking up the tiny sail of the lifeboat. In 20 minutes or so the *Brookwood*'s survivors were aboard the Clan ship for a hot meal and dry clothing. Next day Harry Wright volunteered to help her gun crew of three stewards, who had only completed a short gunnery course. They were closed-up at the gun that evening but did not fire at the faint blur of a distant U-boat on the surface charging her batteries. Harry Wright returned to a shore job being no longer fit for sea service, an MSM added to the DSM he had won landing at Zeebrugge (Belgium) in 1918.

Other Marines serving in DEMS were also held in high regard by the crews of the ships they defended. The gunner aboard SS *Avoceta* (3,000 tons) fired his machine gun at an approaching torpedo although he failed to explode it. He held his fire on another occasion 'despite the German bullets coming straight at us' as a German bomber flew in low over the ship. 'Then he let them have a drum'[8] and smoke streamed from the aircraft. A month or two later, when the afterdeck of *Avoceta* was set ablaze during an air raid on Liverpool docks, the gunner was the first man to get a hose playing on the ammunition in the ready-use lockers. Later he is believed to have been drowned when the ship was sunk on her next voyage, after being 'torpedoed in a gale in the Atlantic'. His old shipmate, a merchant seaman, honoured his memory in a letter: 'Arthur never turned a hair' whatever happened.[9]

Major sea and air battles would be fought off Norway in April 1940, but before then HMS *Royal Oak*, an R-class battleship, was sunk on 14 October 1939 in the Fleet anchorage at Scapa Flow. U47, on the surface, penetrated the barrier of blockships, dived into the Sound and made three attacks, the last of which put three torpedoes into *Royal Oak*.[1] She capsized 13 minutes later with the loss 833 lives, including many from her Royal Marine detachment. The fleet base was then moved to Loch Ewe (Ross and Cromarty) on the West coast of Scotland, as anticipated by the Germans, who mined the approaches, seriously damaging HMS *Nelson* and the cruiser HMS *Belfast* before early December. Other German naval initiatives were to put the pocket-battleship *Admiral Graf Spee* and a number of other raiders among the shipping routes of the South Atlantic and Indian Ocean. German capital ships also made several sorties into the Atlantic, sinking the auxiliary cruiser HMS *Rawalpindi* on 23 November 1939.

Graf Spee was hunted by several groups of warships, including Force G – HMS *Ajax*, HMS *Achilles* and HMS *Exeter*. Patrolling along the Atlantic coast of South America, they were 1,000 miles from the nearest British base. Under the Geneva Convention they were only allowed to call in a neutral port once every three months for fuel.[2] On 13 December 1939 the Force was concentrated 150 miles off the estuary of the River Plate, the south-east wind was moderate and the sea slight – the day dawned as a pleasant morning. Commodore (later Rear-Admiral Sir) H.H. Harwood, RN, his flag in *Ajax*, had planned the tactics for a daylight battle: the Force would divide into two divisions, each swinging to a flank so that they could spot each other's fall of shot, and give the German gunnery control the problem of dispersed targets. On 12 December they had a trial run and the Commodore's final words to his captains were to act in the coming battle 'without further orders so as to maintain a decisive gun range'.[3]

At 0608 on 13 December *Ajax* reported smoke to the north-west and *Exeter* was sent to investigate, reporting in a few minutes: 'I think it is a pocket-battleship'. Action stations were sounded on all three cruisers. Sergeant Sammy Shale of *Ajax* saw a great column of water erupt just astern of the ship, before he swung through the door of 'B' turret to his action station.[4] But *Exeter* was taking the brunt of *Graf Spee*'s fire as both the battleship's 280-mm triple-gun turrets opened up at 19,400yds. *Exeter*, nevertheless, continued on her westward course, while her smaller consorts – following the plan – moved towards the north-east, as *Graf Spee* headed towards them.

Graf Spee's 280-mm turrets – one forward, one aft – took 20 to 25 seconds to reload, and were therefore fired alternately to get a bracket on the fast-moving cruisers.[5] But a few early salvos of 280-mm were apparently also fired at *Achilles*.[6] All the ships were weaving their courses to confuse enemy fire controls, *Graf Spee* also dropping smoke floats to add to the confusion. The German main armament fire was accurate, helped by ranges from *Spee*'s radar, although it was not carried primarily for gunnery; and this was to be one of the last major actions in which British ships did not carry such equipment. *Exeter*'s fire opened at 0620 within two minutes of *Spee*,[7] the two forward twin 8-inch firing at about 19,000yds with the range closing rapidly; 2½ minutes later the two after turrets could bear and fired. With her third salvo, *Spee* straddled the *Exeter*, and 5 minutes from *Spee* opening fire a shell burst abreast of *Exeter*'s midships torpedo tubes. The splinters killed the port torpedo tubes' crew and damaged the ship's communications. One minute later a 280-mm shell hit 'B' turret between the guns, killing or wounding the gun's crew.[8] Splinters from the shell also killed or wounded all but the Captain and two others on the bridge. *Exeter*, however, got three 8-inch shells in direct hits on the battleship. Then, at 0632, after 12 minutes of intense action, *Exeter* fired her starboard torpedoes.[9] They went wide as *Graf Spee* turned 150 degrees to steam north-east behind a smokescreen. Five minutes later as *Exeter* turned to bring her port torpedoes to bear, a shell hit forward.

In the shell room of 'B' turret, Marine W. (Bill) T. Austin 'heard a loud crack and smoke issued from the voice pipe'.[10] He was sent to report to the T/S that 'B' turret was out of action. The 'B' magazine was cleared of its crew, and with the shell room hands, they joined the firefighting parties. Bill Austin was with one of these on the Marine mess deck when 'an 11-inch shell came through the port side forward below the Marines' mess deck ... travelled aft ...' and exploded in the POs' mess, the flash travelling up through a hatch. Being nearest to this hatchway, Bill Austin was badly burnt on his hands and face, his blue serge jacket turning brown. Two Marines got him to the comparative safety of the upper deck, where he met Sergeant W.A. (Tubby) Russell. The last man out of 'B' turret, despite losing a hand and severe wounds to both arms, Tubby Russell 'was standing around bright and cheerful as always'.[11]

Another shell had hit the forward 'A' turret, leaving only *Exeter*'s after turret still in action. Control was difficult, as there was a 7-degree list to starboard,[12] and messengers carried what little communication was possible aboard, but *Exeter* continued at full power to maintain contact with the enemy. The after turret was in action until its magazine flooded, but by then she was falling behind in what had become a chase; for since the action began, *Achilles* and *Ajax* had striven to cripple – if they might not sink – the *Graf Spee*. Despite her secondary armament of 150-mm guns firing steadily, if inaccurately, at the two 6-inch gunned cruisers, they kept up a spirited fire. About a quarter of an hour into the action *Spee* had brought one of her 280-mm turrets to bear on *Ajax*, which was also controlling the fire of *Achilles*. Straddled but not hit, *Ajax* had given some relief to *Exeter*, and when *Achilles* had a heavy shell fall nearby and in line with her bridge, the Germans had clearly been forced to divide the targets of their main armament. Splinters from this last shell, although it fell short, penetrated the director control tower, and it 'resembled a busy day at the slaughterhouse'.[13] Concussion and six pieces of shell had caused the damage – the Gunnery Officer, Lieutenant-Commander Richard Washbourne, RN, was wounded, as was his 'spotter' Sergeant S. (Sam) J. Tribble and the operator of the PIL FT 27 which was part of the gunnery controls. Three men were dead, both telephonists and the range-to-elevation-and-deflection (R to ED) operator, whose natural position where he sat led to several rounds being fired before the Gunnery Officer realised he was dead. The after control position (ACP) took over briefly until replacements could take over from the main director's crew, but, despite a severe wound, Sam Tribble remained at his post.

Fire from both cruisers continued at a high rate.[14] the range at times falling to 8,000yds, and *Ajax* catapulted off her aircraft despite the buffeting the pilot and observer took from the blast of the ship's guns.[15] When *Achilles* had a brief breakdown in 'B' turret, its crew fired a solid-shot practice round, later – by one report – found in *Graf Spee*'s wardroom.[16] More serious was a wireless breakdown, and during the ensuing misunderstanding, both ships' gunners lost accuracy for a time, but the range, now 16,000yds, was found again at 0708. *Ajax* was hit twice in the next half-hour, and she, like *Achilles*, was running out of ammunition, having fired most of her 6-inch shells and several torpedoes. Therefore, Commodore Harden disengaged the Force, *Achilles* and *Ajax* taking station to shadow the *Graf Spee*. The Commodore hoped that the battle might be renewed when there was a better chance of close action after dark.[17] The day then passed with minor incidents: *Ajax* skilfully recovered her plane, and *Achilles*, at one time too close for *Graf Spee*'s liking, was fired on but not hit. Towards dusk Captain J. Lampen, HA Director of *Achilles*, could 'clearly see the *Graf Spee* against the red of the evening sky' as his ship closed the range 'and an exchange of shots took place at 11,000yds'.[18] But just before midnight the chase was called off as *Graf Spee* was entering Montevideo (Uruguay). Four days later her crew blew her up in the estuary. By then the British wounded had been evacuated to the Falkland Islands, where sadly Tubby Russell died of his wounds.

The damage to the *Graf Spee* had been less than expected, for only one of her 150-mm guns had been knocked out,[19] with 36 men killed and 60 wounded.[20] Once again the heavier gunned ship had proved decisive in a sea battle, for only half the three cruisers' main guns were still in battle trim. The expected approach of HMS *Renown* with her 15-inch guns, and the planes from HMS *Ark Royal*, persuaded Kapitan Langsdorf to destroy his ship. She had in her raiding sunk nine ships totalling 50,000 tons,[21] and might well have destroyed the three cruisers of Force G had not Commodore Harwood and his Captains – Captain F.S. Bell, RN (*Exeter*), Captain C.H.L. Woodhouse, RN (*Ajax*) and Captain W.E. Parry RN, (*Achilles*) – handled their ships with great skill and daring. The Commodore made, for example, small alterations of helm *towards* each salvo as it fell, causing the next one to miss.[22] In a further piece of fine seamanship, *Exeter*, made watertight by some remarkable damage repairs, sailed for the UK, arriving on 14 February 1940.

In his report to the Admiralty the Commodore commented: 'The main impression left in my mind is of the adequacy of our peace training. Little that had not been practised occurred'.[23]

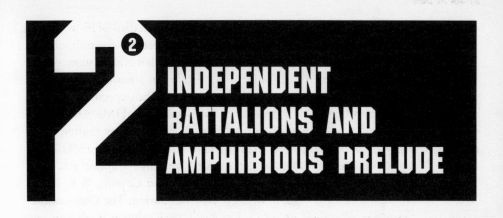

2 INDEPENDENT BATTALIONS AND AMPHIBIOUS PRELUDE

The icy wind continued to make breathing difficult and chilled the bones despite Lt Stephens's Arctic clothing.[1] He and Lieutenant R. C. Carvell were with their CO, acting-Captain C. R. Lane, who commanded an advanced party of 50 Marines. They were travelling by rail to Kandalaksha on the White Sea to set up a ski-training centre for the RM Field Force. This Force had been sent to north Russia in May 1918 when the Admiralty feared that German submarines might operate during the summer from ports on the Barents Sea.[2] In the confused situation of the northern campaigns, which included *Dauntless*'s actions in the Baltic, the Field Force had been in action against pro-German and pro-Bolshevik forces in the Murmansk region north of the Arctic Circle. By January 1919, these Marines were to form one of seven mobile columns[3] and were equipped with Arctic gear. They carried Westinghouse American rifles using .300-inch ammunition, considered more suitable than the SMLE for use in temperatures often 40 degrees Centigrade below zero.

The distances this Force had covered in 1918 show something of the vastness of Russia, although they were only in the Murmansk region, where the principal town, Murmansk, is 400 miles by air from Archangel to the south-east, and almost as far from Moscow at 1,250+ miles as is Berlin. In this relatively small corner of Russia, however, elements of the Force: had restored order in Kem,[4] over 300 miles south down the single railway track from Murmansk; led Karelians and Finnish troops in skirmishes some 100 miles west of Murmansk; and served with the Naval force on the Dwina river, navigable for several hundred miles in the summer from its estuary near Archangel. The Force's main task in 1918 had been to guard 500 miles of railway tracks running south to Soroka (near modern Belomorsk),[5] nearly sufficient railway line to join Paris and Berlin. The five control points they set up on this line included two as far apart as Plymouth and Portsmouth. Yet the Force never had more than 360 Marines in the field, with four 12-pdr and six Lewis guns.

On New Year's Day 1919 the officers of the advanced party for the ski-training centre had got off the train to stretch their legs when it unexpectedly moved on. They had no choice but to march along the railway, a 7-hour trudge through the sharp cold until a passing engine picked them up. Their destination,

Kandalaksha, turned out to be 'rather chaotic' but by mid-January ski-training was under way with two experienced instructors, Lieutenant Stephens and Sergeant Jordan.[6] The training area 8 miles south of the town was in a heavily wooded locality and a more suitable site was later found on the frozen sea at Popoff, the port of Kem. Here, during the next three months, 200 Marines became passable skiers able to fire their rifles on the move or take more accurate aim when their ski-sticks made a bipod. They 'lived like Eskimos' during snow warfare exercises and at other times 'platoon drill [on skis] was carried out as if on parade'.[7] The Force was concentrated for this training but the last men from guard duties in Murmansk did not arrive until 10 March.

The extreme cold must have limited the skiers' exertions, for in these temperatures you cannot take off a glove for a couple of moments without risking frostbite and the wind-proof hood of the Burberry suits had to be drawn closely around the face to protect a man's ears.[8] But the weather was often dry, with little or no wind. Before they could operate as ski-troops, however, over half the Force was called away to garrison Kem, and although the expected attack did not develop, the thaw set it. Nearly 40 years would pass before Marines again trained as ski-troops, but the Field Force had shown how adaptable a Marine can be in Arctic cold.

By April 1919 the Murmansk Allied Command had been organised as a division of 15,000 men – 7,000 British, including the Marines, with some 8,000 French, Italian, Serbian and Karelian troops. Three columns from the division were to advance in May on a 60-mile front in two 'bounds', with the object of making a limited advance to Lake Onega,[9] blocking possible Bolshevik advances towards Murmansk and providing a narrower front to guard, for the Finnish frontier was only 50 miles from the north-west corner of the lake. The GOC, Major General Sir C. Maynard, also felt that more recruits would join the White Russians from the peasantry of this farming country south of the tundra and forests. The RM Field Force in the central column came under the command of the Army's Colonel Leeky, and were brought by train with a company of French infantry and one of White Russians to a destroyed bridge an hour's ride from Urozery. American engineers were working to repair it. The column then marched down the track, thick forest hemming them in on either side. The 20 Marines helping a Royal Artillery gun team with the column's single 65-mm field gun had heaved it across broken bridges and damaged track before they all halted at midnight, 2–3 May, for a meal from their 48-hour ration packs.

They moved off again at about 0130 hours in pitch darkness, the White Russians leading.[10] When this company brushed against a Bolshevik patrol, the column was halted and waited for daylight. In moving forward after dawn two Marine platoons took the first Bolshevik outpost at about 0800. The going was tough, for the men had to march on the awkward pitch of railway sleepers, which give you an uncomfortably short stride, or force their way through the tangle of timber when seeking cover in the forest. Every time a man lay down and often as he marched, mosquitoes swarmed to sting his face and hands. In the early afternoon all four Marine platoons were in action clearing the second

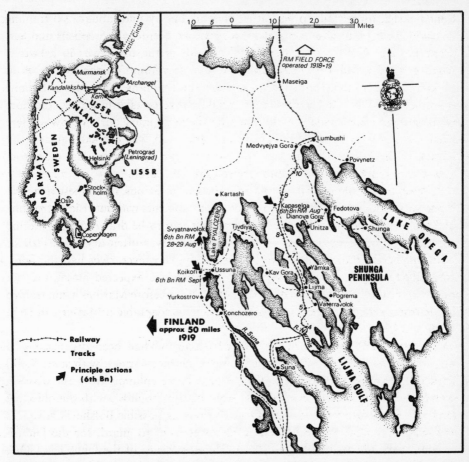

Murmansk region of North Russia in 1919 showing Lake Onega area of operations by 6th RM Battalion.

outpost by 1600 hours, when a bivouac camp was established. The pickets had hardly been put out when an armoured train appeared, its machine gunners killing two Allied sergeants as they attempted with great courage to fling grenades under the engine. It then retired, leaving four of its crew dead.

Next morning the White Russian company was put in reserve, the French took the right flank, the Marines the centre and left of the advance. They had advanced about 3 miles when the train reappeared; the French had lost contact in the thick forest and the Marines were preparing to assault their first major objective – Maselskaya. When the train was about 600yds from the Marines' positions, however, the 65-mm gun got some rounds off over their heads to force it to retire. Then, moving through the forest, they reached the clearing around this small railway centre, in time to see a large engine shed blown up before the Bolsheviks retired. After the column had entered the village, food was found to be short, but the Americans rebuilt 27 bridges in four days to get the first trainload of food into the town since the operations began. While this centre column made its first 'bound', the western column of White Russians and Karelians had acted as a flank guard and reached Karelska Maselga, some 25 miles due west of the RM Field Force. Here on 10 May 30-year-old Major L.A. Drake-Brockman RM was killed leading his Karelian Battalion.[11] He had commanded the RMLI Company of the Field Force before being seconded to the Karelian Regiment with its several battalions of volunteers from independently minded people living west of the White Sea. The Major 'was much loved'[12] by the 4th Battalion he commanded and who successfully drove off Bolshevik counterattacks on the day he was killed.

Twenty miles to the east of the railway, the third column had taken Tolekina and a party of 'White' partisans were even further east by some 30 miles. But this broad front was narrowed to 35 miles for the next 'bound', which moved forward on 15 May.[13] The Marines in the centre column – which had been reinforced by a company of the Middlesex Regiment and one from the King's Royal Rifle Corps – forced the enemy from their outposts after 30 were killed. The enemy then withdrew to a series of entrenchments sited where marshes protected the flanks. The column came up to these defences, and with an improvised armoured train gave covering fire for an attack; the Middlesex and KRRC companies made a successful frontal assault.

Mounting this action had taken 14 hours, exhausting work for men living on meagre rations, so the column rested the next day. The country south of the marsh was better ground for movement but by no means easy to cross, for there were only dirt roads where there was any road at all; patches of marsh were interlaced with the forest fringes and deeper into the woods there were few tracks to follow. The cover of the trees, however, was needed when the enemy's train appeared after the column had moved forward during 17 and 18 May, but once again the 65-mm gun went into action and the train withdrew. Following the train towards its base, the leading RM platoons came in sight of Medvyejya Gora (modern Medvezh' Yegorsk) station,[14] on the northern tip of Lake Onega, a stretch of water over 150 miles long and 50 miles wide in places. This station was taken by the RM Field Force in an action of manoeuvre in tactical stalking rather than direct assault, for the Marines outflanked the Bolshevik outposts and took no casualties in forcing the enemy out of the station buildings. Although these Russians 'were badly trained and led', they left crude booby-traps of dynamite in the fire places of several buildings.[15] In the main village, to the west of the station, the Bolsheviks made a resolute stand but on 21 May were forced out of their positions by an Allied force that included British, French, Italian, Serbian and White Russian troops.

The northern shores of Lake Onega then provided bases for a Naval flotilla, and the advance – timed so enemy gunboats were still iced-up in the lake – held two Russian divisions preparing to advance on Murmansk. But supplying these forward Allied troops had many problems, for nothing but trees and moss grew in the north of the region, so all food had to be shipped to Murmansk before being railed 500 miles to the forward areas. As the single railway line built in 1916 crossed many wooden bridges and passed over innumerable culverts, sabotage was all too easy. Marines mounting guard on food trains might also find they had to keep off Korean and Chinese labourers in Murmansk, hungry Letts or other refugees, and roving bands of ne'er-do-wells who might be fighting for the Allies one day and seeking plunder the next. All food stocks in Medveyeja Gora had been destroyed with the forest around the station set on fire as the retreating Russians followed their customary scorched-earth policy.

The Allied operations had, nevertheless, kept the Germans out of northern Russia in 1918, as a small but active unit like the RM Field Force helped to create the impression that a large force was in the area. The Allied intention had also been to continue operations in the east on other fronts against the Germans after the Russian defences collapsed in 1917, although only at Archangel were there large stocks of Allied war supplies.[16] On these fronts – in the Caspian Sea, in Central Russia and on the Black Sea – Marines were committed in 1918 (see Appendix 4) but after the Allied victory in the west their intervention in Russia changed to 'full-scale support of the anti-Bolshevik forces'.[17] The political implications of this are by no means as clear cut as has sometimes been suggested, for the Bolsheviks seized power and were not an elected government.[18] After the White Russians failed in their attempts to drive south from Archangel, west from Perm in Central Russia and north from the Crimea, the Allied intervention was directed at the evacuation of refugees. Yet long before this final phase, the Allied Command in Paris was understandably hesitant to commit forces to Russia except to cover a final withdrawal.

The RM Field Force had shown signs of indiscipline in the early summer of 1919. These included: 55 men who signed a petition to their CO (Captain Lane) which can only be described as mutinous in tone; a company of the King's Royal Rifle Corps claimed that the Royal Marines had refused to support them in one attack; and later the officer commanding the Force offered to resign his commission. General Maynard commanding the British forces in north Russia signalled to the War Office that he was 'very disappointed in the behaviour of officers and men [of the RM Field Force]' and he sent them to Murmansk 'to await [the] first opportunity for embarkation to England'. The RM Field Force was then withdrawn from northern Russia in July 1919.

These events must be set against a background of broken promises, as the Army staff had on several occasions promised that the RM Field Force would be sent home. A Royal Navy Board of Enquiry later found that these Marines had been 'unsympathetically handled and exploited by the Army'. The Board also recorded that the RM Field Force had been split up under very junior and inexperienced officers.

The 6th Battalion was sent to Murmansk, where it landed on 8 August 1919. It was part of a brigade-sized force sent to relieve the garrisons in northern Russia. This brigade also included two Army infantry battalions, two machine gun companies, a tank detachment and 600 French infantry.[19] The 6th Battalion had been raised for less arduous duties (see Appendix 4). While the Army units were mostly volunteers, the '6th' included many men who had joined for the war with Germany and had expected to be demobilised after the Armistice, they were given a mere three week of training. Their unhappiness was aggravated, no doubt, by fighting in a campaign that was not a full-scale war;[20] and, moreover, a campaign for which there was little or no enthusiasm in most Allied quarters. The Battalion's first major action was on the night of 28–9 August, when C Company moved out of Svyatnavolok in the opening stage of an assault on two Bolshevik concentrations at Koikori and Ussuna.[23] The first contact with the enemy force was made at the junction of the road leading south-west to Koikori and south-east to Ussuna, the enemy withdrawing to the south-west. The Battalion CO, Colonel Kitcat, led 'C' Company after them and reached a hill overlooking the open country that surrounded the village of Koikori. Heavy machine gun fire held up the platoons attempting to get around the village, and a frontal assault would have led to unacceptable casualties, for the few guns supporting the company failed to silence the strongpoints. By nightfall, having lost three killed and 18 wounded, including the Colonel, the company withdrew to its starting point north of the road junction, for its first hot meal after 22 hours in action.

At a meeting on 28–29 August[24] the Army's plan was first explained to the Battalion's officers: General Maynard hoped to drive the Bolshevik forces beyond the line of the river Suna and so leave the White Russians with a sound line of defence when Allied forces withdrew.[25] The Marines were to form a column to the westward of the main drive down railway line, and the assault by 'C' Company had been a preliminary to this. 'B' and 'D' Companies were then moved into the area and were rowed across lakes where possible. Allied planes bombed the road junction – the RAF had been flying six patched-up RE8s and a few other planes since the previous November – in one of the many successful air attacks which they mounted. The enemy withdrew and a firm base was established for renewed assaults on the two defended villages. In addition to the Marine companies there were some 300 Allied troops, five guns, some Army machine gun teams and a Russian battalion of 600 men in reserve, making a force General Maynard felt could roll up the Bolsheviks, allowing White Russians to pass through the Marines to Konchozero. In these actions the Marines were to carry much of their kit with them in full marching order, which in those days included a big pack, and each man carried 'two blankets rolled in a waterproof sheet'; but their steel helmets, and other gear had been left in Kapaselga. There were no portable wireless sets,[26] few permanent telephone lines except along the railway, and the local carts carrying machine guns and ammunition could only move slowly over the dirt roads. The weather, however, was generally pleasant despite the mosquito swarms.

'D' Company moved out from the junction at 0600 hours and was fired on as it neared Ussuna, a few miles south of the road junction. The Marines seized some high ground and the Battalion HQ with two rifle sections attempted to infiltrate eastward around the strongpoints. In doing this, however, they lost contact with the other platoons in the thick woods and fired on some of their own Sections; two Marines pluckily stopped this fire by coming out of their cover. The HQ party was to pass behind the village after Allied seaplanes bombed the defences at 1030 hours, but the Marines were held to the east of the village, and the Company formed a skirmish line by 1330 hours, along the forest edge overlooking open ground around the village. Sergeant J. C. Mumford with a recce patrol got within 80yds of the enemy's positions, which he found defended with barbed wire, concrete machine gun posts and prepared with all the hallmarks of German advice on their siting, good use having been made of hedges. From these positions, despite the party's Lewis gun fire from the left flank and the field guns' shelling, the defences maintained a steady fire. No further advance, therefore, was prudent in view of the orders to company commanders: 'Operations should be taken slowly, casualties can and should be avoided.' The Marines held their positions through the hours of darkness but the enemy had brought up two field guns during the night, and their fire forced the Marines' right flank deeper into the wood.

Meanwhile 'B' and 'C' Companies had attacked Koikori, suffering an equally frustrating day. Their flanking platoons were ambushed when their 'guide' turned out to be an enemy agent.[27] A frontal assault failed to breach the defences – not surprisingly, perhaps, for these two villages were held by 'Red' (pro-Bolshevik) Finns with German advisers.[28] The Marines withdrew at 1700 hours to an outpost line, having lost 10 killed and 23 wounded, including Captain (later Brig, OBE) E.J. Noyes, the second-in-command of 'C' Company.[29]

After these actions a number of men in two companies refused duty, a minor mutiny among several at that time which had nothing to do with ideologies but were in part the result of the Government's ill-considered scheme for demobilisation. Nevertheless the Corps felt the disgrace of this dishonour for many years, after two officers and 89 men had been found guilty by courts martial. Their sentences, which had included 15 death penalties, were later substantially reduced, and the death sentences commuted to terms of imprisonment.[21] No one served more than 15 months but for the long-service Marines of the Battalion, there were also some unfair repercussions, as the list of those who had obeyed orders did not cover men at headquarters many miles from the trouble, all of whom had carried out their orders. Yet for years afterwards some men who had served in the 6th Battalion, although with not the remotest connection to the mutiny, felt their promotion blocked, and one at least took another 10 years to attain the rank of corporal.[22]

Such actions in the campaigns that politicians hope will be fought without somehow becoming full-scale wars are bedevilled with difficulties. Yet there is seldom any way in which you can fight a half-war successfully, and these young Marines of the 6th Battalion had in the main done more than most could achieve in difficult circumstances. Their CO, Colonel Kitkat had not seen active service ashore before taking the Battalion to Russia and a number of his officers and NCOs had not previously been in action. The next 70 years found many a Marine unit faced – as they were even in the late 1990s – with political constraints never imagined by those who fought in the World Wars, when winning the battle took precedence over the finer points of civil liberties.

There are times, nevertheless, when to be effective a government's foreign policy needs some show of military strength. The Bosphoros, Ireland, Turkey and Shanghai each thrust Marine battalions into such a role (see Appendix 4) between the World Wars. It was not always an unpleasant task, for in January 1919 on the shores of the Bosphoros 170 men of the 3rd RM Battalion sunned themselves, ready to man guns in Turkish forts should the Russian civil war spill into the Mediterranean. They had prepared these forts in October 1918 and returned in January 1919, passing a pleasant enough summer despite the heat, before being withdrawn to the UK on 4 November.[30] Soon after this, the Admiralty was to set the Corps different problems, as advanced Naval bases would be required in any major conflict.

General Godfrey, when a Colonel in 1919, lectured on 'Combined Operations' at the Naval Staff College, pointing out that at that time 'without the fleet to assure communications, no British Army can safely leave its native shores'.[1] However, the British, after their experiences in the Dardanelles during 1915–16, were reluctant between the World Wars to consider major landings in planning their future strategy. Yet cooperation between the Army and the Royal Navy in modern concepts of combined operations goes back at least to 1911, the year a joint committee began work on what became the *Handbook of Combined Operations* in 1913.[2] This dealt in eight chapters with the tactical problems of disembarking troops in opposed and other landings. There were other joint services' committees and cooperation that included the Royal Air Force in later years, culminating in the creation of the 1936 Inter-Services Training and Development Centre (ISTDC) described in chapter 3. Meanwhile the Royal Marines' roles in amphibious and other warfare were being examined, for 'their functions . . . [had] never been defined' to quote from one of the 1924 papers submitted to the Madden Committee.[3]

This Committee had been set up after the Adjutant General of the Royal Marines, General Blumberg, had urged in 1922 and again in 1923 – the year the RMA and RMLI were amalgamated – that the roles of the Corps be defined. Indeed Lord Fisher, when Second Sea Lord, had questioned the need for any Marines at all, but a mutiny of sailors in the Naval barracks at Portsmouth caused this enquiry to be dropped.[4] Points raised in the various papers prepared for submission to the Committee bring out a number of revealing truths which indicate the senior Marine officers' awareness of the Corps' problems in 1924 and their determination to solve these difficulties. 'The Marine is trained efficiently in the use of the rifle, Lewis gun etc . . . [but] owing to the time spent at sea, he lacks the practical application in the field.'[5] 'Examination of the services of the Royal Marine officers who held the ranks of Lieutenant-Colonel to General in 1914 . . . [shows that] few proved equal to the leading of men in action on land . . . [because] from the age of say 30 years they were condemned by the system to serve on without opportunities of developing their qualities of command or . . . initiative.'[6] This state of affairs many RM officers had foreseen in 1914, and it was only substantially changed during World War II. To overcome these and other difficulties, including that of finding postings ashore for Marines between their tours of duty at sea, the Adjutant General proposed that Marines should undertake the defence of certain Naval bases.[7] From these units a striking force could then be drawn on to provide 'a most useful reservoir of trained men ... to establish bases in the Pacific when getting to grips with Japan'.[8] These proposals envisaged an increase in the Corps' strength to some 16,000, with only a third at sea at any one time, when 5,333 of the total of 8,588 Marines were currently serving at sea.[9] They also included the strengthening of the Marine element in the embryo Mobile Naval Bases, which we will come back to. Several other aspects of Marines' roles were brought out in the submissions. The landing of Marines, for example, 'has always implied defensive and protective measures of a temporary nature', making them more suitable than Army units 'for policing the Empire';[10] and the need was emphasised for a Marine force in the absence of any decisions in 1924 on the unity of command for future combined operations.[11]

The Committee was chaired by Admiral Sir Charles Madden, a man of intellectual gifts who later became First Sea Lord.[12] Its recommendations broadly followed the Adjutant General's proposals, concluding that 'if the Navy is to be adequately equipped for meeting its liabilities, it must be provided with an efficient Corps of Marines'.[13] Then followed a summary of duties for the Corps that included manning 'their share of ships' gunnery armament' in capital ships and light cruisers, the landing in peacetime of specially trained detachments to protect British interests during disturbances ashore, and the suggestion that in wartime similar forces could 'make use of the command of the sea ... [in] small scale operations'. On mobilisation the Corps could provide a strike force to seize advanced bases and attack enemy lines of communication, supply the Army with units for operations where 'Naval experience is necessary', and take part in landing an Army on a hostile shore.[14]

However, the Government refused to sanction the necessary expenditure,[15] although work on the Mobile Naval Base experiments was allowed to continue. This work originated in a scheme prepared by the Admiralty's staff in April 1920 for a Mobile Naval Base Organisation which 'would permit of advanced bases and war anchorages in any part of the world being occupied and placed in an adequate and efficient state of defence.[16] The strength of one such organisation was envisaged as 259 officers and 3,118 men, including the crews of base ships, and the Royal Marines were to provide its defence force; but the variety of the Corps' operations was little changed, even if they did not have a strike force.

The Corps set up an experimental 'X' Unit[17] to develop techniques for landing heavy guns to defend these advanced bases; their original exercises in a similar role just before World War I had been considered unsatisfactory by Winston Churchill, at that time First Lord of the Admiralty (its political chief) but the Great War had begun before the exercises could be repeated.[18] By 1924, however, there was more suitable if extemporised equipment for landing heavy guns. The experiments were made on a shoestring of £10,000 a year for the years 1924 to 1930, when a Hathi (Elephant) tractor cost £3,000.[19] These tractors, quantities of scaffolding which had, by one report,[20] been rejected by the Army's Royal Engineers, and expertise, were accumulated in the 10 years to 1935. The first experiment, however, was in 'landing weights up to 7 tons or possibly 12 tons on a normal beach' near sites for a base's coast defences.[21] This trial was made on the 1:5 sloping beach of Langstone harbour (near Portsmouth) where a scaffolding jetty had been built with a gyn-type lifting structure of scaffolding which could lift a 4-ton old gun barrel from a horse boat (one of the forerunners of landing craft).

The lessons of this early trial in October 1925 show clearly the unit's awareness of amphibious problems: beach inclines, tidal states, and the structure of landing craft for concentrated loads were all studied. Exercises were held in the following years and by 1932 the unit was landing a light tank from MLC 10 (an early Motor Landing Craft), using a form of beach roadway made from cross-timbers joined by continuous chains, for this tank to cross shingle.[22] Landing the tank through 4ft 6in of water, however, appears to have given difficulties but about 1ft 6in water depths gave no problems. A major exercise was held in 1935 at Lamlash (Isle of Arran) by the unit now called MNBDO Nucleus, with a Captain RN commanding the Base Defences, an RM Lieutenant-Colonel commanding three batteries of coast defence guns – one with 6-in guns, one with 4-in and one with 3-in – and a searchlight section.[23] A Marine Landing, Transport and Workshop company and a Signals Section also served in the Nucleus with a Naval unit for controlled minefields and other specialists. The Hathi tractor drivers needed great skill to push a heavy trailer down the narrow piers, for these vehicles were 5ft wide and a pier might be less than twice this width. Yet few Marines, except those who had served in the transport units of World War I, were used to motor vehicles. But they were keen and tough, all ranks working together without sleep until a pier was built and the guns landed, their language at times on exercises causing visiting 'brass hats to raise their eyebrows'.[24]

In the summer of 1935 the Organisation was brought up to strength within four days on being called to build coast defences for Egypt, 1,600 Marines arriving in Alexandria on 23 September, as part of the inter-service Base Defences Mediterranean commanded by a 'live wire' Royal Marine, Brig W.H.L. Tripp DSO, MC.[25] The force was equipped with boom-nets, controlled sea mines laid by lighters and fired electrically from on shore, four 6-in guns, 33 searchlights and communications equipment.[26] They had completed the main defences by mid-October, and were then held in readiness for the possible occupation of an advanced base, but returned to the UK in July 1936. After their return more money was allocated to the MNBDO and greater emphasis put on anti-aircraft defences. They built defences at Scapa Flow, and elements returned to the Mediterranean briefly in the autumn of 1939 (see Appendix 4), but their first operations were in Norway in 1940.

Both Allied and German operations in Norway were planned to start in the same 24 hours. The British were to lay three minefields in Norwegian waters.[1] The Germans were to invade Norway to secure continuing supplies of Swedish iron-ore shipped in substantial quantities through Narvik, and to establish coastal bases and airfields. The German invasion would eventually comprise over

100,000 men and some 800 aircraft, while the initial British plan 'R4' to counter this threat held 18,000 men in readiness to land once 'the Germans had violated Norwegian neutrality'.[2] To cover the mine-laying and possible landings, a force of British battleships was also available early in April.

The Allied operations have been described as a 'ramshackle campaign', in official reports, but few if any of the routine military intelligence sources appear to have been established, nor should they have been in the days when the implications of total war were not understood by many of Britain's allies. The resulting shambles arose when ships were expected to quickly unload heavy equipment but there were no dockside cranes, or the proposed harbour was even too small for a troopship to come alongside. Events leading up to the main Allied landings[3] foretell the likely confusion and difficulties for an amphibious operation that did not have adequate air cover:

Wednesday – 3 April: Seven freighters, to load fish ostensibly, sail from Hamburg for Narvik, Trondheim and Stavanger, each carrying German military stores, troops and artillery.[4]

Friday – 5 April: RN mine-laying force and escorts leave Scottish waters for Norwegian coast.

Saturday – 6 April: Cruiser HMS *Birmingham* and escorts, looking for German fishing boats off Vest Fjord, move to join mine-laying forces.

Sunday – 7 April: German naval forces, including the battleships *Scharnhorst* and *Gneisenau*, put to sea to cover the invasion; they are first sighted at 0848 hours and subsequent reports during the day lead to British battleships and escorts sailing at 2015 hours to intercept the Germans.

Monday – 8 April: Destroyer HMS *Glowworm*, having become detached from the fleet, is sunk by superior forces but radios their position. A German troop transport is sunk by a Polish submarine but the Norwegian parliament takes no steps to warn its only mobilised forces – the Navy and coast defence units.

The British abandon plan 'R4' and warships of the strike force sail without troops.

Tuesday – 9 April: Germans land in the early hours, surprising the Norwegians at Narvik, Trondheim, Bergen, Kristiansand, Arendal and Oslo, where *Blücher* is sunk by shore batteries in the only setback to the landings, but Oslo is virtually captured by midday.

Gallant resistance at various landings by individual Norwegian ships and units are quickly overwhelmed.

HMS *Renown* had sighted *Scharnhorst* and *Gneisenau* off Vest Fjord in the early hours of the morning, but in the ensuing action these German battleships escaped to the north.

Off Bergen during the afternoon British warships are heavily attacked by German planes and to the north the main Allied Fleet is bombed later this afternoon. An RAF attack on Bergen only achieves some near misses.

Wednesday – 10 April: Many smaller British ships return from the group off Bergen to Scottish bases to refuel.

At 0430 British destroyers begin first of three attacks on ships up the fjord at Narvik – the First Battle of Narvik.

Sixteen Skuas sink *Königsberg* in Bergen at 0700.

At 0730 the battleship HMS *Warspite* and the carrier HMS *Furious* join the group west of Bergen, but priority is given to retaking Narvik.

Thursday – 11 April: *Furious* flies off planes for night attack on Trondheim, but principal target, the cruiser *Admiral Hipper*, has slipped south in heavy seas a few hours earlier. Cruiser HMS *Penelope* is badly holed near Bodö on rocks when searching – as other ships were – for German transports.

Scharnhorst, *Gneisenau* and other German warships avoid British Naval concentrations in the Lofoten Islands and the Trondheim areas. These German ships reach their home waters safely.

First convoy of British Naval ships sails for Narvik.

Friday – 12 April: Warships escort British troop convoy towards Narvik; here *Furious*'s planes launch an attack through heavy snowstorms in the evening but do little damage.

Germans lose 900 men in British submarine attack on a reinforcement convoy for Oslo.

Saturday – 13 April: *Warspite* and nine destroyers enter Narvik Fjord, supported by Swordfish from *Furious*, and drive German destroyers and supply ships aground or sink them in Second Battle of Narvik.

Faroes occupied by 250-strong RM force.

Sunday – 14 April: Force Henry, 350 seamen and Marines, landed with no opposition at Namsos during the evening. Two companies of Guards Brigade land to join Norwegians near Salagen north-east of Narvik.

Monday – 15 April: Germans advance north from Oslo along railway line to Trondheim where other units had earlier seized the port and coast batteries.

HMS *Rodney* and HMS *Renown* return to Scotland, while HMS *Warspite* and *Furious* off Lofoten Islands cover initial landings of Rupert Force – with 6,000 troops, including elements of the Guards Brigade, coming ashore at Harstad.

Tuesday – 16 April: Maurice Force, a British brigade, begins landing this night at Namsos 150 miles north of Trondheim.

Wednesday – 17 April: Primrose Force, over 700 Royal Marines and seamen, land initially to secure the railhead at Åndalsnes, 150 miles south of Trondheim.

Thursday – 18 April: First units of Sickle Force, the reinforcements for Åndalsnes, land.

These events, so briefly summarised, cover two weeks of confused activity. Although Narvik remained a principal prize in the contest, Trondheim was for a time thought by Winston Churchill, among others, to be an equally desirable goal, as the rallying point for Norwegian resistance. The fact that the terrain in northern and central Norway limited all movement by conventional vehicles to the few mainly coast roads of that time does not appear to have been realised, and when available forces were landed north and south of Trondheim, for example, they were never likely to complete a pincer movement. Furthermore, these troops had no training in mountain warfare and – as the Marines of 3 Commando Brigade know in the 1990s – such warfare needs expertise as well as the right equipment. In mid-April 1940, the approach of many staff officers and some senior commanders suggests that they expected the expeditionary forces to land through well-equipped ports. They were then expected to deploy, much as the BEF might do in France or Belgium. Norway, however, poses much more difficult military problems, as we shall see. The Germans mounted their campaign with a speed that astounded many strategists and denied the Allies' later attempts to counter the invasion. Yet the British had their opportunities earlier in the Naval victories at Narvik and elsewhere, which might have been quickly exploited by a trained amphibious striking force.

Renown had been steaming slowly into the great seas west of the Lofotens on the night of 8–9 April. The nine destroyers of her escort plunged down great walls of water as their captains tried to keep their 'boats' from shipping green seas, for life-rafts, whalers, radio masts and even the bridge superstructure can be torn from a small ship in the conditions of that night, if she attempts any turn of speed. So Admiral Whitworth in *Renown* was weathering the storm at a gentle 12 knots to nurse the destroyers through the night.[1] After midnight, however, the weather began to ease, although a heavy swell was running and the Admiral waited until the predawn half light before turning eastwards to resume his patrol of Vest Fjord. Dawn came early in the northern latitudes during April, and the destroyers kept contact in the grey twilight despite occasional snow squalls, lookouts keeping their neighbours in sight, for none of the ships had radar. (Only *Rodney*, *Suffolk* and the anti-aircraft cruisers had radar in the British fleet – Type 79, or Type 279, probably the most advanced anti-aircraft radar of that time.)[2] German surface radar was ahead of the British, although it could only give *Scharnhorst* a bearing within 2° of a target and the aerials had some mechanical slackness in their traversing gear which did not help accurate plotting.[3] Nevertheless *Gneisenau*'s radar picked up the British ships at 0349 hours[4] some 12 miles on her port bow. *Renown*'s lookouts, however, had spotted the German ships coming out of a snow squall 12 minutes earlier. Both squadrons maintained their approaching courses until *Rodney* swung on to a parallel course to the Germans before opening fire at 18,600yds with the guns that would bear – her 'A' arcs just open. *Scharnhorst* fired at the same time, 0405 hours, and *Gneisenau* first fired six minutes later.

The action began some 40 miles west of Skomvaer Light, *Renown*'s heavy guns concentrating on *Gneisenau* and the 4.5-in on *Scharnhorst*.[5] All nine destroyers joined in, although their fire was probably none too effective, as the crews and gunnery control were blinded by spray, if not by the occasional green seas coming around the bucking gun platforms. Indeed, as the action developed, *Renown* reached 29 knots for a brief period, the destroyers falling astern of the chase, since the seas were too great for them to make use of their speed. 'The German gunnery was very good',[6] and they got two hits on *Renown* within the first six minutes of the action: 'one [280mm] shell hit the after end of the ship, plunged through a deck and out of the ship's side without exploding, another went straight through the mast',[7] also failing to explode and there was little damage.[8] *Gneisenau*, however, had her main fire control put out of action when a 15-in shell hit her foretop, and she turned to break off the action at 0418 hours. *Scharnhorst* covered her with a smoke screen, but the chase would continue for another two hours, and *Renown* damaged *Gneisenau*'s 'A' turret, where green seas sweeping her focsle flooded the guns' electrical gear, putting them out of action.[9] A third hit damaged her port anti-aircraft gun aft.

Both squadrons were by now steaming hard into mountainous seas, and *Scharnhorst*'s 'A' turret also became flooded, although she was not hit.[10] At 0500 hours *Renown* lost sight of the German ships in a rain storm, and although they were seen again 20 minutes later, both squadrons successfully avoided the other's shots and at 0615 contact was lost. Had the Germans chosen to bring the full force of their eighteen 280-mm guns into action against *Renown*'s six 15-inch guns, they might well have achieved a notable victory, but they chose to draw the British ships away from the coast.

There, at the time of the big ships' action, the first German troops were landing from destroyers in the Narvik area. These were men of 3 Mountain Division[11] and with them was its commander, Major-General Dietl, a keen skier and experienced mountaineer.[12] The destroyers were at the limit of their range, and without fuel would be unable to leave the fjord. This may not have concerned the Higher Command, and their plan to surprise the Norwegians might have succeeded, had not King Haakon and many of his government minister escaped into Central Norway, to lead a Norwegian resistance, which would continue underground at home and grow in strength overseas until the final victory. As for Allied intervention in the early stages of this German onslaught, only the Royal Navy successfully blocked some enemy moves. The RAF bombed Bergen but did little damage.

Just before dawn on 10 April five British destroyers of the 2nd Flotilla moved through the narrow waters of the entrance to Ofot Fjord, about 30 miles west of Narvik.[13] Some carried small detachments of Marines. Had the sea-mine fields been laid as was planned, ore-carriers would have been forced into international waters. There they might become prizes and the Marines would have guarded the crews. In the event the Marines acted as messengers and ammunition numbers when HMS *Havoc* and *Hotspur* began the first hour of an action that sank two German destroyers and six merchant ships, without loss to the Flotilla, before 0530 hours. In their second and third attacks destroyers again approached Narvik harbour to sink another two merchantmen. The destroyers' captains, under the Flotilla commander Captain Warburton-Lee, RN, then took their ships out into the fjord for a brief consultation before they saw three German destroyers speeding down the fjord from the east. The British ships increased their speed to 30 knots to escape, but two more German destroyers appeared, heading to meet them from the west. These five destroyers carried 125-mm guns, 25 in all,[14] outweighing the 21[15] British 4.7-inch guns, to sink *Hunter*, disable *Hotspur*, the flotilla leader, which beached, and damaged *Hostile*. *Hostile* and *Havoc* turned back some two miles to help, adding to the damage already suffered by the German 'boats', which withdrew at about 0630 hours. The three surviving British destroyers had not finished, however, for they sank an ammunition ship as she came up the fjord about half an hour later. Captain Warburton-Lee was post-humously awarded the VC for this daring Naval action, and among other awards two Marines received the DSM for their part in this First Battle of Narvik.[16]

On the same morning at 0700 hours, sixteen Skuas[17] arrived over Bergen and sank the light cruiser *Königsberg* in a dive-bombing attack. These planes had flown 280 miles from the Scapa Flow Naval airfield at Hatston, the two squadrons being led by Lieutenant W.P. Lucy, RN, and Captain R.T. (Birdie) Partridge. The Captain was one of the few Royal Marines in the Fleet Air Arm, and – like all these Skua pilots – was familiar with flights over the Atlantic, for these pilots were from 800 and 803 Squadrons, which at the time were disembarked from HMS *Ark Royal*. Their attack, therefore, was pressed home with the determination of experience, the planes coming in a 60° dive from 8,000ft[18] to get three hits, two fractional misses, and other semi-armour-piercing 500lb bombs close to the target. *Königsberg* had been seriously damaged by Norwegian batteries early in the landings but now capsized and sank. The Skuas turned away to fly back to Scotland, losing only one plane and this on the return flight, although they were operating to the edge of their range.[19] This was 285 miles and allowed a 25 per cent margin, so that they could also be used in a fighter role, carrying four .303-in machine guns and a fifth which the observer could fire to the rear. But the pilots of HMS *Glorious* considered the Gloster Gladiator superior as a fighter to the Skua.[20]

In the Norwegian campaign air power was a third dimension of warfare, in which the Allies were woefully outmanoeuvred, not for lack of the skills of their pilots, but because the Germans seized the few existing airfields on 9 April and made good use of them, as Allied airmen, sailors and troops ashore were soon to discover. In North Norway, however, the Royal Navy was to have another resounding success before the fog of war, as much as enemy aircraft, slowed down the Allied counteroffensive.

On 13 April HMS *Warspite*, with a screen of destroyers, was to force her way up the 38 miles of Ofot Fjord and by the afternoon would be within striking distance of Narvik.[21] Early in the battle, as *Warspite* passed the narrows, the squadrons of *Furious* were to make a synchronised approach, working to a timetable that could be – but was not – altered. The planes were on time crossing Baroy Island at the mouth of the fjord, but the weather was very thick; and those intended to bomb the north shore batteries at Rammes and the opposite coast defences at Hamnesholm failed to find the fjord entrance, which was hidden in snow squalls. However, the ten Swordfish in the strike force, led by Captain A.R. Burch, came in under the 500ft cloud ceiling,[22] with visibility in the snow flurries reduced to a few yards at times. Buffeted by squalls, they kept formation, rising to 2,000ft in the clearer weather of the open fjord. Then they came down to less than half this height, to drop some 100 bombs on the wharfs and a destroyer alongside. The bombs, mostly 20-pounders with one in three of 250lb, did little damage, despite the number of near misses achieved. Two Stringbags, as the Fleet Air Arm called these open-cockpit Swordfish, were lost; having a top speed of only 139mph,[23] this biplane was at considerable risk if it came within the range of German fighters.

Not that German aircraft in general were all that better quipped or handled than British planes in 1940. The high level bombers of both sides achieved indifferent results against ships at sea or entrenched troops. However, Captain Burch's pilots believed they had hit two destroyers in Narvik,[24] and German dive-bombers were to have their success, as we will see. They had been trained to hit at pinpoint targets ahead of troops, coming down in a near vertical dive. This also proved effective bombing against ships at sea, but these Stukas were vulnerable 'to even the obsolete fighters with which the Fleet Air Arm were equipped'[25] in 1940. Had sufficient carriers been available, therefore, the outcome in Norway might not have been so expensive a defeat for the Allies, but the seeds of these shortcomings were sown in the naval treaties of the 1920s. In these circumstances the British warships, including their submarines, were to achieve a remarkable dominance of Norwegian waters. During the first few weeks of the campaign they not only cleared Narvik Fjord of German warships but also the Norwegian Leads, those inshore channels between the island and the coast, sinking many German supply ships. Such successes raised false hopes perhaps in the minds of senior staffs, but did enable them to plan for unopposed landings through which possibly adequate forces could be built up to defeat the Germans.

Trondheim in Central Norway might have been invested in such a stratagem, had there been an amphibious force to seize it. This railhead lies over 30 miles from the open sea past a narrow entrance to the broad Trondheim Fjord, which continues north-east of the town, in a series of narrows and lochs for another 40 miles or more. Unlike Narvik, which is isolated by mountains from the rest of Norway, Trondheim has rail links to Oslo, and as the ancient capital of Norway, had added political importance in 1940, when Norwegian army units some 200 miles south of the town were fighting in the hope that this area could become a bridgehead for major reinforcements. With these points in mind, although unsure of the disposition of Norwegian troops and without time for careful study of the topography of the region, the British Chiefs of Staff – to some degree against their better judgement – made hasty plans for landings in the Central Region, of which Trondheim was the principal town.[1]

The Germans had landed 1,700 men of 3 Mountain Division[2] in the town on Tuesday 9 April, and two days later *Hipper* slipped south through the Inner Leads. Four days after the landings, therefore, when two British destroyers made a reconnaissance of the Trondheim Inner Leads, they found no German warships but were fired on by batteries on the shores of the narrows. As they were not hit, their captains believed that the batteries did not have modern fire-control instruments, so possibly British ships could force a passage into the fjord.[3] On the Saturday Namsos was reported clear of German ships, and the Admiralty suggested the landing of Marines and seamen to hold this small port, 150 miles north of Trondheim.[4] The senior captain on the spot, Captain Pegram RN, was given the final decision and while considering suggestions from the Norwegians that a landing 150 miles south of Trondheim might be a better bet, he delayed the final decision. The same day, however, his destroyers in the south had been attacked by aircraft. Captain Pegram therefore decided to land his force at Namsos – a small port of wooden houses and timber jetties – although he had waited until the late afternoon of Sunday 14 April before committing it.

This force for Operation 'Henry' was drawn from Marine detachments and seamen of the Captain's cruiser HMS *Sheffield* and the cruiser HMS *Glasgow*. It totalled about 300 all ranks commanded by Captain Edds, and was transferred to two destroyers 12 miles off Namsos, to land at dusk and establish a perimeter defence of the port by about 2300 hours.[5] The force's orders were to hold the port for some 72 hours until the advanced guard of a larger force could arrive on Wednesday, 17 April. Each ship had provided two platoons of seamen, two of Marines, a Royal Marine machine gun section and a Naval demolition squad. The men from *Glasgow* were sent some seven miles further south to hold the road from Trondheim by a road block at the bridge and by covering the quay at Bangsund, and they arrived there about midnight 'in two river steamers'.[6] As there was no information on local conditions, Marines were sent out to contact the villagers, most of them were evacuating their homes and generously told the Marines to help themselves to anything that was left. Firing positions were scraped from the crisp dry snow with a few branches laid to keep themselves dry, as the Marines took up positions to cover the bridge and road tunnel beyond it.[7]

The demolition party of seamen, torpedo ratings by 'trade', prepared the bridge for demolition, should the German troops come up the road. Air sentries were posted, but, on reflection, the houses occupied by the force might have been obvious targets for Stukas. The machine guns in the upper windows were sited to cover the bridge, and sentries stopped all cars from crossing it. In the next two days obstacles were cleared from the lines of fire in front of section posts, which were improved. The seamen mined the road beyond the bridge, but they were short of demolition stores and had only half a mile of telephone cable for communications. The Lewis machine guns – they had no Brens or mortars – 'would have decreased the mobility of the Force'[8] had mobility been required before they were relieved by two Army platoons on Tuesday night, 16 April. The Company and the *Sheffield*'s men returned to their ships next day, for without them the main armament was virtually out of action.

A week had passed since the first German landings, and the British command was finding difficulty in controlling the situation. Nor were the Germans overconfident of success at this stage, for the Norwegians had not capitulated in a few days, as the Germans had expected. The *Luftwaffe* was also reporting shortages of petrol and bombs[9] in the critical second week of its campaign, and had found that bad weather limited operations; for supply by air in Norway during the long winter was – and is – much less reliable than movements by inshore craft. Hitler, thinking of his coming offensive in France, was for cutting his losses[10] when the

Allied landings in Central Norway seemed likely to succeed in reinforcing the Norwegians, but he did not realise how fragile this operation was. At Namsos, in addition to the snow, the staff officer making a reconnaissance for the main force found that there was only cover along the road south to conceal a battalion, and any larger formation's movements would attract air attacks. The planned landing here of 5,000 men to move south was therefore likely to meet difficulties;[11] nevertheless 146 Brigade's ship convoy was diverted to Namsos, as its intended use at Narvik appeared unnecessary in the optimism after Naval victories there. The 1,000-strong advanced elements of the Brigade were landed on Tuesday, 16 April, the platoons relieving *Glasgow*'s company being among them. But their ammunition and supplies were meagre, for the force had transhipped to destroyers in Lillesjond anchorage while under air attack 100 miles north of Namsos.

At the time of the landings in Narvik and Namsos, a direct assault near Trondheim was considered, to capture Vaernes airfield 28 miles from the port. Desirable as this venture might have been in balancing the relative British and German air-cover, a trained amphibious force would have been hard put to dislodge the Germans, who had been established in the area for over a week. The risk from bomber attacks on the Naval covering force was then realised, even if they overcame the coast batteries, and the operation was cancelled, for an unopposed landing 150 miles south of Trondheim in the Åndalsnes area was a better prospect.

On 12 April the Adjutant General, General Bourne, who had been studying maps of the area, received permission to land a force of Marines to hold Åndalsnes – familiar to 3 Commando Brigade in the 1990s – until the Army could land there.[12] This force for operation, 'Primrose', named by the Adjutant General after the flag-day of this name, was 725 strong, drawn from crews of three warships under repair (HMS *Hood*, *Nelson* and *Barham*) and the 21st Light Anti-Aircraft Battery (Independent) of Marines. The 11th RM Searchlight Regiment should also have gone with them, but the Force Commander, Lieutenant-Colonel H.W. Simpson (later Major General, CB, DSO) found that there was no room for them in the four sloops[13] which would carry the force to Central Norway. Lieutenant-Colonel Simpson later wrote that 'a delay of some hours in the sailing might have been justified to allow a reasonable loading plan'[14] As it was, the sloops were drawing a foot more than their normal draft and had heavy gear, including two 4-in coast guns and the 21st Regiment's eight Pom-Pom 2-pdrs, loaded on their upper decks. These light AA guns were not complete, as some had string in place of wires for their sights,[15] nor, when they were landed, did the coast guns arrive with all their gear. Nevertheless the unit formed in haste after the German invasion was at sea within 72 hours. The penalties of hasty action here and elsewhere in Norway, however, would prove severe.

Lieutenant-Colonel Simpson's orders were changed several times during the voyage as the sloops made a mere 10 knots through heavy weather; 'any greater speed and "Primrose" would have been a very wilted flower',[16] for most of the men were seasick. The final orders were to land at Ådalsnes, where the sloops came in at 2200 hours on Wednesday, 17 April. Each was unloaded in turn, a

5-ton travelling crane on the quay helping to complete the job in nine hours. Next day the coast guns were taken to the little island harbour of Ålesund, south of Romsdals Fjord on which Åndalsnes lies. The expectation was that these guns would be able to prevent German supply ships using the Inner Leads, but Major H. Lumley found that the locals feared the guns would attract German bombers. This would also make the gun sites vulnerable, for there were no air defences, so while pits were dug by the Marines, despite the almost daily bombing, further anti-aircraft guns – two 3-inch – were sent. They arrived a few days later, but were incomplete, and the coast guns were never mounted before the Marines were evacuated on 1 May.

One factor contributing to the 'Primrose' landings being unopposed was a bombardment of Stavanger seaplane base and aerodrome earlier that Wednesday morning. The cruiser HMS *Suffolk* and four destroyers had contacted the submarine marking the start line for their approach at 0414 hours, and a Walrus seaplane was catapulted off. Half an hour later the second Walrus was launched and the ships began the first of three bombardment runs, but were unable to make radio contact with the Walruses. Steaming at 15 knots, the ships delayed firing in the hope that wireless contact could be established with the spotting planes – while a torpedo passed close astern of the cruiser at about 0500 hours by one report – but no radio contact was made. The fall of shot would have to be corrected by observation from the ship and what help the planes might give by lamp-signalled reports. HMS *Suffolk* opened fire at 0513 hours when the range was 20,000yds. Before the sunlight became too bright at 0604 hours to observe the flashes of her shells exploding, she had fired 202 rounds, 51 from the Marines' 'X' turret. 'Installations are badly damaged and four seaplanes destroyed' was one German summary of the result.[17]

Suffolk had only been steaming for an hour or so from the coast when she was diverted to look for German destroyers and came under the first of 33 air attacks that dogged her until mid-afternoon. She jinked under full rudder and avoided the first nine attacks, but at 1037 hours was hit, probably by a dive-bomber's 250kg bomb 'just forward of X turret . . . the bomb exploding just abaft the bulkhead of the after engine room'.[18] Its blast killed all but one man in the Shell Room, Cordite Handling Room, and Shell Handling Room, and a number of 'X' gun crew were also killed or wounded. 'Y' turret was damaged but its magazine crew escaped. Damage to the engine roam caused water to flood in, 1,500 tons of it in 20 minutes, and 'Y' magazine was flooded. *Suffolk*'s speed was reduced 11 minutes after she was first hit; she was then attacked by a plane from 150ft that may have launched a torpedo, and for the next 4½ hours further dive-bombing and high level attacks put both steering motors out of action, though they were repaired in 20 minutes. The first air-cover did not arrive until the afternoon, about 1415 hours, and even then attacks got through, one bomb falling within 5 yards of the ship.[19] Several had earlier fallen within 20yds and the last – at 1512 hours – was only 10yds off target from high-level bombers. But *Suffolk* survived to reach Scapa Flow with her quarterdeck awash. She had fired 1,197 rounds of 4-in. Eighteen Marines had been killed and 15 injured, including the lieutenant who was in charge of 'X' turret, and the ship's total casualties were 70 killed or injured.

That Wednesday night 'Primrose' Force landed at Åndalsnes, for which they had been unable to get maps. Simpson found that the narrow roads out of the port were only kept open by snowploughs, and to bring Norwegian ammunition and stores from Molde in the west, trucks had to cross two ferries. More serious was a landing of German paratroopers which had cut communications between the port and the main Norwegian Headquarters some 200 rail- or mountain-road miles to the south.[20] The day after the Marines and seamen landed, the Army's 148 Brigade of 'Sickle' Force came ashore; the Brigade's original orders were to attack northwards but they were rushed south to reinforce the Norwegians,[21] for the Norwegian General Ruge had stressed the need for British troops to be seen helping in the defence of his country.

The Brigade – two Territorial battalions of civilian reservists with only four Bofors guns – would fight for the next two weeks, most of the time in a foot of wet snow, through forests and over steep hill sides. Their own motor transport, and most of their AA guns never reached them, for these were lost when the transport *Cedarbank* was sunk by a torpedo. The companies were put under the command of various Norwegian battalions, and their difficulties with requisitioned transport, poor communications and fragmented command made this one of the most harrowing of operations in Norway. Their first reinforcements, 600 men, arrived the following week, and two days later (on 24 April) 2,700 men of 17 Brigade came ashore. They had been in France but in Norway were now sent south to reinforce the Norwegians. With this Brigade came a battery of Bofors AA guns, nine anti-tank guns, an RM searchlight and men for the Naval base. But already the Germans were pushing back the southern defence line, for they were concentrating their efforts on relieving the Trondheim garrison.

Lieutenant-Colonel Simpson's Marine companies became part of 'Sickle' Force, with the task of holding the port. As there was no base organisation and little equipment, the seamen made up port working parties. The Marines established six platoon posts at vital bridges, at Verna power station 28 miles inland and at the airstrip on the frozen Lake Levaskos. The platoon at this furthest outpost, 40 miles from the port, did what it could with Lewis guns and rifles to break up air attacks. A battery of Naval Oerlikons had been landed at the same time as a maintenance party for the airstrip.[22] Whether or not these guns were intended for airfield defence has not been traced, but when 18 RAF Glouster Gladiators flew in from HMS *Glorious*, they found that the ground party did not even have a petrol bowser. Only four Gladiators survived by the end of the second day of their operations, 26 April, and they left the airstrip as German bombs had broken up the ice – moving nearer Åndalsnes to a hastily prepared airstrip, over which they flew several patrols until the evacuation.

Åndalsnes had been bombed frequently from 20 April, although the RM Pom-Poms, the Oerlikons and Army Bofors broke up some low level attacks, the Marine Pom-Poms reporting that their fire kept dive-bombers from destroying the railway station. Bad weather on 21 April and on other days gave some respite from the attacks, but the brunt of high-level air defence fell on ships, whose expenditure of ammunition gave cause for concern. The sloop *Black Swan* alone fired some 2,000 rounds of 4-in and 4,000 Pom-Pom rounds on 26 and 27 April.[23] Yet there were only 7,000 rounds of ammunition in the UK for the destroyers' AA guns and a supply of a mere 2,000 rounds a week promised up to mid-May, so that there were grave risks of these ships and those elsewhere being exposed without adequate AA defences. The Fleet Air Arm 810 Squadron (led by Captain N.R.M. Skene RM) wrecked three hangars at Vaernes airfield (25 and 28 April) and among other attacks on communications destroyed railway installations near Narvik on 9 May. Nevertheless the heavy German air attacks continued on Åndalsnes until only the concrete quay remained. The wooden jetties – like the town – were destroyed by fires, and ships could only unload while it was dark. 'Sickle' Force, or at least what was left of it, had therefore to be evacuated, and plans were made for this to take place over nine days from 1 May.

Meanwhile the Norwegian gold reserve, which Simpson had shipped on its railway trucks to Molde, was taken off by HMS *Glasgow*, which had come alongside with hoses playing on the burning jetties, for the town was blazing with a brilliant light. With her went the King and his ministers. She was bombed as she left the quay, her two gangways having been manhandled aboard.[24]

German forces from Oslo linked up with their Trondheim garrison on Tuesday, 30 April, some 75 miles north-east of the Allied line of retreat. Already most of the British troops had been withdrawn, but a battalion of the King's Own Yorkshire Light Infantry only escaped from Dombås in the nick of time as their train came under fire that Tuesday night. An hour or so after midnight the train hit a bomb crater and the men marched 18 miles under air attack at times, to hole up in a railway tunnel near Verma. Norwegians, and the RM Platoon that had fallen back from the ice-lake airstrip, were defending the hills around this point, and in the afternoon German patrols made contact with the outposts, which were withdrawn. However, Lieutenant E.D. Stroud did not receive the revised orders to withdraw, and with four Marines and a couple of Lewis guns was at the head of the Rauma Gorge. As the German advanced guard appeared about 1800 hours up the valley, Lieutenant Stroud and his party opened fire.[25] In a classic example of the fire power of a small, well-led group, they held the Germans till after dark, retiring as originally ordered at 2130 hours. Meanwhile the KOYLI had been safely on their way in a train from the tunnel, although this set off on the last 30 miles to Åndalsnes half an hour before nightfall. Other Marines worked there with the Naval Port Parties and held defence posts in the dock area, where Lieutenant-Colonel Simpson was wounded. The Navy's determination in getting warships alongside the quay enabled 1,300 troops to be embarked, despite the first night bombing of the port, on the Tuesday night. Next night, 1–2 May, the last of the troops, a further 2,200, were brought off. The expected nine days for the evacuation were not to be.[26]

Namsos would be evacuated on the nights of 1–2 and 2–3 May, although French reinforcements had been committed on 19 April before the little port was completely destroyed by German bombers next day, when all the civilians evacuated the town.[1] Further French reinforcements landing on 22 April could not bring ashore all their anti-tank guns nor an AA battery, for their transports could not get alongside the stone pier. There were no warehouses left for cover, the streets were cratered and blocked by debris and the decision to evacuate the town had been made, when the RM 3.7-in Howitzer Battery landed on 26 April. They were met 'by a very harassed [Army] staff officer, who was not at all pleased to see us' and when their ammunition arrived in an MFV (Motor Fishing Vessel), she was ordered away by an Army staff officer and not unloaded. The men and guns had been safely landed from a destroyer, but the Battery's quartermaster was killed by a bomb splinter while coming up the fjord in the ammunition MFV. The Marines found billets 3 miles outside the town and collected 'tinned hams, tasty biscuits and bottles of rum' from the French supply dump.[2] The Battery mostly comprised young Marine recruits but with experienced NCOs, and, under the leadership of Captain G.W. Wilson, the unit's discipline and high morale led the Army HQ to place them among the rearguard for the evacuation. In this some 5,400 men[3] were brought out. Finally the Bangsund bridge was blown shortly after midnight and the rearguard's trucks reached the quay in time for them to sail in the dawn half light, their destroyer's guns shooting up the trucks left on the quay. Further air attacks sank several ships, and over 100 seamen were lost, but only a dozen or so Army personnel.

Narvik by early May was once again the focus of Allied attention, but to appreciate the campaign there, its isolation must be understood, for no roads went south and the only road going north ran from the shore opposite the port. The electric rail link to the Swedish orefields could be – and was – easily disrupted. By 1979 the total population in the three northern counties of Norway was only 250 000,[1] about as many people as lived at that time in Portsmouth (Hampshire) or a quarter of those in Boston (Mass). These Norwegians live in the relatively few small towns and villages of this region, which is an area of mountains and fjords the size of Denmark, Belgium and Holland together. Although the British services in general knew little of this region in 1940, the Army's Independent Companies had been formed and fully equipped to operate as guerrillas in the region, if they were not to be employed in Finland.[2] However, the first troops to land in the area on 14 April had been from the Brigade of Guards, and by May a force of nearly 30,000 British, French, Polish and Norwegian troops would be investing the small German garrison,[3] whose only means of supply – after some medical and ration trains reached them through Sweden – was by seaplane and air drops. For their counter-offensive the Allies developed a base in the Lofoten Island harbour of Harstad, from which the attack on Narvik would be mounted. There were, however, conflicting views on the likely success of the Navy's plans for an amphibious assault on the peninsula, and the Army's wish for its slow investment.[4] These differences in approach by the Admiralty and the War Office caused the Admiral commanding Naval operations[5] to be at variance with the Army General initially in charge of the land forces.[6] In the event the campaign became a sideshow, for on 10 May the Germans thrust through Belgium and Holland to outflank the French, and within two weeks were in the Channel ports across the Straits of Dover 21 miles from England.

Before May Winston Churchill wrote of Narvik that the British 'hoped to establish ourselves there almost as strongly as at Scapa . . . [with] at least 30,000 men brought to bear on the Gallivae orefield . . . questions of Swedish neutrality need not be settled yet . . .'[7] This posed many problems: two divisions would need 15-ship supply convoys every nine days or so; more carriers were needed; ships not berthed alongside were 'virtually impossible to camouflage'; the waters were too deep for controlled sea-mines; and anti-aircraft defences would need at least 104 heavy and 96 light guns when only one Army battery and 6 Naval Oerlikons were ashore by late April.[8] Senior Royal Marine officers were on the short-lived 'Narvik Committee', and the Mobile Naval Base Defence Organisation, for which only Marine fighting units had been raised, was strengthened with Naval anti-submarine and medical units when put at a month's notice for overseas service from 12 April.[9] The actual use of Marines ashore, however, was small, the Fortress Unit of MNBDO I arriving on 10 May at Skånland. Here the mainland airstrip was being built some 10 miles south of Harstad. Their depot ship *Mashobra* carried some coast defence guns, a landing craft and pier-building equipment; in addition, 300 Anderson air-raid shelters were loaded and would be used for the protection of base personnel ashore.[10] She was also equipped with workshops and other services, making the Unit self-contained.

After the withdrawal from Central Norway, a number of Allied landings were made in attempts to stem any further German advance northwards.[11] At Mosjoen 100 French Chasseurs were ashore for a week but found that there was little to live on unless they could be supplied by sea or air. South of Mo, guardsmen and the British Independent Companies were outflanked by Germans landing from ships and seaplanes; the British fought their way out and by mid-May were concentrated in the Bodö area. This lies some 100 miles south of Narvik, across mountains at that time under 4ft or more of snow; and by sea, around the rugged coast with innumerable inlets, the distance was greater. Brigadier Gubbins, who had formed the Independent Companies, commanded the Allied forces at Bodö, where the German attacks were held until the final withdrawal of British troops from Norway. The Brigadier, incidentally, made good use of ten Puffers – fishing boats that became known as the Gubbins Flotilla.[12]

The Fortress Unit prepared coast and AA sites, and off-loaded RAF stores for the airstrip and Army supplies for the base[13] (see Appendix 4). On 22 May Captain H.G. 'Blondie' Hasler, who commanded the Unit's Landing and Maintenance units, took two Motor Landing Craft with additional crews to assist in the French and Polish troops' assault on Narvik, although secret orders for the withdrawal of British ground forces had been given on 25 May. One of these, MLC 18, was an old waterjet-propelled craft with an intermittent maximum speed of 4 knots and she was frequently stopped by weeds in her jets.[14] The other craft, MCL 20, was a prototype of the LCM Mk 1 and drew considerably less than the 4ft of No.18, on which 'armour plates [were] rigged in front of the control platform' but the crew aft were considerably exposed. With each craft was a Puffer, the *Skoyter* local boat, heavily built, with a single cylinder engine which was reliable 'but a most unpleasant shipmate in every other way'. These Puffers were superbly handled by the local fishermen who in a typical piece of fine seamanship towed No.18 through a narrow channel marked 'navigation prohibited' on Naval charts. Captain Hasler emphasised in his report that these landing craft operations were 'not typical of an opposed landing or of an opposed withdrawal'; nevertheless they have interesting features. The MLCs landed 13-ton French tanks, often having to probe for a suitable landing point on beaches that had not been reconnoitred. They worked at times with three of the early ALCs (later, Landing Craft, Assault) whose heavy camouflage of brushwood – while moored near the shore – hid them from air attack.

When French and Norwegian companies to the north and Poles to the south assaulted the Narvik peninsula on 28 May, the landing plan provided for the first wave to be taken from Saegnes, a point round the coast 'more or less covered from enemy observation'. At this time of year it was light throughout the 24 hours, but the assault was made at 2350 hours, heading for a point east of the town. The Naval bombardment had been directed at targets suggesting a different landing point, and therefore only scattered shots greeted the LCAs. MLC 18 following in with 100 Foreign Legionnaires aboard, and 'no opposition whatever . . .', which was just as well as there was 'little protection from plunging fire' of mortars or howitzers. The morale of the Legionnaires was magnificent, and their second flight of three craft was brought to a point nearer the landing. This saved time, but the landing craft, the same craft being used in repeated flights, came under shellfire on this exposed loading point, for the Germans had a gun back in action. Not for the last time had heavy and accurate Naval gunfire failed to destroy well-protected shore guns, and several shells fell near MLC 20, the RM's beach officer was wounded and several Frenchmen killed. Naval anti-battery fire soon silenced this gun, which had been run out from the railway tunnel, but the Norwegians appeared to Captain Hasler to have been shaken by this shelling. Nevertheless they were ferried across to support the French, although he felt that they might well have been a handicap to the Legionnaires.

The seamen crews of both MLCs and ALCs were scheduled to make eleven crossings in some 7 hours, bringing in the assault and follow-up forces, the seventh flight including a 13-ton tank in each MLC. Some weeks earlier an MLC had capsized while trying to load a tank from the ramp of a jetty, but this time both were safely taken aboard and landed through 4ft of water, guns blazing, although the shore was in Allied hands by this time! In the air, however, German planes were active, with the bombing of MLC 20 and a Puffer as they off-loaded at one point. The Puffer put out into the fjord as a means of dispersing the craft. Almost immediately she was machine gunned from 100ft, two seamen of the MLC's reserve crew were injured and the deck load of petrol cans set alight. Nevertheless Captain Hasler managed to beach her before 'she disintegrated rather rapidly'. When the craft finally returned under the tow of their remaining Puffer to Harstad, they found *Mashobra* had been bombed and beached, and the

Fortress Unit had returned to England; later the ship was blown up to avoid her capture after the final evacuation. Captain Hasler with two MLCs and an armed trawler took part in this faultless operation, the trawler destroying with her 4-in gun all the landing craft, except for an ALC she attempted to tow back home. She had to be sunk, however, because the tow prevented the trawler keeping station as she left with the last Allied ships on 8 June. There would not be another land action in Norway until the winter of 1941, when Army commandos raided the Lofoten Islands.

The lessons of the 1940 campaigns are obvious perhaps, but each military generation appears to learn anew the more difficult tricks of their trade. And unless combined operations are regularly practised, as they are in the 1990s, amphibious landings become a very difficult trick indeed. The lack of military co-operation from the Norwegians before World War II, when they kept clear of any military contacts with the British and French,[15] led to these nations' armies having to establish liaison missions from scratch at a time of great stress. There was also little appreciation apparently of the effect of bombing on the civilian population, who understandably evacuated towns, leaving Allied military personnel to operate ports and other local services; while the gaps in the British topographical intelligence would not be filled until 1943, when Colonel S.J. (Sam) Basset of the Royal Marines set up a unit for worldwide coverage of this vital information on the state of beaches, strength of bridges and much more besides.[16] Of the glaring misunderstandings between the commanders in the Narvik combined operation, despite the pre-War Staff College work and ISTDC papers on conducting such campaigns, General Moulton has written: 'The principles of joint command at the time were well understood . . . in ignoring them . . . it can only be supposed that the chiefs of staff . . . reverted under stress to lifelong habits of thought on their own service as independent of the others.'[17]

Marines would play an important part in the subsequent development of a Combined Operations Directorate, which would help to mount some of the largest amphibious operations of all time. Although the expertise they brought to these headquarters is sometimes forgotten, officers like Captain Hasler knew the critical factors of beach gradients, beach reconnaissance, the limitations of naval bombardment against well-sited defences and the need for air-cover,[18] knowledge used by Captain Hasler in particular for some remarkable operations and by the Corps in general to further their amphibious tradition.

The Marines of 'Primrose' Force and other detachments ashore, reporting after the campaign on their equipment, stressed the need for more mobile light machine guns. There is no criticism in Marine records of the bolt-action SMLE rifle with its 18-inch bayonet; and reports of the time suggest that a trained Marine could fire 15 rounds a minute in rapid fire, or take more carefully aimed shots at ranges up to 1,000yds. The Lewis gun, however, as we have seen, was thought to reduce mobility. It weighed 27lb against the Bren's 22+lb, their rates of fire were 450 and 500 rpm respectively, while each had an effective range of over 1,500yds.[1] More important in close quarters work was the ease with which a Bren could be fired from the hip; the Lewis, even if a man could fire it without using its bipod, would almost certainly jam. This notorious propensity for the Lewis to jam occurred because – among other things – the round had to tilt in passing to the chamber from the drum magazine,[2] a feed mechanism not helped by the fact that most of these guns had been used in World War I. The German Schmeisser on the other hand, was envied in one report, as 'guns of the "gangster" type were used by the Germans with marked success'.[3] The Marines, however, did not even have 2-in mortars or the Boys anti-tank rifle. This .55-in rifle was reported by the Finns rather surprisingly to have been effective against all but the heavier Russian tanks.[4] However, reports from Norway indicated that it was only 'effective . . . against the tracks of a vehicle . . . [a] target much larger than the slits . . . [but] the bullet would not pierce the front of the tanks being used' by the Germans.[5] Not till later would this 'ear buster',[6] with its mule's kick be issued to RM platoons.

Although, as General Godfrey and others had foreseen in 1922, the Marine of 1940 lacked practical training in the field, there can be no more cogent argument for keeping a strike force available, as the Corps had persistently wished to do, than the failure to capitalise on the Naval victories at Narvik in April 1940. In all their economies, the politicians failed to realise that any future war is as likely as not to be fought by unusual means in the most unexpected places, as in Norway in 1940, 'where there is no great mystery why difficulties of terrain and climate affected the Germans less than the British and Norwegians . . . there were a great many more of them, and they had much better weapons'.[7]

Although the Marines had no trained striking force available early in 1940, they were in the process of forming one, as described in the next chapter. Meanwhile most of the action was seen by Marines afloat, although a number of detachments were landed for specific tasks. The Marines of HMS *Penelope*, for example, had spent long and often boring hours closed up at action stations while she searched for enemy transports on 10 and 11 April, 48 hours after the German invasion of Norway.[1] Her Captain, Captain G.D Yates, RN, was unable to find a pilot, and as she moved into the outer fjord approaching Bodö, she ripped a great gash in her hull on submerged rocks. She was towed to Skjel Fjord in the Lofotens where repairs were made by concreting the gash, but she could only fire one AA gun at a time for fear of shaking loose this large patch.

At first no enemy planes interfered with this advanced fuelling and repair anchorage, which was called 'Cripple Creek',[2] as it became full of disabled ships before the first air attack late in April. *Penelope*'s Marines, however, were landed briefly on shore, they found that their equipment took time to prepare – Lewis guns had to be degreased, and the old khaki service dress with the long puttees and 1908-pattern webbing had not been worn for some time. Ashore, in deep snow, they made slow progress towards a defensive position on a steep hill side, but were recalled before any action took place, and sailed home in *Penelope* on 11 May.

Other detachments landed during these operations had varying fortunes, as we have seen with the force in operation 'Henry' and the force codenamed 'Primrose'. Of the smaller operations, the landing of a reinforced company from HMS *Resolution* on 9 May is interesting for the close support given to the Marines by the armed trawler HMS *Northern Spray*, in which the Marines had mounted their Vickers medium machine gun.[3] Several of the trawler's crew had been killed or captured earlier when they went to investigate a German plane's crash. Her crew, therefore, were keen to help when they landed the Marines that afternoon from lifeboats in the fjord west of this crash. From there the platoons moved to make an approach from three sides – No.3 Platoon struggling through deep snow over a crest, taking an hour to cover a mile – but the Germans had left the plane, although their abandoned camp had been found on the crest beside empty British bivouacs. The Germans were finally found further up the fjord, in a village below so steep a hill side that the houses could only be approached by two platoons in single file, slipping and sliding over the dark cold rocks by the narrow foreshore, while No.1 Platoon moved into the hills behind the village. As the Marines neared the houses, Germans ran out and 'took up defensive positions at the base of the hill'. *Northern Spray*'s 4-in gun, with the Marines' Vickers, drove them out, before Nos 2 and 3 Platoons swept through the village, the Germans retreating over the hill. There No.1 Platoon captured eight of them and killed one, and the Germans' prisoners were released before the detachment returned to *Resolution*, taking with them their German prisoners from a Jaeger battalion. No references are made in this ship's action report to the use of radio and there does not appear to have been one ashore with the company, although pre-war practice was to land a set from a ship for her detachment's exercises. Light (Aldis lamp) and flag signals were no doubt used, and although ship-to-shore radio was practical, the interference of headlands and mountains did make radio communications extremely difficult in North Norway.

HMS *Curlew*, while acting as anti-aircraft guardship off Skånland, also landed a detachment, this time to look for paratroops.[4] The platoon of Marines came ashore in the evening of 25 May and in the next 24 hours sent out a number of patrols, but next night (26 May) they saw their ship, short-handed with over 30 men ashore, was hit and sinking. As one of the three AA cruisers fitted out in the late 1930s, she carried eight 4-in High Angle guns, installed when she was built at a time (in 1936) when the need for convoy air defence was realised. She and her sister ships carried radar of a primitive kind to detect the approach of aircraft, for not until late in 1940 would the British have an effective ranging and directional radar for controlling anti-aircraft guns. The AA cruisers and AA sloops took the brunt of the enemy air attacks in Norway, often being forced to keep their crews closed up for days rather than hours, when men took meals in snatches as a few at a time left their action stations. They slept, if they slept at all, in the occasional lull when one Watch (half the ship's company) might be allowed to go below.

The Director Trainer of *Curlew*, Corporal C. Drury, had not been allowed to join the landing party, and was in the Watch below, for after 72 hours of action the Captain had decided that one Watch must have some sleep. The

Corporal was woken by the guns opening fire again, and lay on the mess stool for a while, then 'the lights went out . . . our mess tables folded . . . the cupboards came down . . . , the ladder disappeared . . .'.[5] In moments the deck opened up and harsh smelling black oil rolled around his legs. The side split open and in rushed the sea. He and five of his messmates pulled themselves through the gap against the weight of water pouring in, and then came up over the outside of the ship to get on the upper deck. It was awash and there was just time to cut a Carley float free as *Curlew* heeled over. There were no paddles so the men 'paddled with our hands like mad in case the ship took us with her', before they were picked up by a destroyer, but over 200 were lost. This might have been more had a number of Marines not been ashore when the bombs 'dropped right down the side of the Marines' mess deck'.

The survivors acted as a guard for Naval staff before joining HMS *Cairo*,[6] the other AA cruiser in Narvik. She too had suffered severe bomb damage. Her guns, like most AA guns at Narvik, were worn smooth, not only affecting the guns' accuracy but making them dangerous. In the event Corporal Drury and the makeshift gun crews fired smoke shells 'to make the enemy believe we were alright'.[7]

The *Curlew*'s Platoon ashore found themselves with unsought provost duties 'fighting their way into canteens when drunken troops fired rifles at each other',[8] for the French had access to almost limitless supplies of rum, which they dispensed with some generosity. In addition, wood alcohol was being distilled illicitly. The Platoon was made up mostly of young Marines, 'but the NCOs kept a good hold on them',[9] a point we will come back to. The Platoon was among the last to be evacuated.

The Army and Royal Air Force units withdrawn from Narvik on 8 June 1940 were successfully brought home, despite a battle at sea.[10] Although the secret of the planned withdrawal had been securely kept, *Scharnhorst*, *Gneisenau* and *Hipper* were in these waters looking for supply ships on that day. After jamming the SOS messages of the first two ships they sank, *Scharnhorst* and *Gneisenau* came on the carrier HMS *Glorious*. Only two aircraft were up on anti-submarine patrol; one later crashed but the other reached Hatston. No other aircraft were up, as in the last 48 hours her flight deck crews had been flying on two squadrons of Hurricanes.[11] These had been flown off Bardufoss airstrip on 7 June by their RAF pilots rather than destroy their planes. *Scharnhorst* opened fire at 1631 at 27,800yds in good visibility.[12] Destroyers immediately laid smoke to screen the carrier but she was hit and a major fire started; further shells fell on her bridge and on the stern and one carried away a main aerial, before she was abandoned about 1720 hours. Her escorting destroyers were sunk, but one of them, HMS *Acasta*, hit *Scharnhorst* with a torpedo. Damaged by this, the battleship was forced to put into Trondheim, and the Allied Narvik convoys were saved; but few were rescued from the carrier and her escorts, 1,515 men being lost, including all but one of the Hurricane pilots. Some men spent over two days in boats on the ice cold water (temperature 5 C) before rescue ships arrived.[13]

The many misfortunes and setbacks suffered in these campaigns were over-shadowed at the time by German victories in France, but the Prime Minister – Winston Churchill became PM on 10 May – rallied the British for a long war that would mobilise virtually all British resources. For the Corps an expansion to more than 78,000,[14] in a multitude of roles, was only possible because the long-service Marines, the regulars, provided many competent and able NCOs. Through all the reports on the Norwegian actions runs a theme of high praise for NCOs that foreshadows this potential. Many of the young regular Marines themselves later became NCOs in their turn, enabling Hostilities Only ('HO') officers to create disciplined units that would include commandos, artillery, landing-craft crews and gunners in support craft, to name a few Marine roles of World War II. An incalculable debt is owed, however, to the regular officers, who – despite the difficulties of the inter-war economies – created a force of such quality that its chief asset, the Marine, was able to train flexible and diverse forces and willing to lead them through many a difficult operation.

3
EXPANSION, IMPROVISATION AND WITHDRAWAL

The last notes of 'General Assembly' died away early one Saturday evening in May 1940,[1] and in answer to this bugle call, the Marines of Chatham barracks came to the parade ground, from cleaning their kit for next day's church parade, from the NAAFI, from the Junior NCOs' Club and the Sergeants' Mess. Some were in blues, ready to step 'ashore' for an evening's celebration, as a King's Squad of recruits had passed for duty that morning. From these men on the parade, 200 were picked for 'a defence landing', the company including many a pensioner, the oldest being 54.[2] By early next morning, Sunday, 12 May, they were taking up defensive positions with Dutchmen to defend the quays at the Hook of Holland. There, under repeated air attacks and some rifle fire, they held the Germans for 4 days (see Appendix 4) before coming off, with a few Guardsmen helping to form the rearguard, before boarding HMS *Malcolm* just as a further bomber raid came overhead. They returned without having lost a man and were 5 anti-tank rifles and two Bren guns to the good.[3] The next week a similar party left hurriedly for Boulogne, to cover the Naval demolition parties at that port and spend two lively days ashore (see Appendix 4) before returning to Chatham on Friday, 24 May.

The German XIX Corps commanded by General Guderian had scythed north, cutting off Boulogne from Calais and the other Channel ports further north.[4] There seems no doubt that Winston Churchill saw opportunities for the RM Brigade to harass the flanks of these German forces,[5] much as the RM Provisional Brigade had done on this coast in 1914. The Brigade had a warning order for Calais, but lack of suitable shipping, the fluid situation and need to retain forces for the defence of the UK, all probably contributed to the decision not to commit them. Nevertheless Naval parties were being brought to Dover, ready to cross to France to operate Channel ports, for the Royal Navy was well aware of the problems in trying to supply Lord Gort's British Expeditionary Force (the BEF), which needed 2,000 tons of ammunition and stores every day.[6] These could not be taken over open beaches, as there were only about a dozen landing craft available, so Dunkirk was to be a supply base, and a fleet of small ships was assembled to ferry stores across the Channel.[7] When British counter-attacks on

Tuesday, 21 May, failed to halt the panzers' northward thrust, however, the prospects for supplies coming through any port looked grim.

By dawn on Thursday a German armoured group was 18 miles from Calais. Its 1 Panzer Division had been on the move for nearly two weeks, the men were tired and at half strength, owing to many breakdowns, but they managed to force back British outposts south-east of the town,[8] although these troops, mostly Territorial searchlight and AA gun crews, put up a spirited resistance. The men of 1 Panzer Division were then ordered to by-pass Calais and move north, leaving 10 Panzer Division to capture the port. At 0300 next day, Friday, the War Office ordered the evacuation of Calais, but there was a complication.[9] The British 30 Brigade in the town was under the command of the French Corps holding this north-west region of France, and General Fagalde, its commander, was insistent that Calais be held.[10] Then, about midday, Hitler halted the panzers on the Aa river, telling General Guderian to leave Dunkirk to the *Luftwaffe* and limit his forces to the capture of Calais, provided this did not entail many casualties;[11] for Hitler looked for a swift and fairly bloodless victory, like the one his armies had achieved in Poland. On Thursday night, therefore the Germans only probed the Calais defences. The Royal Marine Boulogne party had not been back at Chatham many hours when orders were received from the Adjutant General to form another landing party that Friday afternoon. Captain G.W.A. Courtice (aged 25),[12] who had been second-in-command of the Boulogne party, was to command this unit, and a number of men who had been at Boulogne joined it. The orders were quickly executed and two platoons, a Vickers Machine Gun Section, and a Signal Section were mustered, with a Surgeon-Lieutenant and his medical orderly.[13] This company included the blacksmith, Marine Tom Connelly, old hands like Marine Bannerman and young recruits. Some were in blues,[14] and by 1730 hours the four officers and 81 men were on their way in buses. Their police escort passed them through traffic lights at red and gave the convoy priority to reach Dover just before 1900 hours. Here they had an unplanned wait, as the destroyer intended to take them to Calais had already sailed. They therefore went to the local barracks for a meal and met some 200 sailors waiting to go to France,[15] although none of them were clear what they were to do there; they were probably intended to operate Calais harbour or demolish its installations if it was evacuated. The Marines left them in the barracks, and about the time the Marines were loading stores on another destroyer, HMS *Verity*, the War Cabinet decided that Calais must be held. This decision was passed to the garrison at 2323 hours, and the Marines' destroyer sailed from Dover a few minutes later. She carried ammunition, iron rations and life-belts for the garrison, and reached Calais in just over an hour.

She was making fast to the North Quay by the harbour station inside the port when 'six small shells' fell 10yds from her bow.[16] A German battery was firing on this target and no doubt had ranged on it (registered) the previous day. *Verity*, therefore, moved back to the harbour entrance as more shells fell by the station. In half an hour the Marines and seamen had the stores ashore, sentries were posted at 0115 hours and the men told to get some sleep.

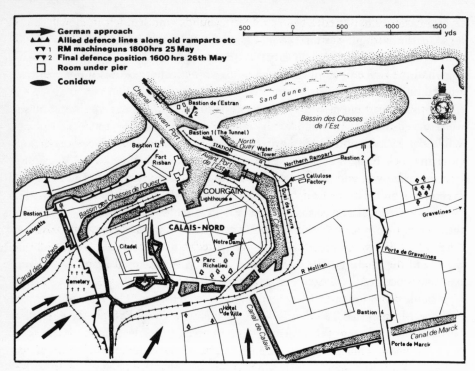

Legend:
- German approach
- Allied defence lines along old ramparts etc
- RM machineguns 1800hrs 25 May
- Final defence position 1600 hrs 26th May
- Room under pier
- Conidaw

Town map of Calais showing operations in 1940.

Calais was a town of narrow streets in the older parts by the docks, which was known as Calais Nord. This is surrounded by basins, canals and locks over which several bridges give access to the old town, while the Citadel blocks the western end. The newer suburbs run south from the docks, and in 1940 a narrow canal system ran around the south-east and east side of the town, following the line of the moat to the old ramparts. The British 30 Infantry Brigade held a line of some six miles round the Citadel and this southern canal system on the evening of 24 May, with some 3,000 British and 800 French troops (mostly French Marines). But Germans had infiltrated into the old town, some had crossed bridges in civilian clothes before hiding in the homes of Nazi sympathisers.[17] The outer defences to the south-east and east were held by the 1st Battalion of the Rifle Brigade, and Territorials of the Queen Victoria's Rifles, the first 'motor battalion' in the British Army but landed without its vehicles and a third of its men only armed with pistols. Some Searchlight and AA units were also still fighting as infantry on this eastern flank.

Around the Citadel and the north banks of the nearby canals and docks, the 2nd Battalion KRRC (the 60th Rifles) had fortified many houses, having smashed all the windows to avoid shattering splinters, and were firmly established to block the southern bridges into the old town.[18] Three tanks, all that remained of the 3rd RTR's 48 landed four days earlier, and a few anti-tank guns were used in the defence, but support from artillery was needed, for the French gunners at several batteries had fired off most of their rounds, and had left in French naval tugs. In the harbour station, in cellars and air-raid shelters, several thousand unarmed French and Belgian troops stayed out of the battle. German 105-mm guns had the range of ships in the harbour, as we have seen, making any evacuation difficult.

In this uncertain situation, under the smoke from many fires, the Marines were turned-to at 0125 that Saturday morning,[19] after a very short sleep indeed. While the MG Section covered the immediate area, both platoons struggled to close the lock bridges to shorten the marching distance from the North Quay into the old town, and in the next few hours requisitioned all the transport that they could find, before being ordered to the Citadel at 0700 hours. Brigadier Nicholson had just moved his 30 Brigade's headquarters there, as he feared that the French troops around the harbour station would be showing white flags ere long. The solid walls offered reasonable protection in this old fortress, built on the site of the English castle begun in 1347, which had been the French garrison barracks since 1660. It covered a vast ground area some 500yds by 250yds, with high banked bastions to the west and south.

The Marines' MG Section took up positions at the top floor windows of a barrack block, though they could find no sandbags or other barricades as they got their medium machine guns and a few Brens firing at the advancing Germans, the 86th Rifle Regiment of 10 Pz Division, attacking a company of the 60th Rifles west of the Citadel. The fire of the machine guns attracted an accurate and increasingly heavy response, but the Marines persisted in firing at rifle positions beyond the Citadel walls. The War Diary of 10 Pz Division records: 'The Citadel and Fort Risban [on the west of the harbour entrance] still being defended with toughness.'[20]

The Germans concentrated their artillery fire on the Citadel about 0930, for if they could force its surrender, the spirit if not the resolve of men in other strongpoints would be weakened. The Marines saw many Frenchmen killed or wounded on the rampart below the MGs. A French officer came up to the top floor and advised the Marines to take cover, and, leaving one gun team 'aloft', they came down to the shelter of the southern ramparts.[21] The noise was stunning; dust, fumes and smoke blotted out the bright day, adding to the heat and the men's thirst. German dive bombers attacked the old town and the quays, when German mortars were worked forward early in the afternoon and the last Royal Marine MG team was brought to the comparative safety of underground dungeons. About this time Anthony Eden, the British Foreign Minister, signalled to the Brigadier, 'The eyes of the Empire are on the defences of Calais'.[22] The BEF, whose headquarters had been at St Omer, 25 miles south-east of Calais, moved its last elements north this Saturday to join the nine divisions concentrating around Dunkirk, seven of which had been in action on the Scheldt and could not be disengaged to turn south.[23]

In the middle of the afternoon the mayor was sent to demand that the Brigadier surrender the town. He got a firm reply: 'If the Germans want Calais, they'll have to fight for it'.[24] After his parley, the MG Section, like other defenders, took advantage of the lull, and with No.1 Platoon were moved in vehicles to the eastern flank defences about 1615. They had hardly reached their new positions, when a large scatter of bombs fell on the Citadel, casualties being caused 'more by the violence and intensity of the bombing'[25] than the size and weight of the bombs and shells.

All afternoon the Rifle Brigade companies had been falling back, their platoons on the outer canal having been overrun by midday.[26] A plan to break out along the shore was thwarted by wrecked vehicles blocking roads to the beach. The regrouping for this move, however, caused some disruption of the battalion's organisation, although the men kept on fighting in independent groups. The bombing of the Citadel had by now set alight most of its buildings above ground, which were now under more or less continuous mortar and shell fire. Choked by dust, short of water, the Citadel's defenders were numb with fatigue. The Brigadier could not be contacted by radio, the last of his two No.9 sets having been smashed, and the telephone exchange was in German hands apparently, for the lines which the staff had been using to contact Dover were cut.[27] By 1900 hours German tanks were probing across the western bridges, but the 60th held them, although French engineers failed to blow the bridges. In a lull 40 minutes earlier Captain Courtice had taken his remaining platoon from the Citadel to the North Quay, where they could help stem the German encirclement threatening to move in from the east. The many fires and rubble-strewn streets made the move difficult, for, with most house doors being locked, there was no easy way to find cover. At one point there was a cry of 'gas' – most troops and civilians had expected and trained for such attacks in 1940 – which split up the platoon, only 17 Marines, a corporal, two sergeants, Lt David Hunter and his Captain reaching the quay. Although crossing one of the bridges they had closed that morning proved hazardous, for it was burning fiercely.

They regrouped and were sent to positions on the east of the Rifle Brigade, ready to cover the forward companies' withdrawal – or so they thought. Here on a ridge of sand dunes they were facing south, and from 2130 'waves of enemy bombers ... carried out low dive bombing and machine gun attacks ... in a systematic manner ... [they] approached in line abreast then each turned and dived along the line of the ridge'.[28] Fortunately the soft sand absorbed most of the blast and there were few casualties. No British troops came through, although they were expected; among them might have been the RM machine-gunners. In fact, the machine-gunners and No. 1 Platoon earlier that evening had dug in across the railway line, their backs to the artificial lake called Bassin des Chasses. On their left was the cellulose factory held by the QVR, a four-storey building surrounded by stacks of timber. There was a reasonable field of fire for 1,000yds up the railway track and to the east from the Marines' positions. As they dug these, 'the Royal Marines discipline was inspiring', one army narrative reports,[29] and the positions would be held until Sunday morning.

Back on the sand dunes an hour after the strafing began all was relatively quiet, for at 2145 hours 10 Panzer Division broke off the attack.[30] The Germans were expecting British reinforcements to arrive, and their own forces would be much stronger next day, when troops and artillery moved up from Boulogne. The lull gave the British a chance to reorganise or at least for individual groups to do so, for any co-ordinated final stand would be difficult as companies were isolated and down to handfuls of men – 30 here holding an old rampart, 20 there in a fortified house. The 60th Rifles still held the line of houses near the Citadel, but the sheer heat of blazing buildings had forced some Sections to shift their positions; they were nevertheless cheerful 'but very done'.[31] Most of the British troops in the old town expected to be evacuated that night. A final decision was made, however, by the War Cabinet at 2100 hours, and the Brigadier was sent a signal, 'Every hour you continue to resist is of the greatest help to the BEF'. There would be no evacuation that night except for the wounded, and a hospital ship came in at 0230 fully lit to take off casualties, including the CO of the Rifle Brigade's battalion, Lieutenant-Colonel Hoskyns, who later died of his wounds.[32]

The night was warm and clear, and a lieutenant of the QVR from near the Marines' positions could see searchlights on the English coast and make out the dark forms of ships offshore. The red, orange and yellow glares of many fires in the port were reflected on the still waters of the Bassin des Chasses, reminding him of the sacking of a walled medieval city.[33] About 2230 hours Captain Courtice brought No.2 Platoon back to the quay and posted double sentries along an 180-yard stretch behind (east of) the station. These were joined by stragglers of different units, who of their own accord stiffened these meagre defence posts.[34] The Captain sent two sergeants to look for other men of the Company further out along the quay, while his own small force remained near the station. At midnight the destroyers, which had been giving close support as best they could all day by shelling German positions, began an hour-long bombardment, and a number of small boats had also been sent over by Admiral Ramsay. Sergeant Mitchell, who was looking for Marines detached from the Company, found several with Lieutenant H.G. Bruce in a tunnel near the outer end of the quay, No.1 Bastion, and with them were several soldiers. The Lieutenant took these men back with Sergeant Mitchell towards the railway station, but in the dark they were mistaken for Germans who might have crossed from the sea dyke on to the quay. Two soldiers were killed and a Marine wounded by other British troops on the quay, before Lieutenant Bruce gave up trying to contact the Marine platoon, and decided to make another attempt next morning.

At 0330 hours that Sunday the 60th's platoons stood-to, and as it grew light in the next hour, they made the last preparations to defend their fortified houses. The Rifle Brigade's companies, mere handfuls of 30 or 40 men, held the ramparts along the north-east shore. Under their command were the remaining troops of the QVR, some dangerously forward in positions south of the factory, the search-light crews and AA gunners fighting as infantry. In all there were about 490 men with 18 officers,[35] to whom were added 30 or so Marines. These were the machine-gunners and riflemen Captain Courtice had brought forward again, to positions at the south end of the station quay.

Sharp at 0500 hours Guderian's Corps artillery began its bombardment of the 60th's platoons and the Citadel, a situation report from 30 Brigade at 0800 stating: 'Germans hold greater part of Northern Town [the old port] ... they have plenty of ammo ... quay and harbour under MG fire ... troops dead beat, no tanks left ... water essential ... reinforcements would have to be on a considerable scale ... [and] probably a forlorn hope'.[36] These messages were passed through *Conidaw*, an RN survey yacht which would remain in the harbour till that afternoon, or through a wireless truck of the Rifle Brigade in touch with Dover from its position near the station. Dive-bombers then added to the fires and by 1040 hours heavy smoke from burning oil tanks made all targets hard to see. The British wounded in the Bastion tunnel at the outer end of North Quay made bets on when the next bombing would be.

Sergeant Mitchell set out at first light to rejoin Captain Courtice but found that the RM platoon had gone, no one could tell him where. So he returned to the Bastion, passing Lieutenant Bruce without realising it, as the young officer made his way towards the Rifle Brigade's positions. About this time Lieutenant-Commander P.F. Cammiade, RNVR, commanding a group of minesweeping trawlers, towed in several boats, one of which Sergeant T.H. East – the second sergeant sent to look for isolated Marines – helped to load with wounded and ferry out to the Lieutenant-Commander's trawler. There the sergeant was given 'an important message for the OC Allied forces', which he volunteered to deliver himself if the Brigadier could be reached.[37] The Sergeant then went ashore, being left by the Lieutenat-Commander 'with very much regret', for the trawler was under machine gun fire and shells were falling on the harbour entrance. A number of unwounded French soldiers were also boarding the boats, as these came into the long pier stretching out to the lighthouse, and to the quay on the west harbour entrance.[38]

During the morning the Germans crossed the bridges into the 60th's positions but their resistance caused the German commanders concern, for their own casualties were increasing. A heavy artillery battery was then brought up to shell the Citadel area, but the British soldiers and French Marines put up such tenacious resistance that, even though they withdrew into the old town, the Germans thought reinforcements had landed,[39] although only 200 Frenchmen still held the Citadel by lunchtime. What rations these men had is not clear, but they probably grabbed what they could from the townsfolk's larders, and certainly they drank wine when the last supplies of water ran out.

Shelling of the tunnel Bastion on the quay was 'both heavy and accurate'[40] as it was on any Allied movements, for the German observation posts could see most of the town despite the smoke. Sergeants Mitchell and East, nevertheless, gathered some dozen Marines and a few soldiers and led them to the Battery No. 4 on the outer sea wall. They had hoped to get its gun firing, but a direct hit had made it useless, and while in this fort they were heavily shelled. Further air attacks on the quays made 'the situation fairly desperate',[41] in the laconic understatement of an action report, but no enemy could be seen. The virtually unarmed *Conidaw* was still berthed alongside,[42] when further air attacks forced the 12 Marines and some 30 soldiers to get under the pier, where the piles and supports gave them some protection. The *Conidaw*, however, grounded by the pier on the falling tide 'despite frantic efforts to refloat her . . . was temporarily abandoned . . . and became the target for two very persistent aircraft' attacking from 500ft.[43] Aircraft also attacked many other targets. The QVR were driven from the cellulose factory about 1300 hours, Captain Courtice with Lieutenant Bruce getting the RM machine guns back to the tunnel Bastion, where they covered the withdrawal of the last two Rifle Brigade platoons moving down the quay to the station.[44] This was a shambles of broken glass, with dead British soldiers lying on its platforms, which were swept by machine-gun fire when visited by the wounded Lieutenant Airey Neave of the Searchlight Regiment, who had been fighting for over three days.[45] Early that afternoon the north quay and station platforms were again swept by deadly mortar fire, the Rifle Brigade's signal truck going off the air at 1356 hours. Yet remnants of the Rifle Brigade's platoons held the dyke until mid-afternoon. They brought Major Hamilton-Russell (OC, B Company) down to the shore about 1300 hours.[46] Sergeant Mitchell then improvised a stretcher of oars and oilskins to carry him to the pier, and six volunteers with the Sergeant made the dash across the sand dunes to collect the Major; one soldier was killed and another wounded, but both wounded men were brought to safety. At 1545 hours the French battery on the west entrance was heavily shelled and the French surrendered.[47] In the town, although casualties had been kept down in the Citadel by keeping men underground during dive-bombing, the Brigadier capitulated at 1600. The last resistance by men of the 60th was in the old town, but when tanks came towards their few defended houses, they were ordered to scatter. Calais Nord was in ruins.[48]

Captain Courtice and most of the Marines were captured, along with many others – Guderian claimed 20,000 French, British, Dutch and Belgians. *Conidaw*, however, on a rising tide and helped by two bombs that fell near enough to lift her from the mud, sailed out of the port with 165 men aboard, including Sergeant Mitchell. During that Sunday night more men found safety under the pier, where a small room hid them from the Germans now occupying the town. A Royal Marine Sergeant (probably Sergeant East) signalled out to sea, as the Navy's yacht HMY *Gulvar* passed inshore looking for survivors.[49] She had been machine-gunned earlier and despite the guns on the pier, her skipper, Lieutenant-Commander C. Brammall, RN, called on his loud hailer (bull horn): 'I cannot stop . . . I'll go out . . . turn . . . and you must jump for it as I pass.' Four officers and 47 men did this as she ran past, despite the machine gun fire.

The previous evening most of the prisoners were marched away, with some ironic cheers when at 1800 hours destroyers shelled the German batteries. Next morning, Monday, 27 May, 38 Lysanders flew over the Citadel and dropped water, grenades and ammunition supplies. Several Lysanders were lost, as were Hawker Hectors bombing the German anti-aircraft batteries, all to no avail, as the Germans held the town. None of these Lysanders had radios and some crews were straight from flying school, furthering the strong support the RAF had given throughout the battle. Such close support, however, by ships or planes requires adequate communications, a lesson that had in some respects to be relearned.

Before leaving Calais, Marine Bannerman saw 'a lot of French soldiers, suit-cases packed, waiting for Jerry to pick them up'.[50] The blacksmith, Tom Connelly – holding all soldiers in something of amused contempt for he was a Royal – was a prisoner for 4 years, never losing his conviction of the Allies' ultimate victory. His 1940 belt, 'a horse's girth', went round his waist twice after years in prison camps. Poor food and hard work took their toll, but he managed to get coal when no one else could do so.[51] A 2nd-Lieutenant of the QVR crossed the Channel in a dinghy to escape,[52] others got away in a motor boat, and an RM corporal and two Marines swam for 4 hours before being picked up by an MTB.[53] Marine S.F. Smith escaped during the journey to a prison camp, although he had seen a man shot in an earlier attempt. Befriended by a Belgian family and reaching Marseilles (southern France), where he was imprisoned, he escaped again but was recaptured 500yds from the Spanish border, being later repatriated as being unfit for active service.[54]

The 4-day battle of Calais has been viewed by some historians as a wasted effort. But the German War Diaries of the Panzer Division, quoted by Airey Neave,[55] show that artillery, men and tanks were delayed those vital hours which enabled the BEF to move closer to Dunkirk, when on the Sunday, 26 May, I Pz Division was still on the Aa River sending units to reinforce the 10 Pz Division investing Calais.[56] But from this time Winston Churchill could never speak of Calais without emotion[57] for probably under 1,000 men were evacuated.[58] Yet Dunkirk is only some 25 miles from Calais and might well have been taken by the Germans on the Sunday, had they overrun Calais the previous day. In the event the British that Sunday sent their ships to bring off the first contingents of troops from Dunkirk,[59] and the Army began organising its perimeter defences. The harbour was used, although latterly under shellfire, until the final evacuation; even on 1–2 June records show that of those reaching the UK, 19,561 had been lifted from the harbour and 6,695 from the beaches. In the next 24 hours, 26,175 men came off, many from the harbour before British block ships sealed Dunkirk channel in the early hours of Monday, 3 June. If Guderian had been able to destroy the harbour, even though he might not have held it, considerably fewer of the BEF would have been rescued. Further evacuations of 4 June brought the total rescued to 338,226 during this operation 'Dynamo', and nearly 28,000 had already been brought back in the previous week.[60]

The naval losses in this evacuation were six British and three French destroyers sunk, and 19 other RN destroyers damaged, but destroyers brought off nearly a third of the men who were rescued.[61] Nine of the 45 troop carriers were also lost, including the SS *Clan Macalister* carrying eight ALCs. The largest warship inshore during the evacuation had been the cruiser HMS *Calcutta*, which took aboard men brought out mainly in fishing drifters, these had in turn been loaded by smaller boats going to the beach. Other men were brought out by destroyers from the west mole of the harbour.

Among the units warned for, but not sent to, the Dunkirk perimeter was the RM QF Regiment,[62] which, late in May, was building improvised mountings for its guns (see Appendix 4). Like so many of the improvisations that summer, creating a unit was relatively easy in comparison with the difficulties in co-ordinating such units into a cohesive force. In this, communications were at the heart of the problem. At Dunkirk, for example, there were difficulties in controlling shipping until a destroyer was sent to act as a wireless link with Dover;[63] for in the Dunkirk evacuation, as in Norway and at Calais, the great problems of modern amphibious operations were first experienced by planning staffs, and the importance of co-ordinating naval and air support with ground forces became clear, because – for all the bravery men might muster when armed with rifles – infantry weapons alone are totally inadequate defences against an organised force with supporting arms.

Yet out of this defeat came a marvellous determination, known to the British as the 'Dunkirk spirit'.

The Royal Marines' plans for a strike force to seize a beachhead, for landings or withdrawals, had taken shape in the winter of 1939–40 with the formation of the RM Brigade (see Appendix 4). Initially its three Battalions had nothing more powerful than 2-in mortars, but plans were soon afoot for organic artillery and air defence.[1] In September 1939 the possibilities for amphibious raids had been considered by service Chiefs to be so remote that even the ISTDC was disbanded, although in a matter of weeks it was re-formed.[2] The only unconventional Naval expedition at that time was the proposed incursion into the Baltic, operation 'Catherine', with warships reinforced with extra deck armour against air attack and several converted Glen-line ships as a fleet train of supply vessels. Work on these fast merchantmen's conversion was begun, but they were later reconverted to carry landing craft when operation 'Catherine' was cancelled. Whether the Marines could have raided the German coast successfully, as one contemporary study paper suggested,[3] seems doubtful, even if they had confined their landings to areas within the range of Naval guns and remained ashore only 24 hours; for the Battalions were almost entirely drawn from recruits, trained – as mentioned earlier – by the small number of long-service Marines available from the drafting margin for sea service (the additional number of men trained for this service, over and above the total of all specific detachments). Nevertheless the Brigade expected to be ready for operations by July 1940, despite the prior claims given to the MNBDO for men and weapons.

Many of the men joining both the MNBDO and the RM Brigade had been called up for National Service, with an initial six weeks' disciplinary training at the Reserve Depot (Exton – Appendix 4). They were taught their infantry skills in their units during 1940. However, those serving in the MNBDO anti-aircraft and searchlight regiments, and later those with the RM Division's artillery, went with their Regiments to train at Army schools. While the squads of recruits for continuous service (CS), the regulars, were trained for sea service at the Divisions, having completed their initial training at the Depot in Deal (Kent). An increasing flow of volunteer recruits and conscripts came forward for service during the period of 'hostilities only', these 'HOs', who, even if conscripted, had opted for the Royal Marines. In a number of cases they came into the Corps despite colour blindness, which at that time was not a bar to joining the Marines, although it prevented them taking their first choice as seamen.[4]

The recruits given initial training in 1941 and 1942, plus the first 800 Special Reservists[5] trained at Eastney (Portsmouth Division) included about 3,400 who were posted to MNBDO units and over 5,000 to the Division. Each recruit squad was on average 40 strong. The total numbers trained mainly through Exton (later known as Lympstone, the Infantry Training Centre (ITC) and in the 1970s the barracks of CTCRM) show remarkable increases in the early years of the war, when you consider the Corps' total strength, including reservists, in September 1939 was 16,146.[6] In the 13 months to December 1940 over 4,000 'HOs' were passed for duty, in 1941 about 7,400, in 1942 about 8,600, and in the 11 months to November 1943 about 11,500.[7] The disciplinary training had by then been increased to an 8-week course (from May 1943), and further training was given to all recruits at the Infantry Training Centre (ITC) established at Dalditch near Exton from April 1941. A contemporary report shows that the concept of training numbers of men for specific types of unit ceased by November 1943.[8]

Although more recruits were passed for duty with the Division than for MNBDOs, the men of some Battalions in the Division were later transferred to the MNBDOs. By March 1944 51,500 'HOs' had been trained at Exton,[9] and 3,500 'HOs'[10], 4,400 continuous-service recruits[11] and some 750 bandsmen[12] had also been trained at other establishments in these 4½ years. (Included in these figures are the RM Engineers, see Appendix 4.) All these brought the Corps' strength to over 78,000 by early 1944,[13] despite heavy losses in 1941 on Crete and in 1942 at Singapore, Dieppe and Tobruk.

Although the Infantry Training Centre did not take its first squads for training until April 1941, before that date and for most of 1941 recruits joining the Brigades were given infantry training in either the 20th Training Battalion at Hayling Island – from which the ITC naturally evolved, as explained in Chapter 5 – or in the training companies of battalions, some of which were stationed at Exton for several months from October 1940. The shortage of manpower before the end of 1942, however, led to many postings of men from battalions to the MNBDOs and the formation of cadres for new battalions with the Brigades which were to form a Division, as the Unit History Summaries show (Appendix 4). The plain truth was that 12,600 officers and men with 3,500 reservists – all men on whom the Admiralty had first call for sea service, with 10,000 at sea and in Naval establishments by March 1940 – could not create two MNBDOs requiring some 10,400 men, and a Division which on paper at least by June 1941 had an establishment of over 7,000 all ranks. By the end of 1942, however, the situation had improved, as will be seen. Many British formations after June 1940, however, had been in a similar plight, and the Marines' catch-as-catch-can in forming Brigades had Army parallels.

The informality of Marine companies flung together for operations in the Channel ports worked remarkably well for small units. Even after the Germans swept through France, ships' companies were helping to evacuate the Polish President, 'his wife, his aides, French officers, British Consuls, British officers including a Rear Admiral in khaki . . .', to name but a few of those who boarded HMS *Arethusa* in Bordeaux on 19–20 June 1940.[14] An elderly consul and his wife were bedded down by the Marines' gun crew of one of the 4-in HA turrets. Later, when a German plane flew over, the old couple were forgotten as the great crack of twin 4-in reverberated through the gun deck, but apologies and cups of tea made amends. Such commitments at sea, and such forces as the one laying river mines in the Rhine (see Appendix 4), must not be forgotten in the press of events surrounding the Brigade's formation, but for battalions and higher formation the problems of organisation and communication militate against *ad hoc* compromises. Nevertheless the RM Brigade's establishment was raised a few weeks after its formation to four battalions, in January 1940,[15] but the prospects of its employment in the Mediterranean or elsewhere were curtailed, General Bourne being told this specifically by the Chiefs of Staff.[16] (In modern terms, the Corps was not allowed to task them.) The Chiefs of Staff had direct operational command of the Brigade, an unusual command structure for a relatively small field formation, and the Admiralty administered the Brigade 'as agents for the Chiefs of Staff Sub-Committee'.[17]

In order to provide separate headquarters for different operations, the RM Brigade had already been split into 101 RM Brigade and 102 RM Brigade, each with two battalions. Both Brigades were held by the Chiefs of Staff for landings in Ireland, should the Germans invade there. At the same time they were to be in readiness for seizing the Azores (Operation 'Accordion') and/or the Cape Verde Islands (Operation 'Sackbut').[18] Both these groups of Atlantic islands were seen as possible bases to replace Gibraltar, should Spain join the Axis powers, although finding escort ships would be difficult if supply convoys were needed for the islands' garrisons, since every available escort was needed for food and supply convoys to the UK. Yet, with the Azores some 1,000 miles west of Lisbon, and the Cape Verde Islands far to the south, 500 miles west of Dakar in French West Africa, their supply would need long voyages. There was also the possibility that the Germans might seize the Spanish Canary Islands, a few hundred miles off the Atlantic Coast of Morocco, as Admiral Raeder suggested to Hitler when proposing the seizure of Gibraltar in September 1940.[19]

In the summer of 1940 Marines in the depots and camps were formed into *ad hoc* rifle companies, for local defence in the event of invasion,[20] and from time to time orders were detailed for each formation's part in the defence of the localities in which it was training.[21] The Brigade's gunners, for example, had established positions from which killing-areas behind a beach could be saturated with shellfire.[22] Others were set to build beach defences, 50 men, for example, digging slit trenches at St Margaret's Bay,[23] where these defences protected the cross-Channel gun sites. The commitment of the RM Brigades and later of the RM Division to possible landings in the Atlantic islands meant that they could not be used in other operations, although the 2nd RM Battalion went to Iceland. However, when the Free French under General de Gaulle were trying to establish themselves and a landing was planned at Dakar, the Marine Brigades were a natural choice for their support, as, with Dakar in Allied hands, the Cape Verde

Islands would not be needed as a base. General de Gaulle saw Dakar, the capital of French West African territories with a 14.8 million population, as a prestigious setting for his government, and believed he had support there.[24]

The Army's Lieutenant General N.M.S. Irvine commanded the land forces, which included the Marines. An able man, he had won an MC, DSO and three bars, the Croix de Guerre and five mentions in despatches before he was 26 at the end of World War I. He was concerned at the few landing craft available, for only 15 ALCs, one Support LC with a mortar and medium machine guns, and two MLCs were carried by the transports. At least 15 ALCs were needed to land a Marine battalion (one contemporary report optimistically suggests 60 were required for the two brigades and the headquarters),[25] but in 1940 ships' boats had to be used as an alternative, being towed inshore. The Brigades, nevertheless, carried out a rehearsal in Scotland, of which General Irvine wrote, 'the battalions of the Royal Marines impressed me most favourably and their officers and NCOs seemed excellent'.[26] The men carried ashore their weapons, reserve ammunition and in the haversack of one MOA were two bottles of good wine. His officer, the novelist Captain Evelyn Waugh, is said to have drawn much from his experience with this Brigade for the amusing novel *Men at Arms* (1952).

Several schemes were worked out for the landing to suit different likely receptions for the expedition, but any bombardment was to be limited so that there would be minimum damage.[27] The plans were code-named 'Rufus' for a landing 15 miles east of Dakar, 'William' for a landing in the centre of the defences, and 'Conqueror' was a combination of the two. But before any of these kings could be played, the Vichy French trumped this operation 'Menace' with a force of cruisers and large destroyers. These sailed through the Gibraltar Strait on 11 September as the British convoys were nearing Freetown.[28]

Two days later the HQ ship HMS *Devonshire* was among the Allied naval forces looking for these cruisers and the operation was briefly postponed. This gave the battalions in Freetown – some could not be landed because accommodation was scarce – time to study each company's part in the proposed operation.[29] But the absence of the HQ ship with the Brigades' Headquarters aboard underlined the mistake of giving an HQ ship dual roles, one of which might lead it into operations away from the landing area. Despite the enforced delay, however, the British convoys sailed at dawn on 23 September 1940 in a wet, warm tropical fog. There was, therefore, no sudden appearance of an armada to shake the resolution of Vichy forces ashore.

Various Free French emissaries were rebuffed and the defenders opened fire about 1000 hours. The British ships replied, but this only made the defenders more resolute, 'for blood is already flowing',[30] and the action was broken off after an hour. In the afternoon some Free French ships in the convoy set off to make a landing at Rufisque, some 15 miles east of Dakar across Hann Bay. But this convoy became 'lost' to *Devonshire* in the mist, which had thickened, and there was a breakdown in W/T communications at this time, producing a confusion of late signals and unanswered queries. Three Free French sloops then got 180 French Marines into Rufisque Bay but failed to land them and a second attempt was not pressed home, although it was only faced by isolated rifle shots. So the first day ended in fiasco; and a good deal of puzzlement among British forces as to why their former Allies were firing on them.

Any 'continuance of "Menace" would undoubtedly commit us to a great effort and great risks' Churchill wrote later,[31] and so the operation was abandoned, but not until HMS *Resolution* was torpedoed by a Vichy submarine three days before the British ships withdrew. The Force Commanders – General Irvine and Admiral Cunningham – had decided that a landing was not practical. Certainly with the inadequate craft that were available, only the slightest opposition could have been overcome.

'We must give the French full credit for a gallant and effective defence',[32] to quote Professor Arthur Marder, whose detailed study of these actions in his book *Operation 'Menace'* (London, 1976) provides a reasoned analysis for the failures. The gross lack of military intelligence on Dakar, no mention of likely fogs, the misappreciation of local French support for Vichy and the misguided fear of Germans in the port, and the advanced warnings of an attack through de Gaulle's broadcasts to the people of Dakar, are readily appreciated in the 1990s as likely reasons for an amphibious operation to fail. But in the long haul to ultimate victory several lessons of Dakar would be the basis of later successful landings. The first specially adapted Combined Operations HQ ship, HMS *Bulolo*, would not be completed until 1942, but the problems of *Devonshire*'s dual roles lent urgency to work on *Bulolo*. The Landing Ship Tank (LST), designed by the British and built in great numbers by the Americans to land tanks on a beach after an ocean voyage, also came into being largely as a result of the Dakar operations. The concept of a nucleus HQ staff available to plan and then accompany amphibious forces – as would be seen in Madagascar – was born out of General Irvine's report, as was some of the work on Combined Operations' signalling techniques.[33]

The setback at Dakar – for it was no more than that – had little effect on the war. For the RM Battalions, however, their commitment to the Atlantic islands precluded them from raiding operations, which may well have suited the War Office. By the time the first Army commando raid was made on the Lofoten Islands in March 1941, a few weeks after the 2nd and 5th RM Battalions returned home, the Marines of the Brigades were angered that their traditional roles had been usurped.[34] But as the senior RM officers later explained to the Director of Plans, they did not want the RM Brigades (by then in the RM Division) 'turned over to the Army', as had happened in World War I, 'when we left trained artillery batteries and RMLI battalions in the line in France, while raising a special unit of Batteries and a Battalion *ad hoc* from the Fleet'.[35] The RM Division would take a thorny path we will tread later, for the roses of sentiment are difficult to disentangle from the briars of professional jealousy. It is sufficient to say at this stage that the Royal Marines battled in Whitehall to keep their amphibious force firmly in the Royal Navy's jurisdiction, to be used for operations which did not entail remaining 'in [an] Expeditionary Force when more suitable [amphibious?] employment arose'.[36] Meanwhile other Marines would be shooting at the enemy with very large guns indeed.

On 22 August 1940 the first half-ton shell was fired from St Margaret's Bay across the Channel. It fell 300yds beyond (over) the target and to its left. The second round was miscorrected and fell short. The third was closer but still 'over' the target, a battery of German heavy guns on Cap Gris Nez 12 miles south of Calais. Enemy fighters came up from airfields nearby, the RAF Anson spotting for the gun was ordered home and the shoot ended. Minutes later 50 German fighters were over the gun site.[1]

The preparations to get this shot 21 miles across the Channel went back only some ten weeks. Yet mounting the 14-in Naval gun on the golf links above South Foreland cliffs was a major feat of civil engineering, completed despite air attacks and the many calls on Britain's slender resources after Dunkirk. The Prime Minister initiated the project when the War Office was closing down its Super Heavy Railway Artillery, the reason the Admiralty had received the PM's entreaty: 'Pray install gun to shoot across the Channel'.[2] The first gun installed was a Naval 14-in intended for *King George V*-class battleships cut from the Navy's building programme. Two proof mountings, normally used in testing Naval guns, were adapted by Vickers-Armstrong to carry this and a second gun, so these could be positioned in concreted gun pits from a railway track laid across the golf course. Later this track was used to bring ammunition from magazines up to 2 miles away, for storage near the gun in heated ready-use magazines.

A Siege Battery of Royal Marines, commanded by Lieutenant-Colonel (later Major General) H.D. Fellowes, was formed to man the first gun, and although golf was being played when the Colonel visited the site on 25 June, a month later the RM Lewis gunners shot down their first Me 109 and two RM Pom-Pom 1½-pdr crews from the MNBDO had been added to the big gun's defences.[3] The Germans had brought super guns to the French coast, including the two 210-mm Kanone (E) railway guns which had been built in 1935,[4] and by the autumn of 1940 their big guns were spread from Calais to some 10 miles south of Cap Gris Nez ready to support an invasion of England. They included 12 280-mm railway guns with a range of 22 miles, 11 170-mm with a range of 17.4 miles and six 240-mm with a range of 18.3 miles.

Later, as the Pas de Calais positions were strengthened by 1944, another 11 great guns of 305-mm to 405-mm were added and the bombproof reinforced concrete casemates of all the large coast guns were little affected by high-explosive shells. These guns would be in action that year but the V3 'Millepede'[5] with a potential range to reach Oxford was not fired operationally before the Allies captured it.

The RM Siege Battery was expanded to a Regiment on 1 September 1940, and during the four years to September 1944 was strengthened from time to time with the arrival of new guns, although few rounds would be fired at the enemy until that September. With its new guns, the Regiment was made up as follows:

'A' Bty of	static 14-in guns with		
	'Winnie' at St Margaret's	from	7 August 1940;
	'Pooh' 1,400yds from		
	'Winnie'	from	17 December 1940;
'B' Bty of	Railway 13.5-in guns with		
	'Sceneshifter'	from	c22 September 1940
	'Peacemaker'	from	November 1940;
	'Gladiator'	from	8 May 1941.

Some brief facts indicated the power of these guns, for three 50-ton cranes – half the heavy railway-cranes in the UK in 1940 – were needed to position the static guns, each with its mounting in two parts, the heaviest of which weighed 75 tons.[6] Their maximum range was 27 miles, using a pre-heated cordite supercharge of 485lb against the normal 14-in charge of 400lb and super supercharges were available weighing 516lb for use when the barrel became worn.[7] This wear was at first calculated as sufficient after each round was fired to reduce the next one's range by 200yds but in practice the wear proved not as great as this and in September 1944 the charges were not pre-heated.

The Royal Engineers had surveyed the site in 1940 and found that the French map grid was several hundred yards 'out by comparison with British maps';[8] for the first time Britain and France were then correctly related cartographically. Some idea of the complexities in ranging these guns on a target can be seen in calculations of that time. These show the factors included in calculating a range were: the co-ordinates of gun and target; target bearing (with adjustments); range with adjustments for differing heights of gun position and of the target; adjustments for drift (due to shells' rotation in flight for calculated time in flight); 'Meteor' information to allow for wind at different heights during a shell's trajectory; Earth's rotation during flight; temperature of Cordite which 'lost' range if too cold; and dial sight readings which allowed for the difference in the angles between the reference point and the alignment of a gun's barrel. Air spotting was used but the hazards for aircrews over the French coast were emphasised in a shoot on 7 May 1941. The fighter – a Defiant – observing shots that day over Calais lost Radio Telephone (R/T) contact with the guns. Then the Blenheim from the RAF's No 1 CACU[9] which took over, using W/T (with Morse), was shot down and the crew killed.

Enemy shellfire damaged buildings from Folkestone to the north of Kent, 2,284 heavy shells[10] falling in Dover alone, and with air bombing they caused nearly 1,000 casualties. The St Margaret's gun sites had been first dive-bombed on 14 August 1940, and 50 shells fell near the site on 24 November. A year later one of the railway guns, 'Peacemaker', was slightly damaged by shellfire, but all three railway guns had only fired registration (ranging) shoots before 'they were handed over to Army crews in the autumn of 1942'. Nevertheless these guns, taken from an interned Vichy warship, had been developed by the Royal Marines, with track laid near 'Winnie' and a railway system around which a gun could be moved for major changes in the direction it was aimed. With sixteen bogies and the railway track acting as a bearing race when the gun recoiled, the drill for firing a round was to align the gun-carriage's yellow arrow mark with a matching mark on the sleepers. The brakes were then fully applied before easing them with 'one turn of . . . the large brake wheels'. The ammunition wagon was towed away, the elevation checked by 'a clinometer-type sight' and the angle of aim checked against a known reference point, before the crew took cover in nearby slit trenches.[11]

On the command 'Fire' the Battery Sergeant Major – well back with a long line to the firing handle – yanked the cord. There was a flash and a bang, the great carriage slid back a few feet and the 1,250lb shell winged its way towards France. These guns could be reloaded in seven minutes,[12] although much of the work was done by muscle as they had few hydraulics and the shell was rammed by hand.[13] The crews lived in the guns' trains – 'Sceneshifter's' was 207yds long and weighed 591 tons – which after some modification could travel on main line tracks. 'Lay back' firing positions at Ashford, Canterbury and north-west of Canterbury were selected, where existing railway curves enabled a gun at each site to give the Regiment an arc of fire from Sheerness to Dungeness, in the event of an invasion. The track at these sites was strengthened, magazines and shellrooms being built in nearby cuttings.

The RM Siege Regiment in March 1943 also fired the experimental 13.5-in 'Bruce', with its 8-in liner that took a ribbed shell to achieve a range of 65 miles;[14] but this barrel wore badly after firing a few rounds. In their build-up after Dunkirk, however, the Allies had put their resources into ships and more conventional weapons than super guns, the more pressing need having been for anti-aircraft guns to defend the south coast in the summer of 1940. Marines were there.

The two guns of a Section from 'B' Battery of the 1st RM (Heavy) AA Regiment opened fire on a fine summer's night at 2230 hours.[1] Their 'hostile plot' was a lone plane passing in and out of the clouds over Eastleigh aerodrome. At this target, the gunners – 'helped with the bearing by the GL', an early radar set – got off 21 rounds with fuses Type 21, one shell being near enough to knock the plane down for their second kill in 36 hours of 11–12 July 1940. This small action was one of many which foreshadowed the major part played by the Corps in anti-aircraft gunnery by late 1944. By then 'D' Battery in several shoots on one day alone fired 561 rounds,[2] with 300 rounds a day being the probable average for most heavy-gun RM batteries. Some batteries might have been in action all night before moving next day to new sites, where they opened fire within minutes at Vl flying bombs. There was a long way to go, however, technically – and geographically for the RM batteries – before such shoots became routine. Back in 1940 many RM anti-aircraft gunners had been in uniform weeks rather than months before being in action. And there is significance in the first National Service recruits being posted to these batteries in the winter of 1939–40; for the fleets' advanced bases were expected to come under heavy air attack. Therefore two regiments, 1st and 2nd RM Anti-Aircraft Regiments, were raised, each with two batteries of 3.7-in mobile guns as these became available, and a battery of light anti-aircraft Bofors guns. The '3.7' was the standard British gun to replace the 3-in 20cwt anti-aircraft gun used in forward areas.[3]

The 3-in of which a number were later taken to Crete by the MNBDO had been the only World War I anti-aircraft gun retained in peacetime. Its mobility made it more useful to the BEF than the 3.7-in, but most of the Army's 3-in were lost during the retreat to Dunkirk. As for the 3.7-in, it met most of the requirements for an effective anti-aircraft gun, and when introduced in 1936, 'was in advance of anything else in the world',[4] although its original concept of 1928 had been held in abeyance for 8 years before the first guns were tested. By the 1940s the Mark III had an effective ceiling of 32,000ft,[5] some 5,000ft above the operational height for bombers of the early 1940s. It fired up to 25 rounds a minute, a rate sufficient to put a reasonable number of rounds in the sky for the short period a plane was in range, even though the plane flew at only 250mph. Yet the lethal area of the 28lb shell was only a few thousand cubic yards for one-fiftieth of a second, and there are 5,500-million cubic yards in a cubic mile of sky,[6] a feature not always fully understood in the three-dimensional aspects of anti-aircraft gunnery.

Another factor was the physical strength required to lift ammunition – the fixed round weighed over 70lb – in maintaining a high rate of fire. In this respect the Marine gun crews were fit men by comparison with the Army's anti-aircraft batteries of men in lower medical categories, giving the Marines a marked advantage when firing for long periods. Many of them were Scotsmen, for the early batches of recruits came from Glasgow, and although in 1940 they had been only a few weeks with the Army's training regiments, they were keen and tough.[7] The young officers of the RM batteries were mostly 'Hostilities Only' recruits, like Lieutenant Sandy Kinnear, who had joined with a Direct Entry commission after leaving Cambridge University in 1939.[8] The Direct Entry officers had been each personally interviewed by General Bourne before they were finally accepted by the Corps in the early months of the War, and among them were a number who later served as senior officers in infantry and landing craft units. After six weeks' initial training, Sandy Kinnear, however, had joined 'B' Battery at Arborfield (205th AA Training Regiment RA) and stayed with RM anti-aircraft units throughout his service, as did many others in these RM Regiments. In 1940 'B' Battery had only two long-service officers, but the young temporary officers had been given as good a training as was possible, their instructors including such fine soldiers as Major (later General Sir) Campbell Hardy.

The most significant improvements the Lieutenant – as a Major, he later commanded 'D' Battery – saw in his five years of service was the introduction of radar. The night before the shoot of 12 July 1940, fourteen RA gunners commanded by a sergeant had arrived not long after midnight with a 'GL', the code-name for 'Gun Layer' or early radar.[9] Up to this time the Army had used sound locators to little effect, but the control of the guns evolved around a predictor. This box of gears, small electric motors and several thousands of parts, was swung by its operator as he tracked a plane through the predictor's telescopic sight. As the height and range of the target were fed into the machine, it interpreted its own swing in tracking the plane, to calculate the speed and therefore the aim-off required. The necessary elevation (range/height) and bearing then passed electrically to the layer's and the trainer's dials. No further corrections were needed, as they followed the pointers on the dials, a task made difficult in the jarring blasts of 20 rounds a minute. Later in the war, American developments of the 1930s would be used to provide automatic aiming, the predictor's data electrically controlling motors – not men – on the '3.7' and other AA guns. But the dial-and-pointer methods of 1940 had made the manual controls festooned on a 3-in unnecessary, so that most of an AA gun's crew were freed to handle ammunition.

Each Marine 'heavy' anti-aircraft Troop had a predictor and associated height/range finder but a week after the radar set was installed, 'B' Bty received a Sperry predictor, which could be electrically linked to the radar. The predictor operators could then follow a plane in response to radar-received data, overriding this if the telescope tracking gave different configurations. The logical next step of radar-controlled gun elevation and training would follow in 1943.

As the predictor operator in 1940 had to see his target (there were no women in Marine batteries, although the Army had many 'mixed' ones), searchlights were necessary for night actions. The MNBDOs raised two RM Searchlight Regiments, the 11th and 12th, but at Eastleigh Aerodrome near Southampton the 'light' with 'B' Bty in 1940 was manned by the Army. After a couple of false starts its crew of Lancashire Fusiliers had it 'working to the GL' radar within a few days,[10] for it and a second light were brought in to work with the radar rather than independently, as searchlight Sections usually worked on sites away from the guns at that time.

Gun efficiency and gun control were only two factors, however, in the complex art of anti-aircraft gunnery. Another was the setting of the shell's fuse to burst it at the height required. A firework-like gunpowder fuse of the 1920s was not replaced in British service by a mechanical fuse until the late 1930s, although the Germans had used a clockwork fuse in World War I.[11] The Marines pre-set their Type-21 fuses in batches for a number of different heights and drew ammunition from the appropriate stack of shells laid around each gun. They had at this time a 'mechanical fuse-setter to speed up this work', the last one being fitted in late July. But by 1944 on static '3.7s' the whole operation would be automatic, after a round had been put on the loading tray, radar controlled predictors not only aiming the gun but also controlling the fuse-setter integrated into the gun's loading system. Such luxuries for a high rate of aimed fire were all in the future, however, when 'B' Bty brought its efficiency up to a peak with muscle and sweat in the hard school of action against the enemy.

During the height of that summer the men of 'B' Bty did a great many things. They worked with searchlights on 'dazzle schemes' to illuminate bombers for the night fighters. They sand-bagged protective walls to the gun sites. They did infantry exercises with the Local Defence Volunteers, who, in the trigger-happy scares of paratroop landings, killed at least one pilot parachuting from his plane.

They got drunk, they went to socials, and closing-up for action became almost as routine as any job of work. Although the first bombs to fall on the gun site caused only four casualties, a gun barrel was damaged when these were in short supply, and for a time 'B' Bty's firing was restricted to conserve guns and ammunition. They calibrated the GL radar with a Lysander flying on set courses at known speeds.[12] They moved briefly to Plymouth, the predictor crews manning Vickers MGs in case of an invasion, before convoying the guns to Bexley (Kent). This was a long slow journey as two of their three guns 'had no brakes' – the fourth gun was with a second convoy – and the loss of brakes was no doubt due to wear and tear in trailing around southern England. But the Battery was in action before the evening on the day it arrived (13 September).

Some idea of their shoots in the next two weeks can be gathered from the number of rounds fired: 16 September 127, next day 433, 288 (by 3 guns), 280, then a breather with under 100 rounds a day, 23 September 161, 26 September 198 and so on.[13] The pre-war concept of AA gun crews having time to sleep between engagements only at night, was shattered, as the men must have been after being closed-up most of the time they were at Bexley. And their first full night's sleep came only when relieved and – like many batteries – given a rest by Sections in a camp at Havant. The Marines' batteries were integrated into Army units, with the whole gunnery defences for an area being controlled by a Royal Artillery anti-aircraft regiment, which was itself working to a district control (part of the Air Defence of Gt Britain (ADGB) Command). Royal Marine batteries would operate within this command structure throughout much of the war, except when both MNBDOs were overseas in 1941–4 (see Appendix 4).

The commander of 'B' Bty, Major Ralph Garrett, had served in the 1st RM Anti-Aircraft Battery[14] at Alexandria in 1939 where they had '3.7s', and his part in the development of the Marines' anti-aircraft gunnery was perhaps only matched by his daring escape from Crete in 1941. (He would command 1st RM (Heavy) Anti-Aircraft Regiment from September 1943). Some of his fellow senior officers had less technical interest in gunnery. Although they could be delightful at mess dinners, they brought an edge of discipline to their RM Regiments which may not always have been appreciated by their temporary officers, the HOs, until in reminiscence: they reflected on the efficiency of these units; for they grew from RM Batteries serving under Army command, and only administered by the RM Regiments' Headquarters, to an RM Brigade of three Marine Regiments with its own operations room and Marine-manned technical services. At one stage this 5 RM Anti-Aircraft Brigade would have operational command of 15 Royal Artillery regiments and other Army troops – in all over 25,000 men[15] (see Chapter 7).

In 1940, however, technical trades associated with radar and other advanced equipment were largely new to the Corps, as they were to most military services, and although 'B' Battery received advice on camouflage from Fort Cumberland (MNBDO), on the surveying of gun sites, and on air raid precautions (PAD, passive air defence), their radar and predictor work, and major maintenance for the guns, were carried out by the Army's technical services. We shall come to the technical training of Royal Marines in a later chapter, but in 1940 at Fort Cumberland, the MNBDO base, there was a technical section – later the Technical Training Depot – in which Lieutenant-Colonel G.F. Haszard, DSC and bar,[16] designed some remarkable gun mountings.

The problems of moving coast guns into position once these were landed for the defence of an anchorage had been one of the first problems solved by the Colonel. His experience with the RMA Anti-Aircraft Brigade in 1914–15 undoubtedly helped him in developing the light-gun mountings for the Pom-Pom. This 1½- and later 2-pdr gun, derived from the Maxim 2-pdr of the 1890s, was a Naval gun and had been included in MNBDO weapons because its use aboard ship made it a 'common' weapon for ammunition supply, but by 1942 the Oerlikon and later the Bofors had largely replaced the 2-pdr ashore. These light anti-aircraft weapons were intended to protect the heavy batteries and anchorages from low-flying attacks, but in 1940 they were not deployed in mutual support, the light batteries being sent to serve the Air Defence Command in river estuaries, where the Admiralty was concerned at about mine-laying by *Luftwaffe* planes. Like most of the Navy's quick-firing weapons, they were designed with sights for aiming-off at MTBs, and not until January 1940 was the 100-knot aiming-off ring added to some gun sights.[17] There may well have been some lack of appreciation of just how difficult it was to shoot down a plane, although enquiry into the loss of ships through bombing found that AA guns and crews were not always 'in a fully efficient state'.[18]

Links between Army and Naval anti-aircraft gunnery were chiefly maintained by Ministries' ordnance and development departments, but in October 1940 'B' Bty provided crews for an experimental anti-aircraft battery at Fort Cumberland,[19] set up with the approval of the Admiralty and the War Office. Six months before then, on 30 April, the interlocking interests of both the Admiralty and the War Office had been evidenced by German planes mining the Tyne estuary in the north-east of England,[20] a move anticipated by the forming of the independent 21st RM Light Anti-Aircraft Battery, sent north by the MNBDO some 12 weeks earlier.

This first RM light AA Battery had no doubt been planned to protect the heavier anti-aircraft guns. In the event, the piecemeal deployment of batteries provided a wide-ranging experience of anti-aircraft gunnery, though initially with some makeshift gear. The eight 1½-pdr Pom-Poms sent to the Tyne, for example, were apparently of World War I vintage and used open sights in firing their shells to 6,000 ft, 1,000ft higher than the Bofors. They had been there some 8 weeks when they moved to Norway with 'Primrose' Force. The 22nd RM LAA Battery, after moving its four Troops to Naval air stations,[21] was typical of other RM light-gun batteries, who before going overseas with MNBDO I were equipped and trained on the 40-mm Bofors. This gun and the 20-mm Oerlikon became two of the most widely used light anti-aircraft guns of World War II, and the Oerlikon with the 2-pdr Pom-Pom would be in action with Royal Marine manned support craft from 1942.

The Swiss Oerlikon, in which the gunner strapped himself under the shoulder fittings, was swung with the body, the concentric metal rings of its open sight indicating the aim-off necessary according to the estimated speed of a plane's approach. It fired over 460 rounds[22] a minute with solid, tracer and explosive shells. This shell was too small, however to do much damage unless one caught a plane with a burst of fire. The 40-mm (2lb) shell was more effective and the earliest Marks – it was first produced in Sweden in 1930 – fired 120 rounds a minute to an effective height of 5,000ft.[23] Marines of the light anti-aircraft batteries found the Bofors a highly efficient gun and its successors continued to be used by many armies into the 1990s.

The 22nd RM Battery fired its Bofors during the series of January 1941 attacks by the *Luftwaffe* on the Royal Navy's air base at Lee-on-Solent, and after these raids the Marines did their share of fire-fighting.[24] They were only a few of the many Royal Marines who took part in those years in what was termed Civil Defence, often when on leave, rescuing neighbours from the rubble of their homes, or going into the bomb-damaged neighbourhood in rescue operations mounted by units around the UK. Several earned gallantry awards in these actions, and the Royal Marine bases were not without their casualties: Fort Cumberland had 84 HE and incendiary bombs in its immediate area in 37 seconds on 26 August 1940, killing seven officers and men;[25] a shell fell in front of the officers' mess at Deal, killing an officer and causing several other casualties; and there were many other incidents – the hut serving as sleeping quarters for 'B' Bty's officers took a direct hit from an 'oil' bomb, the officers getting clear through the windows.[26] Indeed many a youth of the 1940s, all over Europe, would join up for military service not necessarily having been 'shot over' in the accepted military sense of being in action, but certainly used to bomb blasts and having seen people die in a hail of steel fragments.

Coast artillery, although rarely in action by comparison with anti-aircraft batteries of World War II, was one of the principal arms of the MNBDO in the 1920s and 1930s, and when they were sent to the Far East. Their role turned out, with a few spirited exceptions, to be one of patience in the boring remoteness of such places as Addu Atoll, requiring a determination to keep fit to fight despite the lethargy of inactivity in remote islands. These coast batteries, each of some 100 all ranks – 145 in a 6-in battery – were controlled from a Command Post. This in turn was linked to Observation Posts some 4,000 to 10,000yds apart,[1] which in MNBDO I worked on the Tarnow system, the range-finders, tide gauges (to adjust ranges according to the 'height' of water), time-of-flight indicators, and clock-code decoders[2] being among the coastal gunners' instruments. The time-indicator sounded a buzzer seconds before a salvo splashed in, and the decoder converted grid references to bearings and range, for this gunnery had many elements of ship-to-ship gun control, with, for example, the QF 4-in Mk IV guns of 'Y' Battery in Iceland using electric dial repeaters for the layer and trainer 'following the pointers', to give ranges and elevations set by the Battery Command Post.[3] Radar would later be used for ranging on to a target, but in 1940–1 searchlights were needed – a series of remotely controlled 'lights' were installed by Marines at Scapa Flow, for example, and these could sweep nearby seas, but some skill and luck were needed to see a small stationary ship at the extremity of the beam.

The MNBDO RM Coast Batteries were able to install their heavy guns with lifting tackle and other help from the Landing and Maintenance (L & M) Units (among whose senior WOs was the Quay Foreman). What took time was the landline installations, which for an advanced base included twelve telephone exchanges,[4] and would not be completed until D+30 or later. (In January 1940 the date of an operation was designated D-day,[5] previously Z-day, and each successive day was D+1, D+2 and so on.) The World War II actions by coast batteries were almost entirely fought from such well-established fortifications as the Norwegian defences of Oslo, German batteries in Normandy, and Japanese, Russian and Italian batteries elsewhere. A Royal Artillery Battery in Italy fought off E-boats in 1944, but the most renowned coastal forts were those of Manila Bay, where Americans held out for several months after being by-passed in the initial Japanese assault, the disadvantages of all static defences. This danger, no doubt, was in the mind of the commander of the RM Devon Battery when he left gaps in this site's wire defences 'so that his guns' crews could get out and attack [any] German paratroops that landed'.[6] The Army Brigadier commanding these south of England defences, however, insisted that the site be totally ringed with barbed wire. It was a matter of opinion perhaps, but in Crete coast guns would be seized by paratroops and not be by-passed.

The whole conundrum of siting advanced bases was riddled with the imponderables of an enemy's ability to seal them off from taking any effective part in a campaign, as the Japanese were to find in 1942 at Rabaul (New Britain), and the Germans in the fortified ports of Normandy in 1944. An amphibious or airborne force can all too easily land elsewhere before moving inland to shut off a base from its hinterland, while enemy ships and planes block any access to it from the sea. As far as the Royal Marine Group in an MNBDO was concerned, the concept of an advanced base meant deployment over 'a large part of the countryside surrounding an anchorage'. This 'district' was divided in MNBDO nomenclature[1] into four 'areas' for administrative purposes, each with an Administrative Centre, the HQ of an Area Commandant. Each area would contain a number of units and detachments, such as an RM Battery of coast guns or the 17-man detachment on a single Bofors site, each responsible for its own defensive perimeter. In all a district might have up to 70 such posts, each responsible for anti-aircraft or other defence of Naval working parties and/or store dumps. The searchlights, for example, were in clusters of three with eight clusters – 24 lights – administered by an RM Battery, but operationally under control of the gun operations room. An interesting comparison can be made between the two batteries of an RM Searchlight Regiment with its headquarters, giving a strength of over 900 all ranks, and an Army Commando, which at this time had about 450 men. Although the searchlight crews were only partially trained in infantry tactics, they were expected to form 'a small blockhouse with its own garrison', with the cable joining the generator post and the trio of lights buried so the line it followed was a shallow V between these two defence positions. A second line of wire above ground then served as a trip-wire, as well as indication of the live cable's position. The V-configuration enabled both posts to fire at night along opposing arms of the V into the flank of advancing infantry, without the risk of firing into each other. This small but important feature of the thought that went into the intended deployment of an MNBDO accepted that there would be many miles of undefended ground – 'open space' was the term – in which searchlight crews in particular would be outside any perimeter defences manned by infantry.[2]

The Land Defence Force, an RM Infantry Battalion, was 'not intended to deal with formed bodies of the enemy'.[3] An Army force was to accompany the MNBDO for this task, while the Marine Battalion was 'to deal with minor riots . . . prevent sabotage' and protect the beach area from amphibious raids. Another interesting feature of MNBDO I's plans was the landing of '3-in' rather than '3.7' anti-aircraft batteries in the early stages of an operation,[4] for the 3-in AA gun of 1940 was considered – as the BEF had considered it – to have a better rate of fire than the 3.7-in, its ammunition required less shipping space, it could be used against fast surface craft, and the RM Batteries with '3-in' had a Vickers predictor to every two guns. Against this the 3.7-in guns had a better range and were more easily moved. Since low-level air attacks were expected in the initial phase, a Bofors battery (12 guns) was also to be landed early in an operation.

The signal organisation in an MNBDO also differed in some respects from an Army-type division, for these RM signallers not only linked the various unit headquarters but also linked unit HQs to their sub-units or posts.[5] In Army organisations, however, the signallers within a unit were men of that unit – gunners, tank crew, riflemen – with a basic signals training but not specialist signallers who worked only in battalion headquarters and higher commands. But with MNBDO sub-units of gun Troops, searchlight clusters and so on, often intermingled around one location, men of the Signals Company were the only people able to lay a rational system of networks.

The Admiralty's choices[6] for advanced bases in the Mediterranean were also studied by MNBDO I. They included Tripoli (Libya), Moudhros (on the island of Limnos, Greece), Suda Bay (Crete), Salonika (Greece), and eight other possible bases. In each case the procedure might vary slightly but an advanced recce party was to land with a platoon of infantry from a destroyer. Senior officers of this party were to contact the local civil authority,[7] and mark out the initial landing point for MLCs and the location of the main supply dump (the Depot). The water supply would be tested, local communications noted and sketch maps of routes to dumps etc. prepared. The main reconnaissance group, consisting of the advanced MNBDO HQ and the 1st Echelon – some mobile AA batteries, signallers, a rifle platoon to lay defensive wire, and the tented hospital's advanced section – were to land on D+1. With them were 430+ officers and men of the Landing and Maintenance Unit with two or four MLCs. This somewhat large reconnaissance group made surveys for various base headquarters, gun sites and other accommodation; for, when established, an advanced Naval base had a

Naval HQ of 179, accommodation for relief crews of ships and possibly those many and varied facilities from canteens to heavy workshops found in any major Naval base.

At least this seems to have been the peacetime concept, for the landing of an MNBDO was not expected to face more than enemy air raids for some days, if not weeks. With only a few landing craft, the policy was to land personnel from ships before their equipment was brought ashore. But each unit had sufficient rations, ammunition and 'fighting equipment'[8] to be self-sufficient for 14 days. In this period the protective mounds (not unlike: sangars) round heavy anti-aircraft guns would be built, and camouflage frames and nets would have been taken ashore with each unit. The time-scale for landings indicates the need for this self-sufficiency: D-Day, advanced recce party, 83 all ranks; D+1 main recce party with four 3-in AA guns, 328 men; D+2, 394 men with Bofors guns and four more '3-in'. There would therefore be only some 800 men ashore in the first few days, and the main body, some 3,200 more Marines, would be landed in the following days. A prolonged time scale by the standards of the 1990s. The main convoy bringing in MNBDO personnel was expected within 48 hours of D-Day,[9] so major landings could commence, while the reconnaissance force 'would install and bring into action the armaments . . . establish communications' and the command headquarters to maintain the force,[10] defending the 1,000 Naval personnel landed once the base was established.

The reality turned out to be something quite different.

While the Corps had been establishing both MNBDO I and II, and the RM Division of three brigades, more mature age groups were being called up. The coast artillery batteries formed in January 1941, for example, had many more 30-year-olds[1] than those formed in 1940, mainly composed of 18-year-olds. It was these young men who at 19 or 20 would first see action in Crete. By this date other elements of the Corps – at sea, in the Fleet Air Arm, protecting Channel port demolition parties, with the AA batteries in Anti-Aircraft Defence Great Britain (ADGB) Command – had been in action, and the Unit History Summaries (Appendix 4) show other operations in which they were engaged. The RM Boom Scaffolding Unit launched wire-trailing balloons to damage German electricity cables, a detachment floated mines down German rivers, and others operated Dutch schuytes (fishing boats) in the English Channel (two of the three boats were commanded by RM officers and acted as Q-ships to catch E-boats unawares), fired anti-aircraft guns on sea forts, served in the Harwich Auxiliary Patrol, and provided ground defences for Naval air stations. A number of senior officers were also detached on important duties outside the Corps.

The Chiefs of Staff decision to send MNBDO I to Egypt was prompted by developments in Greece and Albania, for the Greeks were in favour of a British Naval base being established at Suda Bay in Crete some weeks after the Italian invasion of Greece late in October 1940.[2] The Germans at this time had adopted a neutral position over the Italian-Greek war, and the Greeks were not anxious to have the support of a British force ashore at that time; but the 2nd Battalion

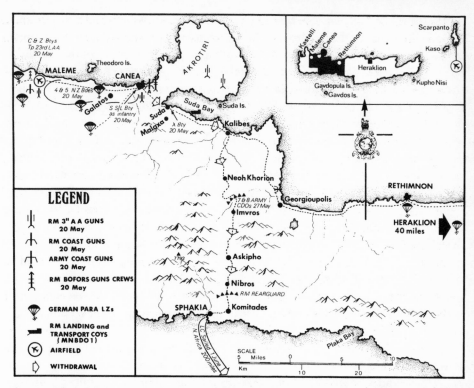

Crete and Suda-Sphakia areas with principal deployment of units in the island's defence in May 1941 and actions by Royal Marines of the Mobile Naval Base Defence Organisation I.

York and Lancaster Regiment was landed in Crete before the end of October and an infantry brigade was to be deployed there.[3] Earlier the Marines from HMS *Liverpool* had mounted two batteries each of two 6-in Naval Mk VII guns – although they were considered to have an inadequate range from the sites available – at Suda Bay to protect the entrance and at Canea, to the west of its protective headland, covering waters a bombarding fleet might use. The navy was also installing some 4-in gun batteries. The '6-in' were set in concrete with 4½ft bolts holding the base plate; and magazines, dugouts, and communications were installed by December with OPs that could be linked to the monitor HMS *Terror* when she was in the anchorage. Magazines were also cut into hill sides with 10-ft narrow tunnels to the 12-ft by 6-ft chambers.[4] Later when HMS *York* was sunk by Italian explosive boats, she settled on the bottom in shallow water and some of her guns were landed.

The British Army became heavily committed in Greece, although the Chiefs of Staff on 8 January 1941 had decided that any intervention there would court a second 'Dunkirk'. Even the Greek General Papagos – who commanded the Greek armies in 1941 – thought that the British expeditionary force's three divisions would have been better employed in Africa, for nine British divisions were needed in Greece if any strong Balkan front was to be established.[5] For political reasons not military ones, therefore, the force was built up in Greece. Meanwhile from Crete 50 and 52 (Army) Commandos – who had been raised in North Africa – mounted a raid on Kastellorizon, an island near the Turkish coast. They were landed there in December 1940, as the Navy hoped to use it as an MTB base, but the Italian garrison on Rhodes counter-attacked with vigour in a landing that largely destroyed '50' and '52'. Admiral Cunningham 'sent 25 Marines bristling with machine-guns in [the river gunboat] *Ladybird* ... but some fool ordered them to re-embark'.[6] The Commando survivors were brought back some days later, after their wireless had failed – so the Royal Navy received no news of the Italians' attack until British destroyers visited the island.

When the Germans invaded, the British obligations under treaties with Greece were partly met by 6 and 7 Australian and the New Zealand Divisions with an armoured brigade and ancillary troops.[7] The Germans – to retrieve the Italians' failures, for the Greeks held the Italians throughout the winter – had launched 32 divisions on 6 April 1941 through Yugoslavia and Greece. The Yugoslav government capitulated on 17 April but RM commandos would fight in support of Yugoslav partisans some three years later; and in Greece the Allied forces were defeated in 10 days, the last formal evacuation to Crete being made on 29 April.[8] Although 14,700 British and Dominion troops had been casualties, many of them prisoners-of-war, the Royal Navy evacuated over 50,000,[9] many from open beaches, and landed 30,000 on Crete.

This island, about the size of Yorkshire or Puerto Rico, is mountainous and largely barren away from the coast, its half-million population, tough peasant farmers and fishermen, many of whom had been serving in Greece that spring of 1941. The German *Fliegerkorps* XI was at this time preparing 500 transports and gliders to carry 4,000 airborne and paratroops from Greece to Crete, after *Fliegerkorps* VIII, with 600 bombers and fighters and 50 reconnaissance planes, had spent some weeks softening up the island. The German airborne troops, having carried out extensive exercises after their victories in Norway and Holland, were to meet MNBDO I on Crete, the Marines having been in transports at sea for much of the previous 12 weeks.

The prelude to the invasion of Crete included an Axis advance in the Western Desert of North Africa where six months earlier the Italians had been driven back by a swift British advance, supported on its right flank by strong Naval forces. These were Force A of the monitor HMS *Terror* and three river gunboats; Force B of four destroyers; Force C of HMS *Barham*, HMS *Malaya*, a cruiser and seven destroyers; and Force D of the carrier HMS *Eagle*, three cruisers and seven destroyers.[1] During mid-December 1940 Force A bombarded Italian positions and supply routes, the 15-in turret of HMS *Terror* manned by Royal Marines, bombarding Halfaya and Sollum in day-long shoots to hamper the Italians' use of these passes.[2] The British Army reached Tobruk in five days, *Terror*'s last major bombardment being on the port's western defences. Then, as the Army continued to advance, she sailed some 200 miles further west to Benghazi. This port, in range of the Axis airfields in Tripolitania, was bombed and mined intensively, and without adequate anti-aircraft protection could not be regularly used by the Royal Navy,[3] although a number of ships were in the port on 22 February when *Terror* was hit in a dive-bombing attack.[4] By this time her guns were worn smooth, having fired more shells than any other 15-in turret in the Royal Navy. Nevertheless she was taken in tow for Alexandria but next day (23 February) she sank off Derna. General Rommel had landed in Africa earlier that month with Panzer formations which would become the *Afrika Korps*. His influence became far greater in these campaigns than the British had expected early in 1941, although his later victories were helped by the British fragmentation of their divisions; for unco-ordinated counter-attacks by brigade groups of armour and infantry were dealt with in turn by the relatively small panzer divisions, each at times with only 20 to 30 tanks.[5] Not until these British brigade groups were re-formed into divisions was the Axis advance finally checked near El Alamein.

As the British Army withdrew in the Mediterranean area, the Royal Navy came under increasing pressure from the shore-based Axis planes. However, there were British successes at Taranto, in a Fleet Air Arm attack on this Italian naval base on 11–12 November 1940, and at Cape Matapan on 28 March 1941, when Royal Navy ships and planes damaged the Italian flag ship, and sank three heavy cruisers[6] and several smaller ships. In this battle the radars of HMS *Warspite* and *Ajax* gave the British a much clearer picture of their targets than the Italians could make out when the action continued after dark; and 3,000 Italians were killed or drowned. Next day an attack by 16 Ju 88s failed to prevent the British fleet returning safely from their pursuit of the Italians towards Taranto.[7] By May, however, with the *Luftwaffe* established in Sicily, Greece and on island airfields, the Royal Navy's operations in the eastern Mediterranean were severely restricted. See chapter 6 for RM aircrews' participation in these earlier actions.

In addition, before the battle for Crete began in the Mediterranean, the German battleships *Bismarck* and *Prinz Eugen* broke out into the North Atlantic, threatening not only convoys from America but also British reinforcement of the Middle East. They had been reported on their passage from the Baltic to northern Norway, and were shadowed by British cruisers' radar as they passed south through the Denmark Strait between Iceland and Greenland on 23 May. At this time HMS *Norfolk* came within 6 miles of the *Bismarck*, and the battleship opened fire in the late evening, before the British cruiser disengaged, to report the German presence to the British Battle Fleet 600 miles to the south.[8] This Fleet steamed northward, with HMS *Hood* in the van, although this battle-cruiser after a long refit had not fully worked up her efficiency. She also had only 7-in deck armour, making her vulnerable to plunging fire at ranges over 12,000yds. Her consort, HMS *Prince of Wales*, on the other hand, as a modern battleship was safe from vital hits by heavy shells from extreme ranges down to 13,000yds.[9]

As they closed the German ships, wireless silence was maintained and radar not used in the hope of surprising the enemy, the British ships steaming in the last few minutes at high speed to close the range, before all the ships opened fire at 0553 hours on 24 May. Approaching in this way, only the forward British guns could bear, with four of *Hood*'s 15-in and six of the *Prince of Wales*'s 14-in able to fire at *Bismarck*. The intention had been to concentrate fire on this battleship but *Hood* appears to have mistaken the cruiser *Prinz Eugen* for *Bismark*. As a result, in the vital opening minutes, the Germans had clear shots at *Hood*, with all their turrets able to bear as they steamed across the line of the British approach. *Prince of Wales*, her radar not registering, was forced to use her small range-finder on the director, as the larger turret range-finders were obscured by spray. She therefore took six salvoes to straddle *Bismarck*, and by then fatal hits had been made on *Hood*. The Germans had concentrated on her, and, using their accurate optical range-finders, were able to score the first hit within minutes of opening fire at 24,000yds. These hits started a fire among the 9.4 tons of rocket-wire projectiles for use against low-flying aircraft and exposed on *Hood*'s upper deck, minutes later at 0600 hours she was straddled by *Bismarck*'s shells as the British battle-cruiser turned to port to bring her after guns to bear. *Hood* then 'blew-up in a huge explosion',[10] all but three of her 1,420 complement being lost, including 151 Royal Marines.

As *Prince of Wales* avoided the wreckage, she was hit several times by accurate German fire before breaking off the action at 0613. Mechanical breakdowns in two turrets, which her builders' men aboard worked to repair – her armament having not been fully tested – contributed to this decision.[11] *Bismark* had not avoided damage, hits forward having contaminated her fuel tanks and two hours after the battle the German admiral[12] abandoned his Atlantic foray, heading for the French coast ports. But she was hit by aircraft torpedoes, her rudders jammed, and she was caught later by HMS *King George V* and *Rodney*. The opening German fire aimed at these ships was accurate but fell away, no doubt because the crew had spent much of the night fighting off destroyer attacks. Nevertheless they fought to the end, *Bismarck* going down with her colours flying about 1035 hours on 27 May with the loss of 2,100 men.

These Naval actions were fought in protection of British convoys, for they were only given close escort by April 1941 to 19W, some 500 miles from Ireland, and as far as 47N,[13] some 200 miles south of Land's End (Cornwall). Not until 27 May would the first convoy, HX 129, be escorted all the way from Halifax (Nova Scotia) across the Atlantic.[14]

The transports of MNBDO I had sailed north about Ireland heading for South Africa the previous February, a journey which for one LAA battery[15] had begun badly – over 48 hours in the train and transit camp and a 6-hour wait in river lighters, before embarking on one of the three transports that would take them from the Clyde to South Africa. Such delays were almost inevitable when dock installations had been bombed, the rail network was overloaded, and ships were anchored while an estuary was swept of mines. Whether or not these problems affected MNBDO I's morale is doubtful, but the cumulative effect of air raids over the previous year made any troop movements a slow business, and getting 5,174 troops[16] embarked was no easy task. The ships were overcrowded, and, following the usual practice of the time, would not revictual until they were in an overseas port. Even water was short aboard *Rangitata*[17] and the last breakfast sitting was at 1000 hours, but the conditions improved somewhat as the Royal Marine officers got things organised. Among the training instructions was RBW 16, 'Local Protection against Parachutists or Airborne Troops',[18] issued nine weeks before many of the men would put this lesson into practice. During a six days' stay in Durban, the MNBDO marched past the mayor before boarding a convoy for Egypt, where they were stationed in Tahag Camp. Major General E.C. Weston of MNBDO I flew to Crete on 21 April 'to superintend the arrival of troops from Greece'. The 'camps' these soldiers took over were no more than areas pegged out among the olive groves, while some platoons had only one razor between 30 men.[19]

At 0830 hours on a fine Tuesday morning (20 May 1941) a German troop glider crash-landed outside Canea on the north-east coast of Crete. A Section of Marines, with their company commander,[1] held their fire as the airborne troops clambered out, then killed them with a volley of shots.[2] Three more Germans were found dead in the crashed aircraft along with two wireless sets. These glider troops were well equipped, each man with his *Schmeisser* (more correctly MP38),[3] five or more grenades and some 100 rounds apiece for this initial assault by three Independent Companies of 7 Air Division's Assault Regiment, who had flown into the Canea area. One company overran two 3-in AA guns of the RM 'C' battery on the Akrotiri peninsula north-east of Canea, when the gliders landed to take out the anti-aircraft defences before the paratroops of the Division were dropped. The first counter-attack by a composite force of Marines and other troops was stopped about 1245 hours, when Captain A.L. Laxton was wounded trying to get within grenade-tossing range. He stayed near enough to the battery's site, however, to indicate the Germans' positions when a second attack was mounted a couple of hours later. In this two platoons of 'S' Searchlight Battery – its 450[4] Marines fighting as infantry – joined companies of 9th KRRC and the Greek 2nd Regiment to recapture the guns intact and release their crews, about 30 men.[5] Most of the other glider companies around Canea had equally brief successes or were mopped up during the next day. It was reported that 'the pilots seemed to disregard [the unsuitability of] the ground'.[6] Elsewhere they had better fortune, the German command, following the proven axiom of reinforcing strength, putting their reserves into Maleme airfield some 8 miles west of Canea.

'S' Battery's HQ and an RM Section,[7] all with rifles but no Bren guns, was sent there as soon as paratroops were seen to be dropping near the airfield, which had two of its three runways unfinished near the sea. A New Zealand battalion held the perimeter and a hill (south of the airstrip) on which two 3-in AA guns of the RM 'C' Battery were sited close to the hill top at about 100ft, with 'Z' RM Battery's two 4-in coast guns on a lower ridge. There was also a Troop of RM 23rd LAA Regiment's crews with the Army Bofors batteries ringing the airfield, and near the beach, where they could fire on invasion barges. The New Zealanders, cleverly camouflaged and dug in around both the hill and airfield, were from 22nd New Zealand Battalion, a well-disciplined unit which initially had no trouble holding the German attacks, for the paratroops were dropped amongst them and the New Zealand Division's other battalions to the east were in positions south of the coast road. In fact, many Ju 52 pilots, fearing that their parachutists might float down into the sea, did not release them as intended over undefended areas, although the dropping zones they chose probably appeared to be safe, because these New Zealanders' positions were also well camouflaged.

Heavy bombing of the airfield at breakfast time had caused few casualties,[8] but the dust and smoke obscured the Bofors gunners' aim; while the air transports' 'dropping' height of about 300ft was below that for effective '3-in' fire, and some low level attacks from 100ft were even below the height of 'C' Battery's two guns. Each stick of paratroops, with 12 to 15 men in a stick,[9] took 5 seconds to hit the ground, and then were spread over several hundred yards and needed to reach their weapon containers quickly; so among the New Zealand battalions east of the airfield they never got a major force assembled. To the west they had more success, however, where some 50 gliders put down, many in the dry river bed just west of the airfield. This glider force accounted for most of the Bofors batteries, five gliders coming close to the coast guns of 'Z' Battery, where only 20 of the 100 or so Marines of the gun crews survived to be eventually captured. Other gliders later came in to the airstrip, inside the New Zealand perimeter, for ten Hurricanes had been expected that morning and the runway had not, therefore, been blocked.

The New Zealanders, in 4 and 5 Brigades, are referred to in Marine reports and orders as the New Zealand Division, although they probably had never more than 3,000 men. They were defending the 8 miles of the Suda-Maleme road, expecting a seaborne assault as well as airborne landings to their south.[10] New Zealand patrols accounted for many of the paratroops who had not been killed when falling into the battalion positions, there was little that could be done about the build-up of Germans to the west of the airfield. Further west Greek irregulars around the little port of Kastelli had disposed somewhat ruthlessly with the men of II Battalion of the Assault Regiment landed there on 20 May,[11] and in the style of the natural law of vendetta, here and elsewhere, took few prisoners. Many shot at any body of soldiers on the assumption that Germans could be wearing British uniforms,[12] others 'stripped the dead of their clothes . . . [despite] the bodies decomposing rapidly in the fierce heat . . . in some cases slitting their throats presumably to make sure' that they were dead. But not all the airborne forces General Student had planned to land at Maleme that Tuesday could be flown there, because the airfields in Corinth (Greece) were congested and flight schedules ran late.[13]

The plan of attack was now becoming clear, with four separate but related sorties:[14] the Assault Regiment (roughly equivalent to a British Brigade) would mainly land west of Maleme; 3rd Para Regiment, reinforced by a parachute engineer battalion, would land in the Canea-Suda Bay area; 2nd Para Regiment at Rethimnon, over 30 miles east of Canea; and 1st Para Regiment further east still at Heraklion; altogether there would be some 17,000 para and airborne troops. They would be followed by 6 Mountain Division's 9,000 men[15] to be landed on captured airfields. On Tuesday evening, 20 May, Major-General B.C.

Freyberg, VC, commanding the Allied forces in Crete, signalled to the General Headquarters in Cairo that the airfields – Maleme, Rethimnon and Heraklion – were being held he thought, but the margin was small, as it was at the harbours at Canea and Suda.[16]

General Freyberg tended to leave his commanders to judge situations for themselves, but when asked to reinforce a brigade with troops to hold the area west of Maleme airfield, he did not want to weaken the line south of the coast road in case of seaborne landings. Yet the Germans had only a tenuous hold on the airfield, as General Student later confirmed: 'Had the enemy made an all out effort to counter attack that [Tuesday] night of 20 May . . . the Storm Regiments suffering from lack of ammunition, could have been wiped out'.[17] An analysis of military decisions long after the event can often produce an easy solution, standing out from the map on your study floor. You are not struggling with scraps of dubious information, eyes blurred with fatigue; there is no dust, no thirst, no pounding of the adrenaline as mortar bombs fall closer to the HQ dugout. All forces at first glance are judged to be at full war establishment. The reality is different, and in Crete the improvisation of units after their evacuation from Greece left an average New Zealand and Australian battalion some 350 strong,[18] less than half their war establishment. They had few light machine guns and a hotchpotch of supporting artillery, but they were in good heart. There was little or no transport, although the battalions were still strung along the Maleme-Suda road, and in the two other concentrations, at Rethimnon (Retimo in 1941 orders) and Heraklion. For these defence forces the MNBDO had expected to provide only coastal and anti-aircraft batteries as the C-in-C Mediterranean had kept the Land Defence Force and other units in Egypt 'in view of the uncertain situation then prevailing in Crete'.[19]

The Organisation was therefore split into sub-units over a wide area, as the table below shows in their dispositions on 20 May.[20] They had not been landed, however, to the tactical plan they were expecting to follow as laid down in the MNBDO operational plan, with a main reconnaissance force and so on. In fact, the units had all been landed on the island on 10 May, except for the 23rd LAA Regiment and the searchlight battery, which landed 5 days later. These latter units were intended to relieve the gunners of 7th Australian LAA Battery and 304th Searchlight Battery RA, respectively, but neither unit could be replaced before 20 May.

The landed strength of the MNBDO on the island at this date was as follows:

	Officers	Other ranks (enlisted men)
MALEME		
'Z' Coast Battery, 2 × 4-in (102mm) on Hill 107	4	88
'C' Battery's 2 × 3-in (76mm) AA on Hill 107	2	55
One Troop Bofors from 23rd LAA Regt by airfield	2	40(?)
SUDA–CANEA		
Advanced Group HQ, Air Defence Bde HQ, survey		

(3 + 26) and Signals (8 + 200) at various sites	22	286
'A' Battery, 8 × 3-in with 2 at Aroni, 2 Sternes, 2 Melaxa and 2 Stada Point	10	249
'C' Battery's 2 × 3-in at St John's Hill	2	55(?)
Two troops Bofors of 23rd LAA Bty at various sites	4	98(?)
'S' Searchlight Bty and 11th S/L Regt HQ in infantry role	17	437
Landing Company in dock area	7	138
Transport Company based in Suda	5	118
Tented hospital	7	30
Air Defence Bde units with 4 × 2-pdr Pom-Poms and three Lewis (DELS) on Suda Island		
COVERING RETHIMNON		
'X' Coast Battery, 2 × 4-in at Georgioupolis	4	84
HERAKLION		
'C' Battery's 4 × 3-in AA with Bty HQ near airfield	9	128
One Troop Bofors from 23rd: LAA Bty, sites not known	2	40(?)

A small number of individuals from other units of MNBDO I were also on the island for reconnaissance and other specialist duties. Much of the stores, however, were still in ships at Haifa (Palestine), including the mountings for three 6-in coast guns.

The only major-counter attack at Maleme was launched on the Thursday morning, 22 May, after the experienced 2/7th Australian Battalion was moved west to hold the coast road, releasing the 20th New Zealand Battalion to join the 28th Maori Battalion. By this time any possibility of an amphibious assault was out of the question, for the Mediterranean Fleet caught 6,300 Germans in two fleets of caiques north of the island on Wednesday night and Thursday morning (21–22 May). The German losses were only 297,[21] although at the time reported as 'many thousands', but the small fleets were scattered and no seaborne German reinforcements reached the island during the battle.

At the time the sea action was being fought, the Australian 2/7th was delayed by bombing, by losing its way after dark in Canea, and those mishaps to be expected in a hurried move along difficult roads. The battalion reached the New Zealanders about 0300 hours and the two assault battalions began their attacks with some 3 miles to their objectives. They were checked at Maleme cemetery and the sun was rising before they reached the perimeter of the airfield. About this time a Ju 52 made a trial landing and successfully took off immediately from the airstrip, and within a few hours, at 0800, the first 40 men of 6 Mountain Division were off-loaded from a Ju 52 in 70 seconds. Already the New Zealanders had pulled back, for not only had their assault battalions – despite spirited bayonet fighting – been repulsed, but the whole brigade was likely to be cut off by a para regiment (probably equal in strength to the brigade, for both had taken casualties) established on the flank at Galatos. The withdrawal had begun, although many German mountain troops would be killed on the airstrip before the makeshift units of New Zealand artillery virtually ran out of ammunition, and by the Army crews of the 6-in battery – installed by Marines that spring – shelling the airstrip. But the guns could not stop the incoming planes.

Some Marines from the gun crews on Hill 107 had found themselves that Wednesday morning, 21 May, alone with a handful of Fleet Air Arm and RAF ground crews. Several days before they had seen the last Gladiator crash-land after shooting down an Me 109. The Marines had been firing Brens, Lewis guns and a Hurricane's Browning over the dry river bed[22] from positions on Hill 107, with much success when the paratroops began to land, but the gunners reported the silencing of the Bofors on the airstrip early in the battle. Gradually during Wednesday, however, they were forced back to the road; they helped to protect the New Zealand artillery's guns for much of Thursday, 22 May, before moving back along the Canea road in good order, with a Captain RM commanding the 140 men, including some Army personnel.

The Marines of 'S' Battalion, its Regiment's HQ and MNBDO I HQ Company, scattered by this time over a wide area, were part of the composite garrison of Canea, with men of the 9th KRRC, some Greeks, military police, Army drivers and the 'Royal Perivolians', 700 men – survivors from 24 different regiments – who had been in Perivolia transit camp.[23] During Wednesday and Thursday they spent much of their time trying to run supplies up the road to Maleme, 'clearing the road of debris and unexploded bombs, by day'[24] before escorting the supply trucks forward at night. As the Germans infiltrated into positions to block this route, setting up machine-guns on fixed lines of fire, a Section or two of Marines or Army privates went down the road in two trucks. When they had drawn the enemy's fire, other Marines worked down the flank to take out the machine-gunners. There were many acts of bravery during the battles around Canea, but as this is a history of Royal Marines, only examples of their daring are given, although the acts of courage among all services on the island are recognised.

The RM Bofors crews stuck to their task, using dummy guns in some pits so they could switch around from position to position, in attempting to avoid the close attention of dive-bombers. They probably shot down some 20[25] of these before the crews joined the infantry, as their guns were knocked out. The AA gunners had taken the brunt of the German air attacks at all the airfields and ports, and General Weston felt that they found this more unnerving than casualties from infantry attacks.[26] However, the guns of 'A' Battery, firing in this barrage, were exposed on St John's Hill, taking 18 per cent casualties before being moved into the olive groves to fire at opportunity targets. Elsewhere Marine B.V. Jones improvised his own anti-aircraft defence,[27] shooting down one plane by firing his Bren gun from the shoulder. Not long afterwards seven German paratroops dropped near his slit trench, and he chased them away with a lone bayonet charge. Another AA gunner, a corporal, stayed with his Bofors despite repeated attacks, and kept it in action, claiming 20 planes, according to a press release.

Sergeant C. Bowden RM, a patient in the Army's tented hospital between

Maleme and Suda, was turned out of his ward by paratroopers. The 300 patients[28] were then marched south into some olive groves, one man being shot for lowering his arms when his trousers fell down, no doubt making all the patients cautious. They encountered a New Zealand patrol, and were caught in Bren-gun fire, but the patients' shouts warned the Bren-gunner, who with his next burst killed three of their guards. Going back to their tents, the patients found most of them burnt to the ground and they were therefore moved to Suda.[29] From there Sergeant Bowden – in pyjamas, boots and his Royal Marine cap – rejoined 'S' Battalion after nearly being shot by wary British sentries. The bombing and strafing added to their difficulties in identifying friend from foe, since sentries or others in the open had to stand 'perfectly still with heads down trying to disguise ourselves as trees',[30] for the slightest movement in daylight when a plane was overhead brought down a burst of fire. The Marine drivers of the MNBDO Transport Company, half of which had been landed before the battle, had even then been put at needless risk, as were despatch riders, by troops – jumpy after air attacks in Greece – firing on any light they saw at night. They were also particularly exposed to air attacks, and on occasions from infiltrating German patrols.

The driver of one Matador, at least, successfully drove out of a German ambush, despite the machine-gun fire.[31] Others were not so fortunate and the Naval staff of the MNBDO Tented Hospital – 7 doctors and 30 medical orderlies – dealt with over 500 casualties of all services in the first week of the battle, '200 being dealt with in one batch'.[32] Later they safely transferred all their patients to the main military hospital before being evacuated.

At Heraklion the first paratroops had landed at 1700 hours[33] on Tuesday evening, 20 May, but no gliders were reported. The Australian Bofors gunners, with those from 23rd RM LAA Bty, and the four '3-in' of 'C' (RM) Bty's anti-aircraft guns with their Battery Headquarters, caused many casualties, one troop plane bursting into flames and each parachute silk exploding in a fire-ball before the jumpers plummeted to the ground. Those that escaped the shellfire were caught in the fire of Brig B. Chappell's brigade: coalminers from Leicestershire, Scots of the Black Watch, RA gunners fighting as infantry, 2/4th Australians, and two Greek battalions. Although some Germans got into the port, most landed where they were expected, near 'C' Bty's HQ at the airfield. By next day, therefore, this 1st Para Regiment had been largely destroyed, enabling the Greek King and his Cabinet to be evacuated to the south coast; before further German attempts to consolidate a ring round the town were broken up by artillery fire, half a dozen light tanks and an 'I' (Infantry) tank, over 1,000 German dead were counted. But as the Germans decided to put their reinforcements into Maleme, Heraklion was not directly attacked by airborne forces, who began to concentrate in the undefended areas a mile or so south and west of the town.[34] A few Hurricanes were flown in but the German air bombardment now intensified. 'C' Battery's two 3-in guns had most of their fire-control gear damaged but, using improvised sights and pre-set fuses, claimed seven planes;[35] they also fired low-burst HE against ground targets to good effect. But the town had been destroyed before two companies of 5th Argylls [36] came into the perimeter from the south

– they had landed on Monday, 19 May.[37] German troop planes, however, were landing their reinforcements on the shore 17 miles west of Heraklion.

The battle for Heraklion lasted 9 days, 'C' Bty and the 23rd's Bofors remaining in action till the last,[38] with only two Bofors out of action through mechanical defects, before Brig Chappell's force was evacuated on the night of 28–29 May. At this time, according to one report, a Marine flyer attempted to fly off the only Hurricane left on the airfield, but he was shot down. Later some 50 men[39] of 'C' Bty aboard the destroyer HMS *Hereward* were brought back to the island after she was hit by dive-bombers, and most of them became prisoners-of-war. The Navy, as it did elsewhere on Crete, had added to the risks of sailing in these waters by staying that extra hour to embark more troops.[40] The cruisers HMS *Dido* and *Orion* were then badly damaged and several destroyers hit, for they were not beyond the *Luftwaffe*'s range before daylight after leaving Heraklion.

At Rethimnon the Australians had even less opportunity to escape from the island. They had killed some 700 Germans in 10 days of fighting, and when 6 Mountain Division came in from the west, there was only a day's rations and little ammunition left. The local Greek battalion, raised three weeks earlier, had melted into the hills. Of the 1,000 Australians[41] here, 160 had been killed, 140 refused to surrender and the rest were captured. The men of RM 'X' Bty, who with their 4-in guns and their Lewis-gun detachment had been covering the Bay west of Rethimnon, were not called on to fire and had withdrawn into the Suda perimeter about 27 May.[42]

General Weston commanded the forces in the Suda-Canea area, including the New Zealand brigades when these withdrew further eastwards on the Friday, 23 May, pulling 5 Brigade back another 2½ miles towards Canea;[43] but by this time its strength was only about 1,200 men. This left the Germans with the unchallenged use of Maleme airfield, for the exhausted New Zealanders had no reserves to draw on. The 'two platoons of Marines', in much the same state after their pounding at Maleme, have been criticised for withdrawing,[44] but it seems likely that they were the gunners we have seen earlier falling back towards Canea in good order, and there is no purpose served in the fragmented losses of any troops. The map on the study floor suggests that somewhat different concentrations of strength early in the battle might have swayed the outcome in Freyberg's favour, but that is only conjecture. He certainly intended to attack again, but his forces were now weaker than the Germans, who had fresh mountain troops coming in every day. The New Zealanders held them at Galatas but, though they might be checked, the Germans were determined to take the island regardless of losses.

General Weston, 'a man of almost irritating fearlessness,'[45] intended to check the Germans again, in order that the rear area troops could be evacuated, but the Royal Navy's operations north and east of the island were by now severely limited, for the few RAF fighters were driven from the island, after brave attempts to fly in reinforcements, and ships were exposed to continuous daylight attacks. Nevertheless the *Luftwaffe*'s airfield on Scarpanto Island, some 15 minutes' flying time from the main battle areas, was bombarded on the first night of the landings and bombed five nights later by planes from HMS *Formidable*.[46] There had been a plan for Marines – drawn from those who had installed the 6-in guns during the winter – to float in rafts with a 4-in gun on to Kaso an island a few miles west of the Scarpanto field, which they planned to bombard at night and hide up in caves during the day,[47] but the scheme was abandoned in March, when commando-style raids had not proved successful. HMS *Kelly* (Captain Lord Mountbatten RN) and HMS *Kashmir* bombarded Maleme on the second night, Wednesday, 21–22 May,[48] but by 26 May there seems little likelihood that the RAF or Royal Navy could operate on the island's north-west coast. Holding the Germans on Greece and Crete, however, delayed the opening of their campaign in Russia, leaving them too few months to reach Moscow before the winter freeze and the Russian army stopped them.

On Crete after the first five days of battle the MNBDO HQ Company and the reorganised Canea/Suda garrison were in the line of defences by the coast west of Canea. 'S' Battery and the HQ of the 11th RM Searchlight Regiment, as part of the Suda Battalion were on the garrison's left. In four days of fighting these Marine units had taken some 400 prisoners 'and killed many Germans'.[49] The Searchlight Battery, as an infantry battalion, had then been moved to Mournies on Friday, 23 May. Here the Australians they were to relieve 'were clearing the olive groves with bursts of fire and much shouting',[50] no doubt to make sure that they did not kill each other. Men of the RM Signals Company laid the Battalion's telephone lines, as they did for other units of the MNBDO, keeping the lines repaired despite the bombing and stray German parachutists. The Battalion also found that good slit trenches had been dug here, and the men set about establishing themselves in these positions. On their left were Greek irregulars, and the Marines were joined by men of 23rd LAA Battery, whose guns had been destroyed in the bombing, and by an enterprising sapper. The mines he armed from a German supply container were laid for the expected German tanks. Later, when an Australian gun team arrived, they fired on the prison, a German strongpoint,[51] this fire brought heavy air attacks in counter-bombardment on the Marines. A day or so later (Sunday, 25 May) the Greek irregulars left for the hills when civilians evacuated Canea, and the Searchlight Battalion now found there were gaps between its defended areas and its neighbours, a situation for which MNBDO units were prepared. They also joked about General Weston's car, ditched in one open space after dodging a bomb.

By Monday afternoon, 26 May, 'the firing had intensified',[52] the farm where the Suda Battalion had its HQ was bombed, and an Australian battalion – 2/7th – filtered through the Marines to form up as a reserve. Although General Weston had the New Zealand Division under command, he was in a difficult position, for he had General Freyberg's orders to hold the line; and so, when the New Zealand Divisional Commander asked for permission to withdraw his brigades, Weston would not give his approval without reference to Freyberg. There were inevitable delays, as General Weston was obliged to walk to Freyberg's head-quarters to discuss the proposal.[53] But as no orders had been received by 1030 hours,[54] the New Zealand Division's commander withdrew eastwards, through the centre of the reserve battalion's defences. Freyberg's confirmation of the order not to retreat did not reach the Division until the early hours of the following morning, when they had already fallen back. The New Zealand official historian of 'Crete' analyses the timing of orders from General Weston's headquarters, and comes to the conclusion that there were inexplicable delays not only in issuing orders to the New Zealanders but also to the Force Reserve, a point we shall come back to.

Courage is not an inexhaustible commodity, and many companies of the battalions which had fought superbly during the previous week became disorganised, for no co-ordination of routes or times for all the troops' moves appeared to have been arranged.[55] The Marines, in good order, also withdrew when ordered to by their brigade commander. Another composite brigade, the Force Reserve, had been sent forward to relieve the New Zealanders. But was now exposed by the New Zealander's withdrawals, despite General Weston's attempts to recall the Reserve. Its 1,200 men[56] of the Welch Regiment, Hussars, and the King's Royal Rifle Corps lost three-quarters of their strength fighting their way back to Canea in the evening of Tuesday, 27 May. This was the day after General Weston issued formal orders for the withdrawal. There has been criticism of the General's and other senior officers' loss of control at this time, but a man on his feet with no radio communications and few staff cannot control a mobile battle. The Allies' difficulties in Crete stemmed from wider issues than any sudden withdrawal: one analysis,[57] not long after the battle, implied a criticism of the GOC, Wavell, for not clearly defining the roles of the original Crete garrison. Was Crete a staging post for the RAF? Was it a defended island? Not until three weeks before the Germans landed was the garrison's task defined as denying 'the enemy the use of air bases'. What is sometimes overlooked, however, is that Crete is Greek territory and excessive British interest in early 1941 was discouraged.

For some of the Searchlight Battalion, however, there had been little chance to deny the enemy anything, for the Germans never attacked their positions, 'most unfortunately some of us thought'.[58] Others remember digging in, building tank traps[59] and hearing the rumours of thousands of Germans killed at sea. Major R.W. Madoc (later Major General, CB, DSO, OBE), remembers the move eastward in the early hours of Tuesday, 27 May; the Marines were bombed and companies split up as troops pushed in from the side roads, but the Marines reached Neoh Khorion before dark. This road junction, some four miles south of Suda Bay, lay at the northern end of the only route for wheeled vehicles going south through the mountains, often climbing in sharp S-bends. Near here was the supply point set up that morning by men of MNBDO's Transport Company, when they ran several lorry loads of rations down the road from Suda, as General Weston intended to set up an assembly area, to form what scratch units he could bring together from men who had lost their companies.[60] Thousands of small but welcome rations were issued, each man getting at least one tin of 'Meat and Veg' and a packet of biscuits.[61]

On the road from Suda 'S' Battalion was to have met the Army commander of its Suda Brigade, but he did not arrive.[62] The Battalion's commanding officer

– considering that there were less exposed positions – declined to form a rearguard here, but moved the Battalion up the road into the hills. The Lewis guns were abandoned as the young Marines slogged up the mountain road; they were strafed but not as often now, for they were clear of the north coast, and once over the main pass they halted nine miles from Sphakia (Khora Sphakion), where they could see the south coast. On this road men of the Army's Commando Brigade – 7 and 8 Commandos – were preparing defence positions. They had landed early that morning from a fast mine-layer in Suda Bay,[63] and during the next few days made dusk raids with small fighting patrols to discourage the Germans from probing forward at night.

The Marines were gathered together in a gulley as they came south down the road, and *ad hoc* units formed before they moved five miles further south through Imvros, to positions on the south-west slopes of a pass overlooking the road. Some units went further south, but late on Wednesday afternoon, 28 May, they were reorganised into a battalion of four infantry companies: No. 1 from 23rd RM LAA Battery; No. 2 from 'X' and 'Z' Coast Batteries; No. 3 from 'S' Battery (searchlight crews); and No. 4 from 'A' Battery of AA-gun crews. 'S' Battery-company had a precipice on its right; the Coast Battery's company on their left was lower down the slope, and the AA and Searchlight Companies further left, where they also overlooked a gorge running westwards. Two of the Companies, Nos 3 and 4, came into this line on Thursday morning, 29 May, but the others took up their positions on Wednesday night and on Thursday recce patrols went out.[64] On the opposite slope of the pass Australians were also dug in. The Thursday was spent improving the positions, and a mobile company was formed with machine-guns from this rearguard. They went forward at dawn on Friday, 30 May, to break up German concentrations, with long-range fire.[65] The Marines had acquired a water truck, but rations were more difficult to bring up through the long jam of vehicles where the road was unfinished, a couple of miles short of the coast.

On the coast south of the vehicle jam the smell of undisciplined men who had relieved themselves indiscriminately, the looting of rations – until these were put under guard – and the chaos of men in defeat were all too apparent. Eventually Rex Madoc and the Australians got one truck load through, although the Germans had begun mortaring their positions. An earlier attempt by Germans, west of the road, to encircle the traffic jam, was driven back by the spirited attack of 28th Maori Battalion, and the Marines settled down to hold their positions for 3 days, 30 May to 1 June, after the 'A' Battery-company had been sent to the east to stop a German probe trying to outflank the positions and were later relieved by Army commandos. But the evacuation by the Royal Navy ended at 0300 hours on 1 June, General Weston being ordered to fly out in a seaplane sent to fetch senior officers on the night of 1–2 June. General Freyberg had been flown out the previous night. The only serviceable warships available with the speed to reach Sphakia and come out before daylight were the battleships, which were not put at risk 'in view of the situation in the Western Desert'.[66]

Post-mortems on military defeats always bring recriminations, and for the

92 officers, 112 senior NCOs, 1,747 corporals and Marines of MNBDO I in Crete on 20 May[67] there were some brickbats but more praise. Their Commander-in-Chief, General Wavell, in a message to Weston wrote: 'Freyberg has told me how gallantly your Marines have fought'.[68] Their losses were mostly taken as prisoners-of-war, some 900 of the 1,114 casualties. These included 431 all ranks of the rearguard holding the enemy at the pass. Although, like all the forces in retreat, they were thirsty, tired and without cigarettes, they caused a diversion with grenades so that they could disengage from the enemy while under heavy fire from machine guns when ordered to withdraw. But all the boats had sailed.

Men of the Landing and Maintenance Unit, working to off-load ships in the early stages of the battle, 'did not come into active contact with enemy'[69] as a unit, but a platoon was sent to Komitades, 3 miles east of Sphakia, to secure the rearguard's line of retreat on the last full day of the evacuation, 31 May. They had formed the guard of General Weston's HQ in a cave above Sphakia; and after the evacuation was ended, they were ordered to capitulate on 1 June, 15 days after the German first landings. Many thousands of Allied troops did the same. Some waited for evacuation in the great ravine, with its stifling heat, between towering rock cliffs above Komitades a few miles east and inland from Sphakia, while others were trekking across the mountains west of the road where there were only tracks and little cover on the barren hill sides. In all the Allies lost over 15,700 men on Crete and had a further 2,011 casualties in the Royal Navy. The Germans had 6,580 casualties,[70] and never again used massed parachute drops. For the Royal Marines, the defeat was a setback and there would be others before the Allies' major offensives began. In such defeats, however, individual acts of courage and leadership maintained the Corps' reputation.

Crossing the flat calm sea on 1 June 'under the eye of the *Luftwaffe*, seemed the clearest suicide'[1] to one watcher that morning. But Major Ralph Garrett called for volunteers, with water bottles (for many days more important than a rifle for survival in Crete)[2] to sail with him to Africa. After dismissing the rearguard battalion, before swimming to a derelict MLC, he found the volunteers to go[3] with him – 4 officers and 134 other ranks, including 56 Marines.[4] They found sufficient rations, some diesel oil, petrol and water containers before casting off at 0855 hours. Four Australian corporals and an Army commando sergeant manned the engines. They had the starboard one working before they sailed, but the port propeller was fouled by a cable. In the slight mist and with their slow speed they were apparently not seen by German planes bombing Sphakia, and in three hours reached a cave on the small Gavdopula Island, having made over six knots for the 20 mile trip. A patrol checked the island for Germans before the men had their first good meal for three days or more. They were already working to free the port screw, clean up the boat, and take on water from a well, before having a second good meal.

They sailed that night and steered south-west to avoid Gavdos Island, and then due south. Steering breakdowns, the failure of the petrol engines to work on dieselite, rough seas – nearly all were seasick – did not stop their steady progress south. Water was rationed the third day out to one-sixth of a pint per day for each man, and they then distilled seawater successfully. They had rigged a sail on a single spar, and when both engines were out of action, this just kept the MLC on course.

Flares, waving clothes, the smoke of burning diesel oil, all failed to attract the attention of RAF planes or RN ships. They were passed by another MLC making for Africa, which promised to report their position but had insufficient fuel to give them a tow. They experimented with rafts, fitted new sails, and rigged a canoe but it would only take one man. On day seven, 7 June, they rigged a larger sail, as all attempts to get a tow by using a light boat to sail ahead, seemed impractical. To wear ship (change tack) six men went over the side to push the 20-ton craft around as they swam against her side. By now the men were weak from exposure and exhaustion, two men of the 52nd Light AA Battery RA dying on the eighth day, prayers were said.

The sails were by now a jib and main, which drove the craft slowly south-ward, although 'the ship made several efforts to swing to the east',[5] before they sighted land 12 miles distant on the evening of 8 June. They sailed those last miles at little better than 1¼ knots, the half-walking pace they had made for some 200 miles. With proper attention to the likelihood of being on German-held beaches, a patrol went out to scout on a compass course for the Sollum road, and they found they had beached 17 miles west of Sidi Barrani (Egypt). By instinct two Maoris found a water hole, and the last of the rations were sufficient for one more day; but after they marched to the road they were picked up by trucks of 1st RM AA Regiment stationed in Sidi Barrani. Unfortunately, the next day one of the escapers, Marine C. Bradford, was killed by a bomb while waiting for a train to Cairo. It was his 21st birthday.

A second MLC also sailed to North Africa, but its voyage is not so well known as Major Garrett's although she also made a remarkable passage. Two Naval officers had this craft in a cave near Sphakia, with some 60 men aboard, including at least two RM Lieutenants.[6] They sailed on the night of 1–2 June for Gavdos. Here they watered, and ate a good meal of mutton, chicken, bread and cheese, which the islanders provided, with some food for the voyage. Their intention was to use the engines to get clear of Cretan waters and find a Naval patrol, but on the third day, not long after passing Major Garrett's MLC, they ran out of fuel. There were then some 150 miles to sail to North Africa, and a jury rig of blankets on boathooks gave them steerage way for a time, although at other times they drifted north-west, away from Africa, in a steady breeze. Distilling up to 2 gallons (9 litres) of water in 12 hours saved their lives, however, for the last rations for each man were down to a knob of butter dipped in cocoa powder on the sixth day. They were by now so weak that anyone standing needed to support himself by holding on to the craft's side decks or elsewhere. In fact, they were almost finished on the eighth day when the African coast was sighted. In a few hours they were ashore, near the Army camp at Sidi Barrani.

Admiral Cunningham, in his report[7] to the Admiralty on the evacuation, summed up the feeling after Crete: 'There is rightly little credit or glory to be expected in these operations of retreat, but I feel that the spirit of tenacity shown by those who took part should not go unrecorded'. As for the delays and withdrawals on the night of 26 May,[9] General Weston – an honest and straightforward man – gave Australian and New Zealand units full credit for their resistance. But on the battlefield he probably seemed a remote figure to them. Nevertheless about 14 July, after the evacuation, he had 'a very pleasant forenoon' with their senior brigade commander. He would not have mentioned that his headquarters – depleted by all the men he could arm as infantry – contained fewer than five officers against a rifle brigade's advanced HQ of ten or more.

4

COMMANDOS WITH A COURAGE TERRIBLE TO SEE

For six months after the loss of Crete to the so-called Axis powers (Germany, Italy, Japan and their allies) and set backs in the Western Desert, the Allies made few amphibious raids, although small raids in search of military intelligence by Army Commandos and other special forces continued on the French Channel Coast. The first major landing had been made in March 1941 by equal parts of 3 and 4 Commandos, when 500 men landed unopposed in the Lofoten Islands. Late in December, however, 3 Commando and two Troops of 4 Commando, 576 all ranks, made the first opposed landing in a classic fighting raid on Vaagso in south-west Norway. By this date 'Layforce' – 7, 8 and 11 (Army) Commandos – had made several raids in the Mediterranean; they lost many men in rearguard actions in Crete, where 'Nos 7 and 8' were landed on the fifth day of the battle. 'No. 11' later lost a quarter of its strength in Syria capturing Vichy French redoubts on the Litani River (9 June 1941).[1] Marines had joined No.10 Troop of 8 Commando, along with Royal Engineers and Royal Artillery gunners, and this specialist Troop trained with Folbot folding canoes, but most of the Marines had returned to sea service before 'No. 8' came to Egypt, in March 1941. Individual Marines continued to serve with the Army Commandos, Special Boat Section and a few were in the Middle East Commando of some 60 men, who did not rejoin their regiments when 'Layforce' was disbanded in the late summer of 1941. This Commando raided a German headquarters in the Western Desert, coming ashore from submarines and making their approach march of 125 miles to their objective in a little over two days to capture the HQ. Lieutenant-Colonel Geoffrey Keyes (Royal Scots Greys) was awarded a posthumous VC for his part in this operation, and Colonel R. (Bob) E. Laycock (Royal Horse Guards) and a commando sergeant made a remarkable trek across the desert, living on berries for many of the 41 days they took to reach the British Eighth Army's lines.

'Layforce' had been sent to the Mediterranean in the three Landing Ships, Infantry (LSIs) converted from fast Glen Line cargo ships. Each could carry two Commandos and put one ashore in a single lift by the LCAs she carried; but these ships were taken from the Commandos and used as troopships in the evacuations of Greece and Crete, where their landing craft brought men off open beaches. There were many other demands on the Mediterranean Fleet that summer, when supply convoys were run at great risk into Malta, a mere 50 miles from Axis airfields in Sicily. Conditions in mid-March 1941 on the island had been critical, but a small supply convoy had reached the capital Valetta, on 23 March with desperately needed food and ammunition.[2] The Naval covering forces for these operations included carriers that flew off reinforcements of fighter planes, and on 6 June 35 Hurricanes flew in, followed by 43 eight days later.[3] In all, 700 fighters were flown in from fleet carriers between August 1940 and October 1942.

The island's garrison included some Marines in the Naval Headquarters, St Angelo, whose *ad hoc* light anti-aircraft battery is described in the Unit History Summaries (Appendix 4). Other Naval commitments included the supply of Tobruk (invested by Rommel's advance that April), and support for the right flank of the retreating Eighth Army and for Allied forces occupying Vichy French Syria. On 22 June German forces attacked Russia, and the war was becoming global, with the likelihood of Japan entering the ring.

Pre-war Naval plans had seen the French fleet controlling the Mediterranean if the Royal Navy had to sail in strength to the Far East.[4] Now the German attack on Russia eased the Japanese fears of any attack from the north, and more Japanese were sent to Indo-China, where the Vichy French had been forced to accept a joint Franco-Japanese defence for that country. British plans had then to be reviewed and a Naval force was to be sent to Singapore.

Meanwhile a fuelling anchorage was to be developed as a base on Addu Atoll, most southerly of the Maldive Islands and 600 miles south-west of Ceylon (Sri Lanka). MNBDO I's 1st RM Coast Regiment and the Landing and Maintenance Unit, in all some 500 men, reached this triangle of islands in September 1941, 'in glorious sunshine and cloudless skies . . . impressed by the green palm trees, undergrowth and very blue sea'. But an old hand took a longer look and decided the islands were 'miles and miles of damn all'.[5] In this remote spot near the Equator and later elsewhere in the Indian Ocean, MNBDO I units would establish not only coast defences but build roads, bases and complete installations (see Appendix 4). The apparent paradox of a Coast Defence Regiment's operations appearing in the Commando chapter of a Royal Marines' history will be seen later to be part and parcel of the Corps' versatility, but for these Marines on the Indian Ocean islands there were many months of hard slog in clearing jungle, building gun emplacements, laying telephone lines, bridging and road-building. They helped to keep down the numbers of flying foxes – one could eat as much fruit as a child – and by early December 1941 they had established base services at 'Port T', the code name for Addu Atoll, with roads to the battery positions from landing points on the atoll's islands. Nowhere did these roads rise more than a few feet above sea level; and water, which had to be shipped in, was rationed at times to 1 gallon per man per day. The atoll's southerly island of Gan was developed as a supply base and would later be an RAF staging post, but in their first three months on these hot, damp islands some 23 per cent of the Marines were evacuated to the hospital ship HMS *Vita*.[6] Other ships could only be unloaded when the tides were right. Heavy rain washed away roads, scrub typhus caused men to drop unconscious without any previous symptoms of sickness, giant land crabs infested one swamp over which a road was laid on a foundation of palm fronds – these were just a few of the difficulties faced in mounting the guns and establishing a means to supply them. The Admiralty had expected the installations would be completed in 1943–4, but after the spring of 1943 the island would again only be used as an occasional fuelling base[7] until it became a staging post for aircraft. (A small detachment of Marines was serving on Gan in the 1990s.)

On 7 December 1941 the Japanese 1st Naval Air Fleet struck at the American Pacific Fleet in Pearl Harbor (Hawaii). Over 300 Japanese planes came in at 0600 hours, sinking five battleships and badly damaging three more; many other ships were damaged but the US carriers were at sea.[8] Some time earlier – the International date line making it 8 December, however – in Thailand, Japanese forces came ashore unopposed; but during landings further south at Kota Bahru (Malaya), the RAF sank a transport and damaged two ships. The Indian troops of the ground defence force, however, were driven back. The British Royal Naval Force Z – the new battleship HMS *Prince of Wales*, the battle-cruiser HMS *Repulse* and some destroyers – left Singapore to intercept the Japanese. On the same day, 8 December, HMS *Peterel*, the last gunboat of the pre-war Yangtze Flotilla, serving as the Shanghai consul's radio link to the Foreign Office, was attacked as she tried to scuttle, one long burst of her single Lewis gun answering the Japanese fire before she drifted ablaze across the harbour, capsized and sank.[9] In Hong Kong the Canadian, Indian and British defence forces were withdrawn into Hong Kong island after 48 hours when the Kowloon defence line was likely to be overwhelmed. Naval parties, including a Marine detachment, were put ashore and in the next two weeks fought in a series of defensive actions and counter-attacks before the colony was surrendered on 25 December.[10] But some British nurses were killed.

When *Prince of Wales* and *Repulse* with four destroyers – Force Z – had steamed north on 8 December, Admiral Phillips expected to have land-based fighter cover and the element of surprise on his side when he reached the Japanese landing areas.[11] Next day he was told there would be no fighters, and that afternoon Japanese submarines and reconnaissance planes found Force Z. Shortly before midnight the capital ships turned southwards on reports of more Japanese landing over 120 miles to the south of Kota Bahru. No enemy were found here, but a Japanese bomber force, returning from its search for Force Z passed over these capital ships coming away from the coast. Bombs began falling before action stations were sounded aboard *Repulse*. One young Marine officer climbed into his gunnery control position to be asked 'Do you think they'll hit us, sir?' by his lads: '. . . just then a bomb hit the port side . . . [our] aircraft sitting on the catapult was damaged and since it was full of petrol . . . they decided to catapult it over the side. I wondered whether it would explode with bombs and depth charges still attached to each wing; it was just below my control position . . . two steam pipes burst and clouds of steam were pouring from the hatches . . . making everyone think that the ship was on fire. All this while the *Prince of*

Wales and ourselves were pumping out shells ... two planes burst into flames ... but we soon saw the *Prince of Wales* had quite a big list to port ... [then] the Japanese concentrated on us ... and started torpedo attacks instead of high level bombing ... As I say, we were pumping out all the fire we could ... twisting and turning in our tracks as we kept dodging the things ... but it was only a matter of time as every few minutes a torpedo hit us and with a shuddering lurch the ship shook, quivered, keeled over and [then] righted herself ... after we had been hit by five torpedoes, the poor old lady keeled right over.'[12]

The order was given to abandon ship, and after 93 minutes in action *Repulse* had been sunk by 1233. Some 40 minutes later *Prince of Wales* turned turtle and sank.[13] Whether or not these capital ships should have been put at risk is debatable, after the carrier HMS *Indomitable* had grounded, with the resulting damage preventing her sailing to the Far East. However, many of the ships' companies were rescued by the destroyers, though 503 men from *Repulse* and 327 from *Prince of Wales* were lost, including the Admiral and her Captain. Among those lost were Marines and Musicians from the detachments and RM bands.

Some of the Marine survivors taken to Singapore were drafted to complete the complements of ships, others had duties with the Naval headquarters and in the ordnance depot.[14] The bands' survivors were embarked on 19 December for evacuation, leaving 6 officers and 204 general service ranks, who formed the guard for the wireless station, for Naval ammunition dumps and acted as a mobile anti-paratroop force in the Naval base. This mobile force also patrolled the base at night to deter pro-Japanese 'fifth columnists' firing flares during air raids to help the Axis forces as these hostile infiltrators did elsewhere. Their flares guided planes to the Naval installations. When the base's personnel were evacuated, these Marines moved to Tyersall Camp and continued the field training that they had been doing for the benefit of 'HO' Marines in the detachments while in Singapore.

On Christmas Eve a Special Service Platoon of Marines drawn from *Prince of Wales*'s detachment left by train to join 'Roseforce' under Major Rose of the 2nd Argylls.[15] There was great secrecy over the purpose of their move, and Lieutenant R.J. (Jim) Davis from *Repulse*, who commanded them, did not know until he reached Port Swettenham exactly what would be their role. It turned out to be 'co-operation with Naval river and patrol craft, to carry out raids on west coast of Malaya in the rear of Japanese lines'[16] in a commando type of operation.

Jim Davis found the Perak Flotillas had been divided, with half the force of motorboats sent to counter Japanese movements to Sumatra across the Strait of Malacca.[17] The boats from the flotilla still available in Swettenham, however, were used in a raid on Sunday, 28 December. Although several of them broke down on the passage to Trong, 140 miles north-west of their base port, 'Roseforce' got ashore. They set up a series of ambushes on the coast road, destroying a number of trucks with their loads of supplies for the Japanese 5 Division, 20 miles to the south. Half a world away men of the Army's 3 Commando had landed the previous day at Vaagso (Norway). For 'Roseforce' in Malaya the prize catches were two Japanese staff cars with senior officers, who were killed in resisting capture before the force returned safely to Swettenham.[18] Two days later they had their first direct air attack and the Flotilla's depot ship was sunk, and soon afterwards five launches on their way north to reinforce the Flotillas were sunk or driven ashore by Japanese aircraft.

'Roseforce's' role was now changed to that of a covering party protecting demolition squads, and operations against the Japanese divisions moving down the west coast trunk road. On 1–2 January 1942 the Japanese 11th Infantry Regiment (about 2,000 men) made an amphibious right hook to land at Telok Anson, forcing the British 11 Division to withdraw from positions north of this small port, as the British lines of communication were threatened.[19] Further Japanese landings at Port Swettenham and south-eastward along the coast were expected, for successful landings would force the British Division to abandon Kuala Lumpur. 'Roseforce' then came under command of Brig Mair, whose force protecting his lines-of-communication prepared to block any amphibious landings. These came on 2 January, (the Thursday after the 'Roseforce' raid) when artillery fire repulsed a landing at Kuala Selangor, and the next day a second landing was broken up by field batteries' fire; but by Saturday a Japanese battalion was ashore north of Kuala Selangor and driving east to cut the trunk road.

On the Monday morning, 5 January, the Japanese were 12 miles inland and had made their first contact with 1st Independent Company reinforced by 'Roseforce'. They were in positions to cover the bridges across a river only 11 miles from the road, the British were also threatened by other Japanese, who, coming down tracks behind the beaches, had then swung east to outflank the bridge positions. The bridges were therefore blown, but as a Japanese column forced its way down the trunk road and across the Slim river some 45 miles north of the 'Roseforce's' positions, resistance began to crumble in central Malaya. In the following week the Marine Special Service Platoon helped to cover the withdrawal by elements of 11 Division[20] now down to battalions of a few hundred or less, several of which had retreated 200 miles in three weeks.[21] There were a further 250 miles or more of fighting retreat to go to reach Singapore.

The Special Service platoon returned there on 14 January, and on 29 January, after the causeway linking Johore to Singapore had been cut, the Marines joined two companies of the 2nd Argylls.[22] These Scotsmen had fought in the rearguard of 11 Division and had lost half their strength; and so were formed into A and B Companies of what became known as 'The Plymouth-Argylls' – after Plymouth's local football team, known as Plymouth Argyle – with C Company of Marines mainly from *Prince of Wales* and D Company from *Repulse*, both Plymouth ships. Marines also took their full share in the Battalion's HQ Company, with two armoured cars, two Bren carriers and two 3-in mortars manned by Royals. At this time the Battalion's Tiger Patrols of an officer and two Marines or privates, or sometimes two officers and one other rank, also practised their stalking tactics. Time was made for some sport, C Company winning the Battalion football competition.

On Sunday night, 8–9 February, a preliminary bombardment began and, as Japanese troops landed on the north-west of the island, the Battalion therefore took up positions near Panjang village as part of the command reserve. Although they took some casualties from air attacks during this move, it was completed by the time the Kranje oil tanks were set ablaze, when every man then became 'black from head to foot, making recognition, even of your friends, extremely difficult'.[23] The Japanese were expected to drive up the road from Tengah airfield, and the Battalion 'fought for the road from the road', even though the Japanese might make wide flanking movements. During Monday the cars patrolled the road and A Company was moved forward, with orders to withdraw before becoming too closely engaged. That night no movement was expected as in the wet and cheerless gloom enemy aircraft could not support their ground forces. But many Australians came through the positions, making for the docks some 10 miles to the rear. The enemy renewed his air attack at dawn and by 0700 hours Japanese infantry were probing the positions. C Company caused them many casualties as the Japanese tried to outflank the road positions. The Marine corporals commanding standing patrols outside B Company's defended area at this time, extracted their sections 'although pressed by considerably superior numbers of the enemy', on whom they inflicted casualties, catching an unwary Japanese patrol with Tommy gun bursts. Although the Japanese were by now only 150 to 200yds from the Marines' slit trenches, there were few casualties, owing to the enemy's poor marksmanship. Yet they continued to probe the Marines' positions, for there were defiles between the companies' defended areas. The Japanese were held until 0930, when the company was 'leapfrogged' back to defend positions they held for the rest of the day, despite air attacks.[24]

Enemy tanks appeared down the road at 1345, and were fired on by the Section covering the road – the only one allowed to fire, so as not to give away positions or hit friendly troops. Any infiltrating Japanese were to be bayoneted. The anti-tank rifles of the Section on the road, drove off these tanks and a road block was hastily improvised; but tanks following up the initial reconnaissance smashed through these trucks and headed for the dock area. By remaining absolutely silent through the night the companies remained hidden, while Japanese patrols moved across the front calling in English, 'Hullo, is anyone there?' No infiltrators came into the positions, however, and just before first light the now combined 'C' and 'D' companies withdrew along a pipeline. Tiger Patrols stayed in position to catch the incoming enemy and discourage them from following the Battalion. Although the Marines stopped for three hours at the planned RV (rendezvous), Battalion HQ had moved back to Tyersall Camp and the Royal Marine company – their OC not pleased to find no one had been left to direct them from the RV – reached the camp that afternoon. In the next few days, when it was hoped to reorganise the Battalion, the camp and adjacent Indian hospital were completely destroyed by bombing. During this, the Marines moved ammunition from the magazines and rescued patients.

On 11 February the senior officers were ordered to embark for Java, and Captain Lang – whose narrative of 1945[25] is the basis of much of these paragraphs – took command of the Battalion. Lieutenant Jim Davies led a small tank-hunting patrol, the remaining armoured car patrolled the roads, and in heavy shelling a lance-corporal of the Argylls repaired the only telephone link to Brigade HQ. Marine P.G.E. Back carried on alone cooking the Battalion's meals, despite shelling that had everyone else in slit trenches. No organised infantry attack followed this shelling and at 2000 hours on 15 February the Battalion was ordered to cease fire.

In concluding his report after 3½ years as a prisoner, Captain Lang wrote: 'I respectfully submit that some token of our esteem be communicated to Brig Stewart and men of the 2nd Battalion Argyll and Sutherland Highlanders whose comradeship did much to sustain us during these dark times'.[26] The medical officer in charge of the Base hospital's mental and nerve section reported that shell-shocked patients in large numbers came from regiments in which the discipline was bad or poor.[27] The Marines had two or possibly three desertions when many troops were falling back without their weapons and in general disarray. 'The bearing of [RM] Junior NCOs stood out', contributing to the Marines' steadiness, and throughout their captivity the morale of the Marines was high, Captain Lang reported.[28]

Other attempts at infiltration along the lines of 'Roseforce' were made in January 1942, when Major Fergusson Warren, a Royal Marine officer attached to the Special Operations Executive (SOE), left Singapore in charge of the 80-ton *Himlee*, a diesel-engined Chinese coaster.[29] By February he had two parties working in Malaya. Led by rubber planters, these parties of Chinese had varied success, and Fergusson Warren was organising escape routes through the Dutch East Indies as well as operating an intelligence network before he was captured in Sumatra on 17 March. But the British plans for the main defence of Malaya had been flawed, by optimistic hopes in some political circles that much of the defence of the Empire could be left in the hands of locally raised forces, until such time as British troops could be rushed to the area. Yet in Singapore – to mention a relatively small example – in February 1915 a native infantry regiment had mutinied and was only contained by an improvised company, including the Admiral's RM orderlies and base staff.[30] Such unreliability, however, did not account for the loss of Singapore – anticipated as this may have been by 1930s' staff exercises for recovering the base after its initial loss – for reinforcements were arriving in growing numbers, with 45,000 fighting troops and 51 Hurricanes being landed at Singapore between 1 January and 8 February 1942.[31] Indeed the Allied troops in Malaya greatly outnumbered the Japanese landing forces. But many of the Australian and Indian battalions had been brought up to strength with troops only partially trained,[32] and although there was an Army Commander-in-Chief, he did not control Naval forces, and the general officers commanding Malaya, Hong Kong and Burma continued to be responsible to the War Office.[33] Yet the most striking flaw was the lack of British sea power in the area, as we have seen in earlier chapters; and the Admiralty was well aware of the likely outcome. Had British and American sea power been adequate – despite the loss of two capital ships – it is unlikely the Japanese could have ventured so far on so many fronts as they did in the winter of 1941–2. That they subsequently overreached themselves by extending the areas they had originally intended to conquer, was a piece of good fortune for freedom rather than the result of any strategy of the Allies.

What naval forces the Allies could assemble in the East Indies fought a series of desperate actions against superior forces. They were forced to commit ships without adequate air reconnaissance, as happened on 26 February when a cruiser squadron – HMS *Exeter*, refitted after the River Plate action, HMAS *Perth*, USS *Houston* and two Dutch ships, *De Ruyter* and *Java* – with ten destroyers sailed to intercept the Japanese invasion force heading for the north Java coast, a 600 mile shoreline on which there were a number of suitable landing points. The Japanese were already established on Bali, close to the eastern coast of Java, having completed the airstrip by the day Singapore fell (15 February), and had landed in Sumatra to the west of Java the week before. The Allied squadron of ships had 'been driven hard . . . were old . . . their men approaching exhaustion'[34] and there were understandable problems of communication between ships of different nations, with methods of signalling that could not be easily co-ordinated without some practice.

In the event the Japanese cruisers of about equal strength, on paper, crossed the T of the Allied ships approaching in line astern on the late afternoon of 26 February. *Exeter*, 'every tank in the ship leaking'[35] after previous actions against Japanese bombers, opened fire at some 26,000yds with her forward 8-in turret. She had turned with the squadron and in the following hour of sporadic firing, with the Allied 6-in cruisers still out of range, two torpedo attacks were made on the Allied ships, but only one of the 120 torpedoes fired hit and sank a Dutch destroyer.[36] As the last torpedo attack came in about 1700 hours, *Exeter* was hit by an 8-in shell which exploded aft, severed the main steam pipe, and killed all but one of the men in the boiler room, and he was terribly scalded. *Exeter* limped eastward to reach Soerabaya (modern Surabaja) after dark. The damage to *Exeter* broke the squadron's line, and in the difficult circumstances of ships not worked up as a cohesive force, some captains turned to follow the ship ahead, thinking an alteration of course must have been signalled. Such confusion and the Japanese flares lighting up the ships when the action was resumed that night, led to the loss of both Dutch cruisers and several Allied destroyers.

Exeter, escorted by a British and an American destroyer, sailed from Java on 28 February, her engine-room staff having made such effective repairs that she could make 23 knots. At dawn next day they came on the Japanese cruiser squadrons covering the Java landings. 'From about 0730 it was just one long succession of load and fire' aboard *Exeter*, 'with the odd lull' when shifting target or taking evasive action behind a smoke screen. For a time this smoke laid by the destroyers skilfully shielded *Exeter*, but as four Japanese cruisers closed in, she was hit: 'a particularly heavy shaking and shuddering of the ship was felt'.[37] The forward boiler room had been hit, steam power was cut off and the ship's machinery failed. Working in the dim emergency lights, the Marines were preparing to wind shells up the hoist manually when they were ordered to abandon ship. The shell room was cleared and the magazine hatch opened, and the men 'without pushing, came through this hatch by a spot of organised hurry' before the magazine was flooded.[38] The ship then sank within 10 minutes, probably with her seacocks opened to ensure she was not captured although she was hit again several times. The British destroyer, HMS *Electra*, was also sunk by shellfire and USS *Pope* by dive-bombers.

The survivors were taken prisoner, after drifting on Flotta nets and rafts for 28 hours or so. 'The absolute lack of pessimism of any sort'[39] during this long time in the water was a tribute to their courage, all the more remarkable in the great dangers at this time in South East Asia, when any hour a Japanese plane – if not a landing party – could be expected and not all the natives were friendly. The distances are vast – Singapore to Soerabaya in Java is nearly 900 miles, Rangoon (Burma) to the Indian frontier is at least 450 miles and Guadalcanal, where the Americans first struck back with landings in August 1942 is some 6,000 miles from San Francisco on the American west coast. The men of the lst RM Coast Regiment had sailed into this great arena in February 1942.

In January 1942 Marines of 1st RM Coast Regiment sailed for Ceylon, leaving behind the intense heat of Addu Atoll and a monotonous diet of tinned food and biscuits. Not long after reaching Ceylon they had a call for men for 'special service of a hazardous nature' and some 100 men were picked from the volunteers, their selection being made on the basis of their fitness, their age, their experience and suitability for operations requiring personal initiative. By 8 February, after three weeks of intensive infantry training, they sailed from Colombo in the cruiser HMS *Enterprise*, and their OC, Major Duncan Johnston, learnt for the first time that they were off to Rangoon. Although conditions were crowded aboard *Enterprise*, they continued their training, but the details of their intended role were not yet known to this Force 'Viper'. Duncan Johnston had named them 'Viper' after the only poisonous British snake, as these three Platoons, with some machine guns and a few 2-in mortars, were expecting 'to bite the enemy hard'.[1]

When they disembarked, each man received a welcome 50 cigarettes from the ship's store, but ashore the job for which they were intended could no longer be carried out, since the Japanese were already established on the southern coasts of Burma, east of the Irrawaddy Delta, and the Force's original task of reinforcing the Navy's coastal patrols in the Gulf of Martaban, at the head of the Andaman Sea, was therefore cancelled. No immediate job was found for them by GHQ, for Rangoon was practically deserted 'with a derelict appearance – piles of garbage in the streets'.[2] Most of the townsfolk had fled after 4,700 were killed in the first two air raids of many in the previous two months. The Fourteenth Army at this time was pulling back to the Sittang river, and two small recce patrols from 'Viper' were sent to 17 Indian Division and I Div (Burdiv) headquarters in search of boats, although their use on the Sittang and Salween rivers seemed unlikely to Duncan Johnston. A proposed raid with four companies of Gloucesters was discussed at this time, but no pilot could be found to take boats by night up the Moulmein river to the Japanese divisional HQ, their intended target, and crossing the Gulf would have attracted enemy aircraft, for the round trip was some 300 miles.

After being in Rangoon for a week, the Major acquired a 35-ft diesel-engined boat for training, and Lieutenant W. Guthrie Penman, Burma RNVR, joined them. Fluent in Burmese and Hindustani, he was a keen yachtsman who had been working as a senior engineer with a teak company. Sub-Lieutenant Wikner, BRNVR, joined a few days later and was sent by Major Johnston to Mandalay, where, with a corporal and four Marines, he fitted out armoured boats and a depot launch with workshops. During the next couple of weeks the Force provided patrols for the town after the civil police had evacuated the area, and guards were required on the demolition charges set at the oil refinery three miles up river. On 18 February the Force had been ordered to form a Flotilla for river work, and Lieutenant Penman, BRNVR, requisitioned four government touring launches, which became the nucleus of the Flotilla, and some smaller motorboats. The launches' crews, natives of Chittagong, came with them, and their 'loyalty was to stand us in good stead throughout the campaign'.[3] Each launch also had a Vickers machine gun, an Aldis signal lamp and a 'China' Mk I W/T Set 8. The Marines in the boats had some hair-raising moments 'in the racing tides of Rangoon river . . . but the troops were intelligent and keen to learn'.[4] Many of them were in for the 'hostilities only' but the Sergeant-Major, Harry Wonfor, and most of the NCOs were long-service Marines. Their boat training had to be fitted into their guard duties, in which Brens were fired to keep looters from the docks, and 'offenders caught by the patrols were flogged in the town square'.[5] But as 2,000 civilian prisoners and criminal lunatics had been released to fend for themselves,[6] such action hardly stemmed the reign of terror, although it cut down the cases of arson to one big fire every other night. The effects of the Japanese successes, however, had emboldened those Burmese who wanted the British to quit Burma. They and other nationalists, therefore, helped the Japanese; and in the coming months throughout south-east Asia and the Dutch East Indies, local populations' cooperation with the Allies could be fickle.

The Force began to patrol the river in its launches on 4 March, covering also the docks and Twante canal; with each launch was a motorboat crewed by Marines, and all sailed under the White Ensign. Their orders – subsequent changes only by chance passed to Major Johnston – were to carry demolition parties to a transport ship on 7 March after oil installations, dock services and stores were destroyed, including 20-million gallons of aviation fuel at one refinery. There was considerable confusion in the dark as launches came alongside this transport, and only with difficulty were the launches of the Flotilla collected together to anchor until the moon rose. But by 0300 hours (8 March) the fires from the successful demolitions gave sufficient light to see the marker buoys of the channel and the launches headed up-river for Prome. On this passage up the Irrawaddy the Marines established their routine. After reveille at 0600 hours, it was scrub decks till 0645, by which time there was sufficient light to get underway. (They did not normally attempt night passages, as the navigable channels could not be seen.) The forenoon continued with breakfast, 'quarters clean guns', and the routine called for lookouts to be on watch at all times.[7]

Among the rations they had acquired before leaving Rangoon were 50 crates of beer and some Australian hock, by courtesy of Captain Herbert Alexander, the second-in-command and OC now of the demolition party with him in the stores launch *Delta*. But later, difficulties in getting hold of diesel led to some reorganisation of the Flotilla: *Delta* was scrapped and replaced by *Cynthia*, a steam launch; two of the diesel motorboats were replaced by armoured boats prepared up-river by Sub-Lieutenant Wikner's party; and the motorboat *Snipe* was added to the flotilla. Their first job in protecting 17 Indian Division's right flank along the river was to support Burma II Commando, 30 men under Major M. (Mike) Calvert, RE, who were sailing some 100 miles back down-river[8] to demolish Henzada oil rigs. Their double-decked steamer *Hastings* and the launch *Rita* arrived together at the rigs and the Commando sent a patrol ashore. The men had gone barely 200yds[9] towards the village, when they were called on by a Burmese civilian to surrender. He was given a gruff refusal, whereupon Japanese appeared all round the patrol. The commandos had no choice but to fight their way down to the river, as *Rita* – pulling out into the stream to get a clear view of the village – began firing when large numbers of Japanese appeared. Her Vickers and five Brens were aided by the crew's Tommy guns, firing on single-shot settings to conserve ammunition but nevertheless getting in some rapid fire, while the Vickers gunner, Lance-Corporal Marriott, caused many of the 100 or so enemy casualties. *Hastings*, skilfully handled by her skipper, also put off early in the action, going back twice to pick up commandos and men of the Marines' demolition party who had landed. The raiding craft came away under mortar fire, having had two commandos and a Marine killed.[10] Burma II Commando then went north for further demolitions, but the remainder of 'Viper's' Flotilla came down-river, and for most of the next week patrolled to within 6 miles of Henzada.

The action by *Rita* had given Duncan Johnston confidence in the launches' ability to engage shore targets, since, among other reasons, he found that Japanese bullets had poor penetrating power, 'being stopped by such unlikely things as a rolled blanket and a tin of sausages'.[11] Patrols were made at irregular times, the launches obliged to keep to the main channels; motorboats then followed river boats into creeks to destroy them, as all boats were a potential means for the Japanese to infiltrate across the river. But the river was falling in the first two weeks of March, and its navigation became more restricted, especially when buoys were cut adrift and crossing markers cut down on the banks – shades of the Yangtze in the 1930s. Ambushes, especially by field-guns, were a distinct possibility, as the launches were slow, making only a few knots against the swifter current, which at times set a launch down stream as the crew used a sounding pole to feel for the channel where it crossed from one bank to the other.

At the time when some 2,000 Japanese and Burmese nationalists (Thakins) were coming north up the river during mid-March, Lieutenant-Colonel G.S.

Musgrove (an Army officer) took command of 'Viper' and Burma II. He later interrogated three Burmese civilians caught by *Stella* when they were carrying Japanese grenades – they were shot as spies. Others picked up by the patrols included wounded and stragglers from 17 Division who were taken to the comparative safety of the next Indian army unit which the Flotilla visited. During all these patrols they had been able to buy vegetables and chickens from villagers along the river, but there were increasing signs of the activities of Burmese nationalists, who welcomed Japanese advanced parties into several villages. Attempted ambushes on these units came to nothing because the launches ran aground in difficult conditions or the enemy by-passed the ambush area – as they did when two platoons and a Vickers section were landed at one village.

On 26 March 1942 the Flotilla landed the commandos and a company of Burmese military police at Padaung, ferrying the men ashore in canoes, 'a slow ... tiresome business'.[12] The next day, therefore, when Force 'Viper' sent two platoons and a Vickers section to this small town, they marched down the west bank some 6 miles, with the machine gun in a bullock cart. They were 8 miles south of Prome, and on the opposite (east) bank a major battle was in progress, but the villagers welcomed them and all was quiet. Lieutenant Cave took his platoon down the river bank, the Vickers was mounted near the police compound by a bungalow just outside the town and sentries were posted. At 0030 hours there was a burst of Tommy gun fire, the Major dashed down the bungalow steps and made out three Japanese on the road. Dodging behind a latrine, he made his way back to the compound. It was filling with Japanese troops, and after a quick word with Lieutenant-Colonel Musgrove, Duncan Johnston led No.2 Platoon as they raced 50yds to a dry gulley.[13]

Firing from this position they took the attention of the Japanese machine gunners.[14] Meanwhile Lieutenant Douglas Fayle (OC, No. 2 Platoon) had rolled under the compound huts, which stood 3ft above the ground; with him was Corporal Harry Winters with a rifle and Marine R.J. Shaw with his Bren. They lay quiet while the men in the gulley were firing, then the Lieutenant opened fire with his Tommy gun, supporting the Bren and rifle, which at this close range killed many Japanese. They fought off a Japanese attempt to rush their position, held their fire when cattle were stampeded through the compound, fired on an officer who shone a torch, and stopped another rush by tossing grenades, all the time shifting their position to keep in the shadow as the moonlight spread under the huts. They found some ammunition but by 0430 hours – they had been under the huts for 4 hours – with ammunition again getting low, they slipped away unnoticed to the river. The main party had disengaged from the fight some hours earlier, as its men had only one magazine of Bren ammunition and not much else after being attacked from two sides. Other small groups made their way back to the launches and the Platoon did not have a single casualty. But fifteen commandos were missing and all Lieutenant Cave's No.3 Platoon.[15]

No. 3 was moving back towards the firing when a large body of Japanese were found between it and the compound.[16] Cave then followed his orders to make for the hills if cut off. The Platoon lay low at daybreak, and then moved north, met six Gurkhas and was running short of food on the second day when three Indian Army 15cwt trucks appeared down the road heading for Prome. Having shared out the rations, the party, numbering now about 40, camouflaged the trucks by the roadside, and, after posting sentries, had some sleep. Late in the afternoon they were motoring north, however, when two Japanese planes machine-gunned the road, killing some ten men. The remainder then went on in two trucks, and were told by some Burmese that Prome had been captured.

Peter Cave led them north again, hoping to rejoin the river beyond the enemy's lines, and the trucks were immobilised. They carried the more seriously wounded and men who had gone down with malaria – the anti-malaria mepacrine supplies were long gone, and two of several cases died. Others died of their wounds, which quickly festered in the heat. By now they were moving by night and hiding up during the day. After eight weeks they reached Toungoo, over 80 miles east of Prome, and at dawn on 26 May they found some defence works. Here Peter Cave hoped that they would be able to join Indian units, as by this time there were only ten Marines and three Gurkhas, the Sikh truck drivers having left quietly one night and others having died or been left by the track too weak to go on. While a reconnaissance was being prepared from the new positions, a mortar and machine gun opened fire on them, for this had been a Japanese defence system and they were in strength in the area, but after the Marines returned what fire they could, all was quiet. That night two Gurkhas went out and silenced the machine gun, coming back just before dawn with their enemy's ears. With the sun came more mortar fire and the Lieutenant was hit in the knee, but despite the obvious pain, he continued to direct the defence. Suddenly Japanese burst from dense cover on the left, ending the resistance, and mortally wounding one Marine. The others were taken off in a lorry, their feet roped together. Several of them died later of their wounds but Chinese troops released six survivors some 11 months later, when their prison camp north-east of Mandalay was recaptured.[17]

Force 'Viper' had reorganised after being ambushed. The Japanese had been hidden in the houses of villagers before the Marines arrived at Padaung, and *Rita* went down river to machine gun the village. *Stella* went upstream on 31 March to destroy all boats on the river for 10 miles. The launches now came under fire in the river off Prome, and although there were no orders for them, they later destroyed all the launches and boats they could find in the area. They were then ordered to patrol from Kama to within two miles north of Prome, and an Army W/T set was taken aboard so they could be on 17 Division's 'net'. Early in April a number of volunteers 'for river commando work' joined the flotilla from the Army's inland water transport companies, and about this time a commando NCO who had escaped after being captured at Padaung reported that several Marines had been bayoneted while they were prisoners, but one had escaped inland.[18]

The retreat was now moving jerkily northward, and the launches came up river burning boats along the banks; but a few miles south of Allanmyo they were fired on. The culprits were from Burdiv, coming in to relieve 17 Indian

Division, and Force 'Viper' was to act as the river link between Burdiv's three brigades. As it withdrew, the Flotilla destroyed more boats, but now ran into its first serious engine breakdowns and devised a substitute for the 'high speed' diesel – 2 parts light diesel and 1 part kerosene. The Flotilla made forays down river – 30 miles on 11 April 1942. A standing patrol, so to speak, was maintained by one launch, which was often withdrawn up river only when the Japanese were in sight. They were machine-gunned and bombed from the air, they ferried troops across the river, acquired replacement boats and blew up oil barges. On 20 April the Chittagonians who wished to leave were paid off, as they were near the Chindwin, a tributary of the Irrawaddy leading to the Indian border. The boats ferried rations to the brigades, Marines by this time were manning the engines, with some consequent reduction of fire-power up-top; but now in late April the river was at its lowest and the last major job they did on the Irrawaddy was to ferry Burdiv's 320 carts, 640 bullocks and some 500 mules across the river at Sammeikkon. The Royal Engineers had made good jetties, with a large flat barge each side of the river, but the job took some 36 hours. During this time the troops were brought out by a separate ferry, and the motor transport by 'a very odd contraption' of local boats with a platform lashed over them and towed by a launch. Next day, 30 April, the big launches and other boats acquired by Force 'Viper', all too deep-draughted for the shallow Chindwin, were sunk to block the Irrawaddy channel.[19]

Force 'Viper' eventually came out of Burma after working on the Chindwin. Three 47-mm Breda anti-tank guns were added to the Force at one time. The Force worked again with men of Burma II Commando, and gave out silver rupees to refugees and not to the District Officer, when these could not be delivered. On one of these ventures Lance-Corporal Parratt and Marine Lough were last seen in small motorboats on the Chindwin 'firing their Bren guns into the Japanese motor transport' which was coming down to the road by the river with seven tanks. Brave acts such as these must often have gone unrecorded, for some small parties just vanished into areas known later to have been strongly patrolled by the Japanese.

While Force 'Viper' was operating in Burma, other men of MNBDO I were in Ceylon, 1st RM Anti-Aircraft Regiment being stationed at the Royal Navy base of Trincomalee. The crews for its thirty-two 3.7-in guns and the twin-Lewis behind 3/8-in steel shields for low level air defence, the command post with telephonists and plotters, were all trained to a high pitch of efficiency despite the ravages of malaria. They were in action only occasionally, however, once against planes that bombed this anchorage. These gunners would mostly remain in their specialist anti-aircraft roles but Marines in the UK were asked to volunteer early in 1942 for The Royal Marine Commando. During the following months there were some changes in this Commando's title (see Appendix 4), and it was not designated 40(RM) Commando until 29 October 1942. The Commando was originally raised for operations in South East Asia, where raids were planned on the Andaman Islands,[1] similar to those of Burma II Commando, Force 'Viper' and other 'commando' volunteers. In the event there were insufficient landing craft and escorts to mount such raids even a year later, in 1943.

The RM Commando, under its Commanding Officer Lieutenant-Colonel J. Picton Phillipps, began amphibious training with an HQ, three specialist Platoons – signals, demolition and close-support – and 'A', 'B' and 'X' Companies, lettered in the style of a three-turreted ship. By April they were in Scotland and those who had volunteered expecting extra pay or were otherwise unsuitable had been returned to their units.[2] In fact, the commandos received no special pay rates but were allowed from time to time to live in civilian billets, for which the men received an allowance of 6s. 8d. (37½ p.) a day and officers received 13s. 6d (67p).[3] The Royal Marines only made use of this practice on occasions, although Army Commandos had followed it since 1940, when it was administratively convenient, and there were not enough barracks to house all the service units being raised. The practice had the advantage of encouraging individual commandos to be self-sufficient while giving them some 'perks' for undertaking hazardous operations.

In the Mediterranean by this spring of 1942 11th RM Battalion, the Land Defence Force of MNBDO I, had been practising amphibious landings for the best part of two years, and was becoming frustrated at the misuse of Marines by 'continuously employing the Battalion in fatigues for the Army'.[4] In November 1941, however, they had some opportunities to train for specific raids, but it was not until April 1942 that they were able to mount what their Commanding Officer, Lieutenant-Colonel E.H.M. Unwin, regarded as a training raid. The objective was the radar installation on Kupho Nisi, a small island off the southeast coast of Crete. The destroyer HMS *Kelvin* took B Company, about a third of the Battalion's full strength of 27 officers and some 400 Marines,[5] to the island on the night of 15–16 April 1942.

On passage to the raid, Unwin met Lieutenant-Commander Nigel Clogstoun-Willmott, RN, who – not by accident, one suspects – was aboard *Kelvin*. He had made a reconnaissance of Rhodes in 1941, swimming ashore at night from an Army Special Boat Section's canoe, and later would be the founder of Combined Operations Assault Pilotage Parties, responsible for the pre-landing surveys of the 'Torch' (North Africa) beaches, and for surveys of Sicily, Italy and Normandy.[6] On this April night in 1942, however, he was rowed ashore in a skiff. The difficulties of these early raids becomes apparent in the lack of proper equipment, for before the skiff had left *Kelvin*, the signal sergeant's 18-set was put out of action by 'a discharge of water from the ship's side'.[7]

The Company, having been dropped 1,000yds from the landing beach, followed the skiff inshore, a 25-minute pull on a calm star-bright night, 'although there was no moon'. With one Section in each oared whaler line abreast, the cutter followed astern with the support platoon and the Company HQ. A channel was found through reefs off the beach by Clogstoun-Willmott sounding the bottom with an oar, and only one whaler got hung up for a while on the rocks. The other boats, however, became dangerously bunched together on a patch of beach no larger than a tennis court and its surround (30yds × 30yds). But the landing was unopposed until the leading Platoon moved off the beach, when, at the first burst of machine gun fire, their Greek guide bolted. He had been in the skiff with Nigel Clogstoun-Willmott and does not appear to have known much about the coast with which he was supposed to be familiar. They pushed on, outflanked the machine gun, and were in sight of the radar station when their guide was 'recaptured'. They now met sporadic firing, but the Sections became disorganised, as there was no track to follow. The Lieutenant-Colonel, having sent the Platoon sergeant to collect in all the Marines he could find, then seized a light anti-aircraft position, putting a Bren-gunner to cover the Platoon sergeant's men from its sandbagged emplacement. The Platoon commander then, following the plan, charged the building from the south with some 15 men. Three were wounded but the rest broke into the building. When he heard the cries of their charge and bursting grenades, the CO led in the remaining men from the west. The second Platoon by this time was in position covering a road from the nearby village, after coming under some fire. It would later cover the withdrawal, blowing up the reserve of Italian ammunition found in the building. A safe, books to fill two suitcases and radio sets damaged by the grenades were also found, and these were carried back to the boats – there is no mention of radar in the reports.

Of the withdrawal the Lieutenant-Colonel wrote, 'the vulnerability at the point of re-embarkation was extreme ... it was difficult to re-embark the wounded ... [the] boats had to back out in turn, a fairly long process for an overloaded whaler ... there was no communication between the forward troops and the beach'.[8] The second 18-set had been damaged in a fall and could not be easily netted into any radio sets on the destroyer, and there was the problem of non-standard batteries linked by external leads to the 18-sets. The suitcases and safe were left in the cutter to be hauled aboard with this boat as *Kelvin* gathered stern way, for there was no time to lose: she had been clearly visible from the shore and fired on by machine guns. But the boat's falls jammed or broke, the cutter tilted, and what might have been an intelligence coup in code-books from the safe fell into the sea and sank.

The limitations of oared boats in amphibious operations has been mentioned before.[9] Although the Lieutenant-Colonel did not labour the matter in his report, on 11th Battalion's next landing the problems of powered boats would prove even more hazardous and cost many lives.

The RM Division, still frustrated in its commitments to operations for the Chiefs of Staff, as we shall see later, had nevertheless been promised a crack at Madagascar. In training for this landing the division 'defeated', in the view of the umpires, 29 Independent Infantry Brigade during an exercise early in February 1942. Following the recommendations made after Dakar, the RM Major General Sturges had formed a planning team – the nucleus of an HQ – which worked in Combined Operations Headquarters and the Royal Marine Office. On 23 December 1941 General Sturges (GOC of the RM Division) and Rear-Admiral Drew were appointed as joint Commanders for operations in Madagascar, as this French island off the East African coast was a potential base for the Japanese, who had already forced the Vichy French to accept their troops in Indo-China. The original operation, cancelled when Ceylon's defences were given priority in January 1942,[1] was revived in March; and as 29 Independent Infantry Brigade was already aboard the three LSIs *Kerens*, *Karanja* and *Sobieski* in preparation for an exercise, it was committed to the operation in place of the RM Division.[2] Attempts by the Chief of Combined Operations, Lord Mountbatten, to have this decision reversed, were unsuccessful.[3]

General R. (Bob) G. Sturges was held in great respect by all who served under his command,[4] his good-humoured wisdom sparkling in his reports even 50 years after they were written. He had only eight weeks between the date of the decision to mount the raid and the landings on 4–5 May (1942), with the convoys leaving the UK on 23 March.[5] This gave neither 29 Brigade nor 5 (Army) Commando any time to acclimatise while they were brought 9,000 miles to be landed through reefs off the west coast of the island. They came ashore in tropical conditions and found the bush country easily set alight in difficult going, as they crossed the 21 miles from their landing point to the main Vichy French defences at Antsirane. The British tanks sped along the hot dusty road but moved too far ahead of the infantry for mutual support, and were then knocked out by the French before the advance finally stalled on the morning of 6 May (D+1), after a night infiltration by 2nd South Lancs was blocked 200yds behind the French defences.

General Sturges wanted 'something to take their eyes off the ball',[6] and going back to the flagship, HMS *Ramillies*, early in the afternoon, he arranged with the Admiral for her detachment to land in the enemy's rear. In an hour 50 Marines commanded by Captain Martin Price were aboard the destroyer HMS *Anthony*.[7] She sailed north to round the tip of Madagascar and be off Diego Suarez by 2000 hours. This anchorage, 8 miles across and the size of Scapa Flow, has a narrow entrance which *Anthony* passed through at 22 knots, such coast-battery fire as she met being silenced by two '8-inch gunned' cruisers lying off the coast. In the harbour there was a strong offshore wind at the landing point and her Captain[8] skilfully forced the destroyer stern-on to the quay for the Marines to get ashore. Some of 5 Commando had been expected to help moor the ship but they did not arrive, and she withdrew with little damage. The Marines had only a map from the Naval book on coastal pilotage, and lost their way to their intended objective: the Artillery Commander's House. Nevertheless they achieved the aim of causing 'the maximum noise and confusion in the enemy's rear'.[9] Ignoring the French 3-pdr firing at the destroyer – its gunner later did not believe he could have missed such a target at 200yds – and some machine gun fire passing over their heads, the Marines reached a steep bank. Scrambling up some 100ft to a strong fence, they broke through it to find that they were in a cattle pen full of water-buffaloes – 'probably our toughest opposition' – on the outer perimeter of a military barracks.

They had been lucky, for a parallel road to the one they had taken was mined and booby-trapped. The few occupants surrendered, the telephonists at the exchange phoning around to say that they were being overrun. A strong patrol then went out to find in a naval barracks in which a company from the South Lancashire battalion, two Swordfish pilots and a British resident (due to be shot as a spy next day) were all prisoners. The patrol released them, but not before Lieutenant H.J. (Jimmy) Powell had accidentally jammed a cell door in shooting off the lock 'in accordance with the best wild west movie principles'.[10] They set fire to a house only to put it out hastily on learning a Swordfish had crashed on its roof with a 500lb bomb still aboard. They then consolidated their hold on the barracks and collected an assortment of weapons, with which the Lancashires were rearmed. The remaining 'liberated weapons' were taken back aboard, where later Vice-Admiral E.N. Syffret considered them to have been looted, and all but eight French light machine guns had to be landed.

The French surrendered as Brig Festing's troops pressed home their attack from the south; and by 0300 hours, seven hours after the Marines had landed, the port was in British hands. The lessons General Sturges drew from this operation are of interest. On the passage out there had been doubts 'whether we would have to assault Diego S. or not' until the convoy reached South Africa; and of the three brigades that eventually came under the General's command 13 Brigade was 'not fully under command until we reached Durban', 14 days before the landing.[11] The Prime Minister had wished to commit a minimum of forces to the campaign and there was no intention of capturing the whole island.[12] However, the General commanding East Africa and a 'political general' both wangled their way on to the expedition, with a result that there were a Rear-Admiral, a General and two Major-Generals for the control of what amounted to two assault brigades. 'The less said about this the better – it couldn't and didn't work'.[13] The command structure of any amphibious operation needs men of tact and understanding, in the way General Sturges described the need for inter-service co-operation with commanders in 'complete understanding ... with commanders (Army, Navy and Air Force) on terms of intimate friendship ... with one staff'.[14]

Ramillies's detachment occupied the dockyard and provided guards for Vichy French prisoners, before coming back aboard on D+2 about breakfast time. Tired and sweaty, they just had time for a shower and a shave before returning ashore in their best tropical rig to form a guard of honour for the formal surrender.[15]

At Combined Operations HQ during the winter of 1941–2 plans were made to test the theories for capturing a defended port.[1] The Combined Operations' planners chose Dieppe, a French Channel port set in a wall of cliffs easily defended. This Combined Operations' plan was to divide the RM Division into two forces, one to land and swing south-west, capturing the airfield 3½ miles south of Dieppe before linking up with the second force, which was to swing north-east; neither force would make a frontal assault.[2] At this time, in May 1942, Lord Mountbatten made clear to the Chiefs of Staff that bombarding a town was an essential preliminary to its capture by an amphibious assault, for such towns were likely to be in the 'front line'.[3] There were, however, doubts as to whether bridges on the routes encircling the town were strong enough to take the new Churchill tanks, and the Army, therefore, favoured a frontal assault for this and other reasons.

For political reasons 2 Canadian Division replaced the Marines, while General Montgomery rejected the concept of flank attacks.[4] Nor were heavy warships to be risked in the raid, so that only a relatively light bombardment was possible. But 40 RM Commando's role was retained: it would assault the docks and cut out German landing barges, and its Commanding Officer, Lieutenant-Colonel J.P. Phillipps, was to 'take charge of all fighting required on the dockside and the capture of all craft . . . He will also be in charge of final demolition work'.[5] Some of the Marines were to be landed from HMS *Locust*, a river gunboat carrying part of the Commando and the RN Dockmaster's party, who were to force lock gates to inner basins. Seven French *Chasseurs* (submarine chasers) carried the remainder of the Commando, No. 2 RM Demolition Party, the Assistant Dockmaster's Party, No. 3 Royal Navy Demolition Party and an RN Engine Room party to start up captured craft.

The troops' movements were concealed on the night of 18 August in the guise of another exercise,[6] an earlier raid on Dieppe having been cancelled.[7] As the ships crossed to France, however, those craft carrying 3 (Army) Commando were scattered by fire from a German coastal convoy.[8] Nevertheless Major Peter Young, Bedfordshire and Hertfordshire Regiment, got ashore with 19 commandos and successfully harassed the easterly heavy battery with small arms fire in a cool piece of determined courage. To the west Lord Lovat's 4 (Army) Commando took out another heavy battery in a classical flank operation. On the main beaches, however, the assault engineers came ashore without covering fire from the tanks running in late. Over two-thirds of these engineers became casualties and could not therefore breach the seawall, with its anti-tank defences; so – caught on the shingle beach – the tanks were immobilised by German 37-mm anti-tank guns, which could knock off the tanks' tracks though not penetrate their armour. Infantry landings were also delayed by heavier gauge German barbed wire than was expected. The final horror for the attackers was anti-tank guns and machine guns wheeled out of caves in the cliff face. Concealed from air reconnaissance, these unexpected defences effectively put paid to any chance of success.

The RM commandos aboard *Locust* – Commando HQ, the A Company and No. 1 Demolition Party – in all 172 all ranks,[9] arrived off Dieppe about 0530 hours, 10 minutes after H-hour on the main beaches (0520). Thick smoke had greatly reduced visibility, although it was a fine day. As *Locust* tried to pass the mole into the harbour, she was hit twice, two men being killed and six wounded. With the guns on the east side of the entrance still effectively covering the channel, *Locust* came out to join destroyers bombarding the shore batteries. Meanwhile all but one of the *Chasseurs* – 'B' and 'X' Companies, No. 2 (Rear) Commando HQ (the second of the HQ parties afloat), Nos 2 and 3 Demolition Parties, in all over 190 Marines – had arrived off Dieppe. *Chasseur* 43 broke down and arrived late.

On the landing beaches the Canadians had failed to make a lodgement, although this was not known on HMS *Calpe*, the Hunt-class destroyer fitted with 32 additional radios and navigational aids as the HQ ship; for these communications had broken down, since the Beach Signals Sections had been landed with the first flights of assault troops and soon became casualties, their wireless sets damaged beyond repair. A Royal Marine provost party under Lieutenant-Colonel R.G. Parks-Smith, a pioneer of parachute landing, was landed on White beach 'to maintain discipline and order over all personnel'.[10] The party came ashore in the first flights but Parks-Smith was mortally wounded not long after it landed. He was with the Beach Party, mainly responsible in this raid for preparing 'the beaches for a smooth and expeditious withdrawal',[10] but in the event this was organised from the HQ ships with a mixture of craft. (There was, incidentally, a second destroyer as a duplicate headquarters.) At a conference about 0630 hours aboard *Calpe* the cutting-out plan was abandoned and the RM Commando placed at the disposal of the Canadian GOC, Major General Roberts. After passing through White beach, they were to join the Essex Scottish, believed to be in the town.

Commando HQ and A Company transferred to two LCMs, the open craft intended to land trucks or a single tank, and B and X Companies transferred from their *Chasseurs* to LCAs from a pool of boats that had already made at least one landing. The LCA were formed up by about 0830 hours for the 4,000yds run to the beach, with the *Chasseurs* giving them fire support on each flank, and the Marine gun-crews of two major support craft and HMS *Locust* adding to the counter battery fire. The submarine chasers then laid smoke but the landing craft came under 37-mm and heavier fire. Colonel Phillipps, in order to get a clearer view, had perched himself on the wheelhouse roof at the stern of his LCM. From there, breaking out of the smoke just before the craft beached, he saw his Marines 'landing with a courage terrible to see'.[11] Intense machine gun and mortar fire was coming down accurately on the leading craft as they hit the shore.[12]

Royal Marine Bren-gunners, standing exposed for a clearer shot, fired back, despite the bursts of enemy bullets which repeatedly hit their craft.[13] Then a hurricane of fire from rifles and machine guns added to that of heavier guns. Nevertheless Major Houghton got ashore from the Rear HQ's LCA, and No. 8 Platoon landed in an LCA, two Marines being hit as the doors opened for the Marines to charge across the beach to the cover of a tank. This Churchill was immobile but still firing. Only one LCM and LCAs had beached, but by now the Colonel could see that the Germans still held the beach in strength, and putting on his white string gloves, he waved back the boats coming in, so saving 200 of his commandos. Shortly afterwards he was killed but 'his personal courage led and inspired his subordinates'.[14] Lieutenant Smale and the survivors of his platoon, No. 8, did what they could to bring out their wounded at 1130, and then the Lieutenant went back to the tank; he was last seen firing from the shelter of a beached LCT and his small party were all probably killed or taken prisoner in the next hour. One small group on the beach was last reported 'digging a

Channel Tunnel',[15] as they kept their sense of humour in desperate attempts to find some cover in shallow trenches.

Those who came out through the smoke were by no means out of the hail of fire, for German bombs falling nearby sent shock waves through the water and more than one Marine 'felt that his stomach had gone'.[16] Marine gunners on the *Chasseurs*' Hotchkiss guns engaged targets as their boats came inshore, the RM Demolition Parties patching up the shell damage to keep them afloat, and rigging jury steering as they picked up survivors. The OC of the A Company then reported the conditions on White beach, to dash an unfounded optimism aboard the HQ ship.

The major support craft, in action for the first time in daylight at Dieppe,[17] had RM gun crews and were developments of LCF No. 1, at first designated a Beach Patrol Craft (BPC), with twin 4-in dual-purpose guns. This craft carried almost as much fire-power as cruisers of the 1930s, and off Dieppe she successfully engaged the German coast convoy which had scattered 3 Commando's craft. Other major support craft – the LC Flak (LCFs), each with four Oerlikons and eight 2-pdr Pom-Poms, and the LC Gun (Large) (LCG(L)s), each with two 4.7-in guns in open gun houses – had come into service during 1942. At Dieppe LCF No. 2 closed White beach 'with great gallantry . . . to point-blank range . . .' and gave close support until she was disabled, her Captain killed, her guns put out of action one by one until she finally sank'.[18] Another LCF (No. 5) came close to 'shooting down an RAF Mustang, the first we have seen of this type',[19] as she neared White beach, while providing anti-aircraft cover for LCTs heading inshore with their Churchill tanks. The LCF cruised some 400yds off the beach, getting its first Heinkel 111 soon after the tanks had been landed, although the craft was already under fire – 'great holes . . . torn in the bulkheads and terrible screams . . . from the poor lads who were mangled. I felt terribly sick', one gunner writes 'but God was with me, and I held out'. The arrival of Spitfire squadrons about this time cheered everyone up, and the LCFs withdrew into the smoke about an hour after the landing. They lay a mile offshore for a short while, before going back in to spend the next three hours near the beach. Shelled, machine-gunned and taking casualties, they nevertheless were still inshore when the RM Commando was being withdrawn, 'scores of unfortunates . . . struggling in the water 200 yards from the beach . . . most commandos and a few Canadians'.[20] The Marines' gunnery officer of one LCF called for two volunteers when she was nearing the end of 'what seemed like years, picking up survivors',[21] for he had seen wounded survivors, one with a leg blown off, clinging to a raft. Their rescuers took a dinghy through the heavy fire, reached the raft and rowed back with the survivors.

A major air battle over the landing area resulted in greater RAF losses than German, but by this date the Germans were trying to conserve their aircraft. Several were shot down by the minor support craft's Naval crews after they had gone close inshore supporting the LCAs. (These small and medium LC support would later be manned by Marines.) The German reaction ashore had been swift enough, although the German 302 Infantry Division did not order action stations until 0501 hours, 19 minutes before H-hour and after the Army commandos were ashore. Nevertheless the Canadians had 3,369 casualties, mostly prisoners,[22] and the commandos lost 247 men including 75 from 40 RM. RM casualties among the support craft were probably over 50, including a number hit by German aircraft's cannon fire.[23]

A Provost sergeant, Sergeant T.J. Badlan, took charge of one landing craft when all the crew had been killed, and some hours after the evacuation a Royal Marine was picked up a mile from the beaches, swimming with his rifle across the Mae West life jacket he was pushing towards England.[24] This Marine epitomised the Allies' determination to survive and return. But there were many lessons to be learnt from Dieppe, including the impossibility of capturing defended ports – a discovery which in Normandy two years later would save many thousands of lives. The Allies towed their own Mulberry harbours to the Seine Bay beaches, while the Germans, massed to defend harbours, were by-passed in June 1944. But before then Royal Marines would have one most traumatic experience of failure in an amphibious raid.

After its raid on Kupho Nisi in April 1942, the 11th RM Battalion trained hard for a raid on the Sollum Pass (modern Salum). But the raid was cancelled, probably because of the scarcity of shipping and adequate air cover. A raid was then planned on Tobruk, 300 miles west of the Allied lines in Egypt. For this raid Lieutenant-Colonel J.E. Haselden, an Army officer with the British Intelligence Services, had originally planned an overland foray by 12 men who would included some Palestinians,[1] to destroy the petrol and other supply dumps near the port. In the event the raid was carried out by three formations.[2] Force A, 350 Royal Marines of the 11th Battalion with some Army specialists in destroyers; Force B, special service troops of the Middle East (Army) Commando and clandestine forces guided by a patrol of the Long Range Desert Group; and Force C, 150 infantry (Argylls and a platoon of Northumberland Fusilier machine-gunners) carried to Tobruk on 18 Motor Torpedo boats and three motor launches.[3] Other raids would be co-ordinated to disrupt Axis supplies.

The two large destroyers HMS *Sikh* and *Zulu*, disguised as Italian warships, were off Tobruk in the early hours of 14 September 1942, when after an hour's delay lighters were launched. These had been built of unseasoned timber with only one in three having an engine. Each engined barge should have towed in two dumb lighters, each trio of craft carrying a platoon, but the stems of lighters pulled away from the hulls, engines failed and the craft took in water. The CO, Lieutenant-Colonel E.H.M. Unwin, found his barge was foundering some distance from the shore and the only radio was damaged. He could not, therefore, warn the destroyers of the difficulties and they came back inshore, expecting to find empty lighters returning from the beach. They were to have landed the second flight, including men with mortars and drivers whom B Company had hoped would handle captured transport in their drive into the town. But this was not to be, for Major Jack Hedley and two tows – two Platoons – were the only Marines still able to make for the shore. They were 800yds from the beach when coast searchlights snapped on and lit up the destroyers.

These 70 Marines nevertheless got to the beach, but many were drowned or crushed between craft and rocks, for they were 2 miles west of the correct beach.[4] Jack Hedley dispersed his men among the rocks, mortar bombs came down on the lighters,[5] destroying one which fortunately was clear of troops. At sea they could see *Sikh* engaging the shore batteries and 'being shelled at terribly close range'.[6] There was no time to lose as dawn was only an hour away, and there would not be the planned three hours ashore before sunrise at 0645. Major Hedley searched for the wadi, the dry bed of a flash-flood river, he expected to find behind the landing beach, but then realised that they were on the wrong beach. He nevertheless led his Platoon (from A Company) off the beach, hearing firing to his left where the other Platoon ashore (from C Company) was putting in an independent attack. As Jack Hedley's men advanced in extended line, Germans and Italians were firing from the surrounding rocks 'at anyone in a [British] steel helmet'.[7] The way from the beach led to a wadi now bright with the light from star shells. The platoon winkled out machine-gunners, passed through a tented camp which they suddenly realised was a field hospital and moved towards another wadi's head. One machine gun on a lorry was silenced by a grenade tossed by Jack Hedley and he killed five Italians in a defence post – he was a crack pistol shot – before reaching the steep bank at the wadi's head. This was under machine gun fire but the Marines outflanked these guns and got over the bank, before pausing in a deserted building, as it was now daylight. They checked their weapons and redistributed ammunition, as they expected a long march before they could reach Allied lines.[8] *Sikh* by this time was on fire, her steering jammed, and *Zulu* had been unable to pull her clear after a freak shot had parted the tow line. Only *Sikh*'s 'X' turret and her Oerlikons were still firing, but she stayed in action until this turret's ammunition ran out and she was scuttled.[9]

By 0830 there were only 11 Marines alive from Jack Hedley's Platoon as he led them towards another wadi, where Lieutenant C.N.P. Powell and 10 survivors from C Company joined them.[10] They found some caves where they lay up, hoping to hide there through the day and move out after dark. All attempts to contact other Allied forces failed.[11] Major Hedley put his foot through the 18-set, 'something I had always wanted to do', he later wrote, for these sets were not powerful or robust enough for this type of operation. A couple of hours before nightfall enemy patrols found the Marines and they were captured. John Haselden had been killed earlier in the day, only three of his men eventually reaching the Eighth Army's lines; the few machine-gunners and Argylls who had landed were killed or captured. The Allies also lost *Zulu*, the anti-aircraft cruiser HMS *Coventry*, and six coastal craft sunk by bombing as they were returning from Tobruk. After this only 90 Marines reached Egypt, many having died as *Zulu* was trying to pick them up from the lighters.

Captain S.W. Roskill, DSC, RN, has summed up the operation: 'Today one cannot but feel that, even making full allowances for the circumstances which caused it to be carried out, the operation was rash ... and that an assault on a strongly fortified port must require far stronger forces'.[12] There is also reason to believe that the Germans expected a raid, for Major Hedley was told by the local commander that a regiment had been brought back the previous day from the German front and 'had been waiting since 0130 hours for the landing'.[13] There was a later report that one of Haselden's Palestinians was pro-German.

The Allies were moving over to the offensive in the autumn of 1942, when commandos would be required in large numbers to spearhead invasions, and although raids would continue they would not be on the scale of St Nazaire, Dieppe and the early raids in Norway when entire units of Commandos or larger forces took part. The small-scale raids, however, including those by the RM Boom Patrol Detachment, would be co-ordinated from early in 1942 by Combined Operations Headquarters. These raiders landed from canoes in many cases, but in May 1940 three reconnaissance parties had landed near Dunkirk by dinghy.[1] Each party – a hydrographer (RN), an engineer (RE) and a Royal Marine officer – had surveyed suitable beaches for small-boat landings to evacuate troops from Dunkirk. A few Marines also served in the Army Special Boat Section,[2] and a landing by two Marines from a flying boat for clandestine operations has also been reported at this time.[3] 'T' Troop of the RM Commando (later '40 Cdo RM') trained for similar operations, and was serving aboard HMS *Fidelity*, equipped with fast motorboats,[4] when she was sunk with the loss of all hands on the night of 31 December/1 January 1943, before she could carry out any raids.

Small-scale raids could be broadly divided into three groups: intelligence gathering in beach surveys, sabotage raids, and deception raids which cloaked the true intentions of beach surveys. Major Hasler's Boom Patrol canoeists were trained in sabotage to sink enemy shipping, the Detachment's title being deliberately misleading in its association with harbour booms. They used limpet mines capable of blowing a 6-ft hole below a merchant ship's waterline.[5] Therefore when fast blockade-runners were reported to be preparing to take the latest German fuses, radio and radar equipment to Japan, they were an ideal target for these RM canoeists, for the ships were moored 70 miles from the sea up the Gironde at Bordeaux. A conventional raid would have required two divisions, as Germans held this southern part of the French Atlantic coast in depth, and air bombing would have caused unacceptable civilian casualties.[6]

Outline proposals for the raid were passed by the Combined Operations HQ committee, who checked all such proposals for their practical value and relationship to strategic aims at the time, although this check took three weeks (22 September to 13 October); finally revised plans were completed five days later. The raid is famous through Brig Lucas Phillips' book *The Cockleshell Heroes* and the film of that name. What are not so well known are the details of raiding techniques Major Hasler developed, with plans to 'sink between ten and twenty of the cargo vessels ... in the Bordeaux area'.[7] Initially they were going to use three Cockle Mk II canoes but this was increased to six in the final plan, with a timetable which by the fourth day at 2000 hours would give them some 2–3 hours paddling to the Bordeaux quays. There they would place limpets before escaping overland or paddling down stream, having started their escape not later than 0230 hours on the fifth day. The limpets should then explode 3½ hours later at 0600, as they were fitted with sympathetic fuses to ensure that they all went off virtually at the same time. Yet Major Hasler doubted if the canoeists would be able to paddle all the way down river, as the weather would probably deteriorate during the five days, setting back their planned timetable. The operation, code-named 'Frankton', would be launched after preparations were completed on 7 November, on a date that would ensure that Day 4, the evening of the attack, was within two days of a New Moon.

No written orders were issued but a later summary of the verbal orders[8] included the operation of the canoes in two divisions, with targets on named quays, as follows:

	'A' DIVISION	'B' DIVISION
Bordeaux, west bank	*Catfish*	*Cuttlefish*
	(Maj Hasler, Mne Sparks)	(Lt McKinnon, Mne Conway)
Bordeaux, east bank	*Crayfish*	*Coalfish*
	Cpl Laver, Mne Mills)	(Sgt Wallace, Mne Ewart)
Bassens, north and south quays	*Conger*	*Cachalot*
	(Cpl Sheard, Mne Moffat)	(Mne Ellery, Mne Fisher)

'B' Division would proceed independently after the first night's passage, and would place its limpets downstream on ships. 'A' Division would place their's upstream to avoid confusion, when the attacks were made by both Divisions at slack water before the turn of the high tide. Each canoe carried a marked chart showing the areas likely to be free of German lookouts, but their orders included the posting of concealed sentries at all times when they lay up during daylight. Directions were also included for independent action if a canoe lost touch with its Division, and an escape procedure for travelling overland in pairs. Instructions in the event of different forms of enemy action broadly aimed at evasion during the passage, but if the action came during the attack, 'boats will not withdraw but will use their own initiative to press the attack at the earliest opportunity'.[8]

On the night of 7–8 December, after two days of flat calm, there was a deceptive ground swell as the submarine HMS *Tuna* lay south of the Gironde estuary. While *Cachalot* was being brought through the submarine's hatch, her rubberised canvas skin was slit and she could not be launched. The other canoes were then put over the side by means of a 4-ft extension girder in the muzzle of the submarine's gun, with a tackle on the end of it to lift the canoes – 480lb with two men aboard – which could then be traversed outboard.

In three hours they had paddled inshore and were moving northward to round the estuary mouth, when they heard the sound of broken water ahead and

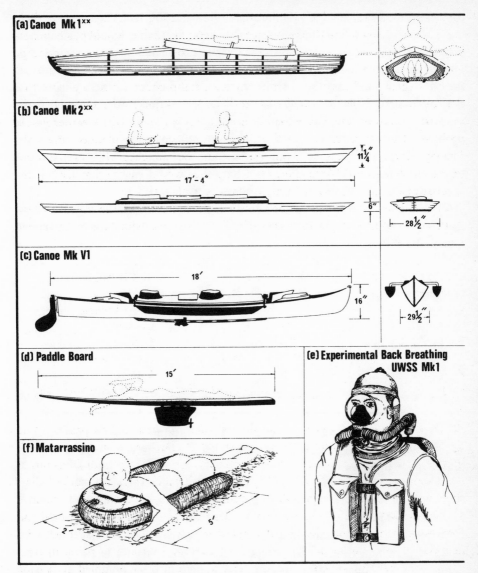

(a) Canoe Mk 1[xx]

(b) Canoe Mk 2[xx]

(c) Canoe Mk V1

(d) Paddle Board

(f) Matarrassino

(e) Experimental Back Breathing UWSS Mk1

Equipment used by RMBPD and other canoeists.

(a) The Mark 1** canoe developed from the 16ft (5m) Folbot with setionalised wooden frame covered by rubberised canvas. This could be packed into a canvas bag with the frame in sections of 4ft 6in (1.3m). Load: 2 men + over 150lb.

(b) Mk 2** canoe with one-eighth inch plywood deck and bottom, could be dragged over beaches. Sides were of 3-ply rubber-proofed canvas, and could be collapsed when the hinged struts supporting the gunwale were 'down' to give a depth of only 6in (15cm) for stowage. Load: 2 men + 250lb.

(c) Mk VI canoe of moulded one-eighth inch 'aircraft' plywood covered in fabric and treated with sealer (dope). A lining of heavy rubber-proofed stockinette kept the hull watertight if the wooden skin was fractured. The outriggers were of fabric covered wood on alloy arms. Load: 2 men + 350lb or 3 men + c 150lb. Engine: 4 HP 2-stroke and retractable, giving 68 miles (105 ~ km) at 7 knots or 90 miles (140 + km) at 5.6 knots. Equipment: included mast and sails, double paddles and fabric sea anchor.

(d) Paddle board with compass in bow normally propelled by a swimmer's arm strokes but here with Welburn propulsion unit of engine-and-propeller with could be detached.

(e) Experimental back breathing apparatus of October 1943 some types of which proved unreliable. The nose-and-mouth seal can be seen behind the glass piece worn with this Type C-Hood.

(f) Matarrassino inflated to 5ft (1.5m) by 2ft (.6m) by built-in-bellows and used to increase a swimmer's range and ability ti navigate. Weight 10lb and rolled into 16in x 10in x 6in package when deflated.

Note: The paddler, usually No. 2 and aft in a canoe, wore a suit with an inflatable stole and kapok belt but not waterproofed. The surface swimmer, No. 1 and forward in the canoe, wore a 14lb rubberised Grenfell fabric suit with rope-soled shoes, sealed at the cuffs etc and with urination valve. In tropical waters the swimmers could carry a fish scarer containing copper acetate and black dye tablets, sufficient for 10 hours discharge during swimming.

came across the first of three unexpected tide races. They could see it clearly 1½ miles off, and, keeping the bows into the rollers and the cockpit cover fastened, the men in four canoes weathered these overfalls, which, with a strong flood tide under the canoes, could not be avoided. *Coalfish*, however, was missing when they got through, and although the other four turned back, she was not seen again. A short time later *Conger* capsized in a second race: she was scuttled and her crew towed to a position 1½ miles from shore, where the lighthouse at Pointe de Groves had suddenly been switched on and 'lit up the scene quite brilliantly for a time'.

As time had been lost, they were forced to take a short cut, and altered formation to pass a line of moored boats. They had started out in two close arrowheads of boats, with the leader *Cuttlefish* of 'B' Division just astern of the two outlying canoes of 'A'. Now they were in line astern, with the three remaining boats several hundred yards apart. Using single paddles for a cautious approach, *Catfish* and *Crayfish* got through, but there was no sign of Lieutenant McKinnon and Marine Conway in *Cuttlefish*.

The two canoes came ashore and were visited by Frenchmen, but they could not get under way next evening until 3½ hours after they had hoped, because the fully loaded Cockle Mk IIs had to be dragged three-quarters of a mile across mud; that this could be done at all, however, was an indication of this type of canoe's strength. They crossed to the east bank and lay up for Day 3. The weather had been cold but this dawn the water froze as it splashed on to the cockpit covers. That night there would only be three hours of flood tide to help them towards the advanced base they had hoped to set up next dawn, so they launched the boats early at dusk and were seen by a French farmer, 'who was rather upset when we declined to go to his house for a drink'.[10] However, he was not so upset that he gave them away.

They had to wait for the tide and were not near enough to Bordeaux at dawn on Day 4 to establish a base from which to launch the attack and get away in darkness. They therefore postponed the attack to the next day, and made a further 9 miles that evening before settling down in their advanced base. At many of these layovers, the boats had to be manhandled over banks before the lightweight camouflage nets were put over them, and at others the canoes were forced with difficulty behind thick reeds to dry out when the tide ebbed. They spent the day well concealed, arming their limpets, restowing their gear in only two bags and preparing for the attack. The matter of fact tone of the official report only hints at their obvious enthusiasm, for opposite their little base two ships were moored, some 800yds away across the river.

At 2100 they set the limpets' time fuses for 9 hours (9 o'clock next morning), and 15 minutes later *Catfish* set out for the west bank quays. *Crayfish* went to the east bank. It was 2115 hours before they set off as they had waited until the moon was setting although this was later than suited them for the tide's flood. Drifting quietly on this flood, *Catfish* reached half-way along the line of ships to put three limpets on a large cargo ship and two on a *Sperrbrecher* mine destroying ship, before the ebb set in; and in order to avoid the disturbance of even stealthy paddle strokes against a stream, they swung back on the ebb. A sentry, for some breath-holding moments, caught them in his torch beam. Still, camouflaged and silent, they watched him, but he did not realise what they were. A floating log? Some other flotsam? When the stream swung them from his view, they waited five minutes, then attached the limpets to the stern of a merchantman; the current was by now too strong to get at her bow, for an oil tanker was moored outside this target and the canoe would have been swept under if she had got between them. In all they placed eight limpets, three on this cargo ship, two by the Sperrbrecher's engine room, two on the merchantman and one on the stern of an oil tanker. *Crayfish* had found no targets on the Bordeaux east quays and returned on the ebb to put eight limpets on the ships that they had seen opposite the advanced base. Then both canoes paddled downstream with less caution then they had been using before, taking double paddles to get well down by 0600 hours. They beached a quarter of a mile from each other and sought separate escape routes. They had paddled 91 miles since leaving HMS *Tuna*.[11]

A party of French Resistance workers, planning to sabotage the ships, saw the flash of the limpets' explosions. The ships that were damaged – *Alabama*, *Tannenfels*, *Dresden* and *Portland* – were all flooded and out of action for several months.[12] The other ships attacked do not appear to have suffered damage, because the limpets failed to explode, or, in the case of the *Sperrbrecher*, her sides having been reinforced for her job of mine clearing, the limpets probably caused only minor damage. Major Hasler and Marine Sparks came out through one of the French Resistance's escape routes, but the fate of the other crews was not known until after the war. Sergeant Sam Wallace and Marine R. (Bob) Ewart in *Coalfish* had carried on all the first night until swept inshore, when they were capsized in surf and captured – in uniform – by a flak battery's crew. Despite interrogation, they did not reveal their objectives but their canoe was found. During the next five days, after further interrogation, they were shot in Bordeaux just after midnight on 11–12 December,[13] some five hours before the limpets exploded. *Conger*'s crew were numb with cold, and despite their life-jackets were probably unable to swim through the inshore current, for Marine David Moffat was drowned, his body being washed ashore some time later. Corporal G.J. Sheard's body was never found, and he must also have drowned. *Cuttlefish* carried on towards Bordeaux for three days after losing touch with the others, but the canoe was badly holed and sank quickly when she hit a submerged obstacle not far from the quays. In the next two weeks, the crew made their way towards Spain, reaching La Reole, over 30 miles south-east of Bordeaux, where they were put in a civilian hospital, having been befriended by various French families. But here they were betrayed.[14] They were in civilian clothing, when German soldiers took them from the hospital, for interrogation.

Crayfish's crew, Corporal A.F. Laver and Marine W. (Bill) H. Mills, having landed after the raid, made good progress in their escape during the next two days but were picked up by French police, passed to the German security police and imprisoned in Bordeaux.[15] Although attempts were later made by the Germans to hide any evidence of what subsequently happened to the four prisoners, they were shot in Paris, probably on 23 March 1943. They all knew that this was a risk they ran when in civilian clothes, but there is no doubt that at least two were in uniform when captured, and they were shot. Men captured from landings by the Small Scale Raiding Force were also shot, in accordance with Hitler's directive: 'All enemy troops taking part in the so-called commando operations . . . in uniform or not . . . whether in battle or escaping . . . will be destroyed to the last man'.[16] The determination and dedication of these young Marines, who were in their early twenties except for Sam Wallace, who was 29, set an example that would be followed by Marine canoeists in later decades. Despite the difficulties and dangers, each crew had continued towards their objectives although out of touch with others in the raid.

The watershed of Allied fortunes came in 1942. During the next year the Royal Marines took on new roles that would require all their individual discipline and dedication, as we shall see in the next chapter.

5 SWEAT SAVES BLOOD – ORGANISATION, TRAINING AND AMPHIBIOUS FORCES

The Royal Navy did not learn as much as they might have done from World War I, for only two of several proposed committees sat to analyse aspects of the war. The Mitchell committee reported, March 1919, on the Dardanelles and Admiral Phillimore's committee – specifically barred from comments on Naval air power – reported on different types of ship,[1] but no scientific analysis of 1917–18 convoys was made until World War II. But the Royal Marines had clearly learnt their lessons, and World War II would prove them to be the correct ones. As explained in Chapter 2, the Marine was a highly efficient soldier, but neither he nor his officers were allowed sufficient time ashore to practise large-scale land actions. These points, as we have seen, were pressed on the Madden committee in 1924.

Before then the RM Artillery and RM Light Infantry had been amalgamated, after being separate formations with their own promotion rosters since 1862, 58 years after the RMA's formation. General Blumberg, the Adjutant General from 1920 to 1924, revived a proposal of 1912(?) for their amalgamation in 1920, after proposals had once again been made to disband the Corps. The Admiralty resisted the proposals but was forced to accept the Treasury's view that some reduction could be made even if the Corps was not abolished, for two Portsmouth Divisions of Marines – the RMA at Eastney Barracks and the RMLI at Forton – were hard to justify.[2] In writing to the First Lord of the Admiralty General Blumberg explained that to abolish Portsmouth RMLI Division at Forton Barracks would lead to many difficulties in manning ships and on mobilisation. He went on to say that to disband the RMA 'though feasible was opposed by sentiment and the probability that a small force of land gunners would always be required ... it was decided that the best solution was to amalgamate the two branches into one Corps for which the following advantages are claimed:

(1) The Corps will be more homogeneous, their thoughts and ideas would be the same, and a certain amount of friction done away with;
(2) Common recruit training at Deal for all Marines as well as for officers;
(3) Equalisation of promotion (for) officers;
(4) A wider field of selection for higher gunnery ratings and for officers' appoint-

ments eg: The RMA out of 2,100 men have to provide 80 gunlayers 1st Class, the RMLI out of 6,900 only 10; and a distribution of the special duties would be possible;

(5) Each Capital ship would be manned from its own port [previously RMA from Portsmouth served in all capital ships];

(6) The whole RM Force would be on an equality as regards serving on foreign stations;

(7) If Land Service Artillery [men] are required, it will be possible to concentrate on specialists, and a proportion of LS would be available on each station [where ships were based].

(8) One type of uniform'.[3]

This reasoning was accepted by the Admiralty and an Order in Council of 11 October 1923[4] confirmed the amalgamation with effect from the previous 22 June. On 3 August the former RMLI companies marched out of Forton Barracks (later HMS *St Vincent*), where they had been stationed since 1848. The local newspaper stressed Gosport's regret, at their going and described the eight companies' march to the ferry, and their later march along the Southsea front with their colours.[5] These were welcomed at Eastney in official speeches, but, so the story goes, former RMA officers in their mess at Eastney sniffed at the 'bits of bunting', for traditionally their guns are the equivalent to artillerymen of the infantry's colours.[6] What these rather proper gunners thought of having the NCOs of the Colour Party in to the Mess for the customary drink, though in a side-room, can be imagined.

The organisation of the Corps from that time until 1946 was based on three Divisions, no longer officially termed 'Grand' Divisions but numbered 1st, 2nd and 3rd,[7] with, for example, two black rings on a Portsmouth Marine's kitbag[8] (these ordinals, however, were seldom used in everyday references to Chatham, Portsmouth and Plymouth). Initial training for recruits was then concentrated at the Depot (Deal), all men being subsequently trained as infantry 'in accordance with the Army Training Manuals' and in Naval gunnery as they had been before the amalgamation, while the Corps' small technical branch of armourers and other tradesmen continued to be based at Fort Cumberland. Officers and Marines were also trained in other specialised skills by the Corps' instructors at Schools of Land Artillery (Portsmouth), Physical Training (Deal) and Signals (Chatham). Others were trained as butchers, printers and 'for special ratings required by HM Fleet'.[9] Musicians continued to be trained at the Royal Naval School of Music in Eastney Barracks.

Eastney carried on the RMA traditions for hospitality, Plymouth maintained its former RMLI reputation for field operations and planning, while Chatham continued to provide many ceremonial guards and bands for parades in London. There were changes in uniform but the Marine's dress (see Appendix 3) retained features which can be traced to the original RMA and RMLI uniform. Keeping such kit clean and smart still meant burnishing bayonets and the steel tips on boot soles; the brass butt-plates of rifles were a gleaming gold colour as were buttons and cap badges. Boots were treated with liberal coats of polish and a hot fork that burnt off the natural blebs (blisters) on the toe caps by removing the oil in the leather, to get a patent-leather finish, after Army boots became standard issue in the Corps during World War II. Before the war each Division had its own tailors' and shoemakers' shops, and without getting too deep into the intricacies of cleaning kit, these oiled boots without toe caps required applications of 'spit black', followed by Cherry Blossom boot polish boned with a handle of a toothbrush into the leather.[10]

Some reorganisation was necessary between Divisions, for RMA gunners from Eastney had previously provided men for all capital ships, but these would now be manned entirely by detachments of Marines from their home ports. Volunteers and some single men, therefore, changed their Divisions, which in many cases meant moving their homes. For some years recruiting was virtually at a standstill but by the late 1920s some 700 recruits were joining each year.[11] They began their training in squads of 40 at the Depot (Deal), where they completed their initial drill training, small arms course, field training and drill revision before going to one of the Divisions (not necessarily the Division to which they were assigned). During the twelfth weeks of training, four or six Section Leaders would be chosen for extra tuition in the evenings. These 'red diamond men' – they wore a red diamond on the top left sleeve – were considered to be the best recruits and from their number a King's Badgeman would later be selected. The 'red diamond men' of 'HO' (Hostilities Only) squads were selected on a similar basis; but the King's Badge was only awarded to the best recruit in continuous service squads, and only to those considered of the high standard required, not necessarily to the best recruit in every King's Squad. To complete the training before World War II, squads at the Divisions learned seamanship, advanced field craft, Lewis gun drills, surveying and repository (building piers, bridges and crane-type hoists). Royal also had to gain his 3rd Class Certificate of Education in English, mathematics and general subjects before he completed his training.

With the necessary recommendations of his commanding officer after a minimum of six months' sea service, but more often after three or four years' service, Marines could be accepted as candidates for promotion. A candidate at his Divisions learnt to take his part as a corporal in charge of a shell-room party or other NCO's duty at sea and as a sub-section leader of an infantry platoon. The successful candidates, however, might have to wait 3 or more years before they were promoted, for each Division had its own promotion roster and a Portsmouth Marine, for example, was not promoted to NCO's rank in another Division. After 9 or so years' service since he joined, and having taken further education qualifications (2nd Class Certificate), a corporal with appropriate recommendations from his commanding officer might take the 16-week Senior NCOs' course. Again a successful candidate might have to wait some years for a vacancy on his Division's roster for sergeants before promotion. Many NCOs were also trained as instructors at the various RM Schools and as gunnery instructors (GIs) at the Royal Navy's gunnery school, HMS *Excellent* (Whale Island, Portsmouth).[12]

Promotion to Colour-Sergeant (C/Sgt), Quartermaster Sergeant, QM Sergeants as CSMs and Warrant Officers (at the time equivalent to this Naval rank) was highly competitive. Less than half-a-per-cent of those who joined as recruits were eventually to reach Warrant rank and fewer achieved further promotion to Commissioned Quartermaster. Yet in other branches of the Navy not less than 2 per cent of recruits and as high as 5 per cent in some years achieved these ranks, a comparison that caused senior RM officers great concern, for the senior NCOs were of exceptional quality.[13] The few Warrant Officers – Staff (Parade) Sergeant-Majors, Orderly Room Sergeant-Majors and Superintendent Clerks – at each Division had a status similar to those of Royal Navy warrant officers, with their own Mess, although the senior Warrant Officer acted as non-resident president of the Sergeants' Mess in each Division. They wore a similar uniform to commissioned officers, with a Sam Browne belt but no star badges of rank. But the badge 'WO' surrounded by a laurel wreath was introduced early in World War II, and when the WO was wearing battledress, with a collar and tie, he could be easily confused with a far more senior rank. There were also commissioned WOs at this time.

Opportunities for promotion from Warrant Officer to commissioned rank were limited in the 1920s and 1930s by changes in the appointment of Commissioned Gunners and a bias in the 1934 (and later) promotion examinations towards Quartermaster's work.[14] Many senior NCOs with powers of leadership in the field had no bent – if QMs will excuse the term – for keeping records and other QM duties.

Band masters and school instructors were also appointed to Warrant rank from Musicians and other specialists, but their promotions were regulated by different procedures from those for general service NCOs. However, with the expansion of World War II, many senior NCOs were given temporary commissions in all sectors of the Corps. The Army equivalent rank of Regimental Sergeant-Major had been reintroduced as Sergeant-Major RM, with one serving at each Division and at Deal. The complications of Royal Marines as Naval warrant officers serving with the Army had led in 1935, during the London duties, to the RM Staff Sergeant-Major being saluted by his Army opposite number. Under the system of Sergeant-Majors RM, with promotion seniority equated to their counterparts, the Orderly Room Sergeant-Major and Superintending Clerks, the problems of RM senior non-commissioned ranks were resolved, but in 1946 the rank of Sergeant-Major RM was replaced by the rank of Regimental Sergeant-Major, who wore the same badges of rank but was an NCO under the terms of the Army Act.

Young officers for continuous service in the Corps have usually been recruited (after December 1838) at 18 by examination and interview. Between the World Wars successful candidates then completed 3 years of courses, including nine months studying military theory and such varied subjects as land artillery, seamanship and the use of searchlights. Before 1930 they also spent six months at the Royal Naval College (Greenwich) studying mainly mathematics, but this was dropped, as were courses on both equitation and electrical mines.[15] Probationary 2nd-Lieutenants were promoted Probationary Lieutenants for the last six months before being confirmed in their rank. There were also a few graduates commissioned by direct entry, each being given courses designed to suit their individual training. Two Marines – fewer if none were eligible – were commissioned each year from the ranks; opportunities to gain these Corps commissions were given to successful candidates under 23 and with three or more years' service and the Higher Education Certificate. After 1932 some reduction was made in the length of service required and 'one slip by a spirited youth' no longer disbarred him for consideration.[16]

The opportunities for promotion beyond Captain were comparatively small, and not until January 1936 could Royal Marine officers take the 'long' gunnery course at HMS *Excellent*, qualifying them as the principal gunnery officer, big 'G', in a major warship. Others who passed the 'short' gunnery course were – in the style of Naval nomenclature – little 'g's'. Both these courses were indicative of the Corps' principal specialisation in Naval gunnery during the years 1919 to 1939, yet there were limited promotion prospects, with 201 Captains and Lieutenants in 1932 mainly at sea, but only 52 Majors, 21 Lieutenant-Colonels and Colonels and 6 more senior officers.[17] In these decades the intake of officers was small. For example, in 1932 only 30 officers were under training: four of 1929, ten of 1930, seven in 1931 and nine in 1932.

In 1923 only two officers had been accepted – C. F. Phillips and B. G. Ralfs. They were both to have remarkable careers: Major General Phillips, KBE, CB, DSO, commanded 47 (RM) Commando in 1944–5 before his later promotion to General; and Major General Ralfs attained the highest rank open to technical gunnery officers, as President of the Ordnance Board, which was responsible for all services' ordnance and successor to the Board of earlier centuries although shorn of political power.[18] There were a number of other officers who served outside the Corps in the inter-war years. Major General A. R. Chater, CB, CVO, DSO, OBE as a young officer began a distinguished career in the Sudan; in 1937 he commanded the Somaliland Camel Corps and in World War II led the force that captured Italian colonies in this part of east Africa.[19] Brig B. W. (Jumbo) Leicester, who would command 4 Commando Brigade in World War II, was seconded in the 1930s to the Sudan Defence Force, in which British officers commanded desert and other patrols in keeping the peace among warring factions.

Before leaving the 1920s and 1930s, a new development of those decades drew the Corps into police work. Policing the Royal Navy's dockyards had been an RM duty on and off since 1764, if not before, when Marine sentries were posted and pickets provided security checks. By 1922, however, a trained force was required, and under the Adjutant General's command 70 senior NCOs took over some police duties in the dockyards, as the RM Police, a body under Army discipline, with a few civilians – former civilian police – as detectives for the Criminal Investigation Department (CID). This force was later established and expanded, with a Chief Constable on the Adjutant General's staff to command it. Men of the force relieved Metropolitan civilian police on security duties at

Admiralty property in London, and by 1939 the force had expanded to 900. During World War II the Admiralty civilian police – men not serving under military discipline – were for a time also commanded by the Royal Marines' Chief Constable, but after the war these bodies became part of the Ministry of Defence's security forces.[1]

Royal Marines served, at times, under Royal Navy or Army discipline. The Navy's regulations limited a commander's powers of punishment to standard punishments only varied according to an offender's past record, and this power of punishments could only be delegated to a senior Naval officer's second-in-command, so that on a ship the Naval Captain could only give these powers to his Commander (or his First Lieutenant in a small ship). While the Captain of a ship was in general vested with wider powers of authority than his counterpart in the Army, under the Army Acts more junior officers, including company commanders, had powers to punish their own men, a system 'more suitable for the Corps' organisation'.[1] The Naval disciplinary code meant that officers commanding an RM detachment afloat could not punish his men but must bring them before the Commander, yet an RM Company or Commando Troop commander serving with the Army could give various punishments, including small fines and confining a man to barracks for seven days. Although Marines in Naval establishments ashore were under the Naval code, the RM establishments at Divisions and the Depot were administered under the Army Acts.[2] But apart from these Divisions, as Marines between the two World Wars seldom served elsewhere than in Naval bases or at sea, there were few senior commands where Marine officers had the disciplinary powers you might expect. Not that this gave detachment officers any difficulties, for there was an understandable affinity between officers and men when they formed a small part of a ship's complement or were otherwise faced by a large 'mass' of the Navy; and, paradoxically, Marine officers have always followed in the tradition of Nelson, who paid particular attention to the care of his men, rather than in Wellington's approach, which appeared to treat other ranks with some disdain. In the war years the long-serving officers' care for their men – in today's terms, man management – would be passed on to the officers with temporary commissions.

The traditions of the Corps were also passed on to many World War II recruits by the trained soldiers – the title given to senior Marines, many of them pensioners – who were responsible for the recruits in each barrack room. For example, there were tales of stealing on to Persian destroyers to disable them in 1906. Or was it 1909? The dates did not matter. What was remembered was the quiet description of getting aboard undetected, the quick rush for the bridge and the scramble down ladders to the engine room. To imbue some 60,000 'Hostilities Only' Marines in this and other ways with the Spirit of the Corps was one of the great contributions the long-service Marines made to the war effort. They taught the 'HOs' to appreciate the value of discipline and how to get by in the ways of the service, with many a comparison of what it was like in the 'old' days. In 1906, for instance, there had been only issues of meat, bread and potatoes, and men had had to buy such essentials as butter, jam and veg-etables out of their own pocket.[3] And take the heavy coal tubs! Handling these had officially been considered 'detrimental to a Marine's health' in 1804,[4] but they were still in use in the 1950s.

Mobilisation went smoothly, as the official Naval histories record, so far as can be judged from letters and narratives of men who were recalled. Ships' detachments were brought up to strength, men were found for Defensively Equipped Merchant Ships (DEMS), the MNBDO expanded and steps were taken to raise a Strike Force. The use of Marines in the essentially defensive role of MNBDOs has been criticised, but these formations were principally anti-aircraft and coast gunners, as we have seen. A pointer to the Royal Navy's concern for the air defence of bases in the winter of 1939–40 is shown by Admiral Somerville's letter of the previous January,[5] in which he writes to the Adjutant General express-ing concern at 'the poor standard of gunnery among Army crews – whose officers did not let training interfere with polo – while serving in defence of Naval bases.'[6] With Marines manning them, the Royal Navy would have control of these defences.

There were many such problems, chief of which was the small number of Marines, no more than 900,[7] available to train the new intakes. Steps were taken to shorten the courses for long-service recruits with 369 King's Squad and 370th both passing for duty on the same day in April 1940.[8] Signallers 1st-class in ships were replaced by signallers 2nd-class and general service Marines[9] (trained in the fleet), enabling a number of experienced men to join special units ashore – the MNBDO, Admiralty shore stations and similar important communication centres. By 1942 there would even be a shortage of buglers; the age limit for their sea service was therefore raised and restrictions placed on their transfer to general service.[10]

Other administrative changes came when Marines manned landing craft and the problems of discipline under the Navy Acts was resolved by a special Admir-alty order,[11] enabling commanders of training companies in LC Units to have some powers of punishment. Other expedients would include training Marines on the RN Air Station at Yeovil, where some anti-aircraft gun crews did part at least of their basic as well as their gunnery training in the early months of 1940, under RSM 'Hickie' Hickman, while the airfield was under construction. The Marines were not the only British force which was dangerously extended in the 1940s, for by the height of the war 55 per cent of the British people were engaged in war work, and 44 per cent of the Americans.[12] Something of the Corps' work in training the many young officers, signallers and other specialists can be seen in Appendix 4 on the Officer Cadet Training Unit, the NCOs School and so on. But much of this training was supervised by many of the 2,000 pensioners recalled, including one of 72,[13] who replaced younger men in jobs at camps and the Divisions. Others were replaced by 'Marens', Women's Royal Naval Service wearing the globe and laurel cap badge on a red flash, which made the girls 'feel extra special'.[14] They filled many clerical, administrative and storekeepers' posts, and also acted as transport drivers, stewards, cooks and pioneers.

Much was accomplished by the help of pensioners and Wrens, the compromises in shortening courses, and above all the hard work of the few staff officers. General Bourne's day began at 0700 hours in the RM Office at St James's, and about 1000 he moved to Combined Operations HQ where he worked until the late evening before returning to the RM Office, where his day would often end after midnight.[15] As a result of such efforts in the 21 months to May 1941, the Corps had expanded to more than 36,000, being deployed as follows:[16]

MNBDO I in Egypt and Crete (with 5,200 all ranks)
Siege Rgt under XII Corps (with 280)
32nd How. Bty in Shetland (35)
Detachments with static minefields (415)
Recruits under training at Divisions etc. and their staffs (8,770)
RM OCTU, including cadets (370)
RM Signals School (90)
RM Engineer Battalion (1,280) building Scapa defences
RM Auxiliary Battalion of tradesmen, pioneers, etc. (890)
RM Division HQ with nucleus of several special duty battalions and reinforcements (1,340)
101 RM Bde in Scotland (1,400)
102 RM Bde in Scotland (1,360)
MNBDO II in formation, mainly anti-aircraft and coast gunners (4,400)
RN School of Music at Malvern (550)
Home Base Ledger (40)
Detachments at sea (including bands) and in Royal Naval establishments (9,800)

This strength of over 36,000 includes a number of formations and units not mentioned before or only briefly. The detachments with static minefields, for instance, were lookouts working with controlled minefields of the type originally to be used in Mobile Base Defences. The Engineer Battalion was recruited from tradesmen, its officers being civil engineers, whose squads completed a short disciplinary course and introduction to the Royal Marines at the Depot Deal or the Divisions before being drafted to build defence works at Scapa. These engineers, the RME, would later (see Appendix 4) be deployed in a wide range of civil engineering tasks, from building camps to building bases for coastal forces' MTBs in Ceylon.

The RN School of Music had been created in 1903 to provide musicians for ships and RM establishments.[17] A brief history of the Band Service is given in Appendix 5, but there was a distinction between the three Divisional bands, with different heritages and administrations, and the Band Service until they were amalgamated in 1950. The Corps of Buglers continued as a separate organisation until 1979, although, in the 1940s and before, all three musical formations enjoyed some autonomy within the Corps. The Band Service had a Training

Wing for boy musicians – not included in the above strengths – and its senior wing provided 84 bands from its 1,955 musicians, some 1,400 of them at sea.[18] In addition to their gunnery-control duties in the T/S, they played each day at such ceremonial occasions as daily colours, when the White Ensign was raised. Admiral Cunningham's flag-ship band was playing on a deck with a list of 15 degrees 2 hours after she, HMS *Queen Elizabeth*, was damaged by delayed action mines planted by Italian swimmers. The Admiral wanted to know 'after the Commander has finished salving the ship, why there is only one drummer with the band'.[19] By this time, December 1941, the Band Service had lost 100 musicians at sea, including the 17-man band of HMS *Hood*.

The administration of pay and allowances for Marines had been controlled by paymasters at each Division, but in the expansion, a small pay office, the Home Base Ledger, was set up. With only five officers and a few Marines, this office was largely staffed by Wrens to handle the pay records of the MNBDOs, the RM Division and recruits in training. Equipment for all services was in desperately short supply and while any study of the Marines' supply problems inevitably encompasses the whole gamut of military stores, only a few examples are needed to illustrate the difficulties. There were 40 rifles between 400 recruits at Exton in July 1940,[20] makeshift anti-tank guns were used by the QF Regiment, and there was a lack of artillery pieces, from which much of the RM Division's difficulties stemmed. But supplies had improved in many respects by 1943, the No.4 Rifle having been introduced in 1942 and standardisation of such things as .303-in ammunition made supplying the forces easier. (The red-labelled boxes of this ammunition specially made for synchronised guns, for example, were no longer required, as all '303' ammunition could be used in aircraft guns, provided it was less than 3 years old.[21]) There were changes in uniform, HO recruits not receiving 'blues' unless they were going to big ships' detachments, and the fore-and-aft cap being replaced by the blue beret; and there were changes in the style of battle dress and other personal equipment, as described in Appendix 3.

Through all these changes of organisation, equipment and personnel, the RM Division soldiered on. But in 1943 the Corps found new roles, and there were changes that undoubtedly ensured its future for the next 50 years, and probably for much longer.

Before the men of the RM Infantry Division and the MNBDOs were remustered in new amphibious roles, there were major changes in the way landings and raids were planned and the methods by which they were carried out. The British introduced a Combined Operations Headquarters, as described in the next chapter. New types of craft and ships were built to carry tanks and vehicles from sally ports and land them over open beaches, and the Americans developed those fleet trains of supply ships which enabled fleets to stay at sea over 1,000 miles from any base. Plans were made to use the fast New Zealand ship *Rangatira*, carrying 450 Marines,[1] on raids in the Far East, and to place British Marines under American command for raids in the Pacific, but these were abandoned when 'the Admiralty believed that the plan was no longer feasible',[2] after the

Allied losses in escort warships, no doubt. Nevertheless 8th RM Battalion had been reformed as 41 (RM) Commando in October 1942 and 'No. 40 (RM)' rebuilt after the losses at Dieppe. The anti-aircraft and coast-defence elements of MNBDO I were deployed in South East Asia; and those MNBDO II units not deployed in the air defence of Great Britain were improving techniques for loading landing craft, marking beaches and so on.

At sea the first ten 'HO' lieutenants, after passing appropriate courses, had proved successful, judging by their confidential reports,[3] but most of the men in ships' detachments were long-service officers, NCOs and Marines. Although a few 'HO' Marines had served in ships' detachments since 1941, in all there were probably no more than 3,500 'HOs' in major warships.

For all these ship's detachments – in the Atlantic, in the Mediterranean, in the Far East and in the Arctic – there could be long periods of routine, as we have seen, but at other times there were days of relentless action, especially in the Arctic. The first convoy had sailed from Iceland to North Russia with seven ships on 21 August 1941, and 10 days later docked safely at Archangel without any contact with the Germans,[4] and other convoys fared reasonably well on this route until the spring of 1942.[5] But as the hours of daylight lengthened and the Polar ice had not melted sufficiently for the route to pass well clear of the North Cape, it was only a matter of time before the Germans would use their northern airfields to attack these ships. Their heavy warships in Norwegian waters were also a threat, but ships of the British Home Fleet could not all be concentrated to protect the Arctic convoys, as other German battleships in French ports threatened Atlantic convoys to the south. The result was that close support for the convoys was often limited to cruisers and smaller escorts, while the British battle squadrons were deployed to block any moves by the German capital ships from Norwegian fjords.

This was the situation in March 1942 when the cruiser HMS *Trinidad* sailed with two destroyers to pick up the convoy PQ13, which would pass the westbound QP9 south of Bear Island (between Spitzbergen and north Norway). This homeward-bound convoy (QP9) had only one brush with German forces, when a minesweeper acting as escort rammed a U-boat.[6] *Trinidad* had her first mishap, however, when taking on fuel from her oiler off Iceland, and in a rising gale bounced this supply ship, damaging several of her own life-rafts, before she picked up her 19 charges. She steamed in the centre of this convoy during Tuesday, 23 March, with the weather worsening all day. That night *Trinada* moved south of the convoy to cover the likely approach of German destroyers from their base at North Cape. The weather continued to deteriorate and by daylight the convoy was becoming scattered over 150 miles of raging seas south of Bear Island. Even the 8,000-ton *Trinidad* had to heave to, rolling and wallowing as she kept four knots steerage way into the heavy weather. She had only found one of the merchantmen, but in these conditions – she rolled to 40 degrees at one time – she could do nothing to find the others during Wednesday and Thursday. They were taking a buffeting, their deck cargoes of tanks and crated planes making them difficult to handle. When the gale eased on Friday, down came the snow, as the cruiser gathered in two more ships, and by the dog watches there was a foot of snow frozen to her upper deck.

Saturday, 27 March, was calm and the *Luftwaffe* found the scattered ships, but only sank a tanker with the cruiser's group and a straggler. *Trinidad* then turned westward, leaving destroyers to escort to Murmansk the two remaining ships in this fragment of the convoy. Action stations were sounded that evening, as she searched for her charges, but the expected German destroyers were not found, for *Trinidad*'s main radar scanner aerial was frozen up. The men were stood down but these destroyers sank a Panamanian ship, and were given information by the survivors that sent them on a fresh sweep into a different area.[7] This brought them in sight of *Trinidad* about midday, and within three minutes her gun crews opened fire at 6,000yds 'and the leading destroyer blew-up with the first broadside'.[8] This was a supremely good shot in such poor visibility, although aided by the cruiser's short-range '284' radar, which was still working despite the flying spray freezing solid as it came aboard. The other two German destroyers turned away as *Trinidad* launched torpedoes but half an hour into the action she was hit. The T/S was flooded, much of the electric power cut and she took on a 20-degree list to port. The Marines of 'B' turret now switched to working the guns by hand, but it took half an hour to swing them through 90 degrees against the list. Her speed was down to 10 knots and further mechanical trouble in the engine room soon cut this to four knots, but she limped into Murmansk two days later. There the debris was cleared from the hull to reveal that she had torpedoed herself, for the severe cold no doubt had made the torpedo's steering erratic.

Fourteen of the convoy reached Russia. There was little chance of survival for any crews of ships that were sunk, although Sergeant Noble, a DEMS gunner, was one of very few who were saved in these waters after spending four days in an open boat.[9] He was in hospital for six weeks in Murmansk recovering from the rigours of such exposure, and was to be rescued for a second time when he was aboard the cruiser HMS *Edinburgh* which was sunk on his first passage home. Most of her crew were also rescued.

Murmansk in 1942 had good anti-aircraft defences which included Russian-piloted Spitfires; and from the air the outline of the docks was hard to see, as ashes had been spread on the snow up to 900yds from the quays. With ships under camouflage nets, this gave the appearance of the water's edge being further inland than it was, and HMS *Trinidad* was undisturbed. In the next six weeks the 40 × 20-ft gash in her port side was patched, while the crew lived in the cold of an unheated ship, slinging their hammocks in undamaged spaces but unable to get away from the throat-catching stench of oil fuel. She was fit for sea by mid-May and sailed late on 13 May with an escort of two destroyers. Next day she was making 21 knots in bright weather – the forecast was for snow – but air attacks did not begin until the evening, as the weather clouded over. For several hours *Trinidad* and her escorts fought off sporadic attacks, and at 2245 hours her anti-aircraft (high-angle) control officer was concentrating her fire against six Ju 88s flying in for a torpedo attack over the starboard quarter, when one or two other Ju 88s came out of low cloud to drop a bomb on her deck alongside 'B' turret. This bomb exploded near the magazine, its crew being lost, but the shell-handlers managed to scramble into the turret from their room above the magazine, and all made their way forward. A near-miss loosened the patch on her hull and she began to flood; the fires in the upper decks could not be controlled and by midnight were 'burning like a large furnace'.[10] The crew had to be taken off and she was sunk by a torpedo from one of her escorts.

The losses of escorts had become so serious that the Admiralty pointed out the danger in continuing these convoys, but political considerations outweighed the military ones and in the next two years convoys continued to fight their way through. Some, like PQ17 in July 1942, were scattered, and 3,350 vehicles, 430 tanks and 210 crated aircraft were lost when three-quarters of that convoy were sunk.[11] In attempts to reduce the strength of German air attacks two Army Commandos, Nos 12 and 14, were raised for raiding the supply dumps of aerial torpedoes and bombs, but all attempts at such raids were frustrated by appalling weather conditions. However, a party of Norwegians were landed on Spitzbergen in May 1942, where they were supplied by flying boat or convoy escorts diverted to visit this island of polar wastes, and this small force prevented the Germans becoming established on the island.[12]

Equally fierce battles were still being fought to bring supplies to Malta throughout 1942, with April as the island's greatest time of trial. In that month repeated bomb attacks largely destroyed the docks, the airfields were damaged, 146 British planes were lost and the cruiser HMS *Penelope* had so many holes in her plating she was known as HMS *Pepperpot*. She came out of the harbour on the evening of 8 April after several weeks in the central Mediterranean, many of them under repeated air attacks. The last of these was fought off before she reached Gibraltar two days later, with her magazines once again practically empty.[13] Her Royal Marine Band had made a fine reputation for itself on the Island, by playing for the stevedores off-loading cargo ships under air attack, and if the notes were occasionally off key, musicians watching incoming bombers with one eye cannot be blamed for not following a score exactly.

By the middle of the month only Malta's underground workshops were in use, and all the other installations badly damaged. The carrier USS *Wasp* flew off 47 Spitfires but many were lost in the next week, and a further 61 Spitfires were flown in – most of them from *Wasp* – to help balance the odds and make possible a run by six ships of a revictualling convoy in June, but only two of them reached the island. In August fourteen ships, including the tanker *Ohio*, slipped through the Straits of Gibraltar in a fog, and the same day a dummy convoy sailed westward from Alexandria. That their cargoes were needed in Malta there can be no doubt, for the 10-day ration for a family of four was 3½lb of bread, 2 tins meat, 2 tins fish, a little lard, a little butter and 2 boxes of matches. No sugar, no cooking oil, no rice was available.[14] Fuel reserves were low.

Axis aircraft did not find the *Ohio* group till the afternoon of the day they entered the Mediterranean. Aboard HMS *Nelson*, one of the two battleships in the covering force, Marines of one of the 16-in turrets went through the hatchway of the armoured deck into the shell-room and heard the chain pulley rattle as the heavy cover was lowered into place. They could not then get out until someone raised the hatch for them. There followed a long wait of many uncertainties, the men feeling rather than hearing the high velocity crack of 6-in guns, as they lay among the heavier shells – these only caused a low rumble when they were fired.[15] Here they would spend much of the next day or two, 'the sweat running from our bodies down the sides of the shells'. They came up from the heat and the sickly cordite fumes for an occasional breather, and were about to do so at 1315 hours on the second day out (11 August), when they heard three or four distinct bumps. Coming up top they saw the carrier HMS *Eagle* sink in eight minutes, after being hit by four torpedoes in the first of several U-boat attacks. This was her tenth ferry trip to Malta, and although 900 of the 1,160 ship's company were saved, eight Marines were lost. HMS *Furious*, however, had flown off 37 Spitfires an hour earlier some 550 miles from Malta and she returned to Gibraltar.[16]

This convoy, building on the lessons of the losses in June, was protected by Allied cruisers and submarines deployed to prevent surface attacks, minesweepers from Malta clearing the approaches, and a barrage of anti-aircraft fire that drove off the first of seven air attacks. The second, mounted from airfields in Sardinia, only succeeded in sinking one merchantman,[17] and later, in well-disciplined evasive actions, the ships weaved their way through torpedo attacks and sank an Italian submarine. Renewed air attacks were more successful, however, and two heavy bombs damaged the carrier HMS *Indomitable*'s flight deck, forcing her planes to land on HMS *Victorious*. The convoy was now approaching the shallows north-west of Cape Bon, and the capital ships, including HMS *Nelson*, turned westward. The convoy had to change from four lines to two before passing through the channel in these shallows, and during this manoeuvre they lost formation. They were also at the extreme range of fighter protection from Malta, and without the cover of co-ordinated anti-aircraft fire, several ships fell easy prey to Axis bombers; others were sunk by E-boats in the next few hours. But *Ohio* got through, although hit several times and virtually unmanageable for the last two days of the voyage, when she was towed by destroyers which continued to fight off air attacks.

The aviation fuel *Ohio* brought to the island enabled sorties to be flown against Axis convoys supplying Rommel in North Africa; and the four other ships reaching the island brought the desperately needed rations. The island was now secure and although air raids continued, they became fewer: 57 in September against 282 in April.[18]

For Marines at sea the war continued for another two or three years, often in long vigils guarding convoys, but there were several decisive ship-to-ship actions, as we shall see. The range of oceans covered by these Marines is exemplified by Boy Bugler Kenneth Saunders, who first went to sea in 1942 at the age of 15. By the time he was 18 he had served in the Atlantic, the Indian Ocean and the Pacific.[19] Something of the extent of service by Marines at sea can be seen in Appendix 4 on ships' detachments, but after 1942 Allied navies expended more ammunition in barrages and bombardments supporting amphibious landings than in ship-to-ship actions.

Throughout 1942 the RM Division, its headquarters reformed after General Sturges's original staff went with him to Madagascar, was training for such landings, but unbeknown to the rank and file the Chiefs of Staff had decided to set up a permanent Expeditionary Force.[1] In this would be an Army Division, an Independent Brigade Group and the RM Division. The Admiralty, supported by senior Royal Marine officers, insisted that the Marine formation be attached rather than embodied in the force, to maintain its own characteristics and not merely be another division on a War Office Establishment. Here lies the nub of the Adjutant General's fears, for if the Marines formed what was nothing more than an Army division, there was every reason to believe that history would repeat itself, when – as in World War I – this field force would virtually become part of the Army. General Bourne, the Adjutant General, has been criticised for adopting this view and there is no doubt that a non-standard Division would never fit into any major scheme for an invasion. It had suited the War Office, therefore, to keep Marines earmarked for the Atlantic Island operations.[2] In all its dealings over the Marines, the War Office put pressure on the Admiralty to allow the RM Division to be assimilated by the Army.

There have been through the centuries Marine officers who leant towards closer links with the Army, and others who saw the advantages of being a Naval force. Perhaps parts of each argument are irreconcilable, but there is no doubt politically that Marines have a different status to any other branch of the services. Foreign governments did not regard the landing of Marines as likely to be so permanent as an invasion of soldiers, but enemy commanders respected Marines' military abilities ashore as superior to those of seamen. After World War I some threads of this argument appear to have been lost, as the few long-service officers and men returning from RM battalions – which had been mostly 'HO' Marines – 'were regarded by their brothers in arms with some envy . . . [for] in battleships and cruisers . . . there had been little opportunity for honour and glory and none for actual command of [large formations] in battle'.[3] During the 1930s the pro-Army Marine officers were in the saddle, and some at least regarded the job of getting ashore as purely the Navy's headache; and out of this thinking in part at least came some Royal Marine officers' wish to have an Army division commanded by Royal Marines, but the Adjutant Generals were Navy orientated.

During April 1942 it became clear that the Army was unable to provide supporting arms, but before then the Chief of Combined Operations, Lord Mountbatten, had 'made friends with' the RM Division in Wales. He also had need of more Commandos, which the Army could not provide, but the Adjutant General resisted all attempts to break up the Division.[4] Nevertheless some changes were made after a meeting at the RM Office – the AG's department – on 8 May 1942. It was accepted that the Division should consist of two brigades, to which later (June 1942) some supporting RM artillery was added, though in something of a hotch-potch, with each brigade group to have a six-gun 3.7-in howitzer battery, a six-gun troop of Bofors, and two 12 gun AA/AT batteries with Oerlikons (or Hispanos).

Lord Mountbatten explained to the Chiefs of Staff Committee the following October that he had discussed the Division with General Eisenhower and the Adjutant General, and one RM Brigade Group 'was instantly available for assault operations with its supporting arms'.[5] If necessary this Group would be reinforced in the event of casualties by breaking up the second RM Brigade. Behind these statements lay a series of events which probably saved the Corps from extinction, for General Bourne and other senior RM officers had remained vehemently opposed to any changes in their proposed use of the RM Division as a single landing force, for the Division had now become their sacred cow. But, aware of the pending operations in North Africa, Bourne had approached General Eisenhower and asked if he could use the RM Division. Eisenhower then telephoned Lord Mountbatten as Chief of Combined Operations, telling him that the Marine Division could not be used as 'they hadn't got a tail',[6] that is: they did not have the transport, ordnance and other services of an Army division. But CCO urged him to accept them, so that later they could be passed over to Combined Operations Command, which at that time had eight full Commandos and some specialist Commando units.

On 3 October, the G-3 (responsible for operations) on the staff of Allied Force HQ had written to the Under Secretary of State for War: 'Mobilisation of RM Division ... it is confirmed that the units ... will be provided as required ... from Allied Force resources when the time comes to employ that formation'.[7] The units were pack-howitzer batteries that General Eisenhower had offered to *supplement* artillery, promised by the War Office, which also in September 1942 had agreed in principle to provide Army transport, field ambulances and other supporting troops.[8] The intention was to mobilise the Division's two brigades for use as reserves for the 'Torch' North African landings, but the War Office was unable to spare these necessary supporting troops. General Eisenhower then promised to find them from his American resources,[9] but Allied Force Headquarters, which was responsible for the 'Torch' landings, later could only offer a few howitzer batteries. The Brigades were not therefore used in North Africa, but other plans were afoot.

In early 1943 there was a plan in which the Division would recapture the Channel Islands (this operation 'Blazing' was to have been preceded by a heavy Naval bombardment, but the ships were required for landings in Sicily). And later a plan was mooted for the Division to isolate the Cotentin Peninsula with Cherbourg at its head;[10] both schemes were intended to provide jumping-off points for further operations in 1944. In retrospect they appear ambitious, in view of what is now known of the German coast defences on the Channel, although these were far from complete in 1943. But such projects indicate something of the RM Division's keenness, efficiency and daring. In the event neither was possible, owing to the shortage of landing craft as well as Naval support after operations in the Mediterranean, and also a shortage of landing-craft crews.[11]

Further meetings were held to discuss organisation and the Division was brought into closer contact with Combined Operations' facilities – Lord Mountbatten held a meeting on 3 January 1943, at which he explained to senior officers of the Division the likely roles of the Brigade Group[12] – and during the next six months it was affiliated to Force J for training.[13] This Naval force had been retained, with squadrons of support landing craft, after Dieppe in order to develop the techniques for close support and amphibious assault.

On 14 January 1943 General Sturges again assumed command of the RM Division; and General R. H. Campbell, who had been a protagonist for retaining a full division, was subsequently to command the RM Training Group.[14] The stage was set for the Division to change its role, and on 7 June the First Sea Lord asked the Prime Minister's permission to break up this 7,000-strong formation and, with 3,000 Marines from other sources, to use 4,000 in Commandos and 6,000 as landing craft crews.[15] Mr. Churchill replied that he would need time to consider the proposal, but by July the plan was finalised. Lord Mountbatten, from 1965 until his death the Life Colonel Commandant of the Corps, had piloted the Corps from the verge of extinction to roles they would play with their traditional élan for amphibious operations. But a final condition had to be made by Mountbatten: provided the Marines were transferred to Combined Operations as *Commandos*, he would appoint a Royal Marine Major General to command all the Special Service Brigades. This came about in October when General Sturges became the General Officer Commanding the Special Service (Commando) Group, with its four brigades.[16]

By this date there were also changes being made in the organisation of Army Commandos, as will be seen later, but the impact of so radical a change for the Corps placed 'a very large commitment and a big responsibility'[17] on General T. L. Hunton, who in 1943 had succeeded General Bourne as Adjutant General. General Hunton, in writing to Lord Mountbatten, pointed out that 'providing boats' crews was something the Corps had never undertaken before' and that he welcomed the co-operation of CCO's staff. The fact that some 10,000 Marines would successfully man landing craft within a year, is an obvious tribute to their versatility. But what is sometimes forgotten is that such capabilities in a force that can be deployed to suit the needs of the Nation, would probably not have been possible and certainly not as quickly executed, had the Marine division been assimilated into the Army. There was also the difficulty that several RM Generals were serving outside the Corps, and could not be recovered. For example, General Hunton was unable to obtain the release of General Dallas Brooks, who was Deputy Director and Military Head of the Political Warfare Department, as his Director, Sir Bruce Lockhart, refused to release him,[18] – but for what job?

The RM battalions serving in the UK that summer of 1943 were remustered as Commandos as follows: 1st Battalion as 42(RM) Commando, 2nd as '43', 3rd as '44', 5th as '45', 9th as '46' and 10th as '47'. The 7th RM Battalion would become 48(RM) Commando in March 1944, but in the meantime it was the nucleus of a 'beach brick' formation in the British Middle East Forces, responsible for the defence of a beach area and the movement of stores across it. For this Battalion, as for the other RM battalions, there was no fundamental change in the principles of amphibious warfare – men still landed from craft to cross beaches – for which they had prepared for several years, although techniques were improving. They were familiar with the problems of off-loading landing craft, of beach gradients and beach exits.

The Marine Commandos – in each battalion volunteers, in the sense that these were the type of operations most 'HOs' expected to do, indeed RM drafting orders of 1943 stated 'volunteers if possible' – took a 2-week course at the Commando Basic Training Centre at Achnacarry (Inverness-shire), renowned for the toughness of its training. The Marines found this Centre the finest infantry training school for motivating men for battle, where they learnt to keep going or they failed the course. But the reduction in the size of battalions to the 450 or so men of a Commando had allowed Colonels to weed out their less resolute men, as some 30 per cent failed the course. Not that hard marching and the tough climbs were new to men of the Division, for several battalions as part of a large force had slogged through an exercise, one of many, in the Black Mountains of South Wales when there were over 300 British and American casualties.[19] One RM Colonel had, therefore, wanted to keep his men with their own officers, at Achnacarry, but the Commandant of the Centre insisted that Marines were trained by his own staff.[20]

These changes had little effect on the organisation of the Royal Marines Headquarters staff at the Royal Marine Office (RMO) in Queen Anne's Mansions, St James's Park (London SW1). Here the Adjutant General was assisted by a Deputy Adjutant General, with the rank of Major General, as his Chief Staff Officer. A Lieutenant-Colonel as Military Secretary (MS) was responsible for the appointment of officers to units and formations, and he advised the Adjutant General on the promotion of individual officers. A general staff (known as G Branch), responsible for implementing the policies of the Adjutant General, training and general supervision of the work of the Corps, was headed by a Brigadier (the Brigadier General Staff) with a Lieutenant-Colonel as his General Staff Officer Class 1 (Gl); the G2s on this Colonel's staff were two Majors – the G2 Staff Duties and G2 Training – who were assisted by a Captain G3 Staff Duties and a Captain G3 Training. A third Captain (G3) was responsible for security and censorship. The administrative staff was headed by the Brigadier Administration and divided into A and Q branches. An Assistant Adjutant General (an Army term), who was a Lieutenant-Colonel, was responsible for personnel matters, with two Majors as staff officers – SO(A) 1 and 2, and a Captain as SO(A)3. The Quartermasters (Q) Branch was headed by a Lieutenant-Colonel as SO(Q), with an assistant – a Captain SO(Q)2. There was also a Major in charge of records (the Registry). In all there were two Generals, two Brigadiers, four Lieutenant-Colonels, six Majors and five Captains. Three Superintending Clerks, who were equivalent to Naval Warrant Officers, headed the office staff of three departments: the Military Secretary's department, the A and the Q Branch.[21]

*   *   *

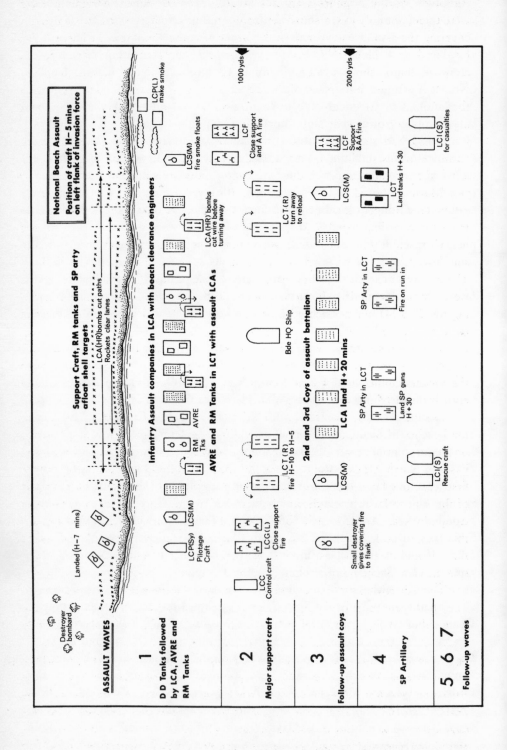

Notional Beach Assault

Position of craft H−5 mins on left flank of invasion force

Destroyer bombard

Landed (H−7 mins)

ASSAULT WAVES

1
D D Tanks followed by LCA, AVRE and RM Tanks

LCP(Sy) Pilotage Craft
LCS(M)

Support Craft, RM tanks and SP arty afloat shell targets

Infantry Assault companies in LCA with beach clearance engineers

LCA(HR)bombs cut paths
Rockets clear lanes

RM Tks
AVRE

LCA(HR) bombs cut wire before turning away

LCP(L) make smoke

LCS(M) fire smoke floats

AVRE and RM Tanks in LCT with assault LCAs

2
Major support craft

LCC Control craft
LCG(L) Close support fire

Small destroyer gives covering fire to flank

LCT(R) fire H−10 to H−5

LCT(R) turn away to reload

LCF Close support and AA fire

3
Follow-up assault coys

LCS(M)

Bde HQ Ship

2nd and 3rd Coys of assault battalion

LCA land H+20 mins

LCS(M)

LCF Support & AA fire

4
SP Artillery

LCI(S) Rescue craft

SP Arty in LCT

Land SP guns H+30

SP Arty in LCT

Fire on run in

LCT Land tanks H+30

5 6 7
Follow-up waves

LCI(S) for casualties

1000 yds

2000 yds

Although Marine Brigades were not landed in North Africa, Marine gunners were there, not only in warships' detachments, but also in the close-support craft covering the assault waves' run to the beach – as they had done at Dieppe. For by this date, 8 Nov 1942, Marine gunners had replaced some seamen in the crews of minor support craft, including the gunners of LC Support Medium No.31. A detailed description of these craft is given in Chapter 7, but in covering the landings by American Rangers at Arzew, 30 miles west of Oran, there was an example of these little ships' versatility.

No.31 had shepherded the American Rangers' craft to a beach near the entrance to this small port, before crashing the boom to go up the harbour for a fighting reconnaissance. Finding a freighter moored to the outer quay, she put two Marines aboard and they had just got the crew – about 18 men – lined up aft, when a Ranger officer called to the Marines to dislodge a sniper. Two bursts from the boarding 'party's' stripped Lewis then brought a fierce reply from a heavier machine gun. The two Marines were ordered back aboard 'No.31' before she moved from her prize, to go up the harbour firing her twin 0.5-in Vickers. The enemy's next burst of fire put a line of holes along her side just above the water line and wounded Marine Westwood, and so the Sub-Lieutenant commanding the LCS(M) put her behind another moored ship. There the crew reloaded the guns, dressed Westwood's wound and checked the damage, before venturing out into a smoke screen, which they had laid with their 4-in mortar and CSA smoke jets – canisters carried to make chemical smoke. As they cleared this screen the Vickers gunner fired several long bursts, silencing the defences, before more craft brought troops into the harbour.[1]

Marines in these LCS(M)s would also cover assault waves the next July on the beaches of Sicily, and by then – indeed since late January 1943 – Marines on major support craft (LCFs) had been providing air defences for advanced bases in North Africa.[2] The four craft of the LCF Squadron in Force J spent the first week of May 1943 searching shallow inlets off the Tunisian Coast, as part of the Allied Naval blockade which prevented any major evacuation of German troops by sea.[3] At Sicily they would be joined by several LC Gun (Large), for this type of craft had originally been designed for coast bombardment, when there would clearly be insufficient numbers of cruisers and destroyers for this role, in view of the number of coast guns in Sicily.[4]

The 7th RM Battalion would also play a valuable part in these landings. They had spent most of the November and December 1942 in South Africa, but were called to Egypt to develop the beach organisation for the Sicily landings.

Fig. 7. The first 4 waves in a beach assault were followed on occasion by: Wave 5 of LCI(L)s at 8,000yd (H−5 mins) bringing in the infantry companies of the second assault battalion to land at H+45 mins; Wave 6 at 10,000yd with priority vehicles and tanks to land at H+55 mins; and Wave 7 of LCI(L) and LCT to land the reserve battalion of the assault brigade at its commander's discretion. Large destroyers on the flank at 3,000yd gave support while further off shore on the flanks heavier warships had bombarded the coast defences and lifted their fire to inland targets by H−5 mins. These techniques used in 1943/4 were later improved by the use of amphibious tracked vehicles (LVTs).

In the Mediterranean with only a 6-in tide, the problems of getting men, vehicles and stores ashore were different to those in cross-Channel operations, although making gaps (gapping) the lines of beach obstacles, lifting mines and securing beach exits are preliminaries to amphibious assaults the world over. After the beachhead is captured, the assault infantry break out, and then come the complex problems of supplying the Army with ammunition, drinking water, rations, fighting stores, petrol and thousands of other items. In 1943 many stores had to be humped by working parties over open beaches, after small craft had brought in vehicles, crates of rations and boxes of ammunition, all of which had first to be laboriously hoisted out of the transports' holds and lowered into landing craft alongside the ships. There were better and faster ways of getting stores ashore, but not many of these could be used in Sicily because there were relatively few Landing Ships Tank (LSTs), each capable of beaching to off-load vehicles, and there were 'few bull dozers and cranes but plenty of beach roadway, and roller runway in the Middle East'.[5]

Rear Admiral L. E. H. Maund was Chairman of the Directorate of Combined Operations in the Middle East (DCOME), and had been associated with such operations since before World War II. There was also a staff at Kabrit on the Suez Canal from early 1941, to train troops for landings, but not until the spring of 1943 did this Amphibious Centre become fully active. Admiral Maund had approached General Weston with a view to employing elements of MNBDO I in beach work, as the Army could now install AA and coast guns, a job they had been doing for some years on the African coast. 'The MNBDO [General Weston] asked whether it was quite certain that it would never be required again in the Med', to which the Navy did not say 'Yes'. And the idea of the MNBDO forming a beach organisation 'became less popular'.[6] It was at this point that 7th RM Battalion was called to Egypt.

On 5 January 1943 the Battalion's Colonel, Lieutenant-Colonel F. W. (Dolly) Dewhurst, was asked by General Headquarters Middle East for his proposals as to how the Battalion might be employed within the framework of a beach organisation. The Lieutenant-Colonel had seen the RM Division's Beach Battalion on exercises and knew the way an MNBDO was intended to operate, and from these concepts he and his staff devised initial proposals that were subsequently raised to a 'Brick' of 2,500 men.[7] The name 'Brick' has no clear origins, but was the name passed to Maund by Combined Operations HQ in London, with whom he and his staff worked closely. The 7th RM then became No. 31 Brick, numbered reportedly to imply that there were many bricks.[8]

Within four days the Battalion began developing the methods, function and training of such organisations, not without some argument between the Director-

---

Right: The early stages in establishing the maintenance area with its beachhead supply dumps are shown on the right above, with – below – subsequent developments of the area after the main battle lines moved inland. These schematic illustrations give a simplified view as almost invariably a beachhead maintenance area's development in practice involved compromises on traffic flow and the siting of dumps etc.

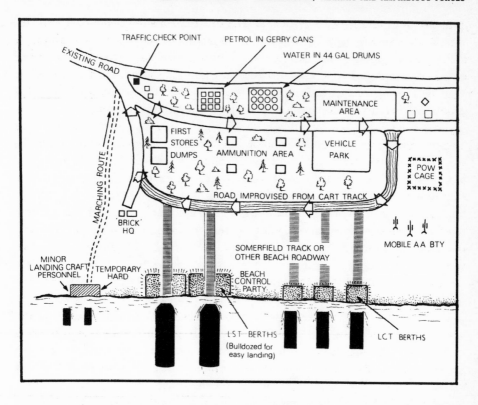

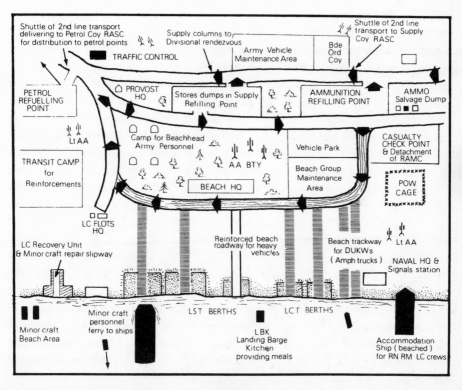

ate, the Kabrit Staff and the Marines. But in a matter of weeks the Marines and Combined Operations Staff had established methods to off-load stores from craft across the water-gap – that stretch of shallow water between the ramp of a craft and dry beach. They laid roadways to pass laterally above sea level beside the two or three berths at a landing point, continuing the road to the left, say, through a beach exit to the areas of supply dumps, then looping back so empty lorries could rejoin the lateral road at its right end. They learnt to locate and disarm mines in the thorough way the Eighth Army did, with small teams using detectors and marker cones, and trios of engineers systematically clearing a lane which was then boldly marked. They learnt to handle bulldozers and cranes, to waterproof vehicles, to recognise different stores by their crate markings etc., and to stack different types of stores. No.31 Brick was joined in this training by various specialist troops and nine companies to provide working parties, while the Brick also provided a team of advisers and a 50-man demonstration squad to visit other Bricks being formed in Palestine: No.32 based on 2nd Highland Light Infantry, No.33 on 1st Argylls, No.34 on 1st Welch, and No.35 on the territorial 18th Durham Light Infantry, who did not land until the Salerno operations of September 1943. All the Bricks but No.35 took part in rehearsals for the landings after they had joined the assault brigades, No.31 Brick as part of 231 Brigade Group landing near Port Safaga in the Red Sea.

At the end of June, No. 31 Brick embarked in three Landing Ships Infantry, carrying the landing craft which would put the Brick ashore, with its 2,700 all ranks, and 1,345 RAF personnel attached for the construction of advanced airfields. Some measure of the complexity of this Beach Brick can be seen in its final composition. The HQ was small, being that for a battalion, and the HQ Company contained motorcycle despatch riders, signallers and a few trucks (the Quartermaster and most of the transport remained in Egypt to be landed over a month after the Brick). The HQ Defence Company included 3-in mortars in six tracked carriers, and there were three rifle companies for working parties. These were the principal RM units in the Brick, but half the Provost Company were Marine 'redcaps', 52 out of 104. Other units under command of this RM Headquarters included six Companies – three from the Baluchi Rifles – for working parties, an AA Group with its own operations room, a Field Company of engineers with a detachment to operate bulldozers, Royal Army Service Corps transport platoons with workshops, a vehicle recovery and repair unit, ordnance and medical unit. The Royal Navy's Beach Party, Boat Repair and Naval Signals Sections were also under command.[9] For the moment we will leave No. 31 Brick aboard its transports.

MNBDO II arrived in Egypt in April 1943. A small number of Army personnel[10] had been seconded to the Headquarters from the Royal Army Ordnance Corps, Royal Electrical and Mechanical Engineers and the Royal Corps of Signals; these attached personnel, working in small mixed headquarters of Army and Marine staffs, would enable the Organisation to draw on Army depots for supplies rather than on the Naval sources normally used. This MNBDO also had minor but important differences in its supporting units from those of MNBDO

1 In 1919 Murmansk was a town of warehouses and workmen's log houses. There were few brick buildings. The quays were dilapidated and without cranes. Royal Marines serving there wore Arctic clothing but when patrolling the dockside great-coats, wooly hats and Shackleton boots were the order of the day.

2 The battle cruiser Repulse fires her main armament in a practice shoot, 1938. Note the gun director on the tripod mast above the bridge and below the fighting top.

3 A Royal Marine Guard in No. I ceremonial dress march through London, exercising the Corps' privilege to march through the capital with fixed bayonets, during a tour of London duties in 1935. The officers and many of the men of the London duties battalion rose to senior rank in World War II.

4 Named after Sir Winston Churchill, the RM Siege Regiment's 14 inch gun 'Winnie' fires from St Margaret's Bay, Kent. The second such gun was called 'Pooh' after the eponymous bear. Both fired on targets in occupied France.

5 A famous still from a captured German film: a Ju 52 crashes in flames over Suda Bay during the German parachute assault on Crete, 20 May 1941.

6 The MLC which Major R. Garrett and his crew with RMs escaped from Crete in June 1941, using different sail arrangements.

7 Men of 11th RM battalion, engaged in river crossing exercises, launch a Goatley canvas boat, Colombo, Ceylon (Sri Lanka), 1943.

8 'B' gun's crew of LCG(L) 1007 engage shore batteries at Courselles, Normandy, 6 June 1944. Both guns in an LCG(L) were manned by Royal Marines who also manned the gunnery control instruments on these and other support craft.

9 Men of 48 RM Commando advance behind German beach defences in June 1944. Note the sergeant's lightweight motorcycle, the signaller's set in a 'pram' and the steel helmets over green berets.

10 A Centaur of No.2 Battery RM Armoured support Group in the Normandy beachhead, June 1944. The markings on the turret were used by one gunner to lay his gun parallel to that of his neighbour, after reading the bearings through his dial sight in the armoured box on the left of the turret top.

11 RM Commands advance towards Westkapelle Lighthouse after landing at Walcheren, 1 November 1994.

12 One of the many support craft sunk during the bombardment of the Walcheren coast defences, LCG(M) 101 began to founder when pulling off the beach after engaging her first target. Her RM detachment is unlashng the flotta nets, preparing to abandon ship.

13 The open country around Lake Commachio were Corporal Tom Hunter won the Victoria Cross while in action with 43 RM Commando in 1945.

14 Royal Marines of Detachment 385 were landed by Catalina flying boats for reconnaissance and clandestine operations in the Far East, going ashore by inflatable or canoe carried on a platform fitted above the aircraft's hull.

15 Hill 170 captured by 3 Commando Brigade at Kangaw, Burma in January 1945. The landing was intended to cut the Japanese line of retreat.

I, for in addition to its air defence brigade, the landing and maintenance units, coast regiment and signals, there were field bakeries, a petrol depot and transport to service these.[11] In short, MNBDO II was organised to operate in a Naval base supplied by the field Armies and did not therefore need its own land defence force, although the Adjutant General's staff considered the 7th RM Battalion would become part of the MNBDO II,[12] though it was not shown as such in the Eighth Army's order of battle until 7 August 1943.[13] This is a minor point perhaps, but indicative of the way the disposition of even large formations of Marines overseas, under command of an Army Group, were little influenced at that time by senior RM Staff, although they were 'kept in the picture' by regular reports from commanders: Col Dewhurst, for instance, sent personal reports at least every month to the Adjutant General.

On the voyage to Egypt many of MNBDO II's coast guns were lost when the freighter *Marcella* was sunk, and therefore 'Dorset' battery spent several weeks in May at the Army's Captured Equipment Depot where they 'mastered the German 88-mm, Italian 90-mm and 104-mm plus . . . 20- and 40-mm automatic weapons'.[14] They would then land in Sicily and use captured equipment to provide coast defences for the Naval base at Augusta. Meanwhile the heavy and light anti-aircraft Regiments were deployed in Malta, whence they would come out of action at dawn on 9 July, waterproof their vehicles the next day and embark in LSTs during the afternoon.[15] Other elements of the MNBDO served with the Eighth Army's supply echelons during May and June before embarking.

Among the Royal Marine Officers flying with the Fleet Air Arm in the Mediterranean was Major Alan Newson, leading 821 Squadron's Albacores.[16] They earned a considerable reputation in the Western Desert for their skill in finding targets and illuminating them – as the 'pathfinders' did over Europe for RAF bombers. They also flew in raids against shipping and laid mines, as explained in the next chapter.

Not long after midnight on 9–10 July LCF 12 was one of the escorts for the American convoy from North Africa as it approached Licata, the westerly landing area of the Sicily invasion. Overhead the Marine gunners heard the aircraft of the Americans' 82 Airborne Division heading for the hills behind Gela, some 15 miles east of the Licata landings, while the gun flashes of the Naval bombardment could be seen along the coast. A heavy swell was running, which would give the men in the small assault craft a turbulent run to the shore. As these craft were assembled off 'Joss' beach (Licata) the LCFs put on speed to escort them to the beach.

The 3rd Ranger Battalion – American Commandos – got ashore with little opposition, and in the next few days would operate on the left (west) flank of the US 3 Division.[1] The LCFs' gunners when dawn broke could see that the beaches, narrow in places where vineyards ran down to the sea, were clear of the enemy. Amphibious DUKWs ferried in stores, crossed the beach and drove inland to the supply dumps. LCF 12 dropped her anchor as the LCF Squadron took up position to provide cover against low flying aircraft.[2] About 0800 two

ME 109s came in low over the hills to the west and were gone away to the east in seconds, having hit an LST that had just beached. In the subsequent fire and explosions the Americans had their greatest casualties on 'Joss' beach, and for the LCFs the lesson was again underlined – as it had been for anti-aircraft gunners in the Norwegian hills – that there are only fleeting moments when a target is in view if planes can use hills for cover. As more men and stores came in to reinforce the Licata landings, the LCFs moved inshore from time to time, escorting the craft ferrying in these forces, and on more than one occasion fire from German artillery in the hills behind the town forced the LCFs to keep on the move as they lay offshore waiting for the next run of ferry craft to the beaches.[3]

The landing plan was to put the American Seventh Army ashore at Licata and Gela, and, some 40 miles to the east, the British Eighth Army was to land around Cape Passero. The beaches on this south Sicilian shore are interspersed with long stretches of rock-bound coast, and there were, therefore, not only long gaps between the main landing areas, but also within each area distances of 10 or more miles between landing points. Therefore the Ranger battalions and Commandos were used in the role of flank forces, expecting not only to capture coast and other guns threatening landing beaches but also to effect the link with troops further up or down the coast. The American airborne troops dropped north of Gela would cut off this small port from reinforcements, and the British 1 Airborne Division was to drop at the extreme right (east) flank to seize key points in the hills south of Syracuse. Preliminary bombardment of the beaches before the landing was sacrificed in order to achieve surprise, but close support of the assault waves was to be provided by LCG(L)s and destroyers, while cruisers gave support from offshore.[4] The Allied air forces, meanwhile, concentrated their bombing effort against enemy airfields.[5]

At Gela, where Ranger battalions were landed each side of the pier, the first Marines in action near this beach had been in the LCS(M) with the British LCA flotilla landing the Rangers. She forged ahead of the plunging and bucking line of craft in rough water, for the coast was more exposed to the dying gale here than on the British beaches further east. As the little support craft surged towards the beach, her gunners shot out an Italian searchlight.[6] From further offshore the larger LCG(L)s engaged what targets they could make out. The gunners had the separate cordite charges ready for loading stacked by each 4.7-in gun, so the skippers of these craft had to be wary of coming under mortar fire, when one bomb could easily set off these charges. The 'G(L)s', nevertheless, had varying degrees of success but the difficulties experienced in controlling indirect fire, and the slowness with which some craft ranged on other targets, were 'largely due to lack of experience and training'.[7]

To the east the British Commandos had flank roles, with the Army's 3 Commando landing on the right flank of 5 Division, to clear heavy guns covering 'Acid North' beach, before a rapid advance over open country for 2 miles to take a battery inland. The Royal Marine Commandos, landing on the left flank of 1 Canadian Division, were to capture coast gun positions covering 'Bark West' beach, and then – as the extreme westerly flank force of the British landings –

hold the flank until the Canadians were ashore. The two Commandos, 40(RM) and 41(RM), had made their last practice landing with the Canadians at Troon (Ayrshire) late in June, before returning aboard the transports *Derbyshire* and *Durban Castle*, which sailed from the Clyde on 28 June.[8] By this date all Commandos, Marine and Army, had or were being organised with a Heavy Weapons Troop of 3-in mortars, some jeeps and other trucks,[9] for now, as they spearheaded invasions of Continental Europe, they would no longer be only raiding from their ships. They would need to be self-sufficient when, for example, they were isolated from the main force as they held flank positions, and at other times they would need to move overland from one area to another on a battle front. There were other changes in Commando organisation, described in the next chapter, but both 'Nos 40 and 41' worked to a small Special Service Brigade HQ sent out from Combined Operations Headquarters, with Brig R. (Bob) E. Laycock of the Royal Horse Guards and an experienced commando officer commanding the force.

An ill-tempered gale on 9 July caused concern that the operation might have to be cancelled, but the command ship, HMS *Hilary*, dropped a black ball from her yard arm at 1700 hours. This signal, on which watches were synchronised in the assault ships, gave the order that the operation would go ahead. Aboard *Durban Castle* the men of 41 Commando turned in for a nap before supper at 2100 hours, and then they dressed for action. Feet – 'a soldier in battle is just as good as his feet'[10] – had been hardened by marching over Scottish moors; nevertheless they were cosseted in clean socks without a darn, well-dubbined boots soft as gloves, and short puttees to protect ankles from the inevitable twists in crossing rough ground. Drill slacks and a bush shirt would keep the malaria mosquitoes at bay. As these men were making a last weapon check about midnight, the ship's engines stopped, and a sudden silence prefaced the ship's loudspeaker's bark: 'Naval personnel and commandos to operation stations'.[11] Men hitched up their packs, climbing ropes were eased, and there was a clinking from the climbing irons (the piton spikes to hold ropes) of leaders expecting to scale the cliff below the Italian guns. Making their way along the dimly lit passages to the brass-bound ladders of the boat decks, and in a well-rehearsed drill, the commandos climbed aboard LCAs. The night was starlight bright and there was still a swell, although the gale had blown itself out. The craft swung on their davits for a tense few minutes. Oh, for a fag at this moment! But the boiled sweets had to suck away the tension before the craft were lowered down the long fall of the ship's side, to heave and toss on the swell as they circled for what seemed an eternity to the commandos. At last the control craft shepherded the LCAs into positions in line astern as they headed for the start line, after much flashing of blue signal lamps. The coxswain opened the throttles and away the craft went towards the shore.

The dim outline of support craft could be seen on the flanks and the looming mass of Sicily's mountains was away on the starboard bow. There was a sense of isolation for crews and cargo personnel, apparently alone in the dark as the flotilla buffeted through the swell, the blunt bows of the heavily loaded LCAs smashing their way through the waves. Aboard several craft water came over the floorboards, as spray and the lop of green water washed over the side decks. In 10 minutes what was a trickle was ankle-deep, and the hand pump was needed if the craft was not to be swamped; but there was no room in the tightly packed mass of men to work the pump handle, until several men climbed aft to lie exposed on the small stern deck, and others heaved themselves on to the side deck, lying outside the protective armour, as the pump sucked up the water. Other men bailing with steel helmets also struggled to keep down the level of water but all to no avail. The coxswain dropped the speed, less water now came inboard, and its level went down, but the craft was falling back from her station. A searchlight probed the night, but went out before its sweep crossed the flotilla; the men on the deck pressed themselves flat at the sound of heavy gunfire but this was from an escort firing 'at bombers overhead',[12] maybe mistaking the Allied airborne troops for enemy planes. About this time the flotilla moved into line, the water was more sheltered and the craft gathered speed as an enemy machine gun fired a few bursts from the left. Like angry wasps the bullets swished overhead – at night gunners tend to fire high and these Italians were no exception. The craft slowed to feel their way through unexpected shelves of rock off the beach, and there were no tell-tale bow waves to aim at.

Coming inshore, the craft touched down with a gentle bump, half an hour late at 0300. Ramps down, the doors opened and the commandos of '41' quickly left the chilly water in their craft's wells, to feel the tepid surf around their knees. But where was the cliff? Several moments passed as officers and NCOs searched in the gloom for landmarks. The Italian machine guns fired again as the commandos dashed forward to cross a long limestone shelf, before finding the safety of a small valley in the sand dunes. Some Marines were caught on the rock shelf by this fire but among the dunes only a few bullets kicked up sand high on the banks, the rest passing harmlessly overhead.[13] Here Lieutenant-Colonel B. (Bertie) J. D. Lumsden reorganised his Troops, and scouts found the footpath leading to the cliff tops. Shouts and cries in Italian, the burst of a grenade and then silence marked the first outpost's capture. Bren fire silenced a machine gun on the point overlooking the beaches, and then in quick succession the strongpoints were taken as '41' moved forward along Punta di Castellazo and Casa Della Marza. The sun rose suddenly, the bright clear light revealing the white walls of Caso and the bay far below where the Canadians were coming ashore.[14] The brief battle was over except for the occasional burst of Bren fire at a sniper's window and the few rifle shots of Marines encouraging Italians to surrender quickly.

40 Commando RM (Lieutenant-Colonel J. C. (Pops) Manners) and Brig Laycock's staff, should have landed to the right of '41', but, just as '41' had been carried east of its cliff objective, so '40' was also landed eastward of its intended beaches, its craft scattered among the Canadians. By the time the Commando was assembled it was daylight, and '41' had already taken all '40's' objectives, which turned out to be coast battery positions in which no guns had been mounted.[15] Both Commandos remained ashore for a couple of days before being withdrawn. They were later embarked for several further operations but these

were cancelled. They would, however, take part in further Mediterranean landings, but on 10 July other Marines had landed in Sicily.

About 0445 (H+2 hours) the LSIs carrying '31 Brick' moved inshore to Bark East – on the eastern tip of Cape Passero, near the village of Marzaemi – and the Colonel with his advanced HQ in an LCP(L) left the HQ ship HMS *Kerens*, which had stopped to drop them before she moved closer to the beach. The assault battalions – men of the Dorset, the Hampshire and the Devon Regiments – seized the beaches, meeting little resistance, and the troops of '31 Brick' began to prepare the beach area to receive supplies and reinforcements. There were only some 200yds of beach roadway needed, and a 100-yard stretch to link this to the coast road, using rubble from houses damaged in the limited pre-landing bombardment, with a top surface of earth mixed with salt from nearby dried-up lagoons. But only 40 tons of stores arrived on D-Day.[1] Meanwhile the Defence Company cleared snipers from the beach area, and patrolled in carriers some 10 miles inland to Noto, mopping up pockets of resistance by-passed by the assault battalions. The Provost Company controlled traffic, which by D+3 was heavier than planned, as this beach proved more convenient than others, where there were water-gaps of up to 200yds and amphibious DUKW trucks had to be used.

After much of the build-up forces had been diverted to 31 Brick's area, its Maintenance Area was expanded to be XXX Corps' Field Maintenance Centre, and although the heavy workshops had remained in Egypt, there was far more traffic to control than had been expected. Some 5,000 prisoners-of-war passed through the Brick's 'cages', 2,000 of them volunteering to work on the beach and having to be escorted in parties to the various dumps. By these means on D+3 1,490 tons – equivalent to some 500 lorry loads – of ammunition, petrol, water and other stores were moved across the beach, and the tonnage was increased when a neighbouring beach area was closed, 20 Beach Group, the UK equivalent of a Middle East 'Brick', moving in to help 31 Brick. About this time a train was found in a village siding, and an RM engine driver 'helped' its Italian crew bring it nearer the stores dumps, from which it was loaded with materials for Syracuse.[2]

Although ships were attacked, there were, surprisingly, no air attacks on this beach until the night of D-Day, by which time men had dug themselves foxholes – sweat saving blood – despite the time this took: 90 minutes of pick-and-shovel labour was needed to get down a foot in the hard ground.[3] There were few casualties on the beach from the first raid, but a petrol dump was set alight; Allied losses were small – although the hospital ship *Kalamba* was sunk – in subsequent raids, when the *Luftwaffe* by day concentrated on the ships and by night bombed the beaches. The enemy's ground forces, not expecting an Allied landing after the gale of 9 July, were slow to recover from the initial surprise, except in the American sector around Gela, where the Rangers and the US 1 Division had a 4-day battle before the beachhead was secure.

As the build-up continued over the beaches controlled by 31 Brick, the Detailed Issue Depot (DID) was moved into open country beyond the beach. In addition to the original command of the Brick's personnel and the Air-fields Group, the landing-craft crews and a dock-operating company also came under the command of 7th Battalion's Headquarters, bringing the total strength of the command to 4,600.[4] The Battalion's War Diary for 10–15 July refers frequently to the quantity of stores being 'far in excess of the estimated weight' which had been in the original landing plans for the first few days of the assault.[5] The weather remained fine but 'very hot for working',[6] and as more materials were landed, the original key plan was modified – it had worked well up to D+3 – for the men off-loading craft into lorries were filling them too quickly for separate parties to empty these vehicles at each dump. Men were therefore moved from dump to dump, speeding the off loading of lorries after each particular type of stores had been landed, and the dumps were enlarged.[7]

On D+7, 17 July, XXX Corps provided lorries – 7th RM with 30 officers and 560 other ranks had only three 3-tonners and six 15-cwts – to take the Battalion some 30 miles to the hill town of Buccheri. Here Col Dewhurst, as Military Governor, organised the civic authorities – Italian army mules were allowed to each family to gather the corn harvest, petrol was found for the corn-grinding machines, the streets cleaned (there were no drains), curfew times arranged, undesirables locked up, rates of exchange fixed and several dozen other details settled, including who might wear their Italian police and other uniforms.[8] Forty-eight hours later the Battalion moved on, to be fed and rested while acting as a guard for XXX Corps HQ. That night, 19 July, they were taken to make an attack across shallow Dittaino River and its bridge at Catenanuova, coming under command of 51 Highland Division for this operation.

The Battalion's organisation was for work in a Beach Brick, and it therefore had no supporting arms other than units which were attached: four carriers – two had been lost – with 3-in mortars; and three Sherman tanks; seven 6-pdr anti-tank guns; an MG platoon; and a Royal Engineer recce party.[9] The plan was to make a silent approach until surprise was lost; two Companies (B and X) would cross the river and move left and right, with 'A' Company then crossing in the centre to take enemy strongpoints on the hill and beyond the road, and Y Company forming the reserve. The road ran east-west beyond the river and was being used by the Axis forces to reinforce defences along a line that reached to the east coast south of Catania.

The only maps available were small in scale and inaccurate, and the night was pitch dark, but by 0500 hours next day, 20 July, the companies had crossed the river, meeting only light machine gun fire. They took some casualties, however, in trying to dislodge enemy machine guns covering the road. The tanks were unable to reach the river and the anti-tank guns were knocked out, as heavy mortar and artillery fire came down on the Battalion's positions. Although A Company had crossed the road and B Company had reached it, the others were held as 'the enemy were firmly dug-in on rising ground',[10] enabling them to enfilade the Marines' positions. They also prevented the tracked carriers making any headway, when these came forward in an attempt to get the 3-in mortars into action with observed fire, not relying on wireless links from an OP. Under increasingly heavy shellfire the Companies were ordered to withdraw back across the river. B Company had 150 prisoners but could not bring them out, for the withdrawal was over open ground between the Companies and a ridge. Neverthe-less the Platoons and Sections extracted themselves, and by midday the Battalion had reformed at the ridge and that evening sent out patrols. It had lost 76 men, including 14 killed.

The Battalion, reinforced with supporting arms, stayed in these positions for the next nine days, sending out patrols, and suffering three or four casualties a day from shelling. Before daylight each morning they moved back to the reverse slopes of hills after standing to on the forward slopes during the hours of darkness. The Colonel, who was over 40 at the time, had spent 20 hours in action on 19–20 July without the opportunity of a proper meal, and has written, 'after the heat of the day and mental strain directing the fighting . . . I felt quite exhausted'.[11] As the Beach Brick role of 7th RM was now over, the Middle East Command's age limits were applied to the Battalion's CO, and the Colonel handed over command to Major J. T. O. Waters. The 7th Battalion was among the first troops into Catania but met no opposition, although there were mines and booby traps; they remained in Sicily and carried out landing exercises. But to go back to the landings in Sicily: some MNBDO II units had come ashore on 10 July.

The gun crews of 'Dorset' Battery had orders to find some guns to defend Syracuse, and were landed from LCI(L)s – the 250-ton shore-to-shore craft carry-ing infantry. At midday on 10 July, they waded chest-deep to cross the water-gap. They followed the signposted route cleared through minefields beyond the beach, before halting for 'a carefree picnic lunch', despite the sound of small-arms fire a mile or two inland. They marched north that afternoon and were dive-bombed; the men learnt in an hour or so not to rush for cover every time planes could be heard, but to wait until these could be seen to be diving in their direction. They were close to the infantry action by nightfall, but had orders not to join in the battle, and so went to ground in an olive grove, 'digging ourselves shallow scrapes' before having supper.[12] Nearby was an American pioneer unit, and its men became somewhat jumpy when enemy troops came within 400yds of the olive grove. The Marines stood to but the danger passed.

Lieutenant-Colonel A. J. Harvey and a small reconnaissance party from MNBDO II HQ joined the battery before daylight, moving with them along the coast tracks, about midday, over the rising ground at the base of Cape Murro Di Porco. Here, by a lighthouse, an Italian battery of Vickers 3-in QF screw-breech guns had covered the southern shore of the entrance to Syracuse harbour. By dusk four of these old guns were ready for action, and the other two had been repaired by next morning. It was not as difficult a task as expected, for the Italians after dismantling the breeches had 'laid the parts out with a screwdriver and spanners alongside'.[13] A few crude booby traps were dismantled, along with the fuse of a mine on the approach road to the battery; this mine had failed to go off because the handfuls of damp hay left to ignite it had not caught alight.

In the next few days patrols from 'Dorset' Battery visited the sites of six Italian coast-gun positions they had been given, looking for possible acquisitions for the harbour's defence, but all the guns had been effectively destroyed before their gunners had retreated. The QF Battery by the lighthouse was undamaged because the local reservist crews had changed into civilian clothes before going home after air attacks on 9–10 July. These dual-purpose guns could be used against aircraft, and the Marines received permission from the local Royal Artillery Operations Room to 'join in the nightly firework display by firing fixed barrages',[14] using the good supply of time-fused ammunition stored by the guns. They remained several weeks at Casteluccio before an RA Battery took over the guns, and 'Dorset' Battery moved north to man what had been Italian 155-mm coast guns on the headland overlooking the north shore of Augusta.

Syracuse fell on the night of D-Day (10 July), although the British 1 Air Landing Brigade lost 69 gliders in the sea, and the other 59 were strewn over 20 miles of rough country. Nevertheless small parties of airborne troops held the vital bridge across the Anopo river, 2 miles south of Syracuse, until elements of 5 Division reached them during the first night ashore, when the defence of Syracuse collapsed.[15] In the next 48 hours Augusta was invested, and at 1930 hours on 12 July the LSI *Ulster Monarch* landed the Special Raiding Squadron of the 2nd Special Air Service Regiment (SAS) in the port. The Naval party that landed with them had to be briefly withdrawn, and attempts to bring other ships into the port were repulsed by artillery fire.[16] However, during D+3 (13 July) the reconnaissance party from MNBDO II coming overland was able to signal Group HQ late in the afternoon that it had completed the recce despite enemy shellfire.[17] On the night of 13 July 3 Commando had landed 10 miles north of the Eighth Army to seize a bridge, and 1 Para Brigade was dropped 20 miles north of the Army to seize a second bridge. Both were overrun after initial successes, for the German forces were in greater strength than expected,[18] but by next morning (14 July) 5 Division was north of the town.

At 1100 hours on 14 July LSTs from Malta brought in MNBDO II's anti-aircraft guns: 24th LAA Battery's Bofors were in action within a couple of hours, during the afternoon the heavy batteries' 3.7-in were brought into action, and 25th LAA Battery was the last to join the barrage at 2230 hours.[19] Meanwhile the remainder of the MNBDO were landed, and several Italian guns were acquired to add to the barrage, while others were mounted on barges for harbour defence. The MNBDO was to operate in Augusta for the next six months, providing signals, medical and security forces. Half the ships' unloading parties in the port were Marines, and for some weeks MNBDO II handled all the petrol brought in for the Eighth Army, while its Detail Issue Depot (DID), organised to handle rations for 7,000, was supplying 35,000 men.[20] The bakery of MNBDO II, staffed by some 40 Marines and seamen, turned out 10,000lb of bread a day in Augusta. In the first weeks they were there, the dough was kneaded by Italian prisoners, but, later, electric mixers were found to speed the work. The bakery and the Oerlikons its bakers manned for air defence were handed over to the Army on 6 January 1944 before most of MNBDO II returned to the UK.[21] Later that year the administrative and provost units would be sent to Taranto (southern Italy), and this relatively small command under Lieutenant-Colonel E. J. Woodington was subsequently relieved by an Army Brigade.[22]

The invasion of the Italian mainland had opened with the crossing of the Messina straits, followed a few days later by a full-scale assault on the Salerno Bay beaches.[1] The Commandos, 3 (Army) and 40 RM, with the Special Raiding Squadron of 250 paratroops trained for amphibious operations, were under the command of the Eighth Army for the operations in Calabria (the Toe of Italy), while 2 (Army) and 41 RM Commandos formed a separate force to operate with X Corps at Salerno.[2] Each pair of Commandos had a small headquarters staff provided from the original Special Services Brigade's HQ. A number of reconnaissance raids were carried out by Army commandos early in September, when '40 RM' was in reserve and suffered casualties – 14 killed and 58 wounded – when bombs hit their LSI *Queen Emma* while at anchor.[3] The first operation for '40 RM' in Italy was a landing at Porto Di S Venere, 3 miles south-west of Pizzo, when on the night of Tuesday/Wednesday 7–8 September it formed part of a force under command of 231 Brigade, which was landed to take this port near Route 18, the main coast road to the north. By this amphibious left-hook the Brigade would also prevent the Germans forming a defence line across the base of the 'Toe'.

In this Operation 'Ferdy' 3 Commando was to seize one beach and 'A', 'B' and 'X' Troops of '40 RM' to take an adjoining beach. But in the dark with a sea running, the LCAs could not find the low mole of Venere harbour, and at 0417 hours (H+77 minutes) 'Pops' Manners asked the flotilla officer to run his six LCAs on to the beach. They were some 800yds west of the intended landing point but found no opposition. 3 Commando had been in some difficulty transfering from its LCI(L)s to LCAs and was also late in landing, but the remainder of '40 RM' came into the harbour on time aboard LCI(L)s before moving quickly into the town. 'Their speed was commendable for immediately after landing, the quayside and town were subjected to heavy mortar and shell fire',[4] but the Marines pushed on, cleared the town and joined the rest of their Commando. 'Y' Troop had been a floating reserve and when it followed in at 0540 hours, it could not establish wireless links with the Commando's HQ, and therefore moved inland across the coast road. Here it came under machine gun and mortar fire from low hills behind the beachhead, but drove off the German infantry, although the Germans' supporting artillery continued to shell the town, and its defence perimeter had to be reorganised.

Battalions of the Dorsets and the Devons were also ashore before a battle group of 26 Panzer Division came south down Route 18. Its leading elements, 3rd Battalion 4th Para Regiment, came into action about 0815 hours, supported by a number of 75-mm and 88-mm guns with a Panzer Grenadier Company. As these guns shelled the eastern perimeter of the beachhead, 40 RM Commando suffered 40 casualties before 'B' Troop was sent to deal with the '88' in the hills opposing the Dorsets and the Devons.[5] 'B' Troop located its battery and brought back nine prisoners, 'A' Troop found its battery but was withdrawn for Kittyhawk bombers to neutralise it. The air activity was by no means one-sided, however, for about 0940 hours six dive-bombers attacked the craft offshore and were given a warm reception by two LCFs. By mid-morning the whole German battle group was embroiled in the battle, and 'X' and 'Y' Troops of '40 RM', with the Commando HQ, were moved eastward to help a battalion of the Hampshires; here 'X' Troop got a fighting patrol into Pizzo some 2 miles from the beachhead. They came across a German patrol and in the close fighting which followed half of the Marines slipped quickly around a pile of brick rubble to take the enemy in the rear; the Germans were then forced from the railway station by a barrage of grenades, before the Marines withdrew despite heavy machine gun fire as they crossed the open ground to the Hampshires' positions.

German counter-attacks broke through the Hampshires' defences but two LCG(L)s successfully put down a bombardment which broke up further attacks, despite the cone of fire falling on 'X' and 'Y' Troops, before they were withdrawn 200yds. This was the Germans' last attack on the port, but they shelled it periodically until the late evening. When dawn broke next day (Thursday) a patrol from 'X' Troop found Pizzo deserted. Within 24 hours 20th Beach Group had made the small port a forward supply base and 5 Division came up the road from Vibo Valentia, 3 miles south of the beachhead.[6]

On Wednesday, 8 September, the Italians had formerly surrendered. Nevertheless 2 Army and 41 RM Commandos and the American Ranger Battalions heading for Salerno were prepared to meet resistance when they landed on Thursday morning at Salerno Bay. This has a 20-mile shoreline divided by the Sele River, which runs out of the hills overlooking the bay. The British X Corps was to land on the left (north) of the Sele, with the Rangers and Commandos on the extreme left to seize two defiles. Through these ran Route 18 northward to Naples, some 30 miles from the Bay. Along this route 46 Division, landing on the left of the X Corps, would advance, and the Army Command hoped to have it in Naples by D+4.[7] The VI (American) Corps would be on the right, landing to the south of the river. Meanwhile during the landings a Naval force was at sea to prevent any possible 'heroics' by the Italian fleet, and a second Naval force provided continuous air cover, the carriers' Seafires flying 715 sorties in 42 hours of daylight. Other planes of these carriers – there were in all 134 aircraft, some with RM pilots – flew frequent sorties, the operation had taken longer than expected when the Germans succeeded in holding Montecorvino airfield. An airstrip was preparted in a tomato plantation, to which a Naval Wing flew in from the carriers, being serviced by No. 3202 RAF Servicing Commando which had landed on D-day, RAF planes later flying in from Sicily to use this airstrip.

The American Rangers, who landed 7 miles north of the main beachhead, quickly had their three battalions established six miles inland on the hills of the Nocera defile overlooking Route 18. The Commandos to the south of the Rangers were on the left flank of the main landing and had first to take out a coast battery before securing the defile at La Molina. This landing was made with that part of the Commando Brigade HQ which had operational command of these Special Forces, whereas '40 RM' and 3 Army Commando had landed under the command of 231 Brigade HQ at Venere. At Salerno Brigadier Bob Laycock with his Chief of Staff Lieutenant-Colonel T. (Tom) B. L. Churchill MC – an Army commando officer and brother of Jack Churchill who commanded 2 Army Commando – landed with '41 RM'[8] and the composition of this half-brigade illustrates the growing complexity of these flank operations.

The LSI *Prince Albert* with six LCAs on her davits carried 2 Commando and the Brigade HQ, two LCI(L)s carried 41(RM), another craft carried a troop of eight 6-pdr anti-tank guns attached to the force, and a third carried an American mortar company, also under the Brigadier's command, with its six 4.2-in mortars.[9] Two detachments of a Field Ambulance were also in the force aboard the LSI. The Naval escorts were the destroyer HMS *Blackmoor*, an LCG(L) and a minesweeper, the destroyer had exercised with a Forward Observation Officer (FOO) who would be in radio contact with the ship, and after landing with the Commandos could direct the destroyer's guns on to targets when the Commandos needed fire support. They were also in radio contact with a field regiment of artillery landing with 46 Division, through a second FOO – both these Forward Observation Officers were from the Royal Artillery and were accompanied by Naval or Army signallers, as appropriate.

The techniques of close-fire support are explained in Chapter 7, and at Salerno such co-operation between ships and forces ashore would prove invaluable. Among the officers landing with assault battalions were two RM officers, one from HMS *Warspite* and the other from HMS *Valiant*, who had similar tasks to the FOOs, although known to the Royal Navy as Forward Officers Bombardment (FOBs).[10] In the early stages of the landing, however, there was little resistance, the minesweeper clearing the approach, and the destroyer and the LCG(L), as they ran in towards the beach, opening fire at 0320 (H-10 minutes) on the battery at Marina and the beach defences.

Five LCAs came in to put 210 men of 2 Army Commando on the beach unopposed at H-hour. One Troop quickly deployed to defend the beachhead, setting up their mortars, while a second Troop moved under cover of this mortar fire to capture the battery from the rear, and found it undefended. Meanwhile 41 RM's LCIs and the LCA carrying Brig Laycock's small headquarters came ashore without incident at 0350. Lieutenant-Colonel Lumsden's 41(RM) Commando, 400 strong as the LCIs could not carry the complete commando in the initial landing, sent two Troops to clear Vietri, east of the beachhead, while the other four Troops headed inland up the road to La Molina. Within minutes the Marines, led by Major John R. Edwards, advancing quickly and silently in their rubber-soled boots, were among the houses of Vietri;[11] they moved so quietly that they could hear the plip plop of leaking taps outside every house, it seemed. Here they found some 20 bemused Germans, but most of the enemy from the barracks fled towards the town of Salerno, a mile or so further east. A heavy tracked vehicle came rumbling through the village, and the Marines took cover in the doorways and alleys until it was in range. Then, as it passed, they caught the crew and half-track of a 155-mm gun in a burst of Bren-gun fire. The half-track's driver was killed and the gun ran off the road, its crew of 12 being captured.[12] Half an hour after landing these Troops had cleared the village and were relieved after dawn by men of 2 Army Commando, who then occupied the village; Brigade HQ was set up in German barracks which showed signs of having been evacuated in a hurry.

Meanwhile the leading Troop of '41 RM', padding through the dark before dawn, hurried to be in position by daylight. They suddenly came on a Panzer MkIV[13] with its crew asleep by the road. The leading section dived for the cover of a ditch and had killed the crew with automatic fire before other Marines climbed to the turret, dropped a 36-grenade through the open hatch and were away before the tank's ammunition exploded. Minutes later they were over the crest of the hill and were digging in on the high ground to the right (east) of the road and railway. Here the hill side was well wooded and fell steeply down to where the road turned sharply eastward. Each man carried a Mark V anti-tank mine slung on his chest, and necklaces of these were laid across the road; while Piats – anti-tank weapons with a range of 100yds – effectively covered this road block.[14] The day was by now bright and pleasantly sunny.

The Demolition Section of '41 RM' had been further down the narrow valley to blow up the railway line, and had removed the German charges on a road viaduct that ran high over the valley south of Molina.[15] RSM Norman Tierney had his Vickers medium machine guns cleverly concealed on a hill some 500ft above the road, dominating the approach up the defile to the col where the road went south to the beachhead. Although these positions were only a mile from the beach, the Marine machine-gunners had to sweat and heave their four guns – each weighing over 100lb with its tripod – up the embankments of the terraced vineyards to their positions. Their ammunition, water and rations also had to be manhandled into their defences – a back-breaking, arm-aching job they had completed before sun-up. But each man of 'Q' Troop on his way from Vietri had helped by carrying a box of ammunition up to the guns.

The remainder of 2 Army Commando were landed by *Prince Albert*'s LCAs on their second run to the shore; the anti-tank guns and American mortars also came in at this time, about 0500. The Commandos established two firm base lines, with 'No.2' holding Vietri and the beachhead, and '41 RM' now established on both sides of road at the head of the narrow valley, where they had been joined by the Marines from Vietri.

The main landings, however, were not making such rapid progress, for the German 16 Panzer Division had four battle groups in the hills overlooking the bay, and other elements of the 76th Panzer Corps were prepared for the landing. In the town of Salerno they offered stout resistance to 46 Division, and were not dislodged when attacked by two Troops from 2 Commando supported by anti-tank guns moving east from Vietri. But these Troops successfully held subsequent attempts by the Germans to break out down the coast road to the Commando's beachhead. During the morning of D-day this came under heavy mortar fire, when the LCAs on their third run were bringing in the big packs in which each commando had his great coat, shaving tackle and spare clothing. The craft turned back and reported incorrectly that the beachhead was lost. If it had not been for the stout efforts of the main beach's '35 Brick' later in the operation, the Commandos would have run out of ammunition. This and the rations were brought in through Salerno once this town was secured, but before then there were several crises. By midday '41 RM' had a Troop on a spur at the mouth of the valley overlooking La Molina from the east, and a second across the valley on a hill of rock outcrops, rough grass and stunted trees. Two Troops were in position lower down the hill side, covering the blocks on the road and railway.[16] A fifth Troop climbed to a position further back from the leading Troop and to the west of the road, ready to counter-attack if there was any break through, and opposite them were the machine gun Sections. All these positions were isolated on hill sides slashed by deep gullies and in places covered by patches of dense scrub.

They saw five enemy tanks that morning but none got through the defile, and although the advanced elements of 46 Division were expected by that Thursday afternoon of D-Day, the Division was so heavily engaged in Salerno that the lower part of the town was not cleared until the evening. This enabled the armoured cars of 44 Reconnaissance Squadron to reach the Marines' position and pass through them about 2030 hours. The cars were soon back to report that Germans held La Molina with anti-tank guns, confirming reports of Marine patrols, and bringing with them an Italian prisoner.[17] He had told of the enemy's presence in strength at La Molina and in Cava di Turreni, with 20 tanks about 1½ miles from the Marines' positions. But all was quiet in the valley that night and the armoured cars laagered near the Marines' rear Troop, after making a second reconnaissance, this time across the valley, where concentrations of Germans were found in hills to the west overlooking 41 (RM) Commando. The cars withdrew to Salerno before dawn,[18] but night listening patrols ahead of the defensive positions were not disturbed by any enemy.

At 0730 on Friday, 10 September, the Commandos were told that they could not be reinforced as 46 Division was threatened by Germans moving south down a road parallel to Route 18. The hot sun burnt down, and the sweat ran in trickles down men's backs as they washed down American biscuits with nearly the last of the water. The men had not been able to stretch their legs since just after dawn, for 'now the swish, swish, swish of mortar bombs falling some way away had given place to the sshh, sshh of those coming in to burst uncomfortably close'.[19] About 1000 hours, forward on the left of the road, 'A' Troop saw two German scouts ahead of an advanced guard coming up the wooded slope.[20] These two men moved cautiously through the patches of sunlight back into shadows, their faces and hands painted green, their green and yellow camouflage jackets making them hard to see as each slowly scanned the ground ahead of him. The small groups advancing behind them came forward with the same well-drilled caution, spread out so as not be an easy target for mortars or machine guns, and most of them armed with sub-machine-guns. Heavy mortar fire fell around the Marines' slit trenches to burst in fierce fragments on the hard ground, but not a Marine made a sound or showed his position. Men took a closer grip on their rifles and Bren-gunners took aim. When the Germans were no more than 20yds away one crashing burst of fire cut them down. But there were too many to stop some infiltration along the gulleys between the Commando Troop positions, and

'A' Troop was almost completely surrounded. Bursts of close-range fire, and the cries of 'Hoch! Hoch!' as Germans rushed the forward slit trenches, could be heard by 'Q' Troop, positioned for a counter-attack. They now charged down the hill, one Section to the left, one to the right of 'A' Troop. The Germans first checked and then retired, but 'Q' Troop's commander and a lieutenant were both killed. The other Section OC, Lieutenant Peter Haydon, was badly wounded but refused to be evacuated and put the few men left of 'Q' Troop under 'A' Troop's commander. They braced themselves for the next attack and held the position, Peter Haydon killing ten or more with rifle shots, although he fainted twice from loss of blood, and was wounded for a second time, before the Marines' defended area was re-established 200yds back from 'A' Troop's original positions. Lieutenant Haydon became at 19 the youngest Marine to receive the DSO.[21] The men by now were parched with thirst, and patrols were sent out to fill water bottles down in the valley.

Across the valley some Germans – men of the Hermann Goering Division by one report[22] – worked their way along the terraces above the Marines' machine guns. As their positions were now revealed, RSM Tierney decided to move the guns, but this would take some minutes. Sergeant D. C. Bullock reacted quickly and counter-attacked the Germans, and although he and four others were wounded, they gave the RSM the time needed to reposition the machine guns. By lunchtime the attacks had subsided, although two Troops of 2 Army Commando on the hills above Vietri had been in action, giving added depth to the defence, and they were in contact with 46 Division's troops on their right. To the west commando patrols were in touch with the Rangers, but there were by now less than 500 men in Brigadier Laycock's command and all the Commandos – including the sixth Troop of '41', which had been in the Brigade reserve – were committed. A sharp counter-attack by 2 Army Commando restored the position after Germans outflanked the Marines on the right, in the last action of the morning. But mortaring continued and Lumsden, among others, was wounded when a direct hit demolished his HQ bunker. In the early evening the commandos on the right were relieved by a battalion from 46 Division, and the three Troops were moved to the west flank. Here at dusk they put in an attack on Dragone Hill and drove the Germans from positions overlooking 41 RM Commando. Next morning, Saturday (D+ 2), two companies of the King's Own Yorkshire Light Infantry added depth to the western flank and that evening the Commandos were relieved.

Twelve hours later there was a major crisis pending in the beachhead, with a strong possibility that 76th Panzer Corps would drive the Allied army into the sea. When the Commando Brigade again took up its positions about 0930 that Sunday, 12 September (D+3), there were no reinforcements available and the Brigade had taken over 100 casualties – 11 officers and 74 Marines of '41', one officer and 33 other ranks from 'No.2'. The Commandos therefore spread their defended areas each some 100yds apart, with 2 Army Commando on the left flank at Dragone and on hills above Vietri, while '41RM' held the valley and the hills east of it. During the day there were only mortar attacks, although these could be vicious enough and caused some casualties. But on Monday morning the Germans made their supreme effort, heavy mortar and artillery fire falling on all the positions. Early in the battle two forward Troops of 2 Army Commando were cut off, but did not give any ground, and when Germans infiltrated through the gulleys between '41' and 'No.2', they succeeded in establishing machine guns on Dragone Hill. Accurate fire from the 71st Field Regiment's guns was called down and prevented the Germans reinforcing this success, but they also reached the terraces above the Marines' machine guns, before RSM Tierney led a counter-attack that drove them off, although he was killed in this action. X Troop was then sent across the valley to join a Troop of 2 Army Commando for a counter-attack on Dragone Hill, led by the Army Commando's second-in-command, Major Lawrie. He was killed early in the advance, but Major John Edwards led the small force up the hill, and cleared it of enemy machine-gunners. This was the decisive final attack, for afterwards the German pressure eased.[23]

The losses of 2 Army Commando were 22 killed and 50 wounded in the morning's fighting, and '41' had taken further casualties. They would fight other battles in the Salerno area but the defence of the Molina valley and Vietri had been a soldiers' battle, where men had fought the enemy off from all sides of the foxholes or scrapes, seldom knowing if the next attack might come from in front or behind, and frequently under mortar fire. Bewildered by doubts – Has the section withdrawn? Should I go back up the hill? Is Sarge dead or just keeping quiet? – they nevertheless stayed put, although often alone in a foxhole or slit trench.

After a day for the men to catch their breath, so to speak, '41' was reorganised into four Troops, 'P' and 'Q' being absorbed by the others. Both Commandos were taken by lorries to Mercatello, a couple of miles east of Salerno. Here on Wednesday night (D+6) '41RM's' objective was a high crag on the roadside 3 miles from the coast. This and two high points further north had been used by the Germans to dominate the coast road with observed artillery fire, if nothing stronger; '41RM' took this hill, suffering only slight casualties, although the three tanks supporting them failed to get within 2 miles of the objective. An hour later 2 Army Commando made the first of two sweeps to clear the valley road leading to these high points, known as 'The Pimple' and 'Whitecross Hill',[24] but was only able to clear the valley and a village, Pigoletti. For the next two days both 'No.2' and '41RM' had steadily mounting casualties from the Germans' 88-mm and mortar fire.

At 0200 hours on Thursday (D+7), just over a week after they had landed and after days without proper sleep, under incessant fire, even during the few hours they had been in rest areas, '41RM' had moved from the crag to the start line for an assault on 'The Pimple'.[25] The planned artillery barrage from 46 Division came down – 11 minutes of concentrated 25-pdr fire that fell, not on the thickly wooded slopes of the Pimple 300yds to the north, but among the Marines. Major Edwards was killed, he had commanded '41RM' since Lieutenant-Colonel Lumsden was wounded, and as there were other casualties, the Commando moved back to the crag, by now known as '41 Commando's

Hill'. But 'B' Troop did not receive the order to retire and about 24 men set off in a speed march along a stony track, across a field, through the skeleton trees of an orchard – peaches here stemmed the men's hunger for they had not had a meal that night – and into a dense wood. The voices of Germans could be heard 'as though they were shouting "last orders" in a crowded pub',[26] a burst of fire ripped through the trees but the Marines pressed on towards the hill top.

Daylight now flooded the hillside and accurate German fire held the Marines at a crest on the hill, while a sergeant and two men went to find a route forward around the Germans' flank. This was exposed but their officer led them to the right, from the open, through woods to terraced vines. From here the 60-ft 'Pimple' could be seen topping the rising ground. The Marines took up positions along the top terrace, and several Germans moving across the hill top were fired on. In the next couple of hours the commandos held several probes by Germans trying to shift the Troop from the ridge. Grenades, rifles and a single Bren held the attacks until the commandos were ordered to retire. They dropped quickly from terrace to terrace, 6ft on each fall, 12ft at times, and stumbled through woods, uncertain of their direction, but reaching Pigoletti before midday, carrying their wounded.

After the fighting around the crag the previous day or two, there is no doubt that both the officers and men of '41RM' were extremely tired and that 'preparations for the attack were therefore somewhat sketchy'.[27] What is not clear, however, is just how the artillery came to use the map reference for the start line instead of the co-ordinates for the objective. Such mishaps are perhaps inevitable over nine days of often confused fighting, in which the two Commandos had suffered nearly 50 per cent casualties, losing 367 all ranks of the 760 or so who had landed on D-Day. They were finally relieved on their ninth night on the Salerno Bay coast, on Friday, 18 September. For both Commandos their defence of La Molina and their tenacity on the hills around Pigoletti had tested their endurance and courage, proving they had both in great measure, and for '41RM' to prove – if this was necessary – that Marines were capable commandos in sustained actions, where a few resolute and well-trained men can defeat larger forces.

In the next two months, October and November 1943, the reorganisation of the Commando Brigades was completed, and those men from the Marine battalions who formed 42, 43, 44, 45, 46 and 47 (RM) Commandos[1] undertook further training. But after their experience with the RM Division, there were few innovations in their training, although – as has been mentioned – the course at Achnacarry added to individual Marine commando's determination to keep going when the odds were against success in a battle, and the less resolute were weeded from the Commandos' ranks. The Army and RM Commandos were then organised into four Special Service Brigades with a Special Service Group Headquarters replacing the single Brigade HQ which had been responsible for the Army Commandos. When the Special Service Brigades were not 'handed over to a commander for operations', they were under command of the Chief of Combined

Operations,[2] as part of his responsibility laid down by the Chiefs of Staff on 5 November 1943. The 1st SS Brigade (the only one with an ordinal number from its units' early association with the Guards) was formed in the UK with 3, 4, 6 (Army) Commandos and 45 RM Commando; 4 SS Brigade was also formed in the UK with 41, 46, 47 RM Commandos and 10 (Inter-Allied) Commando. In November 1943 3 SS Brigade with 1 and 5 (Army) Commandos and 42 and 44 RM Commandos sailed for the Far East, and the same month 2 SS Brigade was formed with 2 and 9 (Army) Commandos and 40 and 43 RM Commandos in Italy.

General Sturges commanded the Group, its SS title being redesignated Commando in November 1944, with responsibilities for training and the development of commando techniques. The Group's supply and services 2nd Echelon was largely personnel from the RM Division, as was the Group's signal unit. Each Brigade had its own signals Troop, a Light Aid Detachment of REME personnel to service vehicles, and a medical detachment at that time attached for particular operations and often of RAMC personnel as well as RN medical staff with the RM Commandos. Also under command of the Group were small operations units, including the SBS and COPPs (Combined Operations Pilotage Parties), when not attached to a field force.

RM detachments continued to serve at sea, with men often on watch for four hours at a stretch. Lieutenant B. B. Ramsden aboard the cruiser HMS *Jamaica* spent his watches exposed in the AA Director dressed in 'khaki trousers over blue serge, then blue pullover underneath blue battle dress jacket, padded yellow overalls over that . . . scarf . . . seaboots . . . and the final black oilskin covering all . . . balaclava, black gauntlets, extra pair in pocket, fur cap, lifebelt and sweater tied round the waist'.[3] *Jamaica* in company with the battleship HMS *Duke of York* spent an uncomfortable Christmas night in December 1943. Nothing would stay put as she steamed through an Arctic gale and the Lieutenant when off watch slept on the floor of his cabin, as the lee-board did not prevent him being thrown out of his bunk on such a rough night. On Christmas morning the German battle-cruiser *Scharnhorst* had put to sea from North Norway, her destroyer escort being unable to stay with her in the south-westerly gale, but when this moderated, they were sent ahead to look for an Allied convoy south of Bear Island.

At 0840 hours the cruisers HMS *Belfast* and *Norfolk* made radar contact at 25,000 yards with *Scharnhorst* but lost her until around mid-day, when British destroyers attempted to position themselves for a torpedo attack but could not reach a firing position. HMS *Belfast*, *Sheffield* and *Norfolk* fired for some 20 minutes, getting a few shells on target but being hit themselves, and for the next three hours the German battle-cruiser steamed south at 28 knots,[4] unknowingly headed towards a British battleship and her escorts. At 1600 hours aboard *Jamaica* came an order over the secondary armament director telephone 'Look out, bearing Red Five O.' Lieutenant Ramsden was told by the gunnery officer: 'Stand by for your low angle procedure', which meant that his 4-in LA/HA guns would be firing at less than 4,000yds. Admiral Fraser was indeed closing the enemy, for although *Duke of York*'s radar had picked up *Scharnhorst* at 44,000yds (40km), he did not illuminate her with star shells until the range was 12,000yds at 1650 hours.

In the hard white light the German battleship could be seen at full speed, her guns still fore-and-aft, before a great wall of water momentarily hid her as *Duke of York*'s salvos fell near, if short. *Scharnhorst* turned north but was prevented by the cruiser squadron from breaking free, although her superior speed enabled her to open the range as she steamed eastward. *Jamaica* fired several broadsides from her 6-in guns but the battle developed into a slogging match between *Scharnhorst*'s nine 280-mm and twelve 150-mm guns and *Duke of York*'s ten 14-in and sixteen 5.2-in secondary armament. Ramsden, seated rigidly among the voice pipes and instruments, the open face of the director towards the enemy, found that 'the clearance of my head above the binocular sight assumed abnormal proportions',[5] and his steel helmet must have seemed little protection as German star shells illuminated *Duke of York* and *Jamaica*. These were closely followed by the great whip-cracks of falling heavy shells, one a few yards off the starboard side abreast of *Jamaica*'s 'B' turret. It sent up a column of water high enough to deluge Ramsden's director, the bridge and after decking, but the 'whizz of shell splinters were the nastiest of all'. *Jamaica* ceased firing early in the action, however, to avoid confusion over *Duke of York*'s fall of shot. Her 14-in shells began to strike *Scharnhorst* repeatedly and at 1820 hours, 90 minutes into the action, the German battle-cruiser ceased firing for a time and lost speed.

Duke of York's shells were fired from comparatively close range and so did not have the high trajectory which might have enabled them to penetrate *Scharnhorst*'s deck armour. Four British destroyers therefore began torpedo attacks, and although two met heavy fire, two more coming up from the south (the only ships between the battle-cruiser and a run to Norway) were undetected until their torpedoes hit. The British cruisers and *Duke of York* then resumed their action but *Scharnhorst* did not sink until 1945 hours, when only 36 of her 2,000 crew were picked up from the icy waters.[6] The tension aboard *Jamaica* now relaxed, men of the 4-in gun crews 'busily striking down the ammunition which had never been used'. Twelve weeks later they would again be in action in these northern waters when carrier planes attacked the *Tirpitz*.

Lieutenant Ramsden was to serve ashore in 1945 with the British Army of the Rhine; Major John R. Edwards had served in ships before joining the Commandos. They were but two of the many Royal Marines who served both afloat and ashore, changes that came unexpectedly fast for many wartime recruits, but then Her Majesty's Jollies 'ain't no limpin' procrastitutes – soldier an' sailor too'.[7] And their experience of amphibious roles in MNBDOs, Beach Bricks and with two Commandos put them in 1943 in a position to undertake great changes in their commitments.

LANDING CRAFT AND CLOSE SUPPORT BY SEA AND AIR

The Royal Marines played a major part in the development of amphibious operations, as has been seen in the work of the MNBDO between the World Wars. A Royal Marine officer was also secretary of the Inter-Service Training and Development Centre, based in Fort Cumberland from its creation in the summer of 1936, when studies were made not only of amphibious landings but also of air supply and similar logistics.[1] The first Marines supplied by air were, incidentally, an RMLI battalion near Le Barque (France) in August 1918.[2] The ISTD Centre maintained close contacts with the RM Brigade in 1940 when proposals were first made for RM crews to man minor landing craft, and among other schemes which Marines devised was one to land the small Austin 7 motorcar from LCAs.[3] RM officers also attended courses at the Centre and by the summer of 1940 the RM battalions were training in boat-work off Hayling Island. Much of this work and experience gained in the early months of World War II, would later be used when they were serving with Combined Operations Headquarters (COHQ), created on 14 June 1940. Ranks in the Royal Marines continued throughout World War II to parallel those in the Army.

General Bourne, the Adjutant General of the Marines, was appointed 'Commander of Raiding Operations . . . and Advisor to the Chiefs of Staff on Combined Operations';[4] but a month after his appointment, the Prime Minister replaced him with Admiral Sir Roger Keyes. Mr Churchill's letter of 17 July went on to express his high opinion of General Bourne, who graciously remained as the second-in-command of the Combined Operations Headquarters.[5] Admiral Keyes unfortunately came up against what he felt was a lack of aggressive urgency in the Chief of Staff's support for Combined Operations, although in 1940–1 all Britain's resources were gravely overstretched in providing escort ships for convoys and maintaining air defences. When the old Admiral resigned, he told his successor, Captain (later Admiral of the Fleet) Lord Mountbatten, that his appointment on 27 October 1941 'had brought him to something of a backwater'.[6] But if it had been such a neglected command in the previous 12 months, it would soon come into the mainstream of the Allied war effort. Mountbatten's abilities changed COHQ's position in some six weeks. He was given a free hand to select staff, and was promoted by March 1942 to Chief of Combined Operations (CCO) which carried 'with it the rank of Vice-Admiral in the Navy,

Lieutenant-General in the Army and Air Marshal of the Royal Air Force' and full membership of the Chiefs of Staff Committee.[7] CCO and his staff were to advise on planning, equipment and training for mounting the invasion of Europe. Also, as an executive command, it was to mount raids in pursuit of the Prime Minister's policy of harassing the Germans along the coast of Europe and to gain military intelligence.

By 1 April 1943 CCO could call on some 50,000 personnel[8] – commandos, landing-craft crews, 1,132 RM gunners in support craft, specialist beach commandos, ships' crews and maintenance personnel – with 90 assault ships and 3,600 craft. Mountbatten then reorganised the headquarters, delegating more executive responsibilities to a small committee under the chairmanship of Brigadier (later General) G. E. ('Peter') Wildman-Lushington (a former RM pilot and Chief of Combined Operations Staff since 1941). Major General J. C. Haydon, who had commanded the Army's Special Service Brigade in 1940, Air Vice-Marshal Orlebar and Rear-Admiral Daniel made up this committee. They had discretion to deal with matters concerning their own service, matters concerning more than one service being referred through General Wildman-Lushington to the CCO in the final stages of any decision.[9] The Headquarters would also work closely with the staff of the Supreme Commander, General Eisenhower, on plans for 'Overlord' – the landing in Normandy. The many facets of Combined Operations Headquarters included in May 1943 the Combined Operations Experimental Establishment (COXE), where the RMBPD among others carried out experiments at Westward Ho! (Devon) with different craft and landing methods. There were also under command four major Combined Training Centres (CTCs), some 30 landing-craft bases and a major supply depot. Staff of the Headquarters also served as liaison officers with Allied forces, and the Headquarters had associated authorities in Australia, Canada, India and the Mediterranean (the Directorate at Kabrit). But later in 1943, the craft and bases were returned to the Admiralty's control. The planning and advisory staffs – signals, intelligence, engineering, topography and the liaison officers – remained in Combined Operations HQ, with many RM officers serving on these staffs, including Colonel R. A. R. Neville (later Major General Sir Robert Neville, KCMG, CBE) who was responsible for co-ordinating planning. The Headquarters was independent of service ministries, the Prime Minister as Minister of Defence being its ministerial head and answerable for it to Parliament.

In the summer of 1943, when the RM Division was to be re-formed as Commandos and with other RM formations was to provide personnel for landing-craft crews, the Corps' role was revised, with the Royal Marines to provide: '(1) detachments for service in HM Ships . . . capable of manning their share of the gun armament . . . and trained to undertake such land operations as the Naval C-in-C may . . . order; (2) Units to undertake . . . special amphibious operations; and (3) Units for the rapid establishment and temporary defence of Naval and FAA [Fleet Air Arm] bases'.[10] Among the special amphibious operational roles was the entirely new task of manning landing craft, and the speed with which the Corps mastered this task – in nine months it trained sufficient crews to man two-thirds of the minor craft in the Normandy invasion – has already been cited as an example of the ability of the Royal Marines to undertake new ventures with adequate but not cumbersome staffs.

The Combined Operations HQ was also reorganised about this time as a result of studies by Air Marshal Bottomley's committee. The staff was slimmed down to meet the changed circumstances of 1944–5, when there would be considerably fewer raids in Europe, and the planning for the invasions in France and in South East Asia would be largely in the hands of the respective Supreme Commanders' staffs.[11]

There were again few changes[1] in the Royal Marine Office, for the landing-craft crews provided by the Corps were viewed by the Admiralty in much the same way as gun crews, although landing craft were obviously going to serve much of their operational time away from their parent ships. In the coming months there was to be a good deal of discussion over the question of command of landing-craft bases; and in the changing circumstances of the Corps' new roles: the title Adjutant General was felt to be an anachronism; therefore on 23 October 1943 the title was changed to General Officer Commanding Royal Marines.[2] However, there were many GOCs and a more fitting title was later given to the commander of the Corps as Commandant General RM, by an Order in Council of 28 May 1945.[3] By this date the question of command of landing-craft bases had been satisfactorily settled, although in the summer of 1943 the Admiralty had wished to limit the Adjutant General's responsibility for crew training until 'they were required to train in landing craft'.[4] There was also the possibility that RM officers might command major landing craft, as some did after 1946.[5] These major craft were defined as vessels under 200ft long which could not be hoisted aboard ships,[6] and the Admiralty authorised RM officers with appropriate qualifications to command LCFs, LCG(L)s and LCTs as well as minor craft.[7] The assault ships – vessels over 200ft – were formed into Assault Groups (with support craft) of sufficient size to lift a reinforced brigade. A number of these Groups with their Naval escorts formed an Assault Force able to lift a division or larger formation.[8] There were some differences between the sub-formations of those years and later practice, for in 1943–4 the British had six ships in a Division as did the Americans, but a British squadron of 12 assault ships was equivalent to the Americans' Group. Although craft in both navies were divided into divisions of six craft, a British LC flotilla had 12 craft usually and an American flotilla of minor craft had 36.[9] However, the precise number of craft was varied in 1944 to suit the lifting capacity – the number and type of davits – of the Landing Ship Infantry (LSI) in which the flotilla was embarked.

The training of RM officers and landing-craft crews began for many men from the battalions and MNBDOs with an introductory course at the holding camps in North Wales forming RMTG(W), which were built in 1943 and became part of the RM Training Group (Wales). Men arrived at 'Matapan' camp (Towyn) from Dalditch or elsewhere for six days' kitting up and selection, did two weeks' elementary seamanship and infantry drill at 'Gibraltar' camp (Peniarth) before going to 'Burma' camp (Llwyngwril), where 'U' Squads did seamanship and gunnery while 'V' Squads studied elementary engineering for two weeks before going to Hayling Island (HMS *Northney*). The 'U' Squads after their two weeks at 'Burma' did a further two weeks' training on craft at 'Crete' camp (Barmouth) or 'Iceland' camp across the Mawddach estuary from Barmouth.[10] In the selection of men for these new tasks, a small team under Sub-Lieutenant (later Lieutenant-Commander) W. S. Porteus, RNVR, interviewed all men drafted to RMTG(W) for retraining. The men completed questionnaires, were given a short interview and completed objective paper-and-pencil tests, with particular emphasis being given to relevant past experience. An ex-fisherman's request to train as a deck-hand, therefore, would not be lightly overlooked whatever the other evidence showed. A man was then assigned to a specialist course with 'desirably his acceptance if not his total agreement'.[11] Follow-up visits by the psychologist to the training camps led to 'continuous refining of the selection criteria and the procedure'[12] in selecting these signallers, gunners, stoker-mechanics, deck-hands and other rates ('trades').

Before the introduction of this selection process, all Marines had been given non-verbal psychological tests at the time they were recruited; but after the success of the selection team in North Wales, their work was continued by a team visiting camps in Scotland to interview men of the MNBDOs returning from overseas, and a selection unit was set up at Lympstone to advise on a Marine's suitability for different roles. Another team was also used in the later stages of the war to interview returning prisoners-of-war, among others,[13] and by June 1945 these teams had interviewed some 30,000 men at Lympstone, 'representing careful and individual enquiry into the intelligence and aptitude of nearly half of . . . the [Corps'] strength'.[14]

The selection of officers from the 'Hostilities Only' ranks was largely on the recommendation of unit officers, although some recruits joined under the Navy's 'Y Scheme' – 'X, Y, ff'ing, Z Scheme' as one CSM called it. These recruits served in the ranks for their initial training but were considered as potential candidates for the Officer Cadet Training Unit (OCTU) set up in an hotel at Thurlestone (Devon) in 1941 – see Appendix 4, RMTG (Devon). Before being accepted for OCTU, however, the candidates had to pass pre-OCTU courses, which varied over the years[15] but in 1943 included small arms instruction (at Browndown) and discipline at Deal. At Deal there were, in retrospect, some foolish elements in the training, for a fire poker might be burnished bright but cadets received an extra parade 'because it was not straight'. Such possibly misplaced instruction made candidates aware of the effects of giving men unjustified punishments, but it also led to a number of senior NCOs who were candidates asking to be returned to their units.

Having passed his pre-OCTU courses, an officer candidate received his military training at Thurlestone, supplemented by tuition on seamanship, signals and elements of Naval law. Those candidates thought likely to pass for promotion after further instruction – the N-Y'ed (Not Yet) cadets – were sent as rear-rank drill instructors to Lympstone before doing a further course at Deal. But the majority of successful candidates for a commission, about a quarter of those who had started the pre-OCTU courses, were posted from Thurlestone to specialist courses. Typically they might go in 1944 to HMS *St Matthew* (Burnham-on-Crouch) for seamanship and signals training, before joining LC Training Flotillas.[16] Their crews had also completed specialist courses: stoker-drivers at *Northney II*, deck-hands at *Northney III*, and coxswains at *Northney I* where they learnt simple pilotage – all three camps being on Hayling Island. The pattern of training as crews varied, with some Marines training at HMS *Dartmouth III*, as did 802 Flotilla when formed under command of its RM officers.[17] Others completed their training at HMS *Westcliff* or, like the LCM crews of 652 Flotilla, worked up at Felixstowe (Suffolk) and Itchenor.

Marines manned LCAs, LCM Mark 1 and Mark 3, and served as gunners in various support craft described later. In operations the flotillas of minor craft were normally embarked on LSIs, but for the Normandy invasion a number sailed from the UK for France under their own power. Nevertheless they all formed part of the British Eastern Task Force, which was made up of three Assault Forces: Force S landed on 'Sword' Beach; J on 'Juno'; and G on 'Gold'. The American Western Task Force landed troops on 'Omaha' and 'Utah', the most westerly assault area. These Task Forces would put ashore 130,000 men by midnight on 6 June 1944 and 23,000 airborne troops would have landed by that night.[18] The Royal Marines in this invasion numbered some 16,000 in landing craft, Commandos, port and other parties, compared to 3,690 at Trafalgar (1805) and 5,800 at Jutland (1916).[19]

The administration of such large numbers of Royal Marines in a single operation was simplified by an RM chain of command within the Eastern Task Force, but in action the RM units and formations came under the direct command of the Army as did the Commandos, or under RN command as did the LC flotillas. In the Eastern Task Force the senior RM officer, Brig St Clair Morford, who had commanded 101 RM Brigade in 1940, was on the staff of the Task Force Commander, with three Lieutenant-Colonels reporting to him from each Assault Force.[20] The disciplinary and administrative command of Force J was typical, divided as it was into the Groups J1, J2 and J3, each with a headquarters ship, assault flotillas and support squadrons. The RM command in Force J had responsibility for some 3,200 Marines. But this did not include Marines in the LCA(HR) which were designed to destroy shore-mines with their special mortars fired from the sea close to the shore, and which were something of a secret weapon that June. The senior RM officer, as Fleet RM Officer (RMO), had both an administrative and a training officer on his staff and Majors or Captains as RM Group Officers.

The composition of each Assault Force varied[21], as did the LCA flotillas in them (see footnote 1).[22] Not all the RM flotillas were in the Assault Forces, several

Note 1: Force J1 had 10 LSIs carrying 72 LCAs and 4 LCS(M); and J2, with 9 LSIs, had the same number of LCAs and LCS(M)s. There were 16 LCAs and two LCS(M)s forming 558 Flotilla aboard SS *Clan Lamont* and 19 LCAs of 544 and 556 Flotillas aboard SS *Monowai*. The Build-Up LCM and LCVP (Vehicle, Personnel) Flotillas sailing from the

working independently for local Naval commands, as did the RM Engineer Hard Parties standing by on 6 June to repair slipways in the UK. Of the Ancillary Flotillas, 441 with the LCP (Small) Mark 2 craft provided 'liberty boats' and messenger services for ships anchored off Cowes (Isle of Wight). One of these light plywood craft had to go alongside a moving merchantman on 5 June, delivering an urgent signal – no doubt the message postponing D-Day for 24 hours.[23]

While the LC flotillas were working up for the Normandy landings, the Landing Craft Obstruction Clearance Units (LCOCUs) described later, were training to clear beach obstacles. Seven of these Units were drawn from the RM Engineer Commando and the other seven from Naval personnel. All had taken part in the experimental work of the Combined Operations Experimental Establishment (COXE) in the Appledore-Instow area, where the beaches and tidal conditions are similar to those in Normandy.[24] The trials at COXE included tests on Bailey bridges to unload LSTs, rigid and flexible bangalore torpedoes to destroy underwater obstacles of designs similar to those in Normandy, and launching a 'snake' pipe filled with nitroglycerine from LCTs for the same purpose. But none of the methods of destroying obstacles proved as effective as teams of assault engineers placing charges on obstructions. Remotely controlled tracked carriers were also tried, and Typhoon aircraft carried out rocket-firing shoots at the largest obstacle, element-C a heavy gate-like structure.[25] Tests were made with the American 'Reddy Fox' 50ft jointed chain of explosive containers, but the spigot mortars on the LCA (Hedgerow) were preferred for clearing a path through beach mines and wire. After October 1943 COXE concentrated on methods and equipment for the Far East,[26] and in 1979, the eventual successor to COXE became an RM establishment.[27] But in 1942–3 not all the Corps' development work was related to amphibious warfare: for example, an analysis of air attacks on the 1st RM Anti-Aircraft Regiment in Crete led to improvements in low-level defences, with mobile 20-mm Oerlikons protecting heavy batteries.[28]

After trials the LCA (Hedgerow) was built in numbers, some 40 craft setting out for Normandy towed by LCTs. Even in training there had been fatal accidents when a crew did not take cover in the armoured cabinets used at the moment of firing.[29] Nevertheless the LCA(HR) Flotillas practised their approach, firing

---

UK included 'A' Squadron of four LCVP Flotillas and 'F' Squadron of six LCM Flotillas for Force J. These minor craft had assembled at Itchenor (Sussex) and Birdham (Sussex), while other RM Build-Up squadrons assembled in other south coast ports. The size of these squadrons varied, with 96 LCVPs in 'C' Squadron in Force S, and the same number of LCMs in 'E' Squadron with Force G and of LCMs in 'F' Squadron with Force J. Squadrons 'A' and 'B' (both LCVP) and 'D' (LCM, including Naval crews in June) were smaller, 'D' Squadron having only 48 craft. Force J also had three Ancillary Flotillas of RM craft for work with headquarters ships and shore parties. The latter included several hundred Royal Marines in the 'Juno' assault area alone, where 144 Marines ran two camps, and there were 188 signallers, 32 RM military policemen, 9 radar plotters, 3 bomb disposal engineers and a transport section of 34.

then turning away before they grounded. The bombs could be set to fire underwater against beach obstacles or on impact with a beach.

Royal Marines also manned many of the LC Support (Medium), a craft with a crew of six, twin 0.5-in machine guns in a powered turret and a 4-in smoke mortar in the bow. These craft also had chemical smoke pots and added to the smoke cover provided by LCP flotillas specially equipped to make smoke. Some of the LCS(M) were also fitted out with extra wireless and other facilities for Forward Observation Officers, and some served as LC Control, providing links between the LCS(M) with assault flotillas and Force HQ ships. The other minor support craft, the LCS(L) Mark 1, had a 2-pdr – four of these in 900 Flotilla had RM gunners at Normandy – but the majority of LCS (Large) by June 1944 was the major landing craft LCS(L) Mark 2 with a 6-pdr gun in a turret forward, power-operated mounting for twin 0.5-in machine guns aft and two Oerlikons abaft the bridge. This LCS(L) Mark 2 was a converted wooden LCI (Small), and although partially protected by armour, it was vulnerable to enemy fire, especially as it had petrol engines. The 10 Mark 2s in 310 Flotilla each had 8 Marines manning the guns in a crew of 25 under Naval officers. Both the 2-pdr and 6-pdr guns were included in close support weapons to attack German tanks, which might have been dug in among the defences, and to attack the armour-plated machine gun cupolas which topped many defence positions.

The principal support craft were the LC Gun (Large) and the LC Flak, briefly described in Chapter 4; by June 1944 a number of these had been built as modifications of the Mark 4 LCT, a beamier craft than the Mark 3 hull used for earlier LCG(L)s and LCFs. The Marine detachments on G(L)s – 31 NCOs and men with two junior officers[30] – manned the QF or the BL 4.7-in guns, which in the Mark 4 craft were mounted so that both could fire over the bows. In the Mark 4 LCFs the detachments – two Lieutenants and 48 other ranks – manned the Pom-Poms and 20-mm guns. But in both of these support craft the Marines also provided the major portion of the crew – 33 of the 52 in a G(L), 50 of the 62 in a Flakker[31] – and therefore the detachments carried out many of the routine seamen's duties in these craft, which were usually commanded by a Lieutenant RNVR with a Sub-Lieutenant as his First Lieutenant. Each flotilla was commanded by a Commander RN who, with his staff, including the senior RM officer for gunnery control, an RM administrative officer, and specialist Naval engineer officers, all in an LC Headquarters. The LCH was a modified LC Infantry (Large) equipped with extra radio and control room facilities. She also carried the engineers' staff, who could assist a craft's stoker-mechanics with major repairs.

In the Normandy landings these major Support Flotillas included three or four LCFs, three G(L)s and an LCT Mark 5 with ammunition reserves. With them in a Support Squadron would be a flotilla of LCT (Armoured) carrying RM tanks, a flotilla of LCT (Rocket), a flotilla of LCA (Hr) and a minor landing-craft flotilla equipped with smoke pots.[32] With this last flotilla were the LCP (Survey), equipped for accurate navigation and used to locate the landing points. The Support Flotillas worked up at the Assault Firing Establishment, HMS *Turtle*, in Poole, where American crews for nine LCG(L)s and 11 LCFs were trained, their RM officer instructors going to Normandy with them.[33] In the British sectors there were 16 G(L)s and 18 LCFs. The LCT(R)s were naval-manned, although Marines helped to load these craft and some are reported to have served aboard these Rocket craft.[34] Mark 4 LCTs carrying self-propelled RA guns loaded in these craft, so that the guns could be fired on the run in, were also in some support squadrons, and several LCFs were with LCT flotillas to provide anti-aircraft protection. The support flotillas in Force G also included eight Army-manned Landing Barge Flak, each with twin Bofors and machine guns to protect the anchorage.

Further offshore the heavy bombardment ships included the monitors HMS *Erebus* (covering 'Utah' targets) and *Roberts* ('Sword'), with RM gun crews, and the covering warships included HMS *Warspite* with an enlarged RM detachment manning two of her main turrets; the third was manned by seamen and the fourth had been out of action since she was hit by a German bomb some months earlier. Marines also manned their share of the 6-in and 4.5-in secondary armament on battleships and cruisers. The fire of these Naval guns and of those of the G(L)s could be directed by Forward Officers Bombardment landed with the assault flights of minor craft, while Forward Observation Officers of the Royal Artillery – some in LCS(M) – could direct the fire of the SP guns in LCTs. Others landed with the assault flights to direct artillery fire as guns were brought into action. The capital ships practised long-range bombardments with both RAF and Fleet Air Arm planes spotting the fall of shot.[35] With all this fire-power the plan was to co-ordinate the warships' fire with breaks for low-level air attacks, and to use the close-support craft to cover the expected 20-minute gap between the lifting of the Naval barrage and the landing of the self-propelled artillery. High-level air bombardment was also part of the plan, as this was expected to neutralise the coast defences on 6 June.[36]

The introduction of air warfare had by 1944 changed the fundamental principles of naval strategy, and the battleship was no longer the all-powerful mistress of the seas. The few Royal Marines with the Fleet Air Arm had seen dramatic changes.[1] On the formation of what was intended to be a unified air service, planes and crews from the RN Air Service were transferred to the RAF in 1918, and a number of RM officers transferred to this new service. There followed a long inter-service squabble over who should control planes in the fleet, and in 1924 a compromise was reached in which a Naval arm of the RAF was created with RAF and Naval pilots.[2] Among the Naval volunteers were 20 RM officers, who renewed the RM connection with the Fleet Air Arm which was to be continued through the 1990s, with RM helicopter pilots flying in amphibious and other FAA operations.

The planes of the inter-war years – the Blackburn Dart and Ripon, the Fairey III D, III F and Flycatcher – were able to land on carriers with comparative ease (according to those who flew them). The 'III F', for example, with 'a deck landing speed of only 44 knots could take some time to catch up with a carrier steaming into a 15 knot wind'.[3]

In 1920 Major R. Gordon, an RAF officer who had transferred from the RMLI, was in charge of the air operations in Somaliland.[4] An RM detachment helped to open the airstrip at Hong Kong, later Kai Tak aerodrome, when in 1925 two Flycatchers and two Fairey III D with floats flew anti-pirate patrols.[5] One of these Flycatchers was piloted by 'Wings' Day, who commanded these flights in 1926. Group Captain H. M. A. Day, to give him his proper title, had joined the Corps in 1916 and the FAA in 1924, but in 1934 transferred to the RAF because there were limited promotion prospects for RM fliers.

During World War II 31 FAA pilots and two observers were RM officers, and nine NCOs transferred to the Navy to fly as Petty Officer pilots. They served in Norway (as mentioned in Chapter 1), flying Skuas and Swordfish, Captain Burch leading the first squadron torpedo attack on 22 August 1940. Captain Patch led the torpedo attack by three planes on ships in Bomba Bay (North Africa). Sighting a submarine four miles offshore while the formation was flying 200yds apart 'fan-wise' low over the water, Olly Patch attacked, jinking to port and starboard before levelling off his Swordfish at 30ft and dropping his torpedo at 300yds range. The submarine blew up. The other Swordfish then hit two ships in the bay, one of them exploding to sink a third.

Captain Patch also flew at Taranto (Italy) on 11 November 1940 when the Fleet Air Arm proved the 'Royal Navy's most devastating weapon . . . [when] in about six and a half hours – carrier to carrier – twenty aircraft had inflicted more damage upon the Italian fleet than was inflicted upon the German High Seas Fleet in the daylight action at . . . Jutland'.[6] This battle finally shattered any illusions of battleships being akin to cathedrals, as, in the opinion of one historian, they were at one time viewed by Admirals. Two years later Major Alan Newson led 821 Squadron's Albacores in pathfinding raids from airstrips in the Western Desert, as mentioned earlier. Their flares would illuminate the target for an hour or so, after being dropped from 6,000ft in sticks of two after the first four had located the target. On several occasions these Albacores were the last planes to leave a forward airfield as the battle surged towards Egypt. During April to November 1942, the Squadron flew 471 sorties, including mining operations against Tobruk. By 1944 Royal Marine pilots were flying Hellcats, Seafires and Wildcats, in the Mediterranean, against the *Tirpitz* in Norway and in the Pacific.

The air support on 6 June 1944 in Normandy was the culmination of weeks of Allied bombing raids, which had been directed against all the potential landing areas so as not to give any indication that the Bay of Seine was the intended one. On the night of 5–6 June heavy bombers raided ten of the principal coast defence batteries, and medium bombers attacked six other batteries shortly after daylight. Forty-five minutes before touchdown (H-45) heavy and medium bombers would drench the beach defences, forcing the enemy to keep his head down as the support craft and assault waves moved towards the beach.[7]

A number of the gunners in the major support craft had been in the RM Division's artillery regiments, and their special training – chiefly on 8-week gunnery-and-seamanship courses at the Sea Service Battery, Eastney[1] – was straightforward, since the Corps was able to provide instructors. The minor support craft crews learnt their gunnery at one of the Combined Operations bases, as their RM officers did at *St Matthew* (Burnham-on-Crouch) in 4-week gunnery courses from 1944.[2] But the majority of the Division's gunners embarked on an entirely new venture in 1943, when they were formed into the Armoured Support Group. They had, however, experience of land gunnery techniques, for the men in the field batteries had manned 25-pdrs, used tracked carriers for forward OPs and were familiar with gunnery communications. Their 22-sets on exercises were on the infantry net, their 21-sets linked to the Division's artillery headquarters, and orders were passed to gun-position officers by LSDSR (Lamp Signal Daylight Short Range) when not on the radio net. They had done their stints of sleeping by day and firing at night, in camouflaging gun positions and convoying their guns behind quads.[3]

When the original fire-support plan for Normandy was being considered in 1943, an LC Gun (Medium) was designed to beach with two 25-pdr or two 17-pdr guns in turrets, providing a series of field batteries on the beach; but sufficient numbers of these craft could not be built in time for the Normandy landings.[4] As a substitute for these, Centaur tanks without engines were mounted in pairs on Bailey bridging, tandem-fashion with the aft one firing over the second gun, in a Mark 5 LCT (Adapted). The Centaur's 95-mm gun-howitzer was able to fire on the run in, and when beached to serve as field artillery, able to lob shells in indirect fire when necessary. The 95-mm was similar to the 25-pdr (with a 3.45-in, 87mm, bore), both guns having many common parts, and it was a logical step for the Division's gunners, with some Marines trained for 'G(L)s', to form the RM Support Craft Regiment to man these Centaurs.

In exercise 'Savvy', some 14 weeks before D-Day, this Regiment 'showed to considerable advantage',[5] but its LCTs blocked some of the best beaching points for follow-up craft. Therefore, when King George VI had queried the likely role of these tanks 'after they have landed', General Montgomery ordered that the role be changed. The Regiment was re-designated the Armoured Support Group, engines were replaced in the tanks, Royal Armoured Corps maintenance crews and Royal Artillery drivers were drafted to the Group, and five batteries were formed for the 1st and 2nd Regiments and the 5th Independent Battery of the Group. The last training in the original static role was completed on 16 March. The methods of fire control had to be reshaped quickly, as half the Group had to be concentrated before mid-April in its pre-invasion assembly areas. Sherman tanks were found for the Troop commanders. They would provide armoured OPs for the four Centaurs of a Troop, which were now mounted in pairs forward in the LCT Mark 5, refitted and retitled LCT (Armoured). Each Sherman, unable to fire on the run in, was further aft in the well of one of a Troop's two LCT(A)s.

The Centaur had not been used before in battle, probably because its 1917-design of Liberty aero engine was unreliable and required non-standard spare parts, but the Armoured Support Group's success demonstrated once again the Corps' ability to improvise. Most of the tanks' RM crews were 'HOs' but their commanding officer, Brigadier D. C. W. Sanders, OBE, AFC, was seconded from the Royal Artillery; his second-in-command was an RM officer, Lieutenant-Colonel A. J. Harvey, OBE, and Royal Marine Lieutenant-Colonels in their early thirties commanded the two Armoured Support Regiments and the 5th (Independent) Armoured Support Battery.[6] They developed techniques for firing at targets on the run in, with the Troop commander on the bridge, and for aligning their guns in concentrated fire when conventional methods could not be used on an enemy held beach. The signallers learnt to cope with the high-pitched oscillations from five radios on the Troop's B net[7] (an Army Troop had only three tanks and therefore fewer radios on its net). They waterproofed their vehicles, although much of the material for this only arrived two weeks before D-Day.[8]

Their intended roles were changed several times, adding to the difficulties in the few weeks for special training and rehearsal in their finally agreed role: the 80 Centaurs and 20 Shermans would land with one Troop supporting each assault company from 'Gold' in the West, through the Canadian sectors of 'Juno' to 'Sword' beach. They were not expected to go more than a mile from the beach or to be ashore for more than a few days. Therefore they would land with a small Headquarters staff, the COs of the regiments and of the Independent Battery each being accompanied by his Adjutant, an NCO signaller and a driver in a jeep or other vehicle. By a private arrangement[9] the 2nd Regiment's tactical Headquarters used a borrowed Canadian Bren carrier.

Before LCT(A) or any other craft could beach safely, gaps had to be made in the beach defences, and this task was allotted to some 150 underwater swimmers trained at COXE (Appledore) and known as 'Loc-Us' (LCOCUs). They were formed into twelve units – six of Naval commandos and six of RM Engineer commandos – each with an officer or NCO commanding 11 men.[10] These Landing Craft Obstruction Clearance Units were allocated in pairs to each Force, and would clear two lanes to the initial landing points on a beach. The RM Engineer Commando evolved as is shown in Appendix 4 from the RM Brigade's Demolition Company of 1940,[11] and by 1944 included men who had trained in Egypt with Royal Engineer mine-clearance and demolition specialists. Some had landed with the 7th RM Battalion in Sicily and had also seen active service in Italy.[12] In 1943 there were two companies of RM [Assault] Engineers and these were re-formed into four Commando Troops or Sections. No.2 Section and good swimmers from Nos 1 and 4 were selected for the LCOCUs. No.3 Section by this date was in the Far East with 3 Commando Brigade, and Nos 1 and 4 would join the 1st (sic) and 2 Commando Brigades.

The underwater swimmers in rubber suits, fins and a modified Davis submarine escape apparatus[13] practised placing charges on the element-C at COXE, needing 36 charges to demolish this 10ft × 10ft × 14ft structure of 6-in steel girders and weighing 2½ tons.[14] They also practised clearing stakes and hedgehogs of angle iron, built like those expected on the Normandy beaches. After some confusion in 1943 as to the responsibilities for clearing obstacles above and below the tide line, a scheme was finally worked out in May 1944 for the LCOCU parties to co-ordinate their work with that of the Royal Engineer companies clearing obstacles above the tide line.[15]

The breadth of the Royal Marines preparations for the Normandy landing, from LCOCUs in the van of the invasion to the detachments on battleships and cruisers, encompassed more than Commandos and landing-craft crews, more than combined operations signallers and gunners. A most important aspect of any major amphibious operation is the speed with which forces can be built up in the beachhead, and in Normandy the build-up would be massive: 183,000 tons of stores, 81,000 vehicles and 557,000 men in the 11 days to 16 June.[16] This would be achieved through two 'Mulberry' harbours – designated 'B' in the British and 'A' in the American sectors – floated in with their blockship break-waters, Army engineers and Naval port parties. These parties included RM anti-aircraft gunners,[17] and the eight Naval Port Communication parties included 12 RM officers with their 650 Marine signallers, including telephone linesmen, VHF (Very High Frequency) radio operators, Don-Rs (despatch riders) and some units specially trained in long-distance communications from mobile centres.[18] Other RM personnel in Naval parties provided provost companies, dock-clearance companies of RM Engineers, and men for the Naval Headquarters ashore. In these HQs were Marine radar plotters, who 'were among the few "other ranks" ... who were fully briefed about the plan for the invasion, before D-Day'.[19] The Marines in all these parties were more often working in small groups with other services than in a major unit of Marines, for the Marine's ability to get on with the job and other services was expected – and later proved – to be invaluable in the inevitable difficulties of even the most carefully planned landings.

The last of the night bomber force were leaving the coast, having dropped their heavy bombs on the batteries at Ouistreham, when HMS *Warspite*, *Ramillies* and *Roberts* followed the minesweepers to the anchorage on the flank of S Force. It was growing light as they took up positions – dawn was at 0600 hours (British Summer Time, GMT plus 2 hours in 1944) – and they opened fire in the pre-dawn half-light about 0530, Aboard the cruiser HMS *Diadem* the gun crews engaged the Moulineaux battery above Courseulles. *Diadem* had steamed slowly across the Channel, the Marines manning both her X and Y turrets. As she moved through the dim light before dawn, her Captain took her with care through the landing craft preparing to make their run to 'Juno' beach, then she opened fire about 0530 silencing the Moulineaux guns with five direct hits.

As the naval bombardment proceeded, HMS *Warspite* engaged Villerville battery at 30,000yds (27+km), HMS *Ramillies* and *Roberts* took on batteries at Benerville and Houlgate[1] – most of the batteries fell silent. But at Longues, despite HMS *Ajax*'s bombardment, the four guns reopened fire just before 0600 and were not finally put out of action until nearly three hours later, after 179 shells had been fired by cruisers, HMS *Argonaut* having joined HMS *Ajax*. Other batteries reopened fire during the morning, but the only German attempt to attack the bombarding warships had been made by E-boats from Le Havre, coming through the smoke laid by Allied aircraft to screen the launching of D-D swimming tanks. Only one ship was lost, the Norwegian destroyer *Svenner*, and no air attacks got through the Allied air umbrellas of fighters. Nor was there

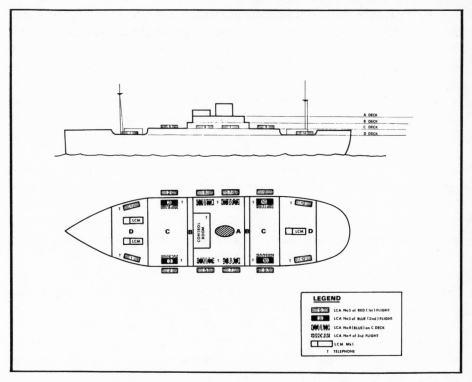

The arrangement of minor craft on a typical Glen ship. LSI had two LCM mk I forward on D deck and one aft, launched by derricks. The starboard LCAs were launched as follows:

No. I from single gravity davit forward on D deck; No. 2 from starboard stowage on luffing davit, this davit's beam was then swung inboard to lift No. 3 and later No. 4 craft from cradles one over the other on C deck; Nos. 5 & 6 and 7 & 8 were in pairs on double gravity davits on C deck; Nos. 9, 10 & 11 were on a second luffing davit on C deck; and No. 12 on a single gravity davit aft on D deck. Craft Nos. 5 & 7 could be loaded from B deck and others were loaded from C and D decks. Men were assembled in waiting positions near their craft, those on B and C decks moving up forward ladders and then aft to the starboard waiting points and those on the port hand moving in the opposite direction. The first flight of craft launched was Nos. I, 2, 5, 7, 9 and 12 both port and starboard, the port hand davit arrangement mirroring that to starboard. The second flight of 8 craft was Nos. 3, 6, 8 and 10 from both sides, and the third flight from the lower cradles of the luffing davits (Nos. 4 and 11) of 4 craft.

any major difficulty apparently for the 160 USAF, RAF and FAA fighters spotting for the bombarding squadron's big ships, although radio contact was sometimes lost and seven planes were shot down.[2]

The Landing Ships Infantry (LSIs) *see above* had sailed on the late evening of 5 June, except for those from the west of England ports, which left earlier for the American beaches. Convoy 7 with HMS *Glenearn*, carrying two flotillas of Marine-manned LCAs, passed out of the Solent through the northern 'gate' in Spithead boom at 2145 hours.[3] On passing the Nab Tower a quotation from Henry V, Act 2 was read over her Tannoy. It begins:

> Now, Lords, for France! the enterprise
> whereof
> Shall be to you, as us, like glorious.
> We doubt not of a fair and lucky war . . .
> We doubt not now
> But every rub is smoothed on our way.

As *Glenearn* came up to the first light buoy, lit so convoys could check their positions, the Captain found it a mile out of position, and as he was responsible for the convoy's navigation, he increased speed from 12 knots to 13 to be on time at the next light buoy: but he found his 'QH' navigation aid – an early form of beamed navigation signal – was subject to interference, possibly by enemy jamming. Nevertheless they were on time at the next buoy before *Glenearn* entered the swept channel through the mine barrage, led by two of the destroyer escorts. She anchored three minutes late at 0533 and 'broke' her anchor cable from the winch, ready to slip instantly. The four LSIs in this 'lowering position' then showed blue lights, one for *Glenearn*, two for *Empire Cutlass* and so on, for easy identification. (See Map Normandy 1944.)

The light was growing stronger and smoking was allowed on the upper deck, a relief for some, as the men had been at action stations for over an hour. The seamen were ready to lower the craft, having taken off 'the guys of gravity davits, all grypes and securing pendants', and on telephoned orders from the control room, would lower them. The men of the 2nd East Yorks boarded the craft and the first flight of ten craft from 543 Flotilla was lowered to the water at 0555 hours. 'There was a bad sea running', but all these craft moved away from the ship in time for the inboard line of craft to be launched 15 minutes later. Meanwhile the first flight set course for its start line and *Glenearn*'s two LCMs were launched to move across to the Force S headquarters ship HMS *Largs*. The second flight of LCAs (from 535 Flotilla) left for its start line at 0625 hours, carrying the 1st Battalion South Lancashire Regiment. Only one hoist had jammed and the craft on it were late leaving the ship. The fortunes of the others we shall follow in due course, but as the craft passed the Headquarters ship, a bugler of the East Yorkshires sounded the General Salute.[4]

All the other LSIs of the Eastern Task Force also reached their 'lowering positions' on time, and despite the short, sharp seas, got their craft away on time except for some minor mishaps. The LCAs carrying Marines of the LCOCU teams – as one craft did from *Glenearn* – had their problems in the rough water, but LCOCUs 9 and 10 heading for 'Gold' beach were on time.[5] The coxswains could see this flat, sandy beach, with low-lying dunes behind it, and as they came inshore the craft grounded some way from the tide line.[6] But there was as yet only occasional fire from the strongpoint at Le Hamel, although this group of fortified houses would prove a point of stout resistance later that morning, as its defenders had not been subdued by an air attack with 1,000-lb bombs.

The craft were on the beach at H-hour (0725), and the swimmers began clearing a path through the obstacles. D-D amphibious tanks should have landed before them at H-4 minutes, but in the rough seas these tanks might have foundered – as many did when launched the planned distance from the shore – for there was little freeboard to the canvas of their flotation screens, and on 'Gold' beach they were brought ashore in their LCTs after the first landings. Nor were the RM Armoured Support Group tanks any more fortunate: only five out of ten got ashore on 'Gold' beach, and all but one of those ashore were soon knocked out by fire from Le Hamel. The obstacles ashore were awash in surf far heavier than expected, but the divers defused the Teller mines and shells with pressure fuses, before placing the demolition charges. Many of the obstacles proved to be more heavily constructed than expected[7] and in places to be more numerous – on 'Gold' beach alone there were 2,500 in 3¼ miles.[8] They were also in deeper water, because the onshore wind had caused the tide to flood 30 minutes ahead of the almanac time. Despite these difficulties and steady fire from Le Hamel, gaps were cleared at both Jig I and 2 landing points on 'Gold' beach. But on the beach these were narrower than the planned width of 200yds, because fewer Royal Engineers and their Assault Vehicles (AVREs) got ashore than were expected. In the water the surge of incoming craft made diving increasingly risky, and the greater weight of explosive needed to demolish obstacles increased the hazard of injury to the swimmers, despite the Kapok jackets under their diving suits as protection from underwater explosions.

Other Marine LCOCU parties on 'Juno' and 'Sword' were landed 20 minutes late but blasted gaps at their landing points.[9] Their work went on through the day and after high water they widened the seaward gaps, Sergeant K. Briggs defusing 100 mines singlehanded despite being under rifle fire;[10] but the gaps were not wide enough on the first tide to take all the incoming craft, although at 'Juno' and 'Sword' there were fewer obstacles at the landing points than on 'Gold'.[11]

The flotillas of LCA (Hedgerow) in tow behind LCTs suffered badly in the Force 5 Westerly – a fresh breeze whipping foam crests off the large waves built up in the previous day's storms. Of the 45 that set out, only a dozen or so are believed to have reached the beach area, and in some craft their spigot mortars punched through the floor as the 60lb bombs were fired. Six of the 45 craft in these flotillas had been under repair on 5 June, and this brave effort was undoubtedly made in the flimsiest of the support craft. The only reports of their operations that have been traced suggest that the spigot bombs did not cut completely clear paths through mines and wire on the beaches,[12] but one group successfully fired 'near Bernières "Juno" beach ahead of the infantry ... and delivered its bombs across the beach'. However, only one craft of a second group intended to fire here survived the crossing.[13] The LCT(R)s' rocket proved more successful, not least in their effect in boosting the assault troops' morale, for each rocket craft fired a pattern of quick salvoes over a stretch of beach 750yds by 160yds, in which nearly 800 rockets – the size of 6-in shells – burst.

The Armoured Support Group's LCTs wallowed in the rough sea, the added armour to their sides and the weight of the tanks making them low in the water. The tank crews had slung their hammocks wherever they could, on the mess decks, in the wheelhouse and between the tanks. Just before 0500 they lashed-up and stowed the hammocks, as the craft approached the assembly areas – the 1st RM Armoured Support Regiment with 50 Division heading for 'Gold' beach, the 2nd Regiment with 3 Canadian Division for 'Juno', and the 5th (Independent) Battery with 3 Division for 'Sword'. Water slopped around the tank wells, on some craft a foot deep. Many of the men were seasick, but some managed to wash down bread and marmalade with hot tea, before they checked the guns on

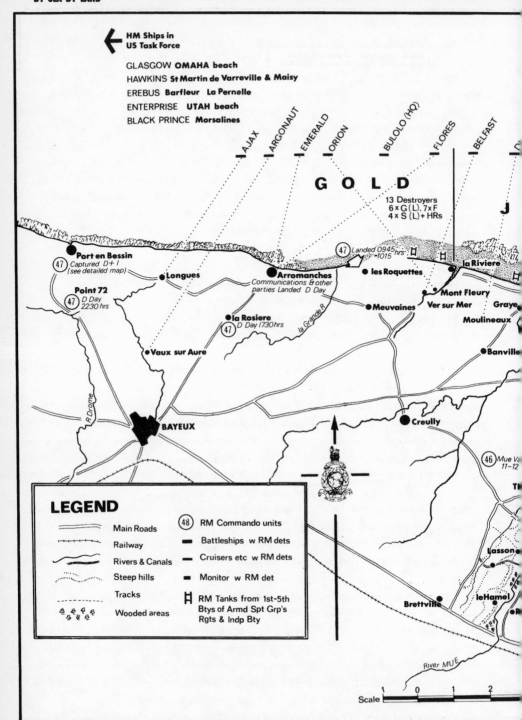

Deployment and principal actons of RM forces in the Normandy invasion, on 6 June 1944. RM gunners were in the following supportcraft: 'Gold'– LCG(L) 1, 2, 3, 13, 17, 18, and LCF 19, 20, 25, 26, 35, 36, 38, and LCS(L) 251, 252, 258, 259 and 591 Flot of LCA (HR); 'Juno' – G(L) 680, 681,

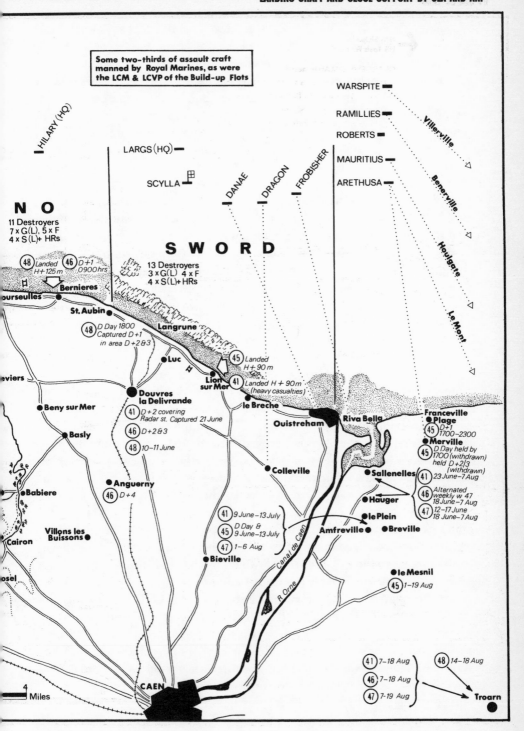

Some two-thirds of assault craft manned by Royal Marines, as were the LCM & LCVP of the Build-up Flots

HILARY (HQ)

LARGS (HQ)

SCYLLA

DANAE

DRAGON

FROBISHER

WARSPITE

RAMILLIES

ROBERTS

MAURITIUS

ARETHUSA

Villerville

Benerville

Houlgate

Le Mont

N O
11 Destroyers
7 × G(L), 5 × F
4 × S(L)+ HRs

S W O R D
13 Destroyers
3 × G(L) 4 × F
4 × S(L)+HRs

48 Landed H+125 m
46 D+1 0900 hrs

Bernieres

ourseulles

St. Aubin

48 D Day 1800 Captured D+1 in area D+2&3

Langrune

Luc

Lion sur Mer

45 Landed H+90 m

41 Landed H+90 m (heavy casualties)

le Breche

eviers

Douvres la Delivrande

41 D+2 covering Radar st. Captured 21 June

46 D+2&3

48 10–11 June

Beny sur Mer

Basly

Anguerny

46 D+4

Babiere

Villons les Buissons

Cairon

osel

Ouistreham

Riva Bella

Colleville

Franceville Plage
45 D+1 1700–2300

Merville
45 D Day held by 1700 (withdrawn) held D+2/3 (withdrawn)

Sallenelles
41 23 June–7 Aug

Hauger

46 Alternated weekly w 47 18 June–7 Aug

le Plein

Amfreville

Breville

47 12–17 June 18 June–7 Aug

41 9 June–13 July

45 D Day & 9 June–13 July

47 1–6 Aug

Bieville

Canal de Caen

R Orne

le Mesnil

45 1–19 Aug

4 Miles

CAEN

41 7–18 Aug

46 7–18 Aug

47 7–19 Aug

48 14–18 Aug

Troarn

764, 831, 939, 1007, 1062 and LCF 1, 21, 32, 33, 37, 24, 29 and S(L) 202, 203, 204, 205 and 590 RM Flot LCA (HR); 'Sword' – G(L) 9, 10, 11 and LCF 30, 34, 39, 42 and S (L) 253, 256, 260 and 592 RM Flot of LCA (HR); various beaches – S(L) 254, 255 and 257.

the Centaurs.[14] About 0630 the crews climbed into their tanks and the RM Lieutenant commanding one Troop of tanks approaching 'Sword' beach helped the skipper check the panoramic pictures for landmarks: the harbour at Ouistreham, the tall factory chimneys of Caen. 'The battleships' barrage, flashes running up and down the beaches as the RAF let go their bombs, the whole coast seemed to swirl out dust and clouds of smoke, the sky was darkened by it and a smell of gunpowder came right out over the sea.'[15] Four hundred yards from the shore the tanks opened fire, each LCT(A) carried ammunition under the tanks' mounting and this was fed to the open turret by a hoist, to save the tanks' ammunition for use ashore.

A few moments later, as the skipper ordered 'full speed ahead', the Lieutenant came off the bridge and climbed into his Sherman; as he did so machine gun fire rattled the sides of the LCT, and the Centaurs' guns trained quickly to silence this strongpoint. The LCT's ramp came down and the tanks slid into the sea, weaving their way through the mines on obstacles before clearing the water. The assault infantry companies were landing at the same time, and the tanks remained just clear of the water, firing at the targets they could see up the beach. 'Two craft went up in flames and several were bumping up and down on the beach with holes in their waterlines; the dust and smoke made the whole thing seem quite unreal.'[16] The Troop Commander could see the top of the beach and that the infantry had a long way to go to reach it, but he found that targets were hard to see. The tide flooded in over his tank's tracks, while the Troop fired into a large house. The Troop Commander then decided to press on up the beach, in the lead, although, 'knowing the Germans' love of mines, these moments were nerve-racking', before the Sherman topped the sand dunes and white handkerchiefs appeared from the German dugouts. Yet a few remained to snipe at the beach through the day, while the tank mopped up positions around the beach.

Twenty of the Centaurs were lost when their LCT(A)s foundered in the Channel crossing – two LCT(A)s capsized – or were hit on landing. Their waterproofing of thick grease around turrets, raised plates to the hatches, Bostik on every rivet,[17] was damaged in some cases before they were ashore, and the heavier bits of the waterproofing kit could be blown off by charges controlled from inside the turret. Nevertheless 34 were ashore by 0830 hours.[18] Many were late because of the rough weather, which upset the timetable for the LCT(A)'s landing. The plans to work with FOOs in forward observation posts of the assault companies were also limited by the difficulties these Royal Artillery officers faced on landing. On 'Gold' beach, for example, the Colonel of the 1st Hampshires and their two FOOs were all killed soon after landing, and therefore not only was the remaining RM tank on this beach without forward contact, but so too were the self-propelled artillery in LCTs and the major support craft.

The RM tanks were in action throughout D-Day. One had to charge the jammed ramp of its LCT(A), others were landed late in the morning, and 12 were put ashore even later, after their craft had undergone repairs.[19] They would be ashore three weeks and support the Commandos, Canadians and others up to 10 miles from the beaches despite their limited facilities for maintenance and the casualties among the RA drivers, who were replaced by Marines.[20] In the words of the official history, 'those RM tanks that were not quickly put out of action did good service, the Marines showing their characteristic enterprise'.[21]

The minor support craft on the flanks of the assault flotillas came inshore around H-hour. The two LCS(M) Mark 2 from HMCS *Prince David* of Force J Group 2 were launched at 0617 hours, and came inshore with an LCA assault flotilla carrying Canadians and an RM Clearance Unit to land near Bernières on 'Juno'. Both support craft foundered on beach obstacles, having gone as far as they could towards the tide line, although they were not expected to beach.[22] The crews, including their RM gunners, got ashore. The other LCS(M)s fared better than might have been expected in view of their stations just off the beach. One skipper flew a White Ensign from his radar mast alongside the coxswain – not the correct position for an ensign but it was his treasured acquisition. Minor craft did not in fact fly battle ensigns, but this one was flown until enemy fire began to cut holes in it. The Naval Lieutenant then hauled it down, at which HMS *Warspite* signalled: 'Why are you lowering your battle flag?'

The LCS (Large), with their anti-tank guns, had been allocated to support several landing points where the LCA flotillas did not have their own minor support craft. On 'Sword', for example, there were at least three LCS(L) Mark 2s to cover the final run in of the RM tanks' craft and *Glenearn*'s LCAs, among other assault flotillas, for behind this beach were many fortified houses. The protection given by the support craft and destroyers coming inshore during the run in 'was so effective that there was little enemy fire till the shore was neared'.[23] *Glenearn*'s LCAs had put their Yorkshire men ashore on the most easterly landing point, the flooding tide lifting the craft clear. But in an onshore wind and surging surf the craft could only be brought out by good seamanship, as the coxswains steered their way back through the menacing black stakes and mined obstacles. The current was setting craft towards the seaside resort of Ouistreham, a mile or so to the east of the Yorkshires' landing point, but only four of *Glenearn*'s craft were reported lost – one hit by enemy fire, which wounded the second-in-command of 543 Flotilla, and the other three caught on beach obstacles. On 'Sword' beach the flooding tide had made the work of clearing these obstacles more difficult, and only one narrow channel was marked to the landing point. As more craft came in the congestion on the water line built up.

The intention here was to land three brigade groups on a narrow front and if possible to break inland as far as Caen, some seven miles from the beach. But by the time 41 RM Commando came ashore to fight its way westward and link with '48 RM' some three miles along the coast, there was growing opposition as the Germans recovered from the initial shock of the assault. More craft all along the coast were lost on withdrawing among the obstacles, including 'hedge-hogs', as they now came under fire, than had been lost on the run in,[24] and the major support craft were brought back into action after ceasing fire during the first landings. As the fire increased on 'Sword', a lone RM redcap seemed to be the only man alive at one time, as he directed vehicles to beach exits.

The LCFs and G(L)s had come inshore with the assault waves. LCG(L) 1007, a Mark 4 of 333 Support Flotilla, had been in a typical action off 'Juno' beach: at 0700 hours she had been 6,000 yards out and closing the beach near Courseulles. Her first target was four German 75-mm guns in a concrete emplacement, which her skipper and his RM gunnery officer identified from aerial panoramic photographs. The gunners got several hits on this target before shifting aim to a row of fortified houses overlooking the landing beaches.[25] Whether or not they silenced these, is not clear, for shortly afterwards their Headquarters ship gave them a fresh target: a strongpoint in an isolated house near Bernières. The first ranging shot fell short, but 'up 400' for the second put shells on the target.

Although '1007' suffered no serious casualties, LCG(L) 831 of this flotilla was repeatedly hit. One shell killed a Marine after it had passed through the gun shield to explode between 'A' and 'B' guns, but it did not set off the ready-use magazines behind their sandbag protection on the upper deck. Her RM gunner officer remained 'cool and collected',[26] the guns continuing to fire.

G(L) 681 also engaged targets on 'Juno' beach,[27] as did LCF No. 1 – the original Flakker with a pair of twin-4in being four dual-purpose HA/LA guns – which neutralised a quartet of 88-mm guns in a concrete emplacement and blew the machine-gunners from a water tower.[28] The crews had been sweating to get the rounds off in rapid salvoes from their guns, the magazine numbers on '681' handing up the separate charges and shells for the guns. These Marines had not been allowed 'up top' when all the major support craft ceased firing as the assault troops landed. They did come up for a smoke, however, some hours later, but had only been watching the shore a few minutes when the action began again, as gun flashes were seen from a church belfry. This they demolished.[29]

There were few German planes for the LCFs to engage, for only 36 German aircraft were seen at wide intervals over the first 24 hours of the landings. But at least one LCF engaged shore targets, clearing Germans from the upper floors of houses near Bernières.[30]

Most of the Commandos were ashore by 0900 hours, having landed to pass through the flanks of each beachhead, and effect the link-up between landing points which in some cases were 10 miles apart.[31] The 1st Commando Brigade – 3, 4, 6 (Army) Commandos and '45 RM', with two Troops of 10 (Inter-Allied) Commando – were landed on 'Sword' beach. The Brigade plan read: 'The Intention: The 6 Airborne Division and 1st Commando Brigade will be responsible for holding the left flank on the Allied bridgehead. The Method: . . . to land on 'Sword' and cut inland to join forces with two brigades dropped inland overnight by glider and parachute. No.4 Commando to destroy a battery and garrison in Ouistreham then later rejoin . . .'[32] With some help from an RM tank, 4 Commando fought its way west and cleared Ouistreham, finding no coast guns mounted, although the battery was stoutly defended. (With No.4 Commando's French Troop was an RM Signaler, Marine Pat Churchill, who would be with them throughout their advance into France, and was one of several Marines attached to Army Commandos.) The remainder of the Brigade, led by 6 Commando, had three hours to fight its way through enemy-held country, and the enemy was prepared for and expecting an attack along the 4½ miles to the bridges over the Orne River, and a further 1½ miles to the line of low hills they would hold. If the bridges were destroyed, 45 RM Commando was prepared to cross the river in rubber boats.[33]

No.6 Commando passed through the beach defences where 4 Commando had blasted a path, clearing German concrete bunkers that should have been taken by the East Yorkshires. The airborne still held the bridges and their wireless signals spurred on the Brigade – 'No time to hang about or proceed with caution'.[34] The leading Troop of 'No.6' were a mere two minutes late. The commandos got across the bridge in no time, but Lieutenant-Colonel N. C. Ries was picked off by a sniper; his '45 RM' was counter-attacked but fought its way forward, and Major W. Nicol Gray led it over the bridges. The Brigade was regrouped in dead ground out of sight and shot from Germans in Le Plein village above the bridges.

'There was a good man in Nicol Gray',[35] who was given an awkward assignment: '45 RM' was to push north to the coast at Franceville Plage, 'disrupting German communications and to contain the enemy'.[36] Lord Lovat, the Brigade Commander, expected '45 RM' back in the line the following night. During the afternoon enemy pressure had suddenly become dangerous, for the Airborne's hold on the ridge was weak and the Commando Brigade stretched to establish a defended line over the three miles along the ridge. The assignment of '45 RM' would plug the gap on the northern flank, where the coast road ran through Sallenelles. 'C' Troop, with their cycles, pedalled ahead to find this small town firmly held; it was therefore by-passed while a company of machine-gunners kept the Germans' heads down. The Commando then dug in near the Merville battery, 500yds short of Franceville, for the Germans had reoccupied this battery after the paras had left it, and '45 RM' formed a tightly defended area in isolation from the Brigade. That evening more formations of 6 Airborne Division flew in, and during the night the Orne positions were established in a smaller perimeter, to which '45 RM' would later have to fight its way.

Coming ashore in heavy fire on 'Sword', 41 RM Commando was landed from wooden LCI(S), as 1st Commando Brigade had been. The craft of '41 RM', however, were on the right flank of 'Sword', and were under fire as they beached 300yds west of their intended landing point. As the Marines came ashore, 'everything appeared the same grey', a few houses, blobs of men taking cover behind tanks. Despite casualties, one Troop reached a strong point near Lion-sur-Mer to find it deserted.[37] Two Troops with a company of the South Lancashires attacked further west and lost more men 'in a series of hand-to-hand fights among the houses'. Their objective was a château west of this village, but both Troop commanders, the two artillery FOOs and their signallers were casualties early in the attack. No artillery support could be contacted, therefore, and three AVRE tanks were knocked out before the attack stalled.[38] Some of the Marines of '41 RM' after landing 'had lost their officers and NCOs, but pushed on gallantly, then missed direction, veered inwards and were brought to a halt', finding cover from fire and bombs in a deep drain. Lord Lovat found them somewhat demoralised, 'boys who looked absurdly young and only lacked for leadership'.[39] When the Cycle Troop commander from 6 Army Commando appeared with a cheery 'I'd rather be shot-up on the road ... than do this sort of thing', every man leapt out of the ditch to follow him, and '41 RM' regrouped that night near Lion-sur-Mer.

Other Commandos of 4 Brigade had similar flank roles, '48 RM' coming ashore on the left flank of 'Juno'. Two of its LCI(S) were caught on obstacles and held by this 'Rommel's asparagus' with its 'hedgehogs' made of heavy pieces of heavy girders some 100yds or more from the beach. Lance-Corporal Wilkinson, RAMC, a commando medical orderly, was dressing a man's wounds at this time, and although hit in the leg, the Lance-Corporal continued his work in full view of the shore; a second bullet hit him in the shoulder but he did not seek cover, and was killed by a third shot.[40] Several commandos were drowned while trying to swim ashore in the strong current. The other four craft beached with difficulty, their cat-walks not square to the beach and plunging the men waist-deep into the sea. Canadians were still firing from the water's edge as the Commando's 2-in mortars laid a smoke screen from the bows of the craft, through which the men advanced past 'the human debris of the assault: some dead, many wounded, some bewildered'. The CO of '48 RM', Lieutenant-Colonel J. L. Moulton, was wounded by mortar fragments, but continued to assemble his men before they advanced inland 1,000yds to form a base from which they could assault the Langrune strongpoint and clear houses along the shore. They cleared the houses, losing an officer and a Marine when a support craft fired into the house in an attempt to give close covering fire. '48 RM' was then held at the strongpoint, but with the help of two RM Centaurs broke into one corner of the fortified block. At dusk, about 2100 hours, the Commando was withdrawn from the houses, to take up positions around Langrune, as an armoured counter-attack was expected.[41] That night German mobile patrols reached a point between '48 RM' and '41 RM' but no serious counter-attack developed.

Lieutenant-Colonel (later General Sir) Campbell Hardy's '46 RM' was at sea that night. The Marines had trained and equipped for a cliff climb to the batteries east of the Orne estuary at Houlgate or Benerville, depending on which was firing to cause the most trouble to the anchorages. The plan was for this Commando to destroy the guns and then – although only lightly armed, as their demolition and cliff-climbing gear precluded full assault equipment – they were to have fought their way to join 6 Airborne Division, if they could not be brought off after four hours ashore. But they were not used for this role because the batteries were not firing with any effect into the smoke shrouded anchorage. Nor was 6 Airborne strongly established in the area of the Dives River; its men had been scattered and were fighting in small pockets, much of their equipment lost in marshes along coast and rivers.[42] So '46 RM' were not landed on 'Juno' beach until the morning of D+1, when – re-equipped with assault weapons by the Canadians – they would fight a series of bold actions in support of the Canadians.

Further west on D-Day, LCAs carrying 47 RM Commando had been launched, with scramble nets for men to climb down to the craft. 'Quite a trick getting down these nets ... in a fairly heavy swell',[43] before the craft set off for the westerly landing point of 'Gold' beach. (Those who have experience of scramble nets, express a preference for pre-loaded craft.) The craft would eventually land near the gaps cut by 9 and 10 Clearance Units, but in the approach the commandos were fired on 2,000yds out by 75-mm guns above Le Hamel. As they neared their intended westerly landing point, they saw it was deserted except for four tanks under heavy fire. The Commanding Officer, Lieutenant-Colonel C. F. Phillips, decided to take the craft eastward to the second landing point on 'Gold'. As they ran parallel to the shore, one LCA was hit, and 'suddenly it wasn't fun any more'.[44] They turned shorewards and came among obstacles 400yds from the beach. 'It was a case of every craft for itself', for the beach was crowded with LCTs and other craft, 'drowned' vehicles and dumps of equipment. A terrific explosion blew off the bows of one craft, which started to sink; the mortar men went over the side into water over their heads and swam in full kit – one-piece jacket with pockets which was supposed to be easily slipped off – but they had to abandon the mortar's base plate and dial sight as they struggled ashore.

Three craft were lost on mined obstacles, and elsewhere these Marines had difficulty getting ashore – their average load was 88lb[45] – many in that panting urgency for a gasp of air as equipment dragged them under the next wave. They had been landed on a 1,500yd front, not the expected 200yds. The beach had not been secured by this time (H+90 minutes) and the way to their rendezvous by the church in Le Hamel was blocked. Nevertheless by 1100 hours the second-in-command, Major P. N. Donnell, had them sorted out and was in contact with their liaison officer, who had landed with the 2nd Devons. The Colonel's craft had been sunk and he would catch them up later, but gathering up German weapons, including four MG42s, and salvaging what heavy weapons they could from the wrecks of LCAs – one 3-in mortar less sight, one Vickers Medium machine gun – they set off inland.

Their objective was Port-en-Bessin, a small harbour between two high features, strongly defended from a frontal attack, which the Marines were to take from the landward approaches. They now planned to make a wide detour around Le Hamel, led by X and B Troops, who had landed 'reasonably dry and equipped'.[46] There were three officers and 73 Marines missing at this time, but an advanced HQ moved with the leading Troops and the remainder of the Headquarters with Q Troop, A and Y Troops followed, with the heavy HQ wireless sets on 'prams', The Colonel rejoined them during this move, having come through Le Hamel riding on the ammunition sledge towed by a self-propelled gun. In a brief halt while the Hampshires moved across the line of march, four carriers of a Recce Troop from 50 Division joined the commandos, each carrier loaded with ammunition. The Commando had been mortared and one Marine killed by a sniper, but their first real opposition came just outside La Rosière. 'A' Troop moved to a flank and took a German machine gun post, X Troop fought through the village[47] and the other Troops went south of it. As they did so, another machine gun they had passed, caught Q Troop in single file, but using smoke and determination they had cleared the village by 1730 hours.

An FOO joined them here to replace the Royal Artillery officer lost in the landings. After two hours' rest and a meal of sorts, they moved off again for 'Point 72', a hill top a mile south of the Port and dug in for the night.

LCMs that had followed the assault waves in had been launched by derrick from the landing ships. The two from SS *Empire Lance* took a buffeting as they slipped the shackles from their hoist and circled, waiting for a corvette's signal telling them to land. When the Marine signaller read this 'go-in' signal to one LCM, her coxswain headed her for 'Gold' beach, checking the shore line against his aerial panorama of the beach. There were still landing craft everywhere looking for a place to land, the noise was deafening, and brave men admitted their fear but overcame it. The LCM was nearly run down by an LCT, then the coxswain had an idea: he followed the LCT through the obstacles offshore, as the choppy water exposed them for brief seconds. The tide had risen over these obstacles and as the coxswain swung his craft clear of the LCT's stern to beach, the stoker-mechanic appeared from the engine room shouting, 'We're sinking'. The craft had hit an obstacle and settled on the bottom, and a sledgehammer was needed to force open the ramp before her cargo of beach roadway could be manhandled ashore.[48] In the deafening noise the coxswain had not heard her hit a mine!

The LCMs and LCVPs of the build-up flotillas, including the Marines of 'A' and 'B' Squadrons of 'VPs' and 'E' and 'F' of LCMs, had sailed from UK sally ports at first light on D-Day. 'B' Squadron was escorted by the motor yacht *Sister Anne*, with two Lewis guns only, not adding much defensive fire to the eighty Lewis guns – one per craft – of the Squadron. It reached 'Gold' beach in the evening of D-Day. 'A' Squadron arrived on 'Juno' about the same time, its 'VPs' carrying stores, metal pipes and beach roadway matting.[49] Also heading for 'Juno' were the LCMs of 'F' Squadron, including LCM 1114 with a DUKW Amphibious Truck and the two soldiers of its crew. By the time this LCM was in mid-Channel she had so much water through the packing – or lack of it – in the ramp, that the Marines' kitbags were floating in the well, and likely to break loose the sixty 5-gallon cans of diesel she carried aft of the DUKW. Eventually the lashings on these cans broke, and those of the crew who were not already seasick vomited in the stench of diesel oil. Nevertheless they landed their DUKW at the beach near Courseulles.[50] Most craft survived the rough crossing, one of them even making the passage on her own. The Mark 3 LCM 1066, christened 'Happy Landings' by her crew after a Derby racehorse of that name, had gone aground in the Solent. The sergeant coxswain got her off the unexpected bank, but this took a couple of hours, and the sea was still rough as she made the passage to 'Gold' beach.[51]

These craft of the build-up flotillas ferried in supplies and stores in a shuttle service from the transports throughout the next few days. And many of them would operate in these services for 12 weeks or more. But on the night of D-Day most crews slept in their craft and were supplied with meals from several Landing Barge Kitchens. Some crews, unable to get along the beach to the kitchens, ate their compo rations 'and weren't these good at that time!'[52] Other crews swopped these 48-hour rations and cigarettes for corned beef.[53] Base camps and depot ships would be used in later weeks, although many preferred to sleep aboard while shells from Le Havre were falling in beach areas, even if these caused no serious damage.

The Naval Headquarters ashore would become a major organisation, but on D-Day only RM and other reconnaissance parties were landed to survey sites – shades of MNBDO – and make contact with the various Naval Beach Parties, some of which had landed in the assault waves. These beach Commandos on 'Juno' included an RM lieutenant, for liaison with RM flotillas.[54] The first of eight Port Communication Parties had also landed, and these Marines began establishing the communications for the Naval Operations Control Centre ashore and radio-telephone links.[55] The beam radio telephone (VHF) link was established by nightfall, RM operators on 'Gold' beach talking to Wren operators in London.[56]

To round off the report of the day's actions, only two of '47 RM's' 14 craft returned with their crews to the LSIs.[57] *Glenearn*'s craft had fared better and were hoisted aboard by 1130, except the four that were lost and the two expected to stay on the beach, with the LCOCUs that had been with '543' and '535'. But *Glenearn* did not sail until early afternoon, having been taking on wounded with some difficulty, since the sally ports could not be opened with the seas that were running.[58] When she sailed, she headed for Cowes to collect 3,000 troops for the build-up. In another LCA flotilla, a 19-year-old corporal coxswain had hung over the stern of his LCA with one foot on the rudder-guard and one on the rudder, after her steering gear was damaged on launching. He steered the craft seven miles to the beach, clinging grimly to a small cleat on the stern and shouting orders to the stoker. One minute the corporal was high out of the water, the next up to his armpits in buffeting waves. He landed his troops, nevertheless, only three minutes late. Then he steered in the same way back to the LSI to be hoisted aboard after 4½ hours in seas that had numbed his body and crunched him painfully against the stern.[59]

The LCFs and G(L)s formed the 'Trout' line, moored 200yds apart in a line running seaward from inshore shallows on the eastern flank of the anchorage. Here they could intercept any attacks by explosive boats or swimmers each craft carried small anti-personnel depth-charges, and they blocked any inshore approach by E-boats. Further out, patrols of MTBs and destroyers kept watch and frigates patrolled within the anchorage.[60]

Among the cruisers, HMS *Diadem* had silenced a second battery early that morning and got nine hits on an ammunition dump. That night she would be attacked by six aircraft, her crew manning the anti-aircraft guns for they were not to get any proper rest or a shave for 52 hours. (*Diadem* also bombarded Carpiquet Aerodrome, the base of a Panzer Division, among other targets. She was to move to the area of Sword Beach in the last week of June to bombard the Caen area and gave support to 46 RM Commando among other units.)

Ashore on D-day there was the first opportunity to look more closely at the beach defences. 'Every strongpoint had been hit but in many cases the loopholes were sited to enfilade the beach',[61] and therefore with the guns firing diagonally across the shore, the bombardment had fallen on well-protected bunker sides facing seaward. Had this been realised before D-Day, the fire plan would have been designed differently, for counter-enfilade fire. More detailed analysis later concluded that only heavy guns of battleships and monitors firing armour-piercing shells penetrated strong concrete-protected emplacements, but against open field-gun positions the bombardment had been more effective, with rockets and self-propelled artillery fire from LCTs proving the most effective close support. The fire of other close-support craft contributed to the Germans' unexpected inefficiencies in counter-ship fire, as it lowered their gun crews' morale.[62]

Around Point 72 as D+1 dawned a bright June day, 47 RM Commando had dug in during the night and extended German defences they had found unoccupied around the hill (see map 9). There was as yet no solid line of German defences behind the beachhead, and although none of these commandos had had more than a couple of hours' sleep that night, patrols went out to find German positions. These were in strength at Fosse Soucy, some three-quarters of a mile to the south, but there were none to the north until the high ground round Port-en-Bessin, known as the 'western' (left) and 'eastern' features, while a few hundred yards south-west of the Port was a strongpoint known as the 'weapon pits'. No contact, however, could be established with the American 1 Division, which had suffered heavy casualties getting ashore on 'Omaha' and by midnight on D-day was some 2¼ miles west of the Marines' positions, for '47 RM' was isolated from the main assault forces.[1]

During the night a second FOO had arrived in his carrier 'after a hectic journey due to bomb craters', but the four carriers from 50 Division had not been able to stay with the Commando. The assault on the Port was then organised for that afternoon, with two troops, A and X, attacking the weapon pits and hill on the left (west) of the harbour, and B Troop attacking the right-hand hill. Q Troop, only half of which had got ashore the previous day, was in reserve and Y Troop protected the firm base around Point 72.[2] A Forward Officer Bombardment was in radio contact with the cruiser HMS *Emerald* and one of the FOOs in touch with the artillery of 231 Brigade. However, only one of the Commando's 22-sets was in working order to contact Brigade, Division, the artillery and the Navy.[3] About 1100 hours that morning two young Frenchmen came on to the hill and offered their help as guides. One took a message to the garrison of the Port demanding its surrender, but 'this produced no results'.[4] During the morning, when not out on patrols, the commandos spent their time checking over equipment and keeping a wary eye out for any signs of a German attack.

About 1400 the Navy began bombarding the seaward defences of the Port, and as this was earlier than planned, it caused some concern that the timetable was awry; but the ships did not appear to be shelling the high ground each side of the port – in fact, these hills protected the landward defences from the direct fire of the ships. Two LCG(L)s, and probably a destroyer, joined in this bombardment, shelling houses on the sea front. The help of six American LCT(R)s, how-

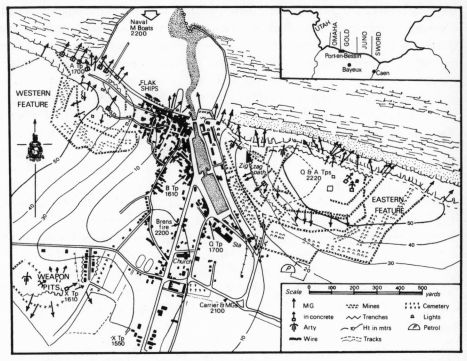

Port-en-Bessin area in Normandy with principal actions by 47 RM commando in their capture of this port on 7 June 1944.

ever, was declined for fear of rockets falling among the Commandos. An hour after the bombardment began HMS *Emerald*, directed by the FOB as planned, shelled the 'eastern' (right flank) feature for 60 minutes; until 10 minutes before the start time (1600 hours) when the first of two ground-support squadrons made an accurate low-level attack with rockets and cannon fire. The roar of diving planes and the rattle of their cannons drowned for 10 minutes the sound of sporadic firing from Germans in the village south of the Commando. Then the second squadron flew in with equally devastating fire. On time the field-guns fired smoke to screen the Troop movement from the start line, and the two medium machine guns of the Support Troop – on the right-hand edge of the wood to the east of Point 76 – put in two minutes of concentrated fire on the 'eastern' feature. They would protect the right flank from any counter-attack, but as a grass fire and the artillery's smoke shells hid the German defences, the machine-gunners stopped firing. The commandos' solitary mortar – without its sight[5] – fired mainly smoke bombs at the weapon pits south of the western feature, but the bombs fell too short and the mortar team was ordered to cease firing. The assault troops by then had dumped their rucksacks and heavy kit by two deep dugouts south-east of Point 72, and had begun moving to their start line about 1530.

As one Troop was moving to this start line along the edge of the orchards north of Escures, the village below Point 72, they had come under fire from the south. For about this time 'these Germans were beginning to show their mettle'. All three assault Troops, A, B and X, were drawn into the fire-fight but X Troop moved towards the coast. B Troop, which would attack the 'eastern' feature, covered A Troop's advance at this point, and Q Troop moved up to help B. The A Troop set off after X Troop along the deep ditches either side of the road going to the coast, guided by a French gendarme. They were 400yds from the Port when the planes came in, and the Troops resumed their advance after the smoke thickened in the artillery's screen. Passing through the streets west of the harbour, they turned left up a track by the seawall and were just where the houses ended and the cliff-top slopes began when they met barbed wire. Bangalore torpedoes with 12-second fuses cut a path through this, and the Marines were soon out on the exposed hill side, in clear view of Germans in trenches above them and two German flak ships in the harbour.

Nos 3 and 4 Sections on the right of the track moving up the cliff edge took many casualties, but No.2 Section on the left suffered most heavily. No.1 Section – Lieutenant Goldstein, Sergeant Fletcher and Corporal Amos with some twelve Marines – scrambled on beside the track to a second line of wire, the Lieutenant and Sergeant squeezed through a gap they made, and the Section quickly followed. But heavy fire from a German machine gun, which a 36-grenade failed to silence, fell on the Section. Grenades wounded the Lieutenant, the Sergeant was hit, and A Troop became disorganised. Captain T. F. Cousins led what men he could find back to the church in the town. Lieutenant Goldstein, recovering from his wounds – 'found himself alone'.[6] He moved back down the slope, found five men (three of whom were wounded), and as they made their way towards the church, came on half a dozen Germans. Fortunately the Marines got 'their blow in first'. By this time the Lieutenant was faint from loss of blood and was carried into a house, where a Frenchwoman looked after him. Throughout the coming battles these French civilians took great care of wounded commandos despite the risks as bullets and heavier fire fell on their homes.

X Troop, after the air attacks, had reached a point 200yds from the 'weapon pits', by using the cover of hedgerows. Two sections then attacked some billets near these gun pits and 19 Germans surrendered. On being interrogated by the German-speaking sergeant attached to the Troop from 10 (Inter-Allied) Commando, the prisoners revealed that no one else was in these positions. So X Troop moved into the Port. On their way the Marines met an American officer in a jeep, about 1745 hours, the commandos' first contact with US 1 Division. The Troop OC, Captain D. H. Walton, then decided to follow A Troop up the 'western' feature but saw the flak ships. By this time his support Sections – two 2-in mortar crews and two snipers – had gathered in some extra men. They were armed with four Brens, a captured MG34, a Piat, another 2-in mortar, and had been joined by two more snipers. This healthy support fire did not go into action, however, for Captain Walton, believing the 'western' feature was held by A Troop, was further misinformed by a Marine that the flak ships were held by commandos. The Troop, therefore, moved back, as it was dusk, and took up defensive positions around the main crossroads south of the Port. They would be in action later.

B Troop had followed A Troop after the afternoon's fire-fight and reached the inner basin without being fired on. Their interpreter from '10 (I-A)' then went forward when the first 10 Germans were seen, and persuaded them to surrender. They were being interrogated when machine guns opened fire, seemingly from all directions. The Marines dived for cover in the houses but one man lay dead in the street, before Nos 6 and 8 Sections were sent to the right, but they were not able to make much progress. Meanwhile Colonel Phillips had come into the Port in a tracked carrier, and left the four recce carriers of 50 Division – which had turned up again after refuelling – by the Commando's kit dump, with a carrier detachment of the Devons. He moved Q Troop into the town about 1700 hours from its defence positions in the wood west of Point 72, to support B Troop's attack on the 'eastern' feature after they had first neutralised the flak ships. Just short of the church, however, Q Troop came under machine gun fire and it took time to work its way to the harbour through back-gardens and yards, but most of the Sections reached houses overlooking the south-west end of the inner basin.

Captain Cousins, having brought the survivors of A Troop off the 'western' feature, led a reconnaissance of the 'eastern' feature, gathering on his way from the church some scattered parties, including a lieutenant and sergeant of B Troop's Nos 6 and 8 Sections, who were somewhat disorganised. Once a Section has been split up by the men taking cover in different houses, getting control of it again proved difficult. The Captain, two Lieutenants, three NCOs and seven Marines followed a zig-zag path up the 'eastern' slope. Although the path was not mined, they came under fire at the bends where the otherwise steep banks gave less cover. They were within 20yds of the flat top of this hill, when heavy fire forced them to withdraw behind their own smoke screen. Cousins reported back to the Colonel: 'If you can give me 24 or 25 men, I'm quite certain I can get to the top'.[7]

Fire support was arranged – by means of the Recce and Devons' carriers with Brens mounted in them, along with Y Troop – who had been called to the Port. Y Troop, however, was under attack, as was the Commando's rear HQ near Point 72. The Colonel had lost contact with the Heavy Weapons Troops in the early evening, but the medium machine gun Section had made its own way to the Port, and also covered the final assault on the 'eastern' feature until it was too dark to distinguish the commandos from the enemy.

The 'self-propelled Brens', 2-in mortars laying accurate smoke cover, and Brens of X Troop in houses near a cemetery below the 'eastern' feature, all gave supporting fire as A Troop led off up the zig-zag path. They were followed by the two Sections of Q Troop. They tossed a few No.77 smoke grenades for cover but no fire came from the crest, nor from the flak ships. There were some delays and it was getting dark before they reached the top of the path and formed a skirmish line. A great shout, heard down by the harbour at 2220 hours, went up as the Marines charged the crest and broke on to the plateau. Captain Cousins then fired a red Very light, the signal for A Troop to wheel left towards the sea and Q Troop to wheel to the right. Sub-Sections of A Troop each dealt with several concrete pillboxes, lobbing grenades and firing Tommy guns through the slits. The Troop had regrouped before it reached the seaward end of the defences – this was a coast battery site – where the men were silhouetted on the cliff top and several hit. Ordering them into empty German slit trenches, Captain Cousins went forward down the cliff path with a Bren-gunner and three men. Those behind the crest could hear this party – the rip of Schmeisser and the deeper but rapid thuds of Tommy guns – in an exchange of fire. There were shouts of 'Kamerad' and Captain Cousins's shouted orders. Then a silence. The A Troop followed the Captain down the path. He was dead, killed by a grenade, and others of his party were wounded. The Germans, however, had surrendered.[8]

Q Troop, having wheeled right, cleared 100yds of the site, firing from the hip as they went. By now it was too dark to see mines or trip wires, but they took the surrender of an *oberleutnant* and seven men. The German officer spoke good English and was persuaded to go further along the site perimeter, ordering Germans hereabouts to surrender, before the process was repeated in the pitch dark for 600yds along the cliff top.

During the early evening the destroyer HMS *Ursa* and the Polish ORP *Krakowiak* had been some 700yds off the harbour entrance. They had seen men of Q Troop on the west mole moving to clear its seaward strongpoint. The destroyer, using her loud-hailer (bullhorn), warned the commandos: 'Attention Royal Marines! There are enemy behind you.' The ships were fired on and mortared, but as the tide came in, they closed to within 300yds of the west mole and fired into one flak ship's bridge. They then sent away two armed motorboats, crashed the boom and came into the harbour. There they saw two flak ships, not one, but found them abandoned except for a dog and the bodies of three Germans. Marines heard the swearing of one boat's crew and signalled by lamp – it was now dark – 'British here' from the houses by the harbour.

Firing from the 'western' feature had stopped by this time, but Germans had overrun Y Troop in the area of the base dump west of Point 72 and the Rear HQ in the wood east of it. Despite a spirited resistance by this rear party – two of its Marines from the Intelligence Section manning a German MG34 – a company of Germans cleared Point 72 and were in the wood to the east of it. Thinking at first that they might be Americans, the rear party in the wood had held their fire, then – realising they were Germans – they held it until the leading 8-man point Section was in range for a clear shot in the dusk. The attack stalled, a flanking move was halted, and German star shells lit the positions. The HQ documents were deliberately burnt and radios turned off the Commando's frequency, in case the HQ was overrun. More than 30 Germans came towards the wood as the flares guttered out. They were allowed to reach a point 40yds from the Marines' slit trenches, then every weapon the rear party had – some dozen rifles and a Bren or two – opened fire. The Germans still came on, and when they were 10yds from the slit trenches, the Marines threw a couple of smoke grenades and slipped away into the woods. Some reached the Colonel about 2330, but several others were casualties.

While the Rear HQ was fighting its little battle, Y Troop – down the hill at the stores dump and its nearby orchard – had been pushed eastward when enemy fire intensified at dusk. One Section moved north, however, and took up a position for the night outside Escures, while the remainder of the Troop – thinking the Port was surrounded by the amount of German activity west of Escures – moved eastward in a night march to Brigade HQ. Two Marine stretcher bearers and two RAMC lance-corporals slept in the bunker by the Commando's dump. This dugout they were using as a Regimental Aid Post to tend the wounded but it was not searched when the Germans overran Point 72. To the stretcher party's surprise, when they emerged, the kit had been pillaged but the dump was deserted. A gendarme appeared and all five set off on bicycles for the Port. Along the road they were captured, and found some 300 German cycle troops and a self-propelled gun in Fosse Soucy. Next day the stretcher-bearers were released by Americans who attacked the German cycle company six miles south-west of Fosse Soucy, as the Germans moved inland.

A number of individual Army commandos and Army units were attached to '47 RM' during the Port-en-Bessin and later operations. These soldiers and gun-ners came or would come from seventeen different regiments including the Irish Guards, the Buffs, the South Lancs, the Highland Light Infantry, Kings Own Yorkshire Light Infantry, and the Welch Regiment.

Near the Port on D+2, Corporal Amos, who was also a prisoner on the 'western' feature, was awoken at 0400 hours by his captors. They wanted to surrender and he led 23 Germans into the Port. The harbour was already in use and over 1,000 tons of supplies a day would soon be coming over its quay. The commandos also found Point 72 had been evacuated and spent some hours clearing up the dumps.[9] With a touch of nostalgia for some commandos, no doubt, the old paddle-steamer *Golden Eagle* later came into the harbour to land reinforcements.

D+1 for 48 RM Commando had been a morning of continued attacks, aided by three tanks – one from the RM Armoured Support Group – clearing Langrune. As the Allied armies were streaming inland from the beach exits, the beachhead by now was some 5 miles deep in many places. The Marines of '41 RM', with the help of two RM tanks, contained the garrison of the Douvres Radar Station, one of the most heavily fortified areas on the coast; and '45 RM' was dug in near the Merville battery, where two heavy German counter-attacks were driven off despite shelling and mortar fire, which became more intense as the morning passed. More German troops had linked up with those bypassed at Sallenelles, and by 1700 hours the Commando was ordered to fight its way back to the Amfreville area, where the 1st Special Service Brigade had firmly established itself. It took three hours to effect the breakout, in which two medium machine guns and a heavy mortar were captured.[10]

As 46 RM Commando, under Lieutenant-Colonel C. R. Hardy, came ashore on D+1, the men exchanged their pistols and demolition charges for more usual battle loads, and by midday were moving to their start line for an attack on the coastal strongpoint of fortified houses facing the sea at Petit Enfer. This seaside village, three-quarters of a mile east of Langrune, overlooked the landing beaches of 'Sword' some 1½ miles further east of it. The village merged into Luc-sur-Mer just to the south. To seaward were offshore rock reefs, which on this stretch of coast had prevented any assault craft landing along the beaches for 5½ miles from Lion-sur-Mer to Bernières. Naval bombardment kept the enemy's heads down in the strongpoint, which was 400yds long and 150yds deep, an area for which some reconnaissance was needed before the final attack. Therefore A and B Troops secured several observation points on the western rim of these defences, while the bombardment covered their movement. From these OPs the western defence system was seen to centre on an anti-tank gun, protecting the seafront houses and pillboxes. There were also a minefield, wire and a trench system on the east side of the strongpoint. The next phase of the attack was timed so that B Troop, followed by an RM tank, drew the enemy's fire, enabling A Troop to clear the way for another RM tank behind them to get a clear shot at the anti-tank gun, which was destroyed. B Troop then gave covering fire from the south while A Troop cut its way through the wire and gained a foothold in houses overlooking the sea, from which the Troop worked their way into the strongpoint and by 1830 hours had taken 65 prisoners, from the German 716 Division.[11]

Also during D+1 the Naval Communications Parties began to improve the telephone and radio links ashore, the signallers of the RM party at Courseulles being responsible, among other things, for all naval telephone systems in the beachheads. There would be eight Naval Communication Parties operating in north-west Europe – two entirely manned by Royal Marines and the other six with RN and RM personnel – all eight coming under the title of Party 'Funshore'.[12] They were one of the three principal types of Naval landing party. The second were personnel of the shore bases with each Assault Force; in these, for example, Force J's RM units included the Communications Party at Courseulles.[13] Thirdly there were the Naval Port Parties, with Marines to provide air defence, help man the operations rooms, clear mines, including those in harbours, and provide transport.[14] Of these parties, one – Naval Party 1500 – was preparing to land at Arromanches on D+2, when instructions to land all Royal Marines with as much small arms ammunition as possible were given.

The men came ashore at 1500 hours to take up defensive positions against an expected German thrust from the west towards 'Gold' beach. That night Marine patrols went out but made no contact with the enemy. Their work, like that of the Provost Company and other RM parties, was stretched far beyond their intended roles; for these Marines of the Port Parties would pump-out landing craft, feed LC crews, purify water and run virtually all the routines of the Naval camps in the beach areas. They would be helped by elements of the RM Engineers in adapting slipways, making diving surveys and clearing mines from harbours,[15] a job in which an RM LCP(L) flotilla used mini-paravanes. The shallow-water RM divers with Naval Party 1500 found such work more hazardous than collecting three buckets of golf balls from a pond in Hadley Wood golf course, one of their training areas.[16] (Some more formal aspects of these parties are set out in the Appendix 4.)

By the time these parties began operating in their full roles, the beachhead was largely secured, and the first blockship 'Gooseberry' breakwaters were in position. Some of these provided accommodation for HQs of RM minor landing craft squadrons, each of a dozen or so men. At least one flotilla officer was killed[17] and there were a number of casualties among these ferry crews in air raids and shelling of the anchorages. Ashore the casualties were still mounting, and on D+5 46 RM Commando fought one of the roughest battles in the beachhead. Under the command of 3 Canadian Division, '46 RM' was given the task of clearing the Mue valley. The Mue River flows into the sea at Courseulles, and five miles inland the valley floor is that combination of orchards, small fields and shoulder-high steep banks topped by hedgerows known as the *Bocage*, where a tank could be ambushed in a bank-sided lane, and a man had good cover from enemy fire and from view. To the west of this valley runs higher ground of open cornfields with little or no other cover.

On 11 June the plan was for tanks of A Squadron of 10th (Canadian) Armoured Regiment and a Troop of RM tanks to move down the open right flank, while the Commando and men of the Chauds (*le Régiment de la Chaudière*) of Canada cleared the valley. A company of machine-gunners would later take up positions on the hill west of the village of Cairon; and also in support was a field artillery regiment with 75-mm guns.[18] The line of advance was from Barbière to Cairon, moving south up the valley, further south and across the valley to Rosel, and then a further 2 miles to take two villages: Le Hamel (not to be confused with the coastal strongpoint) and Rots. By 1100 hours the Commando had cleared the woods between Barbière and Cairon, taking eight prisoners. The Chauds had occupied this village, but fire from a 105-mm gun up the valley at Rosel delayed the attack on that village until 1320 hours. Two artillery concentrations and the machine gun company's fire covered X and Y Troops' advance first to clear Lasson and then Rosel, an advance closely supported by the tanks firing from the western hill side into the *Bocage* and woods ahead of the assaulting Troops. There was little response from the enemy and Rosel was secured by mid-afternoon, although no trace was found of the 105-mm gun, which must have withdrawn.

The final phase of the attack was meticulously planned to make the best use of co-ordinated tank and artillery support. The A and B Troops occupied the west bank woods just short of Le Hamel, while artillery fire on Rots covered their movement. From these new positions the two Troops engaged in a fire-fight with Germans on the left of the assaulting Troops, drawing considerable fire that otherwise would have enfiladed the assault. Tanks on the high ground also moved to positions where they could 'shoot' Y and S Troops into Le Hamel after a concentration of artillery fire on this village. Y and S Troops closed to within 150yds of this barrage and formed a line in the waist-high corn.

'The tanks plastered the houses beyond the cornfield, with their 6-pdrs and Besa machine guns',[19] from positions hull down in a re-entrant fold in the hill side. Y and S Troops then moved forward steadily in line abreast and were some 200yds from the village when five machine guns opened fire on them. At such a moment the urge to hit the ground is almost overwhelming, but the young Marines kept on, firing from the hip. There were two hedges to get through, the first one 30yds from the German weapon pits. As the Marines broke through it, the Germans flung grenades before smartly moving back to defended houses in the village. A number were cut down as they withdrew before Y Troop's continued advance towards strongpoints in houses at the north-east corner of the village, as S Troop on the left was making for the road through the village.

These Germans, men of the 26th Panzer Grenadiers (12 SS Hitler Jugend Division) were well-trained, determined troops, not to be shaken from their hold on the village without battling for every house and each yard of garden. For two hours the commandos edged their way through Le Hamel. The men moved in pairs well apart, dodging from door to door, while a well-sited Bren group gave them covering fire until a street was cleared and this support group could move forward. At times a white Very light fired at a low angle towards a house marked it for the tanks. A few rounds then shifted the defenders, and the commandos found that if they 'could get a tank close in, we could shift the enemy out of the most strongly defended houses'.[20] Two 88-mm guns which might have knocked out the tanks were put out of action, probably by artillery fire. The strongpoints in fields west of the village proved more difficult to clear; they were well camouflaged in open fields, their defenders lying low as tanks passed, then opening fire on the commandos once these supporting tanks had moved away. Nevertheless, the enemy was forced out of Le Hamel. Meanwhile A and B Troops were putting in an attack on Rots.

The A and B Troops had moved off the western hill, once the other commandos were in Le Hamel and clearly going to make progress for 'one felt we were on top, dominating the enemy and with our superior material support dictating to him the terms on which the battle was to be fought', in the words of the Major leading Y and S Troops.[21] A and B Troops crossed the river bridge and, led by a Troop of tanks, followed behind an artillery barrage on Rots. The leading Section of A Troop had reached the crossroads in the centre of the village when the first of two Panther tanks came round a corner 20yds away, killing most of the leading sub-Section. The Shermans' 6-pdrs were no match for these Panthers' 88-mm guns, and in a tank versus tank battle two Shermans had been knocked out before a 17-pdr Firefly Sherman arrived. B Troop meanwhile had reached the edge of the village and were under fire from behind (to the north) and both flanks. The men endeavoured to fight their way across the open ground to the east in encircling the village but took heavy casualties. Their attempt, however, and the arrival of X and Z Troops, caused the enemy to begin to withdraw; the 17-pdr Sherman and other tanks then destroyed the Panthers and took a heavy toll of the retreating infantry.

Le Hamel that night 'was a city of the dead; not a soul was to be seen and only distant firing broke the silent night; a burning tank added a further flicker to the pale moonlight',[22] as the commandos prepared for a counter-attack. About

0400 hours that 12 June a company of the Chauds with carriers and anti-tank guns arrived, but progress on the commandos' flanks by other elements of the 3 Canadian Division had made only limited gains – the commandos and the Shermans had come 7 miles – and in view of their isolation the Division withdrew '46 RM' along with the remaining tanks and the Chauds.

Casualties in '46 RM' had been 20 killed, 9 wounded and 31 missing, the last mostly from 'B' Troop, many of whom had been wounded and captured. The losses might have been greater, but the German machine gunners had held their fire until A Troop was 100yds off, then the Germans had fired high 'owing to the corn'.[23] Such casualties in all the Commandos had been difficult to estimate in the scattered fighting up to D+1, but '47 RM' had lost over 200 men killed and wounded in taking Port-en-Bessin, '48 RM' had lost some 220 all ranks by D+5;[24] '41 RM' had lost its second-in-command and the RSM on landing, and Lieutenant-Colonel T. M. Gray, with other officers were wounded by one of the few German bombs dropped on D-Day.[25] Almost all the Commando Colonels had been wounded. By mid-August, when the Commando Brigades moved forward from the Orne line, the RM Commandos had lost some 50 per cent or more of the Marines who had landed on D-Day.[26] Their defensive role as line infantry was not one for which commandos were equipped, but by aggressive patrolling and steadiness under repeated mortaring, artillery and infantry attacks the young Marines were forged into a formidable force. In the first few weeks some lacked, perhaps, the spirit of the older Army commandos – 'bold lads who joined up for the hell of it and the roving life'.[27] Yet after a few fighting patrols and some days in the Orne defences boys became men, ageing beyond their years.

The Orne line, as mentioned earlier, was at first a series of defended areas running along a low ridge of hills east of the canal and river. Woods and orchards were liberally spread around the slopes, which at the seaward (north) end overlooked the marshy ground stretching to the Dives River. Franceville Plage, the original objective of '45 Cdo RM' on D-Day, was a summer resort, where the coast road turned north, skirting the Orne estuary to pass through the resort of Sallenelles. Here a fork in the road led due south up the hill through Hauger and Le Plain (a key village on relatively high ground) to Amfreville and Breville. Back on the coast near the outskirts of Franceville Plage was Merville, where '45 RM' had been halted on D-Day. By D+3 the 1st Commando Brigade had been forced into a tighter perimeter, and when '45 RM' fell back from northern positions, 4 (Army) Commando restored part of the line with a fierce attack across recently lost slit trenches. But after this D Troop of 'No.4' was only 15 strong.

The men were red-eyed with tiredness: a man lying back in the next few days would fall asleep in the middle of a conversation. They held on with the help of Naval fire support, well-dug weapon pits roofed over against mortar and air-burst HE, and above all the Brigade's experienced Army commandos' ability to hold their fire and catch advancing troops unawares. On D+4 6 (Army) Commando did this, allowing advancing infantry over a hill crest into an orchard, where the Commando had a killing ground; and 6 Airborne Division held the southern end of the line with equal skill. About D+10 4 Commando Brigade came into this line, and took over positions around Hauger. Few of the commandos of the two Brigades will forget the next 2 months – the raiding and counter-raiding, the stench of dead cattle, the smell of Camembert cheese, which comes from this district – and some may remember the new G Mk III tracer, which ignited 100yds from the gun firing it.[28] Out of all the memories, those of night raids could be among the sharpest.

A night raid mounted by 45 RM Commando on German platoon positions on the western edge of a wood, was made by Lieutenant E. H. Thomas with 20 NCOs and Marines from a 'firm' base. This was held by a sub-Section (an officer and 15 men) and advanced Troop HQ, signals and the artillery FOO. They were positioned in an orchard on the road passing Longuemare, some 700yds east of Amfreville. From this point the road snaked eastward to a crossroads, beyond which stretched open fields to a wooded area where the Germans had positions. At 0245 hours the base party was in position and a covering party – two officers, 20 men including a signaller and two medics – moved through the start line to a position by the crossroads where they would be able to cover the raiders' withdrawal. From these positions some 400yds from the Germans, the 21 raiders crossed the road and moved into a field of high corn. In this it was difficult to keep in contact with the man next to you, and so Lieutenant E. H. Thomas led them along a hedgerow beside the field for several hundred yards, before they fanned out to 'beat' the ground in front of the German positions. Soon they came across well-prepared wire defences, which they skirted until they came to a lane and two houses. The commandos tossed grenades through the windows, as they nipped past the houses and began working their way through dugouts and fox-holes, firing their Tommy guns. Two concrete strongpoints were also cleared, when 'a generous supply of grenades were fed through the apertures'.[29]

Having cleared their objective with time in hand – it had taken some 30 minutes from leaving the cover party to clear 16 weapon pits and the two strong-points – the Lieutenant fired a green Very light, to signal that he was going forward into the wood behind these positions. Here there were some damaged and two undamaged buildings and a truck. The undamaged buildings were set on fire, as was the truck. German voices could be heard nearby and those Germans who had been in the next forward defended area came to life. But they were not expecting Marines to be coming from behind them and a sentry's call of 'Muller?' was answered by a bullet. German grenades and rifle fire erupted all round the positions, but in the dark it was wild and inaccurate as the raiders slipped away into the cornfield. They suffered three casualties, but all were brought out, and 50 minutes after setting out on the raid they were back with the covering party.[30] The general practice was to keep away from hedgerows at night to avoid fixed (pre-set) lines of machine gun fire and the noise of breaking twigs – the reasons '45 (RM)'s' patrol first moved into the cornfield. They were lucky perhaps; but they succeeded through another golden rule of night patrols, by keeping together. They had a specific objective and had not wandered aimlessly trying to 'dominate an area'.

In the Orne line the Marine commandos learnt to cope with German snipers, but as one commando sniper remarked of the enemy: 'It isn't right to regard every mediocre rifleman the Germans leave behind, as a trained sniper.' The true German snipers showed lots of ingenuity – one house had a chalked notice on the door that read, 'Danger – booby traps. Do not enter', and it was D+10 before an English-speaking German sniper was discovered upstairs. The commando snipers worked in pairs, and often were transferred from their Troops to the central control of a Commando HQ. They worked in all weathers, a few pieces of wire and a square foot or so of rubber making an umbrella for the sight, and armourers gave the snipers' rifles special attention.[31] The men knew the ground in front of each Commando's position, having crawled over this ground to find good positions nearly always at some height in trees, in buildings or even standing upright in bushes. From such positions they fired usually at 300 to 400yds. They killed several soldiers using a latrine before the Germans realised they were being observed. Most snipers only rejoined their Troops from the central sniper control when these moved forward in August. Snipers and reconnaissance patrols – usually an officer and three men – learnt to shuffle slowly through the grass under orchard trees, so as not to send up a flock of birds; and when a cow shambled over with loud 'Moos' to lick the Marine hiding on the edge of a field, 'the only solution was to lie on one's back and milk the damn thing'.[32] The 346th Fusilier Battalion, opposite '41 RM's' positions, was their 'pet German unit', which had been prodded and probed by '41 RM's' patrols;[33] 46, 47 and 48 RM Commandos had all done their share of such work before the Germans began to withdraw on 18 August. The Commandos would follow them, and some of their actions later in North West Europe are explained in detail in the next chapter and Appendix 4.

The Troops (or Sections as they were at first called) of RM Engineer Commandos with the 1st and 4 Special Service (Commando) Brigades were assault engineers. They also were the only commandos with sleeping bags, which is perhaps not surprising, for RE Commandos in the 1990s were renowned for the comfort of their snow-holes in Norway. During D-Day the 39-man Section with 1st Commando Brigade was to demolish bridges at Franceville Plage and Garneville (east of Sallenelles), but neither was captured because of the Germans' defences. These engineers and those of the 2nd Section with 4 Brigade, therefore, laid defensive minefields and other devices in front of the Commandos' positions. These 'other devices' included bangalore torpedoes buried where German patrols were expected, and later triggered off with spectacular success.[34] The Marine commando engineers also cleared German anti-tank minefields in preparation for the breakout. First they looked for the pair of S-mines each in a small wooden box, making them difficult to locate with a mine detector. They were laid with their trip wires to fire a canister of lethal steel balls waist high over an area of 100yds, if the engineer was careless. With these anti-personnel mines made safe, the first few anti-tank mines could be lifted and the pattern of the field paced out, and then the rest were lifted quickly. On the design of defensive positions, these engineers had few equals, one 'huge hole near Troarn . . . covered well with

sandbags reinforced with steel girders, [had lights powered by] a battery from
... a crashed Spitfire', which the Signals Troop charged up when required.

Despite their efficient use of kit, these Sappers did not have rubber soled
boots until later, and the metal studs of their leather ones were apt to make a
noise that could attract unwanted attention on patrols.

During this high summer and from the early days of the invasion the capital
ships had refuelled and re-ammunitioned and had come back to the anchorage.
HMS *Warspite* had supported the 'Utah' force on 10 June, and the next day she
broke up enemy concentrations behind 'Gold'. The cruisers had also made a
major contribution to this fire support, by 14 June, for example, *Belfast* had fired
almost 2,000 rounds and *Diadem* 1,748 (her main gun barrels were worn out
before the end of the month). 'The effects of heavy Naval bombardment are so
powerful that an operation with ... infantry or armoured formations is impossible in an area commanded by this rapid firing artillery,' Rommel reported.[35] The
area commanded was vast. *Nelson* and *Rodney* had been held in reserve but fired
more than 900 rounds between 11 and 18 June, including one shoot by *Rodney*
that annihilated a concentration of tanks 17 miles inland from 'Gold' beach.[36]
During this week the first flying-bomb V1s had begun to fall on England, but
only stray ones fell on the anchorage. More serious was a summer gale which
blew up in the early hours of D+12 (19 June). Six foot waves swept the anchorage,
and before the gale blew itself out three days later, many craft had been lost and
the protective floating breakwater of the Americans' 'Mulberry' harbour was
destroyed. During this storm LCF 1 had sheltered behind a 'Gooseberry' breakwater; she and some 45 other support craft survived the storms, the shelling from
Le Havre and German air attacks, to form the Support Squadron Eastern Flank.
They and heavier ships, like the monitor HMS *Roberts*, supported the Army by
day and the Support Craft also provided a protective inshore screen for the
anchorages at night. About dawn on 17 August LCF I was hit 'amidships by a
torpedo and literally blown out of the water'. There were a few survivors, and,
after being in the water some time, they were picked up by two motor launches
– 'one boat returned the fire from the cliff top, the other boat picked us [the
survivors] out of the water drenched in oil'.[37]

The cruisers and destroyers were to be in action that August and early
September with three Naval Forces in the Bay of Biscay. Typically Force 28 –
which included the light cruiser HMS *Diadem* – made six sorties. During these
Diadem was attacked by a glider-bomb, she shelled a ship which destroyed mines
(*Sperrborecher No. 7*) off La Rochelle before this mine-hunter was torpedoed by
the Polish destroyer *Piorun* of Force 28. The Force went on to bombard four
coast batteries near St Jean de Luz and landed arms for the Free French Maquis.
The attacks near and on the Biscay coast had continued through August at a
time when General Patton's US army was sweeping eastward towards Paris.

The minor landing craft were worn out after the pounding of summer storms.
The constant battering they took alongside ships and on the beaches in their
ferry work of several months took its toll of seams and joints, and on occasions
caused heavier damage to hulls. A bulldozer might give the craft too heavy a

shove after it was grounded on the beach. At other times a nudge from a 3-ton truck might push a craft off, for although the crews were trained to drop a kedge anchor as they came in – and might later haul the craft out to it – this practice proved of doubtful benefit. All these bumps took their toll. Kedges were not used in the assault, although they had proved useful for clearing obstacles, 'and when the obstacle astern has a tellermine on it!'[38] The minor craft flotillas' engineers, the engineer repair shops in special major craft, and the beach *transport* maintenance teams, all played their part in keeping the craft operational. But eventually many succumbed to the conditions and were towed home behind LCTs, or the unserviceable ones were taken aboard landing ships. F Squadron was reduced to three flotillas, with the most serviceable craft being kept from all six. Those craft likely to make the passage to the UK were gathered together in 601 Flotilla and sailed on 21 July, but in fog off the French coast their LCT escort lost them. As so often happens in the Channel, the fog cleared and a sudden storm blew up. The craft foundered one by one, each crew and other survivors being taken aboard its neighbour. One craft sank with only a sergeant surviving, when he was picked up by an MTB.[39] Only five craft out of 16 survived the crossing and 32 all ranks were drowned

The trucks with Naval Port Parties were run with strict supervision of their maintenance, no RM truck was off the road for more than a day.[40] The RM crews of the boat company with Naval Party 1500 – they had 23 launches and motorboats – with a few seamen, suffered many hardships in the rough weather. They were used as berthing boats, taking ships and craft's lines alongside 'Mulberry' quays, and in the small harbours they acted as despatch and work boats.

The 'Mulberry' at Arromanches was still in use to a limited extent during October and November, but in the next few months the Port Parties would be regrouped. The Communication Parties were regrouped also, and by November these signallers were in 20 cities and towns throughout France, Belgium and Holland.[41] For example, before 4 September the Royal Marines of Naval Party 1501 entered Antwerp; they had followed closely behind 11 Armoured Division's thrust north, travelling from Arromanches in a drive of some 250 miles, and 'stopping their engines only to rig their masts' to report their position periodically.[42] The Communications Party with the Allied Naval Forces' headquarters at Rouen (Seine-Maritime), which had moved there from Courseulles, was provided with telephone, wireless and other networks by RM Signallers. Their despatch riders would travel almost daily to Brussels (220 miles), Arromanches (120 miles), Cherbourg (200 miles) and other long journeys, when they were often the first to report isolated German resistance. The linesmen found many German telephone networks which could be used with little difficulty, as these had been noted from aerial photographs; but the technical equipment in the U-boat headquarters at Rouen had been partially destroyed and RM Signallers 'had a ticklish job . . . sorting out . . . the cable head'. These and other signallers were eventually moved to Antwerp, where, in the early days, the main Naval Communications Centre was only 800yds from the enemy. By November the Centre was the largest in the command of Allied Naval Command of Expeditionary Force (ANCXF), with 78 per cent of its personnel from the Corps.[43] Their work is explained in the next chapter.

The RM Provost Company had landed with the assault forces, and since then had directed traffic on the beaches, patrolled to counter looters, and inspected the records of 700 prostitutes in Rouen – perhaps not a routine chore but necessary to keep down disease. The redcaps had to do more than was originally allowed for in the plans for routine military police work: running POW camps, making security checks, preventing pilfering, providing VIP motorcycle escorts, assisting stray French children; and one once acting as midwives.[44] They rounded up arms and ammunition, liberated 4,000 cases of Benedictine and had a 'patch' – as policemen call their district – from Cherbourg to the Dutch frontier. A large area for 144 policemen. Perhaps one of their greatest achievements was the off-duty patrols which they made with Army redcaps to prevent the pilfering of petrol from the pipelines run forward to supply points. The losses dropped from 33,000 gallons a week to almost nothing.[45]

The Royal Marine Engineers (RME) cleared harbours, sent divers to survey wrecks, used bulldozers to haul small blockships upright, put up the 105-ft radar towers at Courseulles. Each tower was 15ft wide at its base, 3ft wide at the top and prefabricated in America. They worked with Naval salvage teams to raise the 10,000-ton whale-oil ship sunk to block the Seine, mixing 300 tons of concrete in 30 hours with only 46 men, and none of the 1990s style of automated equipment. Typical of harbour clearing work was that done in Rouen's Bassin aux Bois, where 24 small ships of some 500 tons each were cleared from the 800-yard by 100-yard basin. Here, as elsewhere, a variety of mines had to be made safe, and the debris of burnt-out tanks, field transport and the jetsam of war to be bulldozed from the quays.[46] The live ammunition in many of these vehicles made this more dangerous than it may sound; and it was not a job for the squeamish, as there were many dismembered bodies. The work was epitomised for one RME crew by the four burnt chicken carcases alongside the burnt bodies of the German tank crew who had caught them.

In the Normandy landings and the subsequent battles through North West Europe, Royal Marines successfully carried out a wider range of jobs, many of them highly specialised, than they had ever been called on to fulfil before 1944. Maybe they will never be called on again to meet such a variety of challenges, yet military history shows that in all major conflicts new techniques evolve and often the scenes of major battles – as has been said – are fought in localities with terrain very different from that for which armies have trained. Yet Royal Marines, by the nature of their training and experience in the 1920s and 1930s, were able to adapt to new demands in 1944, as they had done in 1914 and 1804 and would do again should this be necessary. They were also in action in the Mediterranean and Burma in the year of the Normandy campaign, indeed 'I met 'im all over the world, a-doin' all kinds of things'.[47] In 1943 just what he was to be doing in the coming Far East campaigns was already being broadly planned, as the strategies were developed for the British participation in the invasion of Japan. This was to be based on first eliminating the Japanese forces from Burma and then Malaya, although in the spring of 1944 alternative strategies had been considered, and plans made for advanced Naval bases to support a thrust north-ward from Australia.[48]

For the longer term, Air Marshal Sir Norman Bottomley's committee, which included Lieutenant General Sir Thomas L. Hunton, General Officer Command-ing Royal Marines, made recommendations on inter-service responsibilities for future amphibious warfare organisation.[49] Sir Norman had chaired the 1943 committee which had recommended changes in the organisation of Combined Operations and its headquarters. In June 1944 his committee's terms of reference were:

> To consider future Inter-Service responsibilities for amphibious war-fare with particular reference to the employment of the Royal Marines; it being recognised that the retention of a Combined Service element on the lines of that already existing in COHQ will be essential to any future amphibious warfare organisation.

Their recommendations included the retention of a Central Organisation, inde-pendent of the three Service ministries but inter-service in character, broadly on the lines of the Combined Operations Headquarters of the period, for 'we cannot afford to rely on improvisation in the event of war'. They envisaged a Ministry of Defence perpetuated after the war, to which the central amphibious organisa-tion would be responsible, with its facilities to train one Army division a year. Although they considered 'a standing specialist [amphibious] assault force is . . . not required . . . effective combined training in peace can only be assured if there are available certain specialist units under the control of CCO [Chief of Combined Operations] and a permanent assault force under Admiralty control but available to CCO during the training season'.[50] They suggested that 'the Royal Marines should find the greater part of the specialists . . . under CCO's control'. The scheme would require some 8,000 Marines – 1,070 in a Commando group, 900 in training bases, 3,000 manning minor landing craft, and 3,000 providing two Beach Groups each with an RM infantry battalion as its nucleus. The Army specialists of REs, RASC, RAOC and REME personnel totalled some 3,800, the Navy would provide 14,000 men principally for the major craft's and LSI's crews, and there would be 300 RAF personnel for fighter direction and liaison units of the assault force.

If the proposals were accepted, those affecting the Royal Marines were to be implemented as soon as possible without waiting until the end of the war, but the timing was to depend on the strategic situation.[51] This in turn would be governed by political situations which were to develop in a substantial reduction of Allied peacetime commitments in the Far East, as explained later. Meanwhile there were many battles to be fought after June 1944 before final victory. In many of these, the Marines would be fighting a type of war for which they were fitted by tradition and training.

7 ISLANDS, RIVERS AND JUNGLE WARFARE

The heavy casualties suffered by both Army and RM Commandos during their operations in southern Italy in September 1943 left them substantially below strength. For example, '40 RM' was over 100 men below its war Establishment of 450.[1] But after a few weeks of rest and re-organisation '40 RM' with 3 (Army) Commando were landed in a right-hook at Termoli on the west bank of the Biferno river, where the Germans early in October might have formed a defensive line to hold the British XIII Corps, now switched to the Italian east coast. This landing had been planned by Lieutenant-Colonel John Durnford-Slater, DSO, RA, commanding '3 Cdo', with a practised simplicity, for the commandos were brought to the beaches by the 22nd LCI(L) Flotilla's four LCIs and seven LCAs which had been operating with the commandos for many months. The orders, therefore, for the whole operation could be set out on half a sheet of paper in what was the last sizeable commando landing for which such informal – although far from casual – methods were used.[2]

There were some delays in the passage to the beach, however, as craft grounded on unexpected sand bars, the penalty paid for mounting raids perforce rapidly and therefore without adequate beach surveys. But a beachhead was quickly formed, the Marines of 40 RM Commando and the Special Raiding Squadron entering the town at about 0330 hours (Sunday, 3 October 1943) to find that two buildings by the railway station were fiercely defended. One proved to be the German HQ, but 'after close fighting, the resistance was overcome and the defenders killed or captured'.[3]

During the next three days the commandos fought in a battle to hold off elements of the German 16 Panzer Division, as the British intention of holding Termoli with elements of 11 Brigade and the Commandos came under increasing pressure. But the Germans do not appear to have realised that the British hold on the town was precarious, for few tanks and anti-tank guns could be brought across the river and the position was not stabilised until another infantry brigade was landed on Tuesday night.[4]

Then 41 RM and 3 Army Commandos returned to the UK, as 2 Special Service (later Commando) Brigade was formed that November in Italy, with 2 Army and 40 RM Commandos joined by 9 Army Commando from Gibraltar and 43 RM Commando from the UK. The Army Commandos were brought up to strength by volunteers from Army units serving in Italy, but Royal Marine reinforcements came mainly from the UK. Some Marines in the Mediterranean Fleet, however, were exchanged for RM commandos and the return of commandos from North African hospitals brought '40 RM' up to strength by the end of 1943.[5] The commander of 2 Special Service Brigade was Brigadier T. (Tom) B. L. Churchill, an Army staff officer with commando experience. His Headquarters included Army and RM officers and by the summer of 1944 had been strengthened to over 50 personnel for administering the handling of stores, supplies and reinforcement when the Brigade was operating independently in support of Yugoslav partisans in Dalmatia.

Before the Brigade went to the Dalmatian coast it was in action several times in Italy, where in December 1943 it was joined by No.2 Belgian and No.6 Polish Troops of 10 (Inter Allied) Commando. For these actions the various Commandos were attached to Army commands, as was '40 RM', which was under command of X Corps to exploit 167 and 169 Brigades' crossing of the Garigliano river on the Italian west coast in January 1944.[6]

B and Q Troops crossed the river on the night of 14–15 January and followed a white tape laid by 2nd/6th Battalion Queen's Royal Regiment. They followed it for some 700yds until the tape came to an abrupt end; the commandos then suffered three casualties in a minefield as they tried to work their way forward. They also came under fire from a hill which had been one of the Queens' first objectives. But as this was still held by German machine-gunners, the Marines not long before dawn put in a successful attack under covering fire from their own Bren groups, before consolidating a defended position on the hill top. Their patrols made contact with the 2nd/6th Queens and a co-ordinated defence was established. The next night the Commando Troops advanced a further 2,000yds, capturing machine guns and establishing another defended hill top 1½ miles ahead of the main British positions. From this hill they dominated the surrounding country; patrols captured 30 Germans having an evening meal, and located machine gun positions for the artillery to blast, before Army units relieved them after four days.

A, F and X Troops crossed the river on the Monday night (17 January) and No. 5 Platoon of 30 men ('40 RM' called its Sections in the infantry style: Platoons)[7] cleared the enemy from forward slopes of Mont Salvatito, and maintained an artillery Forward Observation Officer in this good OP for the next three days. On Tuesday morning the other Marines mopped up a number of German positions in a series of small but sharp actions. Although they had been under heavy fire frequently since crossing the river, they continued to maintain contact with 8th Battalion Royal Fusiliers of 167 Brigade, and on Wednesday (19 January) the Marines were ordered to infiltrate through German positions to capture the key heights of Mount Rotondo. They were also to interrupt traffic on the road east of this hill, which – with the Rotondo heights secured – would be the Army's main objective in their advance at dawn on Thursday.

Moving in Sections, this large fighting patrol of three Troops led by Captain Marshall, set out at 30-minute intervals. They had to cross rugged hill sides broken by steep crags over which it was hard to keep direction. Nevertheless on Wednesday night they had passed through the German lines by 0500 hours to the valley beyond Monte S Cosmo and below their objective. As they regrouped here, Marshall realised that the planned main attack was not being made that dawn, since the front was quiet. Reconnaissance also suggested that the Marines could not hope to hold the hill top all through Thursday, and Captain Marshall therefore decided to attack traffic on the road. Two civilians, brought in from a commando outpost, gave the Captain a better idea of the lie of land than could be gleaned from maps. With this help the Marines reached the road three-quarters of a mile north-west of Castelforte, which lay east of Rotondo and below the hills where B and Q Troops were operating.

As a guerrilla raid this attack on the road proved most successful: telephone wires were cut, despatch riders killed, two guns destroyed, and a vehicle park attacked. In an exchange of fire with an armoured car, the Marines avoided firing at a Red Cross truck, although it later drove off with a machine gun firing from the back. A road block was started but a Pz Mark IV put a stop to this, although Captain Marshall climbed on to the tank and it was partially set alight by grenades before it withdrew. Three more tanks appeared and the commandos came out along a convenient gulley, before withdrawing that night (20 January) to the main British lines.

During February '40 RM' took its turn as line infantry, demonstrating 'the versatility and quality of these troops in, for them, unusual circumstances'.[8] They would have similar roles in the Anzio beachhead where '43 RM' and 'No 9' had landed unopposed on 22 January.[9] The Army and Marine commandos spent another three weeks in the Anzio line in March, but by then this amphibious left-hook had become a battle of attrition in trench warfare not unlike the battles of World War I.

Elements of 2 Commando Brigade had been sent in January 1944 to Vis, an island off the Dalmatian coast, as part of an Allied force, Force 133, aiding partisans. This Force contained 132 second-generation Yugoslav and Greek Americans of the Office of Strategic Services (OSS) and known in Vis as the US Operations Group.[1] The British had been welcomed with great enthusiasm but relationships deteriorated and the seeds of misunderstandings with the partisans were sown in the first few weeks.[2] For although the British had agreed to provide Marshall Tito's forces with arms, their communist government was not officially recognised.[3] These partisans had been fighting the Germans since 1941; but on the Germans' so-called Sixth Offensive, they had been driven into the mountains and only Vis and Lagosta islands had not been occupied by the Germans in January 1944.[4]

Lieutenant-Colonel Jack Churchill (brother of Brigadier Tom Churchill) was an Army commando officer who had landed at Vaagso (Norway) in 1941 and was renowned for his daring leadership. In a series of raids during early 1944 he was able to bluff the Germans' island garrisons into believing that there were far stronger forces than his 2 (Army) Commando based on Vis.[5] But the partisans could not understand the commandos' methods in detailed planning for raids, which the Yugoslavs mounted with little attention to logistics. Then, on 22 February, when the British considered that an attack on Vis was imminent, the partisans embarked on a week of celebrations. They also shot two of their women for becoming pregnant, an act of barbarism in the view of many commandos. Nevertheless relationships between senior commanders remained reasonably good until about June 1944 and between the rank and file until a much later date.[6] On 29 February '43 RM' and 2 SS (Cdo) Brigade Tac HQ arrived on the island. 'The sight that came to our eyes ... carried one back centuries ... the island was mountainous, rising steeply out of the blue Adriatic ... the two ports, the only towns of any size, Vis in the east and Komiza in the west, were like toy towns – or Hollywood's idea in technicolour – of Balkan fishing villages.'[7]

An airstrip was being built on the central plain, with its vineyards surrounded by mountains, and in their foothills the commandos would make their home for the next eight months. During this time they would make many raids on German-held islands. These operations can be broadly divided into four types: reconnaissance in force, work with Naval patrols, actions supporting specific partisan landings, and standing patrols to gain information and harass the enemy. Each had its risks and difficulties, as will be seen from the following examples. But the co-ordination of the Commandos, Royal Navy and RAF forces was effectively established.

After several small raids, 2 Army Commando, reinforced by men of B and F Troops of '43 RM' with heavy weapons[8] and the American Special Operations Group landed on Solta. They killed or captured the garrison of Grobote village and returned to Vis, having lost two men killed. The raid had been supported by 36 Kittyhawk bombers working to an RAF Ground Control Unit with the commandos,[8] making this a model of co-operation between all three services at a time when Lieutenant-Colonel R. W. B. Simonds RM was the Brigade's G1 Planning for offensive operations.[9]

The following week the Marines made an equally successful raid on Hvar, with a force of '43 RM' (about 280 all ranks) and 400 men of 1 Dalmatian Brigade.[10] Major N. G. M. Munro, who commanded '43 RM' on this raid, had spent 36 hours on Hvar in reconnaissance of the island, with its 1,500ft mountain peak. On Sunday, 19 March, a Marine patrol of 30 men secured the small Scedro island south of Hvar and learnt that the Germans were evacuating the larger island, so plans for the raid were brought forward and '43 RM' landed on Hvar the next evening. It was followed by partisans in a slow convoy of schooners.

The Marine commandos set off for Jelsa, the island's north-coast port, which the RAF had bombed. Their route led over the mountains, avoiding the main tracks, although the steep rocky hills, with crags and outcrops, made this a difficult march for the loaded commandos, yet they took only 4½ hours to cross the mountains and invest Jelsa by 2200 hours. But as A Troop in reserve and the Commandos' HQ moved towards the town, they bumped into some 180 Germans also moving north, and a fire-fight ensued in the dark when 'both sides became somewhat mixed'.[11] Nevertheless the Marines of '45 RM' held their ground, forcing the German column to break off the battle and move eastward, leaving their mule train of ammunition, wireless sets and baggage which A Troop captured.

Lieutenant-Colonel Simonds had originally planned to make the attack on Jelsa once the exact German dispositions were known, playing the action off-the-cuff after investing the town. He was therefore quickly able to redirect his force now that the enemy were clearly moving eastward. The partisans were positioned to block the German moves and the Commando set up ambushes on the line of the German retreat but most of the enemy managed to escape through the hills and along the north shore. The next night '43 RM' was withdrawn after being at sea or on the move for over 36 hours, the partisans being given the job of investing the island and its easterly redoubt. The commandos had accounted for 130 Germans killed or captured in country more suited to defence than attack, and might have taken more prisoners had the Germans not been afraid of retribution from the partisans.[12] These Allies were excitable and at other times deeply depressed when a battle did not go their way, yet under Simonds' leadership they had effectively driven the Germans into an enclave through 'quick planning and bold execution',[13] removing any threat to Vis from Hvar.

In April the Germans re-established their hold on both Solta and Hvar, building heavily defended posts often blasted out of mountain sides. The Commando raiding policy was, therefore, reviewed after several reconnaissance raids had proved that the new defences were too strong to be broken by light raiding forces. But during April (1944) the Royal Navy's patrols had their greatest successes, for they had found the routes used by German schooner convoys and their E-boat escorts.

A Troop of '43 RM' had had experience of working with MTBs during September 1943, when in exceptionally rough weather four or five commandos were aboard each of several MTBs intercepting German shipping off Norway. There, although not in action, they learnt how these small craft pitched and rolled, becoming accustomed to keeping more than their feet aboard the craft, for many at first were confined to their bunks through sea-sickness.[14] Six months later they captured Axis schooners by boarding them from Motor Gun Boats (MGBs) off the Dalmatian coast.

In one such action, on 12 March 1944, two MGBs skilfully got inshore of a northbound convoy and MGB 661 prepared to put on a so-called 'I' boat, a boarding party of an officer and four Marines from '43 RM'. The Marines came on deck and slid up into the bow, the MGB's 2-pdr banging away over their heads as the boat surged into the tracer fire from the 'I' Boat. The noise was deafening and the men clung to any cleat or other firm fitting that would steady them as the deck tilted in tight turns or bucked a larger wave. The MGB grazed the stern of the fourth enemy ship, cutting the convoy's line before she came round quickly and alongside the 'I' Boat. The two ships touched but the bow of this German ferry craft struck amidships, too far aft for the boarders to jump to her deck. On the MGB's second pass, they were able to jump, a drop of some feet for the ferry was low in the water, holed by accurate 2-pdr fire. As she sank, the Marines made eight Germans prisoner and had barely hauled themselves back aboard the MGB when the 'I' boat finally went under.[15]

The Marines from MGB 661, Tommy guns at the ready, were next put aboard a schooner and made her a prize, while the party from MGB 647 boarded another schooner and then a motorboat. A third schooner blew up, and a fourth was rammed and also sank before the sea raiders began their 6-hour passage back to Vis. Aboard the prize were: men of 118 Jaeger Division who had been going on leave; and bundles of British uniforms,[16] not as useful a find as the barrels of Danish butter later taken from another of the 36 schooners captured or sunk that spring.[17] On 5 May '40 RM' joined the Vis forces at this time,[18] four LCAs of 561 RM Flotilla having come to the island during the previous month. These craft – with canvas 'dodgers' to keep out heavy seas, and reinforced floors – were often towed long distances before their run-in to a beach. They landed all manner of cargoes at different times: partisans' guns on Korcula (22 April), ammunition, mules, two 75-mm guns, and three 20-mm for beach anti-aircraft defences. On one occasion they had also to man borrowed Brens and the craft's Lewis guns to defend a beach under air attack, for 'the partisans had no training in this respect . . . and obeyed their first impulse'.[19]

The Vis force – by this date Force 266 – did not have the resources to mount raids in strength on the northern islands, and a substituted raid on Mljet failed to capture its garrison; although 2 Army Commando and '43 RM' had a torrid 24 hours on the raw rock heights of this volcanic island, with 1,000ft cliffs near the German positions, which the enemy abandoned before the commandos could reach them. Searches through the 'luxurious undergrowth'[20] in the valley also failed to trace the defenders. But in the Bosnian mountains of central Yugoslavia, other German forces had encircled Tito's stronghold. A major diversion was therefore planned. Some 6,000 partisans and 2 Commando Brigade were to land on Brac (pronounced 'Brach') where the Germans held well-fortified positions on a razor backed hill top above the south-west coast of the island, protecting four 105-mm coast guns, with an observation post 2,000yds to the east overlooking the harbour at Bol. In addition to the 500 Germans defending this battery, there was a defended area 13 miles east of the coast battery and another 4 miles north of it, each garrisoned by several hundred men with artillery. The first phase of the operation was successful in landing parties on D-1 to lie up until midnight on D-Day, 1–2 June These partisans and British soldiers successfully blocked any reinforcement of the 105-mm battery by Germans from the north, but failed to capture the observation post in its concrete defences protected by mines and wire. The attacks were stopped when 2,000ft below the OP the main force could be seen landing in the moonlight, and none of the 105-mm guns were firing on them. Later the guns fired on the beach but only indiscriminately, without help from the OP.

Rocket-firing Hurricanes attacked the battery area at 0610 hours, after which the guns fired less frequently. The men of '43 RM' saw this attack but needed another 80 minutes to climb to positions near the wire on the west hill side of this point '542'. They had climbed some 1,500ft humping their loads as no mules were available and Jeeps could not land. The men each carried a 3-in mortar bomb and some bangalore torpedoes. The Germans' defence posts looked formidable, with stones heaped over concrete and log-roofed bunkers, and under this protection they had soon recovered from the rocket attacks. All the scrub and other natural cover had been cleared from the hillsides by the Germans, giving their machine-gunners a clear field of fire over the mines and wire. This fire made any approach from the west impossible without concentrated artillery support. The ten 75-mm guns ashore had been also firing 'on call' to the partisans attacking points '622' and '648', south of the commandos, but these attacks had also failed. During the afternoon the hills were to be attacked in succession, with time for the guns to concentrate on each in turn. The attack by '43 RM' on '542' came from the north this time, but a partisan battalion due to attack from the south in a co-ordinated assault on the hill top cried off 15 minutes before H-hour (1630). This was too late for Lieutenant-Colonel Simonds to recall his leading Troops, which were out of wireless touch with the Commando HQ. For 15 minutes under intense fire, the Marines cut their way into the wire, but had not made much progress after this as they began clearing a path in the minefield. The Germans by this time had worked machine guns – Spandaus – round the open flanks, and the lengths of bangalore torpedo charges were too few to cut much further into the minefield. The artillery, whose accurate fire would help the commandos on several occasions, put down a concentration with smoke, and, using their fieldcraft to take advantage of every slight fold in the ground, the forward Troops extracted themselves with few casualties on being ordered to withdraw. As they came off the hill, they were attacked by RAF planes for the second time that day, but no one was hit.

The partisans had declined to attack after their comrades earlier that afternoon had again been repulsed at hills '622' and '648'. The heat and tough going had exhausted many Marines after the day's attacks and plans were made to rest '43 RM' that night, while the partisans put in night attacks. The reserves were called in from Vis: three Troops of '40 RM', 300 partisans, two 25-pdr guns and 50 tons of ammunition. These arrived early next morning, but despite accurate fire from the 75-mm guns, the partisans' attacks failed. Radio communications broke down that night owing to local atmospheric conditions,[21] a pointer to future difficulties in co-ordinating night attacks.

During the second day on Brac Lieutenant-Colonel Jack Churchill made a long reconnaissance of the island. The OP of the coast battery had been captured at the third attempt after a rocket attack, and was found to be held by only 20 Germans, 'a good indication of . . . [the enemy's] determination to fight to the last'. The forces to the east had taken prisoners and guns and were now investing the garrison in Selca. While to the north the Supertar garrison was contained. Lieutenant-Colonel Jack Churchill, commanding the Brigade as his brother was visiting the Special Service Group Headquarters in England, formulated a plan for '40 RM' and '43 RM' to attack the point '622'. The Lieutenant-Colonel judged this point to be the key that would unlock the entire defence position. While the commandos attacked this hill, partisans were to fire into points '542',

500yds to the north, and '648', about the same distance due south. Ammunition was in short supply, however, since four mules had collapsed while carrying much of the reserve ammunition and some of it did not reach the commandos, there being no porters to heave it the six or more miles from the beach.[22]

The plan was signalled by wireless to '43 RM' but no reference in this message was made to '40 RM's' attack.[23] Lieutenant-Colonel Simonds had moved his Marines by 1930 hours to their forming-up area facing the west hillside leading to '622'. The mortar barrage came down on time and '43 RM' moved into the attack at 2030. In 45 minutes they were at the edge of wire, cut their way through it and with the help of Captain J. Pirie RE, got through the 20yds of minefield in 20 minutes. The partisans had failed to neutralise the two flank positions – '542' on the left and '648' on the right – and as the Marines broke into the German defences, they lost several men: all the officers and four NCOs commanding sub-Sections of C and D Troops on the left became casualties. There was a stretch of open hill side inside the wire across which the Marines charged, led by two sergeants.[24] They cleared all the pill-boxes on the crest, and although both sergeants were wounded, they held the hill top for some 20 minutes, before being forced off their objective by mortar and machine gun fire about 2215. At this time a German counter-attack was expected and the Marines had little ammunition left.[25]

B Troop on the right became separated from C and D Troops, their OC was twice wounded, and Lieutenant Barnett, an assault engineer, led them through the minefield, cutting the trip wires in making S-mines (aka Schu-mines) safe ahead of the advance. B Troop had taken many casualties before it came on 40 RM Commando also working its way up this wide shallow valley. Why '40 RM' was late was in part at least due to the difficulties of communications on this island. The Marines had only received their orders 45 minutes before the attack was due, and as they had a number of miles of difficult country to cross, they were not on their start line until 2130, a mere 20 minutes before '43 RM' was on the crest. Lieutenant-Colonel Jack Churchill joined '40 RM', and as he felt complications were likely, because the timetable had gone adrift, he spent half an hour briefing Lieutenant-Colonel 'Pops' Manners and his Troop commanders. Jack Churchill then led them in the final attack at 2230, 15 minutes after '43 RM' had left the crest.

Covered by B Troop of '43 RM', which knew where most of the enemy strongpoints were positioned, '40 RM' got through the wire, and Y Troop charged 'all in line and shouting and firing from the hip as if on an assault course at Achnacarry'.[26] The hill top was won for the second time, Jack Churchill playing his bagpipes and firing Very light success signals. Within minutes the Germans counter-attacked, the Lieutenant-Colonel Jack Churhill was knocked out, Lieutenant-Colonel Manners badly wounded, and the radio set put out of action. This had not been in touch with Brigade HQ for some hours, communications having broken down again owing to atmospheric conditions. 'B' Troop ran out of ammunition, but its wounded CO made a further attempt to lead a charge before he was hit again and killed. Germans now drove all the commandos off the hill top.

The withdrawal was a wearying haul for tired men carrying their wounded, but more men from '40 RM' and 2 Army Commando had arrived from Vis to help in the evacuation. The Brigade had been prepared to withdraw that morning whatever the outcome on hill '622'. As success on Brac depended on the Germans reinforcing it at the expense of their mainland forces, and such reinforcements were likely to arrive in the next day or so. The men came down the steep paths to the beach and were brought off by LCI(L)s, 'LCI 260 a great favourite of the Commando [43 RM] remaining to take off the last of the wounded'.[27] The Marines of '43 RM' had had a difficult final route from their covering position to the withdrawal beaches, and were not taken off until that evening. By then the Navy, with strong cover from the RAF, had brought out all the other commandos, the partisans and most of their stores. The Brigade had lost 51 killed and 76 wounded or missing, of whom ten officers had been killed or were missing, among them Lieutenant-Colonel Jack Churchill and Lieutenant-Colonel 'Pops' Manners. The partisans had 260 casualties.

Brigade HQ had anticipated the breakdown in radio communications, sending Captain E. Roger Wakefield – the G3 and an experienced commando officer – to establish a link between '40' and '43 RM'. But in the difficult terrain he and his guide missed the way and the Captain was later killed,[28] underlining the difficulties of such operations in mountainous country where communications were almost as difficult in the 1990s as they had been 50 years earlier, before the widespread use of satellite communications.

A small party from 2 Army Commando was left on the island to search for survivors and recapture if they could any that were prisoners, but 'Pops' Manners died of wounds while a prisoner on the island, and Jack Churchill was flown out as a prisoner. Three Troops of 2 Army Commando were landed on 5 June to act as a support party and with them were two 75-mm guns of the Special Raiding Squadron, all landed from LCAs of the RM 561 Flotilla. During the previous days' operations on the island, to which they had made a 27-mile voyage under their own power, each craft carrying two 40-gallon drums as a reserve of petrol, they had been shelled while ferrying stores from schooners to the beaches, acting as general duty boats, searching the coastline for survivors, and helping to evacuate wounded to Vis. The men of 2 Army Commando had been having a swim when they were called in the late afternoon of 5 June to go in three craft to Vis.[29] This support force was successfully landed and made a number of attacks on German patrols; they also directed the 75-mm guns' fire on to several enemy positions. But on the morning of 6 June a 27-man patrol was caught napping, only 12 escaping to the beach. Lieutenant Peter Davis, who commanded the LCAs, took six volunteers back up the hill, leaving his LCA crew to cover the beach and sending the other two craft to Vis with the guns, when these had fired their last rounds in the direction of the Germans. After a 2-hour climb Lieutenant Davis found a wounded commando Lieutenant who was safely brought down to the beach; Davis's Marines then sailed back to Vis. The advantage of Marine crews in landing craft was highlighted by this and other actions of the flotilla.

On 3 June, one craft from 561 Flotilla had landed a signals officer on Hvar, and he, after reconnoitering the coast, reported back on his radio the absence of Germans from several positions where he had to land by 'jumping on to rocky shore . . . [because] the coast was heavily mined'.[30] A week later the whole Flotilla landed four 75-mm guns on Solta not long after midnight, and these guns carried out a night shoot on map grid references, firing 800 rounds into German defences on the other side of the island.[31] In July three LCAs landed the American OSS Group on Peljesac peninsula before lying up in a cave on Hvar, two Marines having been left on the mainland with an 18-set to radio reports of any enemy movement in the channel or near the beach.

By early June the airfield on Vis had become an important base for giving air support to the partisans, and the garrison came under command of the RAF.[32] The HQ of 2 Special Service (Commando) Brigade then became the garrison's HQ and the commandos had a period of rest; 2 Army and 40 RM Commandos were sent to Italy in mid-July after sending patrols to several islands, and the RM landing craft flotilla carried out several further operations before being withdrawn from Vis early in September. But '43 RM' remained on the island until 13 October, making several sallies onto German-held islands, and losing 36 men in one action on Solta.

In retrospect the Brigade Major considered that attacks mounted jointly with the partisans were almost inevitably going to break down. Neither they nor the commandos fully appreciated the difficulties in co-ordinating their quite different tactics; the commandos' careful planning to anticipate every eventuality, the partisans' reliance on numbers, did not and probably could not be integrated in a joint assault.[33]

While 2 Special Service Brigade had been active on the Dalmatian coast, RMBPD (RM Boom Patrol Detachment) – whose cockle canoes had raided Bordeaux – was also operating in the Mediterranean. Since its first raid, RMBPD had been reorganised into four operational Sections, each commanded by a Lieutenant, with a Sergeant, two Corporals and three Marines; there was also a four-man RM crew for its motor-barge HQ, which carried its Naval Engineer Lieutenant and his shipwrights. A formal selection procedure was introduced and standards set for qualifying to join the Detachment: men had to be able to swim a mile in full kit and to strip down a car engine, as well as pass initiative tests.[1] Their work on explosive motorboats and other special equipment ran into difficulties, in that it was not easy to find a suitable means to launch these boats by parachute from a bomber. They worked with the RN Canadian Reserve officer who later formed the Sea Reconnaissance Unit of men who used a Paddle Board (not unlike an enlarged surfboard).[2] These Marines also completed a parachute course.

One Section had come to the Mediterranean in February 1944 bringing the latest Cockle MkII** canoes, after plans were cancelled for a second limpet attack on Bordeaux shipping. Two new attacks were now planned for this detachment (code-named 'Earthworm'): they would put limpets on destroyers in Portolago harbour (Leros) and against ammunition ships in Crete. For these operations they joined the Middle Fast Raiding Force, which included the Special Boat Squadron of the SAS Regiment, the Long Range Desert Group and some clandestine units, training near Haifa (Palestine). They learnt the Middle East Commandos' practices for signals, and some were trained to use the high-powered 'attaché case' radios for direct communication from island OPs to General Headquarters in Cairo.[3] An emergency operation interrupted this training, when some Greek warships, including a cruiser, became involved in the political warfare between Royalists and Republicans, but the limpeteers were not finally required, as the mutinous cruiser surrendered.

Early in June one party of limpeteers in the submarine HMS *Unruly* completed a cruise of 17 days, but no targets were found in Cretan harbours.[4] In mid-June the canoes *Shark*, *Shrimp* and *Salmon* were taken first to an anchorage on the neutral Turkish coast, where local caiques under camouflage nets 'lying up under the cliffs by day'[5] provided a raiding base. They slipped out of this base in HDML 360 for a night raid against shipping in Portolago Bay, Leros, when the weather was ideal, dark and moonless with sufficient star-glow to see silhouettes. *Shrimp*, Corporal E. Horner and Marine Eric Fisher, entered the harbour first, followed 15 minutes later by *Shark*, Lieutenant J. Richards and Marine W. S. Stevens, with *Salmon* five minutes behind them, crewed by Sergeant J. King and Marine R. N. Ruff. Each craft moved to its target. *Salmon* was challenged as she crossed the harbour boom, but the patrol vessel did not follow them. *Shrimp* was less fortunate, being challenged from the deck of her target ship; Corporal Horner called back 'Brandenburger! Patrola! Patrola!'.[6] The crew threw a rope ladder to them, but they turned away and paddled into the shadow of a cliff – just in the way a German canoe from their Special Boat Section of the Brandenburger Regiment might behave.

Although *Shrimp* had not laid her limpets, *Shark* and *Salmon* had placed theirs on two destroyers and three escorts, with the fuses set for a 4½-hour delay. They had been in the harbour 2½ hours by 0230 when *Shark* began to paddle quietly for the entrance; in 40 minutes they were over the booms and hugging the coastline before crossing the half-mile channel to Kalymo where they would lie up. *Shrimp* appeared that evening, the crew having been further along the cliffs during the day and hearing search parties among the rocks, but they were not discovered. *Salmon*, a canoe with persistent leaks, had been so waterlogged that she did not reach Kalymo until daylight. Her crew were found by a friendly Greek but not by German patrols. At 2300 hours Sergeant King heard the radio call-sign transmitted by the ML and the other canoes' replies. He in turn gave his call-sign and despite a flooded canoe managed to reach the ML, which brought all three teams back to the raiding base.

After this raid both destroyers had to be towed to Greece for repairs and were sunk by Allied bombers before these were completed, a loss to the German naval forces which enabled the Allies' small vessels to move more freely in the eastern Mediterranean. The three escort vessels had been sunk.

* * *

In Normandy, 1st and 4 Special Service Brigades had advanced from the Orne and the Americans had made a sweeping advance from the south. Cherbourg was then reopened as a major port, handling 12,000 tons of stores a day by mid-September.[1] At the time of its capture the previous July, the 30th Assault Unit's A and B Troops had entered this port with advanced elements of the American VII Corps. This Assault Unit was the force of Naval engineers and other specialists with RM commando guards, trained to search enemy headquarters for military intelligence. In Cherbourg on 22 June they had found 'masses of material and an excellent wine cellar'. They searched files, dustbins of burnt paper, desks and lockers frequently in the next 10 months, operating in the van if not ahead of the Allied advances.[2] In the late summer of 1944, the German enclaves at Le Havre, Calais and other Channel ports, which had been by-passed in the main advance, were captured. In one such action the Canadians' advance on Cap Gris Nez was supported by the RM Siege Regiment's 14-in guns, which fired all their remaining ammunition between 18 and 20 September – some 120 rounds.[3]

Le Havre came under attack from 51 Highland Division after air, land and sea bombardment in which HMS *Erebus* and *Warspite* took part, and a four-man patrol of 30th AU – a captain, a Bren gunner and two riflemen – went into the port to find the German naval HQ, but were unable to fight their way through the town square, where the Bren gunner and the captain were killed. The latter was an experienced officer who had served in North Africa with the Unit (then 30 Commando), Captain H. O. Huntingdon Whitely, who was greatly respected. One of the survivors of his patrol later brought the German commander's surrender to the HQ of I (British) Corps. After the surrender of the port on 12 September, it was found to be so damaged from bombardment and German demolitions that the main dock basin was expected to take three weeks to clear. But 'G' Company of the RM Engineers had it cleared in seven days,[4] although the port installations were not fully operational until 9 October. Meanwhile the Guards Armoured Division had made a spectacular advance of over 200 miles in five days to Brussels, and 11 Armoured Division had seized part of the Antwerp docks undamaged on 4 September.[5]

Two weeks later attempts were made by the British Second Army to force its way some 65 miles to join airborne forces dropped at Arnhem across the Lower Rhine. These attempts failed despite the airborne troops' gallant stand. By then the invasion of Germany became a matter of logistics rather than dashing advances against crumbling defences. Major ports had, therefore, to be brought into operation, but Antwerp could not be used until German forces were cleared from the Scheldt estuary islands and from the 40 miles of northern river bank from the sea to this port. The I Canadian Corps had cleared much of the southern coastal strip – the Breskens pocket – by October, as well as much of the south Beveland peninsula, some 11 miles long. They could not, however, force their way across the 1,200yds of causeway, flanked by mud-flats with reed-beds, joining the peninsula to Walcheren.

Walcheren, a saucer-shaped island, had batteries around the rim of soft sand dunes and centuries-old dykes. Batteries of coastal guns covered the shallows of the estuary, and where the dykes had been breached by RAF bombs the water had flooded in to inundate almost all the saucer of low-lying ground. Conventional warships could not approach these shores, although the support landing craft of the Eastern Flank Force could do so, for the LCFs, for example, had a draught of only 6ft 9in and the LCG (Medium) drew less when trimmed for beaching. The G(M) had been the craft conceived for close support after the Dieppe landings, and as insufficient numbers had been built by the time of the Normandy landings, they had been replaced there by the craft of the RM Armoured Support Regiment. This Group had been disbanded that September (1944), and the tank crews remustered as 34th Amphibian Support Group for operations against Japan; 1st Special Service Brigade had also been withdrawn from France on 7 September, to prepare for operations in the Far East, but would return to North West Europe in January 1945.

Throughout the Allied campaigns in Europe, care was taken to avoid casualties among civilians, but at Westkapelle, where the commandos would land, the first breach in the dykes was made by 259 Lancaster Bombers[6] in the early afternoon of 3 October, when many civilians were killed. Leaflets and radio warnings had been given the previous day but in two hours of bombing 'houses crashed and sometimes totally disappeared in the craters'.[7] Families in hand-built shelters were buried alive, 45 civilians in the cellar of a mill were drowned, and 85 per cent of the houses in the village were damaged after further raids on 17 and 19 October. By then three further gaps had been made in the dykes, near Vere and Flushing. Despite such preparations and sacrifices by the Dutch, the German defences on the dykes were little impaired by these attacks, as the guns were in casemates. Although the batteries' communications had been cut, most of these had been repaired by D-Day here, 1 November.[8] Bad weather prevented aircraft sorties on D-1 but limited bombing was carried out on the seafront defences of Flushing that night by 35 Mosquitoes of Second Tactical Air Force (2nd TAF).

The inundation of the island, however, would hamper the movement of German reserves, flood some 36 gun emplacements inland and expose the coast batteries on the dunes to assault from the rear by amphibians. This enabled plans to be made for the operation, with covering parties on foot from 41 RM Commando to land on the left of the gap by Westkapelle village, '48 RM' to land on the right. These Marines would secure the dyke faces each side of the gap, and give covering fire. Under one plan – later modified – the LVTs (Landing Vehicles Tracked) would have passed through the gap to land from the flooded areas. In the event each Commando was to land from the west side of the dykes to seize enemy batteries: '48 RM', having secured the dunes south of the gap, was to attack W13 battery; '41 RM' was to take the village, and batteries W22 and W14 behind it, if these were active, before moving north towards W17 at Domberg, probably on D+1. '47 RM' was to pass through '48 RM' to take Zoutelande and batteries W12 and W11, some 2½ miles further south. The commandos in these assault Troops would come ashore in amphibious LVTs or Weasels, except for the covering parties, which would land in LCI(S) – those wooden craft which had given little protection to commandos on 6 June at Normandy. The LVTs and Weasels were to be put near the shore by LCTs, while the support craft of the Eastern Flank Force would engage the batteries, to cover this approach.

After 3 months in the 'Trout' line off Normandy, these support craft had been sent to the UK to prepare for their part in the landing. They were divided into two groups: North Group, with three LCG(L)s, three LCFs, an LCG(M) and three LCT(R); and South Group, with similar numbers of these craft but one less LCT(R). Each Group was commanded from an LCI(L) adapted as an LC Headquarters, which each carried the Squadron's two gunnery officers, Captains L. W. B. Fisher and G. R. H. Maddan.[9] They would co-ordinate the bombardment of their respective Groups. Once the Support Squadron had divided to cover the north and south sides of the main assault force, each support group would find an ML marking the start line for the final approach. The time for H-hour was fixed at 0945 (GMT+1 hour), as the tide at this time would be low enough to expose obstacles yet provide sufficient depth of water for support craft to come close inshore.[10] Although no detailed beach reconnaissance had been possible, one of the 'Tarbrush' reconnaissance units had managed at the third attempt to get a Dory near the Westkapelle gap;[11] the crew saw the outline of obstacles but were forced to withdraw under fire before making any survey of the conditions in this 100-yd gap through which a 6-knot tide ran during the ebb.

An interesting point in the planning of this landing is that no written directive or formal plan was produced either by II Canadian Corps or the Canadian First Army, nor indeed by the Force Commanders. That is not to say that there was no plan, but its initiation was not formalised in the way most of the these plans were, i.e. written to a brief from the Force Commanders. 'However, the personal relationships between the Naval and military Force Commanders was very good . . . and more than made up for any inherent difficulties.'[12] The Naval Force T, including the Support Squadron, was commanded by Captain A. F. Pugsley, DSO, RN; his support craft were commanded by Commander K. A. ('Monkey') Sellar, DSO, DSC, RN; and 4 Special Service Brigade by Royal Marine Brigadier 'Jumbo' Leicester. The Brigadier later reported that 'the Headquarters of Force T and 4 SS Brigade were sited near each other at Bruges . . . from the start relationships were easy . . . an over-riding requirement for joint command . . . for the commanders must be personally friendly and must have complete confidence in each other's professional ability and integrity.'[13] Although a seaborne assault had not been completely ruled out, the Canadian Army's appraisal in September had assumed that it would be impractical. But when Captain Pugsley was called from leave to the HQ of the First Canadian Army on 20 September, he considered it possible and probably essential. Admiral Sir Bertram Ramsey, Eisenhower's Naval Commander-in-Chief, agreed with this view and a Naval staff was brought together.

In the planning for Walcheren there were practical difficulties because liaison with the RAF demanded visits to the Army HQ at Ghent, and 'the lack of a responsible RAF commander below Army level in the planning stage was a handicap'.[14] Brigadier Leicester considered that the economic use of aircraft demanded control from the highest levels, but it was unusual for there to be an air commander at the tactical level except in airborne operations. The Brigadier felt that a single overall commander or joint sea and land commanders made little difference in practice. In joint-commands, disagreements were more likely to be resolved mutually, without recourse to a higher authority, which might question a commanders' willingness to co-operate; while under a supreme commander, he believed, disagreements could be overridden at the expense of harmony. The fact that decisions had to be made during the operation, when the Naval Force Commander was only able to contact the Brigadier ashore, led to no difficulties at Walcheren. But, the Brigadier has written, 'there was no competent military authority or staff left aboard the HQ ship ... and had a major crisis arisen ... it would have been impossible to arrive at a joint solution ... with none too good communications'. He went on to propose that an amphibious brigade should have a colonel as second-in-command, and he, with two staff officers, would remain on the HQ ship to read the land battle for the Naval Force Commander.

4 Army Commando was to land as part of a separate but related operation by 155 Infantry Brigade to capture Flushing on the south-east of Walcheren. It came ashore at 0545 hours,[15] and with the leading Section was a 'Tarbrush' party, including Captain A. B. Jackson and CSM D. J. R. Morss of the LCOCUs, which had landed in Normandy. Their two LCP(Sy) and an LCA felt their way inshore, one becoming stuck 30yds out, but the men swam ashore and found a suitable landing point for the assault Troop, up the slipway used by garbage lighters. Lieutenant Harry Hargreaves, DSC, RNVR, who had been a Beach Master at Dieppe and in Normandy, set up the beach control point, while the Marines, 'despite the mud often up to our knees', cleared the obstacles with minutes to spare before the first assault troops' LCAs touched down. 'The longest seven and a half minutes that I ever experienced', Lieutenant Hargreaves has written.[16] As 4 Army Commando fought to clear the western end of the town's defences, including fortified houses overlooking the landing area, the 4th Battalion of the Kings Own Scottish Borderers came ashore, though their 5th Battalion could not land until the early afternoon. Forty-eight hours later, after mouseholing their way into German positions by blasting holes in house walls, and battling over rooftops, 4 Commando and other units of 155 Infantry Brigade[17] had taken the town.

About 0815 HMS *Warspite* and *Roberts* opened fire on the Westkapelle defences, but HMS *Erebus* had trouble with the motor training her turret, and this was not repaired for an hour or so. *Roberts*, therefore, took on her targets at 0830. *Warspite*'s targets, an anti-aircraft and two coast batteries near Domburg, were bracketed on the second salvo at 26,000yds (24km). The aircraft to report the fall of shot had been unable to leave their UK airfields, however, because of fog; and although light aircraft of an Army Air OP Squadron were later in radio contact with *Warspite*, their method of reporting caused some confusion, for they worked on the 'cardinal points system', which differed from

Naval methods[18] The monitor *Roberts* first engaged the radar station (W154) before switching to the battery just north of Westkapelle (W15), which comprised what were believed to be 155-mm guns but turned out to be captured British 3.7-in anti-aircraft guns mounted for coast defence. The Allied artillery across the estuary had also bombarded W15 for 70 minutes before H-hour, with 179 shells from the 155-mm guns of 1st and 59th Medium Regiments. However, only two nearby AA guns were knocked out by the Allied gun fire, and all along the coast the Germans maintained a steady fire against the incoming support craft. The bombing and Naval and artillery bombardments had been far less effective than might have been expected, a point considered later.

In the early evening of Tuesday, 31 October, Lieutenant George Flamank RNVR, Captain of LCG(M) 101, briefed his crew on the operation: the craft would go in to point-blank range of the enemy gun position W267, north of the gap, and her sister ship, LCG(M) 102, was to engage W266, south of the gap.

They had all had a reasonable passage in convoy from Ostend, although '101' began to roll a bit as she turned eastward about 0700 hours.[19] G(M)s had a low centre of gravity and tended, therefore, to gather momentum as they rolled, and with only 1½ft freeboard aft and with the bows 6in clear of the water, they sailed in this unusual bow-up trim which gave them an uncomfortable corkscrew motion.[20] Destroyer commanders have been sick on a G(M)'s bridge, and anything not wedged in a storeroom or lashed down shifted position. A bottle of sauce plopped all over one wardroom when the cork came out, although the craft was not in rough water; and more dangerous damage could be caused if ammunition was not securely clipped in the magazines' bottle racks. The practice in a heavy swell was to batten down the deckhouse, as crews did on LCI(L)s in heavy weather, and no one worked on the upper deck. As they were approaching Walcheren, however, the sea eased, and the Support Squadron moved at about 8 knots (15kph) towards the outer shoals, picking up the landmarks of the Westkapelle lighthouse and identifying two major batteries near Domburg (W17) and Westkapelle (W15). The Squadron zig-zagged to put off the coast gunners' aim but continued to make for the shore. At 0725 hours the G(L)s were ordered 'to make smoke', by means of their chemical smoke generators; and duels began at 0809 hours between batteries and support craft. The first shells from W15 fell around one of the MLs marking the position where the Squadron was due to deploy.[21]

Warspite and the monitors had engaged the radar stations and the anti-aircraft battery (W5) protecting the coast battery (W17) at Domburg. This Domburg battery, with its four French 220-mm guns, was engaged by *Warspite* throughout the day but did not seriously interfere with the landing. W15 was a more organised adversary, and its British 3.7-in guns caused considerable damage from their concrete emplacements north of Westkapelle. At 0830 the fire of *Roberts* on W15 was supplemented by fire from G(L)s 9, 10 and 11 before they deployed with the southern group, and other craft engaged it from time to time. Seventeen minutes later (0847) the Squadron split, the Groups moving out to allow the LCTs to head towards the beach, and W15 engaged LCF37 some

3,750yds from the shore. This was beyond the effective range of the Flakker's 2-pdrs and 20-mm Oerlikons, but she continued towards the beach in the van of her Group, although hit on the water line. The hole was successfully blocked with hammocks, and W15 had found fresh targets as the northern Group came closer inshore. LCT(R) 457 of the northern Group ranged with smoke rockets on W15, then fired her pattern of explosive rockets, but the main point of impact was short.[22] This was due to an error in her navigation, and LCT(R) 378, probably taking her timing from an LCT(R) in the southern Group, which also fired 2,000yds short.

LCG(M) 101 was expecting to beach at H-5 minutes, and her gunners saw Typhoons sweep in low. Visibility was a mere 1,000yds, giving pilots about 5 seconds to react as they approach a target, under the very overcast sky, by one report;[23] yet their rockets hit the dykes around both '101's' and '102's' targets, among other defences. The blast effect of these rockets 45 minutes before '101' was due to beach, would, the planners hoped, stun the gun crews, and certainly '101' was able to move inshore from her last position, fixed by bearing on Westkapelle lighthouse.[24] She opened fire as targets became distinguishable in the November light. The pill-box W267 above her beaching point on the north shoulder of the gap did not respond to her fire, which was 'as fast as the guns could be loaded' with their 17-pdr armour-piercing shells. She was firing for most of the last mile towards the beach, the South African Lieutenant T. (Theo) Tuffin RM directing the fire from the armoured control room where he and his sergeant-major, Sergeangt D. Russell-Taylor, could take the bearing of targets through the 2-in slit above their control platform. Several shells hit her at this stage and the bow jack staff was shot away, but no serious damage was done. The trainers spun the double handles of their gear to bring the turrets on to the gyro-compass repeater's bearings, before the hair-line of their telescopic sights crossed a target. The layers 'pressed the tit' of the electrical firing button when they were also 'on target', and several hits were reported on beach strongpoints. LCG(M) 101 was flooding down as she neared the beach, for once she was securely grounded, the guns would have a firm firing 'platform'. She was nearing the beach, at 0955, when LCT(R) 331 fired her rockets, and these fell to the north of '101', among the strongpoints in the village.

She was coming in under the guns in pill-box W267, and let go her kedge some 75yds out. It was H+5 minutes, but the main landing force were still some minutes behind her, as they had delayed to allow the rocket craft to fire. About the time she dropped her kedge, she was hit by a 220-mm shell from W15, 1,000yds north of the gap. This holed her astern but no rounds hit forward, as the turrets and bow were screened from W15 by the dyke. Further hits aft damaged her unprotected stern but did not penetrate the armour protecting her magazines and engines. The gunners in 'B' turret felt her ground, and fired a few more rounds, but machine gun bullets slapped the side of the turret, and one destroyed the dial sight periscope the corporal was using to direct the fire. The circuits from the control room had 'been cut by a shell and each turret was working independently. Bullets then came through the sighting ports, and the layer was hit. Other bullets ricocheted around the turret 'like angry insects . . . several struck the gun loader in both arms and he fainted'.[25]

Bullets and shell splinters also bounced up from the deck through gaps around the turret's underside, a shell splinter damaging 'A' gun's recuperator. The crew in 'B' turret fitted the armoured covers to the sighting ports before they lifted the floor grilles to lower the injured loader to the magazine crew, with blood dripping down into the magazine, and the corporal took the loader's position on the gun. The sight slit-covers were removed and the gun came back into action. They had been on the beach 15 minutes, when the skipper began to bring her off.

The kedge had held her from broaching to on this dyke wall with a 1 in 10 gradient,[26] but she had now to be hauled off by the aft capstan as her high-speed pumps emptied the ballast tanks. The first lieutenant, a leading mechanic and a seaman went aft to work the capstan, but the anchor's cable had become jammed. Continuous fire from machine guns swept the small quarterdeck; nevertheless the first lieutenant took an axe to chop the wire free, but he was killed before he could cut the anchor loose, and his two companions were wounded, one mortally. The heavy fire then severed the cable and '101' came out.

In the 15 minutes she had been beached other support craft had also drawn the enemy's fire. Of the other northern craft, LCG(L) 1 was hit while engaging W15, her survivors coming off in LCS(L) 254, which had tried to take her in tow. LCG(L) 2 was also hit heavily 10 minutes later, at 1010 hours, by the same battery. LCF 36 came inshore, and when LCF 38 caught fire, took her in tow, but she had to be abandoned. The LCS(L)s, Nos 254, 259 and 260, made full use of their speed, firing their 6-pdrs as they zig-zagged inshore to take on strongpoints just north of the gap. Their fire was seen to have little effect on these pill-boxes, however, and they were ordered out to cover the approach of the incoming LCTs.

South of the gap LCG(M) 102 forced her way on to the beach at 0943 hours, two minutes ahead of her intended grounding at H-hour. She was hit forward of the control room. Her Captain remained on the bridge until she was beached or nearly so, for he signalled '101' that he 'preferred the open air' to the control room. One turret was quickly out of action but a Corporal and a Marine kept the other one firing, although they had to push the gun back after each recoil, for the recuperator was damaged. After 20 minutes she was on fire and the only survivor, the Marine who had helped to keep the gun firing, swam ashore. He was taken prisoner but later released by commandos, probably of '48 RM'.[27]

The LCT(R)s of the southern Group had fired at about 0937 hours, eight minutes before the first LCTs were due to beach: '363' drenched the radar station (W154) but was later hit when withdrawing and had to be towed clear; and '334' was hit as she fired her ranging rockets. She reopened fire 5 minutes later and drenched the beach, before taking '363' in tow.

The LCG(L)s of the southern Group fought a series of actions against W13, a battery of four 150-mm guns in concrete casemates, some 2,500yds south of the gap. The battery damaged more craft than any other in the first 90 minutes or so of the action. Its reserves of ammunition were low, however, for the guns had been firing at Allied troops across the Scheldt, and the battery commander probably made the vital error of using his 800 rounds against the support craft and not the LCTs. Although his guns had disabled six support craft, five of which later sank, the first LCTs grounded at 1010 hours and their LVTs, carrying Lieutenant-Colonel J. L. Moulton's 48 RM Commando, were moving ashore seven minutes before W13 ran out of ammunition.[28] The turning point, as General Moulton has pointed out, came hours earlier when *Robert*'s shells and fighter-bombers knocked out guns by W15's Bty. The battery was disorganised by these attacks about 0830, and when the Germans could be seen to be engaging the support craft, the order was given for the landing craft to start their run-in.

The craft nearest to W13, '48 RM's', beached about the same time as '41 RM's' three LCI(S)s. There is some variance in the reported times at which these flotillas landed, but certainly there were only minutes between them,. The craft carrying '41 RM' had been hit several times, causing commando casualties as splinters passed through the wooden hulls, but once they reached the dyke, enemy guns could not be depressed far enough to fire into them. The Commando's advanced HQ and three Troops clambered up the slippery stone blocks of the dyke, with B Troop covering the tiny beachhead. P Troop moved along the dyke and fired into battery W15 north of the village, and S Troop set up its Vickers machine gun to fire south over the gap if necessary. Accompanying these assault Troops, the only ones landed on foot that day, were Army assault engineers, the Naval Beach Master with his Landing Unit of RN commandos, and the A Landing Craft Obstruction Clearance Team of seamen under a Naval Sub-Lieutenant.[29] A shell destroyed their breathing gear, which they were not using, as the tide had not yet covered the obstacles, but later the Lieutenant and a Petty Officer cleared 15 obstacles by duck-diving without air tanks. Four LCTs carrying RAC and RE armoured assault vehicles, flail tanks, and D7 armoured bulldozers, should have landed at the same time as '41 RM's' Troops on foot. But the steep slippery dyke was impassable for tracked vehicles, and only one flail tank got up the incline despite efforts to push others up with a bulldozer. All but one LCT had turned away however from the beach. Some of the assault tanks had been damaged by the enemy on the run-in, and those that could not be landed north of the gap on Red beach were taken south of it.[30]

The battle along the northern dyke developed as A Troop, with 41 RM Commando HQ and X Troop, landed in LVTs and Weasels. These Marines were ashore some six minutes after the first wave, and A Troop moved quickly to the gap, where it came under fire from the lighthouse tower. The lone flail tank, from the 1st Lothians, put eleven 75-mm rounds into this observation post, and the Marines then cleared the main street and confirmed that two batteries (W14 and 22) were inundated by floods and not in action, before regrouping as the reserve Troop and 10(I-A) Commando's two Troops of Belgians and Norwegians came ashore.

Landing south of the gap, 48 RM Commando was shelled during its approach, but landed without casualties until it reached the beach, for this was coming under increasing fire. B Troop dismounted from its LVTs to find the pill-boxes on the south shoulder of the gap unoccupied, as was the radar station (W154). X Troop panted on through the sand dunes and took several prisoners in the strongpoint W286. Y Troop then prepared to attack W13, the battery 1½ miles or so from the beachhead. The Troop had been under some rifle fire around W286, but now met resolute fire from machine-gunners defending W13 battery. Nevertheless Y Troop put in an immediate attack, without any heavy support fire, and Major D. R. W. de Stacpoole was killed in the assault and most of a sub-Section of riflemen wounded but W13 was taken in a second assault.

On the south dyke, 48 RM held a firm footing, although the beach was under fire and several of their amphibian tracked LVTs and Weasels had been knocked out, after these LVTs – known as 'Buffaloes' with cleated tracks for swimming and Polsten 20mm guns – had crossed to the shore from the LCTs. (The LVTs were manned by 6th Assault Regiment RE, with detachments from 11th Royal Tank Regiment, and the Weasels had RM commando drivers who had trained while the Brigade was in Ostend.) LVTs would later prove their worth, but in the shell-cratered shores around all three Commando beaches, several Weasels and LVTs came to grief. Although 4 Special Service Brigade had a foot-hold, some batteries were still in action at mid-day and able to fire into the beachheads.

At sea HMS *Warspite*, *Roberts* and *Erebus* continued to fire 15-in shells as frequently as targets could be safely engaged. Now the commandos were ashore, the warships and support craft needed either aerial observers or their Forward Officers Bombardment to direct fire safely on to targets away from the troops, yet batteries like W17 'seemed to revive easily after shelling'.[31] When LCG(L) 2 was hit by W17 about the time the first wave of assault troops was landing (1010 hours), the damage was serious and she was too heavily flooded to be towed. The LCH 98, the northern Group's HQ craft, therefore pushed the LCG(L)'s stern to bring her 4.7-in guns to bear on the ever-troublesome battery W13, and she continued firing. Later she had been sufficiently pumped out to be towed by an LCT, but both tow and towed craft sank on hitting mines. LCG(L) 17 was firing on W15 for at least half an hour after the landings, but began to flood through holes in her hull and was also towed out by an LCT. The LCF and LCS(L)s each had their difficulties but persisted in the close support.

LCG(M) 101, having come off the north shoulder of the gap, was sinking despite the efforts of her seamen and Marines to plug holes in the hull. The after mess deck flooded, and airburst HE from one of the field batteries ashore made the upper deck unhealthy. The men were therefore ordered to abandon ship. Most took off their boots. The coxswain PO and a Marine got the wounded out of the wardroom which had been the emergency sick bay; others helped wounded men from the turrets. Lieutenant Tuffin remained on the craft until she was on her side, making sure all his gunners were clear before she sank.[32] The survivors were later picked up by rescue craft, three LCI(S) and an LCI(S) converted to carry casualties.[33]

Of the original 25 craft in the Support Flotilla, some nine were still in action at midday. The three LCT(R)s of the North Group had come back inshore at 1130 hours to lay smoke rockets, screening the beach from batteries W17 and W19 – five captured 3.7-in, three in casemates – on the north of the island. The weather and wind did not help this screen, however, and the LCT(R)s withdrew. The six LCG(L)s and LCS(L)s still in action had not been able to subdue W15, W13 and W11, which had four 150-mm guns in concrete casemates some 8,000yds south of the gap.[34]

As 47 RM Commando moved in towards the beach south of the gap, the LCTs came under fire after they were called in to land at 1230 hours. An LCT Mark 4 which had brought in five LVTs and six Weasels took a direct hit, which killed one LVT's driver and its wireless operator, before this shell exploded under a Weasel. 'A fair blaze resulted as only one LVT had gone ashore, [the LVT] crews and their passengers got out [of the amphibians] as things were very uncertain'.[35] An RE corporal drove his LVT clear and Lieutenant-Colonel C. F. Phillips, DSO, the CO of '47 RM' was then driven ashore in his LVT. As some of this Commando's LCTs had landed north of the gap instead of south of it, they had 'to say the least of it, an untidy landing'.[36] But on D+1 they passed through '48 RM' to take positions east of Zouteland, and the following day only took W11 on their second attack, for this battery was well defended and still firing before '47 RM' successfully broke its defences.

Shortly after midday on D-Day, Y Troop of '41 RM' had worked its way round the east flank of W15, the battery that had sunk five craft and contributed to the damage of 15 others.[37] P Troop provided concentrated fire and smoke cover to keep the battery defences occupied as Y Troop put in its attack. In half an hour of grenade and close-quarters fighting, the battery was cleared, with 120 Germans surrendering. While this battle was in progress, the Brigade Tactical HQ came ashore and Brig Leicester ordered '41 RM' to halt on the line gained so far.

Later on D-Day, at 1300 hours, Typhoons attacked W17 near Domburg, and at 1500 hours '41 RM's' advance restarted, W17 surrendering after slight resistance in the gathering dusk. Domburg was ablaze, from *Warspite*'s shelling and air attacks. To the south '48 RM' put in an attack on W13, after regrouping, when heavy mortar fire killed or wounded many of the first assault Troop before the attack was underway. But air support and an artillery barrage enabled B Troop to assault through the wire, and clear the major part of the battery's defences by dusk. All three Commandos – 41, 47 and 48 – remained on Walcheren until it was secured, and the river Scheldt was later opened for supply ships. The first of these reached Antwerp before the end of November, after 80 miles of estuary and river channels had been swept clear of mines.[38] For the Royal Marines of the support craft this was the last major battle in World War II.

Any analysis of this Support Force's achievements, hinging as it must on some subjective opinion, can only point to their success in drawing the enemy's fire which might have hit the meatier targets of LCTs carrying troops. Had the Germans resisted the temptation to take on the support craft, they might well have rebuffed the Commandos. But the Germans did attack the support craft, and 20 of the 25 were sunk or damaged; 297 of the 1,030 seamen and Marines in these craft became casualties, 172 of them killed.[39] The RM Commandos lost many of their Troop commanders, including Lieutenant P. H. Haydon, who had won a DSO at Salerno; and 68 commandos were killed and 233 were wounded or missing in the 7 days of operations on Walcheren. Losses in part because of the physical damage to the concrete-protected batteries had been small. For example, the LCG(M)'s 17-pdr fire achieved 15 direct hits on '101's' target some 30yds from its landing point, and other shots had glanced off the upper faces of this pill-box. The shots, however, had only penetrated some 6ft of the 10ft reinforced concrete walls. Fire from '102' had entered but not breached her target's seaward face, for – like the guns on the Normandy beaches – this strong-point was sited to enfilade beaches to the north.[40] The Eastern Flank Support Force had, therefore, been matched against far stronger defences than it could destroy, and only two out of 26 German guns (mostly in concrete casemates) had been knocked-out by aerial bombing.

While 4 Cdo Brigade was securing its hold on the islands in the Scheldt estuary, the Royal Marine gunners of 5 RM Anti-Aircraft Brigade were in action in the defence of Antwerp. These batteries, now equipped with 3.7-in heavy anti-aircraft guns and in the light batteries with 40-mm Bofors, included many gunners who had served in the defence of the UK in 1940 and in Ceylon, and some were survivors from Crete. In February 1944, when the MNBDOs had returned to Scotland, their anti-aircraft regiments were to be broken up, but the Air Defence Great Britain Command asked for some units to be retained, and 5 RM Anti-Aircraft Brigade was formed on 22 March[1] from the AA Brigade HQ, Operations Room and a Signals Section, all from MNBDO II, with 1st RM Heavy Anti-Aircraft Regiment (ex-MNBDO I), 3rd RM HAA Regiment (ex-II) and 4th RM Light AA Regiment (ex-I). Commanded by Brigadier J. E. Leech-Porter, OBE, the Brigade mobilised (drawing their operational stores) and retrained during May and June. Drawing stores and re-equipping units while trying to complete practice shoots can be a recipe for muddle, but the Brigade put its Regiments in such good order that during July and August they destroyed 122 V1 flying bombs on the south coast of England before sailing to France.

In early October the Brigade took over the anti-aircraft gunnery defences of the Scheldt estuary, and, in addition to RM formations, had under command, 111 HAA, 114 LAA, and 133 LAA Regiments RA, and 76 and 105 AA Brigades (12 Army regiments altogether) plus 6/2 and 415/54 Searchlight Batteries RA and 202 Fixed Coastal Defences RA. Makeshift accommodation was improvised with shacks and 'huts' along dykes, often in flooded areas which could only be approached by boat. Communications were also difficult in these conditions, with over 2,000 miles of telephone line laid by the signallers in a duplicate system connecting all the sites – guns, searchlights, smoke-generating units, operations rooms, stores and headquarters. The duplications proved invaluable after later air raids. All major units were also in wireless contact and the strength of the Brigade's signal units was raised from 80 to 200 personnel.[2]

The heavy gun batteries fired on occasions in support of ground troops during the first few weeks of October, but their principal role was to counter air attacks on the 7,000yds circle covering Antwerp and the area to the west. When V1s began coming over on 27 October[3] two zones or 'belts of AA fire' were organised around Antwerp and Brussels, with a corridor between. The 1st RM HAA Regiment moved to Brussels, where American AA units had SCR 584[4] radar-linked predictors and proximity fuses. They operated in what were known as the east and south-east zones code-named 'Diver' belts, which also contributed to Antwerp's defence.[5]

The Brigade's Operations Room at Antwerp recorded 483 V1 and 313 V2 (rocket) incidents in the month to 12 December 1944. Units of the Brigade also formed rescue squads, with equipment to help civilians buried in wrecked buildings after V1 and V2 explosions. When German air activity increased before their Ardennes offensive, the *Luftwaffe* flew a low-level attack against Antwerp on New Year's Day 1945. Twenty-four fighters came in at 150ft to be met by such intense fire – D Battery alone firing 140 rounds in half an hour during four separate engagements[6] – that later waves flew in higher, and four were shot down. The Army's *Textbook of Anti-Aircraft Gunnery* points out that the true criterion of the efficiency of the AA defence guns is not the number of aircraft shot down, but rather what more could the enemy have accomplished in the absence of AA artillery?[7] That 5 RM AA Brigade met this test of efficiency there seems little doubt, for had German planes been able to disrupt shipping in Antwerp, then the Allied advance into Germany would have been delayed and many more lives lost. Antwerp handled the major portion of stores landed in Europe, with, for example, 28,760 tons landed there on 3 January out of the 57,060 landed in Europe on a typical day.[8]

The V1s and V2s continued to fall in the area, however, with growing intensity during February, 160 exploding in one 24-hour period to 0600 hours on 16 February, almost 5 years to the day (15 February) since the 1st RM Anti-Aircraft Regiment (later 1st HAA) was formed. That Regiment, like the Brigade, had taken part in their last major shoot against aircraft on the previous New Year's Day, but after leaving Antwerp early in March 1945 they were only in action briefly, although one target at the time the Brigade provided coast defence batteries was believed to be a submarine.[9]

The anti-aircraft regiments were Royal Marine formations with no direct descendants in the Corps of the 1990s, although 3 Commando Brigade has its air defence Troop. And of the other wartime formations, such as the Naval Port parties, there are no exact equivalents, although the Mobile Landing Craft Advanced Base (MOLCAB) organisations could be said to have somewhat equivalent organisations in advanced bases for landing craft of the 1990s. The first MOLCAB formed in January/February 1945 was to provide facilities for landing craft crews ashore, when they were operating ferry services away from their parent ship LSIs.[10] This MOLCAB I, under Colonel C. M. Sergeant, OBE, DSC, sailed for the Far East in February 1945 and was followed by MOLCAB II (Colonel C. N. Smith) in March. MOLCAB III (Lieutenant-Colonel E. C. Hoar) was sent from its assembly base (HMS *Dragonfly*, Hayling Island) to Antwerp. There it was joined by engineer ratings of Mobile Base Naval Unit No 6 and LC Repair Unit No 8, with a Naval crane party which had four Bay City mobile cranes. These maintenance units served the five flotillas of Force U which ferried stores on the Scheldt and other waterways. The Marines requisitioned schools and other accommodation, set up kitchens and provided administrative staff for the crews and maintenance personnel, as well as internal security and defence units for these bases. When Force U's flotilla was transferred to the Rhine as Force T, MOLCAB III moved to Nijmegen, but the original scheme to provide six of these mobile bases was curtailed the following September.[11] As victory came sooner than expected in the Far East, many such plans were never tested in action. The RM bomb disposal teams – usually a senior NCO and five or six men – who had served with Naval Port Parties, for example, trained for operations in the Far East during the spring of 1945 but were not sent there.[12]

The Royal Marines' commitments in 1944 to the Far East were mainly in the ships' detachments of the British Eastern Fleet and the two Commandos, '42 RM' and '44 RM', with 3 Commando Brigade. The Fleet had been in action during August against Japanese shore installations, and on 25 August carrier aircraft from HMS *Victorious* (Lieutenant-Colonel R. C. Hay commanding 47 Wing)[1] and HMS *Illustrious* attacked airfields near Sabang on the northern tip of Sumatra. Although there were few targets found on these airfields, the subsequent air and sea bombardment of the port destroyed repair shops, set fire to oil-storage tanks and sank two small ships, with only superficial damage to the Eastern Fleet.[2]

The passage of 3 Commando Brigade to India had been interrupted when one troopship was nearly hit by a bomb in the Mediterranean; this near-miss loosened many of the ship's plates and several months were spent over its repair in Egypt. The transport carrying 5 Army and 44 RM Commandos reached India, however, without incident. These Commandos were landed at Alethangyaw (Arakan) in a series of major raids, to dominate the coastal strip west of the Mayu hills and some 15 miles south of the main Allied offensive by XV Corps.[3] Here the Marines learnt at first hand the battle tactics of the Japanese, for although their weapons and equipment were in many respects inferior to Allied guns, planes and ships, they relied on what they believed were their superior fighting qualities in the exploitation of surprise, speed, tactical ruses and deceptions.[4] When '44 RM' landed in the dark from three flights of leaky old assault craft, the commandos found these tactics were used against them. They first landed at 2330 on 11 March 1944, and found that around the bamboo-mat huts of the village (Alethangyaw) were Japanese defence positions. In the next few days the Japanese spoke in English on the Marines' radio net, made excellent use of camouflage in, for example, lying along the limbs of mangrove trees. They called out in English to mislead if they could any isolated Marine sentries, and in attacks would make a great noise from one direction while riflemen came in quietly on a different line of approach to the defences.

The Marine commandos proved equal to all these stratagems, and not only were more than a match for the Japanese in fighting tactics, but outplayed them in the deceptions. Lieutenant-Colonel F. C. Horton, commanding '44 RM', made bogus 'we are staying in the village' radio messages, while his men waded inland down a *chaung* to set up a box defence on a hill top from which they made fighting patrols.[5] Later the Marines evacuated these positions so quietly that the Japanese put in attacks on the empty defences, when the commandos were several miles to the west re-embarking in their landing craft.[6] This and subsequent raids by '44 RM', with those of 5 Army Commando, proved the value of amphibious forces in the mangrove swamps of the Arakan. This was a strip of Burmese coast west of the Irrawaddy where 3 Commando Brigade, early in 1945, would play an important part in blocking the escape of the Japanese 54 Division from Burma.

By January 1945 the Corps would be well along the road to reorganising its forces for this type of warfare, and to take a major part in the strategy of a Pacific war with vast distances to be covered. Although the Admiralty before 1939 had 'dreamt of a major battle fleet operating 10,000 miles from home despite the uncertainties of operations against Germany',[7] the events of 1941 had forced a revision of this concept. Under the new strategies the Royal Marines would undertake eight principal roles in operations in the Far East.

Over 2,000 would be required for detachments of the British Pacific and East Indies Fleets. Some 9,000 would man the landing craft of three Naval assault forces. About 850 in 34th Amphibian Support Regiment with tracked rocket, flame-thrower and other LVTs mounting 75-mm gun-howitzers (LVT(A) Mark 4s) were intended to provide close support on beaching; this Regiment also had Army maintenance and other support services personnel.[8]

The Marines of the Small Operations Group (SOG) – some 60 canoeists – would work with other reconnaissance groups, and the Corps also provided the administrative back-up for this unit. The six MOLCABs, mentioned earlier, would require some 2,400 men, and the sixteen Mobile Naval Air Base (MON-ABs) some 2,000 men in their defence forces. The Royal Marine Engineers required for construction work with MONABs and other units would number 20,000; while the four RM Commandos in the two Brigades intended to be deployed in the east, each with two RM and two Army Commandos, would need upwards of 2,500 Marines, and eventually many more. No precise figures for these intended deployments have been traced, and as the plans were not finalised before the end of the war, the requirements were never fully met.[9] Although many of these plans were not realised, their composition was to be of interest for the future. There were also plans to form six Beach Groups, along the lines of 7th RM Battalion's Beach Brick in Sicily, with two Groups to each Naval assault force. The battalions which would be the nucleus of each Group were formed in two Brigades – 116 Brigade with 27th, 28th and 30th RM Battalions and 117 Brigade with 31st, 32nd and 33rd RM Battalions – drawn mainly from landing craft crews, but the 27th RM Battalionn was formed from anti-aircraft gunners who had served with MNBDO I. The Landing craft crews would not be required in the Far East, since the main landing forces would make ocean passages in LCI(L)s and their heavy equipment would be landed over beaches from LSTs rather than being ferried in from transports. The equipment of these Battalions, however, was raised soon after their formation from the light scales of beach parties to that of Army Infantry Battalion War Establishments, and they fought as infantry in Europe.[10]

These Beach Groups, among other units expected to serve in the Far East, would require many more vehicle drivers than were available in the Corps, although there were already some 1,000 RM drivers on Naval Air Stations[11] and the MT Company in Sydney was responsible for the Navy's motor transport throughout Australia.[12] An estimated additional 4,000 drivers were to be trained by the end of 1945, and HMS *Excalibur* was opened as the RM Motor Transport School at Alsager (Cheshire), training 288 drivers a month by March 1945.[13] But the whole question of converting the Corps to a fully amphibious role was in debate. While General Hunton, the GOC RM, was pressing for all tracked amphibians to be manned by Marines, the Naval Staff considered that these amphibians, especially the LVT (Armoured) with guns controlled to Army methods and likely to move inland, should be an Army commitment.[14] Nevertheless the 29th RM Battalion, containing many former tank crews from the Armoured Support Group, which was originally to be the nucleus of a Beach Group, was re-formed as the 34th Amphibian Assault Regiment, mentioned above and later renamed 34th Amphibian Support Regiment.

Such questions as the proper use of the Corps' resources were considered by the Golden Committee during the spring of 1945. This committee under Rear-Admiral Golden, with the RM Major-General H. T. Newman and Captain H. P. K. Orason RN, reported on the 'revised instructions to the GOC RM and ... closer co-operation ... between [Naval] Departments and ... the Royal Marines [in] amphibious tasks'.[15] Their reports provided specific suggestions for Royal Marine commitments in the Naval assault force proposed by the Bottomley committee. They recommended that Naval assault forces should include the two Commandos, the two Beach Groups, the LC Obstacle Clearance Units, LC and Vehicle recovery units, and all the minor landing craft crews, but not the gunners on LCG(L)s, since the size of these detachments outweighed the Naval complement.[16] The GOC RM appended to the report a series of proposals to meet the likely need for Naval Commanders-in-Chief 'to have at their immediate disposal a small force which can be airlifted ... [as] future developments may make it economical to use carrier aircraft ... [and] Beach Groups may have to bridge an air-to-ground gap'.[17] This forward thinking anticipated the commando carrier warship, but in the winter of 1944–5 the Corps was stretched to find the manpower for its existing commitments in North West Europe, Italy and the Far East. Reinforcements were being trained for 5 RM AA Brigade.[18] In addition, 3,000 men from landing craft crews originally intended for the third Naval assault force in the Far East were diverted to 117 RM Brigade, and therefore Marines could not man all minor craft in the Far East assault forces. The Corps did not therefore take over the drafting of these crews. The shortage of 'HO' officers also led to recruiting offers to RNVR and RAF personnel, but only seven RNVR officers transferred to the Corps and none joined from the RAF.[19]

Two examples illustrate the complexity of the Corps' commitments at this time. When Colonel E. St J. Brockman was appointed Senior Officer Royal Marines (SORM) Australia, his directive specifically stated that 'you will have the same relation to other branches of the staff of VA(Q) BPF [Vice-Admiral (Q) British Pacific Fleet] as the GOC RM has to other Admiralty Staff Divisions and Departments'. This gave the Colonel the authority to promote officers up to the rank of acting-major in his command and above that rank with General Hunton's approval; the SORM could also make cross-posting within the Pacific Fleet as required by its Commander-in-Chief, authority which, being clearly stated in his directive, 'proved of value in practice'.[20] The second example is one showing diversification. Small groups of Marines, in Carrier Borne Air Liaison Sections, were landed 'to talk planes from carriers on to targets'.[21] Commanded by an army major, with an Army captain doing a similar job to an FOB, each CBAL had an RM NCO and a Marine as drivers and signallers. These 'Seaballs', as they were known, were to include Royal Marines until 1961, by which date they were called Carrier Borne Ground Liaison (CBGL) Sections and thereafter were drawn entirely from Army personnel.[22]

Something of the administrative problems of command and the highly diversified nature of some RM roles, as seen in these examples, led to careful appraisals by General Hunton of the Corps' commitments for the Far East; for on 3 December 1944 the Prime Minister had written to the First Sea Lord asking where all RM formations were deployed, the first step in a search for 10,000 Marines who might be transferred to the invading armies poised to enter Germany, transfers the GOC RM was able to insist should be in formed units.[23] Now that plans were crystallising for the invasion of Japan, General Hunton rightly maintained a similar policy in proposing the use of Marines in formations of adequate size to control their own operations, at least at the level of a brigade or Naval squadron.

The GOC RM's staff was strengthened early in 1945 to carry through the retraining necessary for Pacific operations: the G1-training became a Colonel's appointment, and an additional G2-training and a signals officer (Lieutenant-Colonel or Major) were also authorised for the staff.[24] The Signals Branch was to train for the RM Beach Groups alone some 100 signal officers and 3,000 trained signallers.[25] This was a heavy demand on its training resources, but the Corps had been able through the war years to build up its own training staff in this Branch, as in Naval gunnery. (RM Signallers had not only provided their own instructors, but from the 1870s probably – and certainly since the inception of the Branch in August 1886 – had provided some instructors for the Army Signals School from time to time.[26]) By early 1945 RM Signallers were 'given a working knowledge in all types of communications equipment used in the Royal Marines . . . because of the wide variety of commitments in which [they] may be employed'. These by early 1945 included field cable routes and switchboard installation; brigade and regimental wireless nets; signals instruments and their maintenance; a working knowledge of Naval visual and wireless procedures; and the ability in the case of RMS(3)s – 3rd Class (lowest) – to send and read lamp at 10 words a minute, semaphore at 15 wpm [words per minute] and radio buzzer at 18 wpm.[27] These may not sound too exacting, but a Marine signaller might be working ashore to Army routines on radio networks, and be posted to a support craft the next week on which he would be reading lamp signals in a convoy at sea, as well as operating Naval wireless routines.

The RM Engineers at this time were about 7,300 strong, and serving with these civil engineers and tradesmen were 1,072 general duty Marines of all ranks. At one time this force of RM Engineers was expected to reach 20,000, with 3,000 attached RM ranks. The GOCRM's responsibilities included discipline and military training, and 'by implication these duties included pay, morale, clothing and welfare',[28] but although training facilities were to be expanded during 1945 the RME was not increased in strength much beyond 8,000.[29]

Apart from such schools for specialists as the Signals School at Saundersfoot (Pembrokeshire) and the MT School, the Corps also set up an Eastern Warfare School, Brockenhurst, where officers and senior NCOs did a 10-day course 'on the special form of warfare . . . in the Far East Theatre.' In addition, in the UK and abroad, there were 'jungle warfare' schools. The standards for 'physical efficiency tests', as they were called, were also raised to the following: 10-mile march in 2¼ hours, before firing five rounds, three of which must be hits at 30yds; leopard crawl 45yds in a minute followed by pitching two out of three grenades into a 10ft circle; running two miles on roads in 18 minutes; jumping a 9ft ditch; and various climbing feats.[30] All these were aimed at making every Marine fit – not only those serving in Commandos – and for detachments in the Pacific Fleet: such applied physical training was a routine. This aimed at not only keeping men fit but enabling them to pass these battle efficiency tests.

In July 1944 the fleet aircraft carrier HMS *Illustrious* was joined by the fleet carriers HMS *Victorious* and *Indomitable*; all three, with HMS *Indefatigable*, would later form the core of the British Pacific Fleet (BPF), but that summer they were in the Indian Ocean. Their planes, as mentioned earlier, made several raids against targets in Sumatra and the Nicobar Islands before 19 October, when they were re-equipped with American Grumman Avenger torpedo-bombers, more effective planes than their Barracudas.[1] Most of the fighter aircraft in the BPF were also American, and revised tactics to suit the higher cruising speed and attack characteristics of the Avenger were practised before *Illustrious* and *Indomitable* attacked oilfields in Sumatra, as a rehearsal for their intended roles. These for the BPF would be to destroy Japanese aircraft, oil installations, airfields and communication lines. Operations for which the Fleet Air Arm had trained since 1943, largely at the prompting of two RM captains;[2] and the low flying techniques in conjunction with CBAL Sections would prove effective in ground attacks.

In January 1945, 92 planes of the combined Air Groups from the carriers attacked Pangkalan (near Belwan Deli, Sumatra) with success, destroying 32 Japanese aircraft, many on the ground. Of the two FAA planes lost (one flown by Major V. B. G. Cheeseman, leading 1770 Firefly Squadron) both crews were saved. Much of the success[3] of this raid was achieved by the use of an Air Co-Ordinator, Lieutenant-Colonel R. C. (Ronnie) Hay RM, leading a special flight of Corsairs; and his call sign 'Father' is indicative of the Co-Ordinator's role in these techniques.

The British Pacific Fleet was to be based in Australia, and early in 1945 the nucleus – the four carriers, joined by the battleship HMS *King George V*, three cruisers and ten destroyers – under Rear-Admiral Sir Philip Vian, sailed for Fremantle. Their voyage was routed from Ceylon to pass within air-striking distance of the southeast Sumatra oil refineries at Palembang. These two large refineries, the largest in south-east Asia, could provide three-quarters of Japan's needs for aviation fuel,[4] and their destruction was to hamper the Japanese war effort seriously. Admiral Vian's planes made two attacks: on 24 January, despite heavy anti-aircraft fire and a balloon barrage, the 43 Avengers and 80 fighters destroyed oil tanks and installations, halving one refinery's output; five days later, having refuelled and rearmed, the carriers were back, and their aircraft stopped all production at Soengi Gerong refinery for two months and damaged a large tanker beyond repair. In between photographing the results of this raid, Ronnie Hay shot down two aircraft and had a share in the destruction of two others.[5] In the two raids 130 Japanese planes were destroyed, against 48 FAA planes lost from all causes, some 50 per cent of them in deck landings. Nine of these FAA crewmen were later murdered by the Japanese, after seven months' captivity.

Other elements of the Pacific Fleet were assembling in Australia, and the work of the East Indies Fleet had moved from primarily escort cover for convoys during 1943 to supporting amphibious operations in the Arakan, before Admiral Vian's carriers raided the oil refineries. This East Indies Fleet included escort carriers – converted merchant ships' hulls each with a squadron of fighters flying anti-submarine patrols and giving air cover to convoys. Among them was HMS *Battler*, which had come to the Indian Ocean after several operations: two of her Seafires had shot down a shadowing FW Condor in the Atlantic, and her planes had supported the Salerno landings and helped to sink a U-boat supply ship in the Indian Ocean – under her Commander Flying, Major A. R. Burch RM, who had led the 1940 Fleet Air Arm attack with torpedoes against destroyers in Trondheim Fjord. The escort carriers HMS *Rajah*, *Khedive* and *Ameer* also had RM majors as Commanders Flying at different times, and Majors A. E. Marsh and W. G. S. Aston commanded the planes of *Khedive* and *Ameer* supporting 3 Commando Brigade's landings in the Arakan in the winter of 1944–5.[6] In all, eight RM officers served as Commanders (Flying) in World War II.

The four Commandos of 3 Brigade, Nos 1, 5, 42(RM) and 44(RM) were concentrated at Teknaf in December 1944.[7] The commandos who had landed at Alethangyaw the previous March had been joined by '1 (Army) Cdo' and '42 RM', who had spent some weeks in the line near Maungdaw, operating with 74 Brigade during November 1944. A Troop of '42 RM' had also gone to reconnoitre Elizabeth Island, when it lost one Marine who was cut off from the raiding party, but continued to fire, covering the withdrawal.[8] His position had been revealed after 'one of the "friendly" villagers had run across the island ... to warn the garrison'.[9] '5 (Army) Cdo' had also made a similar raid on Ramree Island. The Brigade Commander, Brigadier Campbell Hardy (who had commanded '46 RM' in Normandy), and his staff had been planning a landing on the western tip of the Akyab peninsula across the Mayu River estuary, an operation expected to meet resistance in February 1945. But on Boxing Day 1944, the Brigadier was called to XV Corps' headquarters and the operation was brought forward, as elements of XV Corps were already east of the peninsula. The Brigadier's small planning staff – the Brigade Major, the DAA and QMG (responsible for supplies, movements and administration), the Intelligence Officer and Brigade Signals Officer – organised the assault in the next few days. And on 4 January the Brigade made an unopposed daylight landing on the peninsula.

The Corps commander[10] had pressed his 25 Division along the coast, as part of his overall plan to prevent the Japanese divisions in the Arakan and those in central Burma, who might use the An pass, being evacuated by sea from the An River delta. The Japanese on the Myebon Peninsula, 70 miles south of Akyab, had first to be isolated from their defence system around Kangaw to the east.[11]

The operational orders for the Brigade were 'to seize and hold Myebon peninsula as a base for further operations against enemy lines of com-munication ...' These orders had been drawn up after the Brigadier had made a personal reconnaissance of the beach in a Naval launch, which, despite coming under fire, did not alert the Japanese to the possibility of a landing. The plan was for 42 RM Commando to land in two flights, one at H-hour (0900) and the second at H+3 minutes; 5 Commando was to land at H+25 minutes, then pass through and secure the village of Agnu and high ground. 35 minutes later 1 (Army) Commando would land, with '44 RM Cdo' as a floating reserve in a craft offshore.[12] Air strikes, bombardment by a sloop, and the demolition of obstacles by a Naval Combined Operations Pilotage Party prepared the way, and 42 RM Commando's craft ran inshore, supported by mortar fire from two LCS(M) adding to the smoke cover, and 5 (Army) Commando were put ashore. The craft carrying later waves on a falling tide, grounded 500yds offshore . The commandos came over the bows, nevertheless, into 4ft of glutinous mud and water, and it was 1700 hours before '44 RM' were cleaned up and ready for action. A naked lieutenant having rescued most of their heavy stores 'and half the heavier personnel'[13] from the slime. There had been little opposition and with difficulty several tanks of 19th Lancers, Indian Army, were brought into action.

Next day in the advance into the hills north of the peninsula, Lieutenant-Colonel H. D. Fellowes, CO of '42', (he had commanded the Siege Regiment in 1940) being well forward with his intelligence officer, was caught in a burst of machine gun fire. Although he was wounded and the wireless hit,[14] the Lieutenant-Colonel got back to his Commando's main positions beyond the village of Myebon, having established that the Japanese held hills to the north in some strength. These were cleared by 42 RM and 1 (Army) Commandos with the very welcome help of a Sherman tank of the Lancers. The nights turned unpleasantly cold for men in tropical rig, but during D+2 the final attacks were made on the three hill positions across the north of the peninsula – '44 RM' having formed up 'under the cover of the hill side opposite our objective ... the first wave streaked across a hundred yards of "paddy" which ... was burning furiously [after] smoke bombs from our mortars had been fired into it'.[15] The Japanese were seen retreating from their bunkers and the Marines secured the hill: 'We "boxed" there that night [forming a defended area] and rum was issued with the evening meal ... a fraction of a tin of self-heating soup' for each man.[16] Later they found a store of Japanese tinned salmon, but were always wary of booby traps on such finds. On 20 January they marched back to the landing beaches, and next day the Brigade was ferried out to LCI(L)s for the Kangaw landings.

The junction of tracks at Kangaw was important, because once these were cut, the Japanese would be left to die in the high Arakan or be killed by the advancing Fourteenth Army. To reach Kangaw, however, involved three choices: to advance along the river banks from Myebon with Japanese holding the high ground ('not attractive'); to fight north and then east, a long operation in which the Japanese would have time to withdraw through Kangaw; or to mount a surprise attack up the river from the south, although this approach would have to be made in daylight. The third and boldest course was chosen, the Brigadier and his second-in-command making a night reconnaissance to find a beach. After approaching the coast in a Motor Launch, they transferred to an LCA with a COP Party whose canoes were lashed to the LCA's gunwales. They then reconnoitred the 'beach', although on the high spring tide they were in the upper branches of mangrove trees! Nevertheless they had found the places to land at low water, after which 'we had a rather adventurous trip back to base'.[17] Kangaw could not claim, however, to have a beach in the accepted sense, among the mangroves.

Kangaw's road runs out of forested hills to the east, but to the west of the village there were *chaungs* and waterlogged paddy fields, with decayed mangrove stumps and thorn in places. The steep, 45-degree, clay banks of the *chaungs* often had 60ft belts of mangrove roots 'with mud not more than 9 inches deep before the firm ground' of a paddy field bund with its banks some 3ft high. At low water the *chaung* banks were 5ft high and the exposed mangrove roots difficult to cross. Nevertheless the Brigade's intention was 'to secure a bridgehead on Daingbon *Chaung* preparatory to establishing a road block at Kangaw'.

There were several small hills west of the village, however, including the key feature Hill 170, a wooded ridge running north-south above the paddy fields. This would be secured, if there was no serious opposition, 'with all possible speed' by 1 (Army) Commando, while '42 RM' secured the beachheads. Surprise was an element in all these landings and therefore the approach was made by the Thegyan River, 27 miles from the sea up narrow waterways that led to Daingbon *Chaung*, with 5 (Army) Commando following the assault flights and having 'the probable task of moving in support of 1 (Army) Commando' and '44 RM' in reserve. H-hour, 1300 on 22 January, would be preceded by strikes by the strategic air force and bombardment support of fire from two sloops and a battery of RA 25-pdrs on Z lighters; to direct this fire two FOO and two FOB parties were to land in the first flight.[18] Also in this first flight were Army Beach Parties with reconnaissance parties from No.3 RM Engineer Commando Troop, which had cleared mines from Myebon beach and provided flame-thrower teams (each of a junior NCO and a Marine) at Akyab.[19]

As the convoy moved slowly up river that sunny Monday morning, 'the line of boats stretched as far as the eye could see', but there was no sign of human life on either bank, 'just muddy mangrove swampland'.[20] The assault Troops of '1 Cdo' moved quickly to Hill 170 and by nightfall held all but its northern end, with '5 Cdo' and Brigade HQ on the southern slopes. '42 RM' found the beach areas waterlogged where 'the whole area had been under water two days before, when the Brigade Commander made his recce'.[21] Nevertheless the RM engineers established landing points in a triangle of land on the east bank of the *chaung* between two small streams running into it. Their recce parties came under machine gun fire and not all the possible landing points could be surveyed. They began to construct roads, but these could only be built by a 'long term policy of digging shallow trenches . . . and throwing up the spoil to dry out in forming a raised roadway'.[22] At this time '44 RM' dug in on the southern slopes of Hill 170, about a mile from the beachhead, where '42 RM' were in water-logged defence positions, yet drinking water was scarce. That night Japanese wandered quite close to the forward positions of 1 Army Commando, then suddenly charged their slit trenches but were driven off; the Japanese officer with a drawn sword leading one such 'Banzai' suicide attack was killed.

On Tuesday morning (D+1), '42 RM' occupied hill 'Milford', and a patrol from '44 RM' reached the small hill known as 'Pinner' east of the main positions. The patrol was followed by this Commando moving in bounds, with one Troop ready to cover the movement of the next and so on. 'The afternoon was calm . . . no Japs . . . no firing', the Marines could see the road running into Kangaw village below them, and away to the north-east they 'could see clearly the heights which were the enemy's stronghold guarding the pass'.[23] The commandos had dug in twice that day and about 1600 hours began digging for the third time, 'until darkness prevented further progress',[24] for perhaps the lack of enemy activity had made these Marines incautious. Certainly they had not occupied enemy bunkers on this hill because they thought these positions would be known.

The moon was up about 2000 hour, when a mortar opened fire on the northern slopes of the hill. Then, 20 minutes later, the sounds of a truck and mules could be heard in the paddy below but nothing could be seen down the densely wooded slopes. Japanese orders were heard, a red Very light shot sky-wards, and the first attack started.[25] An hour later the first shells of a 75-mm gun fell on the hill, the Japanese having brought it up the slope to almost point-blank range. The flashes of the gun and the shells' bursts were almost simul-taneous, while machine gun fire continued to tear through the trees and mortar bombs fell among the commandos' trenches.

'The first wave of Japs were not very persistent and were soon tumbling down the hill again', but the Japanese could be heard calling to each other down the hill side, as they reorganised. The commandos waited motionless. The second attack met steady Bren fire and lobbed grenades, while the Japanese grenades fired from rifle-cup dischargers could be seen silhouetted against the moonlight before they dropped through the trees in among the commandos. Casualties were mounting and the Section guarding the track behind the northern Troop areas was brought forward. Its Bren-gunners were killed but a third man got this machine gun quickly into action and, although wounded, remained with the gun. An attack on the Troop in the right (southern) positions, who had held their fire so far, also failed to break in. Each commando continued to hold his fire till he could clearly see a target coming out of the undergrowth into the moonlight. Throughout these attacks the CO of '44 RM' walked up and down among his men with admirable *sangfroid*,[26] and the Marines still held the hill. One sentry told his Troop commander during a lull, 'Don't worry, Sir, they will not get up here', and an hour later shot the Japanese soldier who was trying to get up a path behind the defence positions. When the moon set about 0300, the Japanese withdrew.

One irony was the amount of ammunition they had used from a dump at the foot of the hill, which the Marines had not found time to explode before they dug in – or at least made scrapes, which were inadequate protection, and there were some 80 casualties.[27] The only intruder which got through the defences was a large porcupine, badly shaken before it fell into the RSM's slit trench, leaving a few quills in his skin.[28] The next day the RM Engineer commandos blew up the remaining dumps and laid booby traps in the approaches to them. The Troop's bulldozer attracted fire from Japanese artillery as the men built rock roads south of Hill 170, but they completed these, using corrugated iron and teak floors from local huts as great duck-boards to reinforce the Sommerfield and coir-matting roadways.

The Japanese kept the beach and hills under shellfire during the following week – 400 shells most days, 800 on some – but many shells failed to explode.[29] Then came the most determined counter-attack, on 31 January, when the Brigade was about to be relieved. After shelling and repeated attacks on No.4 Troop of 1 (Army) Commando holding the northern tip of Hill 170 – Lieutenant G. A. Knowland (Royal Norfolks) won a posthumous VC for his part in this defence – the Troop's forward Sections were overrun, although an LCA with 13 Brens had attempted to break up Japanese attacks by sailing up the small *chaung* north of Hill 170, and firing into Japanese positions on two low hills further north, known as the 'Fingers'.[30] W Troop of '42 RM' moved up to reinforce these forward positions, and 13 Marines under Captain Smith, described as two under-strength Sections, lost half their number trying to clear the north-west slope. One Troop of 5 (Army) Commando also attempted to clear the east slope, but after reaching the paddy fields was forced to withdraw. Further counter-attacks were made by X Troop of '42 RM' and a Troop of 1 (Army) Commando, X Troop taking heavy casualties from three machine guns on the 'Fingers' before it was withdrawn.

The Brigadier, forward on the start line for each assault, kept close control of the battle, and not for the first time his cool courage steadied the men he commanded. The Troop from '1 Cdo' met equally strong defences east of the Commandos' original positions, and despite further attacks by 5 (Army) Commando, the Brigade was held. Although Japanese engineers had knocked out two of 19th Lancers' three tanks early in the battle – they were attacked before the assault began – the remaining tank was in action all day; but the first heavy air attack by Allied planes did not go in until the early evening, when they caused heavy casualties to the enemy, who were withdrawing. The Japanese had shot their bolt and were all off the hill by the morning. Hill 170 had been held, although the Brigade had suffered 135 casualties in the last action alone, including 43 from '42 RM'.[31]

In a special order of the day to 3 Commando Brigade after the battle, General Christisson wrote: 'Your courage and determination in assault . . . your tenacity and aggressiveness in defence . . . have won the praise and admiration of all other formations . . . who fought beside you. The battle of Kangaw has been the decisive battle of the whole Arakan campaign . . . won largely due to your magnificent defence of Hill 170'.[32] General Sir Campbell Hardy has commented: 'None of these successes would have been possible but for the gallantry of other troops under command, notably the 19th Hyderabads and 19th Lancers to both of which units the Brigade later presented green berets which now remain in their respective museums'.

Brigadier (later Major General) Hardy later wrote: 'It would appear that if full advantage is to be taken of initial surprise, every effort should be made to provide sufficient craft for the follow-up brigade to land early . . .' He also suggested that there would be great advantage in having a Beach Command and staff with each assault brigade to speed up planning, and having given due credit to the naval, air and artillery support, he pointed out the advantage of 'having a Forward Tank Officer with leading sub-units', as this made it possible to switch a whole Squadron or Troop on to one target.[33] Such techniques had become increasingly important in Commando tactics, as they expanded their roles from spearheading amphibious landings to operations in closer support of the main Allied armies' advances, as will become apparent later in this chapter.

Royal Marines of the East Indies Fleet also made a landing on Cheduba Island with 500 Marines from ships' detachments, supported by planes from HMS *Ameer* and gunfire from three cruisers. The landing was unopposed, which might have been as well, for Colonel Peter Picton-Phillips (brother of '40 RM's' Colonel, killed at Dieppe) as Fleet RM Officer had the young bugler from '385' Detachment as his bodyguard. The boy was a volunteer and writes of the Colonel: 'He was a real fiery little man but able to inspire his men.'[34] This landing on 26 January, although it met no enemy opposition, when made through heavy surf, was one of the few occasions during World War II when Marines from a fleet had the opportunity to show their abilities as a force ashore. By comparison, the fleet Marines in World War I had made a number of such forays, particularly against the Turkish coast.[35] But late-twentieth century warfare seems inevitably to have brought about a more specialised form of raiding, and the deployment of fleet Marines in, say, Mediterranean landings would have seriously impaired the ships' ability to provide the bombardment support which by 1944 was a feature of all invasions from the sea.

The LCG(L)s and LCG(M)s were being moved to the Far East to join a support squadron of Force 'W' for the landings to capture Rangoon. This was at first planned for 2 May 1945[36] and to be followed subsequent operations. LCG(L) 1062, a Mark 4, visited Ramree Island not long after its capture by 26 Indian Division in mid-February,[37] but the LCG(M) flotillas were not due to sail until midsummer, although several craft set out for the Far East before then, three in the Landing Ship Dock HMS *Highway* and had reached Aden before being recalled. Minor craft had also been shipped out to Burma in the winter of 1944–5, but in the next few months the principal British actions were in Italy and north-west Europe.

During the winter of 1944–5 2 Commando Brigade was in the Mediterranean theatre. The Germans had evacuated Brac, leaving 250 men in hilly strongpoints which '40 RM' and '43 RM' had attacked that summer; and it later took over a week for 2,000 partisans with artillery and air support to take these positions. The losses on Solta, mentioned earlier, had come in the last major raid in force, and 43 RM Commando had been in dangerous isolation on the island before its German garrison was evacuated by sea, an operation in which all the Germans were drowned when British MTBs sank their lighters. The eastern Mediterranean war then moved to Albania, Greece and Montenegro (southern Yugoslavia). In command of 40 RM Commando now was Lieutenant-Colonel R. (Bob) W. Sankey DSC, who had been a company commander in the 11th RM at the time of the Tobruk raid. He spent some months rebuilding '40 RM' after its losses on Brac, and on 23 September the Commando sailed with 2 Special Service Brigade HQ and a troop of RSR 75-mm guns for Albania. They landed near 'Commando Valley', where 2 Army Commando had established a base the previous day.[1] This pass through the high coastal mountains, rising in places to 2,000ft, took 3 hours to march through, for like the many steep-sided valleys of this coast, there was thick scrub and extremely thick woods with no paths. Where the ground was rocky, it was 'so uneven that anyone walking on it was in danger of breaking an ankle', and beyond the valley: the road running south to Sarande crossed a mass of tiny hillocks, 'the ground rough and broken like a giant file'.[2]

The Brigade's two Commandos in Albania – 9 Army Commando was in Greece and '43 RM' going to Montenegro – spent eight days in continuous rain; many men suffered from exposure, before four LCI(L)s were used in the beach-head for them to dry their clothing during 24-hour rest periods. The commandos patrolled and stood-to in this valley for over a fortnight, aware that over 2,000 Germans were within striking distance – 500 of them in Sarande – with heavy German guns bombarding the valley and the beachhead, only 6 miles from the German coastal batteries on the nearby island of Corfu. For the attack on Sarande, two LCG(L)s and two destroyers would supplement the artillery fire. This, from early October, had included 25-pdrs among the 16 guns of the Brigade's organic artillery. The partisans, belonging to a left-wing organisation which later seized control of Albania, created a diversion by firing into the inland garrison's posts around Delvine, before the attack on Sarande went in at 0430 hours (9 October) after a preliminary bombardment.

Having seized the strongpoint north-west of the town, in four hours '40 RM' had cleared the defences from two nearby landing points, which were immediately used to bring in ammunition to resupply the assault force. The Commando pushed on into the town[3] and Lieutenant-Colonel Sankey found that the main defence point was a hospital. He is remembered by many of '40 RM' for 'his jolly way of life, always good for a skylark, yet always treating you as a man and a friend,' and that afternoon he led '40 RM' with a great dash. His .45 revolver in hand, he made a personal close reconnaissance of the defences before the final rush to capture the hospital, after he had organised its bombardment. But the street fighting continued until late afternoon, as '40 RM' cleared pockets of resistance; and many booby-trapped houses were found in the town. The men of 2 Army Commando and No.1 Para Company of the RAF Levies, and 500 Albanian partisans, took their objectives, but the hardest share of the fighting had fallen to '40 RM'.[4]

The Commando then crossed the strait to occupy Corfu, from where Lieutenant-Colonel Sankey wrote to General Sturges (GOC Commando Group) who responded with informal letters. Both officers had much in common in their outlook, and in congratulating the Lieutenant-Colonel on his DSO for the Sarande action, the General commented on his own visits to commandos in north-west Europe: 'being shot at in an Anson [aircraft] . . . or being sick in an MTB . . . there is probably nothing in it either way'.[5] A later letter from the General, dated 3 March 1945, explains in colourful language the difficulties in getting NCO volunteers released for commando service, 'for hells bells some stupid [ass] finds out they are coxswains' or otherwise required for specialist duties. Good NCOs were needed on Corfu, for the Lieutenant-Colonel had more political than military problems; but he dealt with them effectively, although he had to split up his Troops in maintaining an uneasy peace between warring Greek factions. Problems of currency inflation, no pay, no mail and disarming the irregulars were all dealt with by the Lieutenant-Colonel, whose administrative ingenuity matched his military skill. A King's Badgeman before the War, he had been a stockbroker before rejoining the Corps in 1940. His patrols, led by commando officers with 10 Marines, 10 Greek soldiers and a policeman, each disarmed partisans in their strongpoints about the island, to the relief of the local people.[6] The Commando was withdrawn in December but returned in January 1945 to defend the island for the next seven weeks against Albanian and Greek communist.[7]

At this time '43 RM' spent three months in Montenegro, where the German XXI Mountain Corps, 30,000 men, was cut off from its main Army Group – which had retreated further east – and was entangled in partisan defences among the mountains on the line of its retreat. The commandos formed infantry protection parties for 111 Field Regiment's guns, spread in the support of different partisan actions. But the partisans here, in the same way that their attitudes had changed in the Dalmatian islands, no longer welcomed British help. Lieutenant-

Colonel (later General Sir) Ian H. Riches took over command from Major N. G. M, Munro late in November 1944, when the Troops were widely dispersed, and winter had set in, with snow several feet deep in the mountains. The Marines had no adequate cold-weather clothing, and although various plans were made to use the commandos in raids, few were mounted. A small party, an officer and 20 men, unsuccessfully tried to infiltrate German road bridge defences, but a Troop had more success in crossing a river and protecting engineers laying a Bailey Bridge, as the partisans followed the Germans northwards. A party from C Troop came down the steep 2,000ft road from their posts protecting a battery of 111 Field Regiment, to cut the busy coast road to Risan (Gulf of Kotor). Their 300lb of explosives was carried in sacks by villagers for part of the journey, and stacked under a culvert, despite ice-cold water pouring through this under-road drain, the water building up at the dam of explosives to provide a better blast. A truck appeared down the road in spite of a block of mines laid to protect the approach, and the explosives had then to be fired before the party had withdrawn as intended. Nevertheless they all got safely away up the steep roadside bank, just as the enemy truck passed and the culvert exploded with a flash and ear-splitting roar.

Throughout its time in Yugoslavia 43 RM Commando had difficult marches, especially when getting the artillery observation posts forward in rugged mountain country. It solved part of the difficulty of supplying such positions by forming one Troop into muleteers. A second Troop also took over four 75-mm guns, which the muleteers transported, but such added fire-power could not be tested in battle before Tito's partisans insisted on the Commando's return to Italy.[8]

Headquarters of 2 SS Brigade had been reorganised during the winter, and Brigadier Tom Churchill returned to the UK to command an infantry brigade. A number of officers who had served in the Brigade's Commandos were appointed to the staff, including Major I. D. De'ath, DSO, appointed to Brigade Major, before the Commandos were concentrated at Ravenna. During March they served in turn in V Corps' line along the southern shores of Lake Comacchio, some 15 miles long, with shallows in its eastern lagoon. When not in the line, they trained in storm boats for their crossing of this lagoon, with its dykes breached to flood the surrounding countryside. This stretch of shallow water, a mere six inches in depth over large areas, was separated from the sea to the east by a narrow spit of sand dunes containing well-prepared defences. These were held by 1,200 Turkoman Russians from Asia Minor and a German battalion, for this was a key defence on Field Marshal Kesselring's left flank of defences along the line south of the Po valley.

The plan was to send 2 and 9 Army Commandos in storm boats from the peninsula west of the spit to land on its western shore, while '43 RM' attacked up the spit's eastern shore along a tongue of land, before crossing the River Reno's estuary on to the spit; '40 RM' would provide one Troop to create a diversion at the base of the spit by crossing the Reno. Another Troop, under command of a half squadron of the North Irish Horse, was to cross the Reno upstream on rafts, to clear the narrow strip of land between the river's north

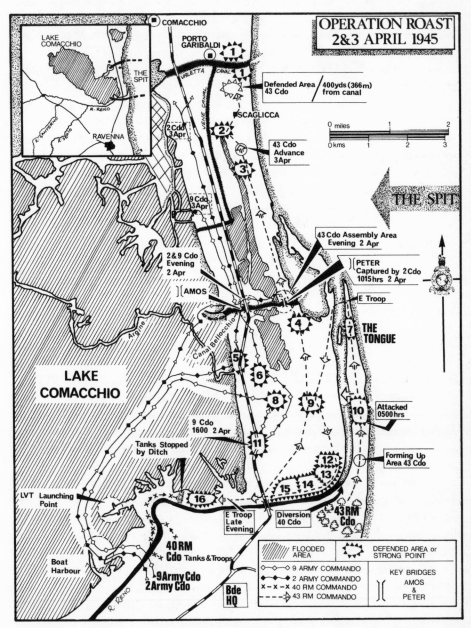

2 Commando Brigade's assault on the eastern coastal defences of Lake Comacchio 2–3 April 1945 against defended areas with biblical code names: 1 north of Valetta canal – 'Samuel'; 1 south of the canal – 'Exodus'; 2 'Jeremiah'; 3 'James'; 4 'Genesis'; 5 'Ezra'; 6 'Isaiah I'; 7 'Numbers'; 8 'Isaiah II'; 9 'Acts'; 10 'Joshua'; 11 'Leviticus'; 12 'Hosea I'; 13 'Hosea II'; 14 'Matthew II'; 15 'Matthew I'; and 16 'Mark'.

bank and the lagoon, while the rest of '40 RM' was held in reserve.[9] The assaults were to be made at night under a strong artillery barrage from seven field and medium RA regiments, and two heavy RA batteries. Reconnaissance by SBS and COPP canoe parties had found the lagoon exceptionally shallow after weeks of dry weather.[10]

The Brigade had been given a free hand by V Corps in the detailed planning of the operation, which would extend the German defences before a general Allied offensive further west. For a week before the operation each night a great deal of noise had been made by – among other diversions – '40 RM' playing Wagner loudly over loudspeakers. This accustomed the defenders to a great hullabaloo, at the same time as '43 RM' made night recce patrols to get specific information on the enemy's defences on the tongue. On D-Day night (1–2 April) the great noise covered the sound of 2 and 9 Army Commandos assembling just before midnight, when their leading LVTs – known here as Fantails – moved across the river and out along a narrow peninsula. The LVTs, however, bogged down; launching storm boats through 1,500yds of glutinous, stinking mud then took several hours; and the first light of dawn was breaking, at 0430 hours, before the Army commandos were afloat. The leading Troop of '43 RM' was 1,000yds from its first objective, but both A and B Troops had to be brought back to maintain surprise as daylight came.

The Brigade Commander, the Army Brigadier R. J. F. Tod, DSO, decided that the assault must go through, and a smoke screen was laid to cover the Army Commandos' crossing of an artificial dyke several hundred yards from the shore. At 0500 hours A and B Troops of '43 RM' moved forward again as '40 RM's' diversion drew much of the enemy's fire. X Troop of '40 RM' had driven stakes into the river bank the previous evening, under cover of mortar fire, and now hauled rubber boats over the bank. Although 'unfortunately the ground was too rough and not all the boats reached the water';[11] but the system of pulleys worked well, rifles attached to dummies were fired and the Troop's Brens, Piats and automatic weapons added to the realism of the attack. Meanwhile A and B Troops had moved out of the wood where 43 RM Commando had been concealed and began a 1,400yds advance.[12] Rockets, artillery and machine gun fire swept the flat ground in front of their objective 'Joshua' (all the enemy's defended areas had been given biblical code names). This company-strong area was heavily defended by machine guns, which continued to fire despite the Brigade's barrage, holding A Troop on the right 300yds from the defences.

Following A Troop along the seashore, and 200yds back, was D Troop in tanks converted to carry personnel, but these Kangaroos stuck in soft sand and the men went forward on foot. German rockets were accurately ranged on this beach, for the defences were prepared for a landing from the sea, but not for one by the back door on to the west of the spit, where 2 and 9 (Army) Commandos had now begun to land behind the southern half of the defences. B Troop of '43 RM' reached 'Joshua' in one long rush and fought its way into the strongpoints. A and D reorganised, and then, in the face of heavy fire, assaulted the right-hand positions, A Troop passing through these to clear the Tongue while D Troop mopped up.[13] By 0738 hours the positions were clear of the enemy, 50 being dead and 30 prisoners.[14]

A few minutes earlier the commandos of A Troop of '40 RM', had begun moving eastward towards 'Mark', but a deep ditch stopped the tanks' advance. Fascines (bundles of wooden stakes) were dropped into this gap and a dense anti-personnel minefield was negotiated; this took time and more fascines were brought up as the tanks bogged down.[15] But '43 RM' had found better going, B Troops covering the river as C Troop prepared to cross from the tongue to the spit, where the river was some 30yds wide. The Marines assembled their assault boats – three of the five Mark 3 boats were holed but the two 10-man inflatable dinghies survived their journey on Kangaroos – under continuous shelling and mortar fire. Nevertheless the Troop crossed the river and made a small bridgehead in flat open country. At about this time E Troop crossed in LVTs from the northern point of the tongue and met slight opposition, before turning south towards C Troop's bridgehead, which was being reinforced by D and B Troops. The intensity of the enemy's resistance to their crossing is underlined by the casualties to the seven men organising the boats: four were killed and one seriously wounded. But the bridgehead was enlarged and when Lieutenant-Colonel Ian Riches had four Troops across the river by 0845 hours, he put in '43 RM's' attack on position 'Acts'. This was a company position with an 88-mm and an Italian 47/32 anti-tank gun in scrub above the dunes, where there was a clear field of fire.[16] A prolonged artillery smoke screen and accurate shellfire enabled B and D Troops to take the position with little resistance by about 1100 hours, for their assault had been perfectly co-ordinated with the artillery barrage.

By midday engineers attached to 43 RM Commando were building a Class-2 raft, and A Troop was clearing positions on the north bank of the river towards 'Hosea'. They had several casualties 700yds upstream on anti-personnel mines, but 'very good use was made of the Piat by firing at dugouts in the bank', and one bomb was usually found sufficient to cause the immediate surrender of the machine gun crews in them. An attack on 'Hosea I' by B, D and E Troops was successful, and these commandos – now temporarily as a single force under Captain B. I. S. Gourlay, MC – swept down the north-west bank of the river and cleared 'Hosea II'. From these company positions the enemy began surrendering in numbers, and the Commando prepared to have its first meal since the previous evening. But 9 Army Commando had been unable to pass 'Leviticus', after three accurate mortar attacks had caused many commando casualties and they had not taken 'Matthews I and II'. These were well protected from any approach from the sea, that is: from the east. Therefore when '43 RM' was ordered to take them 'some considerable time was taken . . . owing to extensive minefields, dykes and strongly held Spandau positions', which had to be overcome before forming up for the attack.[17] The plan was for '43 RM' to blast the front door of these heavily defended positions. These extended 500yds north from the river and several hundred yards along its northern bank. The attack succeeded and both positions were secured by mid-afternoon, despite commando casualties on anti-personnel mines. E Troop then 'exploited 300yds to the west facing "Mark", the only remaining enemy position on the southern spit'.[18]

The A Troop of '40 RM' with the tanks had worked its way along the river bank, the wounded being brought out under cover of the Commando's 2-in mortar's smoke screen, but this obscured the tanks' line of fire and Marine Williamson therefore 'stayed out in the open with absolutely no cover at all for a full 18 minutes', firing his Bren to protect the further evacuation of wounded.[19] Marines also continued to clear enemy foxholes and a Section worked with each tank to help bring them forward. Fire from 'Mark', a platoon position, continued, however, into the late evening, when E Troop of '43 RM' made a wide detour, 'essential to avoid casualties from the minefields', before finally clearing the position by 2000 hours.

That night '43 RM' assembled around 'Peter', the bridge at the seaward end of the Belocchio canal, half-way up the spit, by which time 9 (Army) Commando had taken 'Leviticus', although its protective smoke screen had cleared when there was still 150yds of open ground to cross. The 2 (Army) Commando had also cleared positions on the south bank of the canal that morning, but any attempts to move north were met by sharp enemy fire, including shells from an 88-mm gun firing over open sights.[20]

Once the north-west bank of the Reno had been cleared, the river could be bridged, and tanks were brought up. But the 'Amos' bridge over the canal had been damaged, and that morning passed before an Ark bridge on a Churchill tank could be positioned to span it. The Commando Brigade was not to advance until this tank support was available, as the country north of the canal was flat and open for the four miles to the Valetta canal, its objective.[21] Therefore, '43 RM' did not cross 'Peter' bridge until 1400 hours (3 April) to move up the seaward (east) side of the spit. C Troop led, with the point section moving in bounds – 'one foot on the ground', with the Bren group covering the rifle group, then rifles covering the movement of the Bren – when approaching 'James' and again near 'Jeremiah', but neither locality was defended.

The point Section – Sections of C Troop had each taken spells at the 'point' – moved steadily along the coast track. They passed through an extensive mine-field, a slow and exacting task in their advance over low dunes and scrub, which took a couple of hours. Then three Spandaus opened fire from the few houses in Scaglicca. In an instant the corporal of the leading Bren group, Corporal Tom Hunter, charged the houses. Firing from the hip, he raced the 200yds completely exposed to Spandaus' fire and fire from other machine guns 400yds away on the canal bank north of the houses.[22] He knew that C Troop coming up behind his Section was in the open, and this fire would cause heavy casualties. But as he charged, the enemy gunners concentrated most of their fire on him; those in the houses panicked, and he was through the first door without being hit.

In the first house he captured at least one machine gun crew; he then changed his Bren magazine before bursting into the house next door, where more enemy surrendered. The others 'scuttled across a footbridge on to the north bank of the canal'.[23] C Troop was now sprinting up towards the houses, and as the six

Spandaus north of the canal began to get their range, Corporal Hunter again offered himself as a target, moving quickly out of the houses on to a pile of rubble. From there his accurate fire knocked out several Spandaus. He called for more magazine, which were thrown to him, as he shouted encouragement to the Troop to get on.[24] This they did, and some Marines had reached the canal bank before Hunter was killed.

The Troop then attempted to consolidate its hold on the south bank, but the Troop commander, among others, was wounded. E Troop got one Section forward on the right, but despite their covering fire no further advance was possible, as German machine gun fire swept the flat ground below the canal bank. After dark these forward Troops were able to withdraw into the cover of some scrub and dunes. The Commando then established a defended area 400yds from the canal. The following day not only enemy mortars but also their coast artillery brought down 'harassing fire especially on the forward Troops, the mortars of F Company and Tac HQ'[25] before the Coldstream Guards relieved '43 RM' that night. Supported by tanks, 2 Army Commando had advanced along the east side of the spit, but had been held 1,000yds short of the canal by artillery fire.

In 43 RM Commando's advance the Allied line had been pushed forward 7½ miles in two days; the Commando had taken 450 prisoners for the loss of 53 all ranks, nine of whom had been killed – among them Corparal Hunter, who was awarded a posthumous Victoria Cross. The Brigade's advance had also achieved the intention of the Eighth Army's Commander, Lieutenant-General Sir Richard McCreery, by drawing German reserves to the Comacchio sector, thereby easing the passage of the main offensive. This was to be at Argenta some 20 miles up stream from the Reno's estuary, where the Eighth Army would drive a gap through the German lines. To the right (east) of the gap was low-lying land to the lagoon and the flooded valley of Comacchio, which 167 and 169 Brigades were to cross in outflanking the Argenta defences.

The first of these Brigades had crossed the Reno and advanced to the Umana canal, and 169 Brigade, with '40 RM' under its command, was to exploit this success. The Commando was to make a night advance along a stone dyke, the *argine*, which ran from the Umana pumping station; and at dawn attack the Menate pumping station and it nearby bridge. If successful, the Commando would then 'exploit westward' along a road to protect 169 Brigade's right (north-east) flank. At the time the Marines were to attack the bridge, two battalions (2/5 and 2/6 Queen's) of 169 Brigade would cross the flood-waters in LVTs to attack Menate, and the commandos were expected to link with them about 0830 hours.

The Commando set out along the dyke – some 15 miles west of their earlier operations – with two FOOs and a section of REs in the leading Troop. They had marched some 500yds along this *argine* before launching storm boats, after much trouble pushing and pulling the trucks carrying these boats to the launching site. The time lost during these efforts would have to be made up, for in daylight this dyke was swept by enemy fire from across the lake, but by 2145 hours the assault boats had been assembled, and the storm boats launched.[26] These were then loaded with ammunition reserves, rations and two Little John anti-tank projectors firing a 2lb missile. Each storm boat towed two assault boats, but those carrying the Little Johns drew too much water to get along the dyke's side.

Flares from Allied planes bombing defences across the lake and at Menate 'caused some embarrassment', but Y Troop reached a gap blown in the dyke at 0130 (11 April). 'They tested the depth and found it too deep and muddy to wade . . . [and] commenced to ferry men . . . 50yds beyond the "blow"'.[27] They had brought up inflatables for this crossing, but the first boat had hardly put its commandos over the gap, when the leading Marine snagged a trip wire, and two officers, six Marines and a sapper (RE) were wounded as anti-personnel mines exploded. Nevertheless the assault engineers cleared a path through this minefield, a 2-hour task, as there were many mines. When Y, P and X Troops, with the Tactical HQ, were through this lane, 'they pushed forward with all possible speed, leaving the remainder of the unit to be ferried across the gap'.[28] About this time, as the first signs of daylight began to appear, accurate 88-mm and other defensive fire fell round the leading Troops. But Y Troop reached the canal at the end of the *argine* and P Troop advanced. Men of Y prepared their toggle ropes to get themselves across the canal. These 4ft ropes, with an eye in one end and wooden toggle at the other, could be joined to form 100ft or so of continuous rope, which Captain G. C. Belbin later took across the canal which had a depth of about 3ft of water and nearly as many feet of mud.[29]

At the canal mouth a sentry challenged the leading scouts of P Troop, who killed him. But the light was already strong enough to see the outline of buildings and the commandos were 200yds away still on the dyke. The enemy, firing on pre-set lines, now brought down heavy fire on P Troop, which was isolated and 'desperately short of ammunition when an enemy self-propelled gun followed by infantry crossed the bridge'[30] to the south, before moving towards the pumping station. X Troop was held until aircraft had attacked the pumping station, for although the FOOs had called up heavy counter fire on the German guns, these were still causing many Marine casualties, Y Troop alone losing 30 men.[31] P Troop, 200yds from the bridge, hung on, and its fire prevented the Germans setting off their demolition charges. The Troop's Piat anti-tank weapon had been destroyed, however, and so the Marines could not prevent the armoured Semovente 75-mm gun moving in front of them. Nevertheless Lance-Corporal Vickers, leading the assault Section, tried to get across the bridge, but the Troop commander Major Porter and Lieutenant Wedgewood were both killed, as were many of the Section trying to cover Vickers' men. Vickers was wounded, 'but Marine Punton, firing a Bren, had apparently cut the demolition wires . . . and if they were to blow it [the bridge] the Germans must counter attack'.[32]

By now it was fully daylight and an attack by fighter-bombers at 0920 hours distracted the pumping-house defenders. X Troop waded the canal during this lull and rushed the station, taking 33 prisoners. Q Troop crossed to join them before X Troop, who 'were still fresh with no casualties', captured the bridge and the SP gun; 'this was [then] used with some effect against the enemy'.[33] The commandos could see the LVTs of the 2/5 and 2/6 Queens churning across the flood-water west of the dyke as they advanced towards Menate, a mile south of the Commando's bridge, and they were able to give the Queens' covering fire. However, commando patrols could not make contact with these elements of 169 Brigade until the early hours of the following day (12 April), and late that afternoon they were withdrawn in 20 4-tonners through Menate to Ravenna.[34]

In the following weeks, along with the Army Commandos of 2 Commando Brigade, these Marines of '40 RM' and '43 RM' fought in the watery wastes west of Argenta, patrolling flood banks that dominated the flat country around this town. General McCreery congratulated the Brigade 'on their splendid share in the battle, after your successful "Spit" operation your troops showed a magnificent fighting spirit . . . in difficult operations which enabled V Corps to break out of the Argenta defile'.[35] And General Sturges wrote to Lieutenant-Colonel Sankey, '. . . our service together has been fun, make no mistake about it you did a good job of work'[36] with 40 RM Commando.

In North West Europe the Marines with 1 and 4 Commando Brigades had spent some weeks in the islands along the northern banks of the Scheldt estuary; and, later on, the Maas, where '47 RM' for a time came under the command of 116 RM Infantry Brigade. By April 1945 902 LCS(M) flotilla was also patrolling with its small support craft between the north Scheldt estuary islands, to prevent German midget submarines and/or explosive motorboats attacking shipping on its passage to Antwerp.[1] The commandos raided island garrisons and moved in the van of Army advances, frequently in areas where wet ground or heavily wooded areas were impassable to tanks. At other times they worked with tanks where mutual support was necessary, as when – to go back a few months – 1st Commando Brigade came under the command of 7 Armoured Division (the 'Desert Rats') for operation 'Blackcock' in January 1945.

The British XII Corps had been advancing into a triangle of defences bounded on the west by the Maas and on the east by the river Roer, capturing Echt on 17 January. Here the 1st Commando Brigade spent an uncomfortable night in the cold among the battle-scarred houses on the night of 22 January. Next morning at 0745 hours 6 Army Commando led the advance along the road to Maasbacht. The crisp snow crunched under foot in the dazzling white of that bitterly cold morning, as '45 RM' followed them, reaching the town in a couple of hours before the Royal Marines took the lead on the next leg, as the Brigade swung eastward to Brachterbeek. Here the Dutch were lining the streets to welcome them for the Germans had left that night. By 1030 'A' Troop were moving out of the town along the straight tree-lined road towards St Joostburg and the railway station beyond. The road ran for 1,200yds across flat open country covered in powdered snow, away to the left was a wooded valley 600 yards north of the village, the stream of this valley carrying the waters from the Montforterbeek dyke which drained land north of St Joostburg. This cut ran several feet below the level of surrounding fields and marsh, entering the woods near the small bridge carrying the country road to Linne.

The leading Section of A Troop were nearing St Joostburg when they came under heavy small arms fire from positions along the dyke. They would not have crossed the last fifty yards to the safety of some houses had not Marine N. J. Patrick remained in the open to counter the German fire with his Bren. The second Section's Bren group then gave covering fire before they too made for the buildings, a dash in which four men were wounded. The jeep of the machine gun Section and the other two rifle Sections found what cover they could, but all of A Troop were pinned down by fire from the dyke and isolated from the Commando. It was in turn isolated from the Brigade by heavy artillery concentrations on Brachterbeek.

Some fifteen degrees (Fahrenheit) of frost had been recorded that morning and without immediate medical attention the casualties would die of exposure. Realising this the Troop's medical orderly, Lance-Corporal Eric Harden RAMC, went forward and dressed their wounds before returning to the Troop HQ in a cottage to report their injuries. He then went back 120 yards across open ground to half-carry Marine Wheeler as they zigzagged between steady rifle fire back to the cottage. The Lance-Corporal was wounded, and told to wait until the tanks – a squadron was under the Brigade's command – could come forward. But Eric Harden insisted on going back for Marine Wales who was bleeding badly. Two Marine volunteers went with him as stretcher-bearers, bringing back Fred Wales who had been hit a second time and was mortally wounded. On the third mercy trip, the Corporal calmly directed his stretcher party as they picked up Lieutenant R. C. E. Cory under increasingly heavy fire, for he lay within 200yds of German positions. About a third of the way back to the cottage Eric Harden was killed, and Troop Sergeant Major Harry Bennett went out to help the party over the remaining hundred yards or so to the cottage.

The A Troop remained cut off all day but Captain John Tulloch RAMC got some Jeeps to the village and evacuated many wounded early in the afternoon. Other casualties were mounting as artillery and mortar fire fell on the Commando's rear positions. Nevertheless B and E Troops advanced along the side of an embankment, to gain the edge of the wood at the north end of the dyke. (With E Troop were six Army commandos seconded to the Corps for six months.) The tanks, painted white or covered in white sheets, neutralised the German positions to the north but the Germans counter-attacked from the dyke. They were held by B Troop who had crossed frozen marshland to reach the wood and now held what had been German trenches. They were joined by D Troop about 1530 hours, and both Troops were shelled and mortared in the gloom of the winter's afternoon. Soon after dark A Troop was withdrawn from their positions some half-mile to the south. Patrols from C Troop had taken up ammunition for B, D and E Troops, before a further counter-attack. Germans in white snow camouflage were seen moving near the small bridge, B Troop stood-to. When the forty or so Germans were within certain killing range, the Troop commander gave the order to open fire – machine guns, Thompson sub-machine guns and even the Piat opened up. Some Germans were seen to retreat, others lay motionless, but some infiltrated into the wood before the Troop commander, Captain Day, called down artillery fire within 40yds of the commandos' positions.

This was the last action before '45 RM' were relieved early next morning and went into reserve. Eric Harden was awarded a posthumous VC, his 'magnificent example . . . cool courage and determination will never be forgotten by those who saw it', the citation read. Captain Tulloch was awarded the MC and Marine Patrick the MM among other bravery awards to '45 RM' for their action at the Montforterbeek canal; they had lost six killed and thirty wounded, and would be in action again with the 1st Commando Brigade.

On 23 March 1945 1st Commando Brigade forced the crossing of the Rhine in a night assault. Led by 46 (RM) Commando in LVTs, the Brigade crossed the river near Wesel with 6 (Army) Commando ferried in storm boats manned by No.1 Troop RM Engineer Commando, which had some casualties on its return trip, before 45 RM and 6 (Army) Commandos crossed in LVTs. As the Brigade made these river crossings, heavy Allied bombing further reduced Wesel and the town was taken in the next two days. General Sturges visited the Brigade there and a 'large barrel of excellent hock . . . slaked many thirsty throats'.[2]

Not all episodes in the final months of the war were so pleasant, however, for although the Germans had been defeated, many men were killed or wounded, more often in minor incidents than major battles. Nineteen men of '48 RM' had been killed when their LVT hit a buried sea mine on one of the last patrols on Walcheren, and Captain Belbin was wounded by a mine the day after he had crossed the Menate canal. Yet the commandos were so expert at their trade, so quick in their reaction to enemy attack, that they dominated any area in which they fought. For example, when '48 RM' took over a section of the line – commandos continued to do their share of purely infantry fighting – they found the battalion that had held it felt that the Germans 'were better not disturbed'. But '48 RM' changed that and quickly, replying to German mortar fire with twice as good measure as they received, and their fighting patrols soon dominated no-man's land.[3]

Here and elsewhere the Green Beret came to be feared by the enemy, not only for courage in the heat of battle, but also for that stern resolution to keep in the fight. On a dark night men alone and cold in some snowbound foxhole must draw on their resources, as many of '47 RM' had done on the night of 11– 12 January 1945, raiding Kapelsches Veer, an island in the Maas.[4] 'One of the most frightening and uncomfortable actions',[5] the battle against young German paratroopers lasted all night. Among the Marines were replacements for casualties lost at Walcheren, and they had their first taste of commando action climbing the ice-glazed 25ft dyke, and moving into enemy fire. Although they did not dislodge these Germans, the commandos came off the island in good order, and when two Canadian battalions took the island a fortnight later, they found 147 German graves.[6]

After crossing the Rhine, 1 Commando Brigade, under command of 11 Armoured Division, crossed the Weser, where No. 1 Troop RM Engineer Commando again manned the assault boats, which were Mark 3s nearly 22ft long

and able to carry 21 men, including the crew, although normally used for bridging.[7] The commandos here reinforced a small bridgehead already formed by the
Rifle Brigade, from which they advanced against little opposition, as the Germans
withdrew. At the next river, the Aller, German naval troops (not exactly Marines
but fighting as such) held their ground.

From the Weser 11 Armoured Division had advanced rapidly to hold a line
from Bremen to Celle against the west bank of the Aller, and 'again 1st Commando Brigade was whistled forward to gain a bridgehead'.[8] The Germans held
the village of Essel on the west side of a loop in the river and protecting its road
bridge. Any direct attack through the village would inevitably lead to this bridge
being 'blown'. The Brigade therefore planned to cross the railway bridge a mile
downstream to the west, before seizing the road bridge from the rear on the
north-east bank. A Troop of 3 Army Commando got across the bridge, which
had only been partly demolished: the leading Section 'in stockinged feet ...
managed to cross the iron bridge undetected and surprise the defenders'.[9] But
machine guns wounded five of the commandos before RM assault engineers
made the demolition charges safe. All the Brigade – 3, 6, 45(RM) and 46(RM)
Commandos then followed the white tape laid by '3 Cdo' up to the bridge,
crossed it and 'noises of tracks were heard and fighting broke out at once in
wooded country'.[10] A patrol of 3 Commando seized the small canal bridge north
of the river and by 0530 hours (on the night of 10–11 April) had dug in 'a few
hundred yards to the rear of the road bridge'. The Brigade Commander, Brigadier
Derek Mills-Roberts of the Irish Guards and an experienced commando officer,
shot a German cyclist. The Brigadier had fired his American Garand automatic
rifle from the hip. The Army commandos of this Brigade had been equipped with
these American rifles since 1942, and the Brigadier considered the Garand rifle 'to
be the best made'.[11] His driver-batman, incidentally, always dug him a T-shaped
weapon pit – 'a lovely slit trench'.

Later in the morning the Germans counter-attacked with three battalions,
from positions some 40yds from the Commandos' positions in open forest, and
making for the same high ground which was the Commando's objective. About
0800 hours they came crawling through the trees and close to Brigade headquarters, the FOO calling down 'deadly fire only 70 yards from his own slit
trench'.[12] Later the German commander, his adjutant, two company commanders
and the RSM, all of the 2nd Marine Fusilier Battalion, were found dead within
100yds of the Commando Brigade's HQ. Originally '46 RM' had been going to
attack the road bridge, but it was committed on the northern sector of the
bridgehead. Then, as 6 Army Commando was not in contact with the enemy, it
was moved down the line of the canal ready to assault the road bridge.

Its medium machine guns gave 30 minutes' effective close support down the
right flank, as the Commando charged through the wood, 'cheering with a verve
that must have chilled the enemy', and following the hunting horns of the four
Troop Commanders.[13] Bayonets fixed, running at a fast double for 400yds the
commandos shot all the Germans who did not flee and were at the bridge soon
after 1130 hours. Yet as 'No.6' reached it, they were immediately counter-

attacked by another German force, before '"46 RM" swung down and engaged them, with great assurance', the Brigadier reported. To keep the defences compact, '45 RM' moved across to cover '46', and had no sooner done so than it and 3 (Army) Commando were also attacked by 'some 120 Germans and a Ferdinand SP (a really outsize model) and we decided', the Brigadier wrote, 'that we were overworked'. But the Brigade's machine-gunners persuaded the SP and another armoured vehicle to withdraw before they could do much damage. The road bridge had been 'blown', although by early afternoon, when 45 RM Commando had been established east of the canal, ferrying and bridging had begun, and during the night tanks were brought into the bridgehead to join an infantry battalion, the 2nd King's Shropshire Light Infantry, which now came under the Brigade's command.

The switch between '46 RM' and '6 (Army) Cdo' had been made on radioed orders, an indication of improved Brigade signals, although the signallers were using 18-sets with a limited range. Their one 19-set was in a large van which 'stuck up above the hedges and made one feel very vulnerable'.[14] In action the signallers of Brigade HQ were near the Brigadier's lovely slit trench, when he left it for a recce during the Aller battle. Some wag told a young FOO that the trench was not in use and this RA Captain's batman began filling in half the trench because it was too big. 'All hell was let loose when the Brigadier returned.'[15]

Next day (12 April) 6 Commando sent patrols eastward, the Shropshires and tanks moved north, and the Marines attacked westward towards Hademstorf. The Marines had moved off from their position by the canal at 1100 hours, and had reached the railway when they met heavy fire. The German reinforcements, another naval battalion, were moving east to counter-attack the commandos' bridgehead, and 'the two forces had met half-way', so to speak. The Brigadier, not wanting 'to have a blood-bath', ordered Lieutenant-Colonel T. M. Gray, MC, commanding this force of '45' and '46 RM', to retire. The force withdrew, therefore, to re-form a line by the canal and patrol towards Hademstorf village. Some Germans tried to infiltrate these positions but were killed or captured, a further 50 prisoners being taken by the Brigade.

On the third day of the battle (13 April) patrols reported that some Germans were withdrawing, and '45 RM' set off at 1000 hours to reoccupy without opposition the high ground they had held on the first day. At the same time '46 RM' moved on the left to attack the village. They were met by a fierce defence in the woods south of Hademstorf, Y Troop losing all its officers and the Troop Sergeant Major – all killed except for one, who was badly wounded. Sergeant S. Cooper, MM, took over the Troop 'and pushed on with great determination', X Troop moving forward to help them, before the left flank was secured. On the right there had been less resistance to B and A Troops as one German platoon fled, and the village fell without further opposition. The Brigadier later reported '46 RM' as 'having taken the place in great style, going in with tremendous dash'.[16] Now 11 Armoured Division passed through the bridgehead, and 1st Commando Brigade found that their well-constructed slit trenches with suitable roofs not only kept out shell splinters but also the rain in the following week.

The commandos would see further action in the next month, but the Aller was their last major battle; the Brigade had 127 casualties, including seven killed from '45 RM' and eight from '46'.[17] The Germans of two naval battalions, an SS Training Battalion, and an anti-tank battalion, had lost over 600 men, half of them prisoners of the commandos. Meanwhile Marines of 116 RM Infantry Brigade had also been in action. This Brigade had been formed originally for Beach Battalions, but – as mentioned earlier – transferred (six weeks after they were formed) to 21st Army Group, on 16 February 1945.[18] Twelve days later these Marines took over the defence sectors on the Maas 15 miles north of Tilburg, from Crevecour to Waalwijk, with 41 RM Commando under command on the right, 27th RM Battalion in the centre and 28th RM Battalion on the left. In good visibility they kept a minimum number of well-concealed observation points forward of their positions, and at night or in poor visibility platoons manned forward slit trenches to prevent German infiltration; but where the stone dykes of the Maas prevented slit trenches being dug, patrols had nevertheless to regularly cover the banks.[19]

In the next few weeks this line was linked to 4 Commando Brigade's sector from the Dintel river to and including Walcheren. At this time 1 Polish Armoured Division, providing fire against any enemy movements on the north bank of the Maas, was one of several fire support units that came under command of this Brigade. The deployments were changed several times in the next couple of months, 30th RM Battalion first coming into the line on 8 April, by which time 48 RM Commando was on their right and under the Brigade's Command. An item in Brigade orders sums up the professional approach of these landing craft Marines to their infantry role: it would be no excuse to say 'that's what the people did, who we took over from'.[20] On the night of 11–12 April 27th RM Battalion was relieved and came under command of XXX British Corps – the Brigade by this date was under command of Netherlands District, which had taken over the Maas defences. Towards the end of April, 30th RM Battalion and the Royal Netherlands Brigade crossed the river; 30th RM took Alem island, cleared the isthmus lying beyond this and between the river Waal and the Maas, and consolidated on Kerkdriel. There was apparently little resistance and only a few casualties were reported.[21]

During its time on the Maas and among the Dutch islands the Brigade had proved its ability as infantry, and in the coming weeks would move forward with the general advance. Originally '27th RM' was transferred to XXX Corps to be used in the occupation of Bremerhaven (Lower Saxony), but on 26 April it was switched to the occupation of Wilhelmshaven further west. (Reportedly the CO having found his American superior somewhat 'difficult', he wangled the attachment to the Canadians, whose GOC he had known at Staff College.) For this operation the Marines were under the command of 4 Canadian Armoured Division, 'an unusual role for an infantry Battalion of Royal Marines'.[22] They were in action when the leading elements of the Division met resistance in the area of Oldenberg, some 25 miles south of their objective, but were the first Allied infantry – the Polish Armoured Division beating them 'by a short head' – to enter Wilhelmshaven, and the Divisional commander paid them high tribute for their part in these actions.[23]

Now 28th RM Battalion came under command of the Second British Army and provided the infantry force for the Royal Navy's occupation of Cuxhaven on the estuary of the Elbe and Syer in the north Friesian islands;[24] and 30th RM had similar duties for the Naval-Officer-in-Charge (NOIC) Hamburg, where numbers of Germans landed after escaping in ships across the Baltic from the Russian advance – on one night alone the Battalion had to deal with 14,000 Germans. By early May companies from these Battalions were also taking the surrender of German warships' crews at Emden ('A' Coy 27th RM), Brunsbuttle-koog (30th RM) and Kiel (28th RM); 33rd RM Battalion of 117 RM Infantry Brigade was flown out to help in this task but the rest of the Brigade, forming in the Margate (Kent) area, did not reach Germany until the second week in May.[25] By then 1st Commando Brigade had advanced to Neustadt, 6 miles north-east of Hanover, and Field Marshal Milch surrendered to the Brigadier the day before the German surrender on 8 May 1945.[26]

Neither the Commandos nor the Marine Battalions met the fanatical resistance some expected, and a mortar Section, a corporal and eight Marines from '28th RM' spent a week on the quays of Monkeberg near Kiel searching thousands of prisoners – 6,000 in one 12-hour period alone – and their ships, as part of the Navy's responsibilities before passing these Germans to the Army. In all, these nine Marines searched 27,000 men, finding concealed knives, revolvers and other assorted weapons. Although they had a full platoon's help only for one day, the Corporal and his men 'did our own cooking . . . between the arrival of the prisoners'.[27] Other Marine guards collected signed declarations of surrender from U-boat skippers.[28]

Something of the military commanders' expectations at this time can be seen in 21st Army Group's orders for punishing those troops who fraternised with Germans. Ogling women and girls or giving small gifts to German children could lead to a man forfeiting seven to 14 days' pay. More serious fraternisation, as in visiting German homes, was a court-martial offence.[29] However, the complete collapse of German resistance led to the occupying Powers spending more effort on feeding, housing and administering the Germans than in purely military operations against potential underground resistance.

Nearly 1,000 Marines of all ranks had been killed in the campaigns in the North West European theatre.[30] Other Marine fatal casualties at sea, in the Mediterranean and the campaigns of 1940 amounted to some 1,500 with the total number wounded in all theatres except the Far East an estimated 3,000.[31] For those who had come through the war with Germany, tempered as any celebration was bound to be by the continuing war against Japan, VE-Day – the Victory in Europe Day – was celebrated with some dancing in the streets. But for men of 546 and 547 LCA Flotillas aboard the LSI *Glenroy*, as for other Marines in the Far East, an extra tot of rum on the order 'splice the mainbrace' was the height of their official celebrations.[32]

With the end of the war in Europe General Hunton, the GOC Royal Marines, in June 1945 stressed the care needed in handling the demobilisation of the 63,000 'Hostilities Only' officers and Marines; for their future attitude to the Corps would depend largely on the way their demobilisation was carried out. Although only a proportion of the men who had been fighting in Europe would be required in the Far East, others would have to be retained as they might be required 'for active service in the political vacuums of Europe'.[33] The rate of demobilisation from the Royal Navy was also expected in June 1945 to be slower than from the Army. Nevertheless, as those older Marines with long service (the early age-and-service groups for demobilisation) were released, a smaller drafting margin would be available, while the RM detachments afloat were maintained at about 6,000. The proposal to have Commando Brigades entirely of Royal Marines was also taking shape, and by June 1945 the Corps expected to provide 4,300 – the new War Establishment for the Commando Group – for the Far East, which meant that no reinforcements would be required for a year, as the Group strength was 6,300 that June.[34] This total included Army Commandos, which were well below established strength. The end of the war in Europe, however, eased the problem of finding officers, and the first 'HOs' were being considered for transfer to continuous service.

The question of senior Marine officers commanding landing craft bases was pursued, and HMS *Quebec* (Inverary) was to be the RM Landing Craft Training Centre. But it closed in the summer of 1946, when all RM landing craft activities were moved to Rosneath. The gun crews from major support craft of the Eastern Flank Force and other flotillas not required in the Far East were in holding camps, so that they could be kept together until a decision was made on their future roles. There would, however, be a reduction in the number of Marine-manned minor craft flotillas. Six were serving with the Royal Indian Navy in the Arakan; an RM flotilla which had been with Force X – the Naval maintenance base in Iceland – had gone to New Guinea in the late summer of 1944; and 563 RM LCA Flotilla was the last in the Mediterranean, and was returning to the UK. The flotillas aboard LSIs would be affected by the proposed 20 per cent reduction in the fleets,[35] and there was also to be a 25 per cent reduction in RM establishments from their 1944 complements.[36] But events would overtake these proposals.

In the Far East during the early months of 1945, many escape routes for the Japanese had been cut in the Arakan, but after the Kangaw battle 3 Commando Brigade was withdrawn to India to prepare for landings at Port Dickson (Malaya).[1] In the Pacific the American Army's campaign in the Philippines was virtually complete by early March, and by 16 March US Marines had captured Iwo Jima island, where in four weeks of bloody fighting they suffered 21,000 casualties.[2] For the Royal Marines in the Far East during these and the succeeding months of 1945 there would be many unusual tasks, even by their own standards; their now conventional landing craft and other roles would be expanded into a great variety of duties.

The six flotillas with the Royal Indian Navy.[3] for example, were operating in the jungle *chaungs*. These creeks were in places only a few yards wide; when the tide was out the mangrove roots were over a man's head, and water snakes and crocodiles infested the jungle waters. Yet in the estuaries the LCAs and LCS(M)s 'found the currents very strong'.[4] They operated with Indian and West African Troops, some of whom had never landed from craft before. In addition to the landing operations at Myebon and elsewhere these craft were often employed independently, carrying reserves of fuel for several days' operations and being towed up to 90 miles to a start line. They became adept at using army maps and taking a recce patrol upstream; or a couple of LCAs and an LCS(M) might provide the base for other troops to block a *chaung* for 4 or 5 days. An LCS(M) with one engine idling would lie under a river bank at night; then as soon as Japanese sampans were seen in the moonlight, the support craft would ghost out into the river and destroy the enemy with her twin .5in machine guns. On other occasions a few soldiers might be carried in an LCS(M) to where opposition was expected, but more often 15 men were carried in an LCA with Army mortars fired from these craft for support. Such raids and blocking parties cut off stragglers escaping from Ramree Island and elsewhere in the southern Arakan. The LCM Mark I was used to land all manner of stores for the build-up after a landing, including 100 goats per craft when carrying 'rations' to Dominion troops.[5]

The crews lived in their craft, the LCAs using their canopies over two-thirds of the well (from the bow) on which bedding rolls were stowed as some protection against small arm fire. These craft, despite their wooden hulls, proved sufficiently armour-plated to stop small arms fire from even 35yds range, and an LCS(M) which had to be sunk survived 40-mm Bofors fire, and was only broken up by 3-pdr shells. Coming out of action, however, craft had to manoeuvre to protect their unarmoured sterns. In this they were helped by mutual support, co-ordinated by the senior coxswain, whose craft had the American CR 300 radios, the 18-set proving not very satisfactory even over open water. After some months, however, all the equipment wore out, and although these had been new craft shipped from the UK, their maintenance was difficult and with many craft 'farmed out to the Army, the Flotilla Officers lost touch with units . . . for some considerable time'.[6] Yet the corporal coxswains took charge of their crews and had on occasions to work on equal terms with army majors, when 'they always manage to hold their own'.[7] This is one of the clearest examples of Marines on detached duties, and mostly 'HO' Marines at that, having the self-confidence that the Corps develops and the professional skills which other services respect.

At the time of these operations in the spring of 1945 the Japanese were preparing for a war of attrition, expecting the Allied governments to be forced by their electorates to settle for peace when casualties mounted.[8] To this end the Japanese Army was to hold Malaya, Thailand and French Indo-China but was to send men and oil fuel back to Japan. While to consolidate their positions in south-east Asia, the Japanese began withdrawing troops into central Burma and Thailand in readiness to hold Indo-China. The race to cut off these forces had begun, and on 13 March the RM Flotillas assisted in the landing of a brigade group of 26 Indian Division up the *chaungs* at Letpan, some 10 miles from the coast, where they landed unopposed. Letpan, opposite Ramree Island and 70 miles south of Kangaw, was the last major landing on the Arakan, for Admiral Lord Mountbatten, Supreme Allied Commander South East Asia, planned to land forces at Rangoon and exploit northwards to cut the Japanese lines of communication into Burma. Originally this operation 'Dracula' had been considered in 1944 as an alternative to 'Capital', the drive from north Burma to secure the supply routes to China. However the likely time necessary to mount an amphibious operation had precluded its adoption and the plan for the reoccupation of Burma from the north was chosen instead.

The advance in the Arakan slowed when air supply squadrons were diverted to divisions of the Fourteenth Army across the Irrawaddy in central Burma.[9] At this time, the British Pacific Fleet (BPF) prepared for its part in operation 'Iceberg', the American landings on Okinawa. The Fleet had been assembling in Australia, around the nucleus of carriers which had raided the oil refineries in January (1945), and its supply system was improvised on the American pattern of a 'Fleet Train' – for the American Task Forces had an efficient routine of convoys of supply ships, oilers and battle-damage repair ships. These 'Fleet Trains' sailed to within a few hundred miles of each operation, and warships could then withdraw briefly from an action to replenish ammunition, fuel and stores before returning to bombard Japanese defences or their other duties. The British, short of ships and men, put together a 'Fleet Train' of merchant ships, Royal Fleet Auxiliaries and some Navy-manned Victualling Stores Issue Ships (VSIs). This 'Train' was not as homogeneous as the American system, with all its 'Fleet Train' transports manned by naval personnel, nor were there sufficient fast British tankers and aircraft transports (carrying FAA spares) to keep up with the British Task Force.[10] (In the American practice of designating fleets and/or squadrons as Task Forces, the BPF became Task Force 57.)

The 'Fleet Train', as explained earlier, had replaced the inter-war concept of advanced bases. For example, in the 92 ships of the 'Train' with the BPF were aircraft maintenance ships, accommodation ships, armament store issue ships, to name but three of the 30 or more special purpose depot and supply vessels.[11] Although the carrier-borne aircraft could be serviced and supplied by this train, five Mobile Naval Air Bases had been formed by January 1945, each with its detachment of RM motor transport drivers and other tradesmen. Four of these were on passage to the Far East at the time the first MONAB was set up near Sydney (Australia) in January 1945.[12]

In mid-March Admiral Rawlings signalled the American Admiral Nimitz from Manus (Admiralty Islands), 'It is with a feeling of great pride and pleasure that the BPF joins the US Naval Forces under your command'. In the anchorage at Manus Island, north of New Guinea, that March lay the converted merchant ship HMS *Lothian*, with an RM flotilla of LCAs, as one of several ships in the 'Fleet Train' which had already seen service in the Solomon Islands and New Guinea landings. She had sailed from the UK in the summer of 1944, passed through the Panama Canal, and crossed the Pacific to reach New Guinea that September, before sailing north with the British Pacific Fleet in March 1945.[13] As an LSHQ(Large) she would be part of an armada of 1,205 ships, which included ten battleships and eighteen carriers in the assault on Okinawa.

These landings, 300 miles from southern Japan, began with the seizure of small islands, to establish an advanced anchorage for the 'Fleet Train' some 20 miles west of Okinawa. This opening phase was carried out on 26 March, and the same day the British Pacific Fleet's Hellcats, and Corsair fighter aircraft led in Avenger bombers against the first of six strongly defended airfields, mainly on Ishigaki and Miyako Islands (half-way between Okinawa and Formosa, modern Taiwan), which could be used in refuelling Japanese reinforcement aircraft flying to Okinawa.[14] Major Cheesman's flying log for the next few weeks is filled with 'Fighter sweeps over Ishigaki', 'Top cover to strikes on Hirara and Sukama', 'Strike on Miyako', 'C.A.P. [Combat Air Patrol] over Fleet Train', etc., as he flew from HMS *Indefatigable*.[15] From HMS *Victorious* Lieutenant-Colonel Hay made daily reconnaissances before strikes, supervised their execution and did his share of strafing. Over Formosa one day in April he saw 'a passenger train skulking in a tunnel but with its engine sticking out . . . most unwise with someone like Ronnie Hay around and the result was catastrophic for the train'.[16] The carriers – HMS *Indomitable*, *Victorious*, *Indefatigable* and *Illustrious* – were accompanied by two battleships, HMS *King George V* and *Howe*, the cruisers *Swiftsure*, *Gambia* (HMNZS a NewZealand ship), *Black Prince*, *Argonaut* and *Euryalus*, and 11 destroyers. This British Fleet with its many RM detachments continued over the next eight weeks to deny the enemy the use of these airfields.[17]

The carriers withdrew at dusk, for they had no night fighters, although the Fleet Air Arm had a development unit working in the UK on night fighter tactics, commanded by Captain L. A. 'Skeets' Harris RM with Captain J. O. Armour RM as senior pilot.[18] During the operations against Okinawa the British Fleet was attacked by suicide bombers one such Kamikaze Zeke 55 bomber hit *Indefatigable* forward of her control 'island'. Nevertheless she was able to continue working her planes, because the armoured deck had protected her hangars. In early April the British ships, joined by an American Task Force, bombarded the airfields, as Japanese working parties had been able to repair several runways, and on 4 May HMS *Formidable* was hit by a suicide plane but was kept in action. Another hit *Indomitable* but slid over the side. Five days later *Formidable* was hit again, and *Victorious* was also damaged by Kamikazes, but the armoured flight decks again prevented major damage. By late May, when the carriers operated for two days together and then replenished their stores in the next two, there was little enemy activity on the airfields, and the Fleet were withdrawn to Manus on 25 May. The carriers had lost 160 planes and 41 aircrew.[19]

Soon after the beginning of operations on Okinawa the Joint Force Commander's plan for the mounting of 'Dracula' was agreed. He, Rear-Admiral B. C. S. Martin, had among his forces for this operation some 900 Marines, including those manning ten flotillas of minor landing craft and the guns of 334 LCG(L) Flotilla.[20] The operation was launched in little over three weeks from the date the plan was approved in outline, and the LCT convoys sailed on D-5. On 2 May, D-Day, the LCAs were lowered at 0200 hours for one of the longest night approach runs to a beach that has ever been made – 28 miles. In heavy showers of monsoon rain and the pitch dark, the craft formed up and followed their respective LC Headquarters. Their beaches – one for two assault infantry battalions on the west bank and one on the east bank – were 18 miles south of Rangoon, and some miles up the Irrawaddy estuary, which was mined. On D-1 a Gurkha parachute battalion landed, and after struggling through creeks in flood – the monsoon had broken two weeks early – they took out the only Japanese coast battery at Elephant Point, losing 84 men in a fierce flamethrowers' battle. The Japanese main force, however, had evacuated the area. A sign painted on the prison roof stated: 'Japs gone . . . Extract digit.'[21]

The Marines put the assault companies ashore despite the heavy swell and 6-knot currents, but as there was no opposition, the battalions on the west bank were re-embarked next day and taken up-river by the RM flotillas to land in Rangoon. (The only casualties on D-Day and D+1 were medical staff on an LCT which struck a mine.[22]) The port could now be opened, assuring the Fourteenth Army's supplies throughout the monsoon, freeing their air supply squadrons for work elsewhere. There were still 100,000 Japanese in Burma, many of whom fought to break through to the Salween river and Thailand. They were completely cut off from any supplies coming by sea, and the East Indies Fleet from its base in Ceylon controlled the Indian Ocean. In mid-May it saw one of its last ship-to-ship actions, when the Japanese cruiser *Haguro* and a destroyer attempted to relieve the Japanese garrisons in the Andaman Islands. She was sunk by the 26th Destroyer Flotilla after an escort carrier's planes found her in the Malacca Straits.[23]

Landings by Australians in Borneo had taken place in early May, and several Marines from the LCA flotillas were killed during these and later Australian landings.[24] The British Pacific Fleet which had made the 11-day voyage of 4,500 miles from the operational areas back to Australia, returned in June with a Task Force including the new carrier HMS *Implacable*. She attacked the much-bombed Japanese base of Truk in the Caroline Islands, which the Americans had by-passed. The air-strikes and the Naval bombardment enabled these ships and particularly the carrier with her 75 planes 'to gain experience of conditions in their new theatre'.[25] The RM detachment aboard *Implacable* had duties which demonstrate the changing nature of sea service, for in addition to gun crews and pilots from the Corps, Marines were in the CBAL Sections and in air-crew briefing and debriefing teams; the RM Band provided damage control parties; and signal officers were familiar with both British and American signal and cipher procedures.[26]

Ashore the headquarters of Admiral Lord Mountbatten's South East Asia Command (SEAC) had many Royal Marines of all ranks, including Major General G. E. Wildman Lushington, who had joined SEAC from Combined Operations Headquarters. The Supreme Commander's strategy for the recapture of Malaya was worked out during the spring of 1945: with plans to capture Phuket Island on the west coast of this peninsula during the summer; and the establishment of a beachhead in southern Malaya, operation 'Zipper', near Port Dickson during October. The plan visualised the recapture of Singapore early in 1946.

The Americans, however, did not agree to 'Zipper', as this would divert resources from any invasion of the Japanese mainland.[27] Various changes were made, but on 18 May Lord Mountbatten advised the Chiefs of Staff that he would be ready to launch 'Zipper' in late August with the resources he had and to by-pass Phuket Island.[28]

Much of the beach reconnaissance work for these landings was carried out by the Small Operations Group, which had been formed in June the previous year (1944) for operations by 'small parties of uniformed troops trained and equipped to operate against enemy coastal, river and lake areas ... providing diversions and seizing intelligence data'.[29] The Group was commanded by Colonel (later Major General) H. T. Tollemache and administered by a small RM headquarters, which included Lieutenant-Colonel Hasler. Under command were four COPPs, three SBS Groups, the Sea Reconnaissance Unit – all with Army and Naval personnel – and RM Detachment 385. This last unit had four Troops of canoeists also trained as parachute troops and was equipped with inflatables as well as canoes. They carried out fourteen independent operations, all but two being successful.

On one operation a party from No.1 Troop with two Mark III** quick-release canoes had been landed from a Catalina on Bilugyn island in the estuary of the Salween river some 50 miles east of Rangoon. Their intention was to suggest that the island had been surveyed as a possible site for an airstrip, and Capt J. F. T. Steele with two NCOs and a Marine launched their canoes successfully about 2100 hours and set off for the island. They probably laid their deception items but when the flying boat returned seven hours later, signal lights from the shore abruptly went out. All four raiders were probably washed off a mudbank in the rapidly rising tide, for no sign of them was seen again.[30] Another casualty while he was serving with '385' was Major Johnston, who had led 'Force Viper' in 1941.

The canoeists of '385' planted damaged inflatables, maps and other decoy material, suggesting beaches had been reconnoitred in the Nicobar Islands and Sumatra, and landed agents on the south-east coast of Johore, north of Singapore. But in March in a reconnaissance of Phuket Island by Marines of '385' and by a Combined Operations Pilotage Party several men were killed, and the rest were captured.[31] Major John Maxwell and Sergeant-Major Smith were later murdered by the Japanese.[32]

The Japanese had made clear in radio broadcasts that they would behead anyone landing in 'war canoes' but the SOG was not the only force using them. A clandestine group under Lieutenant-Colonel I. Lyon, DSO (Gordon Highlanders), had followed up a successful limpet raid on Singapore in 1943 with a second raid early in October 1944, which the Japanese intercepted. The party had many difficulties and a fire-fight in making their escape, but were due to be picked up by submarine when on 4 November they were found again by the Japanese, nine being captured despite their resistance. Among them was Major R. M. Ingleton, He had landed in Normandy in an RM tank and only five months later had been raiding in a canoe. As prisoners, they impressed the Japanese greatly by their calm dignity, and before their execution on 7 July: 'They all stood up merrily and even laughingly in a very harmonious manner, [they] bade each other farewell'.[33] This report may, however, be inaccurate in that they were probably murdered by the Japanese, who created the report as a means of possibly lessening the Allies' retribution against the captors.

On 16 July the British Pacific Fleet was again in the north Pacific to form the fourth Task Group of the American Fast Carrier Task Force, and British carriers' planes attacked industrial targets north of Tokyo in the next few days. HMS *King George V* also joined American bombarding forces shelling Hitachi, 50 miles north of Tokyo. Although hampered by the slowness of their Fleet Train tankers, the BPF kept up with the American Task Force as their planes attacked the last of the Japanese fleet – the final destruction of Kure being undertaken by the Americans, while the British carriers attacked shipping on the Inland Sea. On 29 July '*KGV*' with American ships was shelling Hamamatsu, an industrial town, and Fleet Air Arm planes attacked ground targets again, but typhoons had been raging on and off since mid-July and early in August they prevented any further operations at sea.[34] On 6 August the atom bomb fell on Hiroshima, and 3 days later an atom bomb burst over Nagasaki.

The BPF was now running short of fuel, but carrier aircraft attacks and bombardments continued with a token force of British ships – HMNZS *Gambia* and HMS *Newfoundland* shelled ironworks in daylight, with American planes spotting the fall of shot on 9 August. The final Kamikaze attack in the last action against British ships was on HMS *Indefatigable* on the morning of 15 August. The same day Lord Mountbatten suspended all SEAC operations, and took over responsibility also for Malaya and a large part of the Dutch East Indies.

The last big-ship action with heavy guns had been fought on 25 October 1944, when radar directed fire of American battleships sank one Japanese battleship in 16 minutes.[35] 'A funeral salute to a finished era of naval warfare', was how Samuel Morison expressed it.[36] For Royal Marines this also foreshadowed the end of a major role they had carried out with distinction for almost a century.

Their new roles in manning landing craft, support craft and as commandos were familiar by August 1945. The proposed 'Zipper' landings in Malaya were deferred when General MacArthur (Supreme Commander Allied Powers Pacific) on 19 August ordered that no landings were to take place until an instrument of surrender had been signed. In Rangoon surrender documents were signed on 26 August, and two LSIs carrying 3 Commando Brigade had sailed for Hong Kong; they were delayed until Force 'Roma' – HMS *Nelson*, LSIs and RMs from the fleet[37] – were landed at Penang Island off north-west Malaya, and the cruiser HMS *London* put ashore her detachment at Sabang Island (off Sumatra). Documents were signed by local Japanese commanders in both *Nelson* and *London* on 28 August; the band of *London* had landed in their blues some minutes before the battle-kitted Marines of the detachment arrived.[38] Six days later (4 September) Singapore garrison was formally surrendered to Rear-Admiral Holland aboard HMS *Sussex*, and 5 Division and XV Corps' headquarters were then landed there in the next few days.

The 'Zipper' landings with two assault forces were carried out meanwhile, with assault battalions of 25 Division being put ashore eight miles north-west of Port Dickson. They landed across the Morib beaches, which had been surveyed in great detail by SOG parties the previous June.[39] The number of Royal Marines in landing craft, support craft and escort ships, which included *Nelson* and three cruisers, probably exceeded 2,500 here on 9 September. Those in 'Peggy Force' followed an LC Navigation from the LSI *Glenroy*, the two LCS(M) Mark 3s probing a creek beside the Langat river, as more than 30 LVTs churned behind the leading craft to land two Indian battalions two miles up the river on its north bank near Port Swettenham. (The Force was under an RN commander, and two Fairmile Motor Launches provided escorts, with three LCTs carrying the artillery.) The Indian troops were to form a bridgehead, and 'Peggy' force's LCMs landed their tanks – half a squadron – and two Troops of artillery before forming a ferry service at this 200yd crossing. Although no opposition was met, the craft went in at 0645 hours fully prepared – LCS(M)s had fuel for 275 miles, 9,600 rounds for their twin .5-in, smoke and HE bombs for the 4.2-in mortar (60 rounds of each).[40] That afternoon troops landing further east reached the crossing and Port Swettenham was occupied during the afternoon; next day Spitfires flew in to the airfield. The same day the eastern assault force occupied Port Dickson.[41]

In Hong Kong when 3 Commando Brigade landed on 12 September, Naval, RME and RM Shore parties from the fleet were already ashore, with 3,000 RAF technicians intended for Manus who were restoring public services.[42] The repatriation of prisoners began and the commandos had their hands full in containing over 21,000 Japanese and dealing with 'the evacuation of Chinese forces who at times caused trouble'.[43] Royal Marine Engineer reinforcements in two ships had reached Sydney by September, and were sent to Hong Kong.[44] There they made underwater surveys of wharves and began clearing the shipyards at Hong Kong and Kowloon. Other companies were clearing docks, and repairing Naval base installations in Singapore and Rangoon. Since early in the year (1945) detachments of RME had been with MONABs for airfield construction.[45] For the RM commando engineers 'a new racket emerged: sea time' – as they dismantled Japanese suicide boats.[46] But for many – although by no means for all – this was a time for 'waiting our turn to be repatriated and demobilised'.[47]

8

DEMOBILISATION FOR SOME

For the many young Marines expecting to serve at least a couple of years in the Pacific, the fall of Japan 14 weeks after Germany's unconditional surrender was cause for much celebration. Of these the inconsequential memories remain. A publican in Poole gave away beer, 'but bring your own glass' the notice read, and at a time when beer glasses were in extremely short supply. He is said to have garnered sufficient to run his pub for two years. One exuberant bonfire party burnt the colonel's hat, and one idiot let off his Oerlikon to add to the noise of ships' sirens in East Anglia. There were less dramatic events in coming to terms with peacetime conditions with no blackout – as the officer of one landing craft discovered after searching his chart for the navigation light 'flashing green to red'. When the red and amber showed, he realised it was traffic lights on the coast road.[1] Official celebrations would come later, and time to remember the friends who had not survived. For prisoners-of-war release was sometimes dramatic, although often days and even weeks passed before they could be repatriated.

Captain Guy Griffiths was among the former prisoners returning from German camps. After his capture by a U-boat's crew in 1939, he had been among the first escapers in 1940 to dig a tunnel to get away from one Dulag Luft. But he was recaptured along with Squadron-Leader 'Wings' Day (a former RM pilot) and Major 'Birdie' Partridge.[2] By May 1945 Captain Griffiths was in Hungary, one of 1,142 RM prisoners released from German prison camps.[3] Their lives had been hard: for example, Captain I. P. R. Wilson, captured on Crete, had lived on horsemeat soup and hard biscuits in Salonica, where bug-ridden barracks served as a camp, before being moved to Germany and better rations. By 1945 he was one of 1,500 prisoners in Oflag VII B (Bavaria) where in 'a great feeling of solidarity and friendliness . . . there was no divisiveness'. Yet some prisoners felt that 'in the inevitable wastage of war we had never had a chance . . . to live up to the tremendous traditions of the Corps'.[4]

In Japan Marine Wooding (captured in Hong Kong in 1941) had learnt Japanese and in mid-August 1945 he persuaded Japanese guards to unlock the gates of a camp holding Americans near Kyoto.[5] His story of escape from a sinking prison ship in 1942 and subsequent recapture, is one of many which can only be represented here by a few examples in tribute to the courage of all prisoners of war. Colour Sergeant V. S. King, having spent 24 hours in the Java Sea after the sinking of HMS *Exeter*, was picked up by a Japanese destroyer and met the first 'shouting and bullying antics we were to experience in the next 3½ years'. They lived at first on rice and only rice, although a feast to remember was the day a quantity of prunes 'mysteriously appeared'. While still in the Dutch East Indies, these prisoners were marched – many in bare feet – several miles from ships to a camp. They learnt 'to make the Japs "lose face" but not, repeat not, in such a way that the yellow fellows would regain face at our expense, usually by a walloping [which] though severe did not seem so bad on the person as on the pride ... the sick began to mount ... with one hypodermic for the forty medical men [in a camp of 3,000] ...'[6]

These prisoners later built huge concrete shelters, 'leaving pieces of wood at an angle here or there, so that there were gaps in the cement ... in such a way as to deny them being 100% ... Jap sentries frequently fell over from similar sicknesses as we did', for they also needed more than rice in their diet. The day Colour-Sergeant King disarmed a sentry, he was 'made to stand to attention facing the sun with my hands above my head for the next couple of hours'. These prisoners continued road-building near Macassar (southern Celebes) and felling trees. Some died from beatings, many from malnutrition, and not for the first time the Colour-Sergeant had bones broken by a Japanese rifle butt. The prisoners pilfered razor blades from the docks so they could shave, stropping blades on rounded glass, and defied their prison staff, who lost face, as shaving was thought to be impossible without new blades. 'There was the monotony of work, work, work and weakening all the time ... then one day we went to work as usual ... *lekas*, *lekas* [hurry, hurry] with bamboo sticks to give these words weight', but at midday the prisoners were doubled back to the camp. There the senior Japanese Officer got on a rostrum and said in Malay: *Prang Abis* – War finished'. The guards melted away and Allied officers took command, although Japanese guards were kept in the islands to protect white ex-prisoners from Indonesian nationalists.[7]

Other prisoners of the Japanese included men from HMS *Prince of Wales* and *Repulse*, one of whom wrote home describing the 'excellent' conditions in the camp and finished his letter with 'do not forget to tell it to the Royal Marines'.[8] A phrase which in this context meant the letter was a pack of lies, for Captain Drury had written it with similar implications in a novel. Lieutenant Geoffrey Hulton (to be later knighted) was by June 1942 in a camp for 500 men which housed 30,000 for a time; from there prisoners were sent to Thailand in working parties of companies organised in battalions. They suffered in the stifling heat of closed railway trucks and were chilled by freezing nights. Sir Geoffrey was in hospital for three months with beri-beri. He was later moved to avoid the British advance, marching day after day through the monsoon rains, and not until 1 September 1945 did he leave his last prison camp for repatriation.[9] Major Alan Ferguson Warren of the Special Operations Executive (SOE which operated secret missions), who had been running clandestine forces from Java in early 1942, succeeded in convincing Japanese interrogators that he was a survivor from *Prince of Wales* and worked on the Burma railway. There by June 1943 they were 'burying four men a day' from his work battalion. When news came of the end of the War, the Major commandeered a lorry from his last camp and drove into Bangkok, where four Gurkha companies were being flown in to control the airport.[10] Of the 291 RM prisoners in Japanese hands, more than one in five had died.[11]

Officers and men who had been prisoners-of-war were in many cases long overdue for promotion, but with discretion the Corps allowed them some months of rest before considering them for new appointments.[12] This was one of many wise decisions made at this time by General Hunton, among others, in whose hands lay the future of the Corps. After the formal surrenders and official celebrations, including the Victory march through London, there was much to be done in planning the future roles for the Corps. These would be along the lines that had been considered in 1944 and 1945 by the Bottomley and the Golden Committees. General Hunton submitted a memorandum to the Admiralty in September 1945 in which he stressed the need for a proper balance between the *Per Mare* and *Per Terram* aspects of the Corps' roles by comparison with their pre-war duties. As *Per Mare Per Terram*, the Corps motto since 1775 implies, Royal Marines are essentially soldiers by sea and by land, and the reason they became more heavily committed to Naval gunnery in the 1920s and 1930s has been explained (Chapter 1).

The problems of promotion were also understood by 1945, and in his memorandum, General Hunton made proposals that would 'provide early promotion opportunities for the better junior officers'.[13] There were, however, many experienced officers who had commanded large formations, Commandos and other special forces in battle, yet had to revert to their substantive junior ranks. Lieutenant-Colonels reverted to captains, and many majors to lieutenants. Although many of the 3,200 'Hostilities Only' officers were being demobilised (by June 1946 there were to be only 1,400 of them), the loss of their experience would not turn out to be as serious as was expected,[14] and a number of 'HO' officers transferred to Continous Service. However, plans of June 1945 to integrate the Adjutant General's staff with the Naval Operations staff would still take some years to achieve.

Recruiting young officers in the late 1940s was proving difficult and the number of so called 'direct entry' officers, joining from civilian jobs or studies, proved inadequate. Therefore the Corps tried to increase the number of men promoted from the ranks to hold Corps Commissions, after passing educational qualifications. About 1 per cent of the Royal Marine officers before 1939 had come from the ranks, but in the late 1940s this proportion was increased, as sergeants and others – in some cases specially brought back from the Far East – passed the special education courses which did not recognise the syllabus for School Certificates of education. There were also SNCOs with the appropriate service educational qualifications. who could be granted Direct Promotion to commissioned rank, but this scheme was short lived. And by the late 1950s a large proportion of junior officers in several units would have served as Marines before gaining commissioned rank.

In addition to the Direct Entry and Corps Commissioned officers, there was a list of Special Duty (SD) officers drawn from the ranks of quartermasters. Officers on this SD promotion list – see Appendix 3 – were commissioned by the late 1960s initially as full lieutenants, and the senior captains on the list might be promoted to major. But there were only three – and briefly four – SD majors at any one time in the 1980s. Several of the officers holding Corps Commissions and those who had received Direct Promotion rose to senior rank and one officer who held a Corps Commission retired with the rank of Major General (Major General E.D.G. Pounds).

The lessons of World War II for the Corps had been learnt through the frustrations of 1940, when the setbacks to the Division were fresh in the minds of General Sturges and others; of this he was to write of any explanations he might give, 'the greater the truth, the greater the libel ... with regret'[15]. Plans were therefore made to convert 27th RM Battalion into a training battalion equipped with infantry support weapons including 6-pdr anti-tank guns, to give senior officers the opportunity of handling a fully mobilised and equipped unit, which would also provide practical training for young officers (YOs) and NCOs. The American methods of handling amphibians and training drivers were studied, while the Royal Navy's use of drivers was under review, but the everyday work of transport drivers was not a role the Corps wanted to assume, for the essential nature of their work was to be in the assault phases of operations. The employment of Royal Marines in AA, essential as it had been in 1940 for the anti-aircraft defence of advanced fleet bases, was also seen to have no future in 1945.[16] Two factors at this time also influenced the way the Corps would go: colonels of line regiments disliked losing some of their best officers and men to Army Commandos; and the Admiralty with a greatly reduced fleet was proud to keep its Royal Marines.

The pattern of events in the next two years was dominated, however, by demobilisation. This was based on a qualification by age and length of service for Class 'A' releases; and for tradesmen and others urgently needed for industry there was a Class 'B' release, giving them some priority over other servicemen. In carrying out the Adjutant General's policy for sensibly handling the tens of thousands of Marines who would be going outside, educational and vocational training (EVT) was available; although this was not new to the Corps – the first EVT course had been held in 1908[17] – the scale was unprecedented, as was the care taken to ensure men were kept occupied by sport, social functions and many other non-military interests. The policy certainly created the atmosphere intended and there must be few 'Hostilities Only' Marines, if any, who do not remember the Corps with pride and affection. In 1945 even the fiercest drill sergeants turned out to be among the most thoughtful men – one Jewish Marine who did not regularly go to synagogue was detailed off by his sergeant to do so, and transport provided to get him there every Saturday.[18] In India the 34th Amphibian Support

Regiment was briefly employed on internal security duties. The majority of men were now looking forward to demobilisation. Yet for many of these Marines there would be periods in the Far East when there was no opportunity for EVT courses or relaxation, and they again came under fire.

The situations in countries for which the South East Asia Command, under Admiral Lord Mountbatten, had responsibility during the autumn of 1945 illustrates the problems faced by successive British governments in their wish to foster independence – as they would do in India, Burma and elsewhere. The difficulty was to ensure that extreme nationalists did not repress minorities, nor thugs who indulged in murder, looting and uncivilised behaviour to be allowed free rein by their new governments.[19] In Burma a few British officials, disobeying orders from SEAC, soured relations with the Burmese by attempting to reimpose the pre-war style of administration. In Siam (modern Thailand) a peaceful return to civil government enabled an Allied force to disarm the Japanese, but another party in Indo-China met resistance and the Japanese were ordered to aid the Allied powers until the return of the French.[20] In Java even stronger resistance met the prospect of any return by the Dutch, for here the Japanese had established an Indonesian republic with an army which had some supporting artillery and tanks.

Glenroy's LCAs were sent to western Java in mid-October, landing Gurkhas without trouble at Batavia, but after a second landing further east these troops had several casualties. *Glenroy*'s Marines, 546 and 547 Flotillas, returned with Indian troops later in the month and carried Dutch civilians – mostly women and children in a sorry condition – to repatriation camps in Singapore.[21] On her next voyage the situation had deteriorated. The British government had not intended to intervene except for the evacuation of former prisoners-of-war, but atrocities by extremists against Dutch and Chinese civilians led to the Allied occupation of Sourabaya during November, despite fanatical resistance.[22] *Glenroy*'s LCA crews by this time had been ordered to fly the White Ensign and to carry arms, and each craft had its loaded Bren guns ready for action on landing.[23] The LCS(M) which had landed near Port Swettenham did not return to *Glenroy* but with the LSI *Sansovino* went to the Andaman Islands, where for some weeks they served as duty boats for the Naval-Officer-in-command (NOIC) before re-embarking on this LSI.[24] By December she was one of many ships working in the Far East, landing troops and repatriating ex-prisoners and internees.

On Christmas day she was in Batavia where the Naval provost marshal was Major Jimmie Powell. She and her sister ship, HMS *Silvio*, were both former Liberty ships, SS *Empire Halberd* and SS *Empire Cutlass*, which, with the motor vessel HMS *Persimmon*, had been recommissioned as HM Ships after operations in Normandy. Their RN crews were considerably larger than the merchant navy crews. A comparison 553 RM Flotilla made when – having served on *Crossbow* in June 1944 and later when she was an HM ship – they found the anchor party of four men including the ship's baker, was replaced by a party of seamen including men with flags to signal the stages in lowering the 'hook'. *Silvio* struck a mine off Rangoon but her RM LCA crews and the ship's company were transferred to *Sansovino*, and 525 Flotilla did not return with her from the Far

East until April 1946. *Persimmon*'s 559 Flotilla returned on the first of her trooping voyages to the UK, as did the navigational leaders (LCNs of 597 Flotilla), some of which served in each of these LSIs; but *Persimmon* did not make her last trooping voyage until June 1946.[25] Men of 34th Amphibian Support Regiment were also repatriated that summer. They had not used their amphibians in an assault, although they had been briefly in action as infantry during the troubles in Java.[26]

Many Marines from support craft and other detachments which would not be required for their original roles took part in small operations, of which No.35 RM Provost Company's work in Singapore was typical.[27] Here these former RM gunners, landing craft crews and other Marines broke the illicit trade in a dangerous concoction of wood alcohol being sold through local bars.[28] Such internal security operations – both on the small and large scale – would become part and parcel of the Corps' duties in the coming years. Among other reasons, their commando training fitted them for the self-reliance and skill with small arms required in often difficult and always dangerous situations such as these, where a minimum of force is deployed, since heavy weapons are politically unacceptable. In such situations junior commanders have to make decisions despite the yellow-card syndrome with its Rules For Engagement, for, before opening fire, a Marine has to be sure that he has complied with whatever orders are current, a moment of hesitation which may cost him his life.

By November 1945 the decision to disband the Army Commandos had been taken,[29] but during the next few months 1 and 5 Army Commandos continued to serve with the Brigade in Hong Kong. During this period of reorganisation there were for a while joint RM/Army Commandos but in December 1945 all RM Commandos were redesignated Commandos Royal Marines, although some titles were not formally altered until 1946, and 3 Commando Brigade became 3 Commando Brigade RM. Amalgamations and disbandments left the Brigade with three Commandos which by March 1947 were numbered 40, 42 and 45.[30] Long before then the battalions, batteries and nearly all the landing-craft flotillas had been disbanded (see Appendix 4) and the Corps had begun to take on a predominantly commando role. There were, however, a number of cruisers and capital ships still in service with their large RM detachments. In the following paragraphs these changes of emphasis will be seen to be more those of evolution than sudden redirection. But commando service was not popular with some sea-going Marines and there was some animosity between the wearers of the 'blue' and the 'green' berets.

In 1946 General Sir Dallas Brooks, KCB, CMG, DSO, when CGRM, wrote of the future role of the Corps as he saw it, after the Admiralty had redefined the functions of the Corps in 1945. He pointed out that with 'our traditional role in HM Ships . . . as the Navy's soldiers available for operations ashore . . . this role is basic . . . our second major function is to provide commando Units . . . thirdly, to carry out certain duties within a Naval assault force, including the manning of landing craft . . .'.[31] Sir Dallas Brooks emphasised two other aspects of the Corps' likely development as he saw it: being air-minded and fostering the continued co-operation with the United States Marine Corps. He forecast that the traditional role in ships was likely to diminish as the role of capital ships declined. As regards numbers, he expected the Corps to revert to 14,000 or so after March 1948, 'when the majority of National Service men will have returned to civilian life'.[32] These numbers would be supplemented by a reserve, for which government approval was given that year, with a strength of 1,500 all ranks.[33]

During the immediate post-war years the Commandant General was still in theory responsible to the Second Sea Lord, but in practice CG had direct access to the First Sea Lord. General Sir Dallas Brooks and his successor, General Sir Leslie Hollis, KCB, KBE (CG 1949–52), both had had distinguished war careers outside the Corps – Sir Dallas with the Department of Political Warfare and Sir Leslie in the Cabinet Office – which had brought them in close contact with cabinet ministers and the Chiefs of Staff. We shall come back to the later reorganisation of the services, and in particular the changes which formally recognised the Commandant General's rightful responsibilities to the First Sea Lord as Chief of the Naval Staff. Meanwhile, Corps relationships with Combined Operations Headquarters remained close.[34] The Army had no objection to there being three Royal Marine Commandos, but resisted every suggestion that this force might be increased.[35]

Reorganisation within the Corps had been considered in 1942 by the Hunton Committee (Chairman General Hunton). The Committee's report had included a reference to the tendency for the pre-war Adjutants General not to delegate authority, with the result that 'an officer rather than risk a mistake will refer to higher authority on almost every question'.[36] This view could hardly be held in the light of events after 1942, when senior Royal Marine officers commanded field formations, but the Corps had taken it to heart and it was in the minds of the Lamplough Committee.[37] This had been set up by the Commandant General in August 1946 to suggest ways of reorganising the Corps to implement his proposals to the Admiralty. These would cover the replacement of the pre-war 'Grand' Divisions with more appropriate groupings of units, and the introduction of Major Generals to command these groups and provide for expansion in times of national emergency. Expansion of this type was perhaps the most difficult aspect for any service to put across, as most politicians at that time tended to view any future war as being short and sharp, as perforce do many military planners. Nevertheless by the adoption of this report[38] to provide senior officers with experience of large formations, some essential measures were taken towards what was expected to be the likely wartime expansion.

So far as the introduction of Major Generals as group commanders was concerned, they would each have delegated powers which included collation of financial estimates. They would also have discretion in: the apportionment of any sums allocated for the Group's expenditure; power to write off certain stores; authority to deal summarily with charges against captains and more junior officers; and power to grant certain extra pay and allowances. Their Groups, still with the titles Chatham, Portsmouth and Plymouth, each had under com-

mand units based in the respective geographical areas of the corresponding Naval
Home Commands, with some minor exceptions. There was also one major exception with the Commando Group, which at this date was virtually 3 Commando
Brigade. Colonels and Lieutenant-Colonels commanding units and establishments
were not to have their authority restricted by these arrangements, for the purpose
was to give the Major Generals delegated powers from CG, which would leave
their formation commanders authority under each MGRM. Each General's command had its own staff under a Colonel as Chief-of-Staff, to provide for training
supervision, including allocation of training areas, pay, clothing and other services
to the units within a Group.[39]

Continued pressure from the electorate to reduce taxes by cuts in military
forces led to further reorganisations. In 1947 the Newman Committee[40] put
forward proposals for the organisation of the Corps on functional rather than
geographic areas of command. Its recommendations provided the basis on which
the Corps was organised until the early 1990s, for instead of each RM Group
providing training and administrative services for the different types of military
units within its command, each aspect of the Corps' role would be undertaken
by particular groups. Chatham was to have all pay and records, drafting and
NCOs' promotion; Portsmouth would undertake all aspects of Naval and
amphibious training; and Plymouth would be responsible for all military (infantry) training. In the coming years the functional responsibilities of Groups varied
from time to time but from 1969 Commando Forces were based on Plymouth, and
Training Group with the landing craft and other specialists had its headquarters at
Portsmouth, as explained later.

To move ahead of the chronology of the history, when General Sir Leslie
Hollis was appointed Commandant General in May 1949, he was faced by the
recommendations of the Harwood Committee[41] which – among other service
cuts – proposed that the Corps be disbanded. By 1948 the strength of 13,000
included less than 2,000 Marines at sea in warships; sea service, for those in
Whitehall 'accustomed to think in pre-war terms', was the only justification for
the Corps' existence, and this proportion to the total strength was, they thought,
quite uneconomic.[42] General Hollis persuaded the Board of Admiralty that the
Commando Brigade should be retained but the Corps' strength reduced to 10,300
by closing Chatham Division.[43]

For the Marine these changes inevitably had an unsettling effect, but great
care was taken to keep all ranks informed of the intended changes. When, for
instance, the Corps was reorganised into functional Groups, all men had the
opportunity of expressing their views on having to move house and home. This
followed Commandant General's instructions that the effect of the Newman
Committee's proposals 'on the welfare and morale of the Corps'[44] must be given
a careful consideration. However the introduction of specialist qualifications on
a wider scale than before would inevitably lead to centralised drafting, for ladders
of promotion would be by specialist lists rather than being based on Divisional
rosters. The Corps was then to have general duties Marines with a greater number
of specialist qualifications and a technical branch.

National Service had replaced wartime conscription in 1946 and by 1957 over 300 officers and 9,000 Marines had served with the Corps as National Servicemen. A number transferred to continuous service and as late as 1960 there were five officers and 50 other ranks on National Service engagements still serving with the Corps. Their operational roles, as for the continuous service Marine, were not altered by changes in higher policy at this time, and among the ships' detachments of the late 1940s there were, for example, the Royal Marines in HMS *Bermuda*, who among their ranks included men who had landed in tanks in Normandy, served in a Commando, fired anti-aircraft guns ashore, and coxswained landing craft, and her detachment was not exceptional. They provided their share of ceremonial guards, as Marines had done before World War II, and in Hong Kong they were landed to help the commandos search trains. They patrolled to catch smugglers, these were often half a dozen girls with two large baskets 'who could move fast, it took some running to catch them'.[1] *Bermuda* was the first British warship to visit Hiroshima, and did not return from the Far East until October 1947. HMS *London* was on the Yangtse in 1949 when Chinese communists were blockading British warships, and Band Master F. G. Harwood attended the ship's casualties with great devotion, for which he was awarded the DSM.[2]

In 1956 small detachments of an officer and 21 men were drafted to frigates in the Persian Gulf, where they could provide landing parties in local emergencies.[3] But the days of the capital ships were now clearly numbered, for although Admiral Pound in 1937 had rightly believed in their potential uses after any major war, when he expected they might dominate oceans around the Empire,[4] the technology of naval warfare had changed by 1943, if not before, as we have seen. Of the five *King George V*-class and four *Lion*-class (16-in gun) battleships planned before the war, only the 15-in gun *KGV*s were built, the *Lions* being abandoned in 1942. The only battleship completed after the war was HMS *Vanguard* with eight 15-in guns. The effects of such changes in plan on the Corps were explained in Chapter 1, and when these ships were finally scrapped – *KGV*, *Duke of York*, *Anson* and *Howe* in the late 1950s, *Vanguard* in 1960[5] – with them went the berths for some 1,500 Marines during the last decade of the Dreadnoughts.

Nevertheless some ships' detachments saw action in the operations described later, although most future actions would be fought by 3 Commando Brigade RM. In October 1945 this Brigade had been expected to be 3,000 strong,[6] but by 1948 there were only 2,200 commandos[7] after the Brigade had moved to the Mediterranean, where it was deployed in covering the British withdrawal from Palestine. At this time Brigade HQ was a relatively small body, for the commandos could only afford personnel for military matters.[8]

The situation in Palestine had been deteriorating after the United Nations announced plans to partition the country into Jewish and Arab states, and a date (27 June) was announced for the ending of the British mandate, on 14 May 1948. This led to an increase in the Arabs' conflict with the Jews and the reduction of British forces, which were being gradually concentrated around Haifa to keep this port open for the final evacuation.[9] Although the Jewish 'official' army, the Haganah, had orders to avoid killing British personnel, there was proof of their complicity in murder and sabotage of British forces by other Jews. Not for the first time Royal Marines were sent to try and keep the peace between Arabs and Jews. In 1936 Marine Dennis Jones had been awarded the DSM for gallant service in Palestine between 15 September and 14 October.[10] In late January 1948 40 Commando RM arrived in Haifa and took over duties in the port from 1 to 12 May.

From the first day the Commando was engaged in security operations: a bomb in Wadi Rushmiya the 'no-man's land' between Arabs and Jews; the murder of two British policemen, both ex-Royal Marines, by Arabs; fake alarms that sent patrols to guard a grain ship; arrest of two Jews in illegal possession of arms; and confrontation by Arab crowds when the dockyard gate was closed by 40 Commando. It was 'a very full first day'.[11] In the next few months these commandos were on constant patrol, reducing the pilferage, clearing underwater 'mines', destroying sniper positions. Besides keeping the peace so far as they could between Jew and Arab, on one occasion (27 February), when militant Jews tried to prevent young men emigrating, commandos had to keep Jew from Jew. Although the export of oranges kept the port reasonably free of major clashes until the end of April, there was a general round of bomb outrages, searches in the town for illegal arms and action to prevent illegal war stores being unloaded. Although the Jews made sophisticated attempts to obtain these stores, appearing in British uniforms with what appeared to be the correct documents, in attempts to deceive the port authorities.

The Commando acquired two Staghound armoured cars, which were taken from the military dump for use as armoured static posts, but when one engine started 'accidentally' as one Staghound was being towed, both vehicles were used as mobile bases by the Marines from the mortar Group of the Commando. Early in May, after the arrival of 42 Commando with substantial Army reinforcements, including Comet tanks, the Arab forces were disorganised by internal squabbles.

On 20 April the 1st Battalion Coldstream Guards withdrew from the centre of the town – 40 Commando was under command of 1st Guards Brigade – leaving only the evacuation routes open. That night the Commando advanced in a well-organised secret operation, and was redeployed around the port by daylight next morning 'without a shot being fired'.[12] But hostile Bren teams fired into the traffic and Commando positions, wounding Lieutenant A. H. W. Seed before they could be eliminated – one behind armoured plate being destroyed by a Piat bomb and a second stalked by a small patrol of a corporal and two Marines.

About 0522 hours the following day (22 April) Jews began mortaring the Arab quarter and 'masses of Arab men, women and children rushed from the Suk and milled around No.3 gate'.[13] These were the opening moves of the second Battle of Haifa which caused many casualties among these women and children, even though they were allowed into the port out of the line of fire. Lieutenant P. J. Pitman, one of the last 'HO' officers and due for demobilisation in 1949, was holding back Arab men to let the women and children through the gate, when he was hit by a Jewish Bren-gunner's fire.[14] The Commando's Medical Officer, Surgeon-Lieutenant M. I. Cox, RNVR, was also hit as he attended wounded Arabs. The situation was critical and the Staghound was called to No.3 Gate, and 'after several accurate rounds of 37-mm had been fired at them, the Jewish snipers then lost all interest in this target'.[15] This left the Commando with thousands of Arab refugees who had to be immediately evacuated by sea to Acre, and several hundreds to be fed and given a blanket for the night.

The Jews occupied Haifa and only some 2,500 Arabs remained. This deprived the British forces of dockyard labour and strict pass regulations had to be enforced – 40 Commando was the issuing authority – for the British mandate had ended on 24 May, but the peacekeeping force stayed on. In Libya 45 Commando had been on an exercise near Benghazi, where it had been tactically convenient to protect a United Nations commission discussing the new constitution for this former Italian colony. On 1–2 May it flew into Haifa as a reinforcement, landing in operational order, the first men taking up defensive positions as they came out of the planes.[16] They moved off down the road, machine guns mounted to protect each truck, into the Mount Carmel area, where they protected the radio station and policed the district before they were withdrawn on 12 May.

Meanwhile, 42 Commando, had arrived by sea on 3 May, and guarded the Sheik Jarrah area of Jerusalem until withdrawn to Haifa 11 days later and final evacuation on 27 June. HMS *Phoebe* and *Dieppe* were moored to the breakwater and used as HQ ships – *Phoebe* and HMS *Mauritius* had both intercepted illegal immigrant ships the previous year – and 40 Commando built a cordon around the lighter wharf and cargo jetty. Lieutenant-Colonel R. D. Houghton, commanding '40', passed the message 'F3, F4, F5 withdraw', putting all the ships other than HMS *Striker* under way. Then 40 Commando withdrew from the port gates. The Mortar Group, with four 3-in mortars, covered this tactical movement, setting up their mortars in a series of bounds, and *walking* calmly back each time to a new position. 'The last baseplate position was on the bows of the Tank Landing Ship *Striker*.' These Marines were the last British troops to leave Palestine. Colonel Houghton was awarded an OBE, Captain D. L. S. Aldridge the MBE and two NCOs (Sergeant R. R. Dodds and Corporal D. R. Earr) received the MM. Other awards included a BEM for Sick Berth Attendant A. McGlen, a medical orderly, and ten mention-in-despatches.[17]

During these months in the Mediterranean the Brigade (hereafter 'the Brigade' refers to 3 Commando Brigade) was also employed in policing the Canal Zone (Egypt). It had a brief spell in Jordan on the Israeli border as part of a British garrison force – where heliographs on the beach passed messages for the UK to the guardship – and did other policing duties. Then in the summer of 1949, when the Chinese Communist government was expected to invest British territories, the Brigade was sent back to Hong Kong. There, among more routine garrison duties, it took the first postwar census of villagers in Kowloon.[18]

In May 1950 the Brigade left Hong Kong for what would be a two-year tour in Malaya. Although the Malayan Communist Party's underground army had supported the British in World War II, by the late 1940s these Chinese were attempting to seize a tract of country and set up a government, hoping to attract other Chinese, many of whom were illegal immigrants squatting in small villages on the jungle fringes. The communists' efforts, however, would be frustrated when many squatters were resettled in defended villages, forcing the terrorists to move further away from the jungle in search of food and money.[1] Nor were the Communists able to organise urban terrorists on a scale sufficient to prevent Marines off duty having a normal run ashore,[2] although terrorists shot up trains, ambushed planters and terrorised plantation workers.

The Brigade – once again commanded by Brig Campbell Hardy, who had commanded it at Kangaw in 1945 – was given responsibility for counter-terrorist measures in Perak State (northern Malaya). Perak covers an area about the size of Wales, and about a third of it is a plain with tin mines and rubber estates bounded by swamps to the west and by dense jungles which spread eastward into the mountains. The Marines operated up to the Thai border, where terrorists crossed into safe camps. Many Chinese lived in the area and were indistinguishable from terrorists, which could – and occasionally did – lead to neutral Chinese being killed in mistake for terrorists. Each Commando was given an area to control, 40 Commando RM around Kuala Kangsar in the north, '42 RM' in Central Perak at Ipoh and '45 RM' at Tapah in the south. Troops of these Commandos were spread in areas often 50 or more miles from their Commando HQ, for this would be a war of small units. After a few weeks' kitting up in Malaya before deploying to Perak, Marines began to patrol through the jungle 'in places with trees 250ft in height except where the jungle has been temporarily cleared ... [where] a dense secondary scrub had sprung up'.[3] During the first few months the Brigade also assisted the local authorities in resettling squatters, of whom some 91,000 would be in new villages by the summer of 1951. Army units in other areas played the major roles in these operations, which also provided medical and other facilities for the squatters.

Not long after the Brigade moved to Malay, the North Koreans crossed the 38th Parallel (on 25 June 1950) and detachments of Royal Marines were placed indirectly under United Nations command when the light carrier HMS *Triumph* and the cruisers HMS *Jamaica* and HMS *Belfast* came under UN command the day after this invasion. More Marines would be drawn into the Korean War, as explained later, while the operations in Malaya continued. In these operations much of the patrolling was carried out by Sections of a dozen or so men, but on occasions Troops moved away from their established bases to form temporary camps deep in the jungle. Even when such comparatively large bodies of men, 60 to 80 strong, were moving through the jungle, they had a sense of isolation. And torrential rain for 8 to 10 hours at a stretch debilitated the fittest men and laid others low physically and mentally, as did jungle sores and poisoned insect bites. Through such conditions 'X' Troop of 40 Commando made a 21-day patrol in April 1951.

On 5 April, a Malay Auxiliary reported an attack on his village, an isolated Malay *kampong* (settlement) 30 miles east of the Troop's camp at Grik. The

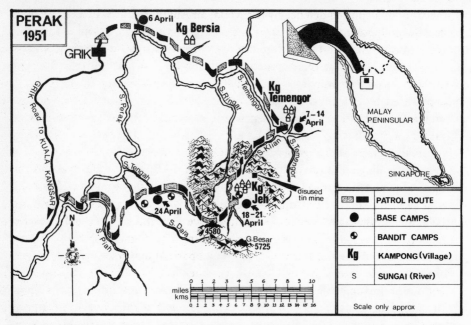

Route of a typical anti-terrorist patrol by 'X' Troop of 40 Commando RM in Malaya during April 1951.

Troop commander flew to the Commando HQ 69 miles away at Kuala Kangsar and there the CO arranged for air support, and for two sections of the Heavy Weapons Group to move up to 'X' Troop's base at Grik for the period that they would be away. Four of their six Sections were brought in from the 12-man patrols they had been carrying out for a week without success. By 0300 hours next day Captain B. P. Elvy, the Troop Commander, and the rest of his force set out to meet them at Bersia.[4] There the porters went 'sick' but doses of No.9s – the pill for the constipated – got them on their feet in a couple of hours and at midday these Sakai aborigines began rafting the men across the Perak river. Some four hours later the first flights of Brigand fighter-bombers began strafing 1,000yds ahead of the point section. There was an almost continual screaming of bombs and rockets as the Troop and a party of police, in all about 80 men, moved up the track, the point Section indicating its position by smoke grenades before each fighter's attack.

Darkness fell at 1930 hours after the Marines had covered some 24 miles, mostly along elephant tracks, the men carrying full loads despite the majority having been on patrol most of the previous week. Leeches, mosquitoes and giant ants are not mentioned in the official report, but were accepted as everyday irritants for all patrols, although they contributed their share to weakening men on such marches. The Troop posted sentries and lay-up that night some 2½-hours march from the Malay village of Temengor, their objective. They reached the village at 0900 hours next day to find the Malays had fled, but as villagers returned, Captain Elvy and the District Police Officer (an ex-RM) pieced together the story of a spirited defence by the Malayan Auxiliaries. They had killed several bandits and wounded others despite three Auxiliaries being killed, for the terrorists had a Bren gun and rifles against the nineteen Malayans' 12-bore shotguns. The Troop then made this village their base, building *bashas* from two supports and a cross pole of timber, with sloping sides of split palm leaves, or with poncho capes used by the less ambitious. From this base they began collecting reports on terrorist activities, all of which were sifted and then radioed to the Commando HQ.

Patrols were sent out to encourage the squatters in the area to move to a defended village. Sadly a Marine on one of these patrols lost the grip of his *oppo*'s – opposite number's – arm and was swept to his death in crossing 50yds of a swift mountain river, and a Sergeant also died during these operations, but helicopters flew out the wounded. After a week in the village the Troop moved base to Jeh, a 3-day march over hills, during which the Saki porters and the guides got disgruntled; but following a compass route brought the Troops over the hills safely into Jeh. There they set up defence posts and in 25 minutes had cut out of the jungle – not light scrub, as expected – a dropping-zone for supplies: 'It is amazing how quickly a hungry Marine can clear jungle', even if the pilot complained that the 'DZ was a bit small'.[5] In three days further contacts were established with the Sakai, many of these friendly people being persuaded to move into safer areas rather than grow crops for the terrorists. The patrol then came out.

'X' Troop had been withdrawn by Commando HQ, for the CO had been advised by intelligence sources that the terrorists had left the area. Sources of information were effectively centralised, so that a patrol could be moved by radioed orders to localities where they would be effective. Operations to saturate areas with troops were carried out later in the campaign, by bringing in Commando Troops and Army companies from their regular patrol areas. These operations were successful in the view of senior officers. But some considered they were of limited success because intelligence on terrorists' movements was disrupted. As informers lost contact with suspects when large numbers of troops were in an area; nor did such large forces create the atmosphere in which others in the local population would come forward with information.[6] The more successful methods were to use small patrols with specific objectives and in the Marines' patrols there were fewer men than in the Army's.[7]

In many of these operations Dyak trackers, Ibans from Sarawak, whose forefathers had been headhunters, worked with patrols. They were long-haired, brave men with gold teeth and tattoos, some of them struck up friendships with several Marines who had learnt sufficient of their language to hold a conversation. And at least four Marines spent a pleasant leave with the Ibans in Borneo.[8] The help of these trackers was invaluable, for they could find trails across tin tailings – the spoil from mine workings, which, incidentally, upset compasses – and over hard ground, and when they had discovered a bandit route, ambushes were carefully laid.

For the many Marines who lay out in the cool and sometimes cold nights of the rain forests, ambushes required almost an infinity of patience, since on many long nights no action resulted. This in part was due to the difficulty of keeping a patrol's departure secret. One Troop dressed as Chinese to deceive distant watchers, and then entered the jungle, but in passing a neutral village they were clapped by an admiring line of villagers. News also leaked out of the 2-in mortar smuggled into a defended village by a Marine carrying it in a pig basket, to beef up the Auxiliaries' defensive fire, but the terrorists did not make the expected attack.[9] 'Y' Troop of 42 Commando, on the other hand, sent a sub-Section commanded by a corporal to ambush the trail alongside a pipeline from tin mines deep in the jungle. As a deception, this sub-Section of some 10 Marines and their Corporal were put into the jungle, as though they were going to operate in the area of a river some days' march from the pipeline. After laying up in the jungle well upstream on the first night, at first light they made their way through thick jungle, crossing a high ridge and innumerable streams. Thorns ripped their olive green shirts and slacks, and they were wringing wet with sweat, hungry and thirsty when they reached a patch of dense secondary jungle, the *belukar*, which screened them from prying eyes. Then the young Corporal gathered his men round him, after they had slipped off their equipment. His orders were reinforced by the knowledge that the pipeline was only a matter of yards away; there was to be no cooking – the smell of hexamine tablets burning in a Tommy cooker could be detected 'a mile away' – and not the slightest sound. Each man carried two water bottles and these would have to be made to last probably for two days. Nor was there much to eat, men usually making two days' rations last for three, so that they could travel light. The Corporal then crawled off in that flat knees-and-belly-to-the-ground manner of a stalker who wants to see without being seen at the edge of the forest. From there he saw the pebble track beside the double lines of black 18-in piping on supports raised some 4ft on stilts. The sun was setting as he made out a shallow re-entrant, a V-shaped depression commanding 18yds of pipeline.

There were too few Marines, he decided, to make a firm base, for all would have to be in the ambush, as the terrorists might approach it from either direction. After he had crawled back into the *belukar*, he briefed the men, marking their positions for them on a sweat-soaked pad with a stub of pencil. The Corporal and Bren team (two men) would be at the head of the 'V' and two rifle groups would be some 20yds on either flank of the depression and above steep banks overlooking the track. The three groups were to be tied together by lines of string on which one jerk meant 'look out somebody's coming', two further jerks told that they were friendly, and three meant bandits. A short pause would follow these three tugs and then each jerk would tell of the number of terrorists approaching. No flank post was to open fire before the Bren, for the killing ground was in the opening in front of the 'V'; but once the Bren fired, no enemy must escape past the rifle groups. They rehearsed the slower wits in the detail of this plan, before all crawling to their positions and laying the strings.

'All night they lay in ambush, a still calm night, whose stars sparkled through the grasses and bushes above their heads. They slept fitfully, in relays, and were thankful when the dawn broke and the mist cleared sluggishly ... the heat of the sun crept through the undergrowth to warm their damp and aching bodies'.[10] As the day grew lighter, tugs on the string increased as Malays and Sakai moved along the track. The heat in the undergrowth grew more stifling the higher the sun rose, the 'sentries' changed places, silently unhitching the strings from the legs of No.2 on the Bren when No.1 took over, sweat running down his face in rivulets. The heat was oppressive and relaxing, and one could fall asleep as if in the lassitude of a steam bath. The sound of guttural Chinese conversation brought a sudden tension, and the lance-corporal in the right picket took an extra turn on the string round his hand. As the loud voices came nearer, he saw two Chinese walking one behind the other, each carrying a large bundle on his back; their khaki shorts and stained white shirts were common enough but each had a rifle. Three sharp tugs, a pause, and then two more, startled the Bren-gunner, he too had heard the voices but had not expected his leg to be nearly pulled off.

The corporal was alert, the Bren-gunner slipped off the safety catch, and brought the butt to his shoulder. Finger on the trigger, he aimed the Bren at a patch of sunlight – the killing ground – and waited. The first terrorist came into this white light talking loudly, his companion next came into view about to say something, when the Bren opened fire, killing him instantly. The first terrorist dodged towards the pipe stilts but died in a hail of bullets, and fine jets of water from bullet holes in the pipes played softly over the bloodstained bodies. The dead were later identified as couriers setting out for a base up above the mines.[11] To make these identifications the patrol had carried the bodies back to the police post, a chore that was heavy work; slicing off heads was not allowed after this practical alternative had received adverse publicity.

In the early months in Malaya the Brigade consisted almost entirely of long-service Marines, but later more National Servicemen joined them. These new-comers had been trained by sergeants and corporals, most of whom were veterans who had fought alongside Yugoslav partisans, or taken a bullet at Walcheren or a mortar fragment in the woods beyond the Aller. 'They wore parachute badges and faded medal ribbons on their tunics of a coveted greenish Canadian cloth not available for recruits ... their faces were "made" of teak ... they were hard and cunning commando soldiers'.[12] Young National Servicemen found them a sharp contrast 'to the screaming primates who taught the Army conscripts disci-pline',[13] when a few of these Marines went to the Army OCTU at Eaton Hall (Cheshire). The 'commando soldiers' taught their temporary charges sufficient of the skills needed to stay alive in a jungle war, and their proteges laid ambushes with a success that would have delighted their instructors.

On one such patrol a young National Service Officer's Section killed three terrorists, the third of whom had turned back from the jungle to rescue a wounded comrade. This act of heroism did not pass unnoticed, although this terrorist was an obscure bicycle dealer from a village in Pahang, not a prominent Communist or a guerrilla officer. Indeed this bicycle dealer was like many terrorists at the time the Brigade arrived in Perak, when there were about 1,000 Chinese in the

Malayan Races Liberation Army with some 500 active supporters. Of these terrorists and those in the south (where 42 Commando served briefly under an Army brigade after May 1952), the Brigade accounted for 221 killed or captured. 'It is a record of hard work, devotion to duty and good comradeship of which the Royal Marines have every reason to be proud', Sir John Harding, Chief of the Imperial General Staff, wrote later.[14] Thirty all ranks lost their lives during these operations, and the Brigade received some 40 gallantry awards, not including 68 mentions-in-despatches.[15]

Ships' detachments during the Malayan campaign took no direct part in the land fighting. Although the cruiser HMS *Newcastle* on one occasion fired a single 6-in shell every few minutes throughout one day, while the ship's company painted ship. Her shells landed on a terrorist route miles away in the jungle.[16]

During the Brigade's two years in Malaya, Marines had been in action elsewhere, as mentioned earlier, and others had provided ceremonial guards and messengers for high-level conferences, as the Corps had done in previous years. In October 1945, 50 Marines were provided for United Nations meetings, and at these UN meetings, in San Francisco, Marine sergeants worked for the British delegation; other NCOs accompanied Prime Minister Macmillan to Bermuda – two examples of a number of such duties carried out by Royal Marines at this time. There were also civic ceremonials such as the granting of the freedom of Deal to the Corps in February 1945.[17] The Corps was represented at the funeral ceremonies for King George VI in February 1952 and, in respect for his late Majesty, HM ships carried out a programme of gun salutes, refrained from playing bugles or bands at the daily ceremony of 'colours', and remained in harbour until after the funeral. Officers wore a black crepe armband on the left sleeve when in uniform until 31 May; and for a week no organised sports took place.[18] A happier occasion was the Coronation of Her Majesty Queen Elizabeth II on 2 June 1953, when Plymouth and Deal bands with RM and RMFVR (RM Forces Volunteer Reserve) detachments were in the procession returning from Westminster Abbey. Portsmouth Group Band supported the Royal Guard provided by the Corps at Westminster Abbey, and other RM bands were positioned along the processional route.[19]

By this date the RM Forces Volunteer Reserve was established in London and a number of major towns (see Appendix 4) and only National Servicemen who had served in the Reserve were accepted into the Corps. One young National Service officer, typical of many, had joined Lympstone from the Reserve and after training in the ranks, he went to the Army OCTU at Eaton Hall (Cheshire).[20] (The period National Service officers spent in the ranks varied according to their date of selection for OCTU and the formation of a cadet batch.)[21] He was commissioned eight months from the day he joined the Corps, and after further training in landing craft he joined the Amphibious Warfare Squadron in 1954. His craft were escorting the Royal Yacht *Britannia* when the Queen left Malta that summer, and the LCAs 'almost blew up their engines keeping station with the Royal Yacht, as she put on speed. One LCA filled when trapped between the wash of two big ships, leaving her crew at attention in a sinking craft as the yacht sailed away. At another time, in a different context, they heard of the Ghost at Eastney, a presence reported by one young officer in No.3 Passage.[22] After two years with many more serious alarms and excursions, these National Service officers rejoined the RMFVR for at least two years, and many served longer in the Reserve; a number also transferred to the Corps with regular commissions.

The Amphibious Warfare Squadron's origins and concepts are explained in the next chapter, but when the Brigade came out of Malaya, it was to be deployed in landing exercises in the Mediterranean with this Squadron from time to time. In May 1953 the Brigade Headquarters, with 42 and 45 Commando, were in Malta. Families were able to join them on 'accompanied tours'. On these occasions the families received every help in making the journey overseas with small children, and after their arrival often enjoyed their stay in foreign countries, with all those experiences which become treasured memories of a childhood spent in exotic places.[23]

The Brigade's role was now becoming clear:[24] it would be moved to the area of likely trouble or within easy striking distance of it, sometimes under the guise of an exercise during the 1950s and 1960s; at other times it would cruise over the horizon off a troubled coast. This is not to say that every exercise had some sinister military purpose but merely that on a few occasions exercises are a convenient cloak – as they always were in wartime – for the movements of large bodies of men.

On 29 November 1952 Prince Philip, Duke of Edinburgh, presented colours to 40, 42 and 45 Commandos on a parade in Malta. The Brigade ships' detachments and landing craft crews 'kept the ground, making in all 67 officers and 1,168 men on parade'.[25] Of this presentation the Prince said, 'These colours are a recognition of the devotion of the wartime Royal Marines Commandos and of the courage and bearing of the Brigade in all the trouble spots of the world since the war [World War II]'. The following year (1953) the Queen honoured the Corps by appointing him Captain General in succession to the late King George VI.

While the Brigade was committed in Malaya, the Korean War broke out across the 38th Parallel, an artificial boundary set in 1945 when Russia occupied industrial North Korea, with its 8 million inhabitants, and American forces occupied the agricultural south (21 million inhabitants). The Americans had withdrawn in 1949, leaving the South Korean Republic with a defence force armed with old World War II weapons. This army could not hold the Communist North Koreans' advance when they crossed the border on 25 June 1950. Before they reached the southern city of Pusan, however, President Truman had ordered the US 24 Infantry Division from Japan in accordance with the United Nations' resolution to send a force to restore peace. This Division was badly mauled, many wounded being taken prisoner and some murdered, but they held Pusan.[1] Two British Army Battalions, 1st Argylls and 1st Middlesex, landed there on 29 August but as no soldiers under 19 were allowed to serve in Korea, these Battalions had

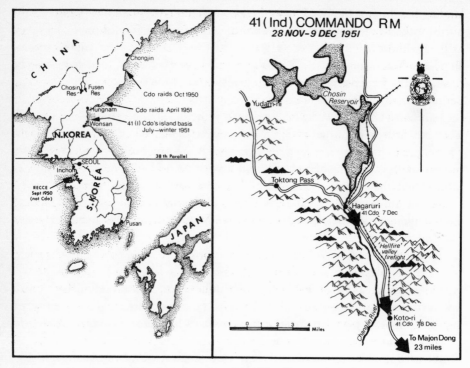

Shows operations in 1950–2 by 41 Independent Cdo RM in Korea, where there were also landings by the detachment from HMS *Ceylon*: 20 May 1951 2 platoons landed 38° 30' N, 125°E, penetrated 1½ miles (2.4k) unopposed and returned without loss; 25 August 7 RMs and 3ABs with beach defence party landed at Songon-ni, surprised an enemy post and withdrew; 30 August 2 RM platoons and one of stokers were caught in heavy fire as they landed after a bombardment at Chonidong, they were re-embarked with 15 casualties.

been reinforced in Hong Kong by men from other regiments. Earlier that month the Admiralty – at the request of the UN Naval Force Commander – had called for volunteers and Lieutenant E. G. D. Pounds (later Major-General, CB) flew from the UK to take command of 10 volunteers from the British Eastern Fleet, who were with the US Marine Corps for 3 weeks' training at Camp McGill (50 miles south of Tokyo).[2] On 8 September they were joined by three Marines from 41 (Independent) Commando (described below) and attached to the American Army's Raider Company. This company of an amphibious battalion was embarked on USS *Whitesand Bay* before sailing for their first operation, intended as a rehearsal raid on the north-west coast of South Korea.

Pounds' Force, as it was unofficially known, had been equipped with American weapons and gear, including two Browning Automatic Rifles (BARs). On this first raid to Robb Island and Kongsoon beaches, the Marines landed on the mainland with difficulty over rock reefs which holed their inflatable rubber boat. Nevertheless, they surveyed 100 yards of beach. The two 'swimmers', the shallow water divers with this Force, made an underwater reconnaissance, leaving evidence of the raid as decoys. These might distract the Koreans from the intended landing beaches for the UN Forces' invasion would be made some 48 hours later north of the Kongsoon beaches. Inaccurate machine gun fire followed the Force as they withdrew without casualties, but on Robb Island, over 1,000yds off the shore, the Americans came under accurate fire and two were killed. At the time of this raid, 12–13 September, the Pusan enclave in the south had a mere 150-miles perimeter and the rest of South Korea had been overrun, but on 15 September the reinforced US 1 Marine Division landed at Inchon after a heavy bombardment. They met little opposition until elements entered Seoul, 20 miles from the beach. This capital city was only secured after heavy fighting, when other battalions moved south to join up with the Pusan force, and a third force secured Kimpo airfield and the border town of Kaesong north-west of Seoul. Pounds' Force arrived on this airfield on 20 September and next day, with its parent Raiding Company, moved to defence positions when North Koreans infiltrated across the Han river.

For the next ten days this small force took part in patrols and skirmishes through the hills. The Naval Petty Officer who acted as Troop Sergeant Major was killed in later operations. They found the shortage of wood in these bleak uplands made cooking meals difficult, and that radio batteries were in short supply so that messages had often to be carried by runners. But the American kit they found to be generally satisfactory, even if the warm sleeping bags could not be used in forward areas, as they were 'difficult to get out of in a hurry' and that half-full water bottles made too much noise for silent patrols at night.[3]

Volunteers from the Fleet were originally intended to form the only Royal Navy force carrying out raids, but early in August 1950 the Admiralty raised an independent Commando. Its CO was Lieutenant-Colonel D. B. Drysdale, who had been on the staff during the Brigade landings of World War II and had considerable experience of raiding. He raised this 41 (Independent) Commando RM at both Bickleigh and Plymouth, which for the majority of Marines was a normal posting, though some also volunteered for this unit. About 200, including some from a draft intended for the Brigade and in transit at Singapore, were flown to Japan, many in Admiralty-issued civilian suits. In the second week of September, they began intensive training with their American equipment. All Marine commandos in Korea had been issued with American weapons and kit, only their green berets distinguishing them from American troops in battle. They worked up at Camp McGill for three raids against the coast railway between Chongjin and Hungnam, as this line carried supplies south from China, and Chongjin is only some 40 miles from the Chinese border. Two of these raids were to be made from American destroyers adapted to carry landing craft, the Assault Personnel Destroyers (APDs) USS *Wantuck* and *Bass*, and another was to be from the submarine USS *Perch*. A certain amount of detailed planning was carried out while the ships were still in Japan, and for the first time these commandos learnt the drills for landing from an APD, before the ships sailed early on 5 October for north-east Korean waters.

Of some dozen possible targets, all north of the 40th Parallel, the two chosen were tunnels on the coast railway. With one Troop in each APD, and Lieutenant

Pounds' men also in *Bass* (with 'C' Troop), having been transferred to her by line from *Wantuck* ('D' Troop). The Marines were to be towed inshore in 10-man inflatables, five or six in a string pulled by an LCP (Ramped). Little was known of the enemy's defences and the raiders would therefore make their own recce just before the final paddle to the beach. The LCP(R)s would carry demolition stores, with American Naval Officers from Underwater Demolition Team No.1 – a unit similar to a LCOCU or a SEAL team of the 1990s – and a USMC intelligence Major, after the APDs and their destroyer escort reached the 'lowering' point some 2½ miles off the coast on the late evening of 6 October 1950.

The tows were assembled and crept at less than 2 knots inshore to the 'bouncer' line 500yds from the beach where the tows were slipped. The inflatables were paddled a further 200yds before the scouts (one boat) from each party went forward. Lieutenant (later Lieutenant-Colonel) Peter R. Thomas then swam the last 100 yards to check the surf; as he left the boat, he found he was on a sand-bar. Then he had to swim through the surf, which, although heavy, could be crossed by the boats. As the shore was also clear, he signalled in the others. The mist shrouding the signal torch light caused some delay before 'D' Troop saw it, but having come in on radar direction, both Troops were landed at the right beach.

Hills loomed in the starlight behind the patch of sand which was used by the small Tactical HQ. The boats were hauled ashore and quickly unloaded, as Lieutenant Pounds led his men towards the long, low building which had been the source of some speculation before the raid. Their rubber and canvas shoes made no noise as they moved into this building, which was empty. Nearby 'in some poor dwellings' women could be heard, but nothing was to be done to civilians provided they stayed indoors, and when the leading Section found refugees from air raids sleeping in the tunnel, they were moved to the beach for their own safety. Two trains passed. Pickets were out beyond the railway and a 3½-in bazooka sited to destroy any further trains that came along before the two tons of explosive had been placed. The men sweated to bring this up the hill from the beach by 0100 hours (7 October), and the fuses were set a few minutes later. The men came back and were through the surf in their inflatables with only one casualty, although Lieutenant Pounds had been burnt by electric cables when these were cut down. They were back with the LCP(R)s when '30 minutes after the fuses were pulled ... a vast orange-red burst of flame was followed by a banging roar, soon a baleful black cloud drifted across the stars'.

This wrecked tunnel helped to block the line for many weeks, as did the second tunnel 'C' and 'D' Troop destroyed south of Songjin. This was a large town five miles from their second landing point, where they also destroyed a bridge. Although they were fired on, there were few casualties.[4] The explosion this time set the paddy fields alight. Another landing had been made earlier from the cruiser-submarine USS *Perch*; a similar raid in World War II by American Marines had been successfully made against Makin Atoll (Gilbert Islands) in 1942,[5] but this was the first time a Royal Marine unit of some size had been landed from a US submarine.

Four officers with 63 NCOs and Marines from '41 RM' were embarked in late September, and had the opportunity to carry out rehearsals. Good aerial photographs and periscope reconnaissance pictures from submarines were available, but the maps and charts were poor. *Perch* carried a light motorboat which could be launched to provide a contact link by telephone to her while she was submerged. The motorboat was also in radio contact with the ten or so inflatables *Perch* had previously launched. The submarine could tow this control boat and the inflatables while she was submerged, but on the night of 2–3 October mines prevented her coming nearer than 4½ miles from shore. The inflatables were therefore towed inshore by the control boat. Periscope reconnaissance on 1 October had been made before the raid, and although this was deferred 24 hours when enemy patrol boats covered the approaches to the proposed railway target, a good secondary target had been selected. This stretch of railway was successfully attacked.

Early in November, the mainly American Eighth Army (including 27 British Commonwealth Brigade) on the west coast was beyond Pyongyang, the North Korean capital, 70 miles north of the 38th Parallel. In the east the American X Corps was at Hungnam, with the US 1 Marine Division advancing north across the Chosin plateau. While the 7 (US) Infantry Division further north (having landed at Iwon on 30 October), and the South Korean Capitol Division were nearing the Chinese border in the north-east. As the coasts were now in United Nations' hands, there was no call for raids. And when I (US) Marine Division asked for '41 RM' as an additional recce company, the Marines were shipped to Hungnam, where they arrived in the middle of November. Just over two weeks earlier China had entered the war, catching many American units on congested roads, for the advance had been something of a mad dash for the Yalu river, the north-west border of Korea with China.[6] On 28 November 1950 the US Marine Division had two regiments 63 miles inland high in the mountains at Yudamni. Their HQ, with a battalion and some 2,000 storeman, clerks and other support services, was 15 miles south-east of Yudamni at Hagaru-ri, near the Chosin reservoir. Covering their line of communications were several battalions based to the south-east at Koto-ri, 10 miles from Divisional HQ, and further south still by 10 miles was a battalion guarding the pass up to the plateau.

Lieutenant-Colonel Drysdale went ahead of the Commando to link up with 7th US Marines in the mountains, but on the morning of 28 November, when 41 Cdo RM was to move north, the Chinese attacked and the Colonel found the road blocked beyond Koto-ri. The Chinese cut off the 7th Regiment from Division HQ and Division HQ from its rearguard at Koto-ri. That night the Commando took up defensive positions at Koto-ri in sub-zero temperatures.[7] The Chosin plateau is 3,000 to 6,000ft high in a climate not unlike that in the Italian mountains. The road snakes through low hills on the plateau, and next morning the Colonel – now commanding Force 'Drysdale' – set out with some 900 men and 17 tanks to force a way through to the Divisional base 10 miles up the road at Hagaru-ri. As the Force now contained not only 41 Commando RM but also a company of US Marines and a US Army Company, they were expected to break through without difficulty. But Chinese troops on the hills were in far greater numbers than had been realised by the Division.

The Chinese were able to shoot into the cabs of lorries, so the Marines and soldiers attempted to clear the heights – a long and bloody process. The Lieutenant-Colonel, having put 41 Cdo RM on to Hill 1, passed the USMC Company on to Hill 2, then '41' on to Hill 3, with the Army Company moving up the road. By early afternoon the Force had advanced only two miles when Division HQ radioed that a break-through that day was imperative.[8] The only thing to do was to get into the trucks, and, with tanks supporting them, to force a way along the road. Although the Lieutenant-Colonel wanted the tanks to operate in pairs throughout the column, their commander insisted on leading the convoy with all his tanks together. Behind them came the American Marines, followed by '41' and the US Army Company, all in transport. Machine gun and sporadic mortar fire harassed the column, which 'made slow progress for three miles', until the tanks were unable to move on in the face of growing resistance. There was only an hour of daylight left when a liaison officer arrived from Division HQ with a message saying again how imperative it was that the Force got through.[9]

All radio communication broke down about this time, probably because of the Force's position in a valley between hills. In the next hour the Chinese made three attacks. Major Dennis Aldridge – commanding '41', as the Colonel was leading the Force – watched the close-support US Marine Corps planes blast the hills. At one point thousands of Chinese, who poured down one hill, had not reversed their khaki/white jackets, and the khaki fronts showed up clearly against the background of snow. The Major, his MOA (batman), a signaller and a runner rolled into a ditch, the MOA shooting two Chinese before the attack was driven off. About 1930 hours the remnants of the Force reached Hagaru-ri, the Divisional base, where the Americans were mighty pleased to see a British Force.[10] One USMC Sergeant later wrote, 'the boot-necks were the only ones . . . to make it and join us in condition and willing to fight some more . . . others [in the convoy] were either killed or surrendered'.[11] Unlike the US Marines, with heads wrapped in towels, scarves and ear muffs, the commandos wore only their green berets. All through the night the commandos kept coming in, however, as scattered parties evaded the Chinese. Of the 200 Marines who had set out, 70 were casualties or missing and most of the Commando's equipment was lost. Force 'Drysdale' in all lost 50 per cent of its strength and 70 vehicles, for three Chinese regiments had succeeded in splitting the rear half of the convoy from the rest. Some of the missing, however, later reached Koto-ri. The two trucks which had reached the base were so loaded with Marines that only the last to climb aboard had been able to fire, for they were sitting on top of others. Nevertheless they sang the marching song of '41 RM' as the men on the truck floors passed up their ammunition.

The Royal Marines were used as a mobile reserve in the base. The next night (30 November) 'B' Troop, worked in the dark over ground which their Troop Commander (Lieutenant G. F. D. Roberts) had not seen. 'They succeeded admirably' in counter-attacking a break-through south of Hagaru-ri village. The perimeter defence was restored by 0400 hours. Meanwhile the USMC Regiments fought their way back to the base from the mountains, and in the next few days the Commando carried out a number of fighting patrols, including a full Commando recce. But they were unable to recover some 155-mm howitzers which had been abandoned earlier when their tractors had run out of fuel.[12] By this time '41 RM' was about equal in strength to an infantry company, and with tank support made these probes to confirm enemy dispositions and recover wounded from a crashed transport plane. 'C' Troop did a spell in the perimeter defences. The Division was to withdraw on the night of 6 December, with the USMC 7th Regiment in the van and all troops marching except for the truck drivers.[13] The intention in what the Division commander called 'this advance to the sea' was to hold the base area of Hagaru-ri long enough for the column – by now some 10,000 men and more than 1,000 vehicles[14] – to break out of the plateau. This, in Lieutenant-Colonel Drysdale's words, 'was carried out in a masterly fashion against very strong opposition'.[15]

That night (6 December) the Commando formed up with the USMC 5th Regimental Combat Team of the rearguard. All day the main column had been fighting its way south after the leading tanks had left the perimeter at first light. Heavy attacks were made about 2100 hours on the troops still holding the perimeter; and with the column stopped, '41' was sent back at midnight into the perimeter line. Some Chinese had infiltrated the old base area and fighting continued until dawn. Then the Chinese withdrew, leaving 600 dead,[16] for the tactical close air support, mainly from USMC and US Navy Squadrons, was effectively preventing any Chinese moves in daylight. 'Air supply, particularly at Hagaru-ri [Divisional Base] was prodigious . . . and the use of helicopters for reconnaissance and evacuation, were all most impressive', the Colonel later reported.[17] The rearguard was therefore able to move out of the old base about 0900 hours that morning (7 December), but it had to break through a heavily defended road block, for it was cut off from the Division. The leading battalion cleared this in a 2-hour battle during the early afternoon. At 1600 hours 'C' Troop was sent to clear machine-gunners from positions dug into a hill overlooking the road. 'A difficult task in which they succeeded in keeping the enemy quiet' before the Marines rejoined the column after dark. The remainder of '41 RM' had by then reached Koto-ri, where they were joined by Captain (later Major General) P. J. Ovens with 11 Marines. Captain Ovens and his men had fought their way through the hills after the convoy battle the previous week.[18] The story of the fight in Hell Fire valley, as the USMC history records 'as nearly as the scene can be reconstructed', was that several defended perimeters held out during the night, when a number of US and Royal Marines made for high ground across the river and 'outdistancing their pursuers, after shooting down several, they reached Koto-ri'.[19] The Marines who came down from Hagaru-ri on 8 December also brought in some bodies from that battle as they retreated to Koto-ri, where they spent the night prepared to take up defensive positions. In the late afternoon '41 RM' was sent to hold high ground on the east of the road. A blizzard blinded the men as they made a stiff climb up to these positions in 2ft of snow, and although there was no opposition, the Commando spent 'a night in the open with the thermometer showing minus fifteen degree (47 degrees Fahrenheit of frost) . . . I thought daylight would never come!'[20]

Next day they were withdrawn from this icy perimeter – there had been no chance for sleep in the past two days – before they began the final march, some 23 miles off the plateau and down the pass. The 5th Regimental Combat Team, of which '41 RM' had been part throughout the withdrawal, moved out of Koto-ri at 0900 hours. The Marine commandos marching with the Regimental HQ, and a Marine was wounded when fire from machine guns held the retreat briefly at the top of the pass. They were down it by about 1800 hours, when artillery and mortar fire fell around the column, probably from United Nations forces to the south, though 'it was none the less unpleasant'. Late that evening they finally reached Majon Dong and were taken by trucks to a tented camp which was a sea of mud, but after 'the march out of the mountains on an empty stomach without sleep for 72 hours, we could not have cared less!'[21]

In all 41 Commando lost 13 killed, 39 wounded and 27 missing after these actions, and 19 had frostbite or were suffering from exposure and pneumonia.[22] The Commando returned to Japan, the mutual respect of Royal Marines and the US Marine Corps strengthened by the comradeship of battle.

The Independent Commando re-equipped during the spring of 1951, and its strength was raised to about 300.[23] They trained for coastal raids once more, as the North Koreans now held the coastlines. Although the Chinese had helped them to cross again into South Korea by the end of March, the United Nations forces had counter-attacked and were again on the 38th Parallel, having recaptured Seoul. Amphibious raids against the west coast, however, were not considered practical because of the high rise and fall of the tides which were similar to those in the Channel Islands,[24] and practically all raiding was therefore made against east-coast targets.

The first of these was a demonstration in force, in which 41 Commando was to be landed in LVTs, for these gave some protection (with pin-on armour)[25] and ensured men got ashore dryshod. This was an important factor in cold weather before an 8-hour stay ashore. Two rehearsals were made during March, but there were some difficulties in assembling the various specialist officers for gunfire support. In part because Colonel Drysdale did not meet the Admiral commanding the Attack Force until D-1, Friday, 6 April 1951, when the Commando was embarked. The intention had been to put the commandos ashore before first light; although this sacrificed the benefit of naval and air bombardment, it maintained the element of surprise. The Attack Force included ships of the American 7th Cruiser Division, the Landing Ship Dock (LSD) USS *Fort Marion* and the APD USS *Begor*, with a UDT (Under Water Demolition Team). Urgently needed stores were brought by helicopter to the ships at sea,[26] a pointer to the versatility of the helicopter, whose role would be developed in the 1950s. (For a decade or so these were colloquially called 'choppers' and later: 'helios', 'helos' or 'cabs'.)

In the early hours of 7 April the LCP(R)s of this Underwater Demolition

Team found the fog so thick off the coast between Songjin and Hungnam, that no landing could be made until daylight. Therefore, the LVT (Armoured) with their 75-mm gun-howitzers led in the LVTs, after *Fort Marion* had flooded down to launch them.[27] The Naval bombardment began two hours before H-hour, 0800, but fog – visibility would be less than 100 yards on and off all day – prevented any air support. The LVTs crawled out of the water only five minutes late and by 1000 hours the first demolition charges had been brought in by LVT and the mortar platoon by LCP(R). Only one 12-man enemy patrol came into the area in the next six hours, and that was easily driven off, while several gaps were blown in the railway line. Two of these were over 100ft long, and mines were laid before the Commando withdrew without casualties, clearing the beach about 1600 hours. The small number of civilian casualties from the Naval bombardment had been treated by the SBAs (Sick Berth Attendants) landed with the Commando.[28]

The following week planning began for a more permanent base for raids and some islands were chosen off Wonsan, 80 miles behind the enemy's lines. Wonsan lies in a great bay, with the high ridge of Kalmaka behind it and a peninsula jutting south from its northern shore making a large area of almost landlocked sea. During May and June the Commando carried out exercises in Japan, and enjoyed the hospitality of the British Embassy, which treated the Commando as special guests, to the displeasure of the Commonwealth Brigade, whose Australian Commander would have liked to have 41 Cdo RM under his command, although it remained under Naval command throughout its stay in Japan. The planned operations, however, were postponed, owing to peace talks, until 8 July, when C Troop landed from an LST on Yodo island off the north-east coast of Korea.[29]

More troops of the Commando moved to these islands the following week, although they were shelled spasmodically from the mainland, and from gun positions on nearby islands. The United Nations forces retaliated by bombarding Wonsan and coast defences from the sea and air. By the end of July 1951 small parties – two canoes (four men), an LCVP with an Officer and four Marines – often 'in unmerciful rain and thick fog-mist'[30] were making successful reconnaissances of enemy positions. Some of the LCVPs had RM crews and some had South Koreans, and one of each brought back parties from Hwangto Do Island, after a useful reconnaissance during which the Commando's support fire-control party – the FOBs of this war – had 'spotted and corrected' the fall of some 200 shells from destroyers. B Troop arrived in the islands during the second week of August, and lived in tents on the high ground of Modo Island, which it took over from South Korean Marines, who passed four 0.5-in heavy machine guns to the Heavy Weapons Troop.

B Troop's first reconnaissance was made by a Section in rubber boats towed by an LCP(L) or possibly an LCVP. Three hours ashore proved this mainland beach to be deserted. Observation posts – small standing patrols – were landed on various islands in the next few weeks, by canoe or inflatables from the LCVPs. The commandos reinforcing their own base islands with mortars registered (pre-ranged) on likely landing beaches in case the North Koreans attacked the islands.

These mortars at other times were put on islands within range of shore defences for brief bombardments before withdrawal the following night. A number of mainland villages were also visited and the locals questioned – these were mostly women and children, for the men of the villages were away in the army – but later the North Koreans began reinforcing the coast.

Towards the end of August, the commandos had their first experience of a typhoon in the islands: heavy winds blew down tents and damaged craft, and torrential rain continued for hours on end. An LCPR went adrift for several days after one such storm, but the crew managed to lie up on a deserted island until the weather improved. D Troop relieved C Troop early in September, and the round of camp improvements, small recce raids, and occasionally being shelled, continued throughout the next few months.[31]

In the last week of September, some 10 weeks after the Commando had arrived in the islands, there was every sign that it was achieving its purpose: for the North Koreans began to reinforce the coast. This was much in the way German forces were deployed in Norway after World War II commando raids. On approaching one coast village, for example, the scouting canoe made three probes to find a suitable point for an LCPR to land a Section of 26 all ranks commanded by Captain 'Lofty' Stoddart for a night raid, but the canoe was fired on and the paddler slightly wounded, so the LCPR withdrew.

Cruisers and destroyers supplying the island garrisons were shelled, and shelled the coast defences in return. These ships included HMS *Belfast* and *Consort*. They brought in mail and received from the Commando intelligence reports on enemy positions. No major raids were mounted in the last few weeks of October while peace talks were in progress, but the Commando occupied more offshore islands and put out defensive minefields and wire. The Marines taught themselves to use the 75-mm recoilless rifle, became proficient with 81-mm mortars, made reconnaissance raids in November, and in December made the last of their landings on the mainland. In two of these, the ambush and recce parties were attacked by North Koreans but successfully withdrew.

The coast railway was by this date heavily defended and few targets were available, as United Nations planes had destroyed most of the bridges. Tunnels were another matter. Blasted out of granite, they proved hard to damage with the demolition gear that could be landed from small boats.[32] Nor were the commandos able to find the North Koreans' high speed boats which had been reported in the area, and the Chinese railway gun which fired on their bases was probably too far inland for a small force to destroy in a raid without causing civilian casualties. Nevertheless, 41 (Independent) Commando RM had ably proved the Royal Marines' skill in raiding. They had received a Presidential Citation for their Chosin operations the previous year, and gained 15 British and 14 American gallantry awards.[33] In 1951 their casualties were relatively light by comparison with losses on Chosin plateau – an officer and a sergeant were killed in canoe raids and some 20 all ranks were wounded.

Although the west coast of Korea was considered impracticable for regular raids, on 20 May 1951 the detachment from HMS *Ceylon* made one of several raids on this coast north of the 38th Parallel, as did the detachment from HMS *Belfast*. In the 20 May landing, the Marines came ashore after a heavy Naval bombardment, and negotiated a beach minefield before searching a coast village and going inland. Although they were ashore for several hours, they met no opposition.[34] For these operations the ships' detachments gained four gallantry awards. HMS *Kenya* and *Jamaica* had also been in action bombarding the west coast and the carrier HMS *Glory* flew off planes with at least one RM pilot, while her band was employed in arming and attaching rockets to the aircraft.[35] Some detachment landings and fleet bombardments were made during 1952, but no RM Special Boat Service (SBS) operations were carried out before an armistice was signed on 27 July 1953.

After the armistice the RM prisoners-of-war returned to the UK, except for one man who deserted. All the prisoners had been under great physical and mental stress during their time in North Korean hands, as this was the first time in the 20th century that prisoners-of-war were subjected to attempts to convert them to their enemy's ideology.[36] At first there had been no proper prison camps, but in January 1951 the first camps were built, mainly along the Yalu river. Life in the prison camps included a routine of lectures on communism, completing questionnaires, compulsory discussion groups and minor privileges for those who attended voluntary re-education sessions. Extra food and medicine were used as rewards for co-operation, but those who were considered 'reactionaries' were punished. Of the 50 or so Royal Marines who were captured, ten died while prisoners-of-war and the others were released when 978 British ex-prisoners were repatriated in September 1953. All had suffered hardships, especially in the early days, when a couple of bowls of cracked corn, millet or sorghum per day was considered luxury. Beating and physical degradation had been endured by all.[37]

By February 1952 41 (Independent) Commando RM had been disbanded, and the Brigade was about to be deployed in Cyprus, as explained in the next chapter. In both Korea and Malaya the value of Marine commandos, with their individual self-reliance, their adaptability and personal dependability, had been proved in actions of small patrols often operating a long way from their Troop base, as they do in internal security operations. The lessons learnt from Korea were not new, particularly the need to co-ordinate clandestine, guerrilla and small force raids by a small staff at the *theatre* commander's headquarters[38] rather than at a lower level. The need for good air photographs, detailed inter-service planning and time for rehearsals, were stressed in reports. A bonus, however, after two years of close co-operation with American forces, was that many Anglo-American friendships were made.

9

COMMANDO CARRIERS

The Brigade's operations in Malaya, like those in Korea, were fought with World War II equipment. The next eight years or so would, however, see fundamental changes in the weapons of war, and by the 1960s Marines would expect more frequently to go into battle from helicopters than from landing craft. There would be organic artillery (artillery under the Brigade's command) by 1962 and battleships' guns would be largely replaced by missiles. Many of these changes came about in part as a result of developments after the Suez landings in November 1956. Other changes in the techniques to defeat terrorism came in the light of the Brigade's operations in Cyprus building on their experience in Malaya. But before considering these and related operations, some explanation is needed of the organisation of the Corps during the early 1950s.

When the experience of Malayan and Korean operations was beginning to crystallise, there was a conference in 1951. There five topics were discussed of particular interest: the training of officers, educational qualifications, the Commando Training Flotilla, recruit training, and pay.[1] The officers' Wing at the Infantry Training Centre (known as the Officers School) had recently opened – only National Service officers were trained at the Army OCTU, Eaton Hall, in the early 1950s – but the question of training afloat had not been finalised. There was a suggestion that perhaps sea service was not expected to figure so prominently in the service of officers, as it had done in the previous generations. At that time the School was hoping to run one-year courses for candidates for the staff college and some longer advanced courses, but staff shortages precluded anything but short courses run by a major and two captains on the School's staff.

The specific question of the qualifications of NCOs in Korea was not discussed. But there is reason to believe that a number of senior NCOs, who had served most of their time at sea in World War II, found that the change to junior command in a Commando was a difficult step – more difficult indeed than it had been for their predecessors joining a battalion of line infantry. This in part was linked to the educational qualification for promotion. About half those eligible for examinations at various levels were taking them, but so few general duty senior NCOs were sitting the higher education test (HET) that young sergeants qualified educationally for promotion to QMS might be promoted prematurely. The meeting agreed that 'although anomalies were bound to occur in the case of older colour sergeants *vis-à-vis* the young QMS . . . the need for obtaining young colour sergeants promoted to QMS early, outweighed those anomalies'.[2] This reaffirmed the Corps' policy of promoting talent after due consideration to other men's length of service.

The Commando Training Flotilla at Plymouth, detached from the Amphibious School (described later), was used to train dory coxswains,[3] dories at that time being considered a better means of landing for raids than inflatable rubber boats, which were comparatively easily holed by rocky ledges offshore.[4] The Flotilla also trained commandos in landings on rocky coats, exercises for which they needed experienced instructors; but the practice – not for the first time – of appointing staff temporarily to this type of training unit put the trainees at risk. The intention was in future to send fully trained personnel for a 2-year appointment to the Flotilla, two years being the usual duration of most appointments for officers and men in the Corps, and 2½ years when overseas.

Recruit training in the early 1950s comprised courses of initial training at Deal, a spell at Lympstone, with field craft and other courses at Plymouth, a period in theory of 38 weeks. But owing to the time taken in moving between establishments and for similar administrative reasons, a recruit spent 41 weeks in training before starting his specialist 'Commando 2' course or higher gunnery training.[5] The developments in recruit training in the next decade were subject to the pressures of economy, leading to constant reviews influenced by reductions in sea-service to obtain the maximum training with the least staff.[6]

Landing craft training was centred on Eastney, but the next major changes in equipment both for craft and LVTs came after the Suez operation, as will become apparent. These changes and the Amphibious Warfare Squadron's origins and development, are examined, therefore, after 1956, and for the moment we will follow the Commandos' story.

By the early summer of 1953, the Brigade was dispersed in the Mediterranean: HQ and '45 Cdo RM' were in Malta; and '42 Cdo RM' in Tripolitana on exercises near Tarhuna Camp.[7] This was located near the possible trouble spots of Britain's ally of those years, King Idris of Lybia. Also that early summer '40 Cdo RM' was returning to Malta from a combined operations exercise in Cyprus, another likely flash point. At this time Cyprus was one of several colonies to which the British wanted to grant independence. Anglo-Egyptian talks were also in progress on the withdrawal of British forces from the Canal Zone, where the British had maintained a military presence since the 1880s. When these talks broke down in May, the Brigade was ordered to Egypt. Within 24 hours Brigade HQ and 45 Commando were at sea in HMS *Ranpura* and *Dieppe*; '42 Cdo RM' had abandoned its exercise, packed its stores and having completed a 60-mile drive to Tripoli, embarked in three destroyers and HMS *Reggio*. The Commando was at sea in a little over 24 hours from receiving the order to move. 40 Commando RM, which had reached Malta the day Brigade HQ had sailed and was expecting to have a spell of garrison duty, was flown to the Canal Zone, arriving in time to welcome the rest of the Brigade. Such rapid deployments were only possible 'due to the close co-operation and efficiency of the Royal Navy'[8], the hall mark of such operations during the next four decades.

On arriving in the Canal Zone the Brigade was deployed in guard duties and convoy protection, its roles in Egypt for the next 15 months. During the spring of 1954 there was an increase in the number of incidents, with attacks on vehicles not travelling in armed convoys, armed hold-ups and murders; although at a typical 'locality, where a company of paratroopers or a Troop of commandos took turns to do duty, life was comparatively unaffected'.[9] They had a routine of three days' duty or standby, and only had one night in four undressed in bed in the nearby garrison town. The food was enhanced by eggs, secretly sold by Egyptian traders coming to the perimeter wire at night. One of whom, nicknamed 'Lofty', warned that the garbage truck would be ambushed next day. To break the humdrum routine of four hours on and two off, the Troop commander decided to ambush the would-be ambushers. A Bren gun behind sandbags was hidden among the waste bins, the escort Jeep's crew were alerted, and the Troop commander (without his captain's badges of rank) rode shotgun in the garbage truck. But before they could set out, Divisional HQ had to give approval, a sign of the cumbersome procedures necessary for even the smallest actions in internal-security operations.

This particular raid foundered on an engine breakdown, for the 3-ton truck had fuel pipe trouble before reaching the dump. The Arab machine-gunners were seen to get bored, and pack their gun on a donkey before the truck could be restarted. Nevertheless the captain went forward and under cover of the Jeep's Bren searched the garbage dump. Nothing was found, even when he fell over his waist in the mire – the origin for several months afterwards of that refrain about 'Sweet Violets' greeting him on mess nights.[10] But such minor matters are the essence of these difficult campaigns, when boredom can make a man careless and the relief of humour in such mishaps leaves the most vivid memories. The British left the Canal Zone in June 1956, by which time the Brigade was again concentrated in Cyprus, with units away on exercises from time to time.

In Cyprus, which the British had ruled since 1878 and which became a colony in 1914, negotiations had been in progress for a new self-governing state. But conflicts between Greek and Turkish Cypriots had delayed the withdrawal of the British administration, and EOKA – a Greek Cypriot terrorist organisation – had committed a number of outrages. Although this force never numbered more than a few hundred hard core activists, they had wide support from the local people.[11] The Brigade had been based in Malta during 1955, as mentioned earlier, against any escalation of violence in Cyprus or elsewhere in the Mediterrean. On 31 August 45 Commando was under orders to move to North Africa, a move expected to follow a routine sequence of preparations, although it was deferred, as a result of which men were on normal night leave that week, when orders were received on the night of 6 September to move as soon as possible to Cyprus. The commandos had to be collected from their homes.[12] Nevertheless the main body was embarked in the Amphibious Warfare Squadron within a few hours, and 450 men followed the next day in HMS *Birmingham*. They had all disembarked in Cyprus by 0900 hours on 10 September, some 1,300 Marines and 150 vehicles and that evening elements were deployed in the Kyrenia mountains. By contrast, the Army battalions usually took several days to settle in before going on patrols.[13]

The terrain in Cyprus is mountainous in the centre of the island, with Mount Olympus rising to over 1,800m. For the Marine the routine patrols were largely a matter of helping the civilian authorities to restore law and order, manning road blocks, removing EOKA flags, dispersing hostile crowds and cordoning off villages to search for known terrorists. The first such cordon a week or so after landing, uncovered nothing startling, but local hostility increased and terrorist reprisals began. On one occasion in November 1955, when a Bedford QL – the standard 3-tonner – was ambushed, 'bullets were flying everywhere and Major H. Bruce (at Calais in 1940) came striding down the road with his walking stick to take charge of its recovery'. The quad was loaded with explosives for a local mine and L/Corporall Maghee, although he had been knocked unconscious when he had leapt down on to the road, recovered sufficiently to scramble back into the cab. There, despite the stream of enemy fire, which had shot away the steering wheel's rim, he drove the quad clear. For his bravery he was awarded the Queen's Commendation. Had this been an international war, he might well have received greater recognition, but operations in a British Colony were by a quirk of legislation regarded as being on the same level as those in the UK, until the legislation was altered in 1967.

The Brigade in Malaya had been used to working closely with the local police, and in Cyprus these techniques would be carried a stage further in the course of the three years or so. During this time Commandos were deployed on the islands at different times (see Appendix 4). In the autumn of 1955, however, the initial difficulties in gathering military intelligence had to be overcome by unit officers, who set up an improvised intelligence service using local civil servants as interpreters and uniformed local police.[14] Later a joint operations room was set up and the co-ordination of police, intelligence and the operational commandos became a highly developed organisation. Major Ian De'ath second in command of '45', also ran a joint military-and-police training course in Nicosia, for in Cyprus the Corps was to play a leading part in the development of such military and police co-operation.[15]

Lieutenant-Colonel (later General Sir) Norman H. Tailyour's 45 Commando that autumn was deployed along the mountains across north Cyprus, with HQ at Aghirds. From there the Commando dominated the Kyrenia mountains to such effect that the hard-core terrorists moved to the central Troodos mountains or into towns.[16] The Lieutenant-Colonel also had under his command for a few weeks a Troop of Marines from the Amphibious Warfare squadron.

When the centre of terrorist activities moved into the Troodos mountains, the EOKA chief, General Grivas paid tribute to the thoroughness of the commandos' searches.[17] The Brigade was redeployed in these 1,000 square km of pine forest, with thick undergrowth and treacherous loose shale in many places. Soon after it took up position General Campbell Hardy, who had been appointed Commandant General earlier that year, visited the Troodos mountains. His tour included Brigade HQ at Limassol; the command post of '40', and its rural police stations in this area; and '45' at Mallia and Platres, with 'A', 'S' and 'X' Troops in the mountains and 'E' Troop at Argos. Typically he made personal air reconnaissances of several areas.[18] Vineyards and hard-surfaced roads ran through the valleys and wound into the hills, with many ambush positions. In these and other areas the Marines making a search might drop down a cliff face on ropes to search a cave, or be lowered into wells 'when the pinprick of light representing the outside would seem many hundreds of feet away'.[19]

After it arrived in the Limassol area, '40 Cdo RM' had built its own camp, working by day and patrolling the town in the evenings. At first the Marines wore steel helmets and used barbed wire barricades to contain rioters, but these tactics were abandoned in favour of more quick-footed methods, the commandos wearing gym shoes and carrying riot sticks. They also patrolled in Bedford ½-tonners ('Pigs') for 20 to 30 miles north of Limassol, and later used scout cars and the sophisticated Humber CT vehicle – a general purpose truck – which is reported to have been difficult to maintain. All patrols and other military intelligence was co-ordinated through the joint military and police headquarters in local police stations.

Heavy snowfalls in February 1956 made patrolling on skis essential. 'X' Troop of '45', for example, were ski-troops and delivered explosives – an obvious terrorist target – to the mines. The weather became so severe that two men died of exposure when their truck was caught in deep drifts. In March, after further political talks broke down, ambushes and counter-ambushes resumed, and there were searches, in one of which arms along with explosives were found in a monastery. The Army also had several battalions deployed on the islands, which carried out joint operations with the commandos. By the summer a hot June sun had made the mountain forests tinder dry when operation 'Lucky Alphonse' was in progress, with Army and Commando troops combing the mountains in a series of great cordons. As these flushed out terrorists, they were bombarded by mortar fire, which on 17 June set the forest alight. The flames running before a strong wind, became completely out of control,[20] and encircled men of the Gordons, the Norfolks and the Parachute Regiment, taking 19 lives. Captain R. Meadows organised the rescue of many men, carrying an injured man over a mile and moving a burning armoured car, and for 'his leadership and courage of high order' was awarded the MBE. The commandos would come back to Cyprus in 1957, but for the first time had already made use of dogs trained by Lieutenant (later Lieutenant-Colonel) P. Montgomery to work with patrols. These Alsatians would later operate in Malaya, Borneo and elsewhere, their RM handlers often going on long patrols when the dogs might lie in ambushes, track enemy forces or carry out the more usual guard-dog and anti-riot duties with their handlers.[21]

On 26 July 1956 President Nasser of Egypt seized the British- and French-owned Suez Canal, and the Chiefs of Staff were asked to prepare a military expedition against Egypt.[1] During these preparations Lord Mountbatten offered an RM formation to the Prime Minister Anthony Eden 'to hold Suez until three divisions or whatever Army formations could be raised to hold the Canal'.[2] The offer was not accepted but the Brigade was to spearhead the seaborne landing, and took part in its planning from early August 1956. The Brigade Commander, Brig R. W. Madoc (who had been in the 1941 rearguard on Crete), flew to London on 4 August for a meeting with General Stockwell commanding II Corps, under whose command the RM Commandos had been placed. No plans had been made to reoccupy the Canal Zone, although the British had left the Zone only some eight weeks earlier. The amphibious assault phase with a landing at Port Said, 'was prepared in hours', on the other hand the main plan was subject to four drastic alterations as the political situation changed over the next three months. There were other planning difficulties, leading, for example, to one destroyer, which had been on detached duties, only reappearing on L-day and firing at targets to an original landing plan which her Captain had not been given any details to update. (L-day, Landing Day had replaced the D-day references in orders and other documents.) While this operation is always known as the Suez Landing, it never extended to a landing beyond Port Said at the northern end of the Suez Canal.

There was time, however, for 40 and 42 Commandos to train with 'C' Squadron, 6th Royal Tank Regiment, whose Centurions would be waterproofed to land near '40' on L-day. An experimental Army/RAF Helicopter Squadron, with six Whirlwind Mark 2s and six Sycamore Mark 14s, joined 845 FAA Squadron's eight Whirlwinds. They were to lift 45 Commando into battle, but a full rehearsal could not be held in Malta for security reasons. Air control, fire control and FOO teams were trained there, however, and an LVT Troop of 16 amphibians with Royal Armoured Corps drivers was also formed, their 16 vehicles being cannibalised to get 15 runners. Three Army anti-tank platoons of 17-pdrs with Stuarts towing them proved difficult to waterproof, although joining the force. And 'on the way to the races': six 106-mm anti-tank guns would also be landed, some by 'chopper' and some by LVTs. On L-7 this force – some 150 officers and 2,000 other ranks of the reinforced Brigade with 550 vehicles – was loaded in 16 hours into three LST (Assault), five LSTs, and eight LCTs.[3] These LCTs were much larger than World War II craft, with bow doors and a ramp, similar to LSTs.

The commandos of '40' and '42' (the latter reactivated after a spell at the training cadre at Bickleigh) were to land in LVTs and LCAs 35 minutes before sunrise. Their objectives were a beach and dock basins at Port Said. Those of 45 Commando, in the carriers HMS *Ocean* and *Theseus*, were originally to land to seize the Interior Basin. But as there were insufficient 'choppers' to lift the whole Commando – shades of Dakar! – and such large-scale helicopter operations were untried, '45' was retasked with the role of floating reserve. Other changes of plan included the limitation of fire support only to guns of less than 6-in calibre. The Brigadier was told only an hour before H-hour that there would definitely be support fire for the landing on 6 November.

The Amphibious Warfare Squadron had been increased to some 20 ships for

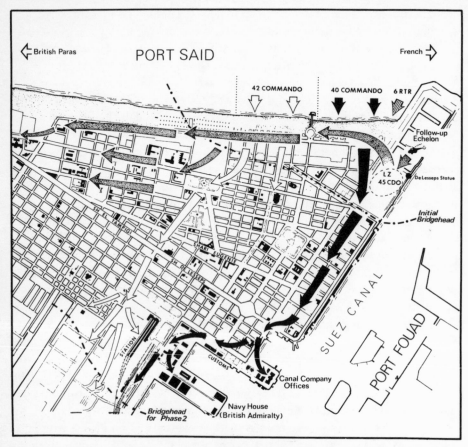

Area of Port Said landings in the 'Suez' operations. this map shows the routes taken by the Royal Marines Commandos and the follow-up through Fisherman's Harbour.

the Suez operation, code-named 'Musketeer', and although this was a daylight landing and therefore expected to be straightforward, in the event there were unexpected problems. The *River*-class frigate HMS *Meon*, adapted as an HQ ship, vectored the LVTs and LCAs some 4 miles to the control Motor Launch's dan buoy for the start point of the last 3-mile run to the beach; and as this ML 2583, commanded by an RM lieutenant with an RM crew, came in to place her marker buoy, she had destroyers on each hand. Their 4-in gunfire set alight a shanty town and the beach was shrouded in smoke. Therefore, after the destroyers peeled away to carry on their bombardment, ML 2583 picked up the craft on her radar screen and then vectored them to the beach. Directions over the radio were given to the Troop leaders' craft whenever a group strayed from the course for their landing point.[4]

As '40' and '42' ran in towards the smoke covered beach, no lights showed from the shore, and a pall of smoke from burning oil tanks hung over the city. Each Commando had two Troops in LVTs as the leading wave, with a second wave of Troops in LCAs. The first line of 15 amphibians churned on to the

16 The Korean War: Commandos move down the mountain pass from Koto-ri to Hungam, December 1950.

17 A jungle patrol from 45 Commando RM searches the swamp for terrorists in one of many such operations in 1952 during the Malayan Emergency.

18 A patrol from 45 Commando RM seen with tracker dogs in the foothills of the Troodos mountains, Cyprus, during the summer of 1957.

19 The commando carrier *Bulwark* (left) with the LPD *Fearless* with her LCMs and LCVPs seen in 1967 off Singapore. Three flights of Wessex 5s from 845 Sqn FAA are followed overhead by a flight of RAF Whirlwinds.

20 The Landing Zone cut out of thick jungle was a small area for RAF and FAA helicopters to land in. Here an RAF Whirlwind is about to land at a typical LZ in Borneo.

21 Members of 41 Commando RM face rioters on the streets of Belfast during 1970.

22 A Rigid Raider of 42 Commando RM intercepts a junk during a tour of Hong Kong in 1979 to assist the campaign against illegal immigration.

23 Commandos training on Ascension Island during the Task Force's stop-over en route for the liberation of the Falklands.

24 SS *Canberra* prepares to be resupplied by an RFA in the South Atlantic, 1982.

25 *Fearless* in San Carlos Water, May 1982. In addition to her complement of landing craft, she carried the Commodore, his staff and the HQ of 3 Commando Brigade as well as 40 Commando RM.

26 Two LCUs carry men ashore during the Falklands landings, HMS *Intrepid* seen in the background.

27 Members of 45 Commando RM advance through San Carlos on a BV202, May 1982.

28 Captain (later Brigadier) David V. Nicholls 'brews up' on the slopes of Mount Kent on East Falkland, May 1982.

29 A local boy helps 40 Commando RM to dig defences at San Carlos, May 1982.

30 Royal Marines patrol along a Falklands beach in 1982.

31 A Blowpipe surface-to-air shouldered by a commando from the Air Defence Troop in the Falklands, May 1982.

beach, with '42' on the right and '40' on the left. The extreme right hand LVT, carrying the OC 'B' Troop of '42', had a driver who was a bit of a wag; with the fastest amphibian. He was determined that the OC would land first, on time at H-hour (0645 hours local time).[5] Fortunately there was not one mine on this beach, although an alternative landing point later proved to be heavily mined.[6] (There had been no SBS recce to check these beaches, probably because of the political risk had such a recce gone wrong.) Behind the beach were five rows of bathing huts, and the LVTs passed through them to reach their objective: the line of houses behind the beach. No one was about as the bombardment whistled overhead and air-strikes kept the Egyptian defenders busy, although a few shots had been fired at the craft on the run-in. Fifteen minutes after the assault wave had touched down, LCTs put tanks ashore in the Fishermen's Harbour on 40 Commando's left. Once the tanks were ashore, '40 Cdo RM' was ready to move off three Troops at H+90 minutes. Their objective was the complex of basins, where II Corps expected to be able to bring ships alongside the quays.

P Troop had the first leg of this advance, having landed from LCAs in the second wave at H+5 minutes and been in reserve while the beachhead was secured. The Troop was supported by tanks. These fired into the windows being used by Egyptian riflemen, and other positions along the Quai Sultan Hussein as far as the police station, which the commandos reached in 15 minutes. At each road junction small-arms fire from side streets swept across the line of advance, but the only injuries were caused when one of the tank's shells exploded when it inadvertently hit some railings close to two commandos. 'Y' Troop, again with tank support, took the next leg to the Suez Canal Company's building. Although they suffered a few casualties from accurate fire, huts on the quay were cleared before the building was taken. The Tanks, machine guns, and the Army platoon of anti-tank gunners, had given covering fire, enabling this advance to be made with few casualties. Resistance now stiffened as B Troop took the lead. The men dodged into doorways but found that many windows had bars from which a tossed grenade could bounce back at the thrower's feet. They then came under heavy fire from the customs shed on the road side north of the arsenal basin. The top floor was cleared fairly easily, but the ground floor's defenders, some 19 men, put up a determined resistance. This long open shed had many small offices leading off it, and long heavy Customs benches provided good cover for the defenders. Two Marines were wounded as two Sections forced their way into the building and radio contact with the tanks was lost about this time.[7] The officer leading the attack, Lieutenant McCarthy, was killed almost as soon as he came into the building, and Lieutenant Ufton, who led the Marines deeper into the building, was killed as he cleared an office at the far end of the complex. Two Egyptians were captured, one having lain low for four hours, but the other defenders were killed.

By now the afternoon was well on, and 'X' Troop made 40 Commando's last attack of the day against the Customs and Post Office buildings of Navy House Quay. The warrens of offices proved difficult to clear, and no more attempts were made to force an entrance into any building until the tanks had blown holes in the walls. This they did at the Customs House, but seven commandos were wounded before it was secured. Eight enemy dead were counted and two captured in these offices, but others escaped across the harbour.

While the main advance had been made during the day, 'A' Troop of '42' with a tank had rescued the British consul. The consulate was in a well-defended square and over 200 rifles were found in the buildings surrounding it.[8] There was also much uncertainty over negotiations for a cease-fire. As early as 0900 hours, '40 Cdo RM's' mortar officer had captured the Egyptian brigadier commanding the garrison.[9] He wanted to arrange a cease-fire and Brig Madoc took him to the Italian Consulate, after its front door was nudged open by a tank. The three senior Force Commanders were brought in by Lieutenant Sharland's Control ML, expecting to be met by Egyptians ready for a cease-fire. But the ML found she was 'running alongside quays and streets from which there was a good deal of small arms fire'.[10] Nearing Navy House Quay, which the enemy still held during the morning, Admiral Durnford Slater's flag no doubt drew more fire – its size being disproportionately large for an ML as flagship – and the Admiral decided they should withdraw. This was no easy task, for blockships and wrecks in the basin left no room to turn, and the ML had to go astern until she reached the LCT berths at Fisherman's Harbour. These blockships also prevented the quays being used by ships bringing in reinforcements, and therefore 40 Commando's objectives no longer had a priority.

That morning 42 Commando RM had moved out of the beachhead about 0930 hours, for what became a dangerous ride down the dual carriageway of Rue Mohammed Ali towards the power station and the Nile Cold storage Company's plant.[11] A tank was leading, followed by the LVT of 'B' Troop's OC, and other tanks interspersed between the other Troops: 'A' and 'X' Troops, with two machine gun Sections and the CO's Tactical HQ (the 'Rover' party). The height of some buildings along this road, many four or five stories high, had not been realised when the first aerial photographs were produced from highflying planes. But a day or so before the landing 42 Commando saw the building heights in oblique angle 'shots' from the Fleet Air Arm.[12] As the convoy now moved off the beachhead, they made tracks as fast as they could for each LVT was packed with over 30 Marines, at least six more than the specified load.

At the start of the dual carriageway 'B' Troop's leading driver asked: 'Do they drive on the left or the right in Egypt?'. On the commandos' right was the Arab town, on the left the tall blocks of flats from which grenades and rifle fire came down spasmodically. 'Look Sir! The light's at red, should I stop?' The wag asked, and was told to press on, for at each crossroads fire from side streets hit the convoy. The vehicles were at 50 to 100yds intervals, with the rear ramps open so that grenades could be kicked clear. They were nevertheless vulnerable because – as they had been loaded into LCTs for an 'exercise' – no pin-on armour had been slotted in the protective screens. Bullets came through the sides and by the types of injury inflicted, they must have ricocheted around inside some vehicles.[13] The wag was wounded, but in the clattering noise this was not realised until the LVT swung violently from side to side; his co-driver took over and at some 20mph they trundled on after the leading tank.

'B' Troop were past their objective, keeping close to the leading tank but both the radio and the tank's external telephone communications broke down, and the OC 'B' Troop was blown off the turret by the tank's 20-pdr firing as he tried to contact the crew. Dusting himself off, he climbed back on the tank, and agreed with the tank commander to pull back to the correct stop – that is, the position where they could protect other Troops from Egyptians to the south and east. X Troop captured the power station when 'A' Troop became embroiled in the stout resistance of Arabs in the market. Although only one LVT had been knocked out in the run to the power station, the CO and his Rover party made several hazardous runs between the beachhead and the power station. At the beach C, Y and A Troops had secured the perimeter, clearing several houses.[14]

The floating reserve, 45 Commando, was called in from its carriers at H+55 minutes, the CO, Lieutenant-Colonel Norman Tailyour, flying in the seven miles to make a recce. 'The first intimation that all was not well was some sinister and much too repetitive "crack" and "thump" . . .'[15] (These frightening noises were caused by enemy rounds passing the aircraft with a crack heard before the thump of a gun firing.) The pilot was undisturbed by this, because – it turned out later – under his helmet he did not hear these noises. The proposed landing zone was fouled by overhead wires, smoke and some enemy fire. But after the Tactical HQ had been landed there, the 'chopper' put down a second time on seeing 'the Egyptian Army [coming] over the surrounding walls'.[16] A landing zone was later found near De Lesseps' great statue and the first wave of helicopters touched down at 0815 hours in the beachhead. This was the first use of British helicopters to land a large formation in a battle area, with 415 men and 23 tons of stores put down in 83 minutes.[17] The three Marines in each Sycamore sat on the floor, the man in the middle holding his companions whose legs dangled over the helicopter's sides. These two each carried a 3-foot 106-mm shell and their 'anchor man' had six mortar bombs. In the Whirlwinds the half-dozen or so Marines were at least in the body of the helicopter but there were few hand-holds, no seats nor doors. With them on an unofficial visit came the Commandant General, General Sir Campbell Hardy, 'because over a third of the Corps were at Suez'.[18] Three helicopters were damaged but some 25 per cent less time had been needed to put this Commando ashore than had they been in LCAs.[19] The expected helicopter losses had been 10 per cent, but were, in fact negligible in the event.

The beachhead was reorganised before '45 Cdo RM' came in, as commandos had cleared the hotels, houses and other buildings up to three streets from the beach, so that '45 Cdo RM' was able to deploy quickly. But as it did so at 1035 hours, British aircraft put in an uncontrolled strike, causing 18 casualties, including the CO who was wounded. Nevertheless the Commando moved west, fighting from tall block to tall block, some seven stories high. The Marines broke through the steel shutters of ground floor shops and up through the building, the break-ins being made with the help of an anti-tank 106-mm 'Rifle' on a borrowed tracked-carrier.[20] Civilian men, women and children as well as Egyptian troops and armed police, crowded many buildings, the soldiers being difficult to trace when they had put on civilian clothing to melt into a crowd. As the commandos cleared each building, they could cover the next from the flat rooftops, but among so many tall buildings this had limited value. Rue La Mahrousa was cleared by 1300 hours and Rue Safia Zaghloul in the early afternoon, before tanks joined the Commando to make the final sweep westward to join with British paratroops. They had dropped the previous day on the airfield. French paratroops had also been dropped east of the Canal at that time.

The Commando's transport was landed from HMS *Lofoten* in time to reach '45 Cdo RM' early that afternoon, but all five Troops were by this time engaged in clearing a route westward towards the shanty town. A major fire broke out, and although this hampered their progress in clearing streets nearby, the commandos killed some 170 Egyptians of whom only 20 were civilians. Every effort had been made to avoid civilian casualties and when the cease-fire came at midnight, with British Army units ashore, there were probably no more than a few hundred Egyptian casualties in a town with a population of over 170,000. The Brigade HQ that night was spread between two blocks on the sea front, the operations room in one having 'the upper floors a mass of aerials and telephone lines common to all HQs'[21] of that time. Navy House Quay had been sealed off by 40 Commando and X Troop had a lively time when an Egyptian ammunition dump caught fire, sending 'live rockets all over Port Said'. '42 Cdo RM' held the beach area, leaving A and X Troops to hold the power station, which could supply most of the town with electricity; and '45 Cdo RM' had been in defensive positions since nightfall (1930 hours), holding the area around Rue El Ghali Moukhtar at the north-west corner of the town. These positions put all the Commandos of the Brigade within a 2-mile radius of Brigade HQ, but it was two miles of city streets with a hostile population and political uncertainties. In the broader political scene Russian tanks were in action in Hungary, Israelis had been fighting on the Egyptian border since the previous week. America was hostile to the Anglo-French invasion, and half the British people did not support this war. Therefore, there were all those difficulties of a 'half-war' compounded by a local cease-fire, which, during darkness, 'seemed somewhat one sided and a good deal of shooting went on through the night'.[22] But the commandos had orders only to return fire if they were directly attacked. Yet a few days later a couple of commando climbers managed to put a green beret on the head of De Lessees' statue some 40ft from the ground.[23] The French and British by this time had been told to stop their advance and not continue the drive on Suez.

The Brigade carried out searches for weapons, patrolled to the airfield and was occasionally sniped at during the next few days. In the Arab shanty town '45 Cdo RM' received an apparently friendly welcome on L+2, although over 57 3-ton truck loads of arms were collected,[24] and '42 Cdo RM' found quantities of arms under the mattresses of patients in the hospital.[25] For the next fortnight '42 Cdo RM' served under 19 Infantry Brigade, before being relieved by Norwegians of a UN force, men they knew from exercises in Norway the previous summer.[26] Brigade HQ with '40 Cdo RM' and '45 Cdo RM', had been withdrawn to Malta on L+8. (For simplicity local times have been used, though in 1956 all British military timings were based on the 'Zulu' [GMT] time-zone, here two hours behind local time.) The Brigade had nine fatal casualties, and this would have been more had not the 60 wounded been efficiently evacuated by helicopter. Of the Army personnel attached to the commandos, two were killed, an LVT driver and an anti-tank gunner of the Somerset Light Infantry.[27] These were in all nearly 50 per cent of the total British and French losses. For their part in the operations the Brigade's commandos received six gallantry awards.

Analysis of the Suez operation provided several lessons. The Brigade needed to keep one Commando, at least, with recent amphibious experience – something they could not get in the Troodos mountains. They needed a nucleus of organic artillery, and a full range of unit anti-tank weapons. Although at Suez the three anti-tank platoons from Army battalions had been very successful, artillery units should be permanently part of the Brigade, as 'borrowing' men would not be a practical proposition in any major conflict. The size of the permanent Amphibious Warfare Squadron also needed to be increased, so that its ships could lift all the Brigade, and there was need of joint planning staffs or the nucleus of them.[28] There had also been a lack of co-ordination by all three services in disseminating military intelligence, the Brigade on one occasion only collecting vital information because a Commando CO accidentally saw a report on a staff officer's desk in Cyprus. The Brigade also needed to improve the administrative back-up for the planning cells in headquarters and to exploit the benefit of helicopter landings. The Suez operation had proved, nevertheless, the value of the Brigade in spear-heading a landing, even if the tempo of its development in conventional amphibious warfare had been slow by comparison with helicopter landings.

The only major ship-to-ship action during the Suez operation had been between an Egyptian destroyer in the Red Sea and the cruiser HMS *Newfoundland*, which found her with engines stopped south of the gulf of Aqaba. As *Newfoundland*'s searchlight picked her out, she started her engines, and despite three calls to stop again, she moved in to the attack. One of her Bofors' shells clipped the support of a director, leaving its crew in some suspended animation for the next few hours. But the *Newfoundland* could fire her 6-in guns in salvos every 10 seconds, and her Bofors aft shot away the Egyptians' bridge and wrecked her fo'c's'le before she sank a few minutes later. After due precautions against submarine attack, *Newfoundland* then picked up survivors. The Marines in the shell room of their 6-in turret remained at action stations, in their boiler suits and gym shoes. Their Corporal checked that the correct rounds of HE, star shell etc. were loaded into the hoist, and keeping an eye on the NAAFI beer stacked nearby.[29] The cruiser put on speed, a sensation not unlike the acceleration of a motorcycle, although she was of 8,000 tons displacement. A few days later the crew were again called to action stations and opened fire at what appeared on the radar screen to be three Egyptian torpedo boats. A good number of rounds were fired, melting the pitch over the armoured deck and warping the teak planking, but the radar blips proved to be a fault in the scanner.

*   *   *

The Royal Marines' connection with big ships' gunnery was drawing to a close in 1956, with only some 20 detachments in major warships beside the dozen or so in small ships,[1] less than 2,000 Marines in all. This had led to a change in the Corps' training commitments, and in 1958 the Gunnery Training Wing at Eastney was closed,[2] although RM officers and NCOs continued to train and instruct at the Navy's gunnery school, HMS *Excellent*, until December 1963.[3] Long before then the effective power of missiles by comparison with a 15-in gun was to have changed the nature of Naval armaments.

Marines, however, retained their roles in minor landing craft, but immediately after World War II only two flotillas were operational, and these – based at the former US naval establishment[4] in Rosneath – were employed in training and had loaded many minor craft into the well decks of LCTs, an operation that covered many months between training spells. At this time in 1946–7 no decision had been made on the role of the Corps in providing landing craft crews, although, as mentioned later, the Corps retained the know-how on Beach Control methods at the Admiralty's direction. While the flotillas, 416 and 461, were still at Rosneath, there was some discussion on the possibility of embarking LCA flotillas in LSTs, but no final proposals were made until much later. A number of amphibians, including DUKWs, LVTs and Weasels were brought together at the Technical Training Headquarters (Fort Cumberland)[5] as their amphibious wing. In the next few years they carried out experimental work with the giant LVT-X capable, if it did not break down, of carrying ashore a Centurion tank.[6] The main amphibious experimental work, however, was carried on at the Amphibious Experimental Establishment (AXE, the successor to COXE).

In February and March 1948 the two flotillas moved from Rosneath and brought their LCAs and LCMs to Fort Cumberland,[7] where they were joined by the Small Raids Wing (SBS canoeists) from Instow. Together they formed the Amphibious School RM which carried out all landing craft training in the Corps until 1954.

The three strands of amphibious warfare – planning, training and execution – took shape in the late 1940s and the 1950s along the lines that would create the commando carrier of the second half of the 20th century. This concept resulted in part from studies by the Joint Services Amphibious Warfare School (briefly known in 1946 as the School of Combined Operations). The history of the School shows some aspects of the developments in so-called 'amphibiosity' after World War II, for as a tri-service establishment at Fremington (north Devon) it later became the Staff Training Wing of the Amphibious Warfare Headquarters, whose head was an RM general,[8] in part successor to the wartime Chief of Combined Operations. Late in 1954 the Royal Marines moved their amphibious training to Poole, taking over the World War II Hamworthy camp, which had been renovated. Two years later the Staff Training Wing joined them to form the Joint Services Amphibious Warfare Centre (JSAWC) known as 'Jaswac'. The Amphibious Training Unit Royal Marines provided the landing craft training and demonstration crews for this Centre. This consolidation of amphibious warfare interests was in line with the recommendations of the Bottomley Committee in

1943, which had also proposed the formation of an Amphibious Warfare Squadron. 'Jaswac' remained at Poole until 1 April 1963, when the Joint Services Staff moved to the Joint Warfare Establishment, Old Sarum (Wiltshire). The Poole base then remained the Amphibious Training Unit RM until 1 July 1973, when most of the Corps' technical training was also moved to Poole from Eastney; and the Hamworthy establishments became Royal Marines Poole.[9]

During the early 1950s the Corps began to provide crews for the Rhine squadron (see Appendix 4), with RM officers commanding major landing craft.[10] Other developments in these years included the introduction in America of the LVTP5 – studied by the staff of 'Jaswac' in 1959. This had a better performance than the World War II LVTs, and its hull could be completely sealed to protect against shell splinters; but its width limited movements on transporters to special routes. It also required skill on the driver's part to manoeuvre this somewhat cumbersome vehicle, although it had a good cross-country performance and could make over 5 knots on water.[11]

Amphibious studies in the UK were largely based on World War II operations, but from 1952 onwards there was an Amphibious Warfare squadron in the Mediterranean, where two converted LST Mark 3s as LST (Assault), with two LCT Mark 8s, arrived for training. An exercise in landing at Tobruk 'was a shambles' and at Brigadier Moulton's recommendation the Squadron was taken over by C-in-C Mediterrean, whose responsibilities included likely rescue operations to bring British nationals out of Alexandria. The Squadron was later joined by the headquarters ship HMS *Meon*, by the control ML 2583 and by other amphibious ships for the Suez operation. During the 1950s they worked closely with the Brigade moving Commandos to exercises or likely trouble spots. In October 1953 they carried out the first major combined amphibious exercise with the US Marine Corps since World War II. This was 'Weld Fast' held in Greece. The previous year '45 Cdo RM' had provided the 'enemy' for another American NATO exercise in Malta.

The Squadron – *Meon*, ML 2583, LST(A)s *Stiker* and *Reggio*, with LCT Mark 8s *Bastion* and *Redoubt* – usually lifted only one Commando at a time. But in the calm summer weather of the Mediterranean, the assault ships could transport over 600 men. However, they were an aging group of ships, most of which had been built in the mid-1940s, and although refitted before their 1960s operations in the Persian Gulf, they did not compare well with American amphibious ships.

There were no aircraft carriers in the Squadron, yet American experience and 45 Commando RM's work with helicopters had shown that these were an effective means of putting men ashore. Indeed, had the original landings in the Suez operation been at Alexandria, helicopters would have been essential, even though the Brigade had rehearsed a Zeebrugge-type landing, storming 'quays' up scaling ladders – practised at sea against the sides of LCTs[12] – from their LCAs. These World War II LCAs were replaced in 1957 by the 'LCA Mark II', capable of landing men and a small vehicle and designated LCVP.[13] They were the craft in general use for the next 20 years. There were also fast raiding craft, the LCR, used by the Raiding Squadron (which had origins in the Dory flotilla) and larger than the 1970s Rigid Raiders although not as fast.[14]

Analysis of '45 Cdo RM's' rehearsals and planning for the Port Said landings had resulted in an initial assault by four waves putting down into the landing zone: 370 men with reduced scales of ammunition but including the mortar, machine gun and anti-tank platoons. Sources differ on the exact number of helicopters used but there were at least ten Whirlwinds and six Sycamores, with probably two experimental Whirlwinds. As a compromise had to be made between the fuel loads carried and the military cargo's weight, each man was loaded to a total weight of 100kg and the planes only refuelled every second flight. This meant that the first 190 men and their heavy weapons could be landed in two flights, as a Whirlwind carried between five and seven men, while a Sycamore carried three of this weight. Uniform 100kg stores' packages were made up, and for the first time 'stick-orbats' were briefed. 'Helicopter loads in order of battle', as this term means, would become more sophisticated as the planning for air landing improved, but at Suez the improvised methods worked well. Once the 'choppers' had made four flights, with two refuellings each and having orbited to form up each wave, they changed to landing 'in a stream', each 'chopper' collecting its load before flying straight to the landing zone. In this way the early landings by waves avoided possible destruction through piecemeal landings, but instead secured the landing zone. While later the 'stream' speeded the flow of follow-up forces, bringing in personnel, ammunition and stores to the full assault scales for a Commando landed from LVTs or LCAs.[15] The commando ship landing men by helicopter was becoming a practical idea.

Further trials and operations were made by '45 Cdo RM' in Cyprus, after it returned to the island on 30 May 1957 to relieve 40 Commando in the Troodos mountains.[16] Although its first big cordon and search operations produced no major arrests, dropping observation parties from 'choppers' at first light: had advantages of surprise and speed which promised well for future operations. Lieutenant-Colonel Jack Richards, who had taken command of '45 Cdo RM' after Lieutenant-Colonel Tailyour was wounded, led a special force the following year (1958) comprising two of his Troops and the RN 728 (Commando) Flight of four Whirlwinds. This 'sky cavalry' carried out several operations before rejoining the Commando in North Africa.[17]

In their various tours on Cyprus the Brigade had suffered over 10 fatal casualties.[18] Included in those killed were a Sergeant and a Marine accidentally killed when their helicopter landed them in a 'killing zone' by mistake. This underlined the dangers in these operations when flying in pre-dawn half-light made identification of landing zones particularly difficult. The Commandos would return to the island in the 1970s as part of the British base area garrisons and at other times as part of the United Nations forces. The operations in the 1950s, however, had been of limited success, for EOKA in Cyprus was supported by nearly all the Greek Cypriots, and therefore the internal-security operations had differed from those in Malaya, where the communists' supporters were a minority of the population. Nevertheless '45 Cdo RM' had captured nearly 70 hardcore terrorists,[19] and '40 Cdo RM' had been equally successful.

The combination of vertical envelopment of a beachhead by helicopter landings, and their value on internal-security operations, emphasized the potential for this aircraft in commando-type warfare. Experimental helicopters had been used in Burma in World War II. In Korea the Americans had used helicopters with success in casualty evacuation (casevac) and in other roles, and by 1955 they had developed the first Landing Platform Helicopter ship, an LPH. By 1962 they had their first Landing Platform Dock (LPD) (developed from World War II types of Landing Ship Dock) which could be used for helicopters and landing craft too heavy to launch from davits. When the British government announced the end of National Service in the Defence White Paper of 1957, placing a greater reliance on nuclear weapons, the Royal Navy and Royal Marines were to provide carrier groups making use of these helicopter developments for limited warfare east of Suez. [20] For these groups the commando carrier was introduced after the Admiralty's proposals to CG and MGRM Portsmouth's staff prepared plans for the use of a light fleet carrier with 8 Helicopters to land RM Commandos.[21] General Hunton had confidently predicted this role for the Corps some 12 years earlier when helicopters were limited in size, but their development seemed promising.[22] At this time he and his advisers thought that gliders might fulfil this role until large helicopters were available,[23] and the suggestion of glider-borne landings from carriers was raised by Lord Mountbatten[24] in 1952. But General Moulton favoured helicopters, and as a result of his 1957 proposals: provision was made in the Navy's financial estimates for a commando carrier.

On 14 March 1960 42 Commando RM would march aboard the specially adapted HMS *Bulwark*, a carrier whose conversion to a commando ship had begun in 1957. She was later designated an LPH; and after refits from time to time she was still in commission in 1980 (see Appendix 4). She had a complement of 980, including the 7th Assault Squadron RM manning her four LCVPs; the anti-submarine/commando 846 RN Squadron with 20 Wessex and Sea King helicopters; and 750 RM commandos or other troops.[25] There were obvious advantages in being able to deploy commandos in this way, as will be seen in the next chapter, for a carrier could remain – that is: loiter – over the horizon from a likely trouble spot with all the advantages of a self-contained 'base' which may be refuelled and resupplied during long periods at sea without the political commitment of landing troops. There was, however, the need to pay particular attention to both physical fitness and acclimatising troops for landings in hot climates, since *Bulwark* was air-conditioned.

Another outcome of the national defence review of 1957 was the raising of two more Commandos despite some senior Army officers' reservations. Lord Mountbatten at this time was Chairman of the Chiefs of Staff Committee, and piloted the commandos' expansion through troubled waters on the formation of a single Ministry of Defence from three separate service ministries. Much as he had done in 1943, he championed the Royal Marines' cause in the next few years while the modern Ministry of Defence (MOD) was created. Recruits also came forward to join the Marines, which put the Corps in a favourable position even when politicians considered defence cuts; although throughout the 1960s the Army's senior staff continued to press for a reduction in the numbers of Commandos to two operational units.[26] Nevertheless as recruits volunteered and could be trained, 41 and 43 Commandos RM were reactivated (see Appendix 4).

The increasing use of helicopters would lead to more RM officers being seconded to the Fleet Air Arm in the 1960s but the last RM 'fixed wing' pilots trained in 1958–9. The World War II pilots had gone back to general duties, as had eight officers trained in the late 1940s, among them Captain P. J. F. Whiteley (later General Sir Peter, KCB, OBE).[27]

Another specialised branch of the Royal Marines service, the Special Boat Sections (or Section) as they were known in the 1950s, continued to train. The hazards of their work was underscored by the loss of four SBS Marines when the submarine HMS *Affray* foundered in 1951.[28] The roles for which the SBS trained in the 1950s covered all the types of operations which had been carried out by the Small Operations Group of World War II: limpet raids on enemy shipping; demolition raids; beach reconnaissance; and landing special agents along with other clandestine forces. Units of the SBS would be attached from time to time to the Brigade or to Army formations, for potential operations in theatres where British interests might require their special talents. In the 1950s the Section was redesignated a Company and about 1975 became a Squadron with its sub-units as Sections, but this elite force never contained more than relatively few personnel, often operating away from their base on detachment.

The Corps provided other small detachments from time to time for internal-security duties in Northern Ireland during the 1950s. A small RM team of advisers on the defence of Naval establishments visited bases in the area in 1954. In December 1956 a composite Troop from the NCOs' school was briefly based in HMS *Sea Eagle* (Londonderry), being relieved by a Troop of 42 Commando in the New Year. Other Troops from '42 RM' were provided from time to time as reinforcements for *Sea Eagle*. They patrolled at night when small IRA (Irish Republican Army) groups were blowing up electricity installations. The commandos' patrols extended to the border, and their assault engineers defused bombs.[29]

Typical of these IRA activities was the planting of carrier bags of explosive alongside electricity transformers and rectifiers on Queen's Quay, one bag blowing up the transformer and cutting the supply to depot ships. Two Royal Ulster Constabulary officers posing as a courting couple saw the bombs being laid, and arrested several men, but a second bomb – 15lb of gelignite with a 9ft fuse and a detonator – did not explode. The only trained explosive experts in the area were the OC of 'B' Troop, an assault engineer, and a Naval sub-lieutenant, who examined the bag.[30] They managed to pull it from a distance with a piece of string to check that there were no booby-trap devices attached to it, before the RM officer dismantled it.[31] Commandos would be deployed from time to time in Northern Ireland from 1957 to the present day, taking their full share of these duties.

Royal Marines were also first detached in 1957 for service in the desert state of Muscat and Oman around the south-east coasts of the Arabian peninsula, which had been an ally of the British since 1798. Their ruler in the late 1950s was a shy reclusive Sultan whose territories in the mountains were taken over by the Imam Ghabia in 1955. The Imam was deposed, however, in an almost bloodless coup but in 1957 reappeared to incite mountain tribes against the Sultan. Backed by Saudi money and Egyptian propaganda, the Imam's brother, Talib then proved a resourceful and brave leader. That December a Lieutenant and six NCOs from detachments with the Persian Gulf Frigate Squadron were sent to help the Sultan, and were later joined for 6-month periods by NCOs from the Brigade. The Marines exchanged their globe and laurel cap badge for the crossed sabres and star badge on the Arab headdresses of the Sultan's army.[32] The senior NCOs commanded platoons of Omani and Baluchi (West Pakistan) infantry, while the RM officers commanded companies. Their forces carried out fighting patrols into the mountains to harass Talib's pickets in a war that would often be fought over arid wastelands, where men in a sangar – a rock-walled strongpoint built where ground was too hard for trenches – might watch a mountain side for weeks. Patrols were supported by a single 5.5-in gun or perhaps a helicopter, and the Sultan's men at times fought the rebels at close quarters.[33] The Oman in this way provided operational experience for officers and NCOs in the field, much in the same way as service in the Sudan Defence Force had done before World War II. By the summer of 1959 20 Officers and 63 NCOs had served in the Oman and two sergeants had been killed.[34] The last Officers to be seconded to the forces in the Oman and Trucial states completed their 2-year tours in 1976.[35] But for some years after this retired RM Officers and SNCOs served on contracts to the Sultan's forces.

The Corps entered the 1960s with the prospect of commando carriers to use in operations and five Commandos for service in Norway, Northern Ireland and those more distant parts of the Commonwealth from which the British were withdrawing. Their training continued to include a series of major exercises in the field, with '40 Cdo RM', for example, having to abandon an exercise in Lybia when torrential rain caused heavy flooding, but their help in the relief work earnt them the gratitude of local people.[36]

In sport the Corps continued to provide proportionately more athletes for Royal Naval teams than its strength might suggest, and in the 1950s had provided the back-up for pentathlon competitors which helped to keep this sport alive at a national level. In competition shooting the Corps maintained its place as a fourth arm of the services. While individual's achievements ranged from riding in the Grand National to participation in international athletics. By 1979–80 12 of the Royal Navy's internationals were Royal Marines, and that year RM units won nine of the Naval inter-command competitions.

10

FIRST IN, LAST OUT

The Marines of 45 Commando RM moved to Aden in 1960, on the first of many tours for individual Marines, as '45 Cdo RM' was in operations in South Arabia during the next 7½ years. These operations would cover internal security in Aden Colony – an area of 75 sqare miles, about the size of central London and with a population of 220,000 – and patrols in desert mountains up to Dhala, 90 miles from the Colony and across the Aden Protectorate near the Yemen border. The protectorate covered an area half the size of France but had a population of only 800,000; and the political background to these operations was complex. By 1960 the independent state of Yemen under its Imam was hostile to the formation of any federation of states, which the British had suggested as one way to political progress.[1] The Egyptians, with support from Russia, encouraged the Yemeni and other anti-British tribes to further the cause of Arab nationalism. They found fertile ground also for the seeds of revolt among the 80,000 Yemeni in the Colony, where trade unions – started by the British to encourage democratic institutions – were becoming increasingly hostile to the feudal nature of Arab states.

Such conflicts of interest were an understandable legacy of treaties made perforce with sheikhs, sultans and kings during the previous 100 years or so, when they were the only authorities in many lands. As the British withdrew their commitments to Aden and elsewhere, therefore, their alignment with feudal rulers sometimes seemed to run contrary to the so-called forces of 'progress'. Yet in hindsight almost invariably these new states can be seen to be military autocracies, at least in the initial periods of their conception. In Aden particularly the Russian interest was a matter of military bases rather than to raise standards of living.

In April 1960 45 Commando relieved an Army battalion, and was based on Little Aden, the oil refinery complex, where men lived in quarters originally built for construction workers.[2] Two Troops that went up to Dhala would be relieved in rotation. At Dhala they strengthened the local forces against Yemeni incursions from the north. The Commando, with the Amphibious Warfare Squadron also based on Aden, was available for operations elsewhere in the Persian Gulf,[3] as was an armoured squadron of the Queen's Own Hussars.

Fourteen months later their mobility would be put to the test, when the commando carrier HMS *Bulwark* was also to fly off Marines as an earnest of Britain's support for Sheikh Abdulla, the ruler of the small, newly independent state of Kuwait. This oil-rich territory at the head of the Persian Gulf bordered to the north on Iraq, whose ruler General Kassim had openly laid claim to Kuwait in the early summer of 1961. By this time *Bulwark* had worked up with 42 Commando and the helicopter squadron 'under the "eye" of FOF (Mediterranean) and the Brigade's headquarters', before sailing to the Far East, where she was based on Singapore. She had carried out hot weather trials the previous year off the east African coast, where her presence was probably a strategic deployment. By June 1961 she was at Karachi (Pakistan) some two or three days' steaming from the Persian Gulf.[4] As Sheikh Abdulla had brought forward the planned date of independence for Kuwait, there was to be such urgency over the final sailing orders that the First Sea Lord called on the RM Major on the Naval Planning Staff – CG's office was some distance from the main Ministry offices – for a brief on the Commando's immediate capabilities.[5]

Bulwark sailed at the end of June and on 1 July put down the first wave of commandos, her sixteen Whirlwinds landing on Kuwait's new airfield, which was still being built. At the time 42 Commando's CO, Lieutenant-Colonel E. R. Bridges, was ashore in Bahrein, where he had been visiting Army headquarters to plan an exercise in the area. Dust storms had prevented him and his Operations Officer flying to *Bulwark* as she steamed north, with a result that knowledge of the local conditions was sketchy. For when commando carriers were first commissioned there was a tendency for the Navy to regard an embarked Commando as simply a large RM detachment in the ship. Captains seeing it as his ship's main 'armament',[6] to be deployed by him with advice from the Commando's CO. The RAF Squadrons flying Hunters into the airfield were somewhat surprised when they found a large formation of helicopters landing out of the dust haze. The Marines had been led in by a Kuwaiti helicopter, while the hot 'Shammal' was blowing at 30 knots driving up clouds of dust which reduced visibility to a mile or less,[7] in temperatures of 40-50°C. This sort of weather reduced the density of the air and therefore the helicopters' ability to lift weight, but '42 Cdo RM' was safely landed and moved north 25 miles into the Bedouins' country, where the men dug in on the 400ft-high Mutla Ridge.[8]

Meanwhile '45 Cdo RM' was being airlifted from Aden. It had been concentrated in Little Aden on 29–30 June, except for the Mobat anti-tank guns. They were with a party several days' journey from the port, and could not be recalled in time for the flights to Kuwait on 2 July. Emergency crews were therefore given a crash course, for the Iraqis were expected to use one or possibly two regiments of tanks on the open ground across which they might invade. Thirty-six hours' non-stop work by the staff produced the flight load plans, known as 'chalks'. But as a variety of planes – Beverleys, Hastings and Britannias – were used in the airlift, the 'chalks' arrived in a different sequence at the new airport in Kuwait, and not in the optimum order to deploy men into action. Nevertheless the advanced elements of '45 Cdo RM' had moved 1,600 miles in a day, with only a brief stop at Bahrein. As they came out of the airport, where the heat and the glare were intense even by Aden standards, they passed from the city's tower blocks and streets with American cars, to an arid wilderness. Across this only

4-wheel drive vehicles could follow the sand track, 'a winding, twisting succession of tyre marks with little signposts at intervals'. This led to the hills west of '42 Cdo RM's' positions, where at nightfall the convoy halted for two hours. Lieutenant-Colonel L. G. Marsh and his machine gun officer were guided by the local sheikh, in a recce of the ground over which the convoy then moved in a nightmare journey. Vehicles bogged down in soft sand and there were sudden flurries of sandstorms, before the commandos reached their defensive positions 12 miles south-east of the main desert road from Iraq. The necessity for safe loads in aircraft had meant that all their entrenching tools were bundled and wrapped before loading, and these bundles had not reached the airfield when this Advanced Party (Tactical HQ and 'X' Troop) set out for the hills. They dug themselves in, using mess-tins and bayonets to make 'scrapes' for cover.[9]

In the next few days the Marines in Kuwait – '42 Cdo RM', '45 Cdo RM' and the detachment from HMS *Loch Alvie* – learnt to survive in the hottest time of the year in one of the hottest parts of the World. Here they built broad pits for the long, low Vickers Mobats, while the only cover for a slit trench was the narrow strip of hessian each man carried to keep out the worst of the sun. As more troops came forward, they extended the defences among hillocks a mere 30ft high in some of '45 Cdo RM's' positions, across which the wind blew like a furnace blast. By 3 July things began to improve – a relative statement, for the blazing sun and high heat never abated – as *Bulwark*'s helicopters flew to both '42 Cdo RM' and the rest of '45 Cdo RM' with supplies. '42 Cdo RM' shared out its large camouflage nets, which gave some effective shade, and also provided ice blocks through its local contact with a sheikh's freezing plant. Two companies of the Coldstream Guards, and a Squadron of the 3rd Carabineers waiting for their tanks, were the only Army presence until 3 July, except for local Kuwaiti troops on the border. But that day (3 July) Army reinforcements began to arrive. The RM Rhino ferry crews of the Amphibious Warfare Squadron rafted ashore tanks and heavy vehicles in a round-the-clock stint of several days' toil. By 5 July the Iraqis were preparing defences apparently not deploying for an invasion and in the next few weeks the threat to Kuwait passed. *Loch Alvie*'s detachment had been re-embarked on the second day, leaving ashore only its Naval Gunfire Forward Observer Team, the FOBs of the 1960s; '42 Cdo RM' went into reserve for a spell before re-embarking in *Bulwark* which sailed on 21 July; and '45 Cdo RM' had flown back to Aden three days earlier.[10] Both Commandos, already acclimatised to tropical heat and trained in desert warfare, survived three gruelling weeks in Kuwait, where troops straight from a European theatre would have been in considerable difficulty through heat stroke and similar casualties. When Army units took over the Commandos' positions, however, they found the slit trenches of a Troop organisation did not readily suit an infantry company's layout for a defended area.

The Kuwait operation highlighted what was already a difficulty with an organisation based on the commando Troop, for – as had happened in World War II – when Army battalions took over a Commando's area, a number of changes were necessary not only in the layout of slit trenches. The whole question of organisation therefore came under review. Four factors had to be taken into account: the need for organic artillery in the Brigade; better anti-tank defences in a Commando; improved helicopter facilities; an organisation which having spearheaded an operation could then hand over smoothly to Army units; and the improved weaponry of the 1960s. In 1959 the Brigade had been equipped with the SLR self-loading rifle,[11] the general purpose machine gun (GPMG) had replaced the Bren, and the Vickers Mobats were in use in each Commando. There was also sufficient transport for all companies to be moved in one 'lift' by the Commando's own vehicles. Studies and exercises in the late 1950s looked at a couple of different forms of organisation the Brigade might adopt, before, in 1962, the Corps' establishment was raised sufficiently to allow for some increased strength in each Commando.

During the 1950s the total strength of the Corps had fallen from nearly 11,000 to about 9,000 in 1959, with in addition over 1,400 reservists. However during these years the number of detachments afloat in major ships fell to less than a dozen. But with the increase in the numbers of Commandos – '41 Cdo RM' was re-formed in March 1960 and '43' in September 1961 – and the commissioning of HMS *Albion* on 1 August 1962 as a second commando carrier, the Corps strength had been increased marginally. By 1963 it would be over 9,000, of which 860 would be in the RM Band Service (see Appendix 5). This strength would include under 1,000 general duty officers and Marines under training, as there were many re-engagements in that year.[12] This seemed to prove that commando service in the Corps was more popular than service in ships. During the late 1950s ships' detachments, especially in fleet carriers, had not had opportunities to exercise that age-old rivalry in competitive gunnery which – among other things – had given Marines of 'X' turret the edge on seamen. And, as in the 1930s, men on shipboard spent more time away from their families than they would have done if they had been in Commando service, whose families moved to bases overseas[13] on 'accompanied' tours.

The reorganisation of Commandos in 1962 had created independent Commando units, with a small HQ of less than 60 (including Naval medical staff), three rifle companies and a support company of 81-mm mortars, a recce Troop in ¼-ton vehicles and assault engineers. Headquarters Companies were also formed with signals, transport and administrative Troops, to provide services to each Commando. A Commando, after various changes over the years, now numbered 640 all ranks,[14] with the term Troop applied to the equivalent of an Army platoon. The size of a Commando was half as big again as the World War II Commandos with an establishment of 450 all ranks. Although the Troop structure was appropriate at the time in the 1940s, it did not give junior commanders – both young Officers and Corporals – specific commands in the day-to-day routine.

Some Naval officers thought that the Commandos should be more or less permanently embarked in commando ships – as these carriers were later called – and that operations would be at ship/unit level. The Admiralty also was of the view that a Brigade Headquarters was unnecessary, if Captains of ships advised by a Commando CO were to deploy these units. A great deal of persuasion was therefore necessary by Brig Norman Tailyour and others to convince the Admiralty that a Brigade HQ was essential and Commandos could not be properly trained without camps ashore.[15] The Navy then provided Sembawang Barracks as the Fleet Amphibious Base Far East, in Singapore, despite what the Admiralty considered to be great expense.[16] Commando carriers, unlike the Amphibious Warfare squadron, had a wider role than merely landing troops, as these carriers had to give a Commando tactical and logistic support.[16] Plans for a '4 Commando Brigade' based in the UK were not carried through; and when in the UK, Commandos were detached under Army command from time to time. They might also be attached to Army commands overseas. However the Brigade HQ was strengthened to command and train its own Commandos, and a Brigade Signal Squadron was formed.

The possibility of raising RM land artillery units to make use of the Corps' gunnery experience was considered, but at Lord Mountbatten's suggestion the Royal Artillery agreed to provide 29th Commando Light Regiment on 1 January 1962.[17] This regiment was commanded by Lieutenant-Colonel (later Brigadier) D. W. O'Flaherty, who as an Army commando had landed at Vaagso (Norway) in 1941. He made a simple rule for his Regiment with their 105-mm pack howitzers: 'where the Commando Brigade went, by whatever means, so too should its affiliated Regiment . . . by helicopter, sea, air or even on its own flatfeet'.[18] This it would do.

From September 1964 a short service commission was introduced, under which officers were trained and served for a relatively short period.

The recruiting of helicopter pilots from RM officers for flying duties had begun in 1961 for what for later pilots would be a year's course, when they learnt not only the commando landing techniques but also anti-submarine warfare – the primary role of Naval helicopters. The first three of these pilots joined 848 Squadron of the Fleet Air Arm in HMS *Bulwark* in 1961, and they would be followed by 23 other long-service Officers and 17 Officers on a short-service commissions. Some of the pilots on short-term commissions, had been recruited under the scheme for RM Special Entry for Flying Duties. This was started with a course in 1965 but discontinued two years later for lack of suitable candidates.[19] In later years the number of RM pilots in Naval Air Commando Squadrons would vary, and some transferred from the Corps to the Fleet Air Arm. In the late-1990s there is a case for having an increased number of RM helicopter pilots who understand warfare on the ground and also bring to the Corps an understanding of operating helicopters.

With sufficient pilots, and Commandos as Commando Groups equipped with a balanced force of all arms, the Commandant General, General Sir Ian Riches, KCB, DSO, planned to use two Commandos with one carrier, or three if there were two carriers on one station in the early 1960s. In this way one Commando could be ashore in order to keep men fit and in proper military training.[20] But '40 Cdo RM' was to be retained in Malta, where it was acclimatised to Mediterranean conditions; '45 Cdo RM' was in Aden; '42 Cdo RM' and the Brigade HQ were based on Singapore. While '41 Cdo RM' and '43 Cdo RM' were in the UK, available for overseas operations. Events in the Middle and Far East would make balanced deployments difficult to achieve in the next few years, beginning in December 1962 with the landing of '40' and '42' in Brunei (north Borneo).

As the British withdrew from Malaya, its newly independent states decide to continue their federation, which was in the early 1960s to include island territories as well as mainland Malaya. The Indonesians of Java and other islands, most of them Mohammedans, opposed the federation of Borneo states which were the territories along the north Borneo coast, Sarawak in the west, Brunei and British North Borneo, with the mainland territories. From this stemmed the first major revolt against this Federation which occurred in Brunei. Here on the coastal plain lived a number of peoples of different origins, among them the Kedayans, an industrious farming community, who had quietly gone about their business. Yet by tradition they were treated as second-class citizens by the local Malays, for the Kedayans were of Indonesian origin having come from Java some centuries before.[1] When the former British protectorate of Brunei – in the late 1990s the Sultan still has a treaty with Britain – joined the Federation, the Kedayans wanted to keep the territory in a North Borneo Union, which would also include the neighbouring territory of Sarawak. To further this in December 1962, the rebels occupied several towns, including Brunei town (modern Bandar Seri Begawa) At Limbang across the border in Sarawak, they also held a number of hostages, including the British Government's Agent – the 'Resident' Dick Morris – his wife and a nursing sister.[2] There were indications that the hostages were to be executed on 12 December.

At this time 42 Commando RM was in Singapore and '40 Cdo RM' aboard HMS *Albion* off Mombasa. On 8 December '42 Cdo RM' was put at short notice to move to Brunei, and two days later 'L' Company flew there.

On landing on 10 December, the Company Commander, Captain (later Major General Sir) J. J. Moore, MC, was ordered to stay in the airport during the night curfew, as the Gurkhas had retaken Brunei town. Information was scanty, but some half dozen hostages were thought to be held in the police station at Limbang in Sarawak, which rebels had captured three days earlier. The Company Commander set about finding craft and was shot at twice, while the CO of 42 Commando RM, Lieutenant-Colonel E. R. Bridges, and his intelligence officer – who had both arrived after 'L' company – flew over Limbang getting 'a brief look at the area through low and heavy cloud cover'.[3] The rebels were thought to be armed with shotguns, an effective close-quarters weapon, a light machine gun and rifles from the police station, and numbered some 150.

Two old 'Z-craft like' lighters were found, one with two great yellow bulldozers aboard ready to push the craft off if they got stuck. That morning the minesweepers HMS *Fiskerton* and *Chawton* arrived in the Brunei river and started preparing the lighters for a voyage up river, for which they also provided the crews. Captain Moore had 2½ rifle Troops, Company Headquarters and a Section of medium machine guns. He assessed that the enemy's the firepower at 100

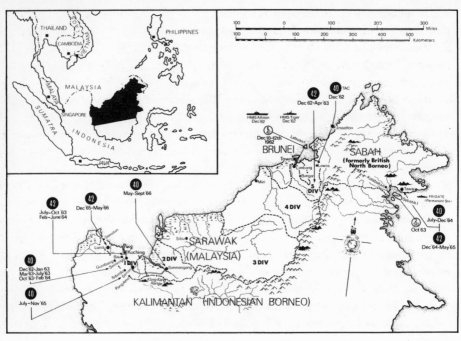

Principal deployments of RM Commandos in Borneo 1962–4 when many minor actions by 'stop' patrols ambushed raiders returning to Indonesia. The commandos also built forts and established good relations with local people.

Date	Cdo	Location
1962		
12 Dec	42 L coy rescue Resident	Limbang
14	42 M Coy with 846 Sqb set ambushes	Bangar
15	40 A Coy ambush laid	Miri
19	40 Tac HQ established	Jessieton
25	40 patrolling area	Lawas
1963		
7 Jan	40 had captured 421 enemy	Temburong
6 Feb	42 Patrols capture two enemy leaders	Tufong/Brunei/Muara area
10 April	40 No. 6 Tp fight attack	tebedu
17	40 with L Coy (42, No. 20 Coy RA, Sqn 1st Division QRIH & 846 Sqn	Sarawak
23	40 BCoy successful night op	Gumbang
27	40 forts & 32 raid posts established	border
13 Aug	42 No. 4 Tp hold off raiders	Gumbang
23	42 last raid of series disrupted by cdo ambushes	Gumbang
31 Dec	40 4-man patrol attack large enemy force, Cpl Marriott killed before enemy forced over border on 6 Jan	Bau
1964		
20 Feb	42 No. 5 Tp attacked Cpl Chappell killed, other enemy forces kill 2 soldiers	Sekabal
21 Feb	42 L Coy in action	nr Biawak
13 April	42 No. 3 Tp ambushed, Cpl Hinds & Mne McCrea killed	nr Padawan
July–Dec	patrolling waterways	Tawau
1965		
Jan	42 small craft patrols as tawau Asslt Grp on rivers	Wallace Bay Area
31 Aug	40 successful ambush	1st Div Border
4 Nov	40 B coy drive enemy back. Cpl P.J.G. Daniels killed	nr Pang Amo
1966		
16 Mar	42 M & L Coys supported by mortars & 105-mm in action against regular troops of Indonesia who suffered heavy losses	South of Biawak

(There were also some other incidents for which details are not available.) Indonesian raids in 1964 into Malaya failed to establish firm bases: (a) seaborne 17 Aug; (b) airborne 2 Sept; (c) seaborne 29 Oct; (d) seaborne 23 Dec; (e) seaborne 24 Dec; and three unsuccessful raids made early in 1965.

yards would not be more than the equivalent to a Section's fire-power. But at close quarters this fire could equal that of the Captain's under-strength Company. Captain Moore decided he must go straight for the enemy's headquarters, which might reasonably be expected to be in the police station.[4] 'We had to get to the hostages before the enemy had time to react', Captain Moore later wrote. The town of Limbag lies on a bend of the river, and, if one approaches up stream, on the left (east) bank were local houses, then shops, the police station and 100yds of open bank to the hospital, with other buildings along the bank beyond. The whole town occupied some 1,000yds of river front where the town area has been cut out of the jungle a few hundred yards from the river's edge.[5]

The Marines sailed from Brunei on the night of 11 December, with Captain Moore, the leading Troop and the Company's Reconnaissance Group in the first craft; and Company HQ, the second-in-command, one and a half Troops and the machine gun section in the second. They lay down river from Limbang for a few hours so that they would arrive at the police station a few minutes after first light. Z-lighters are not the handiest of craft in any waters, for they are flat, raft-like craft and navigating them through the narrow maze of waterways was difficult. Brunei's Director of Marine (the local river and harbour authority) knew of the route, although he had not travelled it, and he went with the leading craft. Despite an engine breakdown and the narrow waterways, they got within a couple of miles of Limbang, when they saw the street lights go out.

When they were 300yds from the police station, and as the leading craft came abreast of the huts south of the town, 'it erupted like a disturbed ants' nest as the rebels stood to'. At 200yds the commando Intelligence Sergeant called through a loud-hailer in Malay: 'The rebellion is over ... you should lay down your arms'. They replied with automatic weapons – an LMG, three or four SMGs – and some dozen rifles, supported by over 100 shotguns. The instantaneous counter-fire from both craft gave the commandos, thanks to their Vickers machine guns, the initiative, enabling the leading craft to beach half a minute later only 30yds from the police station. Two Marines of the leading No. 5 Troop were killed before the craft gained the bank and their OC, Lieutenant 'Paddy' Davis was wounded as he jumped ashore. Sergeant Bickford led two Sections of the Troop against the police station, which was quickly cleared, but the Naval coxswain of the leading craft had been wounded and the craft drifted off the bank. Lieutenant D. O. Willis, RN, drove it hard back ashore; but this shallow draught lighter broached to 150yds upstream between the hospital and the home of the British Resident. Captain Moore sent the reserve Section ashore, with HQ personnel led by TSM McDonald, and they cleared the hospital. As they came through the back of this building, the Troop Sergeant and two Marines were killed 'for the jungle comes literally right down to the back door of the hospital'.[6]

The grounding of the craft up-river had been a fortunate accident, for Captain Moore found some hostages in the hospital. A rebel had fired at them but missed, and no one was hurt. While the ground between the hospital and the police station was being cleared, as was the Resident's house, the Company commander was told of more hostages. Therefore, he organised the clearing of the rest of the town to the south, and by afternoon had released another eight hostages but at nightfall there were still rebels inside the Company's perimeter, two of whom were killed close to the Marines' positions. Next day the town was secured.[7] Five Marines had been killed and six men wounded (including a sailor), but the action here, coupled with those of the Gurkhas and Queen's Own Highlanders elsewhere in Brunei, had broken the rebellion.[8] At Limbang alone 15 rebels had been killed and 50 captured from a force of 350,[9] twice the expected number. They had been taken by surprise, as the commandos now discovered. The Vickers guns in the second craft had been masked by the leading craft, until QMS Cyril Quoins asked the officer commanding this lighter if he could pull out of line to give them a clearer shot. 'Sergeant Major', the officer replied, 'Nelson would have loved you', and promptly swung his craft into a more exposed position.

The success of the operation was due to the first-class leadership of the junior NCOs, two of whom – Corporals W. J. Lester and R. C. Rawlinson – were awarded the MM. Captain Moore was awarded a bar to his MC, and both Lieutenant Willis, RN and Petty Officer P. J. D. Kirwin received gallantry awards. The remainder of '42 Cdo RM' had arrived by plane and warship by 12 December. The Brigade HQ, with most of '40 Cdo RM', landed at Kuching (Sarawak) two days later. They patrolled in this and other areas until re-embarking, as did '42 RM' early in April 1963. But HMS *Albion*'s LCA squadron remained in Borneo, as these craft were ideal for ferrying supplies up the rivers and in coastal waters.[10] The Brigade and both '40 Cdo RM' and '42 Cdo RM' would do further spells in Borneo (see Appendix 4) during 1963. On 1 July the Brigade came under Army command, and would henceforth be under Army codes of military law when ashore or *embarked*; it had previously been under Naval command, and only under Army disciplinary codes when detached ashore under Army command.[11] Nevertheless the Commandos maintained close links with their carriers' crews and staff, for the tendency to think of commandos as Army troops was never allowed to weaken the Royal Marines' bond with the Navy, although in the 1960s, as in other decades, there were a few who advocated closer integration with the Army.

Jungle operations continued during the next 3½ years, when Commandos of the Brigade were to carry out 3-month and later 5-month tours. The campaign became known as 'The Confrontation', for Indonesian sympathisers, like the Kedayans, challenged the rule of the Malay Federal government in North Borneo. These tours led to some medical problems in the early years when a man's health could be undermined in the jungle. When 40 Commando RM returned to Singapore from its first tour, for instance, many men were found to have developed foot-rot and other diseases, and one man died from drinking foul water.[12] The Commando discovered how run down physically a man becomes after weeks in the jungle, and, relearning the lessons of World War II, the officers and senior NCOs went on hygiene courses. They mastered the use of the Millbank bag to filter water, among other precautions, and after '40 RM's' second tour there was considerably less illness. The Marines began to adapt to jungle life and enjoy its challenges, for it had much greater variety than the deserts of Africa and the Persian Gulf. They kept fit, and learnt to avoid streams infected by rats with the often fatal disease of leptospirosis.[13]

A typical tour for the A Company of 40 Commando RM began on 15 December 1962 when they were in reserve aboard HMS *Albion*. That afternoon their Company Commander, Major P. G. Davis – who had commanded LCAs at Brac (Yugoslavia) in 1944 – was called to the Assault Operations Room aboard the ship, not long after the rest of '40 Cdo RM' had been landed. His Company, reinforced by men of the Support Company without their heavy weapons, was to land by helicopter near Miri (Sarawak) to set up an ambush. With them was a cheerful Shell Petroleum Company executive nickname 'Happy' who spoke the local languages, but no one knew if there were any landing sites near the ambush area.[14] Time was short, for the helicopters had to fly in before dusk, a quick calculation of time and distance showing that they must take off as soon as possible. After a short briefing, therefore, the 'sticks' of men filed out of the hangar from their assault stations, put on their life jackets and waited for each pilot's thumbs-up signal to board.

They found an opening in the jungle over marshy ground, to which the commandos abseiled from the 'helios' as these hovered. 'Happy' flung himself flat after leaving the rope, the approved drill in normal circumstances, but in this bog he was covered in mire. The heavy gear was then dropped to the men, their precious wireless set surviving the fall on soft ground. The OC checked that the next three waves of Wessex helicopters knew where to lower their commandos who would form the firm base, with a second Troop to follow the first. This second Troop landed in time to make a 1½-mile speed march to join Major Davis just before nightfall. The ambush was quickly rehearsed and they waited for the 150 rebels that were expected, but although they waited all night, no one appeared. Their first prisoner, 'a very frightened rebel', was captured next morning, after the local headman had suggested where he might be found. The village was without any food and before 'A' Company was lifted out that morning, their 'helios' dropped the villagers some bags of rice.[15] But for 'A' company, already on the go for 24 hours, there was another landing, and 40 minutes after reaching *Albion* a Troop was in the air again. This time they landed near an apparently deserted police station.

'It was suddenly very quiet, very eerie and quite dark' after the helicopters flew off. Within the hour, however, the Marines had contacted a platoon of Sarawak Rangers, with whom they captured 11 rebels. The rest of 'A' Company flew in next morning, and the prisoners were flown out. Major Davis then organised his force, including the Rangers and additional Marines, in four posts at intervals along 30 miles of river, with each post providing a firm base for patrols and a helicopter landing site. A couple of days later, when 100 of his 180-strong force were needed to surround an enemy camp, both RAF and RN 'helios' brought them together from their outpost bases. There was an 8-hour slog ahead, 'through rice paddy, through marsh, from scrub into thick jungle, up hills and across streams', to find the camp had been empty for four days.

On Christmas Eve an air drop of expected presents took three hours to gather in, the parachutes having missed the dropping zone. The containers held not presents but special rations for the Rangers, a disappointment for the Marines, but next day *Albion*'s helicopters flew in with four-course dinners for the men in each of the four bases, and the padre visited them by 'helio' or canoe. The A Company was relieved by Gurkhas on Boxing Day, but were back in the jungle two days later many miles from those outposts. This time they spent two weeks on the coast, one patrol going inland before floating silently down river in local boats to surprise a village at dawn.[16] The A Company collected nearly 300 weapons and some 60 suspected rebels, winning the respect of the locals. Between April and June they spent over nine weeks in the jungle, and were there again that October, for 'Confrontation' continued even after Malaysia had been created the previous August.

During October 1963 '40 Cdo RM' had an area of some 7,000 square miles to patrol, to make sure the Malays' timber trade could continue without harassment. Lieutenant-Colonel John Parsons, MC, who had been with '41 Cdo RM' at Salerno in 1943, had his headquarters in huts at the timber trading post of Kalabakan. This was on the coast, near the south-east corner of what had formerly been British North Borneo. 'Colonel Parsons (red shirt, blue shorts and white sandals) . . . explained that the main threat came from Noenoekan Island', on which detachments of Indonesian Marines were based.[17] Malayan forces and ships provided some defence against these threats, while Marines and Gurkhas did many long patrols, often travelling for 10 to 14 days in the hill country from bases supplied by helicopter, and patrolling the mangrove swamps and rivers in assault boats. By this time they could keep themselves fit despite living on rations of dehydrated foods, although there was little pure fresh water. They survived the high humidity and kept clear of tropical diseases, but they never got used to the thousands of rats which infested camps. The harmless 3-in grasshoppers they brushed aside, while more dangerous insects were treated with respect, as was their enemy. For on the last day of 1963 a Marine Corporal was killed during a terrorist attack on a Malay village.[18] The Commandos served on such tours until the Confrontation ended in August 1966.

In the Borneo campaign the Brigade's logistic support was stronger than it had been in the years immediately after World War II. At that time only an RM Light Aid Detachment (LAD) was available to repair vehicles, and major support came from the Army. By the late 1950s there was a single Commando Mainten-ance Detachment,[19] maintenance in this sense meaning more than servicing vehicles, for this was the first step in setting up an organic logistic unit to serve with a Commando operationally. There was also an RM Stores Park which remained in the Brigade's base area, but the Maintenance Detachment with its vehicles could support a unit in the field. It could also be expanded with additional medical and Army ordnance personnel to service the Brigade in the field, when the Brigade's bandsmen would act as stretcher-bearers. The Detachment, largely drawn from Army personnel, was disbanded in 1960 when the Army in Malta could no longer provide these men. It was replaced in the early 1960s, when the logistical support was further improved by raising the RM Commando Workshops in April 1963, and an Ordnance Field Park company of Royal Army Ordnance Corps (RAOC) personnel with an RM Section handling Naval stores. The Workshops were commanded by a Captain of the Royal Elecrical and Mechanical Engineers (REME) but mainly comprised RM personnel, and Royal Engineers served with the Brigade as part of the support units. They were all deployed in Borneo from time to time and in at least one action, were plucked to safety by the RAF when commando patrols had 'strayed' across the border. Many commandos learnt to speak Malay, asking headmen for information while cordoning and searching villages. In August B Company of '40 Cdo RM' had a large patrol back on the Sarawak border and there the Marines' good marksmanship helped their league table scores in skirmishes with Indonesians.[20]

Royal Marines also served as pilots on an SRN-5 Hovercraft patrolling swamp near the border, but there appear to have been no startling developments at that time from this new vehicle's military use. More conventional canoe patrols by the SBS – if anything they do can be said to be conventional – were carried out to reconnoitre beyond territorial waters of North Borneo, and they served with Army units as well as Commandos.[21] The extent of SBS clandestine operations, if any, is not known, but their patrols among the creeks and rivers of Borneo followed the pattern of SOG's operations in 1945. In March 1966 one of the sharpest engagements took place in pursuing terrorists, for '42 Cdo RM' lost a Lieutenant killed while another junior officer and a Marine were seriously wounded. By this date about 70,000 British, Malay and other troops – including Australians – were in northern Borneo, but in August the Indonesians came to terms with Malaysia and the Commandos were withdrawn. '40 RM' returned to Johore (south Malaya) and '42' to Sembawang in Singapore.

While '40 Cdo RM' and '42 Cdo RM' had been operating in Borneo, '45 Cdo RM' was in Aden in actions described later. The UK-based Commandos took their turn with Army battalions as the spearhead Battalion of the strategic reserve. This entailed having a Company and the Commando's Tactical HQ ready to emplane within 24 hours for an operation anywhere in the World, with the other companies ready to follow within 72 hours of the warning order. In October 1962 elements of '43 Cdo RM' had taken part in a large-scale exercise in North Norway, a North Atlantic Treaty Organisation deployment which was part of '43 Cdo RM's' training, and in the same year '41 Cdo RM' carried out exercises in Lybia. One-sixth of the Corps – some 1,500 officers and men – was serving in ships in 1962. In 1963 '45 Cdo RM' was flown to Kenya as a respite from its tours in Aden, an exercise planned to coincide with elections there. '43 Cdo RM' this year landed in Normandy on an exercise with 29th Commando Light Regiment RA; and '41 Cdo RM' was on exercise in Norway.

Such brief descriptions might suggest a fairly easy year, but the major exercises were interspersed with demonstrations for both recruiting and training, and with ceremonial parades which demanded not only rehearsals but constant practice to keep up drill standards. Among these ceremonies and parades of 1963 in which the Corps took part were two visits by foreign heads of state and the Royal Tournament. A visit by the head of the Indonesian Marine Corps[22] suggests that official relationships between the UK and Indonesia were less strained than might have been expected. But most of the Borneo rebels – communist-inspired by this date, if not so the previous December – were regarded as diplomatically apart from the Indonesian government in Java.

A major part of the work on recruiting displays fell on the UK-based Commandos, although with no formal Brigade HQ in the UK, there was only a small administrative headquarters. Therefore much of the planning for displays and similar activities fell to the Commandos' own headquarters, along with the planning of Company and major exercises.[23] But for some years after Suez and during the operations overseas, press publicity for the Corps brought its reward in recruits. Other RM units also put on displays, and QMSI R. A. Moyse, whose family associations with the Corps went back almost 150 years, produced a tattoo attended by two old gentlemen. They were General Halliday, who had been awarded the VC in 1900, and one of the General's gunners, both in their nineties. When they were reintroduced, the younger man remarking that the General at 97 'was failing a bit'.[24]

Not long after '45 Cdo RM's' visit to Kenya there were a number of mutinies in East African armies, and on 4 January 1964 '41 Cdo RM' – as Spearhead Battalion – was urgently recalled from night leave, and pay-night leave at that, on a Thursday early in January, and flown to Kenya. It landed in Nairobi within 48 hours, and F Company then flew 130 miles to the foot of Mount Kenya; but the expected local mutiny did not materialise, and three weeks later '41 RM' moved to Tanganyika,[25] where '45 Cdo RM' had arrived in helicopters from HMS *Centaur*. These were anti-submarine 'helios' that had been stripped of their radar etc. A landing routine had been worked out for them during the carrier's passage from Aden, with the flight deck 'looking like Farnborough Air Show' – the *Centaur* was a strike carrier.[26] Meanwhile several ships' detachments and seamen platoons were landed to protect British lives.

Although '45' arrived at Dar-es-Salaam on 24 January, it did not land until dawn next day, when helicopters put some 50 commandos down near Colito Barracks. With them was the former commander of the local army, a British Army brigadier. Reveille for the mutineers that morning was sounded by Z Company's fire going into a safe area north of the barracks. HMS *Cambrian* also fired air-burst HE shells high over this waste ground. Some mutineers fired at the commandos, but after a 3.5-in rocket was fired into the guardroom, the barracks surrendered and was cleared. 'X' Company took over the airfield and 'Y' Company, with the Commando HQ, went into the town. That afternoon *Centaur*'s band played in Dar-es-Salaam's city square. Troops meanwhile had flown to other trouble spots and patrols landed in the bush from helicopters to round up small bands of mutineers. Relieved by '41 Cdo RM', '45 Cdo RM' then carried out two hot and dusty exercises from HMS *Albion* before returning to Aden on 25 February. The rear party of '41 Cdo RM' finally left on 6 April after a generous tribute by President Nyerere. The Marines and other British troops – several Army battalions had been landed in Uganda and Kenya – had been relieved by Nigerian troops. The Presidents of all three countries later expressed their gratitude for Britain's prompt response to the requests for help when their armies mutinied.

The speed of reaction 'at the Top' of the Ministry of Defence can only be commended on these occasions, but – as was the case before the Kuwait landings of 1961 – there were practical difficulties when the Commandant General's office was not in the main complex of the Ministry of Defence during the early 1960s, when communications using computers on the Internet, for example, were not as comprehensive as they would be in the 1990s. A more important difficulty could have arisen in the changing nature of Whitehall relationships. For what had sufficed in the decade after World War II, when old friends among senior RM officers and politicians might be able to cut official corners, could not be expected to run smoothly through the 1960s. As the British contracted their overseas commitments, the services could expect cuts in the amount of money available to them. General Riches, CG from 1959 to 1962, and his successor General Cartwright-Taylor (1962–5) both worked to bring about a more practical organisation, with the result that in the Corps' tercentenary year the following changes were made. On 1 April 1964 the Commandant General's staff were integrated with the Naval staff,[27] CG taking his place as head of a department, under the Vice-Chief of Naval Staff, with the heads of other departments for policy, operations-and-air, and operational requirements. Therefore CG's staff would be known as the Department of CGRM, with the Chief of Staff and the General Staff Branch, which moved into the main MOD office complex that April.[28] In this context one aspect of CG's authority, which was sometimes overlooked, was his power to draft Marines and their officers and to promote them, an authority vested in few of even the most senior officers of the services. The organisation would later be changed as of 1 April 1993, with *inter alia* the formation of the Headquarters Royal Marines (see chapter 12).

Royal Marines officers serving on the various planning and other staffs continued to carry out their functions at the higher levels of the Ministry. But with the integration at the top, their work was more effective as events in the next 30 years have proved.

On 7 February during the tercentenary year of 1964 there was a dinner in the Eastney Mess for the Board of Admiralty – a unique occasion, for the Board as such ceased to exist on 1 April, when the Ministry of Defence's Navy Department (MOD Navy) was created with an Admiralty Board of the Defence Council.[29] Other celebrations included ceremonial parades through Chatham, Portsmouth, Plymouth, Exeter and Poole; 'Beating Retreat' on Horse Guards Parade; and a parade for the Lord Mayor of London followed by an official reception in the City. Later the senior NCOs gave a banquet in Portsmouth Guildhall attended by the Captain General; and the tercentenary orchestral concert was also given in Portsmouth. Among the church services were those attended by the RMFVR in Scotland, Merseyside, Tyne and a Corps service in St Paul's Cathedral. Of the many momentous occasions that year the highlight was the Royal review at Buckingham Palace.[30] A dinner was also given by the Corps, at which Her Majesty the Queen granted the privilege to the Royal Marines of

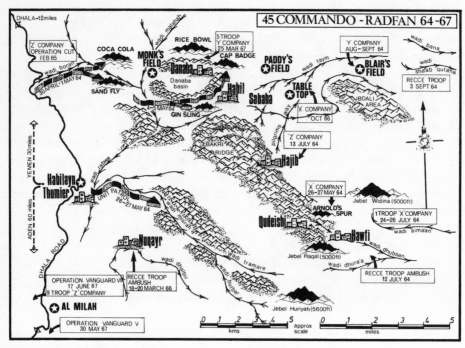

Principal operations by 45 Commando RM in the Radfan (Southern Arabia)

1964

30 April–May	Night infiltration to Sandfly and Coca-Cola with B Coy 3 Para under command.
4–5 May	Assault on Cap Badge.
11 May	39 Brigade formed 'Radforce' with 45 Cdo RM under command.
25–7 May	X Company flown to join 3 Para on Arnold's Spur, the Company moved down Wadi Dhubsan under fire, Mne D. Wilson was killed, Capt. R. Brind and 2 Mnes wounded before the Company successfully cleared the wadi and then withdrew. Heavy rain caused flooding and the further related army operations were cancelled.
July	Patrols and ambushes with X Coy on Jebel Widina, Y Coy on Jebel Haqia, Z Coy on Bakri Ridge and the Sp Coy as riflemen with X Company.
12 July	Recce Troop ambush two men in Wadi Dhura.
23 Aug–18 Sept	Patrols and ambushes in Danaba Bassin and Wadi Taym with Y Coy and Recce Tp on Blair's Field patrolling into Wadi Sha'ab. X Company at Dhala.

1965

Jan–Mar	Work with civil authorities and at one time the Commando's Headquarters had 1,500 all ranks under command. 45 Cdo being also strengthened to a Commando Group with one company at Dhala, one at Thumier, and the 3rd at Monk's Field patrolling area from Cap Badge to the head of Wadi Rabwa.
Feb	Operation 'Cut' in which patrols moved into the area north of the Radfan reaching to within 6 miles (9k) east of Dhala where one enemy base was found, after a fire-fight and aircraft attack the base was cleared. This operation cut the route of enemy reinforcements into the Radfan.
April–May	X Coy and Recce Tp at Ad Dimah (8 miles south of Dhala) using a deserted village of 80 houses as the firm base for their patrols.
June–July	Commando carried out extensive night patrolling during all their tours in the Radfan completing 305 major night patrols in one period of 8 weeks.

1966

Dec (65)	26 incidents were reported.
Jan	
April–May	patrols
Sept–Nov	Increasing activity by tribesmen with attacks on Commando positions, many long range fire-fights.

1967

Feb–Mar	66 patrols during this tour including 'Vanguard VI' operations.
May–June	'Vanguard' patrols including 'Vanguard VI' to keep roads free of tribesmen's ambushes.

remaining seated during the Royal toast when given in RM establishments as well as – following the Royal Navy's privilege – in ships.

A bomb attack on the High Commissioner in Aden on 10 December 1963 had opened a new wave of terrorism.[1] The Yemen border was closed, and to achieve the British government's political commitments in the area, other steps were considered. To recapitulate the position mentioned earlier, the British were responsible internationally for Aden Colony and the Protectorate. They were bound to keep law and order in these territories; and the rulers of states likely to form the Federation supported the British but did not have the formally expressed support of the people, as defined by the United Nations. The tribesmen, however, 'had no true loyalties to Britain or to the Federation, neither of whom had achieved much to show that they had the welfare of these people at heart'.[2] Among these tribes were several hundred fighting men who could be brought together in the Radfan, an area of 400 square miles east of the point where the road winds into the hills up to Dhala at 6,000ft on the frontier. For centuries tribes of the Radfan had exacted protection money from caravans on this road, including pilgrims heading north to Yemen and onwards to Mecca. 'Every tribes-man thinks himself a sultan' is a saying which sums up their fierce independence; and as they had always been 'agin' any government, they readily accepted Yemeni help against the Federation.

A strong force of three battalions of the Federal Regular Army (FRA) sup-ported by a Troop of British tanks, a few guns, some Royal Engineers and six Wessex helicopters from HMS *Centaur*, was sent into the Radfan in January 1964. It overwhelmed resistance and built a road into these hills, and by 31 January had reopened the Dhala road, suffering only a few casualties. It had then to be withdrawn to maintain the guard on the frontier further north, and tribesmen reoccupied their mountain strongholds.[3] This move the Egyptians and others exploited as a great victory, encouraging the tribesmen in the Radfan and elsewhere. Yemeni planes overflew the border in further provocation of the Federation's sheikhs, who on 19 March invoked the treaty terms for British protection.

The Commanding Officer of 45 Commando RM, Lieutenant-Colonel T. M. P. (Paddy) Stevens, had anticipated that his Commando might be called to operate in the Radfan, and had decided that a deep penetration at night offered the most likely chance of success. The Lieutenant-Colonel had served during World War II with 4 (Army) Commando when they led the infiltration in stygian darkness across the difficult *bocage* country east of the Orne (Normandy).[4] He now planned to seize a rocky hill feature known as the 'Cap Badge' in the Radfan. This dominates Danaba village, a tribesmen's stronghold and the fertile strip 3 miles by 9 miles running northwest/south-east. But before any major operation could be mounted, better intelligence was required. Preparatory work on mapping and route surveys was carried out from time to time by Royal Engineers with commando escorts, and in March X Company of '45' spent three weeks patrolling while under command of 4th FRA Battalion at Thumier, some 20 miles south of Dhala. This Arab village 'on the rugged one way track bounded by sunbaked rocky slopes', as the Dhala road has been described,[5] became the base for operations into the Radfan, and an Army camp was built north of Thumier. The Companies of '45 Cdo RM' came north to the village on 29 April, after carrying out rehearsals around the *jebel* (hill side) overlooking Little Aden.

That day a Special Air Service (SAS) patrol – an officer and nine men – had moved from an SAS Troop base established 5,000yds into the Radfan, to mark a dropping zone (DZ) for 'B' Company of the 3rd Parachute Battalion, which was under command of '45'. The paras were to land near 'Cap Badge' at midnight and occupy it by first light, while two Companies of '45 Cdo RM' made a night march to seize 'Rice Bowl', the hill north of 'Cap Badge', and a third company would occupy 'Sand Fly' as a firm base three miles east of Mile Post 26 on the Dhala road. The SAS patrol was discovered by a shepherd as it lay up short of its objective, and the tribesmen attacked it; despite the help of an RAF Hunter aircraft, guided by a hastily improvised ground-control system, the patrol was unable to break out until nightfall. By then its radio had been destroyed and the operator killed, and the patrol leader was killed as it broke out. Meanwhile '45 Cdo RM' had begun its march at last light.

The Arabs did not normally fight at night and this would catch them off guard. A diversionary attack by a platoon of the East Anglian Regiment, armoured cars and Royal Engineers had succeeded in forcing the tribesmen from positions overlooking Wadi Rabwa. From there the guns of 'J' Battery, 3rd Royal Horse Artillery, could get to a position where they could fire in support of the paras on 'Cap Badge'. This fire would be at the extreme effective range of their guns. Lieutenant-Colonel Stevens had appraised the commandos' approach route carefully, choosing Wadi Boran, the rougher and more northerly route, as the least likely to be defended. There had been a plan to use helicopters – 'fathers of grasshoppers' as the Arabs called the Wessex – but there were too few in Aden for logistic support should the operation be prolonged. Instead the Marines marched in, but they only carried three water bottles with 3 litres in all. They would have to be supplied by air next day, although there were only sufficient helicopters to supply two companies, the reason for limiting the number of companies making the infiltration. Some Sections of the Commando had GPMGs,[6] but the men would also have to 'manpack' the Vickers and mortars, and a few of the Recce Troop were attached to each Commando to help with this, the rest of the Recce Troop taking their usual route-finding role.

Four hundred commandos in two Companies had silently gone to ground from their trucks at Mile Post 26, waiting for darkness. They wore floppy hats like the soldiers based at Thumier, as indeed they did throughout the tropics. The ground was rough under foot even before they reached the wadi, and in the last of the daylight the Marines saw the black sides of the mountains towering over a dry river bed with its boulders among the scrub. The long file of heavily laden men moved slowly until they were five miles from the road, where 'Z' Company turned off for 'Sandfly'. Here they would protect the commandos' supply route from a 1,500ft hill, and before dawn they had begun to build their sangars and get the support weapons' ammunition in protected dumps.[7]

About 2235 hours a distorted message was received from Force Head-quarters, only indecipherable snatches as it reached the Commando's tactical HQ which was screened by mountains. The column then stopped, for X company's leading Section had reached the 'Puddle'. This stretch of shallow water had a sheer drop of several feet at its edge, over which two men fell. Once they were fished out, the column snaked along the vertical side of Wadi Boran. The going became easier by midnight as the moon rose to silhouette the hill 'Coca Cola, and on higher ground the Force Commander's message could be received.[8]

During the evening the Army Force Commander, Brigadier R. L. Hargroves (who was also Aden Garrison Commander), had received no news of the SAS patrol, and since all likelihood of surprise in marking the paras' DZ was lost, he cancelled the drop. Although the SAS Troop was willing to do the job somehow and the Para Company was equally prepared to jump into an unmarked DZ, such risks were felt not to be justified.[9] Lieutenant-Colonel Stevens had therefore to change the plan to meet new objectives set by the Brigadier. Major M. (Mike) Banks, a Himalayan climber of great experience, studied the air photograph of 'Coca Cola', the ridge some 1,500ft above the Tactical HQ's position. By the faint light of heavily shaded torches, he and Lieutenant-Colonel Stevens agreed the route was difficult, especially for men carrying the heavy weapons, but shortly after midnight the Major's X Company was on its way.

Followed by Y Company, it crossed two small valleys before entering a steep ravine leading up the side of the mountain out of the moonlight.[10] In only the starlight glow of a clear night, the pathfinder party with Major Banks picked its way neatly up the crags, only the occasional clatter of a loose rock falling and stifled curses breaking the silence. Then came a steep face, a difficult climb, as Major Banks – who was leading – had not had the usual opportunity to study the route beforehand. Strange lights were seen and men could be heard moving below the climbers, but no one followed them towards the upper climb.[11]

The commandos had been equal to this unexpected climb, and the Major was at the top in a short time. (Commandos no longer carried individual toggle ropes, but as some were specialist cliff climbers, lengths of rope were standard kit in mountain warfare.) On this occasion Major Banks, 'knowing that we would be in the mountains . . . took a rather tatty length of manilla rope, just in case'. It was this rope which the 'whole force heaved themselves up'.[12] Y Company followed X and by 0400 (1 May) both companies, Tactical HQ and men of the Recce Troop – over 250 in all – were on the ridge top. With two hours to go to daylight, 'X' Company moved a mile to the south down the ridge, while Y Company consolidated its position at the top of the climb.[13]

As the sun came up, they saw the great bowl of the Danaba basin, several miles from west to east. Around its rim were rock ridges over 1,000ft above the valley floor, and away to the east was the dominant feature of 'Cap Badge' mountain some 9,000ft above sea level. While the Marines were taking in the splendour of the view, five miles to the west eight men of the SAS patrol reached

Thumier and reported their action of the previous evening. Helicopters failed to find the bodies of the two dead.

Brigadier Hargroves reassessed the position. The Marines were established firmly on 'Coca Cola'. The lights they had seen had been flares carried by tribesmen hurrying to stand to in their defence positions. They probably had not heard the commandos because for some weeks Shackleton bombers had been overflying the Radfan at night. This had ensured that the tribesmen thought nothing unusual was happening when they flew over to cover any sound of the infiltration, and ready to drop illuminating flares if necessary. The Shackletons would also have cloaked the noise of the Paras' aircraft, but, as it was, the Company of 3rd Para (known by this date as 3 Para) came up by road to Thumier in the early hours of 1 May.

After five days in their hill positions, '45 Cdo RM's' Companies moved for the completion of their original infiltration with an assault on 'Cap Badge'. This feature could only be approached from the south-west and the south-east, other approaches being up sheer cliffs from the north or running close to Danaba. As so often in the Radfan, the ground dictated the tactics when Lieutenant-Colonel Stevens made his plan. X Company would take the most direct route along the south-west ridge. Y Company would follow and from the ridge's south end ('Gin Sling') give covering fire to X Company or to B Company of the paras, moving in what appeared from aerial photographs to be an easier sweep south of the mountain. Exposure in the heat and sweat of the mountains was taking its toll of the men's stamina, despite the hessian strips over their scrapes and some shade in enemy sangars they had occupied. Lieutenant-Colonel Stevens by one report had used a copy of The Times for shade.[14] The fact that the commandos could operate for days on end in the Radfan was a surprise to many people, not least to the tribesmen.

Although the supply point in Wadi Boran was further down this valley than expected, and despite their tiredness, X and Y Companies reached the Danaba basin some two hours after dark – they had hoped to be there at dusk.[15] But in this sort of country movement times were difficult to judge, for aerial photographs do not show all the difficulties on the ground. Y Company led through the dark after the paras had swung away on their route for the south face of 'Cap Badge'. There were three miles of difficult going, but as Captain Gavin Hamilton-Meikle and his second-in-command, Captain E. (Ted) Goddard both had some climbing experience and the value of '45 Cdo RM' as a mountain warfare Commando was apparent. They led Y Company up a nasty climb of 1,000ft to the top of 'Gin Sling' and were joined by the Commando's Tactical HQ an hour before dawn. Their GPMGs weighed only 2lb more than a Bren,[16] but each 200-round belt of ammunition festooning a gunner made movement difficult when this snagged on undergrowth, rocks or any other projections.[17] X Company, following Y, had also skirted a village, yapping dogs causing the Company to pause for a few moments – 'we were not the only ones around by any means [but] . . . contact was avoided'.[18] Once again X Company scaled pitches of almost sheer rock and as dawn broke had reached its objective: enemy sangars, well-used but unoccupied. Below them the Marines saw the moving flares held by tribesmen.

The Paras had a more difficult approach than expected, and were held up waiting for several batches of tribesmen to pass. Dawn found them in open ground short of their objective and out of radio contact with the Lieutenant-Colonel. They followed orders for this eventuality and fought their way against fierce resistance into the village of Habil Sabaha. Tribesmen on high ground above the village pinned down any movement between the mud huts and forts. Z Company of '45 Cdo RM' was then ordered up from the assembly area. Stripped to a minimum of equipment, the men clambered into an RAF Belvedere. This twin-rotor helicopter in theory carried some 22 men, but was heavily over-loaded by Z Company to get as strong a force forward as possible.

They landed below X Company's positions, for these were above a cliff which shielded the enemy sangars at its base. Hunter aircraft had spent an hour shooting up caves and sangars with 30-mm cannons and rocket fire, before the Belvedere arrived. It hovered long enough for the commandos to land and get their covering fire on the tribesmen's sangars, while the assault troops began a 3-hour climb down 1,500ft to the cliff base.[19] The tribesmen had retreated, leaving several dead, as 'Z' Company secured a landing zone for the Belvedere. This was near a village that would later be called Pegasus Village, El Naquil, close to the sprawling village which the paras had captured. The 'chopper' was on the ground for 10 minutes, while six wounded paras were brought from their uncomfortable shelters in the sticky heat to be 'casevacced' to safety. Two had been killed, including the second-in-command, who was shot as he gave morphia to a wounded Sergeant lying in the open. Z Company's commandos and the weary paras climbed back up the mountain side to reach the top of 'Cap Badge' at dusk.

The tribesmen had lost six dead and many wounded. Their warriors left the basin during the night, and next day, Y Company sent patrols to four villages, including Danaba. An uneasy calm settled in the Radfan and the Companies stayed another three days before being relieved.[20] They marched back to the assembly area 'at high speed partly because of everyone's desire to wash and partly because of the supercharged energy of Major David Langley (OC, Z Company), who had accidentally filled his water bottle with petrol during the night.[21] This company returned to Dhala, proud of its beards and looking forward to cold showers.

Marines would be skirmishing in the Radfan on and off for the next couple of years. X Company was later that May, serving under 3rd Para when the Marines combed the valley floor in the steep-sided Wadi Dhubsan south of their earlier actions. Here, deep in tribal territory, they were under steady fire from six light machine guns and some 40 rifles.[22] Captain Roger Brind was wounded while trying to put out a coloured panel to point the Hunter aircraft towards enemy positions, and a Marine was badly wounded when a 30-mm spent cartridge case fell from a plane, hitting his head.[23]

There were obvious difficulties in the control of a force in the Radfan, where radio communications were difficult in the mountains. Yet the team spirit of units was excellent, often in combined Para/Commando formations, as when Z Company in Wadi Dhubsan fought its way to rescue the para CO, Lieutenant-Colonel (later General Sir) A. (Tony) Farrar-Hockley, whose helicopter had been forced down by damage from rifle fire.[25] Supplies were flown in successfully by helicopter so often that '45 Cdo RM' knew the service as the 'Lloyd Chopper Milk Run' in 1964. In other years the nickname might change, but the service was almost invariably good.

Flying in the thin air of a high evening temperatures could be dangerous and the RAF set strict limits to the conditions in which helicopters could fly. Brought up on Air Marshall Trenchard's dictum that air power must be controlled at the highest level, the RAF could at times take caution to extremes; and – as Brigadier Leicester had experienced in planning the Walcheren landings (1944) – the lower levels of RAF command often needed time to consult higher authority before taking action. This and the Royal Marines' affinity with Naval flyers, led to better understanding between commandos and their Naval support squadrons than with RAF units, but there are many examples of close co-operation between commando units and the RAF. The first night assault by helicopter was made in the Radfan, however, by the Army Air Corps landing on an unlit and unmarked DZ.[28]

Over the next three years a series of terrorist groups emerged in Aden, and from as few as 36 incidents during 1964 there were nearly 3,000 in the 10 months to October 1967. The NLF (National Liberation Front), supported by the tribesmen, favoured violent resistance to the Federation, infiltrating supporters to many government bodies. FLOSY (Front for the Liberation of Occupied South Yemen) was supported by trade unions. For a time it joined with the NLF, but broke away in December 1966.

In the Radfan '45 Cdo RM's' Recce Troop had its first kills when terrorists approached an abandoned village on 12 July 1964. A Recce Troop patrol with eight days' food had been hiding in the overpowering heat by day and had laid ambushes at night.[29] By 1966, on its eleventh tour up country (14 September to 10 November), its members were old hands at the game, or rather the old hands had taught the new ones very well. The Commando's personnel changed over the years, each man doing a year's tour before being posted – with luck to a Commando in the UK – and by means of this 'trickle drafting' a formation could be based overseas almost indefinitely, ready for operations. At one time groups of new arrivals were formed into a Troop with an experienced officer and NCOs and could be together for a year.

On both nights of 13 and 14 October 1966, 'X' Company had been fired on by mortars, rifle fire and blindicide rockets. The Company's position on 'Table Top' was attacked from both sides. The senior NCO commanding the mortar Section, Sergeant Peter Littlewood, then had his 81-mm mortars firing, after an 180-degree switch, with commendable accuracy 'to despatch the leader of the Wadi Bana gang and wound five others'. Mortars by this time were usually placed in circular pits or in similar open sangars – the pits were double the size of the conventional half-circular mortar pits – with an eccentric bipod, giving a longer arm on which to rotate the weapon and its base plate as the 'third' leg formed a tripod. Defence fields of fire were registered all round the position and the known range and bearing of these ensured the subsequent accurate fire either of 81-mm or 3-in mortar bombs. The latter were fired on reduced charges which were liable with smoke bombs to splash phosphorus on the mortar crew, so copper sulphate jelly was kept handy to treat any burns.[30] These mortars each had a dial sight, which could be used to align several on to one target.

The Commandos by 1966 had largely replaced their Mobats by Wombats, the vehicle-borne version of this anti-tank weapon. In addition, the GPMG had replaced the Vickers medium machine guns. Although the GPMG's range of 1,400yds against the medium machine gun's 2,000yds meant that men in defended areas could less easily cover the gaps between them, unless they were sited closer together.[31] Other forms of standardisation, often a relief to Quarter-masters, sometimes led to difficult compromises, not least on footwear. Trials had been made of the Army boot, which had a moulded sole, and the black 'George' chukka-type boot, as replacements for the Marines' Naval boots and shoes, in order to reduce the amount of footwear a Marine had to carry around. This was also necessary because the volcanic rock of the Radfan cut the composite soles of SV boots to pieces. The issued footwear would be standardised on the Army-type boot of the 1960s with a directly moulded sole (DMS).[32] These did not compare – nor were they intended to – with the steel-stiffened climbing boots of that period, which were more suitable than DMS boots for climbing rock faces.

The more sophisticated equipment was also changing, for in mid-1965 the first Sioux light helicopters were with 40 Commando in the Far East. These Sioux were to be used as: 'spotter' aircraft; to lift GPMGs for a form of air cover;[33] and for recces, with both officer and NCO pilots (the first of whom had started training in June 1965). The following year there were three of these light 'helios' with each Commando. In 1968 they were brought together as the Commando Brigade Air Squadron,[34] and they were detached to Commandos as required (see Appendix 4). RM Pilots in this squadron wore the Army flying badge,[35] but there were some pilots in the Squadron who had been trained by the Fleet Air Arm. They were RN aircrew and wore Naval flyers' badges.

In September 1965 the 29th Commando Light Regiment RA was relieved in the Far East by 95th Commando Light Regiment RA, with batteries attached to Commando units from time to time. On one such deployment the 79th (Kirkee) Commando Light Battery RA was with '45 Cdo RM' in the Radfan in October 1966, when it fired its 105-mm pack-howitzers in anger for the first time. At other times commandos taught themselves from old handbooks how to fire an earlier field gun. This was carried around the mountains by local muleteers,[36] where not only helicopters but also the pack mule was a regular form of transport.

The Land Rover ¼-ton vehicles in Aden had armoured plate undersides as protection against the many mines in the Radfan or in town road blocks, and dated mostly from World War II. Assault engineers in the Middle East became familiar with a wide variety of anti-tank and anti-personnel mines, including a few hitherto unknown German experimental mines of the 1940s.[37]

The terrorists and tribesmen of Aden began to feud between themselves, NLF and FLOSY detainees jeering each other during the visit of a delegation from the United Nations in April 1967.[38] They would hurl more serious brickbats at each other and the security forces in the following months. Such disturbances led to the withdrawal from the mountains of '45 Cdo RM', which handed over to 9th Battalion South Arabian Army on 26 June, and left in a convoy of 108 vehicles.

The Company which had been at Dhala was withdrawn on 12 June, leaving defences 'so well dug in that one would have thought we had returned to trench warfare'.[39] Such defences were necessary when, for sound political reasons, a minimum of offensive action could be deployed. Before leaving Habilayn Camp in the Radfan a Beverly had struck a Mark VII mine as it taxied, and was left as a mute reminder of the hazards in this type of limited war. After the Israeli victory in the Six Day War (3 to 9 June) the Arab frustrations had reverberated in more violence in Aden itself. Strikes paralysed the port and FLOSY lost ground as a result of the withdrawal of Egyptian troops from the Yemen. The NLF would eventually negotiate with the British to take over South Arabia, but for '45 Cdo RM' the niceties of political negotiations were to mean some difficult tasks on the ground. In Aden Colony the Commando had carried out internal security duties on and off since September 1964, when not in the mountains. 'X' Company had been the first Commando unit on internal security (IS) duties to enter Sheikh Othman, on 17 April 1966; this trouble spot was north of Aden and had direct communications with dissidents further north.

The previous month (March 1966) the Intelligence Officer of '45 Cdo RM', Lieutenant Andy Moreland, with some of his Section, were attacked by a 36-grenade thrown into the back of the ¼-tonner in which they were travelling. But Marine Gordon Griffin kicked it off the vehicle, which accelerated away, leaving the grenade to explode in the street. This was typical of attacks on British forces, and '45 Cdo RM' knew what to expect when it took over the Crater district from 21 June to 8 August 1966. This great 'rabbit' warren of back streets was peopled by Arabs, Indians Pakistanis, Jews, Somalis and a few sophisticated terrorists. Special Branch Officers were the terrorists' particular targets, and '45 Cdo RM', among other British units, formed its own Special Branch Section, two 4-man teams under Lieutenant Malcolm Macleod moving mostly in plain clothes. Using disguised Land Rovers or smart private cars, they trailed uniformed patrols, or made snap raids. Three major cordon-and-search operations were based on information they had gleaned. But some warning of these got out before Lieutenant-Colonel F. C. E. Bye, the CO of '45 Cdo RM', tightened security within the operational headquarters, with its local police and other forces. Further operations were carried out in Crater[40] as well-practised drills. The terrorists usually worked in pairs with one acting as a lookout, and the other, the 'grenadier', waiting hours and even days for a suitable target. One 'grenadier' frequently stationed outside Sheikh Othman police station chewed *gat* – the red stem stimulant chewed by many South Arabians – ready to lob grenades over the wall.[41]

By September all service families had been evacuated and '45 Cdo RM' moved into their flats after leaving Little Aden, 'home' for the best part of seven years. Lieutenant-Colonel (later Major General) John I. H. Owen, had taken command that July and would have the responsibility of planning '45 Cdo RM's' final withdrawal. Before then in Ma'alla, the town of *Kutcha* huts and shanties, commandos were in heavily protected observation posts, each with four men, and on street patrols. These were all linked to the 'regimental' wireless net. Orders for Lieutenant-Colonel Owen were so repeatedly changed at this time that: while men on patrol, say, were following one set of instructions on when to open fire, he was briefing his company commanders on a second set, just before he was called to Brigade HQ for a third. Hence '45's' jingle:

> Shoot 'em on Monday,
> Don't on Tuesday,
> Withdraw on Wednesday,
> Smile on Thursday,
> Don't on Friday,
> Shot at on Saturday,
> Crisis on Sunday.

A Second Lieutenant of '45' was killed on one of his first overseas patrols in Aden, not long before '42 Cdo RM' arrived aboard HMS *Bulwark* on 11 October. In their distinctive olive green jungle dress, they took up positions in the 'Pennine Chain' north of the airport. This was the line the British had held since September, for its trenches, road blocks and OPs sealed off the peninsula from the north and kept the airfield out of mortar range of the terrorists. The NFL was busy defeating FLOSY; the Southern Arabian Army 'left' the Federation and joined the NLF, and in a final fury at not getting terms agreed at Geneva, mortared '42 Cdo RM' at Tawahi on 11 November 1967. Marine Blackman has the unfortunate distinction of being the last British serviceman to be seriously wounded in Aden during this incident.[42]

Shortly before midnight on 28 November 1967, '45 Cdo RM's' first of 13 Hercules plane loads became airborne; '42' left in their helicopters on 29 November, having been the last unit in Aden. But an RM Landing Craft 'hand' slipping his bow line from the quay was probably the last British serviceman to step off Aden rock, when this craft brought out the last British official to leave Aden.

The epitaph to the servicemen of all British forces in Aden, including the officers and men of the Commandos and ships' detachments killed in this 7-year war, was written by a Fleet Street journalist, Wilfred Sendall, who described the troops in Aden as 'men whose steadfast patience had been tested and found to hold firm on thousands of unrewarded, forgotten occasions'.[43]

From their first commissioning commando carriers proved their worth and from 1968 to 1971 there was usually one in the Mediterranean and another based on Singapore, as the British withdrew from 'east of Suez'. Apart from the RM detachments serving in these ships, the last major detachment from a 'fixed-wing' carrier in the Fleet was withdrawn from HMS *Centaur* which paid off during 1965. Although *Hermes* would later become a commando carrier, for those who served on her in the late 1950s and early 1960s there was the familiar round of guards and port visits.[1] Comparisons between these and the ships' routines of 20 years earlier suggest that the guards were as smart and the evolutions equally well executed, although there was a lot less time needed to keep the uniforms of the 1960s as smart as the brass and blancoed 'gear' of inter-war vintage (see Appendix 3). The major change, however, was the introduction of Lovat uniform in April 1964, when battledress was phased out and later the working rig became a woollen pullover. Lovats were made of cloth in a shade of green and in a style similar to Army service dress. The 'woolly pullies' were not suitable for formal parades, and 'blues' (of an improved material for other ranks from 1974) would be used only for major ceremonial parades, Lovats being worn for other ceremonials.

Accommodation was improved in ships designed in the 1960s: the *Leander*-class frigates, for example, had bunk beds, separate dining 'halls' – men would no longer sleep and eat in the same mess deck – and air-conditioning in all the operational and living quarters of the ship. There was also new weaponry in the frigates, whose twin-4.5in mounting was fully automatic, and the linked fire-control radar had revolutionised the old director control systems. The Seacat ship-to-air missile launcher had its control system in the *Leander*-class and there was an anti-submarine mortar, as well as a helicopter equipped for anti-submarine warfare (ASW) work.[2]

Detachments continued to land from time to time, as they had done in previous decades. In July 1964 the detachment from the frigate HMS *Whirlwind* landed at Georgetown (West Indies) to temporarily reinforce the garrison.[3] In November the survey ship HMS *Protector* put her detachment ashore on the Falkland Islands, which was the start – or rather the restart – in modern times of the Royal Marines involvement in the Falkland Islands, where they had served in the 19th century. Two years later a plane hijacked by 'activists' with more enthusiasm than experience was flown to the Islands. The members of the gang were subdued on discovering that there was no modern airport, and the pilot with great skill had to put this civilian airliner down on a road in bad weather. When they scrambled out of the plane, the hijackers were further nonplussed because the locals stood around smoking and did not flee from the guns. Several Marines were caught up in this incident but with tact and restraint avoided what might have been a nasty little fire-fight.[4] The hijackers eventually surrendered and the plane took off later from the racecourse. After this incident a small RM garrison, Naval Party 8901 served in the Islands and were serving there in 1982 when the Argentineans invaded.

Other units in the 1960s landed in the West Indies. In 1968 the Wasp helicopter of the frigate HMS *Eskimo* landed a Section of her Marines on an island to intercept armed Cuban dissidents, and from this island the Marines in a Gemini inflatable crossed to the Cubans' island, surprising them at first light.[5]

Reference has been made to the short-service commission introduced in 1964 for pilots. The short-service commission for general duties officers wishing to serve only five years on the active list, gave them an option to complete ten. A number of these officers, according to their abilities, were given the opportunity to transfer to the General List, and by 1979 they represented about one-third of the officers recruited. Almost all the General List officers were selected in the 1970s by interview, from candidates with a minimum education qualification of five O-levels and two A-levels, but University Cadetships – the cadet being paid while he graduated – have been awarded since 1968.[6] Other young officers have also been selected for full-time university studies sponsored by the Corps. All General List Captains and Majors normally served in the 1990s until their they were 50, but they were liable to be recalled until they were 60. Corps commissions were also awarded to selected Marines over 21 (the age limit having been lowered from 23), and some were awarded short-service commissions for which they could be selected up to the age of 25. Warrant Officers and senior NCOs up to the age of 34 were eligible for Special Duty List (SD) commissions, but in 1968 the age level was raised by four years and provision made for RSMs to be commissioned up to the age of 44.[7] A proportion of these SD officers have carried out General List duties over the years.

Not surprisingly perhaps the officers of the late 20th century were men of widely different interests and had a dedication to fitness which distinguishes them from earlier generations. Some have felt that the net for their recruitment in the early 1970s may have been cast too widely, but if that was so, the position has righted itself in more recent years. Indeed the standard of intelligence in all ranks equates with the national trend, and the Corps was able in the 1970s to recruit the numbers required. This was not always possible in the 1960s, when full employment and comparatively better pay in civilian jobs made service life less attractive.

Since 1958 the Corps has also recruited a number of juniors over 16 and under 17½ years of age. They receive a similar training to an adult recruit but after April 1971 recruits who joined before they were 17½ had the right to confirm their original engagement of nine years followed by three in the reserves, or of reducing it to an enlistment for three years.[8] The previous year the Corps had introduced a 4-year engagement but all men joining for less than a 9-year commitment were paid lower rates. There were in the late 1970s other option points during a recruit's training at which he could leave the service. While this is an understandable approach for junior recruits, who should not be expected to commit themselves for nine years, there seemed no doubt that the opt-out rate reflected the tendency in the 1970s in all walks of life to try a job and then change it if you did not like it. In the 1990s, as we will see, the Corps could recruit the numbers it required. There was also in the 1990s the opportunity to learn at first hand what the service is like, when potential recruits were given an introductory course of a few days before they signed up. This substantially reduced the opt-out rate during recruit training.

Those who completed their 30 weeks of training as Marines were ready to take their place in the Brigade or other branches of the Corps, unlike the Army recruit, who completes his training in the first three months with his battalion.

As for the glory, there were few campaign medals in the 1960s and 1970s. Yet in Malaya in the early 1950s a day's service in that theatre entitled a man to the General Service Medal 'which was issued with your bedding the day you arrived'.[9] A Royal Marine received the Naval General Service Medal with the bar appropriate to the campaign in which he served, and a few who were seconded to the Army received the Army General Service Medal. The Naval General Service Medal was always awarded with a bar, of which there were 15 from 1915 to 1964 including: Palestine 1936 to 1939 and 1945 to 1948; Malaya; Cyprus; the Near East ('Suez'); the Arabian Peninsula; and Brunei. The Army General Service Medal of 1918 to 1964 had 16 bars including those for the campaigns mentioned above. After the Malayan campaign, longer service in a theatre was required to qualify for a bar, with 16 weeks in Cyprus, for example, to gain the medal with this bar. From October 1964 the General Service Medal was awarded retrospectively in some cases, with bars for Borneo (1962–6), Radfan (April to July 1964, South Arabia (1964–7), Malaya (1964–6), and, from 1969, Northern Ireland, Dhofar and Vietnam. There was also a war medal for service in Korea between 1950 and 1953.[10]

The strength of the Corps fell from 11,000 in 1953 to around 8,500 in the 1960s; and after the 1974 defence review, was reduced to about 7,000, with the RM Reserve at just over 1,000 before the subsequent increase to an establishment of 8,000.[11] In the 1960s and 1970s the numbers of general duty Marines were usually up to establishment but vehicle mechanics, the largest of the Corps' specialist trades, were at times below establishment. Printers, armourers, illustrators (who worked – and work – with the Intelligence Sections of units) and a few senior NCO technicians made the Corps self-sufficient in these specialist trades. And when vehicle drivers were included, the technical branch amounted to some 10 per cent of the Corps' strength.[12] In the late 1970s, however, some drivers were trained in their units, as were some signallers, for no longer were all signallers in lower formations from the Signals Branch. Although training all such specialists away from their units had been expensive, it had proved worthwhile when drivers came to cross a difficult stretch of beach; and Marine drivers on occasions could take their vehicles over routes which the Army found impassable.

The co-ordination between Royal Marines and Army forces in amphibious operations continued, although there were fewer opportunities in the late 1970s for the Army to carry out amphibious exercises than there had been in earlier years. Nevertheless amphibious warfare had a higher priority than it was given in the 1930s, and in 1964 the first Commodore flew his pennant in the flagship of the Royal Navy's Amphibious Force. His chief of staff was a major RM, and a close understanding had been established between the Brigade and this Force by the late 1960s.

Something of the methods employed in the late 1960s by commandos operating from their LPH to establish patrol bases in a jungle well behind an

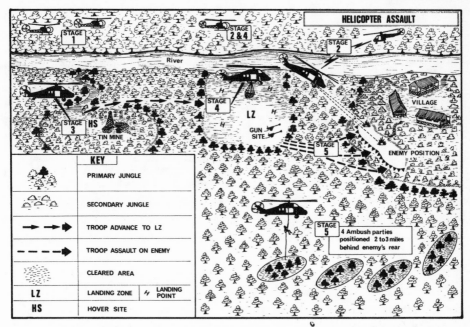

This simplified example of a company exercise with an Airborne Command Post is based on operations in Vietnam, when there were clearings cut for landing zones to bring in guns (in other types of operation the commandos would abseil 200ft (60m) down ropes from choppers above the trees, only cutting an LZ when they needed to be lifted out).

enemy's forward positions, can be summarised in six stages. In stage 1 two Sioux helicopters made a recce of the target area. In one Sioux was the assault Company's OC and the Unit's Air Support Officer (UASO). In the second Souix was the Forward Officer Bombardment. In stage 2: two Wessex with commandos manning GPMGs mounted in the side doors and firing rockets, strafed the enemy positions. Stage 3: Nos 1 and 2 Troops commanded by the Company's second-in-command and joined by the FOO, jumped 6ft down from other Wessex over the 'Hover site', to establish a base from which to set up a landing zone (LZ). They advanced in stage 4 to the intended LZ; cleared it of tall trees and of scrub at four landing points, where tree stumps were marked with panels to warn pilots of dangers to their helicopters' rotors. At this stage the Company OC was still airborne and able to call in No. 3 Troop to the LZ or to the 'Hover site' as appropriate. Stage 5: essential stores and light artillery were landed in the LZ while assault Sections moved against any enemy threatening the LZ from positions outside it. Stage 6, the final stage, involved positioning ambush parties

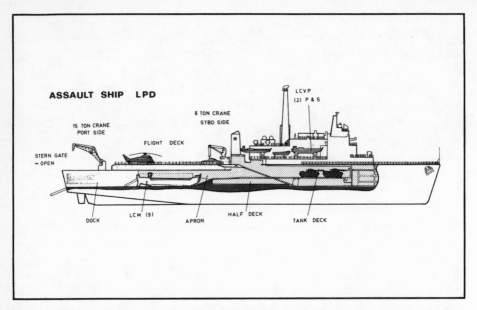

The four LCM are taken aboard by flooding the dock while the ship keeps on steerage way and are launched in the same way, when docking both ship and LC crews require good seamanship. The ship also has headquarters facilities and communications. The quadruple launchers of the Sea Cat missiles are positioned with 3 on the after end of the superstructure and one forward.

who abseiled to these positions some miles beyond the LZ. Naval gunfire was called in by the FOO at any time it was required during the establishment of the LZ. The dogs with the Company had been trained to jump or abseil with their handlers into the LZ and later during such operations to abseil into ambush positions.

Proof came in 1967 that the potential ability to make landings in this way could be maintained below the enemy's horizon – although no doubt on his satellite pictures – for long periods. That year '41 Cdo RM', with a battery of 29 Commando Regiment RA and 848 Naval Air Commando Squadron, spent 100 days in HMS *Albion* off the African coast. Their sailing had been such a pierhead jump from exercises in Scotland that their tropical kit had to be collected from Gibraltar.[13] But for the development of a major assault the Army needed to land tanks and for this the LPDs *Fearless* and *Intrepid* were commissioned, originally largely for use by the Army.[14] Purpose-built to flood down so that they could float out their LCMs, these LPDs each could carry four LCM Mark 9s and four LCVPs on davits[15] (see Figure). They also had flight deck facilities for five Wessex and could carry in a typical load 15 tanks, 7 × 3-tonners and 20 × ¼-tonners. HMS *Fearless* had completed her working up exercises in 1966 and was followed a year later by HMS *Intrepid*.[16] As these ships were originally to work mainly with the Army, they had a high proportion of Army personnel in their complement, but over the years the Amphibious Detachment, albeit smaller than in the 1960s, was drawn almost entirely from Royal Marines.

The LPD was also equipped as a headquarters ship able to control forces ashore in the early stages of a landing (as we will see in chapter 11). The LPHs had a dual role in anti-submarine and amphibious warfare, and therefore might have been expected – as their successors would do in 1982 – to remain in the area of a landing.[17] As a result of cuts in the National Defence budget amphibious shipping was limited but in 1976 the Amphibious Forces' command carried out exercises with car ferries.[18] Ferries present some problems, for the modern car ferry uses purpose-built terminals, but these were overcome by bridging the gap using Rhino-type ferries with inboard/outdrive engines. The LCM Mark 9 had some rudimentary living accommodation and was designed to carry two Centurion tanks or four 3-tonners,[19] these craft were not of the size of World War II LCTs, being only intended for coastal work. The LCVPs could provide mobility for Commandos where vehicles were impractical. The difficulty in protecting crews and their cargo personnel from the weather was largely overcome – as a result of experience and trials in Norway – by a modular canopy fitted over the LCVP's well, and similar protection for personnel in LCMs was developed.[20]

The Beach Unit aboard an LPD was capable of laying so-called 'beach roadways' (trackway) using the Michigan 175 tractor fitted with road laying equipment handled by its driver from his 'cab'.[21] During the 1960s the Beach Unit included some Army personnel, affectionately known – as are all soldiers – as Percy Pongos. The Units have evolved since 1946, when after World War II a few Royal Marines were trained to retain the Royal Navy's know-how on beach control. By the 1970s small RM parties from the Units provided the control for personnel and vehicles crossing a beach, a task which could involve every man in the Unit, the cook on occasions leaving his makeshift galley to direct tanks to taped routes of a beach exit.[22]

Working with the Amphibious Squadron from time to time in the 1960s and 1970s was the Raiding Squadron. During the severe flooding in Bangladesh (at the time East Pakistan), 17 men of the 2nd Raiding Squadron were flown from the UK to assist in the training of Gemini coxswains for local forces.[23] By the end of the 1970s the Raiding Squadron with its Rigid Raiders was carrying out operations in Hong Kong to assist the garrison – including '42 Cdo RM' in 1979 – in stemming the flow of illegal immigrants. The Rigid Raiders with their Cathedral-hulls and high powered outboards, could on occasions sacrifice surprise in the noise of a high-speed approach. But if conditions were right, these craft could put their raiders some way from the water's edge, for they could be driven hard up a beach. Some other aspects of the development of raiding craft are briefly explained in the Squadron's Unit history (Appendix 4).

Among techniques developed during the 1960s and 1970s were: the use of ground radar by reconnaissance Troops; the command and control of ground forces, from helicopters; Forward Air Controllers also working from helicopters over a battle; and new designs of Arctic equipment were developed by Marines. The Forward Air Controller (FAC) as a specialist was a new concept of the late 1960s, although commando officers had carried out such work as part of their general duties. In jungle (the 'ulu' as Marines called it) where you can see nothing if you are on the ground, the helicopter gave the FAC an aerial observation post, from which he could direct fighters onto a target. The close personal liaison between the pilots and their FAC enabled them to use 'the freedom of the telephone conversation', while the FAC kept one eye on the strike aircraft and the other on the target. For example, the information passed to the aircraft might be: 'target immediately to the north of the lone *Kampong*'.[24] In Aden an RM FAC had himself landed when ground communications broke down near the Yemen border, to control a successful air strike only a few days before the final withdrawal. This action ensured that one 'Royal' at least was the last British serviceman out of the Protectorate, as all other British troops had been withdrawn by then into Aden Colony.[25]

One unusual job fell to the RM detachment in the Falklands in the early 1970s. The SS *Great Britain* lay there as a hulk, built in the 1840s her engines had been taken out in 1882. She was the first deep-sea steamship with screw propellers, watertight bulkheads, an electric log and balanced rudder. The old ship was salvaged by taking out her masts, a job needing more than simple work with blocks and tackles, before she was floated on a 2,600 ton pontoon Mulus III. The civilian salvage officer had been a shipwright aboard HMS *Exeter* when she was repaired after the River Plate action, and made use of the Marines' skills. Sergeant 'Yorky' Stott was the first man for over 50 years to climb the main mast with its great iron spar 110ft wide, still suspended from an iron bridle in 1970. Other Marines helped in the salvage work and in three weeks the old ship was ready for her voyage to the UK on the football-pitch sized pontoon.[26] She arrived safely in Bristol some months later.

The political aspects of the conflict in Northern Ireland are too complex to be considered in detail in the last part of the 20th century but here can be recorded a number of factual accounts of the Royal Marines' dispositions in the security effort. (State papers on these operations will not be available for some years, but see writings of D. Barzilay.[1])

The first Commando to go to Northern Ireland in the 1969 emergency was '41 Cdo RM', they were the Spearhead Battalion of the Strategic Reserve when sent to Divis Street, Belfast on 28 September. The garrison Battalions in Northern Ireland had been prepared for trouble during riots, after attacks on electricity and other installations. Through the summer of 1969, however, Civil Rights marchers had continued to clash with Protestants, and in August soldiers had been first sent to riot areas. This for a time quietened the situation, but in serious riots during October from time to time '41 Cdo RM' stood to without shields or other riot gear, until the Commando was recalled to the UK after six weeks. During this deployment the anti-riot drills – known as: internal security drills – used in the earlier decades were found to be totally inadequate for the conditions in Northern Ireland, and were therefore completely revised.

The following year in the first 4-month tour by Royal Marines in Northern Ireland, '45 Cdo RM' arrived in Belfast on 1 June (1970).[2] They were quartered in what would become all too familiar accommodation. HQ and 145th (Maiwand)

Commando Light Battery RA were in police stations. The quartermaster and B-Echelon were in a Territorial Army Camp at Ballykinler (south of Belfast). The HQ Company which administered the Commando and had specialists, not to be confused with the Commando's HQ, along with the Support Company, 'X' and 'Y' Companies were billeted in hutted camps or the gaunt factory buildings ill-suited in those days as living quarters. '"Home" for the average Marine was a sleeping bag in a crowded room, on immediate call should trouble break out.'[2] Trouble all too frequently did break out, but a few examples must suffice for the many incidents in the 1970s.

On Friday, 26 June 1979, '45 RM' had been in Belfast nearly two months and was responsible for a district which included the Crumlin Road as its focus. To the north was the Ardoyne, where Roman Catholics had their Citizens' Defence Committee, and to the south was a Protestant area. From the rows upon rows of small brick houses to the south came a procession of eight Orangemen's Lodges, each group of members headed by a band; and with the crowd following them, there were over 2,000 Protestants. The Commando, with 1st Battalion King's Own Scottish Borderers and 1st Battalion Royal Scots, had stood to that evening, when about 2030 hours the first volleys of stones fell among the leading band. Some 350 young Catholics hurled more rocks but were prevented from closing with the Protestants by No.11 Troop of the Support Company. (All Commando Support Companies were trained and operated as Rifle Companies with infantry roles in Northern Ireland). The Troop's 4-tonner and trucks across the street blocked a side road, but there was little protection against stones, catapulted rivets, iron piping and broken sheets of glass. This glass was flicked to skim below knee height along the street at Marines' shins. Nearly every man was injured and their 2nd-Lieutenant was hit in the mouth by a brick flung a mere five yards. The Sergeant took over while this wound was dressed, before the lieutenant resumed his place in the line.[3] By now there were some 1,000 people battling to get at each other.

Further down the road 400 commandos held 2,000 Catholics from the fray, and the Royal Ulster Constabulary stood off 3,000 Protestants. The confrontation lasted through the night,[4] but as dawn broke on a summer's day, the mobs went home to the south waving Union Jacks as the Republicans carried the Irish tricolour in the opposite direction.

Saturday passed in an uneasy calm until Protestant marches outside the Commando's area sparked off shooting in the Ardoyne: a Marine of Y Company 'was chatting quietly to a Mick ... when all of a sudden shots rang out and he collapsed, dead ... I dodged behind my truck ... letting off six rounds which seemed to do the trick'.[5] The Operations Officer arrived in Y Company's area and the first two close shots clipped past him. Less fortunate was one of '45's' medical staff, PO F. (Freddy) MacLaughlin, for as the bullets flew he was calmly giving first aid to a civilian, and as he got his patient into a clearly marked ambulance, shots ripped through its side and wounded him. The Petty Officer was awarded the George Medal for his courage.

The CO, Lieutenant-Colonel Roger Ephraums, brought in five Companies and his 'Rover Group' from the police station to a patch of waste land by the road. The Companies had subdued the outbreaks of violence by late afternoon, but at 2100 hours a drunk ran a stolen bus into a pub and trouble broke out again. The 23 men of No.5 Troop, with tear gas, arc lights and snatch squads made seven arrests, then drove the mob back 500yds. From this mob a gunman fired about eight shots, one lodging in a Marine's equipment, but finding that the Marines were undaunted, the mob turned to looting and burning. The smell of burning tyres mingled with the smoke of fires drifted along the streets. One group of rioters broke into a wine shop, and, in a wild mood, attacked the police station, where the Commando's Tactical HQ – 20 men, without the 'Rover Group' – held off some 300 people. During the riots, Chief Superintendent Bill Leget RUC, was shot in the neck, having bravely gone into the Protestant crowd to calm them.

On Sunday morning 'Y' Company cleared the bus from the pub and used it as a billet, now that the whole Commando could settle down for some rest. The 'Rover Group' slipped back unnoticed into the police station, and when Protestants again attacked the station, '45 RM' repelled them. In the following weeks the Commando worked hard to establish good relations with both factions, and selected teams – 'with an ability to consume vast quantities of tea'[6] – toured the localities, calming the residents. The RSM[7] organised entertainments, including outings for children to a farm, 'more exhausting than riot control' in the view of some helpers. The Assault Engineers repaired both a 94-year-old's home and a community centre, among other helpful jobs. At this time the Recce Troop, with both 17th/21st Lancers and the Life Guards, formed two of many close and happy relationships between the Commando and other services, before the Marines returned to the UK

These tours demonstrated that Royal Marines could be used in Army roles and the Army no longer opposed there being 'more than two Commandos RM'.[8] Commandos were with Army units in operation 'Motorman', the largest operation since Suez, when some 15 Battalions and Commandos entered the No-Go areas of Londonderry and Belfast on 31 July 1972. But in most daily routines the Section commanders and junior NCOs took the brunt of responsibility. For 'Motorman' the 170 men of a reinforced Company of five Troops were organised into foot patrols of an NCO and five Marines, observation point (OP) lookouts, vehicle patrols, reserves and the Company base guards.[9] In an OP heavily sandbagged and protected from missiles that might be lobbed into it, and from rifle fire, three or four men could watch an area for the unusual event or simply signs of a pending riot. An OP was manned by the same Marines on each duty, so that they were familiar with the daily round on their patch: the milkman's arrival, dustmen, paper boys and regulars going to the pub. When anything suspicious was seen from the OP, the foot patrols in the area would be given the task of investigating it. This was a swift reaction without reference to their Company HQ, when, say, children were causing 'aggro', the vernacular for aggressive behaviour. The observer who had tasked the patrol would continue to watch its movements and pass information on events in the immediate area of the incident in case the children, for example, were bait for a gunman's ambush. In the meantime a second observer would take over the general watch of the area.

When 40 Commando RM was in the New Lodge district in 1972, one OP was placed in the motor room of lifts high on a tall block of flats, with observers cramped between two 1,000-gallon water tanks. Here and in other OPs the observers did spells of duty for 3½ days, while the other half of the Troop made up foot patrols. The patrols might be called in at times to be briefed by Company HQ for a house search, a 3-hour job. During this a gunmen could move into position for a shot at any Marine in the cordon, whose concentration had wandered in the tedium of waiting. If the searchers found a weapon or explosives, then the nearby residents – mostly women and children – would cause distractions in any way they could. One old lady of 72 turned up frequently, as did others on these occasions. The golden rule was never to let anyone leave or enter a house until the patrol commander had sorted out the situation. The attic would be searched early, for many terraces of houses were linked by 'mouseholing' through the dividing walls. Any suspects were taken away in a closed Land Rover or an Armoured Personnel Carrier, when again the OP would keep the searchers informed of what was happening nearby. Searchers themselves would be searched before they entered and on leaving a house to make clear that there was no pilfering.[10]

Patrols always moved with 'one foot on the ground', half the team being in firing positions as the other half moved. At night, patrols had the advantage of the Starlight Scope, among other image intensifiers through which observers and patrols could see at night almost as well as if it was daylight. Areas were normally manned day and night by a Company of 100 commandos who provided the patrols and were also in the OPs. Unless they and other patrols were properly briefed, however, the silent patrols moving without their combat kit could have a nasty accident.

The Assault Squadron had also played their part in these operations, and on the night of 31 July four LCMs from HMS *Fearless* made the 25-mile passage through fog to land the Royal Engineers' armoured vehicles (AVREs). Escorted by the minesweeper HMS *Gavington*, the craft reached their landing beach just before midnight, and the AVREs came ashore over trackway laid by hand so as not to attract undue attention. When they had cleared the barriers in the Creggan and Bogside of Londonderry, their part in operation 'Motorman', they returned to the beach and were taken off before dawn.[11]

For 40 Commando RM there was a significant improvement between 1972 and 1973 tours, reflecting their improved techniques and the increasing difficulty the terrorists experienced in moving weapons and explosives. Three of '40 RM's' Marines had been killed and 17 injured in 1972, but there were no casualties in 1973. In this year nearly four times as many cars (115,000) and 50 per cent more derelict houses (3,133) were searched,[12] and the 91 terrorists lifted out of circulation were nearly twice the 1972 number. But the level of violence fluctuated, and in 1976, when '40 RM' was in South Armagh, six Marines of 'A' Company were wounded when Crossmaglen Police Station was bombarded by a 10-barrelled mortar on a flat truck. This had been positioned out of sight of the OP sangars, and the bombs were fired electrically to give a ripple-effect which reduced the stress on the launch platform. Two bombs lodged in the attic and Staff Segeant Bruce, an army Ammunition Technical Officer (ATO), disarmed them despite his rain-wet hands and having first to prise them from the ceiling. For his work with '40 RM' and 3 Para he was awarded the George Medal.[13]

In their country patrols the commandos were deployed in a familiar style of operations. Patrols and observation were routine work. Each patrol might spend two or three days in the field, being lifted in and out on occasions by helicopter. From their base they could dominate an area, and when the OP saw a pig lorry parked across the road at Finnegans Cross, the CO ordered the nearby railway line closed. Air photographs were taken but by nightfall there was insufficient information to put in a clearance party.

The Recce Troop was therefore brought in, to reinforce the stake-outs watching for any further attempts to place booby-traps. The Troop was landed by a Puma and a Scout helicopter (fitted with an infra-red searchlight) without using lights. Early next day (30 August 1976) a small explosion in a derelict house further up the road drew attention to a possible ambush, and the clearance party was prepared for this after finding no explosives in the lorry. In the house the party found 60lbs of Frangex, a mixture of fertiliser with other readily available ingredients to make a crude but effective explosive. It had been packed in a beer keg with 50lbs of scrap metal and a booster charge, which might be Semtex to set off the 'home made' explosive. The bomb was to have been exploded by radio control, and the early morning blast had been the booster charge going off but failing to set off the main charge. 'C' Company, the 'Railway Children', continued to guard this railway to Dublin until the end of the tour.

In all their operations in Northern Ireland, the Marines have found that 'humour plays a big part ... tight discipline with good humour and a laugh sometimes has more effect than ten rubber bullets'.[14] Typically members of a Republican club, emboldened in their comfortable surroundings, were militant in their non-cooperation when surprised by RM patrols. Surprised, that is, in a raid successfully mounted by a simple stratagem rather than the use of highly technical equipment. Once the first member's bluff of bravado had been called by his arrest, others readily gave their names and addresses. At other times street patrols had to exercise great self-control in the face of screamed taunts from frenzied women and provocation from children. And when a half-brick has smashed his teeth, burst a lip and broken his nose, the personal self-discipline of the serviceman could only be admired when he did not retaliate with the maximum force at his disposal.

The localities of these operations where by no means all mean back streets, as many people imagined. The Turf Lodge estate, for example, was an area of neat modern semidetached houses, where a burning bus was as incongruous as it would have been in a housing estate in Manchester or Birmingham. Also, just as in such operations anywhere in the UK, the actions of a junior corporal came under the eye of government in Northern Ireland. In minutes an incident could be reported to the Secretary of State and within the half-hour be the subject of reports in the Cabinet Office.

The number of British troops in Ireland had been reduced from nearly 22,000 at the time of 'Motorman'[15] to 13,000 in 1979, while the equipment to contain terrorism from extremists of all persuasions had become highly technical. A number of items can be described, as can some riot gear. Of the latter, CS smoke caused something of a furore when first used, but by the mid-1970s it was no longer used in a grenade, although a rubber-cased shell of CS pellets could be fired to lay smoke over a wide area.[16] The Makrolon shield was a major breakthrough, for the holder could see through it while rocks and petrol bombs bounce off it, and it was as effective as the shield of a Roman legionary.[17] The development over the years of helmets made in composite materials with visors, for use in riots, and special boots, protective gloves and associated kit, substantially reduced minor injuries. The flak-jacket protected men from low velocity bullets and blast fragments. The 1.5-in baton round of rubber or PVC proved extremely useful; at 25 to 50yds a good shot could hit individuals, bruising their bodies, and a bad shot could cause more painful bruises. Night could be turned into day for such shots by the 3.8-million candlepower of the Nitesun searchlight fitted to helicopters; it could also be used with infra-red light, when a man with the necessary goggles could see the 'illuminated' area.[18] There were also infra-red cameras which gave pictures that revealed where vegetation had been trampled in laying a mine. For surveillance over riots, helicopter-borne TV cameras transmitted pictures for tape recording to help later identification, and for evidence of what precisely happened in an incident. There was also Radar on vehicles (the Claribel Shot Direction Indicator) which picked up the fire of a sniper, and indicated the direction on a clock dial to show where the fire came from.[19]

Terrorist organisation and equipment had also grown more sophisticated, and, with the international exchange of technology between such groups, continued to do so. The Security Forces, however, recovered many thousands of conventional weapons, including rifles bought in 1909 for the Ulster Volunteer Force, 7.62-mm and other modern rifles as well as the so-called Loyalists' home-made 9-mm sub-machine-gun.[20] In such operations before 1981 11 Officers and Marines of the Commandos were killed and over 80 wounded, in 22 tours.

Yet for many Royal Marines these tours meant longer separation from their families than when they were on accompanied tours abroad. After each Ireland tour many Royal Marines, after a brief spell in the UK, found that an exercise in Norway made a refreshing change.

The north European terrain is as forbidding in the late 20th century as it was in 1919 for the North Russia Force and the 6th RM Battalion. Over many years the prospect of war on what became NATO's northern flank had been considered by strategists, as the Norwegian border was the only region where NATO countries' borders adjoined Russia. But from the late 1940s the Norwegians did not permit large bodies of foreign troops to carry out exercises in their country. Small numbers of Royal Marines, nevertheless, were allowed to join Norwegian army courses, and the Norwegian military always co-operated closely with the Corps.[1] With the advent of NATO and collective defence '45 Cdo RM' was committed to mountain and Arctic warfare in 1969. But at first only Commando Troops without their supporting arms exercised in Norway, no more than 300 or so men being there at any one time. These Troops worked under Norwegian command, receiving generous help in time and advice from them[2] while establishing the commandos' willingness to put themselves under an Allied command. However, during the winter of 1971–2, '45 Cdo RM' served in Ireland where it was able to knit together – to 'shake down' – with its attached units. Only a 150 or so men went to Norway, they were mostly Marines under 18, who were not sent to Ireland. During 1971 this Commando had also moved its base to Arbroath (the old RNAS HMS *Condor*) in Angus, on the east Scottish coast.

As the expected stint of Arctic training had, therefore, been missed, some expertise was lost, but the Corps had sufficient instructors to train fresh troops in skiing and the other skills needed for what was known as Mountain and Arctic Warfare (M and AW). By 1973, therefore, it had been possible to deploy in Norway 45 Commando Group of some 900 all ranks; this Group included: 45 Commando; No. 145 Battery of 29th Commando Regiment RA; Condor Troop of 59th Engineering Squadron; 612 Tactical Air Party; and some service and supply units. For some years before this deployment much thought had been given to forming a Commando Logistics Regiment, and the Regiment held its inaugural parade on 11 January 1972. This Regiment had Medical, Ordnance, Transport and Workshop Squadrons and an RAOC Petrol Company. It could – and can – service the Brigade's many vehicles which include oversnow tracked vehicles as well as 'wheels'.[3]

The Medical Squadron had Royal Naval personnel, while army specialists from the RE, RAOC, and REME – some of whom had served with the commandos in Borneo and elsewhere – served in other Squadrons alongside the Marines. The men of this Regiment were – and are – deployed with Commandos, as are flights of the Brigade Air Squadron. At sea an entire Group could be lifted by the Amphibious Force, with its RN- and RM-piloted helicopters, as happened when 42 Commando Group was first deployed in Norway in the early months of 1977. In 1979, Brigade HQ and 29th Regiment's HQ provided elements for a major exercise in Norway in which nearly 3,000 commandos took part.[4] Among them was Whiskey Company of the Royal Netherlands Marines, who, by a memorandum of understanding at government level in 1972, came under command of '45 RM' should there have been any period of tension. (Their name stems from 1973 when they were attached as 'W' Company to this Commando.[5]) The large exercise in 1979 was the first deployment since World War II of an integrated Commando Brigade as opposed to one with attached units.

In 1977 General Sir Peter Whiteley, a Royal Marine officer with commando experience who had been CG, was the first Royal Marine appointed Commander-in-Chief, Allied Forces Northern Europe, a command which included Norway, Denmark, and Schleswig Holstein.[6] For the Russians, this flank would probably have had to be secured during any general offensive against the West. Because their submarines and ships of the Northern Fleet could not otherwise have reached their bases safely after attacking NATO reinforcements from the USA. Allied Forces North (AFNORTH), therefore, were opposed in the late 1970s by naval forces of considerable power, including 124 nuclear and 74 diesel submarines and by large land forces. The Kola peninsula contained an amphibious Naval Infantry Regiment, two infantry divisions and supporting arms, with special forces for diversionary raids. In the Baltic there were: a Soviet Naval Infantry Regiment; a Polish Sea Landing Division; and up to seven infantry divisions. These forces could be quickly reinforced, depending on the position in central Europe.[7] The parallels to 19th century Baltic deployments are obvious.

Bearing in mind what in the West was seen as the Russians' need to cut Europe's sea communications, and therefore to maintain submarines at sea, any strike against the West was expected to mean an early attack on both North Norway and the Baltic. In a period of tension, therefore, the commandos would probably have been deployed to AFNORTH in readiness for such a battle, in which case the Commando Group would have worked under Norwegian Command at brigade or higher level, or as an independent brigade, 'for there is no doubt that Commando Forces can adapt to any command structure required'.[8] What was expected to be complex was the Command Post – the tactical HQ – and RM experience with LPDs had put them in the forefront of these developments.

The commitment to AFNORTH, however, had not lessened the role of Marines elsewhere in the world, as the operations in 1982 in the South Atlantic would prove. 'Blackshod' mountain training continued in the Highlands of Scotland, that is training without white 'snow' camouflage. In the Mediterranean 41 Commando RM began the Corps' first 6-month tour with United Nations forces in Cyprus (UNFICYP). In November 1974, they took over the Limassol district from the 2nd Battalion of the Guards Brigade. With '41 RM' in this Commando Group were 8th (Alma) Battery and two Troops of the 59th Independent Squadron RE, the Group being the first commandos to wear the light blue beret of UN forces.[9] In this command the regulations were quite different from those in national armies, for the force was under the direct command of the Secretary-General and regarded as representatives of the UN. Breaches of discipline, therefore, were punished severely and the method of operating depended more on tact and parley, the antithesis of a commando's training to take the initiative in any dangerous situation, Nevertheless commandos had to exercise that flexibility for which their commanders had made then famous, with a Marine one day taking the part of a village policeman and next bluffing a would-be aggressor across the peace line – in one case by creating mock machine guns out of drain pipes to appear as though a building was heavily defended.

By the mid-1970s a Commando Group had 'quite a punch' being regarded by the Americans as an effective independent formation. When such a Group was acting as a garrison – as '41 RM' did in Malta in the early 1970s – they had under command civilians handling stores and administration work, a school, a kindergarten and a clinic. The elite Army units serving with Commandos in these deployments became ambassadors for the Corps, when they later returned to service with army brigades. This attitude helped to foster the good relations between the Corps and the Army, so important in many Commando deployments of the 1970s.

In Cyprus 41 RM Commando set a high example of discipline and bearing to other units in the Force, not only in low-key observation of Greek and Turkish activities, but also in humanitarian work for minorities caught on the 'wrong' side of the peace line. One Corporal, arriving in a village to find its inhabitants about to flee, persuaded them to stay and continue farming. He became their surrogate headman who the villagers did not want to leave them when the Commando was withdrawn from the island.[10] In a similar context the Beach Units proved useful in providing military aid to civil communities (MACC), for they could land food in bulk for famine relief more cheaply than it could be flown in by helicopter.[11] On a larger scale, in September 1979 42 Commando RM began a deployment in aid of the Hong Kong government's attempts to stem the flow of illegal immigrants (IIs). These had been arriving in the Colony at the rate of 14,000 to 17,000 a month during the early summer, swelling the already overcrowded population of 5 million in that small colony. Although the return of a Chineses army from its campaign in Vietnam reduced the numbers for a time, there were still many thousands crossing the border when they could, nearly 3,000 being caught by the British Security Forces in October. In making their contribution to these arrests the Marines patrolled difficult country scarred by ravines in the hills on the border, in mosquito-ridden swamps to the west and in seaborne fast patrols.

The work in Hong Kong with its hours in observation posts, dawn sweeps along the border, bicycle patrols, the stalking of suspects and using night observation devices, all had a familiar ring from earlier operations. As does the Commando's readiness to cope with the unexpected, 'for there [was] no copybook solution, no set tactics, every capture [was] different'.[12] At sea the coxswains piloted their variety of fast craft, including Geminis, Rigid Raiders and speedboats, with much success, although there had only been time for a 4-day refresher course in handling the speedboats. They set up bases on small islands some within 800m of the Chinese border, often finding the 'work distressing for many of the "IIs" were women and children . . . most had been in the water many hours . . . and many would not have survived had they not been arrested'.[13] Early in 1980 '42 RM' returned from the Far East to take part in exercises in Norway, to find that the 'training' – as it had regarded the Hong Kong deployment – had kept them fit. A small number of Royal Marines officers and NCOs were also deployed at that time in Rhodesia (modern Zimbabwe).

Nearer home in the early months of 1980, the Corps formed Comacchio Company with 300 Marines to protect Naval installations.[14] It was based on *Condor* and largely worked in small detachments in different locations, much in the way Marines have from time to time been deployed, in this case to protect oil and gas rigs in the North Sea. For many years the Special Boat Squadron had carried out exercises to test the defences of such assets and of Naval installations, in 1963 swimmers twice entering a Naval base undetected.[15] In March 1976 on a similar exercise they 'attacked' an oil rig 82 miles from Peterhead (Aberdeenshire), against a defence provided by commandos from '45 RM' and a frigate's detachment.[16] Their methods of attack and defence will have to be described in a later history, for security reasons. But something of the fire-power of a Commando in 1980 could be seen in the wire-guided Milan anti-tank missile. Its warhead penetrated all armour known at that time and was delivered by the weapon's two-stage rocket motor.

The combination of technical proficiency with military bearing had contributed to the Corps' reputation as a compact versatile force. This had led to the Shah of Persia's decision to base his amphibious force on the Royal Marines, as a result of which Major General Loudoun visited Iran in January 1972 to study what help the Corps might give in training this force. Seventeen Iranian officers and NCOs – like those from other nations from time to time – had been under training at Lympstone, and on the General's advice a team of instructors was sent to Persia (modern Iran). The team was small, as any large number of officers and NCOs might have led to the Iranian Marines being run by the Corps not merely trained by it.[17] (In practice even this small number of RM officers, in essence ran the units they were teaching.) As the situation turned out, the Iranians' original intention to form a commando school and one Commando was expanded, although the precise objectives were never satisfactorily defined. By February 1979 1,500 commandos based at Manjil on the Caspian Sea had largely completed their training; and in the south at Bushire on the Persian Gulf a Commando HQ, three rifle companies and a support company were 70 per cent trained. But when the supporters of Ayatollah Khomeini gained control of Tehran, the Iranian Marines threw in their lot with the new government and the training cadre left Iran. This move took some of them several weeks, and nearly all lost many personal possessions.[18] Despite the outcome of this venture, there is no doubt that the Corps' ability to train its own instructors was used elsewhere to advantage in the last decades of the 20th century, by providing training cadres for some of Britain's allies.

In 1980 the developments in the Corps, including an increasing number of RM helicopter pilots, new weapons and equipment, continued to give the Royal Marines a wide experience of the technology of warfare. This would be put to the test in the next 15 years, when the Corps added further to its high reputation for quiet efficiency and military competence.

11

MAINLY WAR IN THE SOUTH ATLANTIC

> It was 3 Commando Brigade, the thoroughly practised formation led by men of great experience in working together, who were the stars of the campaign [in the Falkland Islands]. There is little the Brigade would have done differently with hindsight . . .
>
> Max Hastings and Simon Jenkins[1]

The history of the Corps continued in the 17 years to 1997 with many deployments in the early-1980s following the pattern of those in the previous decade. But in May 1982 Commando Brigade spearheaded landings in what has been described as 'an old fashioned war'.[2] This was fought as much by foot-slogging marches across East Falkland, as by the high technology of satellite communications, of Exocet missiles and of Harrier Jump Jets. The campaign and associated operations in the South Atlantic began on 2 April 1982 when Marines of the Falkland garrison were in action against invading Argentinian forces and could be said to have ended when the Argentinians surrendered on 14 June. The Brigade returned to England aboard SS *Canberra* and other ships arriving at Southampton on 11 July that year.

In the winter of 1981/2 there had been continued deployments in north Norway (Appendix 4). Also at that time a survey was completed to establish what was needed for the defences of naval bases, of Britain's off-shore oil installations and for the protection of atomic fission material while in transit. The outcome of this survey was the development of Comacchio Company into Comacchio Group (appendix 4). Commandos continued to take their share of duties in Northern Ireland and the Corps also provided individuals for specialist posts in the Province. Also ships' detachments of Marines were by this date much smaller than had been even in the 1970s; by the 1980s there were senior NCOs commanding detachments of ten men in frigates, with larger detachments in the two Assault Ships (Landing Platforms Dock) and the ice patrol ship HMS *Endurance*.

An extension of the duties for ships' detachments came about almost unnoticed, as the naval warships used their helicopters to take boarding parties of Marines to abseil down to any ship requiring interception or to land on a hostile shore. This became a routine operation for Marines of the 1990s. In 1981 the Corps' strength had been about 7,500[3] with some 1,000 in the RM Reserve. A defence review at the time when Mr (later Sir) John Nott was Secretary for Defence led to a number of proposals including the de-commissioning of both Assault Ships (LPDs), but Sir John saw a demonstration at Browndown (Hampshire) and expressed the view that the Navy should retain its amphibious force 'but not the amphibious ships'.[4] Other cuts considered at this time were the phasing out of the two aircraft carriers (one to be sold to the Australians), the removal of naval 4.5-inch guns from new designs of frigates, and other capabilities were to be limited except those related to anti-submarine warfare. Such capabilities as the sweeping of mines by minesweepers were to be provided by other NATO navies.

The war in the South Atlantic stemmed from an ongoing diplomatic dispute between Argentina and the British Government, on behalf of Falkland Islanders, raising the question of sovereignty over the Islands.[5] To most British people the Islands were a distant and unknown territory, unknown that is until March 1982 when there were riots in Argentina and the military government there sought to unify the country by mounting a long-promised campaign to 'recover' the *Malvinas* as they called these Islands, a provocative step encouraged when the British Government intimated that, as an economy measure, they might withdraw the ice patrol ship HMS *Endurance* from the South Atlantic.

In chapter 10 we saw the incidents that occurred with a small detachment of Marines stationed on the Islands and known as Naval Party 8901 (appendix 4). This set the scene for the Royal Marine presence, albeit a small one, on the Falkland Islands in March 1982, when a relief party (known as the '8901 detachment 1982/3') took over from '8901 1981/2'. Also in the South Atlantic that March was a detachment of Marines aboard the ice patrol ship HMS *Endurance*.

In late March the Commando Brigade RM commanded by Brigadier Julian Thompson was at its customary seven days notice; on Friday 2 April this was reduced to 72 hours.[7] That Friday the Brigade's units were spread over many locations: 42 Commando was on leave, having just returned from Norway; its commander, Lt-Colonel Nick Vaux, was expecting to fly to America; 40 Commando was at the firing ranges in Altcar (Lancashire); and one company of 45 Commando was in Brunei (north-west Borneo). The Brigade Major and the Brigade staff were in Denmark, carrying out a recce for an exercise.[8] Major Ewen Southby-Tailyour, who would become a key player in the forthcoming campaign, had commanded Naval Party 8901 in 1978. This cheerful professional was a naturalist with a love of sailing, both of which he had put to good use in 1978. In early April 1982, as an Arabic speaker, he was attending a course on the Middle East at London University.[9] He was called to Brigade headquarters in Plymouth on the Friday morning, having collected his charts and Falkland notes from his office in Poole. There the Landing Craft Branch was being mobilised just before they were due to go on Easter leave.

HQ and Signals Squadron, the Logistic Regiment RM, and 29 Commando Regiment RA were all due to go on leave but were mobilised, as was 59 Independent Squadron RE, commanded by Major Roderick Macdonald RE. The Major, who had a great sense of fun, was at that time Army Hang-Gliding Champion. He was highly professional and had formed in January 1982 a recce troop of engineers which had trained with 40 Commando, and which 'was to pay dividends in the Falklands'.[10] The Brigadier was telephoned by the CO of the 22nd Special Air Service, Lieutenant-Colonel Michael Rose Coldstream Guards, suggesting that one of his squadrons at least might be required. He had put one squadron on stand-by when his HQ at Hereford (in Hereford and Worcestershire County) heard of the invasion.[11] The Colonel was a sophisticated and intellectual Guards officer.

On South Georgia, a British protectorate some 1,500 km east of the Falklands, there was a British Antarctic Base at Grytviken. And at Leith, some 30 km west along the coast, was an abandoned whaling station where a party of over 40 Argentinians had been landed to collect the scrap. They had permission to land but not to hoist the Argentinian flag which they later refused to lower. Whether these men were working to any formal plan by the Junta seems doubtful, but there may well have been some informal offer of support from their navy, as the scrap dealers' ship was chartered from the Argentinian navy. The landing took place on Friday 19 March and two days later *Endurance* sailed from Stanley, having embarked her aircraft and 12 men from '8901' (of 1981/2) in addition to her Marine detachment. By the Tuesday she was off South Georgia where she was to await further orders.[12] Meanwhile the armed Argentinian naval survey ship *Bahia Paraiso* replaced the chartered ship in Leith.

A large number of the Junta's warships were known to be at sea as many radio signals were intercepted; they might have been on a well-publicised exercise with the ships of Uruguay or have a more sinister intent. Subsequently it became apparent that the Junta's plans for an invasion of the Falkland Islands, to be made later in 1982, were triggered by the confrontation at Leith. In London the Prime Minister and her Secretary for Defence countered the Junta's moves by the despatch of three nuclear submarines to the South Atlantic. Aboard these were to be SBS teams although only HMS *Spartan* was immediately available, and she sailed on the night 30 March/1 April from Gibraltar. The other two followed a few days later, as did the RFA *Fort Austin*. The First Sea Lord, Admiral Sir Henry Leach, and his Operations Staff, realising that a full Battle Fleet would be required to face the Junta's powerful navy with six of its ships equipped with Exocet missiles, looked to Rear Admiral John (Sandy) Woodward's 20 or so ships on exercise in mid-Atlantic. Sir Henry's second-in-command, the Commander in Chief Fleet Admiral Sir John Fieldhouse, was with Woodward's 1st Flotilla. Sir John had served some 15 years in the Submarine Service. In the last days of March he came back to London and steps were taken to assemble what would turn out to be the most powerful British fleet to put to sea since World War II.[13]

The Junta now realised that they had to move quickly to get to the Islands before their garrison was reinforced. In London, Sir Henry – 'sharp, erect and an admiral's admiral' – told the Prime Minister on 31 March that he could

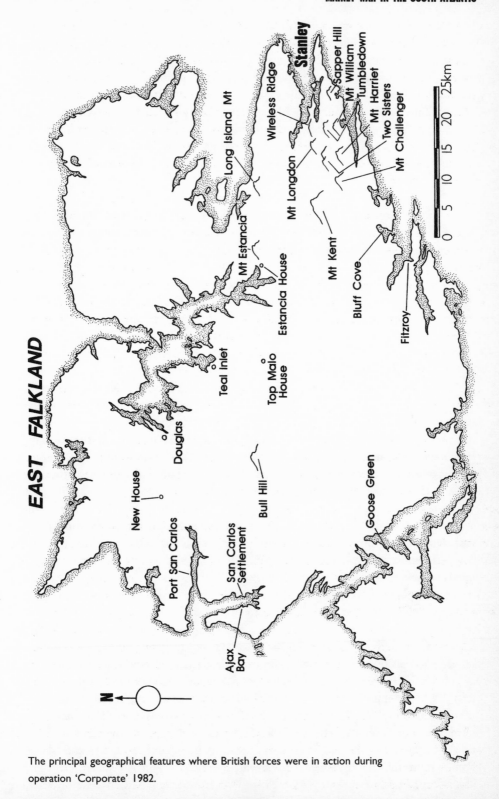

The principal geographical features where British forces were in action during operation 'Corporate' 1982.

raise a task force 'by the weekend'. Further diplomatic contacts were explored. Brigadier Thompson had discussed the possible invasion of the Islands with his Brigade Major, the tall and highly intelligent Major John Chester, when they were in Denmark. Some days previously the Brigade had gleaned a little knowledge of the Navy's intentions through the general commanding the Commando Forces, Major General Jeremy Moore, with his separate headquarters in Plymouth. The General, a Royal Marine officer whom we last met in the East Indies (chapter 10) was regarded as 'a soldiers' General', respected throughout the Corps and had been twice decorated while serving with Commandos. He was about to retire in the spring of 1982.

In London several senior officers in the Army and RAF had major reservations about any attempt to retake the Islands, but the Royal Navy continued to put together a Task Force, later to be designated by the number 317. On 1 April General Sir Steuart Pringle, the Commandant General injured by an IRA bomb who had now returned to duty, chaired a meeting of his senior officers. The Falklands were on the agenda among other items. And various options were considered elsewhere in the Ministry of Defence, 40 Commando receiving orders to the effect that there was the possibility of air-lifting a Commando via a friendly South American state. On Thursday (25 March) the Fleet was put on full alert while further diplomatic efforts were made to deter the Argentinians from mounting an invasion. But no detailed plans were projected by the Ministry of Defence for a recovery of the Islands. Indeed it seems that General Moore's Headquarters Commando Forces and the Brigadier's Headquarters, both in Hamoaze House by 2 April, after the Brigadier had moved his HQ to be 'closer to the source of information and policy', were the first to give any detailed consideration to how this might be done. In peacetime the planners of the Commando Forces tended to concentrate on long term plans for the development of exercises for the Brigade among other aspects of Commando operations.

Major Southby-Tailyour has summarised the nature of amphibious operations in the 1980s and 1990s as being more demanding than the preparation and planning for other phases of warfare. Amphibious Warfare needs careful, detailed, considered and precise planning, practice and execution, with surface, air, sub-surface and land warfare. Each of these facets has to be weighed and balanced against cross-decking requirements (moving men from the deck of one ship to that of another), helicopter and flight deck availability, landing craft launching and loading difficulties in the prevailing sea state and other weather factors. Consideration has also to be given to the gradients of landing beaches, any restrictions on vehicle movements and beach exits (as we have seen in earlier decades) and the surf height at the end of a long undefended water gap must be taken into account. There is the logistic tail stretching back out to sea and loaded in incompatible ships. The whole affair is highly complex and puts a considerable burden on junior leaders, the corporal coxswains and section commanders.[14] But the old adage stands: in amphibious operations the unexpected is the norm however carefully the operation has been planned.[15]

* * *

The Marines of '8901' were based 5 km from Stanley in a camp at Moody Brook maintained under an MOD contract by the Falkland Islands Company (a department of the British Government's Property Services Agency).[16] In 1978 some of the buildings still dated from World War I, including a vast concrete structure built to house generators for a Royal Navy signals station. The block, know as the Belsen Block, had long been unoccupied and the signallers long gone. Indeed in the 1970s the communications with London for Detachment 8901 were by teleprinter; this line was run by the Cable & Wireless Company whose operator only worked office hours. Civilian radio sets were used to link into the Islands' local network.

The detachment was intended as a trip-wire, so to speak, for any invasion force and would most likely have provided some intelligence from patrols escaping to the Camp, the open countryside of East Falkland, its name derived from 'campos' (countryside) which was some 80 per cent peat bog. There was also a body of locals trained as the Falkland Islands Defence Force, with 120 names on its books but considerably fewer active members. They and the Marines might have briefly defended key points but not against a serious assault. Here Major Garry Noott's detachment had been stationed for a year, when Major Mike Norman's 'new' Detachment 8901, 40-strong, arrived on a Monday (29 March). He took command of the garrison detachment at 0900 hours (local time) on the following Thursday. On the Wednesday, men had been deployed to several lookout posts and at the airfield guarded several aircraft of the Argentinian airline (LADE) which flew a regular service to the mainland. By Thursday night the camp at Moody Brook had been evacuated, with sections including some RN personnel in defence positions and at the airfield where obstructions had been placed to prevent aircraft landing. Other sections were covering some beaches likely to be used by landing craft. But Major Noott's detachment had been reduced from its normal strength of about 40, when 12 of its Marines had been added to *Endurance*'s detachment before she had sailed for South Georgia.

At dawn on the 2 April (Friday) firing was heard from the Moody Brook camp area, some 3 km from Government House where the Governor, Rex Hunt, was in communication with London. Garry Noott was acting as adviser to the Governor while Mike Norman had overall command of the detachments, and was at Look Out Rocks. The Governor, as Commander-in-Chief of the Falkland Island defences, had told the Marines that he wanted no fighting in the built-up areas of Stanley.

The Marines withdrew to form a defence perimeter around Government House, having rounded up all the Argentinian civilians from Stanley. Before withdrawing, Sgt Sheppard's section engaged the Armoured Personnel Carriers, in this case Landing Vehicles Tracked (LVTs), advancing down the airport road. Marine M. Gibbs stopped the lead vehicle with a direct hit from his 66 mm Light Anti-Tank Weapon, and Marines S. Brown and Best fired a missile from an 84 mm Carl Gustav into the LVT's cargo hold. An assault on Government House was repulsed about 0615 hours. But two hours later when the Argentinians were known to be ashore in strength, Major Mike Norman told the Governor that although they were willing to try and break out into the Camp countryside, if they remained in positions around Government House they would be overrun. Surrender was arranged.

One section under Cpl S.C. York with five Marines were positioned north of Stanley Harbour. They stayed out in the Camp for nearly four days before surrendering. They had their heads shaved, were placed in solitary confinement and interrogated. But they along with the rest of the '8901s', Royal Navy personnel and some families were repatriated through Montevideo (Uruguay).[17]

The Argentinian commandos were later learned to have landed by inflatables in Mullet Creek almost 5 km due south of Moody Brook. They had come ashore about midnight and advanced at about 0100 hours in two parties: one to attack the Royal Marines' camp; and the other to capture Government House.[18] A party of Argentinian under-water swimmers landed north of the airport about 0330 hours, seizing the beaches at Yorke Bay. There, 15 LVTs landed Argentinian Marines, those in the lead vehicle being caught in the fire of one of the defence sections, as we have seen. Throughout the rest of that Friday (2 April), the Argentinians consolidated their forces on the Islands: two infantry platoons were landed by helicopter at Goose Green; a reinforced company landed at Fox Bay on West Falkland; the airport was cleared of its obstructions; and an Air Warning and Control unit was landed that afternoon to be set up by the following Tuesday on Sapper Hill. This radar unit had a range of 380 km (240 miles) and controlled some 70 anti-aircraft guns and eight missile systems.[19]

On South Georgia the 23 Marines landed from *Endurance* were in defensive positions, under the command of Lieutenant Keith Mills RM. They had laid barbed wire on the beach and put explosives on the jetty,[20] while a Force 10 gale blew throughout 2 April. When, on 3 April, the Lieutenant was called upon to surrender to the Argentinians at Leith, Mills prepared to fight. He had received somewhat contradictory orders in the previous days, reflecting London's anxiety not to provoke an invasion.[21] The Lieutenant attempted to persuade the Argentinians not to land but a Puma helicopter put down some 20 Argentinian Marines some 50 metres from the jetty. Against this assault, Keith Mills and his men were to put up a stout resistance. Soon after midday on Saturday (3 April) the Argentinian corvette *Guerico* attempted to enter Grytviken harbour. With her were two Alouette helicopters and the troop-carrying Puma. The corvette was hit three times by Carl Gustav anti-tank missiles fired by Marine D. Combes[22] and by small arms fire. The corvette now had difficulty in aiming her 100 mm gun and withdrew but the Puma's Marines attacked the defences. The firefight continued for some two hours, before Mills boldly walked forward to make terms for a surrender and was repatriated with his men. *Endurance* sailed north to meet the RFA *Fort Austin* some nine days out from Gibraltar.[23]

That weekend of 2–4 April the British Government resolved to retake the Islands,[24] and the Task Force became more than a diplomatic threat; it might have to fight in the South Atlantic, although even in early April many people believed that the deployment of the Task Force with its Amphibious Group would give Britain the diplomatic muscle to force a withdrawal of the Argentinians from the Falklands, without resorting to war.

The two staffs of Commando Forces and Brigade Headquarters at Hamoaze House in Plymouth have been described as a well-trained team, 'arms and papers waved in the air as [they] ebbed and flowed like an amoeba'.[25] Brigadier Julian Thompson was at the centre of this activity. A cheerful and very experienced senior officer, he was also a military historian, an authority on the Gallipoli landings of 1915. He had no intention of repeating any of the mistakes of earlier amphibious operations, and coolly made decisions on what might be required and what stores could be left behind. His staff took up their various duties, including the loading plans for ships that were being requestioned. About this time the MOD issued instructions for the release of the War Maintenance Reserve from stores in the Midlands of England among other places.

Meanwhile the Navy was bringing together the ships, some of which were requisitioned from merchant fleets, known as Ships Taken Up From Trade (STUFT). What ships were available, their capacity for troops and cargoes all affected the Headquarters' loading tables. These were revised more than once but over the weekend of 3–4 April completed tables were issued. The assault ship HMS *Fearless* was the major ship in the Amphibious Group, commanded by the Commodore Amphibious Warfare (COMAW), Commodore Mike Clapp. He was a Cornishman, 'a practical man with considerable moral and physical courage';[26] a one-time Buccaneer Squadron Commander, he also had wide experience of staff work. He reached Hamoaze House on the evening of 2 April, and would work closely with the Brigadier in the coming months. The Commodore, a rank held during a particular appointment, was the only senior RN Captain of eight such officers with a sea-going appointment at that time.[27]

The command structure would be – after several changes – as follows: [28]

Task Force Commander – Admiral Fieldhouse at Northwood

Maj. Gen Moore became Land Deputy to Adm. Fieldhouse

Cdr Carrier Battle Grp	Cdr Amphib Task Grp	Cdr Landing Force Task Grp
Rear-Adm Woodward	Cdre Clapp	Brig Thompson

Also under Adm. Fieldhouse's command were the South Georgia Task Force and the Sub-Surface Task Group

The Royal Navy staff had put in hand some improvised measures to bring together the shipping that would form the Task Force with its Carrier and Amphibious Groups. On 1 April HMS *Hermes* and *Invincible* were put at 48 hours notice for sea. Both were at Portsmouth with *Hermes* in a period of Dockyard Assisted Maintenance with many major systems dismantled and *Invincible*'s crew on leave.[29] HMS *Fearless* was also in Portsmouth in her role as an officer cadet training ship, with 4 Assault Squadron RM embarked. While *Intrepid* had paid off – she would join the Amphibious Task Group, nevertheless – her landing craft crews of 6 Assault Squadron RM were at the Landing Craft base in Poole (Dorset). There they provided men for training jobs and other duties but were an already practised team.[30] The dockyard and others prepared both *Hermes* and *Fearless* for long voyages with all manner of stores, these arriving on the dockside to be handled by naval and dockyard personnel stowing the Supply Officers' requirements in quick time. Not surprisingly perhaps, the personnel of the dock-yard showed remarkable energy in completing their tasks with almost unheard of alacrity, as the author witnessed. Four of the Landing Ships Logistic (LSLs) were available in docks near Plymouth, manned by Royal Fleet Auxiliary person-nel with British Officer and mainly Chinese crews.[31]

At Gibraltar Admiral Woodward – a Rear Admiral since 1981 and a sub-mariner since the mid-1950s – arranged for the seven ships going south in the first wave to take on stores from ships not initially in the Task Force. Other ships sailed to relieve those on patrol at the entrance to the Persian Gulf. The submarine *Splendid* sailed in the first few days of April from Faslane, the nuclear submarine base in Scotland, followed by the submarine *Conqueror* which sailed from Faslane on the following Sunday (4 April). Twenty fighter aircraft, Sea Harriers, were flown to the carriers as were anti-submarine Sea King helicopters and the Commando Mark 4 helicopters of 846 Squadron. There were spare crews for the nine anti-submarine helicopters but few reserve pilots for the 12 assault helicopters.

During the week ending 11 April a number of ships were taken up from trade[32] including oilers, Roll-on Roll-off (RoRo) ferries and the 'great white whale', the P&O flagship *Canberra*. She had been completing in the Mediter-ranean the last leg of a world cruise, but was diverted to Gibraltar to take on a party of some 60 specialists. They planned, as she sailed across the Bay of Biscay, how she might be fitted with platforms to land helicopters and where troop accommodation might be provided. The officer in this team who represented 42 Commando, Lieutenant Tony Hornby, is said to have 'manipulated statistics' to get more accommodation for '42 RM'.

The Brigade's basic formation of that time was 40 Commando RM, 42 Com-mando RM, 45 Commando RM, Commando Logistics Regiment RM, 59 Inde-pendent Regiment RE, 29 Commando Regiment RA, the Commando Brigade Air Squadron, the Headquarters and Signal Squadron (with its Air Defence Troop and a Raiding Squadron). The Brigade was reinforced by the 3rd Battalion of the Parachute Regiment, commanded by Lieutenant-Colonel. Hew Pike whom Brigadier Thompson had known since their days at Staff College together.[33] 3 Para, like other battalions of their Regiment, had one company specialising in patrol reconnaissance which would prove invaluable in providing information for their Commanding Officer, otherwise they were organised in a similar way to a Commando.[34] Also joining the Brigade was T Battery (Shah Sujah's Troop) of 12 Air Defence Regiment RA with their 12 surface-to-air Rapier missile launchers.[35] They were particularly welcomed as Captain Viv Rowe (the GSO3 Intelligence) and his team had unearthed some stark facts from their researches in the local library(!): the Argentinian Air Force was well equipped and might be expected to put up spirited attacks on any landing force, especially bearing in mind that country's reputation for adventurous polo players and their drivers' successes in racing cars. Such intelligence had to be gleaned from wherever it might be found since the MOD had no such background information available at this time; even the satellite pictures held by the Americans lacked any clarity.[36] Major Ewen Southby-Tailyour put together an informative series of lectures 'with slides', stressing the bleakness of the Islands and their lack of resources which a landing force might need, including drinking water, at least in the quantities a military force might require. Lieutenant R.E. Veal RN with recent experience of South Georgia also gave a talk – a 'brief' – on that island's terrain

Two troops of the Blues and Royals (Royal Horse Guards/Dragoons) with eight light tanks and an armoured recovery vehicle, joined the Brigade; and the Band of Commando Forces RM were to be deployed as stretcher bearers for which they are trained. Meanwhile Lieutenant-Colonel Ivor Hellberg, commanding the Commando Logistic Regiment RM, was pulling out all manner of stops to get some 4,500 tons of war stores required to keep the Brigade in action for some weeks. Among the equipment coming south from Arbroath (45 Commando's Base in Scotland) were 70 tracked Volvo BV202 over-snow vehicles (known as Bandwagons) which were to prove as effective over bogs as they had proved on the snows of Norway. More units would later be added to the reinforced Brigade.

Virtually no information was available on the disposition of the Argentinian forces in the Falklands, intelligence which might have included their order of battle and the state of their troops' morale.

The troops and stores were embarked with surprisingly little, if any, confusion due to the Commando staffs' long experience of mounting such operations albeit in exercises in the late 1970s, in 1980 and in 1981. *Canberra* (44,807 gross registered tons) carried the majority of 40 Commando RM, 42 Commando RM, 3 Para Battalion and the RM Band personnel under their Director of Music, Captain John Ware LRAM RM. The Brigadier had arranged for Colonel Tom Seccombe to be his deputy and this 'much respected and experienced commando officer'[37] was in overall charge of the troops embarked in her. The CO of 42 Commando, Lieutenant-Colonel Nick Vaux, later wrote of the welcome the men received aboard 'this graceful floating hotel'. The fast stores replenishment ship RFA *Stromness* had been brought out of the reserve fleet, her holds fitted with troop accommodation before she embarked 358 men of 45 Commando RM (other companies would join her at Ascension and Z Company sailed in *Canberra*). She also had a flight deck and improvised air defences. In her holds were a month's rations for 7,500 men. *Fearless* was to carry COMAW's and the Brigade's staffs, three Scout helicopters of the Brigade Air Squadron, some Volvo oversnow vehicles with the communications equipment and camouflage tenting for Brigade headquarters. There would normally have been two groups of these BV202s, used by the Headquarters staff when they advanced from one location to a second. They would only move after the second set of vehicles had been set up for immediate operation, ensuring continuous contact with the units, but lack of shipping space meant that only one group of HQ BV202 over-snow vehicles was taken to the Falklands.[38] The majority of over-snow vehicles were at that time stockpiled in Norway and would have required more shipping space to carry them to the Falkland Islands than was available. But later the Brigadier wrote 'in retrospect I wish we had taken more'.

HMS *Intrepid* sailed later and carried her Royal Marine detachment of about 100 from 6 Assault Squadron RM, with its Amphibious Operations Officer (AOO) Major Malcolm Macleod RM. The AOO in an LPD was the captain's advisor on amphibious aspects of an operation. The gunners of 29 Commando Regiment RA, with its three batteries of 105 mm light guns and a battery of Forward Observation parties to control naval gun fire support to the Brigade, were embarked. The Naval Gunfire Support (NGS) parties were in the ships for which they would control the gunfire, at times from the ship's helicopter. The engineers of 59 Independent Commando Squadron RE and the Logistic Regiment with its vehicles sailed in LSLs. This brief summary belies the complexity of the embarkation, for example the Motor Vessel *Elk* (4,190 gross registered tons) was converted from its normal RoRo ferry role when taken up from trade. She carried 2,500 tons of ammunition as well as vehicles, stores and six helicopters.[39] There were to be five other RoRo ferries, each with its ramps modified to lower onto a Mexeflote, and four RoRo container ships of between 10,000 and 20,000 tonnes, which had been modified as aircraft transports, including the *Atlantic Conveyor*. In addition to ten RFA oilers and five fleet replenishment ships (including the RFA *Stromness*) there were ships for minesweeper support, the hospital ship *Uganda* (16,907 gross registered tons), a helicopter support ship, a dozen support oilers and storage tankers taken up from trade and more besides. A number of these ships had a brief opportunity to test their techniques for refuelling ships at sea, routines with which many Marines are familiar from their time with ships' detachments. The last of the first group of ships to sail for Ascension were the MV *Elk* and SS *Canberra*. Both ships cleared the English Channel on 9 April, some 10 days after Sir Henry Leach had told the Prime Minister that the Royal Navy could despatch a force to the South Atlantic.

There was still virtually no hard intelligence on the Argentinian forces ashore on the Islands. On a visit to Northwood (HMS *Warrior*) by Brigadier Thompson, took his party down into the 'Hole', a nuclear-bomb-proof part of the Fleet Headquarters where the orderlies were armed Marines. Here there was a briefing for the Commander-in-Chief Fleet, Admiral Sir John Fieldhouse, which was also attended by Rear Admiral Derek Reffel who was Flag Officer 3rd Flotilla, COMAW's commander, and by Major General Jeremy Moore. The senior officers in the Task Force were to be Rear Admiral Sandy Woodward commanding the Carrier Battle Group, COMAW commanding the Amphibious Task Force and the Brigadier commanding the Landing Force, all reporting to Sir John Fieldhouse. Sandy Woodward was perhaps understandably to assume the leading role through this ex-submariner's seniority in rank, although his methods of command did not endear him to all members of the Task Force, as his naturally aggressive character tended to unnecessarily involve him in detail that was strictly – and logically – in the province of the Brigadier and COMAW. (When in Falkland waters that June there were delays ashore, as the Admiral was later to write, which he had seen as stemming from a lack of skill on the part of the land forces. He continued by expressing his 'lack of insight into General Moore's problems' at that time, when the Admiral's Carrier Battle Group had suffered losses and a number of ships were in need of major overhauls 'as the Battle Group was running out of steam'.[40])

All amphibious landings are improved by proper rehearsals, but there was no opportunity to rehearse a full Brigade landing, although some opportunities for individual units to rehearse the landings in this operation 'Corporate' arose when the Amphibious Group was held at Ascension, *Fearless* having anchored during 17 April. At a Council of War that day aboard *Hermes* the Brigadier was told that his Brigade would be reinforced by 2 Para whose CO was Lieutenant-Colonel H. Jones (whom the Brigadier had known for some years) with attached sub-units (light guns of 29 Battery 4th Field Regiment, a Field Ambulance Clearing Troop, a squadron of Royal Engineers, two Blowpipe Sections and a flight of Army Air Corps Scout helicopters). The Brigade's strength nevertheless was below that considered necessary for a successful assault, when 3-to-1 in favour of the attackers was the accepted ratio. The odds were therefore improved by the addition to the landing force of 5 Infantry Brigade with its headquarters that would report to a Divisional Headquarters commanded by General Moore as Commander Land Forces Falkland Islands.

Good relationships were developed with the journalists from the press and TV despite some initial misunderstandings. In the words of Lieutenant-Colonel Vaux with his 42 Commando RM aboard *Canberra*, writing of the Press: there was 'a mutual understanding and respect, despite wrangling over censorship'. Max Hastings was to spend time on the mountains before being one of the first, if not the first, unofficial representative of the Task Force to enter Stanley. But that was some weeks away. The Colonel, by the way, was amused that he might be described as: an 'ex-steeplechase rider whose wife breeds Connemara ponies in the West Country', but no mention might be made of his Commando.

Elements of the Battle Group were steaming south during these last weeks in April, while the Amphibious Group had an opportunity at Ascension to re-stow stores and equipment which had not been loaded tactically (with items to go ashore first in a landing at the right place in the cargo holds of the right ships). There had been no opportunity for tactical loading and now over 300 movements were made in a day by helicopters often with underslung loads.[41] Some LSLs had arrived with an overload that put them deeper into the water by up to 45 cm below the safe loading marks. But an unloaded LSL arrived from Belize, *Sir Tristram* – in which her Captain, Robin Green, and his crew took great pride[42] – to which loads could be redistributed, including 200 tons of ammunition for the Commandos. And A Company of '40 RM' was transferred from *Hermes* to *Canberra*.[43]

Ascension is an island of volcanic origin lying about halfway between the United Kingdom and the Falklands. It had a substantial runway operate by Pan American Airways, supporting a US satellite tracking station, British communications installations and an anchorage open to Atlantic swells. The Royal Navy's organisation on Ascension was mainly in the hands of Naval Captain Bob McQueen's British Forces Support Unit. He had the seniority and character to turn away men sent from England in specialist parties which were, in his opinion, unnecessarily large for their tasks. However among those sent back was a team from the Brigade which had been tasked with sorting out the mass of stores which had arrived by air. The Captain[44] had arrived in the first week in April and among his many facilities was a pre-fabricated camp supplied and erected by Americans in days rather than weeks. Bearing in mind that the small population of this island had to sustain 1,000 new residents, the need for good relations with these Americans and resident workers (mainly from St Helena) was vital and the Support Unit successfully fostered them. The transport by air of multitudinous items – not least of which were charts for the Falklands – required large quantities of fuel for the nine or so aircraft flying in daily over the 6,500 km from the UK.[45] The Forces Support Unit also organised live-firing ranges, ancillary refuelling services to supplement those of PanAm, and many other facilities. Commando staffs had to keep track of the Brigade's war materials, a chore with which they were familiar and for which they had used chacons – those large containers often shipped as deck cargo – in Norway. A tri-service cell was later successfully set up to handle transhipments.

The intelligence needed for a detailed final plan for the landing would have to be obtained by 'mark one eyeball', to quote the Brigadier. To this end Colonel Richard Preston (a Royal Marines officer) went south with the Carrier Battle Group as Land Force adviser to its commander and the Brigadier's representative on the Battle Group staff. He was in secure-voice communication with the Brigadier over thousands of kilometres to his north. This radio link enabled the Special Forces, teams from both SAS and SBS, to provide critical intelligence for shaping the landing plan.[46]

Also at Ascension, further modifications were made to some STUFT ships, including the clearing of *Elk*'s superstructure to enable her to fly on helicopters, and fitting her with a pair of 40 mm Bofors. Whether or not *Canberra* should be at anchor when she offloaded her troops or be steaming slowly ahead was tested, as was the effect of putting the light tanks forward in an LCU to fire over an opened ramp as the craft approached a target beach. (The luxury of fire support from LCGs and their like had long been a matter of history.) Timings could also be tested as when ten helicopters, landing two at a time, lifted a company from *Canberra*. And in the midst of these trials, *Fearless* was so short of fuel – and therefore so buoyant – that she could not dock down to launch her LCUs for 48 hours until a tanker became available. The re-stow occupied the helicopters and therefore there was only sufficient airlift available for each unit to have one day ashore on the ranges and two other days when they landed from Landing Craft.[47] The Rapier Battery, although landed at the island, had to be recalled before setting up a firing practice, as the Amphibious Task Group had been ordered to sail earlier than planned. 2 Para reached Ascension 12 hours before the Amphibious Task Group sailed on 7 May for the South Atlantic (the LSLs had sailed on the 30 April). Therefore they and the crew of their ferry, *Norland*, had insufficient time to iron out all the snags of loading men into LCUs. X Company of '45 Cdo RM' was flown out to join *Stromness* before she and *Norland* sailed on 8 May to catch up their Group.

There had been no opportunity for the Brigade to rehearse all its units in a coordinated landing, and while the techniques were familiar in general to the Commandos a specific rehearsal had usually been essential in previous major assaults. Meanwhile, the planning staff was still in need of more intelligence, although the first of the Special Forces' teams had landed on East Falkland on 1 May. The staff considered 19 possible landing beaches, whittled down to five areas for closer inspection by the teams of Special Forces.

In early April the Naval Staff had begun to plan the recapture of South Georgia. M Company (Captain. C.J. Nunn) of 42 Commando RM formed the nucleus of this Landing Force from the Brigade which sailed south and was commanded by '42's' second in command, Major Guy Sheridan. The Major had recently led the first party to traverse the Himalayas on skis and was an experienced climber. They flew to Ascension on 7 April and joined the fleet oiler *Tidespring* which was escorted by the guided missile destroyer HMS *Antrim* (5,440 tons), whose Captain Brian Young commanded this Force, and the Type 12 frigate HMS *Plymouth* (a 1961 ship of 2,380 tons). Guy Sheridan sailed in *Antrim* with elements that had been added to his command, including two Naval Gunfire Support Observer parties and a section of SBS. D Squadron (Major Cedric Delves) of the SAS aboard *Antrim* were also under the command of Captain Young, and in communication with the SAS HQ at Hereford. The operation was code named 'Paraquet' which is said to be a corruption of 'Parakeet'. This island was beyond the range of any shore based Argentinian aircraft except C-130s and Boeing 707s, and British submarines screened the Force from surface attack, with HMS *Conqueror* making some inshore reconnaissances, despite the threat of icebergs. An RAF Victor made a 15-hour flight to confirm the submarine's report that there was no Argentinian surface ships in the area.[48]

At dawn on Wednesday 21 April after a helicopter recce, the helicopters with 20 men of D Squadron's Mountain Troop commanded by 29-year old Captain John Hamilton flew to a position on the Fortuna Glacier 16 km west of Leith which lies in Stromness Bay. Their first attempt to land was frustrated by a 'white out' of swirling snow driven by turbulent winds funnelling down the glacier which created down-draughts. Two hours later they tried again, and succeeded in putting the recce party on the glacier. D Squadron's commander had insisted on the landing against the advice of Major Sheridan; that night the weather again deteriorated with force 10 gales. Next day (Thursday) the recce party had to be evacuated as the glacier's crevices – not to mention the weather – had made any movement impossible. They were safely recovered by *Antrim*'s Wessex Mk 3 with its radar and the remarkable skill of its pilot, Lieutenant-Commander Ian Stanley, who flew twice to the glacier after both the other Wessex had crashed in white outs.

On the previous night (Wednesday) the frigate had entered Stromness Bay and launched Gemini inflatables with the SAS Boat Troop's recce parties. Some of their boats had not been adequately maintained and the SAS had difficulties from the start, one being driven by the wind to the edge of the coast just before it was swept into the open Atlantic. This team were recovered on the Friday morning (23 April) by the redoubtable Lt-Cdr Stanley in his single engined Mark 3 Wessex.

The Force received some reinforcement by the Saturday after Admiral. Woodward sent HMS *Brilliant* (a Type 22 frigate of 3,500 tons only a year old) to join the South Georgia Force. She carried two Lynx helicopters. Meanwhile *Endurance*, with the SBS section aboard, was south-east of Grytviken and although at one stage she had been the intended platform for launching an assault on the island, the plan had to be changed. The previous Tuesday the American press revealed that the British were near South Georgia, forcing some re-disposition of ships around this island. Then on the following Sunday morning the Argentinian long range submarine *Santa Fe* was caught on the surface by depth charges from *Antrim*'s Wessex. Although she had seen the helicopter, she did not dive as her Captain wanted to avoid an expected attack by homing torpedoes from a helicopter. She limped back to Grytviken where she had landed troops and supplies the previous day. For the two hours from when she was first sighted, the submarine was harassed by helicopters from the British ships.[49]

Captain Young agreed to Major Sheridan's wish to be put ashore as soon as possible, and the Major assembled his men from elements of M Company (its HQ and Recce Section) but the bulk of this Company was in *Tidespring* 320 km to the north. He also had *Antrim*'s detachment of ten Marines and *Plymouth*'s detachment, the two NGS teams with SAS and SBS making up a force of some 75 highly trained infantry. *Endurance*'s Wasp landed the first NGS team into an area that had been bombarded by *Plymouth*'s 4.5-in shells, ceasing fire just before the Wasp touched down. The spotting officer almost immediately called for fire against defenders on Brown Mountain overlooking Grytviken; and in the next forty minutes *Plymouth* fired short bursts from her twin Mk 6 4.5-in guns to put 40 rounds into the defences. (These 4.5-in guns had a dual purpose: anti-aircraft and surface fire and could fire among other rounds a 25 kg high-explosive shell over ranges up to 16 km and provided extremely effective support fire for the landing force. Elsewhere the Mark 8 4.5s could automatically fire 25 rounds a minute as might be necessary in their anti-aircraft role.) The second NGS team was then landed. The barrage crept closer to the main Argentinian positions. A white flag was run up and the garrison surrendered to Major Sheridan whose men were now ashore after lifting from the warships in an assortment of heli-copters. The position of Argentinian minefields caused the Major some concern but bold steps brought a quick victory, with 137 Argentinians captured and only one man killed; he was mistakenly thought to be scuttling the *Santa Fe*. In London there had been gloom at the initial failures on the glacier because this operation was intended to strengthen British diplomacy, and its subsequent success was welcomed with euphoria;[50] unfortunately, perhaps, as the relative ease with which South Georgia was retaken led to an underestimation in some quarters of Argentinian military capabilities, although 3 Commando Brigade RM never doubted the Argentinians' determination to hold on to the Falklands.

The Brigadier knew that the Argentinian staff officers were largely American trained and might therefore expect an assault on Stanley through Fitzroy with its surfaced road to the capital, or by some other route along which wheeled vehicles might approach the defences of this city. Therefore any assault near Stanley might run into prepared defences and put at risk the civilian population. The Commodore and the Brigadier therefore finally decided on San Carlos Water which provided a number of features which would favour a successful landing. They were out of the range of guns deployed in the defence of Stanley, the beach gradients were suitable for LCUs and Mexeflotes, and the landings could be effected regardless of wind direction. There were suitable positions into which the Brigade might quickly disperse to provide defences from counter-attacks and beach areas where stores could be landed. At this stage in early May, the plan was to keep afloat much of the ammunition and stores which would be used to maintain the Brigade in action. This was expected to be possible as the air threat was considered likely to be minimal by the time of the landing, which was was to made in sufficient time to allow a successful assault on Stanley before 24 May, when the South Atlantic gales might be expected. General Moore was briefed on the proposals while at Ascension and returned to Northwood with this and a couple of other less favourable options.

The distance from San Carlos to Stanley, the key target for victory, was greater than might be normally acceptable, especially as this was over 65 km across extremely difficult terrain. Few outside the Brigade staff seemed to have grasped the difference between the 'going' on the Islands and similar distances in North West Europe. Indeed the presumption that the Falklands were in some way similar to European islands, appears to have confused some of the planners in London. Meanwhile the staff of the Carrier Group pursued some other alternatives, looking for a suitable airstrip that might relieve the carriers of their need to cruise near to the Islands, as they must do if their aircraft patrols were to have adequate time over the beaches and advancing British forces. But the premise was that the Argentinian Air Forces would have been defeated before any landings were made.

During the voyage south various specialists on the Brigade staff were consulted on their aspects of the landings: Major John Chester, the Brigade Major; Lt-Col. Mike J. Holroyd-Smith RA who commanded the gunner regiment; Maj. R. Macdonald RE commanding the engineers; Maj. Gerry Wells-Cole RM, the logistician (DAA & QMG of the Brigade); Major W. David H. Baldwin RM, a former DAA & QMG; Maj. Ewen Southby-Tailyour RM with detailed knowledge of the Islands; Capt. 'Viv' Rowe RM the Intelligence Officer; and the Army's Maj. Hector Gullan who had been on the Brigade's staff for some time and was appointed liaison officer with the Paras. He would later act as the Brigadier's 'eyes and ears' with some assault companies. The success of this staff was in no small measure due to the fact that they had worked together in previous exercises and studies for possible operations. The close friendship which developed between COMAW and the Brigadier also played a major part in the smooth development and execution of the landing plan, despite the disruptions as we shall see.

The difficulties of keeping fit on the various ships during the many weeks they were at sea required physical training often restricted by a ship's routines and adverse weather.[51] For the planners a number of alternatives continued to need detailed work at the request of Admiral Woodward but San Carlos remained the accepted landing area. The intelligence gleaned by the Special Forces had begun to fill out the picture of Argentinian deployments. The teams made their reconnaissances on the inhospitable moorland with no cover for men moving in daylight. Therefore these SAS and SBS teams moved only at night and then in some places at no more than 250 m an hour. They hid during daylight in crevices among rock outcrops or in holes which they had dug, and camouflaged with turfs over chicken wire brought ashore for this purpose. They usually were landed several nights' march from their intended target and marched at least one night away from it before being ex-filtrated. This meant that they spent at least five days in the cold and wet conditions, and some teams were on East Falkland for much longer. There were only four sets of Passive Night Goggles (PNGs) available for helicopter pilots, so that the number of landings which might be made was restricted. These goggles make use of the ambient light, enabling a pilot to see the ground of a landing zone among other things, albeit in a green 'light'. Frigates and destroyers were used later that May to insert teams by boat, reminiscent of beach surveys of forty years previously. The only fatality in the SBS patrols occurred when one strayed into a 'buffer' zone between the SBS and the area patrolled by the SAS, and the leader of the SBS was killed b 'Friendly' fire.

On 9 May an SBS team abseiled from a Mk 4 Sea King to seize the 'spy' ship *Narwal* (a freezer trawler of 1,398 tons). They were covered by GPMG gunners in the doors of two Mk 5 Sea Kings supporting the boarding party. The *Narwal* had been seen by ships of the Task Force on and off from 30 April. She had a crew of fishermen, but was – rightly as it turned out – thought to be spying on the movements of the Carrier Task Force. She had been stopped in the water by bombs from *Hermes*'s aircraft, although these had not exploded due to the fuses being incorrectly set for a low-level attack; the Marines then boarded her without opposition. The Argentinian naval officer aboard the trawler had not destroyed his orders, which not only confirmed that she was a 'spy' ship but gave the names of two other 'spy' trawlers. Her crew were winched to the Mk 5s and the SBS returned to their Mk 4, which was only able to return to *Hermes* after refuelling from *Glasgow*'s flight deck, a landing which had required great skill as there was only a metre between the rotor blades and the Lynx hangar door on the destroyer.

Intelligence for the areas around San Carlos Water pointed to only occasional Argentinian patrols crossing the area in early May. But before the landing an Argentinian company took up positions on Fanning Head overlooking the entrance to Falkland Sound (which divides East Falkland from West Falkland). They also overlooked San Carlos Water which runs eastward off the Sound along the southern shore of this headland.

The risks posed to any landing force should the Argentinian Airforce be still active at the planned time of landing were thoroughly researched by the Brigade's Intelligence staff. Yet Captain Rowe's presentation of these facts was brushed aside by Admiral Woodward at a meeting aboard *Hermes on 16 April. The Carrier Battle Group's approach to the Islands was to make clear that Argentinian pilots had all the dashing courage for which South Americans are renowned.*

The Government had enlarged from 1 May the area around the Islands from which all shipping and aircraft were to be excluded except those authorised by the British (the Total Exclusion Zone, TEZ). This zone was 480 km in diameter and provided some sea-room for the ships requiring maintenance after weeks at sea and frequent actions against Argentinian aircraft. These had seriously damaged HMS Sheffield on 4 May and she sank some days later when being towed. Others attacked British ships with limited success; HMS *Glasgow* was hit by a bomb which failed to explode but left a metre-wide hole in both her port and starboard sides. However the British warships were deterred from their bombardment of the Islands' Argentinian defences, until the Carrier Group could be reinforced. Heavy weather was also taking its toll in some structural cracking of HMS *Arrow*'s hull; and similar damage, although less serious, led to HMS *Alacrity* requiring careful handling. (Such damage would be repaired by teams from the 162 technicians in the repair ship *Stena Seaspread* based at this time at South Georgia.) One difficulty was that the Battle Group did not have adequate long range warning of approaching aircraft, and an attempt to mount a surveillance patrol overlooking the mainland airfields had no luck, when their heavily laden Sea King crashed in Chile.

The Argentinians had an airstrip on Pebble Island north-west of Falkland Sound where in mid-May there were a number of Pucara aircraft. These strongly built twin-engined aircraft were equipped for ground support and capable of flying relatively slowly to attack troops or in counter-insurgency roles. This slow speed and manoeuvrability, with its armament of rockets, cannon and bombs, made the Pucara a particular threat to helicopters. A party from the SAS D Squadron's Boat Troop made a recce of Pebble Island before the remainder of D Squadron was flown in on the night of 14/15 May by Sea Kings from *Hermes*. They landed in a marked-out zone from where they dispersed to attack the aircraft. At the same time the garrison was bombarded by HMS *Glamorgan*, the fall of her shots being checked by Captain Brown RA who was ashore with the SAS. The SAS's 81 mm mortar fired illuminating bombs and Captain Hamilton's party destroyed 11 aircraft including six Pucaras, using prepared charges, after boldly stepping out onto the runway. They withdrew about 0330, later than intended, but *Glamorgan* had remained on the gun line to support them. A counter-attack by the garrison was put to flight, then the raiders were lifted back to *Hermes* before dawn and she sailed east, out of range of any land-based aircraft.

Naval bombardments during this time were frequently directed by officers from 148 Commando Battery RA in ships' helicopters, with teams of the 148 Commando Forward Observation Battery embarked in ships of the Carrier Battle Group. Despite the Argentinian air activity, some 13 shore bombardments were carried out by the Battle Group during the first few weeks of May.[55] The Group also provided air cover, and the Admiral's handling of his meagre force of fighter and ground support Harriers and his skill in keeping his carriers safe from air attack, were greatly respected,[56] for had he lost a carrier it might well have sunk the expedition before it started or worse – left the landing force isolated ashore.

The Special Forces recces and a few other sources – but no aerial photographs – had established that there were some 11,000 Argentinians ashore by 13 May (Thursday). That day the Brigadier issued his orders for the landing which was intended to create a beachhead, presenting these at an Orders Group (O Group). By this date there was no question of the Islands being retaken by the Brigade and once a beachhead was secured they would be joined by 5 Brigade who had sailed from the UK on 12 May. The orders followed General Moore's directive received the previous day: 'You are to secure a bridgehead . . . in which an airstrip can be established and from which operations to repossess the Falklands can be achieved; you are to push forward . . . so far as the maintenance of security allows, to gain information, to establish moral and physical domination over the enemy, and to forward the ultimate objective of repossession.'

The Commando and Battalion Commanders and their key staff officers were packed into the wardroom of *Fearless* for the O Group, plus the landing craft squadron commanders, aviators, liaison officers and beachmasters.[57] There was 'a polite silence', over which hummed the distant generators and creaks of the ship driving south, as the Brigadier and COMAW entered.

The terrain of the San Carlos landing beaches, intelligence reports and the Brigade Major's succinct summary of friendly forces, were covered in crisp presentations. Then the Brigadier set out the Mission: a silent night approach by landing craft to seize high ground before first light and secure a beachhead. There was no ambiguity in these concise orders which were followed by specialists detailing information on: logistics, the naval dispositions, gun fire support and instructions on coordinating the phases of the operation. The Brigadier completed his orders by making clear that this operation would be 'no picnic'. There were no questions, confirming the clarity and comprehensive nature of the orders.

D-day was later set for Friday 21 May with an approach on D-1 to put the Amphibious Task Force in North Falkland Sound, and H-hour for the first touch down on the beach by LCUs was in the early morning of that Friday. (All timings were given in Zulu time, this is Greenwich Mean Time [designated Z time], four hours 'ahead' of local time on the Islands, with midday GMT being 4 pm local time). A final piece of the complex jigsaw of this operation was put in place with a diversion set up by D Squadron SAS. They would land on the night of D-1/D-day (Thursday/Friday) from helicopters and with the support of HMS *Ardent* they were to create a diversion at Darwin. In the event this was so successful that the Argentinians though they were being attacked by a battalion.

A number of changes had to be made since the original O Group after the Argentinians had placed a force on Fanning Head, which overlooked San Carlos Water from the north and could control the entry to Falkland Sound to the west. This headland rises to over 200 m and a well positioned anti-tank weapon could play havoc with any ships approaching the Sound. To counter this threat, a 25-man detachment of SBS with 12 GPMGs supported by naval gunfire would land from helicopters in the early hours of D-day. They would attack from the east of these positions and in the event surprised the 'Fanning Head mob'. An SAS team also took along 'the superb new American 60 mm lightweight mortar'.[58] With the SBS was Captain Rod Bell, an RM officer who had been brought up in Costa Rica. He was a good judge of the various characters making up the Argentinian forces, as we shall see, but this would be the first test of their resolve as he called on them over his loudhailer to surrender.[59]

The political risk of losing *Canberra* and her embarked force became a concern in London and so on D-2 orders were given to disperse '40 RM' and 3 Para to other ships.[60] This would meet a requirement of London that only one major unit should be carried in a particular ship. However it was to be no simple task as helicopter cross-decking would use precious time out of the aircraft's endurance between maintenance periods. Using jackstays to haul men one at a time between ships would take days not hours. The LCUs were the solution and they were favoured with good fortune: it was an unexpectedly calm day for the South Atlantic. Only one man took a ducking when he fell between *Canberra* and an LCU bobbing 3 m or more up and down the ship's side. '40 RM' was taken across to *Fearless*. One company was to live in the wardroom, another in the junior rates dining hall and the CO (Lieutenant-Colonel Hunt) had 'quarters' in Brigadier Thompson's cabin.

3 Para went to *Intrepid* along with J Company. This Company had been formed from men who had been repatriated in the detachments that had served on the Islands and South Georgia in April.

The LPDs were grossly overloaded with their new arrivals jammed into spaces where a cabin floor might already be covered with several layers of boxed compo rations or a small bathroom be the all-purpose-space – cabin and office – of a senior Landing Craft officer. Other movements were required in which there was one tragic accident; the last helicopter flying men of D and G Squadrons of 22 SAS Regiment to *Intrepid* from *Hermes* probably hit a bird in the dusk and crashed with the loss of 22 men. The number of SAS ranks killed in this accident was the largest loss that Regiment had suffered in a single day since World War II.[61]

On D-1 (20 May) the weather turned foul; good fortune had again favoured the brave for no aircraft could locate the ships under a scudding sky. Although the Brigadier would have to secure the beachhead, he had to compromise on the available darkness, as the ships would need some dark hours during their final approach. (It was clear by this time that the Argentinians did not fly their attack aircraft at night.) All commanding officers had now been sent the final times for each stage in the operation, but 2 Para had not received this signal because the decoding equipment on *Norland* was not working. The signal had to be fired to her by way of HMS *Broadsword*'s rocket line.[62] There seemed to be no further hitches during the final approach

To meet the planned H-hour of 0230 on D-day, the assault ships had to enter Falkland Sound from the north at 2300 hours (local time) on D-1 (see map).[63] Dawn in the Falklands at that time of year was about 0630 hours local time and dusk at about 1645 hours. The East Falkland waters of Port San Carlos (to give it its full name) run west to east from Falkland Sound and are entered with Fanning Head – as mentioned earlier – to the north and Chancho Point some 2 km to the south. In broad terms: the San Carlos river enters from the east into Port San Carlos, and San Carlos Water runs to the south of this estuary in an open stretch 2 km wide and 10 km long. On the west of this stretch with its apex at Chancho Point and about half way down this western shore is Ajax Bay with the Red Beach (where '45 RM' would land and later the Brigade Maintenance Area would be established). On the north-eastern shores of the river estuary was Green Beach One (used by 3 Para followed later by '42 RM') and Green Beach Two ('40 Cdo RM'). On the south-eastern shores of San Carlos Water lies San Carlos Settlement just south of Little Rincon, a small promontory. To its north was Blue Beach One ('40 Cdo RM'), and to the south of this promontory was Blue Beach Two (2 Para).

It was 'a typical Falkland morning – calm, cool, clear and starlit'. To Lieutenant-Colonel Vaux aboard *Canberra* – he had paid his Mess Bill tactfully headed 'before disembarking from your cruise on *Canberra*' – the morning scene appeared 'comfortingly familiar, like just another NATO exercise off Greece or Gibraltar, Denmark or Norway'. That was the scene until a Pucara came twisting and turning towards the ship through the anti-aircraft fire before turning away towards the mountains. The next attack was more serious as a wave of aircraft arrived 'like thunderbolts from the blue'. The noise was overwhelming: explosions boomed, there were flashes of light, the crackle of machine gun fire and the shouts of lookouts. The ship lurched and shuddered as bombs detonated in the water. Then the enemy was gone. The pilots concentrated their attacks on the warships and were not apparently able to get a clear run at *Canberra* because of the hills surrounding the anchorage.[64]

The LPD *Fearless* was delayed by mist at the entrance to Falkland Sound and anchored an hour late, outside Port San Carlos. Then Captain Jeremy Larken

– long familiar with the Commandos' needs – had her flooded down despite a fault in the pumps which might have left his ship low in the water after her LCUs were launched. These carried the men of '40 Cdo RM' who had been embarked in the craft after making their way in the darkened ship along passages and down ladders, or up ladders for those making for the LCVPs. The men, in camouflage cream to 'hide' their faces, each carried a heavy Bergen, weapons and ammunition. (Major Southby-Tailyour wore Arctic ski-march boots, gaiters and two pairs of loop-stitched socks with long-johns under denim trousers, a hairy khaki shirt under a white submariners woollen jersey topped with a Special Forces jacket of oiled-cotton that had a hood, and his green beret.[65]). Some men carried radios although these would not be used until after they were ashore. Radio silence was strictly observed, as it was by the ships, to avoid any chance of the Argentinians picking up an indication of the presence of the Force. The LCUs came out of the dock, where they had been buffeted against the wooden-battened dock walls and its centre partition, in the eery red glow of the dimmed lights, as the sea surged in, sometimes lifting the craft and at others 'grounding' them on the dock floor.

Two of these LCUs each had at the bow a Scorpion with its 76 mm gun and a Scimitar with a 30 mm automatic cannon, both of the Blues and Royals, in the way landings had been rehearsed at Ascension. The Commando's A Company were in LCVPs launched from *Fearless*'s davits, and joined her LCUs led by Major Southby-Tailyour with his Passive Night Goggles giving him a view of his charges in shades of green. With him in *Foxtrot 1* was Colonel Seccombe who did not interfere with the Major's orders but offered reassurance when necessary. They had to transfer from the LCU to an LCVP at one stage and finally into *Intrepid*'s leading craft *Tango 1* whose coxswain was C/Sgt Barry Davies. He, like the other coxswains who would come alongside *Norland*, would need all their undoubted skills as seamen, because this ship had no convenient strong points to moor their LCUs alongside; any line had to be long and reach high to the ship's deck bollards.[66]

2 Para from *Norland* came out of the ship's tiny side door which served as a landing port some 3 m above the plunging craft. With none of the usual means of securing these to *Norland* and with less than a square metre of LCU deck for each man to land on as he jumped down, not surprisingly loading was taking time. During such delays commanders can become impatient, but COMAW and the Brigadier refrained from needless signals as the Major sorted out his charges. He agreed with Colonel Jones that the fourth LCU, about to take on her Paras, would have to catch up, and the Flotilla ceased circling before heading down the west side of San Carlos Water. Going flat out, not the planned 6 knots intended for this approach, the craft swept in line astern through the kelp beds. The briefest of radio signals 'out stern lights' had filled a gap in the Major's orders, for he wanted the craft without their usual means of 'preventing collisions at sea'.[67] These no doubt looked very bright in the Major's PN Goggles. The risk of sea mines was always in the back of his mind but they were unlikely to be inshore. COMAW had similar concerns on a larger scale, but Admiral Woodward had sent HMS *Alacrity* (a Type 21 frigate of 2,750 tons) through Falkland Sound

some days before D-day, trailing her expensive hull in looking for any mines.[68] She had found none. In late May two LCVPs would be fitted with lightweight minesweeping gear, shades of the Corps' minesweeping minor craft flotillas of World War II.

The landing craft were not using their radar and the only signals were passed by a pencil thin red light to minimise the possibility of visual sighting from onshore. But no signs of life could be seen as they raced to their forming up positions, with the reassuring bulk of HMS *Plymouth* moving to port of them, where she was acting as escort with her NGS officer landing with the CO of '40 RM'. There were, however, flashes of naval gunfire and tracer of the SBS on the headland to the north, crossing the fire of the Fanning Head mob. The craft covered the 8 km at full speed as the Major searched the shoreline for familiar features. '40 RM' left the Squadron to make the run to Blue Beach One, while 2 Para were to land to the south of San Carlos Settlement where they could approach Sussex Mountain, some 6 km further south, without the need to pass through any area with farm buildings.

Beach Blue Two was to have been marked by an SBS team but there was no red light being shown as the craft approached this beach, having crossed to the eastern shore. Therefore the Major had to go forward on *Tango 1*'s catwalk to warn Lieutenant-Colonel Jones that any armed men on the beach might be the SBS team, as there was no sign of any Argentinians. With that the craft formed up in line abreast and ran onto the beach. Power to the ramp's winch was switched on 50 m from the shore, and 'the harsh wine of its hydraulics' carried further than the throb of *Tango 1*'s engines on this still night.[69] There was an unfortunate water gap of about 10 m through which the Paras splashed ashore. It was 0430 local time and some 45 minutes later than the planned H-hour. 2 Para later reported that some members of the SBS team here had not been expecting them for another 72 hours.

'40 RM' ran in on their Blue Beach One, north of Little Rincon promontory, after receiving the red light signal from an SBS team. Two LCUs carried the HQ and some of Support Company 'crammed in behind the armoured vehicles'.[70] C Company was in a third LCU and the fourth carried a section of Royal Engineers, the rest of Support Company and a Combat Tractor. A Company cleared White Rincon (north of their target beach) and moved on to take up defence positions on the western slopes of Verde Ridge, some 3 km east of Blue Beach One. B Company cleared Little Rincon on the small promontory and then joined A Company. C Company cleared San Carlos Settlement where they hoisted the Union Flag before taking defensive positions south of the Settlement. All the defence positions were on the reverse slope of hills, with observation posts on the crests. In this way any attacking force would be silhouetted as they came over a hill.

The landing craft withdrew without incident having been joined by *Intrepid*'s fourth LCU which had offloaded her troops. For planning reasons it was easier for *Intrepid*'s craft to lift 3 Para from *Fearless* and her craft to take '45 RM' from *Stromness*.[71] Major Southby-Tailyour was to lead in 3 Para's craft to an 'unexplored' Green Beach One at Sand Bay in *Foxtrot 4* (her coxswain was C/ Sgt Brian Johnston who – with his crew – had taken the Major to Norway in the experimental *Black Pig*). There seemed to have been some delays as the exhaust fumes from the LCUs filled *Intrepid*'s dock and men struggled to reach the LCUs but eventually *Foxtrot 4* led off the craft, two of which each carried a pair of the CVRTs of the Blues and Royals. The 8 km run to Green Beach One on the northern shore of the river estuary, took little over half an hour at over 9½ knots, but off the beach the Major's craft grounded in a metre of clear water – too deep for the men to get ashore without wading waist deep. The other craft were ordered to beach some distance away to land their men and the tanks dry-shod. Then the LCVPs had to come out from the beach to take the men from *Foxtrot 4*. The SBS team who had been ashore for days, although they appeared as if they had only been 'on a day's exercise', were taken back to *Fearless* as 3 Para fanned out to secure Port San Carlos Settlement were they encountered half a company of Argentinians who withdrew.

When '45 RM' had been collected by craft from *Fearless,* these had to be overloaded as one LCU had broken down.[72] But it was still a beautiful morning.

As these LCUs were making their way back to *Fearless* the anchorage came under air attack. The various assault ships had now moved into the broad stretch of San Carlos Water and the priority was to lift ashore six light guns from the upper vehicle deck of an LSL, then the twelve Rapier firing posts could be hoisted from her hold to be flown ashore. It would be midday before all the intended sites for these missile launchers could be secured, carefully selected sites based on RA Battery Commander Major T.H.P. Smith's assessments using computer technology.[73] The recce parties were therefore flown in by Sea Kings escorted by pairs of Gazelles from the Brigade Air Squadron, each Gazelle having been armed – in part at Ascension – with SNEB Rockets and a GPMG.

Major Peter Cameron commanded the Commando Brigade Air Squadron. He was a skilled pilot with great courage and compassion. He usually piloted Brigadier Thompson's helicopter 'so he kept fully in the picture on what was in [the Brigadier's] mind'.[74] He and his pilots enjoyed the freedom to land their helicopters as operations required, without any of those restrictions on airspace required at home. As the war developed they would fly forward ammunition and bring back casualties despite the risks of coming, albeit low and fast, close to enemy positions.

The Rapier sites included one on the Knob lying east of Port San Carlos Settlement, which was being approached by the helicopters flying north to the site near the San Carlos river. They were fired on at 0800 hours by the Argentinians retreating before 3 Para along the north bank of the river. Sgt A.P. Evans was mortally wounded but skilfully set his Gazelle down on the water 500 m from the Settlement. His crewman, Sgt E.R. Candlish, managed to inflate Sgt Evans's lifejacket but they continued to be fired on, as the crewman swam with the dying pilot towards the Settlement. The other Gazelle was hit but got back to its LSL parent ship, as did the Sea King.

A third Gazelle flying near the Settlement was also hit and disintegrated;

both the pilot, Lieutenant K.D. Francis RM, and the crewman, Corporal B.P. Giffin RM, were killed. These were the Brigade's only casualties on D-day. But out in the anchorage, where the ships lay between the steep sides of Wreck Point (the headland with Chancho Point at its apex) and the protection of the Verde Mountains to the east, a Pucara attacked *Canberra* at 0855 hours, as we have seen. And throughout the rest of the day Argentinian fighter-bombers – to use an old fashioned but descriptive phrase – attacked the ships. HMS *Ardent* was sunk with the loss of 22 lives. These attacks did not reach the transports, to the relief of the Landing Force staffs, and many of which still carried teams of Marines and soldiers who had provided close anti-aircraft fire with GPMGs. The guardships, however, were hit and all the frigates near the anchorage were sunk or damaged that day, yet the LSLs with the Brigade's stores were still afloat. The helicopters with their underslung loads continued to fly to the beaches and the Mexeflotes' Royal Corps of Transport (RCT) crews continued to carry stores ashore. In the nine hours of daylight *Fearless*'s seven Sea Kings alone picked up 288 loads, tasked by the staff in this LPD, and put ashore 520 men with over 220 tons of stores from eleven different ships taking the loads to 21 different sites.[77] They had landed the rest of the guns from the four light batteries and a good deal of ammunition, although not enough should the beachheads be seriously attacked as the Brigade had expected them to be. There were also some problems with communications as the radios aboard *Fearless* had not always been able to keep in contact with forward units.

The LCUs chugged from ships to shore carrying loads as they would for the rest of the campaign when not involved in specific landings. On D+1 (Saturday 22 May) three LCUs each used their 560-horsepower engines to tow HMS *Argonaut* from west of Doctor's Head to a less exposed position in San Carlos Water. Argentinian planes had achieved some eight near-misses when they attacked her and she had two unexploded bombs lodged in her hull, one in her Seacat missile magazine. Yet the calm steadiness of her crew impressed the Marines. Her Captain, Kit Layman, and his men might have been conducting 'some rather mundane evolution ... in her Devonport Naval Base'.[78] Two craft were secured on each side and a third on a long towline forward gave some steerage, bringing this frigate's loaded 3,000 tons to anchor an hour and a half before sunset. During the tow *Argonaut*'s crew had continued to do what they could to secure their deadly cargo but it would be seven days before the second unexploded bomb could be removed. A claim for salvage in the hope of adding some millions of pounds sterling to the LC Branch Welfare fund was submitted before the LCUs slipped from the stricken ship. Six months later they received a penny 'in full and final settlement'.[79]

42 Commando RM, the Brigade reserve, having left *Canberra* early that afternoon after several more air raids, landed to reinforce the beaches near 3 Para on 'Green One'. *Canberra* signalled the P&O head office: 'Have delivered passengers as requested'[80]. The initial landings were now complete. The Fanning Head mob had been rounded up after seven hours. D Squadron SAS, having successfully distracted the Argentinians by their raid on Darwin, were withdraw-

ing to the area of 2 Para on Sussex Mountain. There, an SAS trooper trained to use the American Stinger shoulder launched missile, had destroyed a Pucara that tried to attack this withdrawal.[81] '42 RM' had landed without their Bergens, left aboard *Canberra* along with most of their stores and the Commando's Main HQ. As they moved eastward, they passed through 3 Para's defences, whose CO, Lt-Col. Hew Pike, was 'looking brisk and warlike'.[82] They continued along the northern bank of the river being offered cups of soup by excited children. As Lt-Col. Vaux was crossing the heather along the hills by the river, a Gazelle landed bringing Brigadier Thompson to visit the Colonel – in the way the Commando Brigadier kept in contact with his COs – and among other news which he brought, the Brigadier warned that *Canberra* would be leaving the anchorage that night, as *Canberra* and *Norland* had been ordered to put to sea out of 'bomb alley' as San Carlos Water was now known. The Commando advanced further along the line of the river bank, had a false 'enemy' contact – Lt-Col. Vaux was furious at the unprofessional way some of his men had 'shot at boulders' – before nightfall led to their taking up defensive positions. (Those who knew the Colonel would have found 'furious' a mild term, for his displeasure at incompetence was renowned but so was his reputation for 'getting things done'.) He did not want his men exposed to possible own-goals through movement outside an ill-defined perimeter in the dark, but at first light next morning they moved quickly to the crest of their objective: the ridge of Cerro Montevideo hill. And that evening their Bergens were flown in, but not the Colonel's![83]

The beefy and cheerful Major Smith commanding the Rapier Battery had warned the Brigadier that it might take until nightfall to get all his Rapiers' electronics working properly, that is 'in' to use the technical term. The journey south in an LSL's hold and the possible tilting of one mounting – said to have disturbed a level of mercury in the delicate control systems – made more than the normal adjustments necessary, but by midday on D+1 (Saturday 22 May) the three sections of Rapiers each with four 'ire units' were in action or ready for it.

The Brigadier's Tactical HQ, having stood-to since dawn on the Friday (D-day), got ashore that evening some 10 hours later than planned, but the air battles around *Fearless* had prevented it being landed earlier.[84] Through these air attacks her captain, Captain Larken, 'fought' his ship in his usual devastatingly calm manner.[85] Brigade HQ, with all the communications equipment needed to coordinate the Brigade's activities, would be landed early on D+1 (22 May). This HQ had seven BV202 over-snow vehicles and a specially constructed tent which could be spread over these when backed into position. In this way each staff had their desks at the back of a vehicle facing the centre of the 'tent', an efficient organisation, again well-practised during exercises in Norway and when suitably camouflaged with netting was difficult to see even from the ground. It was dug into the side of the isthmus joining Little Rincon to the mainland at San Carlos Settlement.[86] The Brigadier and his staff worked there regardless of air raids, although as a precaution slit trenches had been dug and were there if required.

The Brigadier's original intention had been to keep the reserves of stores and ammunition afloat, but the air superiority to warrant this was not achieved, and on D-day these 'bullets, beans and fuel' began to be put ashore beside the Mutton Factory at Ajax Bay. Here also would be Surgeon Commander Rick Jolly's Field Surgical Team, the *Red and Green Life Machine*, which was to serve the Brigade and others so well. This location had a beach that would take several craft at a time and involved only short journeys for the forklift trucks to transfer pallets from these craft to the stores dumps by the factory.[87] Until there were sufficient quantities of combat stores ashore to last 30 days, several thousand tons of them, the Brigade could not fight far from the beachheads without undue risks to the operation. Indeed every battle would need the support of at least one light gun battery requiring eleven lifts by eight Sea Kings to take forward the guns and 500 rounds for each of them,[88] and units outside the air umbrella of Rapiers and cover air patrols could in all probability be seriously compromised by air attacks.

Nevertheless the Brigadier wanted to strike at the Argentinians in order to keep up some momentum and therefore planned with Lieutenant-Colonel H Jones a raid on Darwin some 19 km south from 2 Paras positions on Sussex Mountain, with a further 3 km to Goose Green. But any major movement was going to require more helicopters than were available, a constant drawback to the intended plans for leap-frogging the Brigade's units forward over the Camp – the open countryside – to reach Stanley.

5 Brigade aboard the passenger liner *Queen Elizabeth II* (67,140 tons) sailed south passing the area of Ascension but avoiding the island on about 21 May. She and the ships carrying this Brigade's heavy weapons and stores joined a convoy with its screen of warships. They sailed for security reasons well to the east of a line to her intended destination of South Georgia. General Moore had sailed with 5 Brigade but as the *QE II* had no secure radio satellite communications, the General was to be out of touch with 3 Commando Brigade for some 10 days. He would have preferred to fly to the Carrier Battle Group and parachute into the sea, but until later in the operation this was not thought feasible. A Royal Marine himself, the General was one of many Marines who had no difficulty in working with the Army.

Admiral Fieldhouse by this time had another military adviser, General Richard Trant, who had served in the Royal Artillery. The Admiral was coming under pressure from the Cabinet to get the Landing Force moving towards Stanley and discussed the possibilities with the Brigadier over a secure satellite radio link. The Cabinet's concern was that if a major land area was not occupied quickly, then the diplomatic pressure on the Argentinians would be weakened. Lafonia, the plain covering half of East Falkland, looked invitingly open for attack, as it might have been if it was in north-west Europe. As it was, as one commentator put it at the time: the Argentinians in Lafonia were going nowhere and could be easily cut off by blocking the isthmus. Stanley was the prize.

42 Commando RM were outside the air defence umbrella at Cerro Montevideo, the hill feature some 7 km east of Port San Carlos Settlement. Therefore the Brigadier decided to move them closer to the air cover and on the

night of D+2 (23 May) they were to be ferried by landing craft down the San Carlos River to Port San Carlos Settlement. While this movement was being planned, two LCUs – *Foxtrot 1* (C/Sgt 'Connie' Francis) and *Foxtrot 4* (C/Sgt Brian Johnston) – were alongside the frigate HMS *Antelope* helping to fight serious fires and to pick up survivors, although some of the crew had been taken off earlier. The LCUs remained there despite radioed orders to clear the area, until *Antelope*'s First Lieutenant ordered the rest of his crew to abandon ship and they came away from the flight deck in the LCUs, while an LCVP took the Captain and his party off the fo'c'sle. Ten minutes later the first of several of *Antelope*'s magazines exploded and others blew up during the night.[90] She finally sank at 1300 hours (1 pm) next day.

The transfer of '42 RM' went to plan. Although in the narrow river the lead craft grounded at one point, because such incidents were routine for landing craft crews she was quickly hauled off. Two LCUs made a double trip to bring the Commando back to Port San Carlos Settlement, saving the men a tedious march, and providing 'a good example of the use of LCUs exploiting the water lines of communication'.[91] But when Lieutenant-Colonel Vaux saw the boggy ground where it had been proposed his men should dig in – 'showing the dangers of picking positions from maps'[92] – he arranged with Lieutenant-Colonel Pike that '42 RM' should take up positions at the eastern end of San Carlos Settlement. The Para Colonel agreed to the arrangement with his 'characteristic consideration and flexibility' as his 3 Para moved to cover the west side of the Settlement. Both units were now positioned to prevent any possible Argentinian thrust from the north-east into the area of the bridgehead.

The Raiding Squadron was operating from an inlet at Bonner's Bay using their Rigid Raider craft to insert SBS and other teams along the coast. Some raiding craft on occasion were taken by frigates to make their insertions. The Squadron's Captain Chris Baxter RM was to make this a fine art during the campaign and on the night of D+3 (24 May) the Marines of 6 SBS were landed on the shores of Port Salvador, their movements being cloaked by poor weather. This large stretch of water formed a route from the north coast of East Falkland for some 30 km to within 10 km of the Argentinians' outer defence line of Stanley.

The weather continued to be misty with low cloud on the night of Monday (D+3), preventing planned helicopter insertions, although two teams of commando Mountain Leaders (MLs) were already in observation posts hidden on Bull Hill some 30 km east of San Carlos and on Evelyn Hill a further 12 km to the east. Inserted by helicopter on the night of D-day, from these OPs they could see any movement towards the beachheads and in clear weather they had views to the south towards Lafonia, north towards to Teal Inlet (off the waters of Port Salvador) and eastwards towards Stanley.[93]

The bad weather also prevented any airlift of the light guns which would have been necessary to support 2 Para's intended raid on Lafonia. Therefore the Brigadier wisely cancelled it, despite Lieutenant-Colonel Jones's annoyance at having his battalion remain on Sussex Mountain. He is reported to have said

'I've waited 20 years for this and now some f–ing Marine's cancelled it'.[94] The weather also frustrated the landing of D Squadron SAS and '42 RM' on Mount Kent, although a recce party from the Squadron had seized this high ground (at about 600 m) on D+3 (Monday 24 May). Mount Kent was the key to dominating the defences here in the mountains west of Stanley, as we shall see.[95]

The impatience of Admiral Woodward, as noted earlier, was expressed in some 'hurry up' signals which did not endear him to the Brigadier, but Brigadier Thompson was not a man to be bullied. At this time he still also had to contend with the limitations of helicopter lifts, since they had the unforseen tasks of landing stores to the Brigade Maintenance Area (BMA) at Ajax Bay. This was made difficult because most ships had only one helicopter landing platform, limiting them to lift of about 20 tonnes an hour compared to over 90 tonnes from some of the RN support ships. And the loading ramp heights of some STUFT ships had proved incompatible with LCUs and Mexeflotes, impeding the offloading of stores.

The weather also prevented any landings on West Falkland; it was too rough even for an LCVP to cross Falkland Sound for any attempt to clear a suspected Argentinian OP on Mount Rosalie. From this OP aircraft were being – as it later proved – directed onto ships near the entrance to San Carlos Water. The weather cleared during daylight on that Tuesday and the Argentinians sank the transport *Atlantic Conveyor*. This large Cunard vessel of about 15,000 tons was carrying five Chinook large troop-carrying helicopters, each capable of lifting over 70 men. She also carried other aircraft most of which had flown off before she was sunk but four of the Chinooks were lost, as was the material for a landing strip among other war stores. The Commando Brigade would have to walk to Stanley.

Admiral Fieldhouse expressed to the Brigadier over the satellite link London's impatience for a breakout from the beachhead. General Richard Trant – the military adviser to the Admiral after General Moore had sailed south – overruled any objections which the Brigadier had to undertaking an offensive against Goose Green; therefore the raid was to be mounted.[96] This would be the only time that London interfered with those conducting the campaign on the spot, and in retrospect is an example of 'the risks and complications which can set in when a military operation is being conducted to serve an urgent political purpose'.[97]

Lafonia is the only large plain on East Falkland with undulating ground seldom rising to more than 30 m. It is joined to the rest of East Falkland by a narrow isthmus of about 6 km in length with the Darwin settlement at the northern end near the head of Choiseul Sound; to its east and across the isthmus is Brenton Loch. Lieutenant-Colonel Jones, known as 'H' to his officers and others, was briefed on the available intelligence (which subsequently proved grossly to under-estimate the Argentinian strength on Lafonia.)[98] 'H' gathered some of this infor-mation from the SAS men who had created the diversion on D-day, but nobody in the Brigade knew that the garrison had been strengthened by an Argentinian regiment.

At nightfall on D+5 (Wednesday 26 May) 'H' led his battalion to Camilla

Creek House, the large home of the local farm manager, a kilometre or so north of the isthmus, where they lay up through Thursday concealed in the farm buildings. From here 'H' sent out two patrols which reported that there were enemy positions on a hill south-west of Darwin and at several other positions on the isthmus, but the patrols could make no deeper recces as they were seen by the Argentinians and withdrew under fire.

Much has been written about the exposure of modern military operations to journalistic reports spread worldwide. Indeed two journalists with the Brigade had attempted to use the Island's telephones, surprisingly still connected up to Stanley and totally insecure. The Brigadier had taken them aside to point out the dangers of letting the Argentinians know details of planned operations; and care was taken to limit what journalists were told. Others in London had not heard this warning and at midday local time on Thursday, the BBC World Service announced that 2 Para was advancing on Darwin, an indiscretion which had nothing to do with the BBC's Robert Fox who was with the Brigade. Subsequently the Land Force discovered that an Argentinian mobile reserve had been flown from Mount Kent to Darwin when their command was alerted by this broadcast.[99] 'H' was rightly extremely angry when his men heard this broadcast as they lay at Camilla Creek House. These Paras had been exposed to the weather on Sussex Mountain and already had some cases of trench-feet, the debilitating effect of a prolonged soaking, yet with typical Para determination the Battalion, some 450 men, were keen to follow 'H' into the battle.

Three guns of 8 (Alma) Commando Battery with 320 rounds per gun were flown in that Thursday night to Camilla Creek House area. And at 0230 on Friday morning the Battalion began their attack after a section of 59 Commando Squadron RE had checked that there were no mines laid on the approaches to the defended positions. HMS *Arrow* provided gunfire support until 0520, although first light was due at about 0545 and she would be exposed in daylight to air attack as she came back to San Carlos Water. The rain poured down and Argentinian gun fire became increasingly heavy, but the casualties were minimal and as dawn came up 'H' ordered A Company to assault Darwin. They came under fire from machine guns now able to see any movement in the rapidly increasing light. Some 800 m to A Company's right, B Company was under fire on the forward slopes of a hillock overlooking Boca House on the western shore of the isthmus. Ammunition supplies were running low; already the two 81 mm mortars had fired all their rounds which had been carried in by the Paras.

About 0930 hours 'H', who was with A Company, personally led a deter-mined assault on a slit trench but was hit mortally by fire from another trench. Major Keeble, 'a quiet courteous man',[100] moved forward with the duplicate Tactical HQ; as second-in-command he now took hold of the operation. With him was Major Hector Gullan who continued his commentary over a direct radio link to the Brigadier: 'Bit of a problem here – but we'll sort it' was his reference to the defences of Boca House.[101] Pucaras attacked the companies and the two light helicopters from the Brigade Air Squadron. These were under the command of 2 Para to assist with casualty evacuation among other things. One was shot down as it flew forward to evacuate 'H'. Its pilot, Lieutenant R.J. Nunn RM, was killed and his gunner, Sergeant Belcher, survived the crash but lost both legs when hit by cannon shells. The second light helicopter was deftly flown by Captain J.P. Niblett RM as his gunner, Sergeant Glaze, stood in the back of the helicopter passing information on any attacking Pucara's position.[102]

The battle was to continue for over six hours: B Company moved along the beach out of the line of direct fire to seize Boca House after its strong points were destroyed by the Milans of Support Company. A Company took Darwin Hill and C Company passed through them to attack Goose Green airstrip. D Company skirted a minefield and saw white flags at Darwin; as a platoon commander moved forward to accept these surrenders he and two NCOs were killed. The platoon then cleared several buildings, killing the defenders. By 1530 Goose Green airfield was taken.[103]

Air attacks continued as 2 Para cleared the isthmus, a couple of napalm bombs falling just clear of D Company. Under command of 2 Para were some of the Commando Brigade's Air Defence Troop and 'as if in a butt on a grouse moor' Marine Strange stood up to shoot down a Pucara using his cumbersome Blowpipe. 2 Para's own Air Defence Section was successfully defending the light guns. As light was fading about 1525 hours, three Harriers arrived, bad weather having prevented any earlier flights from the carriers. The NGS officer acting as Forward Air Controller (FAC) brought in two Harriers to drop cluster bombs on the guns firing from the Goose Green peninsula to the east of the airstrip. The third Harrier attacked these gun positions and seemed to silence not only the anti-aircraft guns but also artillery in the area. The companies 'went firm' on positions ordered by Maj. Keeble and Brigadier Thompson sent a signal to the Regimental Colonel of the Parachute Regiment in Aldershot:

> 'You will wish to know that today's battle for Darwin and Goose
> Green was won by the magnificent fighting spirit of 2 Para.'

That Saturday night Captain J.G. Greenhalgh RCT flew his Scout helicopter back to Ajax Bay. With the help of ships' lights switched on briefly to guide him, he brought out several Para and Argentinian wounded. A Harrier strike was also arranged for Sunday morning, when it was put down near the garrison 'to convince them that the British meant business'. Meanwhile Major Keeble issued an ultimatum, translated into Spanish by Captain Rod Bell RM who had advanced with 2 Para. This was taken by two prisoners under a white flag of truce to the garrison commander, and a meeting between Major Keeble and the Argentinian commanders was arranged. When the garrison surrendered, 250 men of Air Force Defence troops, allowed to form up and march away to the prison areas. They were well disciplined troops whose 30 mm anti-aircraft cannons had caused much of 2 Para's difficulties. Then to Rod Bell's surprise almost 1,000 Argentinian infantry shambled onto the airstrip and surrendered. The list of captured artillery was long. Although the victory had cost 20 British dead and 37 wounded, 2 Para were in defensive positions by Sunday night, expecting some possible counter-attack.

* * *

While the battle was being fought on Lafonia, the 600 men of '45 RM' were moved before first light on Thursday (27 May) by LCUs from Ajax Bay to Port San Carlos Settlement. From there – on Sunday, 30 May – they marched ('yomped' – as Marines say) to Douglas on the north-west shores of Salvador Water. ('Yomping' is derived from the name of a Norse deity Yompa, noted for his endurance, athletic ability and tenacity. *Yomp* is also Norwegian for a big jump or stride.) The Argentinians were fully occupied with events at Goose Green and there were no air attacks against the forces crossing the northern Camp. '45 RM' covered the first 20 km – the worst stage – of this march, crossing boggy ground with its tufts of tussock grass that could turn an ankle or worse. The hillsides which they crossed were steep in places, making the men's loads of over 50 kg difficult to balance, and even their CO, Lieutenant-Colonel Andrew Whitehead, 'seemed dwarfed by his rucksack' and he was a big man. Meanwhile, his RSM, Pat Chapman, seemed to have 'his wings clipped' but not his sardonic sense of humour: 'Sorry to see 42 Commando has again been left behind' he remarked to Lieutenant-Colonel Vaux. There was one halt at about 1615 hours for a brew before last light, then the snake of Marines in single file pressed on some 8 km to reach New House at 2200 hours. The rain lashed down as the men lay on the ground to snatch some sleep, although their sleeping bags were soaked despite the plastic covering intended to keep them dry.[104] Next morning (Monday 31 May), they covered a further 12 km to Douglas Settlement, advancing without their Bergens behind a screen of scouts and in tactical formation ready to fight if the enemy appeared. They found that the enemy had left 48 hours earlier, after some vandalising of the Settlement. Not surprisingly, the locals were delighted to see '45 RM' and provide what help they could with tractors to carry some heavier loads. The commandos dried out in the Settlement buildings and next morning (Saturday) their Bergens – in which were their rations – were brought up by helicopters so that they had their first hot meal since Thursday night. ('45 RM' were to devise a compromise between moving in fighting order and carrying more than just emergency rations. Their 'heavy fighting order' worn in future operations weighed some 35 kg, but they would not have to depend on others to bring forward their rations for immediate use.)

3 Para marched ('tabbed' as Paras say) to Teal Inlet a little south of Douglas, crossing 40 km of similar country to that covered by '45 RM'. The Paras left a re-broadcasting unit on Bombilla Hill over 26 km from San Carlos. These radios could maintain contact with the Brigade at San Carlos by clear but secure speech, carried across the hills as signals were re-broadcast. As such radios provided an essential link to the Brigade, they were usually mounted in BV202 Bandwagons. On the Saturday at 0700 hours an SBS patrol reported that they had contacted 3 Para, who were to lay up some 9 km from Teal on Saturday night. The Battalion's Mortar Platoon had followed up on two trailers pulled by local farmers' tractors. The Battalion advanced next morning on the little group of farm buildings at Teal, sending one company to the south to cut off any enemy which might try to escape their advance. There was none but, like '45 RM', the Battalion sent out patrols to ensure that there were no unpleasant surprises.[105]

The limited transport in this and '45 RM's' advance had been dictated by the lack of fuel, after the LSL *Sir Lancelot* had been forced to ditch her load of motor transport fuel when an unexploded bomb lodged in her hull. This shortage had also delayed a troop of Scorpions and Scimitars leaving Port San Carlos, until its enterprising commander hijacked some fuel. An ineffective air attack did not slow their advance and the tanks caught up with 3 Para at Teal. Both 45 Commando RM and 3 Para had been on the move for some 36 hours, but 2 Para at Goose Green had the priority; helicopters had been needed to fly forward light guns for the support of those men marching eastward and with these flights went the Bergens for 3 Para.

With the pending arrival of 5 Brigade, a Task Force Assault Squadron was formed to coordinate all 'boating' assets. Commanded by Major Ewen Southby-Tailyour, it included the landing craft and the Rigid Raiders of the Raiding Squadron which had been part of the Brigade's HQ and Signals Squadron. Captain Chris Baxter commanding the 'Raiders' had considerable knowledge of raiding techniques and was good at staff work. The latter sometimes caused the Major to hurry things along, when he considered that there was not the time for proper procedures.[106] The Assault Squadron pooled the landing craft and Raiders' signal networks, which came under the efficient Corporal Williams, who had no additional radio sets but handled their communications 'with good sense and useful ideas' at their headquarters on Little Rincon, near Blue Beach One and Blue Beach Two. Later the Corporal's duties would be taken over by 'a Warrant Officer, a Signals Senior NCO and a number of corporals'.[107]

At dusk on the Thursday (27 May), Skyhawks had dropped parachute retarded bombs on the BMA and Dressing Station, setting fire to the Milans of 45 RM (each missile costing the price of a small car) and pallets of ammunition stacked for lifting to 2 Para and which were replaced before that Battalion was in action. Half a dozen men were killed.[108] Order was quickly restored by the army officer commanding the Commando Logistic Regiment RM, Lieutenant-Colonel Ivar Hellberg. This quiet Everest and Alpine climber had been responsible for the handling of the Brigade's war and other stores throughout the collection of these in the UK and their eventual accumulation at Ajax Bay. The bombs lodged near the Dressing Station did not explode and the medics worked on, attempts to find a new location for them having failed to produce any suitable building, which was why the dressing station had been placed near the BMA in the first place. Two slit trenches in '40 Cdo RM's' HQ area were hit; in each were two men taking cover. In one trench one man was killed and in the other a man was so badly wounded that he later died after being evacuated. Their companions suffered 'whistling in the ears' from the blast.[107a]

Men of the Logistic Regiment boarded ships each night when they came into San Carlos Water, to be hastily offloaded before the ships returned before dawn to the comparative safety of the Total Exclusion Zone (TEZ). By Sunday however, supplies were dangerously low in the BMA with, for example, only 83 rounds for each 105 mm light gun, and no hexamine fuel for the men's cookers on which they would heat water or snow to reconstitute their dehydrated rations. There were other serious shortages. The LSLs had also to be loaded for the supply of the men on the west shores of Salvador Water, where a new BMA (the Forward BMA) was to be established at Teal, but ships for these cargoes would not be available until later in the week. It had taken seven hours to fly an additional three guns and ammunition to the gunline near Camilla Creek, a round trip of only 38 km,[109] but helicopters were in such short supply due to their many tasks and the loss of *Atlantic Conveyor* that their tasking would become a bone of contention for several commanders.

By Saturday (29 May), men of the M&AW Cadre had been moved to OPs further east after various frustrations in foul weather at night; this had also dogged the SAS's D Squadron on Mount Kent. Nevertheless the SAS would mark out a Landing Zone for men from '42 RM', some 100 m below the summit. The CO, Lieutenant-Colonel Vaux, made the arrangements with Lieutenant-Colonel Rose in the SAS Colonel's Command Post, described by Lieutenant-Colonel Vaux as 'a brigand's cave of specialist weapons and technological devices'. And Lt-Col. Vaux no doubt looked suitably war-like with his sterling sub-machine gun slung on his shoulder. The Commando was to be allocated four Sea Kings and the Chinook for limited sorties over the next few nights. The initial landings – made after an appropriate rehearsal – would be executed by Lt-Col. Nick Vaux, his TAC HQ, K company (less 30 men), a section from the Mortar Troop, a section with Blowpipes and three 105 mm guns securely tethered in the Chinook. The first 'sticks' were flown to the Landing Zone on the night of 30/31 May (Sunday/ Monday) after an initial delay the previous night due to a blizzard. As the first sticks of men came out of their aircraft, they found the SAS engaged in a fire fight with a patrol of Argentinian Special Forces.

As the Chinook, flown by Squadron-Leader Richard Langworthy RAF, was coming back through snow storms it hit the surface of a lake and the aircraft's undercarriage was damaged. The guns had been landed but, without the Chinook, not all the ammunition could be flown forward as was intended. Sea Kings would now fly this ammunition forward but at the expense of not carrying L Company. Indeed there would only be one more lift-of-men that night as the helicopters' fuel was running low and would now be needed to bring up pallets of ammunition. These flights were still controlled by Naval staff aboard HMS *Fearless* and on Sunday morning an RN Movement Control Team had arrived at '42 RM's' Command Post. Their expertise and special communication links had enabled a more flexible tasking for the Sea Kings and as '42 RM's' logistical support – ammunition, rations and radio batteries, etc., – had to be flown forward, the Team sorted this out.

When the last troop flight took off that night (Sunday/Monday) with the 'roar of the engines coughing out the hot, acrid fumes of burnt Avcat',[110] the helicopters were loaded regardless of safety margins. Troops piled in on top of missiles for the Blowpipes, on reserves of ammunition and spare batteries. 'Surveillance devices replaced fuel', there were no seats, no safety belts and the loads were not made tactically; they would have to be sorted out after landing. Colonel Rose flew in this flight with reserves for his SAS on the mountain top, and with them was the large bulk of the reporter Max Hastings, his place, he claimed, to have been personally allocated by the Brigadier. As Lieutenant-Colonel Vaux's flight hovered and the klaxon sounded as the dimmed light at the exit changed from red to green, he and his 'stick' – RSM Chisnall, two radio operators, the Battery Commander of the 105s and the CO's bodyguard – prepared to land. There was always a moment or two when a stick landed in which the men could be disorientated in the down-draught of the helicopter's rotors, the dust these kicked up and the thunderous noise, but the stick leader knew from the pilot in which direction the aircraft had landed. As it flew off the leader could then get his men, and the supplies tossed from the helicopter, away from the landing point and into a defensive semi-circle.

Lieutenant-Colonel Vaux met Major Delves and Captain John Hamilton at the Landing Zone and they confirmed that K Company had moved off with their SAS guides. By first light on the Monday (31 May), the enemy patrol had been driven off by the SAS, as K Company reached the summit. The temperature was well below freezing but when the mist lifted they could see hastily abandoned Argentinian positions and Stanley 15 km in the distance.[111]

That morning the Colonel learnt that Max Hastings had *not* received the Brigadier's permission to fly forward, and he was therefore given a Blowpipe to carry. Col. Rose was in conversation over his SATCOM radio with Hereford, as '42 RM's' headquarters was established in the saddle some 2 km south of the summit of Kent. Further south across this saddle was Mount Challenger, its 'jagged ridges slashed by sharp re-entrants or encrusted with jumbled stone runs'. The HQ would be there for the next 12 days (31 May to 11 June). Lieutenant-Colonel Vaux led his TAC HQ by way of the south-east slopes of Kent towards the summit. As he came through the mist swirling in a buffeting wind near the top, he heard the clash of a weapon being cocked. At this moment the RSM gave his Colonel a hefty push to send him sprawling on the ground, as Chisnell bellowed 'British commandos! Royal Marines!'. The man who had cocked his weapon turned out to be Sergeant 'Dinker' Bell of the SAS in a two-man OP, who recognised the RSM whom he had known when Bell was in the Marines. In the next half-hour Major David Brown RA's 105 mm battery in support of '42 RM' fired some salvoes using 'super charge' ammunition with a range of 17 km. These were directed onto targets by the Battery's artillery observer Captain Chris Romberg RA from the top of Mount Kent.

The Brigadier intended '45 RM' and 3 Para to advance to Estancia House on the southern shore of Salvador Water. From there '45 RM' was to pass through 3 Para to seize Long Island Mountain over 10 km east of Salvador Water and overlooking the east coast of East Falkland. But the same bad weather which delayed '42 RM's' landing on Mount Kent delayed this move and the Brigadier's attempts to visit his commanders. He nevertheless went forward in one of two Gazelles from the Brigade Air Squadron which flew to Teal that Sunday morning.

The risks run by these light helicopters were accentuated by their ground camou-flage which stood out against the withered-white autumn grass of the Camp below and the threat of Pucaras attacking them. The 15 to 20 minute flight, low and fast across the Camp, jinking to see they were not open to any aircraft flying up behind them, passed without incident. The Brigadier gave his orders: '45 RM' were to move to Teal and 3 Para to Estancia House, but it would take several days before they could move into the mountains, with adequate support from light guns. Helicopters again were too few for all the moves which the Brigadier would have preferred to make. He was flown back to San Carlos.

The Commando Brigade Air Squadron's refuelling area was bombed the next Tuesday (1 June) by a high flying Canberra but there were no serious casualties.[112]

General Moore arrived ashore at the Brigade headquarters that Sunday (30 May), having been brought by a destroyer from South Georgia to *Fearless*, in which the Divisional Headquarters would be established. When some concern was shown about the status of 'red' and 'green' berets, the General had a neat touch in wearing his Norwegian Army forage cap. He was being briefed ashore at the Brigade's HQ by the staff when the Brigadier returned from his visit to 3 Para. The Brigadier has written: 'his cheerful presence now allowed me to concentrate on commanding my Brigade'. The General's Division – the Land Forces Falkland Islands – included 3 Commando Brigade and the Army's 5 Brigade commanded by Brigadier Tony Wilson, and took under its command the SAS and SBS Special Forces. The General also took over the twice daily report to Northwood over the satellite communication network operated by a team from the Royal Signals at Ajax Bay. He made reassuring nightly signals to Northwood. This soothed the impatience in some quarters,[113] even if the campaign was continuing to Briga-dier Julian Thompson's original plan. Under this plan, approved by the General, Julian Thompson intended to seize Long Island Mount, Mount Estancia, Mount Challenger and Mount Kent, so that 'the enemy in Stanley would be invested and 3 Commando Brigade would have unrestricted use of the many inlets of Port Salvador'.[114] The execution of the plan could now unfold with Brigadier Thomp-son moving his Headquarters to Teal on 31 May (Monday), the day after the Divisional HQ aboard *Fearless* took command of the Land Force.

The composition of 5 Brigade was mainly of men who had experience of NATO's Central Front in Germany and had been trained to fight using Armoured Personnel Carriers for long movements across a battlefield. In the Falklands they had few vehicles and had to depend largely on the Commando Logistics Regiment RM for the handling of their re-supply. However the General had agreed during the voyage south that 5 Brigade should be – in broad terms – on the southern flank of the advance on Stanley. 5 Brigade was to have a number of mishaps which, in part at least, could be put down to their lack of experience in Cold Weather Warfare, a natural element for the Marine commandos. Their com-mander, Brigadier Tony Wilson, with a distinguished military record having an MC, also 'appeared obsessed with the fear that [Brigadier] Julian Thompson would win the war before Wilson's men could do anything'.[115]. Yet any movement along the line of the south coast of East Falkland would be dependent on helicopters and ships for re-supply, and there were insufficient of either of them to enable both men *and* war stores be moved, so the men might therefore be expected to march.

There now occurred one of those dreaded misadventures which can cause senior commanders a great deal of anxiety: the movement of units without reference to the overall plan. There have been occasions when such bravado has won battles, but this was not to be such an occasion. The General required most of the available helicopters to supply Brigadier Thompson's men strung out in the appalling weather along the mountains on the northern flank. But Brigadier Wilson was to seize a chance to move his Brigade forward, although his northern flank was unprotected by any patrols in the mountains – hills they might be to some not used to the Falkland climate, where a height of say 300 m can be as unforgiving as 900 m in other parts of the world.

At this time 2 Para at Goose Green was to come under command of 5 Brigade in which they had served in Germany. Brigadier Wilson's Gurkha Battalion, 1/7th Duke of Edinburgh's Own Gurkha Rifles, were brought in *Norland* from South Georgia, where they had crossed from the *QE II*. Landing at Ajax Bay on 2 June, they marched to Goose Green, a slog over which these hardy troops from the mountains of Nepal raised 'no difficulty', despite having suffered a good deal of sea sickness in the weeks before they landed.[116] An enquiry over the open civilian telephone link from a house at Swan Inlet to the Fitzroy Settlement, ascertained that no Argentinians were in the immediate area that Wednesday. Therefore Brigadier Wilson used five Scout light helicopters of his Brigade's Air Squadron and the one Chinook, to fly forward men of 2 Para to the inlets at Fitzroy and Bluff Cove on the late afternoon of Wednesday (2 June), after patrols had been landed by the Scouts to confirm that there were no Argentinian positions. There was none. But the Paras due to mark the Landing Zone for the following flights were put down 4 km short (west) of the intended landing site. This was not at first realised and led in the gathering darkness to some companies losing contact until the Battalion was established at Fitzroy during that night.

The Commando Brigade's advances had been carefully protected by a screen of OPs. From one of these, the RM Cadre of Mountain Leaders under Captain Rod Boswell RM had received a report from Sergeant C.R. Stone during the previous week of Argentinian helicopters over his team's OP on Bull Hill (25 km east of San Carlos) from where they had been reporting since D-day.[117] Brigadier Thompson had ordered the Cadre to search out enemy OPs possibly overlooking Salvador Water, especially above Teal. Therefore when Lieutenant Fraser Haddow's team on the lower slopes of Mount Simon some 30 km east of San Carlos reported men landing at Top Malo House, Captain Boswell and 19 of his climbers – all Mountain Leaders are climbers – prepared to patrol the hills and on the morning of 31 May were landed one kilometre from the house. He had been unable to establish radio contact with his OPs when reception proved impossible, a rare occasion in this campaign although *Fearless* had experienced such difficulties on occasions.

The patrol moved forward at dusk, putting seven men to provide covering fire about 150 m from the house while 12 men under the Captain moved round to a position south-east of it. They were exposed to any sentry watching the approaches to the house as their camouflage uniforms stood out on the snow-covered ground. They fixed bayonets and the Captain fired a green mini-flare, the signal for the covering party to fire their 66 mm anti-tank rockets into the building. A man appeared in an upper window and was shot by an ML using a sniper's rifle. The assault party stopped briefly to fire their own '66s', the range being decided by an almost parade ground drill, each man next to the Captain giving his estimate and Rod Boswell averaging these with his own. The rockets hit home. The assault force charged forward again. Out came the Argentinians firing as they tried to escape from the house. It was now burning and their reserves of ammunition exploded in one of the rooms as the house was burnt down.

A couple of rounds from a 40 mm grenade launcher, fired by Corporal M.L. Barnacle, were enough for the Argentinians to surrender. They had lost five men killed and seven were wounded; three of the Cadre were wounded. At this point, Lieutenant Haddow, who had seen the action, came to join the Captain, Haddow's large Union Jack ensuring that there were no mistakes with MLs firing on each other. This was a model action and proved, as other actions would do, that the Marines' basic training for battle would meet the tests now to be confronted. The Argentinian officer in charge of this Special Forces' section had, perhaps ironically, been through a course at CTC, Rod Boswell took him to task for not applying its lessons!

Other Argentinian OPs saw the firefight and two at least surrendered to men of the Commando Brigade after coming down from the mountains.[118] The Commando Brigade's forces could now be reinforced as men and guns were moved forward onto the mountains. L Company (Captain David Wheen) and 2 Troop of 59 Commando Squadron RE advanced to Mount Challenger from where they 'could dominate the track from Fitzroy to Stanley'. They were joined by the rest of '42 RM' in the next couple of nights. The commandos were in range of the 155 mm guns outside Stanley but had limited artillery support themselves, as the shortage of helicopters had meant the supply of ammunition to the British guns limited them to 100 rounds a day for each gun.[119]

5 Brigade's battalions – except the Gurkhas – had landed from *Canberra* by Wednesday (2 June), after the liner had brought them from South Georgia.[120] Meanwhile 2 Para had been coping with 1,200 prisoners and several tonnes of dodgy Argentinian ammunition, some of which was booby-trapped. An explosion on 2 June injured nine and killed three Argentinians who had volunteered to move this ammunition, since it was stored near their camp.[121]

There were now some additional helicopters including some equipped for anti-submarine warfare. Their pilots had no experience of operating with land forces and, despite their undoubted bravery, they could not read maps accurately enough on occasions to put their loads where these were intended. One vehicle, for instance, was left on the eastern slope of Mount Kent far from any track but in full view of the enemy. There it remained until the war was over. They were also apt to land close to the Commando Brigade HQ, parking in neat rows which invited Argentinian air attacks.[122]

The Commando Brigade had established the Forward BMA and a Field Dressing Station at Teal. The Dressing Station would be one of the medical facilities for casualty evacuation. These were at stages along a route stretching some 70 km from the front line Regimental Aid Posts in the mountains, back to the Main Dressing Station and then on to the hospital ship *Uganda*. The Royal Marines' system for informing next of kin of casualties proved effective and every family was visited by an officer as soon as possible after a casualty report was received, or the next morning if a frightening night call was to be avoided. Nevertheless many families had added anxiety for their loved ones when they saw reports on the television.

Enemy fire was not the only cause of casualties on the mountains: some men suffered trench-foot or other injuries from exposure which frequently they did not willingly report. The medical teams were aware of a man's limitations in any prolonged exposure to the harsh conditions, which were also to cause Brigadier Julian Thompson and General Jeremy Moore some concern.

The Commando Brigade Headquarter's BV202s had taken 17½ hours to reach Teal from San Carlos.[123] They were escorted by the tanks of 3 Troop of the Blues and Royals but the journey had been slowed as the Bandwagons, despite their broad tracks, got stuck in the boggy peat from time to time. By Friday (4 June), the Commando Brigade were established in their mountain positions, patrolling at night, observing by day. 3 Para had put in a prolonged attack on Mount Longdon, some 15 km to the east, on the Thursday afternoon but 'had run into well-planned artillery fire and was ordered back'. They then sent out patrols to watch Mount Longdon and Mount Vernet (some 6 km to their north-east).

Sir Lancelot had been the first LSL unloaded at Teal on the Wednesday before, and ships came into Salvador Water despite the lack of Rapier defences during the first few days. As the Forward BMA built up, Brigadier Thompson was concerned by the lack of air defences even though the stores dumps were dug into hills. His concern was made the more anxious on the Friday (4 June) when the BBC World Service announced that 'Teal Inlet is the HQ of the force attacking Stanley'.[124] The source of such leaks has not been established, but perhaps in future producers of programmes which make such life-threatening gaffes should be sent out to join the front line forces.

The Division's Deputy Commander, Brigadier C.J. Waters, an old friend of Brigadier Thompson, brought to bear his 'excellent brain behind large spectacles and benign expression' on the Division's many problems, including those of 3 Commando Brigade.[125] On the Thursday (3 June) afternoon the 1st Battalion Welsh Guards attempted to march south from Sussex Mountain with a view to moving along the southern coast. Knowing the problems of bringing up reserves of food and ammunition: their CO, Lieutenant-Colonel Johnny Rickett, decided that they should man-pack as much as they could, since only three civilian tractors were available to assist them in this move. After 50 minutes, the CO wisely ordered them to return, as they were clearly excessively weighed down by their kit and they returned to Sussex Mountain. At this time the General and others were expecting some counter-attack, possibly by paratroops, on the area of San Carlos water and '40 RM' – now under Divisional Command – were spread fairly thinly around its shores. Their CO, Lieutenant-Colonel M.P.J. Hunt, was not entirely his usual cheerful self, as he considered his '40 RM' was missing the action. But General Moore needed a unit experienced in Falkland conditions for the defence of this pivotal area in the campaign. There was also a strengthening of the air defences, in that Harriers could now refuel (but not rearm) at an airstrip, HMS *Sheathbill*, built by 11 Field Squadron RE despite the loss of the pre-fabricated landing strip aboard *Atlantic Conveyor*. The men of 1 Troop 59 Commando Squadron RE also built a farm of fuel storage tanks from which later over 220,000 litres a day were to be supplied.

The landing craft continued their service in ship-to-shore offloading of the amphibious ships; on one trip C/Sgt Brian Johnston rescued an Argentinian pilot who had come down in the sea.[126] Similar incidents occurred during these round trips across San Carlos Water, as the LCUs went about their hazardous job.

From the Tuesday (1 June) four men of the Mountain and Arctic Warfare Cadre were established on Mount Smoko 7 km north-west of Bluff Cove with a second team nearby. COMAW authorised *Intrepid* to sail along the south coast of East Falkland, but only at night and no further east than Lively Island over 40 km from Bluff Cove. This Cove with its narrow beach was north of a sea-inlet which has Fitzroy near its south-east shore, and could be reached by a bridge on the track from Fitzroy to Bluff Cove.

On Saturday (5 June), a re-broadcasting team and 5 Brigade's Signals Officer, Major Mike Forge, flying east that night, were shot down by a Sea Dart missile fired by HMS *Cardiff* at a range of more than 15 km,[127] as the flight had not been notified to Divisional HQ and was therefore presumed to be hostile. A replacement 're-bro' station was later set up. A similar mishap could have also happened about this time when men of 2 Para were flown – unknown to the Division – in the surviving Chinook to Bluff Cove, had not an observant Captain Boswell RM in his OP noticed that this Chinook had no door. It was the survivor from *Atlantic Conveyor* and was about to be shelled as it landed by several of the Commando Brigade's light guns when the Captain ordered 'Check, Check, Check' over the artillery radio net.[128] Such movements unknown to the Division could cause plans to become pear-shaped through no fault of General Moore's staff.

The Scots Guards were being taken by HMS *Intrepid* from San Carlos Water on that Saturday/Sunday night (5/6 June) to be launched in landing craft into a calm sea off Lafonia with mists obscuring visibility. The intended passage would be some 60 km.[129] Major Southby-Tailyour had no detailed charts and the radar packed up, no doubt because it had to be switched on only intermittently. About 0400 hours the craft were bombed, possibly, or shelled by a shore battery but the explosions caused no damage. (The LCUs had no escorts as the Divisional HQ felt that any ships moving along this coast might increase the risks of the Force's detection.) The LCUs' gunners now stood-to; soon afterwards they were lit up by star shells from two British frigates before these moved off, and the LCUs began to cross the open water at the mouth of Choiseul Sound. Their 600 Scots Guardsmen were exposed to the slop of cold seawater as the craft changed course from time to time and seas came over the sides onto the tank decks. The weather was 'now deteriorating very quickly' with short steep seas slamming against the craft. Rough water forced them to take a course further offshore than the Major had intended, before they ran at full revs through the heavy gusts into Bluff Cove. There they were met by Paras sheltering near the woolshed and who waved them to the slipway.[130] Several companies of 2 Para had by this time taken up positions on the high ground north of the two settlements; the Battalion HQ with the Regimental Aid Post were in buildings at Bluff Cove.

The craft had been buffeted for some seven hours on what the Guards had been told would be a 'two hour voyage' – as it might have been had the craft been launched where COMAW intended – and which the Major was later to describe as 'the worst night of my life'.[131] The Scots Guards established their headquarters in farm sheds, but were out of touch with San Carlos and their own Brigade HQ. The loss of these links was due to the re-broadcasting team's disaster on the Saturday, and would only be corrected when the replacement team was set up. There was to be further confusion, with ammunition dropped at the wrong location and men deposited in full view of enemy positions on Mount Harriet to the north-east.

The South Atlantic winter had now set in, and the attempt on the Sunday (6 June) to land the Welsh Guards from *Fearless* ran into trouble. The intention was that the Welsh Guards were to be landed at Bluff Cove and then move forward through the Scots Guards to take up positions astride the track leading to Stanley. The two pre-loaded craft of *Fearless* carried four Land Rovers and trailers, the Recce Platoon and other sub-units which had inevitably taken time to load into the LCUs. The four rifle companies could then have been quickly loaded into *Intrepid*'s craft when they came from Bluff Cove to meet *Fearless*. But these did not appear. When Major Ewen Southby-Tailyour reached Bluff Cove, after a quick trip by helicopter to San Carlos, all but one of *Intrepid*'s craft had been ordered to move by a major in 2 Para, who seems to have felt it necessary to wave his pistol about, as he wanted to move men from Bluff Cove to Fitzroy, a move made after the COs had decided to concentrate the Para Battalion at Fitzroy and the Scots Guards at Bluff Cove. The craft had to make two attempts at this passage, as the first time they set off for Fitzroy they appar-ently got lost – they had no charts and were expecting to rely on Major Southby-Tailyour's local knowledge – and when the three LCUs from *Intrepid* reached Fitzroy they were storm bound for a time. The lack of communication radio nets between 5 Brigade HQ and their forward units does not appear to have been advised to General Moore at this stage. Meanwhile 9 Parachute Squadron RE and 2 Para's own Assault Pioneer Platoon had worked to remove demolition charges from the bridge on the Fitzroy/Bluff Cove track and to repair it.[131]

The Welsh Guards transhipped to the LSL *Sir Galahad* which was also to carry Rapier firing posts to Fitzroy for the defence of 5 Brigade's Main Headquarters, joining a Royal Artillery Blowpipe Section which was already there. But at Fitzroy the beaches could not be 'worked' for a couple of hours either side of high water, when the track to the beach exits was under water, a period when the landing craft crews could get a shower as best they could from a friendly LSL, perhaps, although there was no place to beach an LSL.[132]

About this time *Intrepid*'s craft were required at San Carlos and set off on an unescorted voyage along the south coast. Therefore there was only one LCU and a small Mexeflote for offloading ships coming into Fitzroy and these could take all of Tuesday (8 June) to offload *Sir Tristram*, even with the help of her Sea King. The LCU *Foxtrot 4*, C/Sgt Johnston, escorted by the local Motor Coaster *Monsunnen* (230 tons), had sailed for Goose Green to collect some of 5 Brigade's Headquarters vehicles. Also that early morning (8 June) the LSL *Sir Galahad* appeared unannounced at Fitzroy, loaded with the companies of Welsh Guards still to be landed. The Landing Craft would unload her after *Sir Tristram*, but Major Ewen Southby-Tailyour argued that first the Guardsmen must go ashore. They could be taken to Bluff Cove that night in a round trip of some two hours. However they would not land, because they had been 'messed around enough since they came to the Islands'.[133] The offloading from *Tristram* continued until the CO of the Field Ambulance unit commandeered the craft and the Mexeflote to land his vehicles from *Sir Galahad*. Meanwhile an RM Captain aboard the LSL continued to impress on the company commanders of the Welsh Guards how advisable it would be to go ashore. They then offered to put men on the upper decks with GPMGs, but this was considered likely to impede the helicopter and craft unloading her.

This Tuesday was bright and clear as Argentinian aircraft attacked the frigate HMS *Plymouth* in San Carlos Water. About 1300 hours she was hit by 30 mm cannon shells and several bombs, none of which exploded. Swinging westward after this attack, these Daggers were followed by the Harriers which had formed the CAP over Fitzroy. Other Argentinian aircraft, five Skyhawks, were flying low and fast, eastward along the southern shores of East Falkland about this time, searching the bays and inlets for British ships. They did not see the LSLs at Fitzroy until, climbing to make their run for home the Argentinians saw the masts of the two LSLs hidden within a bend in the inlet leading to Fitzroy. They flew in to attack the LSLs at about 1315 hours.[134] Their bombs set fire to both ships, *Sir Galahad* blazing fiercely, with the flames being fuelled by petrol she carried ready to be landed for the Rapiers' generators. There were many acts of great bravery in both ships as helicopters, called to the scene by the CO, Lieutenant-Commander Hugh Clark of 825 Squadron, winched men to safety despite the acrid smoke and exploding ammunition. Fires in *Sir Tristram* had been started by cannon fire as well as bombs, one of which tore off her stern ramp, but she still sent lifeboats to her sister ship. The final casualty toll was 50 men killed and 57 wounded,[135] both ships being abandoned although *Sir Tristram* would eventually be shipped back to the UK and subsequently reconstructed.

Helicopters came in to the beach area 'impeccably marshalled by an RM Corporal', while Colour-Sergeant 'Connie' Francis put his LCU alongside the burning *Sir Galahad* and patiently waited to take off survivors.[136] Two more air attacks followed. Further west, *Foxtrot 4* had also been attacked, a brave signaller of 5 Brigade staying with his vehicle chained to the LCU while he reported her sinking. Despite the Major's orders not to sail in daylight, C/Sgt Johnston had told his senior passenger: 'Bugger the orders. The Brigade needs these vehicles forward now. We'll sail.'[137] The Colour Sergeant, three other Royal Marines and two Royal Naval ratings were killed, but the LCU stayed afloat long enough for all her 16 passengers to be taken off.

The naval historian David Brown has pointed out that the losses at Fitzroy, coming close to the end of the war '... were to overshadow the clinical professional achievements of the Marines and Paras in their battles for the hills above Stanley'. He felt that this was due to a number of journalists being unfamiliar with the realities of war, but this publicity was – as we will see – to serve the Landing Force's ends.[138]

Four LCUs, each loaded with 66 tons of ammunition, went up to Fitzroy 48 hours later on the night of Thursday/Friday (10/11 June), as General Moore was determined to keep up the momentum of the advance and in this he was aided by the Argentinians' misunderstanding that there had been 900 casualties at Fitzroy, a misconception which the British talked up, 'despite the anguish it would cause to service families', by not revealing the exact casualties until later.

General Moore had considered that there might be a build-up of Argentinian forces on West Falkland and Special Forces teams were put ashore. The SAS officer we have seen on several occasions in this narrative, Captain John Hamilton, was killed during one of these recces, while giving his signaller covering fire, and the signaller was captured when he ran out of ammunition.[139]

Sufficient 'political' strength could be gained from the Landing Force's strong – well, relatively strong – positions on the mountains, although the deteriorating weather was causing them casualties from exposure, particularly on Mount Kent where '42 RM' had spent the best part of a fortnight with more than occasional attention from Argentinian 155 mm guns. On at least two of these nights the temperature fell to minus 12C on the summit, and although not quite as cold on the lower slopes, '45 RM' in the area of Teal and 3 Para in the area of Estancia House suffered from the almost continuous rain and snow. Yet the Commando Brigade continued aggressive patrolling forward of their positions, each unit gathering intelligence on Argentinian positions on hills forming the outer perimeter of Stanley's defences. '42 RM' had put L Company in one overnight move on to Mount Challenger some 6 km south of Kent. From there aggressive patrolling penetrated as far as Mount Wall on the eastern extremity of another ridge running due east from Mount Challenger.[140]

Orders for attacks on Mount Longdon (3 Para), Mount Harriet (42 Commando) and Two Sisters (45 Commando) were being given by their respective COs on the Friday (11 June).[141] That same day General Moore had flown forward to Fitzroy, where the pilot of his Scout helicopter was later to compare the General's prompting on mountain warfare given to Brigadier Wilson, with his quiet acceptance of Brigadier Thompson's plans devised with a knowledge of the terrain. In a further move, the survivors from *Sir Galahad* were taken back to San Carlos and two companies of '40 RM' replaced them at Fitzroy.

About this time aboard *Fearless* one SBS corporal, shaved and smartly dressed as he crossed the tank deck, was jostled by a few soldiers who chided him for 'living in luxury in this ship'. They had just spent a day or so in what they called 'the front line'. The Corporal had spent the previous 14 days in an OP behind the Argentinian lines, but was restrained from striking his accusers.[142] (There has always been some friendly rivalry between the Guards and the Royal Marines, as seen in the newspaper cutting pinned up in 1943 in Deal Depot's barber's shop, which showed a line of Guardsmen on some ceremonial as anything but 'precisely dressed by the right'. Humorous cracks about 'furry hats' are sometimes heard in the Corps, and the fact that both the 2nd Battalion Scots Guards and the Welsh Guards with 5 Brigade had just completed tours of ceremonial duties in London was a source of some jokes from men who had spent winters in northern Norway.)

The Division now faced some 8,400 Argentinians with four 155 mm howitzers and 30 105 mm guns and other supporting arms.[143] What was not generally known at the time was the low morale of many of these men. They were conscripts from northern Argentina, where the weather can be warm, if not tropical. Their officers and senior NCOs did not have that skill in leadership which could be seen throughout the British Division, and this led among other things to a poor distribution of the plentiful rations stored in Stanley. Other Argentinian units of regular soldiers and Argentinian Marines were to fight tenaciously in the defence of Stanley which was one reason why General Menendez considered that he had made 'Stanley impregnable'.[144]

The build-up of intelligence from patrols had enabled Brigadier Thompson to plan his attacks originally for the night of 8 June, but 5 Brigade had to delay their intended participation for reasons we have seen. They would take part in Phase II: an advance from the Commando Brigade's positions to seize Wireless Ridge, Mount Tumbledown and Mount William. Phase III would involve attacking Sapper Hill and the high ground south and south-east of Stanley. Teams from the M&AW Cadre were sent to recce these areas on the 8 June. Patrolling – as we shall see – was the name of the game at this time, and Major Hector Gullan was appointed patrol master. He knew what patrols were going where and when they would be in particular areas, enabling him to advise the gunners and others where to 'expect our own troops'.[145]

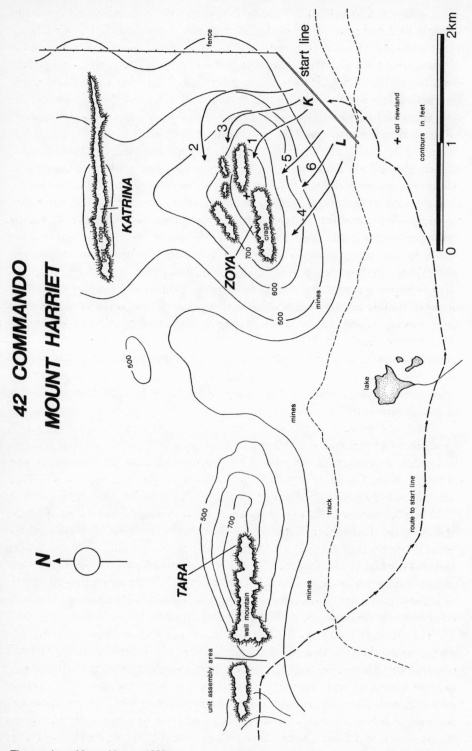

42 COMMANDO
MOUNT HARRIET

KATRINA

boat ridge

ZOYA

crags

700

600

500

TARA

wall mountain

500

700

500

unit assembly area

mines

mines

mines

track

route to start line

lake

start line

fence

K

L

1
2
3
4
5
6

+ cpl newland

contours in feet

N

0   1   2km

The attack on Mount Harriet 1982.

Lieutenant-Colonel Mike Rose was a man with a forceful mind. He and Captain Rod Bell now began a series of contacts with civilians in Stanley, using the Island's radio frequency which had been kept open to provide medical advice to islanders on the Camp. (London had refused requests for PsyOps teams (for psychological warfare) and for some Spanish speakers, a refusal based apparently on a wish that prisoners should not be interrogated. Captain Bell was therefore the only available linguist familiar with Spanish and taken from his job as Adjutant of HQ and Signals Squadron of the Commando Brigade.)[146]

Lt-Col. Hew Pike commanding 3 Para had continued to watch Argentinians on Mount Longdon on the left flank of the Commando Brigade and at the north-easterly edge of the arc of mountains which it was to attack. The defenders' positions were not at first clear, and in the days before the night attack his men had patrolled the 5,000 m or a little more between the opposing armies, across a broad valley along which were stone runs sometimes several hundred metres wide. These were made up of boulders covered in lichen made slippery in the wet. Some were a metre or more in diameter, others were much smaller and prone to tumble together noisily if disturbed. Where there were not stone runs, there was bog. The Para patrols were mainly carried out by Major P.P. Butler's D Company, the Battalion's Patrol Company. They had a base some way east of the Battalion's main positions, giving them longer in darkness on the mountain. They penetrated into the Argentinian defences, coming back unseen or fighting off any opposition, patrolling which Brigadier Thompson considered to be of a very high standard.[146]

After a few days the Argentinians began shelling the patrol base and Lieutenant-Colonel Pike withdrew it, leaving a round trip of 16 km in a direct line but more often three times this as a patrol moved around minefields and other obstacles. On occasion patrols now stayed out for several days at a time, lying up out of sight of the enemy during daylight. The Battalion therefore had good intelligence on the enemy's positions before they moved out on the night of 11/12 June (Friday/Saturday) leaving their established positions at about 1700 hours (sunset was at 1645 hours) and crossing their start line for the attack on Mount Longdon at 2000 hours. The enemy had some 1,000 m of open ground around their positions, with a minefield to the south and enemy positions 1,000 m to the east on Wireless Ridge. The attack was to be made without any preliminary bombardment which would have alerted the defenders.[147]

The Colonel's plan was simple, as are all good operational plans: A Company would attack the spur running north from Longdon; B would attack along the crags of the Mountain's ridge; C Company was in reserve; and teams from Support Company with Milans and GPMGs would be held near the start line until required. The mortar platoon was in firing positions behind the start line. Some slight delays occurred at this very dark time of the night when forming up on the start line defined by the Murrell River, but the Paras moved forward. A man stepped on an anti-personnel mine at the right flank of B Company, and the enemy then fired on them and on A Company to the north. It was about

2100 hours and the Battalion would be in action for the rest of the night, fighting Argentinians in good defence positions. Some held their fire until Para platoons could be clearly seen as the moon rose, others manned a heavy machine gun in a sangar. Corporal Bailey charged 50 m to the sangar that was holding up No.4 Platoon but the Corporal was seriously wounded. Its machine gun was only taken out by a determined attack by Sergeant Ian McKay who, having worked around the position, threw two grenades. He and Private Burt were killed. A second machine gun continued to fire, driving the Paras back until accurate salvoes from the Commando Brigade's 105 mm guns, some falling a few metres from the Paras, gave them the chance to reorganise, with A and C Companies coming into the action. Probing and clearing these enemy positions, using grenades, 66 mm LAW and bayonets, the Battalion at last saw the Argentinians withdraw from the ridge just before daylight. But the casualties were relatively heavy with 23 men killed and 47 wounded, including three men when the Milan team had been struck by a round from a recoilless rifle.[148]

Lieutenant-Colonel Pike had hoped to seize Wireless Ridge to the east of Longdon but Brigadier Thompson ordered the Battalion to consolidate on Longdon, as in daylight Wireless Ridge would be under accurate Argentinian fire, although the Colonel was not best pleased to halt his Battalion's advance.[149]

Lieutenant-Colonel Andrew Whitehead led '45 RM' that night (11/12 June) in an attack on Two Sisters. His Commando had been patrolling the previous week from their positions south-west of Mount Kent. Careful liaison was required with the other units of the Brigade as they were operating in a tangle of rocky hills and boggy valleys with stone runs. '45 RM's' Lieutenant C. Fox with the Patrol Troop had been flown forward to a recce base on the slopes of Mount Kent near Two Sisters. He then led a patrol, with a section of 59 Independent Commando Squadron RE, to look for minefields on the western approach to Two Sisters. The round trip took 16 hours on this first patrol as sappers from time to time probed with their bayonets but found no mines. Part of this route was so boggy that the men sank up to the ankles in peat. On his second patrol made on Sunday 6 June, Lieutenant Fox set up an effective OP hiding his eight men in a rocky outcrop. They were later found there by 20 unwary Argentinians, 13 of whom were killed in the subsequent firefight, before Chris Fox withdrew his men behind artillery support. Another of '45 RM's' patrols led by Lieutenant A.D. Shaw seized a copy of the operation orders with a marked map which had been left on Two Sisters by the Argentinians flown some two weeks previously to Goose Green. The Milan teams of the Support Company were – after the loss of their weapons in the bombing of the BMA – rearmed with machine guns and Carl Gustavs, and '40 RM's' Milan Troop seconded to '45 Cdo RM'.

Fighting patrols were sent in on several nights to harass the defenders of Two Sisters, one such patrol – Lieutenant D.J. Stewart's 3 Troop of X Company – crossed 1,000 m of open ground, killing two sentries and other Argentinians before the Marines withdrew. On the morning of Friday (11 June) '45 Cdo RM' moved to the area of their patrol base, leaving them some 6,000 m to cover that night to reach their start line about 2,250 m north-west of the Sisters and some

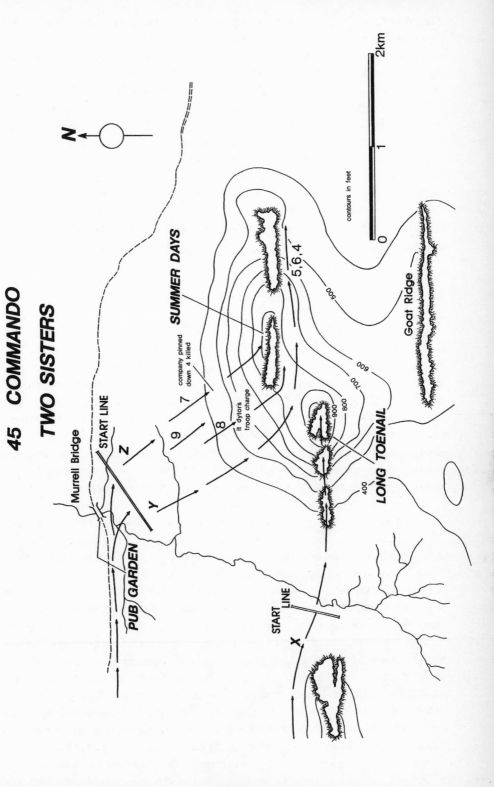

45 COMMANDO
TWO SISTERS

PUB GARDEN

Murrell Bridge

START LINE

Z

Y

SUMMER DAYS

company pinned
down 4 killed

9   7

8

lt dytor's
troop charge

LONG TOENAIL

Goat Ridge

contours in feet

5,6,4

500

600

700

800

900

400

START
LINE

X

N

0   1   2km

800 m from Murrell Bridge. But the 150 men of X Company followed a different route, to be some 1,000 m due west of these crags, intending to be at this start line at 2100 hours. They carried forty Milan missiles and a number of Milan firing posts, as well as their other weapons but they did not arrive there until 2315. Nevertheless Colonel Whitehead told X Company commander Captain Ian Gardiner to 'carry on as planned'. The Colonel's calm voice over the radio would be 'like a tonic to all'. X Company began their assault at about 2325 hours. The whole approach had been made in silence, with no supporting artillery fire to warn of a pending attack, although the companies could see the Paras' tracer as they fought to gain Mount Longdon on the Marines' left.[150]

The troops of X Company found no opposition on the western peak, but about halfway along the 1,500 m of a rocky ridge to the east, two machine guns opened up. There was no artillery support available, since the batteries were supporting other attacks, while Argentinians fired from the eastern peak preventing any initial development by the commandos along the ridge. But by 0030, 2 Troop (Lieutenant Caroe) of X Company had fought their way to the top of the western peak and along its eastern spur, an attack 'like fighting in a built-up area' among the house-size boulders and crags, under Argentinian artillery fire from time to time.

The Colonel now moved forward his Y and Z Companies, a moment after Argentinian shells had fallen on an area in their line of advance. But this, like many other enemy bombardments that night, was fired as a pre-arranged defence barrage on a likely forming up area. The commandos had 1,500 m to go, up the northern slopes of Two Sisters, across bogs, over tussock grass and rock runs. The enemy did not notice this advance and therefore the Colonel held the Companies in dead ground, while X Company completed their attack on the western peak.

An Argentinian flare was thrown near Z Company, while several commandos were picking out enemy positions using their Image Intensifier Sights, although these were to prove not as effective as the American night sights used by the Argentinians. The flare was followed by heavy and other machine gun fire, which swept over the companies in dead ground. Commando Batteries then shelled the feature but enemy mortar bombs began falling around Clive Dytor's troop. He called on his men to dash forward, shouting the battle cry 'Zulu, Zulu' as they skirmished forward to again take cover in a patch of dead ground. Meanwhile mortar fire was brought down on the Argentinian positions and steady GPMG fire from Support Company was backed up with missiles from the 66 mm LAWs and the 84 mm MAWs, the Carl Gustav anti-tank rockets. Colonel Whitehead, moving on the right of Z Company's leading troop – 'he was always where he was needed' – now called Y Company to move up on his right (west). This enabled them to open an angle for fire into the eastern peak, albeit by firing mighty close to their Colonel's head. No.8 Troop now charged forward supported by No.7 Troop. As No.8 Troop skirmished into the enemy positions, acquiring a .50-inch heavy machine gun, No.7 Troop (Lieutenant Paul Mansell) pressed forward and No.9 Troop, depleted by casualties from enemy fire, was held in reserve. It had taken Z Company 2½ hours to secure the eastern peak after crossing their start line. About this time a great glow in the sky out at sea indicated some offshore drama.

155 mm shells began to fall on what had been the enemy positions and mist was creeping over the mountains, when Sergeant J.P. Menghini of the Brigade Air Squadron flew his Scout through the darkness 'to the dim green torch light marking the landing site where 45 Commando's casualties were being collected'. At 0430 on the Saturday the Commando 'went firm', having secured all its objectives for the first phase of the battle. To the Colonel's annoyance he was told to stay in these positions for the same reasons which had held 3 Para on Mount Longdon. '45 RM' reorganised, drawing back men from the eastern slopes of Two Sisters, but covering the 4,000 m across the eastern end of Goat Ridge to Tumbledown, which Whitehead had hoped to take in a second phase of his Commando's attack.[151]

About 0230 hours HMS *Glamorgan,* which had been providing support from her twin 4.5-in guns, had stayed longer than planned and in taking a 'short cut' to be off the coast before daylight, had crossed an area in range of a land-based Exocet. This was fired from the metalled road south of Stanley and hit *Glamorgan* when she was some 27 km south-west of the town, causing an explosion, the great flash seen by the Commandos and Paras fighting in the mountains. With fires in her hangar aft setting alight to the galley and some machinery spaces, she nevertheless maintained 10 knots and by the time she rejoined the Carrier Battle Group she was making 18 knots at 1100 hours next morning. Nine men had died, four were missing and another 14 were injured.[152]

On the Commando Brigade's right, Lieutenant-Colonel Nick Vaux would lead 42 Commando in a bold outflanking movement which brought his assault companies behind the defences of Mount Harriet. This Commando had done some excellent patrolling in the first few days of June and were helped by teams from the ML Cadre in OPs east of Mount Kent. The Commando also received the six Bandwagons for its HQ's secure communications, a chance for the Colonel to rest his back on a hard bench, as an old riding injury caused him discomfort. Major Guy Sheridan, the second-in-command, was now back from South Georgia and he understood the Colonel's problems with his back, but more importantly he concerned himself with the logistics. What was beginning to become serious was the effect on everyone of living in continuously wet and cold conditions. Ammunition had priority over dry clothing, however, and men had to manage as best they could by keeping one pair of socks dry to wear when at rest. Moving on to another task therefore meant stowing away the dry pair and climbing into your wet ones. Nor, in the Colonel's opinion, did the type of boots which you wore make much difference, even the best quality leather boots available becoming porous. It rained most times when it was not snowing or a heavy mist hung deadeningly around the commandos' positions, reducing visibility to less than a metre. If 'ifs-and-ands' have any place in a history, it is surely the difference more helicopters would have made to the Marines' lot. As it was, they had often to hump stores from an LZ to their company areas, sapping the men's strength and adding to their foot sores. However, the junior officers and NCOs – particularly the corporals – kept the Marines going with a joke here and there, making sure rations were eaten and that men paid attention to keeping themselves alert, the whole ably monitored by those experienced Warrant Officers – Dave Greenough, Len Cook, Cameron March, 'Dusty' Miller and Fred Cummings to name a few – who were 'their Company Commanders' mainstay, and the Commanding Officer's reassurance'.[153] When Brigadier Thompson did offer to take '42 RM' back for a chance to dry out, the consensus – and the Colonel had asked around – was that, in the words of Captain David Wheen 'no one wants out of this mountain, Colonel, we just want to hurry on to the next one'.

Like other units of the Brigade, the companies had also been rehearsing their attacks using features, in the case of '42 RM', near Mount Challenger. They moved forward at 1615 hours on the 11 June (Friday) to their assembly area near Mount Wall, the 'granite crow's nest' which was held by J Company. This overlooked the steep valley to Mount Harriet. And this reserve company would also be able to distract the defenders with fire from their GPMGS and other weapons, while Commando Batteries would bombard the defenders just before the final attack.

Lieutenant-Colonel Vaux had gone forward on the Friday morning to meet Brigadier Thompson and Lieutenant-Colonel Whitehead of '45 RM', to a position where they could see both Commandos' objectives and discuss boundaries. Since it was in sight of his TAC HQ, Nick Vaux had not taken his HQ party with him as they were having a well-earned break. As luck would have it, an Argentinian patrol had appeared east of Mount Wall down by the track to Fitzroy and there was an unconfirmed report of an Argentinian company leaving vehicles to climb Mount Wall and defend it. Without his full 'set' of radios, Vaux could hear what was going on and he could see the developing firefight, but he could not contact his forward L Company and the Recce Troop in order to give 'decisive directions'. At this time '42 RM's' Forward Air Controller destroyed his highly secret equipment used to direct aircraft on to targets, just in case this might be captured by this Argentinian company. Meanwhile patrols from the Recce Troop with two fire-control teams had lost much of their equipment in the haste to prevent its capture, as they withdrew from Mount Wall. Vaux would never in future move without his whole TAC HQ. But the position was restored and by the time J Company came up to their intended positions, Mount Wall was again occupied by a troop from '42 RM'.[153]

The outflanking route had been reconnoitred by patrols from '42 RM' during the previous week. They had discovered a minefield in the valley east of Mount Wall and found that the enemy had established strong positions sited on the west slopes of Harriet. On one of these patrols, led by Lieutenant Ken McMillan, Marine M. Curtis – a 15-stone rugby player – stepped on a mine, killing the pain with a self-injected shot of morphine, before Corporal G. Cuthell carried him out of the minefield. (Those man-lift exercises at CTC proved to have their practical purposes.) Enemy shelling and rough going delayed the patrol further and although Medical Assistant Heyworth had attended to Curtis's wounds, it was another seven hours before the patrol carried him to safety. Engineers of '59 RE' and the assault engineers of '42 RM' later cleared a safe route from Mount Challenger to the Fitzroy-Stanley track which ran south of Harriet. Another patrol followed the cleared route to move further east, but had a casualty; Marine K.R. Paterson lost a foot on a mine. He was evacuated by Captain N.E. Pounds who used PN goggles to fly his Gazelle well forward of '42's' main positions and collected the casualty.[154]

Some time before the main action began, Lieutenant-Colonel Vaux had arranged a series of bogus radio calls 'indicating no change in his Commando's position on Challenger or in the logistics for several days to come'. The outflanking route was marked on the night of the attack by Lieutenant Colin Beadon who 'dropped off' two Milan sections: one some 800 m south of Harriet; and the second to cover the Fitzroy-Stanley track. The route lay south of this track and eastward, in all some 6 km – a distance equivalent to perhaps more than 12 km on European terrain – to the forming up positions (FUP) for L company (on the left) and K Company (on the right), south-west of the main defences. K Company would attack the eastern end of Mount Harriet and an hour later L Company would attack the western defences. The companies yomped an hour apart to avoid both being caught in any Argentinian shelling, should they be seen prematurely. In the event L Company lost their way for a brief period, losing the marked track until they found it again.

Captain Peter Babbington's K Company were twice illuminated by flares, but they avoided detection by standing rock still near their FUP. They had expected a recce patrol from the Welsh Guards to join up with them, but in the dark they missed the commandos and it took an hour for them to join up. H-hour was delayed and Babbington took his troop commanders forward to the start line (500 m north of the FUP). There he was able to show them the ground ahead and the line of attack, as the moon was rising and their objectives could be seen through binoculars.

J Company opened fire as planned just before the revised H-hour, firing flares, their rifles, GPMGs and captured machine guns. With them were some Milan teams. They sent up flares, yelling shouts into the night. They certainly created the impression that a major attack was coming from the west, and induced the Argentinians on Goat Ridge to reveal their positions by returning fire. The Commando's mortars, with their bed-plates on Challenger's lower slopes, had been hit by an Argentinian 155 mm shell which had killed a Marine, before an hour or so later they were firing parachute-flares which floated down in sequence to illuminate the western end of Goat Ridge. Moments later the swish of Milan missiles was heard in the TAC HQ, before the warheads exploded among the Goat Ridge crags to silence the enemy positions.

K Company had by now advanced to within 800 m to their objectives on the eastern end of Harriet.[155] The Company's radio net had an unusually large number of stations, as every section leader and more senior ranks were on the net, and therefore knew what was happening. They were 100 m from the Argentinian positions when the defenders could be seen to have spotted them. K Company opened fire. No.1 Troop engaged them, while No.2 Troop skirmished forward and in 45 minutes had cleared the enemy from these defences, but not before Cpl Lawrence Watts, 'a most professional young NCO', was killed. He had taken out a key defence post and the Company had seized four 120 mm mortars. No.3 Troop (Lt J.L. Heathcote) was then passed across the ground held by No.2 Troop, and as No.3 advanced westward, No.1 moved along lower ground parallel to No.3's advance. Cpl Ward reported (over the radio) some enemy positions on the ridge and Cpl Steve Newland responded that he could see these positions. He then climbed some 6 m up a rock slab to find that he was looking down on some 15 Argentinians. He put a fresh magazine in his rifle, flung two grenades and jumped down on the enemy. He killed most of them. Meanwhile, Cpl Ward called out '66', enabling Newland to take cover before this rocket hit the defences. When Newland returned to the enemy positions he was shot in the legs by an Argentinian, before this man was also killed. The Corporal then lit a cigarette and propping himself up against a rock continued to use his radio to report enemy positions. And his Company Commander gave concise situation reports ('sitreps') to Lieutenant-Colonel Vaux as the situations developed.

Captain Babbington with an artillery FOO and an MFC (mortar fire controller) had stood out in the open, the better to control his company. While the artillery fire came down accurately on enemy positions, the sections were in radio contact with Babbington's advanced headquarters and his troop commanders; NCOs and Marines had 'worked like a well-drilled football team as they fought their way forward'. But as they moved westward they were caught in Argentinian shell fire, while to their left – down the slope of the mountain – L Company (Captain David Wheen) had come under fire as they climbed towards the western features of Harriet. Lieutenant Ian Stafford Argyll and Sutherland Highlanders,[156] on secondment as 2i/c of the Company, and Lieutenant Julian Pusey RM, a troop commander, were both hit, as were several Marines. But supported by Milans firing from the south, the Company pressed forward. They took hours to cover the line to their final objectives, making section and troop attacks on one position after another. It was during this time that they saw the great flash of the Exocet exploding as it hit HMS *Glamorgan*. Once on the western end of the main ridge, the Argentinians began to surrender. They were sent down to the rear. Wheen then concentrated 15 machine guns on the ridge to cover No.5 Troop's further advance along the spur running northward. They met heavy fire as they crossed a shallow valley and were pulled back so that Wheen could get concentrated mortar and artillery fire on the new objective, Goat Ridge, before No.5 Troop renewed their attack 'with great determination', killing six enemy as the remainder fled into the mist.[157] K Company were directed towards Goat Ridge.

L Company continued its advanced towards Goat Ridge about 750 m to the north and a similar distance south of Two Sisters. The Colonel brought up his TAC HQ and J Company, led by Major Mike Norman, who took the lead across the mined valley to the western features of Harriet. The Colonel had deemed it safer to 'sprint through the minefield' than to delay by coming along the southern route, as he expected a counter-attack as soon as dawn broke. His companies were quickly organised to defend the heights they had just captured. With L Company fighting the last resistance on the western defences of Harriet, K Company would soon be on Goat Ridge and J Company was on the eastern end of Harriet. The original advance had been followed by 35 men in a Porter Troop of load carriers, carrying six tripods and dial sights for GPMGs. These weapons could be mounted for prolonged fire aimed at possible concentrations of troops in any counter-attack and in the general defence of the newly captured positions; with them was 10,000 rounds of ammunition. In the event there were no counter-attacks but the Brigade's positions were shelled. Brigadier Thompson put down the Commando's success in these night actions to surprise (having outflanked the enemy), the high standard of training and fighting qualities of the Marines.[158] Lieutenant-Colonel Vaux found at the original FUP 'a mass of dishevelled, bemused figures', prisoners under the eye of the wounded Corporal Steve Newland, who had been carried down the mountain by two prisoners. In all '42 RM' was to take some 300 prisoners. And many acts of courage were shown as men helped wounded Marines from positions exposed to shell fire.

So many 155 mm shells burst around '45 RM's' positions that morning that the ridge between the peaks of Two Sisters looked 'as if it had been ploughed by giant moles'. Fire was particularly heavy on 3 Para's positions on Mount Longdon. Although Brigadier Thompson was keen to get his men moving forward, he did not want them to move into open areas where Argentinian artillery would have slaughtered them in the daylight.[159]

When the mists cleared it was a bright frosty morning along the mountains, but further westward it was snowing. The Brigadier in his Commando Brigade HQ, by this morning at the base of Mount Kent, had controlled the battle through the night, ready to move up his reserves or take other action had it been necessary. The success of his Commandos and Battalions was such that they had moved forward without need of any major changes in plan. 2 Para whilst at Fitzroy had organised a platoon of 35 men for ammunition re-supply and to be stretcher-bearers in the next action. Now back with the Commando Brigade, they had been brought to the Mount Kent area from Fitzroy in a series of helicopter lifts, for which the 'sticks' were loaded under the watchful eye of Captain David Constance RM, the Battalion's liaison officer with 3 Commando Brigade. On the Friday (11 June) night, they had moved forward between 3 Para and '45 RM' in a gruelling 15 km march, or 'tab' if you prefer. They could see the battles ahead of them as they snaked forward, with what must have seemed interminable halts for one thing or another. They now dug-in on the north-west slopes of Mount Longdon.

3 Para had found weapons, clothing, rations (some packs of which contained a tot of whisky and 20 cigarettes), blankets, boots, ammunition, sleeping bags, excellent night vision goggles and other goodies on Mount Longdon. 45 Commando found similar comforts on Two Sisters, as did 42 Commando on Mount Harriet. The number of prisoners was growing apace; among them was the CO of the 4th Argentinian Infantry Regiment who told RSM Chisnall that the

commandos had shown great skills in night-fighting. Nick Vaux was feeling the effects of several jarring falls in the dark and his 'gallop' across to the 'mined valley'. With the battle drawing to its close, he realised that they had been on the move for 10 hours and everyone's pace was slackening, except the ebullient Captain Babbington who said that he had 'a real buzz on'. He went off with his company to occupy Goat Ridge. Major Guy Sheridan took over the Commando for a spell while the Colonel slept in 'welcome oblivion', rolled up in his USMC poncho. He awoke to join his TAC HQ in a spartan location as the BV 202s could not be brought forward; a cleft in the rocks covered by a tarpaulin had to suffice as cover for the HQ.

The Brigade was shelled throughout Saturday and that night the men were without their big packs, although some found warmth in captured blankets and sleeping bags. Also that night a figure appeared through the mist at X Company's TAC HQ: 'Hello,' the figure said in a strong Welsh accent, 'It's the Vicar, I've forgotten the bloody password.'[160] The Commando Brigade were to spend Saturday on the mountains, while 5 Brigade made recces of the approaches to Tumbledown and Mount William, helped by some of the ML Cadre who knew these areas. Meanwhile Brigadier Thompson was about to fly forward to visit his Commanding Officers when four Skyhawks came low over the mountains to drop a total of seven retarded 180 kg bombs near the Brigade HQ. Fire from GPMGs and Blowpipes did not deter them, nor did the Deputy Brigade Commander, Colonel Seccombe, waving his stick, described by one commentator as 'more a medieval monk's staff than a walking stick'. The nearest bomb to explode was only 50 m from the HQ's Bandwagons. The Marines had taken cover in slit trenches and the only casualty was a man with concussion whose trench had been close to one of the bombs. Two of these did not explode and the soft peat absorbed the blast and most of the splinters from the others. Nevertheless these damaged three helicopters and shredded the Command Tent which fortunately was not in use at the time.[161] With the location of the headquarters clearly compromised, it was moved over the next 24 hours. During that morning mail was received and distributed.

The first aerial photographs were received by the Commando Brigade that Sunday, reportedly taken from a Harrier with a camera in one wing that could only take pictures of the ground when the aircraft was flown 'on its side'.

On the night of Sunday 13 June, 30 Scots Guardsmen from the Headquarters Company and commanded by Major The Hon. Richard Bethell, with a troop of Blues and Royals, made a diversionary attack on Argentinian positions south-east of Mount Harriet. They at first met no opposition but about 2030 hours one of the tanks struck a mine. The Major and Drill Sgt Danny White were considering where the enemy might have gone as they could see no movement in some nearby sangars. Then they heard snoring. An enemy rifle shot just over a metre away from the Major was the initial spark from the defenders of the sangars who broke into violent action. The Guardsmen fought back and in the next two hours cleared eleven or more sangars and trenches. With the tanks trapped in a minefield, this clearance was made with rifles and grenades before the Major and one of his pipers (serving as a medic) were attacked by a lone Argentinian who had been badly wounded. He was shot, the Major and his piper both wounded. Enemy mortar and artillery fire came down on the Guardsmen who – having completed the intended diversion – extracted themselves carrying the wounded.[162]

The Scots Guards began their assault on Tumbledown at 2100 hours, from forming up positions near '42 RM'. They met no opposition as they advanced through flurries of snow and took their first objectives. But as they moved forward up the higher ground of this mountain, they met strong resistance from some 92 men of the Argentinian 5th Marines. These troops were not to be dislodged by 66 mm or other sangar-busting weapons and were supported by well-sited mortars and machine guns firing on fixed lines. By 0230 hours, after some four hours of heavy fighting, a brief bombardment by 5 Brigade's artillery enabled Major John Kiszely to lead his Left Flank Company in a bayonet charge up the mountain. Only seven men reached the summit and three of them were immediately hit by machine gun fire. But they had broken this sector of the defences, and were soon joined by others of the Major's Company. Further fighting by G Company and others during the next few hours cleared the Argentinians from the eastern slopes of Tumbledown 'inch by inch up the rocks, using phosphorus grenades and automatic weapons'.[163] In all the Guards had eight killed and 33 wounded.

The Gurkhas and Welsh Guards met 'no significant resistance' on Mount William and Sapper Hill, but there was some spasmodic artillery fire falling on the lines of their advance.

While 5 Brigade were attacking their objectives east of the Commando Brigade's positions, 2 Para were to take Wireless Ridge on the same night (13/14 June, Sunday/Monday). They were now commanded by the large and confident Lieutenant-Colonel D.R. Chaundler who had parachuted to the Carrier Battle Group with other battle casualty replacements for his Battalion. He was known to Brigadier Thompson from when the Colonel was a student at Staff College and the Brigadier was on its directing staff. They were to advance from a col north of Mount Kent to their objective: a ridge about 1,500 m east of Mount Longdon and which ran due east a further 3,000 m to overlook the Marines' old camp at Moody Brook. The attack was deferred for 24 hours. Then on the night of Sunday (13 June) it was begun with a first phase being the bombardment of a hill 1,000 m east of 3 Para's position on Mount Longdon. This fire was extremely effective as would be the mortar fire brought down later to support the advance. D Company with the support of the tanks – two light tanks (CVRTs) of the Blues and Royals with superb night vision gun sights – moved down from their start line to the north to attack the Ridge. They met no serious opposition and went firm on their initial objective. A and B Companies (B to the west of A) now moved forward in Phase 2 of the battle, attacking the hill to the north of the Ridge. They had some mishaps with ponds on this hill's plateau but despite several men going into these up to their necks, all were pulled to safety. They found only dead Argentinians but as they were regrouping Argentinian 155 mm air-burst shells showered their positions, and the companies moved 300 m to the east. There was some fire from Argentinian defences but as the Paras moved to clear these, the enemy left in great haste, in such haste in fact that radios were left switched on in this Regimental HQ. The two companies consolidated in the enemy's sangars which gave them protection from the continuing enemy artillery barrages.

In the third phase, D company again took up the advance moving eastward down the ridge and were not at first opposed. Then they met stiffening opposition despite supporting fire from the Para companies to the north, the tanks and Milan teams. The enemy made a fighting withdrawal from bunker to bunker, as D Company fought them at close quarters. The Company called for more fire support but these artillery shells fell on the leading platoons – a blue-on-blue – causing casualties until this fire was re-targeted onto what was left of Moody Brook Barracks. The Paras pressed on, skirmishing forward until they came up against coils of concertina wire. Rightly suspecting these covered mines, they saw some lanes through the wire and safe routes that were not mined. A severe burst of fire halted the Company at this point but the junior officers and NCOs got the momentum going again. They cleared the immediate defences but as they went firm on the eastern end of the Ridge, they came under sniper fire and 'enemy artillery continued to make life uncomfortable'.[164] The Argentinians could then be heard re-grouping near Moody Brook, and so the leading platoons of D Company ceased firing so as not to give away their positions. There were two hours to go to first light. The wounded switched on their parachuting easco light, so that they would not be missed in the dark, as the platoons regrouped.

As dawn broke some 40 Argentinians put in a counter-attack against D Company; ammunition was low as the Company fixed bayonets and used grenades to repulse the attack. '2 Para had fought a model, all-arms battle . . . The Scorpions and Scimitars had stood up to the test brilliantly, as had their crews', to quote Brigadier Thompson. C Company in the fourth phase of the attack had captured a hill north-east of the main objectives, but the enemy had withdrawn from this area in haste.[165]

Brigadier Thompson arrived and with the Colonel planned the Battalion's moves for that day (14 June). They first consolidated along the Ridge then platoons probed forward down the slopes to Moody Brook and the Murrell River, where they rescued some SAS raiders from the shores of Stanley Harbour as we will see. They were well on the way down the road into Stanley when the cease-fire was announced.[166]

The Welsh Guards with their replacements, A and C Companies of 40 Commando RM, had been in reserve from the Friday (11 June). On the Saturday night (12/13 June), the Guards advanced but the Guards Machine gun Company, carrying .5-inch heavy machine guns, found the going difficult and would not catch up with the battalion for some 18 hours. The battalion lay up in daylight on the Sunday and that night the advance continued in a cold clear night, the long snake went *north* of a lake on their line of march, this surprised the Marines who had been warned of a minefield in that area. There were two Royal Marines casualties on these mines, both evacuated by helicopter. The advance was delayed while engineers cleared the route. On the Monday Marines were flown forward to establish a forming up position on a road by the lower slopes of Mount William, 5km south-west of Stanley. But No.9 Troop were inadvertently set down 3km east of the intended landing zone, and were on Sapper Hill. Two Marines were slightly wounded when the Argentineans fired on them as they withdrew; several Argentineans were killed before the order for the cease-fire stopped the fighting. A planned fire mission was cancelled and the Marines with the Welsh Guards quickly occupied this hill.[167]

While these battles were being fought, an attempt to land SAS troopers from G Squadron by the Marines of Captain Chris Baxter's 1st Raiding Squadron was mounted that Sunday night. This bold raid – in part a diversion to help 2 Para – failed, as during their approach to some fuel tanks on the edge of Port Stanley, an Argentinian hospital ship in Port William illuminated them with her search-light. This brought down heavy fire and the raiders had to be picked up by men of 2 Para.[168] Destruction of the runway at Stanley had not been achieved, and the supposed 'bomb crater' was a neat piece of camouflage to make the British *think* that the runway was closed. Cluster bombs, on the other hand, had 'riddled some Argentinian vehicles with numerous small perforations' and buildings had been set on fire.

On Monday (14 June) Brigadier Thompson's flight to see 2 Para had been delayed by a snow storm and when the weather cleared he had been called first to meet General Moore at 5 Brigade's TAC HQ. There the plans were agreed for that night's operations and the Brigadier flew forward to meet Lieutenant-Colonel Chaundler, as mentioned earlier. The enemy's artillery was still active, when three Scout helicopters of 5 Brigade's Air Squadron fired their SS11 missiles into an Argentinian battery east of Wireless Ridge, before scooting off like 'cheeky little boys that had been caught thumbing their noses' as anti-aircraft fire burst near them.[169] General Moore then ordered Brigadier Thompson to take charge of the pursuit into Stanley, which was exactly what the Brigadier had planned to do with his Commandos and Battalions at 30 minutes notice to move.[170] Division HQ next advised the Brigadier that the Argentinians were surrendering and that 'fire was not to be opened unless the British were fired on'.

Max Hastings, the journalist who had come south with the Amphibious Task Force and was to write about the battles with both the Argentinians and British political masters in London, was forward with 2 Para. He describes the way they 'marched east along the battered road which led to the capital sustained only by the euphoria of the moment for they were utterly exhausted'.[171] Leading them were the two Scorpions and two Scimitars of 3 Troop of the Blues and Royals, carrying some men of the Battalion and flying the Para's Regimental Flag. Briga-dier Thompson with his R Group (the gunner Lieutenant-Colonel Holroyd Smith, the Intelligence Officer Captain Rowe, Marine McGuire with a radio and Cor-poral Dean for close protection) joined the Paras on that battered road. They were to be followed by 3 Para. The men of 2 Para exchanged their helmets for

red berets, and led by their Colonel marched on down the road, passing abandoned vehicles, seeing 'at least a regiment's worth' of abandoned artillery on the
hillside, and a litter of ammunition, clothing and equipment jumbled in the mud
by the road. The stench from the slaughter house where the freezers were no
longer working and the smell of smouldering refuse 'rolled over us'. To avoid
any possible suicidal Argentinian attacks, the British were ordered not to advance
'beyond the racecourse' until the peace negotiations were completed.

The Battalion found an extraordinary prefabricated building that had come
from Argentina for the use of their airforce officers. This now served as the
Battalion HQ and Brigadier Thompson stopped to congratulate them on being
the first into Stanley, before he and his R Group continued some 750 m down the
road to the Secretariat. Negotiations were already under way, Lieutenant-Colonel
Rose and Captain Bell having flown in by a Gazelle trailing a white parachute that
served as a flag of truce. They were discussing the details of the surrender with
Major-General Menendez. The R Group did not disturb them, but walking round
the streets among 'so many armed Argentinian soldiers was an uncanny feeling'.[172]

By 1330 hours '45 RM' had been digging in on Sapper Hill, where they and
the Welsh Guards overlooked Stanley. And where they would spend a bitterly
cold night, their last on the 'mountains'. The 105 mm guns of the Commando
Batteries were loaded and targeted on the airport and the eastern end of Stanley
in case any Argentinians decided to ignore the surrender.

42 Commando were still on Mount Harriet and Goat Ridge where the
Colonel and his second-in-command, on hearing of the surrender, discarded their
'uncomfortable helmets which had . . . dangled awkwardly' from their equipment.
There was a lot going on as the Commando Brigade was being redeployed and
a flight of Wessex helicopters arrived at Harriet, unannounced. '42 RM' then
received 'vague instructions to fly to new positions on the north-east slopes of
Tumbledown'. From there they would march into Stanley, to be met by Brigadier
Thompson who told them to 'go firm' at the western end of the town. He called
his COs to an Orders Group in the top floor of a building being used by 2 Para,
and where the Brigade R Group was now located. '42 RM' had retraced their
steps out of the town so that Lieutenant-Colonel Vaux could keep control of the
unit, as there was already some drunken indiscipline among some of those who had
reached the town before his Commando. Now there was some delay before the COs
meeting with Brigadier Thompson could begin, as a confusion in the signals sent
to Lieutenant-Colonel Whitehead and Lieutenant-Colonel Vaux caused them to be
landed by helicopters at Government House 'under the startled eyes of the Argentinians guarding it'.[173] However they reached the O Group and the Brigadier 'tied
up the inter-unit boundaries and areas' working in the light of torches.

During that afternoon Max Hastings – his face still darkened by camouflage
cream – had been walking around the streets, surprised that he met no hostility
as the cowed Argentinians seemed to be lining up for surrender. He walked into
the Upland Goose Hotel: 'like liberating an English suburban golf club'.[174] At
this time Lieutenant-Colonel Rose's negotiations were being confirmed at each
stage through his portable satellite radio link to London. But bad weather delayed

General Moore's arrival and it was 2100 hours before he and General Menendez could sign the surrender documents. The war was over and it seems that the Cabinet in London had been surprised at the final speed of this complete victory. 3 Commando Brigade's R Group heard of the formal surrender through a news flash on the BBC World Service, such is the speed of modern communications. The ever resourceful Major Gullan found some red wine for the R Group to celebrate this victory. Next day there was a ceremonial hoisting of the flag outside Government House, by men who served in '8901'. (This was a flag Major Southby-Tailyour had brought with him, and had been the Governor's standard when the Major – commanding Naval Party 8901 at that time – had borrowed it after the Queen's Birthday parade in 1978.)

An SBS team landed the same day (Tuesday, 15 June) on Pebble Island and accepted the surrender of its garrison, after which 40 Commando crossed the Falkland Sound to take the surrender of West Falkland's garrisons. Among the captured materials on the Islands were Exocets on trailers, radar-controlled anti-aircraft guns and huge stockpiles of war stores. The Argentinian conscripts, unused to proper sanitation at home, had defecated in buildings as they had in their defence positions without any sanitary arrangements. And although there were cases of vandalism out on the Camp, the Argentinians had in general treated islanders with some respect in their attempts to reconcile the locals to the intended occupation. The major task now was to repatriate nearly 13,000 prisoners who were taken to Argentina in British ships to underline the completeness of the victory.[175]

Two Troops of '42 RM's' M Company (the Mighty Munch) had been the garrison on South Georgia. They now formed the Assault Force taken to South Thule, 720 km south of South Georgia, where a small Argentinian force had in 1976 established a weather station. A section of commandos, commanded by Sergeant J. Napier, were landed on 19 June on an ice bound LZ 'behind the weather station', and additional flights by the helicopters of ships accompanying *Endurance* were made to suggest that more than ten men had landed, reinforced with spurious radio messages to suggest that a full company was ashore. The weather was foul and the ships' upper decking 'iced with freezing spray'. The Sergeant's men, wearing 12-point crampons, carried ice-axes and climbing ropes as they jumped down from the helicopter onto an ice slope. Next day, as the ships entered the bay on which the weather station was located, and the Marines ashore came down the hill towards it, the 10-man garrison surrendered to the Marines.[176] M Company continued to garrison South Georgia until mid-July, having enjoyed on the 25 June a successful Southern Hemisphere 'Christmas'.

The rest of the Commando Brigade had left the Islands on 25 June aboard *Canberra* and reached Southampton on 11 July, when she had a tumultuous welcome. Her commandos were landed and carried in lorries back to their bases, journeys which passed cheering crowds at towns and villages as the trucks went to Plymouth and other bases. The ships were cheered as they reached their home ports, all receptions being amply covered by television. But the reception was tinged with sadness because two RM officers and 24 Marines had been killed and 67 wounded during this campaign. In all 255 officers and men in the British services were killed.

The lessons of the Falklands War were studied by both the Ministry of Defence and politicians. Perhaps the first lesson, which came as no surprise to the Corps, was the effective fighting qualities of the Marines and of their commanders. Patrick Bishop of the *Observer* summed up these Para and Commando COs in the words: 'they tended to be practical, spartan men who shared all the discomforts that their men had to put up with'. All the commanding officers of Marine Commandos were later promoted to Major Generals.

The need for amphibious shipping for operations outside Europe led to the commissioning of HMS *Ocean*, and plans for the new HMS *Bulwark* and *Albion* – see chapter 12. The organic air-defence of the Brigade was strengthened, as would be the artillery support with 155 mm heavy guns.

The affinity between officers and men is brought out in many personal narratives with their references to such events as Major Ewen Southby-Tailyour's breakfasts. Can it be true that he ate three one morning? (He has assured the author that it was.) Each was provided by cheerful coxswains of landing craft, who had vied with each other in the sumptuousness of the meal provided from their meagre galleys. Nor – while speaking of meals – did every pongo appreciate the Commando Brigadier's assertion of his men's ability to live off the country, and to tease him, he was presented at one dinner table with a live worm. This he plunged into whisky before devouring it.

The aftermath of this great victory was interesting to students of military-political history in the Corps' refusal to be vainglorious. It is said that Mrs Thatcher was displeased that the Archbishop of Canterbury's sermon on Monday 26 July did not strike a sufficiently triumphant note.[177] But the Brigade was not prepared for any note of triumphalism in a parade in Plymouth nor in a succession of victory parades, for the British losses had been 255 men killed and 777 wounded. Six ships had been lost and 10 others more or less severely damaged. Appropriate memorials to those killed during Operation Corporate have been erected in San Carlos, Stanley, the RM Barracks at Stonehouse and at RM Poole. In all 27 officers and men of the Corps had been killed and over 100 wounded.

There had been some failure of naval weapons in the first week of the campaign. But such setbacks were overcome by the Royal Navy's dogged persistence in the face of adversity. Admiral Woodward was not responsible for the lack of point defence on ships, or the lack of airborne early warning systems and lack of powerful air cover. And in the event the brilliant choice of San Carlos as a landing site was just enough – matched by the power of the Harriers, the Rapier missiles (despite the early set backs in setting these up) and other British weapon systems – to hold the tactical balance against the enemy's air force.[178]

Mobilising scores of ships and 28,000 men to fight and support an operation over 12,000 km from home was something of a political gamble. And while the

Prime Minister was a strong enough character to bear such risks, ably supported by her senior Royal Naval officers, steps were subsequently taken to strengthen Britain's ability to fight such wars. There had been much 'ad hoccery' in putting the second brigade into the field and although Major General Jeremy Moore proved 'a good front-line commander, constantly visiting his units', his Division's staff found great difficulty in grasping the reins at such a late stage,[179] a difficulty that would be offset in future with the formation of a Rapid Reaction Force.

The honours and awards to Royal Marines for operations in the South Atlantic in 1982 included: a KCB; an operational CB; two DSOs; two DSCs; five MCs; two DFCs (the first ever awarded to men in the Corps); a DCM; four DSMs; ten MMs; a DFM; and a QCM (*London Gazette* 8 October 1982).

Brigadier Julian Thompson and his Brigade staff's achievements are hard to overstate, achieved as they were with the close cooperation of Commodore Mike Clapp and his experienced staff, particularly because few British campaigns in this century have been fought with so little military intelligence on the enemy's morale and dispositions. On this occasion the enemy was foxed in part because initially General Menendez believed that the San Carlos landings were a diversion.[180] Two battalions of Argentinian mountain troops were held on the Chilean border throughout the campaign, while the Argentinian army had been taught to rely too heavily on resources rather than human endeavour as we have seen. So although the Argentinians had better equipment, their tactics and military skills on land were lamentable.

Some reflections on 'Corporate' have brought out a miscellanea of interesting facts not widely known. For instance, at Poole WO2 Tony Samson had used his many contacts to track down special items for the SBS. Ammunition loads arrived in trucks, but there was only one crane to load HMS *Hermes*, the loads were therefore man-handled aboard. At sea aboard ships the PT exercises might begin in the early morning dark. Some men landed on D-day on East Falkland after a 4-hour trip in an overcrowded LCU. At other times they flew in helicopters hugging the contours of the mountains, when one error by a 'pilot and that will be it'. There are memories of: crossing the great stone-runs among 'boulders as a big as a man'; of the RSM of the Welsh Guards using his motorcycle to bring forward rations: of one Marine as he followed his Captain literally step by step through a minefield; of delays when the 'satcomms' might take two hours to get the required links; and when a BV driver did not realise his vehicle had begun to float. There were hazards too for the Gazelle and Scout helicopters which were used as high speed 'Land Rovers': in the air they could be turned right over by the down-draft from a larger helicopter flying above them.

Major General Moore has pointed out that 'logistics are everything' in operations involving amphibious assaults on distant shores. And a study of the campaign, *The Falkland Islands Campaign: The Lessons* HMSO December 1982 showed, among other things: the advantage 'in the high state of individual training and fitness of the land forces'. The study also recorded the fitting of some Sea

Kings with early-warning radar. Ammunition stocks were also reviewed and a study made of the censorship necessary in future operations.

Professor Freedman in his book *Britain and the Falklands War* was to point out that the fate of the British had not been at stake in this war, even if the fate of the Conservative Government and national pride had been so. But after one of the 'most remarkable logistical feats of modern times', there followed a swift military campaign. In this the traditional military virtues proved decisive, and served as a corrective to the notions of electronic battlefields. There was a wider purpose served in countering the Argentinians original aggression, for in doing this, the British contributed to upholding the rule of international law and ended the totalitarian regime in Argentina.

KEY EVENTS IN THE SOUTH ATLANTIC – MARCH TO JUNE 1982

19 March (Friday)	'Scrap metal merchants' landed on South Georgia and hoisted the Argentinian flag.
21 March (Sun)	HMS *Endurance* re-embarked her aircraft, the RM detachment and nine ranks of Naval Party (NP) 8901, before sailing for South Georgia.
23 March (Tue)	NP8901 provided overnight guards for aircraft on the airfield at Port Stanley.
27 March (Sat)	NP8901 deployed in defensive positions at the airfield before first light.
29 March (Mon)	Maj M. J. Norman and relief party 8901 arrived Port Stanley in RRS *John Biscoe*. They were known as the '1982/83' detachment.
1 April (Thur)	At 0900 hours – Maj Norman took over operational command from Maj G. R. H. Noott who command the '1981/82' 8901 detachment. 2300 hours – both 8901 parties briefed and deployed.
2 April (Fri)	UN resolution 502 passed demanding Argentinian withdrawal Argentinians invaded the Falklands and captured all but six Marines of the 8901 parties. The captives were flown with the Governor, his wife and three RM wives to Argentina, and on to Uruguay the next day.
3 Apr (Sat)	British Parliament sat in emergency session. Argentinians overran 22 Marines on South Georgia.
5 Apr (Mon)	Task force sails from Portsmouth with HQ 3 Cdo Bde and elements of 40, 42 and 45 Commandos. The six Marines who had avoided capture on the Friday, gave themselves up.

	The 8901 Parties and some RN personnel arrived in England at RAF Brize Norton.
9 Apr (Fri)	SS *Canberra* sailed from Southampton with the main bodies of 40 and 42 Cdos and 3 Para.
12 Apr (Mon)	Britain declares a maritime exclusion zone of over 300km around the Falkland Islands.
17 Apr (Sat)	Adm Fieldhouse, Adm Woodward, Gen Moore and senior officers of Amphibious Force and 3 Commando Brigade have a conference at Ascension.
19 Apr (Fri)	Maj Norman and 8901 (1982/83) flew back to the South Atlantic.
20 Apr (Tue)	Lt Keith Mills, 27 Marines, a Leading Seaman and 13 members of the British Antarctic Survey team repatriated to the UK.
21 Apr (Wed)	South Georgia operation begins
23 Apr (Fri)	Argentinian submarine *Santa Fe* attacked while reinforcing their troops on South Georgia.
24/25 Apr (Sat/Sun)	A landing force commanded by Major Guy Sherridan with M Coy of 42 Cdo, with attached personnel, recaptured South Georgia.
26 Apr (Mon)	Lt-Cdr Aziz signed surrender of South Georgia.
28 Apr (Wed)	Britain declares a total sea and air exclusion zone around the Falklands.
30 Apr (Fri)	Gen Moore flies to Ascension for meeting with Brig Thompson. Total Exclusion Zone (TEZ) enforced.
1 May (Sat)	Initial landings of SBS and SAS recce teams on East Falkland
1/2 May (Sat/Sun)	RAF Vulcan bomber raided Stanley airport and Fleet Air Arm attacked Stanley airport. RN bombarded Stanley airport, submarine attacked Argentinian cruiser *General Belgrano* and RN also sank a coastal craft.
2 May (Sun)	Argentinian cruiser *General Belgrano* sank.
4 May (Tue)	HMS *Sheffield* badly damaged by Argentinian Exocet missile, and later she sank while under tow on 10 May. Vulcan and Sea Harrier raids on Stanley and Goose Green, Harrier lost.
6 May (Thur)	Two Harriers crashed in fog.
8 May (Sat)	War Cabinet dispatched landing force south from Ascension.
9 May (Sun)	Argentinian 'spy' trawler *Narwhal* boarded by SBS before sinking as a result of a previous air attack.
12 May (Wed)	5 Brigade sailed from Southampton in *Queen Elizabeth ll*. Gen Moore issued directive to 3 Cdo Bde 'to secure

bridgehead on East Falkland ... from which operations to repossess the Falkland islands can be achieved'.

14 May (Fri)	SAS raid to destroy Argentinian aircraft on Pebble Island.
18 May (Tue)	Landing Force rv with Adm Woodward's Battle Task Group.
19 May (Wed)	War Cabinet give final approval for assault landing.
20/1 May (Th/Fr)	3 Cdo Bde landed in San Carlos Bay and established a beachhead
21 May (Fri)	Frigate HMS *Ardent* sunk with the loss of 22 men. 16 Argentinian aircraft lost.
22 May (Sat)	Cdo Bde Command Post set up at San Carlos Settlement. Raid by 2 Para planned to attack Darwin and Goose Green but this original plan cancelled on the following Monday due to lack of helicopters and bad weather.
23 May (Sun)	Argentinians lost 7 aircraft. After repeated air attacks HMS *Antelope* had been on fire but most of her crew evacuated (a Warrant Officer RE defusing an unexploded bomb was killed).
24 May (Mon)	SAS recce party seize high ground near Mount Kent's summit.
25 May (Tue)	Type 42 destroyer HMS *Coventry* and the *Atlantic Conveyor* sunk.
26 May (Wed)	War Cabinet questions lack of movement from beachhead.
26/27 May (Wed/ Thur)	2 Para set out to attack Goose Green on basis of revised plan for raid. 3 Para and 45 Cdo set out for Teal Inlet and Douglas Settlement. SAS landed in strength on Mount Kent.
28 May (Fri)	2 Para Bn captured Goose Green and Darwin. 5 Brigade transhipped (crossdecked) from *QE II* for passage to San Carlos.
29 May (Sat)	Goose Green's Argentinian garrison surenderd.
30 May (Sun)	General Moore arrived at San Carlos.
31 May (Mon)	42 Cdo landed by helicopters on Mount Kent. M&AW Cadre capture Top Malo House over 30km east of San Carlos, and eliminated a patrol of Argentinian Special Forces. 3 Cdo Bde command post without its vehicles arrived Teal.
1 June (Tue)	5 Bde began to disembark at San Carlos. 3 Cdo Bde Air Sqn's refuelling area bombed from high level, no serious casualties
2 June (Wed)	2 Para move to Bluff Cove. First LSL offloaded to a Forward BMA at Teal Inlet.
3/4 Jun (Th/Fr)	3 Cdo Bde began patrolling in mountains approaching Stanley.

5 June (Sat)	Scots Guards embarked for Fitzroy.
6 June (Sun)	Scots Guards landed at Fitzroy after transhipping to LCUs for a long, exposed passage in rough weather.
	Welsh Guards embarked for Fitzroy.
8 June (Mon)	LSL *Sir Galahad* and *Sir Tristram* came under air attack at Fitzroy, 51 seamen and soldiers killed.
	LCU *Foxtrot 4* sunk by enemy action with loss of 6 of her crew.
9/10 Ju (Wd/Th)	5 Bde regroup on southern flank of pending attacks towards Stanley.
10/11 Ju (Th/Fr)	LCUs take ammunition to 5 Bde at Fitzroy.
11/12 Ju (Fr/Sat)	3 Cdo Bde mounted night attacks to seize mountain defences of Stanley. 3 Para, Mount Longdon. 42 Cdo, Mount Harriet. 45 Cdo, Two Sisters. All successful.
	By this dates attempts were being made by Capt Bell RM to contact the Argentinian staff over the Islands' medical radio service.
13/14 Ju (Su/Mo)	2nd Bn Scots Guards took Tumbledown (mountain) taking casualties in a 'tremendous battle'.
	1st Bn Welsh Guards and 1st/7th Gurkha Rifles took Mount William and Sapper Hill, and although they came under shell fire they met no significant resistance.
13/14 Ju (Su/Mo)	2 Para took Wireless Ridge and the Argentinians withdrew. A raid by SAS and an SBS team both in 1st Raiding Sqn's RRCs was repulsed in their attempt to destroy a fuel depot.
14 June (Mon)	Argentinians began to surrender this morning and by 1630 the terms of surrender were agreed and signed at 2100 hours.
18 June (Fri)	Argentinian prisoners began to be repatriated.
19 June (Sat)	Recovery of South Thule mounted and successful the following day.
25 June (Fri)	3 Cdo Bde sailed for home in SS *Canberra* and other ships, arriving in Southampton on 11 July.

12 TRAINING, ORGANISATION AND WEAPONS IN THE 1980S AND

At the Commando Training Centre in the late 20th century both officers and men were trained for service in the Royal Marines, it was – and is – based at Lympstone (Devon – see Appendix 4). In the 1980s some 15 per cent of officer recruits failed the course. And of the Marines only 28 per cent passed their 30-week course, the majority failing in the first few weeks. (The numbers dropping-out was reduced by giving potential recruits a week at Lympstone to see if life as a Marine was likely to suit them and if they would suit the Corps.) The course was comprehensive in training basic military skills and in the mid-1980s cost £20,000 to train a man as a Marine before he was posted to a Commando or some other unit. NCOs were – and still are – also trained at CTC which ensured that all officers and men had a common background, and accounts in part for the continued tightly knit 'family' relationship throughout the Corps from the day a man joins.

Young officers found some surprises in the first year of their training: a training session on the second night in the Corps, when one YO in September 1983 was called from his bed for a long session of exercises in 'white shorts and plimsolls', under his instructors, inelegantly known as 'beasting'; and a great number of domestic chores with washing, ironing and hoovering. A full working day left no time for socialising and each night's cleaning intermixed with writing up notes, left only a few hours for sleep. A man could become utterly exhausted after each period in which the YO received an introduction to military fitness. Yet most YO's in the 1980s and 1990s came to enjoy the team spirit of their batch, welded as it was in the rigours of ever changing tasks set by their instructors, indeed in this aspect the 'modern' Corps did not differ from that of earlier decades.[1] In 1983 Lieutenant HRH The Prince Edward RM joined the Corps as a university entrant and did well by all reports during his training, but he was to resign in 1987.

Several features of this training were innovations of the late 20th century. For example: most teenagers of the 1980s and 1990s had worn soft canvas-type shoes – the so-called 'trainers' – before joining the Corps, therefore they had to be given a period in which their feet were toughened up before they wore boots. There were also more stress-factures to limbs than appears to have been the case a few decades earlier, men with such injuries served in a Remedial Troop so that these could heal. And while recruits have always been encouraged to help the local community, in the 1980s they spent a week-end with the disabled as part of their commando training.[2] The Assault Courses looked as fierce as they ever were and the instructors as competent, although there was perhaps some more temperate use of language that reflected changes in the public's attitude to personal relationships in the 1980s.

There had been a systematic approach to training which continually developed to meet new requirements. And in April 1991 the NCOs Training Wing introduced a quality control program which among other things ensured that men were adequately prepared for their roles in the Commando Brigade. In 1993 Quality Control (Internal Validation) at CTCRM – to give the procedure its full title – was extended to recruit courses. This entails several procedures including: the use of test results, interviews, questionaries and unsolicited feedback which has been described as 'constructive "drip" sessions'. After every four or five consecutive courses a 'Trends in Training Report' was produced which highlighted any problem areas as well as reviewing the effectiveness of training. As a result: should a man's training have omitted a technique or a weapon with which he should have been familiar, corrective action was taken. Feed back from the Brigade was also studied, so that a man's failure through some gap in his training would lead to future improvements in training syllabuses.

The training of specialists has tended to move from the Corps' own training centres to centres run for all three services. Although the skills of amphibiosity remained essentially a Royal Marine province. Young officers in the 1990s going into the Landing Craft Branch did a three-month course, longer than those of many of their predecessors. In the 1990s they learnt the rudiments of seamanship and navigation, learnt to land in surf and on rocky beaches. They also practised laying beach roadways, making beach recces [3] and those other skills needed for operations involving amphibious landings.

Tradesmen in the Corps were an essential part of its operations, as they have been since Captain John Judd was the first apprentice in the 1930s. They usually still had a rating according to the proficiency of their training, with Class 2 grades being promoted to corporal provided that they also passed the Junior Command Course. Class 1 specialists had also to pass the Senior Command Course before they might be promoted to Sergeants.

Drivers were the most numerous tradesmen at 565 in 1980 with 189 vehicle mechanics, 13 metalsmiths and 14 vehicle artificers capable of taking charge of major vehicle workshops. Most of these and other tradesmen* were trained by

---

* Tradesmen in the Corps also included in 1980 (and 1997):

27 carpenters who did a 15 week course at TTC RM; (only a few Assault Engineers trained as carpenters in 1997);

18 illustrators whose duties included a great deal of high quality art work and marking operational maps; (18 in 1997);

41 printers trained at HQ TRFRM in Portsmouth in 1980 for service in C-in-Cs offices, major NATO establishments and various Corps HQ's; (this branch disestablished by 1997);

the Technical Training Company RM at Poole,* gaining qualifications – for example as Heavy Goods Vehicle (HGV) drivers – which were accepted for civilian employment in their specialist field. By March 1995 basic driver-training had been transferred to the Army School of Mechanical Transport (Leconsfield near Hull).[4] There was some concern at that time, that drivers in the Marines might loose their mastery of beach crossings but no evidence of this appeared. Also a driver's ability to control BV202s on snow required mastering in the mountains of Scotland, before he was deployed to Norway.

The Clerks Branch in the early 1980s could not be filled by volunteers and a number of men were trained to enable the branch to make up its quota. But by 1987 there were sufficient numbers of volunteers for some of the quota men to be allowed to return to general duties. In 1988 the Service Funds Accounting Course was introduced at CTC (replacing a manual accounting course at the Royal Army Pay Corps' Training Centre at Worthy Down). On each of these new courses six and later nine clerks were trained to run service accounts on computers.[5]

The Cooks Branch had a strength of 228 all ranks in late 1983 when their training had been carried out by the Royal Navy Cookery School. But that year their training was reorganised with a 'new style Specially Enlisted Cook' who did a 30-week course at CTC. This included basic training and preliminary training as commandos. This was followed by seven weeks of basic cookery at the RN Cookery School and a further two weeks of field cookery at CTC. After joining their units, these cooks could sit a Provisional Professional Examination before attending the eight weeks of the K2 Course (the qualification for Junior NCOs in this branch), and from which they could gain a City & Guilds certificate as a recognised qualification in the catering industry. The K1 course included advanced catering management, lead to the highest trade qualification in the catering industry, and to Senior NCO's rank. Both the Army School of Catering and Royal Naval Schools of Cookery were in Aldershot from September 1983 [6]. The standard of cooking and of presentation of meals has steadily improved

---

42 Armourers trained at the Army's School of Electrical and Mechanical Engineering (by 1988 there were to be 44, some running their own small workshops in places like Diego Garcia;[77] this branch numbered 45 by 1997); and

42 Telecommunications Technicians trained to repair and check communications equipment at the Army's School of Electronic Engineering (Arborfield); (this branch numbered 38 by 1997).

A typical establishment for tradesmen in a Commando was: 7 Vehicle Mechanics with a sergeant in charge (12 Vms with a WO2 in charge in 1997), who could recover tracked vehicles and maintain them in the field; 3 armourers with a sergeant in charge (4 armourers with a sergeant in charge and a metalsmith by 1997); one illustrator (in the intelligence section); 3 carpenters with a sergeant in charge (trade with RM Engineers by 1997); 2 Telecom Tecs of which the senior was a sergeant (and an MESM by 1997). Clerks by the 1990s were trained computer operators.[78]

* In 1988 The Technical Training Company became the Technical Training Wing and had moved to CTC by 1997.

in the Corps, reflecting the wider interest taken by the generations of civilians who took regular holidays abroad. And there have been some interesting appointments in this branch whose chefs serve in messes and galleys at home and abroad. (Old 'hands' will note that the *Globe and Laurel* referred in the 1980s to chefs as well as cooks.) One accompanied post in 1990 was that of cook/driver to the Senior Royal Naval Officer in Washington DC.[7] By the late 1990s all Marines with a qualification for cooking, were known as chefs in the Corps, there being 140 of them in 1997. Indeed this change in title had its amusing anecdotes, for on one inspection by a visiting General a Marine when asked said 'he was a cook'. The General told him: 'We only have chefs in the Corps'. A man parading a little down the ranks when asked what he did, replied 'I was a cook Sir, but now I am a chef'.

Specialist courses also include those for Assault Engineers which in the late 1980s were run every three years and for about six students. In the ten weeks of such courses at CTC a man qualified for his AE1's badge, having learnt to design and build a wide range of structures including improvised bridges capable of carrying a fully laden 4-tonne truck with its trailer. Mountain Leaders, after what has been described as 'cruel but fair' selection [8], did a 7-month course including climbing, combat survival and time in Norway [9]. But since the mid-1990s their training has been for Cold Weather Warfare, not just for operations in the Arctic. The RM Police were trained by the Royal Military Police at Chichester, and in 1987 the Royal Marines Troop with the HQ and Signals Squadron included six Marine policemen trained in Close Protection.[10] The Signals Branch, as it had in the past, continued to provide specialist Signallers who 'were well represented in all units' in the 1980s. The signallers' Clansman radios of the mid-1980s provided clear and reliable communications, but the procedures were considered to provide the Russians with more signals intelligence than necessary. Therefore new radio-voice procedures on internal 'nets' were introduced in the British services from 1 June 1984. These methods included a new call sign system and a new low-level code which has proved more acceptable than the old ones.[10a]

Musicians continued to be trained by the RM School of Music – see Appendix 5. There was one significant innovation in August 1992 when women musicians first joined the RM Band Service as detailed in that appendix.

Parachuting in the Corps has been long established, for example, a Marine officer among those landed from craft at Dieppe in 1942 was an experienced parachutist. By the early 1980s R Company had a team of parachutists who gave displays using – among other techniques – Canopy Relative Work (CRW). This was at that time a relatively new technique in which controlled movements enabled one parachutist to hook his feet into the centre rigging lines of a companion jumper and several jumpers might then form a stack [11]. The RM team had taken third place in the World Parachute Championship of 1984 with 8-man stacks and other formations. They had other successes and in 1993 were British Champions in both the 8-man and 4-man. [12] This RM Free Fall Team was disbanded by

1995 but it held a number of records: the largest stack; the largest night stack, the highest abseil/skydive and the largest diamond formation in free-fall.[13] By 1996 the Corps also held the records for the longest continuous abseil, abseiling from the tallest building, the longest and highest death slide,[14] and a team of Marines and Lieutenant Phil Armstrong RN in November 1993 abseiled over 1,100m (actually 3,500 ft) down the shaft of Cleveland Potash Mine in Yorkshire. To these records Marine Steve Anderson and his friend a former Marine, Alan Darvill in 1996 added a 'Descentathon' record when they came out of a helicopter at about 1.5km above Grand Cayman in the Bahamas. They each abseiled down a 30m rope, before parachuting into the sea and diving another 30m to recover a statue on the seabed.[15]

In 1997 the SAS and SBSRM came under the unified operational command of the Director of Special Forces. Each unit had its own commanding officer, and the Regimental and Administrative Command of the SBS remained with the Commandent General who retained the powers of promotion. The SBS maintained their maritime specialisation, although the men of each unit were broadly interchangeable for operations.[16] The SBS ranks were specially selected and trained – their Swimmer Canoeist SC3's course of the 1980s included a 50km-paddle [17] – for deployments in these decades to places no-one mentions and probably have not heard of. They had a regular annual exercise with submarines off Gibraltar, they mounted exercises to test the defences of Britain's oil rigs and other offshore assets but only fleeting glimpses of their passage through history swim to the surface. How did they get wherever they were going? By parachute, swim or paddle canoes, these are the usual answers but there is one technique about which a little has been published: the Maritime Craft Air Deployment System which the SBS has used since the mid-1980s and was bought by the USN Seals (Sea-Air-Land) teams. The two systems bought by the USN cost £50,000 each and allows a rigid-hull inflatable to be launched using a special platform loaded into a C-130 Hercules. The platform grips the boat 'using a scissor-like mechanism' and is pulled from the aircraft at altitude by an extraction parachute of over 6m in diameter. The platform releases the boat into a free fall until four 9.5-metre parachutes open to land the boat safely on water. The system was made by Aircraft Materials Ltd of Devon.[18] There were press reports of the late 1990s describing other possible craft used by the SBS. One of these was an 'Inflatable Submersible Stealth Assault Craft' which was claimed to travel quietly at over 90kmph on the surface, driven by water-jet engines. The craft could also submerge to leave only the coxswain's head above water, as the other nine men in the craft were using underwater breathing tanks while electric motors propelled the inflatable. Its hull was coated with radar-absorbing 'paint' and its overall shape tended to deflect radar waves. There were also reported to be enquiries afoot for a mini-submarine to carry 10 men for beach reconnaissance and similar insertions into hostile areas. However not all RM facilities are quite so ingenious.

Indeed the specific facilities for training had not changed over much in the

1990s. 'There were live-firing ranges and assault courses for realistic training.' There is however the use of 'Simunition' in the 1990s which enables a man to fire a small sabot from a specially adapted weapon. This has a range of 50m and on hitting an 'enemy' the plastic sabot releases a fluorescent non-toxic dye, a 'splat' which can later be washed off. There could be no arguments as to who hit who in these close exchanges; and perhaps the only unreal aspect of such fire fights, was the need to ensure that a man's face and hands were covered.[19] Indeed such battles with paint-ball ammunition had also become a civilian sport.

A typical couple of months at CTC in the winter term of 1989 saw a YO batch (Sept 88) inspected on their passing out parade by the Commandant General, before they each went on to a Commando for Phase II of their training. The Marines of 573 Troop were inspected by the Director General Aircraft (Navy) Rear Admiral D. M. Pulvertaft BSc, who was also father of their Troop Officer, Lieutenant R. J. Pulvertaft. 574 Troop was inspected by Major General R. J. Ross OBE, and Marine A. R. Harker received the King's Badge. The PT2 Course 1/89 passed out with 'a fine display of gymnastics'. The Chief Constable of MOD Police visited to see the MOD Police Instructors Course and the Captain of the Royal Naval College Dartmouth was briefed on the training of YO's. Other visitors included Careers Masters and members of the Combined Cadet Force. The Remembrance Service was followed by the laying of wreaths at the Commando Memorial. The on-going Arduous Training Research Project continued. In sport CTC won the Navy Football Cup and hosted a number of championships including not only those for CTC but also the Corps Fencing Championship and the United Services Cross Country. The term ended with a church service in the gymnasium when 1,000 Royal Marines sang carols.[20]

What did become more sophisticated was the training in the late 1990s when elements of the Brigade might be deployed by helicopters and Combined Arms Exercises could involve a fully integrated 'array of fire support available with ground manoeuvre elements'. On ranges in America this support could include 2,000-pound (900kg+) bombs, napalm, TOW-firing Lynx helicopters as well as light guns (105-mm) and mortars. There might also be American M1 tanks attached to a company to beef-up its support. 4 Assault Squadron RM, which served on an LPD and 539 Assault Squadron RM, which was part of 3 Cdo Bde also took part in many of these exercises when the Commando Brigade practised its full skills. These, as we will see in the next chapter, might be in the frozen wastes of North Norway but Marines were trained to fight in different climates and not only as infantrymen. The embarked Assault Squadron on an LPD, for instance, was fully integrated with the crew and took part from time to time in the ship's Operational Sea Training, before she went on more major exercises.[21]

The Corps continued to have its ski instructors, but in 1997 Steinar Harväg MBE retired as chief instructor. He had run some fifty RM Ski Courses each with some 100 Marines who in turn trained many Marines. Therefore his influence on the Corps' skiing had been wide ranging. The Corps' Jungle Warfare Instructors were trained in Brunei by an inter-service team, when the trainees might have experienced the extremes of temperature from –40°C in Norway and some 14 days later were in Brunei with temperatures which cause one to sweat in almost continuous downpours of tropical rain.[22] Other exercises overseas added spice to unit training. There continued to be other aspects of training in the unit similar to those of previous decades, including black-shod training in Wales,[23] anti-riot training and on various live-firing ranges. While throughout all ranks of the Corps, officers and men learnt to expect the unexpected and that the careful planning of an operation, however detailed, may come unstuck at some point,[24] which was a tenet of combined operations in World War II.

The manpower available to the Corps continued to be set by Parliament after periodic Defence Reviews. These, as we have seen in earlier generations, give rise to the possible disbandments of the Corps. This might well have happened in 1982 had not 3 Commando Brigade RM carried through the professional operation, which contributed a major part to the recovery of the Falkland Islands and other actions in the South Atlantic. At that time senior officers in the Royal Navy proved that Britain could still project power far overseas. Indeed in 1980 there had been concern that there was going to be insufficient numbers of Marines with specialist and trade qualifications (SQ's and TQ's), in part because there was a poor response for these men to re-engage as there were many opportunities for them to take up civilian employment.[25]. In 1981 the disbandment of '41 RM' suggested that Corps would not reach its manpower ceiling until late in 1992.[26] And on 1 October 1991 the R Company of that period and the Youth Visiting Team (YVT) were disbanded.[27]

A number of units were reorganised from time to time, as when Comacchio Group (see Appendix 4) was set up with three companies in 1992 and these provided a roulement tour of six weeks on the west coast of Scotland. Two weeks were spent on operational duties, one week was stand-off, followed by three weeks of training. Royal Marines Protection Parties (RMPP) who boarded ships to safeguard Naval search parties had been drawn from ships' detachments over the years. Then in 1992, when few HM ships carried permanent detachments, two 6-man RMPPs were selected from 45 Commando Group and after pre-embarkation training joined the then new Type 23 frigate HMS *Norfolk*. (The Parties would later form the Fleet Standby Rifle Troop.) *Norfolk* had never carried an RM detachment before and both RMPPs were given a week's exercises, fast roping down from her Lynx helicopter to an RFA and having cleared the ship of any would-be resistance, the Marines were followed by the Naval boarding party. The training was extended to other warships. In early-1993 these parties were found from a Fleet Stand-By Company within 3 Commando Brigade whose Protection Parties might be called on to serve anywhere in the world.[29]

In the years from late-1983 into the 1990s major studies linked to the Royal

Navy's *Oasis* project, were carried out to set up Information Technology (IT) systems not only for pay but for other records. (Meanwhile a centralised bank payment system had been introduced in the Royal Navy, with determination of pay and its issue from a central point.) This system for Naval stores accounting in use throughout the Royal Navy was introduced at CTC in 1984 and after successful trials was extended to all major RM Establishments. It used small personal or mini-computers and through 1986 accounts for Catering and Word Processing were introduced, using this type of machine. It had to be compact enough for its components to pass easily through a ship's hatch, to be assembled in less than an hour and be reasonably robust. The BT Merlin Computer was in use by 1990 following the Navy's second *Oasis* phase. The software programs were designed to give an interface that was readily understandable to personnel who had not been educated with an IT background. But not until the 1990s were applications standardised throughout the Corps.[30]

3 Commando Brigade was to establish integrated IT equipment in the summer of 1987, and all mobile units and headquarters were to be trained and practiced in the use of computers by that December. This made the Brigade the first NATO military organisation (including the Americans) to adopt an advanced world-wide system of IT – if that does not sound too grand!. By June 1988 all major RM bases would be similarly equipped and the RMR would have their installations by March 1990. Larger establishments had 40 or more terminals with pay and personal records on the system by March 1987.

Operational use of IT had been a developing skill since the 1970s if not before; and by the 1990s computerised images of the three-dimensional space involved in a modern battle area could be projected on screens in operation control rooms.[31]

A number of innovations in pay and allowances were introduced in the 1990s with the intention of clarifying a man's entitlement. Boarding School Allowance, Removal Expenses and Separation Allowance, for example, became contingent on whether a man had declared his family to be 'mobile' or 'static'. From 1 April 1990 a married man on his final tour of duty before retirement, could claim removal and disturbance allowances if on this tour he was 'away from his location of first preference'.[28] But the RM Officers Widow's Pension Fund, which had been started in 1766, was closed in 1989 due to lack of support from young officers and the much improved Armed Forces pension scheme.

The Corps has throughout the 20th century had very many unusual duties as this history shows, and that did not change in its last two decades. The appointment of its senior officers has continued to show a high degree of quality in these officers' military abilities, as the battle in the South Atlantic proved. Care is also taken to choose those honorary senior officers who add lustre to the Corps. For instance, in 1981 Crown Prince – subsequently King – Harald of Norway was appointed an Honorary Colonel.[32] In 1988 the post of Corps Colonel was established, the duties of this senior officer were to act as 'Regimental Colonel' with responsibilities for the recruitment of potential officers and supervision of the potential officers' course.[33] And in December 1994 Her Majesty graciously approved the appointment of Admiral of the Fleet The Lord Lewin KG, GCB, LVO, DSC as Life Colonel Commandant of the Royal Marines.[34]

A new post was created for the Corps' Historical Records Officer in the early 1980s. He was responsible for ensuring that Corps and Unit historical records were being kept and for maintaining records of all ranks who had left the Corps. He was – and is – also responsible for the issuing of medals to serving and former Royal Marines.

Changes in the Corps strength were made from time to time. And with effect from 1 April 1995 the Manning Margin was reduced by 131 men. This margin provided a small number men over the total authorised Schemes of Complement and was intended to give some flexibility in drafting men to appropriate units. The only way some flexibility could be retained was by leaving posts unfilled – gapping billets – when men were on long Command and SQ or TQ courses.[35] One possible avenue for increasing the numbers was through extended service and there were those who thought in the 1990s that the retirement age should be raised. But this would have blocked promotions if men had normally served beyond 40 years of age. There were, however, limited opportunities for prolonged service in the Corps, and musicians, normally reaching their prime in their 40s, could extend their engagement.[36] A study in 1992 showed that the Corps had the best ratio of men to officers of any British service. Out of various studies came the Manning Office commanded by the Corps Personnel Officer with six sections: records, promotion, drafting GD, drafting Technical, drafting band and an officer co-ordinating courses.[37]

Two retired officers were employed in the mid-1990s by the HALO Trust for work lifting mines in Afghanistan. They trained Afghans and led teams clearing mines, in what was to become an international issue of the 1990s, when steps were taken through the UN to outlaw the laying of anti-personnel mines.

Several changes in organisation came about as a result of lessons from 'Corporate'. The first of these was the formation of 539 Assault Sqn RM 3 Commando Brigade on 1 April 1984 (Appendix 4) to provide LC and Raiding Craft support for UK/NL landing forces.[38] It comprised: the LC Troop; the Raiding Troop (formerly 1st Raiding Sqn); Support Troop commanded by an RN lieutenant; and HQ Troop; totalling 103 RM & RN ranks commanded by Major Ewen Southby-Tailyour and based at Royal William Yard and Stonehouse Barracks. The title came from 539 LCA Flotilla of World War II, which had distinguished itself on Gold beach on D-day 6 June 1944 (see Chapter 6).

A second change was the creation of the Patrol Troop which was given a year's trial from July 1992 and which had been expanded from the Mountain and Arctic Warfare Cadre. It provided – and provides – the medium reconnaissance teams of 3 Commando Brigade. The ML training cadre now became a separate entity in the Patrol Troop. The Patrol Troop's training included parachuting (in southern France in 1994 with challenging Dropping Zones in mountains), mountaineering at altitude, and snipers courses among others. They made insertions from submarines as well as those from the raiding craft and by other conventional means. Their patrols usually consisted of a sergeant and five Marines.[39]

The Commando Logistic Regiment revised its command and control procedures over the years and by the late 1980s could deploy an Advanced Logistic Group (ALG) of 100 men landing a few hours after H-hour. (The previous concept had been to keep all the Regiment afloat until D+1.) The first exercise in which the ALG landed was in Loch Ryan in November 1987, when the RFA *Sir Percivale* was beached four hours after H-hour, although the beaching of an RFA was always fraught with some difficulties because she needed a dockyard survey afterwards, to meet a peacetime requirement. The ALG went ashore to set up their tents and camouflaged stores area some 8km from the landing point. Three further Beach Maintenance Areas were set up when the rest of the Regiment had come ashore on D+1. In this exercise 'Purple Warrior' a second landing had to be effected on the fifth day with the Regiment dividing in half to set up BMAs on another island, which they did in spite of 50-knot winds.[40]

The tasking of helicopters in 'Corporate' had caused many frustrations among commanding officers, but there would be a number of changes in the organisation of both light and other helios before a scheme which seemed likely to meet the Commando Brigade's needs was established in 1995. In 1987 an exchange programme was set up between 3 Commando Brigade Air Squadron (3 BAS) and Helicopter Light Attack 267 Squadron of the USMC. They flew AH-1W Cobras designed to attack armoured vehicles and other ground targets. And although the Brigade did not get any attack helicopters when economy measures restricted the acquisition of such assets, the exchange scheme continued into the late 1990s.[41]

The problems of tasking helicopters led to the formation of the Commando Helicopter Operations and Support Cell (CHOSC), to coordinate the tasking and operational deployments of the Commando Helicopter Force. It provided centralised support for stores (QM), motor transport and training. CHOSC also had a Mobile Air Operations Team. This Force consisted in 1991 of 845 and 848 Naval Air Commando Squadrons, normally flying Sea King MK IVs in operations with Royal Marines. In addition to the wheeled transport, CHOSC had some BV206s.[42]

The Brigade Air Squadron Support Flight provided the ground handlers from its 'bootnecks, matelots and REME'. On exercises the Flight broke up into three sub-units with the echelon providing the re-supply line for the Squadron. The men of the Forward Operating Base (FOB) and at two Forward Arming and Refuelling Points (FARPs) worked in the field for the quick resupply of the helicopters. Each FARP had seven vehicles including bowsers and 4-tonners, moved around to avoid detection by an enemy and with its commandos trained not only for its defence but also to refuel and rearm the aircraft. The Light Aid Detachment (LAD) with the Squadron had a lieutenant commanding 42 other ranks. They were aircraft technicians who serviced the helicopters, and some of whom had passed the All Arms Commando Course.[43]

On 1 September 1995 the 3 Brigade Air Squadron, which had always trained to Army Air Corps standards and systems, was transferred to 847 Squadron in the Naval Air Command. The manning of the Squadron remained largely unchanged but at the RNAS Yeovilton – where the Squadron had been based since the late 1980s – a number of personnel were transferred to the Commando Helicopter Operations Support Cell (CHOSC) which changed its name to HQ Commando Aviation. The HQ would command four squadrons and up to 1,000 RN, RM and Army personnel The light helicopters of what was '3 BAS' included six Lynx AH7 (some with Tow Missiles since August.1982) and nine Gazelles one of which was permanently in Northern Ireland, and the Commando Helicopter Squadrons, numbers 845 and 848, each had increased the numbers of their Seakings to ten. The light helicopters from this date would train and operate to RN flying standards and routines. Arrangements were also made with the Army Air Corps for a squadron of attack helicopters from its 9 Regiment AAC to be earmarked for the support of amphibious operations. And from the year 2001 two additional Lynx were be equipped for 847 Squadron with weaponry for ground attack roles.[44]

Perhaps the most significant change as a result of 'Corporate' was the recognition that the British needed a modern amphibious capability despite – or because of – the Commando Brigade's professional operations in the South Atlantic. On the 11 October 1995 HMS *Ocean* (20,500 tonnes) was launched, this purpose built Landing Platform Helicopter (LPH) would carry a Commando Group of 830 all ranks on a '42-day mission'. With hanger space for 12 EH101 *Merlin* helicopters which were expected to be in service before 2000, a vehicle deck for guns with light vehicles and a purpose-built Amphibious Operations Room. (In 1997 no final decision had been made as to whether the EH 101 or another aircraft would replace Sea Kings in support of the Royal Marines.) She has been designed with a side ramp for loading from a dockside, a fixed ramp to take vehicles from their deck to the Flight Deck and a stern ramp to take them to Mexeflotes, one of which might be carried by *Ocean*. (See illustration.) Her Assault Squadron RM was to be No. 9 and they were to join her for trials in 1998, when her first deployment with an embarked force was planned for the summer of 1999.[45] Replacements for old LPDs HMS *Fearless* (built in the mid-1960s) and *Intrepid* had been ordered in July 1996. They were to be named HMS *Albion* and *Bulwark* and were expected to be operational in April 2002 and April 2003 respectively. These ships of 15,100 tonnes were to carry an embarked force of 245 personnel with 648 when on overload.

Replacements were being considered for the amphibious support ships (the LSLs), with funds earmarked to replace them with ships specificaslly designed for amphibious warfare, an upgrade from the existing ships which were essentially designed for the strategic movement of cargoes. The new design was expected to provide on/off loading to landing craft in the same sea states at which the new LPD would operate. Funds had also been earmarked for two RoRo vessels to carry the heavy vehicles for the Joint Rapid Deployment Force (JRDF) although not designed for amphibious operations.

The landing craft planned for these new ships were the LCU(10) and LCVP(5). The '10's' were to be RoRo craft capable of carrying a Challenger main battle tank or four 8-tonne vehicles or five BV206D all terrain vehicles. The '5's' were to carry a BV206D or 35 fully equipped troops.[46]

The new emphasis on the British amphibious capability had led to a re-emphasis of the Corps integration with the Royal Navy. Therefore from 1 April 1993, as a result of studies over two years, the headquarters structure of the Corps was changed and the Department of CGRM no longer remained a separate department within the MOD. The Department was combined with HQ Commando Forces and HQ Training and Reserve Forces (HQTRFRM) to form Headquarters Royal Marines under CG, with the rank of Major General. He ranked with his fellow Fleet Flag Officers under the full command of the Commander in Chief Fleet (CINCFLEET). The officers who were serving in the various departments in the Ministry buildings in Whitehall, were to remain there as CG's staff had to some extent been integrated with the Naval staff since April 1964, but the Headquarters RM was to be established at the old school of gunnery, HMS *Excellent* at Whale Island in Portsmouth, albeit in new custom built offices.[47] These changes reflected the likely requirements for the 21st century. They contrasted with the potential major increases in manpower in the event of hostilities that had been envisaged when the old headquarters' structure was created, out of the experience of World War II. See diagram for the 1994 command structure and * below.

As from 1 January 1995 Royal Marines establishments flew the White Ensign in recognition of the status of the Corps, and no longer flew the Union Flag from the mast-heads at establishments. This change did not affect the status of men serving in shore establishments who continued to be subject to the Army Act 1955.[48] The Corps also had an increased number of officers on the staff of CINCFLEET some of whom had taken up their appointments in 1992 to ease the transition. This had entailed a temporary 'home' for the HQRM in what had

---

* From 1 January 1982 the staff titles were changed in the British forces to conform with NATO titles:

Old	New
Brigade Major (BM)	Chief of Staff (COS)
Deputy Assistant Adjutant and Quarter Master General (DAA & QMG)	Deputy Chief of Staff (DCOS)
Staff Captain A	SO3 G1 (Personnel)
GSO 3 (Intelligence)	SO3 G2 (Intelligence)
GSO 3 (Operations)	SO3 G3 (Operations)
Staff Captain Q	SO3 G3 (Logistics)

In both nomenclatures the abbreviations SO and GSO stand for Staff Officer and General Staff Officer. To avoid any confusion in April 1982 during operation 'Corporate' the old styles were used.

been HMS *Vernon* until the new offices were built. DRORM (see appendix 4) became part of the new HQ in May 1995 and was initially renamed the Drafting Pay and Records Office RM (DPRORM) when integrated with the Personnel Branch of HQRM. A number of agencies also were now to be co-located with HQRM, including the Corps Secretariat. Subsequently matters of pay were dealt with by the Armed Forces Pay and Administration Agency within the *Centurion* building, and drafting – no longer under CG's direct control – was carried out by personnel based in CG's department but who were responsible to the Naval Manning Agency.

By 1995 the new HQ building was complete with its integrated IT cabling and other services. (To install these and modernise the old Eastney Barracks would have cost over £12-million and no other existing buildings in Portsmouth were available at that time for a cost effective redevelopment as the HQ.) Portsmouth had been chosen as a location in an area of 'strong Naval influence and was also geographically within easy reach of MOD'. There were also economies in the allowances paid which had always been much higher in London than in the provinces. A SNCO based in London in 1994 received £9,427.95 (tax free!) more than a sergeant serving in Portsmouth and officers received even more, with an average annual allowance of £11, 575.37 for every person serving in MOD compared to their equivalent ranks in Portsmouth. The calculation can be expressed in a different way: the removal of RMHQ outside the capital saved £521,000 a year.[49] While in the Dockyard there was one of the bases for warships and Royal Marines forces were once again one of the Royal Navy's chief weapon systems.

By 1996 the structure of what became the general duties branches was revised with a view to reducing the 30 per cent overtraining that had come about under the existing structure. This had arisen when corporals and sergeants were promoted under the common Promotion Roster and had been appointed to a different branch from the one within which they had experience. Therefore by creating equal opportunities for promotion within each branch, unnecessary re-training was avoided. Also this division between GD (General Duties), Specialist Qualifications (SQ) and Technical Qualifications (TQ) for purposes of promotion, offered more chances for signallers, stores accountants, clerks, drivers and others to become NCOs. A further step in 1996 was the formation of the General Duties Branch, although all Marines had always been trained in such duties. From 1996, therefore, a man with a specialist or technical qualification who might become an NCO, could expect to serve in his branch before and after promotion. Each branch was also restructured to ensure that promotion prospects were similar throughout the Corps with provision for selected NCOs to serve outside their branch in GD-type appointments (billets in the jargon).[50]

There were difficulties in recruiting Marines in the mid-1990s in part stemming from the general public's view that a military career was no longer worthwhile, once the threat from the Soviet Union had largely ceased. Yet there seemed likely to be many minor wars for which Royal Marines would be required, not altogether unlike those fought in the late-19th century albeit for different political reasons, and considerably more occasions for humanitarian help to which Royal Marines have always been particularly suited. Why? The strong character found in most Royal Marines allows a generosity of spirit not found in weaker men.

A number of redundancies arose in 1996 when the Corps' overall strength was reduced by 600 to 7,000 but those not re-engaging exceeded the numbers expected. Therefore that summer a bounty of £2,000 was paid to any man who extended his service by two years. A further £250 bounty was to paid each Marine bringing in a new recruit who was still in training after 12 weeks.[51] Pay was also increased by almost 5 per cent, taking account of the X factor. This additional element in pay awards had covered the special features of military service when rates were compared to those of civilians since the 1970s. There were also improvements in allowances and men were given longer notice of routine drafts, with details of any new location in order to help individuals 'more readily to plan their lives'.[52] The effect of all these changes was improved recruitment.

RM Combat Display Teams, which had replaced the R Company's recruiters, had been 40 all ranks but by the end of 1996 was reduced to six teams each of a SNCO and two Marines. They gave presentations on the Corps' activities and assisted in programmes of the Director of Naval Recruiting. Other recruiting initiatives included the distribution of 3,500 compact discs to schools where this package of information could be shown on computers from these CDs.[53]

The order of battle within 45 Commando Group was revised to include a newly formed command team among other developments. These were tested in Brigade Battle Group Training exercises at Catterick (Yorkshire), including an exercise in Built-Up Areas. During this time (1996) the number of BV206s was increased. Another important addition to the Commando Brigade's organic units was 20 Commando Battery RA with Rapier missiles for air defence (see appendix 4). The Battery was expected to have 10 x FSB2 (Field Standard B2) missile firing posts as part of an area Short Range Air Defence (SHORAD) system. This 24-hour all weather capability with an engagement range of 7.2 km, could be linked to the air defence organization of a formation of which 3 Commando Brigade might be a part.*

---

* 1992 saw the introduction of the world's first operational-ground based infrared search and track (IRST) system: ADAD (air defence alerting system) developed over 15 years from the late 1970s. This system could track a multiplicity of targets in an arc of the sky when they were several kilometres away from air defences, which gave the defenders an increased probability of successful hits with missiles by a factor of three or more times. Displays from the system could be used by men firing shoulder-launched surface-to-air missiles, for missiles fired from Rapier and similar launchers. The ADAD system could provide cuing signals fed into the weapon's sights or the operator's headphones. Its design enabled so-called stealth aircraft to be detected regardless of the presence of smoke, haze or ground clutter, with – its makers claimed – an acceptably low number of false alarms. (This last feature is achieved by soft-ware programs linked to integrated circuits.)[79]

New vehicles in these decades included in 1981 the Bedford 8-tonner for 'GS' cargo, with a CALM (Crane Attachment, Long mounted), winch and tipper variants, not much larger than the old Bedford 4-tonner.[54] While in 1992 the Comacchio Group were using Saxon APCs which weighed 10 tonnes, had a 5.4 litre engine and an automatic gear box. However they had a poor off-road performance, and their cargo area, which could carry eight Marines, was not heated, while the driver had many blind spots from his cockpit. In the Spring of 1994 the Saxon was replaced with the Land Rover Snatch with better brakes, good all-round vision and other improvements on the old APC.[55] Another vehicle which has been in service with the Commando Brigade since the summer of 1994 was the Foden heavy vehicle of which the Recovery Section of the Log Regiment had three. (This Section streamlined this recovery work when a vehicle came off the road or bogged in a mire, work previously done by the Repair Troops in the Workshop Squadron.) A small but perhaps significant additions to the Corps' vehicles have been a number with left-hand drive.

In 1980 infantry weapons and motor transport which might come into service with the Corps and the Naval establishments in the UK, were tested by a small team – Inspector of Motor Transport and Weapons RM (IMTWRM) – based in Poole. These included a new 51-mm mortar in 1981 (but not in service till modified by mid-1984), the SA 80 rifle and the 66mm Light Anti-Tank Weapon (LAW) both introduced in the mid-1980s. All were tested by the Team under WO2 Allan Winterbottom. Some items they rejected, for example, a 6-wheeled vehicle with tracks, the 'Supacat' that was used by the Army and the RAF. It failed five weeks of testing in Norway. However by 1993 this 'beach buggy' with its handlebars, had been modified, a version was incorporated in a special trailer to carry a fully loaded Rigid Raider Craft and from which one man might launch and later recover the RRC. The IMTWRM recommended the Norton Interpol 600cc motorbike, mainly for use by RM Military Police instructors, it had a Wankel rotary engine and could accelerate to 100kmph in under four seconds. The team also visited RN and RM units to train selected men to strip weapons and judge their serviceability.[56]

The need to have weapons and ammunition which were compatible with those of other NATO forces was a factor in the choice of arms during these decades.

By late 1987 the Corps was issued with the SA 80 after various trials. It could be fired on single shots or when on 'automatic fire' it became a light support weapon. Its 5.56mm SS109 rounds had a smaller penetration than the heavier 7.62 mm bullet of the SLR, giving about 60 per cent of the penetration of the larger bullet. Nevertheless the 5.56 was intended to penetrate steel helmets, light armour and body vests. The SA 80 was easy to handle with the right hand holding the firing grip and the left hand manipulating 'all the levers, knobs and catches', those on the right-hand side being reached by tilting the rifle. The recoil gave a 'gentle push allowing the sight to fall back on the point of aim'. There were three settings for the gas plug controlling the recoil: N for normal conditions; E for firing such underpowered rounds as the M193 and for use in extreme cold or when the normal re-cycling action is fouled; and O when firing grenades. A steel magazine carried up to 30 rounds and was interchangeable with those for the M16. The sling was attached in such a way that there was never any need to put the weapon down, but both hands could be free when necessary. An interesting feature was the optical Trilux Sight Unit (Susat) which shows an image magnified four times to that seen by the naked eye and also carried a fixed emergency battle sight. The optical sight was also used to locate potential targets in poor light. The laser range finders, Passive Night Goggles, Handheld Magellan Global Positioning Systems and similar specialised equipment were available, but details of their distribution in the Corps, were not available.

The bayonet followed the late-20th century practice of providing more than a blade weapon. The bayonet scabbard also housed a small saw blade, had a bottle opener feature and could be attached to the bayonet to provide wire cutters. The sharpening steel within the scabbard was for use in wartime when blades were to be razor sharp, although in peacetime they remained blunt.[57] The arms drill with this rifle led to several changes. The position of 'slope arms' was reintroduced and 'shoulder arms' used for the 'stand at ease' position. The shape of the SA 80 and its bulk lead to wear on the shoulder of uniforms, not to mention its weight on a man's shoulder, therefore the order 'Change Arms' had to be used more frequently than it had been in the past. The Corps first used these drills at a major parade in June 1986.[58]

Snipers had the 7.62mm Sniper Rifle L96A1 in 1987, at a time when the Army had again decided to train snipers after discontinuing the art in the late-1960s. But the Corps had maintained sniping skills albeit only in Recce Troops. The L96A1 had an effective range of 1,000m, could penetrate 13mm of armour which was sufficient to knock out the driver's ports and periscopes in an APC, and its muzzle suppressor helped to disguise the sniper's firing position. Its special sight also enabled him to carry out effective observations in daylight or at night and those trained on the Snipers Course became a useful 'force multiplier'.[59]

Competition shooting has always had its devotees in the Corps and in the three years from 1988 a team went to Camp Lejeune, North Carolina for four weeks of training with the USMC. In 1990 the team did further training in this specialist art of competition shooting at the Pirbright ranges and in June won all but one of the prizes at the SW United Services Skill at Arms Meeting. At Bisley that year, team members firing SLRs and at different times using competition rifles, won a number of awards before the team for that year was disbanded. Incidentally the SLR had first been introduced to Bisley shotists in 1960.[60] Over the years the training at CTC has put stress on good marksmanship and in 1995 a 2-man Marksmanship Training Team was established at Lympstone to raise the standard and reduce the training periods required for effective marksmanship.[61] Commandant General's Shooting Badge were awarded to those who were in the Corps Team of eight shooting in the United Services Rifle Match each year. It was first awarded in 1990 but was retrospective in that men who shot in these teams in the previous 20 years were eligible to wear this badge, with its crossed rifles over the letters RM superimposed on VIII. The badge was worn throughout the wearer's career on the lower left sleeve in place of the marksman's badge.

Clothing has seen several changes in the 1980s and 1990s the most important of which were probably in the design of boots. The original Boot DMS, as used by the British Army, had some serious drawbacks for use in mountain regions where the Corps might operate. It was not very water resistant and required to be worn with puttees or anklets, the initial RM Combat High Boot of 1981 was some 10cm higher than the Army pattern but weighing nearly 5kg , almost a kilogram heavier than the DMS Boot.[62] Other new items of Arctic kit were introduced in 1981, after many trials in the 1970s and 1980s by the Corps. These also benefitted equipment for general service.

By 1990 men were familiar with the MK4 NBC suit and the A10 respirator[63] NBC training was highlighted in a typical set of exercises by Zulu Company of 45 Commando RM at Porton Down in the summer of 1996. There the Marines learnt to prevent unnecessary degradation of their respirators, gloves and boots through not decontaminating these as soon as a threat had passed. You knew if it had done so by checking the equipment which measured the level and type of toxin on detector papers and similar agents. The directing staff proved constructive rather than critical in giving their advice, with the emphasis on staying out of the constricting clothing once you were familiar with methods of detecting nerve gasses and similar nasties, so you would only wear the suits when necessary.[64]

As we saw in chapter 11: Landing Craft served many more purposes than those of ferrying stores and men ashore. In 1981 an LCU Mk9 had been adapted for continuous operations in extremely cold weather. She had a protective covering over her tank well among other special fittings; and in September that year had sailed from Poole to Rosyth and then to Norway where she delivered two Land Rovers: one to Trondheim and the second to Ramsund north of the Arctic Circle. The total voyage was over 3,000km and made in about three days, when the total of nine days for delays due to severe weather and Norwegian regulations are excluded. [65] Mention has already been made of the new craft to be designed for the LPDs of the 21st century.

By the winter of 1984 some progress was being made on the concept – foreseen in the Falklands War – of craft operating from a Forward Operating Base in which LC units would be supported by their own mechanical and electric engineers.[66] Similar concepts had been used in World War II (see chapter 7) and in 1971 Lieutenant-Colonel (later Lieutenant General) Sir Steuart Pringle had arranged for craft from HMS *Albion* to set up a Forward Operating Base under the command of Major Ewen Southby-Tailyour during exercises in Norway. This was a bold step for Captain Staveley (later Admiral) commanding the landing craft's parent ship, who allowed these craft to be placed under the command of a Commando major. Subsequent exercises were carried out over the years but not until 1982 was a craft available for such radical changes of camouflage from the greys used by parent ships, to disruptive patterns of black and dark brown the only paint available in quantity in *Fearless*'s paint store. Although Major Southby-Tailyour has teasingly claimed the designs were 'the brainwave of his artistic mind'. The effect was dramatic and the craft 'disappeared' against the edges of fjords . . .[66]

In 1985 the first LCVP Mark IVs were taken into the Landing Craft Branch. These had a number of improvements on the Mark IIIs, with a detachable cockpit cover, a manually raised mounting bar for navigation lights and a mounting for a radar set. The well deck could also be covered by a canopy for use in very cold climates, in this well a band waggon might be carried although not when it was fully loaded, or a light gun, or a 1-tonne Land Rover. Work was being undertaken to improve the crafts' speed of 14 knots.[67] By march 1989 a Slingsby Aviation SAH 2200 Hovercraft was on trials with the Squadron's craft, which was said to have given the crews the pleasure of being able to 'bung something across the briny, up the sandy bit and park it outside the grot [sleeping quarters]' without an inevitable court of enquiry.[68]

In the winter of 1989/ 90 four designs of a new rigid raider craft (colloquially the 'Jumbo' RRC) were tested in Norway. The design in use since the early 1970s was not large enough to carry a Section of commandos with their equipment, especially when they were carrying Arctic Warfare kit; and this 17-foot (5m+) raider was very 'wet' in rough seas.[69] The new design accepted by 1994 as the RRC Mk2 had a petrol driven outboard and reliability in high surf was improved in 1996 with the RRC Mk3 which had a turbo injection diesel power unit.[70] The Light Air Cushioned Vehicle – or as it became: the Landing Craft Air Cushion (Light) – came into service in 1994 with 539 Assault Squadron. The swift insertion and dry landing 'was favoured' but there were some initial reservations about this craft, which could only operate in limited conditions of wind and sea states on the open ocean. Trials on the jungle rivers of Guyana, however, proved that the craft was ideal for crossing shoals and rapids in daylight or at night at speeds in excess of 30 knots when carrying 16 Marines and their kit.[71]

The Landing Craft personnel – known by the 1990s as crewmen – were to enter the 1990s with some interesting kit. In 1989 at Poole they tested new Immersion Suits (IS Boat Operator) of a type used by the SBS which gave a better protection for crews of RRC in Norway. And they tested a new suit for the crews of LCUs and LCVPs, this LC Crewman's Suit gave men improved protection against cold weather, but they were still looking for improved lifejackets. Other trials included hand-held echo sounders and auto-plotting navigational aids.

The Landing Craft Branch was expected in 1996 to leave Poole when this base was due to close in 1999.[72] Before then the Joint Warfare staff that had been based in RM Poole were transferred to the Maritime Warfare Centre opened on 1 April 1996 at HMS *Dryad*. This formed part of the Joint Warfare Team which ran a number of courses for officers who might be appointed to various staffs for: multinational and combined conventional military operations; air/

ground operations; amphibious warfare; and a maritime tactical course.[73] In late 1997 the planned move of the Landing Craft Branch was deferred – probably indefinitely.

The Commando Logistic Regiment RM and 59 Independent Squadron RE moved to a one-time RAF base at Chivenor during November and December 1996. The accommodation at Seaton Barracks with the Workshops at Coypool had proved inadequate, lacked training facilities and had some sub-standard buildings. Therefore the move was essential and would also save money! Near the new barracks were adequate training areas on this flat land on the estuary of the Taw, 6km west of Barnstaple in North Devon.[74] (See also appendix 4.)

In the 1983 a permanent planning group had been set up to co-ordinate British operations outside the NATO theatre. It had its own headquarters with its chief of staff who was an Army Colonel, and with a Lieutenant Colonel RM as senior operations and planning officer. Three Army majors covered operations, plans, intelligence, communications and logistics, a commander RN covered Naval plans, a Squadron Leader advised on air supply and there was a small administrative staff of four. It was expected that a 2-star Officer (a Naval flag officer in the case of amphibious operations) would be appointed with an MGRM commanding any landing force. However if the operation was mainly concerned, say, with the air evacuation of civilians then a senior RAF officer would probably command the operation. All the senior appointments were to be made by the Chief of the Defence Staff as and when an operation was required.[75] A decade later, in 1995 the Rapid Reaction Force was created with 3 Commando Brigade Royal Marines and the Army's 5 Airborne Brigade at the core of an estimated 9,000 all ranks including Naval personnel. The Force was to have its own headquarters (to be opened at Northwood in 1996), obviating the changes of the previous decade. (The Falklands War was commanded from the Naval HQ at Northwood in North London, the Gulf War from the RAF HQ at High Wycombe in Buckinghamshire and Bosnia deployments from the Army's HQ at Wilton in Wiltshire.)[76]

Many changes in Naval organisation took place in these decades, for instance Wrens of yesteryear were integrated with Navy ranks in the 1990s. Other changes took place in the organisation of the Army and the RAF but the Corps maintained its position as a potent fighting force specialising in amphibiosity. Yet there is much more to the history of 'Royal' – the Navy still referred to their Royal Marines by this abbreviated title – than military skills. Although at times the differences between military and recreational skills may have been hard to distinguish. They had a full sporting calendar every year of these decades, with inter-unit competitions in all manner of sports: from the long established association football's Tunney Cup, through orienteering, sailing, fishing matches of the RM Angling Association, Corps Badminton won by HQRM in 1995, and Corps tennis to mention just a few Corps sports. In the Navy's Inter-Command Basketball

Championship an RM team was 3rd in 1994, RM canoeists on a number of occasions paddled their way to win the Devizes canoe-races of the 1980s and 1990s (against more than 370 competitors in 1997, down the Thames for 200km from Devizes to Westminster). The Corps Sailing Club had long been established but in 1988 the musicians had their own sailing club with 10 Topper dinghies. RM yachts took part in races including those around the Three Peaks during these decades, involving both sailing and 'running up mountains'. For those who enjoyed less tranquil sports there was motorcycling with, in 1984, an RM team coming 3rd of 31 teams in the Army Motorcycle Championship in Germany. But not all events proved as successful: the Dragon Boat Team sank in Hong Kong in 1994, and during training in 1995. However the team in these fiercely paddled large canoe-like vessels won two golds and two silvers in the South African championship during the late 1990s.

Marines have always been generous in their support for charities, to list these of the 1980s and 1990s might be invidious and take more than a 'full' appendix but an example was shown in 1997 by RMR Bristol. They organised a Commando Slide (a 'Death Slide') across the Clifton Gorge, raising £25,000 for 'a host of charities'. The Corps Museum is a charity with its own Heritage Fund. It has seen dramatic changes in the 1990s when its buildings were to include further parts of the old officers Mess at Eastney. A new entrance was built giving access from the sea front. CGRM opened the extensions on 30 July 1997. The Museums exhibits and displays had been expanded to include *inter alia* Landing Craft and in 1983 the Museum won a European Commendation for quality. And see notes on the museum p. xviii.

The memorials to their predecessors were respectfully honoured from the Commando Memorial at Lympstone (CTC) to such interments as the single grave at El Alamein (North Africa) of an unknown Royal Marine of 'the 1939–1945 War'. Other memories were renewed in the many parades and visits to old battlefields which took place in June 1994, commemorating the 50th anniversary of the landings in Normandy. Other memorial services honoured those who had died in the Falklands, their names will not be forgotten.

The Structure of the Royal Marines Command in 1998

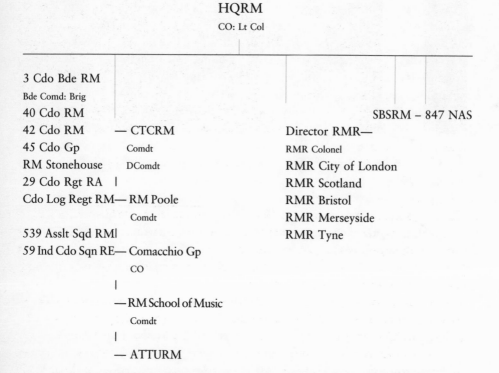

HQRM
CO: Lt Col

3 Cdo Bde RM

Bde Comd: Brig

40 Cdo RM

42 Cdo RM — CTCRM

45 Cdo Gp   Comdt

RM Stonehouse   DComdt

29 Cdo Rgt RA |

Cdo Log Regt RM— RM Poole

     Comdt

539 Asslt Sqd RM|

59 Ind Cdo Sqn RE— Comacchio Gp

      CO

    |

    — RM School of Music

     Comdt

    |

    — ATTURM

SBSRM – 847 NAS

Director RMR—

RMR Colonel

RMR City of London

RMR Scotland

RMR Bristol

RMR Merseyside

RMR Tyne

Notes: 1 All units where the commander is not specified had a Lieutenant-Colonel as CO except '539' with a Major as its officer commanding and ATTURM also commanded by a major.

2 DRORM commanded by DODAR was a separate unit of HQRM until it was merged with Personnel Branch RM as the Drafting Pay and Records Office RM (DPRORM)

(Source: *Globe and Laurel* 1998 p 87)

13

A' DOING ALL KINDS OF THINGS

(From Rudyard Kipling's poem *Soldier an' Sailor too*)

The Corps continued to provide from time to time in the 1980s and 1990s, a Commando as one of the duty battalions in Northern Ireland. And on 17 October 1981 an attempt was made by the IRA on the life of CG, Lieutenant General Sir Steuart Pringle Bt KCB outside his home. He lost a leg in this car bomb but his cheerful determination was an inspiration to his Marines on his return to duty.

Typically on a 4½-month tour in the summer of 1986 advanced parties of 45 Commando arrived in Belfast, followed on 4 July by the main body. This included X Company HQ, with four Troops (one having been brought up to strength by men of the temporarily defunct Support Company and men who had recently returned from Belize) and various specialists including drivers, vehicle mechanics, cooks and signallers, a Company of 230 all ranks. They were based in North Howard Street Mill, a Victorian building on the west side of Belfast and near the surrounding 'green belt'. The ground and first floors housed offices with a medic's surgery, a fully equipped gymnasium and a radio room. On the second and fourth floors was sleeping accommodation, teasingly described by one resident as '60 bedrooms, each one with its leaded window and vaulted ceiling'. On the third floor was the Company OC's quarters, the canteen run by a civilian on contract, and kitchens where the staff were also on contract as reportedly 'were the cockroaches'. Commandos continued to use this billet into the late 1990s, when it still had a 'strong sterile smell hanging in the musty air' as a result of daily mopping with industrial detergent. The lack of natural light – since the windows were high in the walls – made what daylight there was merge into a perpetual gloom.[1]

X Company were to work with four Continuity NCOs (CNCOs) of the 1 King's Own Border Regiment, a detachment of the Royal Corps of Transport with Armoured Personnel Carriers (known to the locals as 'Pigs'), four WRNS and three WRAC cooks. There were also two dog handlers with their dogs.

Two SNCOs were based in the tower of the notorious Davis Flats, Marines provided a guard for the mill and manned various other OP's including one on the top of the local nurses' home. There were two 'bricks', each of four men, in

APVs as a quick reaction force (QRF), ready to attend any incident in X Company's area, and backed up by a similar pair of 'bricks' at 10 minutes notice. Up to 40 call-outs each 24 hours was not uncommon for the QRF. They also provided military escorts to back-up the RUC with a 'brick' in an APC between two police armoured patrol Land Rovers, the vehicles moving at speed with the commandos ready to react if any anti-vehicle missiles were fired at the patrol. This last stint could last some 18 hours with the compensation of lunch in the RUC canteen 'usually served by pretty natives'.

Foot patrols covered the two main areas of the East and West Neighbourhood Police Units. Generally these 'bricks' provided close escorts for policemen enabling them to get on with their duties in as normal a manner as possible, while the commandos kept watch for snipers. Each patrol could be as many as four 'bricks' commanded by a lieutenant or sergeant. But by 1986 times were relatively quiet by comparison with the 1970s and X Troop only had three 'happenings of note' during their tour. A SNCO of the Kings Own Borderers was not hit when fired on by a man with a pistol from 150m, but the 20 rounds returned by the commandos also missed. A bomb outside the Provisional Sinn Fein office in the Falls Road had to be disarmed by a bomb disposal officer (officially: an Ammunition Technical Officer), as was a hoax bomb at the Divis Flats. Commandos were not allowed into pubs except when on duty with an RUC officer. They could not stop and search vehicles and other steps had been taken to ensure that the public could see the RUC had the primary role in anti-terrorist activities.[2]

Other examples of these deployments saw C Company of 40 Commando RM in South Armagh during 1988, manning OP's with one at Glassdrumman, known as the 'Spy Tower', and three other Posts. From these one Troop of commandos built up a picture of the pattern of local life including movements by smugglers crossing the nearby Irish border. While patrols from the company's other Troops were in Crossmaglen and Forkhill carrying out surveillance and escorting RUC patrols. Men on patrols found that field obstacles were somewhat standard: barbed wire as high as a man's inside leg plus two inches (50mm); fence posts that were firm until a man committed his weight against them; and always(?) a stream between the commando and the boggy helicopter landing site with its ankle-straining ruts and potholes (some of which were mortar bomb craters).

The OP's were a target for the local IRA and demonstrators, nevertheless over 20m up high in a 2½m² 'box' on the Spy Tower, a team might spend three weeks, with their off duty time in the bunker below the tower which was 'like accommodation in a submarine'. Three mortar attacks, a bomb in a van, and other attacks against the commandos took place over a few months during the summer and autumn of 1986. The Company was based in accommodation in the centre of Crossmaglen, the ardently Republican town in the centre of this rural area. These buildings were screened from view by corrugated iron, which prevented any IRA sniper taking a clear shot at a Marine, while sangar defences protected the base from rioters. There was little time for much else than the round of work-sleep-eat, the 'spinning dits' of life for a Marine in Northern Ireland.[3]

M Company of 42 Commando RM in the hot summer of 1989 were based on Fort Whiterock north of Adersonstown, for a 4½-month tour. They patrolled in helmets, a sign of increasing tensions.[4] Later that summer on 22 September 1989 a number of musicians were killed in Deal when an IRA bomb was exploded in a recreation room of the School of Music, killing 11 people and wounding many more.[5] The following week the Staff Band marched through Deal, with spaces in their ranks for those musicians who had been killed.

During another tour by '45 Cdo RM' in 1991[6] the patrols from Bessbrook Mill in south Armagh were usually of three 4-man 'bricks' making up a 'multiple' of twelve men, with 28 multiples from the Commando. Each multiple patrol was strongly armed with at least three GPMGs, a 66mm light anti-tank weapon (LAW) and a reasonable supply of ammunition. Although on one occasion there was nearly insufficient for sustained fire. On this occasion a hill-top OP, designated Golf 70, had been attacked from two IRA positions, the response by three patrols put down some 2,500 rounds on these targets at 900m. There were no casualties but the enemy positions were later seen to have been effectively clobbered. In other incidents two patrols were bombed, the RM casualties later returning to duty, a Sapper of 59 Independent Squadron 'crawled almost from the seat of an explosion' but he also returned to duty. Support Company (in the role of S [Rifle] Company) was mortared in Crossmaglen but six of the eight bombs exploded in the barrels, causing damage to surrounding houses. This Company was also fired on by a GPMG, and a Lynx helicopter bringing in its rations in an underslung load was shot up but landed safely 4km away. Z Company was attacked at its base in Forkhill as a Wessex was leaving when this helicopter was fired on by several machine guns including a 12.7-mm medium machine gun. Vehicle check points were attacked and there were hoax bombs. In a new departure for the Marines, a smuggler's tanker lorry was seized and 'its removal from South Armagh' deprived the enemy of a source of funds.[6] This type of action was to become more frequent as the IRA was to be deprived of more of its illegal income.

From the 1980s, if not before, a permanent RM detachment served on Carlingford Loch in operation 'Interknit' and was based at Kilkeel. Its primary operation was to provide boarding parties for the interception of vessels large and small which crossed from the Republic of Ireland, sometimes these carried smugglers and others were considered to be carrying illicit cargoes. The detachment also carried out more usual chores like manning vehicle check points and patrolling.[7]

The operations for over twenty years of fighting terrorism in Northern Ireland – and indeed elsewhere – have shown subtle changes. What were more or less straight forward conflicts between those who wished to remain in the United Kingdom and those who wished that the Province should be integrated with what was once called the Irish Free State, became confused by criminal undertones. Added to these were the often misleading angles which were presented in newspaper reports, while the actions of Royal Marines on the ground continued to be scrutinised in Parliament (see chapter 10). Therefore by the early-1990s service in Northern Ireland had become a 'complex and difficult task'.[8] Before deploying on their tour in 1991, 45 Commando spent 50 days training to meet the special requirements as these duties which required a 'softly, softly' approach when a Marine was often called upon to be policeman, diplomat, social worker and even customs officer. Yet the Commando units' reputation is considered to be high in the Province, known for acting without fear or favour, they apparently have the respect of both Unionists and Republicans. 42 Commando RM carried through a 6-month roulement tour completed in early April 1995. Their HQ was based in Bessbrook, a large village some 65km south-west of Belfast and 95km north of Dublin and beside the main Belfast to Dublin railway line.[9]

In July 1995 one company (Zulu) from 45 RM was withdrawn from Fermanagh after only eight weeks of a four-month tour, and although held at notice to fly back to the Province if required: it was not called on to do so.[10] This withdrawal was a part of the reduction in UK forces stationed in Northern Ireland. The situation was to change further by the late 1990s when a referendum had brought about a political dialogue between some Unionists and the Republicans. Victims of these conflicts were not many but they, like the very few men killed in training over these decades are remembered with those of earlier wars mentioned in chapter 12.

In October 1980 the Hong Kong government ended its 'touch base' policy under which an illegal immigrant (II) having reached an urban area was allowed to remain in the Colony and able to apply for a residents permit. This had enabled successful IIs to seek employment. After the Government decided to end this policy, the number of Illegal Immigrants fell by 90%, also the compulsory ID cards and registration of employees in factories made it difficult for Illegal Immigrants to remain. Before the law changed 3 Raiding Squadron RM (3 RSRM) chased speed boats which charged HK$20,000 (£1,800) per head to bring illegal immigrants into the colony either from mainland China or Macau. Up to the time the new legislation was passed, 3 RSRM had captured 17 speedboats,[11] but one speed boat tried to escape and both of its crew were killed when it hit rocks. The Squadron was operating from a forward base in the New Territories and as an occasional diversion men were sent on detachment to HM ships of the Hong Kong Squadron for visits to Philippines, Japan, Korea, Brunei and Singapore.

After the Squadron was withdrawn in 1983, a lieutenant with a small detachment was posted to the three Hong Kong patrol craft. By 1993 these each carried a Corporal LC2 (Landing Craft rating 2nd class) and two GD (General Duties) Marines who worked the ship. The OC served on the base staff (HMS *Tamar*) with a colour-sergeant and a corporal armourer. The patrol craft – HMS *Peacock*, *Plover* and *Starling* – each carried two fast pursuit craft, these 28-foot Rigid Inflatable Boats were capable of 50 knots, carrying an RM coxswain and a boarding party of three Naval Ratings. (Interceptions were also made by an SRN 6 hover craft with an RN crew.) The duties included intercepting smugglers, some of whose multi-engined 50-foot craft could achieve 70 knots, although other smugglers used small craft. They tried to bring in electrical goods, TVs and the like, and to take stolen motorcars to China.[12] By 1995 the GD Marines had been replaced by Landing Craft rates who were armed with 9mm pistols due to shooting incidents in the colony. Each patrol craft's Rigid Inflatable also carried an SA80 rifle and 18 illuminating flares. But the smugglers had also become more sophisticated by the late-1990s and might carry passive night goggles, GPS positioning equipment and make greater use of OP's to watch the movements of patrol craft.

In 1983 there were what was described at that time as the 'last frigate detachments' in HMS *Battleaxe* and *Yarmouth* in which Marines served as gunners as well as doing the usual detachment duties.[13] But while one posting was curtailed another opened up in the squadron of Falkland Islands Patrol Vessels, Marines once again served in ships with the normal duties of seamen when aboard. This squadron was formed from three oil rig support vessels bought in March 1983, and renamed HMS *Protector*, *Guardian* and *Sentinel*. The shallow draft of these vessels made them suitable to work inshore on the Islands' coasts. Each had a 7-man detachment (a sergeant, two corporals and four Marines) including an LC2 and an LC3. The General Duties Marines provided a team for recces ashore and observation who could be landed from their ships' pair of RIBs. They also provided a 'heavy mob' giving military support to boarding parties searching ships under suspicion of doing something illegal. The ships carried their RIBs in cradles and were armed with twin 40/60 Bofors. Their detachments reported to a Lieutenant RM from the Landing Craft Branch and his Colour Sergeant (LC), who were both on the staff of the Senior Naval Officer in the Falkland Islands (SNOFI).[14]

The first patrol vessels were commissioned in October 1983 and sailed to the South Atlantic after working up in November. These detachments served for a five-month commission and by early in 1984 further detachments were being trained as were detachments for frigates, the LPDs and the ice patrol ship which would replace *Endurance*. The Falkland Patrol continued into 1987 with HMS *Sentinel* visiting Recife (Brazil) and the Gambia on her way home to the UK.[15]

Other Marines aboard ships included from time to time men of the Air Defence Troop who provided the close defences against air attack for ships in various hostile areas, as they had done off the Falklands.[16] There were also ships detachments as that in HMS *Battleaxe*, which served in the Armilla Patrol and HMS *Brilliant* and *Yarmouth* carried detachments in 1985.[17] This RN patrol in the straits of Hormuz was tasked with the prevention of arms going to Iran or Iraq, in support of a UN resolution. The Javelin Detachments from the Air Defence Troop serving in the ships of this Patrol in the late 1980s included Colour Sergeant R. Birkett with a corporal and three Marines serving in HMS *Brazen* for some three months in the winter of 1988. They worked up with the ship's crew at Portland, Dorset, and during the voyage to the Gulf, there they also provided some training for the seamen armed with GPMGs and provided studies in aircraft recognition. One of their firing practices sent a Javelin missile close to a model aircraft some '2 inches longer than a Medium sized gull', the explosion of this missile flying at Mach 1.4 startled the sub-lieutenant who was operating the target's radio controls and showed how accurate the detachment's fire could be at close range. Their voyage, however was not all seamanship and demonstrations, for instance: the detachment had a couple of days ashore in Egypt during the voyage out. During her return from the Gulf she called at a number of ports including Djibouti and Mombasa before landing the detachment in Cyprus.[18]

In 1994 a press report showed a good example of the Corps' seaborne deployments in the way Marines of Protection Parties from HMS *Nottingham*, the Class 42 destroyer, intercepted suspected gun runners off the former Yugoslavia. Six men in two fast rigid inflatable boats (RIBs) that were launched from the destroyer's davits, scaled the side of the suspected gun runner and seized control. They were followed by a specially trained search party who spent some hours going through the ship, diverting it to an Allied port if anything suspicious was found. Other boardings were made from *Nottingham*'s Lynx helicopter, but when the upper deck clutter of aerials and top-hamper prevented abseiling onto a ship, she had to be boarded from RIBs. The boarding party wore combat body armour, carried SA80s and were led by a sergeant with a practised skill. They might board as many as three or more ships in a day, sometimes in a strong wind at night when their target was making 10 knots through a choppy sea. Such tactics deterred the merchant crews trying to evade the UN economic sanctions and embargo on arms to the factions who were recently at war.[19]

The following year a detachment of 10 all ranks were aboard the Type 22 frigate HMS *Campbelltown* and supplemented that year by six members of the Standby Rifle Company. These Marines carried out duties normally associated with seamen and acted as gunners, while the Standby Rifle Company's Marines formed the protection parties boarding ships, but all seaborne Marines were trained in damage control and firefighting in ships. *Campbelltown* was at this time in the Adriatic as part of the Standing Patrol in operation 'Sharp Guard'[20] which was deployed under a UN resolution imposing sanctions on Serbia and Montengro. The following year she went on a seven-month tour from April with the NATO Standing Naval Force Atlantic. This commission with her detachment and men from the Standby Rifle Company, the so-called Protection Party, took her from patrols off the former Yugoslavia to the Caribbean, on along the eastern seaboard of the USA and to Canada. The autumn took her to Scandinavia and 'home for Christmas'. Accommodation had been improved in ships designed in the 2nd half of the 20th century: the *Leander*-class frigates, for example, had bunk beds, separate dining 'halls' – men no longer slept and ate on the same mess deck – and there was air-conditioning in all the operational and living quarters of the ship. There was also new weaponry in the frigates, whose twin-4.5in gun mounting was fully automatic. Some carried Exocet anti-ship missiles with a range of over 25km and surface-to-air missile system linked with fire-control radar like the Sea Wolf.[21] The development of new missile systems had in part changed the nature of warfare at sea but there were still many features that a 19th century Marine would have recognised. He had fought pirates and during the Fleet's Far East deployment in exercise 'Ocean Wave' during 1996/7, elements of the Stand By Rifle Company were deployed on anti-piracy duties when some RM Protection Parties were carried in the RFA *Fort George*.[22]

Two SBS operations in Iraq were highly successful, during the so-called Gulf War. On 23 January 1991 two Chinooks flew to a landing zone 60km to the south of Baghdad and a short distance from the main road to Basra. Here SBS teams opened up the inspection manholes of military telephone lines connecting the Iraqi high command with their front line troops. The cables were buried several metres below the desert and the raiders dug up a length of cable which they took with them for analysis. They also blew-up considerable sections of these telephone lines. Then the Chinooks lifted off, after re-engaging their props which had been idling to keep down their noise. They also brought back with them one of the ground markers which showed where the telephone cable ran, this they presented to the senior American General Schwarzkopf. He in turn reported the success to Washington. With the result that in the words of the British Commander, General Sir Peter de la Billière 'this first raid made a major contribution towards establishing the reputation and capability not only of our [British] Special Forces, but of those of America as well'.[23] The second SBS raid was reportedly successful in reconnaissance of Iraqi beaches.

Royal Marines also served during this war as Air Defence Detachments and Protection Teams in roles that continued those they had in the Armilla Patrol. Others served in the Allied HQ, aboard RFAs and in Naval Helicopter Squadrons flying from bases in Saudi Arabia. M Company was deployed to Abu Dhabi to protect the logistic supply through this port. And the band of C-in-C Fleet served as medical orderlies in the RFA *Argus* treating casualties.

An interesting sidelight on the illnesses reportedly resulting from multiple inoculations against nerve gases, arose from this history. A number of former Royal Marines have claimed to have suffered similar disabilities from problems arising from inoculations in World War II.[24]

A major operation which called on the Marines' skills in mountain country was operation 'Haven', which began in April 1991 shortly after the Gulf War, when 3 Commando Brigade RM moved at short notice to northern Iraq. HQ Commando Forces RM formed the core of the British Joint Forces HQ, with Major General R. J. Ross OBE commanding the Joint Force, which was some 5,000 strong with substantial numbers of Army and RAF personnel as well as the Commando Brigade and the RN Commando Squadrons of helicopters. A complex command but the willing co-operation between the various forces involved, made possible a rapid deployment. This had been made as quickly as possible because disease was spreading among the refugees, who were living in harsh conditions. Winter

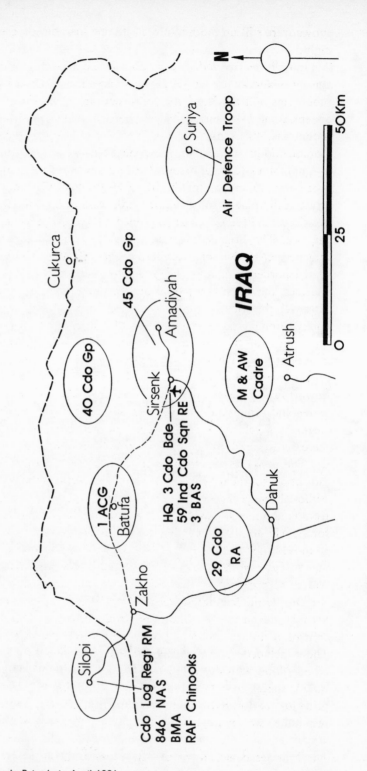

Deployment of 3 Commando Brigade in April 1991.

snows were still on the ground and the temperatures were below freezing every night.

Initially tents, food, water and medical supplies were dropped from C130 transport aircraft to the settlements spread across more than 150km of these mountains and the Kurds beautiful country. The Main Headquarters were at Sirsenk some 25km inside the Iraqi border and in about the centre of the Kurdish mountains. 40 Commando RM were some 12km to the north of the HQ, 45 Commando in an area which included Sirsenk and Amadiyah 12km to its east, 1 Amphibious Combat Group (ACG from the Netherlands) was in the Batufa area some 30km west of the Main HQ, while 29 Commando Regiment were strategically placed some 40km south-west of Sirsenk. Due south of the main positions the M&AW Cadre provided a screen, as did the Air Defence Troop to the east. The Brigade Maintenance Area and 846 Naval Air Squadron with attached RAF Chinooks were established at Silopi (Turkey) some 10km north of the border with Iraq. Then, as the units reached the refugees' camps, the Marines found just how afraid these civilians were of Saddam Husein's regime. However the friendly forces living 'very simply with what we carried on our backs' brought them reassurance. The Brigade's experience of operations in mountains and their knowledge of internal security procedures both stood them in good stead, in what was a volatile situation with some Kurdish factions opposing the local Turkish forces. Yet by the end of May the refugees had been escorted down to the valleys 'where they were provided with decent shelter, food, clean water and sanitation'. Journeys which had taken a heavy toll on the Logistic Regiment's vehicles even though – or perhaps: because of – the Regiment's increased strength to over 800 for this operation.

The presence of Iraqi soldiers in the area needed to be faced with a clear indication to them that neither overt or covert threats would be tolerated. Although on occasions these troops fired at Marines, the greatest danger was from land mines which caused a serious number of injuries among the Coalition forces. The Iraqi Secret Police were another threat which deterred the civilians from returning to their homes, although every effort was made to identify these men and to escort them out of the area, it was not possible to ensure that they had all been caught.

During the five or six weeks of this operation there was close co-operation between the various coalition partners, with some RM units under the tactical control of foreign forces and their units at times serving with the Commandos. These included 75 Australian soldiers who were engineers and medics. Close co-operation with the volunteers of the Overseas Development Administration (ODA) suggested to General Ross that 'operation "Haven" could provide a blue print for the future, in that a combined military and ODA organisation could respond to similar tragedies with even greater speed and efficiency'.[25]

The Marines detached for special duties with the Royal Navy and the Army continued to have a variety of security and other duties, with for example officers, NCO's and Marines in support of the Joint Headquarters at High Wycombe

(Buckinghamshire) and the Joint Forces Headquarters at Riyadh in Saudi Arabia. There were also 100 Royal Marines on security and other duties in Naval units and establishments in the opening months of 1991.[26] That year the Corps provided the Commander British Forces Falkland Islands, with his corporal driver.

Other personnel served with Army units as did Lieutenant S. J. Richards from the Commando Air Squadron who spent a year in 1989/1990 with 4 Regiment of the Army Air Corps flying in Germany. And Lieutenant James Turner RMR was with an Italian armoured infantry brigade – 92PzGrnL Bti – for 16 days in 1992.[27] There have been many officers who served on exchange postings with the USMC which gave the Corps close understanding of developments in the USMC and *vice versa*. For example, in 1990 Captain A. R. Milne was awarded a Letter of Commendation by the United States Navy for his professional leadership as Operations Officer with the 2nd Marine Regiment.[28] Service with Naval Parties continued into the 1990s including that with NP 1002 on Diego Garcia, the Anglo-American communications centre: (This island had been fortified by Marines of MNBDO I during world War II, as one of a series of Ocean Fortresses – see Appendix 4.) In the 1990s the detachment on Diego Garcia was: one officer, one SNCO and 18 Corporals and Marines.[29] However such advanced bases seem likely to be replaced by the Americans who allocated $150-million in 1997 for their first giant Mobile Offshore Base (MOB), which will obviate their need to lease island bases and avoids any problems of sovereignty.

Another Naval Party was No.1042 in Cambodia 1992 under UN sponsorship. In this party were Royal Marines serving in several roles: a military observer, five other officers and 15 NCOs. By the summer of 1993 they were monitoring any cease-fire violations by the various factions in Cambodia who had initially signed the Paris peace Agreement in 1991. The Cambodians were due to have elections in 1993 when over 22,000 UN civilian and military personnel were in their country. In keeping the peace, the Marines were to visit villages and boat-people along the Mekong and other rivers. To make such visits the Naval Party used Rigid Hulled Inflatable boats on occasions, when a patrol might have consisted of men from various nationalities: Canadians, New Zealanders, Filipinos and British in one team of 10 men.[30] Some factions had turned to banditry and the Khmer Rouge withdrew from the peace agreement before the elections.

Training the forces of overseas allies has included work with the Zimbabwe National Army (ZNA). This was formed after the cease-fire of 1980 when that country's forces from what was the Rhodesian Army were merged with former guerillas. The British Military Advisory and Training Team with 60 members by 1984, included six officers and men of the Corps. Typically they were attached to the Battalion Battle School and trained instructors for 1 Zimbabwe Commando Battalion. This battalion had had close contacts with the Royal Marines from its inception in 1980 and by 1984 was operating against poachers in Zimbabwe National Park and able to mount an exercise for an amphibious company assault.[31]

In October 1982 a Regional Security System (RSS) in the Eastern Caribbean was formed by Antigua, Barbados, Dominica, St Lucia and St Vincent, joined in 1984 by St Kitts /Nevis and in 1985 by Grenada. The British and American governments sponsored a training team to bring about a uniform system of defence for forces from these seven islands. This regional security was tested in October 1983 when Marxist fanatics murdered the Grenada Prime Minister, himself a Marxist but not sufficiently Left Wing for some of his followers, before the Americans restored the elected government on this island. By 1988 Royal Marines were serving in the RSS training teams which that year included also instructors from the US Army Special Forces and the Hong Kong Police. The 42 students had to listen to lectures in classrooms when the temperature was over 30°C, and the difference in English as spoken by tutors of differing backgrounds could lead to amusing incidents. Their annual training period was known as exercise 'Tradewinds'. This deployment continued in an advisory form into the late 1990s.[32]

In 1994 a battalion was formed from men trained over the years in the Regional Security System, to provide security in Haiti's main port areas. The Americans were to restore the elected president in this republic but needed the support of Caribbean forces for political reasons, and there was especial significance in the cooperation between forces of the Caribbean in helping to enforce law and order in their part of the world. This CARICOM Battalion had been equipped by the Americans and trained by a British team from the 1st Royal Welch Fusiliers and the RAF Regiment with Major C. V Whiteley RM as the UK liaison officer. Bangladeshis and Guatemalans were also to join the force in Haiti.[33]

In 1990 an RM training team was in Namibia (south west Africa).[34] In the autumn of 1994 there were two officers acting as military advisers to the UNAMFIR Force Commander in Rwanda (part of the UN Trust Territories in Central Africa) and at that time also two officers were helping to train the South African National Defence Force. Another training team of 16 all ranks was deployed for some months in the Baltic States during 1995 and this team's successors continued into 1998. An officer served as a UN Observer in the Republic of Georgia in 1995, raised to two officers 1996.[35]

Units 'showing the flag' so to speak in foreign parts, have included men of 40 Commando RM who were in Belize in October 1985 at Holdfast Camp, where there were 'no mosquitoes, lots of sun, and our own private swimming pool'. The camp was a 2½-hour drive from Belize International Airport and the base for patrols to the north and to the south of the area. Each patrol took two to three weeks and the Company also manned OP's, they were supported by the 14/20 Hussars Armoured Recce Troop with six CVR (T)s, and three light guns of 79 Kirkee Commando Battery RA. After three months at Holdfast, the R&R was taken in America or Mexico although some men flew home to UK for this period. (A squadron of the 14/20 Hussars had supported 3 Commando Brigade in Singapore in 1972 and the following year the Regiment had operated with 40 Commando in Northern Ireland.)[36]

Other units frequently deploying to Belize were Tactical Air Control Parties whose job was linked to the resident squadrons of RAF aircraft. Three Tactical Air Control Parties 605, 611 and 612 from HQ & Signals Squadron and the RMR served there in the late 1980s. The parties from HQ & Signals Squadron in 1986 were deployed with '40 RM'. Each party consisted of an officer – including some from the RAF – each trained as a Forward Air controller, an NCO signaller and a driver/signaller.[37] The role of these teams was to guide Harriers to targets which the FAC could illuminate with Laser Target Marking equipment. In Belize this was practised on a range where 1,000lb (450kg) bombs provided 'most spectacular fireworks', watched by the TACP one of whose officers acted as range safety officer. TAC parties had their own OP's on occasions, often reached along jungle tracks which passed for roads when no helicopter was available to insert the party.[38]

Norway remained the major operational commitment of the Corps in the NATO theatre throughout the 1980s and early-1990s (see chapter 10). There were annual winter deployments designated WD81, WD82 and so on for each year, although the commando carrier HMS *Bulwark* had left Norway for last time in 1981.[39] The annual winter deployment became such a routine that the Commando Brigade Air Squadron had a saying: Must be Norway 'cos its January.[40] The Air Squadron flew around, literally and metaphorically from one deployment to another throughout each year.

These aircrews enjoyed(?) a round of duties each year which took them to to several continents. While individual members took part in those twitchy competitions which flyers seemed to enjoy: Lieutenant D. J. White was the pilot and Corporal A. F. Barnwell was the aircrewman, flying around a course while carrying a bucket of water as their underslung load, the Corporal won the winching competition at this meeting held by the Army Air Corps in 1988. The Squadron's representatives had been eighth that year in the British Open Helicopter Championships. The activities, however, were not all in Competitions. On one occasion in 1988 the Gazelles 'casevacced' men of 2 Para with heat stroke, snake bites and malaria during exercises in Kenya (East Africa), when a further 18 men received injuries jumping onto the baked hard ground.[41] Several men of the Squadron did a 4-week exchange visit that June with the Jamaican Defence Force, whose pilots flew 26 aircraft in operations which included anti-drug recces for fields of illegal crops.

Amphibious operations had once again become a major part of the Corps' operations concentric with its commando roles and continued to evolve in these decades. Indeed the term Assault Squadron had growing significance as the need for out of theatre operations became apparent. 6 Assault Squadron RM was formed on 3 December 1984 and after Pre-Embarkation Training (PET) of six weeks, joined HMS *Intrepid* in mid-February 1985 when she was undergoing a dockyard refit ... The ship completed her refit on 29 March and the Squadron had a final exercise at ATTURM where – among other exercises – the LCU crews practised their drying out drills (on the ebb-tide of course). *Intrepid* completed her trials and working up, taking over from HMS *Fearless* in the Dartmouth Training Squadron (DTS) and sailing to the Med early in June. The Squadron had several runs ashore, at Palma, Villefranche in the Riviera and did intensive exercises in the Cape Teulada Training Area in Sardinia. Having stopped at Lisbon for a final 'run' ashore on this voyage, the ship returned to Portsmouth by mid-July.

In that autumn of 1985 and the following winter the Squadron took part in several exercises including a landing of vehicles for the Commando Brigade HQ and establishing an FOB on the stormy coast of Cape Wrath (Sutherland), and a landing in the Dutch Islands with 45 Commando RM Group.[42] This was followed by their annual exercise in Gibraltar. 1986 saw the Squadron in exercises in Norway followed by a nine week voyage in HMS *Intrepid*, which included a visit to Cyprus on exercises with '40 Cdo RM'. She then went south through the Suez Canal and the Red Sea to Djibouti (in northeast Africa). From there the ship took part in an assault exercise with '40 Cdo RM' landed by helicopter and craft in the Oman. 1987 began with a cruise as part of the Dartmouth Training Squadron, taking Royal Navy cadets to the Canary Islands.[43]

Not all the studies of amphibiosity came to immediate fruition, although the knowledge gained was to prove invaluable on later occasions. As happened in the autumn of 1995 when consideration was being given to the purchase of two roll-on-roll-off ferries for use by the Ministry of Defence. These would enable British forces to be carried in a relatively short time to areas where they might be deployed against military threats. During this passage the heavy vehicles would be adapted to suit the terrain of the target area, and this was claimed to be an advantage over airlifting the heavy vehicles after they had been adapted.

Those security roles which have fallen to the Corps since 1664, were epitomised by the continuing work of Comacchio Group. In September 1986 the Group deployed on exercise *Brave Defender*, to rehearse its war role in the defence of strategically Vulnerable Points associated with nuclear submarine bases in Scotland. It was re-enforced by RMR ranks including assault engineers, as T Company, and Royal Fleet Reserve (RFR). A number of regulars who held dual appointments (mainly from RM Poole and CTC) formed R Company along with two troops of RM recruits, and two platoons of sailors from the Naval bases at Faslane and Rosyth. The air lift of helicopters was provided by a Sea King from 846 Naval Air Squadron and a Gazelle from the Commando Brigade Air Squadron. The men attached for this exercise were kitted out, fed and deployed within two to four hours of their arrival at the Group HQ at Garelochhead, Strathclyde on the west coast of Scotland. This HQ that was defended with sangars and wire around its perimeter.

P Company had an armaments depot to defend with a perimeter of some 11km but the Company was reinforced with the RMR assault engineers to supervise the building of sangars and Naval personnel to help man them. Fire support teams from the RMR also added to the potential weight of defensive fire. The 'enemy' tried to infiltrate into the depot and the Company OC was 'ambushed' when on his way to a meeting at Group HQ. Another Company (O) defended the installations of a torpedo range at Loch Long also in Strathclyde. The accommodation left something to be desired but the 100 or so men of this reinforced Company soon had sandbags filled for their sangars and dannet wire 'sprouting all over' the perimeter, with trip flares set in the approaches to the defences which could not be covered from OP's. The 'enemy' provided a lively variety of attacks from simulated machine gun fire from a passing van to the detonating of a '250kg bomb', there were 'grenade' attacks, bogus ministers of some church, and others who tried to infiltrate the defences. In all this mayhem the defenders got little sleep. And they were constantly wet from the Scots mist, that penetrating rain which fell for the two weeks. However, the defence was not just static, Companies carried out cordons and searches, while patrols sought out the enemy in the nearby forests.[44]

The aid to civil powers in these decades covered not only major deployments but a number of smaller ones. C Company and Support Company of '40 Cdo RM' helped South West Electricity Board in Exeter and Torquay (Devon) after severe gales in the Spring of 1990 had brought down many trees. Men from CTC also helped clear up this damage. Much further afield another example of small scale aid was in 1991 when 18 men and six Rigid Raiding Craft aboard the RFA *Fort George* provided relief in Bangladesh after major floods.[45] When the volcano on Montserrat – a British dependency in the West Indies – erupted in 1995, Major Steve Bruce RM was sent from the RSS in Barbados to advise the Governor. And two Marines climbed the volcano to discover a third vent – two were known to exist – and in the light of this, the island's residents were being prepared for evacuation. M Company of 42 Commando RM, as Fleet Stand-By Rifle Company, assisted civilians on the Island in early August; and 112 all ranks from the Commando Logistic Regiment RM established an evacuation centre for 4,500 refugees on the nearby island of Antigua. Working with the Logistic Regiment were 21 engineers from 59 Independent Commando Squadron RE. In September the Overseas Development Administration and the Foreign and Colonial Office, advised by CINCFLEET's staff among others, decided that a full evacuation seemed unnecessary. However a hurricane blew up early in September and all the military personnel became involved in providing shelter from this weather for civilians. Damage from the hurricane was considerable on Antigua where the Medical Squadron of the Logistic Regiment and engineers with the Regiment, re-established power in the hospital and teams from the Workshop Squadron repaired the airport buildings. Assault Engineers from '42 Cdo RM' also worked to improve Montserrat's sanitation facilities before the Marines were withdrawn in late September.[46]

Nearer home: an LCVP brought by road from RM Poole and an LCU sailed from ATTURM were sent to the Pembrokeshire coast in April 1996 to help with the clearance of a 10,000-tonne spillage of oil from the *Sea Empress*. The craft ferried drums of detergent, men and pumping equipment to various beaches and over the next week brought off sealed drums of waste.[47] In the Mediterranean

32 A Royal Marine prepares to abseil down from a helicopter.

33 Special Boat Squadron canoeists, the SBS, have operated in much the same way as the Small Operations Group of 1945, but with improved techniques and equipment.

34 Not all ski training is as simple as a straight downhill slope: 'how not to negotiate dips and bumps'!

35 Roadway matting is laid ashore from a landing craft, providing instant 'roads' for the beachhead.

36 Marines of the SBS abseil on to the roof of the British Embassy in Kuwait City during the 1991 Gulf War.

37 Royal Marines from M Company, 42 Commando seen in the new-style desert camouflage issued for the 1991 Gulf War.

38 Marines of 45 Commando pull their pulk (sledge) through a snow storm in Norway, 1989.

39 A BV202 tractor with its trailer of passengers, here men of 45 Commando RM, were used in Norway as the primary over-snow vehicle.

40 42 Commando RM training in the Copehill FIBUA complex on Salisbury Plain, 1991.

41 Village elders in northern Iraq welcome a Royal Marine patrol, 1991.

42 A Royal Marine patrol seen in a Rigid Raider on a river in Africa during one of the Corps' special deployments.

43 Operation 'Safe Haven': Royal Marines help move the Kurdish people out of reach of the Iraqi army during 1991.

45 A Royal Marine coxswain from Commachio Group steers close to a submarine, providing part of the security for the base at Faslane.

44 HMS *Ocean* is designed to carry an embarked force of 500 with an additional 303 on overload, with bunks for the total force of a Command Group (Light) and 180 personnel of a helicopter force.

early in 1997 a 30-man team from '42 Cdo RM' was ready to help with the evacuation of British civilians from Albania. They had no sooner returned to the UK than they were redeployed to Zaire. There two LCAC and four Rigid Raiders from 539 ASRM were standing by to evacuate British civilians from Kinshasa. These craft were lifted out from Brazzaville in the Democratic Republic of Congo on 24/25 May 1997.[48]

At the risk of getting the Corps' history somewhat fragmented, the work of Marines in a multiplicity of roles has to be considered. A few instances are, therefore, given here as samples of Booty's off-beat chores. SNCOs served in the mid-1980s with the Joint Air Transport Establishment, this unit at Brize Norton (Oxfordshire) had five sections: one tested new equipment (the Infantry Section); a section which *inter alia* worked with large containers in Hercules aircraft (Airportability); a section which taught personnel to work with helicopters (Helicopter); a section which worked on aid to civilians (Air Despatch); and a section which trained Unit Emplanement Officers (Training). The Royal Marines SNCOs taught abseiling and the drills for attaching underslung loads.[49]

In 1987 Corporal D. Bothwick served with a Close Protection team in Uganda [50] as did other RM police. The Corporal was a member of the Brigade Police Troop of HQ & Signals Squadron, he had been trained by the Royal Military Police for these duties, which entailed protection for the High Commissioner among others. Armed in the Corporal's case with a Walther PKK with which he was an excellent shot, and wearing civilian dress appropriate to whatever occasion the Commissioner was attending, the Corporal was to spend six months in Uganda. The job had its difficulties as many soldiers of the National Resistance Army carried rifles, some only 12-year old boys, and hijackings were common.[51] Also during the late-1980s and 1990s a sergeant Mountain Leader (ML1) ran the Army's Cold Weather cadre on South Georgia and a sergeant or a corporal from the Landing Craft Branch acted as advisor to this Garrison Headquarters, overseeing Royal Engineers' boat operations.[52]

Mention has been made of Naval Parties operating under United Nations' mandates and from time to time Royal Marines served with various NATO and other Army forces also operating under UN mandates. In 1984 a lieutenant served with the British Force in the Lebanon (BRITFORLEB).[53] That year there were a number of Royal Marines with the peace keeping force in Sinai. (This was not a UN body and was distinguished by their orange berets.) The British contingent of 38 all ranks was drawn from 13 different regiments and corps.[54] In 1992 three Royal Marine lieutenants served for six months as military observers with the peace-keeping forces in the former republic of Yugoslavia. They found themselves in such places as Knin, 'a miserable, grey, semi-industrial blob stuck in a bowl surrounded by hills' in a part of Croatia that was controlled by Serbs. From here the lieutenants were sent to patrol as UN Military Observers along various sector boundaries of the UN protected areas. The observers found that the contestants had little respect for the United Nations' forces, and were likely to fire on UN vehicles. However the UN Secretariat had given their observers subsistence to 'live off the land', making these officers independent of battalion and sector organisations, when as the eyes and ears of the Security Council they reported through their own chain of command. They provided escorts for VIPs and for 'ethnically cleansed' families across cease-fire lines, they retrieved the bodies of the dead from the no-man's-lands between front lines. The UN forces had about 30 personnel killed by January 1993 and many more injured by mines. One example must suffice for the many incidents during this time: in July eight UNMOs based on Sinj some 30km north of Split on the Adriatic, patrolled a front line of 60km and monitored a hydro-electric dam which had been prepared for demolition. The dam survived when it was made safe by Croatians under the guidance of British experts sent from the UK.[55]

In May 1993 nine NCOs and seven Marines joined the UK liaison officers working in what became loosely known as 'Bosnia'. These LO's and their teams were drawn from many regiments and initially based at the HQ BRITFOR in Split. They made visits to villages where clashes were expected and found that the local alliances could vary alarmingly: Muslims and Croats against Serbs in one area while 40km 'down the road' the Muslims fought the Croats. On another occasion Serbs and Croats fought Muslims in an attempt to 'cleanse' Maglaj a predominantly Muslim town, setting buildings on fire and shooting the fleeing Muslims. The teams gathered intelligence reporting on their satellite INMARSAT SATCOM systems and using Ground Positioning Systems (GPS) to accurately – well, to 10m if the batteries worked – identify the location of positions on the ground.[56]

There had been some misunderstandings between the European Community Monitoring Mission (ECMM) which did not come under the aegis of the UN, and men of BRITFOR. These were straightened out in the later months of 1994 when Lieutenant General Sir Martin Garrod KCB, OBE was appointed to the hierarchy of ECMM and was to become the civilian governor of Mostar late in 1997.[57] Before then the Corps' involvement with this operation 'Grapple' would embrace two officers and eight signallers/drivers by the summer of 1994 and 29 Commando Regiment RA provided an officer and nine men for artillery monitoring teams, while the Regiment also provided a battery of guns from time to time for service with NATO forces in the former Yugoslavia.

In June 1995 a Rapid Reaction Force (RRF) was sanctioned by the UN as a reserve for operations in the former Yugoslavia. The RRF was to have British elements (from UNPROFOR), a multi-national brigade commanded by the French and comprised mainly of Foreign Legionnaires, 24 Air Mobile Brigade to be deployed if required from the UK, and a planning and co-ordinating headquarters of mainly Royal Marines drawn from HQRM but with other British and French officers. Major General D. A. S. Pennefather CB, OBE with 74 officers and men formed the nucleus of this UNPROFOR HQ. Its personnel of the RRF Operations Staff set up their 'stalls' in the Dalmatia Hotel in the small Croatian town of Kislejak some 20km up the valley from Sarajevo. Working under the command of General Smith, the commander of UNPROFOR the planners became involved in selecting targets for the proposed air strikes against the Bosnian Serb

Army, with the steps needed to prevent that Army from seizing more towns and in particular to prevent them from seizing UN observers and others as hostages, which they had done on a previous occasion. While the logistics and other requirements for the UN forces needed detailed planning for a smooth integration with the RRF.

At this time all peace initiatives had failed after the Bosnian Serb Army had seized 300 UN hostages on the 25 and 26 May 1995. The UN peacekeepers had limited freedom of movement and the credibility of both the UN and NATO forces was in doubt. Lieutenant General Smith, Commander of UNPROFOR needed a planning staff at divisional level but another two-star General's command was not politically acceptable to the French, therefore the planning staff became part of the Rapid Reaction Force. The RRF by this date was a multinational brigade lead by the French. Major General Pennefather, a Royal Marine commanded the RRF Operations staff who would plan for the Force's military operations that would enable the peacekeepers to carry out their task. On the other hand the UN peacekeepers operated on the use of a minimum of force and the use of negotiations.

The RRF was to provide a response to threats at an appropriate level from the use of small arms to air strikes. Its operations were distinct from those of the peacekeepers and it was not intended to enforce peace nor to directly deliver humanitarian aid under resolution 998 of the United Nations. This caused the Bosnian Serbs to attempt to restrict the Force's movement, while nevertheless wanting to obtain the maximum payments for accommodation and other services. The Force's camouflaged green vehicles were all too easily distinguished from the white peacekeeping vehicles in the Serbs' efforts to frustrate the RRF. Nevertheless the Operational Planning staff was set up – as we have seen – in Kiseljak with proper security for the offices, guarded by commandos, and secure radio links established using Ptarmigan communications. There were many complexities in mounting operations which required among other things, the agreement of UN and NATO authorities, and acceptance of the command and control arrangements by the contributing nations. The acceptable likely casualties had to be agreed with contributors, and the planners had to consider the possible effect of an operation on UN forces against which there might be retaliation.

The RRF was deployed to secure Mount Igman after the Serbs had shelled UN forces in Sarajevo, but it was the introduction onto the mountain of 155-mm self-propelled guns with a range of 25km which caused the Serbs to halt their aggression. These guns had brought the Bosnia Serb capital of Pale into range. Also the political chain for initiating operations was streamlined with the decision to execute operations to be made by the senior commanders in the region. On 29 July the NATO Air Commander General Ryan, met General Smith and General Pennefather to set out a concept for a UN/NATO air/land campaign. This was examined next day by senior officers in Naples where a UN/NATO memorandum was drafted and later agreed – after some robust discussion apparently.

The memorandum cleared the way for close co-operation between the UN staffs and the RRF planners. They were then able to develop the air/land war into an effective means of countering aggression. All targets had been scrutinised to minimise civilian casualties and possible losses among UN forces. On the night of 30 August the first waves of strike aircraft were vectored in on the heavy guns surrounding Sarajevo. The staff took cover in their sandbagged hotel apart from those detailed to observe the action. In a planned lull during the bombing, these observers saw the UNPROFOR gunners blast Bosnian-Serb positions making it clear that the UN forces meant business. The air strikes were to continue for a fortnight with 'pauses' and 'extended pauses', then on 14 September the Bosnian Serbs withdrew their heavy weapons from the Exclusion Zone set by the UN around Sarajevo. Meanwhile a Croatian offensive had led to their recovering land to the west and north, areas which had previously been captured by the Bosnians (in 1992). Throughout this period of ever changing battle lines, the planners had worked on the likely future requirements to feed local peoples and what forces might be needed to halt the waring factions

The outcome was successful in contributing to the Serbs acceding to the United Nations' demands. A success due to the air/land operations formulated by General Smith of NATO and General Ryan commanding the NATO Air Forces South working for the UN, with the catalyst of Major General Pennefather's operational staff. In addition to the air strikes a number of artillery and mortar bombardments had kept the Bosnian Serb forces at a distance. They did not counter-attack the Rapid Reaction Force for fear of UK infantry in Warrior APCs attacking the Bosnian Serb HQ near Mt Igman. As a result the casualties were minimal as combat at close quarters had been avoided.

In doing this work they had been confronted by 'attempts to exploit the situation for profit' and in Major F. H. R Howes RM's words 'the lesson to be learnt from all this [the Major served on the Operations Staff] is perhaps that compassion is the highest form of human intelligence'.[58] By November the RRF included 68 RM/RMC personnel. (Royal Marines/Royal Marine Command a title used in the 1990s to embrace all operational, training and reserve units under command of HQRM and including men of 29 Commando Regiment RA, 59 Independent Commando Squadron RE in addition to RM units). They provided – among other duties – a road show to demonstrate the skills required by drivers in snow conditions, before the Marines returned to the UK the following month. However at this time elements of 3 Commando Brigade were 'at reduced notice' to move to the former Yugoslavia.[59]

In the late 1990s there have been SBS teams working with HM Customs and Excise to intercept drug smugglers. At least one 'gun fight' took place in seizing some five tonnes of drugs from a yacht, the *Simon de Danser* (227 tons) in the Atlantic in May 1997. Since the Customs men were not armed, they called on the SBS when 'large drug shipments [were] aboard yachts or oil rig supply vessels'.[59a]

What of the 'buttons and bows'? The Corps could still present a more than adequate turnout on ceremonial occasions. Although to maintain a high standard of arms drill when men had other commitments, required more time than there was perhaps available and not as much as their officers would have preferred. In 1981 Royal Marines had provided some of the street lining parties and several Bands marched in the procession for the marriage of Prince Charles. Such ceremonial necessities involved extra parade-ground drills which were also required in 1983 for the parade associated with the Commando Training Centre being granted the freedom of Exeter.[60] 42 Commando RM trained hard in preparation for their tour of London Duties from 17 June to 15 July 1986. They were the first unit to carry the SA80 rifle on these duties. Bands turned out frequently for parades but the musicians supporting a memorial parade in 1981 were referred to in one press report as the 'Garden Band of the Royal Marines', for which the illustrator Colour-Sergeant Art Hubbard produced an amusing cartoon, which, needless to say, does not include the RM Guard.[61] The Bands and contingents from the Commandos appeared on a number of spectacular occasions at the Royal Tournament in the 1980s and 1990s.

An overview of the Corps' standing in the late-1990s shows a most encouraging picture for the future. Not only has the commissioning of amphibious ships like HMS *Ocean* ensured the Royal Marines' future into the 21st century, but the steps taken in the late 1990s to develop the Corps' training routines showed what manner of Marine will provide these ships' and other assault forces, from a strength of about 6,500. This was some 14 per cent of the Royal Navy's total manpower in 1997, and included some 600 RM officers. Of these around 180 were serving outside Corps.

CTC planned to train 1,200 recruits in 1998, who will complete a 30-week course, regarded by many as the hardest recruit training in NATO. This produced 'professional amphibious commandos prepared to meet whatever future challenges require their unique skills' to quote Brigadier David Nicholls, Commandant CTC in the late 1990s. The Officers' Training Wing trained 50 to 60 young officers each year, 90 per cent of whom were graduates, their course lasting 12 months. This Wing also ran courses for the further training of officers in preparation for posting to Special Forces and similar exceptional appointments. The NCOs Training Wing had courses for all non-commissioned officers from corporals to Regimental Sergeant Majors. This centralisation of 'command training' maintained a high common standard throughout the Corps.

The Common Recruit Syllabus (CRS) was divided into five modules, with assessments at the end of each two- or three-week period to ensure that the recruit had the necessary skills and physical ability 'to merit progression' to the next module. With weeks 23 to 25 including the commando tests on assault courses and so on, leaving the final weeks for the completion of professional training of the General Duties Marine. Other courses were run by several Wings of CTC, for example: the Infantry Support Wing trained Assault Engineers who we saw in chapter 12. This Wing also trained specialist instructors for Heavy Weapons, and trained Platoon Weapons instructors who went back to teach men in their units the latest techniques in the use of small arms, in fieldcraft and other basic skills. A Physical Training Troop not only manned the gymnasium complex at CTC, but also trained the Corps' PT instructors. The Drill Troop (abbreviated as DL Troop, sometimes mistakenly taken for Drill Leaders) trained Drill Instructors who guided the drill training and ceremonial throughout the Corps. The Signal and Clerk Training Wing continued to instruct both signallers, clerks and illustrators. The clerks' roles were changing with the pending introduction of digital radio networks (Bowman) requiring keyboard skills which were expected to take clerks out of the office into the field. There clerks will work in command posts and similar battle stations. This Wing also had a Computer Awareness and Application Training School. Men from other British Services attended a 10-week course at the Commando Training Wing before joining units with 3 Commando Brigade; and some Foreign and Commonwealth students attended these courses. In all over 450 courses were run at CTC in the year to March 1998 with 150 different syllabuses. Consideration was also being given to offering courses in leadership training for civilians which could generate some income, but the capacity for earning such fees was limited.

The medics at CTC have been in the forefront of research on stress factures and impact injuries, leading to men wearing 'quality trainers, the gym floor being sprung and men being individually fitted for boots'. The latest developments in medication for blisters became available. While the diet for men under training was constantly monitored. Yet despite the care that was taken to bring recruits up to a physical standard necessary to complete the Common Recruit Syllabus, in 1997 one in three spent time recovering from injury. Subsequent changes of emphasis in the training programmes was likely to reduce these injuries in future years, as recruits would spend more time on sports in the early part of their course and have their professional military skills honed in the last month or so.

The training staff treated men as individuals and while the trainees' relationships with their instructors were robust, the staff were also expected to be 'benevolent and caring'. To this end families were invited to a day of briefings after the fifth week of training – 'we get Mum to join the training team'. While aspects of good citizenship and moral values were taught so that a man face to face with civilians during an operation, could be expected to make reasoned moral judgements. All these facets of recruit and other training was aimed at making the best use of man-management and associated practices of the late 1990s. At the same time almost half of the training staff might have been called on to reinforce 3 Commando Brigade in a time of crisis.

Consideration to opening some jobs to women recruits was actively reviewed at a time when the Army opened 70 per cent of its posts to women but none were expected to join the Corps, apart from musicians. (An MOD study into the introduction of women into 'teams of frontline soldiers' was initiated in the late 1990s and was due for publication in 2001.) Other studies – in-house and by consultants – had enabled the staff at CTC to improve the design and execution of courses, reduce injuries and give added focus to a Marine's professionalism. These trends have maintained the family ethos of the Corps, while continuing to instill those characteristics taught at Achnacarry in the early 1940s which give a man the determination to 'go that extra yard' when facing up to a challenge.

A sign of the fundemental changes in the political climate in these decades was a visit by Russian Naval Infantry to CTC in 1993.[62] But the concluding pages of the Corps' history in the 20th century have yet to be written, although they will probably retain their single battle honour: Gibraltar. It was given added recognition on 28 October 1996 when the Freedom of Gibraltar was conferred on the Corps. 40 Commando RM's Support Company escorted the Queen's and Regimental Colours of 40 Commando RM, marching through this city with drums beating, colours flying and bayonets fixed.[63]

To the dedication in *Royal Marines 1919–1980* must be added a dedication to Royal Marines of the 1980s and 1990s. Therefore to all ranks currently serving in this hard-working, cheerful and dedicated Corps, and their predecessors, this history is respectfully dedicated. For the ski patrols of 1919 in North Russia, the gun crews in HM ships, the thin blue line on the bunds in China during the 1930s, the landing craft 'hands' and commandos of World War II, the Marines of '41 Cdo RM' at Chosin, the assault force at Suez, the men who patrolled the jungles of South East Asia, those who 'yomped' across East Falkland and those who protected the Kurds in northern Iraq, would be – and are – proud of those now serving in the Corps. Although this history could not cover every action in detail through 75 turbulent years, the author believes that there is sufficient information on the many successes and some mistakes during these decades, to help those serving today to understand events of those years. This history also puts on record the facts for those who played a part in the many campaigns since 1919.

APPENDIX 1

ABBREVIATIONS

Abbreviations over 75 years have varied greatly and may be unfamiliar to different generations of Marines.[1]

AA   Anti-aircraft
AAC   Army Air Corps
AADC   Anti-Aircraft Defence Commander
ACG   Amphibious Combat Group [Dutch]
ACPL   Armed Customs Patrol Launch
AD   Air Defence
AE   Assault Engineer
AFO   Admiralty Fleet Order
AFV   Armoured Fighting Vehicle
AG   Adjutant General (obsolete)
ALC   see LCA
ALSL   Alternative Landing Ship Logistic
AMP   Assisted Maintenance Period
ANCXF   Allied Naval Command of
   Expeditionary Force
ANFO   Ammonium Nitrate/Fuel Oil
   (explosive)
AOO   Amphibious Operations Officer
AOR   Amphibious Operations Room
AP   Armour-piercing
APC   Armoured Personnel Carrier
APD   Assault Personnel Destroyer
AS   Anti-Submarine (warfare)
ASI   Arctic Survival Instructor
ASRM   Assault Squadron Royal Marines
ATO   Ammunition Technical Officer
ATTURM   Amphibious Trials and Testing
   Unit Royal Marines
AVRE   Assault Vehicle Royal Engineers
AW   Amphibious Warfare
AWT   Arctic Warfare Training

BARV   Beach Armoured Recovery Vehicle
BFT   Basic Fitness Test
BL   Breech-loading
BM   Brigade Major
BMA   Brigade Maintenance Area
BOST   Basic Opertional Sea Training (1980s)
BPC   Beach Patrol Craft
BRNVR   Burmese Royal Naval Volunteer
   Reserve
BSM   Battery Sergeant Major

CA   Coastal artillery
CACU   Coastal Artillery Cooperation Unit of
   the RAF
CAFO   Confidential AFO

CAP   Cover Air Patrols
CCF   Combined Cadet Force
CCO   Chief of Combined Operations
CCO   Clandestine Communist Organisation
Cdo   Commando Unit
cdo   commando, individual
CFMU   Coastal Forces Maintenance Unit
CG   Commandant General
CHOSC   Commando Helicopter Operations
   and Support Cell
C-in-C   Commander-in-Chief
CINCFLEET   Commander-in-Chief Fleet
CL   Cliff Leader
CLF   Commander Land Forces
Co-Ops   Combined Operations
COMAF   Commodore, Amphibious Forces
COS   Chief of Staff
'Co-op'   Homemade explosive
Coy   Company
CRS   Common Recruit Syallabus
CS95   Combat Soldier [Dress] 1995
CSM   Company Sergeant Major
CTC   Commando Training Centre
CTC   Combined Training Centre
CVRT   Combat Vehicle Reconnaissance
   Tracked

DAA&QMG   Deputy Assistant Adjutant
   General & Quartermaster General
DAQMG   Deputy
   Assistant-Quartermaster-General
DAR   Dual Appointed Regular (1980s)
D-Day   First day of an operation
DCI   Defence Council Instruction
DEMS   Defensively Equipped Merchant Ships
DL   Drill (formerly MTI, instructors)
DODAR   Director of Drafting & Records
DP   Displaced Person
DP   Distribution Point
DPM   Disrupted Pattern Martial
DRORM   Drafting & Records Officer Royal
   Marines
DTS   Dartmouth Training Squadron
DTP   Driver Training Platoon
DZ   Dropping Zone

EMF   Embarked Military Force

EOD   Explosive Ordnance Disposal
EVT   Education & Vocational Training

FAA   Fleet Air Arm
FARP   Forward Arming and Refuelling Point
FOB   Forward Operation Base
FOB   Forward Officer Bombardment
FOF(1)   Flag Officer, Flotilla (one), etc.
FONAC   Flag Officer Naval Air Command
FOO   Forward Observation Officer
FOST   Flag Officer Sea Training
FSRT   Fleet Stand-By Rifle Troop

GD   Gun Direction Exercise
GI   Gunnery Instructor
GI   General Infantry (US)
GOC   General Officer Commanding
GPMG   General Purpose Machine Gun
Grp   Group
GSW   Gun Shot Wound

HA/LA   High-Angle/Low-Angle (gun)
HALO   High Altitude, Low Opening
    (parachute)
HATS   Harbour Acceptance Trials
H.L.   Home Base Ledger
HE   High Explosive
HGV   Heavy Goods Vehicle
H-hour   Time of launching attack, etc
HF   High Frequency (radio)
HMT   Her Majesty's Transport
HV   High Velocity (weapon)
HW   Heavy Weapons

II   Illegal Immigrant
IMTWRM   Inspector of Motor Transport and
    Weapons RM
INTSUM   Intelligence Summary
IO   Intelligence Officer
IRA   Irish Republican Army
IRC   Inflatable Raiding Craft
IS   Internal Security
ISTDC   Inter-Services Training and
    Development Centre
IT   Information Technology
ITC   Infantry Training Centre

JCC   Junior Command Course
JRDF   Joint Rapid Deployment Force
JS   Joint Services

K-bar   USMC survival knife (slang)
KUA   Kit Upkeep Allowance

LAD   Light Aid Detachment
LADE   *Lineas Aereolineas del Esto* (airline)
LAW   Light Anti-Armour Weapon
L& M   Landing and Maintenance

LC   Landing craft
LCA   Landing Craft Assault
LCAC(L)   Landing Craft Air Cushion (Light)
LCAC(V)   Landing Craft Air Cushion
    (Vehicle) became LCAC(L)
LCA(HR)   LCA (Hedgerow)
LCF   Landing Craft Flak
LCG(L)   LC Gun (Large)
LCG(M)   LC Gun (Medium)
LCM   Landing Craft Mechanised
LCOCU   Landing Craft Obstruction Clearance
    Unit
LCP   Landing Craft Personnel
LCS   Landing Craft Support
LCVP   Landing Craft Vehicle Personnel
L-day   Landing day
LFFI   Land Force Falkland Islands
L-hour   Landing time for first assault wave on
    beach
LMA   Leading Medical Assistant (RN)
LMG   Light Machine Gun
LP   Landing Point
LPD   Landing Platform Dock
LPH   Landing Platform Helicopter
LS & GC   Long Service & Good Conduct
    (medal)
LS   Landing Ship
LSI   Landing Ship Infantry
LSL   Landing Ship Logistic
LV   Low Velocity (weapon)
LZ   Landing Zone

MACC   Military Aid to Civil Community
MAD   Magnetic Anomaly Detector
M&AW   Mountain & Arctic Warfare
MAW   Medium Anti-Armour Weapon
Med   Mediterranean (slang)
Met   Meteorological
MGRM   Major General Royal Marines
Milan   wire guided anti-tank weapon (Missile
    d'Infanterie Leger Antichar)
ML   Mountain Leader
MLC   Motor Landing Craft (of 1930s)
MN   Merchant Navy
MNBDO   Mobile Naval Base Defence
    Organisation
MOA   Marine Officer's Attendant
MOD   Ministry of Defence
MOLCAB   Mobile Landing Craft Advanced
    Base
MONAB   Mobile Naval Advanced Base
MP   Member of Parliament
MP   Military Police
MTI   Military Training Instructor
MVP   Moisture Vapour Permeable [material]

NAAFI   Navy, Army and Air Force Institute
    (canteens)

NAMET   Naval Mathematics & English Test
NATO   North Atlantic Treaty Organisation
NBC   Nuclear, Biological and Chemical (warfare)
NEC   Northern European Command
NES   Naval Examination Service
NI   Northern Ireland

OCRM   Officer Commanding Royal Marines
OCTU   Officer Cadet Training Unit
ODA   Overseas Development Administration
ODMA   Operational Data Material Assessment
OOW   Officer of the Watch
Ops   Operations
ORP   Okręt Rzeczypospolitej Polskiej (Warship of the Republic of Poland)

PE   Physical Education
PE   Plastic Explosive
PET   Pre-embarkation Training
PLCE   Personal Load Carrying Equipment
PM   Prime Minister
PTI   Physical Training Instructor
PVR   Premature Voluntary Release
PWI   Platoon Weapons Instructor
PX   Post Exchange (US) – similar to NAAFI

QF   Quick Firing
QMS   Quartermaster sergeant
QR   Quarters Range Taking (a qualification)
QRF   Quick Reaction Force
Q-ships   Decoy merchant ships with hidden guns

RA   Royal Artillery
RA   Ration Allowance
RAN   Royal Australian Navy
RAPC   Royal Army Pay Corps
R&R   Rest & Recuperation
RBW   MNBDO staff study references
RCL   Ramp Cargo Lighter
RCN   Royal Canadian Navy
RCT   Royal Corps of Transport
Regt   Regiment
RFA   Royal Fleet Auxiliary
RIB   Rigid Inflatable Boat
RL   Recce Leader
RMA   Royal Marine Artillery
RMA   Royal Marine Association
RMC   Royal Marine Command (units commanded by HQRM)
RMBDSU   RM Boom Defence Scaffolding Unit

RMFVR   Royal Marine Forces Volunteer Reserve
RMLI   Royal Marine Light Infantry
RMNS   Royal Malayan Navy Ship
RMO   Royal Marine Officer
RMP   Royal Military Police
RMR   Royal Marines Reserve
RMR   Royal Malayan Rgt
RMRO   Royal Marine Routine Orders
RNAS   Royal Naval Air Station
RNLMC   Royal Netherlands Marine Corps
RNZN   Royal New Zealand Navy
RoRo   Roll on/Roll off
RRC   Rigid Raiding Craft
RRF   Rapid Reaction Force
RRS   Royal Research Ship
RSM   Regimental Sergeant Major
RSR   Raiding Support Regiment
RSRM   Raiding Squadron Royal Marines
RSS   Regional Security Team (in the West Indies)
RUC   Royal Ulster Constabulary

SATCOM   Satellite Communications
SBS   Special Boat Section
SBS   Special Boat Squadron
SC   Swimmer Canoeist
SCC   Senior Command Course
SD   Special Duties
SEME   School of Electrical & Mechanical Engineering [Army]
SITREP   Situation Report
S/L   Searchlight
SLR   Self-loading Rifle
SMG   Sub-machine-gun
SMP   Self-maintenance Period
SNEB   French design of air-to-air rocket
SNOFI   Senior Naval Officer Falkland Islands
SO3   G1 Staff Officer [Grade] 3 General Duties 1 (Personnel)
SO3   G2 Staff Officer [Grade] 3 General Duties 2 (Intelligence)
SO3   G3 Staff Officer [Grade] 3 General Duties 3 (Operations)
SO3   G3 Staff Officer [Grade] 3 General Duties 4 (Logistics)
SQ   Specialist Qualification

TacHQ   Tactical Headquarters
TAOR   Tactical Area of Responsibility
TAVR   Territorial Army Volunteer Reserve
TQ   Trade Qualification
T/S   Transmitting Station (associated with ships' gunnery)

UHF   Ultra High Frequency (radio)

UIF   Unit Institute Fund
UCAV   Uninhabited Combat Air Vehicle
UNPROFOR   United Nations Protection
   Force
USMC   United States Marine Corps

VCP   Vehicle Check Point
VHF   Very high Frequency (radio)

WE   War Establishment
WO   Warrant Officer
WP   White Phosphorus (grenade)
W/T   Wireless/Telegraphy

YO   Young Officer
YVT   Youth Visiting Teams

ORGANISATION IN THE SOUTH ATLANTIC IN APRIL 1982

(for Organisations of World War II and other early 20th century formations see *Royal Marines 1919–1980*)

Task Force Commander:
Admiral Sir John Fieldhouse (at Northwood)

Commander Carrier Battle Grp	Commander Amphibious Task Grp	Commander Landing Force
Rear-Admiral 'Sandy'	Commodore M. C. Clapp	Brig Julian Thompson
Woodward (See note 1)	(See note 2)	(See note 3)

South Georgia Group
Captain of HMS *Antrim*

Sub-Surface Task Group

Note 1: **The Carrier Battle Group** was to consist of –
   2 × Aircraft Carriers – HMS *Hermes* (23,900 tons) as Flag Ship from 15 April; HMS
   Invincible (16,000 tons); 8 × Guided Missile Destroyers; 15 × Frigates; 2 × Offshore Patrol
   Vessels; 5 × Minesweeping Trawlers.

Ships in Support including those Supporting Amphibious Task Group:
   RFA Oilers, Fleet Replenishment Ships, Helicopter Support Ship, Tug – 16 vessels in all; and
   Ships Taken up from Trade included – Hospital Ship; Stores Ships; Personnel and Vehicle
   Transports; Minesweepers Support Ship; Support Oilers; Aircraft Transports; Mother Ship for
   Submersibles; Repair Ships; Logistical Support Ships; etc

Note 2: **The Amphibious Task Group** was to consist of –
   2 × LPDs (HMS *Fearless* as HQ ship and HMS *Intrepid*); 6 × LSL (RFA *Sir Geraint, Sir
   Galahad, Sir Percivale, Sir Lancelot , Sir Tristram* and *Sir Bedivere* which joined at Ascension
   from Vancouver); and STUFT shipping.

Note 3: **Composition of Land Force in April 1982** –
   April 1982 3 Commando Brigade
      Brigade HQ & Signals Sqn RM including 3 Cdo Bde Air Defence Trp RM, 1 Raiding Sqn
      RM, and with attached units; 40 Cdo RM; 42 Cdo RM less M Coy (see operation 'Paraquat')
      plus J Coy; 45 Cdo RM; 2nd Bn Parachute Regt with attached units; 3rd Bn Parachute Regt
      with attached units; Cdo Logistic Regt RM with attached units; D and G Sqn 22 SAS Regt;
      three sections of Special Boat Sqn RM; Mountain and Arctic Warfare Cadre RM; two Troops
      RHG/D The Blues and Royals; 29 Cdo Regt RA and attached units; 59 Independent Cdo Sqn
      RE and attached units; 3 Cdo Bde Air Sqn RM plus one Flight from 656 Sqn Army Air
      Corps; Tactical Air Control Parties (605 RM, 611 RM, 612 RM and 613 with 2 Para); for
      full details of composition of units see Appendix 2 Formation and Unit details.

ORGANISATION IN THE SOUTH ATLANTIC FROM ABOUT 12 MAY 1982

Task Force Commander
Admiral Sir John Fieldhouse (at Northwood)

Commander Carrier Battle Grp   Commander Amphibious Task Grp   Commander Landing Force F1
Rear-Admiral Sandy Woodward   Commodore M.C. Clapp   Major-General Jeremy Moore
(see note 4)
Sub-Surface Task Group

Note 4: Composition of Landing Force Group (also known as Land Force Falkland Islands LFFI) –
3 Commando Brigade and 5 Infantry Brigade (See Formation and Unit details)

FORMATION AND UNIT DETAILS IN OPERATION 'CORPORATE'

Land Force Falkland Islands (LFFI)
Divisional HQ
3 Commando Brigade RM, 5 Infantry Brigade
and Divisional troops

Under command of 3 Commando Brigade RM

3 Commando Bde HQ:
  Brigadier, Brigade Major (Chief of Staff),
  DAA&QMG (Deputy Chief of Staff), Staff
  Captain A (Personnel), GSO 3 (Intelligence),
  GSO 3 (Operations), Staff Captain Q (Logistics) and all-arms advisers.

Brigade HQ & Signals Sqn RM:
  3 Cdo Bde Air Defence Troop RM (transferred
  to Division May 1982), 1 Raiding Sqn RM
  (transferred to Task Force Landing Craft Sqn
  in May); Satellite Communications Detachment Royal Signals; Cdo Forces News Team
  RM; Postal and Courier Communications Unit
  RE which was a detachment of 1 PC Regt;

40 Commando RM:
  Cdo HQ, A Rifle Company, B Rifle Coy, C
  Rifle Coy, Support Coy, HQ Coy

42 Commando RM:
  Cdo HQ, K Rifle Company, L Rifle Coy, M
  Rifle Coy, J Rifle Coy, Support Coy, HQ Coy

45 Commando RM:
  Cdo HQ, X Rifle Company, Y Rifle Coy, Z
  Rifle Coy, Support Coy, HQ Coy

Each Commando rifle company (commanded by
a captain) had an HQ and three rifle Troops of
about 30 Marines (each commanded by a Lt with
a SNCO as 2i/c). Each Commando HQ Company
had a Signals Troop, a Quartermasters Troop, a
Motor Transport Section and a Medical Section.

The Rifle Troops each had an HQ and three rifle
Sections (each commanded by a Corporal). The
standard rifle, with a Trilux image enhancing
sight, was the self-loading 7.62mm (SLR which
did not fire in bursts), and each Marine normally
carried in action L2A2 explosive grenades and/
or No.80 White Phosphorous grenades. Each
Section also had: a 7.62mm L7A2 belt fed
GPMG, a 66-mm LAW and some had magazine-
fed LA4A4 LMG (the Bren gun modified to take
the standard NATO 7.62-mm rounds). Each
Troop HQ had a Carl Gustav 84mm MAW. Each
Commando Support Company had: a Mortar
Troop (with six 81mm mortars); an Anti-Tank
Troop (with 14 × Milans); a Reconnaissance
Troop (with M & AW specialists); and an Assault
Engineer Troop of Marines trained in mine clearing, demolitions and other combat engineer techniques.

Snipers had an L42A1 rifle which was an up-
graded version of the .303-inch Lee Enfield. Also
issued to some officers and other ranks were
9-mm Sterling submachine guns and 9-mm
Browning pistols.

2 Para in 3 Cdo Bde from 15 April (warning order in UK) until 29 May when it reverted to 5 Bde and again in 3 Cdo Bde from 9 June to about 15 June 1982:

  Bn HQ, A Rifle Company, B Rifle Coy, C Rifle
  Coy, D Rifle Coy (one of these companies – C
  Coy in the case of 2 Para – was tasked as
  the Patrol Company and commanded by an
  experienced major, with two platoons trained
  for reconnaissance and with an Assault Pioneer
  Platoon for mine clearing etc, there were also
  in the Recce Platoons a number of sniper-
  observers in direct contact with Battalion HQ).
  The Companies each had three Platoons each
  of three Sections. The Rifle Sections each had
  two GPMGs for this operation. There was also

a Support Coy with its Machine Gun Platoon, Anti-tank Platoon and Mortar Platoon. With attached: 2 × Sections of Blowpipe from 32 Guided Weapons Regt RA; detachment of 81 Ordnance Coy; and 613 TACP. The command of 2 Para was organised to provide the CO with a Tactical HQ forward in a battle with a duplicated Tac HQ under the 2i/c at the rear. The Clansman radios used during this operation had only been issued to the Battalion immediately before leaving the UK.

3 Para in 3 Cdo Bde from early April:

Bn HQ, A Rifle Coy, B Rifle Coy, C Rifle Coy, D Rifle Coy and Support Coy. D Coy was the Patrol Coy (Cp: C Coy in 2 Para). The organisation was in general similar to that for 2 Para (see above). Attached 1 × Detachment from Ordnance Coy.

D and G Squadrons of 22 SAS Regt initially under command of Commodore Amphibious Warfare but later came under command of LFFI in early May but were tasked from Norwood:

Commanded by CO of 22 SAS with a Tactical HQ in contact with the Regt HQ in Hereford, UK over satellite radio link. About 100 all ranks deployed in ships of the Carrier Battle Group for insertion by helicopter or surface craft, and 7 ranks initially with Brigade staff in HMS *Fearless*.

Special Boat Squadron RM

2, 3 and 6 Sections about 20 all ranks based in HMS *Hermes* plus a command element of 11 (some with Battle Grp staff and some with Amphibious staff.)

Mountain and Arctic Warfare Cadre RM

About 35 Marines, all specialist climbers and divided into some eight 4-man teams with a small HQ.

Blues and Royals RHG/D

Two Medium Reconnaissance Troops of B Squadron, with a total of 4 × Scorpion and 4 × Scimitar Combat Vehicle Reconnaissance Tracked (CVRTs) and a Samson Field Recovery Tractor.

Commando Logistics Regiment RM

Regt HQ, Transport Sqn, Workshop Sqn, Ordnance Sqn, Medical Squadron (3 × Surgical Support Teams, 16 Field Ambulance Parachute Clearing Troop, Commando Forces Band) and HQ Sqn.

29 Commando Regiment RA

Regt HQ, 7 (Sphinx) Cdo [Gun] Battery RA, 8 (Alma) Cdo [Gun] Bty RA, 79 (Kirkee) Cdo [Gun] Bty RA each with 6 × 105-mm Light Guns; and 148 (Meiktila) Cdo [Forward Observation] Bty RA with teams to spot Naval Gun fire to bring this fire onto targets ashore either by landing with assault troops or from ships' helicopters. Attached: were 29 (Corunna) Field Bty from 4th Field Regt RA (which joined the Cdo Bde along with 2 Para); and OP parties of 41 Field Bty with the Bty Commander from 4 Field Regt RA; T (Shah Shujah's) Bty of 12 Air Defence Regt RA with 12 × Rapier posts for missile launchers.

59 Independent Commando Squadron RE

HQ, and a number of specialist Troops. Attached were: 2 × Troops of 9 Para Sqn RE; a team of two specialists from 49 Explosive Ordnance Sqn of 33 Engineer Regt; and a team of Explosive Ordnance Disposal specialists from the RAF. (The Squadron's core sub-units in November 1998 were: 3 × Field Troops; 1 Support Troop; 1 Recce Troop; 1 HQ Troop; 1 × Workshop Troop.)

3 Cdo Brigade Air Squadron RM

HQ and Maintenance Flight, 6 × Scout Light Helicopters with SS11 anti-tank wire-guided missiles and 11 × Gazelle Light Helicopters. With one flight of 656 Sqn Army Air Corps flying 3 × Scout and 6 × Gazelle Light Helicopters.

Tactical Air Control Parties

605 RM, 611 RM, 612 RM and 613 (which joined with 2 Para) each party consisted of an officer from the RAF and two driver/signallers. Deployed to direct aircraft onto land targets.

Air Defence Troop of 3 Cdo Bde under command of HQ & Sigs Sqn until under-command of T-Bty

12 × Blowpipe missile launchers and attached two Sections of 43 Bty of 32 Guided Weapons Regt RA (after their initial deployment with 2 Para)

I Raiding Squadron RM under command of HQ & Sigs Sqn until late May when it came under command of the Task Force Assault Sqn

Commanded by an RM Captain with a small HQ and 17 Rigid Raiding Craft

Task Force Assault Squadron formed in San Carlos about 26 May 1982

Commanded by a Major with a small HQ (initially little more than a Corporal Signaller with two radios), the Squadron co-ordinated the 'boating' assets and set up a Forward Operating Base at Bonners Bay (originally Blue Beach II). 1RSRM came under command and sixteen other craft's operations were co-ordinated for LFFI.

Force Reinforcement Holding Unit

Unit through which Battle Casualty Replacements might be channelled.

Field Records Office

Maintained records of casualties etc.

Under command of 5 Infantry Brigade

Brigade HQ
2nd Battalion the Scots Guards
1st Battalion the Welsh Guards
1st/7th Duke of Edinburgh Own Gurkha Rifles
97 Battery Royal Artillery – 6 × 105-mm light guns
HQ 4 Field Regt RA
10 Field Workshop REME
16 Field Ambulance RAMC
81 Ordnance Coy RAOC (some detachments with 3 Cdo Bde RM)
Forward Air Control – 2 × Parties

Units under command of LFFI in addition to Brigades

Air Maintenance Group
Detachment of RAF Special Forces
Detachment 47 Air Defence Despatch Squadron RCT
Detachment 49 EOD Squadron of 33 Engineer Regt RE
Y Troop Detachment Royal Signals – analysis of enemy signals traffic
Rear Link Detachment 30 Signals Regt of Royal Signals providing Satellite and High Frequency radio links.

Units in Ships – see also Ships RM detachments in Appendix 4

3 × Mexeflote Detachments from 17 Port Regt RCT
5 × Landing Ship Logistic Detachments from 17 Port Regt RCT

Associated Deployments

SBS – 3 × 4-man teams with 2-man command cell in submarine HMS *Conqueror*; teams (total 22 all ranks) in other submarines.

UNIFORMS AND ACCOUTREMENTS

The many and varied details of RM uniforms can only be outlined in a short appendix, but the following paragraphs describe the salient features of all ranks' uniforms from 1919 to the 1990s. Items covered in the text have not been repeated in this appendix, however. A detailed study of dress can be made in the RM Museum and see *Uniforms of the Royal Marines 1664 to the present day* by Charles C. Stadden and G & C Newark 1997 ISBN 0 9519342 2 8.

Dress Regulations

Before 1966 these were published as *Royal Navy and Royal Marines Uniform Regulations*. These included, for officers, nine orders of dress, from No.1 Full Dress to No. 13 Lovat Shirt Sleeve Order, each order of dress being assigned a number for combinations of different items of dress. There were also nine orders for wear in hot climates including No.8W Tropical Dress. For other ranks there were 15 orders of dress, including No.12 Tropical combat Dress,[1] plus the snow warfare and various orders of dress for operations in other theatres.

RMA and RMLI

Details of these uniforms are given in earlier histories, although during World War I dress regulations had not been enforced, and both branches of the Corps did not revert to pre-1914 uniforms until the winter of 1918–19. The pre-1914 full dress, however, was only worn by the divisional Bands and by one, or possibly more, detachments in ships on a Royal Tour.[2] The RMA in 1921 adopted a cap badge with a small grenade above the globe and laurel for sergeants and lower ranks. This grenade snapped off easily, making the badge fragile, and in 1922 the RMA reverted to a simple grenade badge with small crossed guns set separately above a silver globe and 'gold' laurel leaves. RMA staff sergeants wore the same badge as junior ranks but from 1921 the grenade was worn separately in the way WO2s wore the Crown and Lion in the 1970s.

Headdress

The Wolseley pattern white helmet was reintroduced after World War I. Although not generally worn between 1939 and 1950 (from late 1940s

for bands), it again became the ceremonial headdress and was worn in the 1990s.

The blue Broderick cap (introduced in 1903) continued to be worn in 1919 by ranks below Staff Sergeant, although the RMA corporals' and gunners red piping in front of the pre-1918 Broderick was no longer used. In 1927 a similar cap to the Broderick was introduced, but had no peak. The semicircle of red serge behind the cap badge was retained, as was the additional blue cloth trim in the front of caps. This trim had gold piping around its upper edge for senior NCOs. Officers and staff sergeants continued to wear a cap with a scarlet band and scarlet piping around the crown. Other ranks were issued from 1933 with a new pattern cap with a scarlet band (but no piping). White cap covers were worn on these various caps during the summer (May to September) in the UK and home Waters and in hot climates, except for some 18 months (30 April 1921 to 22 October 1922). During 1938 a cap with a white duck top (blancoed) was introduced for wear in hot climates, and this was considerably lighter than the normal cap. White cap covers continued to be worn in the UK and in UK-based ships until World War II. They were reintroduced after the war until replaced in 1956 by a white plastic-topped cap in one pattern for officers and one for other ranks.

The blue field service cap of 1897 – the 'fore-and-aft', often incorrectly called a forage cap – was worn by officers in mess dress, and particularly before World War II it was sometimes worn on board ship. In 1942 blue FS caps were issued for wear aboard ship, and withdrawn on disembarkation. A similar pattern of khaki cap was worn by all ranks after the introduction of battledress into the Corps in 1939; it was also worn by some recruits and others wearing khaki service dress, and was an optional item from 1948. Officer cadets in World War II wore a white cloth insert in the front of this cap and white ½-in bands on the shoulder straps of their battledress blouses, probationary cadets wore similar inserts and bands but in blue cloth. Blue field service caps could be worn when not on parade during World War II, but were an optional item a man might buy at his own expense.

The peaked khaki forage cap was worn with khaki service dress, the other ranks' pattern of this cap being similar to that worn by Foot Guards, and had a small, soft ribbed peak. Officers continued to wear their pattern of this cap throughout World War II, although it was not worn on parade after the issue of blue berets. Other ranks in Provost Companies also wore forage caps with red covers on the crown in the same manner as the Army's Military Police. But the khaki forage cap was not generally worn by other ranks after 1940.

The blue beret began to replace the khaki field service (fore-and-aft) cap late in 1943, and had been worn by all ranks of Royal Marines in Combined Operations from that summer. Although it was generally issued, it was not worn throughout the Corps until 1948. In 1995 it is only worn by young officers and recruits (including juniors) under training, for the green commando beret has been worn by all ranks passing their commando course since 1960. This green beret had previously been worn by all ranks in Army and RM commando units since its introduction late in 1942.[3]

The Wolseley helmet was worn between the World Wars in hot climates, as part of a man's non-ceremonial dress, when the brass ball was replaced by a zinc top. In the Mediterranean it was worn with a khaki cover during field training. In World War II many Royal Marines in hot climates were issued with the khaki tropical helmet with a ribbon of Corps colours on the puggaree (left side), and khaki bush hats were also issued when appropriate.

Cap badges

Since 1923 the globe and laurel surmounted by the crown and lion (irreverently, the dog and basket) has been the Corps' cap badge. This was of polished brass for Marines and corporals, but sergeants and above was gilt, needing no polishing. Quartermaster sergeants also had a gilt badge but the crown and lion were a separate part of it. Before World War II a bronze badge was worn by other ranks in khaki service dress, and in World War II a Bakelite cap badge was issued for economy. Officers' cap badges are 'split' but have a silver globe, and although anodised were always polished, before the general introduction of anodised badges for all ranks. Since 1958 all cap badges have been anodised and in the field all ranks have worn a bronze cap badge since 1964.

A red patch behind the badge on khaki caps had been worn from late 1941 by all and the patch was incorporated into the design of the blue beret. But since the training of all Marines as commandos, recruits are issued with the blue beret-with-flash on joining. The only other cap badges worn since 1923 were officers' full dress collar badges, worn in World War II on green berets of officers of 41 RM Commando, and the bands' badges described below.

Blue Tunics

After the Amalgamation a new ceremonial dress was introduced (see Fig. 14), in 1925, but like all new uniforms this took time to become generally available; three years were allowed for its complete distribution, although it was not worn generally after 1939. The tunic featured several items with origins in the RMA and RMLI.

The pattern of both the officers' and other ranks' blue suit ('blues') has been unchanged since the Amalgamation; but between 1941 and 1947 other ranks were issued with utility style 'blues' of lower quality and with no lower pockets, pocket pleats and other features. These were the first blue tunics made by outside contractors in modern times, for the Divisional tailors had previously made all blue suits. The first deliveries were returned, however, because they were black not blue. The buttons on all 'blues' were brass with the 'foul anchor' embossed and polished, but the much prized sets of RMLI buttons of a brighter and softer brass were used by those who could acquire them. Anodised buttons were introduced (to save cleaning) from 1958, and as from 1974 a finer blue tweed cloth was introduced, though the pattern of tunic did not change and after World War II became the Marines' ceremonial tunic.

Before World War II officers wore a ceremonial blue tunic, but since then officers have worn for ceremonial the blue tunic which was their everyday parade dress of the 1930s. This is of the same pattern as the pre-World War II khaki service dress (KSD). During the war a utility KSD was worn which did not have 'pointed cuffs' or the fullness of material in pockets and pleats. Many 'HO' officers did not receive a kit allowance for 'blues' and were not required to wear them, but for those in ships' detachments the blue suit of prewar pattern continued to be worn during World War II.

Badges of Rank

These have followed army styles with chevrons, crowns, etc., but with some exceptions that include:

(a) Colonels Commandant before World War II wore, and senior officers – colonels and above – in 1990s wear, army style dress. However, since 1964 these senior officers have worn RM buttons and a Corps-pattern of mess dress. General officers in the 1990s wear Army styles of ceremonial uniform but with Corps buttons.

(b) Royal Marine officers below the rank of colonel wear the letters RM below the stars and/or crowns on their shoulder straps except when in combat dress or mess kit. The letters 'RM' are replaced by the appropriate cipher for RM equerries to members of the Royal family.

(c) Special Duties (SD) Officers was a change of title, as before 1948 there were Warrant Officers and Commissioned Warrant Officers (see below). SD Officers wore similar badges of rank to general service officer, and the rank of 2nd-lieutenant was discontinued from 1 July 1996. Commissioned ranks in the Band Service had included Bandmasters as 2nd Lieutenants, Lieutenants and Captains on the SD list but they were referred to as Directors of Music or as appropriate for their appointment. RM Gunners in the late 1950s became 2nd Lieutenants on a Special Duties list.

(d) Sergeants on the staff (as opposed to staff sergeants, later QM Sgts) wore three inverted chevrons on the right cuff. The hospital sergeant who ran the infirmary wore a red cross on a white circle edged in red above his chevrons; the armourer sergeant similarly wore crossed hammer-and-pincers. Provost sergeants continue to wear inverted chevrons and leather sword belts.

(e) Colour Sergeants wore above their three gold chevrons in ceremonial dress of 1925–39 a large, gold-wire embroidered badge (globe over crossed union flags with crown above, foul anchor below, the whole surrounded by laurel leaves). A smaller version of this badge was reintroduced in 1956 for ceremonial 'blues'.

(f) Band masters from time to time also wore badges unique to RM bands.

(g) Quartermaster Sergeant Instructors of physical training, gunnery and infantry, the principal specialist qualifications before World War I, each had their SQ badges incorporated in the gold wire badge on their blue tunic from the late 1920s until the mid-1950s. (See also 'Cloth Insignia' below.)

(h) RM Warrant officers were entitled to a salute but wore no badges of rank on their officers' style uniforms, they were few in number and their dress-without-badges caused confusion when approached by men of other services. From 1940, however, Warrant Officers wore 'WO' in a small laurel wreath on the shoulder straps. In the late 1940s there were also Commissioned and Senior Commissioned Warrant Officers. The Commissioned WO wore a small star (of ½-in size) and the Senior Commissioned WO wore a 2nd lieutenant's single star (incorrectly called a 'pip'). On promotion to Lieutenant (Quartermaster) and more senior ranks they wore the same badges of rank as general service officers

(two stars for lieutenants, three for captains and so on). About 1948 these WO's as Commissioned Sergeants Major and Senior Commissioned Sergeants Major were known as Branch Officers. In 1957, when these commissioned WOs came on the SD officers' promotion list (see below), the term Branch Officer was abolished. The classes of Warrant Officer in 1997, as WO I and WO II were distinguished by a badge worn on the bottom of the right sleeve: WO I's badge being the Royal Coat of Arms in a laurel wreath: and WO II's badge being a crown in a laurel wreath

(i) Special Duty (SD) Officers from 1957 were – and are – commissioned Warrant Officers and senior NCOs at one time known as Branch Officers and who usually served as quartermasters but at times carried out general duties. They had a separate list for promotion from other officers.

On the tri-service camouflaged uniform introduced in the late 1990s, all officers badges of rank were worn on a cloth tag on the chest and *not* on shoulder straps.

Cloth insignia

Examples of the shoulder flashes of RM units are given in Fig. 15 of **Royal marines 1919–1980**; other formation signs were worn from time to time, although after May 1942 Royal Marines were not allowed to wear 'Army Area badges etc, and other Army distinctive badges (Signals, Artillery etc) . . .' 'Y' Bty (MNBDO I) had worn the Polar Bear insignia of 49 Division while in Iceland with this division in 1941–2. 27 RM Signals Coy had worn the 2-in coloured strip the army used to distinguish different branches, changing from blue/white for signals to red/blue of artillery, as it came under different commands. When with Twenty-first Army Group, the Coy is reported to have worn – contrary to orders? – the Group's formation insignia. RM Armoured Support Group's personnel also wore artillery distinguishing marks (or shoulder 'bars'). Landing craft personnel wore the Combined Operations' insignia.

Specialist qualifications (SQ) badges are, those currently worn by Army and Navy specialists, with a few exceptions. Since 1945 a great number of specialist qualifications have been introduced, and a system of stars and crowns incorporated into the SQ badges denote the wearer's degree of efficiency. These badges were worn on blues, battledress, khaki service dress and tropical rig before 1964, but since then have only been worn by RMs in Lovats. The position of these SQ badges has varied from time to time, and varied to distinguish specialists from specialist-instructors, in the position of the badge on the tunic sleeve.

Army-pattern badges for good conduct, World War II length of service and wound stripes were also worn by Marines. In the 1990s good conduct badges are awarded to RM other ranks at 4, 8 and 12 years' service with good conduct.

The Commandant General's Shooting badge is designed for the marksmen who shoot or have shot in the Corps Team of eight in the United Services Match, it has crossed rifles over 'RM VIII' and is worn on the lower left sleeve in Blues and Lovats. First awarded to the team of June 1990 and retrospectively to those who had shot in the Corps' team in these matches over the previous 20 years. In the latter part of the 1990s with many units serving overseas, the number of marksmen available from which to pick the 'Eight' has been limited.

Lanyards

Officers of the RMA in khaki dress wore a blue silk shoulder lanyard for a whistle in the top left pocket, and RMLI one of Light Infantry green; after amalgamation the blue lanyard continued to be worn on the left shoulder in blues, KSD, battledress and in Lovats. When the rank of RSM was introduced in 1939, the RSMs also wore the blue lanyard, as they do in 1990.

Other ranks wore a plain cord knife-lanyard on the right shoulder when in marching order with khaki or blue suits until the late 1940s. This, unlike the blue lanyard with slip 'Turks head' slip knot, was similar to a naval lanyard and doubled to form the shoulder loop. Other ranks in Plymouth Barracks are known to have worn a white lanyard on the left shoulder, but no regulation has been traced which authorised these, and the practice had ceased by 1939. Since the 1930s by custom the King's Squad has worn a white naval-type lanyard on the left shoulder and two chin-straps, with one around the cap.

In World War II the 1st RM Battalion wore a white lanyard, and artillery men in the RM Division in 1940–3 wore a plaited knife lanyard (on the right shoulder), as worn by the Royal Artillery.

Unit lanyards are worn by all ranks in Commandos in Lovat Dress, and earlier when in KSD and khaki battle dress. These lanyards, originally naval lanyards dyed, are worn on the right shoulder, and since the mid-1950s have been single cotton braid lanyards with a 'Turks head' slip knot.

The Commando lanyards were: dark blue for those in HQ Commando Forces and the Logistic Rgt; dark green for HQ 3 Cdo Bde; light blue 40 Cdo; old gold 41 Cdo; white 42 Cdo; scarlet and old gold 43 Cdo; scarlet 45 Cdo; old gold/scarlet Comacchio Coy/Grp; old gold/rifle green 539 Assault Sqn; and dark blue/light blue 847 naval Air Sqn. By 1997 these had been lanyards had been varied in some cases: HQRM wore maroon lanyards; Log Regt wore dark blue; HQ 3 Cdo Bde wore dark green; 40 Cdo RM wore light blue; 41 Cdo RM wore old gold; 42 Cdo RM wore white; Comacchio Grp wore old gold/scarlet; and 45 Cdo RM wore scarlet.

Blue Suit Trousers

All officers below the rank of colonel before World War II wore 'overalls' – the tight fitting trousers with a scarlet welt down each side – when not on parade with troops, in what was undress order, and when a frock coat was worn, Since World War II field officers, adjutants and ADCs in ceremonial dress have worn 'overalls' and spurs. ('Overalls' have bands fitted under the leather Wellington boots with which they are worn.) Plain bottom trousers ('slacks'), are worn on parade by all other officers. The scarlet 'stripes' are ¼in wide but colonels and more senior officers have a wider stripe on their trousers.

Other ranks' blue trousers have been the same cloth as tunics, and have a 5/16th inch stripe down each side seam (in the utility suit this only ran to the lower edge of pockets). Blue serge trousers without a stripe were worn until 1964 with a blue tunic for parade drills, orderlies' duties and similar work, but retained only for PTIs from 1964.

Belts

Before 1939 a working belt was worn. This was in the Corps colours: four parts navy blue, one part old gold, one part Light Infantry green, one part Drummer red, and another four parts navy blue. It was replaced during World War II by a blue belt worn when in 'shirt sleeve order'. In mid-1950s a Corps pattern belt – a stable belt – in Corps colours was an optional item of kit, which later became standard issue for wear in working dress and with appropriate dress in hot climates.

For ceremonial parade Marines wore a white web belt (in the current style of webbing equipment), and a blancoed khaki web belt was worn with battledress on drill parades. At other times belts have been blancoed white for drill parades, but after 1948 they were boot-polished black as 3 Commando Brigade had followed this practice, blacking being more suitable than blanco in hot climates. White belts, however, were retained for minor ceremonials in battledress, and in the 1990s commandos wear white plastic belts for parades. RSMs wear Sam Browne belts with an infantry sword, while Warrant Officers, Staff band Masters, Drum Majors, Bugle Majors and Provost Sergeants wear white buff or leather sword belts with appropriate dress.

Khaki and Lovat suits

All ranks wore army pattern khaki suits as issued from time to time, and as a general rule until 1964 Marines had two blue and one khaki suit; although this was varied from time to time and RMs joining the Brigade in the 1950s were issued with an additional battledress. In World War II many 'HO' Marines had only two khaki battle dresses – no blues – and Marines in some units equipped to army scales (as laid down in the appropriate G1098) had only one battledress and no blues.

On the 1 April 1964 Lovat suits were introduced, with the distinctive dark green infill in their khaki weave, and in the 1990s Marines have two suits of Lovats (with bronze RM buttons and badges, both in the pattern of 1923) and one of 'blues'. Lovat suits are unique to the Corps. They are worn as an alternative to 'blues' for certain ceremonial parades, by sentries and other duty men, and for walking out when 'ashore' on duty. Since 1969 a heavy woolen jersey has been worn as normal working dress, with badges of rank and a Royal Marines Commando shoulder flash.

Top Coats

Officers may wear a blue boat cloak with crimson lining and reaching 2in above the knee; it is normally worn with mess dress. This cloak has lion head fastenings with a chain. Army officers' pattern greatcoats are worn but officers may wear British warms of a light khaki colour with leather buttons, on occasions when wearing Lovats. Before Lovats were introduced, officers wore a military-style riding mackintosh with metal badges of rank and the letters 'RM' on detachable shoulder straps but since 1964 they have worn the general issue mackintosh (see below).

Since the Amalgamation the Marine's greatcoat has been double-breasted, with two rows each of four buttons and a large collar. NCOs' badges of rank are worn on the lower arm. In World War II army-pattern greatcoats were the general issue, and since 1968 RM greatcoats for all ranks have been held in central stores and only issued when required for ceremonial parades.

A blue mackintosh for RM other ranks was an optional item of clothing not worn on parades. It was often worn on shore leave after its introduction in 1921, but the practice of wearing these

gradually died out after World War II when civilian dress could be worn for 'going ashore'. Two patterns of Lovat Macintosh have been issued since 1964, and are worn with anodised metal badges of rank for officers, or white embroidered NCOs' badges, on slides over shoulder straps.

Navy Blue Battledress

This was introduced in June 1942 and was of the same pattern as khaki battledresses, which had covered pocket buttons etc. Officers wore it with a blue lanyard, white shirt and collar and black tie; the shoulder title letters 'RM' were at first worn but from November 1943 these were not worn on this dress but woven arm badges 'ROYAL MARINES' (in scarlet on blue) were worn. NCOs' badges of rank were in red and their blue battledress was fastened at the neck, as were those of Marines. This was the dress of landing craft crews and of ships' detachments when not doing dirty jobs. It ceased to be manufactured in 1950 but for many years afterwards was worn for office work, often with trousers from 'blues'. Medal ribbons were not worn on this dress until after World War II.

Combat Dress 1980s and 1990s

The No. 11A Arctic combat dress had: a DPM cold weather cap with velcro fastenings on its crown to which the quilted cotton ear and neck flaps could be folded back, these flaps incorporated nylon fur and the cap had any badge of rank on its front; a DPM windproof jacket; lightweight green or DPM windproof trousers; combat shirt [khaki]; woollen heavy jersey; ski march boots; snow gaiters; ski march toe covers; inner woollen mittens; windproof/waterproof outer mittens. Also available were: a loose fitting two-piece snow suit in white nylon and worn over combat clothing; Du-liner Arctic overalls for technicians; and thermal overboots for sentries and others on static duties. Snow goggles were also available for ski patrols. (See BR81 Dress Regulations for Royal Marines.)

In 1991 a new Desert Lightweight Combat dress in DPM material of various shades of stone and brown was first worn for operation 'Haven'. But to avoid the need to issue special clothing when men were to operate in different theatres in 1995, a new uniform was introduced as Combat Soldier 1995 (CS95). The basic uniform consisted of a lightweight shirt (worn outside the trousers) and trousers, both of cotton/polyester DPM material, under which a cotton T-shirt could be worn or thermal underwear including 'Long Johns' in cold weather climates. A shirt with a zip fastener at the front, in the Norwegian army style with a roll-collar might be worn under the combat shirt. A wind-proof thigh length gaberdine smock in DPM cotton was worn in moderately cold weather, and a fleece lined jacket was available for cold weather. This jacket had a zip fastening, a woollen collar and elastic cuffs, normally worn under the smock. This clothing could be covered by waterproof over-garments of a smock and trousers. These were in a material which allowed perspiration to evaporate to its outside, but prevented water passing through this material from the outside. This Moisture Vapour Permeable material (MVP) was used for other linings. The principle on which this clothing was designed relates to the layers of dress which retain air as an insulator between layers.

The combat boots worn with CS95 dress had shock absorbing soles and a speed-loop lacing system with an eyelet. There was also a Pro-boot which was Goretex-lined (an MVP material) for wear in severe weather. Gaiters in heavy duty nylon or MVP material were worn for added protection against water seeping into boots. The gaiters covered the whole of the upper boot with a strap under the instep and reached to just below the knee.

Gloves issued with CS95 had a pair of nylon inner gloves with rubber grips on the palms, and leather outer gloves with MVP linings. The Mark 6 GS Combat helmet could be worn with a white or a DPM cover, and was made of a bullet-resistant plastic. NBC suits were worn at times when chemical warfare attacks seemed likely. These protective smocks and trousers had patches that could detect chemical vapours, they were worn with black rubber overboots and rubber gloves as well as a respirator.

See also *Webbing and Similar Equipment* below.

Mess Dress

RMA officers wore a dark blue mess dress which after World War I replaced the high-necked, ornate dark blue dress. But after Amalgamation the RMLI scarlet mess jacket, blue waistcoat and blue trousers with red welts were adopted as the mess dress for officers of the Corps. This is the dress worn in the 1990s, usually with a soft white shirt and black tie, although stiff shirts with winged collars were always worn until the late 1960s and are still worn on occasions of particular formality in the 1990s.

Senior NCOs have worn a mess dress as an optional item of clothing since the 1950s, when it was the same pattern as the officers' white tropical mess dress. But in the 1960s the officers' pattern with a scarlet mess jacket was adopted, with a scarlet cummerbund in place of the waist-

coat and miniature gold wire badges of rank on the right sleeve only.

Other Clothing

A blue canvas working dress was worn from about 1925 until World War II, when the army denim suit (of a battledress pattern) became the dress for fatigues and was on occasion worn in action. 'No.8s' of dark blue trousers and a light blue shirt were worn by detachments as 'action working dress' in the 1980s and 1990s but in World War II boiler suits were worn under anti-flash gear at sea. On landing craft in those years 'sea rig' consisted of any comfortable combination of polo-necked jerseys, slacks and fleece jackets under oilskins or a duffle coat (sea boots or puttees were not worn, as a man's boots or trousers filled with water, making him heavy to pull from the sea if he fell overboard). Lightweight nylon trousers (latterly with stay-pressed creases and zip fly) replaced denims in the mid-1960s and were worn with woollen pullovers on occasions. But due to the fire risks with nylon, these trousers were not worn where there was any danger of petrol bombs or similar fire hazards.

Tropical dress has followed army patterns, but there were differences in material, and in style for RM other ranks. Since the late 1960s the ceremonial drill tunic has been replaced by an open-necked tunic, not unlike a bush shirt, and worn with a white helmet on ceremonial occasions in hot climates. Several patterns of olive green walking-out dress with a bush shirt, shorts or trousers, have been worn in the Far East since the 1950s.

The Combat Dress (see above) in the 1990s could be supplemented by various items privately purchased, giving rise to the Army's allusion to 'Millett's Marines'. Milletts were a chain of shops selling camping equipment and clothing in the second half of the 20th century.

Webbing and Similar Equipment

This has followed army patterns for field service, but Marines were also issued with hammocks and other items of naval kit – oilskin, duffle coats, etc. in World War II – when required. As a result even a small Marine detachment of 14 men travelling by rail could be mistaken for the baggage party of an army platoon, for the Marines had seagoing kit bags, army kitbags (with their tropical suits, etc.) and hammocks, taking up considerable space in a luggage van.

By 1995 Marines used the 1990 Pattern of Personal Load Carrying Equipment (90 PLCE) of heavy duty nylon, with black plastic quick-release buckles. A nylon mesh yoke fastened to the back of the waist belt, had wide padded straps which stretched over the shoulders and were attached to two narrower adjustable straps which came up from the two ammunition pouches, one each side of the wearer's chest and attached to the belt. Two further ammunition pouches could be fastened to the belt, as could a bayonet frog, an entrenching tool, a water bottle and a respirator. Two adjustable side straps could be worn for added stability. This PLCE could be worn in three configurations: Assault Order when the weight was kept to a minimum consistent with the projected battle; Patrol Order which allowed for rations to be carried and other necessities for prolonged time in the field; and Marching Order when a Bergen might be carried. This Bergen rucksack usually carried spare clothing, a tent, climbing equipment, rations, a stove, possibly ammunition reserves, and an appropriate shovel. (White camouflage could be added using a cover with elasticated sides.)

Kit Upkeep Allowance (KUA) and its replacement

After World War I a Marine's kit was replaced according to expected 'life' of each item; but if a man did not need a new suit of blues, for example, he could draw a cash sum approximately equal to its cost. Many men, however, preferred to draw the 'replacement' item even though they did not need it, as in this way they built up a wardrobe, so to speak, of clothing and spare kit. During World War II there was a system of survey, when after fair wear and tear an item would be replaced on the basis of new for old without charge. This system was changed, although some items continued to be issued for replacement on survey until the early 1950s, but from 1948 a Kit Upkeep Allowance was paid at set rates per annum for all other ranks, and men had to buy new suits out of this, shirts, vests and so on as required. In addition to basic kit, Marines from time to time have received items – such as combat clothing – on loan, and this issue is known as 'loan clothing'.

From the Spring of 1992 KUA was replaced by a form of survey not unlike that available in World War II.

Band Uniforms

These are a study in complexity and minor variations beyond the scope of a general history, but the salient features were the following:

Ceremonial Dress. The RMA Band wore a navy blue hussar-type tunic with horizontal gold-braided bars, and gold-braided collars, cuffs and back panel seams. Their cap badge was different to that worn by RMLI bands. After the Amalgamation, bands continued to wear their original uniforms until 1925, when new ceremonial dress

was introduced for Divisional Bands. After World War II they wore the general service ceremonial dress of 1925.

Broad red trouser strips from 1925 were the traditional mark of Divisional bandsmen, until the formation of the new Band Service in 1950. Since 1951 all RM musicians have worn trousers with the broad stripe in 'blues' and ceremonial dress. Buglers, however, continue to wear the thin stripe.

Band Service pre-1950 wore 'blues' (with thin red trouser stripes) of general service Marines.

Cap badges and helmet plates have incorporated different features for divisional bands from time to time. But in 1980 the cap badge of other ranks in C-in-C Naval Home Command's band (Portsmouth) was a gilt grenade on which was mounted the cipher GRV and a crown, both in silver, surrounded by a gilt laurel wreath. The silver cipher EIIR/PP with a crown was worn separately above this cap badge. The helmet plate was of standard RM design with the ciphers GRV below the globe and EIIR/PP above it, and incorporated into the full design of the helmet plate. The other ranks of the Band of Royal Marines Commando Forces wear a cap badge with a silver Prince of Wales plume between the globe and the lion and crown. This plume was worn in a similar position on their helmet plates. The directors of both these bands wear helmet plates in the special style of their musicians. These unique badge features were granted to these bands' predecessors at different times for services to the royal family. However, the white rose, which was a feature of Chatham Division Band's badge, had not been incorporated into any badge of a band in 1980.

Distinctive badges included the lyre cap badge and collar badge. The latter were worn from 1906 until 1951 by Band Service musicians, who also wore the lyre cap badge until 1946. Both badges were replaced by general service globe and laurel style badges on the respective dates. The bandsman's 'RMB' on his shoulder straps was replaced in 1946 with the general service 'RM'. Other ranks of the Portsmouth Band wore on the right shoulder a blue flash with 'Royal Yacht' surmounted by a crown, both in gold. By the 1990s the shoulder flash of this band was 'Royal Band' on the change of name when the Royal Yacht was paid off. This band wear a unique Divisional Band tunic.

Badges of rank. There have been a number of changes in the style of these, and until 1968 band masters of Portsmouth, Plymouth and Deal bands wore three inverted chevrons surmounted by an academy-style lyre, on the right cuff of all uniforms; the drum and bugle majors wore four similar chevrons surmounted by a drum and bugle. These chevrons were in gold on ceremonial and best blue uniforms, and in red on working dress. Staff band masters from 1963 to 1972 wore the gold embroidered badge of a lyre enclosed in a laurel leaf, surmounted by a crown, on the right cuff. In 1972 the rank of WO2 (Band Master) replaced staff band masters, who since that date have worn the Corps' WO2 badges of rank. A WO1 (Band Master) has worn the badge of the Royal arms on the right cuff. Band C/ Sgts, sergeants and corporals have worn normal badges of rank since 1968.

Miscellaneous. In 1921 'garter blue' ceremonial uniforms with light blue collar and trouser stripes was briefly issued to one or two bands. After world War II the band service was reissued with white helmets and buff equipment. Since 1965 musicians have worn a ceremonial order of dress in hot climates. This consists of a white drill tunic, blue trousers with broad red stripe, and a white helmet. However, the Royal Yacht Band continued to wear an all white tropical dress; its bandsmen also wore the pre-1939 Divisional Band's ceremonial tunic on other occasions when embarked.

In 1966 the senior NCOs began to wear scarlet mess jackets when performing as leaders of an orchestra or conducting small dance bands. Band orders of dress also included Lovats; and the mess 'kit' with a stiff shirt for officers conducting orchestras, when musicians wear No.1 blue uniforms (1925-style) with a cloth belt and no cap in evening perfomances but the officers may wear frock coats for such daytime performances.

Green beret. This was worn by the band of 3 Commando Brigade when in battledress, but band ranks of the 1990s wear their white-topped caps in all but ceremonial orders of dress, including dress with woollen pullovers.

For bandswomen's uniform see Appendix 5 *Changes and events 1981–1997.*

UNIT HISTORY SUMMARIES

(The source note abbreviations before 1981, here follow those for the main text, but where no sources are given for a unit History this is based on RM Archive files and War Diaries, except for ships' details which have been taken from RMROs and published sources.)

LAND UNITS 1919–38

63rd (Royal Naval) Division and 3rd RM Bde

First called the Royal Naval Division with three brigades, two of seamen and 3rd (RM) Brigade, the Division served in the Dardanelles and Gallipoli campaigns of 1915 and from 1916 served in France and Belgium.[1] The 3rd Bde originally contained four RM battalions, but after losses at Gallipoli they were reorganised in August 1916 into two battalions (see next entry). There were several Marine supply, medical and other units (including 190th MG Coy RM) under the division's command. All were demobilised under army arrangements, the long-service Marines being dispersed to their RMLI Divisions in June 1919.

1st and 2nd RMLI Battalions

Originally four[2] battalions, after losses at Gallipoli the Chatham and Deal Battalions formed the 1st RMLI Bn, and the Portsmouth and Plymouth Bns formed the 2nd RLMI Bn and 3rd Bde HQ was absorbed into the divisional units in 1916. further casualties led to the merging of the 2nd RMLI into the 1st RMLI in April 1918, giving a combined strength of about 1,100 all ranks in November 1918; the unit was disbanded with the RN Division in June 1919.

3rd RMLI Battalion

Raised in October/November 1916[3] to replace army units as garrisons on Greek-administered islands in the eastern Aegean. Gen Sir H. E. Blumberg, KCB, a Brigadier at that time, commanded from June 1918 until November 1919. In the summer of 1919 4,000 Russian refugees were housed in a camp which had been improvised by the Battalion which was now small in numbers. Meanwhile 170 of the Battalion manned Bosphorous forts[4] from January to November 1919,

when all the garrisons were reduced to a total of 194 all ranks, the French taking over when 15,000 defeated White Russians arrived on Mudros, and the garrison finally left the islands on 25 June 1921.

4th RM Battalion

Assaulted the mole at Zeebrugge on 23 April 1918, and in their honour no subsequent '4th battalion' has been raised.

5th RM Battalion

Formed in September 1918 with 20 platoons (907 all ranks), mostly 45-year-olds, to operate electrically controlled sea mines etc. in coastal defences. Disbanded January-February 1919.

RM Field Force

Formed 5 May 1918,[5] the force of 365 all ranks was commanded by Lt-Col R. O. Paterson, RMA, for service in Murmansk to support local forces (see Chap 2). They established control posts along the railway, guarded many wooden bridges, and trained 150 Poles to use MGs. A hundred[6] were sent with an Allied assault force, mostly comprising French troops, landed from British warships on Modyuski Island (River Dwina, near Archangel). These Marines later served with the Naval Brigade landed in that area, until July 1919, having been in action in support of British Army units. Elements of the field force in Murmansk were concentrated for ski training but were not in action until early May 1919 after the spring thaw. They sailed from Murmansk on 10 July and were disbanded on their return to the UK.

6th RM Battalion

Formed[7] during July 1919 under Lt-Col A. de W. Kitkat, RMLI, for supervision of the plebiscite in Schleswig-Holstein (northern Germany), they were diverted to relieve northern Russian garrisons (see Chapter 2). Many of the older men were employed in GHQ and as clerks on the Murmansk railway. The companies, each reduced by these commitments to some 140 or so young Marines, were sent to forward areas on Lake Onega. At Kapaselga some 15 miles south of the Medvyejya Gora base the Marines took over the outpost line, which had been pushed south. General Maynard was moving what forces he could to secure lines of communication to the Shunga Peninsula where a rising against the Bolsheviks had been successful, About this time several[8] small units 'were relegated to the lines of communication', including some Marines after they refused duty.

On 23 August the companies were deployed, and on the night of 28–9 August moved against two concentrations of Finnish[9] troops supporting the Bolsheviks (see Chapter 2). After this action and the subsequent operations, the companies were replaced by White Russians and Serbians (a battalion of these fighters[10] served in the Allied force), and sailed from Murmansk on 8 October, being dispersed a week later. There has never been another 6 Battalion RM.

7th RM Battalion

Formed in the summer of 1919 from RMs landed under Lt-Col J. W. Hudleston, RMA, from the Grand Fleet, the Battalion was to help supervise a plebiscite, but was not used and re-embarked.

8th Battalion RM

The Battalion was brought together in June 1920, sailing to Cork in HMS *Valiant* and *Warspite* before being taken by destroyer to protect coastguard and signal stations around the coast. The three companies were split into detachments, none smaller than 27 strong,[11] allowing for two men to be on leave in the UK, with posts often 100 miles from the companies' HQs. A typical post was at Buncrana[12] on Lough Swilly (Donegal), some 20 miles north of Londonderry. Apart from Lewis gun and rifle practice at a box towed astern of a dinghy, no shots were fired.

Stations were to be defended to the last if attacked.[13] The 1922 *G&L* p 39 refers to 'considerable casualties'. Individuals with the Battalion were relieved for home service from time to time, and the Battalion was not withdrawn until the spring of 1922, after the Anglo-Irish treaty was negotiated. The Marines by that date had been guarding some key points for five years, as the 8th Battalion had taken over these duties from the rear party of an RM Battalion that went to Ireland in 1916.

9th Battalion

This had been formed after the Armistice in 1918 and was one of the Battalions deployed at the time of the coal miners' strike in 1921.

10th Battalion

Formed by the time of the coal miners' strike in 1921, elements were deployed apparently to defend strategic installations.

11th Battalion and RM detachments in Turkey

Turkish Nationalists opposed to the Sultan refused to accept certain treaties negotiated with him by the allies, including the Greeks, who the British government initially supported. Marines and sailors from the Mediterranean Fleet numbering 3,600[14] were landed in Constantinople (modern Istambul) on 16 March 1920[15] and met no resistance. In June ships and planes bombarded the Nationalists occupying the Ismid Peninsula and these Turks withdrew. Early in July strong parties of Marines and seamen were again landed from the Fleet; these were later withdrawn but the Fleet's presence maintained in Constantinople. A Nationalist army in 1921 drove the Greeks back to their enclave in Smyrna and the French and Italians made peace with the Turks.

The 11th Battalion was initially formed during the emergency declared for the 1921 coal strike.

In 1922 the Greeks invested Constantinople, weakening their Smyrna army to do so. A few Marines were landed at Smyrna 'as a calming influence'[16] from the battleship *King George V*, but the city caught fire a few days later and on 13 September was burnt to the ground. Greeks and Armenians numbering 250,000 were then evacuated by sea, and Nationalist Turkish forces of 35,000 moved towards the Dardanelles. Five British Army battalions and some planes blocked the Turks' possible advance across the straits, the troops digging in on the Asian shore around Chanak. The 11th RM Battalion – mobilised in a few days – sailed on 28 September,[17] their transport ship reportedly reaching Constantinople in five days. The Battalion's four companies, some 700[18] in all under Lt-Col J. A. M. A. Clark, CMG, RMLI, included an RMA company sent out as infantry. These gunners were remustered for duty with the RMA Heavy Batteries,[19] for on 21 October Maj W. H. Tripp, DSO, MC, joined the Battalion to command 12 naval guns the Marines had installed by building piers on the northern shores of the Dardanelles,[20] to cover a 30-mile arc across the water. At this time they came under command of GOC Chanak (on Amalgamation they became RM Heavy Batteries).

The infantry companies did guard duties in Constantinople and in the defence of the neutral zone around the city. Their only casualty was a death from malaria[21] before sailing in August 1923 for the UK, where they were disbanded in September.

12th Battalion

This is another battalion which had its origins in a formation for the coal strike emergency.

Disturbances in China led to the formation of the Shanghai Defence Force and other measures that by mid-March 1927 involved 17,700 troops[1] (10,000 of them British) to defend four times this number of foreigners in the city. The Admiralty offered a Marine battalion, available in a matter of days against the Army's need of some weeks,[2] and on 14 January 1927 telegraphed orders were sent to all RM Divisions to mobilise the 12th RM Battalion of 1,000 all ranks commanded by Lt-Col G. Carpenter, OBE, DSC.[3] They were ready by 21 January but their old transport, SS *Minnesota*, had been laid up needing a good deal of preparation, and they could not embark until 26th January. The only wheeled transport taken was some horse-drawn field cookers.[4] (The Companies were originally numbered 1 to 4 but were apparently redesignated A to D by the summer of 1927.)

After a 28-day passage, the Battalion came under the army GHQ's direct command to provide guards, and from 21 March was in the Pootung district, covering almost a 5-mile front along the Whangpo River opposite the city. An area of factories, wharves and warehouses, where most communication was by boat. On 20 August 'C' Company[5] arrived at the British Cold Store in Nanking on a gruelling hot day, where they found the Southern Army's soldiers had briefly occupied the western compound, the most suitable for defence. After taking over from *Dauntless*, 21 volunteers stoked the boilers generating the power for the cold stores, as when the temperature was 32C the cold rooms were needed to keep rations fresh. Nanking lies on the southern bank of a river bend, and was reoccupied by the Southern Army in 1927 without opposition on 3 September and for the next ten weeks the Marines were confined to the compound, before being relieved on 20–21 November by an Army company.

The Battalion embarked on 6 December in SS *Mantua* after Chiang Kai-shek arrived and the tension had eased in Shanghai.

13th RM (Reserve) Battalion

Formed from reservists at the time of the 1920–1 strikes in the coalfields, which culminated in the national coal strike from 31 March to 1 July 1921, the Battalion provided detachments to protect installations and RN personnel manning pumps at mines. Disbanded within a year.

14th Battalion

This was another internal security battalion formed in 1921, but no details have been traced.

RM Battalion for Public Duties (London Bn)

Formed in July 1935 for carrying out these duties, from 17 August to 19 September, in conjunction with the 1st Battalion Scots Guards, this Battalion[6] was honoured as at that time few units other than the Brigade of Guards carried out ceremonial guards in London. The Battalion 281 strong, had a band and drums of 111 musicians. As the King was not in residence at Buckingham Palace, the King's guard was changed at St James's Palace. Guards were also mounted at the Hyde Park Magazine, the Central London Recruiting Depot and the Bank of England. The Battalion, exercising the RMs' right to march through London with bayonets fixed and colours flying, and marched through the City on 19 September. During the month some officers were called back to the MNBDO Nucleus in case gun-mounting parties might be required in the Abyssinian crisis, and Guards' officers in RM uniforms helped out.[7]

INFANTRY UNITS 1939–46

RM Division HQ

The background to the formation of the Division and its subsequent development are explained in Chapters 5; but, briefly, in August 1940 Maj General R. (Bob) G. Sturgess, a Brigadier at the time, was appointed to command the Division at the same as time as the formation of 103 Bde was approved that August.[8] On 23 September the intended order of battle[9] was the following: three brigades – which would become 101, 102 and 103 – each with an HQ, signals and two battalions; a battery of 6 × 3.7-in howitzers (presumably the 31st RM Light Bty); a mobile unit of motorcycles with some carriers and anti-tank weapons; a field ambulance and a Light Aid Detachment to be provided by the War Office; and Army instructors for 'one engineer unit'. The War Office prepared the equipment authorisations (G1098s) for a unit with characteristics of great mobility 'but with great fire and assault powers',[10] capable of operating in temperate or semitropical climates.

During the early winter of 1940–41 101 and 102 Bdes were abroad, but on 21 February 1941[11] the Divisional HQ opened at Alresford (Hampshire); until this time the General, his DAQ and one clerk had been the only staff. The Division (except for 103 RM Bde and ancillary units still being trained) concentrated in Scotland, and in April 1941 was standing by for possible occupation of Grand Canary Island (see Chapter 3). It was mobilised on 30 April[12] before embarking in ships on the Clyde on 5 May for an exercise, the HQ moving to Inverary on 9 May. About this time responsibility for bringing the Division up to War Establishment was taken over by the staff of 103 Bde HQ.[13] During the rest of 1941 and 1942 several amphibious and other exercises were carried out, as part of Force 106 with 29 Bde and army support.

On 10 December 1941[14] the General and part of the HQ staff had begun planning the ship loadings and operations for landings in Madagascar, and from this date there were in effect two HQs: one administering the division and the second planning for the Madagascar landings. The Chiefs of Staff decided early in 1942 to create what was called the Expeditionary Force of a division, an independent brigade group and the RM Division,[15] which – as noted above – was intended eventually to have three brigades. The Admiralty, however, only agreed to the RM Division being attached to the force, so the Division could maintain its own characteristics (see Chapter 5).

The Division's supporting units – 15 RM (MG) Bn, the Anti-Tank Bty and 18 RM (Mobile) Bn – were reorganised, and 103 Bde given a low priority for personnel during the summer of 1942, when the Divisional Artillery HQ was raised in September. There was no available supply of guns and therefore – perhaps now obvious – difficulties in attaching army units to the RM Division, when considerable quantities of equipment had to be provided for the Alamein (Egypt) build-up, among other calls on the War Office's resources. The Divisional Artillery, nevertheless, included three HQs for field, anti-tank and regiments.[16] By late November proposals to employ 101 and 102 Bdes as brigade groups in North Africa had come to nothing (see chapter 5), and the Division continued to train for amphibious operations during 1943. The benefits of three years of this training would not be seen until after the summer of 1943, when its personnel were serving as commandos or in landing craft crews. The Special Service (later Commando) Group HQ opened under command of General Sturges at the RM Division HQ on 15 August 1943 and a month later (15 September) the Division 'ceased to function', after its personnel had been transferred.

RM Division Holding Unit

This unit was opened during 1942 and disbanded 12 October 1943 when its personnel had been transferred.

The RM Brigade, later 101 RM Bde

Formed at Bisley (Surrey) in December 1939[17]

with three battalions – 1st, 2nd and 3rd – under command of Brig A. St Clair Morford, MC, it was originally numbered as 1st RM Bde the number was changed to avoid confusion with Army units and RM Bn, to 101 RM Bde. At the time 60 'HO' officers began training near Deal.[18] The Brigade 'was directly under the Chiefs of Staff Committee'[19] for a role that included seaborne raiding in the Mediterrean should Italy enter the war as expected. Naval gun and air support was expected, but no AFVs were included, as surprise would be lost 'owing to time required to hoist them into MLCs'.[20] Any raid would be limited, therefore, to 24 hours ashore, but plans were discussed with the ISTDC to improve the landing time required for vehicles. In January 1940 a fourth battalion, 5th RM Bn, was added, and the plan was dropped for including an Army battalion when required operationally. The Brigade was split in two, as 101 and 102 RM Bdes before or during May 1940, although 102 Bde's HQ was not formally raised until 12 July, about this time (see RM Circ No. 1659/40S) an RM Bde Reinforcement Depot was established at Sunshine Camp, Hayling Island (see 20th RM Bn Unit History). Although 101 Bde had expected to complete training by July, events overtook these plans.

One of the few fully armed units in the UK that summer, 101 Bde had 66 officers and 1,350 other ranks[21] (an Army brigade had 120 officers, 2,824 ORs and 396 vehicles).[22] The Brigade was temporarily attached to 55 Division for 'reinforcement or counter-attack of any island localities'[23] and as a reserve for action on the mainland. The Chiefs of Staff had agreed in mid-June that both 101 and 102 Bdes should be held at 6-hours' notice for despatch to Ireland[24] should any German invasion begin there, and for seizing the Azores and Cape Verde Islands. But the Brigades were released from their potential commitment for Ireland on 1 July.[25] Having been concentrated near Milford Haven (Dyfed) in late June with Bde HQ and Signals Coy at Tenby, later at Saundersfoot and on 30 June at Pembroke Dock. The Brigade moved early in July to take over 30 miles of coast defences just west of Plymouth, a convenient port for mounting an operation against islands in the Atlantic. The Brigade remained under Home Forces Command but was reduced to three battalions (1st, 2nd and 5th) about July 1940, and was joined by 8th Argylls on 17 July.[26] In August they embarked for Dakar (capital of Senegal, Senegambia) – see Chapter 3. On their return to the Clyde in October 1940, they were held in readiness, training for further operations in West Africa and then for possible landings in the Azores.[27] Although detailed for the December raid on the Lofoten Islands (North Norway), the Brigade was not sent, army commandos making the raid.[28] In April 1941 the 8th Argyls returned to army command.

During 1941–2 a number of operations were considered (see summary of RM Division history) but 101 Bde spent its time in amphibious and other exercises from its ships in Scotland. Brig A. N. Williams later succeeded Brig Morford. The Bde HQ moved to Ystrad Camp (South Wales) during July 1942. Here it developed amphibious techniques, such as employing engineers in the first flight of landing craft, the use of smoke from support craft, and the Beach Bn (see Unit history summary of Beach Units) showing lights to seaward indicating gaps in beach minefields and wire. The problems of clearing stores from beach dumps were realised. In November 1942 the Brigade was back in Inverary (Argyll)[29] doing amphibious exercises, and by January 1943 was in the south of England, with Bde HQ at Chilworth Manor (nr Southampton). By this date the HQ had 161 all ranks,[30] with the Brigadier's command post in tracked carriers and the advanced brigade HQ all in vehicles. The rear HQ and B-echelon had nine vehicles, including the Light Aid Detachment's recovery truck, transport for cooks, signallers and half of the defence platoon, and five motorcycles. In May the Brigade moved to Cowes (Isle of Wight), taking the opportunity to practise landings, and in June and July was in Burley (Hampshire), where by September the HQ was reformed – see RM Circ 1282/43A3, dated 26 August – as part of 4 Special Service Bde's HQ.[31]

102 RM Brigade

Formed when the RM Brigade was divided into brigades each of two battalions, this was at first designated 2nd Brigade in about May 1940,[1] but in August the number was changed to avoid confusion with Army units and RM Bn, to 102 RM Bde. It was commanded by Brig R. H. Campbell, who would later command the Division. His HQ had been formally opened on 16 July[2] at Plymouth and moved to Liverpool on 19 August[3] but part[4] only of the HQ appears to have sailed (with 101 Bde HQ) to Freetown, and this Brigade's 2nd and 3rd RM Bns remained in Freetown (West Africa) until February 1941, when they returned to the UK.[5] The Bde HQ continued to train its battalions until August 1943, when its HQ personnel became the HQ staff of 3 Special Service (Cdo) Brigade.[6]

103 RM Brigade

Formation was approved by Chiefs of Staff in August 1940[7] at the time the RM Division's formation was approved, two battalions – 7th RM Bn and 8th RM Bn – were to be raised at Exton, where the Brigade HQ opened 1 October 1940, but the following month recruits intended for the Battalions were re-allocated to MNBDO II. The HQ continued at Exton, with the Brigade Commander also Commandant of this Reserve Depot, and the battalions were each reduced to 200 all ranks. 7th RM Bn was moved to Hayling Island that December, as a training unit. The 103 Bde HQ was reactivated in April 1941[8] at Exton (CTC Barracks in 1997). It was commanded by Brig N. K. Jolley and its battalions – 7th and 8th – were drawn from recruits at this Reserve Depot;[9] also under command for some months were the 10th RM Bn (see unit history of 10th RM Bn), 31 Lt Bty, 15th RM Bn, 18th RM Bn, RM Division Reinforcement Depot (see 20th RM Bn Unit History) and 1st RM Bn (for administration only). In April the 7th RM Bn came back to Devon, being under canvas at Dalditch. The Brigade took over responsibility for training reinforcements on 2 May 1941[10] and Brig Jolley commanded the Exton Depot until the end of December, when again many men from the battalions were drafted to make up the establishment of MNBDOs.[11]

The 103 RM Bde was rejoined by the 10th Bn on 21 January 1942 before it moved to Dalditch on 27–29 January, when RM brigades of three battalions were planned. But in May 1942 '103 Bde was again reduced to a low priority'.[12] The Brigade HQ's training responsibilities passed to 104 RM (Training) Brigade on 17 June and 103 Bde's HQ was disbanded on 16 July 1942.

104 RM (Training) Brigade

Formed before the summer of 1942[13] as the training brigade of the RM Division, this HQ's responsibilities included the organisation of NCOs' and other courses at Hayling Island, its 20th (Training) Battalion being responsible for recruits' infantry training. (See Administrative Instruction No. 7 for details of formation and unit signs.)[14] From April to mid-July 1942 the HQ was in Exmouth.[15] The Brigade took over responsibility for training at Lympstone and the infantry training of recruits at Dalditch from 17 June 1942, the HQ moving into Lympstone Grange on 16 July. They also liaised with battalions over the provision of reinforcements, including officers for battalions when mobilised.[16] The 22nd RM (Trg) Bn of young soldiers came under command of this HQ in November 1942, before the HQ was absorbed by RM Training Group on its formation early in 1943.

116 Infantry Brigade RM

Originally intended to command beach battalions in the Far East, the Brigade was formed during January 1945 on an Army war establishment under command of Brig C. F. Phillips, with three battalions – 27th RM, 28th RM and 30th RM – a brigade defence platoon, signals section and provost section of RM personnel and an Army unarmoured Light Aid Detachment Type 'A'. Within eight weeks the Brigade was in Belgium and its battalions in action in North West Europe during the last three months of World War II. They returned to the UK at the end of June 1945, and this HQ took under command some personnel from 117 Bde RM, 5 RM AA Bde and 33rd RM Bn during November 1945 as units were run down on demobilisation. The personnel of this HQ were redeployed about January 1946.

117 Infantry Brigade RM

HQ formed 16 January 1945 in Kent on an Army war establishment under command of Brig W. I. Nonweiler, with three battalions – 31st RM, 32nd RM and 33rd RM – and Brigade troops which were similar to those of 116 Bde RM. After further training on the Lancashire coast, the Brigade HQ moved to Germany during mid-May 1945, and from 18 May to 27 June was under Naval command in Keil. It returned to the UK on 1 July 1945 and was disbanded on 31 August.

1st RM Battalion

Formed about January 1940 at Bisley (Surrey),[17] commanded by Lt-Col Wildman-Lushington as part of the RM Bde, with four rifle companies and an HQ Coy (cp: 2nd Bn). In June 1940 it was based at Haverfordwest (south Wales), training for amphibious operations in the summer of 1940 and was in the UK defence forces. In August it took part in amphibious exercises based on the Clyde from the transport *Etteric*,[18] in which it sailed to Freetown on 31 August. The Battalion was in the transport off Dakar on 23–5 September 1940, but did not land and returned to Freetown before sailing to the UK in October. During the next 2½ years the battalion carried out many exercises, while stationed in Scotland from 27 October 1940 to 8 October 1942 standing by for raids on the Atlantic islands, and moved with the Brigade to various training areas for exercises. These included night infiltration, street fighting and a landing from LSIs when moving to Newport (Isle of Wight) on 19–20 April 1943.[19] Lt-Col B. W. Leicester took command during 1942. At the end of July 1943 the Battalion was re-formed as 42 RM Commando,

but some men went to minor landing craft flotillas and other duties.

2nd RM Battalion

HQ began forming about December 1939[1] as part of RM Brigade, but the first recruits did not join until April 1940[2] at Bisley (Surrey). Commanded by Lt-Col A. N. Williams, the continuos service officers and NCOs of the Battalion HQ, its four rifle companies, and the HQ Company, had been training the largely 'HO' recruits in infantry tactics for about three weeks before 3 May.[3] On that day they were put at 2-hours notice for overseas service. Bren guns, anti-tank rifles and 2-in mortars began to arrive next day, to equip the Battalion to its war establishment. Three days later they were aboard the cruisers HMS *Glasgow* and *Berwick*, sailing as part of force Sturges to Iceland, where they landed on 10 May.[4] During the passage the new weapons had been zeroed (their sights tested for accuracy by firing a number of rounds) despite the rough weather. The strength of the Battalion at this time was 28 officers and 280 men.[5]

Although the Battalion had a large area to cover, 'A' Coy's OC prevented the German Consul burning important documents, as the Marines had brought some fire extinguishers ashore.[6] The HQ Coy's Fire Power Platoon, to which most of the Brens[7] had been issued, was sent to Kaldadarnes, where planes carrying 2,000 German troops might land'. The orders to the Platoon were: to hold their fire until troop-carrying planes landed; to fire at paratroops in the air; and should any Germans be caught not in uniform after parachuting in, they were to be shot.[8] (See also Force Sturges's in Unit History Summaries.)

After returning to UK in late May, the Battalion became part of 102 RM Bde.[9] In mid-June 1940 it was in Pembroke (Dyfed). It was the sent to Freetown (West Africa) in the transport *Kenya* for the Dakar operation, and remained in Freetown for possible operations against the Cape Verde islands before returning to the UK in February 1941. During the next 30 months the Battalion took part in various training exercises, being stationed in Scotland.[10] In August 1943 the Battalion HQ and most of the Marines were re-formed as 43 RM Commando.[11]

3rd RM Battalion

HQ formed in December 1939[12] under Lt-Col E. T. Harden as part of RM Bde, and sometimes styled as 3rd (Plymouth) Bn RM. The first recruits joined the Battalion in February 1940, during May the Battalion was transferred to 102 RM Bde and in June was stationed at Manorbier (south Wales). In August it sailed to Freetown in the transport *Sobieski*, with 'A' Coy in *Etteric*. The Battalion remained in Freetown with the 2nd RM Bn (see above) after the Dakar operation.[13] Returning to the UK in February 1941, it went to Scotland and elsewhere in the UK, taking part in many training exercises during the next 30 months. In August 1943 the Battalion and its HQ were re-formed as 44 RM Commando[14] but some personnel went to other units.

4th RM Battalion

Not formed in World War II, see history summary of Land Units 1919–38 above.

5th RM Battalion

Formed 2 April 1940[15] at Cowshot Camp (Brookwood) Hampshire, commanded by Lt-Col H. E. Reading. The Battalion was part of 101 RM Bde. An advanced party went to Hayling Island in preparation for boat training, but the Battalion began to move to Tenby (South Wales) on 19 June. In August it embarked in the transport *Karanja* for the Dakar operations and sailed to Freetown.[16] It returned to Scotland in late October, where it carried out exercises until June 1942. In February that year Lt-Col S. G. Cutler[17] became CO and the Battalion moved to Ystrad (South Wales) on 8–9 June, and on 2 September Lt-Col K. Hunt took command. Some companies returned to Scotland for amphibious training in November/December. These companies and those in South Wales were assembled at Hursley (Hampshire) from 12 December 1942,[18] moved to Ryde (Isle of Wight) in April 1943 and to Burley (Hampshire) on 29 May. Disbanded at Burley early in August 1943, the HQ and most of the personnel were re-formed as 45 RM Commando.

6th RM Battalion

Not formed in World War II

7th RM Battalion

HQ formed during April 1941,[19] CO Lt-Col T. B. W. Sandall, for service with 103 RM Bde. The first three Continuous Service squads joined at Exton about 23 September 1940 and 'HO' squads allocated to 7th RM began training in October. Then 300 men were drafted to MNBDO, and to make more accommodation available at Exton, the remainder went to Sands Camp (Hayling Island), which was taken over by the Battalion's HQ with two recruit squads on 8 February 1941. At Hayling it became a training unit. It moved back to Devon, arriving at a tented camp at Dalditch in April. On 2 May the CO, Col Sandall, also took command of the 8th RM

and 9th RM Battalions – total strength of all three battalions was 28 officers and 797 other ranks.[20] The Battalion was rebuilt after the drafts to MNBDO, although 103 RM Bde was given a low priority from May, when the Battalion apparently became independent.

In June 1942 Lt-Col F. W. Dewhurst[21] was appointed CO before the Battalion moved to the Treglog area in Wales before embarking in September 1942 For South Africa; on passage (in HMT *Empress of Russia*) the Marines manned the ship's guns and helped with the work in other departments. On arrival in Durban the Battalion spent five weeks in a transit camp, their intended role of guarding naval stores dumps having been cancelled on political grounds. In December the Battalion sailed to Egypt in SS *Aronda*, landing at Suez on 1 January 1943, and went to Kabrit Camp north of Little Bitter Lake. The Battalion developed a Beach Brick in the following months, for landing men and stores over open beaches (see Chapter 5). On 27 March the Battalion came under command of GHQ Middle East and under Force 545 (later part of Eighth Army). Final training as '31 Brick' was carried out at Fayid (Egypt) from 25 May 1943 when for a time the battalion was under command of MNBDO II.

The Battalion landed in Sicily at Marzamemi (see chapter 5). On D+6 (16 July 1943) the Battalion was warned for operations under the direct command of XXX Corps in the area of Buccheri, some 70 miles from the Battalion's beach area. On arriving at this hill town next evening (17 July), the CO and his staff undertook the various steps to restore the town's civil administration, the battalion being deployed to guard bridges. But 48 hours later it moved off to secure a bridgehead across the Dittaino River (see chapter 5).

Maj J. T. O. Waters the second in command, took command of the Battalion in action on 30 July, before it was relieved on 7 August and moved to Augusta where it again came under the command of MNBDO II. The Royal Marine Office in London considered the Battalion to be under command of MNBDO II from late June 1943, and briefly before then, but the Battalion's CO did not hear of this until 30 July, and the Battalion had been operating as Corps Troops for some weeks.[22] Lt-Col K. Hunt was appointed CO on 10 August. During the autumn the Battalion carried out guard and other duties, and was embarked several days for an operation that was cancelled at the end of September. The Battalion arrived at Toranto (southern Italy) on 27 November and did routine training and guard duties before sailing for the UK in February 1944. The Battalion was re-formed as 48 Commando soon after its arrival in the UK, and the Battalion was formerly disbanded on 16 March.

8th RM Battalion

HQ forming in April 1941,[1] CO Lt-Col S. G. B. Paine, and the first recruits joined from initial training at Exton, where the Battalion was being formed as part of 103 RM Bde, in the autumn of 1941.[2] In December men were drafted from the Battalion to the MNBDOs and the Battalion HQ moved to open the OCTU at Thurlestone (Devon). The Battalion re-forming at Dalditch, came under command of the CO of 7th RM Bn from 2 May 1942. When the need arose for a second RM Commando in the autumn of 1942, the Battalion HQ and most of the other ranks were transferred to 41 RM Commando, the Battalion formerly disbanding on 29 October 1942.[3]

9th RM Battalion

Formed about January 1942[4] as part of 103 RM Bde. On 2 May came under command of CO of 7th RM while training at Dalditch, and after further training re-formed in August 1943 as 46 RM Commando.

10th RM Battalion

Formed at Crookston (Glasgow) on 18 April 1941,[5] CO Lt-Col F. M. Bramall (promoted from Major 25 April) with personnel from 2nd RM Bn, 3rd RM Bn and 5th RM Bn, and drafts from Divisional reserves on 2 May, as the third battalion of 103 RM Bde.[6] Within a week most of the men from the 3rd RM Bn were redrafted to that Battalion. The Battalion HQ moved to Paisley (Scotland) on 17 May, and two months later was in Dalditch Camp. Here in July/August the Battalion lived under canvas until moving to Fishguard (Wales) on 20 August 1941. By 29 January 1942 they returned to Dalditch, their strength at time being 660.[7] From Dalditch they went on an amphibious exercise on Loch Fyne (Scotland) for four days in March 1942. Lt-Col C. N. S. Smith was appointed CO on 15 May, and Nos 1 and 2 Anti-Tank Btys and 31st Light Bty were attached for discipline while at Dalditch. The Battalion was to move to Hayling Island as beach engineers[8] but in June moved to Tenby (Dyfed) and on 2 December 1942 moved to Freshwater (Isle of Wight). The next move to Hursley (nr Winchester) was use on 7 April 1943 'to practise naval cooperation in a movement'.[9] The Battalion was re-formed as 47 RM Commando in August 1943.

11th RM Battalion (formerly Land Defence Force)

Formed as Land Defence Force of MNBDO (later MNBDO I) with cadres of all ranks at Fort Cumberland in February 1940,[10] CO Maj G. W. M. Grover. In March moved to Plymouth, in May to Hayling Island and in June – CO Col R. Sturges – deployed in defence of Deal (Sub-Area A6 of Home Command).[11] In accordance with RM Circe 5078/408, 13 June 1940, became 11th RM Bn. In September 20 machine-gunners joined the Battalion after training at Browndown.[12]

The Battalion embarked in early February 1941[13] and sailed for Egypt. (See MNBDO I history summary). In Egypt during the summer of 1941, the Battalion was often misused in doing fatigues for the Army, until August. In about this month the Battalion was attached to C-in-C Mediterranean's command 'to be used as required';[14] as MNBDO I was rebuilding after Crete, the unit was an independent Battalion for all practical purposes. On 15–16 April 1942 a 100 all ranks led by Lt-Col Unwin raided Kupho Nisis island near Crete. Although used 'mostly as a training raid',[15] the raiders successfully got ashore to destroy enemy installations (see chapter 4).

The Battalion's first major operation was a raid of 13–15 September on Tobruk (see chapter 4). Here it suffered heavy losses with Lt-Col Unwin and 17 officers, including the MO, and 200 other ranks missing after the raid. Subsequently a number were reported as prisoners-of-war, including QMS R. (Reg) W. Beasant, aged 47, though the majority were 20-year-olds.[16] After this action the Battalion was rebuilt and by January 1942 had a strength of 27 officers, 27 senior NCOs and 371 other ranks.[17]

The Battalion was in Ceylon and India in 1942–3 on various duties until it returned to the UK. It was disbanded in June 1944. (Elements reportedly remained in India until October 1944)

12th RM Battalion

Formed in the UK in 1941[18] as the Auxiliary Bn and later designated the 12th Battalion as the Land Defence Force of MNBDO II. Disbanded in the summer of 1942.

13th RM Battalion

Not formed in World War II

14th RM Battalion

Intended to replace the 8th Argylls in RM Division but not raised.

15th RM Bn and Machine Gun Companies

Early in 1940 plans were being made to provide

support units for the RM Division[19] and in May 1940 the first draft of 62 recruits left Exton for the MG Companies.[20] These were apparently to serve with each RM Battalion and in the Land Defence Forces (11th and 12th Bns). During December there was a reorganisation proposed, the MG Companies (except those with Land Defence Forces) forming the 15th RM MG Bn with an HQ formed in March 1941 at Hayling Island; the Battalion had an HQ Coy and Nos 1, 2, and 3 MG Coys. Further drafts did not join until October 1941 and in January and March 1942. In all over 430[21] recruits were drafted to the Battalion from the Depot for training in Wales.

In the summer of 1942 the Battalion moved to Dalditch for combined training with infantry battalions, the main party arriving on 3 July.[22] Later the Battalion was reorganised into three independent companies,[23] to serve with the Brigade Groups formed for possible operations in North Africa. Although the formation of a Support Battalion for each Brigade was suggested early in 1942, this was not accepted by the Chiefs of Staff.[24] But from December 1942 the Battalion CO was appointed adviser to the Divisional GOC on tactical handling of MG Coys.[24] Although the formation of a Support Battalion for each Brigade was again considered in 1942, this was not accepted by the Chiefs of Staff.[25] In August/September 1943 the Battalion was disbanded,[26] many of the men being posted to the gun crews of support landing craft.

16th and 17th RM Battalions

Not formed in World War II, as ordinals earmarked for Support Battalions of 102 and 103 RM Brigades (see RMOs).

18th RM (Mobile) Battalion and Mobile Companies

Formed in January 1940[1] as the Mobile Coy of the RM Brigade, to be under command of Brigade HQ for reconnaissance, and in June 1940 was in south Wales. The unit was expanded into several Mobile Companies to serve with each RM Battalion in the division. A Mobile Coy had a few tracked carriers and motorcycle combinations with an anti-tank rifle and/or Maxim guns to be replaced by Brens when these became available.[2] By December 1940 the companies had been formed into the 18th RM (Mobile) Battalion, and the ratio of carriers to motorcycles was to be reduced. In March 1941 the Army Reconnaissance Training Centre agreed to help with the training of Mobile Companies,[3] and on 2 May 1941 the Battalion came under command of 103 RM Bde for training.[4] The Battalion had

moved from south Wales, where it had been training in radio communications, to Dalditch in April 1941.

By early 1943 it was also equipped with Scout cars. After the RM Division was disbanded, there was apparently some possibility of employing the Battalion with other formations, but it was disbanded about August 1944.[5]

19th RM Battalion and RM Companies at Scapa Flow

When this Naval base was expanded in 1940, 'W' Company (MNBDO) of 211 Marines – mostly tradesmen, including National Servicemen – arrived on Hoy (9 March)[6] and were followed by 'D' Coy on 25 April. The companies had been known as the Labour Battalion but this was changed to Auxiliary Battalion in April and in September 1942 changed again to 19th RM Battalion.[7] By June 1940 five companies had been living in tents in Lyness (Hoy), and by October 1943 had completed much of the civil engineering work,[8] including: drainage at Hoy and Flotta; roads; canteens; Mill Bay Naval camp; the storage wharf with piers at Rinnigill; and a weather station for the RAF. In April 1940 they had also built, in only eight weeks, the seaplane slipway at Balta Sound in the Shetlands, and they helped to build and guard (from 1940 to 1942), the FAA base at Twatt. They also provided stevedores for unloading ships, with officers experienced in cargo handling, their men loading and discharging some 2,000 tons of stores and ammunition a week from 1940 to 1945.[9]

When the civil engineering work passed to RM Engineer units in autumn of 1942, 19th RM Battalion was reduced to three companies. The others were redeployed with 'X' company becoming No. 3 Coy of Landing and Maintenance Unit of MNBDO II with effect from 1 October 1942. 'W' Company became No. 2 Coy of the Landing and Maintenance Unit of MNBDO I in November 1942. In December 'Y' Company was reformed as RM Boom Defence Scaffolding Unit.[10] The companies at Scapa were then 'A' Coy of 122 all ranks for administration, 'B' Company of 235 all ranks for guards and escorts; and 'C' Coy of 128 stevedores with 12 transport drivers who also worked as stevedores.

The Battalion was formally disbanded on 15 July 1943, but certain personnel, including the stevedores presumably, were absorbed into the complement of HMS *Prosperine* the Scapa depot. But some contact was maintained with Fort Cumberland for administrative purposes, until the Scapa Base contracted in 1945.

20th (Training) Battalion, formerly RM Division Reinforcement Depot

Early in 1940 a Reinforcement Depot for the RM Division was formed at Sunshine Camp, Hayling Island,[11] to give reinforcements their boat and other training, including landing exercises, for which companies were sent to Scotland. The first Marines had joined the Depot in April 1940,[12] and on 16 January 1942 it was redesignated 20th RM Training Battalion, commanded by Lt-Col F. B. Pym. In June 1942, when the Sunshine Camp was taken over for LC crews' training, the Battalion moved to Dalditch under command of 104 RM (Training) Bde. The staff trained recruit companies here until late October 1942, when the Battalion was merged with 21st RM Holding Battalion to form the Infantry training Centre.

21st RM Holding Battalion

Formed early in 1942 to absorb men who could not be posted to operational units after training, this battalion provided camp staff for 20th RM Bn before they were merged in October 1942.[13]

22nd (Training) Battalion

Formed in November 1942, CO Lt-Col D. A. C. Shephard, when government prohibited men under 19 joining operational units. From these young trained Marines – 218 joined on 26 November 1942 – the Battalion trained its own junior NCOs and by the summer of 1943 there were several companies. In the summer of 1944 the Battalion moved to Towyn (north Wales), merging in October with the 23rd RM (Training) Bn to become part of RMTG Wales.

23rd RM Battalion

Formed in April 1943[14] at Dalditch as part of 104 RM Trg Bde, the battalion moved to Towyn in the summer of 1944, and it was merged[15] in October with 22nd RM Bn.

24th RM Battalion

HQ of this Battalion[16] was forming in late July 1943 in Ceylon and drew men mainly from MNBDO I, with a nucleus from 'R' Searchlight Bty, but the Battalion was never brought to full strength[17] before returning to the UK and was disbanded 15 May 1944.

25th RM Battalion

Was formed at Dalditch, CO Lt-Col T. W. B. Sandall and was disbanded on 24 August 1944.

26th RM Battalion

In the summer of 1944 the damage caused by German V1 'flying bombs' and by V2 rockets was considerable, many houses being damaged in London and its suburbs. The Admiralty was approached by the Ministry for Reconstruction, and to provide help with building repairs this 26th RM Battalion was raised at Lower Sydenham (London) in July 1944,[18] the battalion HQ opening on 10 July, CO Lt-Col R. E. S. Jeffries.

Organised in 15 Platoons (16 by 1 August[19]) of about 30 men each, the repair squads 'followed the bangs' and during the next few months patched-up 6,720 houses, made permanent repairs to 1,414 buildings and even built a few houses from their foundations. Three men had been killed by bombs before the Battalion was to be disbanded on 14 March 1944; but after the Ministry had asked for its continuance, 250 men were replaced by those in low medical categories.[20] The Battalion continued its building repair work, covering sites as far apart as Esher, Kew, Ilford and Orpington, until it was disbanded early in 1946.[21]

27th RM Battalion

The Battalion was one of several raised from cadres of former LC crews and recruits, as Beach Battalions for service in the Far East and on a war establishment appropriate to troops in a light division.[1] Formed at Dalditch on 24 August 1944,[2] CO Lt-Col P. W. O'H. Phibbs, the Battalion was trained in Scotland during December. On 4 January 1945[3] the Battalion came under command of 116 Infantry Bde RM for service as infantry and the war establishment was changed to that for an Army rifle battalion. Lt-Col N. H. Tailyour was appointed CO on 8 January 1945.

On 12 April the Battalion was detached from the Brigade, and under US Army command, prepared for the assault on Bremerhaven (Lower Saxony), but about the 26 April the Battalion was switched to the command of 4 Canadian Armoured Division for the assault on Wilhelmshaven further west (see chapter 7). Later 'A' Coy was detached to take the surrender of ships in Emden, 'B' Coy went to Sengwarden where it 'chaperoned' naval personnel in that former German HQ, and the Battalion Anti-Tank Platoon was billeted in Wilhelmshaven Dockyard. In taking the surrender of ships' crews, the Poles of *Conrad* (formerly HMS *Danae*) assisted the Marines.

The Battalion returned to the UK on 27–8 June[4] (see 116 RM Bde history summary), and provided parties that autumn to work on farms while based at Beacon Hill Camp (nr Falmouth).[5] On 27 November it moved to Chedworth (nr Cheltenham), before becoming a training battalion at Windrush Camp (west of Burford, Oxfordshire) early in 1946 and absorbing the 33rd RM Bn[6]. On 1 April the Battalion became the training cadre at the Infantry School RM, Bickleigh (RMRO 323).

28th RM Battalion

The Battalion HQ was forming at Dalditch in August 1944,[7] CO Lt-Col J. M. Fuller.[8] During the early winter the men who had served in the 1st Armoured Support Rgt were drafted to the Battalion.[9] They moved to Scotland on 8–9 December, where the Battalion trained as the nucleus for a Beach Group.[10] But on 4 January the Battalion came under command of 116 Infantry Bde RM and its original war establishment was changed to that for an Army battalion (see 116 RM Bde history summary). After service on the Maas the Battalion continued under army command (see chapter 7).

It returned to the UK in June 1945, and was stationed in August at Okehampton (Devon)[11] in the late summer of 1945. From here it took part in internal security duties, quelling riots in a Polish naval camp. It was later briefly stationed in Plymouth and St Germans (Cornwall), where it provided parties for farm work. In November it was in South Brent (Devon), there it absorbed men from the 30th RM Bn.[12] In rationalisation as demobilisation continued, the Battalion moved to Windrush Camp (see 27th RM Bn history summary) and was disbanded on 21 January 1946,[13] the men being transferred to 27th RM Bn.

9th RM Battalion

When the Armoured Support Group was disbanded after returning from France in 1944, many of its personnel were transferred to this Battalion which was formed on 3 October 1944 at Burma Camp in Llwyngwril (North Wales). On 1 March 1945 practically all its personnel were drafted to form the 34th Amphibian Assault Rgt RM.[14] However, the Battalion HQ was not disbanded until February 1946.[15]

30th RM Battalion

Formed at Dalditch on 15 January 1955,[16] CO Lt-Col T. K. Walker, mainly from former crews of LCs, the Battalion was under command of 116 RM Infantry Bde, and after a brief shakedown in Yorkshire went to France with the Brigade in late February 1945 (see 116 RM Bde history summary). The battalion HQ was disbanded at Topsham (nr Exeter) on 7 November 1945,[17] the personnel leaving Stoke Gabriel on 27 November for South Brent, where they merged with 28th RM Bn.

31st, 32nd and 33rd RM Battalions

These Battalions of 117 RM Bde were formed at Deal late in January 1945. The 33rd RM Bat-talion was flown to Germany to assist 116 RM Bde in accepting surrender of the German fleet, and had some casualties. The 31st and 32nd RM Battalions joined the 33rd in the second week of May 1945. They carried out security duties in the Kiel area until returning to the UK in July 1945, and the 31st and 32nd were disbanded shortly afterwards; the 33rd absorbed some men from the other Battalions before itself being disbanded at Towyn on 7 October 1945.

Other Infantry Units

60th Reinforcement Holding Unit:[18] formed in spring of 1945; mobilised (under Army command) at Aldershot in May before going to NW Europe. Reverted to RM command on return to UK 1 June 1945 and disbanded shortly afterwards. Some Royal Marines for this unit who were under training with the Army in UK that June, also reverted to RM command.

RM Base Defence Unit:[19] formerly 'Y' Company, formed in 1940 for ground defence of naval bases. (See also Boom Defence Scaffolding Unit.) *Plymouth-Argylls Battalion*:[20] formed in Singapore on 29 January 1942 with 'A' and 'B' from men of 2nd A & SH, 'C' Company of mainly Marines from *Prince of Wales*, and 'D' Company from *Repulse*. In action 8–15 February before Singapore troops ordered to cease fire (see chap 4).

Defence Force RN Air Stations: from 1940, and before then in the case of specific stations, RM units were formed to provide the ground defences of Naval air stations, and were organised in companies and platoons.[21]

COMMANDOS 1942–97

Special Service (SS)/Commando Group

Origin and titles:

Before 15 August 1943, when Commandos were not detached to field commands, they were under command of a single SS Brigade. SS Group under command of General Sturgess (GOC SS Group) was formed to take over this single Brigade's responsibilities with four new SS Brigades. The Group's HQ was opened on 15 August 1943, at the RM Division's HQ at Milford-on-Sea (nr Lymington), with the Divisional staff and some Army personnel forming the SS Group's Headquarters. In November 1944 the titles of this Group and its Brigades were changed from SS – which was associated in the public's mind with Nazi Storm Troops – to Commando, although some weeks passed before all the units overseas used these new titles (see RMRO 11 December 1944). In

August 1945 the suffix '(Light)' was added to these titles on the reorganisation of Army War Establishments.[1] The Group was commanded by General Wildman-Lushington (May 1945) and by 1946 by General Campbell Hardy.[2]

Examples of Orders of battle:

September 1943 – 1st SS Bde, 3 Special Service and 4 SS Brigades, Holding Operational Commando at Wrexham, 2nd Echelon (RM personnel) and 43 RM Cdo (other units which would form 2SS Bde were under army commands in the Middle East), 30th Assault Unit, Commando Basic Training Centre at Achnacarry, Commando Mountain Warfare Training Centre at St Ives, the RM Engineer Commando, Small Scale Raiding Force (COPPs, SBS, RMPBD, etc.) Field Provost and Administrative Sections.[3] The Field Security Section and the Postal Unit of the Division had been transferred to the Group.

April 1946 – Commando Training Unit RM, Commando Holding Unit RM, Commando basic Training Unit RM (for recruit), Commando Mountain Warfare Training Centre RM at St Ives, Commando Group 2nd Echelon, service Sections including Repair Section; and a nucleus for re-forming 41 RM or another Commando.

Locations etc:

After moving from Milford-on-Sea, the Group HQ had several bases in the London area, including Hatch End (Middlesex) in September 1943. In the summer of 1944 it was in Petworth (Sussex); on 15 March 1946 the Group's staff merged with HQ Training Group Wales to form a new HQ Commando Group HQ at Towyn, North Wales.[4]

Tactical HQ:

Commanded by the Group's Deputy Commander (an Army brigadier) and formed for planning with General Eisenhower's staff, this HQ landed in France on 7 June 1944, and remained in NW Europe until mid-1945.[5]

Administration in World War II:

The group's GOC kept in touch with his COs by visits and frequently by private correspondence.[6]

Disbandment:

When commando training moved from North Wales to Bickleigh (in RM's Plymouth Group) in 1947, the HQ was in Plymouth and closed on 8 August 1947.[7]

Commando Training Centres since 1947

The training of commandos continued at Bickleigh until 1954 under the staff of the Commando School and then under a cadre of 42 RM Commando except when this Commando was re-mobilised. In 1960 all commando training was concentrated at Lympstone (at one time known as Exton) in Devon. By 1969 it was part of the Training Group RM.[8] On 24 August 1970 Lympstone was redesignated the Commando Training Centre, its name in 1997 is CTC RM.

In 1997 the Centre ran 30-week courses for commando training. It trains some 60 officers each year in the Officers' Training Wing; about 400 NCOs pass each year through various courses in the NCOs Training Wing. The Infantry Support Wing trained officers and men as instructors in specialist equipment. About 500 students attended courses for signalers and clerks in the Signals and Clerks Training Wing.

In the 1990s CTC was a Brigadier's command with some 900 instructors and other staff. (For history of the CTC Barracks see RM Bases, Depots and Training Establishments.)

HQ Commando Forces RM

After world War II the Major General RM Plymouth commanded all Commandos in the UK when these units were not detached to Army or Navy commands. On 31 October 1969 Plymouth Group was redesignated Commando Forces; and when 3 Commando Bde returned to the UK, it came into this command. In 1980 the Bde HQ and all operational Commando Units formed part of Commando Forces. The HQ provided personnel for the HQ of the reinforced 3 Cdo Bde and for General Moore's Division in the Falklands operation 'Corporate'. It remained based in Plymouth during the late 1980s and early-1990s. In April/June 1991 deployed to Iraq for operation 'Haven'.

In March 1993 this Headquarters was closed and its functions taken over by personnel of HQRM as from 1 April 1993.

Miscellaneous

Memorable date for HQ Cdo Forces was 14 June recapture of the Falkland Islands (in 1982).

1st SS/Commando Brigade

General history:

Formed in November 1943, CO Army Brig the Lord Lovat, DSO, MC, with 3, 4, 6 Army and 45 RM Commandos, its ordinal '1st' signifying its association with officers and men from the Brigade of Guards who served in the 1st Cdo Brigade. Landed in Normandy and after 83 days was withdrawn to the UK from France. Although intended to move to the Far East, it returned to Europe in January 1945 with 3 (Army), 6 (Army), 45 RM Cdo and 46 RM Cdo Commandos under command. The Brigade was in action in penetrating the Siegfried line, crossing the rivers Rhine, Weser, Aller and Elbe. Early in May 1945 the Brigade was on the Baltic coast and later returned to the UK to be disbanded early in 1946.[9]

2 SS/Commando Brigade

General History:

Formed from the Commandos in Italy on 23 October 1943[10], CO army Brig T. B. L. Churchill with 2 (Army), 9 (Army), 40 RM and 43 RM Commandos. Units of this Brigade served in Italy, the Dalmatian Islands, Albania and Greece. The staff of its HQ provided a Brigade base at Molfetta (southern Italy) and Tactical HQs for operations with units detached to other formations. During the summer of 1944 they formed the garrison HQ on Vis with several thousand Allied troops to administer; the main HQ landed on Vis 5 March 1944 and returned to Italy on 13 August. It planned operations that autumn and sent a Tactical HQ to Albania.[11] In the spring of 1945 the HQ moved to Ravenna and elements worked with the Brigade's Commandos, which were all detached to Army commands during operations in April and May. Sailed for UK on 19 June. 43 RM Cdo absorbed into 40 RM Cdo as The RM Cdo of 2 Cdo Bde and 2 (Army) melded with 9 (Army) Cdo as The Army Commando of 2 Cdo Bde, disbanded in September.[12]

3 SS/Commando Brigade – see also sub-units 1981 etc

Origin and titles:

Formed 1 September 1943 at Dorchester with personnel of 102 RM Brigade HQ,[13] CO Brig Nonweiler until 26 November 1944, Brig Campbell Hardy December 1944 to October 1945. Title changes as for SS Group but by October 1946[14] the Commandos were all RM units, with some army personnel serving in the Brigade.

The Brigade passed to the operational command of C-in-C India on 23 November 1943[15] and remained overseas until 1971.

Examples of Orders of Battle:

In August 1943 the RM Office had expected 3 Commando Bde to include 42, 43 and 44 RM Cdos.

January 1945 – 1 (Army), 5(Army), 42 RM and 44 RM, Brigade Signals Troop, LAD Type A (for vehicle maintenance) with 'C' Squadron 19th Lancers of Indian Army.

January 1946 – combined 1/5 (Army) Commando, 42 RM Cdo and 44 RM Cdo, with some Army subunits attached.

October 1946 – 42 RM Cdo, 44 RM Cdo and 45 RM Cdo, with some Army subunits attached.

April 1961 – 40 RM Cdo and 45 RM Cdo with some Army subunits attached.

During the decades since 1961 various Commandos have been detached to other commands from time to time but when not detached: all RM Commandos were under the Brigade's command.

April 1982 – see appendix 2.

December 1997 – 40 Cdo RM, 42 Cdo RM, 45 Cdo RM, RM Stonehouse (barracks staff and instructors HQ Plymouth Garrison RM), 29 Cdo Rgt RA, 20 Cdo Bty RA, Cdo Logistic Rgt RM, 59 Independent Cdo Sqn RE, HQ & Signals Sqn RM, Patrol Troop and 539 Assault Sqn RM.

The Brigade became a part of the Rapid Reaction Force created in June 1995 as a reserve for possible operations in Yugoslavia. And in 1997 became a part of the UK Rapid Reaction Force.

HQ locations and principal operations of World War II and in 1946 & 1947:[16]

Canterbury (Kent) in late summer of 1943; 12 December, Egypt; 9–21 January 1944 at sea; February 1944 Poona (India); elements of this HQ remained in India; 17 March to 19 April at Maungdaw; early summer became Area Command Silchar (Surma Valley); 13 August arrived Ceylon (modern Sri Lanka); early October Teknaf; November Maungdaw; December Teknaf; January 1945 Myebon and Kangaw, Tactical HQ in Motor Launch, main HQ aboard HMIS *Narbada*; February Akyabb and later Myebon; 16 March sailed for Madras (India); spring in Poona and later Kharakvasa; 12 September arrived Hong Kong.[17] The internal security duties which the Brigade's units carried out in the next two years included: the prevention of smuggling and illegal exports; raiding opium dens; patrols against armed robbers; and other police duties.

Tactical HQ 1944:

February/March Cox's Bazaar and aboard LCH 261 for Alethangyaw operations.

Formation of RM Brigade:

In 1945–6 most long-service RMs were Naval gunnery rates, and 720 Marines (mostly 'HOs') were drafted to Hong Kong to replace Army commandos in the spring of 1946. Six RM Commandos were to be formed but this was cut by the end of 1946 to three in the Far East; 40 Commando RM (formerly '44'), 42 Commando RM and later joined by 45 commando RM.[18]

HQ locations and principal events 1946–80:

1946 to 17 May 1947 in Hong Kong; June

1947 to August 1949 in Malta (during these years elements of this HQ went to the Canal Zone (Egypt) from January to April 1948); August 1949 to 23 May 1950 Brigade reinforcing Honk Kong garrison; June 1950 to March 1952 in Malaya, taking responsibility for military operations with police from August 1950; March 1952 to May 1953 in Malta (on 29 November 1952 the Duke of Edinburgh presented colours to 40 RM, 42 RM and 45 RM); May 1953 to August 1954 in the Canal Zone, Egypt (some elements stayed until September 1954); August 1954 to April 1961 in Malta except for operational tours (Cyprus in September 1955 to August 1956, 'Suez' operation November 1956, Tripoli exercise April 1957 and other HQ exercises); April 1961 to 1971 based on Singapore with three tours by HQ in Sarawak (July 1963 to October 1963, April to January 1964, January to March 1965); by late 1971 established at Plymouth where this HQ continued to be based; deployed as HQ in Norway January to March 1979 and again in 1980.[19]

HQ locations and principal events 1981–97:

Based at Stonehouse Barracks, Plymouth and mobilised for the Falkland Islands operation 'Corporate' from 2 April 1982 when co-located with HQ Commando Forces RM, landed East Falkland 20 May, fought various successful actions (see Chapter 11) and returned to Plymouth after 11 July 1982. Deployed to northern Iraq for operation 'Haven' in April 1991 returning to Plymouth May/June 1991.

Miscellaneous:

The Brigade commander's pennant was navy blue with inverted red dagger.[20]

4 SS/Commando Brigade

General history:

In August 1943 the RM Office had expected 4 Commando Bde to include 45, 46 and 47 RM Cdos, but formed in UK September 1943, CO Brig B. W. Leicester with 10 (Inter-Allied) Cdo, 41 RM Cdo, 46 RM Cdo and 47 RM Cdo with HQ staff from 101 RM Bde. Raised 48 RM Commando on approval dated 1 February 1944. The Brigade HQ was in France and NW Europe from June 1944 until the winter of 1945.[1] While at Ostend in October its HQ was the planning authority for the Walcheren landings and at this time 46 RM Cdo was replaced by 4 (Army) Cdo. During the winter of 1944–5 this HQ had responsibilities from time to time for sectors of the Allied line in Holland but Commandos were sometimes detached to other commands, as when 41 RM Cdo and 48 RM Cdo were under command of

116 RM Brigade, the remainder of the Brigade under its HQ formed a mobile reserve of 41 RM Cdo, 46 RM Cdo and elements of 10(I-A) Cdo, located south-west of Rotterdam. On 22 April the last of its raids was made by units under command. In late May 1945 the Brigade moved to Minden (Germany), where it was reinforced by drafts from 1st Commando Brigade in preparation for service in the Far East, but returned to the UK and was disbanded in December 1945.[2]

40 RM Commando/40 Commando RM

Origin and titles:

Formed at Deal with 'A', 'B' and 'X' Companies in February 1942 as *The* RM Commando, it was briefly known as 'A' RM Commando (12–18 October 1942) before being designated 40 RM Commando.[3] In August 1945 retitled 40 RM Commando (Light) until personnel disbanded but 44 RM Cdo in Hong Kong was later redesignated 40 Commando RM. On the original formation in 1942 the personnel were mainly volunteers from RM battalions, with an officer and 80 men of 8th Argylls; a USMC officer and two other ranks in the summer of 1942 were the first of several American Marines to serve with 40 RM Cdo.[4]

Principal operations in World War II:

After training in Scotland and Portsmouth Dockyard preparatory to the proposed raid on Dieppe, operation 'Rutter', embarked twice for this raid before it was cancelled. When it was remounted as 'Jubilee' (see chapter 4), the Commando landed at Dieppe on 19 August. Returned to the Isle of Wight, where the Commando had been based since 28 June; in October trained in Weymouth before going to Irvine (Scotland) in January 1943 and two weeks at Achnacarry in April; reorganised into Troops before sailing for Sicily early in June after landing rehearsals on the Clyde. On 10 July landed at Cape Passaro; many of 'B' Troop killed on 1 August when the Commando was aboard an LSI as a floating reserve; 8 September spearheaded 231 Brigade's landing at St Venere, withstood counterattacks and advanced to Pizzo; 3 October landed Termoli (see chapter 7); 14 January to 21 February 1944 supported 56 (London) Division in crossing Garigliano river, later raiding behind enemy lines; 2–23 March patrolled and held sectors of Anzio Beachhead, making one major incursion with 9 (Army) Cdo into enemy defences. Landed Vis on 5 May; provided boarding parties and raided Komiza 23–4 May, Brac 3–4 June (see chapter 7), Mljet 6–

13 July. August/September in Malta, reinforced by seven officers and 160 other ranks; 21 September returned to Italy; 24 September landed in Albania to capture Sarande with 2 (Army) Cdo on 9 October; advanced elements in Corfu on 13 October to garrison and administer the island until 9 November; but 'A' and 'X' Troops remained till 1 January 1945; main body at Turi (nr Salerno) until returned to Corfu 9 January 1945 to 27 February. During 22–31 March held a sector of line south of Comacchio; 1–2 April operation 'Roast' at Comacchio (see chapter 7); 11–13 April operation 'Impact' to cross Menate Canal; 16 April, after casualties, formed into three Troops at Ravenna; guards for prison camps etc. until June when sailed for UK.[5]

Reorganisation:

On return to UK 40 RM Cdo was based at Basingstoke (Hampshire); as of 12 September 40 RM Cdo absorbed men of 43 RM Cdo and became The RM Cdo of 2 Commando Brigade. (On 24 September the Army Commando in 2 Cdo Brigade was formed by 2 and 9 (Army) Cdos at Alresford, nr Colchester.) The men of 40 RM Cdo were posted to Wrexham for demobilisation or to Towyn before the Commando disbanded, early in October 1945. It was re-formed in Hong Kong in the summer of 1947 by redesignating 44 RM Cdo as 40 Commando RM.

Operations 1945–80:

May 1948 in Haifa during the Arab-Israeli battles, and last unit to leave on 30 June; moved from Malta to Cyprus on 1 November 1948 with 3 Bde RM; August 1949 to May 1952 patrolled over 300 sq. miles of Malaya from the Thai border to Pangkor Island on west coast, mainly in Kedah and Perak, an officer and five other ranks killed in these actions. On 1 July 1952 in Malta; February 1953 to October 1954 in Canal Zone (Egypt) guarding installations and on desert exercises; based on Malta 1954–62 and deployed in Cyprus 1955 to 1958 against EOKA guerrillas; 'Suez' operation 6–14 November 1956; returned to Malta, exercises, operations in Cyprus till 1958 and spring of 1959. Based on Singapore May 1962 until October 1971 with tours in South East Asia – December 1962 to January 1963 in Brunei and Sarawak; April to July and October 1963 to February 1964 in Sarawak; July to December 1964 at Tawau; May 1965 in Johore; July to November 1965 in Serian; May to September 1966 in Simmangeang Barracks (Borneo) and elements in Brunei; later moved to various barracks in Singapore until 30 October 1971, with a tour of duty in Hong Kong in September 1970; based on Seaton Barracks (Plymouth) from late 1971. Spearhead battalion to Cyprus on 17 July to 16 September 1974; tours in Northern Ireland 14 June to 18 October 1972, 16 June to 16 October 1973, 16 August to 15 December 1976; from 5 March 1979 for four months; and during part of 1980 in Londonderry.[6]

Some operations and deployments 1981–97:

1982	Landed on East Falkland 20/21 May; provided the protection force for San Carlos area; two companies seconded on 11 June to 1st Bn Welsh Guards to replace the Welsh casualties and later advanced by helicopter to Sapper Hill 14 June; companies to West Falkland 15 June.
1983	move to Taunton (Norton Manor Camp); tour in South Armagh; last Commando landing from *Hermes* for exercise ashore in Turkey (October).
1984	Exercises in Egypt.
	With UNFICYP summer in Cyprus.
1986	February composite company to Brunei for exercise 'Curry Trail'.
	One Troop on raiding exercises from Gibraltar.
	Deployed to Belize.
1988	20 July returned from a successful tour of Northern Ireland based in South Armagh. Fifty Marines of A Company recalled from Christmas leave on 26 December and deployed at Lockerbie to search for wreckage from the PanAm aircraft which had exploded over the town. The search was so thorough that men found themselves searching almost inaccessible woods, thick pine forests and never forgetting to look up every five metres for pieces lodged in trees
1989	April deployed in exercise 'Dragon Hammer 89'
1991	Summer: a company provided an element of the multinational 'Rainbow Battalion' in Turkey, which was part of the air/land deterrent protecting the Kurds.
1992	May the A Company flew to Kuwait for cross-training with Kuwaitis whose weapons included Russian RPG-7 anti-tank rocket launchers, gave fire demonstrations of commando weapons and trained in the desert. Other Companies were in the Caribbean at this time

1993/4	and a Troop from A Company deployed to the Indian Ocean for exercise 'Orient 92'.
	the Commando served a tour in Northern Ireland based in West Belfast. Returned May 1994.
1994	October C Company Group on exercise 'Sandy Warrior'.
1995/6	Commando served a tour in East Tyrone, Northern Ireland
1996	Series of exercises and cross-training in South Africa during 'Ocean Wave' deployment, which took the Cdo to the Far East and a late summer on exercise 'Desert Song' in Jordan.
1997	autumn – provided the Lead Cdo Group/Spearhead for the JRDF.

Miscellaneous

Flag had pale blue background with navy blue centre segment carrying inverted red dagger.[7] Memorable dates: 3 October the landing at Termoli (in 1943); and 6 November the assault on Port Said (in 1956). Companies 'A', 'B' and 'C' in 1997.

41 RM Commando/41 Commando RM

Origin and titles:

Formed 10 October 1942 at Pembroke Dock (south Wales) from 8th Battalion RM; was briefly B RM Commando (12–28 October) before being designated 41 RM Commando,[8] which was disbanded at Llwyngwrill (north Wales) on 20 February 1946. Re-formed on 16 August 1950 at Bickleigh and Plymouth as 41 (Independent) Commando RM for service in Korea, and disbanded 22 February 1952 at Plymouth.[9] Re-formed on 31 March 1960 at Bickleigh as 41 Commando RM. Reduced to a Cadre from time to time. Disbanded at Deal in April 1981 when personnel were merged with other Commandos.

Principal operations in World War II:

After training in Scotland (7 April to 27 June 1943), the Commando sailed for Sicily, landing on 10 July (see chapter 5). On 9 September landed at Salerno to capture a defile (see chapter 5) and withdrawn after suffering 50 per cent casualties. On 19 September returned to UK. On 6 June 1944 landed to capture Lion-sur-Mer strongpoint; served with 4 SS Bde in Orne line and later breakout; 1 November landed north of 'gap' at Walcheren to capture Westkappelle. January 1945 at Bergen-op-Zoom (Holland) and during next few months served as line and reserve troops for time to time in Maas River area; 30 May to 26 November in Hesse (Germany) before returning to UK.

41 (Independent) Commando

Fought in Korean war, initial strength 219 all ranks, including five RN personnel. Landed Japan 5 September 1950 to join US Army Special Raiding Force. 12 September mounted raids near Inchon, west Korean coast (see chapter 8); in November came under command of 1 (US) Marine Division and took part in Chosin operations (see chapter 8), withdrawing to Hungnam by 8 December; strength raised to 300 during 1951; 7 April raided east a coast railway; occupied major islands in Wonsan Bay (east coast of Korea) and raided Korean coastal defences (see chapter 8). Returned to UK early in 1952 and disbanded in February at Bickleigh. Awarded US Presidential Citation.

Major deployments 1960–81

Re-formed 31 March 1960 as 41 Cdo RM. Based in UK 1960–3; 27 January to April 1964 as first Commando RM assigned to UK Strategic Reserve and deployed in Tanganyika and Kenya (February).[9] On return to the UK stationed at Bickleigh from 7 April 1964, and in the following years took part in several major exercises in Norway and the West Indies, between the following deployments: 18 April to 13 August 1969 in Mediterrean; 28 September to 10 November on peacekeeping duties in Northern Ireland; 3 September to 20 October 1971 based on Malta; visited USA in *Bulwark* May-June 1972 for exercise 'Rum Punch' with USMC; returned to Malta on 6 July until temporarily disbanded. The winter of 1974–5 was spent with UN Force in Cyprus; by April 1977 reduced to Salerno Company Group, which was Malta Garrison, leaving 30 March 1979. Meanwhile 41 Commando RM was re-formed at Deal in the autumn of 1977, where it was based until disbanded in 1981; served in Northern Ireland 27 February to 28 June 1978; winter 1978 on London duties; with UN Forces in Cyprus during winter of 1979; on peacekeeping duties in Northern Ireland early summer of 1980. Last trooping of the Commando's colour July 1981.

Miscellaneous:

Flag of old gold background and centre segment as for 40 Cdo RM.[10] Memorable date: 9 September, landing at Salerno (1943). Coys 'E', 'F', and 'G' in 1980.

42 RM Commando/42 Commando RM

Origin and titles:

Formed in August 1943 at Sway (nr Lymington) from 1st RM Bn, the Commando was redesignated: 42 RM Commando (Light) in August 1945[11], and 42 Commando RM early in 1946.

Principal operations in World War II:

After ship damaged 42 RM Cdo reached India by August 1944 and carried out jungle training at Belgaum with 1 (Army) Cdo; later trained at Combined Operations Training Centre (Indian east coast) in temperatures of 45C at times. October 1944 at Teknaf; November relieved a battalion of 74 (Indian) Bde at Maungdaw, patrolling aggressively into Japanese-held areas; December Teknaf; 12 January 1945 at Myebon; 19 January to early February at Kangaw (see chapter 7); early summer, exercise 'Lilliput' with Brigade at Kharakvasa (India); arrived Hong Kong about 11 September, where the Commando remained as part of the garrison after civilian administration restored in April 1946.

Principal deployments 1946–80:

1946 to June 1947 in Hong Kong; July 1947 to early 1948 based on Malta; May 1948 at Jerusalem, then Haifa, before evacuation on 27 June. While based in Malta, the Commando carried out exercises in Tripoli and Internal Security duties in the Canal Zone; returned to Hong Kong in August 1949; 1950–2 in Malaya based on Ipoh (Perak) for antiterrorist operations and later in southern Malaya; June 1953 returned to Malta. With Brigade in Canal Zone May 1953 to September 1954, when the Commando returned via Malta to Bickleigh to staff the Commando School from 4 October. The Commando remained here with exercises in Norway in 1955 and 1956, until the Com-

mando was reactivated on 1 August 1956. Landed in 'Suez' operation 6 November 1956 (see chapter 9), and remained after the Brigade withdrew, until 27 November, later returning to Bickleigh as training cadre and operational nucleus. (One Troop in Londonderry, Northern Ireland, for eight months in 1957).[12] Reactivated in summer of 1958 for Lebanon crisis and embarked for exercises in Libya; returned to Bickleigh and reduced again to a training cadre until 1959; reactivated for commando carrier force; embarked *Bulwark* March 1960 and after exercises in the Mediterranean began 11 years of service based on Singapore; 1 July 1961 landed Kuwait as defence force; December 1962 to Brunei at the time of the Indonesian confrontation, serving there till April 1963. In Sarawak July to October 1963 and February to June 1964; at Tawau December 1964 to May 1965; in Lundu area December 1965 to May 1966; at Aden 11 October to 29 November 1967 and retained until May at various periods in commando carriers; returned to Singapore until October 1971. Returned to UK in the summer of 1971 and spent eight periods of duty in Northern Ireland including: summer 1972, spring of 1973, summer 1974, winter 1975, spring of 1976, and July to November 1978. Also deployed in Norway on exercises in January to March or later, during 1979 and 1980. Company Group to New Hebrides from 13 June 1980 for two months.

Some Operations and deployments 1981–97:

1981	exercise 'Mainspring'.
1982	The only Cdo RM to go to Norway
1982	M Coy elements in recapture of South Georgia 24 April.
	Landed Falkland Islands 20/21 May; advanced by helicopter to Mt Kent and patrolled from the Mt Kent 31 May to 11 June; night attack on Mt Harriet was successful 11/12 June; flown forward to NE shoulder of Tumbledown and marched into Stanley 14 June.
1983	Exercises in Canada.
1984	tour in South Armagh, N Ireland
1985	M Coy in London ceremonies, November.
1986	exercise 'Westward Shift' with 42RM 'opposing' Dutch 1 ACG & Grp.
	Exercise with Spanish amphibious shipping
	London Public Duties 17 June to 15 July
	Exercises 'Sea Soldier' and 'Eternal Triangle'
1987	Recce Trp in N Ireland with Army units.
1988	Deployed in Norway during Spring, WD87.
1989	In Belfast during tour of N Ireland
	M Coy training at Fort Whiteroga.
1990/1	M Coy that winter was aboard the RFA *Sir Diligence* berthed in Dubai's port, the Company providing protection against terrorists attacks on this dock. By January some of the Coy were deployed in RFAs with GPMGs and 20mm Oerlikons. Later the Company provided port protection parties for Bahrein. When the Gulf War started there was a Troop at Dubai and one at Bahrein, for port protection. A third Troop was aboard *Sir Galahad* as a sea-borne quick reaction force.

1992	Tour in N Ireland
1995	In the summer L Coy carried out joint training in Romania with the Romanian 2nd Mountain Brigade in the Brasvo/Predeal region.(Exercise 'Eastern Climb').
	M Coy as Fleet Stand By Rifle Coy assisted civilians on Montserrat after volcano eruptions, helped in the aftermath of a hurricane on Anguilla in September.
	K Coy and elements of HQ in exercise 'French Phoenix' off the coast of South Wales, before gong to Brunei for exercise 'Curry Trail'.
1996	In America on exercise 'Purple Star'.
1997	Norway on WD97

Miscellaneous:

Flag of red St George cross on white cross over yellow ground, with white number '42' dissected by inverted dagger in the centre. This flag is based on a Lt-Col's colour in the Lord High Admiral's Rgt of 1664–89, adopted by 1st RM Bn as their unit flag in World War II.

The Commando raised a pipe band in 1943, which, with only a few breaks over the years, continues in 1997. Since 1968 one of these pipers has been appointed the Commandant General's piper.

Memorable dates: 31 January, the battle of Kangaw (in 1945); and 11/12 June the attack on Mount Harriet (in 1982). Coys 'K', 'L' and 'M'.

43 RM Commando/ 43 Commando RM

Origin and titles:

Formed on 1 August 1943 at Hursley (nr Winchester) from 2nd RM Bn and absorbed in 40 RM Cdo as of 12 September 1945. In 1961, when the Corps was reorganising its Commando Units, 43 Commando RM was reformed (5 September) at Plymouth and disbanded at Eastney in mid-November 1968.[13]

Principal operations in World War II:

After training in Scotland, the Commando joined 2 SS Bde, arriving in North Africa late in 1943; 23–4 January 1944 landed as flank force at Anzio against little opposition; 2 February with 9 (Army) Cdo attacked hill features after night infiltration north of Allied position on Garigliano River; 28 February landed on Vis, joining 2 SS Brigade's force on this island; 22–3 March raided Hvar with partisans; in May carried out unit recces on Uljan and Pasman islands with 9 (Army) Cdo and 43 RM Cdo; 22 May raid on Mljet with other units proved unsuccessful in steep hills; 2–4 June on Brac (see chapter 7); small recce patrol returned to Brac (20 June) but found no suitable positions for artillery to shell garrison; July, recce patrol on Hvar, ambushed Germans (12 July) and visited Korcula; artillery landed after patrols on Korcula and Peljesak Peninsula; 11 September returned to Brac to block possible German threats from the mainland when partisans took control of this island; 16–

18 September landed on Solta and drove garrison into a heavily defended enclave; 27 September sailed from Vis for Italy. From 28 October to 22 December 1944 part of 'Floyd Force' landed at Dubrovnik (at that time in Yugoslavia) as nucleus of force engaged in mountain warfare. After intense training in Italy the Commando took over a sector of the line south of Comacchio Spit for several periods in March 1945; 2 April operation 'Roast', Lake Comacchio (see chapter 7), where Cpl Tom Hunter was awarded a posthumous VC for actions on 3 April; the Commando reached a point short of the Valetta canal; and relieved on 4 April. On 16 April, after moving to Argenta area, the Commando advanced on the Quaderna canal, cutting the Argenta road; 17 April successfully stormed buildings in open country north of Argenta Road and held off strong counterattacks but withdrawn at daylight on 18 April; the next night again advanced to the buildings before moving westwards, clearing the banks of the Reno;[14] this was the Commando's last action, and in June it returned to the UK being absorbed into 40 Cdo RM on 12 September 1945.[15]

Re-formation in 1961:

For the six months after reforming in September, the Commando was training while it was built up to full establishment; 12 Marines from the Commando served as orderlies and guards on Prime Minister Macmillan's visit to Bermuda on 20 December 1961; 1–2 March 1962 reorganised from Troops to three rifle companies, a Support Coy and an HQ Coy.

Major deployments 1962–8:

October 1962 on exercise 'Donald Duck' in Norway; mid-1963 exercise on Normandy Coast; 6–13 September on exercise 'Bar Frost II' in Norway; 7 January 1964 placed in Strategic Reserve at 10 days' notice and organised for air lift, having trained to be air portable; 6 March embarked in *Bulwark* for North African exercise 'Sand Fly II' and subsequently training before being flow back to UK. In January 1965 took part in exercise 'Cold Winter' in Norway; 22 July presented with colours by the Duke of Edinburgh; November, helicopter landing exercise 'Gadfly II'; March 1966 used in exercise 'Morning Glory' to test command and control from HMS *Fearless*; 24 June embarked in *Bulwark* for 'Dry Fly' exercise at Inverary (Scotland); 28 February 1967 elements of the Commando to Nassau (Bahamas) for exercise 'Winter Sun'; spring of 1967 reorganised into special companies for demonstrations etc in recruiting: 'O' Coy in London ceremonies and display; 'P' Coy at Royal Tournament and street lining parties for ceremonial parades; and 'R' Coy providing youth activity teams. On 28 November 1967 to Melville (later Comacchio) Camp in Portsmouth; April 1968 recruiting companies reorganised as 'O' and 'P' prior to rundown during autumn.

Miscellaneous:

Flag with a red background and yellow segment carrying red dagger (cp: 40 RM Cdo).[16]
Memorable date: 2 April, the battle of Comacchio (in 1945)

Companies: 'O', 'P' and 'R' in 1968.

44 RM Commando/44 Commando RM

Origin and titles:

Formed 1 August 1943[17] at Ashurst, Hampshire, from 3rd RM Bn, the unfit and unsuitable members of the Battalion being drafted to other units. The Commando's title having been briefly 44 RM Commando (Light), was changed in 1946 to 44 Commando RM, and the following year, on 16 March 1947, it was redesignated 40 Commando RM, which had origins as the first RM Cdo, and which title the Corps wished to retain,[18] in perpetuating the titles of Commandos which had each served in a principal theatre of World War II.

Principal operations and deployments:

In training at Achnacarry in September 1943;[19] sailed for the Far East, arriving in India for training from December 1943 to February 1944; deployed in Burma from March 1944; 11–17 March made landings at Alethangyaw in rear of Japanese lines; March-April patrolling from Maungdaw; 9 April moved to Silchar (see 3 SS Bde history summary); 13 August at Trincomalee after transit via Bangalore, then to training with 3 Commando Brigade before landings at Myebon etc (see Chapter 7). In 1945 the Commando sailed for Hong Kong, landing on 11–12 September; they remained with the Brigade on garrison duties after the civil administration was restored in March 1946, and were renamed – see 40 Commando RM summary history.

Miscellaneous:

Early in 1946 they cut their crest in a 2ft deep outline 80ft by 54ft on the hill side at Fanling, facing the Chinese border with Hong Kong, but little of this earthwork remained in 1970.[20]
Memorable date: Kangaw 31 January (in 1945). No record of a unit flag has been traced. The companies were designated as: A Troop; B Tp; C Tp; D Tp; X tp; S Tp; and HQ Troop.

45 Commando/Commando RM

Origin and titles:

Formed during the first week of August 1943 from 5th RM Bn at Burley, Hampshire, with five Troops ('A' to 'E'), support Troop ('F') and HQ Troop ('H'), with 500 all ranks. After world War II the Commando was reorganised in the UK, redesignated 45 Commando RM in Hong Kong about March 1946 and continues.

Principal operations and deployments in World War II:

Landed 6 June 1944 in Normandy with 1 SS Bde; in Orne line (see chapter 6); 19 August night infiltration with 1 SS Bde to Angerville; returned to Bexhill (Sussex) after 83 days in France. Returned to Europe and on 23 January 1945 in action at Montforterbeek; March to April in river crossings of the Rhine, Weser, Aller and Elbe; reached Neustadt on Baltic on 2 May; stationed in Germany until June 1945, when Commando returned to Sussex.

Reorganisation:

The commando was reorganised in the autumn of 1945 and retained in preparation for service in the Far East.

Principal deployments 1946–50:

The Commando sailed for Hong Kong in January 1946; served on internal security duties in Hong Kong 1946–7. January 1947 Troops redesignated 'A', 'B', 'E', 'X' and 'Z' to come in line with other units in 3 Cdo Bde; May 1947 to December 1948 based on Malta, deploying to: Benghazi (Libya) March 1948; Haifa (modern Israel) in spring 1948; July last 'HOs' left; August training in Tripoli; January 1949 to Canal Zone catching 40 thieves, many stealing telephone cables; June/July at Aqaba, at that time Jordan's only port. Sailed from Suez for Hong Kong in August to reinforce the Honk Kong garrison for nine months.

Malaya emergency 1950–2:

The commando arrived in Malaya from Hong Kong in June 1950 for jungle training; July at Tapah in Perak to resettle Chinese squatters and conduct anti–terrorism patrols; August 1951 moved to Batu Gajah in Ipoh area, patrolling swamps; 31 March 1952 sailed for Malta.

Mediterranean 1953–9:

Carried out training while based on Malta and deployed from time to time. May 1953 in

Canal Zone protecting ammunition dumps and carrying out amphibious exercises in eastern Mediterranean; returned to Malta in August 1954; training exercises in North Africa; and deployed from Malta to Cyprus in September 1955. Operations against EOKA terrorists in Cyprus, initially at Kyrenia on north coast, then in Troodos mountains; February 1956 formed ski-Troop. Returned to Malta on 16 August, for 'Suez' operation. Landed Port Said on 6 November (see chapter 9), in first helicopter deployment in battle area; withdrawn to Malta in November. Deployed in 1956 to Tripoli for training; in Cyprus May to October 1957 on anti-terrorist patrols; the Commando returned to Malta but 'X' and 'Z' Troops formed 'Heliforce' in Cyprus during June 1958; training in Benghazi before returning to Cyprus from July to December. In 1959 trained in Malta.

Aden 1960–7:

The Commando's main body sailed from Malta and arrived in Aden on 4 April 1960; advanced elements had arrived in March and were in Dhala by 25 March, where the Commando over the next six years would from time to time patrol to the Yemeni border. From 1 to 19 July in Kuwait as part of the defence force. In August first deployed on internal security in Aden Colony; in October patrolling from Dhala. In September 1962 reorganised from five Troops to 'X', 'Y' and 'Z' Companies. Training continued in Aden with some exercises in Kenya (East Africa), when all companies were there for two weeks in 1963 on 'Winged Marine'. January/February 1964 in Tanganyika (central Africa) to aid local government quell a mutiny; March visited Mombasa (at that time in Kenya). First operations in the Radfan 30 April to 28 May, which was followed over the years by: second tour from 3 July to 6 August; third – 20 January to 4 March 1965 (mounted 305 night patrols); fourth – 20 April to May; fifth – 23 June to 28 July; sixth – 22 September to 26 October; seventh 15 December to 28 January 1966;

eighth – 14 April to 22 May; ninth – 14 September to 10 November; tenth and last from 6 February to June 1967. Between tours in the Radfan, the Commando was frequently deployed on internal security duties in Aden Colony. The last elements of the Commando left Aden on 29 November 1967.

United Kingdom 1967–80:

Based on Stonehouse Barracks after returning from Aden, the Commando served in the Strategic Reserve. In June 1968 it was the 'enemy' in Norway for the exercise 'Polar Express'. In October 1968 it exercised in Northern Ireland. In the spring of 1969 'X' coy was in the Bahamas, 'Y' Coy aboard *Fearless* in the Mediterranean and 'Z' Coy in Norway. 13 May 1969 HM the Queen Elizabeth II presented new colours to the Commando; in July 'Z' Coy deployed to the West Indies; September the Commando embarked in *Bulwark* for a month's deployment as part of NATO's southern flank forces in the Mediterranean. In 1970 commenced intensive snow warfare and mountain training, with 845 Naval Air Cdo Squadron and the four Sioux of an RM Cdo Flight. Spring 1971 850 all ranks moved to a new base in the old RNAS HMS *Condor* in Arbroath (Angus) as a Commando Group which in addition to 45 Cdo RM included: a battery of 29 Cdo Light Rgt RA; a Troop of 59th (Independent) Sqn RE; other support personnel; and an RM organisation for the base. The Commando was the first specialist Mountain and Arctic Warfare unit, although retaining general skills. There were tours in Northern Ireland: summer 1970; summer 1971 (when PO F. MacLaughlin was awarded the George Medal in June)[1]; winter 1971–2; autumn 1974; summer 1977; and August 1979.

1980 in September exercise 'Teamwork 80' which included 6-days ashore with the Brigade in various 'assaults' in the areas of Halsafjord and Vinjeford in Norway. Returned to the UK for moutain training in October in preparation for January 1981 exercises in Norway.

Some operations and deployments 1981–97:

1981   late-Summer in Belfast
1982   landed East Falkland 20/21 May; advanced during 30 and 31 May to Douglas Settlement over 30km from San Carlos with loads of some 50kg per man; successful night attack on Two Sisters mountain 11/12 June; advanced to Sapper Hill on 13/14 June joining the Welsh Guards who had been flown there.
1983   Support Trp on NBC exercise Porton Down
1986   Tour in Belfast, N Ireland.
1987   Contingent in Royal Tournament.
1990   North Norway exercises including the landing of 550 men and 35 vehicles in Tovik/Grov area.
        Tour of duty in South Armagh, N Ireland.

1991	In Northern Ireland on a roulement tour of six months]
1992	A team from the Commando took part in the Swiss Commando Raid Competition where they yomped about 30kms up a Swiss mountain within 3½ hours, a Dragon anti-tank shoot, a shoot with a Panzerfaust (equivalent to an LAW), and other firing exercises with Swiss weapons, a 3-minute swim across a fast flowing river, silence shots at two sentries before a house clearance and 'killing' its five occupants in under 30 seconds. This team achieved the highest score not only of any foreign team in that year's competition but the highest by a foreign team since the inception of the competition.
1993	Deployed to Belize for six months.
1994	Deployed to Kuwait in operation 'Driver'.
1995	Deployed as Fermanagh roulement battalion returning at the end of November.
1996	Provided Fleet Standby Rifle Coy from January.
1996	From October the Commando was Spearhead Battalion as part of JRDF into 1997.
1997	Provided Fleet Stand-By Rifle Troop with Marines in West Indies guard ship and RN ships off west Africa.

Miscellaneous:

Flag green ground with red letters '45' dissected by red inverted dagger.[2] Memorable dates: 23 January, the attack on Montforterbeek, near Linne, Holland (in 1945); and 11/12 June attack on Two Sisters (in 1982).

Coys 'X', 'Y' and 'Z' in 1997.

46 RM Commando

Origin and titles:

Formed at Dorchester, West Dorset, in August 1943 mainly from men of 9th RM Bn; its title was briefly 46 Commando RM before being disbanded on 31 January 1946.

Principal operations 1943–6:

Trained in Scotland with two weeks at Achnacarry (23 October to 9 November 1943); mobilisation completed on 24 January 1944, but intended night raiding role cancelled. Embarked 1 June with cliff-climbing and demolition equipment for destruction of Benerville Bty (or Houlgate Bty as alternative target) in Normandy, but unfavourable weather and the fact that neither battery was harassing shipping, led to operation being cancelled. Landed Berniers (Normandy) on 7 June (D+1) capturing strongpoint at Petit Enfer (see chapter 6) before occupying the town. 7/8 June patrols sent inland to La Deliverande, Douvres; 9 June occupied the village of Douvres and came under command of 3 Canadian Division; 11–12 June actions in Mue Valley (see chapter 6); 17 June rejoined 4 SS Bde in Orne line; 'S' Troop re-equipped with support weapons; 17 August patrols entered Troarn to find it deserted but heavily mined; 19 August with 47 RM Cdo attacked Dozule successfully after silent approach at night. On 25 August, having been brought forward in transport, the Commando was south of Beuzeville, the CO Lt-Col Campbell Hardy was wounded but continued in action while the road was cleared as well-camouflaged enemy defences were engaged in a fire-fight, as the Commando and a Para Bn advanced. After three hours the second-in-command, Maj John Lee, MC, and 10 others had been killed and 37 all ranks wounded before the commando was withdrawn. The Commando went into billets – the first in 12 weeks – on 26 August at St Maclou; 11–15 September guarded prisoners near Le Havre; 18 September in Bray Dunes area (Belgium) occupying former German defences investing Dunkirk; 7 October sailed for UK to join 1 SS Brigade. The Commando received 200 reinforcements and reorganised; sailed to Ostend (Belgium) on 15 January 1945 and detached from 1 SS Brigade for deployment to Antwerp. Took over a sector of line Heel to Beegden on the Mass on 2 February, with standing patrols out but little activity. On 12 February the Commando relieved 3 (Army) Commando at Linne, and after spending several weeks here and further west, the Commando trained for river crossings. It crossed the Rhine on 23 March, establishing a bridgehead, helping to clear Wesel next day; in April in actions crossing the Weser, Aller and on 29 April the Elbe. Arrived Neustadt (near Lubeck) on 5 May and returned to UK on 8 June. The Commando spent the summer of 1945 at Tunbridge Wells training for operations in the Far East, but the Commando's strength began to be run down from October.

Miscellaneous:

Memorable date: 11 June, the attack on Le Hamel and Rots (in 1944)

47 RM Commando

Origin and titles:

Formed on 1 August 1943[3] at Dorchester, West Dorset, mainly from 10th RM Battalion and disbanded at Haywards Heath, West Sussex, on 31 January 1946.

Principal operations 1943–6:

After training in Scotland a 32-strong detachment was provided for MTB operations from Lerwick (Shetland Islands), two raids were attempted: one successful in a landing in Norway; and the second aborted due to presence of enemy ships. 8 February 1944 to Herne Bay (Kent); landed Normandy 6 June and next day (D+1) prepared to assault Port-en-Bessin, captured the following day (see chapter 6); 12 June moved to Orne line; 18 June raiding force sent into forward German positions; 19 August crossed Dives River to attack Dozule with 41 RM Cdo; moved to Beuzeville area and on 26 August after night infiltration took Toutanville; 31 August, after brief rest, crossed Seine and on 2 September at Fécamp, closed the last enemy escape route from Le Havre; 18 September in line investing Dunkirk; during October at Wenduine carrying out amphibious exercises and joined by large draft of reinforcements. 1 November 1944 landed at Walcheren but only three of the Commando's amphibious tracked Weasels survived the landing; by D+1 (2 November) afternoon all Troop commanders were casualties but on the morning of D+3 the Commando captured W11 battery and cleared the dunes towards Flushing before returning to Weduine on 10/11 November. 25 November in training at Bergen-op-Zoom; 22 December joined mobile reserve for defensive duties along the Maas, patrolling in anticipation of German counter-attack towards Antwerp, but only enemy fighting patrols crossed the river; 13–14 January 1945 made attack on Kapelsches Veer Island, but, having forced a way into the defences, was withdrawn in face of strong opposition. The island was later captured by 10 Canadian Infantry Brigade. After returning to Bergen-op-Zoom, the Commando was deployed in defence of Walcheren; 12 March to North Beveland, raiding from there to German posts on Schouwen in the Schelt estuary; 7–8 May invested Schouwen. Moved to Germany and by January 1946 were only 100 strong at Minden; brought up to strength in August and had Army Troop under command with 130 army personnel serving in the Commando for a period; 31 August moved to Erkenschwick (Ruhr) to administer displaced persons; 28 November returned to UK shortly after moving to Warburg. (See ADM 202/431 for further details of operations.)

Miscellaneous:

Memorable date: 7 June capture of Port-en-Bessin (in 1944).

48 RM Commando

Origin and titles:

Formed[4] at Deal 2–13 March 1944 from 7th Bn and disbanded at Beeding, near Horsham, on 31 January 1946.[5]

Principal operations 1944–5:

Trained at Achnacarry 13 March to 3 April 1944; 6 June landed in Normandy and captured the strongpoint at Langrune-sur-Mer where the Commando remained on security duties after suffering 50 per cent casualties; 9 June reinforcements arrived, bringing strength to 250, before advance to Douvres for patrolling; 11 June in Orne line and next day advanced 1,000yds to Sallenelles where the Commando in a defence line for 60 days, although the number of patrols was limited so as not to interfere with other Commandos' patrols, since there were four Commandos on a 2,000yds front. On 20 August moved from Troarn, bypassing Dozule to advance in daylight to reach Clermont-en-Auge, attacked German field batteries etc before midday, and later secured high ground overlooking Dozule; 25 August outflanked enemy positions near Beuzeville which were mortaring 46 RM Cdo, and next night infiltrated behind this town to St Maclou with 41 RM Cdo; advanced across Seine to Valmont against no opposition; 5–13 September in Valmont for rest; policed Le Havre for next two days; 18–27 September held front of 10,000yds investing Dunkirk and patrolling. October trained for Walcheren operation; on 1 November landed on Walcheren, clearing south of the 'gap' (see chapter 7) and successfully assaulted W13 battery about 1600 hours; D+1 (2 November) captured strongpoint W288 at first light (0630 hours), 'A' Troop entering Zouteland at 1100 hours before 47 RM Cdo passed through; clearing dunes while other units gave support fire from north of the 'gap'; the Commando moved north to support 41 RM Cdo on D+4 (5 November) before being withdrawn on 12 November. After rest at Haan, moved to Goes (South Beveland) training reinforcements; three Troops, 'X', 'Y', and 'Z' under command of 47 RM Cdo as only infantry in Oosterhout area at the end of December. During March 1945 the Commando mounted five raids against Schowen and Overflakkee, the Commando suffering casualties on mines. On 25 March in defensive positions on the River Maas at Hertogenbosch, a road and rail centre 6,000yds from German positions; enemy artillery and patrols were active; in April on a quieter front of 35,000yds, as reserve to Belgians and Dutch near Kapelsches Veer; raided in dories into the Biesbosch, among marshes and waterlogged islands; 23 April last operation by this Commando to rescue a patrol in the Biesbosch without casualties before ceasing fire, except for defence. From 1 May to 31 August based at Minden (Germany) as defence force for the HQ of Allied Naval Commander Expeditionary Force (ANCXF); September to 21 October at Waltrop and near by controlling displaced persons (DPs). October to November 1945 the Commando on occupational duties at Kreis Buren looking after two camps of DPs, with patrols based on five burgomasters' offices; these patrols stopped 'black market' rackets, rapes and armed robberies; Marine officers organised camp improvements before returning to UK on 29 November and disbanded January 1946.[6]

Miscellaneous:

Memorable date: 6 June, the landing in Normandy (in 1944).

RM Engineer Commando

This unit[7] had developed from units in the RM Battalions which were trained in demolitions and as assault engineers. From 25 October 1943 the first War Establishment was: HQ; Holding Troop; and two fighting Troops (RM Circ 1303/43G dated 26 November 1943). By June 1944 there were 180 all ranks, forming a small HQ with a Training Troop (the Holding Troop?) and two fighting Troops. These were reorganised for the Normandy invasion with HQ and Training Troop in the UK, one Section with 1st SS Bde, one Section with 4 SS Bde, and six Landing Craft Obstruction Clearance Units.

Sections with Commando Brigades:

The Section with 1st SS Bde of 39 all ranks commanded by a lieutenant, landed in Normandy on 6 June 1944 at H+75 minutes to demolish bridges; but these were still in enemy hands and this Section prepared the defences of Brigade HQ; later they were employed in mine-clearing and building strongpoints. They also improvised bridges and fords ('wet bridges' lying below the surfaces of rivers), before returning to the UK on 9 September 1944. The Section with 4 SS Bde. The Section which joined 4 SS Bde arrived in France at the end of June 1944 and served in mine-clearing, demolition and other work of assault engineers. In November 1943 a third Section served in the Far East. This Section had joined 3 Commando Brigade in November 1943 and was increased to a Troop in the late summer of 1944. It built the 'roads' at Myebon (from 12 January 1945) and at Kangaw (from 19 January), under appalling conditions on both occasions.

Landing Craft Obstruction Clearance Units:

In the Normandy landings on 6 June 1944, Nos 7 and 8 were with Force S, Nos 9 and 10 with Force G, and 11 and 12 with Force J. They were all intended to clear paths through beach obstacles, but owing to the conditions of the tide and dangers from incoming craft the men were unable to use their shallow-water diving gear, but nevertheless cleared obstacles.

After World War II:

Royal Marine assault engineers served with various Commandos from time to time and continue to do so, but see also history summary of 59th Independent Cdo Sqn RE.

Commando Logistic Regiment RM

In the mid-1960s the permutations of subunits in Commando deployments, were expected to require a flexibility in logistic support which could not be provided from existing formations. After careful study the peacetime and war establishments of new units were determined, and between July 1971 and January 1972 subunits were brought together to form this Regiment. In operations the Regiment HQ became – and becomes – the HQ for the Brigade Maintenance Area (BMA), controlling the logistics to the Brigade's plan. Among its 400 all ranks in 1980 were army personnel from the RCT, REME, ROAC, RAPC, and personnel of the RN Commando Medical Squadron. The Medics did not provide staff for the sick-bays when in barracks, but were equipped to provide medical services in the field during operations (including those in Arctic areas). The Regiment's Transport Squadron was equipped to move supplies from the areas of a beachhead to the Brigade Maintenance Area and from there to distribution points for the units deployed. The Squadron could also transport personnel. The Ordnance Squadron held 'on wheels' (loaded in vehicles) two months' needs in spare parts and technical stores, including those for the Brigade's aircraft and motor transport. In addition men from this Squadron were responsible for stock control in the Maintenance Area and at distribution points, and they distributed the bulk fresh rations, ammunition, petrol, oil and lubricants. The Workshop Squadron's three Troops repaired vehicles, and electronic and other equipment, including instruments, and was equipped to recover light vehicles. All Squadrons continued to provide these services in 1997.

Deployments and changes in organisation 1981–1997

1981   training in Sillies.

1982   deployed to Falkland Islands in operation 'Corporate' setting BMA at Ajax Bay and later at Teal (see chapter 11).

1985   training in Wales.

Exercise 'Mainspring'.

Belfast tour in N Ireland.

1991   deployed in operation 'Haven' during April to August[?] when strength raised to over 800, but by mid-September returned to 'a more normal strength of 540 men'.

The configuration of the Regiment as originally laid down, had been modified in practice and was at this time brought up to date.

1993   By late 1993 the First Line Troop of Transport Squadron, the Servicing Bay and the LAD joined HQ Squadron, and the Medical Squadron moved to Coypool (Plymouth) where a new building housed the NAAFI and a purpose built galley for RM chefs who served the new mess rooms. The Workshop Squadron's hangar was renovated. During this year the Regiment put on many displays, with a section from the Ordnance Squadron, another from Transport Squadron and one from HQ plus some last minute additions, all climbing Jenny Cliff to show the Regiment's versatility.

1995   Exercise 'Rolling Deep' (where Rgt repaired CVR(T)s of the Household Cavalry).

26 Aug tasked with establishing an evacuation centre on Antigua for deployment of people evacuated from Montserrat.

Elements in Cyprus supporting 29 Cdo Regt RA.

On 26 October the CO formally took over the former RAF barracks at Chivenor (Devon) enabling the Regt to bring together its various units.

Elements deployed with 45 Commando to Kuwait in operation 'Driver'.

In November and December the Regiment moved to RM Barracks Chivenor.

1997   Winter deployment preparations for WD 98

Miscellaneous

Memorable date: 22 May landing at Ajax Bay (in 1982)

Commando Brigade Air Squadron

A light aircraft unit was formed by 42 Commando RM in 1965; this flight and others formed to support Commandos, were brought together to form the Commando Brigade Air Squadron on 12 August 1968.[8] In the early 1970s these flights were each equipped with three Sioux AH1 helicopters for which there were four pilots – an RM OC, an RA second-in-command, an RM sergeant and an RA sergeant. Each flight had two observer/gunners, a signaller and three drivers for its vehicles drawn from RM or RA personnel, and an REME team of six airframe fitters and other mechanics. The flights served with their respective Commandos in Northern Ireland and elsewhere, providing Nitesun illumination, forward air command and air OPs. They landed on darkened LPHs at night, and in October 1978, one flight relieved an Army Air Corps' flight in Belize (formerly British Honduras). Three flights served in Norway in 1979 with six Gazelles and six Scout helicopters.[9]

Deployments and changes in organisation 1981–1997

The Squadron provided flights in Northern Ireland from time to time in the 1980s and 1990s in support of army units on some occasions. They deployed with 3 Cdo bde to Norway. In 1982 they were deployed in operation 'Corporate' (see chapter 11). They also provided flights for operations in Belize from time to time, as in 1992 a typical year of their 1990s deployments: the A Flight, issued with new tropical flying suits, served five months in Belize as the roulement for 25 Flight of the Army Air Corps; their Gazelles were fitted with emergency flotation equipment, but weight restrictions meant that 'the optical aid was not fitted'. Much of the flying required extra concentration to identify landing sites in jungle clearings, when the duties were mainly involved with liaison work.

1991 deployed with 3 Cdo Brigade in northern Iraq flying resupply missions to locations not readily accessible by road and distributing vital humanitarian aid to Kurdish refugees.

1993 Pilots had additional training at Middle Wallop on part of a new syllabus for the Army Pilots, so that they could work in pairs as Aircraft Captains commanding a section of aircraft. In November Sgt Jack Frost won the Hughes Master Pilot's Trophy awarded annually to the pilot who obtained the best results in the Army Master Pilots'

Exam.[10] In 1994 the deployment in Norway only required part of the Squadron but a team also deployed to Kenya to support 3 Para in exercises. On 1 September 1995 the Squadron became a part of 847 Squadron in the Naval Air Command (see below).

Miscellaneous

Memorable date: 14 June recapture of Falkland Islands (in 1982)

Comacchio Company RM/Comacchio Group RM

The origins of this Group were a detachment of 45 Commando (3 NCOs and 13 Marines) stationed at Faslane, the submarine base. Their strength was raised to a Company on 1 May 1980 (as Comacchio Coy based at Arbroath) with 300 all ranks, this company provided detachments for the defence of Naval installations, for Britain's offshore assets in oil rigs and movement of nuclear missiles. The Company took on many of 43 RM's traditions including the red-and-old-gold lanyard. It was renamed Comacchio Group on 1 November 1983 with three rifle companies and an HQ company.

Three troops had continued to carry out security duties in support of the RN and the RAF throughout the 1980s. The Group – by this date reporting directly to CG – was reorganised in 1992 into three companies for roulement on the west coast of Scotland (see chapter 12) And in the early 1990s they were deployed annually for two weeks of training in Cyprus. In 1993 a company from the Group visited the USA for some USMC courses on fighting at close quarters and anti-terrorist activities. They continued to carry out security duties in the 1990s, and one Troop went to Belize in 1990 and one in 1992. Elements in exercise 'Malayan Warrior' during Jan-Feb 1993. In March 1998 elements were again in America with the USMC. The Group continued to be based at Arbroath but was expected to move to Faslane at some later date.

Miscellaneous

Memorable date: 2 April battle of Comacchio (in 1945) and was the memorable date of the disbanded 43 Commando RM.

29 Commando Regiment RA

Royal Artillery units' close association with the Commandos began in 1961 when 29th Field Regiment RA began to re-form as 29 Commando Light Regiment RA with four batteries (220 all ranks). The first battery in action, 145 (Maiwand) Bty, joined the Cdo Brigade and was in Borneo firing the 105-mm pack howitzer for the Battery's first shoot 'in anger' on 23 December 1962.[10] By 1965 the 95 Regiment RA of forward

observation teams had been reorganised for service with the Commandos, but after the economies of 1976 only one headquarters was retained. The batteries served in Malaya, Singapore, Brunei, Sarawak, Cyprus, Aden, Norway and from 1971 were on tours in Northern Ireland with Commandos.

On 1 April 1977 the first TAVR battery joined the Regiment, 289th Commando Battery. In 1978 the three gun batteries of 29 Cdo Regiment were each equipped with six 105-mm light guns, replacing the pack howitzer, and the TAVR battery was equipped with this light gun. The Commando Forward Observation Battery, 148th (Meiktila) Bty, provided parties to control air strikes and naval support fire, the men being trained parachutists and divers. All ranks of the Regiment wear the green beret on completing their commando training.

Deployments and changes in organisation 1981–1997

The Regiment deployed in 1982 to the Falkland Islands (see chapter 11). They trained with the Cdo Bde in various exercises including those in Norway and with Commando units in Belize from time to time. They were involved in other exercises including in 1990 a battle run with a rifle company and helicopters.

Batteries were detached for service in Yugoslavia on roulement tours in the late 1980s and 1990s.

7 (Sphinx) Commando Battery RA

Formed in 1748 as No. 1 Company Bombay Artillery for service in India and later in Egypt, where in 1801 their distinguished service was recognised in award of a cap badge with a Sphinx and the word 'Egypt'. However the Honour Title 'Sphinx' was not awarded to the Battery until 1926. The Battery served in several wars in the Far East during the 19th century and in WW I fought in Mesopotamia (1914–1916) with only 15 other ranks surviving. Reformed in India as 2/86 Heavy Bty RGA, returning to England after 1918. In WW II the battery fought in France in 1940, in North Africa (1942–1943) and Italy (1944–1945). It converted to the commando role in 1964, initially in support of 41 Cdo RM and in 1975 came under command of 45 Cdo RM when the battery replaced 145 (Maiwand) Battery in Arbroath. During service with 45 Cdo RM the Battery gained an expertise in mountain and arctic warfare and in 1982 served in operation 'Corporate' (see chapter 11). In the 1990s elements of the Battery have served in Bosnia, in Ireland and on other deployments with 3 Cdo Bde.

8 (Alma) Commando Battery RA

Raised at Woolwich in 1755 as Maitland's Company, it fought in America, India, in the Napoleonic Wars and the Crimea (1854) where they are said to have been given the nickname 'Black Eight', possibly because their guns were pulled by black horses. The Battery was re-designated 1 Battery 4 Brigade in 1859 and later became 12 Field Battery. They fought in several actions in the Far East and China before serving during WW II in North Africa and north-west Europe as 12/25 Field Battery. In 1947 the Battery was renumbered as 8 Field Battery RA and in 1954 received the Honour Title Alma. After service in Cyprus (1957–1960) and in Aden (1961) the Battery became a Commando Battery. Service in the 1970s included: three deployments in Ireland; and with the UN Force in Cyprus. In 1982 the Battery served in the Falklands (see chapter 11) and in recent years has deployed to Norway and elsewhere in support of 40 Cdo RM.

23 (Gibraltar) Cdo HQ Battery RA

Formed as Capt Strachey's Company in 1757 for service in America where it was in a number of key actions. It served in Gibraltar from 1779 to 1783 during the 180-day siege from which it was to gain the honour title 'Gibraltar'. The Company was renamed 4 Battery 1st brigade Northern ireland Division and based in the Far East from 1885 to 1912. The Battery served in various roles in modern times, but was disbanded for a period before serving as a Coastal Artillery Battery, an Anti-aircraft Battery, then as Guided Weapon Battery, a Missile Battery and later a Self-propelled gun Battery before 1993 when the title was passed to the Headquarters Battery 29 Cdo Rgt. RA.

79 (Kirkee) Commando Battery RA

Formed in 1797 as a unit – 6th Company of the Bombaby Foot Artillery – in the army of the Honourable East India Company. During the battle of Kirkee on 5 November 1817, the Company's 12-pdr guns played a significant part in defeating a large local army. By 1862 the Battery was part of the RA as the 31st Field Battery which served in France and Italy during World War I and in the 1930s again served in India. In WWII the Battery served in Egypt before being overrun by a Panzer force at Tobruk in 1942, when the Battery was virtually wiped out. After reforming in 1944 in England, it served in France and Germany. After 1945 the Battery became the 79 (Kirkee) Field Battery RA and served in Germany, England, Egypt and Cyprus before taking on its commando role in 1962 for service in Borneo, the Aden theatre and Cyprus. In the alte-

1960s the Battery was based on the Far East until joining 41 Cdo Grp in Malta from 1971 to 1974 until it returned to the Citadel in Plymouth. From there it completed two hours in Northern Ireland, a UN tour in Cyprus with 41 Cdo RM, in Belize (1980) and several annual deployments in Norway. It went to the Falklands in 1982 (see chapter 11) and has served with 3 Commando Brigade on various deployments in the 1990s.

148th (Meiktila) Commando Forward Observation Battery RA

Originally raised in 1942 as S Company 2nd Battalion Bengal Artillery in India, became part of the Field Artillery in 1861 and in 1900 became 59 Battery Royal Field Artillery. Served in India and England from 1919 to 1939, gained battle honours in France in 1940 and returned to England that May. Fought in Assam, Manipur and Burma from 1944 to 1945, supporting defence of Meiktila (Burma). From 1946 to 1960 was a training battery and in 1960 converted to the commando role, with operational tours in Malaya (1963–1966), Borneo (1963–1966) and Aden 1960–1967. Served with the Commando Brigade in the Far East until 1971 when the Battery moved to Poole (Dorset) and became the Forward Observation Battery with the Commando Brigade (see chapter 11). By the 1990s there were seven Naval Gunfire Observation teams in the Battery, each with an officer and four men. Elements of the Battery served in operations *Granby*, *Haven* and other deployments in support of the Commando Brigade.

20 Commando Battery RA [an Independent Battery]

This Battery was formed after trials of Rapier missiles for air defence, to support 3 Cdo Bde, and based at Kirton-in-Lindsey [Suffolk?]. Before 1985 a series of trials with Rapiers in Norway led by 1985 to the formation of a cadre which by 1987 (Lt, WO + 3 × Sgts) trained RA gunners for mountain warfare and to work Rapier FSB1. Capt M. G. Flanagan (previously RSM of 29 Cdo Rgt RA) joined Cadre as Project Officer and the Cadre became C Troop, deployed in WD89 with 3 × FSB1 fire units. These gunner officers and NCOs passed the Cdo course but not entitled to wear Green Berets officially. Bty Cmdr appointed in Sept 1989 some months before official formation of the Bty in Apr 1990 as 20 Cdo Bty RA and armed with 24 Javelins as interim measure, as the FSB1s did not work satisfactorily in mountains and cold. In the Spring of 1997 training with Rapier FSB2 but maintained full capacity of 24 × Javelins. To have 10 × FSB2 (an area Short Range Air Defence (SHORAD) system. 24 hour all weather capability with engagement range of 7.2 km.

The Battery used Air Defence Command Control and Information Systems (ALES) which automated the rapid passage of weapon control instructions from an Army Corps level to individual fire units. By 1998 the systems was to be carried in BV206s. These were expected to have two Autonomous Link Eleven Systems (ALES) which would receive and display tactical information from NATO Link 11 in AWACS aircraft, providing warning of aircraft at ranges of over 750km. ALES would also provide additional information such as IFF (identifying friend from foe), speed, heading and position of aircraft. The Air Defence Troop (RM) came under command of 20 Cdo Bty as did the Dutch Air Defence Trp (RNLMC AD TP). The AD Troop was expected to be fully converted to Rapier FSB2 by March 1998, a system which may be replaced in AD 2013 by another SHORAD System.

59th Independent Commando Squadron RE

Formed as a Field Company in 1900, the Squadron served in both World Wars; and became closely associated with 3 Cdo Brigade when stationed in Singapore between 1968 and 1971. Reformed at Plymouth in April 1971 as 59th Independent Commando Squadron, as an integral part of Commando Forces, these engineers were mainly employed in mountain and Arctic warfare. They built bridges, ferried troops, lay and/or cleared minefields, as well as other defences. They could build sophisticated field defences, carry out demolitions, and had a number of general tradesmen among the eight officers and 221 soldiers in the Squadron in 1979. All ranks of the Squadron wear the green beret on completing their commando training. In November 1998 there were the following Troops in the Squadron: 1 × HQ Troop; 3 × Field Trps; 1 × Support Trp; 1 × Reece Trp; and 1 × Workshop Trp.

Other Commando and Special Service Units

SS Platoon:[11]

Formed in Singapore on 24 December 1941 this Platoon raided behind Japanese lines (see chapter 4).

30th Assault Unit:[12]

An intelligence unit had existed since the late summer of 1941 as the special Engineering 30 Commando, included in this unit were RN and RM personnel as well as army troops. In operations in North Africa one Section under an RN lieutenant landed from HMS *Broke* when

she crashed the boom at Algiers. The Commando operated in Sicily and Italy, recovering codes and other documents from German headquarters. In February the Unit was reformed as a Naval intelligence-gathering Commando (wearing green berets and commando flashes). The former CO of 5th RM Battalion recruited many RM guards for Naval specialists in this 30th Assault Unit which was under the command of the Director of Naval Intelligence. The personnel were trained as parachutists, and in such offbeat skills as safe blowing. They were also trained in security duties and street fighting. The Unit was organised in Troops, with 'one' Troop landing in Normandy on 6 June 1944, followed by 'A' and 'B' Troops on 10 June.

During the next ten months these Troops operated close to or ahead of the Allied advanced positions, and by March 1945 'A' Troop was moving towards Leipzig (in eastern Germany), 'B' Troop towards Hamburg and 'X' Troop to Keil, areas they all reached as German resistance crumbled. In April teams were finding minefield charts, ciphers, data on naval technical developments and other intelligence in German HQs. The Unit's HQ had moved close behind the Allied line of advance and was in Minden by May. In June the RM elements returned to the UK and were disbanded.

RM Boom Patrol Detachment:

Formed[13] on 6 July 1942 at Southsea, Hampshire, the Detachment trained in canoes, in long-distance swimming and shallow-water diving.[14] It mounted a raid on shipping in Bordeaux in December 1942 (see chapter 4). A unit went to the Mediterranean and mounted raids in 1943–4 (see chapter 7). The Detachment did development work on air-launched explosive motorboats but these were not used operationally. The personnel were later absorbed into the RM Special Boat Sections.

Small Operations Group:[15]

Formed on 12 June 1944 to co-ordinate small scale raiding parties in South East Asia Command, the Group was based in Ceylon (modern Sri Lanka) with an RM base staff by 1945. Under command were four COPPs, three SBS Groups and four Sea Reconnaissance Sections, all with Army and Naval personnel and RM Detachment 385. Units of the Group had carried out 174 operations by June 1945 and several after this date. The Group was disbanded in the autumn of 1945.

RM Detachment 385:[16]

Formed April-May 1944 at Havant, Hampshire, from volunteers, many of whom had served with MNBDO I and MNBDO II. Seven officers flew to Ceylon (modern Sri Lanka) for instruction from Lt-Col H. G. Hasler and were later to train the main body (112 all ranks) after their arrival in Ceylon on 7 July 1944. Between August 1944 and February 1945 the Detachment completed training. Operations were mounted for reconnaissance, deception and to land clandestine forces in Burma, Malaya, Thailand, and the Nicobar Islands between late February and mid-August 1945, in all 16 operations, some of which comprised more than one raiding party. After World War II some personnel were absorbed into the SBS when this Detachment was disbanded.

Special Boat Section:[17]

Army commandos had been using Folbot canoes since early in 1941 and Special Boat Sections of canoeists were formed. These carried out a number of recces and demolition raids in Europe and the Mediterranean. They were also used to collect agents, deliver clandestine stores and for beach reconnaissance in World War II. By July 1944 the SBS had been formed into 'A', 'B' and 'C' Groups under command of the Small Operations Group. After World War II the SBS became an RM unit, and although political factors have limited their use in peacetime, they are available as the Special Boat Squadron for beach surveys and similar work when required. The Squadron had three operational Sections of selected volunteers in the 1970s and continues.

SBS teams were deployed in the Falkland Islands from 1 May 1982 in operation 'Corporate' (see chap 11). In 1991 they made two raids into Iraq (see chap 13). At other times in the 1980s and 1990s they continued their secretive work but by 1997 their operational command was joined to that of the SAS.

Raiding Squadrons RM

After World War II an RM flotilla of LCP(L)s was based at Plymouth for training commandos in landings at the base of cliffs. They carried out much of their training at St Ives (Cornwall). A larger raiding craft was introduced in the early 1950s. This flotilla did not carry out any operations.

Experimental work in Malta with an inflatable rubber craft (IRC) during the 1950s led to the adoption of the Gemini for seaborne raiding. This craft was based on designs of the French Zodiac. In July 1967 No.1 Raiding Squadron RM was formed at Poole (Dorset) initially with 12 all ranks, to take over the training and operational commitments of 3 Cdo Brigade for raids. A second Squadron was formed on 2 December 1968 under the command of 45 Cdo RM but was disbanded after some months. In 1978 the RMR formed the 2nd Raiding Squadron, which continued in 1980. That year there was also a third Squadron, the 3rd Squadron RM in Hong Kong.

The 1st Raiding Squadron landed men from their rigid-raiders or from inflatables (launched from submarines on occasions). Sections were deployed with individual Commandos in many of the operations noted in the Commandos' histories. Typically in 1979 their exercises included: the Arctic Section's visit to Norway from January to March; a detachment in Holland (June); another in Scotland (September to October); and throughout the year the Squadron provided training facilities for other units

Raiding Squadrons 1981 to 1997

Since before 1981 1st Raiding Squadron had been attached to the Cdo Brigade's HQ & Sigs Sqn. It deployed to the Falkland Islands in 1982 (see chapter 11). And was deployed on exercises in Norway and elsewhere. In April 1994 it came under the command of 539 Assault Sqn.

A 'new' 2nd Raiding Squadron was an RMR unit formed in 1978 (see above). In a typical exercise it was in the Mediterrean in 1992.

3rd Raiding Sqn formed for service in Hong Kong in 1978 (see above). 1 July 1988 ceased operations against illegal immigrants in Honk Kong, but some personnel remained in the Hong Kong for service with patrol boats.

Miscellaneous

Regarded as part of the Assault Squadrons, the Raiding Squadrons had the 6 June (Normandy 1944) as their memorable date.

OTHER SUB-UNITS OF 3 CDO BRIGADE RM 1981–97

Commando Brigade HQ & Signals Squadron

The Squadron had more rough and tumble about its activities than might normally be associated with staff work. Typically in 'Event 80' there was a competition between teams (1 officer, 1 NCO, 1 JNCO + 3 Mnes) from each troop or department in HQ & Sigs Sqn with 5 stages: gym test; orienteering; whaler racing; run with casualty to cross water; and pulling a 4-ton truck.

1982 Deployed with 3 Cdo Bde to Falkland Islands and in other years with the Brigade on Winter Deployments and on operation 'Haven'.

Miscellaneous

Memorable date: 21 May landing at San Carlos Water)in 1982)

Communications Troop

Under command of HQ & Signals Sqn, this Troop operated the main Net for the Brigade's radio communications, and by 1997 also had satellite communications with the Permanent Joint Headquarters of the Rapid Reaction Force.

Tactical Air Control Parties

These were deployed with HQ & Sigs Sqn or independently as TACP 605, 608 (RMR) and 611. They served at various times in Belize, in Norway on Winter Deployments, in operations 'Corporate' and 'Haven'. Each TACP had an officer and two driver/radio operators.

Air Defence Troop

This Troop was part of HQ and Signals Squadron RM although came to be regarded as an independent asset of the Brigade, until late in 1994 when it came – and remains – under command of 20 Cdo Bty RA. It normally deployed with the Squadron and subsequently with 20 Cdo Bty. But had also been deployed independently.

Some examples of deployments

1982	served in operation 'Corporate' summer of 1982.
1988	Detached for operations in support of the Fleet.
1991	Service in operation 'Heaven' during the Spring and annual firing practice in September on the missile range at Tenby (Dyfed) firing the allotted 16 Javelin missiles. Other live firing practice at Tenby included live firing GPMGs from vehicles and other weapons in air defence shoots while wearing full NBC kit for some exercises.
1994	By 1994 – if not before then – the Troop was regarded as a Brigade asset which could operate anywhere in which there was an air threat. In based in an old WW II camp on the Essequibo River in Guyana for jungle training and live firing, then visits to Trinada, Puerto Rico (more live firing) and on to Tortola in the British Virgin Islands followed by five days R & R in Bermuda. In October deployed to Kuwait with 45 Cdo RM when the Troop's demonstrations of their Javelin missiles is said to have boosted British armament sales.
1995	In Norway from first week in January attached to 20 Cdo Bty RA.
1997	Equipped with shoulder-launched Javelin S15 missiles for local air defence.

RM Police Troop

This Troop was part of HQ and Signals Squadron and normally deployed with the Squadron, but from time to time men were detached for special duties with other units. On Brigade operations the RM police provided the Brigadier's bodyguard, co-ordinated vehicle movements, sign posting routes into and out of beachheads and other combat areas.

1988 Detachment assisting with security at HM Prison Alma, Dettingen.

Y Troop of Brigade HQ & Signals Squadron

Equipment with Electronic Warfare devices to interception and monitor an enemy's signals traffic.

Brigade Patrol Troop of HQ & Signals Squadron

This Troop was to take over the M&AW Cadre's functions. It began a year long trial in July 1992. This proved successful and in the summer of 1993 the Patrol Troop was set up with a Recce Troop, the ML Cadre and an Admin section under a small HQ (OC Bde Patrol Tp + 3). The Recce Tp was commanded by a Lt Mountain Leader who had an HQ of 4 men. There were four Sections each commanded by a SNCO with two ML Cpls and three GD Marines. See G & L 1994 p 77 for full details. The Cadre continued to run courses in mountain climbing and cold weather warfare. The Recce Troop deployed to Switzerland in June 1993 for exercise *Ice Flip*. In January 1994 the whole Patrol Troop deployed to Norway. During this six weeks of training the Recce Troop made eight parachute jumps. The Cadre continued that year for a further three week in Norway. The Recce Troop by 1997 reportedly had six 4-man teams providing medium range reconnaissance for the Cdo Brigade.

Amphibious Units

539 Assault Squadron

Formed as organic unit in 3 Cdo Bde on 1 April 1984 at the Royal William Yard in Plymouth (See chapter 12). The Squadron had an Amphibious Beach Unit (ABU) with a Beach Armoured Recovery Vehicle (BARV) and the ability to lay beach trackway with a specially adapted vehicle.

1988/89	Trials with Slingsby hovercraft.
1989	Squadron reviewed in their craft, when the salute was taken by Maj Gen N. F. Vaux CB,

	DSO at Plymouth and he presented them with a new ceremonial pennant.
1989/	After pre-winter training in Snowdonia mountains and craft training at ATTURM,
1990	deployed in Norway in January (later than usual) when the Squadron carried out various training exercises including trials with a new RRC replacement.
1990	LCs off Libya for evacuation if required. Hovercraft trials.
1991	Caribbean training.
1991	Exercise 'Final Nail' landed YO's and their 'enemy' from the Royal Scots on the beaches of Skye (Inner Hebrides) and experienced Force 10 gale which brought the exercise to an abrupt end. It became Force 12 as the LSL *Sir Belvedere* sailed back to Plymouth with 539 Sqn aboard.
1993	In June moved to a custom built base on the banks of the Plym River on the site of the old Turnchappel Wharf. This had 1,000mFD of hard standing, 150m of jetty, 900m of concrete slipway and a careening grid. The workshops and offices were housed in nearby buildings including five of stone and built in the early 19th century by French Prisoners of war. These and other services provided all that the Squadron required to be operational.
1994	By March the Squadron had four hovercraft and the first RRC Mk2s.
1995	The advance party for the winter deployment to Norway in 1995 arrived at Harstad soon after Christmas on the Squadron's 10th deployment to Norway, making recces of sites for various courses. The main body arrived and the new comers completed the Novice Ski and Survival Course, others completed the Winter Warfare Course (Infantry). LCU C2 fouled her kedge on an underwater electric cable, requiring the aid of the Norwegian Coast Guard Service to extract the 'hook' in a sudden storm.
1996	Exercise 'Purple Star' in America and by the winter several craft had major refits.
1997	The Squadron had: LCUs capable of carrying a battle tank or 100 Marines and their equipment; LCVPs which were each able to carry a Land Rover plus a Light Gun (105-mm) or 30 fully equipped Marines; IRC to carry six Marines; RRC to carry 8 Marines; and four LCAC which were hovercraft each able to carry 64 Marines.

Miscellaneous

Memorable dates: 6 June landings in Normandy (in 1944) and 21 May landings in San Carlos Water (in 1982)

AMPHIBIOUS UNITS NOT UNDER DIRECT COMMAND OF BRIGADE

1 Assault Squadron RM

This Squadron was the last of the Assault Squadrons to serve in HMS *Anzio* which paid-off in the early 1970s.

2 Assault Squadron RM

This Squadron normally served in one of the LPDs manning her Landing Craft and when she was under dockyard overhauls these crews assisted with training at RM Poole. The Squadron had an Amphibious Beach Unit (ABU) with a Beach Armoured Recovery Vehicle (BARV) and the ability to lay beach trackway with a specially adapted vehicle.

3 Assault Squadron RM

Served in Hong Kong in the 1950s.

4 Assault Squadron RM

This Squadron normally served in an LPD manning her Landing Craft and when she was under dockyard overhauls, these crews assisted with training at RM Poole. The Squadron had an Amphibious Beach Unit (ABU) with a Beach Armoured Recovery Vehicle (BARV) and the ability to lay beach trackway with a specially adapted vehicle.

1990	Re-embark in HMS *Fearless*
1991	In *Fearless* to Sevastopol 6 October 1991 in first visit to a Soviet Block port for 50 years.
1992	In *Fearless* on exercise with French Assault Ship
1994	In exercises 'Tartan Surprise' and 'Royal Dawn' in Scotland and April/May that year in exercises 'Resolute Response' and 'Dynamic Impact'
1995	with *Hermes* in America on exercise 'Purple Star'
	Caribbean training
1997	Embarked in HMS *Fearless*.

6 Assault Squadron RM

This Squadron normally served in an LPD manning her Landing Craft and when she was under dockyard overhauls, these crews assisted with training at RM Poole. The Squadron had an Amphibious Beach Unit (ABU) with a Beach Armoured Recovery Vehicle (BARV) and the ability to lay beach trackway with a specially adapted vehicle.

1981–89	aboard HMS *Intrepid* at times when she was exercising or deployed – as in 'Corporate' 1982 – in amphibious roles.
1990	in HMS *Intrepid*'s winter deployment from early January when some men undertook the Novice Ski and Survival Course with '' and then a Winter Warfare Course at Krakenes, Harstad. These were followed by NBC trials controlled by scientist from Porton Down. In February landed 45 Commando Group in the Tovik/Grov area. LCVPs operated from an FOB. Later that month landed 1 ACG and all its vehicles in less than 1½ hours. Remained in *Intrepid* until she returned to Portsmouth in October and Squadron retuned to RM Poole. Disbanded 21 December 1990.

9 Assault Squadron RM

The Squadron was at Poole in the summer of 1997 and due to embark in HMS *Ocean* in March 1998. Their craft was to included four LCVP(5)s.

Miscellaneous

Memorable dates for operational Landing Craft Squadrons: 6 June landings in Normandy (in 1944) and 21 May landings in San Carlos Water (in 1982).

Memorable dates

These were revised in 1987 when citations for Unit memorable dates were first published. Units first formed in World War II and still in existence were given two memorable dates: one for their World War II achievements and one for achievements since 1945. In addition to Unit dates the Corps has several memorable dates: 23 April the raid on Zeebrugge (in 1918); 28 April Gallipoli (in 1915); 6 June Normandy landings (in 1944) which is also the memorable date for some units; 14 June recapture of Falkland Islands (in 1982) which is also the memorable date for some Units; 17 June battle of Bunker Hill (in 1775); 24 July capture of Gibraltar (in 1704); 21 October battle of Trafalgar (in 1805); 28 October birth of the Corps (in 1664); and 1 November assault on Walcheren (in 1944).

RN Commando Squadrons

845 and 846 Squadrons

Squadron 845 was flying helicopters in the 1970s and in 1991 846 flew helicopters in operation 'Haven'. The two Squadrons each flew 10 Seaking support helicopters in 1997, which were flown by RN crews.

847 Squadron RN

First formed in 1943 as a squadron of helicopters and absorbed in 810 Squadron on 30 June 1944. Reformed in the following periods: 1956–59; May 1964 to December 1964; March 1969 to may 1971; May 1982 to September 1982. On 31 August 1995 re-formed to take over role of 3 Cdo Brigade Air Squadron (see above) on being re-commissioned as RNAS Yeovilton with six LYnx Mk7 equipped with anti-tank missiles and nine Gazelle AH 1s primarily for observation work. Manned by RM aircrews with RN badges. Command of this unit passed to CINCFLEET on 1 September 1995.

HEADQUARTERS ROYAL MARINES (HQRM)

From 1 April 1993 this Headquarters was formed under the command of the Commandant General and took over the functions of: CG's Department at the MOD; HQ Commando Forces; and HQ Training and Reserve Forces (HQ TRFRM). Initially based in HMS *Vernon* at Portsmouth, the staff moved to new buildings at HMS *Excellent* at Whale Island in 1996. Reporting to CG in this Headquarters were in 1997: the Commander of 3 Cdo Bde; the Commandant of CTC RM; the Commandant of RM Poole; the CO of Comacchio Group; the Commandant of the RM School of Music; trials unit ATTURM; the Director of the RMR; 847 NAS; and the SBS which in 1997 came under a Special Forces HQ for operations but was administered as a unit under command of CG.

MOBILE NAVAL BASE DEFENCE ORGANISATIONS

'X' Organisation, later MNBDO Nucleus

Formed in the autumn of 1923[1] at Fort Cumberland, Eastney in Hampshire, the Organisation experimented with methods of landing guns etc. over scaffolding piers 'mainly by extemporisation, brute force and guts'[2] (see Chapter 2). After a major exercise in 1935 on the Isle of Arran (Scotland), the Nucleus arrived in Alexandria on 23 September, worked on defences in Egypt[3] and Palestine, retuning to the UK in July 1936. The authorised strength was then increased but men were drafted from the unit in 1938 to bring fleet detachments up to war-strength. This was later stopped and the Nucleus organised into eight AA batteries to defend Portsmouth. In August 1939 a battery of eight 3.7-in guns was formed and sent to Alexandria, with some men from the Nucleus and 100 from the Fleet, who were replaced by reservists.

That summer the unit strength was 264 all ranks,[4] 175 of these manning the AA guns in Alexandria. Men from the Nucleus were also drafted to the Fortress Unit (FU I) that summer. Fourteen of the unit's 20 AA and coastal guns were sent to the Army. Skeleton units were left at Fort Cumberland in September 1939, for an air defence brigade HQ, a signals company, fire control for 6-in gun batteries and a Landing, Transport and Workshop (LTW) Company. The unit had a few tractors, six searchlights, training facilities[5] for coastal defence artillery, including indirect fire control gear. It also had quantities of scaffolding and other materials for landing guns over beaches. The experience gained in the 16 years to 1939 gave this Organisation probably the most advanced techniques for the beach landing of heavy equipment of any service in the world. It was situated alongside the ISTDC at Fort Cumberland, so that there was certainly unofficial liaison between these units.

Those remaining at Fort Cumberland joined MNBDO I on its formation. The war establishment of officers and 568 other ranks had been agreed by 17 May 1939, but the unit was not brought up to strength until 1940 as MNBDO I.

'MNBDO Group'

This term was applied to the RM component of a Mobile Naval Base. The Base was commanded by an RN captain and also had RN units for booms and mines (the Under-Water Group) and a Sea Patrols Group. The commanders of MNBDO Groups when under RM command reported to the Adjutant General, and the full title of their commands were Royal Marine Group MNBDO I or MNBDO II.

MNBDO I

Formation was approved as of 12 September 1939,[6] with an establishment of 78 officers and 2,150 other ranks, but the equipment available was only a fraction of that authorised (e.g. six searchlights out of 48, 17 vehicles out of 75).

Arrangements were made to train tradesmen, AA gun crews, searchlight crews, and gunnery and wireless instructors, at Army establishments.[7] The establishment was reviewed by a small HQ set up on 29 January 1940, when a provisional strength of 202 officers and 4,089 other ranks was proposed. During February HQs were also set up for the Air Defence Group, the Land Defence Force and the Coast Defence Group. Brig Weston took command on 1 March and four days later the HQ Wing was formed with a Provost Company, Survey Section, HQ Defence Platoon and some other administrative Sections. The Landing and Maintenance Group was formed in May 1940,[8] absorbing officers and men with experience of building piers, and handling stores and vehicles over open beaches, etc. Other subunits were formed from time to time, as shown in the unit history summaries for beach units, artillery regiments and battalions.

The majority of men in the Organisation were 'HOs', as were eventually nearly all the junior officers. The first 2,010 recruits[9] joining the organisation in mid-February 1940 went from depots and their homes to: 1st RM AA Rgt at Arborfield, Carlisle and Blandford; 11th RM Searchlight Regiment at Taunton and Yeovil; the Land Defence Force (later 11th RM Bn) at Browndown; and the Coast Artillery Brigade with its HQ at Fort Cumberland and Hayling Island camp.

The MNBDO HQ in 1940 provided a training party[10] in June – about the time of the retreat from Dunkirk – to advise Army coastal batteries on techniques and equipment. Many subunits were detached; and, under Army command, were employed in AA and other Home Defence deployments (see subunits' history summaries). During the invasion scare the HQ stood to for 72 hours from 7 to 9 September. On 21 November the AA units with the Army were put at seven days' notice to revert to RM command. Exercises and training continued; then from the strength of 4,501 on 1 December 1940,[11] 500 experienced men were provided for MNBDO II and replaced by recruits.

The HQ at Fort Cumberland was closed on 4 February 1941,[12] and the Organisation sailed for the Middle East. After a five-day visit to Durban (South Africa), the men reached Tahal Camp in Egypt on 23 April and came under command of the C-in-C Middle East.[13] Three ships carrying heavy gear reached Haifa (Palestine) the next day, and the equipment, guns, etc. were reloaded tactically during the next few weeks by men from the MNBDO, Meanwhile General Weston took elements of the Organisation to Crete, where they landed on 9 May and were in action as infantry during the German airborne landings and sub-sequent fighting (see chapter 3). There were nearly 1,200 casualties,[14] mostly prisoners, from the MNBDO units.

During the rest of 1941 the units were brought up to strength and reorganised. General Weston hoped to use the Organisation in the Far East and resisted attempts to have subunits detached,[15] but in February 1942 1st RM (Heavy) AA Regiment went to Ceylon. 1st Coast Regiment with the Landing and Maintenance details, fortified island bases in the Indian Ocean. Various subunits had been in action while MNBDO I was in the Mediterranean, but the majority of time was spent in anti-aircraft defences and in training. All the searchlight units in the Canal Zone came under the command of the RM searchlight group for a time.

The stores depot from Fort Cumberland moved to Geneifa (north of Port Tewfik) in 1941, and its staff, along with other elements then in Egypt, followed the AA Regiment to the Far East in 1943. Major General W. B. F. Lukis[16] took over from General Weston in April 1943; and the HQ of MNBDO I closed in the Middle East on 16 June 1943 and reopened in Colombo (Ceylon, modern Sri Lanka) on 27 June. This HQ commanded two Mobile Naval Base Brigades organised for the defence of Ceylon and training for operations in Burma. The two AA regiments – 1st RM Rgt in India, 2nd RM Rgt in Ceylon – were also administered by the HQ of MNBDO I in Ceylon, until they returned to the UK, along with the personnel of the two Brigades, during the spring of 1944.[17] The personnel were remustered that summer for landing craft, commando and other duties, the HQ finally being disbanded in September 1944,[12] when the principal AA units formed 5 RM AA Brigade.

MNBDO II

Formed about 1 January 1941 under command of Brig H. R. Lambert (later Major General, CBE, DSC) with 500[18] men from MNBDO I, including 130 from Fortress Unit I. Many junior officers were transferred from Army OCTUs[19] and the men were 'HOs'. The Organisation was based on Hayling Island (near Portsmouth), and in April bomb damage[20] caused the HQ to be moved at least once. During the summer many of the men of the subunits were trained in various Army establishments (cp: MNBDO I) including the School of Cookery at Aldershot. The HQ had moved to Bentworth (Hampshire) area in May, and for a short while had an RAF radar and balloon barrage squadron under command. Units were deployed in the air and coast defences of the UK during 1942–3 before being concentrated

in the Nottingham area early in 1943, ready for embarkation for the Middle East, where they arrived in June 1943 just before[21] the HQ of MNBDO I left for the Far East. Subunits of MNBDO II were deployed in AA defences of north-east Malta in April and from 16 June to 9 July[22] before the Organisation was sent to Sicily under command of the Eighth Army. The establishment of some subunits by this date had been brought in line with Army war establishments for personnel and weapons.

After service on detached duties with the Eighth Army, the units of MNBDO II were assembled in Augusta (Sicily) for embarkation and arrived in the UK in February 1944.[23] The HQ was disbanded in May 1944[23] and personnel of all but those AA Regiments forming 5 RM AA Bde were sent to North Wales for selection as landing craft crews, commandos or for other duties.

Fortress Unit I

Formed about August 1939[1] under Lt-Col H. R. Lambert, DSC, as The Fortress Unit from men of the MNBDO Nucleus, it had an HQ and five companies:[2] Landing Coy, Ship Unloading Coy, Gun-Mounting Coy, Boat Coy, and a Transport and Workshop Coy. Men of the Unit modified SS *Mashobra*[3] in Liverpool during that summer, with accommodation and provided deck stowage for two MLCs, one had to be left behind when a derrick jib buckled on hoisting it aboard. The MLC sailed independently for Scapa. Meanwhile Col C. T. Brown had been asked to advise[4] on the preparation of Scapa Flow's defences (see chapter 2), and the Unit, with a Survey Section and a Signals Section, about 450 all ranks, sailed for Scapa in SS *Theseus* on 14 July 1939.[5] Despite incessant gales and mud, the Marines installed their first gun in seven days (mostly with hand tackle and tools), and in 12 Days they had disembarked all the gear, including guns, searchlights and generators. Some searchlights had to be hoisted up a cliff face, ammunition shelters had to be built and proof rounds fired from each gun, before the Unit left on 3 September to return to Portsmouth. The job had been completed in under six weeks, when the Army reportedly said it would take six years.[6]

In October *Mashobra* was in Portsmouth,[7] her fitting out incomplete and her structure based on Transport Regulations which were not suited to MNBDO-type operations. She sailed to the Clyde and during that winter her AA guns were in action, the ship also weathered several gales in practice landings. The Unit also unloaded stores from a number of ships in April, and on 3 and 4 May 1940 the men worked nonstop loading

Mashobra, which had been commissioned as an HM Ship for the coming voyage to Norway. The Unit became independent of MNBDO I at this time but was still administered from Fort Cumberland,[9] and was regarded as a Landing and Maintenance Group.

Mashobra carried Army vehicles as well as MNBDO-type stores, the MLC No. 18, two picket boats and a speedboat being stowed on deck.[8] Warm clothing was issued during the voyage in rough weather to Skånland (near Narvik) where she moored on 11 May. Throughout her stay in Norway all parties worked on unloading ammunition, petrol and other stores from ships that could use Harstad.[10] The MLC was sent to land troops on several occasions. On 23 May *Mashobra* was bombed[11] and had to be beached, the men living ashore for three days in tents while salvaging what they could from her before sailing for the UK. 'All beards were shaved off',[12] before landing on 5 June 1940.

Re-equipped the Unit sailed for Iceland a month later, landing at Reykjavik on 12 July.[13] The Marines had to scrounge tents for their camp ashore. They prepared gun sites, and during September erected huts for the Army when waiting for more guns to arrive. The 2101 all ranks of the Unit were employed in off-loading guns and stores, surveying sites and preparing them – in one case blasting mica-granite – before installing some 18[14] 3-in and 6-in guns. Often these had to be hauled by tractors making little more than 3 mph for long distances, and in one fortnight elements of the Unit travelled 800 miles[15] to prepare sites. They returned to the UK at the end of October and were absorbed into MNBDO II on disbanding early in January 1941.[16]

Fortress Unit II

This Unit was being formed[17] in May 1940 but no records of its composition have been traced. It became the Landing and Maintenance Group of MNBDO II.

Special Gun-mounting Party, RM

On 27 August 1939 orders were received to mount several coast guns, a party of four officers and 50 other ranks (including four seamen) – drawn from Fortress Unit I and with NCO volunteers[18] taking the place of Marines, as few men were available – began dismantling one battery (three guns) at Fort Cumberland and collecting scaffolding etc. Three more guns, packed for shipment, were collected from Coventry (West Midlands), and the installation work began within three days of the orders being received. At Blyth (Northumberland) the first pair of 6-in guns were installed after considerable exca-

vations in sand dunes. These guns were fired on 4 September. The next pair of '6-in' were installed without difficulty at Sunderland (County Durham), along with two coast-defence searchlights and three generators, by 7 September. At Yarmouth (Norfolk) concrete holdfasts had to be built and the guns were installed, despite difficulties, by 17 September. The experience of this Party pointed the need for gun and mounting components to be un-boxed and checked by Fort Cumberland staff, for at Yarmouth considerable work had to be done by armourers on guns collected through Naval stores. The Director of Armament Supplies took up this point, but the difficulties in assembling and specially packing equipment for MNBDO operations continued throughout 1940.[19] The guns were manned by Army crews before the Party returned to Fort Cumberland that September 1939.

3 Mobile Naval Base Brigade

Formed[20] on 24 July 1943, at the time Japanese amphibious and other raids were expected on Naval bases in Ceylon during the summer of 1943. The Commander Brig J. H. G. Wills, OBE, had under command: 1st RM Coast Rgt, from August 1943 to December 1944;[21] and from formation 24th RM Bn, 3rd RM Coast Rgt, 'S' Searchlight Bty, 2nd RM AA Rgt (operationally commanded by 24 (Army) AA Bde), the HQ Defence Platoon, etc. From mid-August 1943 to January 1844 the Brigade was based at Katukurunda,[22] south of Colombo, in a ground defence role. Its higher formation was GHQ Ceylon, until early in 1944 it reverted to Admiralty control, when it was briefly commanded by Brig H. T. Tollemache (who also commanded the Small Operations Group in Ceylon). 3 MN Brigade returned to UK, arriving on 16 March 1944 and was officially disbanded on 17 May 1944 (RMRO 719/44). The HQ had closed on 14 May, when 3 officers and a 100 men went to commando training and other remustered for LC crews etc from a total strength that April had been 927 all ranks.[23]

'MB Group' with XXXIII Indian Corps

The 1 RM AA Brigade HQ, 1st RM (Heavy) AA Rgt and a Landing and Maintenance Unit, were sent to India from Ceylon in April 1943, commander Brig V. D. Thomas, to train for amphibious operations in the Arakan. The 'Group' was under the command of XXXIII Indian Corps. The proposed operations were deferred and the 'Group' disbanded about January 1944.

LAND ARTILLERY UNITS

Artillery of World War I

The RMA formations which had fought in the 1914–18 War were disbanded in 1919[1] and included: RMA AA Brigade, disbanded about February; RMA Howitzer Brigade, disbanded 15 June; RMA gunners from 525 to 528 RGA Siege Btys, disbanded May; and RMA Heavy Siege train, disbanded in March.[2]

Artillery Headquarters of RM Division

During the formation of the RM Division in September 1940[3] a six-gun battery of 3.7-in howitzers was to form the Division's artillery. The first of these had been formed in April 1940 (see RM Circ 2119/40S dated 18 April 1940) and others were to be provided by transfers from the howitzer batteries at that time with the MNBDO. The Army Council drafted – if it was not signed officially – a letter of 8 January 1941 to the Lord Commissioners of the Admiralty, which included the following: 'The principle that the [RM] Division should contain . . . anti-tank and light anti-aircraft guns, is accepted . . . [and these] should eventually be manned by Royal Marines . . . There is little prospect, however, of these weapons being available . . . for some considerable time. If the division is required for action before these units are available the Army accept the responsibility for provision to the scale laid down . . .'[4] When a ceiling was placed on Army manpower, however, 'the War Office found it necessary to cancel the agreement',[5] and the Adjutant general agreed that the RM division should raise its own supporting units.[6]

The HQ of RM Division Artillery was opened in the autumn of 1942 at Lympstone Grange, near Exton Camp in Devon. The commander was Col S. G. B. Paine, an appointment equivalent to CRA in an Army division. Arrangements were made to attach various RM artillery cadres to Army units for training.[7] By mid-October 1942 the establishment was:[8] Division Artillery HQ with 'H' Section of No. 2 Company of Division Signals; a field regiment, a light anti-aircraft regiment and an anti-tank regiment. In December this HQ moved to Brockenhurst, Hampshire, and a number of exercises were carried out. On 27 April 1943 the Royal Artillery Col D. C. W. Sanders, OBE, AFC, TD, assumed command of the RM Division Artillery and was promoted Brigadier on 2 July.

When the Division was disbanded, the Brigadier and many of the Division's gunnery Officers were transferred to the Armoured Support Group and major support craft. The last War Diary entry for this HQ dated 4 July 1943 states that 12 rounds HE and some smoke were the maximum available per Section for practice shoots.[9]

Brigade Artillery Headquarters

In August 1942 part of the Artillery HQ RM Division became a separate Brigade Artillery HQ, and by 27 August were at Dalditch, Devon, where artillery units were being formed. It seems likely that this Brigade artillery HQ, commanded by Lt-Col J. M. Fuller, took over training responsibilities from the RM Division Artillery HQ, for the Brigade artillery HQ moved to Penally Camp in Pembrokeshire, in the last days of August. During practice shoots on Army ranges near Penally the movement of guns and vehicles became impossible in part of the camp, owing to heavy rains and lack of hardstanding gun parks. This HQ was disbanded by August 1943 and the personnel posted to the Armoured Support Group.

Air Defence Brigade of MNBDO I, later I RM Anti-Aircraft Brigade and Headquarters AA Ceylon.

The nucleus of an Air Defence Group was formed by MNBDO on 29 January 1940, with a staff which included Fire Control Instructors.[10] But a Brigade HQ was not formed until January 1941, with 1st and 2nd RM Anti-Aircraft Regiments and 11th Searchlight Regiment under command. An Advance HQ went to Crete in May 1941 (see chapter 3). The main HQ remained in Egypt, but as the MNBDO AA units moved to Ceylon in the winter of 1941–2, a new HQ was formed by redesignating 1st RM AA Regiment's HQ as 1 RM AA Brigade HQ. Although no War Diary entries were made for the Cairo HQ after December 1941, it possibly supervised the re-formation of 'A' Battery, and its staff finally dispersed in December 1942.

The 1 RM AA Bde headquarters in Ceylon had under command a Gunnery Operations Room Troop[11] (March to November 1942), as well as 1st and 2nd (Heavy) AA Rgts from December 1941 until May 1944, and for the period February 1942 to 29 August 1943, this HQ was designated HQ AA Ceylon,[12] with Army units under command, including an RA Operations Room and RA batteries. There is a record of a Brigade HQ Battery from December 1942 to September 1943, no doubt to carry out Brigade (as opposed to Command HQ) functions. The Brigade was disbanded on 7 May 1944,[13] but its official disbandment is given in RMRO 719/44 as 16 May 1944, and after 5 RM AA Brigade had moved to Clacton, Essex, for training.

Air Defence Brigade MNBDO II later 2 RM Air Defence Brigade

On 5 February 1941 the RM nuclei of AA and Searchlight Rgts joined Army training establishments.[14] In March the AD Brigade HQ was established,[15] and by August 1942 had a Gunnery Operations Room which in the next 20 months worked with the Organisation's AA Regiments. This staff, both of the Brigade HQ and its Operations Room, became the HQ of 5 RM AA Brigade in the spring of 1944.

3 and 4 RM AA Brigades

Not formed in World War II, but see below.

Artillery Staff Headquarters MNBDO II

There is a record of this staff's existence from August 1942 to July 1943, with responsibility for artillery units attached to the Organisation.

5 RM Anti-Aircraft Brigade

When the anti-aircraft regiments of MNBDO I and II returned to Scotland in February 1944, they were to be disbanded, but a general of the Army's Air Defence Staff asked that some units be retained and from these – AA Bde HQ and Ops Room MNBDO II, 1st RM HAA Rgt (ex-MNBDO I), 3rd RM HAA Rgt (ex-MNBDO II), 4th RM LAA RGT (ex-MNBDO II) and a Signals Section (ex-MNBDO I) 5 RM AA Brigade was formed on 22 March 1944[16] at Hamilton (Lanarkshire), under the command of Brig J. E. Leech-Porter, OBE. His Brigade came under army command of GHQ AA Troops three days later. It was then mobilised to Army War Establishments. During May and early June the Brigade spent six weeks at the army's AA practice camp at Clacton-on-Sea, Essex. Gunnery practice and mobilisation (with all this entailed in drawing stores) were carried on at the same time, some army HAA Regiments joining the brigade in May.

During July and August the Brigade's regiments were deployed against 'flying bombs' on the south coast of England, destroying 122 of these V1s.[17] The Brigade landed in France early in September (see chapter 7), and took over the anti-aircraft gunnery defences of the Scheldt estuary that winter, and in addition to RM formations had under command 111 HAA, 114 LAA and 133 LAA Regiments RA; 105 AA Brigade (12 army regiments); 6/2 and 415/54 Searchlight Batteries RA; and 202 Fixed Coastal Defences RA.

Makeshift accommodation was improvised with shacks and 'huts' along dykes (see chapter 7). Communications were also difficult with more than 2,000 miles of telephone line laid by the Brigade's signallers in a duplicate system; this connected all sites – guns, searchlights, smoke-generating machines, and operations rooms – the duplications proving invaluable after later air raids. All major units were also in wireless (radio) contact, the strength of Brigade signals units being raised from 80 to 200 personnel.[18]

The heavy gun batteries fired on occasions in support of ground troops during the first few weeks of October, but their principal role was to defend against air attack a 7,000yds circle covering Antwerp and the area to its west. When V1s began coming over on 27 October,[19] two zones or 'belts of AA fire' were organised around Antwerp and Brussels with a corridor between; there were American AA units (with SCR 584[20] radar-linked predictors and proximity fuses) in the east and south-east zones, and as the flight path of V1s brought them near to the Brussels defence zone, that could therefore contribute to Antwerp's defence.[21] The Brigade's Operations Room at Antwerp recorded 483 V1 and 313 V2 (rocket) incidents in the month to 12 December 1944. Units of the Brigade also formed rescue squads with equipment to help civilians buried in wrecked buildings after V1 and V2 explosions.

The German air activity increased in preparation for their Ardennes offensive. The last air attack on Antwerp, on New Year's Day 1945, was initially at low level (500ft), when the Brigade shot down four planes; around this time the V1 and V2 attacks intensified. The Brigade was relieved on 5 March 1945, and moved to Ostend.

The Brigadier took over as AADC for Ostend and Calais on 11 March. The last plot in the Brigade Operations Room was for a friendly aircraft on 6 May, and the Brigade returned to the UK some three weeks later on 28 May.[22] Brig S. G. B. Paine commanded the Brigade in the autumn of 1945.[23]

The Brigade was stationed at South Brent (Devon) in December 1945 when they were disbanded,[24] the HQ having been disbanded at Topsham, Devon, the month before.[25] The continuous service personnel returned to their Divisions and the 'HOs' were absorbed into the 27th and 28th RM Battalions.

RM Siege Regiment

For origins see chapter 3. Lt-Col L. Foster was appointed CO[1] and the Regiment's strength was reduced from some 700[2] to 300 in late 1942. the gun crews – in 'civvy' street a store manager, labourers, lorry drivers, a solicitor's clerk, a policeman, tradesmen and clerks among them – had long periods when the guns were not in action, and these men formed an infantry unit[3] with support weapons (a 74-mm gun, six Blacker Bombards, five MMGs and six 3-in mortars) for local defence in 1942.

The two heavy guns (described in chapter 3) were BL 14-in Mk VIIs.[4] The supercharge of SC 500 cordite,[5] was not available in this standard size after 1944, as loaded in four quarter-charges. In the final shoots as the Allies entered Boulogne and Calais, virtually all the ammunition was used (see chapter 7) and the Germans fired their reserves of ammunition for their big guns, much of it into Dover, Kent.

The Regiment came under the command of the Vice-Admiral at Dover from August 1940 to 15 September 1940, and thereafter under the army command of XII Corps (which in January 1942 became HQ SE District).[6] In September 1941 the CO sought permission to use the guns offensively, for by that time the invasion of England seemed unlikely, and there was ample ammunition:[7] 350 rounds of HE for the 14-in, 400 rounds for the 13.5-in and spare barrels (2 for the 14-in and six for the 13.5-in). When *Scharnhorst* and *Gneisenau* came through the Channel, however, the siege gun crews were doing infantry training and only two 14-in rounds were fired on predetermined coordinates,[8] a spot in the channel previously decided by XII Corps HQ. The ships had been picked up on coastal radar when 38 miles south of Hastings (East Sussex) at 1050 hours,[9] but the coast batteries were not told to fire until the ships had passed through the Channel, when the Army's 9.2-in guns got three hits on a rapidly receding target.

The following month the Regiment manned the experimental 135/8-in gun named 'Bruce', after Vice-Admiral Sir Bruce Fraser.[10] Test firings into the sea south of Hastings were closely monitored, and some useful data collected on the ballistics of high trajectory and high velocity guns.

By 1942 the German long-range batteries were conserving ammunition against the day of an Allied invasion, and there was little activity until the Regiment fired its remaining rounds in September 1944, when the Germans were being driven from the French coats. The siege gun crews were then disbanded, many men going to Dalditch for the School of Mines,[11] a unit set up to train men in clearing Pacific beaches. but in November 1944 they were sent to RMTG (Wales), destined for the infantry battalions or the 34th Amphian Support Regiment. The Siege Regiment HQ was disbanded in March 1945.[12]

RM Light AA Regiment/1st RM Light AA Regiment

Formed in the summer of 1942 when the RM Division was setting up its organic artillery units;[13] 101 RM Brigade's artillery HQ staff provided the personnel for this Regiment's HQ. CO Lt-Col J. M. Fuller[14] from 24 August 1942 to 31 July 1943. While under command of 101 RM Brigade, the Regiment's HQ was in the following locations, with the units commanded shown in brackets:

24 August 1942:	Near Fishguard (with 1st and 2nd LAA Btys and 1st AA/Anti-tank Bty).
November 1942:	Inverary on amphibious training (as for 24 August).
December 1942:	Sandbanks at Poole, Dorset for training shoots (as for 24 August).
about 1 January 1943:	Sandbanks – Regiment redesignated 1st RM Light AA Rgt.
about 31 July:	At Sandbanks Regiment disbanded, HQ personnel to Support Craft Regiment[14].

1st RM AA Regiment

Formed in February 1940 as part of MNBDO I, with a cadre of officers and NCOs who had served in 1st RM AA Battery of 1939.[15] COs included: Maj L. O. Jones (Instructor of Gunnery), 15 February to 14 April 1940; Lt-Col J. E.

Leech-Porter, 15 April to about December 1940; Lt-Col E. H. M. Unwin, January to May 1941; Lt-Col R. Garret, June to December 1941.[16]

The Regiment's HQ was in the following locations, with the units commanded shown in brackets:

15 February 1940:	Fort Cumberland when with COAST DEFENCE GROUP ('A', 'B' and 22 Light Batteries, with RA Trg Rgts in Arborfield, Carlisle and Blandford).
mid-June 1940:	Exton with AIR DEFENCE GROUP ('A', 'B' and 'R' [Searchlight] Btys[17] provided experimental Section and HQ from 'B' Bty[18] 'R' Bty under command June to September and later.
February 1941:	With AIR DEFENCE BRIGADE OF MNBDO I, at sea ('A', 'B', 'R' and 22nd RM LAA Btys).
March 1941:	Egypt (as for February).
May 1941:	Crete ('A' Bty in Crete, 'B' Bty in Sidi Barrani, North Africa).

Summer 1941:	Egypt mainly on internal security duties and aerodrome defence[19] ('A', 'C', 'R' and 22nd RM Light Btys).
21 December 1941:	Ceylon, HQ redesignated 1 RM AA Brigade, see unit history ('A' and 'C' Btys to 2nd RM (Heavy) AA Rgt. 'R' Bty to 11th RM (Searchlight) Rgt).[20]

2nd RM AA Regiment

Formed with 'C', 'D' and 23rd RM Light Btys which were under training with RA Regiments.[1] First CO Lt-Col C. M. Sergeant, 15 April to 21 December.

The Regiment's HQ was in the following locations,[2] with the units commanded shown in brackets:

15 April 1940:	With COAST DEFENCE GROUP, Arborfield ('C', 'D' and 23rd RM Light AA Btys).
8 August 1940:	With AIR DEFENCE Gt BRITAIN Matlock, Derbyshire (Btys as at 15 April).
January 1941:	With AIR DEFENCE BRIGADE MNBDO I, Portsmouth (Btys as at 15 April 1940).
March 1941:	Egypt (Btys as at 15 April 1940).
May 1941:	Crete ('C' Bty. elements of 23rd RM Light AA Bty and advance party from 'D' Bty).
June 1941:	Moascar, Egypt (after the Crete operation this Regiment had only elements of its three Btys with cadres from 'D' joining 'C' and some men from 22nd RM LAA Bty joining the 23rd RM Light AA Bty).
21 December 1941:	Cairo, the HQ became the 1st (Heavy) AA Rgt's headquarters,[3] 'C' and 'D' Btys to that Regiment and 23rd RM Light AA Bty to 2nd RM (Heavy) AA Regiment.[4]
July 1942:	Headquarters re-formed.[5]
1943–4:	Ocean fortresses on islands in Indian Ocean, the staff providing command facilities for AA defences.[6]

1st RM (Heavy) AA Regiment

Formed on the reorganisation of the Air Defence Brigade of MNBDO I in December 1941;[7] personnel of 2nd RM AA Rgt formed this HQ with 'B', 'C', and 'D' Batteries from 1st and 2nd RM AA Regiments ('B' Bty had been 'A' Bty of 1st RM AA Rgt). COs: Lt-Col C. M. Sergeant,

December 1941 to August 1943; and Lt-Col R. Garrett, DSO, September 1943 to November 1945.[8]

The Regiment's HQ was in the following locations, with the units commanded shown in brackets:

21 December 1941:	With AIR DEFENCE BRIGADE MNBDO I, Cairo ('B', 'C' and 'D' Btys).
1 February 1942:	Colombo, Ceylon (as at 21 December 1941).
11 March 1942:	Colombo, although the HQ was in Ceylon, 'A' Bty was re-formed initially under its command, but as the Battery was in Cairo it was transferred to 2nd RM (Heavy) AA Rgt on formation.
9 April 1942:	Tricomalee, Ceylon when Batteries deployed in defence of the island. Malaria caused many casualties, 'D' Battery at one time having 92 per cent of its strength sick or convalescing. RA gunners were attached to make up the Batteries' strengths but all had returned to Army units by June.[9]
October 1942:	Ceylon, the rounds per gun were reduced from 1,250 to 930[3] ('D' RM Heavy AA Bty, 'Devon' RM LAA Bty and 1 RM AA Signals Squadron, 'Devon' Bty handed over sites to 7 Bty Ceylon Garrison Artillery on 5 November 1942, see WO 172/1523).
January and February 1943:	Ceylon, days when petrol not to be used, to conserve fuel.
15 April 1943:	Poona, India, ('B', 'C' and 'D' Btys training with XXXIII Corps for operations in the Arakan, Burma).
28 September 1943:	Bhiwandi, near Bombay training for amphibious operations, practice shoots included low burst HE and at anti-tank targets. Mobile Operations Room with improved techniques. Scales of equipment change to mobile 3.7-in guns

and 22nd RM LAA Bty under command for defence of heavy AA guns ('B'(?), 'C', 'D' and 22nd RM LAA Btys).

January 1944:	Bhiwandi, preparing to return to UK after the Arakan operations were deferred.
February 1944:	Largs, Scotland, Batteries were to be disbanded but retained for future service in Europe.
March 1944:	With 5 RM AA BRIGADE in Scotland all Batteries brought up to War Establishment of a mobile AA regiment on army scales ('A' came under command, 'B', 'C' and 'D').
23 April 1944:	22nd RM LAA Bty to 4th RM Light AA Regiment.
May 1944:	With AIR DEFENCE Gt BRITAIN, Clacton-on-Sea, Essex ('A', 'B', 'C' and 'D' at RA training camps).
August to September 1944:	With TWENTY-FIRST ARMY GROUP, Cherbourg in defence of this French port ('A', 'B', 'C', and 'D' Btys)
19 October 1944:	Antwerp in AA defences of Scheldt see chapter 7, and fired low airburst HE in support of Canadian Division West of Antwerp ('A', 'B', 'C' and 'D' Btys).
21 October 1944:	With US ARMY 101 (AA) BRIGADE Louvain, near Brussels, all Batteries in 'Diver' belt defences, credited with 41 'kills' of V1s ('A', 'B', 'C' and 'D' Btys).
October and November 1944	With CANADIAN DIVISION Schelt area, a Regimental Command Post was formed and FOOs worked with Canadian infantry (detached from time to time in a ground support role 'A', 'B', 'C', and 'D' Btys, in 44 days some 1,300 shoots were made at ground targets, firing air-burst HE).
January 1945:	With 5 RM AA BRIGADE Antwerp in air defence of port, and credited with four planes during low level attack on 1 January ('A', 'B', 'C', and 'D' Btys, except for one Troop of 'D' which was with US Army in 'Diver' belt and credited with 30 V1s [10]).
March and April 1945:	Ostend, all Batteries in coast defence role, on 18 April sank a midget submarine[11] ('A', 'B', 'C', and 'D' Btys).
May 1945:	Topsham, Devon with Batteries in By-Pass Camp near Exeter, personnel being demobilised but 'D' Battery retained as holding battery.
16 November 1945:	Topsham, HQ disbanded and personnel from 'D' Battery posted to 28th RM Battalion.

2nd RM (Heavy) AA Regiment

Formed on the reorganisation of MNBDO I Air Defence Brigade in December 1941.[12] This HQ had only the 23rd RM LAA Battery under command until December 1942, when the heavy AA Battery 'A' came under command while still in Egypt, before the Regiment's HQ provided control staff for anti-aircraft defences in Indian Ocean bases. The Regiment returned to Scotland in February 1944 and 'A' Battery transferred in March to 1st RM (Heavy) AA Regiment. The Regiment's HQ was disbanded with the 23rd RM LAA Bty on 23 May 1944.

3rd RM (Heavy) AA Regiment

Formed as a Regiment of MNBDO II Air Defence Brigade in January 1941.[13] the first CO was Lt-Col J. E. Leech-Porter.

The Regiment's HQ was in the following locations, with the units commanded shown in brackets:

7 January 1941:	With AIR DEFENCE BRIGADE MNBDO II Hayling Island, Hampshire[14] ('E', 'F' and 24th RM Light AA Btys).
Winter 1941:	With AIR DEFENCE Gt BRITAIN on UK south coast ('E', 'F' and 24th RM Light Btys).
3 August 1942:	With AIR DEFENCE BRIGADE MNBDO II in United Kingdom when all heavy AA batteries reorganised into heavy AA regiments ('E' and 'F' joined by 'G' and 'H' Batteries, 24 RM Light AA Bty transferred to 4th RM LAA Regiment).
March 1943:	Batteries concentrated at Nottingham for embarkation.
June 1943:	With various Army commands as CORPS or ARMY TROOPS Egypt batteries at various locations for defence of Suez Canal and other installations, gunners also employed on internal security ('E', 'F', 'G' and 'H' Batteries).

July 1943:	HQ in Egypt with Batteries in defence of Malta prior to landing in Sicily ('E', 'F', 'G' and 'H' Batteries).
15 July 1943:	With AIR DEFENCE BRIGADE MNBDO II Augusta, Sicily in defence of this port ('E', 'F', 'G' and 'H' Batteries).
January 1944:	Augusta, Sicily, Batteries concentrated for embarkation. ('E', 'F', 'G' and 'H' Batteries).
February 1944:	Scotland preparing for disbandment but retained ('E', 'F', 'G' and 'H' Batteries).
March 1944:	With 5 RM AA BRIGADE Scotland, reorganised to a War Establishment of an Army 3.7-in static regiment for Defended Ports Abroad, with Scale III equipment that limited each man to one battledress, one beret and so on until the winter ('E', 'F', 'G' and 'H' Batteries).
May 1944:	Clacton-on-Sea, all Bakeries at army training camps ('E', 'F', 'G' and 'H' Batteries).
June and July 1944:	With AIR DEFENCE Gt BRITAIN at various sites in UK ('E', 'F', 'G' and 'H' Batteries).
August 1944:	With 5 RM AA DEFENCE BRIGADE Cherbourg in defence of this French port ('E', 'F', 'G' and 'H' Batteries).
October 1944:	Antwerp air defences of Scheldt ('E', 'F', 'G' and 'H' Batteries).
March 1945:	Ostend in coast defences ('E', 'F', 'G' and 'H' Batteries).
May to November:	Southern England, Batteries demobilised and HQ disbanded (about November 1945).

4th RM AA Regiment/4th RM (Light) AA Regiment

Formed as a regiment of MNBDO II Air Defence Brigade about January 1941.[15]

The Regiment's HQ was in the following locations, with the units commanded shown in brackets:

January 1941:	With AIR DEFENCE BRIGADE of MNBDO II Hayling Island ('G', 'H' and 25th RM LAA Btys).
Winter 1941:	With AIR DEFENCE Gt BRITAIN on UK south coast ('G', 'H' and 25th RM LAA Btys).
3 August 1942:	With AIR DEFENCE BRIGADE OF MNBDO II, Nottingham, the heavy Batteries 'G' and 'H' transferred to 3rd RM (Heavy) AA Rgt, and this Regiment redesignated 4th RM (Light) Regiment, with 24th, 25th and 26th RM Light Batteries redesignated as Light AA Btys. The '26th' had been the defence unit of AD Brigade's HQ to defend it against low-flying aircraft. (24th, 25th and 26th RM Light AA Btys, preparing for embarkation[16]).
June 1943:	With VARIOUS ARMY COMMANDS Egypt Batteries at various locations (24th, 25th and 26th RM Light AA Btys).
15 July 1943:	Augusta, Sicily (24th, 25th and 26th RM Light AA Btys).
January 1944:	With AIR DEFENCE BRIGADE MNBDO II Sicily Batteries concentrated for embarkation (24th, 25th and 26th RM Light AA Btys).
March and April 1944:	Scotland 24th RM Light Bty disbanded at Motherwell on 11 April (25th and 26th RM Light AA Btys).
23 April 1944:	With 5 RM AA BRIGADE in Scotland put on a War Establishment for light AA regiment of Defended Ports Abroad with Scale III equipment that limited each man to one battledress, one beret and so on until the winter (22nd, 25th and 26th RM LAA Btys).
June 1944:	With AIR DEFENCE Gt BRITAIN Kent, all Batteries 'constantly in action' and by one report credited with 61 V1s, before units embarked for France (22nd, 25th and 26th RM LAA Btys).
August and September 1944:	With 5 RM AA BRIGADE Cherbourg with all batteries in defence of this port (22nd, 25th and 26th RM LAA Btys).
October and November 1944:	Antwerp with guns in flooded areas often in single gun detachments, see Chapter 7. When 'Diver' belts set up the Regiments 54 Bofors defended 26 miles of quays in the dock area[17] (22nd, 25th and 26th RM LAA Btys).

1 January 1945:	Antwerp with Batteries in last action against major low-level attack (22nd, 25th and 26th RM LAA Btys).
March 1945:	Ostend deployed in coast defences (as above)
May 1945:	Ivybridge, Devon preparing for demobilisation (as above)
30 September 1945:	Ivybridge Regiment HQ, 25th and 26th Batteries disbanded, personnel from 22nd Battery to 'D' holding battery.

11th RM Searchlight Regiment/'S' RM Battalion

The coastal searchlight crews of MNBDO Nucleus provided some men for this Regiment's HQ, formed in February 1940 as part of MNBDO Air Defence Group (later Air Defence Bde, MNBDO I).

The Regiment's HQ was in the following locations,[18] with the units commanded shown in brackets:

14 February 1940:	With AIR DEFENCE GROUP later AIR DEFENCE BRIGADE of MNBDO I Yeovil, Somerset with Batteries training from 15 February with 220 Searchlight Training Rgt RA ('S' and 'R' Btys).
about May 1940:	Exton, Devon in tented camp ('S' and 'R' Btys).
June 1940:	18 June at Exton, HQ and 'S' Bty formed 'S' Battalion of infantry, as no searchlights available and on 26 June 'R' Bty transferred to 1st RM AA Regiment.
Summer 1940:	'S' Battalion deployed in UK defences
20 September 1940:	Deal, Kent, the Regiment's HQ and 'S' and 'R' Bd Heries again as searchlight unit.
January 1941:	Portsmouth 'R' Battery reverted to 1st RM AA Rgt, HQ and 'S' Bty prepare for embarkation.
March 1941:	Egypt HQ and 'S' Bty in Canal Zone
May 1941:	Crete where HQ and 'S' Bty formed an infantry unit (see Chapter 3); many were taken prisoner.
summer 1941:	'R' Battery manned flares in Suez Canal defences as well as searchlights.
July 1941:	Batteries became independent, serving with forces on Indian Ocean islands under command of local headquarters.
February 1943:	With VARIOUS COMMANDS in Ceylon, the Regiment's HQ had been re-formed and 'S' and 'R' batteries were again under command.
summer 1943:	Ceylon with Batteries in air defences ('S' and 'R' batteries).
March 1944:	With 1 RM AA BRIGADE Ceylon, Batteries concentrated for embarkation ('S' and 'R' batteries).
May and June 1944:	Scotland where 'S' and 'R' Batteries were disbanded on 15 May and Regiment's HQ in June.[19]

12th RM Searchlight Regiment

A Cadre of personnel from 11th RM Searchlight Rgt formed this 12th RM Searchlight Regiment in January 1941 as part of MNBDO II Air Defence Brigade.[20]

The Regiment's HQ was in the following locations, with the units commanded shown in brackets:

1 January 1941:	With AIR DEFENCE BRIGADE MNBDO II, South Hayling Camp, Hampshire ('N' and 'O' Batteries).
June 1941:	Truro, Cornwall, providing guide 'lights' for Allied airfields ('N' and 'O' Batteries).[21]
winter 1941 and 1942:	With AIR DEFENCE Gt BRITAIN on south coast of UK ('N' and 'O' Batteries).
March 1943:	Nottingham with Batteries concentrated for embarkation ('N' and 'O' Batteries).
Early summer 1943:	With VARIOUS ARMY COMMANDS in the Mediterranean when Batteries deployed in air defence in Egypt and Malta ('N' and 'O' Batteries).
July 1943:	Augusta, Sicily in air defences (as above).
January 1944:	With AIR DEFENCE BRIGADE MNBDO II Augusta where Batteries concentrated for embarkation (as above).

April 1944:   Burbank, Scotland, where HQ and 'N' and 'O' Batteries disbanded.

RM Coast Brigade/1 RM Coast Brigade/1st RM Coast Artillery Regiment

Formed by MNBDO I on 15 February 1940[22] (when briefly known as RM Coast Defence Group) with recruits trained in 'B', 'C', 'G' and 'K' companies.[23]

The Regiment's HQ was in the following locations, with the units commanded shown in brackets:

30 March 1940:	With MNBDO I Eastney ('Kent', 'Devon', 'X' see 14 June 1942 below, 'Y' and Anti-MTB Btys, Land Defence Coy of which a platoon only formed, and Signals Section; 'Z' Bty formed at Harwich 13 May; and 'Y' Bty in Iceland).
May 1940:	'Devon' Bty was to become a howitzer battery, and no longer a part of the MNBDO War Establishment, memo from AGRM No. 2147/40S; but it was to train under MNBDO command and appears to have remained or been re-formed as part of this Regiment, see 31 March 1941 below.
6 August 1940:	Eastney with 'Hampshire' Bty formed ('Kent', 'Devon', 'Hampshire', 'X', 'Y', 'Z' and Anti-MTB Btys, Land Defence Coy, and Signals Section).
1 January 1941:	Portsmouth with Batteries being concentrated for embarkation and Regiment redesignated 1 RM Coast Brigade ('Kent', 'Devon', 'Hampshire', 'X', 'Y', 'Z' and Anti-MTB Btys, Land Defence Coy, and Signals Section).
31 March 1941:	Egypt Canal Zone and party sent to off-load ships in Palestine, 'Devon' Light AA Bty formed from cadres of 'Devon' and A-MTB Btys ('Kent', 'Devon' Light AA, 'Hampshire', 'X', 'Y', 'Z', Anti-MTB Btys, and Land Defence Coy, and Signals Section).
May 1941:	Crete with guns of 'Z' and 'X' Btys mounted, personnel later fighting as infantry; other personnel of this Coast Brigade with advance party in Crete see Chapter 3 ('Kent', 'Devon' Light AA, 'Hampshire', 'X', 'Y', 'Z', Anti-MTB Btys and Land Defence Coy[?], and Signals Section).
1 August 1941:	Egypt after losses on Crete, the Brigade was reorganised with 'Z' Bty now independent of Brigade and 'X' Bty disbanded ('Kent', 'Devon' Light AA, 'Hampshire', 'Y', A-MTB Batteries and Land Defence Coy, and Signals Section).
6 September 1941:	Egypt and Indian Ocean islands, redesignated 1st RM Coast Artillery Rgt ('Kent', 'Devon' Light AA, 'Hampshire', 'Y', A-MTB Batteries and Land Defence Coy, and Signals Section).
winter 1941–2:	Indian Ocean Batteries deployed in island base defences ('Kent', 'Devon' Light AA, 'Hampshire', 'Y', AMTB Batteries and Land Defence Coy, and Signals Section).
5 April 1942:	Ceylon ('Kent', 'Devon' by this date re-formed with 6-in coast defence guns, 'Hampshire', 'Y', A-MTB Batteries and Land Defence Coy, and Signals Section).
14 June 1942:	Ceylon in coast defences ('Kent', 'Devon', 'Hampshire', 'Y', A-MTB Batteries and Land Defence Coy, and Signals Section).
1 August 1943:	Ceylon all personnel to RM Coast Defence Rgt (later 3rd RM Coast Rgt) as infantry except 'Devon' Bty.
January and February 1944:	Ceylon, personnel of HQ to 3rd RM Coast Rgt and HQ disbanded; February 'Devon' Bty disbanded, although see unit history summary of this Battery.

2 RM Coast Brigade/2nd RM Coast Artillery Regiment

Formed by MNBDO II in January 1941, with 'Y' Bty from 1 RM Coast Brigade providing cadres for new batteries.

The Regiment's HQ was in the following locations, with the units commanded shown in brackets:

1 January 1941:	Hayling Island ('Sussex', 'T' and 2nd Anti-MTB Btys).
28 April 1941:	With ARMY COAST DEFENCES FOR UK, Portsmouth ('Dorset' formed this day, 'Sussex', 'T', 'U' formed this day, 'W' formed this day, and 2nd Anti-MTB Btys).
6 September 1941:	Portsmouth redesignated 2nd RM Coast Artillery Regiment.
14 June 1942:	'X' Battery re-formed from men at Geneifa (north of Port Tewfik) the Base Depot in Egypt, for deployment as an independent Battery, although originally intended for this Regiment apparently.
8 September 1943:	HQ personnel provided staff for Coast Defence Station for about 12 months until January 1944.
March 1943:	With MNBDO II UK, Batteries concentrated for embarkation ('Dorset', 'Sussex', 'T', 'U', 'W', and 2nd Anti-MTB Btys).
summer 1943:	Egypt with Batteries deployed in training areas ('Dorset', 'Sussex', 'T', 'U', 'W', and 2nd Anti-MTB Btys).
July 1943:	Augusta, Sicily, with Batteries in coast defences ('Dorset', 'Sussex', 'T', 'U', 'W', and 2nd Anti-MTB Btys).
Late summer 1943:	With ARMY COAST DEFENCE COMMANDS, Italy, ('Dorset', 'Sussex', 'T', 'U', 'W', and 2nd Anti-MTB Btys).
January 1944:	Batteries concentrated for embarkation (as in late-summer 1943).
February 1944:	Largs, Scotland, HQ personnel to 1st Coast Rgt HQ[24] about this time and Batteries disbanded in the next few months but see Batteries unit history summary.

RM Quick Firing (QF) Regiment

Formed by MNBDO I in mid-May 1940 at the time of the German invasion of France.[25] The Regiment was part of 16 land batteries formed by Royal Naval personnel and largely staffed by officers from HMS *Effingham*, which had recently been sunk. The 41st RM QF Battery sailed for Dunkirk but was not landed (25–8 May) and was detached with eight 12-pdr Portees (guns on lorries) to 15 Division at Dunmow, Essex, during June and July. The other two Batteries, equipped like the '41st' were also detached: '42nd' to 5th Loyals at Crowborough, Sussex 20 May to 12 July; and '43rd' to 18 Division HQ at Norwich, Norfolk during May and June. These batteries, each of six officers and 165 other ranks, were all disbanded within 10 weeks of their formation.

RM Field Artillery Regiment

Formed at the time the RM Division established organic artillery units, by 102 RM Brigade's HQ at Dalditch from 10 September 1942.[26] Under command 16 October were 32nd Howitzer Bty, 2nd Anti-Tank Bty, 2nd Light AA Bty and 1st Field Bty forming at St Margaret's Bay, Kent, from men of the RM Siege Rgt. Plans were made to equip the field Batteries with 25-pdrs; two RA Field Btys were to be regimented with these RM Btys, but the arrangement was cancelled. The Regiment's HQ went to Tenby (South Wales) in November, but only elements of the Batteries under command went there for training with the RA. All but the Field Bty were transferred to the RM Anti-Tank Rgt before March 1943, when

1st RM Field Artillery Regiment was stationed at Christchurch, Dorset. a second field battery was formed on 1 June 1943, but on 12 August the first drafts from this Regiment were sent to the RM Siege Rgt as this built up again, and the RM Field Artillery Regiment was disbanded at Wimbourne, Hampshire, by the end of August 1943. Some men from this Regiment joined the RM Support Craft Regiment.

RM Anti-Tank Regiment

On the organisation of organic artillery for the RM Division, 102 Bde Artillery HQ took all but the Field Batteries from the RM Field Artillery Regiment to form the Anti-Tank Regiment at Dalditch, where the Regiment had under command 1st and 2nd Anti-Tank Btys and 31st and 32nd Light Btys. These units moved to Burry Port, South Wales for gunnery training on 6 November, and were mobilised there on 20 November. The Regiment moved to Bournemouth, Dorset, early in December, carrying out practice shoots on nearby ranges. In June 1943 the Regiment was concentrated at Wimborne, Dorset, and the Batteries redesignated Support Craft Batteries, before RM Anti-Tank Rgt HQ was disbanded on 31 July.[27]

ARTILLERY BATTERIES AND ASSOCIATED UNITS

1st RM AA Bty/RM Anti-Aircraft Battery of MNBDO Nucleus: under Army command in Alexandria, Egypt, August to 29 December 1939, see MNBDO Nucleus history summary. This was a battery of eight 3.7-in AA guns from Army sources, in four two-gun Sections. It sailed for Egypt on 28 August 1939, in HMT *Lancashire* and apparently served in Egypt until absorbed into other units.

Fort Cumberland RM AA: under Army/Navy joint command in Portsmouth, September 1939, with 8 × 3.7-in guns from Fort Cumberland.

1st and 2nd RM Anti-MTB: the '1st' with Force Sturges in Iceland, May 1940, with 4 × 2-pdr Pom-Poms; served in air defence Devonport (Plymouth) in October 1940; later equipped with Bofors; redesignated 'Portsmouth' Battery in Ceylon August 1943. The '2nd' when in Falmouth with 2nd Coast Bde in 1941 had 4 × 2-pdr Pom-Poms and was later equipped with Bofors.

1st RM Anti-Tank, 1st RM AA/Anti-Tank and 2nd RM Anti-Tank: these Batteries initially had 2-pdr Portees in four Troops or 2-pdr Pom-Poms; by mid-March 1943 they had some 6-pdrs.

1st and 2nd RM Light AA: equipped on formation in November 1942 with Oerlikons on trucks and later with Bofors.

1st and 2nd RM Field: initially equipped with 8 × 18/25-pdrs and three armoured mobile Observation Posts (the '2nd' only existed for eight weeks in June/July 1943 and trained on 25-pdrs with RA at Harrogate, Yorkshire).

1st, 2nd and 3rd RM Support Craft: the '1st' became the 5th RM (Independent) Armoured Support Bty; the '2nd' became the 1st RM Armoured Support Rgt; and the '3rd' became the 2nd Armoured Support Rgt.

4th to 20th RM: no RM batteries with these numbers have been traced for the years 1919 to 1995.

21st to 26th RM Light later RM Light AA: initially equipped with 8 to 12 Pom-Poms; some subsequently had Oerlikons on lorries, but after Bofors guns became available, these Batteries were re-equipped. For example, the '22nd' when a Light AA Bty had 16 Bofors when serving with 1st (Heavy) AA Rgt in Ceylon during April 1943, at a time when Army Bofors batteries were of 12 guns. The '22nd' were deployed to protect the heavy gun Batteries from low-flying air attacks. Later the '22nd' had 18 Bofors and 12 Oerlikons on Hazard lorry-type mountings when in India in the autumn of 1943.

RM Light Battery: this battery went to Norway in 1940 with 3.7-in pack howitzers of an old design (see Chapter 2). The strength was eight officers and 123 other ranks. A memo from AGRM No. 2147/40S of 13 May 1940 directed that the men of this Battery be deployed in re-forming 'Devon' Battery of coast guns with eight 3.7-in howitzers, and that they were to begin training with MNBDO Group but not to form part of the Group's War Establishment. But see unit history summary of 'Devon' Battery.

31st and 32nd RM Howitzer later RM Light Btys: initially equipped with 3.7-in howitzers, 'A' Section of the '31st' went to the Shetland Islands in May to July 1940. Other Sections, as part of the RM Division, had 3.7-in guns in lorries towing limbers, but this did not prove satisfactory. These units redeployed as 2nd RM Support Craft Bty (from the '31st') and in the 1st RM Support Craft Bty, after the gunners had trained on 25-pdrs.

41st, 42nd and 43rd RM QF: see unit history summary of RM Quick Firing Rgt.

'A' to 'H' RM: these were all heavy AA Batteries equipped with 8 × 3-in AA guns or later with 3.7-in AA guns.

'I' to 'M' RM: no trace has been found of RM batteries with these letters in the period 1919 to 1995.

'N' and 'O', 'R' and 'S' RM: these searchlight Batteries had – for example – six Guy lorry-mounted searchlights in 'N' Bty, at Truro, Cornwall, in 1941. These crews formed infantry units from time to time, and 'S' Bty on the voyage to Crete manned machine gun AA defences of HMT *Nieuw Zeeland* before later serving as infantry on this island No trace has been found of 'P' and 'Q' Batteries.

'T', 'U', 'W', 'X', 'Y' and 'Z' RM: these Batteries were formed by 1941–2 as coast defence batteries, each had 2 × 4-in guns and were in the UK; 'T' Bty of 2nd RM Coast Rgt was at Eypemouth, near Bridport; 'U' and 'W' Btys of the same Regiment were at Bembridge, Isle of Wight; 'X' Bty in 1940 with MNBDO I was at Sunk Island, Yorkshire; 'Y' Bty from May 1940 to March 1941 was in Iceland before returning to the UK; 'Z' Bty was at Harwich, Essex, in 1940. 'X' and 'Z' Btys were in Crete in May 1941 and suffered heavy casualties. 'X' was re-formed in Egypt in June 1942 and later served in Ceylon during 1942–3. 'Z' Bty served in 1941–2 on Addu Atoll in the India Ocean. These Batteries were initially equipped with 4-in guns on special Hazard Mountings, which made them mobile enough to be positioned once they had been landed in 1940–1; later the Batteries had other naval 4-in guns in conventional coast mountings at times.

All Batteries but 'Y' were disbanded as of 15 May 1944 (RMRO 719/44). 'Y' Bty does not appear to have been reformed after personnel served in RM Coast Defence Rgt in August 1943.

Kent RM, Chatham RM, Devon RM, Hants RM, Sussex RM and Dorset RM: these coast batteries initially had 2 × 6-in guns and control posts or rooms; the guns were a Naval type on coast defence mountings. In the summer of 1940 the Batteries were deployed as follows: 'Kent' detached from MNBDO I, sent to Lowestoft, Suffolk, with 3 × 6-in guns later handed over to Royal Artillery; 'Devon' in Iceland without guns, then to Folkestone, Kent, with 2 × 6-in but to be trained as Howitzer Battery May 1940, see 2nd Coast Rgt unit history; 'Hants' at Sheringham, Norfolk. During 1941–2 'Sussex' at Littlehampton, Sussex, and 'Dorset' at Portland, Dorset. Men of 'Hants' in Crete with 6-in guns but no mountings in May 1941. After service in Egypt at different periods, these heavy coast batteries were deployed in Indian Ocean islands bases – 'Kent' and 'Devon' on Addu Atoll ('Devon' on Hitadu Island) in September 1942, but sickness reduced both Batteries from their former strength to 50 men. 'Kent' was redesignated 'Chatham' when in the 3rd Coast Rgt at Katukurunda in Ceylon in August 1943. See also Coast Regiments' unit history summaries for deployment of these 6-in Batteries in Italy and Ceylon. Although some of these Batteries had been disbanded in practice before 15 May 1944, they appear to have continued as 'of record' until all were disbanded as of 15 May 1944 (RMRO 719/44).

Devon RM Light AA: formed from Devon RM Coast Battery's personnel *et al*, see 1 RM Coast Brigade unit history summary.

Portsmouth RM: with 3rd Coast Rgt in Ceylon August 1943, equipped with Bofors.

St Angelo RM Light AA: clerks, MOAs and other RM personnel of Naval headquarters in Malta, manned Lewis guns in air defences from June 1040 to mid-January 1941, when they received two Bofors. The guns were sited near the upper barracks, with a third Bofors for a time in the wardroom garden. These crews worked in the base when not closed up, by May 1941 there were two crews for the pair of Bofors in the barracks. They could change a barrel in a little over 16 seconds. Among the crews' memories were the German G-mines with Bakelite wind baffles, low-flying aircraft and an issue of semi-armour-piercing shells. These shells were intended for use against Italian coastal forces which had raided the harbour on 25–6 July 1941. A 1,000lb bomb hit the Sergeants Mess that autumn, but heavy raids were not renewed until January 1942, the Battery later being showered from time to time with unexploded air defence rockets. The Battery claimed over 50 planes, and crews were awarded a DSC and Bar, four DSMs and five 'Mentions'.

RM Gun Location Battery: formed by 1 RM AA Brigade for accurately surveying gun sites on map grid references, etc. A Gun Location Section for similar work was part of the HQ Wing of the Beach Units of MNBDO I and surveyed coastal as well as anti-aircraft sites.

RM AA Operations Rooms: in March 1942, 1 RM Air Defence Bde formed an AA Ops Room; in August a second Ops Room was formed by 2 RM Air Defence Bde. Personnel of this second Ops Room were later absorbed into the AA Ops Room of 5 RM AA Bde, when the Air Defence Brigade was disbanded in the spring of 1944.

Signals detachments with artillery units: in 1940 RM Batteries' communications were in Army or navy signals networks in the UK, but when overseas the MNBDO Headquarters provided signals detachments. Some of these signallers formed the signals element of 5 RM AA Brigade's Operations Room in 1944–5.

1st RM Survey Company: with HQ of AA Command Ceylon and formerly L & M Unit. In March 1944 absorbed by 5 RM AA Bde HQ and disbanded in December 1945 or soon afterwards.

MNBDO SPECIALIST SUB-UNITS

MNBDO I Units

Landing and Maintenance Group/L & M Unit: Formed in February 1940 but Naval ratings for boat crews and some RM specialists did not join this Group until late in 1940. At that time some units that later became part of HQ Wing were commanded by this Group. Elements of the Group had been with the 6-in gun coast defence RM Batteries that summer, before they embarked for Egypt. The name 'Group' was changed to Unit on 1 April 1941, when the subunits' names were also changed, although their roles remained the same. The **Boat Unit** became the **Boat Company** with Naval cutters and some landing craft when available, they were used for landing stores and equipment. By the summer of 1941 this Company was training with LCMs at Kabrit, Egypt. There were also two Companies equipped with scaffolding, concrete mixers, four Lister (TLC type) lorries, road roller, roller conveyor and other handling equipment for stores, pier building and making short sections of roadway.

In May 1941 the L & M Unit was in Crete, from where the majority of its personnel were successfully withdrawn. Early in 1942 they were deployed in building Naval bases on islands in the Indian Ocean. The Unit formed a **Transport Company** and a **Workshop Company** in addition to **Nos 1 and 2 Companies** and the Boat Company. About this time the Unit moved to Ceylon.

The Unit went to India in 1943 for training with XXXIII Indian Corps and during this time, in October 1943 the **Beach Park Company** was formed. Its personnel prepared sites for stores dumps etc. in a beachhead.

RM Survey Section/Survey and Meteorological Section/1st RM Survey Company: formed in February 1940 as part of L & M Group, this Section provided maps and surveyors who located precisely the map grid reference of the gun positions of both AA and coast batteries, and advised on such matters as the guns' heights above sea-level, for calculation of the guns' ranges etc. The meteorological services for AA and Coast Batteries came under the command of this Section from about September 1943 to March 1944 (it does not appear to have had RM in its title as it included RN meteorologists) when it was attached to 1 RM Air Defence Bde in Ceylon. Before the L & M Unit returned to the UK with this Section, the naval meteorological officers left it, and the Section became the 1st RM Survey Company with HQ AA Command Ceylon (formerly 1 RM Air Defence Brigade HQ).

RM Signals Company/RM Signals Unit: formed in February 1940, its personnel were the signallers in an MNBDO. These specialist signallers served with both higher and lower formations (see chapter 3). Early in 1943 the signals Company was redesignated Signals Unit but continued to provide specialist supervision and training for detachments with various HQs including that of the Survey and Meteorological Section. the Unit came under command of 3 Mobile Naval Base in August 1943, but the detachment with 1 RM AA Bde HQ may have been redesignated Signals detachment AA Command Ceylon.

HQ Wing: formed on 5 March 1940, it eventually was comprised of the following – Camouflage Section; Beach Park Company (attached to L & M Units, see above); HQ Transport Company; Survey Section, which had two sub-Sections – Meteorological and Gun Location – both attached to 1 RM Air Defence Bde; Bomb Disposal Section; and other specialists under command from time to time, including medical units.

Ordnance Depot: formed in the 1920s as a small depot for MNBDO-type stores, it was expanded in the spring of 1940, moved to Egypt in 1941, and in 1943 moved to Ceylon before returning to the UK in 1944. most of the specialist stores were then retained at Fort Cumberland.

MNBDO II Units

HQ Wing: formed in March 1941, by December 1943 the units and sub-units under command included four Street major units – Ordnance Depot, Group Supply Unit, Medical Services and Boat Unit – and a number of specialist smaller units. While in the UK the Wing was deployed in training exercises before embarking for Egypt. The Wing's Units were deployed to various locations before going to Sicily and Italy in support of naval parties as well as MNBDO forces.

Landing and Maintenance Unit: formed in January 1941, and with effect from 1 October 1942, 'X' company of the 19th RM Battalion became No. 3 Company of this L & M Unit. By December 1943 it had four companies – Landing, Ship Unloading, Pioneer/Defence and Engineer – which while in the UK trained both in port operating and in amphibious landings. On arriving in Egypt in the summer of 1943, the Companies were on occasions employed in the roles for which they had trained, but not until they landed at Augusta, Sicily, were they able to make full use of their special training, as they did later in Italy.

BEACH UNITS

RM Beach Battalion/RM Beach Unit HQ/QG RM Beach Group

The RM division formed this Battalion[1] on 7 July 1941 at Warblington Camo, Havant near Portsmouth. First CO Lt-Col J. P. Phillipps whose Battalion had two roles: to land RM Division and its stores, holding the beach area as the Division moved inland; or when elements of the Division were used in a raid, to cover its subsequent withdrawal and to reload stores. In both roles the Division expected to organise the flow of ammunition and stores over an open beach, having cleared paths through mine fields, created beach exits, laid roads and built light-weight piers. Much of the landing concept, however, appears to have been built around the off-loading of ships into MLCs, for the LST and LCT had not been brought into service – the first LCT did her trials in November 1941. The HQ Company of 1941 had an AA Platoon and an Administrative Platoon, and three Beach Companies. Each Beach Company had a Beach Platoon of four Sections and a Ship Unloading Platoon with six gangs to work in holds, its equipment included or was to include: four bulldozers; four dumpers; and 200yds of Briggs Roadway. In all 1,050 personnel, with No. 4 Signals Company attached from the Division's signallers.

While in the UK the Ship Unloading Platoons did stevedores' work in Southampton docks, and 'picked men' supplemented AA gun crews on escort and anti-submarine destroyers. One subsection aboard HMS *Fernie* on the night of 4–5 May 1942, engaged German E-boats with two Brens on Motley mountings, helping the ship's guns to sink one of the boats. After various exercises, it became clear that the Beach Battalion could only land two infantry battalions, but it had few opportunities to practice with LCTs when these first came into service.

The Beach Battalion HQ had been redesignated Beach Unit HQ in September 1942, and in October became HQ RM Beach Group and the Companies formed 1 and 2 Beach Groups, but by January 1943 the special nature of RM Beach Group had become impractical – see below. On 10 May 1943 the name of HQ RM Beach Group was again changed to QGRM Beach Group (at that date the logistical staff was known as Quartermaster General's staff); and its function changed in August 1944 to the HQ for training the two intended beach battalions 27th and 28th RM Bns, before these subsequently went overseas as infantry battalions with 116 RM Brigade. It then acted as their rear HQ in the UK, and remained in existence as QG RM Beach Group until January 1945, if not until that spring.

1 and 2 RM Beach Groups/1 and 2 RM Landing Groups

Both formed[2] in October 1942 from Companies of the Beach Battalion, these Groups did a series of amphibious exercises: at Emsworth, Hampshire; in Scotland; and at Christchurch, Dorset. In May 1943 their names were changed to 1 RM and 2 RM Landing Group respectively; but these Groups needed an Army War Establishment, so that follow-up units could also be handled by these RM Groups and not just RM battalions with their special organisation. Therefore the RM Groups were disbanded at Christchurch on 31 July 1943, the personnel going to the Holding Unit of the RM Division.

1st Middle East Beach Brick/Beach Brick 31

The 7th RM Battalion was the nucleus around which the first Middle East Beach Brick was

created (see Chapter 5); and when the Brick was enlarged in 1943 as Brick 31, they prepared to land in Sicily with 231 Brigade. During the early stages of the build-up, 7th RM Bn remained with the Brick but on D+7, the Battalion reverted to an infantry role under XXX Corps.

Force X/RM Detachment 300

This force initially comprised an RM Ship Unloading Company, RM Engineers and landing craft crews serving under RN command in Iceland from July 1940 to June 1942. There they handled stores and other work at the RN Repair Base at Hvitanes. (The LC Flotilla subsequently went to New Guinea in the late summer of 1944.[3]) In February 1943 another Force X was formed at Deal with 480 RM Engineers, kitted for shore service but with sea kit bags. Each man had a rifle, 50 rounds of ammunition and the Force had three days rations. Its postal address was RM Detachment 300. Having had embarkation leave, the Detachment was ready for overseas service by 12 March 1943 (RM Circ 123/26/43QS dated 3 February 1943). Elements of Force X or possibly men from Detachment 300 were still in Iceland in 1944.

OTHER MOBILE BASE UNITS

MOLCAB I

The Mobile Landing Craft Advanced Base[4] (Naval Party 2400 *Landswell*) was formed January/February 1945, under Col C. M. Sergeant, OBE, DSC, to provide shore base facilities for minor landing craft flotillas and their maintenance units operating away from their parent carrier ships (LSIs) on ferry services, etc. in the Far East. MOLCAB I sailed from the UK for Australia in February and served in Singapore before returning to the UK and being disbanded in the autumn of 1945.

MOLCAB II

Similar unit[5] to MOLCAB I above, formed in February 1945 as Naval Party 2401 *Landlock*, under Col C. S. N. Smith. Due to sail in March 1945 for the Pacific, it was not employed operationally before World War II ended.

MOLCAB III

Similar to MOLCAB I, formed at Hayling Island Camp (Northney II) in February 1945,[6] (as Naval Party 2402) with older personnel than in other MOLCABs. COs were: Lt-Col E. C. Hoar, February to 29 April 1945; and Lt-Col J. P. Kelly. It was joined by No. 6 Mobile Base Maintenance

Unit (MBMU 6). The base personnel were shipped to Antwerp by LST, where they tran-shipped stores to set up, with 'Red', 'Blue', and 'White' Camp teams, three bases in the Boreham area, near Antwerp. From these camps the engineer ratings of MBMU 6, joined by Landing Craft Repair Unit No. 8 and a Naval crane party (with 4 × Bay City cranes), maintained 660, 661, 821, 822, 823 LC Flotillas of Force U, which were ferrying stores. In mid-April 1945 this Force became Ferry Squadron Force T. In May MOL-CAB III moved to Nijmegen to set up camps for the maintenance personnel of the flotillas ferrying men and cargoes on the Rhine. The next month they returned to the UK and were disbanded, as the majority of the personnel were due to be demobilised.[7]

MOBLABs IV, V AND VI

Although 'IV' was formed in April 1945, both 'V' and 'VI' did not complete their formation, begun in July 1945, and all three were disbanded later that year.[8] Only 'IV' has been identified as a Naval Party (NP 2003).

MOLCAB Assembly Base

This RN command on Hayling Island (HMS *Dragonfly*) became an RM command on 12 July 1945, CO Lt-Col T. P. Honnor, but the base was disbanded that autumn.

MOBILE NAVAL AIR BASES (MONABS)

Eleven of these had reached the planning stages by August 1945, and two battalions of RM Engineers had reached Australia to join Naval Party 580, who were to build the intermediate forward air base at Manus, in the Admiralty Islands, and had reached Australia early in 1945. Other detachments were assembling with 79 all ranks, including 30 tradesmen being drafted to MONAB XI that August. But the MONABS IX, X and XI were not deployed. In August most of the others were in Australia, with MONAB I (*Nabbington*) at Nowra (New South Wales), 'II' (*Nabberly*) at Bankstown (NSW), 'III' (*Nab-thorpe*) with the 2nd RME Battalion at Scho-fields, 'IV' (*Nabborrow*) had elements at Manus in the Admiralty Islands, 'V' (*Nabswick*) was at Nowra (NSW) in 1946, 'VI' was with 'III', and 'VIII' (*Nabbatcher*) served in Hong Kong. 'IV' was probably the TAMY (*Nabsford*) at Archerfield. All were disbanded as World War II ended before bases were required. Some of the personnel worked on restoration on harbour or other facilities before returning to the UK.

Ocean Fortresses

In September 1941 Col (later Brigadier) C. T. Brown reconnoitred Addu Atoll, as a result MNBDO I provided 500 all ranks in force 'Overt'. This force was commanded by Brig C. T. Brown until he was killed in a flying accident, he was succeeded by Brig Lukis. The personnel of 'Overt' installed guns on; Addu Atoll; on other islands including those in the Seychelles; and on a tiny atoll in the Chagos Archipelago some 1,000 miles south-west of Ceylon.[10] This small atoll of Diego Garcia would become familiar to Marines serving there in the 1990s with NP 1002. It is hot and humid with no land over six feet above sea level. During 1942 the landing points were blasted in the coral on these islands and roads were built linking the landing points to gun sites. Telephone cables were laid and a number of bridges were built for the Addu Atoll sites. In the autumn of 1942 the L & M Units of MNBDO I and RM Engineers returned to Addu Atoll to build Gan aerodrome.[11] Although this airfield was abandoned after World War II, it was rebuilt in the 1950s as an RAF staging post, and is used by the USAF in the 1990s. (See also Naval Party 1002.)

ARMOURED SUPPORT FORMATIONS

RM Armoured Support Craft Regiment

Formed at Merley House Camp, Wimborne[12], Dorset, during July and August 1943[13] from ranks of the RM Division's artillery units, it was reorganised in September with an HQ, 1, 2 and 3 Batteries, each with three Troops, and a Holding Battery. From 18 October the Regiment was under the direct command of AGRM (see RM Circ 7399/43). The personnel wore combined operations flashes. In each Troop were four detachments for LCGs,[14] but these became the nuclei of units in the Armoured Support Group after the Batteries moved to Le Marchant Barracks in Devizes, Wiltshire, as of 18 October 1943. The HQ was disbanded about March 1944.

RM Armoured Support Craft Group

Formed on 14 March 1944, this Group would command the two RM Armoured Support Regiments and an RM Independent Battery of Centaur tanks. It was commanded by Brig D. C. W. Sanders, OBE, AFC, who had been CRA of the RM Division. He was killed when this HQ was in Normandy in June 1944 and succeeded by the second-in-command Col A. J. Harvey, OBE.[15] See also HQ Wing (below). The small tactical headquarters was staffed by RM officers who developed: first, the techniques for firing engineless tanks on Bailey bridging in LCT(Adapted); and later, the methods of firing and control for these Centaurs with their engines replaced.

The headquarters returned to the UK in late June 1944 after several weeks in action, and on being disbanded that autumn the personnel were transferred to the 29th RM Bn, later forming the 34th Amphibian Support Regiment.

1st and 2nd RM Armoured Support Regiments

Formed in the spring of 1944, each with two Batteries, these Regiments were landed from LCT(Armoured), being LCT(Adapted) that had been modified. The HQs, each of some 40 all ranks, were mainly administrative, and only the tactical portion of two officers and two other ranks landed with the Batteries on 6 June 1944 in Normandy. The Regiments' personnel included RA officers and RA gunner-drivers, with RAC fitters and mechanics, but the majority were RM gunners, including those who had trained for LCG(L)s. Many of the HQ staff transferred ultimately to the 34th Amphibian Support Regiment, after the armoured Support Regiments were disbanded in the autumn of 1944.

1st RM, 2nd RM, 3rd RM, 4th RM and 5th RM (Independent) Support Batteries

The '1st' and '2nd' were in the 1st RM Armoured Support Regt, the '3rd' and '4th' in the 2nd RM Armoured Support Regt, and the '5th' was an independent Battery. Each had four Troops with its Left and Right Sections. Troop commanders were in Sherman tanks, with the two Centaurs of the Left Section, in one LCT(A). The Right Section of two Centaurs were in a second LCT(A). Operationally Batteries Nos 1 to 4 had no tactical HQ, as Troop commanders worked to their local artillery commands, therefore the Batteries' cooks and quartermasters landed in follow-up waves. After the initial landings described in chapter 6, the Batteries were used as independent units. The tanks of the '1st' and '2nd' supported 4 (Army) Commando and 48 RM Commando; the '3rd' and '4th' supported the Canadians, being deployed 3,000yds forward of the Canadian artillery. Troops from these last two Batteries assisted 46 RM Cdo on D+1 (7 June), and a Troop from the 5th RM Battery crossed the Orne river to give counter mortar fire in support of 4 SS (Commando) Brigade, among several independent actions by these Batteries before they were withdrawn on 24 June. By this time some 50 per cent had had mechanical failures. Although they had been intended as purely assault troops, they had stayed in action for almost three weeks and proved a valuable supplement to conventional artillery.

The Centaurs' 95-mm gun-howitzer had many parts in common with the 25-pdr, and as a totally protected gun in a turret was less vulnerable than self-propelled artillery. These tanks were taken over by RA gunners before the Batteries' personnel returned to the UK for disbandment on the formation of 29th RM Battalion on 3 October 1944, this Battalion later became the 34th RM Amphibian Support Regiment.

RM Armoured Support Group HQ Wing and holding Battery

This Wing included 65 RAC mechanics under command of five RAC officers,[16] and 50 RM reserves for tank crews. These mechanics, assisted by RM tank crews, made exceptional improvisations to keep the tanks in action, despite the limited facilities available.

34th RM Amphian Support Regiment

Formed under War Office control from the 29th RM Battalion on 1 March 1945, with a War Establishment of 43 officers and 725 other ranks,[17] including some Army personnel. The Regiment arrived in India on 8 May 1945, and was to have come under command of the Commando Group later that year. The Regiment's 1st and 2nd RM Support Batteries were equipped with LVT(Armoured), the 3rd RM (Rocket) Battery with LVT(Rocket), and the 4th RM Battery with LVT(Flamethrower). But the only operations carried out by this Regiment were in south East Asia, where it was equipped as infantry and employed on internal security operations for a short time in 1945. The Regiment returned to the UK in 1946, after carrying out internal security duties in India, and was disbanded that autumn.

NAVAL PARTIES AND MISSIONS

Naval Examination Service

Marine signallers served in small ships of this Service, which examined merchantmen entering British ports in wartime.

Conferences 1919–1939

Marines served as orderlies for many conferences, including the Washington Conference of 1922, when seven corporals were commended by the First Lord of the Admiralty, as they 'proved themselves equal to every . . . emergency in difficult circumstances'.[1]

North Persian[2]/Caspian Flotilla[3]

A small British Army formation in 1918 had been assisting a local Russian force to hold a Turkish advance, which the Germans had hoped might reach Afghanistan. In August they were joined by an RN force which armed a number of Russian ships and that December prevented the Bolsheviks gaining an ice-free port on the Caspian Sea, a sea of 600 miles from north to south and up to 300 miles wide, with nearly 1,000 sizeable vessels on its waters in 1918. The flotilla flew the Imperial Russian ensign before 2 March 1919,[2] when it came under British command. The ships *Venture*, *Fox*, *Emile Nobel*, *Alla Vardi*, *Salva*, and *Bibi-Abat* had RMA/RMLI detachments, each with 11 to 16 Marines, commanded by sergeants or corporals. Other ships had British gunners – *Kruger* with RA field artillery, and *Zorcaster* and *Asia* with RN seamen gunners. RN crews operated the Flotilla's ships, which also included the *Windsor Castle*, the improvised seaplane carrier *Orlionock*, and *Sergei* which carried some of the Flotilla's 12 RN Coastal Motor Boats. The old ships of the Flotilla, however, were limited to a best speed of 9 knots. Livestock was carried to provide rations for 14 days, but the sheep often died from the cold in the first week at sea.

Ashore a force of Royal Marines had set up coast guns at Petrovsk (Makhachkala in 1980) on the western shores of the Caspian, several hundred miles north of Baku, and from 1918 had garrisoned this advanced base. After January 1919 the 160 Marines of this defence force were attacked several times, but held the port after street fighting.[4]

At sea a typical action by *Emile Nobel* (3,799 tons) on 21 May 1919, when she was making a reconnaissance of Alexandrovsk (Fort Shevchenko in 1980). It began with her being hit by a 15-in shell. This killed 11 of her crew of 84[5] before she opened fire with her two 4-in QF guns. The flotilla then attacked the port and sank nine vessels. Allied aircraft – some 40 RAF planes supported the Flotilla – later drove the remaining Bolshevik ships from this port, and by the end of May the only armed Russian ships were in their Astrakhan base on the Volga estuary. But 13 improvised warships and a small force of aircraft could not control this sea, although they captured several Russian ships in August 1919 before handing the Flotilla over to the White Russians. The last Marines left Petrovsk on 2 September,[6] but before handing over the *Emile Nobel*, the breechblocks of her guns were thrown over the side, to disarm them.[7]

Naval Mission to Siberia/Kama River Flotillas

In 1917 some 600,000 tons of Allied war materials were a Vladivostock waiting to be shipped on the Trans-Siberian Railway, when an armistice was signed by Russia and Germany. A token Allied force was landed briefly in April 1918 to protect these supplies, and that summer more British, French, Japanese and American forces were landed.[8] By the autumn an armoured train was equipped by HMS *Suffolk* with one of her 6-in guns and 4 of her 12-pdrs. this train, with Royal Marines from *Suffolk*'s detachment, was in action in support of Czech forces fighting the Russians at Tischima, after the train had made a journey of 6,105 miles from Vladivostok. When the guns were frozen up, the train withdrew to Omsk in Central Russia, where in March 1919 another 6-in gun was fitted. This gun, from HMS *Kent*, had been brought to Omsk by a Canadian unit. The *Suffolk* detachment was then replaced by Capt T. H. Jameson (later Major General, CBE, DSO) with 29 RMLI NCOs and privates. All were volunteers, accompanied by four RN specialists including a doctor.

They reached Perm on the Kama River on 28 April just as the ice was breaking, and within a week had mounted the 6-in gun from the train in a Russian steamer renamed *Kent*, and the second '6-in' in a barge named *Suffolk*. The steamer *Kent* sank three armed Soviet steamers on 23 May,[9] in an action 300 miles south of Perm. She fired Lyddite shells from an opening range of 8,100yds and closed to 4,000yds before the remaining Bolshevik ships retired. The barge *Suffolk* was moored to support the steamer *Kent* and six ships of the Omsk government which were with her. But once the Czech Legion decided to withdraw, resistance crumbled. The steamer and barge's guns were in action against artillery positions on the river bank during June, after the river levels fell. Later they withdrew to Perm. A Bolshevik agent in the steamer *Kent*'s Russian crew added to the RM Detachment's difficulties, for 'a small force . . . in a foreign country . . . [can find] that any lack of security may quickly undermine morale'.[10]

The British Government withdrew its support for the Omsk Government, and the Marines with great ingenuity and little help put the guns on railway flat-trucks, requisitioned an engine and set off for Vladivostock. Despite typhus and small pox among refugees, train wrecks and marauding bands of guerrillas, they reached this base in 52 days, on 18 August 1919, having suffered only minor casualties. The Japanese held the base until October 1922; but when HMS *Carlisle* left the port that November, she reported that there were no disturbances when Soviet forces entered the port.[11]

Black Sea Operations

A naval garrison of seamen and Marines was landed in December 1918 at Sevastopol in the Crimea, and was strengthened to nearly 500 all ranks by men of the 3rd RM Battalion[12] before being relieved by French troops later that month. Allied support for the White Russian forces continued into the spring of 1919, but after April the RN ships' help was limited and by June they were observing a strict neutrality.

Upper Yangtse Guard

Formed on 15 November 1927 with an officer and 10 other ranks from HMS *Vindictive*'s detachment, the Guard sailed up river to help protect merchant ships passing through the rapids of the Upper Yangtze (modern Chang Jiang).[13] Other small detachments served in this Guard until 1928 or later.

Harwich Auxiliary Patrol

Formed from trawler crews in June 1940 with trawlers and other small vessels, the Patrol was in action against E-boats and German planes.[14] The crews were instructed in small arms and gunnery by nine RM sergeant pensioners.

Dutch Schuytes

Three of these[15] were commandeered by the Admiralty and two were commanded by RM officers – the first to command HM ships in World War II – with RM crews. They acted as Q-ships to counter E-boat attacks on shipping in the English Channel.

Force W Fire Control Unit

A number of Marines served in this unit as signallers in the latter part of 1945, if not before.

Naval Port Parties (Normandy and North West Europe 1944–5)

Four of these[16] were formed with RM personnel as well as Naval ratings in March 1944, to operate captured ports and for boat duties, etc. in the Mulberry harbour; they also manned Naval bases ashore.[17] They each had a repair element and communications parties.

The large party '1500' landed at Courseulles on 7 June 1944 with its repair element (NP 1526) and communications (NP 1518) – see chapter 6. The RM Passive Air Defence Section of '1500' was responsible for precautions against and

repairs after any air raids, but also worked on salvaging craft. Marines of '1500's' Administrative Section fed men in the Naval camp, while those who were telephonists and those who plotted movements on the HQ maps, worked in the HQ of '1500'. The boat crews were mainly RMs and the RM bomb disposal team cleared mines

The second of the large parties, '1501' was based at Ouistreham with its repair element (NP 1528) and its communications (NP 1518). Later its personnel went to man the Naval HQ at Rouen, and then moved to Antwerp.

The first of the smaller parties, '1502' with a repair party '1531' and communications '1520A, B & C', was at Calais, but some elements were at Port-en-Bessin (1502A) and others at Ostend and Zeebrugge. The second of the smaller parties, '1503' was at Boulogne with its repair element '1530' and communications as NP 1521.

NP 1686 with Naval ratings and some Marines cleared Dieppe harbour of mines and obstructions in July 1944. NP 1715 when later in North West Europe included 324 RM Engineers. NP 1747 dismantled a V1 flying-bomb launching site in February 1945, and sent it to Chatham. NP 1749 with RM signallers was in Germany in the autumn of 1945.

Naval parties – ships' names 1944–50s

Port parties at major bases were given ships' names and RM detachments, RM Landing Craft flotillas and SBS served in these formations, which often commanded more units than the numbered Naval Party, or the Port Party initially clearing a port or setting up a headquarters. The names were:

Princess Amelia, 1945 Europe; *Princess Irene*, 1946 Berlin; *Princess Louisa*, 1945–6 Brunsbüttel on river Elbe; *Royal Adelaide*, 1945–6 Tonning, on Eider estuary; *Royal Albert*, Berlin in 1945 and later, but by the 1950s had become the depot in an ex-German ship at Cuxhaven, near Hamburg; *Royal Alfred*, Kiel in 1945 and later; *Royal Caroline*, 1945–? Lübeck on the Baltic; *Royal Charles*, port parties at Le Havre and later at Calais in 1945; *Royal Harold* (NP 1742) in April 1945 at Kiel, later merged with NP 1743; *Royal James*, parties at Boulogne 1944–5; *Royal Prince* in 1945–6 at Emden, Lower Saxony and later name of a parent ship for all RN forces in Germany; *Royal William*, port parties at Cherbourg, France 1944–?

Naval Party Operation 'Grapple'

In 1956 this party, No. 2512,[18] included a flotilla of RM LCMs and other Marines, about 56 in all, who were deployed in landing stores, and building roads, camps and other installations for the testing of the British hydrogen bombs in 1957 on Christmas Island in the Pacific. Their LST *Messina* had been modified to carry six LCMs launched by a boom crane.

Falkland Islands
A small detachment of Royal Marines was maintained on these islands from the 1960s to 1982 as NP 8901 – see also chapter 10.

Other Naval Parties in World War II
There were many naval parties in which RMs served as specialists or guards from time to time, and some included complete RM units described elsewhere in this Appendix. For example, Party 2402 included MOLCAB III.[19] Almost all Naval Parties are formed for a specific task lasting a relatively short period but occasionally – as in the Falklands up to 1982 – they are in commission for many years. In World War II the '800s' were mainly deployed in the Mediterranean, the '1500s' (see above) and '1600s' in North-West Europe, and the '4000s' included landing craft ferry crews in India and SEAC. The large NP 31 in India became '1031' in Rangoon, in a typical example of the renumbering of a party on its redeployment.

Carrier Borne Air (later Ground) Liaison Sections
These[20] were formed in 1943 to carry out similar duties to those which Forward Observation Officers carried out in directing Naval guns, but CBALs (Seabals) directed aircraft on to ground targets or worked in intelligence teams. The RMs in these units were trained at Yeovilton RNAS by 1946. There were CBALs numbered in the 60s by this date, when 20 of them returned to the UK from the British Pacific Fleet. CBAL 51 was formed on 22 September 1944 but by 1947 CBAL 70 was an HQ at Yeovilton. The Army had sponsored these Sections in 1943 and many included Army officers, but by 1961 the Corps was unable to provide officers for training in this role, and the units continued as purely Army Sections.

Beach Control Parties
These Parties in World War II had been Royal Navy Commandos operating under command of a Beachmaster RN, who controlled the berthing at landing points and was in general responsible for the organisation of craft's beaching, coordinating this with the operational requirements as a beachhead developed. In July 1946 three officers and 37 other ranks were in training as half of a beach party to learn from RN experience. They were moved to Rosneath on the Clyde estuary but were reduced to a cadre of eight,[21] from which the knowledge of Beach Control Parties' work was retained and later expanded. The Parties had their equivalents in the LPDs of the 1990s, as a part of the Beach Units in Assault Squadron.

SHIPS' DETACHMENTS

Many ships were laid up immediately after World War I, or, in the case of older vessels, had been stripped of their guns, but the lists below of capital ships and cruisers existing in 1919 but disposed of by 1932 indicate the Corps' commitment to Naval gunnery at the end of that war. Details are given of displacement tonnage and the date of a ship's first inclusion in government financial estimates. See any standard reference books of Naval ships, for details of the armament, but Royal Marines almost invariably manned at least one main turret and a number of secondary guns.

Detachment sizes are indicated by letter 'd' and RM band sizes by 'b', where these have been estimated the item is starred (*). These figures are indicative only of the size of these units for several reasons. In the 1930s many detachments were as much as 25 per cent below their establishment strength, due to the shortage of manpower. The approved strengths for wartime service were some 35 per cent above those of peacetime. In some cases the actual strengths were even increased by 50 per cent after the outbreak of World War II as additional armaments were added. Further increases in weaponry during that War, led to further increases in detachment sizes and no doubt in band sizes, where musicians were needed for increased instrumentation in the T/S. Detachments were further increased on those ships acting as flagships.

The dates of a ship's completion and of its disposal are shown in parentheses, except for those disposed of before 1932. Not included are a number of ships on which Marines served briefly, including the gunboats in China, destroyers at Narvik, and depot ships and submarines on which individual Marines occasionally served.

Battleships and Dreadnoughts of 1919, disposed of by 1932
Majestic-class (14,900 tons) of 1894 – d-and-b 80*, in *Caesar, Hannibal, Jupiter, Magnificent, Prince George* and *Victorious*.
Canopus-class (12,950 tons) of 1896 – d-and-b 100*, in *Albion, Canopus, Glory,* and *Vengeance*.

Formidable-class (15,000 tons) of 1898 – d-and-b 100* in *Implacable*.

London-class (15,000 tons) of 1898 – d-and-b 100* in *London* and *Venerable*.

Duncan-class (14,000 tons) of 1898 – d-and-b 100* in *Albermarle*, *Duncan* and *Exmouth*.

Queen-class (15,000 tons) of 1901 – d-and-b 100* in *Queen* and *Prince of Wales*.

Purchased from Chile *Swiftsure* (11,800 tons) of 1902 – d and b not traced.

King Edward-class (16,350 tons) of 1902 – d-and-b 100* in *Africa*, *Commonwealth*, *Dominion*, *Hibernia*, *Hindustan* and *Zealand*.

Lord Nelson-class (16,500 tons) of 1904 – d-and-b 100*

Dreadnought (17,900 tons) of 1906 – d and b not traced.

Temeraire-class (18,000 tons) of 1907 – d-and-b 96 in *Bellerophon*, *Superb* and *Temeraire*.

St Vincent-class (19,250 tons) of 1909 – d-and-b 99 in *Collingwood* and *St Vincent*.

Neptune (19,900 tons) of 1909 – d-and-b 97.

Colossus-class (20,000 tons) of 1909 – d-and-b 99 in *Colossus* and *Hercules*.

Orion-class (22,500 tons) of 1912 – d-and-b 97 in *Conqueror*, *Monarch*, *Orion* and *Thunder* (see also post-1932).

King George-class (23,000 tons) of 1911 – d-and-b 97 in *Ajax*, *Centurion* (in 1913 used as radio controlled target ship, see also post-1932) and *King George V*. When these were flagships the d-and-b was 107.

Iron Duke-class (25,000 tons) of 1912 – d 109 and b 24 in *Benbow*, *Emperor of India*, *Iron Duke* (see also post-1932) and *Marlborough* (see also post-1932).

Battleships 1932–1960

Iron Duke – see above – (1912–46 but disarmed c1922)

Centurion – see above – used as a Mulberry blockship in 1944.

Queen Elizabeth-class (31,100 tons) of 1912–13 – d 115 and b 24 in *Barham* (1915–41, sunk), *Queen Elizabeth* (1915–48), *Warspite* (1915–47, with a d 200 and b 24 at times in World War II), *Malaya* (1916–48) and *Valiant* (1916–48).

Royal Sovereign-class (29,150 tons) of 1913–14 – d 125 and b 22 in *Resolution* (1916–48), *Revenge* (1916–48), *Royal Sovereign* (1916–1943 when secondary armament was reduced, 1944 to USSR) and *Ramillies* (1917–48).

Nelson (33,500 tons) and *Rodney* (33,900 tons) both of 1922 – d 185 and b 20 (1927–49 and 1927–48) respectively.

King George V-class (35,000 tons) of 1936–7 – d-and-b 350 in *King George V* (1950–48), *Duke of York* (1941–58), *Prince of Wales* (1941 and sunk that year), *Anson* (1942–58) and *Howe* (1942–58).

Vanguard (44,500 tons) of wartime (1940) but not built until later – d-and-b 350, for Royal tour in 1947 the band was increased to 50* (1946–60)

Battle-Cruisers

Invincible-class (17,250 tons) of 1906 – d-and-b 86 in *Indomitable* (1908–21) and *Inflexible* (19808–21).

Improved Invincible-class (18,750 tons) of 1909 – d-and-b 86 in HMAS *Australia* (1912–24) and *New Zealand* (1912–22).

Lion-class (26,350) of 1909 – d-and-b 88 in *Lion* (1919–24) and *Princess Royal* 1912–22. When these were flagships, the d-and-b was 94.

Tiger (28,500 tons) of 1911 – d-and-b 115 (1914–32).

Renown-class of world War I – d-and-b 157* in *Renown* (1916–48) and *Repulse* (1916–1941 sunk).

Hood (42,100 tons) – d 135* and b 17 (1920–41 sunk).

Capital ships' service in World War II

Barham was torpedoed while on Atlantic patrol on 28 December 1939, but reached Liverpool. In November 1940 she joined the Mediterranean Fleet and was in action at Cape Matapan in March 1941. She was later sunk by torpedoes while exercising off Egypt when doing 17 knots, only 300 of her crew of 1,150 were saved.

Queen Elizabeth was in action off Crete in May 1941, but on 19 December that year was heavily damaged while in Alexandria, Egypt, by 'human' torpedoes. She was recommissioned at Devonport (Plymouth) in July 1943 after returning from extensive repairs in America. She arrived at Ceylon on 28 January 1944, to support air strikes against Sabang and Sourabata, before going to South Africa for a refit that winter. As flagship of the 3rd Battle Squadron, in January 1945 she again bombarded Sabang and operated against other Japanese island defences, before sailing for the UK on 12 July 1945.

Warspite sailed from the Mediterranean to join the Home Fleet in 1939, returned to the 'Med' in 1940, but was recalled for the defence of Norway. In the 2nd Battle of Narvik she bombarded shore batteries. In May she again returned to the 'Med'. During early 1941 she bombarded North African ports, but in May her starboard secondary armament was wrecked by bombs. After refit in the USA, she was flagship of the Eastern Fleet, and early in 1943 she covered convoys to Australia. Later she supported landings at Sicily and

Salerno, but on 16 September she was hit by a German glider-bomb, flooded and had to be towed to Malta. During 1944, despite having one turret out of commission, she covered the Normandy landings but on 13 June when returning to UK to replace her worn gun barrels, she hit a mine. When repaired she took part in the Walcheren landings among other bombardments.

Malaya covered the third Canadian troop convoy, arriving in the Clyde on 7 February 1940. She went to the Mediterranean to cover Malta convoys and take part in North African bombardments. On 9 February 1941, with *Renown*, she bombarded Genoa. When escorting convoy SL68 to Sierra Leonne in West Africa, she was sighted by German capital ships, which then left the area. After refitting in the USA, she joined the Eastern Fleet in 1944 and was serving in the East Indies during 1945.

Valiant completed an extensive refit in December 1939 before sailing to the West Indies. She covered Atlantic convoys and the passage of troops from Norway in June 1940, before sailing to the 'Med' in August. In December she bombarded Valona. In March 1941 she was in the battle of Cape Matapan, where she fired 62 15-in shells and got about 20 hits on Italian ships. On 21 April she fired more than 200 shells into Tripoli, and later escaped any major bomb damage off Crete and attacks from 'human' torpedoes. After refitting in the USA, she joined the Eastern Fleet in January 1944, and that spring through to the summer, she bombarded Japanese defences on various islands. But on 8 August she was accidentally sunk while in a floating dock at Trincomalee. Refitting after this mishap was not completed, although she reached to UK after temporary repairs.

Resolution covered the escorts of bullion convoys to Canada, then served with the Halifax Escort Force before going to Dakar, in West Africa in September 1940. There she was hit by four heavy shells and a French torpedo. After repairs she joined Force H in 1941, escorting convoys in the Mediterranean. By March 1942 she was in Ceylon with the Eastern fleet. In February 1943 she covered troop convoys to Australia, before returning to the Clyde to become the Depot Ship in the Gareloch which leads to the Clyde estuary.

Revenge was also in the bullion convoy of October 1939, sailing to Canada and later covered Atlantic troop convoys. In October 1940 she bombarded Cherbourg, while she was being held in home waters for some months, against the possible breakout of German capital ships from Brest. She joined the Halifax Escort Force

in the summer of 1941, and later sailed to join the Eastern Fleet, arriving in Ceylon in March 1942, and early in 1943 she covered convoys to Australia.

Royal Oak was in the Home Fleet based on Scapa Flow, when *U-47* torpedoed her at anchor on 14 October 1939. She capsized and sank in 13 minutes with the loss of 834 officers and men, including most of her RM detachment.

Royal Sovereign was in the Home Fleet in 1939 and joined the Halifax Escort Force in 1940. She was with the Eastern Fleet in 1941–2. Her secondary armament of 12 6-in guns was reduced to 10 in 1943. She was lent to the USSR from 30 May 1944 until she was returned to the UK in 1948 or 1949.

Ramillies was in the Mediterranean Fleet in September 1939, but escorted Australian troops to the Red Sea in January 1940. On 8 February 1941, after joining the Atlantic force covering convoy escorts, she was covering convoy HX106 when *Scharnhorst* and *Gneisenau* sighted her and broke off their intended action. She supported the Madagascar landings and her Marines were put ashore behind the French lines (see chapter 4). Shortly after these landings, she was torpedoed by a Japanese midget submarine, but there was only one minor casualty. After temporary repairs in Durban, South Africa, she sailed for a refit in Plymouth. On 6 June 1944 she took part in the Normandy bombardment and later bombarded Toulon and Port Cros in support of landings in southern France.

Nelson was built to limits set by the Washington Treaty. In September 1939 she was flagship of the Home Fleet. On 4 December she struck a magnetic mine while entering Loch Ewe on the west coast of Scotland. Repaired by September 1940, she was searching for enemy raiding ships in Norwegian waters. In March 1941 she covered the Army commandos' second series of landings on the Lofoten Islands, then she escorted troop convoys to Cape Town, before returning to Gibraltar to join Force H in July. On 27 September she was hit by an enemy aircraft's torpedo, forcing her return to the UK for repairs and a refit. The following April (1942) she joined the Home Fleet; in May she escorted a convoy to Freetown, West Africa, and in August she escorted the last convoy to Malta, before its relief from constant air attack. She briefly returned to home waters before joining Force H, and was its flagship during the Sicily landings. In November she returned to the UK. In June 1944 she carried out 21 bombardments in support of the Normandy landings, being slightly damaged by a mine during the last of these. On 24 June she sailed for an extensive refit in the USA. On its completion in January 1945, she returned to the UK, and arrived in the Far East early in July to support operations in Malaya. On 3 September the surrender of the local Japanese in the Penang area was received aboard *Nelson*; and on 12 September at Singapore, the surrender of Japanese forces in South East Asia was signed aboard her. She sailed for home on 13 November.

Rodney, like *Nelson*, was built to limits set by the Washington Treaty. She was with the home Fleet in September 1939, and on 8 April 1940, while with *Valiant* off Bergen, Norway, she was hit by a 500kg bomb during three hours of air attacks. In June she was in the covering force protecting convoys from Norway, and the following November she joined a force covering Atlantic convoys. She was detached from this work in late May 1941 to join *King George V* in hunting the *Bismark*. After this she refitted in America, returning to the UK in November. During the following months she operated off Norway, positioned to capture raiding ships in Hvalfiord among other waters. During 1942 she covered convoys to Malta, bombarded Fort Santon and in 1943 was with Force 4 to cover the landings in Sicily. In June 1944 she was one of the bombardment force off the Normandy coast, successfully breaking up counterattacks on the British 3 Division; in July she supported an Army offensive near Caen; and later that month destroyed much of the battery of heavy coast guns on Alderney in the Channel Islands. By September she was covering convoys to Russia and from 30 November 1944 to April 1945, she was the flagship of the Home Fleet.

King George V, like others of her class, had 14-in guns with a better penetrative power, range and rate of fire than the older 15-in guns. She joined the Home Fleet in October 1940, covered the March 1941 landings on the Lofoten Islands, North Norway, and was Admiral Tovey's flagship in the action against the *Bismark*. During 1942 she covered Atlantic convoys and searched for raiders before joining Force H in May 1943 at Gibraltar. Later that year she covered the Sicily landings and carried out shore bombardments. After a refit in the UK during February to July 1944, she sailed to join the Pacific Fleet in October. Early in 1945 she was in a force bombarding Japanese island aerodromes as part of the Okinawa operations, in July she bombarded installations on the Japanese mainland, and on 2 September she was in Tokyo for the Japanese surrender. After refitting in Australia, she took the Duke and Duchess of Gloucester to Tasmania

in January 1946, before returning to the UK. She was flagship of the Home Fleet during the latter part of 1946. After a long refit she became a training ship but in 1950 she was laid up, being one of the first capital ships to be 'sealed for preservation'.

Duke of York she – like the *KGV* – had powerful 14-in guns. She joined the Home Fleet on 6 November 1941 and carried the flag of the second-in-command, taking the Prime Minister to America in December. During early 1942 she covered convoys to Russia, before joining Force H. She was flagship of this Force during the North African landings in November 1942 but returned to the UK for a refit that winter. On 8 May 1943 she became the flagship of the Home fleet. That December she was in action against the *Scharnhorst*. She supported aircraft carriers in strikes against *Tirpitz* in a Norwegian fjord before she began a long refit in September. This was to prepare her for operations in the Far East. In July 1945 she arrived at Sydney and was at Manus on 15 August. She returned to the UK in summer of 1946 and that December became the flagship of the Home Fleet. She was transferred to the Reserve Fleet in April 1949.

Prince of Wales was in action against the *Bismark* in May 1941, before she had competed her work-up cruise. In August she took Prime Minister Churchill to Newfoundland for meetings with President Roosevelt. She returned to the UK, then had a brief spell in the Mediterranean, where on 24 September 1941 she shot down seven planes. She again returned to home waters, before sailing for Singapore as flagship of the Eastern Fleet. On 10 December, within days of her arrival, she was sunk by Japanese aircraft.

Anson joined the Home Fleet in April 1942, and, as flagship of the second-in-command, she covered convoys to Russia. She also protected aircraft carriers during strikes in 1943 against shipping in Norwegian waters, and in February 1944 against the *Tirpitz*. In April 1945 she sailed from Scapa to work-up in the 'Med' before going to the Far East. There she was with the force reoccupying Hong Kong and returned to the UK in July 1946. After a spell as flagship of the Training Squadron she was laid up.

Howe arrived in Scapa in August 1942 for her work-up. After covering convoys to Russia and patrolling northern waters against potential raiders, she joined Force H in the early summer of 1943. She was based on Algiers (modern El Djazair) with *KGV*, she covered Mediterranean convoys and carried out shore bombardments. In October 1943 she returned to the UK for a refit in preparation for sailing to the Far East. She arrived there in June 1944, and that summer bombarded Japanese railway workshops in Sumatra, in modern Indonesia. In December 1944 she sailed from Ceylon as flagship of the Pacific Fleet. In the late spring and early summer of 1945 she took part in the bombardments of aerodromes and other Japanese island defences, sailing in June, via Australia, for a refit in South Africa. In late September 1946 she relieved *Nelson* in the East Indies Fleet before sailing for the UK that December. She was later flagship of the home Fleet's Second Battle Squadron before joining the Training Squadron, and was laid up in 1951.

Vanguard was not completed until after World War II, she took part in a major Royal tour in 1946–7.

Battle-cruisers in the 1920s carried out a number of tours showing the flag around the World. Lord Jellicoe and his staff had a year-long cruise from 21 February 1919 to 2 February 1920 in *New Zealand*. She sailed 33,000 nautical miles visiting India, Australasia, USA, Cuba and other countries on this tour. *Renown* took the Prince of Wales on his tours to the USA, Canada and Australia in 1920–21, and the following year took him on visits to India and Japan, in one of several major cruises before World War II.

Renown in 1939 was modernised with new engines. In the early months of World War II she was based on Freetown, West Africa, and with *Ark Royal* was searching for surface raiders making for the South Atlantic. She reached Montevideo, Uruguay, soon after the *Graf Spee* was scuttled. In 1940 she was Vice-Admiral Whitworth's flagship off Norway and on 9 April was in action against the *Scharnhorst* and *Gneisenau* (see chapter 3). She later joined Force H as Admiral Somerville's flagship. In April 1942 she escorted the carrier USS *Wasp* with 41 RAF Spitfires aboard, from the Clyde to Malta. She took Prime Minister Churchill to the Quebec conference in September 1943 and in November took him to the Teheran Conference. She sailed in December to join the Eastern Fleet. During 1944 she bombarded Japanese installations, including on 25 July those at Sabang on Sumatra and others in the Nicobar Islands bombarded in November. She had returned to the UK by August 1945 when King George VI met President Truman aboard *Renown* in Plymouth Sound.

Repulse carried the Prince of Wales on his South American tour in 1925. She had a major refit from 1936 to 1938 but was not 'modernised'. In September 1939 she and *Hood* formed the Home Fleet Battle Squadron. By mid-February 1940 she had been at sea for 130 days in covering Atlantic convoys. She was in the Far East at the time of the outbreak of hostilities with Japan, and was sunk by aircraft on 10 December 1941.

Hood in 1939 was with the Home Fleet, she was transferred to Force H as Admiral Somerville's flagship on 24 May 1941. On 24 May 1941 she blew up after being hit by a salvo from *Bismark*. There were few survivors and all the RM detachment was lost.

Cruisers in 1919 disposed of by 1932

Detachment sizes are indicated by letter 'd' and RM band sizes by 'b', where these have been estimated the item is starred (*).

Endymion, Gibraltar, Grafton, Theseus (7,350–7,700 tons) of 1891 – d 50* b 15*.

Crescent and *Royal Arthur* (7,700 tons) of 1891 – d 50* and b 15*.

Astrala, Charybdis, Forte, Fox and *Hermione* light cruisers (4,360 tons) and *Sappho* (3,440 tons) of pre-1894 – d 30* and b 15*.

Eclipse-class (5,600 tons) of 1894 – d 34* and b 15* in *Diana, Doris, Eclipse, Isis, Juno, Minerva* and *Talbot*.

Diadem-class (11,000 tons) of 1895 – d 60* and b 15* in *Amphitrite, Europa* and *Diadem*.

Pelorus, Prosperine and *Pyramis* (2,135–2,220 tons) light cruisers of 1869–9 – d 30* and b 12*.

Cressy-class (12,000 tons) of 1898 – d 60* and b 15* in *Bacchante, Aerialist* and *Sutler*.

Drake-class (14,100 tons) of 1898 g d 60* and b 15* in *King Alfred*.

Challenger, High flyer and *Hyacinth* (5,600–5,915 tons) light cruisers of 1900 – d 40* and b 15*.

Monmouth-class (10,000 tons) of 1900 known as 'County' class – d-and-b 100* in *Berwick, Cornwall, Cumberland, Donegal, Essex, Kent, Lancaster* and *Suffolk*.

light cruisers *Amethyst, Diamond, Saphire* and *Topaze* (3,000 tons) of 1902 – d-and-b 40*.

Devonshire-class (10,850 tons) of 1902 – d-and-b 80* in *Antrim, Caernarvon* and *Devonshire*.

Attentive (2,895 tons) **light cruiser** of 1903 – d-and-b 40*

Foresight and *Forward* (2,850 tons) **light cruisers** of 1903 – d-and-b 40*.

Sentinel and *Skirmisher* (2,895 tons) **light cruisers** of 1903 – d-and-b 40*.

Duke of Edinburgh-class (13,550 tons) of 1903 – d-and-b 80* in *Duke of Edinburgh*.

Warrior-class (13,550 tons) of 1904 – d-and-b 82* in *Achilles*.

Minotaur-class (14,600 tons) of 1905 – d-and-b 98 in *Minotaur* and *Shannon*.

Bellona and *Boadicea* (3,300 tons) **light cruisers** of 1907 – d-and-b 35*.

Bristol-class (4,800 tons) of 1908 – d-and-b 45* in *Bristol, Glasgow, Gloucester* and *Liverpool*.

Blanche and *Blonde* (3,400 tons) **light cruisers** of 1909 – d-and-b 40*.

Weymouth-class (5,250 tons) of 1909 – d-and-b 50* in *Dartmouth, Weymouth* and *Yarmouth*.

Active and *Fearless* (3,440 tons) **light cruisers** of 1910–11 – d-and-b 40*.

Chatham-class (5,400 tons) of 1911 – d-and-b 60* in *Chatham* and *Dublin*.

Lowestoft (5,400 tons) **light cruiser** of 1912 – d-and-b 60*.

Aurora, Galatea, Inconstant, Royalist and *Undaunted* (3,520 tons) **light cruisers** of 1912 – d-and-b 40*. *Aurora* to Royal Canadian Navy in 1920.

Conquest and *Cordelia* (3,800 tons) **light cruisers** of 1913 – d-and-b 40*.

Cruisers 1919 to 1979

(Several of these are not ships in a 'class' and therefore appear in italics with **cruiser** on first lines.)

Caroline-class (3,750 tons) of 1913–14 – d-and-b 40* in *Crayford* (1915–31), *Cleopatra* (1915–31) and *Conquest* (1915–30).

Cambrian-class (3,750 tons) of 1914–15 – d-and-b 40* in *Calliope* (1915–31), *Champion* (1915–34), *Cambrian* (1916–47, latterly, RNVR Depot ship), *Canterbury* (1916–34) and *Constance* (1916–36).

Centaur (3,750 tons) **cruiser** of 1915 – d-and-b 40* (1916–33).

Concord (3,750 tons) **cruiser** of 1915 – d-and-b 40* (1916–35).

Improved (World War I) *Birmingham*-class (9,996 tons) of 1915–16 – d 94 and band 15 in *Vindictive* (1918–46 completed as an aircraft carrier but converted in 1925), *Hawking* (1919–48), *Raleigh* (1919–22, wrecked), *Frobisher* (1919–48) and *Effingham* (1925–40, wrecked).

Caledon-class (4,180 tons) of 1916 – d-and-b 50* in *Caledon* (1917–48, modified as AA cruiser), *Calypso* (1917–42, sunk) and *Caradoc* (1917–46 latterly as depot ship).

Dauntless-class (4,850 tons) know as D-class of 1916–18 – d 51 and b 13 in *Danae* (1918–44, Mulberry blockship), *Dauntless* (1918–47), *Dragon* (1918–44, Mulberry blockship), *Delhi* (1919–48), *Dunedin* (1919–41, sunk), *Durban* (1921–44, Mulberry blockship), *Despatch* (1922–46) and *Diomede* (1922–46 with Royal New Zealand Navy).

Carlisle-class (4,200 tons) – d-and-b 60* in *Car-*

lisle (1918–45, modified as an AA cruiser), *Cairo* (1919–42, sunk), *Calcutta* (1919–1941, sunk), *Colombo* (1919–1948, modified as an AA cruiser) and *Capetown* (1922–46, modified as AA cruiser).

Ceres-class (4,290 tons) of 1917–18 – d-and-b 60* in *Cardiff* (1917–46, training ship from 1940), *Ceres* (1917–46, modified as an AA cruiser), *Curlew* (1917–40, sunk had been modified as an AA cruiser), *Coventry* (1918–42, sunk had been modified as an AA cruiser) and *Curacao* (1918–42, sunk).

E-class (7,550 tons) 1918 – d 90* and b 11 in *Emerald* (1926–48) and *Enterprise* (1926–46).

Cruiser-minelayer (6,740 tons) of 1921–2 – d 30* in *Adventure* (1926–47, became repair ship in 1944).

Kent-class (9,800 tons) of 1924 – d 70 and b 15 in *Berwick* (1928–48), *Cornwall* (1928–42, sunk), *Cumberland* (1928–59), *Kent* (1928–48), *Suffolk* (1928–49), *Australia* and *Canberra* both with Royal Australian Navy from 1927).

Dorsetshire-class (9,000–9,925 tons) of 1926 – d-and-b 92 in *Dorsetshire* (1930–42, sunk) and *Norfolk* (1930–50).

York (8,250 tons) **cruiser** of 1927 – d-and-b 80* (1930–41, sunk).

London-class (9,750 tons) of 1928 – d-and-b 100 in *Devonshire* (1919–45), *London* (1929–50), *Shropshire* (1929–49, with Royal Australian Navy from 1943) and *Sussex* (1929–49).

Exeter **cruiser** (8,300 tons) of 1928 – d-and-b 86* (1931–42, sunk).

Leander-class of 1929 – d 61 and b 17 in *Achilles* (1933 48), *Leander* (1933–49), *Neptune* (1934–41, sunk), *Orion* (1934–48), *Ajax* (1935–49), *Sydney* and *Hobart* (both with Royal Australian Navy from 1934).

Arethusa-class and Improved *Arethusa*-class of 1932 – d 52 and b 13 in *Arethusa* (1935–50), *Galatea* (1935–41, sunk), *Penelope* (1936–44, sunk) and *Aurora* (1937–48).

Amphion-class (7,000 tons) of 1932 – d-and-b 65* in *Amphion* (1936–9 transferred to Royal Australian Navy as HMAS *Perth*, sunk 1942) and *Apollo* (1936–9 transferred to Royal Australian Navy as HMAS *Hobart*).

Southampton-class (9,000 tons) of 1933 – d 60 and b 18, with wartime detachment raised to 80 in *Southampton* (1937–41, sunk), *Birmingham* (1937–60), *Glasgow* (1937–58), *Liverpool* (1937–58), *Newcastle* (1937–58), *Sheffield* (1937–67), *Gloucester* (1938–41, sunk) and *Manchester* (1938–42, sunk).

Belfast-class (10,000 tons) of 1936 – d-and-b 100* in *Belfast* (1939–c40) and *Edinburgh* (1939–42, sunk).

Dido-class (5,450 tons) of 1936 – d 65* and b

18 in *Dido* (1940–58), *Aerialist* (1940–58), *Hermione* (1940–2, sunk), *Phoebe* (1940–56), *Charybdis* (1941–43, sunk), *Cleopatra* (1941–58), *Sirius* (1941–56), *Scylla* (1941–50), *Argonaut* (1942–56) and *Bonaventure* (1940–1, sunk).

Mauritius- and **Fiji-classes** (8,000 tons) of 1937–9 – d 104 and b 18 in *Fiji* (1940–1, sunk), *Kenya* (1940–62), *Mauritius* (1940–65), *Nigeria* (1940–54 to India), *Trinidad* (1940–2, lost), *Bermuda* (1942–65), *Gambia* (1942–3, to RNZN), *Jamaica* (1942–60); the following of 3-turret design (8,800 tons) *Ceylon* (1940–57), *Newfoundland* (1942–59 on her last cruise d 90 and b 25) and *Uganda* (1942–44 to RCN).

Cruiser-minelayers (2,650 tons) of 1938 – d-and-b none in *Abdiel* (1940–43, sunk), *Latona* (1940–41, sunk), *Manxman* (1940–63, became a support ship), *Welshman* (1940–43, sunk), *Apollo* (1943–65) and *Ariadne* (1943–65).

Later Dido-class (5,770 tons) of early 1940s – d-and-b 80* in *Bellona* (1942–48, to RNZN), *Black Prince* (1943–48, to RNZN), *Royalist* (1943–58, to RNZN), *Spartan* (1943–44, sunk) and *Diadem* (1944–56, to Pakistan).

Minotaur-class (8,000 tons) of early 1940s – d 100* and b 20 in *Minotaur* (1944 to RCN), *Swiftsure* (1944–62) and *Superb* (1945–60).

Tiger-class (8,885) of early 1940s but completion deferred and redesigned with 40 Sea-cat missiles – d-and-b 30* in *Lion* (1958–74), *Tiger* (1958–77) and *Blake* (1959–79).

Fleet and Light Aircraft Carriers

Furious (22,450 tons) of 1915 – d-and-b, no trace
Courageous-class (22,500 tons) of 1915 – in 1938 d *c*100 b 19 in *Courageous* (1917–19, sunk) and *Glorious* with 115 Mnes (and Band?) (1917–40, sunk).

Argus (14,450 tons) of 1916 – d-and-b 80*
Hermes (10,850 tons) of 1916 – d-and-b 60* (1923–42,sunk).

Eagle (22,600 tons) of 1917 – d100* and b 20* (1923–42, sunk).

Ark Royal (22,600 tons) Fleet Carrier of 1934 – d 100* and b 20* (1938–41, sunk).

Illustrious-class (23,000 tons) Fleet Carriers of 1936–37 – d 34 and b 19 in *Formidable* (1940–53), *Illustrious* (1940–56) and *Victorious* (1940–61).

Indomitable-class (23,000 tons) Fleet Carriers of 1937–39 – d-and-b 128 in *Indomitable* (1941–55), *Indefatigable* (1944–55) and *Implacable* (1944–55).

Hermes-class (23,300 tons) Fleet Carriers of early-1940s, but completion deferred – d-and-b 62 in *Centaur* (1953–64), *Hermes* (1953 and see Commando Carriers), *Albion* (1954 and see Commando Carriers), *Bulwark* (1954 and see Commando Carriers).

Ark Royal-class (36,800 tons) Fleet Carriers of early-1940s – d-and-b 60* in *Eagle* (1951–70) and *Ark Royal* (1955–78)

Colossus-class (14,000 tons) Light Fleet Carriers of early-1940s – d-and-b not traced in *Colossus* (1944–46, to France), *Glory* (1945–58), *Ocean* (1945–56), *Venerable* (1945–48), *Vengeance* (1945–56, to Brazil), *Theseus* (1946–57), *Triumph* (1946–54) and *Warrior* (1946–58).

Majestic-class (14,000 tons) Light Fleet carriers of early-1940s – d-and-b not traced in *Magnificent* (1944 to RCN), *Hercules* (1946–61, to India), *Leviathan* 1946, not completed), *Sydney* and *Melbourne* (1949 and 1955 both to RAN), *Powerful* (1956, completed as *Bonaventure* for RCN).

Escort Carriers

These did not normally carry RM detachments but RM officers with FAA squadrons were embarked from time to time. the first five ships were converted merchantmen or supply ships, including *Avenger* (sunk 1942), *Audacity* (sunk 1941) and *Dasher* (sunk 1943). Later escort carriers were C-35 cargo ships converted in building at American yards, 36 of these ships came into service in 1942–3 and were returned to America in 1945–6.

Monitors

Ex-Brazilian order (1,260 tons) of 1914 – d-and-b 40* in *Humber* (1914–20), *Mersey* (1914–1919) and *Severn* (1914–22).

14-inch class (6,150 tons) of 1914 – d 80* in *Abercrombie* (1915–27), *Havelock* (1915–27 and *Roberts* (1915, used for trials after 1919).

Marshal-class (6,670 tons) of 1914 – d 80* in *Marshal Ney* (1915–57) and *Marshal Soult* (1915–46), after 1920 both monitors used as depot or drill ships.

12-inch class (5,900 tons) of 1915 but several later fitted with 18-in guns – d 80*in *Earl of Peterborough* (1915–22), *General Wolfe* (1915–22, latterly 18-in gun), *Lord Clive* (1915–22, latterly 18-in gun and used for gun trials after 1920), *Prince Eugene* (1915–22), *Prince Rupert* (1915, depot ship *Pembroke* from 1922), *Sir John More* (1915–21) and *Sir Thomas Picton* (1915–21).

Ex-Norwegian order (5,700 tons of 1915 – d 40* in *Gorgon* (1918, used for trials after 1920).

9.2-inch class (540 tons) of 1915 – d not traced in M16 to M26 (11 monitors built 1915 and all decommissioned by about 1922).

6-inch class (355 tons) of 1915 – d 30* in M29

to *M 33* (five monitors all built from 1915 and sold or converted in 1920–22).

2nd 15-inch class (8,000 tons) of 1915 – d 90* in *Erebus* (1916–46, additional guns added in World War II) and *Terror* (1916–41, sunk).

3rd 15-inch class (7,200 tons) of 1939–40 – d-and-b 120* in *Roberts* (1941–65, latterly as drill ship), *Abercrombie* (1943–54, latterly as drill ship, etc.).

Landing Ships

See Minor Craft Unit history summaries for examples of World War II LS Infantry, as their detachments were LC Flotillas. Marine LC crews also served on detachment to LSTs in 1945–6, and from time to time after World War II on Landing Ships such as: *Rocksand* (1944–46); *Sir Hugo* (in 1945 renamed from 'Empire' ship of world War II); and such former LSTs as *Attacker* (1947–54), *Avenger* (1947–49) and *Charger* (1947–56). many of these former LSTs were modified and by 1956–57 were carrying the following craft:

Ben Lomond, Ben Nevis, Messina and *Narvik* – one LCT and 5 LCAs, but no permanent RM detachment in 1957.

Reggio and *Striker* as LST(Assault), each with 8 LCAs, and carried 3rd Assault Squadron RM with the captain RM in *Striker*.

Anzio, Battler, Bruiser, Charger, Chaser, Hunter, Puncher, Pursuer, Ravager, St Nazaire, Slinger, Stalker, Thruster, Tracker, Trouncer, Trumpeter, Tromso and *Vaagso* – with 4 LCAs had no permanent RM detachment but some of these ships were later converted to LST(Assault) with RM Assault Squadron LCAs embarked.

By 1960 most of the World War II LSTs had been sold or scrapped, but the following continued in service, although at times in the Reserve Fleet, and RM Assault Squadrons served on several of them after they were converted to LST(A)s:

Anzio (1945–70+), *Ben Lomond* (1947–60), *Ben Nevis* (1945–70+), *Chaser* (1945–62), *Messina* (1945–70+), *Narvik* (1945–65), *Puncher* (1945–62), *Messina* (1945–65), *Narvik* (1945–65), *Ravager* (1944–61), *Reggio* (1944–60), *Stalker* (1944–70+), *Striker* (1944–70+) and *Tracker* (1945–70+).

Destroyers and Frigates 1959–1980

From 1959 to 1980 detachments served in frigates and latterly in destroyers; in the early 1960s these detachments were of 20 to 22 but by the late 1970s they were as small as 10-man detachments commanded by a sergeant with a flotilla RM officer. the following classes of ship carried or might have carried RM detachments from time to time:

Loch-class (1,435 tons) of early 1940s – d 20 (but not until 1959) in *Loch Alvie* (1944–1960s), *Loch Fada* (1944–60s), *Loch Insh* (1944–64), *Loch Killisport* (1944–60s), and *Loch Ruthven* (1944–66).

Leander-class frigates (2,300 tons of 1958) – d 10 in late 1970s, see below.

The practice in 1980 was to maintain detachments in a given number of ships, moving detachments from one to another so that all ships in a class did not necessarily carry a detachment but might have done so on any commission. The last of the 22-man detachments was serving on *Phoebe* in January 1980, other detachments were in training, with 10-man detachments in *Eskimo, Kent, Ashanti, Bristol, Scylla, Antrim, Berwick, Gurkha, London* and *Rothesay*.

Various ships 1981–1997

During the 1980s and 1990s 10-man detachments served in the following ships at different times. There were also detachments on the Falkland Islands patrol ships and other vessels. The ships included HMS *Rhyl, Herald, Battleaxe, Yarmouth, Danae, Brazen, Sentinel, .Invincible* (aircraft carrier), *Brogan, Hecali, Ambuscade* (embarked a detachment from *Fearless* in 1991 for operations in Carribean), RFA *Geraint* for operations in 1993. See also Commando Carriers and LPDs.

Commando Carriers

Bulwark (23,300 standard tons) originally a carrier with fixed-wing aircraft of 1944 but completion deferred until 1954 for the Korean War, served two commissions before a major refit when she was converted to an amphibious assault ship on its completion in 1959. Later designated a Landing Platform Helicopter (LPH), she could carry a Commando Group to land them by helicopter or assault craft, and keep them supplied in the field. She also had an anti-submarine role for her helicopters. Affectionately known as the 'Rusty B', she was finally paid off in 1981.

Albion of similar class to *Bulwark* she was refitted as an LPH in 1961 and was the companion carrier to *Bulwark* throughout the next two decades, she finally paid off in 1973.

Hermes (28,700 full load) completed 1959, was converted to an LPH by March 1971, and had a further refit in 1977, but was principally deployed in an anti-submarine role. She embarked her first squadron of Harrier aircraft in 1980. She had a crew of 1,350 plus a Commando in an emergency, but in 1982 – see chapter 11 – she was required to carry Harriers to the

South Atlantic, and only carried a company of commandos.

Landing Platforms Dock *Fearless* (11,060 tons standard) completed November 1965 and *Intrepid* (11,060 tons standard) completed March 1967 (12,120 tons loaded, 16,950 with dock flooded) were similar to American LPDs (see chapter 10), carrying in their dock four LCMs or larger vessels, and with four LCVPs on davits. There were flight deck facilities for five helicopters, see chapter 11. Continued in service in 1997.

New construction in 1997 was the Landing Platform Helicopter (LPH) HMS *Ocean* (21,500 tons) was to be launched by Her Majesty the Queen on 20 February 1998; and designed to land by helicopter or landing craft, Marines and their supporting artillery. Her AOC joined her in the summer of 1997 and elements of 9 Assault Sqn RM were forming at Poole. She has been designed to carry:

Four LCVP(5);

A Cdo Group (Light) of up to 803 men (500 as standard load and 303 at overload) with bunks for all the embarked troops;

A helicopter force with 180 personnel to fly and maintain: 12 Support Helicopters and six Light Helicopters; or six Attack Helicopters; or four Chinook helicopters.

39 BV 206D to be accommodated on the vehicle deck which will have a side ramp and a steep stern ramp for offloading to LCVPs in sheltered waters; and

The AOR is designed for Command Support Systems for the ship's staff and a Cdo HQ but *not* COMAW and Brigade command systems;

In July 1996 two replacement LPDs (as LPD(R)) – HMS *Bulwark* and *Albion* each of 15,100 tons displacement – were ordered with a view to their becoming operational from 2000 with *Albion* and 6 Assault Sqn being commissioned first, when *Intrepid* was expected to pay off. *Bulwark* was expected to become fully operational (with 4 Assault Sqn) in April 2002. Meanwhile *Fearless* was expected to stay in commission. The LPD(R) will each carry an EMF of 245 personnel (648 on overload), with four Mk 10 RoRo LCUs and four LCVP(5)s. The flight deck will accommodate EH101 Support Helicopters. The operations room has been designed to include extensive command and control facilities (designated C41) to support COMAW and the Brigade staff.

The Landing Ships Logistic were planned to be replaced by ALSLs specifically designed for amphibious warfare with two to be operational by 2003.

Other vessels

Royal Yachts, *Victoria and Albert* (4,700 tons) embarked a band of 20 or more musicians from time to time (1899–1954). *Britannia* (3,990 tons) completed in 1954 and in service in 1995 but due for disposal, carried a band of 25 musicians from time to time.

Caledonia, ex-liner *Majestic* used as RN training ship (1937–39, damaged by fire).

Fidelity (2,450 tons BRT) converted for clandestine raids from French cargo boat, carried two aircraft and high speed power boats, but lost on second mission with all hands including 'T' Troop of 40 RM Commando about 31 December 1942.

Glory IV former Russian cruiser was captured in 1918 and used as the depot ship in Murmansk in 1919, providing facilities for men ashore from the battleship *Glory*.

Martial was name of Mobile Naval Base I in 1941–43.

Mashobra was supply ship of MNBDO from before 1938, sunk 1940.

Menace was name of Mobile Naval Base II in 1941.

Meon (1,375 tons) a converted *River*-class frigate she was the HQ ship of the Amphibious Squadron and carried an RM detachment in the 1950s and 1960s (1943–66).

Protector (2,900 tons) a net layer built in 1934, converted for Antarctic patrols in 1955, carried small RM detachments in the 1960s and was replaced by *Endurance* see below.

Endurance (3,600 fully loaded) completed as Antarctic patrol ship in 1968 from the *Anita Dan* purchased in 1967, originally built in 1956. Carried RM detachments from time to time and in service in 1982, see chapter 11. In late 1987, her 20th year of service in the RN, after a major refit sailed to the South Atlantic. Continued in commission in 1997.

Victory, first rate of 100 guns built 1759, and continues in dry dock at Portsmouth since 1922, from 1980s RMs attached as guides who are on the books of the barracks, HMS *Nelson*.

RN DEPOTS AND BASES

While a comprehensive list of these is beyond the scope of a Royal Marines' history, many Marines including transport drivers, ground defence forces and specialist trainees of World War II, have served in many of these establishments, although only the major establishments are listed below with examples of some smaller establishments:

Actaeon Torpedo School, Kent 1905–22;

Afrikander Base, Simonstown, South Africa, pre-1919–75; *Antrim* Base, Belfast, Northern Ireland, WW II; *Appledore* RN Commandos, North Devon, 1946; *Ararat* see *Brontosaurus*; *Ariel* Training Centre, see also RNAS of World War II; *Astraea* Base, Lagos, Nigeria, WW II;

Bacchante Base, Aberdeen, Scotland, WW II; *Badger* Establishment at Harwich, Essex in WW II; *Bahadur* Base, India; *Baldur* at Reykjavik, Iceland, WW II; *Barbrook II* Boom Defence Depot, Freetown West Africa, WW II; *Basilisk* Base, Port Moresby, New Guinea, 1943–46; *Beaconsfield* British Pacific Fleet Base, WW II; *Beaver* Base, Humber, Yorkshire, WW II; *Beehive* Base, Felixstowe, Suffolk, WW II; *Bellerophon* Reserve Fleet, Portsmouth, 1950; *Benbow* Base, Trinidad, WW II; *Bonaventure* Base, South Africa, WW II; *Boscawen* Establishment at Portland, Dorset. where ships worked up, 1932–47; *Braganza* Base Chittagong, modern Bangladesh, WW II; *Bristol* Base, Gloucestershire, WW II; *Britannia* RN College, Dartmouth, Devon, 1940s to mid-1990s; *Brontosaurus* Amphibious Training Centre for Royal Armoured Corps, Castle Howard, Yorkshire 1942–46 (briefly *Ararat* before 1942); *Bruce* Training establishment Crail, Fife. WW II; *Brunswick* Base, St John, New Brunswick; *Bull* Base Nassau, Bahamas, 1942;

Cabbala Education & Vocational Training, Staffordshire, 1947; *Cabot* Base, Bristol, Avon, WW II; *Caledonia* Base Oban, Scotland formerly *St Andrew*, 1943 and continued until 1980+ as Engineer Training School, Rosyth, Scotland; *Calliope* Base, Tyne, Durham, WW II; *Cambridge* Gunnery Training School, Wembly, London, 1956; *Canada* Base, North America, WW II; *Cannae* Barracks, Phillipville, (modern Skikda), Algeria, WW II; *Canopus* Training Establishment, Alexandria, Egypt, 1940–45; *Carleton* Base, Ottawa, Canada, WW II; *Caroline* Base, Belfast, Northern Ireland, WW II; *Carrick* Base, Clyde, WW II; *Cartier* Base, Montreal, Canada, WW II; *Catariqui* Base, Kingston, Ontario, WW II; *Centurion* RN Pay & Records where Drafting & Record Office RM (DRORM) was based near Portsmouth until early 1993; *Ceres* Supply School, Weatherby, Yorkshire, 1947-?; *Chembaur* Camp, near Bombay, India, 1944–46; *Chippawa* Base, Winnipeg, Canada, WW II; *Chrysanthemum* Establishment, London 1940s; *Claverhouse* Base, Leith, Scotland, WW II; *Clio* Base, Barrow-in-Furness, Cumbria; *Cochrane* Depot ship and later Establishment, Rosyth, Scotland, 1937 and continued to mid-1990s; *Collingwood* Training Establishment, Fareham, Hampshire, 1940 and continued 1980 as RN

Weapon & Electrical Engineering School; *Commonwealth* (Naval Party 2504) Base Kure, Japan, 1946–48; *Conestoga* Base, Galt, Ontario, WW II; *Conway* Training Establishment, Mersey, 1940s; *Copra* Co-Ops Pay & Record Office WW II; *Cormorant* Base, Gibraltar, 1889–1946, renamed *Rooke*; *Cornwallis* Base also RNAS training, Deep Brook, Canada, WW II; *Cressy* Base, Dundee, Scotland, WW II; *Cricket* Landing craft Base, Southampton, Hampshire, 1945–46 (RM command from 1945); *Curlew* Harbour Defence Depot, Inellan, 1943–46;

Dalhousie Establishment, Bombay, India, WW II and after; *Dartmouth* Landing Craft base, Dartmouth, Devon, WW II and see *Britannia*; *Dauntless*, WRNS Training Depot, Reading, Berkshire, 1947 and continued training 1997; *Defiance* Establishment, Devonport, near Plymouth, WW II; *Defender* Base, Liverpool, Lancashire, WW II; *Defiance* Base Devonport, Plymouth, WW II; *Dilawar* Base, Karachi, modern Pakistan, WW II; *Diligence* Small Ships Base, Hythe, Isle of Wight, 1953; *Dinosaur* Base, Troon, Ayr, WW II; *Discovery* Base, Vancouver, British Colombia, WW II; *Dolphin* Submarine Base, Gosport, Hampshire, since about 1912 and continues; *Drake* Depot Devonport, near Plymouth, 1934 and continues as parent ship of Devonport; *Dryad* Navigation School, Southwick Fareham, near Portsmouth, 1919 and continues as School of Maritime Operations; *Dundonald I* and *II* Naval Wing of School of Signals, Inverary, Argyll, but at Auchengate 1942–46; *Duke* Establishment, Great Malvern, Worcestershire, WW II.

Effingham Co-Ops Training Base, Dartmouth, Devon, 1943–46; *Eland* Base, West Africa, WW II; *Europa* Base, Lowestoft, Suffolk, WW II; *Excellent* RN Gunnery School, Portsmouth, 1891–1980s, HQRM established here in 1996; *Exmouth* accommodation ship, Scapa, northern Scotland, 1942–45;

Ferret Base, Londonderry, Northern Ireland, WW II; *Fervent* Base, Ramsagte, Kent; *Fisgard* Training Establishment, Portsmouth, 1910–32, later an establishment at Torpoint, near Plymouth, 1946 and continued in 1980; *Flinders* Depot, Australia, WW II; *Flora* Base Invergordon, Scotland, 1939; *Forte* Base, Falmouth, Cornwall, WW II; *Fortitude* Base, Ardrossan, Scotland, WW II; *Fortune* Base, Newhaven, Sussex, WW II; *Forward* Base, Newhaven, Sussex WW II; *Fox* Base, Lerwick, Shetland Islands, WW II; *Fullarton* Landing Craft Base, WW II;

Ganges Boys Training establishment, near Harwich, Essex, c1906–75; *Glendour* Establishment, Pwllheli, North Wales, WW II; *Golden Hind* Base, Sydney, New South Wales, WW II; *Gordon* Base, Gravesend, Kent, WW II; *Gould* Barracks, Ceylon, 1946; *Grasshopper* Coastal Forces, Weymouth, Dorset, 1943–44; *Griffin* Base Port Arthur, Ontario;

Hamilcar Landing Craft Base, Algiers, WW II; *Hasdrubal* Base, Algiers, 1943–46; *Harrier* Aircraft Direction Centre, Pembroke (modern Dyfed), Wales, 1948; *Hawk* Upper Yardman (see *Temeraire*), Exbury, near Southampton, 1946–50s; *Helder* Co-Ops Training Establishment, Brightlingsea, Essex, 1942–46; *Helicon* Base, Aultbea, Australia, 1941–45; *High flyer* Base, Trincomalee, Ceylon, 1943–59+; *Hornet* Coastal Forces Base 1925–34, and at Gosport, Hampshire 1939–57;

Imperieuse Training Establishment, Devonport pre-1919-?; *Impregnable* Training Establishment, Devonport, 1920-? and at St Budeaux, near Plymouth, 1943–48;

Jufair HQ Persian Gulf, at Aden and later Bahrain, after 1946 to 1960s; *Jupiter* Reserve Fleet, Gareloch, which leads to the Clyde estuary, 1950s;

King Alfred RN Officer Training Establishment, Hove, Sussex, and in last year at Exbury, near Southampton, 1939–46;

Landswell Landing craft base, Singapore, c1945–46; *Leonidas* Base, Takoradi, Ghana, West Africa, 1941–45; *Lizard* Landing Craft Base, Cornwall, 1942–45; *Lochinvar* Base, Port Edgar and later Minesweeper Trials Establishment, 1940–57+; *Lucifer* Base, Swansea, South Wales, WW II; *Lynx* Base, Dover, Kent, 1939–46;

Malabar nominal depot, Bermuda, 1919 and continued 1980; *Marlborough* Torpedo School, Eastbourne, Sussex, 1942–47; *Medway II* Base, Beirut, Lebanon, and later at Malta, 1942–46; *Melampus* Base, Bathurst, Canada, WW II; *Melville*, Darwin, Australia, WW II; *Mentor* Base, Stornoway, Scotland, WW II; *Mercury* Signals School, Leydene, 1941 and continued in 1980 at Petersfield, Hampshire; *Mercury II* Signals School at Portsmouth WW II; *Mersey* Depot, Liverpool, Lancashire, 1940–46; *Midge* Coastal Forces Base, Gt Yarmouth, Norfolk, WW II; *Minos* Base, Lowestoft, Suffolk, WW II; *Miranda* Base, Gt Yarmouth, Norfolk, WW II; *Monck* Carrier Training and *Monck II* Landing Craft

Base, Port Glasgow, 1942–46; *Montcalm* Base, Quebec, Canada, WW II; *Montserrat* Base, Londonderry, Northern Ireland; *Moreta* Establishment, Palestine, WW II; *Mosquito* Coastal Forces Base, WW II; *Mount Edgcomb* Barracks, Devonport, 1945; *Mount Stewart* RN Commandos, Devon, 1945–46, became *Appledore*;

Naden Base, Esquimault, WW II; *Nelson* RN Barracks, Portsmouth since 1 August 1973 and continues, see also chapter 11; *Neptune* Base, Faslane, on Clyde, 1974 with Marine detachment 1975–80; *Nile* Base, Alexandria, Egypt, dates not traced; *Nimrod* Establishment, Castletown, Isle of Man, 1940–46; *Niobe* Establishment, Glasgow, WW II; *Nonsuch* Base, Edmonton, Alberta, WW II; *Northney I, II, III* and *IV*, Landing Craft Training, Hayling Island, Hampshire, WW II;

Osborne Parent Establishment, Cowes, Isle of Wight, 1941, renamed *Vectis*; *Orion* Reserve Fleet, Devonport, 1950; *Orlando* Base, Greenock, Scotland, 1940–46; *Osiris* Base, Canal Zone, Egypt, 1949–54; *Osprey* Base, Portland (see also RNAS) 1928 and continued in 1980, but in 1941–46 was at Dunoon, Scotland;

Pembroke Base and HQ Chatham, Kent, 1891 and continued 1980; *Penguin* Base, Sydney, Australia, WW II; *Philomel* Base, Auckland, New Zealand, WW II; *Phoenicia* C-in-C Mediterranean Staff WW II to 1950s; *Phoenix* RN Defence School, Stamshaw, 1949–57; *Pomone* Boom Defence Depot, Scapa, 1943–46; *Porcupine* Landing craft Base, Stokes Bay, near Portsmouth, 1944–46; *Prosperine* Base, Lyness, WW II; *Powerful* Training Establishment, Devonport, from before 1919 but in 1920 renamed *Impregnable* – see above; *President* RN Staff, London, formerly RNR Drill Ship, 1862 and continued in 1980; *Prometheus* Depot for local defence vessel in the Mediterranean, 1942–44; *Pursuivant* Base, Falkland Islands from 1946; *Ryramus* Base, Kirkwall, Orkney Islands, WW II;

Quebec Co-Ops and LC Base, Inveraray, Argyle, 1940–46; *Queen* Base, Regina, Saskatchewan, WW II; *Queen Charlotte* AA ranges, Ainsdale, Lancashire, WW II;

Racer Base, Larne, Northern Ireland, WW II; *Raleigh* Training Establishment, Torpoint, near Plymouth, 1939–45 and continued as new entrants training establishment in 1997; *Resolution* Base, Christmas Island in Pacific, 1958; *Robertson* Camp and LC Base, Sandwich, Kent, c1941–46; *Rooke* Boom Defence, Rosyth, Scotland, 1940–45 (see *Safeguard*) and Base Gibraltar, 1946 and continued 1980; *Rosneath* Base, Scotland, WW II; *Royal Anne* Depot Ship, Arromanches, Normandy, 1944–45; *Royal Arthur* Training Establishment, Skegness, Lincolnshire, WW II, later School for Petty Officers at Corsham, near Bath; *Royal William* Dockyard Establishment, Plymouth, in 1980 closed early 1990s (see also WW II Naval Parties;

Safeguard Boom Depot, Southampton, WW II and at Rosyth, 1946–50s; *Saker* RN Staff, Washington, District of Columbia, USA, 1950s; *St Andrew* Base, Oban, Scotland, renamed *Caledonia*, 1941–43; *St Angelo* Base, Malta, formerly *Egmont*, 1933 and continued 1980; *St Christopher* Coastal Forces Base, Fort William, Scotland, WW II; *St George I* and *II* Training Bases in Isle of Man, 1940–45, at Gosport, Hampshire, 1946–48 and later RN SD-Officer School, Portsmouth in 1970s; *St Matthew* Landing Craft Training Base, Essex; *St Vincent* Training Establishment (formerly Forton Barracks) Fareham, Hampshire, 1927–60s; *Sandfly* Coastal Forces Base, Peterhead, Scotland, WW II; *Salsette* Co-Ops Base, India, 1943–45; *Sandragon* Base, Seychelles, 1946–?; *Saunders* LC Training Camp, Kabrit, Egypt, WW II; *Scipio* Base, Oban, 1943; *Sea Eagle* Training establishment and Base, Londonderry, Northern Ireland, 1947–60s; *Sea Serpent* Landing Craft Base, Bracklesham Bay, near Chichester, WW II; *Sheba* Base, Aden, 1944–67; *Skirmisher* Base, Milford Haven, Dyfed, WW II; *Spartiate* Base, Glasgow, 1939–46; *Sphinx* Base, Egypt, 1941–46; *Squid* Base WW II; *Stagona* Base, Halifax, Nova Scotia, WW II; *Stag* Depot, Suez Canal, 1940–49; *Standard* Naval Camp, Hexam, Northumberland, 1941–45; *Star* Base, Hamilton, Ontario, WW II; *Sultan* Depot, Singapore, 1940 and 1945–46, later Training establishment, Gosport, Hampshire, 1956 and continued 1980;

Talbot Base, Sardinia, WW II; *Tamar* Depot Ship, Hong Kong, 1937–41, sunk, HQ and base Hong Kong 1945 and continued 1980; *Tecumseh* Base, Calgary, Alberta, WW II; *Temeraire* Upper Yardsman College for other ranks officer candidates (attended by some Royal Marines), Port Edgar, 1955–60s, continued 1980 as RN Physical Training School at Portsmouth; *Terror* Base, Singapore, WW II to 1971; *Thunderer* RN College, Keyham, near Leicester, 1946, later as RN Engineering College, Manadon, (Devon) until closed in mid-1990s; *Caledonia*, until closed in late 1980s; *Toreador* Base for ferry services, 1944; *Tormentor* LC and Raiding Base, Hamble river, Southampton Water, 1940–46; *Tower*

Auxiliary Patrol Depot, London, 1940–46; *Turtle* Co-Ops Base, Poole, Dorset, 1942–46;

Unicorn Base, Saskatoon, Canada, WW II;

Valkyrie Radar School, Isle of Man, 1941–46; *Vectis* Base, Isle of Wight (formerly *Osborne*), 1942–45; *Vernon* Torpedo School, Portsmouth, 1876 and continued 1997 as seamanship, diving, etc. school, RMHQ based here temporarily 1993–96; *Vivid* Devonport Barracks, from before 1919 to 1934, renamed *Drake*; *Volcano* Bomb Disposal School, Holmrock, WW II;

Wasp Coastal Forces Base, Dover, Kent, WW II; *Warren* Base, Greenock, Inverclyde, WW II; *Warrior* HQ C-in-C Fleet, Norwood, London area, continues; *Watchful* Base, Gt Yarmouth, Norfolk, WW II; *Wellesley* Training Establishment, Liverpool, Lancashire, 1940–46; *Westcliffe* Landing craft Base, Essex, c1942–46; *Wildfire* Gunnery Ranges and gun testing, Sheerness, Kent, before 1919 to 1924 and 1937–50; *Woolverstone* Landing Craft Base, Suffolk, c1943–46.

York Base, Toronto, Canada, WW II.

ROYAL NAVAL AIR STATIONS AND RN AIR SERVICE ESTABLISHMENTS

Main Air Stations

Royal Marine personnel from the Royal Naval Air Service Defence Force (RNASDF), as of 28 June 1943 when a Depot was formed at Towyn, North Wales, under command of Commander RM Training Group Wales (AGRM Circ 25 June 1943). In August they came under the direct control of AGRM, as advisor to the Admiralty (AGRM RM Circ 2126/43 10 Aug 1943). The Depot was closed in October/November (RM Circ 8969 2 Nov 1943) and its personnel transferred to RMTG(Wales). The air defence units with the RNAS became known as RM AA Companies RN Air Stations from about August 1943. Other Marines served as drivers in many stations, as ground defence forces in those likely to be attacked, and as security forces in others. From 16 August 1943 Marines in the AA Companies were administered by RM Headquarters as shown below by stars – Chatham*, Portsmouth** and Plymouth*** – (RM Circ 314/10/43A 23 Aug 1943):

*Condor*** Arbroath, Angus, 1940–60s, later 45 Cdo RM base; *Cormorant II* Gibraltar, 1940–

46+; *Daedalus*** Hull 1915–20, Lee-on-Solent, Hampshire, 1939 and continues; *Kai Tak*, Hong Kong, 1926–41 and 1945–60s; *Fulmar* Lossiemouth, Scotland, 1940–75(?); *Gadwell* Sydenham, Belfast, 1941–65(?), see also *Caroline* below; *Goldcrest I* (see below for *II*), Dale and Brawdy, both Dyfed, 1940–65(?); *Heron**** Yeovilton, Somerset, 1940 and continued 1997; *Jackdaw*** (see Home Air Station); *Kestrel**** Worthy Down, Worcestershire, 1919–50s; *Merlin** Donibristle, Fife, 1940–1960s (RM AA detachment to *Peewit* Sept 1943); *Osprey* Portland, Dorset, (seaplane base in World War I), WW II and continues; *Owl* *** (see Home Air stations); *Phoenix* Fayid, Egypt, 1940 and returned to RAF about 1946; *Peregrine* Ford, Sussex, 1939–46; *Raven* Eastleigh, Hampshire, 1937–47(?); *Seahawk* Culdrose, Cornwall, from about 1940 and closed in the mid-1990s; *Simbang* Sembawang, Malaya, 1945–50s; *Vulture* (see Home Air Stations)

Home Air Stations (UK) of World War II

During World War II the Corps provided ground defences (RNAS Defence Forces) and some AA defences from time to time for some of the following stations, a number of which had RM transport drivers in small detachments commanded by sergeants:

Blackcap, Stretton, Lancashire; *Buzzard* Lympne, Kent, from 1944; *Caroline* satellite station, see *Gadwell* in Main Stations; *Condor II* Dundee, Scotland; *Corncrake* Ballyhalbert and Kirkston, Northern Ireland; *Daedalus II* Sandbanks and Lawrenny Ferry, Pembroke (modern Dyfed); *Dipper* Henstridge, Somerset; *Drake II* Ruborough; *Fieldfare* Evanton, Scotland; *Flycatcher* Middle Wallop, Cheshire, and later Ludham, Norfolk; *Fulmar II* Milltown, Moray; *Gamecock* Bramcote, Warwickshire; *Gannet* Eglington, West Midlands(?); *Godwit* Hinstock, Staffordshire; *Godwit II* Weston Park; *Goldcrest II* Angle, Dyfed; *Heron II* Charlton Horethorne, Somerset, and Haldon, Devon(?); *Hornbill I* Culham, Oxfordshire; *Hornbill II* Beccles., Suffolk; *Humming Bird* Zeal, Somerset(?); *Jackdaw I* **, Crail, Fife; *Jackdaw II* Dunino, Scotland; *Landrail I* Machrihanish and Strabane, Northern Ireland; *Mentor II* Stornaway, Outer Hebrides; *Merganser* Crimond, Scotland; *Nighthawk* Drem, Scotland; *Nightjar* Inskip, Lancashire; *Nightjar II* Macmerry, Scotland; *Nuthatch* Anthron, Scotland; *Owl**** Fearn; *Peewit* (***from September 1943) near Carnoustie, Scotland; *Pintail* Nuts Corner, Antrim; *Ringtail I* Burscough, Lancashire; *Ringtale II* Woodvale; *Robin* Grimsetter; *Sanderling* Abbottsinch; *Shrike*

Maydown, Londonderry; *Siskin* Gosport, Hampshire; *Sparrowhawk* Hatston, and from 1944 at Halesworth, Sussex; *Tern* Twatt, Orkney; *Urley* Ronaldsway, Isle of Man; *Vulture I**** Cornwall(?) and *Vulture II* Thrall, Cornwall and Bushbarn, Hampshire; *Wagtail* Ayr, Scotland.

Home Establishments (UK) of World War II

During World War II the Corps provided defences and security from time to time for many of the following stations, most of which had RM transport drivers in small detachments commanded by sergeants:

Ariel Warrington, Lancashire; *Daedalus* Newcastle-under-Lyme, Staffordshire; *Daedalus III* Bedhampton, near Havant, Hampshire; *Eaglet* Liverpool, Lancashire; *Fledgling* Eccleshall and Millmeece, Staffforshire; *Gosling* Warrington, Lancashire; *Harrier* Kete, Dyfed; *Macaw* Bootle, Cumberland; *Medina* Puckpool, Isle of White; *St Vincent* Gosport, Hampshire; *Seaborn* Dartmouth, Devon; *Shearwater* Yarmouth, Isle of Wight; *Turnstone* Fulham and Watford, London area;

Overseas RNAS Establishments and Air Stations of World War II

During World War II the Corps provided defences from time to time for those establishments in hostile areas, and security for others of the following stations:

In Argentina (offices?) *Avlon*;

In West Indies including *Buzzard* 1940–44; *Goshawk* Trinidad; and *Malabar II* Bermuda.

In Mediterranean including *Grebe* Dekheila; *Falcon* Hal Far, Malta; *Goldfinch* Ta Quali, Malta.

On the Indian sub-continent including *Bambara* China Bay, Trincomalee, Ceylon; *Bheruda* (Race Course) Colombo, Ceylon; *Garuda* Coimbatore; *Kalugu* Establishment, Cochin; *Monara* Establishment, Marhagama, Ceylon; *Rajalaya* Puttalam, Ceylon; *Scruna* Establishment, Ratmalana, Ceylon; *Ukussa* Katukurunda, Ceylon; *Valluru* Tambara, Madras; *Vairi* Sollur; *Valru* Establishment, Sollur.

In Malaya including *Rajala* Penang.

In East Africa and Indian Ocean establishments including *Ironclad II* Andrakaka; *Kaiton II* and *Maragas* Addu Atoll; *Kipanga I, II* and *III* Port Reid and Voi; *Korongo* Nairobi.

In Australia establishment at HMAS *Albatross* Nowra.

In South Africa establ'ts including *Malagas*, Wingfield; and *Samur I* and *II*.

In the Gold Coast (modern Ghana) establishment *Wara*, Komenda.

In Siera Leone Spurwing Establishment, Hastings.

MAJOR LANDING CRAFT OF WORLD WAR II

LC Gun (Large)

RM detachments of two officers and 31 other ranks served in these modified Mark 3 LCTs, which had a total complement of 47, commanded usually by a lieutenant RNVR. The craft carried two 4.7-in BL or QF guns on a reinforced deck over the tank well, with large quantities of ammunition above the water line. They also carried two or four 20-mm quick firing cannons. The craft numbers were:

1–4, 6–7, 9–10, 12–14, 17–25 of which Nos 1, 2 and 15 were sunk.

The G(L) built on a modified Mark 4 LCT, had a slightly larger complement and the two 4.7-in guns were mounted so that both could fire forward, with the second turret superimposed to fire over the forward turret. They also carried three 20-mm cannons. Intended for operations in the Far East, these craft had better accommodation, a ship-type bow and improved armour, compared to the Mark 3 modifications. Few were completed before August 1945, but the following were commissioned:

26, 27, 330, 334, 371, 424, 426, 449, 500, 680–687, 764, 811, 831, 893, 939, 1007, 1062, and probably some others, as there is reference in one record to No. 251. Nos 764, 831 and 1062 were lost in action.

LC Flak

LCF No. 1, formerly Beach Patrol craft (BPC) No. 1 was built experimentally in the summer of 1942, as the forerunner of a monitor-like vessel to bombard Sicily's defences. She had twin 4-in HA/LA guns with several 20-mm cannons in a modified LCT Mark 2. Her gun houses were on a deck over the well. She accompanied several night raiding parties before her first daylight operation at Dieppe, on the French Channel coast. She was in action on 6 June 1944 during the Normandy landings. Sunk by a torpedo while in the 'Trout' line on 17 August, there were few survivors from her RM detachment of 50 all ranks.

LCF No. 2 carried 12 or more light AA guns as an experiment in 1942, using a modified LCT Mark 2 hull. On 19 August 1942, she closed the beaches during the operation at Dieppe, and was sunk by shore batteries, with few survivors from her RM detachment of about 50. Some LCFs were built as modified Mark 3 LCTs, with an RM detachment of two officers and 48 other ranks. These LCFs carried 2-pdr Pom-Poms and 20-mm Oerlikons as follows: Nos 3–6 8 × 2-pdr + 4 × 20-mm; Nos 7–18 4 × 2-pdr + 8 × 20-mm.

Later craft were built on a modified LCT Mark 4 hull with 4 × 2-pdrs and 8 × 20-mm guns.

LC Gun (Medium)

These purpose-built craft carried an RM detachment of a lieutenant and 13 or 14 other ranks, as part of the total complement of 31. The RMs manned two 25-pdr or two 17-pdr guns in single turrets. The two craft in action at Walcheren in November 1944, were lost. The remainder were preparing for the invasion of Japan when World War II ended. The craft numbers were: 101–112, 114–125, 127, 129 commissioned in September 1945, 144–150, 175–181, 184–186, 192–196, of these Nos 101 and 102 were lost at Walcheren.

There are records of what were probably experimental G(M)s: Nos 4, 53, 54 and 68. Nos 91 and 93 are also recorded but probably commissioned as LCR(M), these rocket firing craft did not carry an RM detachment.

LC Support (Large)

These were converted LC Infantry (Small) with armour over wooden hulls and in the LCS(Large) Mark 1 carried a 2-pdr anti-tank gun in the type of turret used by Daimler Armoured cars. The Mark 2s were similar but carried a 6-pdr anti-tank gun in the turret. Both Marks carried an RM detachment of eight other ranks, part of a total complement of two RN officers and 23 other ranks. On 6 June 1944 one flotilla of four Mark 1 craft, was in action off Normandy. The craft numbers included:

Mark 1 Nos 202–205 and Mark 2 Nos 251–260. At least four were lost. Records suggest that one LCS(L) flotilla, became RM LCS(L) Flotilla 900.

LC Headquarters

These were converted LC Infantry (Large) equipped as flotilla flagships and had first been deigned as LC(Flotilla Flagship). The staff on these craft with Support Flotillas included the RM Flotilla Officers, their administrative staffs, and gunnery control staffs, as well as the Flotilla Flag Officer's personnel.

MINOR LANDING CRAFT OF WORLD WAR II

These craft were normally carried on Landing Ships infantry, which were a variety of converted merchantmen; some – like the Glen ships – were given a major refit to carry landing craft, and some were Liberty ships using their lifeboat davits and with little major alteration. A wide range of steamers, motor vessels, oilers and ferries were adapted in various degrees as LSI (Large), (Medium), (Small), and (Hand Hoist). The last were LSI(HH)s with their craft lowered by hand-worked falls normally used for ships' lifeboats.

Training Flotillas

These initially were all manned by seamen rates, although at Eastney in Portsmouth, there were craft in 1940 manned by Marines for training purposes. In 1943 RN officers and ratings continued to carry out the major part of the crews' instruction but by the end of World War II there were RM training staffs, with flotillas of various types of landing craft, including the following:

400–435, 437 and 490 of 1945.

In a typical change over to RM staff, 235 RM LCP Flotilla relieved the training staff of RN Training Flotilla 188 as early as 18 June 1943.

Some training flotillas also served in operations as Ancillary flotillas.

LC Assault

These wooden craft were 41ft 6in overall, with a well to carry troops. Flotillas were commissioned in the early 1940s with RN officers and ratings. But by the end of 1943 the RM flotillas began to assemble, although not all became 'formed units' appearing in the Admiralty Green Lists of ships and craft locations, until later. Some had been commissioned by RN officers and ratings before being taken over by the Marines, but most early RN flotillas were disbanded. There had also been some LC Support with RM gunners and seaman crews attached to LCA flotillas manned by seamen. For example Flotillas 504, 505 and 507 were initially manned by seamen but each had an LCS(M) attached, other flotillas had two support craft.

The sizes and therefore the complement of flotillas varied according to the lifting capacity of the LSI to which they were attached. Of these the following have been identified as RM LCA flotillas:

504–510, 521, 524–529, 533, 535–565, 570–579, 590–594, 597 and 780.

A number of these – like '780' – were manned by seamen on 6 June 1944 but later became RM flotillas. The records are incomplete, as, for example, with '126', which may latterly have been RM-manned. There were also two flotillas of LCAs among those converted to LC Navigation, with RM crews as 340 and 597 Flotillas.

LC Personnel and LC Vehicle Personnel

There were several types of LCP and LCVP, which were wooden assault craft or used for ferry work and ancillary services. The following have been identified as RM Flotillas at some stage in their existence:

LCP Ancillary Flotillas with either LCP(Large) of 36ft 8in or LCP(Small) of under 30ft, and sometimes with other LCP-types: Nos 441–449, 452, 477, 478, 469, 470. 476, 481, 490, 493, 495, 498 and 780. Others existed for short periods with RM crews.

LCP(Ramped), similar to an LCP(L) but with a ramped bow, and used to land personnel and stores. Those identified as manned by RMs were: 454 and 480

LC Vehicle, a wooden craft used to land 36 troops or 4½ tons of stores. Those identified as manned by RMs were:

455 at Kabrit, Egypt, originally manned by seamen, 456 and 491,

LC Vehicle Personnel, an improved LCV, used in ferry services from ships to shore. The RM Build-up Flotillas included:

459, 800–814 and 823.

LCP(Large) was originally a raiding craft but by 1944 many were being used as ferry craft etc. in Ancillary Flotillas. Those identified as manned by RMs were:

704, 708–711, 713 and possibly 700–702 and 705–707, although these last six flotillas were manned by seamen cres on 6 June 1944.

LCP(Medium) a clinker built coble, this craft was intended for landings on rocky coasts, but an RM LCP(M) flotilla landed Marines from the Fleet in January 1945 at Cheduba Island.

LC Mechanised

Designed to carry vehicles or tanks, these were steel craft either Mark 1s of 44ft 8in overall or Mark 3s of 50ft overall. They could be hoisted out from many LSIs or used in ferry services after a sea crossing, for example, of the English Channel. A Mark 7 was designed for use in surf on Far East beaches. Some craft were built for RM Flotillas, but the programme to build 250 Mark 7s was not completed. The following RM LCM Flotillas have been identified, but there were more which did not become operational:

600, 601, 604–607, 609, 640–642, 665–669, 672–675, 680–683, 690, 691, 698, 901 and 903.

One flotilla might often be carried in several LSIs, with a couple of craft attached to the LSI's flotilla of LCAs or LCPs, and several LCM flotillas had both Mark 1 and Mark 3 craft. In June 1944, the RM LCM Flotillas on ferry work in Normandy each had 16 craft.

LC Support (Medium)

These craft provided fire support and smoke cover for assault flotillas, and had been manned by seamen crews with a small RM detachment of gunners, until they were taken over by all-RM crews. The LCS(Medium), of which both Mark 2s and 3s were in action on 6 June 1944 off Normandy, with twin-.5 machine guns, a 4-in smoke mortar (later firing an HE bomb) and smoke generators. The following RM LCS(M) Flotillas have been identified:

901 and 903–6, and there is one reference to No. 902 as an RM Flotilla of 1945.

LCA (HEDGEROW)

These adaptions of LCAs carried four rows each of six Spigot mortars; they were kept 'on the secret list' until 1944, and do not appear in many records of that time including RM Force orders. Three flotillas manned by Royal Marines from their inception, covered part of the Normandy landings on 6 June 1944. They were:

590 with 18 craft on 'Juno 2' beach, 591 also with 18 craft on 'Gold' beach and 592 with 9 craft on 'Sword' beach.

There are also records of 593, 594 and 595 Flotillas in training during 1944.

LC Control

These flotillas were deployed as individual or pairs of craft to control minor landing craft flotillas. They carried RM staff from time to time before the autumn of 1944, when some of these modified LCS(M)s were entirely manned by Marines.

LANDING CRAFT 1946–1997

Manning

Since 1945 most British landing craft have been manned by Royal Marines for operations, and have included the LCA(Large), able to land a Jeep or its equivalent as well as personnel. The LCA(Large) was later designated the LCP and the LC Mechanised Mark 9 – sometimes 'Mechanical' – replaced the LCMs of World War II. In broad terms these LCMs were larger than their forerunners, providing temporary living quarters for the crew. Craft were grouped in Assault Squadrons, the equivalent to World War II flotillas.

Rhine Squadron

In 1946 there were RM landing craft flotillas and SBS with the RN Rhine Flotilla. This had the role of moving Allied tanks behind the Rhine, if that

had become the 'holding line' in Germany against an advance from the Warsaw Pact countries. The Marines at times had many types of boat for demolition work, had this been necessary in a withdrawal. In the early 1950s, the chiefs of staff decided that this squadron should become a Royal Marine commitment, and in 1953 Marines began to replace sailors in the Squadron which they would operate for the next ten years. RM officers captained LCTs and the Squadron's second-in-command was a major RM, its commander was a captain RN. Its craft included a Naval Servicing Craft Engineers (NSCE), equivalent to the world War II LCE which was equipped to do emergency repairs. The Squadron also had many former German air/sea rescue and torpedo-recovery craft carrying demolition parties. In the early 1960s this squadron ceased to be an RM commitment.

Elbe Squadron

In 1945–6 a squadron of craft with mainly captured German vessels, operated on the Elbe. It included many RM personnel manning small craft, for intelligence gathering and internal security of activities on the river.

Assault Squadrons

After 1946 the run-down in landing craft numbers led to a much smaller amphibious capability being developed, although these Squadrons were each capable of lifting more personnel and stores than their equivalent flotillas of World War II. And from the introduction of Commando Carriers in the 1950s, LC Assault Squadrons were embarked in LPHs and LPDs as part of the ship's company. A Royal Marine officer commanded the Motor Launch (ML) in an Assault Squadron, as its forward control craft. The Assault Squadrons by the late-1990s included '539' which was organic to the Cdo Bde and two which were deployed on the LPHs (see Other sub-units of 3 Commando Brigade RM 1981–97 and Amphibious Units NOT under direct command of Brigade).

The Assault Squadrons had 6 June (Normandy 1944) as their memorable date by 1980.

Amphibious Warfare Squadron

In the 1950s and 1960s the Mediterranean fleet had an Amphibious Warfare Squadron which was employed in landing commandos and Army troops for operations and exercises. The Headquarters Ship HMS *Meon* carried a Naval and RM operational staff. Ships serving in the Squadron included at various times: LST(Assault)s *Reggio* and *Striker*, each with an RM Assault Squadron of eight LCAs; and the Mark 8 LSTs

Bastion and *Redoubt*. In the Suez operation and elsewhere, the Squadron was reinforced being joined by other LST(A)s and LSTs.

The Squadron and its successors operated in the Persian Gulf landing tanks and Army troops as well as RM Commandos. But once the LPDs and LPHs were established as the Royal Navy's principal assault ships, the Mediterranean Squadron was disbanded. However, a number of LSTs were operated by the Royal Corps of Transport until the late 1970s.

Forward Operating bases 1971–1997

In 1971 the Assault Squadron from *Fearless* established procedures for craft operating independently from a parent ship (cp: MOLCABs of world War II). They landed at night by LCUs and four LCVPs from *Albion*, to set up a base with radio communications, service and repair facilities. Such operations in the Arctic required – and require – special procedures. These bases were more mobile than their predecessors and were integral parts of RM landing craft operations. In 1982 the landing craft operating with 3 Cdo Bde formed an *ad hoc* squadron (see chapter 11) with its own base. And in the 1990s elements of 539 Assault Sqn could operate from a forward base.

DEFENSIVELY EQUIPPED MERCHANT SHIPS (DEMS) OF WW II

The organisation of DEMS – known as 'Churchill's Gunners' – began in June 1939,[1] and by the following winter some 2,000 RM and RN pensioners were providing the initial gun layers and instructors for Merchant Navy crews. Their ships were armed[2] with as little as one or two MGs in coasters and fishing boats. Coasters and other vessels up to 2,000 tons had a 12-pdr High Angle or HA/Low Angle (HA/LA) gun. Most cargo ships had a single 4.7-in or 4-in but those of 15,000 tons had a single 6-in gun. Larger vessels had a range of HA/LA guns to meet both close and other air attacks and attacks by surface vessels. By 1944 there were 24,000 Naval and Marine gunners in the Navy's DEMS Department, with 14,000 Maritime Regiment Royal Artillery gunners;[3] and although these Naval and Army personnel were to some extent interchangeable, the soldiers manned the 40-mm Bofors and machine guns. Additional anti-aircraft equipment might include: the Holman Projector, which threw No. 36 grenades by a jet of steam at 150–250lbs pressure,[4] or by compressed air to a height of several hundred feet; and the PAC (Parachute

and Cable) equipment that launched a rocket which carried a parachute with wires to trail when it opened, against low flying aircraft.[5] In a ship of 9,000 tons or smaller, the pensioner colour sergeant or sergeant was the senior gunner. He cleaned and maintained the guns, supervised the storage of ammunition, and trained his MN crew. They usually had only a week's course in gunnery at one of the DEMS schools. In liners and large transports the DEMS detachment might number 30 or more. For example, the MV *Circassia* (11,136 tons), a former auxiliary cruiser, carried 28 DEMS ratings, as she retained much of her armament when carrying troops in 1942–3.[6] These larger detachments were usually commanded by a lieutenant RNVR.

The Marines and other DEMS personnel signed on as 'deck hands' for the purpose of maritime law, and were paid 6d (2½p) as principal gunner or 1d (½p) as gunners in detachments, in addition to their service pay. Detachments frequently transferred from outward bound ships, on their leaving a danger zone, to inward-bound ones.

Lloyd's War Medal for Bravery[7] was awarded to: C/Sgt W. E. Jewell, who was wounded in action in 1941 against a U-boat his gun crew drove off; Sgt W. C. Prescott who continued to fire at aircraft as his ship sank, also in 1941; and to Cpl John Hartridge, who 'although his foot was shot away . . . continued to man his gun . . .', in 1945. At least 15 Marines in DEMS received the BEM.

ROYAL MARINE ENGINEERS

Origins and Organisation

A force of RM Engineers served in World War I and were disbanded, but by an Order in Council of 19 March 1940 the RM Engineers (RME) were to be formed. RME had dual headquarters, the Technical Officer being responsible to the Naval Civil Engineer-in-Chief, and an Administrative Officer responsible to the Adjutant General RM for military matters and discipline; but from July 1941 the command was headed by an RM Colonel who was also a civil engineer and given the dual responsibilities.[8] By 1945 the prospect of a major commitment of these engineers in the Pacific area, led to the appointment of an RM General to command them, who was supported by operational, technical and administrative staffs. The Admiralty, however, continued to allocate RME units to various commands. The initial strength was two companies, each with five technical and two administrative officers and

500 other ranks and had an HQRME at Portsmouth, see RM Circular 1214/40s of 10 April 1940, for full details of the formation of the RME. A camp was established at Freshwater on the Isle of Wight. This original unit was expanded by May 1945 with a War Establishment of battalions commanded by Lieutenant-Colonels RM and each 1,500 strong. Although the full establishment was never reached, on 1 August 1945 there were 257 officers and 7,764 other ranks in the battalions, but the intended increase to 20,000 was cancelled.

Officers received pay and allowances at RM rates, and the tradesmen and pioneers received the rates paid to Royal Engineers. Most of the tradesmen were recruited from civilian skilled labour, and the technical officers (203 of the 257 in 1945) were civil engineers. In 1943 two companies ('T' and 'U') were formed to build airfields for the Mobile Naval Airfield (MNAF) Units. 'T' company on 23 August 1943 came under command of the Training Group at Dalditch, Devon, for administration and discipline. Both Companies were given training in demolition, in military operations and technical requirements for building airfields. Most of the RME training was carried out at the RME Depot, by this time, at Farrington, Berkshire. Advanced military training was also given at Eastney, Portsmouth.

Technical Equipment

By early 1943 each Mobile Naval Air Base Group (which controlled the MNAF units) had Mechanical Sections from the RMEs, equipped with special earthmoving and other plant for preparing difficult air strips. There was high investment per man in equipment, and by August 1945 approval had been given for expenditure of nearly £2½ million (perhaps equal to £25 million in 1995) on further equipment. However there was understandable difficulty in obtaining equipment, which was much in demand for rebuilding European cities.

HMT *Matiana* (9,000 tons) was used in the Far East for transporting RMEs and their equipment; they also had MNBDO Landing Craft attached from time to time to land stores from her and other ships.

Principal deployments

UK and Home Waters:
Heavy engineering at Dover, Kent, and with airfields on the islands of Orkney; destroyer repair bases at Dunstaffnage, on the west coast of Scotland, and Corpach on Jura, Argyll; RN Air Station at Dale, Scotland; assembling American equipment for air stations and building Naval landing pontoons at Eastham, Cheshire; repair

of air raid damage and building Sandridge Camp near Plymouth; preparing hards (slipways) etc. in the spring of 1944 at embarkation ports and standing by for emergency repairs.

Mediterranean:
RMEs were frequently the only people available to restore captured ports. At Ferryville, Tunisia, Detachment 375 restored Nos 1 and 2 Docks; in Naples RMEs worked on clearing docks and built 3-skid slipways for the repair of minor landing craft, as they did at Anzio. In May 1944 with equipment from MNBDO II, RME personnel repaired and improved the naval oil fuel installations at Maddalana. The RME also built oil tanks in Tunisia, bridging and drainage at Leghorn docks, and guarded an important caustic soda plant, while under shell fire at San Vincenzo, Italy, before repairing it. The majority of RME personnel deployed in Italy were withdrawn by the end of 1944.

North West Europe:
Detachments in Mulberry Harbour's installation crews at Arromanches, June 1944; work on clearing the port at Le Havre, working with US Navy's CBs; various camp and accommodation sites completed before units moved to Hamburg; work in the late summer of 1945 on Naval HQs at Minden and Berlin; and maintaining installations in several German ports.

Far East:
RMEs built: an MTB base in Ceylon; the Gan airfield at Adu Atoll; and after the ports were liberated, RMEs went in to repair docks and installations at Akyab, Kyaukpy and Rangoon. One RME unit landed with the first Allied troops at Singapore in September 1945, and by December 1,460 men of the 3rd RME Battalion were working on dockyard repairs and the RM Electrical and Mechanical Engineer Company was helping to restore the supply of electric power to the dockyard. The RMEs were withdrawn in April 1946, from Singapore.

Two battalions (Detachment No. 580) were in Australia by the summer of 1945, preparing to develop the Naval intermediate base which was to have been built at Manus in the Admiralty Islands, but this was abandoned in August.

RMEs did not leave the Far East until May 1946, after completing work in Hong Kong.

Other deployments:
Special units erected Wireless/Telegraphy (W/T) masts at major stations, and others assembled refrigerators. Fuel Gear Assembly Parties (called 'OFGAPS') trained to install fuel tanks, jetties

etc. RME units were drafted to MOLCABs, as their versatility made them particularly useful for these mobile bases.

General

The RMEs included divers for underwater work, frequently made use of local labour to speed reconstruction work, and their versatility ran from infantry skills to building major civil engineering projects with foundations on the sea bed. They were disbanded in the summer of 1946, as tradesmen had a priority in demobilisation.

RM SIGNALS UNITS

RM Signallers had been attached to ships' detachments and land forces since the late 19th century, and many served in World War I. By 1919 the Signals School at Chatham, Kent, was training each year some 40 signallers of all ranks. During world War II the Signals School moved to Trecwn, Wales. Signal units served with all higher RM formations, see other unit history summaries and references to the units to which they were attached.

In August 1945, a Line Signals Unit was briefly formed in Hong Kong. In the 1950s many signallers after completing basic training (see Signal Training Wing in unit history summary for Training Establishments), trained as Naval W/T operators, but later took courses as commando signallers at the Signals Training Wing.

RM PROVOST UNITS

RM Provost Sections served with higher RM formations of World War II, including those landed at Dieppe in 1942. The RM Division Provost Company on 10 September 1943 came under command of RM Division Holding Unit and was based at Foxholes in Southbourne, Dorset. Half of a Section was temporarily attached to each of 3 and 4 SS Brigades HQs by 6 Oct 1943. On 8 Oct (two days later) the Provost Company came under direct command of AGRM, and was noted in RM Circ 282/9/43A3 (dated 12 oct 1943) as SS Group Provost Company at Southbourne.

Detachments landed in Normandy with the initial assault waves on 6 June 1944, and in the next 14 days they carried out far more than their intended role as Naval military police, after working with the Army to direct traffic, etc. (see chapter 6). They provided patrols against looters, and moved with the Naval HQ to Rouen disarming local groups. Men from the Company

later served in Provost Units at Naval HQs in Germany.

Other RM Provost units were formed from time to time for Naval police duties, including those in Singapore in 1945–46. The RM Provost Company was reformed in the 1960s and continues as RM Police Troop, one of the 'Other sub-units of 3 Cdo Brigade RM 1981–97' noted above.

ROYAL MARINES RESERVE

Origin and Units

Proposals for an RM Volunteer Reserve in the 1890s came to nothing, as did the RM aspects of the 1903 Act setting up the RN Volunteer Reserve. But when the Corps' commitments to commando and landing craft roles were established, Parliament in 1948 approved an RM Forces Volunteer Reserve of 200 officers and 1,300 other ranks.

Two centres were opened, the City of London and Glasgow, which began recruiting on 1 November 1948 and started training in the following January. There were a large number of applicants who wanted to join, but the numbers accepted were severely limited in order to give the volunteer reservists proper training.

The Merseyside Centre opened in February 1949 and the Bristol Centre the following month. All four centres – called Units from the 1950s – had considerable help from the RNVR, which provided accommodation for provincial Centres, and the Territorial Army (Finsbury Barracks) provided accommodation for the City of London RMFVR's drill nights. RMFVR Tyne was the last Unit formed, on 1 October 1954. By the 1960s, however, all but the Merseyside unit, had their own premises and considerable facilities.

Over the years the names of the Units have been changed from time to time, but they retained their geographical location in their titles. They have also raised detachments, to recruit reservists over a wide area, the first being at Portsmouth in September 1950 as a subunit of 'City of London'. On 1 October 1966 the words 'Forces Volunteer' were dropped from the Reserve's title. Several detachments were set up but later closed – St Ives (1954–69), Birmingham (1957–60), Sunderland (1974–78) and Edinburgh (1958–69) – and in 1980 the RMR consisted of:

RMR City of London with detachments at Portsmouth and Chatham; RMR Scotland in Glasgow with detachments at Dundee and Greenock; RMR Bristol with detachments in Cardiff, Poole, Lympstone and Plymouth; RMR

Merseyside at Birkenhead with a detachment in Manchester; and RMR Tyne.

The RMR was also responsible for three reserve operational units – 608 Tactical Air Control Party (Reserve), 4 SBS (Reserve) and 2nd Raiding Squadron (Reserve) – each of which could be independently mobilised.

Organisation

The RMFVR Headquarters was set up in 1948 as a department of the Royal Marine Office. This RMFVR HQ was responsible for equipping, training and directing reserves, and had a staff of serving (regular) officers. The Director who commanded the Reserve until 30 November 1979 – a Colonel or Lt-Colonel RM – had direct responsibility to the Commandant General, with MGRM in the different commands having powers of command for discipline. But on 1 December 1979 the RMR HQ became the responsibility of the Major General Training and Reserve Forces (MGTRFRM) based at Eastney in 1980. A Lt-Colonel GSO1 Reserves was the senior officer of the RMR staff.

Each RMR Unit had a permanent staff of serving officers, which in 1949, for example, comprised a Captain RM as adjutant, eight senior NCOs, including instructors, and an orderly. The Units were usually commanded by a Lt-Colonel RMR, with other RMR officers commanding Companies or Troops.

By 1962 the Units were organised in Companies and Troops. At that time there were usually a company of men doing initial training, one of trained soldiers and a rifle Troop of general duty reservists (the largest subunit despite its title), a Landing Craft Troop, Sea Service Wing, a Signal Troop and a special Boat Section. In the mid-1960s, however, the Sea Service Wings and Landing Craft Troops were phased out.

Each reservist from September 1953 signed on for four years – previously it was five years – and in the 1950s National Service men completed three years in the reserve. Reservists normally attended Unit training periods on one night a week and on nominated weekends each month. For these they were paid at rates similar to those for the serving Corps, and receive similar payment for other duties. Each year they also carried out two weeks annual training with the Corps, and until the mid-1970s there were also RMR exercises. A tax-free bounty was paid to those who completed this training and 80 other 'drills' (a full day's training counted as four 'drills'), which by 1980 was £100 for the first year, rising to £300 after three years.

Training

In 1950 the reservists who were training for sea service, spent two weeks at the Gunnery School at Eastney, and others attended specialist courses at RM establishments. In 1951 the Amphibious Wing spent two weeks with the Rhine Squadron. But over the years the 'annual' training had become far more integrated with the regular Corps, and reservists have served worldwide wherever Commandos RM were stationed. By 1956 some reservists were regularly taking part in parachute exercises, and in the late 1960s RMR Company Groups (reinforced Companies) were in Germany on major NATO exercises. During 1979 men from the RMR took part in exercises as far a field as Belize in South America, Hong Kong, Norway, Cyprus, Gibraltar and Germany.

The RMR has a creditable sporting record and RMR Scotland won the Comrie to Stirling race of 1953, in 9 hours, to the amazement of the organisers, who had expected the winners to take 14 hours! In the Devizes, Wiltshire to Westminster canoe race, a City of London crew in 1959 won the Reservists class in a then record time of 23 hours and 17 minutes, and an RMR Team won this class again in 1962.

Ceremonials and Dress

The Units have provided guards and street-lining parties for many local events, including visits of foreign prime ministers to London. They provided guards for the Prince of Wales' investiture and Sir Winston Churchill's funeral, to name only two of their major ceremonial parades from 1950 to 1980. For such parades they wear 'blues' and on other occasions wear orders of dress identical to those of the serving (regular) Corps, but with a shoulder flash including the letter 'R' below the general service flash. A reservist on completion of his training, wore – and wears – a green beret.

Awards

Some measure of the courage, resource and ability of these reservists can be seen in the number of awards they have earned by 1980: six OBEs; three MBEs; 11 BEMs; the Queen's Gallantry Medal to Mne J. Crawford for saving a man's life during a parachute drop; two bravery commendations from the Commandant General; and two Royal Humane Society Testimonials.

Changes in 1981–1997

In 1986 T Company Group was formed to defend the rear areas of 3 Cdo Bde, and the former T Coy became V Coy for UK defence. And in 1990 RMR Tyne was granted the freedom of Newcastle at the time its HQ moved into Anzio House. In 1993 the RMR came under direct command of CG with its Director at HQRM and five regional commands: RMR City of London; RMR Scotland; RMR Bristol; RMR Merseyside; and RMR Tyne.

FORMATIONS WITH CODE NAMES

A number of *ad hoc* forces are described in the main text. From time to time over the years commandos and other Marines' units have been named after their commander as a code-name, for particular operations. For example, 'Wool Force'. 'Pike Force' and 'Curt' Force were Troops and Sections of 30th Assault Unit in Normandy, commanded in 1944 by Lt-Col Woolley, Capt Pike and Lt-Cdr Curtis RN. There have been many others, such as 'Force Sturges' described below. Other forces were named after the location in which they operated.

OTHER UNITS AND AD HOC FORMATIONS

Island Garrisons
In 1815 Royal Marines were sent to garrison the two Atlantic Islands of St Helena and Ascension, against possible French attempts to rescue Napoleon. They were not withdrawn from what became HMS *Acsension* until 1922; and continued to serve as a regular garrison on St Helena until the 1930s.

Faeroes Force (operation 'Valentine')

A force of 13 officers and 180 men,[1] with two 3.7-in howitzers, all commanded by Lt-Col T. B. W. Sandall, landed on these islands from HMS *Suffolk* on the afternoon of 12 April 1940. They landed with a month's stores which took seven hours to unload.[2] The Danish Governor made only a formal protest. The Marines were made welcome and there were no incidents during the six weeks on the islands, before they were relieved by the Lovat Scouts on 27 May.

'Hook of Holland' Company (Force A)

A force of 200 Marines with some machine guns, under Lt-Col B. G. B. Mitchell[3] was landed from destroyers at the Hook of Holland at 0515 hours on 12 May 1940. They were to defend Naval demolition parties.[4] Early next morning a composite battalion of guardsmen landed;[5] they set out for the Hague but met Queen Wilhelmina of the Netherlands and her Government Ministers already near the Hook, before boarding destroyers that afternoon. A German mobile column appeared from Rotterdam and dug in at 1330 some 2,600yds from the Marines, but remained there. That evening, during an air raid, guardsmen manning a Bren on the roof of the RMs' HQ were killed. The raid also started fires near ammunition dumps, but these were quickly put out through Mne S. Glenn's prompt action. Next day, 14 May, further raids at 0545, 0645 and 0930 hours led to the Dutch evacuating the town at 1100 hours, but they still refused to allow the British to block the harbour.[6] Fog delayed the evacuation ships before the Guards came off, and as soon as their ships were clear of the harbour, the Marines embarked at 1305 hours.[7] Offers to bring off Dutch troops were not accepted, before the last RN ships left at 2000 hours, just before the Germans entered the port area.[6]

'Boulogne' Company (Force B)[8]
Some 100 Marines,[9] commanded by Maj C. Holford, the Instructor of Naval Gunnery, with Capt G. W. A. Courtice as second-in-command and Lt Peter Hellings, Adjutant, left Chatham at 0645 hours on 23 May 1940, joining seamen demolition parties; and reached Boulogne in HMS *Vimy* at 1100 hours that morning. Numbers of men were on the mole, their weapons scattered about, they were tired and many were in rags; some were drunk, wandering in the town among refugees. There was no radio link with the UK, and the guards defending this port did not know that the Marines were coming. But their Brigadier quickly extemporised a defence plan: the Guards units were withdrawn to form a perimeter around the post, while French destroyers were heavily engaging German positions; and the Marines held two bridges 1½ miles from the station.[9]

From 1530 hours the dock and the mole coming under aerial bombing, artillery and small arms fire, before the Marine Platoons were withdrawn to the fish market,[10] their reserve Sections searching unsuccessfully in houses, looking for snipers, who were possibly civilian '5th-columnists' who were supporting the Germans. Throughout the day demolition parties calmly prepared 40-ton cranes, lock gates and the main harbour bridge for demolition, and, except for the bridge, these were blown up that evening. Destroyers came in under an 'umbrella' of RAF fighters, while German tanks and artillery opened fire to good effect from positions in the hills beyond the port. At 1800 hours the quays were also under mortar fire, although in the next couple of hours, the troops were withdrawn across the bridge and the first 1,000 men were taken off at 2020 hours. Twenty-five minutes later Lt Hellings watched destroyers 'put up a heavy barrage of fire'. The din was appalling as the ships' guns fired an almost continuous barrage at close range. Several German tanks were hit and 'buildings were smashed as the V- and W-type destroyers' 4-inch burst among the XIX Corps' panzers'.[11] Guardsmen and Marines were marched over the bridge to impress the now unruly mob on the mole, before two destroyers embarked 900 men.[12] The ships then fought their way out of the harbour, despite grounding on the mud, the Marines being back in Chatham at 0230 hours next morning. Capt Courtice was 'especially recommended'[13] for coordinating the RM Platoons while often under heavy fire.

'Calais' Company

Capt G. W. A. Courtice commanded 81 men[14] in the action at Calais, 25–27 May 1940 (see Chapter 3). Much of the fighting was in the final defence of the old town and harbour area, where some 600 men of 30 Infantry Brigade and several hundred Frenchmen held out against 10 Panzer Division. Sgt P. M. Mitchell was awarded the CGM for bringing many wounded to a pinnace in Calais harbour, and Sgt T. H. East for courage during the withdrawals from both Boulogne and Calais.

War Cabinet Guard (Churchill's Guard)

RM guards and orderlies were provided for the War Room,[15] where the War Cabinet and senior officers co-ordinated the mobilised civilian effort with the fighting services in campaigns in every theatre of war. This special detachment included men with medical training[16] who attended the Prime Minister's personal needs, lifting him in a special chair up steep stairs when doctors forbade him to climb them. From time to time Royal Marines also travelled abroad with the Prime Minister.[17] RM Party 'Argonaut' of 57 other ranks commanded by Maj A. H. R. Buckley, were sent to the Yalta conference, and a guard paraded for President Roosevelt and Marshal Stalin to whom Churchill remarked 'Some of my Marines – representatives of one of the finest Corps in the World'. (source: Policy & Progress Letter No. 2 dated 1 Apr 1945)

Force for Mining the Rhine (Operation 'Royal Marine')

After the Germans had mined the Thames with magnetic mines dropped from aircraft, a force of RM and Naval personnel was trained in the use of river mines.[18] These fluvial (R-mines) were of four types:[19] contact-fused 'floaters' below the river's surface, suspended from floats; 'slippers' near the river bed, dragging chain; anchored mines with contact fuses; and 'slugs' which rolled along a river bottom to be fired by clockwork fuses. The majority had 25lb of explosive and could be set to self-destruct in one to six days, before reaching neutral waters. A few giants with 380lb of explosive were used as 'slippers' and 'slugs', but needed trolleys to launch them, all other types being launched by hand.

The Force was ready to operate by 12 March 1940 and launch 1,000 mines a week, but the French fearing retaliation,[20] refused permit the Force to operate until 10 May, when 407 mines were streamed in the River Moselle on the Franco-German border, and a canalised tributary of the Rhine.[21] The Force's night operations were hampered by bright moonlight, exposing the launching sites to German emplacements on an opposite banks of rivers, and within range of the teams launching R-mines. Nevertheless the first night's operation was followed by about 50 mines a night until 13 May, when the number was reduced. The operations had successfully deterred traffic on the river.

This mining was seen by the French as defensive, but the original concept of mining 100 miles of the Rhine was not possible, as the river levels were too low by May and breakwaters broke the river's surface. The Meuse on the Belgian borders with Germany and Holland, was mined from 18–23 May, when the German armies were already at the English Channel. For the next three weeks the Force operated under French command, but the mines were unsuccessful when launched to destroy bridges, a job they were not designed to do. The Force had moved west by 10 June, their final operation on 13 June was streaming mines west of Paris,[22] when the French army was evacuating the area. Two days later the force sailed from St Malo for the UK.[23]

Force Sturges

The Force commanded by Col R. G. Sturges, totalled 40 officers and 775 other ranks, including RN crews for two Naval 3.7-in howitzers, and RM crews of 'Y' Battery of 4-in coats guns and four Pom-Poms (later the Anti-MTB Bty). They landed in Iceland's capital Reykjavik at 0620 hours on 10 May 1940. They had been brought ashore by destroyers, after transferring from two cruisers during a snowstorm.

The advance guard was met by guides from the British consul, and deployed on a nine mile front within an hour. Vehicles were then requisitioned and by 1800 hours the Force was deployed in positions across a 75-mile front protecting two airfields, a seaplane base and three roads leading into the capital, as well as key points in the city. By this time HMS *Glasgow* and *Berwick* had sailed, as they were urgently needed for possible operations elsewhere, as that morning the Germans had entered Belgium.

The Icelandic Government protested against the landing but did cooperate, as the British had come in a spirit of goodwill. There was no violence – see Chapter 2 – and some 60 Germans, mostly off a ship in the harbour, were rounded up. Over the period the Force occupied the island, the attitude of the local people changed, because they feared the British presence would attract German naval bombardment and/or bombing by aircraft. They were also apprehensive of friendships between Marines and Icelandic girls, but no untoward events occurred before the force was relieved by the Army's 147 Infantry Brigade on 17–19 May. Two days later the 2nd RM Battalion and the Force HQ returned to the UK, but the artillery units remained in Iceland and were joined by Fortress Unit 1.

Thames Estuary Special Defences

Luftwaffe planes laying mines in the Thames Estuary had operated with little opposition until the early summer of 1942, when four forts[24] were floated into positions on shoals[25] from which they took their names as HM Ship Forts: Roughs, 10 miles off Felixstowe, Suffolk; Sunk Head, about 10 miles off Clacton, Essex; Tongue Sand, 13 miles off Margate, Kent; and Knock John, 12 miles off Southend, Essex. When in position, a fort could be flooded down in 15 seconds. At low water Sunk Head Fort, for example, was in 30ft of water.

A fort's complement of 120 to 130 included about 70 Marines[26] under its Naval officers. The Marines served for four weeks in the fort followed by two weeks ashore, and when at sea 'had a fair amount of night action and . . . quite a few kills'. They fished, had quiz nights, and ran regattas when tides were not running.[27] Plans to reinforce the forts for defence against V1s were not put into effect in 1944, but they accounted for a number of these flying bombs.[28] (Army manned inshore forts also came in these defences, off the Isle of Sheppy, Kent.)

The forts were paid-off in July 1945.[29]

RM Boom Defence Scaffolding Unit

Formerly 'Y' Company of the 19th RM Bn, reformed as RM Boom Defence Scaffolding Unit on 14 December 1942, moved to Deal in the winter of 1942–3 to build the sea-fire coast defences, designed to spread petrol on the sea's surface in the event of a landing; and a Section worked on the boom defences of the Clyde. In the summer of 1943 they launched 20ft diameter hydrogen balloons, each trailing 200ft of wire, intended to short-circuit overland power lines in German occupied France. These balloons were launched from Felixstowe, Suffolk and the Unit also flew balloons from Palling, Norfolk, carrying sabotage materials.

Force Viper

This Force was Formed late in January 1942 from 107 all ranks of 1st RM Coast Regiment, who volunteered for hazardous service (see chapter 4).[30] After operating as a river patrol aiding Allied forces to cross the Irrawaddy in Burma and raiding Japanese units on river banks, the Force transferred to shallow-draft boats on the Chindwin until reaching the Allied final crossing point. Survivors of the force then marched out through the jungle, and the Force was disbanded in India in the summer of 1942.

International Danube Commission

Some 40 Royal Marines – from *Ajax* and 3rd RM Battalion – served as guards and escorts for the commission, which was based on Budapest, Hungary. They were joined by 50 seamen in October 1919, when a Rumanian Army retired across the bridge between Buda and Pest. Advancing Hungarians marched in, saluting the British guard.[31] The last 20 of these Marines did not rejoin the 3rd RM Bn until January 1920, and the last RN gunboat was withdrawn in 1925.[32]

Observation Minefields

These Units by May 1941 totalled 14 officers and 410 men[33] who were deployed in small detachments to watch harbour minefields controlled electrically from on shore (cp: MNBDO naval units). Trained to pass headings and speeds of approaching ships using coast artillery instruments, they also were trained in ship recognition. Their shore stations were at Liverpool, Exmouth, Blyth, Southampton, Harwich, London, Humberside, Lowestoft, Yarmouth, Aberdeen, Brightlingsea, Dartmouth, Torquay, Llanelly, Fishguard, Salcombe, Peterhead, Newcastle, and Newhaven.

RM BASES, DEPOTS AND TRAINING ESTABLISHMENTS

Chatham

Marines were based in this town from the 17th century,[1] and in 1906 also occupied the converted Naval hospital (Melville Barracks) until June 1950. The barracks were then used by PRORM, the Pay and Records Office RM, until the 1960s. From 1775 the Grand division of Chatham RMLI companies had occupied the main barracks, and on the Amalgamation in 1923 it became the 1st division, continuing to provide detachments for Chatham ships. On the reorganisation into Groups in 1947, the Chatham Groups became responsible for RM establishments in the area and was commanded by a Major General until the Group HQ closed in 1950.

Portsmouth (Eastney)

A company of Marines was billeted in Portsmouth in September 1668,[2] and in the next 200 years Marines were based from time to time in the town (see Forton Barracks below). The major part of the barracks at Eastney was built between 1862 and 1867, when they were first occupied by the RM Artillery as their division's HQ, with holding companies and training facilities.

On Amalgamation this barracks became the 'home' of the Portsmouth Division (the 2nd Division), with particular emphasis on Naval gunnery and seamanship training in World War II. In 1947 this Division took over responsibility for RM establishments in Hampshire and nearby, under command of a major general, as RM Group Portsmouth. This Group became the training Group RM in October 1969 and on 1 December 1979 it became the RM Training and Reserve Forces HQ. In 1975 the RM Museum was opened in the original officers' mess; by 1980 offices in the Barracks were occupied by the small staffs of various Corps services.

During the 1980s the HQTRF remained at Eastney until this Barracks was closed in late 1991, although the RM Museum remained on the site. The RM Cadets left the Barracks as of 8 December 1991. And civilian development of the site began in 1992.

Portsmouth RMLI (Forton)

In 1755 on the formation of the Grand Divisions, the Portsmouth Division was billeted in the town,[3] and first occupied Clarence Barracks in May 1765. In 1848 the division moved to Forton Barracks which was subsequently enlarged, but on Amalgamation in 1923 the Portsmouth RMLI Division was disbanded and the men moved to Eastney.

Plymouth

Although Marines serving in Plymouth[4] ships had been billeted from time to time in the town since the 17th century, companies were not permanently based there until May 1775, on the formation of the Plymouth Grand Division. The Stonehouse Barracks were built in 1781–3 and first occupied on 8 December 1783, Considerable additions and rebuilding had been undertaken by 1980, the last major one being in 1960–1.

The officers' mess was hit by a bomb on the night of 11–12 March 1941 and three people were killed. Throughout World War II this Division followed its custom of concentrating on infantry training, although there was a training battery of Naval guns as part of the establishment. One of these gun positions could be made to 'roll' as if at sea.

In 1946 this Division became Plymouth Group, which for some years from 1949 had responsibility for commando training. In 1967 '43 RM' was stationed there; they were replaced by '45 RM' until the spring of 1971, when these Barracks became the 'home' of the Commando Logistic Regiment and the Brigade HQ, with Commando Forces HQ nearby at Mount Wise, as they were in 1980. For 1981 to 1997 see Unit histories.

Deal

A platoon of Marines was stationed at Deal, Kent, in 1665.[5] The Infantry (North) and Cavalry (South) Barracks were built about 1795, and a naval hospital (largely rebuilt in 1806) became East Barracks. On 7 May 1861 the RM Depot was established at Deal, at first in East Barracks; North and South barracks were taken over in 1869. The Depot was training mainly RMLI recruits, with an RM Bicycle Unit in training in 1889. After 1923 the Depot trained all continuous service recruits.

In 1930 the Royal Naval School of Music moved to these Barracks, and continued in 1980 as the RM School of Music, by 1997 it had moved see Unit histories. The Depot had also been the physical training centre for the Corps, with a Physical Training Wing from 1957 to 1978.

The Depot was closed for a short time after bomb and shell damage in 1940, but except for this short break, pre-OCTU, NCO and other courses were run at the Depot throughout World War II. And throughout 1942 and 1943 the Deal Depot, known to most old 'hands' as the 'Depot Deal', continued to draft men from its Holding Battalion to units overseas such as those of the MNBDOs and the RME. The establishment at Lympstone in Devon, became the principal recruit training depot during World War II, see Lympstone below. This enabled considerable rebuilding to take place at the old Depot Deal, which from 1977 was the 'home' of '41 RM' until disbanded.

Fort Cumberland[6]

First built in 1746[7] on the eastern tip of Portsea Island, protecting the flank of Portsmouth some miles west across the marshes, the fort was later rebuilt in a star-shaped design. RM Artillery were stationed here from time to time in 1817, landing guns across the beach, and from 1858 to about 1867 it was the RMA's HQ. From that time gunnery training and developments were carried out there: in 1895 there was a High-Angle Fire Battery,[8] and many developments over the years were carried out in conjunction with other service departments. The MNBDO experimental unit was formed there in 1923–4, the ISTDC was based there in 1938, and the Corps' technical training was carried out there from its inception.

In World War II some 4,000 personnel were trained at the Fort for MNBDOs, which had their Depot there. By early 1945 the Technical Training Depot ran courses for 20 trades, including drivers (five weeks), surveyors (16 weeks), gun fitters (10 weeks) and many civilian-type trades. This training was transferred to Poole, Dorset, in the 1970s when the Fort was no longer an RM Establishment.

RM Special Reserve (Exton)/ Depot RM Lympstone/CTC RM

Exton Depot was built for Royal Marines conscripted under the National Service (Armed Forces) Act, which called up the 'militiamen' of 1939. The first 400 joined Eastney on 12 October 1939, but on 22 February 1940 these National Service recruits began to join at Exton.[9] During that year the camp – although a Depot, Marines called it 'Exton camp' – provided a 'home' for several units, including the Junior Wing of the RN Band Service, the staff from the Deal Depot, the 7th and 8th RM Battalions, and facilities for MNBDO personnel living in the nearby tented camp. Intakes were reduced from September 1940 until early in 1942, when these Battalions had been moved.

The name RM Special Reserve was changed to the Depot RM Lympstone on 5 September 1941.[10] By 1943 the Corps had decided that Exton should become the main RM Depot allowed under its Peacetime Establishment. Therefore, after World War II, when the Corps was reverting to peacetime strengths, Lympstone, not Deal, was regarded as *The* Depot. (And see RM Circular 2208/430 of 7 September 1943.)

Intakes rose to 800 recruits a month in 1942 and by May 1943 the initial course was increased from six to eight weeks. The following October recruit squads began an 18-week course with the same instructors at Lympstone and at Dalditch,

nearby, which had become the RM Infantry Training Centre.

The Depot was under various commands – its own Lt-Colonel early in 1940, the Commandant of Deal that summer, 103 RM Brigade and other higher formations – until the reorganisation of 1947, when it became part of the Plymouth Group. Two years later it was under the command of the Training Group at Portsmouth. But throughout these changes Lympstone Barracks, as it later became, has remained the centre for training new recruits to the Corps, latterly as the Commando Training Centre RM.

These barracks have been almost completely rebuilt since World War II, and house the most sophisticated training equipment. (For details of 1997 courses see Commando Histories – CTC.)

Tented Camp, Exton

Opened in 1940, literally 'across the road' from the entrance to the Exton Depot, personnel of MNBDO I and two Squads of continuous service recruits, used it a different times before it was closed in August that year.[11]

Dalditch

This was a camp on Woodbury Common, near Lympstone, in the 1940s the RM Infantry Training Centre. The camp opened initially with tents accommodating the first recruits to train there from 1 May 1940 and elements of the 7th RM Bn. In August arrangements were made to find temporary accommodation for the personnel forming 101 RM Bde and 102 RM Bde in Army camps and 103 RM Bde in a Naval camp. The first huts were completed in November, although the internal lighting was not completed before the following spring, and the camp was eventually laid out for 5,000 Marines at a cost of £220,000.[12] In 1941 and 1942 several units were stationed there, but for many trainees it will be remembered for the unfortunate effects of having the sewage disposal above the water table levels. Before steps were taken to improve this situation, the drinking water could be contaminated.

In 1944 the School of Mines with former gunners from the Siege Rgt, was opened at Dalditch in the autumn. The School was to train men in clearing Pacific beaches. but in November 1944 it was apparently closed.

In September 1946 the last trainees completed their 10-week course here, and the camp was pulled down, but since then this has been a training area used by CTC.

RM Snipers School/ RM Snipers Wing

The Corps maintained its special training of snipers over the years, and by 1943 had the RM

Snipers School which moved from Penally near Tenby in South Wales to Browndown, Hampshire, in July 1943. Subsequently it was redesignated RM Snipers Wing.

RM Small Arms School, Browndown

A small arms range on the heath by the sea near Gosport in Hampshire, was first used by the RMs in the early-1850s, and in 1857 the Admiralty acquired the nearby Browndown camp for the RMLI.[13] The ranges were considerably extended and in 1923 the Corps' Small Arms School was established here, for the instruction of NCOs and others who would return to their units as instructors. The camp was further extended in 1937 and used throughout World War II to train various specialists in small arms. By 1957 the power of infantry weapons had made the ranges too small for some platoon weapons and the School moved to Lympstone, although the ranges were still in use in 1980.

Poole

In World War II HMS *Turtle*, a joint British-American base in 1942 and 1943, was established at Hamworthy near Poole, in Dorset at that time.[14] The Assault firing establishment (formerly the Assault Gunnery School) used the base from 1943 until it closed in 1946; and crews of major support craft among others, were trained in ship-to-shore bombardment, firing into the beach ranges of Studland Bay, west of Poole. The camp site, slipways and other facilities were not used again until 1954 when the Corps' amphibious training unit moved here.

In the 25 years to 1980 new buildings and installations were put up, when various units were based here (see Chapter 9). By 1980 the establishment was known as Royal Marines Poole, and was part of Training and Reserve Forces RM. The World War II landing craft associations were continued, as in 1997 this was the principal base of the Landing Craft Branch. (See also Technical Training Wing below.)

Sandwich (HMS *Robertson*)

This camp between Ramsgate and Deal in Kent was reopened by 1943[15] as HMS *Robertson*, a holding camp for major landing craft detachments. RM Flotillas were also based in the nearby port of Richborough, and immediately after World War II they loaded many hundreds of minor landing craft on to American ships for return to the United States, under the Lease-Lend agreements. The camp closed in the summer of 1946.

Seaton

These were Army barracks briefly occupied by 116 RM Bde in the summer of 1945.[16] From the winter of 1971 they were the barracks of 40 Commando RM until 1983.

Bickleigh

This had been a Royal Navy camp,[17] just north of Plymouth, and was first occupied by the Corps on 1 April 1946, as its Infantry Training School as an establishment of RMTG Devon, based at Plymouth. It had an HQ, an Officers' Wing, and a Training Cadre from 27 RM Bn. This organisation developed to include an OCTU Wing, the Commando School RM and a Cliff Assault wing based at St Ives in Cornwall. Later it became simply the Commando School RM. Drafts for 41 (Independent) Commando RM were assembled here in 1950 and in 1954 '42 RM' (when its strength was reduced to a training cadre) provided the staff for the School except when this Commando was remobilised in 1956 and in 1958. After '42 RM' remobilised again in the spring of 1960, the Commando School was moved to Lympstone by June. Bickleigh barracks were completely modernised and continues to be the barracks of 42 Commando RM.

Chivenor

The Cdo Log Regiment moved to this former RAF base in November and December 1996. The workshops were housed in hangars and modern accommodation blocks included some single rooms with built-in furniture, spacious Squadron offices and a gymnasium built in 1988. At nearby Braunton Sands was an ideal location for 'local low-level training'. The airfield near the Squadron lines was used by an RAF Search and Rescue Flight, and provided opportunities for demonstrations of the Regiment's new concepts of operations.

RM Small Arms School Plymouth[18]

The 'Small Arms School Plymouth' was at Blarrick, opened in 1940 and which provided ranges for the Division/Group until the mid-1950s. When this site was used by the Americans in 1944, the School moved to a tented camp at Harford Bridge, a few miles east of Plymouth.

RM Officer Cadet Training Unit (OCTU)

An hotel at Thurleston near Kingsbridge in South Devon, was taken over as the RM Officer Cadet Training Unit (OCTU) in January 1941, as part of RMTG(Devon); and staffed by personnel from the nucleus of the 8th RM Bn who moved from Exton, see also **Military School** below. By February the RM OCTU was functioning, with the first course of cadets 'HO 7', completing its 12 weeks' training by mid-April. Before this time some 'HO' cadets were trained in Kent. When the 8th RM Bn mobilised in August, Thurleston became the RM Military School, initially under command of 103 RM Bde. The School's establishment included an Officers' Wing (which ran military courses), the Cadet Wing, and the NCOs' Wing (which had been the NCOs' School at Exton). The Commander of RM 103 Bde was to interview over 1,000 candidates for commissions, during his frequent visits to London. By this date continuous-service officer recruits were also under going their initial training at the School. 'HO 15' arrived in October 1942, being the 15th set of cadet officers to be trained in World War II, and the first to have completed preliminary training at Browndown. By then the Cadet Wing occupied most of the complex, as the NCOs' Wing had moved to Deal. In 1943–4 officer cadets came to Thurleston after six weeks at Browndown, followed by six weeks on a pre-OCTU course at Deal. After April 1945 'HO 39' and '40' did their pre-OCTU training at Lympstone, before all officer cadet training moved to Bickleigh in August 1946.

Establishments of RMTG (Wales)
The camps in North Wales[19] were all built in 1942–3 for training Royal Marines at a time when the Corps had expanded considerably, and were officially:

Group HQ at Llanegryn, Towyn (modern Tywyn); Camp 'A' *Matapan* in Towyn where men were remustered for LC crews, before it was used for commando training; Camp 'B' *Iceland* at Arthog on the south bank of the Mawddack's estuary, where crews did landing and field exercises; Camp 'C' *Gibraltar* in Peniarth NNW of Towyn, used for elementary seamanship courses; 'D' *Burma* at Llwyngril on the coast, it was the gunnery training camp with a range on the beach for 25-pdr and light AA guns; 'E' Barmouth *Crete* at the mouth of the Mawddack, with requisitioned houses and used as the base for the training craft.

Also in the Group were the assault engineers training camp at Llanegyrn, and the RM Snipers School at Penally near Tenby.

Other camps
Over the years from 1919, when RMLI and RMA personnel were stationed at the Naval Division's Depot at Blandford, Dorset,[20] to 1979 when a company base for 40 Commando RM[21] was in the Creggan Camp high above Londonderry in Northern Ireland, Royal Marines have been sta-

tioned in many Navy, Army and RAF camps at home and abroad. The following few camps have to suffice as examples of the many:[22] Beacon Hill in Falmouth, Cornwall, a former US Services camp, was used by the 27th RM Battalion in July 1945; Sandridge Camp, Stoke Gabriel in Devon, was used by landing craft crews training at 'Dartmouth II' in 1943–4, and in July 1945 30th RM Bn was stationed there; South Brent near Totnes, was a former Army camp where 5 RM AA Brigade was stationed in the winter of 1945; Windrush in Oxfordshire, a former RAF station, was used by the 33rd RM and 27th RM Battalions before it again became an Army camp in January 1946. Army training camps were also used by RM AA Regiments and other RMs.

Amphibious Trials and Training Unit RM
COXE was succeeded by the Amphibious Experimental Establishment (AXE),[23] a Royal Navy establishment which worked alongside the Army's Fording Trials unit, but in 1979 these establishments at Instow, North Devon, were reorganised as an RM establishment.

The Military School[24]
This was established at Exton as the RM OCTU before it moved to Thurleston in 1941 – see **RM Officer Cadet Training Unit (OCTU)** – and on 7 April 1946 it became part of the RM Infantry School at Bickleigh.

Signals Training Wing[25]
By 1919 signals training had been established at Portsmouth and other Divisions since before World War I. But in July 1943 all signals training was to be concentrated at the RM School of Signalling in Saundersfoot, near Tenby in South Wales, which had opened in 1941. On 9 September 1943 an RM Signal Holding Company was established at Letterstone, Dyfed, from which trained signallers could be posted to units. The School moved from Saundersfoot in 1945, to stay briefly at RAF Templet Camp before moving to Ringswould Camp, near Deal. It moved – as the Signals Training Wing? – to Eastney Barracks in 1948, and was later amalgamated with the Clerks Training Wing. In 1973 the **Signal and Clerk Training Wing** moved to Lympstone where it continued in 1997.

Physical Training Wing[26]
As the RM School of Physical Training, it was based at Deal from 1868 until it moved to the Portsmouth Division in June 1940. After World War II the School returned to Deal before moving in 1978 to Lympstone where the School, the PT

Wing from Portsmouth and Lympstone's Physical and Recreational Training Troop, were amalgamated to form the PT Troop RM, which continued in 1997 as the centre of the Corps' physical education, training PTIs.

Motor Transport School[27]

Opened on 9 March 1945 at Excalibur Camp at Alsager in Cheshire, when driver-training facilities at Fort Cumberland were inadequate for the number of LVT, DUKW and vehicle drivers which were needed for the Far East. The School started with 144 RMs under instruction, and was to turn out 288 drivers a month from some 570 trainees. It the autumn of 1945 the School moved to RM Training Group Wales, and subsequently to Poole. It became a part of the Technical Training Wing in about 1973, and when this Wing was disbanded on 31 March 1995 the Driver Training Squadron – as it was known by this date – moved to the Army School of Mechanical Transport at Leconfield near Hull, where it continued in 1997 as the RM Division of the School.

Technical Training Wing

Originally the Technical Training Company which moved to RM Poole in 1973 and was subsequently renamed in the late 1980s to the Technical Training Wing. In 1995 it had a Driver Training Squadron (qv Motor Transport School), and a number of other sub-units which were or had been transferred on the closing of the TT Wing on 31 March 1995 as follows:

Vehicle Mechanics Coy transferred in September 1977 to SEME at Bordon;

Armourers & Metal Smiths training transferred in 1977/78 to SEME;

Carpenters' Training for what had been an SQ until 1991/2 was reassigned as an additional qualification taught in the Assault Engineer Branch. This training was subsequently transferred from 31 March 1995 to the Royal School of Military Engineering at Chatham. The training managed by a WO2 RM.

Illustrators' Training and the Corps' central production facility had been part of TTW since 1973. The Training moved to the Signals & Clerks Training Wing at CTC by 31 March 1995, the central production facility being closed.

R (Cdo) Company disbanded in 1991 had elements which then became part of the TTW. These included: the RM Free Fall Team which later moved to CTC; the Cdo Display Team transferred to HQ Coy RM Poole by 31 March 1995; and the PT Visits Team transferred before March 1995 to CTC.

On the closing of the TTW the work it had done in servicing RM Poole's vehicles, the services of a PO (Photographer), a unit illustrator and an equipment repairer were transferred to HQ Coy RM Poole.

Drafting and Records Office RM (DRORM)

When the Corps was organised in Grand Divisions at the Navy's home ports of Chatham, Portsmouth and Plymouth, a man's pay and records were administered by his division. Drafting rosters were also handled by each Grand Division, as men were posted to detachments in ships based on these home ports. During World War II, with many units overseas, the divisional records had to be supplemented by offices handling particular units, with, for example, Combined Operations Pay and Records Administration (COPRA) handling the records of personnel in landing craft and units in Combined Operations. By 1947 Col (later Maj General) H. T. Tollemache devised and then installed a pay and records department for the Corps, known as PRORM it was based at Chatham Division. In 1960 as PRORM it was re-located at Eastney (Portsmouth) but in order to include the drafting functions of this office it was renamed the Drafting Pay and Records Office (DPRORM) on 17 January 1966. When the computerised systems were introduced for Royal Navy records, DPRO moved to HMS *Centurion* (the Navy Records Office at Gosport) as from 1 April 1973. The Office remained responsible to the Commandant General, the 'P' was dropped from the title when the Navy took over responsibility for pay. In May 1995 the office moved to HMS *Excellent* and became part of the Personnel Branch of HQRM.

Home Base Ledger Office

Had been established to keep the pay and records of Marines not on the books of a particular ship or 'stone frigate' (Naval barracks). On 17 September 1943 the offices at Bournemouth (then in Dorset) were closed and reopened next day at Ilfracombe, North Devon. This work was later taken over by PRORM, the Pay and Records Office RM, based until the 1960s at Chatham.

ROYAL MARINES ON DETACHMENT OUTSIDE THE CORPS

The number of RM officers and other ranks who have served on detachment to British and foreign forces are too numerous to detail, and only examples can be given: Lord Hankey – when a Major in 1908 was appointed assistant Secretary to the Committee of Imperial Defence, he became its Secretary in 1912 and subsequently became Secretary to the Cabinet, a post which he held until after WW II; General Chater and Brig Leicester with the Sudan Defence Force; three or four senior officers with the Egyptian Army in 1920s; General Sir Leslie Hollis as a Major in 1936 appointed Secretary to a sub-committee of the Chiefs of Staff Committee, subsequently he held various posts in the War Cabinet Secretariat until May 1949 when he returned to the Corps as CG; Maj Gen Dallas Brooks was Deputy Head of the Political Warfare Executive in the early 1940s before he returned to the Corps as CG until 1949; Lt-Col V. C. Brown – in many peoples' opinion one of the Corps' finest soldiers – killed in France in 1940 when CSO 3 Division; officers and men with the Sultan of Oman's forces from 1957 to 1976.

CADET UNITS

Marine Detachments with Sea Cadet Corps

These were first formed ion 1955[28] and by the mid-1970s over 50 detachments were active in most major cities and larger towns in the UK. A number of these cadets joined the Corps each year.

RM Volunteer Cadets

These have their origins in cadet units for children of Senior NCOs attending schools, which in the early 1900s were run by the Corps in various barracks. Although no longer confined to children of members of the Corps, the Cadet Units enjoy encouragement and facilities from the various headquarters in the areas where they are based.[29] The Units have a broad aim in helping youngsters to grow up with a knowledge of citizenship, and they run sporting activities and hold annual tattoos.

There are also RM Girl Ambulance Companies at Plymouth, which were first set up about the time of World War I,[30] and continued in 1980. The title of Cadet Corps was changed to Boys Corps in the late 1970s, and in 1980 there were RMVBC Units at Portsmouth, Plymouth, Deal and Lympstone[31] (a Unit at Chatham was closed in the 1970s). Those Cadet Units with girls in their ranks retained their title of Cadet Corps.

RM ASSOCIATION (RMA)

In 1945 Col Nichol Gray and others proposed the formation of the Association, which the Corps supports. By 1980 there were 40 branches with 7,000 members and 1,400 members without specific branches. In 1997 the Secretary coordinates the day-to-day work from offices at Eastney, to overall policies guided by the Council to promote *esprit de corps* and comradeship between serving and retired Royal Marines.

APPENDIX 5

ROYAL MARINE BANDS

The following paragraphs are based on information in the privately published *Operation Music-Maker* by kind permission of its author, Mr John Trendell.

ORIGINS

In 1919 there were two distinct organisations of RM musicians: the so-called Divisional Bands and the RM Band Service of the Royal Navy School of Music. The former had been established at the Grand Divisions since 1772, if not earlier, and were successors to the musicians like the few drummers and players of hautboys impressed into service with the 1st Marine Regiment of 1693. The RM Band Service of the Royal Naval School of Music had been formed by an Order in Council of 20 May 1903, under which Naval Band ratings were gradually transferred to the Corps, which from time to time would provide musicians for service in ships and Naval establishments. This Band Service was based at Eastney, Hampshire, where its staff trained boy recruits to be musicians for the 50 bands provided in 1914, when the established strength of the Service was 1,450.

DIVISIONAL BANDS

Organisation

An Order in Council of 10 June 1921 authorised five commissioned Directors of Music in the Corps, each responsible for the musical direction and discipline of his band. These Directors had virtually complete authority over recruitment of their bandsmen, who were almost invariably trained musicians and often had served in other military bands. They usually joined one of these bands because it provided a permanent base with relatively few commitments that took a man away from home, and so he was able to undertake private engagements in his free time. Another attraction was the corporal's rate of pension which musicians received on retirement.

The bands each developed along separate lines, but were influenced by the Royal Military School of Music at Kneller Hall in Twickenham, Middlesex in those years. Here British military band masters were trained, as after 1880 all band masters were required to have military rank and training. The instruments for RM Divisional bands were provided in part by the officers surrendering one day's pay each year for the band funds. These amounts were supplemented by grants from the Admiralty, from RM non-government funds and by 10 per cent of the profits from private engagements. The Portsmouth Band (see below) also received sums from the Privy Purse – Parliament's allowance for the monarch's private expanses – as a contribution towards its costs in serving in the Royal Yacht. The number of musicians in each band varied slightly from time to time, but in 1950 Chatham and Plymouth bands were each 35 strong and Portsmouth had 50 musicians. Each man could play at least two instruments – one in the military band and the other in the orchestra – as in addition to ceremonial parades the bands provided orchestral music for formal events in the officers' mess and on other military occasions. They also took engagements for non-service functions, when fees would be paid into the bands' funds, from which musicians received payments over and above their service pay.

The Divisional bands were amalgamated with the Band Service in 1950, but before then they underwent a number of changes, as shown below. (The colloquial titles are used in 'Portsmouth Band' and so on, although the full title of this band for example, was 'the Band of HM Royal Marines [Portsmouth Division]' and after 1947 the word 'Group' replaced 'Division' on the restructuring of the Corps.) The extent of their activities over the years can only be briefly indicated, but the programmes of ceremonial and orchestral work required considerable rehearsal, and when in barracks, the musicians rehearsed during most mornings. The preliminary work on musical scores, extending the repertoire and checking the drill for particular ceremonials – Is there room to countermarch outside the Guildhall? Will the bass drum 'fit' into this motor coach? What formation is needed to pass through that arch? – all require and required administrative as well as musical skills on the part of the officers and NCOs.

The Bands

Chatham Band, being based near London, frequently performed in the capital, not only for ceremonial parades but also for other events: the Wembly Tattoos of 1924 and 1925, and the Football Association Cup Final of 1925, were typical of many such engagements. It also gave bandstand concerts in the Royal Parks, playing one series of these in 1940 despite the 'blitz'. Overseas engagements included the funeral of the King of the Belgians (1934) and the victory parade in Berlin (July 1945). Its last ceremonial parade was on 6 August 1950 when the Colours of Chatham Division were laid up in Rochester Cathedral at the time this Division was disbanded.

Portsmouth RMLI Band was based at Forton Barracks from 1919 to the Amalgamation of the RMA and RMLI after which the majority of its musicians were transferred to the Depot (Deal) and the band disbanded.

RM Depot Band since 1900 had been organised as a Divisional band, and in 1923 it was strengthened by the musicians transferred from the RMLI at Portsmouth. Two years later they served in *Repulse* during the Prince of Wales' tour of West Africa, when – as on most tours – the band not only performed in ceremonies aboard ship but also took part in parades ashore and provided orchestral music at receptions. The band was disbanded in August 1930, a few months before the RN School of Music moved to Deal.

RMA Band was based at Eastney and had provided musicians for the Royal Yacht since the early 1900s, King Edward VII selecting them in 1904 as the permanent source of the Yacht's band, a duty that their successors carried out into the mid-1990s. On the Amalgamation of the RMA and RMLI this band remained at Eastney and was redesignated 'the Band of HM Royal Marines (Portsmouth Division)'.

Portsmouth Band was formed by the redesignation of the RMA Band in 1923. Among the ceremonial duties it carried out were those at the wedding of the Duke of Kent (1934) when – while marching back to the railway station – the Drum Major threw his Staff (known colloquially as his mace) to the level of the second-floor windows of the Army and Navy stores in London, a height of 40ft. During World War II the Band visited many RM establishments, played in 11 August 1948 'Savings Day' parades, had a full broadcasting schedule and in 1945 toured Scotland. Two years later it served in *Vanguard* during the Royal Tour of South Africa, then visited Canada in 1949. Its last major ceremonial was at the launching of *Ark Royal* in

May 1950, before becoming part of the new Band Service.

Lympstone Depot Band was formed during World War II with some 25 pensioner musicians whose average age was nearly 55. They provided a military band for morning parades by recruits, a small orchestra and a concert party.

RM Far East Band was formed from 60 selected musicians from the Divisional Bands, toured India and South East Asia in the winter of 1945–6.

Plymouth Band in 1919 and 1920 served in *Renown* during the Prince of Wales' tour of Canada. It was little affected by the Amalgamation of the RMA and RMLI. In 1935 it began the first of a series of regular British Broadcasting Corporation (BBC) broadcasts, which only ceased on the outbreak of World War II. It had visited Paris, France, in July 1939 and was returning from Canada when war was declared. It went back to France in 1944 and later gave an open-air concert in the Champs-Elysées in Paris.

Royal Yacht Band, with some 20 musicians and four buglers was provided by the Portsmouth Band based at Eastney. In addition to its ceremonial duties, it provided a small orchestra and contributed to the ship's concert party. The extent of its engagements varied over the years, but it spent some four months in the Yacht during an average year. The musicians selected for this duty greatly appreciated the opportunity for personal service to the Royal family.

Changes and events 1981–1997
See details below.

THE ROYAL NAVAL SCHOOL OF MUSIC

Organisation

The Jerram Committee in 1919 made several recommendations which led to major changes in the Band Service, for this became a self-contained unit with its own administrative staff for work previously done by the RM Artillary band. Two general list officers, however, continued to serve as the Superintendent and his assistant, when the rank of commissioned warrant officer was introduced at this time to provide a link between commissioned and noncommissioned ranks, and the rank of commissioned band master was introduced to the Band Service. Civilian instructors at the School were replaced by NCO instrumentalists and other steps were taken to provide more opportunities for band ranks in this Service to have spells of duty ashore. In 1921 the ranks of Band Master 1st and 2nd Class replaced Band Colour Sergeant and Band Sergeant; then in 1947 the ranks of Band Master 1st and 2nd Class were altered to Band Master and Band Sergeant respectively. From 1920 to 1951 Staff Sergeants, equivalent to Quartermaster Sergeants, carried out the administrative work; this rank became Staff Band Master and included musical appointments. Later, when the Naval rank of warrant officer was discontinued in 1949, the Warrant Band Masters became Commissioned Band Masters and the existing Commissioned Band Masters were appointed Senior commissioned Band Masters. But since 1972, when senior ranks were restructured in the Royal Navy, Band masters have held the rank of Warrant Officer.

Aboard ship the bands provided ceremonial music at 'colours' each workday morning when the White Ensign was hoisted, and at 'Divisions' they often paraded with the guard, accompanied church services, and played orchestral music at formal functions in the wardroom. They practised wherever they could find a free space – in the engineers' workshop, perhaps, the canteen flat or their mess. The size of bands varied with the class of ship, a capital ship carrying some 15 musicians, but in D-class cruisers in the early 1930s, for example, the band complement was only 11 musicians under a band Master 2nd Class. By 1942 a typical band aboard a cruiser was no larger, although one musician might be a corporal. Their instruments for military work were typically a piccolo/flute, two clarinets, an alto saxophone, three cornets, a euphonium, a trombone, a bombardon and a drum. They could also muster a tiny orchestra, but the larger string instruments were withdrawn from smaller ships.

RM bands' casualty rate was probably the highest of any British service in World War II, as they worked in the T/S (see below) which was usually on the lower decks of ships.

In 1929 before the School moved in October 1930, to Deal in Kent, the Band Service had an establishment of four officers (at the School), 11 commissioned or warrant officer band masters, three staff sergeants, 63 band masters, 66 band corporals, 723 musicians and 195 band boys. The boys joined at 14 or a little older, and were trained to play in both military bands and orchestras. But the trained musicians spent so much time at sea that few signed on for the full 22 years' service to qualify for a pension. This led to a shortage of musicians, and in April 1937 360 boys were under training in a major effort to increase the strength of the Service. Their training also included a gunnery-control course at HMS *Excellent*, as these musicians' action stations were in the Transmitting Station (T/S) of their ship, operating gunnery-control instruments. Those selected for promotion to corporal had

also to have a working knowledge of the Infantry Drill Book, hold a First Aid certificate, have the necessary educational qualifications, and undertake studies in musical theory and instrumentation. Band masters did a year's course under the personal supervision of the musical director.

During World War II the School was evacuated from Deal, first with the Boys' Wing at Lympstone in Devon and the musicians at Plymouth. The musicians were sent from Plymouth to supplement other bands or to stand by ships being built in the summer of 1940. That September both the Senior and Junior Wings were reunited at Malvern in Worcestershire; but the following summer the boys moved to the Isle of Man and the seniors to Scarborough in Yorkshire. From 1946 the RN School was based at Burford in Oxfordshire, before returning to Deal in 1950 where they remained until March 1996 when they moved to HMS *Nelson* barracks in Portsmouth (see *Changes and events 1981–1997* below).

Performances

Every ship's band carried out a wide range of musical work, from ceremonial to providing jazz groups for private entertainments; the Prince of Wales (later Edward VIII) joined sessions held in his cabin during the 1921 Royal tour. A 1938 list of engagements for ships' bands shows them playing at functions on every continent. During World War II, when 170 'HO' musicians were recruited, the Band Service strength was just under 2,000, with 84 bands, of which 13 were composed of pensioners in 1941. Bands from the School continued to provide ceremonial music at military parades, with, for example, two bands each of 50 musicians taking part in parades publicising the National Savings Week of 1944. By August 1945 there were 20 bands in the British Pacific Fleet.

Ships' bands from various fleets had been brought together from time to time to play as massed bands, and by 1946 – when there were too few musicians to fill the complements required – a central band of 40 musicians was formed at Malta. This band provided musicians when these were required for ships' visiting the Mediterranean ports for ceremonial occasions. They also played at various functions in Malta. Only the cruiser *Birmingham* of the Mediterranean Fleet had a band permanently embarked at this time. In the Home fleet only the flagship *King George V* carried a band.

The RM Band Service had provided bands for a wide range of official functions ashore throughout its existence, and 60 musicians from the Service played outside Westminster Abbey during ceremonies at the wedding of Princess Elizabeth and Prince Philip in November 1947. Three years later, on 1 May 1950, the bands of *Liverpool, Gambia, Ceylon, Euryalus, Glory, Forth* and the Malta shore base (*St Angelo*) 'Beat Retreat' before the Princess and the Prince, in one of the last major ceremonies before the RM Band Service was amalgamated with the 'Divisional' bands. By this date the Band Service was providing bands for Lympstone (formed 1946) and for 3 Commando Brigade. The Brigade's band had been formed in 1948 and by about 1950 had 23 musicians and some buglers.

ROYAL MARINES SCHOOL OF MUSIC

Formation

When General Hollis was faced with major cuts in the Corps' establishment during the early summer of 1949, he put forward recommendations for an amalgamation of all RM musical services. These proposals had been prepared by a committee under the chairmanship of General Leech-Porter, who had commanded 5 AA Brigade in World War II, and before 1939 had been a superintendent of the RN School of Music for several years. As a result of these recommendations the new Band Service was formed on 1 September 1950.

During the period before the formal amalgamation there were a number of moves to forge closer links between the RN School of Music and the 'Divisional' bands, which since 1947 had been 'Group' bands. Since 1944, for example, vacancies in 'Divisional' bands had been filled where possible by musicians from the old Band Service, a number of joint programmes had been performed and in August 1950 Maj Vivian Dunn prepared a concert with 85 musicians drawn from his Portsmouth Group band and the old Band Service units in the Portsmouth area. The intention was for the new Service to provide two Group Bands, each 38 strong, five class 'A' bands of 24 musicians each, and 16 class 'B' of 18 men each.

Organisation

There were a number of major changes in the detail of the organisation. These included the appointment of civilian instructors in 1950, after a period of 25 years in which senior NCOs had carried out this work. Pay was increased (by 60 per cent for band masters). And later, on changes in Naval regulations, bands would normally serve in a ship for a commission of 1½ years, of which 12 months might be on overseas service,

whereas before 1954 commissions were for 2½ years.

Within two years of its formation the new Band Service had 280 boys under training, and this was increased until 380 were at the School in 1955. That year 100 trained musicians were drafted to bands, and by 1957 there were 1,000 all ranks in the Service which expanded from the original establishment of 1950. Some National Servicemen were recruited, and as these were mainly from civilian music colleges, they contributed considerably to the music standards of this Service. The number of bands afloat was reduced, however, from eight in seagoing ships at the end of 1954, to five in 1968 and one in 1973, as the number of major warships in the Royal Navy declined. Nevertheless, from the mid-1950s until 1968, the Service provided some 20 bands.

In 1958 the established strength of the Service was reduced from 1,000 to 800. This was further reduced by 1 April 1973 to 540 all ranks. In the 1970s each band normally had 25 or more musicians, with a greater proportion of juniors in the horn, oboe, bassoon and cello/tuba sections, which had not usually formed part of the smaller bands. Six of these 25-man bands, each with five buglers, were serving in 1973, and there were four staff bands each of 43 musicians and 15 buglers. At sea there was the band of HMS *Ark Royal* with 18 musicians and six buglers.

Staff bands were the equivalent to the old 'Divisional' bands, but various changes had been made in the titles of bands at shore establishments. Since 1969 some staff bands had been attached to Naval commands as well as those which were in RM Groups. In 1980 there were the following Royal Marines Bands: RM School of Music (Deal); C-in-C Naval Home Command (Portsmouth); Commando Forces (Plymouth); C-in-C Fleet (Chatham); Flag Officer Scotland and Northern Ireland (Rosyth); Flag Officer Plymouth (Torpoint); Flag Officer Naval Air Command (Yeovilton); HMS *Britannia* Royal Naval College (Dartmouth); and the Flag Officer Third Flotilla.

Since 1968 all officers holding musical appointments have been Directors of Music, with the Service being led by a Principal Director of Music since 1953. In 1953 the then Principal Director, Maj Vivian Dunn, was promoted Lt-Colonel, the first RM Band officer to attain this rank. From 1978 the Principal Director also held the appointment of Commandant of the RM School of Music. His staff at the School in the late 1970s, included: a Director of Music (Training); an Assistant Director; a Supply Officer (Music); an Assistant Drafting Officer (Band), who worked in the Pay and Records Office; and one junior officer at the Royal Academy of Music doing advanced studies. The Directors with the C-in-Cs' bands held the rank of captain as did the Training Officer but other officers were lieutenants (the rank of 2nd-lieutenant was discontinued from 1 July 1966 in the Band Service, as it was for all SD officers).

From 1970 band masters who by 1980 were WO2s, completed a year's course in the musical aspects of their duties and might also have taken an advanced command course. Prospective band sergeants took an 8-week practical course in music studies (aka the 'MI' course) and a Senior Command Course; some capable corporals who had passed these courses were promoted straight to WO2 after also passing the band masters course. As corporals they had passed their 'M2' music examination after training within their band, and also had passed the general service Junior Command Course of five weeks. (These Junior Courses before 1970 had been considerably longer.) The band sergeant instructors serving with Voluntary Bands of seamen and other ratings in naval establishments, had to pass the 'MI' examination.

Junior musicians – the term 'boy' was discontinued in 1956 – were still trained by civilian tutors, and after the age of entry was raised to 15 in 1966 and later to 16, their training lasted two years and eight months, covering eight school terms. During this time they were taught to play two instruments, although a few potential soloists might concentrate on one instrument. Typical combinations were clarinet/violin, flute/tenor saxophone and cornet/piano. This training also included general education, drill and PT, and before a junior completed it he became a Musician 2nd Class at 17 years of age. He might have been sent for short periods to serve with bands in order to gain experience. On reaching the musical standard to pass the 'M3' examination, he was promoted to Musician 1st class.

Duties

Queen's Regulations laid down 'the primary duty of Royal Marines Bands is to fulfil its threefold role as a military band, an orchestra or a dance band'. In the last of these functions one band was engaged to play for a 'season' aboard the liner *Queen Elizabeth*, in an unusual but an effective example of the way the Band Service helped – and helps – the Crops' good name through civilian engagements.

Some measure of the bands' versatility is shown by the 1968 programme for the Royal Tournament: the 80-strong Corps of Drums and Bugles opened the display; a 90-piece orchestra followed; then came a 16-piece dance band; and

a marching band for the finale. In the concert theatre the bands were – and are – famous, and in 1997 gave their 23rd annual concert for RM charities at the Royal Albert Hall. In the ceremonial of 'Beating Retreat' – with origins in the military drum beats which signalled to the 16th century soldier that nightfall was near and he must disengage from battle – the Corps has a high reputation and from 1950 they 'Beat Retreat' every few years on Horse Guards Parade. A notable ceremonial 'Retreat' was performed for Prince Philip on the 25th anniversary of his appointment as Captain General of the Corps, with five separate parts of the ceremony, including fanfares and marches in slow and quick time.

Some Major Engagements 1950 to 1980

Plymouth Band presented outdoor concerts for the Festival of Britain in 1951, visited Germany in 1956 and 1957, played at the Edinburgh Tattoo in 1959, in America in 1960 and later. From 1968 the musicians of this band were based at Lympstone for four years before returning to Plymouth to take over the role of the 'Band of HM Royal Marines, commando Forces'. They had engagements in Northern Ireland, ceremonials with NATO Forces, and in 1977 made a major contribution to the musical support for the silver Jubilee of Her Majesty Queen Elizabeth II. The following year they visited Iran.

Portsmouth Band continued to provide the band for the Royal Yacht. In 1953 it provided the band for the guard of honour at the Queen's coronation. In November that year a band of 29 musicians and buglers accompanied the Royal tour aboard SS *Gothic* and *Britannia*, when they were directed by Lt-Col Dunn who had retained command of the Royal Yacht band. The tour lasted six months and visited the West Indies, Australia, New Zealand, Malta and Gibraltar. The Royal Yacht Band was to provide musical support for tours in later years. In 1959, for example, this band played 500 pieces of music at 57 functions and took part in 50 military band programmes during a five-month tour visiting Australia. In the next two decades the Portsmouth Band with its Royal Yacht connections, was the most travelled of the RM Bands, albeit as the band of C-in-C Naval home Command from April 1972.

Deal Band, as the Staff Band of the School of Music from 1950, it took part in 1953 in the Coronation procession, and among its overseas tours was a visit to North America in 1965, when it played in a mass band with the Band of the USMC. It was usually conducted by the Principal

Director of Music. It was almost invariably the core of massed band performances in concerts and ceremonials, playing its part in the training of senior musicians.

Chatham Band was formed as the band of C-in-C Western Fleet in January 1969, and replaced the 'ship's band' which had been serving at Chatham. This Staff Band provided small bands for duties afloat in County-class guided-missile destroyers, frigates and Royal Fleet Auxiliary ships, as and when bands were required by a ship visiting foreign ports or for other ceremonies. Nevertheless the Band could play a full repertoire even when sections had been briefly detached for sea service. It made a number of overseas tours. On reorganisation of Naval commands these musicians became the Band of C-in-C Fleet in 1971.

CHANGES AND EVENTS 1981–1997

The annual concerts at the Royal Albert Hall which had started as an event on a single night in 1973, continued during these years with increasing success and by the late 1990s included three evening performances. These concerts raised substantial sums for the Sir Malcolm Sargent Cancer Fund and for other charities. Concerts in the Guildhall were also held annually from 1996 and were concluded with Beating Retreat in the Guildhall Yard.

During the Falklands War of 1982, bandsmen were deployed as medical orderlies in *Canberra* and provided working parties to help in the offloading of stores for the Commando Brigade. On 22 September 1989 a bomb planted by the IRA in the recreation Room of the School of Music killed eleven people and wounded many other members of the Staff Band.

On 31 August 1992 ten women joined the Band Service. They were aged 17 to 24 and formed the New Entry Squad 2/92. They completed 15 weeks military training before starting their music training which would take up the rest of their first two years in the Corps. However during their music training they had further periods of military training, all of which parallelled a recruit's basic training at CTC. They found the military course demanding especially in bad weather during two of their four field exercises.[1] Two girls came 2nd and 3rd in the Cassel annual music competition held at the time when they had completed their first year of training.[2] Their dress code followed that of bandsmen except that the bandswomen's blue peaked caps had a narrower shape to the white tops of their

caps. In Lovat dress they could wear a skirt which might also be worn in barrack dress and shirt-sleeve order. Their dress regulations included: barley-black tights; a black plastic shoulder bag; Navy issue black court shoes; and 'Pantees' (sic).

During the Gulf War of 1991, the band of C-in-C Fleet served as medical orderlies in the RFA *Argus* treating casualties.

In the summer 1994 the Band of C-in-C Fleet was disbanded.[3]

In March 1996 the RM School of Music moved from Deal to HMS *Nelson* Barracks in Portsmouth. The first trainees joined the re-established RM School of Music in September 1996. On 28 October HRH The Prince Edward formally opened the new buildings for the School which were – and are – at HMS *Nelson* in Portsmouth. The Deal band was disestablished and work with the School was undertaken by the Portsmouth Band. The School continued to run courses for musicians and formed close links with the Music Department of Portsmouth University.

Men and women in the RM bands continued to be Royal Marines first and musicians second. But in 1997 there were only five full-strength bands: the Band of HM Royal Marines Portsmouth (who also provided bandsmen for the Royal Yacht); the Band of HM Royal Marines Commando Training Centre; the Band of HM Royal Marines Plymouth; the Band of HM Royal Marines Scotland; and the Band of HM Royal Marines *Britannia* Royal Naval College.

THE MUSIC

Directors

So many distinguished musicians have held senior band appointments in the corps since 1919 that any summary must in its brevity do scant justice to their service to the Corps. Among them were the three O'Donnell brothers, who between them had directed each of the five 'Divisional' bands at different times in the 1920s and 1930s. Maj J. C. J. Hoby, MBE, Mus Doc (Oxon), LRAM, ARCM, who was appointed in 1908 to the Chatham Band as its WO Band Master. He retired 20 years later with the rank of major, and took up the post of Professor of Military Music at the Royal College of Music. Maj F. J. Ricketts wrote many famous marches under the name of Kenneth J. Alford. These included 'The Thin Red Line', 'On the Quarter Deck' and 'Colonel Bogey' (reportedly written after meeting his Colonel on a golf course). He turned down the musical directorship of Kneller Hall, the Royal Military School of Music, to move from the Deal Band to the Plymouth Divisional Band in 1930, which he would direct for the next 14 years until ill-health forced him to retire in 1944. He was commissioned in the Band Service in 1927 but had served with the Argyll and Sutherland Highlanders, which he had joined in 1908.

In 1931 Lt F. Vivian Dunn, ARAM, was appointed at 22 years of age Director of the Portsmouth Divisional band. Four years later his abilities were recognised when he directed seven bands massed for King George V's birthday parade. He directed Portsmouth Band until 1953, when he was appointed the first Principal Director of Music Royal Marines. He had been a major influence on the reorganisation of the band Service; had served four Sovereigns in the Royal Yacht, which was recognised by the award of the Royal Victorian Order; and found time to write several marches, including 'Cockleshell Heroes', 'Commando Patrol' and 'The Captain General'. On his retirement in December 1968 he was appointed Knight Commander of the Royal Victorian Order. Sir Vivian continued to take an interest in and support the Corps' activities until his death in April 1995.

Sir Vivian was succeeded as Principal Director of Music by Lt-Col P. J. Neville, OBE, MVO, FRAM, who had trained as a band boy in the mid-1940s, was commissioned in 1958 and had held several appointments as a Director of Music. The Principal Director of Music in 1980, Lt-Col James Mason OBE, MVO, LRAM, had also joined the band service as a boy in 1946, was commissioned in 1959 and for seven years directed the Portsmouth band as well as holding senior staff appointments at Deal. From 1 November 1982 Lt-Col Graham Hoskins OBE, MVO, ARAM was Principal Director and was succeeded by Lt-Col John Ware BA, ARAM from 1989 to 1994. From 1994 the post was held by Lt-Col R. A. Waterer LRAM.

Instruments and Instrumentation

From December 1921 saxophones were introduced into British military bands, and over the next six years were brought into RM bands. But the major change did not come about until the 1950s and 1960s, when symphonic style arrangements were introduced, although the small ships' bands of those years did not have the range of instruments required. Nevertheless, enterprising bandmasters got around this by judicious arrangements for the instruments, a cornetist, for example, playing second alto parts or an E flat saxhorn.

American influences and compositions in the 1970s called for some strengthening of the upper woodwinds and the saxophone sections for concert bands. But no doubt following Sir Malcolm Sargent's advice on his appointment in 1949 as honorary adviser in music, the bands played more serious pieces in this decade, the days of 'oompah' music and light overtures had passed. By this time the RM military bands were playing more transcriptions from orchestral works, from the theatre, film themes and from other popular music.

Recordings and Broadcasts

Ten RM musicians from Chatham made the first record of RM music in 1893. The first broadcast by an RM Band was made in Canada in 1925 by the band of HMS *Calcutta*. Reference has been made to the Divisional Bands' broadcasts of the 1930s. Several RM bands have taken part in making films. And the Deal Staff Band auditioned successfully for BBC broadcasts in 1950, from that year RM bands broadcast regularly up to 1960. After 1960 there has been less military music played for BBC radio programmes but all the Staff Bands have broadcast occasionally since then.

Before World War II the Plymouth Divisional Band made some recordings for HMV, and in 1953 the Portsmouth Group Band made its first long playing record. Five years later the School of Music made a contract with HMV (EMI in 1980) for regular recordings each year. Commando Forces (Plymouth) Band had a similar arrangement with Decca from 1972. Other RM Band recordings have included those by C-in-C Fleet Band (Chatham) for RCA in 1975.

BUGLER BRANCH

This Branch of the Corps was an independent unit until 1979 when it became part of the Band Service. In 1980 it was about 100 strong, it trained drummer/buglers at Deal, and a trained bugler had similar promotion prospects to those of musicians up to the rank of WO. Warrant Officer and senior NCO buglers were eligible for appointment as Drum Majors and Bugle Majors.

NOTES ON SOURCES

The three-figure numbers after correspondents' names refer to letters to the author which at one time were in the RM Museum under Archive 11/2/17. These are held in 1997 by the RM Historical Society. The 'Arch' numbers are Archive references to the Museum's files of 1980; where no single source has been used from such a file, its reference number alone is given. PP references corresponding to Archives are private papers lent to the author in the course of his research.

xi Author's Note
1 Sir Bruce Lockhart, *The Marines Were There*, London 1950, p 4 – hereafter Lockhart
2 Sir H. E. Blumberg, *Britain's Sea Soldiers*, Devonport 1927 – hereafter Blumberg

Pages 1–5
1 Blumberg, p. 468
2 Major General J. L. Moulton, *The Royal Marines*, London 1972, p. 66 – hereafter Moulton *RMs*
3 *Instructions for RM Divisions quoted by General Bourne*, Arch 2/14/1
4 Kipling, 'Soldier an' Sailor Too' from *Rudyard Kipling's Verse*, London 1958, p. 433 – hereafter Kipling
5 General Lamplough's letter (675)
6 A. J. Marder, *From the Dardanelles to Oran*, London 1974 – hereafter Marder
7 S. Roskill, *Naval Policy Between the Wars*, London 1968, Vol. I, p. 331 – hereafter Roskill *Policy*
8 G. Haines, *Gunboats on the Great River*, London 1964, Macdonald, pp. 72–3 – hereafter Haines
9 ibid, p. 73
10 Mr Flambard's letter (706)
11 Mr Hoskin's letter (835)
12 Haines, p. 88
13 Arch 7/18/2 (2) narrative
14 Haines, p. 142

Pages 5–6
1 Mr Hopkins' letter (835)
2 *The Nautical Gazette* of HMS *Revenge*, privately published 1921, pp. 3–22, Arch 2/22/1 – hereafter *Nautical Gazette*
3 ibid, p. 6
4 ibid, p. 28

5 F. C. Bowen, *The King's Navy*, London 1925, p. 192
6 Mr Eggo's letter (793)
7 Arch 11/2/7, item 5232 and Arch 2/22/1
8 J. D. Ladd, *Assault from the Sea 1939/45*, London 1976, p. 65 – hereafter *A from S*
9 Maj Kelly's letter (905)
10 General Leathes' notes, Arch 11/2/7, item 5202
11 Lord Mountbatten's comments, Arch 11/2/7, item 5173 – hereafter Lord Mountbatten's comments

Pages 7–11
1 Detachment Orders HMS *Sussex*, Arch 2/2/20 – hereafter DO, HMS *Sussex*
2 Mr Eggo's letter (793)
3 Mr Bayle's notes, arch 11/2/7, item 5201 – hereafter Bayle
4 *G and L*, XXXVI, p. 251
5 Conversation with Maj A. G. Brown
6 Bayle
7 DO HMS *Sussex*
8 ibid
9 Bayle
10 ibid
11 Maj Kelly's letter (905)
12 *G and L*, XXXVII, p. 251
13 ibid
14 Bayle
15 *G and L*, XXXVII, p. 264
16 General Leathes' notes, Arch 11/2/7, item 5202

Page 12–13
1 Maj Kelly's letter (905)
2 Col Shepherd's letter (788)
3 CAFO 1552/22
4 Charles Owen, *No More Heroes*, London 1975, p. 120 – hereafter Owen
5 ibid
6 Mr Eggo's letter (793)
7 Order in Council, 10 June 1921
8 Arch 7/18/5
9 Mr Hopkins' letter (835)
10 Arch 7/18/5
11 Owen

Pages 13–14

1 N. H. Gibbs, *Grand Strategy*, London 1950, Vol. I, p. 61 – hereafter Gibbs
2 Owen, p. 142
3 Subsequent detachment strength on ships built
4 Calculated on detachment numbers with drafting margin
5 Godfrey correspondence, Arch 15/13/1
6 ibid
7 S. W. Roskill, *The War at Sea*, London 1954, Vol. I, p. 14 – hereafter Roskill *W at S*
8 Marder, p. 37
9 Godfrey correspondence, Arch 15/13/1
10 Arch 15/13/1
11 Arch 9/2/G1
12 General Leathes' notes, Arch 11/2/7, item 5202
13 Gibbs, p. 193
14 Maj Wall's notes, Arch 11/2/7, item 5176
15 Mr Round's letter (812)
16 Marder, p. 37
17 RM General Standing Orders 1922 – hereafter GSO 1922
18 Admiralty 'Pink' Lists
19 Gibbs, p. 27
20 Mr Eggo's letter (793)
21 Mr Fisher's letter (723)
22 See Unit History Summaries (Appendix 4) for detachments

Pages 14–15

1 Arch 7/19/1
2 J. Rohwer *et al*, *Chronology of the War at Sea 1939–45*, translation, London 1972 Vol. I, pp. 2–3 – hereafter Rohwer
3 Winston Churchill speaking of Jutland
4 Mr Drury's letter (809)
5 Rohwer, pp 2–3
6 Notes on the RMs in the FAA by Maj Alan Marsh – hereafter Marsh notes
7 Arch 11/2/7, item 5001
8 Roskill *W at S*, Vol. I, p. 106
9 Marder, pp. 46–7

Pages 16–17

1 CAFO 36/40
2 Correspondence of C/Sgt Wright, Arch 2/12/2 – hereafter Wright
3 Mr Hopkin's letter (835)
4 Wright
5 Rohwer, Vol. I, p. 44
6 Album and notes Arch 13/1/80
7 ibid
8 Arch 2/12/2
9 ibid

Pages 17–20

1 Roskill *W at S*, Vol. I, p. 74
2 ibid, p. 116–8
3 *The Battle of the River Plate*, HMSO 1940 – hereafter *BRP*
4 Arch 7/19/20
5 Padfield, p. 299
6 *G and L*, XLVIII, p. 79, 1940
7 *BRP*
8 Mr Kelly''s letter (905)
9 Padfield, pp. 299–300
10 Mr Austin's letter (875)
11 ibid
12 Arch 7/19/20
13 Padfield, pp. 299–300
14 ibid
15 *BRP*
16 *G and L*, XLVIII, p. 79
17 *BRP*
18 *G and L*, XLVIII
19 Padfield, pp. 299–300
20 Rohwer, p. 14
21 Roskill *W at S*, Vol. I
22 Padfield, pp. 299–300
23 *BRP*

Pages 21–27

1 Blumberg, pp. 198–205
2 ibid
3 Sir C. Maynard, *the Murmansk Adventure*, London *c*1928, p. 162 – hereafter Maynard
4 Blumberg, pp. 198–205
5 ibid
6 ibid
7 ibid
8 Maynard, p. 194
9 ibid, p. 277
10 Blumberg, pp. 198–205
11 *G and L*, XXVI, p. 86
12 Blumberg, pp. 198–205
13 Maynard, p. 228
14 Blumberg, pp. 198–205
15 ibid
16 Roskill *Policy*, Vol. I, p. 155
17 ibid
18 A. J. P. Taylor, in the *Listener*, August 1978
19 Maynard, p. 295
20 Roskill *Policy*, Vol. I, p. 142
21 ibid
22 Mr Eggo's letter (793)
23 Blumberg, pp. 207–11
24 ibid
25 Maynard, p. 304
26 ibid, p. 230
27 Blumberg, pp. 207–11
28 Pro-Bolshevik forces driven from Finland in 1917–18 by 'White' Finns who were pro-

German. The 'Red' Finns appear to have acquired German advisers by 1919
29 Blumberg, pp. 207–11
30 ibid, p. 432 – men of 3rd RM Bn

Pages 28–30
1 Arch 6/4/1 (1)
2 ibid (2)
3 Arch 15/3/1 (18), an archive of working papers
4 N. 1707/23, quoted in Arch 15/3/1 (17)
5 Arch 15/3/1 (18)
6 Arch 15/3/1 (8)
7 ibid (various)
8 ibid (7)
9 ibid (11)
10 ibid (13)
11 Arch 15/3/1 (18)
12 Roskill Policy, Vol. 1, p. 46
13 Arch 15/3/1, notes from this report
14 ibid
15 Lockhart, p24
16 Roskill Policy, Vol. I, p. 113
17 Arch 2/12/2
18 Arch 2/12/2 (2)
19 ibid
20 ibid
21 Arch phot 13/11/40(A)
22 ibid, phot 145
23 Arch 2/11/4
24 ibid
25 Moulton RMs, p. 68
26 Marder, p. 72

Pages 30–31
1 Arch 7/19/19
2 ibid
3 Arch 7/19/19 (2 and others), Arch 2/12/2 and Rohwer, pp 21–7
4 Major General J. L. Moulton, The Norwegian Campaign of 1940, London 1966, p. 64 – hereafter Moulton Norway

Pages 33–36
1 Arch 7/19/19
2 Moulton Norway, p. 78
3 Padield, p 297
4 Arch 7/19/19. Note that all times in this Section are British Summer Time (BST), being Greenwich Time Zone less one hour
5 Arch 7/19/19
6 Mr Kelly's letter (905)
7 ibid
8 Rohwer, p. 24
9 Arch 7/19/19
10 ibid
11 Moulton Norway, p. 63
12 ibid, p. 214

13 Arch 7/19/19
14 ibid
15 Hardy had five
16 Arch 5/2/6
17 Arch 7/19/19
18 Moulton Norway, p. 109
19 ibid, p. 301
20 ibid, p. 304
21 Arch 7/19/19
22 ibid
23 Moulton Norway, p 159
24 Arch 7/19/19
25 Moulton Norway, p. 159

Pages 36–41
1 Arch 7/19/19
2 Moulton Norway, p. 63
3 Arch 7/19/19
4 ibid
5 Operation report Arch 7/19/19 (10)
6 ibid
7 Conversation with Mr J. Stuckey
8 Operation report Arch 7/19/19 (10)
9 Moulton Norway, pp. 162–3
10 ibid
11 Arch 7/19/19
12 ibid, 1961 letter from General Bourne
13 Black Swan, Flamingo, Auckland and Bitterne
14 Arch 7/19/19
15 ibid
16 ibid, quoted from Capt Poland RN's report
17 Rohwer, p. 26
18 Action report of OCRM suggests this may have been 500kg, Arch 7/19/19 (5)
19 Arch 7/19/19
20 Moulton Norway, pp. 173–9, analyses the operations south of Åndalnes
21 Arch 7/19/19
22 ibid
23 ibid
24 Converstaion with Mr J. Stuckey
25 Arch 7/19/19
26 ibid

Page 42
1 Arch 7/19/19
2 Operation report, ibid (1)
3 Moulton Norway, p. 212

Pages 42–45
1 General Pringle's notes, Arch 11/2/7, item 5169
2 Marder, p. 149
3 Arch 7/19/19
4 Moulton Norway, pp 200–1
5 67-year-old Lord Cork and Orrery
6 Major General Macksey, DSO, MC

7 Admiralty messages 1939/29, Arch 7/19/19 (8)
8 Arch 7/19/19
9 Arch 7/19/19 (8)
10 ibid
11 ibid (general)
12 Action report by Capt Hasler from which the action details have been taken for these paragraphs, ibid (6)
13 ibid
14 ibid
15 Moulton *Norway*, p. 150
16 Col Bassett's papers
17 Moulton *Norway*, p. 149
18 Arch 7/19/19 (6)

Page 45–46
1 Jane's *Fact Files*
2 *Arch 11/2/17, item 5239*
3 *Report from Sheffield*, Arch 7/19/19 (11)
4 Information circular from RMO, Arch 14/5/6 1940
5 Report from *Sheffield*, Arch 7/19/19 (11)
6 Mr H. Evans' letter (768)
7 Moulton *Norway*, p 191

Pages 46–49
1 Arch 7/19/19
2 Maj A. Dron's notes, Arch 11/2/7, item 5240
3 Action report, Arch 7/19/19 (10)
4 Action report, ibid (4)
5 Mr C. Drury's letter (809)
6 This was the only other AA cruiser in Narvik at the time
7 Mr C. Drury's letter (809)
8 narrative, Arch 7/19/19 (4)
9 ibid
10 ibid (various)
11 Moulton *Norway*, p 251
12 Arch 7/19/19
13 ibid
14 Figures mainly from Arch 5/13/1

Pages 50–59
1 Narrative, Arch 7/19/24
2 Action report, ibid (1)
3 Arch 7/19/24 (1)
4 Airey Neave, *The Flames of Calais*, London 1960, p. 39 – hereafter Neave
5 Arch 2/13/1
6 Roskill *W at S*, Vol. I, p. 212
7 ibid
8 Neave, pp 38–9
9 ibid, p. 88
10 ibid, p. 102
11 ibid, p. 38–9
12 Arch 9/2/1

13 Action summary dated June 1940, Arch 7/19/24 (4)
14 Neave, p. 178
15 Arch 7/19/24 (4)
16 ibid
17 Neave, pp 128–32
18 ibid
19 Arch 7/19/24 (4)
20 Neave, pp 140–7
21 Arch 7/19/24 (4)
22 Neave, pp 140–7
23 ibid, p. 30
24 ibid, p. 140–7
25 Arch 7/19/24 (4)
26 Neave, pp. 140–7
27 ibid, p. 158
28 Arch 7/19/24 (4)
29 Neave, pp 176–8
30 ibid, p. 167
31 ibid, p. 162
32 ibid, p. 176–8
33 ibid, p. 174
34 Arch 7/19/24 (4)
35 Neave, p. 162
36 ibid, p. 176–8
37 Letter of June 1940, Arch 7/19/24 (4)
38 Arch 7/19/24 (4)
39 Neave, pp. 193–7
40 Arch 7/19/24 (4)
41 ibid
42 Roskill *W at S*, Vol. I, p. 215
43 Arch 7/19/24 (4)
44 Neave, pp. 193–7
45 ibid, p. 186
46 ibid, p. 202
47 Arch 7/19/24 (4)
48 Neave, pp 193–7
49 ibid, p. 206
50 Mr A. Bannerman's letter (901)
51 Mr A. R. Harding's letter (837)
52 Neave, p. 207
53 *The Royal Marines: The Admiralty Account of Their Achievements 1939–43*, HMSO London 1944, p. 33 – hereafter *RMS 1939–43*
54 ibid
55 Neave, p. 19
56 ibid, p. 213
57 ibid, p. 162
58 Roskill *W at S*, Vol I, pp. 216–18
59 ibid
60 ibid, p. 227
61 David Devine, *The Nine Days of Dunkirk*, p. 130
62 Lockhart, p. 41
63 Roskill *W at S*, Vol. I, p. 224

Pages 59–64

1 Arch 2/13/1
2 Arch index card
3 Arch 2/13/1
4 Mr Porteous's letter (647)
5 Arch 2/12/35 (2)
6 Roskill *W at S*, Vol. I, p. 25
7 These figures are based on an average of 40 men in a Squad and the records of Squads passed for duty in arch 2/12/25 (2)
8 ibid
9 Based on estimate for number of Squads passed for duty from Exton
10 Calculated from P & P letter, June 1945, and Squad records
11 Calculated from arch index cards for C/S Squads
12 Calculated from sources used for Appendix 5
13 No comprehensive returns for recruit training have been traced, but the numbers given below are estimated from various sources.
14 Mr D. Thompson's letter (772)
15 Archh 2/13/1 (13)
16 ibid, quoting COS (40) 179th meeting, 14 June 1940
17 Arch 2/13/1 (13)
18 ibid
19 Eric Halder, 'Fuhrer Conferences on Naval Affairs', *Brassey Naval Annual*, 1948
20 AG's letter, Arch 2/12/2
21 Arch 2/13/1
22 Mr G. Collard's letter (892)
23 Mr C. Drury's letter (809)
24 A. Marder, *Operation 'Menace'*, London 1976, p. 6 – hereafter Marder *Menace*
25 ibid, p. 27
26 ibid, p. 48
27 ibid, p. 55
28 ibid, p. 63
29 Bde's War Diary, ADM 202 34
30 Marder *Menace*, pp. 108–9
31 Winston Churchill, *The Second World War*, London 1948, Vol. 2, p. 435
32 Marder *Menace*, p. 160
33 ibid, p. 172
34 Capt George Belbin, 2nd RM Bn, in conversation with the author
35 Manuscript notes of 2 March 1942 meeting, initialled by Col Grover, Arch 2/13/1 (13)
36 ibid, annotation by General Bourne on above

Pages 64–66

1 1940 despatches, Arch 2/15/5 (16)
2 Ian Hogg, *The Guns of World War II*, London 1976, p. 76 – hereafter Hogg *WW II*
3 General Fellowes' notes (622)

4 Hogg *WW II*
5 Experimental 150-mm weapon system aimed at London, in which a series of charges fired in succession along a barrel accelerated the shell. The 50-barrelled installation 2 miles from Cap Gris Nez, however, was captured before it fired, Arch 2/15/5 (20)
6 Arch 2/13/5 (16)
7 Arch 2/12/5 (1)
8 ibid, (20)
9 ibid, (16), Coast Artillery Command Unit
10 ibid, (15)
11 ibid
12 ibid
13 Arch 2/12/5 (16)
14 Arch 2/12/5 (20)

Pages 66–71

1 Bty Officer's personal diary, Arch 11/2/17 item 5193
2 'D' Bty's informal War Diary in RM Arch and RM Circ 5244/40A dated 24 June 1940
3 Hogg *A-A*, p. 78
4 ibid, p. 90
5 ibid, p. 166
6 ibid, p. 105
7 Maj Kinnear's notes (5162)
8 ibid
9 Arch 11/2/17, item 5193
10 ibid
11 Hogg *A-A*, p. 78
12 Arch11/2/17, item 5193
13 ibid
14 ibid
15 Arch 11/2/17, item 5164
16 Had been a temporary officer in WW I, became a regular officer at Fort Cumberland and for a time was attached to the Royal Artillery as a senior instructor in AA gunnery, *G and L*, 1967, p. 144
17 AFO 52/40
18 AFO 935/40
19 War Diary, ADM 202 and 149
20 Rohwer, p. 28
21 Mr Colenso's letter (801)
22 Handbook of Oerlikon
23 Hogg *A-A*, pp. 80 and 166
24 Mr Colenso's letter (801)
25 Arch 17/15/2
26 Arch 11/2/17, item 5193

Pages 71–72

1 Coast Artillery Handbook, Vol. I, 1938
2 Arch 2/12/3 RBW 23 – the instruction 'RBW' were a series of notes for guidance and *not* orders
3 Maj E. Beven in conversation with the author
4 Arch 2/12/3, RBW 23

5   Arch 2/12/3, MNB 158/2/4 (G)
6   Maj E. Beven in conversation with the author

Pages 72–74

1   Arch 2/12/3, RBW 1
2   ibid, RBW 16
3   ibid, RBW 1
4   ibid, AA Appreciation
5   ibid, RBW 16
6   ibid, RBW 7
7   ibid, RBW 10 and 11
8   ibid, RBW 16
9   ibid, AA Appreciation
10 ibid, RBW 24

Pages 74–76

1   Arch 11/2/17, item 5172
2   J.H.Spencer, *Battle for Crete*, London 1962, p. 8 – hereafter Spencer
3   ibid, p. 9
4   Gun mounting report, arch 7/19/7 (5)
5   Spencer, p. 13
6   ibid, p. 25
7   ibid, p. 31
8   ibid, p. 72
9   Rohwer, p. 94

Pages 7–79

1   Rohwer, p.63
2   *RMs 1939–43*, p. 13
3   Roskill *W at S*, Vol. I, p. 423
4   Rohwer, p. 81
5   C. E. Lucas Phillips, *Alamein*, London 1962, p. 53
6   Roskill *W at S*, Vol. II, p.89, *Fiume*, *Zara* and *Pola*
7   ibid, p. 89
8   ibid, Vol. I, p. 397
9   ibid, p. 398
10 Arch 2/22/16
11 Padfield, p. 306
12 Admiral Lutjens
13 Roskill *W at S*, map opp. p. 93
14 Rohwer, p. 104
15 Mr Colenso's letter (801)
16 Arch 2/12/3
17 Mr Colenso's letter (801)
18 MNBDO I War Diary, ADM 202, 131–2; the instructions 'RBW' described as a series of notes for guidance and not orders
19 Reports and narratives, Arch 7/19/7 (III)

Pages 79–89

1   Spencer, p. 165, Maj Willis Farrier
2   Narrative of 'S' Bty Sgt Maj G. Hughes, Arch 7/19/ (2)
3   P. Chamberlain *et al*, *WW II Fact File* –
Machine Guns, London 1972, p. 15 – hereafter Chamberlain *Machine Guns*
4   Approximate Order of Battle, Arch 7/19/7 (13)
5   Spencer, p. 168
6   Arch 7/19/7 (2)
7   ibid
8   Spencer, p. 133
9   ibid, p. 128
10 General Weston's report, Arch 7/19/7 (18g)
11 Spencer, p. 130
12 ibid, p. 130
13 ibid, p. 181
14 ibid, p. 98
15 ibid, p. 99
16 ibid, p. 153
17 ibid, p. 153
18 ibid, p. 111
19 Arch 7/19/7, (18g)
20 Arch 7/19/7, on the basis of figures that only differs by some 40 men
21 Arch 7/19/7 (15)
22 Arch 7/19/7 (3)
23 Spencer, p. 102
24 Arch 7/19/7 (2)
25 ibid
26 Arch 7/19/7 (18g)
27 Arch 7/19/7 (2)
28 Spencer, p. 262
29 ibid, p. 276
30 Arch 7/19/7 (2)
31 J. M. Worrall's article, Arch 7/19/7 (18d)
32 Arch 7/19/7 (18g)
33 Spencer, p. 173
34 ibid, p. 237
35 Arch 7/19/7 (18g)
36 Arch 7/19/7 (13)0
37 Spencer, p. 240
38 Arch 7/19/7 (18g)
39 ibid
40 *Naval Operations of the Battle of Crete*, BR 1736(2) No. 4 (1942) – hereeafter *Naval Operations – Crete*
41 Spencer, p. 281
42 Arch 7/19/7 (18g)
43 Spencer, p. 250
44 ibid, p. 252
45 Arch 7/19/7 (22)
46 *Naval Operations – Crete*
47 Operation notes, Arch 7/19/7 (22)
48 *Naval Operations – Crete*
49 Spencer, p. 274; other sources give 317 as recored tally
50 Maj Maddoc's narrative, Arch 2/12/3
51 ibid
52 ibid
53 Spencer, p. 273
54 ibid, p. 277

55 ibid, p. 173
56 ibid, p. 277
57 ibid, p. 88
58 Capt L. R. P. Wilson's letter (766)
59 Mr J. Grandfield's letter (888)
60 Arch 7/19/7 (18g)
61 ibid
62 Arch 2/12/3
63 J. D. Ladd, *Commandos and Rangers of World War II*, London 1978, p 118 – hereafter Ladd *Commandos*
64 Arch 2/12/3
65 Arch 7/19/7 (18d)
66 *Naval Operations – Crete*
67 Arch 7/19/7 (18g)
68 ibid
69 ibid
70 Rohwer, p. 103

Pages 89–91

1 Capt L. P. R. Wilson's letter (766)
2 Arch 7/19/7
3 ibid (14), Maj Garrett's action report on which these paragraphs are based
4 *RMs 1939–43*, p. 38
5 Mr J. M. Worrall's article, Arch 7/19/7 (18d)
6 Lts Macpherson and Hope
7 Arch 7/19/7 (10)
8 D. M. Davin, *Crete*, the New Zealand Army's official history
9 Arch 7/19/7 (III)

Pages 92–100

1 Ladd *Commandos*, p. 118
2 Roskill *W at S*, Vol. I, pp. 423–5
3 Rohwer, Vol I, pp. 106–7
4 Roskill *W at S*, Vol. I, p. 553
5 narrative, Arch 17/11/9 (1)
6 ibid (3)
7 Ladd *Commando*, p. 118
8 Rohwer, Vol I, p. 156
9 Haines, p. 158
10 Naval action report, Arch 7/19/23
11 Roskill *W at S*, Vol I, pp. 564–7
12 Sir Geoffrey A. Houlton Bt, correspondence 1941–2
13 Roskill *W at S*, Vol I, pp. 564–7
14 Arch 7/19/22
15 S. Woodburn Kirby, *War with Japan*, London 1957–65, Vol. p. 233 – hereafter Kirby
16 Report of Capt Lang, Arch 7/19/22 (1)
17 Kirby, Vol. I, p. 233
18 ibid, p. 245
19 ibid, p. 272
20 Arch 7/19/22 (1)
21 Kirby, Vol. I, p. 281
22 Arch 7/19/22 (1)

23 ibid, (2)
24 Kirby, Vol. I, p. 245
25 Arch 7/19/22 (1)
26 ibid
27 medical report, ibid (4)
28 7/19/22
29 Arch 11/2/17, item 5000, notes by Maj Warren
30 Blumberg, p. 433
31 Roskill *W at S*, Vol II, p. 8
32 Kirby, Vol. I, p. 403
33 ibid, p. 51
34 Roskill *W at S*, Vol. II, p. 13
35 Mr V. S. King's letter (802)
36 Rohwer, Vol. I, p 195
37 V. S. King's letter (802)
38 ibid
39 ibid

Pages 100–105

1 A. Cecil Hampshire, *On Hazardous Service*, London 1974, p. 95 – hereafter Hampshire *Service*
2 Maj Johnson's action report, Arch 7/19/2 (1)
3 ibid
4 ibid
5 ibid
6 Hampshire *Service*
7 Arch 7/19/2
8 Hampshire *Service*, p. 95
9 Arch 7/19/2 (1)
10 ibid
11 ibid
12 ibid
13 ibid
14 Hampshire *Service*, p. 114
15 Arch 7/19/2 (1)
16 Narrative by member of No. 3 Platoon on which this paragraph is based, Arch 7/19/12 (3c)
17 ibid
18 Arch 7/19/2 (1)
19 ibid

Page 105–107

1 Narrative history, Arch 2/14/5
2 40 Cdo War Diary, ADM 202 87
3 Ladd *Commandos*, p. 167
4 11th RM Bn War Diary, ADM 202 180
5 Action report, Arch 7/19/7
6 Ladd *Commandos*, pp. 57–67
7 Arch 7/19/7
8 ibid
9 Arch 2/13/11

Pages 107–109

1 Roskill *W at S*, Vol. II, pp. 186–7
2 Narrative, Arch 7/19/6 (1)

3 COS meeting, May 1942
4 General Sir Campbell Hardy's notes (621)
5 Arch 7/19/6 (1)
6 narrative, ibid (5)
7 Notes from Maj A. J. Powell, Arch 11/2/17, item 5109
8 Lt-Cdr J. M. Hodges
9 notes, arch 7/19/6 (3)
10 Arch 7/19/6 (1)
11 General Sturges' notes, ibid (4)
12 Roskill *W at S*, Vol. II, p. 187
13 Arch 7/19/6 (4)
14 Roskill *W at S*, Vol. II, p. 187
15 Arch 7/19/6 (5)

Pages 109–113
1 Notes by General Sturges, arch 7/19/6 (6)
2 BR1887, *The Dieppe Raid*, Combined Ops HQ report, 1942 – hereafter BR1887
3 Various notes, Arch 7/19/12 (22)
4 Terence Robertson, *Dieppe, the Glory and the Shame*, London 1963, p. 79 – hereafter Robertson
5 BR1887, p. 72
6 Mr G. H. Atkinson's letter (843)
7 Lord Mountbatten's comments
8 BR1736, Battle Summary No. 33, Naval Staff 1946
9 Action reports, Arch 7/19/12 (19)
10 BR1887
11 ibid, p. 173
12 Arch 7/19/12 (19)
13 Mnes R. B. Singleton, L. C. Bradshaw, Breen and others, arch 7/19/22 (19)
14 ibid, comment by unknown RM officer
15 Sir Campbell Hardy's notes (621)
16 Mr I. Jackson's letter (786)
17 *RMs 1939–43*, p. 73
18 BR1739, p. 23
19 Unsigned narrative, arch 7/19/12 (4)
20 ibid (4)
21 Mr G. H. Atkinson's letter (843)
22 Ladd *Commandos*, p. 92
23 BR1887, p. 211
24 Ladd *Commandos*, p. 92

Pages 113–115
1 Ladd *Commandos*, p. 122
2 L. S. O. Playfair *et al.*, *History of the Second World War: The Mediterranean and Middle East*, Vol. IV, London 1966, pp. 20–3 – hereafter Playfair
3 Roskill *W at S*, Vol II, pp. 310–11
4 Arch 2/13/11
5 G. Landsborough, *Tobruk Commando*, London 1956, gives a detailed account of these operations – hereafter Landsborough
6 Narrative by Maj Hedley, Arch 2/13/11

7 ibid
8 Playfair, Vol IV, p 22
9 Reports by former prisoners of war, Arch 7/19/4 (2)
10 Landsborough
11 Playfair, Vol IV, p. 22
12 Roskill *W at S*, Vol. II, pp. 310–11
13 Arch 2/13/11

Pages 115–120
1 Col Sam Bassett, *Royal Marine*, London 1962, p. 156 – hereafter Bassett
2 Mr W. J. Goodwin's letter (777)
3 Unsigned letter (912)
4 Arch index card *Fidelity*
5 Ladd *Commandos*, p. 242
6 General Horton's notes (634)
7 Outline plan for 'Frankton' and reports, Arch 7/19/13 (1)
8 ibid
9 ibid
10 ibid
11 C. E. Lucas Phillips, *The Cockleshell Heroes*, London 1956 – hereafter Phillips *Cockleshell*
12 Roskill *W at S*, Vol. II, p. 275
13 Phillips *Cockleshell*, p. 236
14 ibid, p. 231
15 ibid, p. 230
16 Ladd *Commandos*, p. 55

Pages 121–125
1 Marder, p. 34
2 Correspondence AG/First Lord of the Admiralty, 1922–8, Arch 15/3/2
3 ibid AG's letter, 23 April 1923
4 Arch 15/3/2
5 *Hampshire Telegraph*, 3 August 1923
6 Corps tradition
7 AFO 1643/23
8 Mr Eggo's letter (793)
9 AFO 1643/23
10 Mr Hewitt's letter and Maj A. E. Marsh
11 Estimate as 94 Squad (1924) and 399th (August 1940)
12 Various conversations with the author
13 Arch 9/2/18
14 ibid
15 Various reports, Arch 6/9/2
16 Committee report, Arch 15/3/1 (31)
17 Navy List, 1932
18 RM Hist. Soc. *Letter IV*, pp. 59–61
19 Arch 15/3/2

Page 126
1 W. E. Davey, *Watch and Ward*, privately published

Pages 126–129

1 RM P&P Letter, August 1945, p. 8
2 *RMs 1939–43*, p. 8
3 Arch 11/2/17, item 5009
4 Mr Eggo's letter (793)
5 Correspondence with AG, Arch 15/3/1
6 ibid
7 Estimated on basis of men drafted to ships
8 Mr W. Jackett's letter (727)
9 AFO 46/40
10 AFO 2487/42
11 RM P&P letter, August 1945, p. 8
12 Owen, p. 178, quoting Corelli Barnett
13 *RMs 1939–41*, p. 4
14 Mrs Amy Blake's letter (792)
15 Bourne correspondence
16 Figures mainly from Arch 5/13/1
17 John Trendell, *Operation Music Maker*, privately published, Southampton 1978, p. 45 – hereafter Trendell
18 ibid, p. 68 and estimated on basis of 550 at Malvern in 1945
19 ibid
20 Corps folklore
21 AFO 1082/40

Pages 129–133

1 Letter January 1942 re COS (40) 32nd meeting, Arch 14/2/10
2 *RMs 1939–43*, p. 72
3 P&P letter, October 1945
4 Rohwer, p. 127
5 Roskill *W at S*, Vol. II, p. 119
6 ibid p. 126 – U655 sunk by *Sharpshooter*
7 ibid, p. 126
8 narrative by Cadet Feltham, Arch 7/19/20
9 Mr G. W. Nobel's letter (773)
10 Arch 7/19/20
11 Roskill *W at S*, Vol. II, p. 126
12 ibid
13 ibid, p. 58
14 Handbook of Malta Museum, arch 7/19/21
15 Mr R. Hewitt's letter (881)
16 Rohwer, p. 242
17 Roskill *W at S*, Vol. II, p. 307
18 ibid, p. 126
19 Mr K.C. Saunder's letter (878)

Pages 134–137

1 COS (42) meeting 6, quoted in Arch 2/13/1 (13)
2 Arch 2/13/1
3 ibid (10), notes by Major General Neville
4 Lord Mountbatten's comments
5 COS Committee 148th (42), quoted in DEFE 2/3
6 Lord Mountbatten's comments
7 DEFE 2 984, letter T/900/4

8 ibid, CCO's letter 12 November
9 COS 314th (42) meeting
10 General Sturges' notes, Arch 2/13/1
11 COS 358th (42) meeting
12 Combined Ops HQ War Diary, DEFE 2
13 Divisional War Diary, ADM 202 9
14 Arch index card
15 COS 120th (43) meeting
16 COS 144th (43) meeting
17 DEFE 2 1041, AG's letter to CCO, 1 July 1943
18 Lockhart, p. 101
19 Mr F. S. Ross's letter (846)
20 Donald Gilchrist, *Castle Commando*, London 1960
21 Navy Lists

Pages 139–143

1 Mr C. W. Westwood's letter (914)
2 Mr W. H. Smith's letter (919)
3 RM Hist. Soc. *Newsletter*, Vol. III, No. 3
4 Ladd *A from S*, p. 175
5 Adm L. E. H. Maund, *Assault from the Sea*, London 1949, pp. 217–18 – hereafter Maund
6 ibid
7 Col Dewhurst's narrative, Arch 2/13/7 (1)
8 Maund, p. 219
9 DEFE 2 282 Planning for 'Husky'
10 Mr H. J. Gray's letter (707)
11 Maund, p. 219
12 ibid, p. 217–18
13 ibid, p. 219
14 Narrative, Arch 7/19/6 (2)
15 Movement reports, Arch 2/12/4 (1)
16 Notes on RMs in the FAA prepared by Maj Alan E. Marsh – hereafter Marsh notes

Pages 143–146

1 Ladd *Commandos*, p. 129
2 RM Hist. Soc. *Newsletters*, Vol III etc., articles by Mr H. Playford – hereafter Playford
3 ibid
4 Roskill *W at S*, Vol. III, Pt I, p. 115
5 ibid, p. 117
6 Ladd *Commandos*, p. 130
7 Notes from Co-Ops HQ, Arch 7/19/16 (7)
8 ibid, narrative reports
9 DEFE 2 1051, role of SS Bde
10 Arch 7/19/16 (16)
11 ibid
12 ibid
13 ibid
14 ibid
15 40 Cdo War Diary, ADM 202 87

Pages 146–151

1 Narrative by Col Dewhurst, Arch 2/13/7 (1)

2 Narrative, Arch 7/19/16 (1)
3 ibid
4 Arch 2/13/7 (1)
5 7th RM Bn War Diary, ADM 202 62
6 ibid
7 ibid
8 Arch 2/13/7
9 ibid
10 7th RM Bn War Diary, ADM 202 62
11 Arch 2/13/7
12 ibid
13 Notes made in 1962, Arch 7/19/16 (2)
14 ibid
15 C. J. C Malony, *History of the Second World War: The Mediterranean and Middle East*, London 1973, Vol. V, p. 81 – hereafter Malony
16 Roskill *W at S*, Vol. III, Pt I, p. 137
17 7th RM Bn War Diary, ADM 202 62
18 Ladd *Commandos*, pp. 133–4
19 Movement Report, Arch 2/12/4 (1)
20 Press release, Arch 7/19/16 (5)
21 E. Parsons, *Bible Back*, privately published in New Zealand, pp. 120–4
22 Arch 22/12/4

Pages 151–158
1 Malony, Vol. V, p. 235
2 ibid, p. 81
3 *The History of Commandos in the Mediterranean, September 1943 to May 1945* – probably prepared for COHQ *c*1946, p. 8 – hereafter *Med Cdos*
4 ibid
5 40(RM) War Diary, ADM 202 87
6 Malony, Vol. V, p. 241
7 Ladd *Commandos*, p. 139
8 *Med Cdos*, p. 37
9 ibid
10 Arch 7/19/17 (2c) Capt Crombie and Capt P. Wall
11 Narrative, Arch 7/19/17 (2b)
12 R. Mitchell, *Marine Commando '43*, unpublished narrative (Arch 2/14/6), p. 68 – hereafter Mitchell
13 Arch 7/19/17 (2b)
14 Ladd *Commando*, p. 141
15 Narrative, Arch 7/19/17 (12)
16 ibid
17 Mitchell, pp. 70–4
18 *Med Cdos*, p. 42
19 Mitchell, pp 70–4
20 Arch 7/19/17 (12)
21 ibid
22 Mitchell, p. 79
23 Arch 7/19/17 (1)
24 *Med Cdos*, pp. 55–6
25 ibid

26 Mitchell, pp. 168–70
27 *Med Cdos*, pp. 53–6

Pages 158–160
1 War Diary Co-Ops HQ, DEFE 2 17
2 Amphibious Warfare HQ, *History of Combined Operations*, 1956 p. 70 – hereafter *History Co-Ops*
3 *Blackwood's Magazine*, November 1944, article
4 ibid
5 ibid
6 Roskill *W at S*, Vol. III, PtI, pp. 79–89
7 Kipling

Pages 161–163
1 Maund, Chapter 1
2 Blumberg, p. 357
3 RM/ISTDC correspondence, Arch 6/4/1 (11)
4 COS (40) meeting 468
5 *History Co-Ops*, pp. 13–17
6 Lord Mountbatten's comments
7 ibid
8 *History Co-Ops*, p. 59, details 44,000 naval crews, to which must be added some 5,000 commandos
9 ibid, p. 60
10 Co-Ops Directory, May 1943, Arch 2/15/1
11 *History Co-Ops*, pp. 112–14

Pages 163–168
1 Navy List, June 1944 and June 1945
2 P&P letter, June 1945
3 ibid
4 DEFE 2 984, Miscellaneous RM papers
5 In Rhine Sqn, 1950s for example
6 AFO 2189/43
7 AFO 3795/43
8 AFO 2189/43
9 ibid
10 *G & L*, 1976 pp. 42–3 and *RM Business*, January 1944
11 Mr W. Porteous's notes (648)
12 ibid
13 Mr Heigham's notes (647–8)
14 P&P letters July 1945
15 *G and L*, February 1980
16 Maj A. J. Donald in conversation with the author
17 Mr F. Humphries' letter (842)
18 L. F. Ellis, *Victory in the West*, London 1962, Vol. I, p. 223 – hereafter Ellis
19 Blumberg, p. 53 and estimates for 6 June 1944:
commandos 2,000
ships' detachments 3,315
major support craft 1,550
Armoured Support Grp 600+

minor craft crews 8,000
port parties, signallers *et al.* 1,000
LCOCU, provost, radar plotters and HQ staffs 450
20 *RM Business*, Oct 1944
21 Green lists – Admiralty disposition of vessels – and Maj D. L. Burge's loetter (797)
22 Force J reports, Arch 7/19/5
23 Mr J. H. Lowe's letter (890)
24 *History of Co-Ops*, pp 151–9
25 Notes on COXE reoprts, Arch 11/2/17, items 5135–42
26 *History of Co-Ops*
27 Amphibious Trials and Training Unit RM
28 Lt-Col Sergeant's report and War Diaries of MNBDO I in the Far East, Arch 7/19/7 (III)
29 CAFO 242/44
30 Force 'J' reports, Arch 7/19/5
31 ibid
32 Green lists at 5 June 1944 and notes thereon, Arch 11/2/17, item 5145
33 Maj P. Wall in conversation with the author
34 Mr J. W. Gate's letter (859)
35 *RM Business*, No. 3 October 1944
36 Ellis, p. 233

Pages 168–9
1 Maj Marsh's notes are the basis of these paragraphs
2 AFO 1058/24
3 Marsh notes
4 Blumberg, p. 480
5 Arch 11/2/17, item 5011
6 Adm Cunningham, quoted in Padfield, p. 307
7 Roskill *W at S*, Vol. III, Pt II, p. 30

Pages 169–172
1 RM Hist. Soc. *Newsletter*, Vol. III, p. 22
2 Maj A. J. Donald in conversation with the author
3 R S. Collard's letter (823)
4 *History of Co-Ops*
5 *RM Business*, October 1944
6 Maj Britton-Johnson's letter (702); he commanded the 2nd Rgt at 32. Lt-Col V. Peskett at 30 was CO of the 1st Rgt; and Lt-Col Freeman at 33 commanded the 5th (Indpt) Bty
7 Mr G. Collard's letter (892)
8 *RM Business*, October 1944
9 Arch 14/3/2
10 *RM Business*, March 1945
11 Maj E. T. Gilbert's letter (931)
12 Mr R. Brooks's notes, Arch 11/2/17, item 5140
13 Maj E. T. Gilbert's letter (931)
14 Ladd *Commandos*, pp. 177–8
15 ibid and *RM Business*

16 Ellis, Vol. I, p. 264
17 ibid
18 Unsigned narratives, Arch 7/19/5 (25)
19 *RM Business*, March 1945

Pages 172–186
1 Ellis, Vol. I pp. 162–86
2 ibid
3 Reports from *Glenearn*, Arch 7/19/5
4 Ellis, Vol. I, pp. 162–86
5 *RM Business*, October 1944
6 Ellis, Vol. I, pp 162–86
7 Ladd *Commandos*, pp. 172, 180–1
8 Roskill *W at S*, Vol. III, Pt II p. 47
9 *RM Business*, October 1944
10 Arch 7/19/5 (9); Sgt Briggs awarded DSM
11 *RM Business*, October 1944
12 Ladd *A from S*, p. 173
13 Ellis, Vol. I, pp. 162–86
14 Eyewitness reports, Arch 7/19/5 (10)
15 Lt Badenock (Arch 7/19/5)
16 ibid
17 Mr G. Collard's letter (892)
18 action report, Arch 2/16/3
19 ibid
20 Correspondence of 1968, Arch 14/18/6
21 Ellis, Vol. I, pp. 162–86
22 Maj Donald in coinversation with the author
23 Ellis, Vol. I, pp. 162–86
24 *RM Business*, October 1944
25 Eyewitness reports, Arch 7/19/5 (12)
26 ibid
27 Mr Smith's letter (919)
28 Mr H. R. Neville's letter (877)
29 Mr W. H. Smith's letter (919)
30 Brig Morford lecture, Arch 7/19/5 (24b)
31 Roskill *W at S*, Vol. III, Pt II, p. 62
32 Lord Lovat, *March Past*, London, 1978, pp. 393–319 – hereafter Lovat
33 *RM Business*, October 1944
34 Lovat, pp. 293–319
35 ibid
36 ibid
37 Ellis, Vol. I, p. 202
38 ibid
39 Lovat, pp. 293–319
40 MO's letter of 1944, Arch 11/2/17, item 5015
41 J. L. Moulton, *Haste to the Battle*, London 1963, p. 186 – hereafter Moulton *Battle*
42 Ellis, Vol. I, pp. 152–6
43 Mr F. Wildman's letter (933)
44 ibid
45 *RM Business*, October 1944
46 Narrative history of 47 RM Cdo, Arch 2/14/12
47 ibid
48 Mr R. Hewitt's letter (881)
49 Mr F. Humphries' letter (842)

50 Mr A. Burns's letter (821)
51 Mr B. Murray's letter (862)
52 Mr F. Humphries' letter (842)
53 Mr B. Murray's letter (862)
54 Force J Operation Orders
55 Arch 7/19/5 (25)
56 *RM Business*, October 1944
57 Arch 2/14/12
58 Arch 7/19/5
59 Arch 7/19/5 (3), re Cpl G. E. Tandy
60 Ellis, Vol. I, pp. 211–12
61 Arch 7/19/5 (24b)
62 Roskill *W at S*, Vol. III, Pt II, p.53

Pages 186–201
1 *RM Business*, October 1944
2 Narrative history of 47 RM Cdo on which theese paragraphs are based, Arch 2/14/12
3 *RM Business*, October 1944
4 Arch 2/14/12
5 Mr F. Wildman's letter (933)
6 Action reports on which much of the deatil of these paragraphs is based, Arch 7/19/5 (2)
7 ibid
8 ibid
9 Arch 2/14/12
10 Arch 7/19/5 (2)
11 *RM Business*, October 1944
12 Narrative history of 46 RM Cdo, Arch 2/14/11
13 Reports on signal parties, Arch 7/19/5 (25)
14 *RM Business*, March 1945
15 Force J orders, Arch 7/19/5
16 Maj J. P. Kelly's letter (905)
17 ibid
18 Arch 7/19/5 (2)
19 ibid
20 Narrative history of 46 RM Cdo on which these paragraphs are based, Arch 2/14/11
21 Maj John Lee
22 Arch 2/14/11
23 Arch 7/19/5 (2)
24 Hilary St George Saunders, *The Green Beret*, London 1949, p. 269–72 – hereafter *Green Beret*
25 Roskill *W at S*, Vol. III, Pt II, p. 47
26 50 per cent is an estimate from casualty reports
27 Lovat, p. 299
28 *RM Business*, June 1944
29 Arch 7/19/5 (2) and *RM Business*, various
30 ibid
31 ibid
32 ibid
33 Arch 2/14/11
34 Mr R. Brooks' notes, Arch 11/2/17 item 5140
35 Roskill *W at S*, Vol. III, Pt II, p. 62
36 ibid

37 Mr H. R. Neville's letter (877)
38 Arch 7/19/5 (2)
39 Maj J. Powell's notes, Arch 11/2/17 item 5109
40 Arch 7/19/5 (2)
41 Arch 7/19/5 (25)
42 ibid
43 ibid
44 *RM Business*, October 1944
45 ibid
46 ibid
47 Kipling
48 J. Ehram, *Grand Strategy*, Vol. V, pp. 460–1
49 Bottomley Report and papers, Arch 2/15/1
50 ibid
51 ibid

Pages 202–204
1 *Med Cdos*, pp. 57–77
2 Ladd *Commandos*, p. 146
3 *Med Cdos*, pp. 57–77
4 ibid
5 ibid
6 Malony, Vol. V, pp. 434–6
7 *Med Cdos*, pp. 94–100
8 ibid
9 ibid, p. 107

Pages 204–211
1 The Office of Strategic Services was the American department organising clandestine warfare, Malony, Vol. V, p. 830
2 *Med Cdos*, pp. 139–40
3 ibid, annexe No. 3
4 Malony, Vol. V, p. 830
5 *Med Cdos*, p. 144
6 ibid, p. 140
7 Narrative history of 3 RM Cdo, Arch 2/14/8 (3)
8 *Med Cdos*, pp. 164–9
9 Arch 2/14/8 (3)
10 *Med Cdos*, pp 172–9
11 ibid
12 ibid, p. 181–94
13 ibid, p. 172–9
14 Operational reports, Arch 2/14/8
15 Lt D. B. Clark's action report, Arch 2/14/8 (5)
16 ibid
17 Arch 2/14/8
18 War Diary 40 RM Cdo, ADM 202 87
19 War Diary of 561 Flot., Arch 11/2/17 item 5103
20 Arch 2/14/8 (3)
21 Sir Alfred Blake in conversation with the author
22 Arch 2/14/8 (3)

23 Col Simonds' comments
24 Sgts Gallon and Pickering were both awarded the MM for this action
25 Arch 2/14/8 (3)
26 Col Jack Churchill quoted in *Green Beret*, p. 252
27 Arch 2/14/8 (3)
28 Sir Alfred Blake in conversation with the author
29 Lt-Col P. Davis's notes, Arch 11/2/17 item 5108
30 Arch 11/2/17, item 5103
31 *RM Business*, August 1945
32 *Med Cdos*, p. 295
33 Sir Alfred Blake's notes (504)

Pages 211–212
1 A. Cecil Hampshire, *The Secret Navies*, London 1978, pp 122–72 – hereafter *Secret Navies*
2 Ladd *Commandos*, p. 272
3 Mr E. Horner's letter (607)
4 *Secret Navies*, pp. 122–72
5 Mr E. Horner's letter (607)
6 ibid

Pages 213–223
1 Roskill *W at S*, Vol. III, Pt II, p. 70
2 Narrative histories of 30th AU, Arch 2/16/4 and 7/19/3
3 Action reports, Arch 7/19/3
4 *RM Business*, March 1945
5 Ellis, Vol. II, p. 5
6 ibid, p. 110–24
7 Dutch narrative, Arch 2/11/17, item 5137
8 Army Research Report No. 299, Arch 7/19/3 (4)
9 *RM Business*, March 1945
10 Brig Leicester's report, Arch 7/19/3
11 ibid
12 ibid
13 ibid (2) notes by Brig Leicester
14 ibid
15 Ladd *Commandos*, pp. 199–204
16 J. T. Waldron *et al*, *The Frogmen*, London 1950, p. 109 – hereafter Waldron
17 Ladd *Commandos*, pp. 199–204
18 Arch 7/19/3 (4)
19 ibid, (12), Cpl J. Rutland's report
20 Ladd *A from S*, p. 188
21 Roskill *W at Sea*, Vol. III, Pt II, pp 148–52
22 arch 7/19/3
23 ibid, (9)
24 ibid, (12)
25 ibid, (12)
26 *RM Business*, March 1945
27 Conversations of 1944
28 Arch 7/19/3 (4)

29 Sub-Lt I. A. P. Rumsey, DSC, RNVR, Waldron, p. 108
30 Ladd *Commandos*, pp. 199–204
31 Arch 7/19/3 (4)
32 ibid, (12)
33 ibid, (4)
34 ibid, (4)
35 ibid, (20) Action report of 80th Assault Sqn RE
36 ibid, (9)
37 ibid, (9)
38 Roskill *W at S*, Vol. III, Pt II, pp. 49–52
39 Arch 7/19/3 (4)
40 *RM Business*, March 1945

Pages 223–225
1 War Diary, ADM 202 271–91
2 *RM Business*, August 1945
3 Hogg *A-A*, pp. 132–4
4 ibid
5 *RM Business*, August 1945
6 'D' Bty War Diary
7 Hogg *A-A*, pp 132–4
8 Roskill *W at S*, Vol. III, Pt II, p. 265
9 'D' Bty War Diary
10 P&P letters from RMO, February-August 1945
11 ibid
12 Narrative, Arch 2/12/1

Pages 225–229
1 March notes
2 Roskill *W at S*, Vol. III, Pt II, pp 202–3
3 Ladd *Commandos*, pp. 209–11
4 *RM Business*, June 1944
5 Ladd *Commandos*, pp. 209–11
6 General Horton's notes, Arch 11/2/17, item 5183
7 Gibbs, Vol. I, p. 775
8 P&P letter, RMO February 1945
9 The figures estimated for each of these requirements are based on assumptions of the like commitment for each role
10 116 Bde War Diary, ADM 202 120, and other War Diaries
11 P&P letter, March 1945
12 This MT Company was to be raised to a battalion but War Establishment not confirmed
13 P&P letter, RMO April 1945
14 ibid, February 1945
15 Golden Committee report, Arch 6/4/1
16 ibid
17 P&P letter, RMO April 1945 and Arch 6/4/1
18 P&P letter, February 1945
19 ibid, May 1945
20 ibid
21 Mr D. Thompson's letter (772)

22 *G and L*, May 1977, p. 186
23 P&P letter, RMO February 1945
24 ibid
25 ibid, April 1945
26 *G and L*, December 1966
27 Signals School Syllabus, Arch 6/7/4
28 P&P letter, RMO February 1945
29 Narrative history of RME, Arch 2/12/5
30 *RM Business*, March 1945

Pages 229–236
1 Roskill *W at S*, Vol. III, Pt III, pp. 309–15
2 Marsh notes – Capt A. E. Marsh and Capt H. A. G. H. Beal
3 J. Waterman, *Fleet Air Arm History*, London 1962, pp. 124–5
4 Roskill *W at S*, Vol. III, Pt III, pp. 309–15
5 Marsh notes
6 ibid
7 Narrative history of 3 Bde HQ, Arch 2/14/4
8 Ladd *Commandos*, pp. 212–217
9 Mr F. Allison's letter (781)
10 Lt General Sir A. F. P. Christisson
11 Ladd *Commandos*, pp. 212–17
12 Action reports and narratives, Arch 7/19/8
13 ibid
14 General H. D. Fellowes' notes (622)
15 Mr F. Allison's letter (781)
16 ibid
17 Sir Campbell Hardy's notes (621)
18 Arch 7/19/8
19 Op report No. 3 Tp, p. 70 ibid, (17)
20 MO's narrative, ibid
21 Op report No. 3 Tp, p. 70 ibid, (17)
22 ibid
23 MO's narrative, Arch 7/19/8 (17)
24 Troop Commander's narrative, ibid, (16)
25 MO's narrative, ibid (17)
26 *Green Beret*, p. 342
27 Arch 7/19/8 (17), Lt-Col Stockley
28 ibid
29 Op report No. 3 Tp, ibid, (17)
30 Op report, Arch 7/19/8(a)
31 Arch 7/19/8
32 ibid
33 ibid, notes of 1945
34 Mr K. C. Saunder's leter (878)
35 Blumberg, pp. 215–18
36 Roskill *W at S*, Vol. III, Pt III, pp. 309–15
37 Mr H. M. Green and Mr L. M. Green's notes (848)

Pages 236–245
1 *Med Cdos*, p. 295
2 ibid, pp. 306–23
3 Sankey private papers
4 *Med Cdos*, pp. 306–23
5 Sankey private papers

6 Op report, Arch 7/19/29
7 *Med Cdos*, pp. 352–74
8 ibid, pp. 339–51
9 *RM Business*, August 1945
10 *Med Cdos*, pp. 384–422
11 War Diary 40 RM Cdo, ADM 202 87
12 Op report 43 RM Cdo, Arch 7/19/26
13 Arch 7/19/26
14 *Med Cdos*, p. 450
15 War Diary 40 RM Cdo, ADM 202 87
16 *Med Cdos*, p. 450
17 Arch 7/19/26
18 ibid
19 *RM Business*, August 1945
20 *Med Cdos*, pp 384–422
21 ibid
22 Citation report, Arch 7/19/26
23 *Med Cdos*, pp. 383–422
24 ibid
25 Op report 43 RM Cdo, Arch 7/19/26
26 War Diary 40 RM Cdo, ADM 202 87
27 ibid
28 *Med Cdos*, pp. 384–422
29 *RM Business*, August 1945
30 War Diary 40 RM Cdo, ADM 202 87
31 *Med Cdos*, pp. 384–422
32 *RM Business*, August 1945
33 War Diary 40 RM Cdo, ADM 202 87
34 ibid
35 *Med Cdos*, p. 450
36 Sankey papers

Pages 245–252
1 P&P letter, RMO August 1945
2 *Green Beret*, p. 325
3 Maj D. J. Flunder's notes (633)
4 *RM Business*, August 1945
5 Mr F. Wildman's letter (933)
6 *Green Beret*, p. 314
7 Chris Ellis *et al.*, *Handbook of the British Army 1943*, London 1975, original edition 1943, TM30–410 – hereafter *Army 1943*
8 *RM Business*, August 1945
9 'Five Rivers', a narrative *c*1945–6, Arch 7/19/10 – hereafter, 'Five Rivers'
10 ibid, Brigadier's report
11 ibid
12 ibid, 'Five Rivers'
13 ibid, Brigadier's report
14 Mr D. E. A. Roby's letter (932)
15 ibid
16 Arch 7/19/10, Brigadier's report
17 ibid, 'Five Rivers'
18 Joslen, *Orders of Battle in the Second World War*, London, 1965 pp. 308–9 – hereafter Joslen
19 116 Bde Op orders etc., Arch 7/19/10
20 ibid

21 Mr J. Bawden's notes and diary (655)
22 General Sir Norman Tailyour's letter (915)
23 Lockhart, pp. 173–5
24 116 Bde Op orders, etc., Arch 7/19/10
25 ibid
26 *Green beret*, p. 331
27 Lockhart, p. 173–5
28 Arch 7/19/31
29 Arch 7/19/10, (ref. 21 AGp/ 3732/111/A/ PS1), 30 March 1945
30 Other ranks 804, Arch 2/12/1; estimate of officers killed 180
31 Based on estimates from incomplete casualty reports
32 Mr F. Humphries' letter (842)
33 P&P letter, RMO June 1945
34 ibid
35 ibid, August 1945
36 ibid

Pages 252–259
1 Narrative history, Arch 2/14/4
2 Roskill *W at S*, Vol. III, Pt II, pp. 328–55
3 *RM Business*, August 1945 – 901 and 903 LCS(M), 570 LCA and 780 LCP(Large), 682 and 690 LCM Mk 1 Flotillas with RM LCN 340
4 Op report, Arch 7/19/11
5 ibid
6 *RM Business*, August 1945
7 Arch 7/19/11
8 Kirby, Vol. IV, p. 3
9 ibid, p. 342
10 Roskill *W at S*, Vol. III, Pt II, pp. 328–55
11 ibid, p. 427–30
12 Arch 7/19/11
13 Mr L. Jones's letter (820)
14 Roskill *W at S*, Vol. III, Pt II, pp. 328–55
15 Marsh notes
16 ibid
17 Roskill *W at S*, Vol. III, Pt II, pp. 328–55
18 Marsh notes
19 ibid
20 *RM Business*, August 1945
21 Kirby, pp. 394–5
22 ibid
23 Roskill *W at S*, Vol. III, Pt II, pp. 317–19
24 Correspondence with Museum Archivist, 1974
25 Roskill *W at S*, Vol. III, Pt II, p. 363
26 Lt-Col G. P. D. Pease's notes (739)
27 Lord Mountbatten's comments
28 Kirby, Vol. V, pp 5–9
29 Ladd *Commandos*, p. 208
30 Note of 1965, Arch 7/19/11
31 '385' unit history, Arch 2/15/7
32 Intelligence report, Arch 15/2/2

33 Translation of Japanese report, *G and L*, 1946, p. 333
34 Roskill *W at S*, Vol III, Pt II, pp. 374–82
35 Padfield, pp. 312–13
36 S. E. Morrison, *History of the US Naval Operations in World War 2*, Washington 1947, Vol. 5, p. 241
37 Arch 7/19/27
38 Letter to the author
39 Ladd *Commandos*, p. 219
40 Arch 7/19/28 and notes by Maj A. J. Donald
41 Kirby, Vol. V, pp. 265–75
42 ibid
43 ibid
44 Col H. Scrutton's letter (918)
45 Narrative history of RME, Arch 2/12/6
46 *Third Jungle Book*, Arch 2/14/4
47 Narrative history of 3 Bde Headquarters, ibid

Pages 260–267
1 Unconfirmed stories of 1945
2 Marsh notes
3 Notes and reports on prisoners-of-war, Arch 15/15/5
4 Capt L. P. R. Wilson's letter (766)
5 Lockhart, pp. 204–5
6 C/Sgt V. S. King's narrative (802)
7 ibid
8 Sir Geoffrey Hulton's notes (744)
9 ibid
10 Col Warren's notes, Arch 11/2/17, item 5000
11 Arch 15/15/5
12 Arch files RM officers, Col Warren's papers
13 P&P letter, October 1945
14 ibid, June 1945
15 Letters from General Sturges, Arch 2/13/1
16 Various reports,
17 *RMA History*, Vol. 2, p. 680
18 Mr A. Goldberg's letter (717)
19 Kirby, Vol. V, p. 406
20 ibid, p. 289–306
21 Mr Humphries' letter (842)
22 Kirby, Vol. V, pp. 289–306
23 Mr Humphries' letter (842)
24 Maj A. J. Donald in conversation with the author
25 Naval Historical Branch notes, Arch 14/2/11
26 *G and L*, 1948, p. 134
27 Lockhart, p. 198
28 Mr H. Playford in conversation with the author
29 45 RM Cdo HQ War Diary, DEFE 2, and Hansard 25 October 1945
30 Arch 11/2/17, item 5158
31 *RUSI Journal*, Vol. XCIII, May 1948
32 ibid
33 Arch index card reference to Hansard
34 *History of Co-Ops*

35 General P. R. Kay's notes (690)
36 General Chater quoting Hunton Committee, Arch 2/15/1
37 Col C. R. W Lamplough, CBE, MSM, Lt-Col . W. Lawson, MSM, and Capt A. E. Marsh
38 Lamplough report, Arch 6/4/1
39 ibid
40 Major General H. T. Newman, CBE, Col P. R. Smith Hill, CBE, with six others. See arch 6/4/1 for their report.
41 This committee reviewed service commitments
42 Moulton *RMs*, p. 84
43 ibid
44 Arch 6/4/1

Pages 268–270
1   Mr C. Drury's letter (809)
2   DSM awards, Arch 5/2/8
3   PP 7/20/3
4   Marder, p. 118
5   Ships' chronologies, Arch 11/2/17
6   Hansard extract, 25 October 1945, Arch 2/18/1
7   Moulton *RMs*, pp. 84–8
8   General John Owen's notes, Arch 11/2/17, item 5194
9   Research notes of Lt D. K. Tong, Arch 7/20/15
10 DSM awards, Arch 5/2/8
11 Booklet *40 Cdo in Haifa*, Arch 7/20/15
12 ibid
13 ibid
14 Mr Pitman's letter (622)
15 Booklet *40 Cdo in Haifa*, Arch 7/20/15
16 Capt G. Montgomerie in conversation with the author
17 Extract from *London Gazette*, Arch 7/20/15
18 Capt G. Montgomerie in conversation with the author

Pages 271–277
1   Maj A. Crockett, *Green Beret, Red Star*, London 1954, p. 12 – hereafter Crockett
2   Maj H. J. Hawley in conversation with the author
3   Narative and informal reports, PP 7/20/3
4   Narrative of Capt B. P. Elvey, ibid
5   ibid
6   PP 7/20/3
7   Sir Campbell Hardy's notes (621), Arch 11/2/17
8   Crockett, p. 53
9   Sir Campbell Hardy's notes (621), Arch 11/2/17
10 Crockett, pp. 86–91
11 ibid

12 *Blackwoods Magazine*, No. 1889, march 1973 – article
13 ibid
14 Moulton *RMs*, p. 88
15 PP 7/20/3
16 Capt D. Oakley in conversation with the author
17 Various papers, Arch 2/18/1 and 7/20/1
18 Foreign Office Gibraltar signals, Arch 3/5/4
19 Various programmes, Arch 3/13/4
20 Capt J. M. Brandon's letter (856)
21 Maj A. J. Donald in conversation with the author
22 Capt J. M. Brandon's letter (856)
23 Mrs June Barry and family in conversation with the author
24 Various conversations with the author
25 Moulton *RMs*, p. 88

Pages 277–287
1   P. Gaston, *The 38th Parallel*, Glasgow 1976, p. 76 – hereafter Gaston
2   General Pounds' notes (678)
3   Reports, PP 7/20/6B
4   ibid
5   Ladd *Commandos*, pp. 97–100
6   Gaston, pp. 20–23
7   Reports, PP 7/20/6B
8   *G and L*, 1951, pp. 58–9, quoting War Diary
9   ibid
10 Maj D. Aldridge's notes (692)
11 Letter, Arch 7/20/6
12 Lynn Montross *et al.*, *USMC Operations in Korea*, Washington 1957, Vol. 3, p. 302 – hereafter Montross
13 ibid
14 ibid
15 Reports, PP 7/20/6B
16 *G and L*, 1951, pp. 58–9
17 PP 7/20/6B
18 *G and L*, 1951, pp. 58–9
19 Montross, pp. 231–6
20 Reports, PP 7/20/6B
21 *G and L*, 1951, pp. 58–9
22 ibid
23 Reports, PP 7/20/6B
24 Maj D. Aldridge's notes (692)
25 Ladd *A from S*, p. 167 etc.
26 Reports, PP 7/20/6B
27 ibid
28 ibid
29 Narrative, Arch 7/20/6
30 Reports, PP 7/20/6B
31 ibid
32 ibid
33 Various papers, Arch 7/20/6
34 ibid

35 Mr H. Playford in conversation with the author
36 *Treatment of British POWs in Korea*, HMSO London 1955
37 ibid
38 Reports, PP 7/20/6B

Pages 288–292
1 Notes, arch 15/3/1 (32)
2 ibid
3 ibid
4 Narrative reports, PP 7/20/6B
5 Notes, Arch 15/13/1 (32)
6 PP 7/20/6B
7 Narratives and other papers, Arch 7/20/7
8 Reports, PP 7/20/7
9 Lt-Col P. Davis's notes (602)
10 ibid
11 *Times of Cyprus* article, 24 October 1956, Arch 7/20/8
12 Notes etc., PP 7/20/8
13 D. Young, *Four Five*, London 1972, pp. 218–38 – hereafter Young
14 ibid
15 General P. Spurgeon's notes, arch 11/2/17, item 5196
16 Young, pp. 218–38
17 ibid
18 Printed article, Arch 3/17/5
19 Young, pp. 218–38
20 Notes etc., PP 7/20/8
21 Printed article, Arch 3/17/5

Pages 292–99
1 Selwyn Lloyd articles in *Sunday Times*, June 1978
2 Lord Mountbatten's comments
3 Lecture notes, PP 7/20/5
4 Major A. C. J. Sharland
5 Capt D. Oakley in conversation with the author
6 Lecture notes, PP 7/20/5
7 *G and L*, February 1975
8 ibid
9 A. J. Baker, *Suez*, London 1964, p. 205
10 Major A. C. J. Sharland
11 Capt D. Oakley in conversation with the author
12 ibid
13 ibid
14 *G and L*, February 1975
15 ibid
16 ibid
17 Lecture notes, PP 7/20/5
18 General Sir Campbell Hardy's notes (621)
19 ibid
20 Lecture notes, PP 7/20/5
21 *G and L*, February 1975

22 Lecture notes, PP 7/20/5
23 Capt D. Oakley in conversation with the author
24 *G and L*, February 1975
25 Capt D. Oakley in conversation with the author
26 ibid
27 *G and L*, February 1975
28 Lecture notes, PP 7/20/5
29 Capt J. Parry's notes

Pages 300–305
1 Estimated numbers from Archives chronologies
2 Various notes and reports, Arch 6/2/3
3 Newspaper articles, Arch 6/7/29
4 Maj A. J. Ayre in converstaion with the author
5 Capt John Judd in converstaion with the author
6 ibid
7 Maj J. Powell's notes Arch 11/ 2/17, item 5109
8 General Moulton's comments
9 *G and L*, 1961, p. 48
10 Arch index card
11 Report, Arch 14/3/3
12 Maj A. C. J. Sharland in conversation with the author
13 PP reports
14 PP reports
15 *G and L*, February 1957
16 Newspaper and other reports, Arch 2/18/8
17 Narratives, Arch 7/20/6
18 Casualty books
19 Young, pp. 239–49
20 General Moulton's notes
21 General Moulton's letters
22 Submission to Golden Committee, P&P Letters, etc
23 Arch 2/15/1 and P&P Letters
24 General Moulton's comments
25 Jane's *Warships of the World*, various dates
26 General P. R Kay's notes (690)
27 Arch index cards
28 Newspaper reports, PP
29 ibid
30 Capt D. Oakley and Sub-Lt J. W. King, RN
31 Capt D. Oakley in conversation with the author
32 *G and L*, June 1959
33 ibid
34 ibid
35 ibid, 1976, p. 169
36 ibid, June 1959

Pages 306–310

1 J. Paget, *Last Post Aden 1964–7*, London 1969, pp. 24–8 – hereafter Paget
2 Maj A. J. Donald's notes (601)
3 ibid
4 Various papers, Arch 7/20/14
5 General P. R. Kay's letter (690)
6 ibid
7 Various papers, Arch 7/20/14
8 Young, pp. 290–303
9 ibid
10 ibid
11 PP reports
12 Various papers, Arch 15/41
13 Arch 11/2/17, item 5097
14 Notes, Arch 2/18/1
15 General P. R. Kay's notes (690)
16 ibid
17 Lord Mountbatten's comments
18 Brig O'Flaherty in a letter to the author
19 PP reports
20 ibid

Pages 311–319

1 Tom Harrison, *Background to Brunei*,Brunei 1963. Booklet written at GOC's request
2 Various printed articles, Arch 7/ 20/11
3 Capt Moore's report, ibid
4 ibid
5 Various printed articles, Arch 7/20/11
6 ibid
7 Capt Moore's report, ibid
8 Various printed articles, ibid
9 Capt Moore's report, ibid
10 PP reports
11 ibid
12 Maj-Gen P. J. Spurgeon's notes, Arch 11/2/17, item 5196
13 General Sir Peter Whitely's letters, Arch 11/2/17
14 Col Davis's narrative, ibid, item 5089
15 ibid
16 ibid
17 Various printed articles, Arch 7/20/9
18 Newspaper report, Arch 6/7/10
19 PP reports
20 Various printed articles, Arch 7/20/9
21 Newspaper report, Arch 7/7/10
22 PP reports
23 Maj A. J. Donald in conversation with the author
24 Lt R. A. Moyse's letter (716)
25 *G and L*, April 1964
26 ibid
27 PP reports
28 General P. R. Kay's notes (690)
29 Owen, p. 201
30 PP reports

Pages 321–329

1 Young, pp. 324–415
2 Paget, pp. 44–6
3 ibid
4 Ladd *Commandos*, p. 197
5 *G and L*, 1964, pp. 156–7
6 ibid
7 ibid
8 Young, pp. 324–415
9 Paget, pp. 62–72
10 Young, pp. 324–415
11 ibid
12 Maj Bank's notes Arch 11/2/17
13 Young, pp. 324–415
14 ibid
15 ibid
16 Comparisons of published weights
17 PP reports
18 *G and L*, 1964, pp. 156–7
19 ibid
20 Paget, pp. 62–72
21 *G and L*, 1964, pp. 156–7
22 Paget, p. 93
23 *G and L*, 1964, p. 258
25 *G and L*, 1964, p. 258
28 Paget, p. 131
29 Young, pp. 342–68
30 *G and L*, 1967, pp. 120–1
31 Jane's *Fact Files*
32 PP reports
33 ibid
34 Marsh notes
35 ibid
36 *G and L*, 1964, p. 258
37 ibid
38 Paget, p. 193
39 *G and L*, 1967, p. 262
40 Young, pp. 379–415
41 ibid
42 Paget, p. 250
43 *Daily Express*, 5 September 1967, Mr W. Sendall served in the Royal Marines in World War II

Pages 330–336

1 Col Davis's notes, Arch 11/2/17, item 5108
2 *G and L*, 1967, p. 336
3 PP reports
4 Maj P. Troy's notes (500)
5 PP reports
6 Lt D. Tong and other graduate officers
7 PP reports
8 ibid
9 Lt D. Tong and other graduate officers
10 D. Hall, *British Orders, Decorations and Medals*, London 1973
11 PP reports
12 *G and L*, 1967, p. 249

13 ibid
14 Comments to author by Maj J. Powell
15 Jane's *Warships of the World*
16 Arch index cards
17 Comments to author by Maj J. Powell
18 Newspaper articles, Arch 7/20/1
19 *G and L*, 1964, p. 101
20 Comments to author by Maj J. Powell
21 *G and L*, 1967, p. 239
22 *G and L*, various articles and Arch 2/3/4
23 Arch 1/2/5
24 *G and L*, 1968, p. 280 and Capt D. Oakley
25 Capt R. Priddle in conversation with the author
26 Capt M. L. A. MacLeod's notes (693)

Pages 336–341
1 David Barzilay, *The British Army in Ulster*, three vols, Belfast 1973, 1975 and 1978, Vol. III, p. 9 – hereafter Barzilay
2 Young, pp. 429–36
3 2nd-Lt E. Cooke and Sgt D. Carman, ibid
4 ibid, p. 430
5 Mne R. Thomas
6 Young, pp. 429–36
7 Mr Harry King
8 General Kay's notes (690)
9 Barzilay, Vol. II, pp. 215–19, quoting 40 Cdo RM comments
10 ibid
11 *Commission of HMS Fearless 1972–3*, privately published
12 Barzilay, Vol. II, pp. 215–19
13 ibid, pp. 69–70
14 ibid, pp. 215–19
15 ibid, Vol. I, p. 71
16 ibid, Vol. II, p. 79
17 ibid
18 ibid
19 ibid, Vol. III, p. 231
20 ibid, Vol. II, p. 196

Pages 342–345
1 General Pringle's notes, Arch 11/2/17, item 5169
2 ibid
3 PP reports
4 Arch 11/2/17
5 ibid
6 Arch index cards
7 *International Defence Review*, No. 6, 1979
8 Arch 11/2/17
9 Various conversations with the author
10 Col M. Marchant in converstaion with the author
11 Maj A. Parker's notes (522)
12 *G and L*, 1979, pp. 341–3
13 ibid

14 Hansard
15 *Suinday Times*, May 1963
16 Press reports, Arch 6/6/7
17 Lt-Col B. H. C. LeMesurier's notes, arch 11/2/17, item 5171
18 Maj M. R. L. Ward's notes, ibid, item 5233

Pages 346–407
1 *The Battle for the Falklands* by Max Hastings and Simon Jenkins – hereafter Hastings
2 ibid
3 *Pictorial History of the Royal Marines* by Derek Oakley et al – hereafter Oakley
4 *Reasons in Writing* by Ewen Southby-Tailyour p 103 – hereafter Southby-Tailyour; and correspondence with Lieutenant General Sir Steuart Pringle, Bt, KCB
5 *The Falkland Islands* by Ian J. Strange – hereafter Strange
7 *No Picnic* by Julian Thompson p 11 – hereafter Thompson
8 Hastings p 105
9 Southby-Tailyour
10 Thompson p 8
11 Hastings p 106
12 ibid p 77
13 ibid p 83
14 ibid p 87
15 *The Royal Navy and the Falklands War* by David Brown – hereafter Brown
16 Southby-Tailyour p 23
17 Globe and Laurel various articles
18 Brown p 57
19 ibid p 60
20 ibid p
21 Hastings various
22 Brown p 63
23 ibid p 63
24 Hastings p 100
25 Southby-Tailyour p 105
26 Thompson p 12
27 Brown ref p 68
28 Thompson p17
29 Brown
30 Southby-Tailyour
31 Brown p 68
32 ibid various
33 Thompson p 12
34 ibid p 12
35 ibid p 13
36 Hastings
37 Southby-Tailyour p 120
38 Thompson p 172
39 Brown p 240 & p 369
40 *One Hundred Days* Admiral Sandy Woodward p324 – hereafter Woodward
41 Brown p 87
42 Southby-Tailyour p 87

43 Brown p 87
44 conversation with Capt Bob McQueen RN
45 Brown p 87
46 Thompson p 20
47 ibid p21 and the General's letter of 17 March 1999 to the author
48 Hastings p 150
49 ibid
50 ibid p 155
51 G & L p 365
52 **final list to be revised – this not used 1 April 1999**
53 – do –
55 Thompson p 35
56 Southby-Tailyour p 139
57 ibid p 174
58 Hastings p 227
59 Capt Bell in conversation
60 Hasting p221 & Southby-Tailyour p 183
61 Thompson p 52
62 ibid p 55
63 ibid
64 *March to the South Atlantic* by Nick Vaux p 81 – hereafter Vaux
65 Southby-Tailyour p 307
66 ibid p 194
67 ibid p 195
68 Woodward p 303
69 Southby-Tailyour p 199
70 Thompson p 59
71 Southby-Tailyour p 201
72 Thompson p 61
73 ibid p 62
74 ibid p 105
77 Brown p 189
78 Southby-Tailyour p 212
79 ibid p 213
80 Vaux p 88
81 Thompson p 64
82 Vaux p 86
83 ibid p 91
84 ibid p 67
85 Southby-Tailyour p 113
86 ibid p 217
87 Thompson p 68
88 ibid
90 Brown p 210
91 Thompson p 76
92 Vaux p p3
93 Thompson p 71
94 Hastings p 271
95 Thompson p 77 & p 80
96 Hastings p 271
97 ibid p 362
98 Thompson p 81
99 ibid p 83
100 ibid p 21
101 ibid p 89
102 Thompson p 90
103 For a detailed study of 2 Para's battle see *2 Para Falklands* by John Frost, published by Buchan & Enright, London 1983.
104 Thompson p 102
105 ibid p 104
106 Southby-Tailyour p 237
107 ibid p 237 to p242.
107a letter from Maj General M. P. J. Hunt
108 Vaux p 99
109 Thompson p 97
110 Vaux p 107
111 Vaux pp 106–110 and Thompson p107–108
112 Thompson p 245
113 Hastings p 307
114 Thompson p 105
115 Hastings p 308
116 ibid p 309
117 Thompson p 110
118 ibid p 112
119 ibid p 114
120 Southby-Tailyour p 255
121 Frost p 102
122 Thompson p 116
123 ibid
124 ibid p 119
125 ibid p 120
126 Southby-Tailyour p 213
127 Brown p 286
128 Capt Rod Boswell in conversation
129 Southby-Tailyour p 266
130 ibid p 274
131 Frost p 112
132 Southby-Tailyour p 291
133 ibid p 296
134 Brown p 301–3
135 ibid p302
136 Southby-Tailyour p 305
137 Brown p 305
138 ibid p 306
139 Hastings p 327
140 Vaux p 122
141 Southby-Tailyour p308
142 ibid p 309
143 Hastings p324
144 ibid
145 Thompson p 136
146 ibid p 128
147 ibid p 160
148 Hastings pp 337–9
149 ibid p 338
150 Thompson pp 141–169
151 ibid
152 ibid
153 Vaux154 ibid
155 ibid
156 This secondment was made to commemor-

ate the link beween RM troops and the Lieutenant's Regiment in Singapore in 1941.

157 Vaux
158 Thompson
159 ibid p 165
160 ibid
161 ibid
162 Hastings p 341
163 ibid p 341–343
164 *The Falklands Military Machine* by Derek Oakley – hereafter Oakley
165 Frost p 146
166 Thompson p 177
167 Conversation with Brig. A. Pillar
168 Thompson p 183
169 Hastings p 343
170 Thompson p181
171 Hastings
172 ibid p 347
173 ibid p 348 and Thompson p 184
174 Hastings
175 ibid p 350
176 Oakley p 343
177 Hastings
178 Hastings p 356
179 ibid p 359
180 ibid p 365

Pages 412–431

1 Globe and Laurel (G & L)1983 p 369
2 Maj Mike Wooley, lecture of 1986
3 Globe and Laurel 1996 p 89
4 G & L 1994 p 93
5 G & L 1987 p 90 and 1990 p242
6 G&L 1983 p 234
7 G & L 1990 p 25
8 G & L 1983 p 305
9 G & L 1994 p 286
10 G & L 1987 p 238 & 1989 p 149
10a G & L 1984 p 100
11 G & L 1983 p 25
12 G & L 1993 p 331
13 G & L 1984 p 388
14 G & L 1996
15 G & L 1996
16 *Sunday Telegraph* 28 December 1997
17 G & L 1981 p 155
18 *Telegraph* 17 August 1996
19 G & L 1996 p13
20 G & L 1990 p 19
21 G & L 1990 p 18–19 and 1996 p 204
22 G & L 1981 p 206
23 G & L 1985 p12
24 G & L 1988 p 366
25 G & L 1980 p 379
26 G & L 1992 p 98
27 G & L.1992 p 281

29 G & L 1993 p 22
30 G & L 1985 p245 and 1990 p 242
31 *Connect* 23 September 1997
32 G & L 1981 p 137
33 G & L 1988 p 26
34 G & L 1995 p 5
35 G & L 1995 p 95
36 G & L 1993 p 145
37 G & L 1994 p 26
38 G & L 1984 p 140 *et al*
39 G & L 1994 p 77
40 G & L 1988 p 16
41 G & L 1988 p 16
42 G & L 1990 p19
43 G & L1989 p 83
44 G & L 1995 p 226
45 G & L 1995 p 368
46 G & L1997 July issue
47 G & L 1991 p 338 and 1992 p 355
48 G & L 1995 p 2
49 G & L 1991 p 338 ,1992 p 355 and 1994 p 311
50 G & L 1996 p 24
51 *Mail on Sunday* 9 June 1996 & G & L 1996 December issue
52 G & L 1996 p December
53 G & L 1996 p December
54 G & L 1981 p73
55 G & L 1994 p 160
56 G & L 1985 p386
57 G & L 1986 p 42
58 G & L 1988 p 161
59 G & L 1987 p 161
60 G & L 1990 p 304
61 G & L 1996 p 31
62 G & L 1981 p 206
63 G & L 1990 p 104
64 G & L 1996 p 337
65 G & L 1981 p 353
66 G & L 1984 p 220 and Southby-Tailyour p 101
67 G & L 1985 p 301
68 G & L 1989 p 289
69 G & L 1990 p 151
70 G & L 1996 p 342
71 G & L 1994 p 146 & 288
72 G & L 1996 p 21
73 G & L 1996 p 166
74 G & L 1996 p 10
75 G & L 1985 p 96
76 *Sunday Times* 22 May 1995
79 Press release by Thorn Emi Electronics 1992

Pages 433–453

1 Globe and Laurel 1994 p 8
2 G & L 1986 p 303
3 G & L 1988 p 136 and 1994 p 362
4 G & L 1989 p 209

5   G & L 1989 p 269
6   G & L 1991 p 148
7   G & L 1997 p 15
8   G & L 1991 p 151
9   G & L 1995 p?
10 G & L 1996 p 9
11 G & L 1981 p 74
12 G & L 1993 p 152
13 G & L 1983 p 21
14 G & L 1983 p 380
15 G & L 1983 p 381, 1984 p 28 and 1987 p 30
16 G & L 1984 p 374
17 G & L 1984 p 17] [G & L 1985 p 301]
18 G & L 1989 p 149].
19 Sunday Express Classic 13 November 1994
20 G & L 1996 p 78 and 1995 p 166
21 G & L 1996 p 221
22 G & L 1997 p 2
23 Storm Command by Sir Peter de la Billière p 222–3
24 telephone call to JDL in 1997
25 G & L 1991 p 350 and 1991 p 209
26 G & L 1991 p 2
27 G & L 1992 p 103
28 G & L 1991 p 2
29 G & L 1986 p 62 and 1998 p 70
30 G & L 1992 p 334 and 1994 p 16
31 G & L 1984 p 388
32 G & L 1988 p 233 and 1990 p 294 and 1998 p 70
33 G & L 1994 p 384
34 G & L 1991 p 3
35 G & L 1996 p 2 and p 130
36 G & L 1985 p 358]
37 G & L 1988 p 224
38 G & L 1986 p 28
39 G & L 1988 p 82
40 G & L 1988 p 82
41 G & L 1988 p 81
42 G & L 1985 p 380
43 G & L 1987 p 30
44 G & L 1986 p 18
45 G & L 1991 p138
46 G & L 1995 p 357
47 G & L 1986 p 18 and p 144
48 G & L 1997 p 138
49 G & L 1986 p 29
50 G & L 1987 p238
51 G & L 1987 p238 2nd reference
52 G & L 1986 p 18 and 1995 p 138
53 G & L 1984 p 195
54 G & L 1984 p 86 and 1984 p 155–6
55 G & L 1993 p 100 and p 199
56 G & L 1994 p 100
57 G & L 1986 p 18 and Telegraph 13 November 1997
58 G & L 1955 p 308
59 G & L 1995 342, 1996 p 91, 1996 p 2 and p 262
59a The Sunday Telegraph 17 May 1998
60 G & L 1983 256
61 G & L1982 p 51
62 G & L 1993 p 218
63 G & L 1997 p 5

Appendix 1: Abbreviations

Information taken mainly from World War II and contemporary published sources.

Appendix 3: Uniforms and Accoutrements

Information taken from notes compiled by Maj A. J. Donald from his personal collections of data on uniforms, and from notes prepared in 1980 by Maj A. G. Brown.

1   Dress Regulations, January 1980
2   Mr Eggo's letter (793)
3   Ladd, Commandos, p. 169

Appendix 4: Unit History Summaries

Note that ADM 202 refers to the War Diaries of subject unit unless otherwise stated.

Pages 471–472

1   Blumberg, pp. 311–88
2   ibid, pp. 127–84, 311–88
3   ibid, pp. 259–66
4   ibid, p. 432
5   ibid, pp. 198–205
6   ibid, p. 83
7   ibid, pp. 206–12
8   Maynard, p. 276
9   ibid, p. 305
10 ibid, p. 117
11 Arch 2/11/3 and Blumberg, pp. 419–20
12 Mr Eggo-s letter (793)
13 Arch 2/11/3 and blumberg, pp. 419–20
14 Roskill Policy, pp. 188–90
15 ibid, p. 196
16 Arch 7/18/3
17 Men from ships in UK ports made up these numbers
18 arch 7/18/3 (4)
19 ibid
20 ibid
21 ibid

Pages 473–475

1   Haines, p. 72
2   Conversations of the 1940s
3   G and L, 1927, p. 32
4   Report, Arch 7/18/2 (5)
5   G and L, 1928, p. 92
6   Booklet and notes, Arch 3/1/3
7   Sir Campbell Hardy's notes (621)

8 Official notes quoting COS (40) 258th meeting, Arch 2/13/1 (13)
9 ibid
10 ADM 202 1–9
11 File quoting COS (42) 6th meeting, Arch 2/13/1 (13)
12 Memorandum from General Hollis in the Cabinet office, ibid
13 Lord Mountbatten's comments
14 Arch 2/13/1 (13)
15 ibid
16 ADM 202 1–9
17 Various contemporary papers, Arch 2/13/1
181950 notes of Lt-Col Digby Hall, ibid (12)
19 RMO files of 1940, ibid (13)
20 Minute dated October 1939, ibid
21 GHQ Home Forces letter 1184/ Ops, May 1940, ibid (4)
22 *Army 1943*, p. 24
23 Arch 2/13/1 (4)
24 Document quoting COS (40) 172nd meeting, Arch 2/13/1
25 ibid
26 Document quoting COS (40) 208th meeting, ibid
27 RMO files of 1940, ibid (13)
28 ADM 202 34–7, opens 1 July 1940
29 War Diary of 1st Bn, ADM 202 40
30 ibid
31 ibid

Pages 475–476
1 contemporay notes and reports, Arch 2/13/1
2 ADM 202 46–9
3 ibid
4 Marder *Menace*, p. 55
5 Arch 2/13/1
6 ADM 202 46–9
7 Various papers, Arch 2/13/1
8 ADM 202 59
9 War Diary of RM Div, ADM 202 1–9
10 ibid
11 *G and L*, 1978, pp. 304–5
12 Various papers, Arch 2/13/1
13 Contemporary papers, ibid (13)
14 ADM 202, opens January 1942
15 Arch 2/13/1 (13)
16 Correspondence July 1942, Arch 2/13/7
17 RM Div papers, Arch 2/13/1
18 Arch 7/19/25
19 ADM 202 38–41

Pages 476–477
1 Based on date 3rd RM Bn formed
2 Lecture notes, Arch 7/19/18 (4)
3 ibid
4 Various papers, ibid
5 ibid (5)

6 ibid
7 Unpublished text by Maj D. Bittner, USMCR
8 Arch 7/19/18 (5)
9 Based on date 3rd RM Bn formed
10 ADM 202 50–3
11 No War Diary entries after 31 July 1943
12 ADM 202 4–7, opens December 1939 and closes July 1943
13 Marder *Menace*
14 ADM 202 50–3
15 ADM 202 42–5
16 Marder *Menace*
17 ADM 202 42–5
18 *ibid*
19 ADM 202 62–5
20 *ibid*
21 *ibid*
22 *Col Dewhurst's narrative, Arch 2/13/7 (1)*

Pages 478–479
1 RM Div papers, Arch 2/13/1
2 *G and L*, 1978, p. 164
3 ADM 202 60, and 41 RM Cdo Diary ADM 202 103
4 ADM 202 61
5 ADM 202 58–9
6 War Diary RM Div, ADM 202 1–9
7 *G and L*, 1978, p. 304
8 War Diary RM Div, ADM 202 1–9
9 ADM 202 58–9
10 ADM 202 180
11 ibid
12 War Diary MNBDO, ADM 202 131–6
13 ibid
14 Operation narratives of *c*1942 and other papers, Arch 2/13/11
15 ibid
16 ibid
17 ADM 202 180
18 ADM 202 232
19 RM Div notes, Arch 2/13/1 (13)
20 Arch 2/12/25 (2)
21 RM Div notes, Arch 2/13/1 (13)
22 *G and L*, 1978, pp. 304–5
23 RM Div notes, Arch 2/13/1 (13)
24 War Diary of RM Div, ADM 202 1–9
25 RM Div notes, Arch 2/13/1 (13)
26 ADM 202 73

Pages 479–480
1 ADM 202 66
2 RM Div papers, Arch 2/13/1
3 War Diary RM Div, ADM 202 1–9
4 ibid
5 ADM 202 66
6 ADM 202 181
7 ibid
8 Narrative history, Arch 2/12/10

9 Arch index cards

10 Mr B. A. York's letter (845) and Mr A. N. Boalch's letter (743)

11 RM Div papers, Arch 2/13/1

12 Arch 2/12/25 (2) and ADM 202 115

13 *G and L*, 1978, p. 304

14 ADM 202 118

15 *G and L*, 1978, p. 304–5, and Arch 11/2/17, item 5148, notes on unit dates by member of Hist. Soc., gives 31 July 1943 as date disbanded; companies may therefore have been under command of 22nd RM Bn before moving to Towyn.

16 Brigade War Diary, ADM 202 190

17 ADM 202 194

18 ADM 202 302

19 Arch 11/2/17, item 5148 (see 23rd RM Bn)

20 P&P letter, April 1945

21 Arch 11/2/17, item 5148

Pages 480–481

1 Narratives, Arch 2/16/2

2 ADM 202 121

3 Joslen, p. 308

4 Note – reference to Pioneer Platoon lifting mines in Arch 11/2/17, item 5148, April 1945

5 Joslen, p. 308

6 ibid

7 ADM 202 122

8 Various papers, Arch 2/16/2

9 Arch 11/2/17, item 5148 (see 23rd RM Bn)

10 ibid

11 Unpublished article by A. J. Perret, ibid , item 5243

12 ibid

13 Various papers, Arch 2/16/2

14 Arch 11/2/17, item 5148 (see 23rd RM Bn)

15 ADM 202 72

16 ADM 202 123

17 Arch 11/2/17, item 5148 (notes)

18 ADM 202 313

19 Correspondence, Arch 11/2/17

20 Arch 7/19/22

21 Various correspondence

Pages 482–484

1 ADM 202 74–6

2 Narrative history, Arch 2/14/4, and *48 RM [Cdo] History*, privately published

3 Various War Diaries

4 Minutes of meetings, Arch 2/14/4

5 ADM 202 74–6

6 Private correspondence lent to the author, and War Diaries

7 Various papers, Arch 2/14/4

8 Various *G and L* articles

9 Ladd *Commandos*

10 Notes on operations, Arch 7/19/32

11 *Med Cdos*, history

12 ADM 202 86

13 Summarised histories of operations in WW II, Arch 2/14/4

14 History of 45 RM Cdo, Arch 2/18/8

15 War Diary SS Gp, ADM 202 74

16 Various War Diaries and *G and L* articles

17 History notes, Arch 2/14/4

18 Arch 2/18/2 and *G and L* articles

19 ibid

20 Notes on flags, Arch 3/2/13

Pages 484–489

1 War Diary SS Gp, ADM 202 74–6

2 ADM 202 98–102

3 Contemporary WW II papers, and various press releases etc., Arch 2/14/5 (WW II) and Arch 2/18/3

4 Various press reports, Arch 2/19 /12 and unit history

5 ibid

6 Various *G and L* articles, and press reports etc.

7 Notes on flags, Arch 3/2/12

8 Contemporary WW II papers, and press releases and booklets, Arch 2/14/6 (WW II), and Arch 2/18/4 (1946–80)

9 Arch 2/18/4

10 Notes on flags, Arch 3/2/12

11 History of 3 SS Bde, Arch 2/14/4 (WWII), and mainly press cuttings in arch 2/18/5 (1946–80)

12 Arch 2/18/28

13 Narrative history, Arch 2/14/8 (WW II), and various press cuttings, Arch 2/18/6 (1946–80)

14 *Med Cdos*

15 ADM 202 88

16 Notes on flags, Arch 3/2/12

17 History and notes, Arch 2/14/9

18 *G and L*, 1947, pp. 113–14

19 History narrative (typescript), Arch 2/14/9

20 Press articles, ibid

Pages 489–496

1 Citation, arch 5/2/4

2 Notes on flags, Arch 3/2/12

3 Narrative history and other notes, Arch 2/14/12

4 *48 RM History*, privately published

5 Arch 2/14/3

6 ibid

7 Narrative history and various correspondence, Arch 2/12/6

8 Marsh notes

9 *G and L*, 1979, p. 62

10 Arch and news Team sources

11 Narratives, Arch 2/16/4

12 Operation reports and correspondence on Museum files (1980), Arch 7/19/3
13 Arch 2/15/4
14 ibid
15 Bulletin 1945, Arch 2/15/1
16 Unit history, Arch 2/18/24
17 WW II operation reports, Arch 2/18/4 and Arch 7/19/3

Pages 500–502
1 Lecture notes, Arch 2/12/2 (2)
2 ibid
3 Arch 2/12/2 (2)
4 ibid, (14)
5 ibid
6 Extract from letter RM 881/39Q, ibid, (2)
7 Notes, ibid, (23)
8 ADM 202 131–6
9 Arch 2/12/2 (23)
10 ADM 202 131–6
11 Arch 2/12/2 (23)
12 ADM 202 131–6
13 Reports of 1941, Arch 7/19/7 (18)
14 Moulton *RMs*, p. 72
15 Col Archdale's notes, Arch 11/2/17, item 5241
16 Various papers, Arch 2/12/3
17 Arch 11/2/17, item 5241
18 War diary of MNBDO I, ADM 202 131–6
19 Narrative report, Arch 2/12/3 (2)
20 ADM 202 195–213
21 Arch 2/12/3 (2)
22 Action report, Arch 2/12/3 (1)
23 ADM 202 195–213

Pages 502–503
1 Various notes and papers, Arch 2/12/11
2 ibid
3 Col Archdale's notes, Arch 11/2/17, item 5241
4 Arch 2/12/2 (2)
5 Diary of Ship Unloading Coy, Arch 2/12/3 (1)
6 Diary note, Arch 2/12/11
7 Operation reports, Arch 7/19/18
8 Arch 2/12/3 (1)
9 Diary note, Arch 2/12/11
10 ibid
11 Arch 2/12/3 (1)
12 ibid
13 ibid
14 Operation reports, Arch 7/19/18
15 ibid
16 Arch 2/12/3 (1)
17 Arch 2/12/46 (6)
18 Arch 2/12/11
19 Arch 2/12/4
20 ADM 202 192

21 See Rgts' histories
22 ADM 202 192
23 ibid

Pages 503–505
1 Arch 11/2/17, item 5148 (see 23rd RM Bn)
2 Blumberg, p. 248
3 Official notes of 1942, Arch 2/13/1 (13)
4 Letter with note from General Haining, Vice-CIGS, stating letter referred to had not been signed officially, ibid
5 Memorandum from Brig Hollis, Cabinet Office 2 November 1942, ibid
6 AG to First Lord, 16 November 1942, ibid
7 ADM 202 14
8 ibid
9 ibid
10 War diary of MNBDO I, ADM 202 131
11 ADM 202 145–9 (incomplete)
12 ibid
13 Arch 11/2/17, item 5148
14 War Dairy of MNBDO II, ADM 202 195–219
15 ADM 202 234–7 and 249
16 ADM 202 271–91
17 *RM Business*, No. 5
18 ibid
19 Hogg *A-A*, pp. 133–4
20 ibid
21 *RM Business*, No. 5
22 ibid
23 Arch 22/2/17, item 5243
24 ibid
25 ibid, and item 5148

Pages 505–506
1 Arch index cards
2 Calculated from nominal roll, Arch 2/12/5 (18)
3 1940s despatches, ibid (3)
4 Letters etc. of 1941, ibid (9)
5 1944 Narrative, ibid (1)
6 ibid (9)
7 ibid
8 ibid (16)
9 Hogg *World War II*, p. 147
10 Arch 2/12/5 (16)
11 *G and L*, 1978, p. 305
12 ibid
13 Arch 11/2/17, item 5148
14 ADM 202 16 (incomplete)
15 War Diary MNBDO I, ADM 202 131–6
16 Arch 11/2/17, item 5148
17 ADM 202 149
18 Arch 11/2/17, item 5148
19 ADM 202 131–6
20 ibid

Page 506–512

1 Arch 11/2/17, item 5148
2 ibid
3 War diary MNBDO I, ADM 202 131
4 ADM 202 157
5 ADM 202 131
6 Arch 11/2/17, item 5148
7 ibid
8 Lt-Col Eagles' letter (921)
9 'D' Bty's War Diary, Arch
10 *RM Business*, April 1945
11 ibid
12 Arch 11/2/17, item 5148, and ADM 202 157
13 War Diary MNBDO II, ADM 202 195
14 ADM 202 238
15 ADM 202 244
16 ibid
17 *RM Business*, No. 5
18 War Diary MNBDO I, ADM 202 131
19 ADM 202 162
20 War Diary MNBDO II, ADM 202 195
21 Capt J. Judd's notes, Arch 11/2/7, item 5165
22 War Diary MNBDO II, ADM 202 131
23 ADM 202 167
24 War diary MNBDO I, ADM 202 131
25 War Diary MNBDO I, ADM 202 131, and operation reports, Arch 2/13/2
26 War Diary 102 RM Bde Arty, ADM 202 20, and Bty War Diaries, ADM 202 21–2
27 ADM 202 23–5

Pages 513–518

1 ADM 202 67 and 70–1
2 ADM 202 68 and 69
3 ADM 202 312
4 P&P letter, No. 1
5 ibid
6 ADM 202 326 and P&P letters
7 Arch 11/2/17, item 5004
8 P&P letter, October 1945
9 ibid, No. 6
10 Report 1940, Arch 17/11/19 (11)
11 ibid, (3)
12 Arch 11/2/17, item 5148
13 ADM 202 303
14 Contemporary note on organisation Arch 2/13/2 (5)
15 Various correspondence, Arch 2/16/3 and ADM 202 304
16 Arch 2/16/3
17 2/16/5

Pages 519–521

1 Arch, letter of 1922
2 Blumberg, p. 430
3 Roskill *Policy*, Vol. I
4 Research notes of Lt-Col P. G. Davis
5 Mr Pegg's letter (796)

6 Blumberg
7 Mr Pegg's letter (796)
8 Blumberg, p. 431
9 Narrative report by general Jamrson in 1926, Arch 7/17/4
10 ibid
11 ibid
12 Blumberg, p. 432
13 Roskill *Policy*, Vol. I, pp. 156–7, 160
14 Correspondence, Arch 11/2/13
15 Col D. B. Drysdale
16 Reports, Arch 2/12/9
17 ADM 199 1553
18 Mr R. J. Oldfield's comments to the author
19 re Party 2402, ADM 202 326
20 Notes in possession of Maj A. Marsh
21 1946 correspondence, Arch 2/15/6

Page 537

1 Roskill *W at S* , Vol. I, p. 21
2 CAFO 36/40
3 Roskill *W at S* , Vol. I, p. 21
4 CAFO 1643/40
5 Roskill *W at S* , Vol. I, p. 21
6 D. W. Bone, *Merchantmen Rearmed,* London 1976, p. 143
7 Arch 5/1/3
8 History and satistics prepared in 1947 and correspondence as referenced in main text, Arch 2/12/6

Pages 541–543

1 *RMs 1938–1943*, pp. 15–16
2 CO's report, Arch 7/19/19
3 Narrative report, Arch 7/19/24 (4)
4 Roskill *W at S*, Vol. I, p. 209
5 ibid
6 ibid
7 Arch 7/19/24 (4)
8 Action report, Arch 7/19/24 (1)
9 ibid
10 ibid
11 ibid
12 Roskill *W at S*, Vol. I, pp. 213–14
13 Arch 7/19/24 (1)
14 Action report, ibid (4)
15 *RMs 1939–43*, p. 7
16 Letter to author
17 Various papers and correspondence, Arch 2/12/8
18 Sir Winston Churchill, *The Second World War,* London 1948, Vol. I, pp. 454 and 570 – hereafter Churchill
19 Action reports, DEFE 2 532
20 Churchill, Vol. I, pp. 454 and 470
21 Action reports, DEFE 2 532
22 ibid
23 ibid

24 Mr A. J. Smith's letter (836)
25 Press reports, Arch 11/2/17, item 5037
26 ibid
27 Mr C. G. Willis's letter (806)
28 Hogg *A-A*, p . 127
29 Mr A. J. Smith's letter (836)
30 CO's report, Arch 7/19/2 (1)
31 Blumberg, p. 432
32 Roskill *Policy*, Vol. I, p. 77
33 Reports, Arch 2/13/1

Pages 543–549
1 Narratives, Arch 2/7/2
2 History brochures and correspondence, Arch 2/7/7
3 Newspaper reports and narrative histories, Arch 2/7/6 and 17/2/6
4 Newspaper reports and history brochures, Arch 2/7/4
5 Narrative histories and various notes, Arch 2/7/8
6 Various histories, Arch 2/12/5
7 ibid
8 WO 78 4164

9 Arch 2/12/25
10 *G and L*, 1978, p. 163
11 ibid, p. 164
12 ibid, p. 302
13 Arch 17/4/2, and other sources
14 Arch 2/18/23, and index cards
15 Arch record cards
16 ibid
17 *G and L*, February 1980
18 ibid
19 Capt J. Judd's comments, Arch 11/2/17
20 Blumberg, various
21 *G and L*, 1978, p. 102
22 Unpublished article, Arch Arch 11/2/17, item 5243
23 Comments by Maj J. Powell
24 Arch record cards
25 ibid
26 ibid
27 P&P letters
28 Arch 21/1/1
29 Arch 21/7/2
30 Arch 21/7/7
31 Training Grp, sources

BIBLIOGRAPHY

Histories:

Baker, A.J. *Suez* London 1964

Barzilay, D *The British Army in Ulster Vols 1-III*, Belfast 1973, 1975 & 1978

Blumberg, Sir H. E. *Britain's Sea Soldiers* Devonport 1927

Bowen, F.C. *The King's Navy*, London 1925

Brown, John *The Royal Navy and the Falklands War* London 1987

Crockett, A. *Green Beret, Red Star* London 1965

Davey, W.E. *Hail and Farewell* RM Historical Society, Portsmouth 1978

Davey, W.E. *Watch and Ward*, Privately published

Davin, D.M. *Crete*, New Zealand Army Official History

Ellis, L.F. *History of the Second World War: Victory in the West*, London 1962

Field, C. *Britain's Sea Soldiers*, Liverpool 1924

Fraser, E. et al *The Royal Marine Artillery* , London 1930

Freedman, Lawrence *Britain and the Falklands War* London 1988

Gaston, P. *The 38th Parallel*, Glasgow 1936

Gibbs, M.H. *History of the Second World War: Grand Strategy Vol 1*, London 1950

Haines, G *Gunboats on the Great River*, London 1964

Hampshire, Cecil *The Royal Marines Tercentenary 1664-1964*, privately published London 1964

Hampshire, Cecil *On Hazardous Service*, London 1974

Hampshire, Cecil *Secret Navies*, London 1978

Hastings, Max & Jenkins, Simon *The Battle for the Falklands* London 1983

Hogg, Ian *Anti-Aircraft: A history of Air Defence*, London 1978

Kirby, S Woodburn *History of the Second World War: War with Japan Vols I to IV*, London 1957-1965

Ladd, J.D. *Assault from the Sea 1939/45*, London 1976

Ladd, J.D. *Commandos and Rangers of World War II*, London 1978

Lansborough, G. *Tobruk Commando*, London 1956

Lockhart, Sir Bruce *The Marines Were There*, London 1950

Lovat, the Lord *March Past*, London 1978

Maloney, C.J.C. *The History of the Second World War: The Mediterranean and Middle East Vol V*, London 1973

Marder, A.J. *From the Dardanelles to Oran*, London 1974

Marder, A.J *Operation Menace*, London 1976

Maund, L.H. *Assault from the Sea*, London 1949

Maynard, C. *The Murmansk Adventure*, London 1928

Montross, Lynn et al. *The Chosin Reservoir Campaign*, Washington 1957

Morrison, S.E. *History of United States Naval Operations in World War II, Vols 1-15*, Boston USA 1947-51

Moulton, J.L. *The Norwegian Campaign of 1940*, London 1966

Moulton, J.L. *The Royal Marines*, London 1972

Moulton, J.L. *Battle for Antwerp*, London 1978

Neave, Airey *The Flames of Calais*, London 1960

Nicholas, Paul H. *Historical Record of Royal Marine Forces*, London 1845

Oakley, D. *The Falklands Military Machine*, Tunbridge 1989

Owen, Charles *No More Heroes*, London 1975

Padfield, P. *Guns at Sea*, London 1973

Padget, J. *Last Post Aden 1964-7*, London 1969

Phillipps, Lucas C.E. *Alamein*, London 1962

Phillipps, Lucas C.E. *The Cockleshell Heroes*, London 1956

Playfair, L.S.O. *History of the Second World War: The Mediterranean and Middle East Vols I to IV*, London 1957-66

Robinson, T. *Dieppe the Glory and the Shame*, London 1963

Rohwer, J. et al. *Chronology of the War at Sea 1939-45*, (translation) London 1972

Roskill, S. *Naval Policy Between the Wars Vols 1 & 2*, London 1968 & 1970

Roskill, S. *History of the Second World War: The War at Sea Vols I, II & III*, London 1954, 1956 & 1961

Saunders, Hilary St George *The Green Beret*, London 1949

Stadden, Charles et al *Uniforms of the Royal Marines from 1664 to the present day*, Romford 1997

Spencer, J.H. *The Battle for Crete*, London 1962

Trendell, John *Operation Music Maker*, privately published Southampton 1978

Waterman, J. *Fleet Air Arm History*, London 1962

Whitehouse, A. *Amphibious Operations*, London 1964

Young, D. *Four Five Commando*, London 1972

Memoirs and Bibliographies:

Basset, S. *Royal Marine*, London 1962

Billière, Sir Peter de la *Storm Command* London 1992

Chilchrist, *Commando*, London 1960

McManners, H. *Falklands Commando*, London 1984

Mitchell, E. *Marine Commandos*, unpublished (Arch 2/14/6)

Moulton, J.L. *Haste to the Battle*, London 1963

Parsons, E. *Bible Back* Privately Published in New Zealand

Southby-Tailyour, Ewen *Reasons in Writing* Barnsley 1993

Strange, Ian J. *The Falkland Islands* Newton Abbot 1983

Thompson, Julian *No Picnic* London 1985

Vaux, Nick *March to the South Atlantic* London 1985

Woodward, Adm Sandy with Patrick Robinson *One Hundred Days* London 1992

Proceedings and Papers:

Dieppe Raid, Combined Operations HQ report (BR 1887 of 1942)

History of Combined Operations, prepared by Amphibious Warfare HQ 1956

History of Commandos in the Mediterranean 1943 to 1945, prepared by Combined Operations HQ c1946

Jungle Book, magazine of 3 Commando Brigade RM

Naval Operations of the Battle of Crete, (BR1736(2) of 1942)

RM Business Vols 1–5, issued by RM Office 1945–6

Treatment of British Prisoners in Korea, HMSO London 1955

Articles and References:

The Nautical Gazette of HMS *Revenge*, 1921

The Globe and Laurel, the journal of the Royal Marines

RM Historical Society Newsletters and special publications

Jane's *Fact Files*

Battle of the River Plate, HMSO London 1940

The Royal Marines: The Admiralty account of their Achievements 1939–43, London 1944

Ellis, C et al. *Handbook of the British Army 1943*, originally US Army publication, republished London 1978

Hall, D. *British Orders, Decorations and Medals*, London 1973

Hogg, Ian *The Guns of World War II*, London 1976

Joslen, J.A. *Orders of Battle: Second World War*, London 1965

Kipling, Rudyard *Rudyard Kipling's Verse*, London 1958

Partridge, C. *Hitler's Atlantic Wall*, Guernsey 1976

Paterson, H.L. *The Book of the Gun*, New York 1962

Rogers, H.C.B. *Weapons of the British Soldier*, London 1960

Stadden, Charles et al. *Uniforms of the Royal Marines*, Romford 1997

INDEX FOR GENERAL SUBJECTS

INDEX FOR ROYAL MARINE ACTIVITIES, UNITS AND UNIFORMS